STRUCTURAL SAFETY AND RELIABILITY
VOLUME 3

PROCEEDINGS OF ICOSSAR'97 – THE 7TH INTERNATIONAL CONFERENCE ON
STRUCTURAL SAFETY AND RELIABILITY/KYOTO/24-28 NOVEMBER 1997

Structural Safety
and Reliability

Edited by

N. Shiraishi
Maizuru National College of Technology, Kyoto, Japan

M. Shinozuka
University of Southern California, Los Angeles, California, USA

Y. K. Wen
University of Illinois, Urbana, Illinois, USA

VOLUME 3

© 1998 A.A.Balkema, Rotterdam

A.A.BALKEMA/ROTTERDAM/BROOKFIELD/1998

Supported by The Commemorative Association for the Japan World Exposition (1970).

Cover photo: By the courtesy of Honshu-Shikoku Bridge Authority

The texts of the various papers in this volume were set individually by typists under the supervision of each of the authors concerned.

Published by
A.A. Balkema, P.O. Box 1675, 3000 BR Rotterdam, Netherlands
Fax: +31.10.413.5947; E-mail: balkema@balkema.nl; Internet site: http://www.balkema.nl
A.A. Balkema Publishers, Old Post Road, Brookfield, VT 05036-9704, USA
Fax: 802.276.3837; E-mail: info@ashgate.com

For the complete set of three volumes, ISBN 90 5410 978 5
For Volume 1, ISBN 90 5410 979 3
For Volume 2, ISBN 90 5410 980 7
For Volume 3, ISBN 90 5410 981 5

Structural Safety and Reliability, Shiraishi, Shinozuka & Wen (eds) © 1998 Balkema, Rotterdam, ISBN 90 5410 978 5

Table of contents

Earthquake engineering

Geotechnical engineering

Geotechnical engineering (ongoing research)

Bridges

Bridges (ongoing research)

Offshore structures

Offshore structures (ongoing research)

Earthquake engineering

Structural Safety and Reliability, Shiraishi, Shinozuka & Wen (eds) © 1998 Balkema, Rotterdam, ISBN 90 5410 978 5

Engineering simulation of ground motions using a seismological model

T. Ohsumi & H. Darama
Planning and Research Department, Research and Development Center, Nippon Koei Co. Ltd, Takasaki, Ibaraki, Japan

T. Harada
Department of Civil Engineering, Miyazaki University, Japan

ABSTRACT:This paper describes a digital simulation method of ground motions using a seismological model. The method is based on the spectral representation of stochastic waves in conjunction with the stochastic summation of the small ruptures in making use of the representation theorem of elastodynamics of the far field seismic waves. Numerical example demonstrates the effect of the directivity of seismic waves on the acceleration time histories.

1 INTRODUCTION

In order to simulate high frequency ground motions ($\geq$ about 1 Hz) at an average site from an average earthquake of specified size, Boore (1983) presented a stochastic method in which the Fourier spectrum amplitude of simulated ground motion approximates the acceleration spectrum with ω^{-2} property and a single corner frequency (Hanks and McGuire, 1981).

It is well known that the rupture plane of large earthquake is too large to be treated as a point source, and the slip motion as well as stress drop are not uniform (irregular) over the extended rupture plane. These heterogeneities of the rupture process may cause the significant departure from the self similar ω^{-2} model of source spectrum (Aki and Richards,1980; Papageorgiou,1988).

In order to represent a type of heterogeneity of the extended rupture, the effects of source-station geometry, and the effects of propagating rupture in a simple model, Joyner and Boore (1986) considered a model where many small rupture areas are added together with their start times distributed randomly with uniform probability over the rupture duration.

In this paper, we apply the above Joyner and Boore method to the general empirical Green's function method proposed by Harada, et al.(1995, 1996) which is the generalization of the Irikura formulation (Irikura, 1988). Consequently, we pro-pose an average spectrum of ground motions at a distance from an extended rupture where a type of heterogeneity of the extended rupture, the effects of source-station geometry, and the effects of propagating rupture are taken into account.

2 SPECTRUM OF GROUND MOTION FROM STOCHASTIC SUMMATION OF SMALL EARTHQUAKES

2.1 Starting Equations

The starting equations in this paper belong to the empirical Green's function method initially suggested by Hartzell (1978). This method, which has been discussed in detail by Irikura (1988), is a method to simulate ground motions from an extended rupture on the basis of the representation theorem of elastodynamics. Here, a brief discussion of the relevant mathematical formulation is presented in the frequency domain, and a new transfer function is presented, which accounts for the difference of the slip time functions between extended rupture and small rupture area.

The extended rupture plane with length L and width W is divided into small rupture areas with length ΔL and width ΔW, as shown in Fig.1. Using the representation theorem of elastodynamics, the far-field displacement $\boldsymbol{u}(\boldsymbol{x},t)$ in a homogeneous, isotropic, and layered medium can be expressed in the following integral form (Aki and

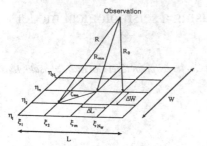

Fig.1 Schematic diagram of the Green's function method and its notation

Richards, 1980; Somerville, *et al.*, 1991):

$$u(x,t) = \sum_{m=1}^{N_L}\sum_{n=1}^{N_W}\int_{\xi_m}^{\xi_m+\Delta L}\int_{\eta_n}^{\eta_n+\Delta W}\dot{D}(\xi_m,\eta_n,t-\tau_{mn})$$

$$*G(x,\xi_m,\eta_n,t-t_{mn})d\xi d\eta \qquad (2.1)$$

where $x = (x,y,z)^T$ is the observation station, $\dot{D}(\xi,\eta,t)$ is the velocity of the source time function at position (ξ,η) on the extended rupture, $G(x,\xi,\eta,t-t_{\xi\eta})$ is the Green's function (the impulse response of medium), and $*$ represents a convolution. τ_{mn} is the rupture propagation time from the hypocenter of extended rupture to the $(m,n)^{th}$ small rupture area, and t_{mn} is the propagation time for S waves to travel from the $(m,n)^{th}$ small rupture area to the observation station, which are defined by:

$$\tau_{mn} = \frac{\zeta_{mn}}{V_R}; \quad t_{mn} = \frac{R_{mn}-R}{C_S} \qquad (2.2)$$

where ζ_{mn} is the distance from the hypocenter of the extended rupture to the $(m,n)^{th}$ small rupture area, R_{mn} is the distance from the $(m,n)^{th}$ area to the observation station, R is the hypocentral distance of the extended rupture, V_R is the rupture velocity, and C_S the S wave velocity of the medium.

The Fourier transform of Eq.(2.1) yields the following equation:

$$u(x,\omega) = \sum_{m=1}^{N_L}\sum_{n=1}^{N_W}\int_{\xi_m}^{\xi_m+\Delta L}\int_{\eta_n}^{\eta_n+\Delta W}\dot{D}(\xi_m,\eta_n,\omega)$$

$$G(x,\xi_m,\eta_n,\omega)e^{-i\omega(\tau_{mn}+t_{mn})}d\xi d\eta \qquad (2.3)$$

In order to take into account the difference of the slip time functions between the extended rupture and the small rupture, the transfer function is introduced, which is defined as:

$$T_{mn}(\omega) = \frac{\dot{D}(\xi_m,\eta_n,\omega)}{\dot{D}_{mn}(\xi_m,\eta_n,\omega)} \qquad (2.4)$$

where $\dot{D}_{mn}(\xi_m,\eta_n,\omega)$ is the Fourier transform of the velocity of the slip time function at position (ξ_m,η_n) of the small rupture. By using Eq.(2.4), Eq.(2.3) can be written as:

$$u(x,\omega) = \sum_{m=1}^{N_L}\sum_{n=1}^{N_W}T_{mn}(\omega)u_{mn}(x,\omega) \qquad (2.5a)$$

where

$$u_{mn}(x,\omega) = \int_{\xi_m}^{\xi_m+\Delta L}\int_{\eta_n}^{\eta_n+\Delta W}\dot{D}_{mn}(\xi_m,\eta_n,\omega)$$

$$G(x,\xi_m,\eta_n,\omega)e^{-i\omega(\tau_{mn}+t_{mn})}d\xi d\eta \qquad (2.5b)$$

In Eq.(2.5b), $u_{mn}(x,\omega)$ is the far-field displacement due to the small rupture. Equation (2.5) indicates that the motions from the extended rupture is the summation of the motions from the $N_L \times N_W$ small rupture areas with the weight of $T_{mn}(\omega)$.

Based on Eq.(2.5), an approximate method can be obtained, using a single record $u_0(x,\omega)$ due to the $(m_0,n_0)^{th}$ rupture area. By assuming that the slip time function of each small rupture and the Green's function from the position of each small rupture to the observation station are approximately equal to those from the $(m_0,n_0)^{th}$ rupture area, then Eq.(2.5a) can be reduced as:

$$u(x,\omega) = \sum_{m=1}^{N_L}\sum_{n=1}^{N_W}\frac{R_0}{R_{mn}}T_{mn}(\omega)e^{-i\omega\tilde{t}_{mn}}u_0(x,\omega)$$

$$(2.6a)$$

where

$$\tilde{t}_{mn} = \tau_{mn} + t_{mn} \qquad (2.6b)$$

In deriving Eq.(2.6) the effect of the hypocentral distance on the Green's function has been considered approximately because the S wave attenuates inversely proportional to the hypocentral distance in a homogeneous isotropic medium.

From the similarity conditions of earthquakes (Kanamori *et al.*, 1975), the following relations are derived:

$$\left(\frac{M_0}{m_0}\right)^{1/3} = \frac{L}{\Delta L} = \frac{W}{\Delta W} = \frac{D}{D_0} = \frac{\tau}{\tau_0} = N \qquad (2.7)$$

where $N = N_L = N_W$, and M_0 is the seismic moment of the extended rupture; m_0 the seismic moment of the small rupture area; D and τ are the final offset of the dislocation and the dislocation rise time of the extended rupture, respectively; D_0 and τ_0 those of the small rupture.

The transfer function $T_{mn}(\omega)$ defined by Eq.(2.4)

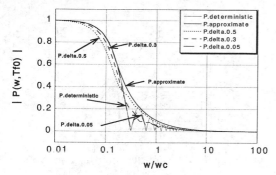

Fig.2 Frequency variation of $|P(\omega, T_f)|$

can be obtained by specifying a slip time function. The following transfer function is used in this paper:

$$T_{mn}(\omega) = \left[\frac{i\omega + \dfrac{N}{\tau}}{i\omega + \dfrac{1}{\tau}}\right]\left[\frac{1 + \kappa(\dfrac{\omega\tau}{2})^2}{1 + (\dfrac{\omega\tau}{2})^2}\right] \quad (2.8)$$

where κ is a parameter that controls the value of the transfer function in high frequency range($\omega \geq \omega_c = 2/\tau$). Although several physical models exist (Aki and Richards, 1980), the generation process of high frequency seismic waves due to extended rupture may be quite complex. Therefore, without the use of physical models, one parameter κ has been introduced here, which has to be empirically estimated. For $\kappa-1$, the transfer function is equivalent to that obtained by assuming the exponential function for slip time functions of the extended and small rupture areas (Harada *et al.*, 1995).

2.2 *Average characteristics of the source spectrum of an extended rupture obtained from a stochastic summation of small rupture areas*

We consider here a simple model for a simulation of the many patterns of irregular propagation of a coherent rupture front from a specified hypocenter on a given extented rupture plane. For each pattern of irregular ruptures, the small rupture areas can be considered to be distributed on the extented rupture plane with later start times at progressively greater distances from the hypocenter. However, in considering the collection of many patterns it may be appropriate to assume approximately that the start times of small rupture areas are randomly distributed with uniform probability over the observed rupture duration T_f of the

given extended rupture. It is noted here that the duration T_f depends on the size of the extended rupture and on the rupture velocity, but it also depends on the orientation of the observation relative to the rupture (see subsection 2.3). It is also noted that the duration T_f is assumed to be a random variable with uniform probability. By considering the practical situation, the small rupture areas are assumed identical. For the attention of the source characteristics, we neglect the correction of the hypocentral distance.

With the above assumptions the Fourier spectrum of the uni- component waveform $u_S(\omega)$ from the extended rupture may be written such as:

$$u_S(\omega) = \left[\sum_{m=1}^{N}\sum_{n=1}^{N}T_{mn}(\omega)e^{-i\omega t_{mn}^*}\right]u_{S0}(\omega) \quad (2.9)$$

where $u_{S0}(\omega)$ represents the Fourier spectrum of the uni-component waveform from a small rupture area, and t_{mn}^* the time delay uniformly distributed over T_f. By taking the expectation over the ensemble, the average source spectrum $|u_S(\omega)|$ is obtained as:

$$|u_S(\omega)| = SUM_N(\omega)|T(\omega)||u_{S0}(\omega)| \quad (2.10)$$

where $|T(\omega)|-|T_{mn}(\omega)|$, and $SUM_N(\omega)$ is the coefficient of random summation given by:

$$SUM_N(\omega) = \left[N^2\left\{1 + (N^2 - 1)|P(\omega, T_{f0})|^2\right\}\right]^{1/2} \quad (2.11a)$$

where

$$|P(\omega, T_{f0})| = \frac{1}{4\sqrt{3}\delta_{Tf}\left(\dfrac{\omega}{\omega_{f0}}\right)}\left[(Si[\varpi_1] - Si[\varpi_2])^2\right.$$

$$\left. + (Ci[\varpi_1] - Ci[\varpi_2] - \ln[\varpi_1] + \ln[\varpi_2])^2\right]^{1/2} \quad (2.11b)$$

where

$$\varpi_1 = 2(1 + \sqrt{3}\delta_{Tf}\frac{\omega}{\omega_{f0}}) \quad (2.11c)$$

$$\varpi_2 = 2(1 - \sqrt{3}\delta_{Tf}\frac{\omega}{\omega_{f0}}) \quad (2.11d)$$

In Eq.(2.11a) T_{f0} is the mean of the observed rupture duration T_f, and δ_{Tf} is the coefficient of variation of T_f. The functions Si and Ci represent the sine and cosine integrals. The first corner frequency ω_{f0} is defined in this study such as:

$$\omega_{f0} = \frac{2}{T_{f0}} \quad (2.11e)$$

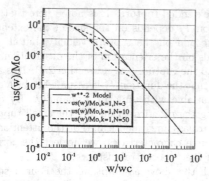

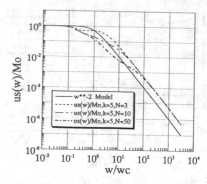

Fig.3 Normalized spectra of large earthquake by the Joyner and Boore stochastic summation of small earthquakes, compared to the ω^{-2} spectrum (heavy line). (In the case of $\kappa = 1$)

Fig.4 Normalized spectra of large earthquake by the Joyner and Boore stochastic summation of small earthquakes, compared to the ω^{-2} spectrum (heavy line). (In the case of $\kappa = 5$)

The frequency variation of function $|P(\omega, T_{f0})|$ is shown in Fig.2 for $\delta_{Tf} = 0.05$, 0.3, and 0.5. For small value of $\delta_{Tf} = 0.05$, the frequency variation of $|P(\omega, T_{f0})|$ indicates a wavy form with peaks and troughs, similar to the behavior in the case of deterministic rupture duration ($\delta_{Tf} = 0$) where the function $P(\omega, T_{f0})$ is given by:

$$|P(\omega, T_{f0} = T_f)| = \left| \frac{\sin \dfrac{\omega}{\omega_f}}{\dfrac{\omega}{\omega_f}} \right| \qquad (2.12)$$

The function of Eq.(2.12) is the same derived by Joyner and Boore (1986), and also shown in Fig.2. For large value of $\delta_{Tf} = 0.5$, the frequency variation of $|P(\omega, T_{f0})|$ is smooth. By considering the fact that the variation in the first corner frequency ω_{f0} may be large, we propose the following simple function for $|P(\omega, T_{f0})|$:

$$|P(\omega, T_{f0})| =$$

$$\begin{cases} 1 - c_1 \left(\dfrac{\omega}{\omega_{f0}} \right)^2 + c_2 \left(\dfrac{\omega}{\omega_{f0}} \right)^4 & 0 \le \dfrac{\omega}{\omega_{f0}} \le \dfrac{\pi}{2} \\[2mm] \dfrac{1}{\dfrac{\omega}{\omega_{f0}}} & \dfrac{\pi}{2} \le \dfrac{\omega}{\omega_{f0}} \end{cases}$$

$$(2.13)$$

where $c_1 = 0.16605$, and $c_2 = 0.00761$. The function of Eq.(2.13) is also shown in Fig.2.

By introducing the second and third corner frequencies defined by,

$$\omega_c = \frac{2}{\tau}, \qquad \omega_{c0} = \frac{2}{\tau_0} \qquad (2.14)$$

the transfer function of Eq.(2.8) can be rewritten as:

$$T(\omega) = T_{mn}(\omega) = \left[\frac{N + i(2\dfrac{\omega}{\omega_c})}{1 + i(2\dfrac{\omega}{\omega_c})} \right] \left[\frac{1 + \kappa(\dfrac{\omega}{\omega_c})^2}{1 + (\dfrac{\omega}{\omega_c})^2} \right]$$

$$(2.15a)$$

where,

$$N = \left(\frac{M_0}{m_0} \right)^{1/3} = \frac{\omega_{c0}}{\omega_c} \qquad (2.15b)$$

The source spectrum of the small rupture is assumed to be ω^{-2} model such as:

$$|u_0(\omega)| = \frac{m_0}{1 + \left(\dfrac{\omega}{N\omega_c} \right)^2} \qquad (2.16)$$

In the two extreme frequencies where $\omega \to 0$ and $\omega \to \infty$, the source spectrum of an extended rupture is found from Eq.(2.10) to be given by:

$$|u_S(\omega)| = \begin{cases} N^3 m_0 = M_0 & \omega \to 0 \\[2mm] \kappa M_0 \left(\dfrac{\omega_c}{\omega} \right)^2 & \omega \to \infty \end{cases} \qquad (2.17)$$

Figures 3 and 4 show the average source spectra of extended rupture normalized by the seismic moment M_0 for the cases of $\kappa = 1$ and 5, respectively. In each figure, $\omega_{f0}/\omega_c = 1/10$ is assumed and the variations with the summation parameter N are shown. For comparison, the ω^{-2} source spectrum model with the second corner frequency ω_c is shown by the heavy line in each figure. It is found from Fig.3 (for the case of $\kappa = 1$) that the source spectrum of extended rupture follows the ω^{-2} model at the lower frequency (ω_{f0}) and the

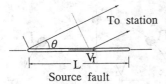

Fig.5 Geometry of a rupturing fault and the path to an observation station

higher frequency (ω_{c0}) ranges, but at intermediate frequency range its spectral amplitude is lower as the summation parameter N increases than that expected from the ω^{-2} model. These characteristics observed from Fig.3 are also observed from Fig.4 (for the case of $\kappa=5$), but the source spectral amplitude is amplified by a factor of κ at higher frequency range ($\omega \geq \omega_{c0}$).

By comparing these characteristics shown in Figs. 3 and 4 with those obtained from the various irregular source models (for examples, Izutani, 1984; Papageorgiou, 1988) where the heterogeneity of either slip or stress drop on the extended rupture plane is taken into account, the parameter κ may be found to be equivalent to the ratio of local stress drop to global stress drop or the ratio of dynamic stress drop to static stress drop.

2.3 *Average rupture duration observed at a station*

The observed rupture duration T_f depends on the size of the extended rupture and the rupture velocity, but it also depends on the orientation of the observation station relative to the extended rupture. For simplicity we adopt the simplest model for the geometry of a rupture and the path to an observation station as shown in Fig.5. The observed rupture duration ($R \gg L$ where R is the hypocentral distance and L is the strike length of the extended rupture) is given such as (Ben-Menahem, 1961):

$$T_f = \frac{L}{V_R}\left(1 - \frac{V_R}{C_S}\cos\theta\right) \quad (2.18a)$$

where θ is the azimuth angle from the strike of extended rupture to the observation station. V_R and C_S are the rupture velocity and the S wave velocity. In Eq.(2.18a), L, V_R, C_S, and θ may be considered as random variables. However, for simplicity, we use the rupture duration of Eq.(2.18a) as an estimate of the average rupture duration observed at a station:

$$T_{f0} \simeq T_f \quad (2.18b)$$

3 SAMPLE GROUND MOTION FROM STOCHASTIC SUMMATION OF SMALL EARTHQUAKES

A sample acceleration time history of ground motion is generated using the spectral representation of stochastic waves proposed by Shinozuka (1974); Shinozuka *et al.*(1987). In this method, the power spectrum of ground acceleration have to be given, then the stationary acceleration time history is generated by the following equation:

$$a_s(t) = \sqrt{2}\sum_{j=1}^{N_\omega}\sqrt{2S_{aa}(\omega_j)\Delta\omega}\cos(\omega_j t + \phi_j) \quad (3.1a)$$

where,

$$\omega_j = j\Delta\omega; \quad \Delta\omega = \frac{\omega_u}{N_\omega}; \quad j = 1, 2, \ldots, N_\omega \quad (3.1b)$$

An upper bound of the frequency ω_u in Eq.(3.1b) represents an upper cut-off frequency beyond which $S_{aa}(\omega_j)$ may be assumed to be zero for either mathematical or physical reasons. In Eq.(3.1a), ϕ_j are independent random phase angles uniformly distributed over the range $(0, 2\pi)$. Note that the simulated time history is asymptotically Gaussian as N_ω becomes large due to the central limit theorem.

The nonstationary acceleration time history $a(t)$ is obtained by multiplying an envelope function $W(t)$ into the stationary time history $a_s(t)$.

$$a(t) = W(t)a_s(t) \quad (3.2)$$

In this study, the following expression for the envelope function is used:

$$W(t) = \begin{cases} \left(\dfrac{t}{T_b}\right)^2 & 0 \leq t \leq T_b \\ 1 & T_b \leq t \leq T_c \\ \exp[-c(t - T_c)] & T_c \leq t \leq T_d \end{cases} \quad (3.3)$$

where the duration (effective duration T_e)of the stationary strong portion ($T_e = T_c$ - T_b) of ground motion is assumed equal to the average observed rupture duration in Eq.(2.18).

$$T_e = T_c - T_b = T_{f0} \quad (3.4a)$$

Then, the duration of nonstationary ground motion (T_d) can be given using the empirical relations by Ohsaki(1994):

$$T_d = 2.63T_{f0} \quad (3.4b)$$

$$T_b = [0.12 - 0.04(M_{JMA} - 7)]T_d \quad (3.4c)$$

$$T_c = [0.50 - 0.04(M_{JMA} - 7)]T_d \qquad (3.4d)$$

$$c = -\frac{\ln 0.1}{T_d - T_c} \qquad (3.4e)$$

The power spectrum $S_{aa}(\omega)$ of ground acceleration appearing in Eq.(3.1a) is constructed using the spectrum of chapter 2. Then, $S_{aa}(\omega)$ with the effective duration $T_e = T_{f0}$ is given by:

$$S_{aa}(\omega) = \frac{1}{2\pi T_e}|A(\omega)|^2 \qquad (3.5)$$

where $|A(\omega)|$ is the spectrum of ground acceleration which is given by:

$$|A(\omega)| = SUM_N(\omega)|T(\omega)||A_0(\omega)| \qquad (3.6)$$

where $|A_0(\omega)|$ is the acceleration spectrum of small earthquake observed at a distance R (the hypocenter of a small earthquake is assumed to be the same place of the extended rupture) with seismic moment m_0, which is given by:

$$|A_0(\omega)| = CA_{S0}(\omega)A_D(\omega)A_A(\omega) \qquad (3.7)$$

where C, $A_{S0}(\omega)$, $A_D(\omega)$, and $A_A(\omega)$, represent a scaling factor, a source spectrum, a diminution factor, and a local soil amplification factor, respectively.

The scaling factor and the source spectrum of the small earthquake are given by:

$$C = \frac{R(\theta, \varphi)FV}{4\pi\rho C_S^3}; \quad A_{S0}(\omega) = \frac{m_0\omega^2}{1 + (\omega/\omega_{c0})^2} \qquad (3.8)$$

where $R(\theta, \varphi)$ is the average correction factor for radiation pattern, F accounts for free-surface amplification, V accounts for the partitioning of the energy in two horizontal components, ρ is the density of the material at the source, C_S is the S wave velocity at the source, and ω_{c0} is the corner frequency of the small earthquake.

The diminution factor and the local soil amplification factor are given by:

$$A_D(\omega) = \frac{1}{1 + (\omega/\omega_{max})^n}\frac{1}{R}\exp(-\frac{\omega R}{2QC_S}); \qquad (3.9a)$$

$$A_A(\omega) = \sqrt{\frac{\rho C_S}{\rho_0 C_{S0}}}\frac{\sqrt{1 + 4h_g^2(\frac{\omega}{\omega_g})^2}}{\sqrt{(1 - (\frac{\omega}{\omega_g})^2)^2 + 4h_g^2(\frac{\omega}{\omega_g})^2}} \qquad (3.9b)$$

The first factor in $A_D(\omega)$ is the high-cut filter that accounts for the sudden drop that the spectrum exhibits above ω_{max}. It is assumed here $n = 1$. The

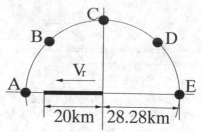

Fig.6 Plane view of the rupturing fault and the 5 stations with equal hypocentral distance

second factor is the geometric spreading factor of the S wave. The third factor is the effect of the material damping on wave propagation in which Q is a frequency-dependent attenuation factor.

The local soil amplification factor $A_A(\omega)$ is composed of the deep soil amplification from the deep ground level near the source with the density ρ and the S wave velocity C_S to the engineering ground base with ρ_0 and S wave velocity C_{S0} of about 0.5 to 1 km/s, and the shallow soil amplification from the engineering ground base to the ground surface. The first factor in $A_A(\omega)$ of Eq.(3.9b) corresponds to the deep soil amplification factor proposed by Boore (1987), and the second factor to the shallow soil amplification represented by the Kanai-Tajimi spectrum (Kanai, 1957; Tajimi, 1960). ω_g and h_g control the peak position and the peak value of the amplification factor; $\omega_g = 15.6$(rad/sec), $h_g = 0.6$ for a firm soil.

4 NUMERICAL EXAMPLE OF SAMPLE GROUND MOTIONS

Numerical example is given now in order to demonstrate an applicability of the simulation method using a stochastic summation of small earthquakes to an artificial generation of strong motions for aseismic design. The example is also given to visualize the effect of directivity of seismic waves on the ground motions.

In this numerical example, the horizontal ground acceleration time histories on rock site are generated from an earthquake with magnitude $M_{JMA} = 7.0$ and hypocentral distance $R=30$ (km). A strike slip fault with length $L=20$ (km) and width $W=10$ (km) is considered. The hypocenter is assumed to be at the bottom edge of the the extended rupture area.

The determination of the magnitude of small earthquake may be arbitrary. In this study the magnitude of small earthquake M_{JMA0} is assumed

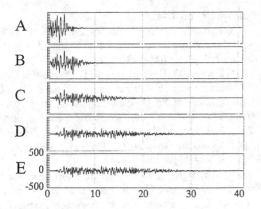

A

B

C

D

E

500
0
-500

0   10   20   30   40

Fig.7 Sample ground acceleration time histories at 5 stations on rock site with equal hypocentral distance (M_{JMA}=7.0, R=30 km)

to be 5.0, because the many empirical relationships in the parameters are usually obtained for the magnitude greater than about 4.0 to 5.0.

We determine the seismic moments of the earthquakes with M_{JMA}=7.0 and M_{JMA0}=5.0 by the following empirical relation which is obtained from the earthquakes occurred under the sea area around Japanese teritory (Sato, 1989):

$$M_0(\text{dyne-cm}) = 10^{(1.5M_{JMA} + 16.2)} \qquad (4.1)$$

From Eq.(2.7) the summation parameter N is determiend using the seismic moments, M_0 and m_0, of large and small erthquakes such as:

$$N = (\frac{M_0}{m_0})^{1/3} = 10 \qquad (4.2)$$

In evaluating the acceleration spectrum $|A_{A0}(\omega)|$ of ground motion from small earthquake, the following values are used:

$$R(\theta,\varphi) = 0.63; \quad F = 2.0; \quad V = 0.5; \qquad (4.4a)$$

$$\rho = 2.7\text{gr/cm}^3; \quad C_S = 3.6\text{km/sec}; \qquad (4.4b)$$

$$\omega_{c0} = 9.3\text{rad/sec}; \quad \omega_{max} = 28.7\text{rad/sec} \qquad (4.4c)$$

$$Q = 10^{(q_1 \log(\omega/2\pi) + q_2)} \qquad (4.4d)$$

where q_1=0.64, q_2=2.1.

The soil amplification of deep soil layers is assumed constant as:

$$\sqrt{\frac{\rho C_S}{\rho_0 C_{S0}}} = 2.0 \qquad (4.5a)$$

The soil amplification of shallow soil layers is evaluated using the following parameters:

$$\omega_q = 5.56\text{rad/sec}; \quad h_q = 0.6 \qquad (4.5b)$$

The ground acceleration time histories at 5 stations on rock site in Fig.6 are generated, with time interval Δt =0.01 sec, and $\omega_u = 2\pi \times 50$ rad/sec, N_ω=1024. The sample of acceleration time histories at 5 stations (M_{JMA}=7.0, R= 30km, on rock site) are shown in Fig.7. It is observed from Fig.7 that even in the same hypocentral distance R= 30 (km), the acceleration time histories are quite different from station to station in peak amplitude and duration. The higher acceleration and the shorter duration are observed in the stations A and B which are located in the direction of propagating rupture of the fault, while the lower acceleration and the longer duration in the stations D and E located in the oposite direction of the propagating rupture. The phenomenon observed in Fig.7 is well known as the directivity of seismic waves.

5 CONCLUSIONS

This paper describes a digital simulation method of strong earthquake ground motions using a seismological model. It can be concluded that:

(1) Based on the representation theorem of elastodynamics for the far-field seismic waves in the frequency domain, the Fourier spectrum amplitude of ground acceleration motion from an extended fault is constructed by the stochastic summation of small earthquakes proposed by Joyner and Boore (1986), where the rupture start times of each small earthquake are distributed randomly with uniform probability over the rupture duration which is also random variable with uniform probability.

(2) In the stochastic summation, a new transfer function is introduced which originally takes into account, not only the difference of the slip time functions between the extended rupture and the small rupture, but also the irregular slip motion over a heterogeneous extended rupture plane.

(3) One parameter κ introduced into the new transfer function is found to be equivalent to the ratio of local stress drop to global stress drop or the ratio of dynamic stress drop to static stress drop in the available irregular source models where the heterogeneity of either slip or stress drop on the extended rupture plane is taken into account.

(4) The source spectrum of an extended rupture by the stochastic summation have three corner frequencies, ω_{f0}, ω_c, and ω_{c0} which are related to the observed rupture duration of the extended rupture, the rise time of the extended rupture, and the rise time of the small rupture.

(5) Based on the spectral representation of stochastic waves, the simulation method of the nonstationary ground acceleration time histories is summarized.

(6) Numerical example is given in order to make clear the procedure and the evaluation of the model parameters for the generation of ground acceleration time histories.

(7) Numerical example also demonstrates the effect of the directivity of seismic waves on the acceleration time histories.

ACKNOWLEDGMENT

We thank Messrs. Kurokawa, T. and Shigenaga, M., Students of Miyazaki University, for their help in drawing the figures.

REFERENCES

[1] Aki, K., and Richards, P.G. (1980), *Quantitative Seismology, Vols.I and II*, W.H. Freeman and Company.

[2] Ben-Menahem, A. (1961), Radiation of Seismic Surface Waves from a Finite Moving Source, *Bull. of Seism. Soc. of Am., Vol 51*, pp.401-435.

[3] Boore, D.M. (1983), Stochastic Simulation of High Frequency Ground Motions Based on Seismological Models of the Radiated Spectra, *Bull. of Seism. Soc. of Am., Vol.73*, pp.1865-1894.

[4] Hanks, T.C., and McGuire, R.K. (1981), The Character of High-Frequency Strong Ground Motion, *Bull. of Seism. Soc. of Am., Vol.71*, pp.2071-2095.

[5] Harada, T., and Tanaka, T. (1995a), Digital Simulation of Earthquake Ground Motions using a Seismological Model, *Journal of Structural Mechanics and Earthquake Engineering, JSCE, No.507/I-30*, pp.209-217.

[6] Harada, T., and Tanaka, T. (1995b), Digital Simulation of Ground Motions using Stochastic Green's Function and Its Verification, *Proc. of the 3rd Japan Conference on Structural Safety and Reliability*, November, Tokyo, pp.527-534.

[7] Harada, T., and Tanaka, T. (1996), Engineering Simulation of Ground Motions From an Extended Fault, *Proc. of the 11th World Conference on Earthquake Engineering*,

[8] Hartzell, S.H. (1978), Earthquake Aftershock as Green's Functions, *Geophys. Res. Lett., Vol.5*, pp.5.

[9] Irikura, K. (1988), Prediction of Strong Accelerations Motions using Empirical Green's Function, *Proc. of 7th Japan Earthquake Engineering Symposium*, pp.37-42.

[10] Izutani, Y. (1984), Source Parameters Relevant to Heterogeneity of a Fault Plane, *J. Phys. Earth, Vol.32*, pp.511-529.

[11] Joyner, W.B., and Boore, D.M. (1986), On Simulating Large Earthquakes by Green's Function Addition of Smaller Earthquakes, in *Earthquake Source Mechanics*, Geophysical Monograph 37, Edited by Das, S., Boatwright, J., and Scholz, C.H., American Geophysical Union, Washington, D.C., pp.269-274.

[12] Kanai, K. (1957), A Semi-Empirical Formula for the Seismic Characteristics of the Ground Motions, *Bull. of Earthquake Research Institute, The University of Tokyo, Vol.35*, pp.309-325.

[13] Kanamori, H., and Anderson, D.L. (1975), Theoretical Basis of Some Empirical Relations in Seismology, *Bull. of Seism. Soc. of Am., Vol.65*, pp.1073-1095.

[14] Ohosaki, J. (1994), *Introduction of Spectral Analysis of Earthquake Ground Motions*, Kajima Publication, Tokyo, Japan, pp.199-201.

[15] Papageorgiou, A.S. (1988), On Two Characteristic Frequencies of Acceleration Spectra: Patch Corner Frequency and f_{max}, *Bull. of Seism. Soc. of Am., Vol.78*, pp.509-529.

[16] Sato, R. (1989), *Handbook of Source Parameters of Earthquakes in Japan*, Kajima Publication, Tokyo, Japan, pp.82-92.

[17] Shinozuka, M. (1974), Digital Simulation of Random Processes in Engineering Mechanics with the Aid of FFT Technique, In *Stochastic Problems in Mechanics*, Edited by Ariaratnam, S.T. and Leipholz, H.H.E., University of Waterloo Press, Waterloo, Canada, pp.277-286.

[18] Shinozuka, M., Deodatis, G., and Harada, T. (1987), Digital Simulation of Seismic Ground Motion, *Stochastic Approaches in Earthquake Engineering*, Edited by Lin, Y.K., and Minai, R., Springer-Verlag, pp.252-298.

[19] Somerville, P., Sen, M. and Cohee, B. (1991), Simulation of Strong Ground Motions Recorded during the 1985 Michoacan, Mexico and Valparaiso, Chile Earthquakes, *Bull. of Seism. Soc. of Am., Vol.81*, pp.1-27.

[20] Tajimi, H. (1960), A Statistical Method of Determining the Maximum Response of a Building Structure during a Earthquake, *Proc. of 2nd World Conference on Earthquake Engineering, Vol.2*, pp.781-797.

Structural Safety and Reliability, Shiraishi, Shinozuka & Wen (eds) © 1998 Balkema, Rotterdam, ISBN 90 5410 978 5

Stochastic interpolation and mapping of earthquake ground motion displacements

Masaru Hoshiya
Musashi Institute of Technology, Tokyo, Japan

Kinya Yamamoto
Kogyokusha College of Technology, Tokyo, Japan

ABSTRACT: Under the condition that the mean field and the covariance matrix of a stochastic field are considered to be unknown a priori, but the variogram can be estimated with sample values at observation points, a stochastic simulation theory which predicts a sample field at non-observation points has been applied to a simple example of predicting ground displacement distribution.

First, necessary formulas are presented, and then the vertical ground displacements have been conditionally simulated with observation data at Port Island on the 1995 Hyogoken-Nanbu Earthquake. And the probability distribution that the vertical ground displacement is greater than or equal to h (cm) have been mapped by the Solow's Indicator Kriging.

1 PROBLEM SETTING

Consider a Gaussian field $Z(x)$ of a discrete spatial coordinate x, where the mean field and the covariance matrix are unknown. When n sample realizations $(\underline{Z}(x_i); i = 1 \cdots n)$ are observed, the variogram of the Gaussian field can be estimated with these n sample realizations. Here it notes that the variogram is defined as : $\gamma(d) = \frac{1}{2} Var[Z(x+d) - Z(x)]$ which means that $2\gamma(d)$ is the variance of the difference between $Z(x+d)$ and $Z(x)$ separated by a distance d. With this estimated variogram, we generate a sample realization $\underline{Z}(x_r)$ at a non-observation point x_r, under a condition that when this non-observation point x_r coincides with one of observation points $x_i; (i = 1 \cdots n)$, $\underline{Z}(x_r)$ must be completely identical with the corresponding observation value. We suppose that the expected value of a stochastic field $Z(x)$ is expressed with coordinate functions as follows.

$$E[Z(x)] = \sum_{j=1}^{p} \beta_j f_j(x) \tag{1.1}$$

where β_j = an unknown weighted coefficient

$f_j(x)$ = a coordinate function.

It is assumed that, the best unbiased estimated value and the sample realization value at a non-observation point x_r are respectively given by

$$\hat{Z}(x_r) = \sum_{i=1}^{n} \lambda_i(x_r)\underline{Z}(x_i) \tag{1.2}$$

and

$$\underline{Z}(x_r) = \hat{Z}(x_r) + \varepsilon(x_r) \tag{1.3}$$

where $\hat{Z}(x_r)$ = best unbiased estimated value

 $\varepsilon(x_r)$ = error of estimation.

In Eqs.(1.2) and (1.3), it is too difficult to estimate the $\varepsilon(x_r)$, as $\hat{Z}(x_r)$ and $\varepsilon(x_r)$ are not mutually independent because of the non-homogeneous stochastic field. Therefore, we express the stochastic field $Z(x)$ with Eq.(1.1) as follows.

$$Z(x) = \sum_{j=1}^{p} \beta_j f_j(x) + W(x) \tag{1.4}$$

where $W(x)$ is a stochastic field which varies around the expected value of $Z(x)$, and the expected value of $W(x)$ becomes zero. In order to estimate the sample realization value at a non-observation point x_r, we must estimate the expected value of $Z(x)$ and generate $W(x)$.

2 THE EXPECTED VALUE OF $Z(x)$

In order to determine $E[Z(x)]$, we must estimate the coefficient β_j of Eq.(1.1) with the sample realization values at observation points such that the mean square error is minimum. When we assume the variance of the stochastic field $Z(x)$ is invariant of x, we have an objective function

$$\Delta^2 = \sum_{i=1}^{n}\left\{\underline{Z}(x_i)-\sum_{j=1}^{p}\beta_j f_j(x_i)\right\}^2 \tag{2.1}$$

However, if we can release the above condition and assume the coefficient of variation of the stochastic field $Z(x)$ is constant, we have more rationally

$$\Delta^2 = \sum_{i=1}^{n}w'\left\{\underline{Z}(x_i)-\sum_{j=1}^{p}\beta_j f_j(x_i)\right\}^2 \tag{2.2}$$

where $w' = $ coefficient of weight ($w' = 1/E[Z(x_i)]^2$). The coefficient β_j can be estimated with Eq.(2.1) or Eq.(2.2) by putting $\dfrac{\partial \Delta^2}{\partial \beta_l}=0 ; (l=1\cdots p)$.

3 CONDITIONAL SIMULATION OF $W(x_r)$

As a Gaussian stochastic field $W(x)$ with zero mean value, the best unbiased estimated value $\hat{W}(x_r)$ is given by the linear estimation with sample realization $\underline{W}(x_i); i=1\cdots n$, ($\underline{W}(x_i)=\underline{Z}(x_i)-E[Z(x_i)]$) as follows.

$$\hat{W}(x_r)=\sum_{i=1}^{n}\lambda_i(x_r)\underline{W}(x_i) \tag{3.1}$$

where $\lambda_i(x_r) = $ unknown coefficients

$x_r = $ arbitrary spatial coordinate point.

And $W(x_r)$ is expressed by

$$W(x_r)=\hat{W}(x_r)+\varepsilon(x_r) \tag{3.2}$$

where $\varepsilon(x_r)$ is the error of estimation.

We want to estimate $\lambda_i(x_r)$ so that the error variance ($\sigma^2_{\{\varepsilon(x_r)\}}=E\left[\left\{W(x_r)-\hat{W}(x_r)\right\}^2\right]$) is minimum. If we carry out the minimization, we have

$$\sum_{i=1}^{n}\lambda_i(x_r)\left\{\gamma_{il}-\frac{1}{2}\sigma^2_{\{W(x_i)\}}-\frac{1}{2}\sigma^2_{\{W(x_l)\}}\right\}=$$

$$\gamma_{il}-\frac{1}{2}\sigma^2_{\{W(x_l)\}}-\frac{1}{2}\sigma^2_{\{W(x_l)\}} \tag{3.3}$$

where $l=1\cdots n$

$\gamma_{ij} = $ variogram of $W(x)$ formulated as

$$\gamma_{ij}=\frac{1}{2}Var[W(x_i)-W(x_j)]=\frac{1}{2}E[\{W(x_i)-W(x_j)\}^2]$$

$\sigma^2_{\{W(x_i)\}} = $ variance of $W(x)$ at coordinate x_i. We can estimate the variance of $W(x)$ at discrete points with Eq.(2.1) or Eq.(2.2). $\lambda_i(x_r);(i=1\cdots n)$ are given by

$$\sigma^2_{\{\varepsilon(x_r)\}} = \sigma^2_{\{W(x_r)\}} - \frac{1}{2}\sum_{i=1}^{n}\lambda_i(x_r)\sigma^2_{\{W(x_r)\}}$$

$$-\frac{1}{2}\sum_{i=1}^{n}\lambda_i(x_r)\sigma^2_{\{W(x_i)\}}+\sum_{i=1}^{n}\lambda_i(x_r)\gamma_{il} \tag{3.4}$$

$\lambda_i(x_r)=1$ with $i=r$ and $\lambda_i(x_r)=0$ with $i\neq r$. These relations are consistent with Eq.(3.3). And $\sigma^2_{\{\varepsilon(x_i)\}}=0$ with $i=r$. Again this is consistent with Eq.(3.4). From the nature of $\lambda_i(x_r), W(x_r)$ coincides with a sample realization value at an observation point if $r=i$. We have also the following properties (Hoshiya 1995).

$$E[W(x_r)\varepsilon(x_r)]=0 \tag{3.5}$$
$$E[W(x_i)\varepsilon(x_r)]=0 \tag{3.6}$$

The correlation between $\varepsilon(x_r)$ and $\varepsilon(x_s)$ (x_r and x_s are discrete coordinate points) is given as follows.

$$E[\varepsilon(x_r)\varepsilon(x_s)]=\frac{1}{2}\left[\sigma^2_{\{W(x_r)\}}+\sigma^2_{\{W(x_s)\}}\right]$$

$$-\sum_{i=1}^{n}\lambda_i(x_s)\left\{\frac{1}{2}\left[\sigma^2_{\{W(x_r)\}}-\sigma^2_{\{W(x_i)\}}\right]\right\}+\sum_{i=1}^{n}\lambda_i(x_s)\gamma_{ri}-\gamma_{rs} \tag{3.7}$$

We can simulate $\varepsilon(x_r)$ from Eq.(3.7). And we can simulate $\varepsilon(x_r)$ with zero mean value and the variance as Eq.(3.4) by the Hoshiya's method (Hoshiya 1995, Hoshiya1994). The best unbiased estimated value (the conditional mean) $\hat{Z}(x_r)$ and the sample realization value at the non-observation point x_r are given as follows.

$$\hat{Z}(x_r)=\sum_{j=1}^{p}\beta_j f_j(x_r)+\hat{W}(x_r) \tag{3.8}$$

$$Z(x_r)=\sum_{j=1}^{p}\beta_j f_j(x_r)+\hat{W}(x_r)+\varepsilon(x_r) \tag{3.9}$$

4 NUMERICAL EVALUATION

Before we apply the above theory to real data, we numerically evaluate the conditional simulation theory with a one dimensional Gaussian field with the mean field

$$E[Z(x)]=3.0+0.391x-0.114x^2+0.026x^3$$
$$-0.0020x^4+0.0000641x^5 \tag{4.1}$$

and the covariance is

$$Cov[Z(x_l)Z(x_m)]=\exp\left[-\frac{|x_l-x_m|}{2.0}\right] \tag{4.2}$$

We use a sample set of 11 sample realization values ($\underline{Z}(x_i); i=1\cdots 11$) standing in line at same space. They are made by the Choleski's decomposition method.

The raw variogram estimated from the sample realization values $\underline{W}(x_i); i = 1 \cdots 11$ is shown in Fig. 1. Also shown is a continuous variogram fitted with the raw variogram. The correlation between discrete points whose distance is near is stronger than one whose distance is far so that we use the reciprocal of a distance of two discrete points x_i and x_j as a weight coefficient. The continuous variogram is obtained as follows.

$$\gamma_{ij} = 0.680 \left[1.0 - \exp\left(-\frac{|x_i - x_j|}{2.5} \right) \right] \qquad (4.3)$$

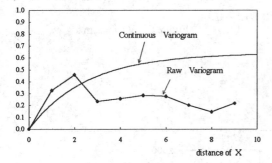

Figure 1　Variogram

And we use the expected value and the variance value given by Eq.(2.1). The conditional mean by Eq.(3.8), the conditional standard deviation by Eq.(3.4) and the non-conditional standard deviation by Eq.(2.1) are shown in Fig.2. The conditional standard deviations stay between the non-conditional standard deviations in Fig.2.

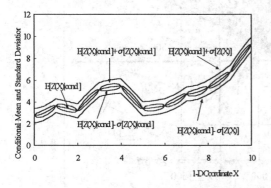

Figure 2　Analytical Solution

This means that the uncertainties in the sample stochastic field was decreased by the information from sample realization values. The simulated

values by the Hoshiya's method are shown in Fig.3.

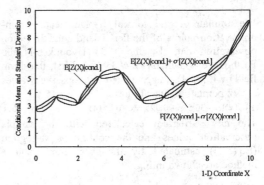

Figure 3　Simulation

We simulated 1000 values at each point and calculated the conditional mean and the conditional standard deviations. The statistics in Fig.2 and Fig.3 are almost agreed. Fig.4 shows a few sample fields that always pass through observation points.

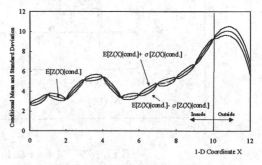

Figure 4　Conditional Sample Fields

It is observed that the conditional mean and the conditional deviations where the estimated points are outside of the sample realization points turn out to be close to the mean and standard deviations given by Eq.(2.1) in Fig.5.

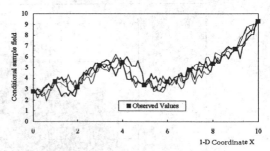

Figure 5 Inside and Outside of the Observation Points

5 SIMULATION OF GROUND DISPLACEMENT

We simulate ground vertical displacements at non-observation points of the Port Island conditioned on observation data by the 1995 Hyogoken-Nanbu Earthquake (Hamada *et al* 1995). First, the mean field by Eq.(2.1) was estimated with observed values at 672 points(Fig.7) as follows.

$$E[Z(x)] = -30.585 + 0.02522x - 0.04141y \qquad (5.1)$$

The raw variogram calculated with the sample observation values and the continuous variogram (Eq.(5.2)) estimated by the least mean square method are shown in Fig.6.

$$\gamma(d) = 3427.7\left[1.0 - \exp\left(-\frac{d}{231}\right)\right] \qquad (5.2)$$

where d = distance between two discrete points. Then the conditional mean $\hat{Z}(x_r)$ at non-observation points x_r were estimated and error of estimation $\varepsilon(x_r)$ were generated by Eq.(3.7).

Figure 8 shows a sample field of the ground vertical displacements.

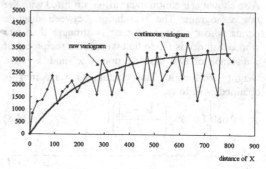

Figure 6   Variogram

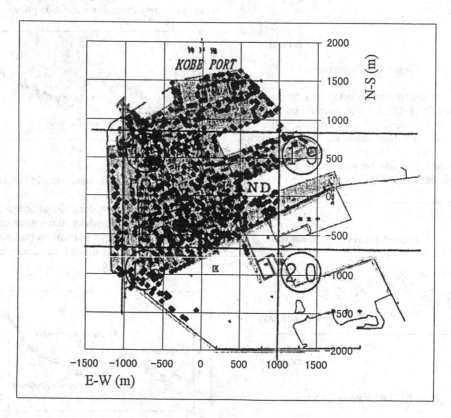

Figure 7   Observation Points at Port Island

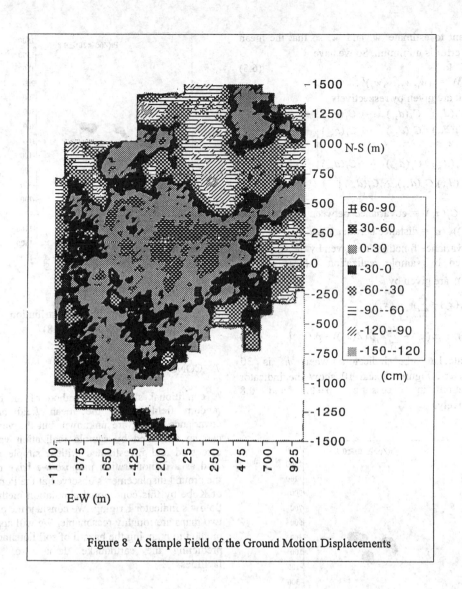

Figure 8 A Sample Field of the Ground Motion Displacements

Legend (cm):
- 60-90
- 30-60
- 0-30
- -30-0
- -60--30
- -90--60
- -120--90
- -150--120

N-S (m) axis values: -1500, -1250, -1000, -750, -500, -250, 0, -250, -500, -750, -1000, -1250, -1500

E-W (m) axis values: -1100, -875, -650, -425, -200, 25, 250, 475, 700, 925

6 MAPPING THE GROUND DISPLACEMENT BY INDICATOR KRIGING

We map the Solow's indicator distribution based on the aforesaid ground displacement data. We define the indicator as follows.

$$I(Z(x)) = 1 \quad if \quad Z(x) \geq h$$
$$= 0 \quad if \quad Z(x) < h \qquad (6.1)$$

where h = a specified ground displacement value.
The probability that $Z(x)$ is greater than or equal to h is given by

$$\Pr(I(Z(x)) = 1) = p_1(x) \qquad (6.2)$$

When sample values at n points are observed, the conditional probability that $I(Z(x_r))$ is 1 at a non-observation point x_r is given by

$$\Pr[I(Z(x_r)) = 1 \mid I(Z(x_i)) = j_i, i = 1 \cdots n]$$
$$= E[I(Z(x_r)) = 1 \mid I(Z(x_i)) = j_i, i = 1 \cdots n] \qquad (6.3)$$

where $j = 1$ or 0.
We estimate an indicator at a non-observation point x_r by the linear minimum variance unbiased estimation. The best unbiased estimated value $\hat{I}(Z(x_r))$ is expressed by

$$\hat{I}(Z(x_r)) = w_r + \sum_{i=1}^{n} w_i I(Z(x_i)) \qquad (6.4)$$

where w_r = unknown weighted coefficient

w_i = unknown weighted coefficient $(i = 1 \cdots n)$.

1483

We want to estimate w_r and w_i so that the mean square error is minimum. So we have

$$\mathbf{W} = \mathbf{K}^{-1}\mathbf{k} \qquad (6.5)$$

where $\mathbf{W} = (w_1, w_2, \cdots, w_n)^T$.

$\mathbf{K}$ and $\mathbf{k}$ are given by respectively

$$\mathbf{K} = \begin{bmatrix} C_I(d_{11}) & C_I(d_{21}) & \cdots & C_I(d_{n1}) \\ C_I(d_{12}) & C_I(d_{22}) & \cdots & C_I(d_{n2}) \\ \vdots & \vdots & \ddots & \vdots \\ C_I(d_{1n}) & C_I(d_{2n}) & \cdots & C_I(d_{m}) \end{bmatrix} \qquad (6.6)$$

$$\mathbf{k} = \left[C_I(d_{r1}), C_I(d_{r2}), \cdots, C_I(d_{m}) \right]^T \qquad (6.7)$$

where $C_I(d_{ij})$ = covariance between $I(Z(x_i))$ and $I(Z(x_j))$. d_{ij} = distance between x_i and x_j.

The covariance functions are given by the variogram estimated by sample realization values. w_r and $\hat{I}(Z(x_r))$ are given by

$$w_r = p_1(x_r) - \sum_{j=1}^{n} w_j p_1(x_j) \qquad (6.8)$$

$$\hat{I}(Z(x_r)) = p_1(x_r) + \sum_{j=1}^{n} w_j \left[I(Z(x_j)) - p_1(x_j) \right] \qquad (6.9)$$

We calculate the indicators when h is 30 centimeters. Figures 9 and 10 show the indicator distribution in excess of $p = 0.7$ and 0.8 respectively.

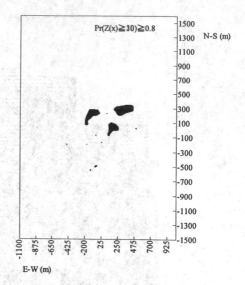

Figure 10   Indicator Distribution
(h=30(cm), $p_1 \geqq 0.8$)

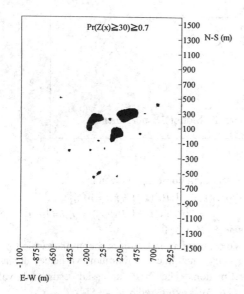

Figure 9   Indicator Distribution
(h=30(cm), $p_1 \geqq 0.7$)

7   CONCLUSION

A conditional simulation method of an intrinsic random field where the mean field and the covariance matrix are unknown, but the variogram can be estimated by sample realization values is discussed and investigated with a simple sample. And as a demonstration purpose we have mapped the ground displacements observed at the Port Island of Kobe by this conditional simulation method and Solow's Indicator Kriging. We consider the obtained two maps are roughly reasonable. We will apply this method to mapping the hazard of soil liquefaction or predicting the earthquake damage of lifeline facilities.

REFERENCES

Yamamoto,K. and Hoshiya,M. 1996, Application of conditional stochastic field to mapping of ground vertical displacement, Proceeding of the sixth Japan-U.S. workshop on earthquake registration design of lifeline facilities and countermeasures against soil liquefaction, Tokyo, Japan, June 11-13, 1996, pp.153-162

Hoshiya,M. and Yamamoto,K., 1995, Conditional simulation of an intrinsic random field, Proceedings of the 50th annual conference of JSCE, pp.1290~1291

Hoshiya,M., · 1995, Kriging and conditional simulation of Gaussian field, Jour. of Eng. Mech. ASCE, Vol. 121 No. 2, pp.181~186

Hoshiya,M., 1994, Conditional simulation of a stochastic field, ICOSSAR '93, pp.349~353

Delhomme,J.P., 1978, Kriging in the Hydrosciences, Advances in Water Resources Vol.1 No.5, pp.251~266

Bastin,G. and Gevers,M., 1985, Identification and optimal estimation of random fields from scattered point-wise data, Automatica, Vol.21, No.2, pp.139~155

Ang,H-S. and Tang,H., Probability concepts in engineering planning and design, translated by Itoh,M. and Kameda,H., Maruzen corporation

Solow,A., 1986, Mapping by simple indicator kriging, Mathematical Geology, Vol.18, No.3, pp.335~352

Hamada,M., Isoyama,R. and Wakamatsu,K., 1995, The 1995 Hyogoken-Nanbu(Kobe) Earthquake, Liquefaction, Ground Displacement and Soil Condition in Hanshin Area, published by Association for development of earthquake prediction

Structural Safety and Reliability, Shiraishi, Shinozuka & Wen (eds)© 1998 Balkema, Rotterdam, ISBN 90 5410 978 5

Segmental cross-spectrum in microtremor spectral ratio analysis

M.R.Ghayamghamian
International Institute of Earthquake Engineering and Seismology, Geotechnical Division, Tehran, Iran

H.Kawakami
Saitama University, Department of Civil and Environmental Engineering, Japan

ABSTRACT: The aspects of spectral analysis for site response evaluation are investigated. The segmental cross-spectrum is introduced in spectral analysis of microtremor as an effective tool in compensation of unknown effects (e.g., source effects). The performance of segmental cross-spectrum in contrast with the conventional methods, i.e. Fourier or power spectra, is investigated through the mathematical modeling and numerical simulations. Furthermore, in numerical simulations the effect of averaging the spectrum is also accounted. Results of investigation indicate that segmental cross-spectrum gives more reliable results for both amplification factor and predominant resonance frequency of the site than the conventional methods. Therefore, the proposed method can eliminate the main restriction in application of microtremors for evaluation of site response.

1. INTRODUCTION

The effects of local site condition on ground motion characteristics are clearly revealed in past earthquakes. Therefore, the site response is an important factor that should be considered in microzonation study for aseismic design and prevention of seismic disaster. For this purpose, numerical and analytical methods are available. However, detailed geotechnical studies as well as geophysical investigation are necessary for such an analysis, which restricts the application of them. To avoid these hindrances, microtremors can be utilized as an effective tool. The application of microtremors to determine dynamic characteristics of sites was pioneered by Kanai and his associates (Kanai and Tanaka, 1954, 1961). The use of microtremors is convenient because of its simplicity, ease of operation, economy and minimal disturbance to other activities. On the other hand, source effects can obscure microtremors response of the site especially for short period microtremors addressed in this study. The microtremors, less than two seconds in duration, are mainly excited by human activities such as traffic or machinery noise. Aki (1988) reviewed the problems associated with the determination of site effects using microtremors. He identified the strong dependence of microtremors on the very local sources that excited them. In addition, the difficulty

in separation of source from site effects is mentioned as a main disadvantage in interpretation of microtremors since the source is different for various sites. As an example, Udwadia and Trifunac (1972) found that spectral analysis of microtremors does not correspond to site response estimated from earthquake data. Consequently, the compensation of the source effects is the main problem in microtremor response of a site.

In this study, segmental cross-spectrum is introduced as a new method in spectral ratio of microtremors. In order to show the advantages of segmental cross-spectrum in comparison with conventional Fourier or power spectra, two kinds of investigation are carried out by using mathematical and numerical simulations. First, the comparison between segmental cross-spectrum and power spectrum was made through derivation of the mathematical model . Second, the system identification by microtremor data was numerically simulated considering the noise and source effects. Moreover, the effect of averaging the spectra is considered in both segmental cross-spectrum and conventional methods.

2. SPECTRAL RATIO ANALYSIS AND PROPOSED METHOD

Cross-correlation function can detect and recover the

signal (here the site response) buried in extraneous noise, where the signal is not necessarily of a periodic form. However, autocorrelation function is useful for this application when the signal is periodic and cannot extract a random signal from extraneous noise. Specifically, if a noise free replica of the signal (either random or periodic) which one wishes to detect is available, then a cross-correlation of the signal plus noise with a stored replica of the signal alone will extract the correlation function of the signal. Furthermore, in the case of periodic signals, the cross-correlation function will provide a greater output signal-to-noise ratio than will the autocorrelation function for any given input signal-to-noise ratio and sample record length (Bendat and Piersol, 1971 & 1984).

This substantial concept of cross-spectrum in comparison with Fourier or power spectra can play a considerable role in spectral ratio analysis of the site. Research has been done on the effectiveness of cross-spectrum in spectral ratio of sediment site to rock site by using earthquake motion (Steidl 1993, Field et al. 1992, Safak 1991). An explanation of the segmental cross-spectrum application presented in this study will be preceded by a brief review of previous cross-spectrum application.

Considering the input, $x(t)$, and output, $y(t)$, to the linear system, the relation between input and output can simply be written as:

$$|H(f)| = \frac{|Y(f)|}{|X(f)|} \quad (1)$$

where $X(f)$ is the Fourier transform of the input at the base of sediments, $H(f)$ is the transfer function, and $Y(f)$ is the Fourier transform of the output at the surface of the sediment site (Fig.1). Accordingly, the site response can be evaluated if the output and input motions for the given earthquake are known exactly. If random noise is present in the observations, which will always be the case in practice, the smoothing techniques will be applied to both numerator and denominator spectra before taking the ratio. The spectral ratio, $|H(f)|$, is then given by:

$$|H(f)| = \frac{<|Y(f)|>}{<|X(f)|>} \quad (2)$$

or

$$|H(f)| = \frac{<|S_{xy}(f)|>}{<|S_{xx}(f)|>} \quad (3)$$

where $S_{xx}(f)$ and $S_{xy}(f)$ are the two-sided power spectral and cross-spectral density functions respectively which is defined as:

$$S_{xx}(f) = \int_{-\infty}^{\infty} R_{xx}(\tau) e^{-i2\pi f\tau} d\tau$$

$$S_{xy}(f) = \int_{-\infty}^{\infty} R_{xy}(\tau) e^{-i2\pi f\tau} d\tau \quad (4)$$

and $< . >$ denotes a smoothed estimate determined by one of the many smoothing schemes employed in spectral analysis. In Eqs. (4), $R_{xx}(\tau)$ $R_{xy}(\tau)$ are autocorrelation and cross-correlation functions respectively. The definition of cross-spectrum in Eq. (3) was used in site effect identification using earthquake records (Field et al. 1992, Steidl 1993, Safak 1991). Field (1994) believed that there is no significant difference between cross-spectrum and Fourier spectrum. However, Bendat and Piersol (1971,1984) as well as Steidl (1993) suggested that the cross-spectrum should be calculated together with Fourier or power spectra for better understanding of site effects. In the discussion on the application of cross-spectrum by the above researchers, the earthquake motion was used in analysis.

Here, for evaluation of site effects by using microtremors a new method in spectral ratio analysis is introduced as a segmental cross-spectrum. Accordingly, the system response is calculated by:

$$|H(f)|^2 = \frac{<|S_{yy'}(f)|>}{<|S_{xx'}(f)|>} \quad (5)$$

where $S_{yy'}(f)$ and $S_{xx'}(f)$ are the two-sided cross-spectral functions of two different segments of output and corresponding input records respectively. The basic physical concept behind this definition is that in microtremors the unknown effects (difference in source and/or noise) vary in the whole length of the record. Consequently, segmental cross-correlation of two different segments of the input or output compensates the random noise and source effects for accurate evaluation of the site response by microtremors. This new definition and its

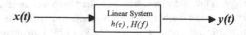

Fig. 1 Single input-output linear system

effectiveness on microtremors are investigated by analytical and numerical analyses. Once more, the attention to the different definition of site response evaluation in Eqs. (3) and (5) is emphasized here to the better understanding of analytical and numerical investigations in the next sections.

3. MATHEMATICAL MODELING OF TRANSFER FUNCTION USING SEGMENTAL CROSS-SPECTRUM AND POWER SPECTRUM WITH NOISE

Considering a linear system with a weighting function $h(\tau)$ and a frequency response function $H(f)$, as shown in Fig. 1, the output $y(t)$ can be given by:

$$y(t) = \int_{-\infty}^{+\infty} h(\tau)x(t-\tau)d\tau \tag{6}$$

Introducing the unknown effects in output and input as $y_n(t)$ and $x_n(t)$ respectively in Eq. (6), the recorded output, $y^*(t)$, and input, $x^*(t)$, can be written as:

$$x^*(t) = x(t) + x_n(t)$$
$$y^*(t) = y(t) + y_n(t) \tag{7}$$

Substituting Eqs. (7) in (6) yields:

$$y^*(t) - y_n(t) = \int_{-\infty}^{+\infty} h(\tau)[x^*(t-\tau) - x_n(t-\tau)]\, d\tau \tag{8}$$

The product, $[y^*(t) - y_n(t)][y^*(t+\tau) - y_n(t+\tau)]$ for a pair of times t and $t+\tau$, is given by:

$$[y^*(t) - y_n(t)][y^*(t+\tau) - y_n(t+\tau)]$$
$$= \iint_{-\infty}^{+\infty} h(\xi)\, h(\eta)\, [x^*(t-\xi) - x_n(t-\xi)]\, [x^*(t+\tau-\eta)$$
$$- x_n(t+\tau-\eta)]\, d\xi\, d\eta \tag{9}$$

The expected value of Eq. (9) yields:

$$R_{y^*y^*}(\tau) - R_{y^*y_n}(\tau) - R_{y_ny^*}(\tau) + R_{y_ny_n}(\tau)$$
$$= \iint_{-\infty}^{+\infty} h(\xi)h(\eta)[R_{x^*x^*}(\tau-\eta+\xi) - R_{x^*x_n}(\tau-\eta+\xi)$$
$$- R_{x_nx^*}(\tau-\eta+\xi) + R_{x_nx_n}(\tau-\eta+\xi)]d\xi\, d\eta \tag{10}$$

where $R_{yy}(\tau) = E[y(t)\, y(t+\tau)]$, $R_{x^*x_n}(\tau) = E[x^*(t)\, x_n(t+\tau)]$, etc. represent the autocorrelation and cross-correlation functions. The stationary segmental cross-correlation function between two output segments, $y(t)$ and $y'(t)$, corresponding to input segments, $x(t)$ and $x'(t)$ respectively, can be derived as:

$$[y^*(t) - y_n(t)]\left[y'^*(t+\tau) - y'_n(t+\tau)\right]$$

$$= \iint_{-\infty}^{+\infty} h(\xi)h(\eta)\, [x^*(t-\xi) - x_n(t-\xi)][x'^*(t+\tau-\eta)$$
$$- x'_n(t+\tau-\eta)]d\xi\, d\eta \tag{11}$$

where $y'^*(t)$ and $x'^*(t)$ are another set of recorded motions. The expected value of Eq. (11) gives:

$$R_{y^*y'^*}(\tau) - R_{y^*y'_n}(\tau) - R_{y_ny'^*}(\tau) + R_{y_ny'_n}(\tau)$$
$$= \iint_{-\infty}^{+\infty} h(\xi)h(\eta)[R_{x^*x'^*}(\tau-\eta+\xi) - R_{x^*x'_n}(\tau-\eta+\xi)$$
$$- R_{x_nx'^*}(\tau-\eta+\xi) + R_{x_nx'_n}(\tau-\eta+\xi)]d\xi\, d\eta \tag{12}$$

The Wiener-Khintchine transform of Eqs. (10) and (12) yields the conventional spectrum and segmental cross-spectrum density relations respectively, as follows:

$$S_{y^*y^*}(f) - S_{y^*y_n}(f) - S_{y_ny^*}(f) + S_{y_ny_n}(f)$$
$$= |H(f)|^2 [S_{x^*x^*}(f) - S_{x^*x_n}(f) - S_{x_nx^*}(f) + S_{x_nx_n}(f)] \tag{13}$$

and

$$S_{y^*y'^*}(f) - S_{y^*y'_n}(f) - S_{y_ny'^*}(f) + S_{y_ny'_n}(f)$$
$$= |H(f)|^2[S_{x^*x'^*}(f) - S_{x^*x'_n}(f) - S_{x_nx'^*}(f)$$
$$+ S_{x_nx'_n}(f)] \tag{14}$$

where $S_{y^*y'_n}(f)$, $S_{x^*x'_n}(f)$, etc. show the two-sided spectral density functions.

By introducing the independence of known effects (site response) from unknown effects (noise or source effects), Eqs. (15) can be written from Eqs. (7) as:

$$S_{x^*x_n}(f) = S_{x_nx^*}(f) = S_{x_nx_n}(f)$$
$$S_{y^*y_n}(f) = S_{y_ny^*}(f) = S_{y_ny_n}(f) \tag{15}$$

Moreover, considering the independence between unknown effects, the transfer function by using power spectrum and segmental cross-spectrum can be given respectively as:

$$|H(f)|^2 = \frac{S_{y^*y^*}(f) - S_{y_ny_n}(f)}{S_{x^*x^*}(f) - S_{x_nx_n}(f)} \tag{16}$$

$$|H(f)|^2 = \frac{S_{y^*y'^*}(f)}{S_{x^*x'^*}(f)} \tag{17}$$

As can be seen in Eq. (16), the noise spectral density functions affect the transfer function. However, in Eq. (17), the noise spectral density functions are effectively removed . Then, comparing Eq. (16) and (17) shows that unknown effects can be strongly compensated by segmental cross-spectrum, but

1489

contaminate power spectrum. Hence, segmental cross-spectrum can reveal the transfer function of the system more accurately. This is an important result for spectral analysis of weak motion where the signal is buried in extraneous noise and especially microtremor data. In addition, for our purposes, we will consider that there is no fundamental difference between Fourier amplitude and power spectral density spectra.

In the above paragraphs, the known effect or signal refers to the site response and the unknown effects are considered as a noise in input and output or the difference in the source of microtremors. In the following, the validation of mathematical models for segmental cross-spectrum in contrast with power spectrum will be proven via two types of numerical analysis.

4. NUMERICAL ANALYSIS (1)-NOISE EFFECT

In this part, the noise effects in input and output of the soil system are investigated. Here, the term noise is referred to the noise measurements in input and output that do not pass through the system. The analysis was done through the response of microtremors to a simple soil model. Fig. 2 shows the soil model and its analytical transfer function.

The model is subjected to microtremor data as an input motion. The computer program is developed to calculate the output at the soil surface . In the computer code, vertical propagation of shear waves through the linear viscoelastic soil system is considered. Noise effects are considered by adding a different white noise to input and output motions.

The response of site is calculated by spectral ratio (output/input) using segmental cross-spectrum and power spectrum and smoothed using moving average spectral window with 0.4 Hz width. Additionally, in calculation of transfer functions, the square root was taken as can be understood from Eqs. (16) and (17). The calculated transfer functions are shown in Fig. 3. As expected from Eqs. (16) and (17), the transfer function using segmental cross-spectrum is in better agreement with the analytical one (Fig. 2). However, the transfer function using power spectrum is affected by noise effects especially in the predominant frequency which is of more interest in engineering applications.

It should be mentioned that in microtremor response of the site, mostly, the identification of the system would depend on peaks of transfer function.

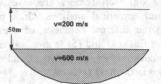
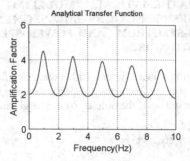

Fig. 2 Simple soil model and its analytical transfer function

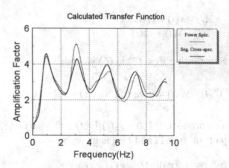

Fig. 3 Results of numerical modeling (1): Soil transfer function using segmental cross-spectrum and power spectrum while adding white noise to input and output motions.

Practically, the first peak in transfer function would be considered as predominant resonance frequency. In actual case, the shape of transfer function is more complicated. Then, according to the results in Fig. 3, the identification of system using power spectrum would be different from actual one.

Therefore, the results of numerical analysis (1) support the application of segmental cross-spectrum in microtremor data analysis. In the second numerical analysis, the source effects will be accounted as the main disadvantage factor in system identification using microtremors.

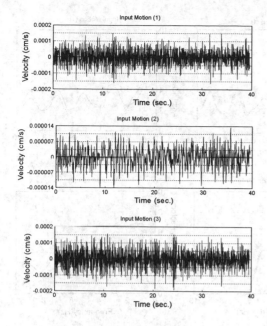

Fig. 4 Time histories of microtremors for 20 s of horizontal component (N-S direction)

5. NUMERICAL ANALYSIS (2)-SOURCE EFFECTS

In the second numerical analysis the unknown effects are considered as a difference in the source of microtremors. For this purpose, the soil model shown in Fig. 2 is subjected to the three sets of microtremor data with 40.96s length as an input motion (Fig. 4). The different microtremor input motions were considered to make the results more reliable and account for possible difference in frequency content of input motions. The motion at surface layer was calculated for each set by computer program. Then, the input and output motions were divided into four segments with 10.24s length. The segmental cross- and power spectra were calculated on input and output motions with smoothing to get the transfer function of soil. In calculation of transfer function using spectral ratio of output to input motions, three cases are considered in selecting the segments:

I. Selecting same segments for input and output motions to simulate the same source for microtremors.

II. Selecting different segments for input and output motions to simulate the difference in the source of microtremors.

Fig. 5 The pattern of selecting segments in numerical analysis (2) (C and A for segmental cross-spectrum and power spectrum respectively).

III. Selecting two sets (four segments) of different input and output motions and averaging between them to show the averaging effects in microtremor response of the site.

The pattern of selecting segments and the calculated amplification functions for each case are shown in Figs. 5 and 6, respectively.

In case I, when there is no difference in source of microtremors, the system can be accurately defined by either method (Fig. 6.a). However, by comparing between calculated and analytical transfer functions in case II (Figs. 2 and 6.b), it is clear that the segmental cross-spectrum gives reliable results for the predominant frequency and amplification factor, which are important in engineering application.

As shown in Fig. 6.b, the transfer functions evaluated by power spectrum show higher amplification than the actual one at the second and forth resonance frequencies for input motions one and two respectively. Furthermore, for input motion 3 in Fig. 6.b, the calculated transfer function using power spectrum cannot even identify the predominant resonance frequency. However, transfer functions evaluated by segmental cross-spectrum are in significant agreement with the analytical one.

In case III, an attempt was made to account for the effect of averaging of transfer functions derived from different sets of data for better identification of the system. As can be seen in Fig. 6.c, the averaging of transfer functions improves the results. However, still, the averaged transfer functions using segmental cross-spectrum are in better agreement with the analytical transfer function.

The other important parameter for system identification is the amplification factor of the system.

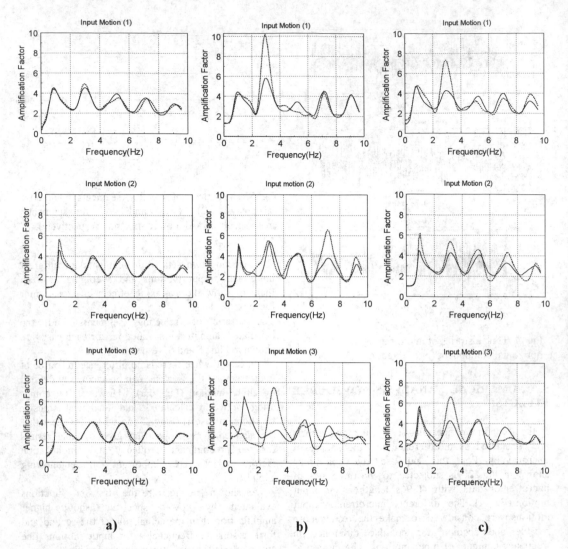

Fig. 6 Results of numerical modeling (2): transfer function by using segmental cross-spectrum (continuous line) and power spectrum (dotted line): a) case I, b) case II, c) case III

As mentioned in section 2, researches have been done for accurate determination of this factor for weak earthquakes (Field et al. 1992, Safak 1991). Here, from Fig. 6, it is clear that amplification factor can be evaluated more accurately for microtremors using segmental cross-spectrum than conventional Fourier or power spectra. Therefore, in conclusion of our second numerical analysis the results testify the application of segmental cross-spectrum in comparison with power spectrum for microtremor data.

6. CONCLUSIONS AND DISCUSSIONS

The aspects of spectral analysis for earthquake and microtremor data for site response evaluation are studied. The segmental cross-spectrum is introduced in spectral analysis of microtremors as an effective tool in compensation of source effects and noise in the input and output measurements that does not pass through the system.

The performance of segmental cross-spectrum in contrast with the conventional Fourier or power spectra is investigated through the analytical modeling and numerical simulations. Results from the above analysis indicate that the segmental cross-spectrum gives more reliable results for predominant resonance frequency and amplification factor of the soil system.

It is clear that the above study should be accompanied by the investigation on the application of segmental cross-spectrum and power spectrum to the actual microtremor measurements. These have been done by Ghayamghamian (1997). But, due to space limitation they will not be given here. However, some results of investigation will proceed in brief.

The effects of segmental cross-spectrum and power spectrum in spectral ratio analysis of microtremor measurements which were simultaneously recorded at nine soil and rock sites were investigated by using the following two techniques:

1. The spectral ratio of horizontal components that were recorded at sedimentary (Hs) and rock (Hr) sites.

2. The spectral ratio of the horizontal (H) to vertical (V) components (Nakamura, 1989).

For spectral analysis one part of a 20.48s long simultaneous recording was selected from the stationary part of a 180s recording. The amplification function was calculated by using H/V and Hs/Hr spectral ratios.

The segmental cross- and power spectra were applied in spectral analysis for both cases. Vertical and horizontal spectra were calculated and smoothed three times by using moving average spectral window. Hs/Hr spectral ratio was next calculated for soil sites using the records of reference rock stations. Then, the H/V spectral ratio was calculated for all sites (Figs. 3.6-3.9 in Ghayamghamian, 1997). Additionally, in calculation of spectral ratios, square root was taken from the original horizontal and vertical spectra as can be understood from Eqs. (16) and (17).

The results of microtremor data analysis also confirm the application of segmental cross-spectrum in microtremor data. Furthermore, the results demonstrate that segmental cross-spectrum together with H/V technique can strongly compensate for the source effects in microtremor response of the sites (Ghayamghamian, 1997). This is an important conclusion regarding the possibility of removing source from local site effects in microtremors.

One deficiency of microtremor analysis to obtain soil transfer functions for seismic analysis or microzonation studies is the influence of the excitation amplitude on soil response. This effect may result in a frequency shift or in a reduced system band width. The transfer function of the sites with different excitation levels demonstrates more appropriate results than conventional methods using segmental cross-spectrum and H/V technique (Figs. 3.7 and 3.8 in Ghayamghamain, 1997). This may also verifies the efficiency of segmental cross-spectrum in eliminating the effect of difference in excitation level on soil response. Finally, the application of H/V technique together with segmental cross-spectrum was emphasized by the outcome.

REFERENCES

Aki, K. 1988. Local site effects on strong ground motion , *Proc. 2nd Conf. on Earth. Eng. and Soil Dyn.*, 103-155.

Aki, K. and Irikura, K. 1991. Characterization and mapping of earthquake shaking for seismic zonation. *Proc. 4th Int. Conf. on Seismic Zonation* 1: 61-110.

Bendat, A. S. & Piersol, A. G. 1971. Random data: analysis and measurement procedures. *John Wiley and Sons:* New York.

Bendat, J. S. & Piersol, A. G.1984. Engineering application of correlation and spectral analysis. *John Wiley and Sons*: New York.

Field, E. H., Jacob, K. H. & Hough, S. E. 1992. Earthquake site response estimation: a weak motion case study. *Bull. Seis. Soc. Am.* Vol. 88 No. 6: 2283-2307.

Field, E. H. 1994, Discussion of variation of site response at the UCSB dense array of portable accelerometers by J. H. Steidl. *Earth. Spectra* Vol. 10 No.2: 451-455.

Finn, W. D. L. 1991. Geotechnical engineering aspects of microzonation. *Proc.4th Int. Conf. on seismic zonation* vol.1 : Stanford: California: 199-256.

Ghayamghamian, M.R. 1992. The comparison of 2-D finite elements site response analysis and microtremor measurements for evaluation of site amplifications. *Int. seminar on earthquake prognostic*: Tehran-Iran.

Ghayamghamian, M.R., Kawakami, H. and Mogi, H. 1995. Microtremor data analysis for seismic microzonation in north of Tehran, *Proc. of 1st. Int. Conf. on Earth. Geot. Eng.*: Japan: 561-566.

Ghayamghamian, M. R. 1997. Non-linear and linear response of the site with evaluation of actual dynamic soil properties using vertical array accelerograms and microtremors. *Ph.D.*

Dissertation: Saitama University, Japan.

Jafary, M. K. and Ghayamghamian, M. R. 1991. Seismic hazard assessment and risk analysis in Tehran. *Internal Report*, International Institute of Earthquake Engineering and Seismology: Tehran: Iran.

Kanai, K. 1983. Engineering seismology. *University of Tokyo press*: Tokyo.

Kanai, K. & Tanaka, T. 1954. Measurement of microtremor. *Bull. Earth. Res. Inst. 32:* Tokyo University: 199-209.

Kanai, K. & Tanaka T. 1961. On microtremors VIII. *Bull. Earth. Res. Inst. 39:* 97-114.

Lermo, J. & Chavez-Garcia, F.J. 1994. Are microtremors useful in site response evaluation?. *Bull. Seism. Soc. Am.* 84: 1350-1364.

Mogi, H. Kawakami, H. & Ghayamghamian, M.R. 1995. Probability distribution of spectra and spectral ratios. *Proc. of 1st. Int. Conf. on Eart. Geot. Eng.:* 573-578.

Nakamura, Y. 1989. A method for dynamic characteristics estimations of surface using microtremors on the ground surface. *QR of RTRI:* Vol. 30, No.1: 25-33.

Ohmachi, T. & Nakamura Y. 1992. Local site effects detected by microtremors measurements on damage due to the 1990 Philippine earthquake. *Proceedings of the tenth world conference on earthquake engineering.*

Osaki, Y. 1992. Principal of earthquake spectral analysis. *Kajima Inc.:* Tokyo (in Japanese).

Safak, E. 1991. Problems with using spectral ratios to estimate site amplification. *Proc. of 1st. Int. Conf. on Seis. Zonation:* United State of America: 277-283.

Steidl, H. J. 1993. Variation of site response at the UCSB dense array of portable accelerometers. *Earth. Spectra* Vol.9, No.2: 289-302.

Udwadia, F. E. and Trifunac, M. D. 1972. Investigation of earthquake and microtremor ground motions. *Earth. Eng. Res. Lab:* 72-02.

Structural Safety and Reliability, Shiraishi, Shinozuka & Wen (eds) © 1998 Balkema, Rotterdam, ISBN 90 5410 978 5

Physical patterns in characteristics of spatially variable seismic ground motions

Aspasia Zerva
Department of Civil and Architectural Engineering, Drexel University, Philadelphia, Pa., USA

Ouqi Zhang
Center for Building Envelope Design, Drexel University, Philadelphia, Pa., USA

ABSTRACT: A methodology for the investigation of the spatial variation of seismic ground motions is presented. The application of the approach to data recorded at the SMART-1 array in Lotung, Taiwan, suggested that the amplitude and phase variability of the seismic motions over extended areas around a common, coherent component are correlated; i.e., increase in the variability of the amplitudes of the motions recorded at each individual station around a common amplitude identified from the consideration of data recorded at a number of array stations implies increase in the variability of the phases at the individual stations around the common phase, and vice versa. The variabilities of amplitudes and phases around the common component appear also to be, qualitatively, associated with physical parameters. Thus, the approach sets bases for the possible physical modeling of spatially variable seismic ground motions.

1 INTRODUCTION

The spatial variability of seismic ground motions has an important effect on the response of lifelines, such as bridges, pipelines and communication transmission systems. It results from the apparent propagation of the waveforms on the ground surface and the differences in their shape at the various locations. The description of the spatial variability is based on probabilistic, regression, analyses of data recorded at dense instrument arrays. Commonly, the more well understood phenomenon of the apparent propagation of the motions on the ground surface is considered independently of the other spatial variability causes. The main descriptor of the remaining spatial variability causes is the coherence, defined as the ratio of the cross spectrum of the motions at two recording stations divided by the product of the power spectra at the two stations. In coherence estimates, the power spectra of the motions, which are proportional to the square of the Fourier amplitude, are eventually canceled, and are subsequently assumed to be the same at all locations. Consequently, the variability in the motions described by the coherence is attributed mainly to their Fourier phase differences between various locations. Simulations of spatially variable seismic ground motions are also, generally, performed according to this same amplitude-variable phase concept.

The analyses of recorded data has indicated that the coherency (square root of coherence) is a function exponentially decaying with separation distance and frequency. However, different expressions and degrees of exponential decay fit data recorded at different sites or at the same site but for different earthquakes; as a result, there is a multitude of spatial variability expressions in the literature (e.g., Refs. [4]-[6], [8]-[12]). It is being examined recently whether generic models can reproduce the spatially variable nature of seismic motions at different sites and various events. Some studies [5], [11] suggest that such models may be feasible, whereas others [12] that they may not.

This study investigates whether an alternative approach than the conventional estimates can answer this question. Because conventional approaches evaluate the coherence of the motions, which is based on regression analyses of data with large scatter, any correlation of phase variability with earthquake and site characteristics may be difficult to recognize. Also, the assumption that the phase and amplitude variability can be examined independently, when they may be attributed

-in part- to the same physical causes, or that phase variability only contributes to the spatially variable nature of the seismic motions may not be totally realistic. Therefore, the approach adopted deals directly with the recorded time histories, and analyzes the amplitude and phase variation of the seismic motions simultaneously.

The methodology [14], [15] is applied to seismic ground motions recorded during the earthquake of January 21, 1981, (Event 5, $M_L = 6.3$) at the SMART-1 array in Lotung, Taiwan. At the time of the earthquake, the array consisted of a center instrument C00, and 36 additional ones arranged on three concentric circles, the inner denoted by I, the middle by M and the outer by O, with radii of 0.2, 1.0 and 2.0 km, respectively.

In the approach, the seismic motions are modeled as superpositions of sinusoidal functions, described by their amplitude, frequency, wavenumber and phase. Signal processing techniques are initially applied to the recorded data in order to identify their apparent propagation characteristics. A computationally efficient least-square minimization scheme, developed in the course of this study [14], [15], is then utilized to estimate the amplitude and phase of the signals. Common signal characteristics (amplitude and phase) in the seismic motions are identified from the application of the approach to a number of array stations. The common signal represents a coherent wavetrain propagating with the identified velocity on the ground surface and approximates to a very satisfactory degree the actual motions. The differences between the recorded data and the coherent estimates of the motions are caused by spatial arrival time delays associated with the upward traveling of the waves through the site topography, in addition to the broad-band wave propagation delays, and by variabilities in both the amplitudes and phases of the sinusoidal signals, identified from the application of the least-square minimization scheme to the data recorded at one station at a time. It is shown that the variabilities in amplitudes and phases identified at individual stations around the common component amplitude and phase are correlated and associated with physical parameters.

2 PROPAGATION CHARACTERISTICS OF THE MOTIONS

The conventional method [3], [7], used with slowness stacking [13] is first applied to the data for the identification of the propagation characteristics (azimuth and apparent propagation velocity) of the broad-band waves in the analyzed windows. For illustration purposes, only the strong motion S-wave window (7.0-12.12 sec actual time in the records) in the N-S direction of Event 5 is presented herein; the duration of the analyzed motion is 5.12 sec with a time step of 0.01 sec. The slowness spectra of the motions are presented in Fig. 1. Figure 1 is a contour plot: the darker the area, the higher the elevation of the spectra. The slowness stacking process identified the slowness of the dominant broad-band waves in the window as $\vec{s} = (0.1 \text{ sec/km}, -0.2 \text{ sec/km})$. Since body waves are essentially nondispersive, they have the same slowness $\vec{s}$ at all frequencies, which specifies the direction (azimuth) of the signals through the ratio s_y/s_x, and the magnitude of their apparent propagation velocity (v_{app}) on the ground surface, since $|\vec{s}| = 1/v_{app}$. The identified slowness suggests that the waves impinge the array at an azimuth of 153° with an apparent propagation velocity of 4.5km/sec; these results are consistent with the source-site geometry and the apparent propagation velocity of shear waves at the site. The (horizontal) wavenumber, $\vec{\kappa} = \{\kappa_x, \kappa_y\}$, of the motions is related to the slowness through $\vec{\kappa} = \omega \vec{s}$.

3 LEAST-SQUARES MINIMIZATION SCHEME

For the complete identification of the signals it is necessary that, in addition to their propagation characteristics, their amplitude and phase be known. Let the seismic ground motions be de-

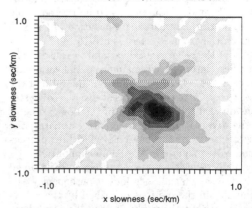

Figure 1 Slowness spectra of the motions

scribed by p sinusoidals and expressed as:

$$\hat{\psi}(\vec{r}, t) = \sum_{m=1}^{p} A_m \sin(\vec{\kappa}_m \cdot \vec{r} + \omega_m t + \phi_m) \qquad (1)$$

in which $\vec{r}$ indicates location on the ground surface and t is time. Each sinusoidal component is identified by its (discrete) frequency and wavenumber $(\omega_m, \vec{\kappa}_m)$; A_m and ϕ_m are the amplitude and phase shift, respectively, of the signal. It is noted that, at this stage, no noise component is superimposed to the ground motion estimate of Eq. 1. The amplitudes, A_m, and phases, ϕ_m, of the signals can then be determined from the system of equations resulting from the least-squares minimization of the error function between the recorded time histories $\psi(\vec{r}, t)$ and the approximate ones $\hat{\psi}(\vec{r}, t)$ (Eq. 1) with respect to the unknowns A_m and ϕ_m [14], [15]:

$$E = \sum_{i=1}^{L} \sum_{j=1}^{N} (\psi(\vec{r}_i, t_j) - \hat{\psi}(\vec{r}_i, t_j))^2 \qquad (2)$$

evaluated at discrete locations (stations) i and times j; $N\Delta t$ is the duration of the window analyzed and Δt is the time step. Any number L of stations-ranging from one to the total number of recording stations-can be used for the evaluation of the signal amplitudes and phases. A computationally efficient approach to determine the amplitude and phase of the signals (A_m, ϕ_m), $m = 1, ..., p$, has been developed in the course of this study [14], [15]. When $L > 1$ in Eq. 2, the identified amplitudes and phases represent the common signal characteristics at the number of stations considered; when $L = 1$, the amplitudes and phases correspond only to the particular station analyzed.

4 RECONSTRUCTION OF SEISMIC MOTIONS

Five stations ($L = 5$) are used in Eq. 2 for the identification of their common amplitudes and phases (Eq. 1); the stations are C00, I03, I06, I09 and I12 -center and inner ring (radius of 0.2 km) stations of the array-. Once the common characteristics are identified, they are substituted in Eq. 1, and an estimate of the motions at the stations considered is obtained. The comparison of the recorded motions with the "reconstructed" motions, resulting from the superposition of the identified signals at the stations (Eq. 1), are presented in Fig. 2; no noise (random) component is added to the reconstructed signals. Since amplitudes and phases at each frequency are identical for all stations considered, the reconstructed motions rep-

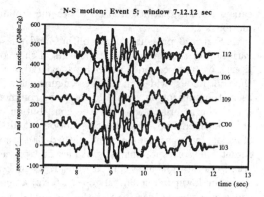

Figure 2 Comparison of recorded and reconstructed motions

resent a coherent waveform that propagates with constant velocity on the ground surface.

Figure 2 indicates that the reconstructed motions reproduce to a very satisfactory degree the actual ones, and, although they consist only of the broad-band coherent body wave signal (Eq. 1), they can describe the major characteristics (overall apparent propagation, amplitude and zero crossing rate) of the data. The details in the actual motions, that are not matched by the reconstructed ones, constitute the spatially variable nature of the motions.

5 CAUSES FOR THE SPATIAL VARIATION OF THE MOTIONS

When only one station at a time ($L = 1$ in Eq. 2) is used in the evaluation of amplitudes and phases at different frequencies for that particular station, the reconstructed motion is indistinguishable from the recorded one. This does not necessarily mean that the analyzed time histories are composed only of the identified broad-band waves, but rather that the sinusoidal functions of Eq. 1 can match the sinusoidally varying seismic time histories, i.e., Eq. 2 becomes essentially compatible to a Fourier transform. However, significant deviations in the values of the amplitudes and phases evaluated at each station from the common ones suggest the effect (amplification and phase modification) of the upward propagation of the waves through the site topography, the contribution of wave components other than or in addition to the broad-band wave and/or the presence of scattered energy. Thus, the comparison of the results at the individual stations with the common ones provides insight into the causes for the spatial variation of seismic ground motions.

Figure 3 presents the amplitude and phase variation of the sinusoidal components of the motions up to a frequency of 15 Hz ($\approx$94 rad/sec); the continuous, wider line in these figures, as well as in the subsequent ones, indicates the common signal characteristics, namely the contribution of the identified body wave to the motions at all 5 stations, whereas the thinner, dashed lines represent the corresponding amplitudes and phases when one station at a time is considered in Eq. 2. In the lower frequency range (< 1.5 Hz) amplitudes and phases identified at the individual stations essentially coincide with those of the common component. As frequency increases, in the range of 1.5 - 4 Hz, the common amplitude represents the average of the site amplification and phases start deviating from the common phase. It should be noted that the values of the phases were restricted in the range of $[0, 2\pi)$, and, therefore, jumps of approximately 2π are not indicative of a drastic variation in the phases. At higher frequen-

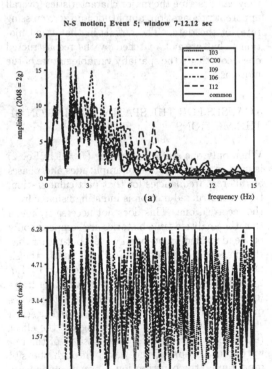

N-S motion; Event 5; window 7-12.12 sec

(a)

(b)

Figure 3 Amplitude and phase variation of motions at inner ring stations and C00

cies, the common amplitude becomes lower than the ones identified at the stations and phases vary randomly.

Part of the variabilities around the common components in Fig. 3 -in addition to possible scattering effects and the contribution of wave components other than the broad-band wave- may be due to the fact that an absolutely constant slowness was used for the propagation of the sinusoidal components at all frequencies, due to inaccuracies in the estimation of the slowness $\vec{s}$ of the motions, and also because the time history approximation (Eq. 1) does not allow for small time delays in the arrival of the waves at the various stations due to their upward traveling through horizontal variations of the geologic structure underneath the array. The use of the actual slowness of the waves identified at each frequency would reduce the variability, but, due to its detailed and event specific nature, would not be helpful in establishing general description for the spatial variation of the motions. Inaccuracies in the slowness estimate may be difficult to avoid, due to limited recorded information in space and the dependence of the results on the array configuration. However, the contribution of the time delays due to the upward propagation of the waves can be partially eliminated by aligning the seismic motions.

6 ALIGNMENT OF TIME HISTORIES

The alignment of the time histories at the array stations was performed with respect to the center station of the array, C00; in the process, the time delays corresponding to the maximum cross correlation between the motions at each station and C00 are determined, and the motions are shifted, so that the propagation effect is removed. The arrival time delays evaluated from the alignment process were not compatible with those determined from the apparent propagation of the motions identified from the constant slowness of the broad-band waves, and exhibited a random behavior [15]. The reason for the differences is that the broad-band wave characteristics obtained from the slowness stacking analyses represent the average propagation of the motions over the entire array. On the other hand, the alignment process identifies possible delays in the arrival of the waves between two stations that are caused by their average propagation pattern, by their upward traveling through the site topography and by random effects, i.e., the alignment presents a detailed, local picture of the wave propagation differences between stations.

1498

7 COMMON COMPONENTS IN ALIGNED MOTIONS

For the identification of the amplitude and phase variation of the aligned motions, the error function (Eq. 2) is used again in the minimization scheme but, in the sinusoidal approximation of the motions (Eq. 1), the term $\vec{\kappa}_m \cdot \vec{r}$ is set equal to zero, since the motions arrive simultaneously at all array stations. When the motions recorded at one station at a time are used in the minimization scheme, Eq. 2 reduces to the Fourier transform of the aligned motions.

Figure 4 presents the variation of the amplitudes and phases determined from the application of the least-square minimization scheme to the aligned motions at four inner ring stations (I03, I06, I09, I12) and the center station C00, together with the amplitude and phase variation identified using one station at a time. The variability range of amplitudes and phases around the common component is reduced in the aligned data results compared to those of the actual motions (Figs. 3 and

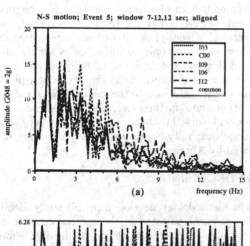

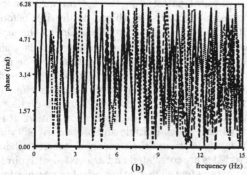

Figure 4 Amplitude and phase variation of aligned motions at inner ring stations and C00

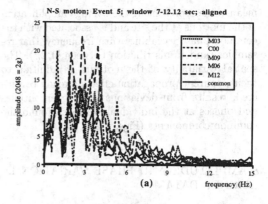

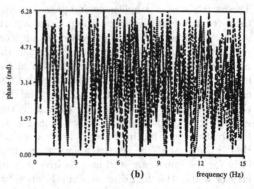

Figure 5 Amplitude and phase variation of aligned motions at middle ring stations and C00

4), indicating the significance of the consideration of the spatially variable arrival time perturbations in the approach. Figure 5 presents the results of the application of the approach to the middle ring stations, M03, M06, M09 and M12, together with the reference station C00.

The common amplitude and phase identified from the inner and the middle ring stations (Figs. 4 and 5) are very similar -same trend, almost identical phases, slight variabilities in the values of the amplitudes-, particularly considering the facts that separate analyses were performed for the two sets of stations, and that the longest separation distance for the middle ring stations is 2 km whereas that of the inner ring ones 400 m. Their differences are an expected consequence of the larger scatter in the data at the further away stations due to attenuation of the waves and more significant variations in the site topography. The agreement of the common amplitudes and phases over an extended area of radius of 1 km strongly suggests the existence of the coherent component in the data. The common amplitude can be viewed as a mean value representing the average amplification of the motions at the site and is associated with the common phase variability with frequency, that resembles random distribution between $[0, 2\pi)$. The spatial variability of the motions, in addition to their apparent propagation effects already considered, results from deviations in both amplitudes and phases at the individual stations around the common components (Figs. 4 and 5).

8 AMPLITUDE AND PHASE VARIATION IN ALIGNED DATA

The variabilities of amplitudes and phases around their corresponding common components appear to be correlated and associated with the physical parameters: In the lower frequency range of the motions amplitudes and phases identified at the individual stations essentially coincide with those of the common component for the inner ring data (Fig. 4) and vary only slightly for the middle ring ones (Fig. 5). This is attributed to the long wavelength of the contributing waves at low frequencies, that do not "see" the site irregularities, particularly for the inner ring stations. As frequency increases within the dominant site amplification frequency range, the common amplitude and phase represent the average (mean) of the values identified at the individual stations. The variability of both amplitudes and phases around the common component increases consistently with frequency and separation distance. The rate of increase is slower for the inner ring motions than the middle ring ones. The fact that the common amplitudes reproduce the average of the site amplification (Figs. 4 and 5) implies that the motions are controlled by the signal that is transmitted upward through the horizontal variations of the layers underneath the array and is, consequently, amplified with some modifications in its phase. The increase in the variabilities of amplitudes and phases around the common component as frequency increases may also be associated with the decreasing wavelength of the signals at increasing frequencies, which is more obvious for the middle ring results, and to the initiating contribution of scattered energy. At higher frequencies, wave components in addition to the broad-band signal, and, mainly, scattered energy (noise) dominate the motions. Because these higher frequency wave components propagate at different velocities, phases at the individual stations (Figs. 4 and 5) deviate significantly from the common phase, and the com-

mon signal amplitude no longer represents the average of the site amplification and becomes lower than the amplitudes identified at the individual stations. Thus, although the approach does not consider noise directly, it recognizes it implicitly. Similar results, not shown, have been obtained for the vertical and E-W motions of the same event, as well as for the vertical and horizontal motions of other events.

It follows then from the above considerations that the amplitude and phase variability of the motions around their common, coherent characteristics are correlated and associated with the physical parameters. The differential phase variability can also be associated with coherency estimates: in the low frequency range, where the phase dispersion range around the common phase is small, coherency assumes values close to one; within the dominant site amplification frequency range of the motions, where the phase variability increases with frequency, coherency decreases, and, finally, in the higher frequency range, where phases vary randomly and noise dominates, coherency assumes zero values. It appears then feasible to associate coherency with physical parameters. It is emphasized, however, that the results of this study indicate that spatial variability estimates based on phase variability only do not suffice for the realistic modeling and simulation of spatially variable seismic ground motions: both amplitude and phase variability contribute to the spatial variation of the motions, and, furthermore, they are correlated. It should be noted that the relation of coherency with phase variability between stations has been recognized by Abrahamson [2].

9 CONCLUSIONS

The methodology developed in this study identifies physical patterns in the spatial variation of the seismic motions, which was not feasible before with commonly used approaches. One of the new perspectives introduced in the approach is that the spatially variable seismic motions can be expressed in terms of their common, fully coherent component and variabilities in the arrival time of the wavefronts, and in the amplitudes and phases that are particular for each recording station. It is shown that the amplitude and phase variability of the motions around their common, coherent characteristics are correlated and associated with physical parameters. The mathematical representation of the identified correlations in the amplitude and phase variations and the quantitative description of the physical causes underlying the spatial variability in the seismic motions are currently underway. Based on the results of this study, it should be also strongly emphasized that the consideration of coherency -based on phase variability only- as the sole descriptor of the spatial variation of the motions is insufficient both for their modeling and their simulation.

ACKNOWLEDGMENT

This study was supported by the National Science Foundation (NSF) under Grant No. BCS-9114895. The SMART-1 array data were made available by the Seismographic Station of the University of California at Berkeley and the Institute of Earth Sciences of the Academia Sinica in Taipei.

REFERENCES

[1] N.A. Abrahamson, "Spatial interpolation of array ground motions for engineering analysis", *Proceedings, Ninth World Conference on Earthquake Engineering*, Tokyo, Japan, 1988.

[2] N.A. Abrahamson, "Generation of spatially incoherent strong motion time histories", *Proceedings, Tenth World Conference on Earthquake Engineering*, Madrid, Spain, 1992.

[3] N.A. Abrahamson and B.A. Bolt, "Array analysis and synthesis mapping of strong seismic motion", in *Seismic Strong Motion Synthetics*, ed. B.A. Bolt, Academic Press Inc., 1987.

[4] N.A. Abrahamson, B.A. Bolt, R.B. Darragh, J. Penzien and Y.B. Tsai, "The SMART-1 accelerograph array (1980-1987): A review", *Earthquake Spectra*, Vol.3, pp. 263-287, 1987.

[5] N.A. Abrahamson, J.F. Schneider and J.C. Stepp "Spatial variation of strong ground motion for use in soil-structure interaction analyses" *Proceedings of the Fourth US-National Conference on Earthquake Engineering*, Palm Springs, CA, pp. 317-326, 1990.

[6] N.A. Abrahamson, J.F. Schneider and J.C. Stepp, "Empirical spatial coherency functions for applications to soil-structure interaction analyses", *Earthquake Spectra*, Vol. 7, pp. 1-27, 1991.

[7] J. Capon, "High - resolution frequency - wavenumber spectrum analysis", *Proceedings of the IEEE*, Vol. 57, pp. 1408-1418, 1969.

[8] H. Hao, C.S. Oliveira and J. Penzien, "Multiple-station ground motion processing and simulation based on SMART-1 array data", *Nuclear Engineering and Design*, Vol. 111, pp. 293-310, 1989.

[9] R.S. Harichandran and E.H. Vanmarcke, "Stochastic variation of earthquake ground motion in space and time" *Journal of the Engineering Mechanics Division, ASCE*, Vol. 112, pp. 154-174, 1986.

[10] C.H. Loh, J. Penzien and Y.B. Tsai, "Engineering Analysis of SMART-1 array accelerograms" *Earthquake Engineering and Structural Dynamics*, Vol. 10, pp. 575-591, 1982.

[11] O. Ramadan and M. Novak, "Coherency functions for spatially correlated seismic ground motions", Geotechnical Research Centre Report No. GEOT-9-93, The University of Western Ontario, London, Canada, 1993.

[12] J.F. Schneider, J.C. Stepp and N.A. Abrahamson, "The spatial variation of earthquake ground motion and effects of local site conditions", *Proceedings, Tenth World Conference on Earthquake Engineering*, Madrid, Spain, 1992.

[13] P. Spudich and D. Oppenheimer, "Dense seismograph array observations of earthquake rupture dynamics", in *Earthquake Source Mechanics*, Geophysical Monograph 37, S. Das, J. Boatwright and C.H. Scholz, eds., American Geophysical Union, Washington, D.C., 1986.

[14] A. Zerva and O. Zhang, "Estimation of signal characteristics in seismic ground motions", *Probabilistic Engineering Mechanics*, Vol. 11, pp. 229-242, 1996.

[15] A. Zerva and O. Zhang, "Correlation patterns in characteristics of Spatially variable seismic ground motions", *Earthquake Engineering and Structural Dynamics*, Vol. 11, pp. 19-39, 1997.

Structural Safety and Reliability, Shiraishi, Shinozuka & Wen (eds) © 1998 Balkema, Rotterdam, ISBN 90 5410 978 5

Seismic hazard analysis of nonlinear multi-degree-of-freedom structures

Takashi Inoue
Technical Research Institute, Hazama Corporation, Tsukuba, Japan

Jun Kanda
Department of Architecture, University of Tokyo, Japan

ABSTRACT: The seismic hazard of nonlinear multi-degree-of-freedom structures was studied by incorporating nonlinear response factors in a conventional seismic hazard analysis equation. Simulated ground motions were generated using a proposed response spectral attenuation relation. Six structural models were analyzed and spectral reduction factors, F, were evaluated. The values of F decrease as magnitude increases for the most cases. The standard deviations of the seismic risk evaluation functions are almost the same as those of the attenuation equation. The annual probability of failure of the structures in Tokyo and Osaka was evaluated.

1 INTRODUCTION

A method to evaluate the seismic risk of nonlinear multi-degree-of-freedom (MDOF) structures by incorporating the spectral reduction factor and a MDOF response factor in a seismic hazard analysis equation was proposed by one of the authors (Inoue 1990). In the study, ten ground motion records were used to evaluate the nonlinear response of four simple structural models. However, it is often difficult to obtain ground motion records of large magnitude and small epicentral distance, and the recorded motions inevitably reflect specific site conditions. In this study, ground motions corresponding to four magnitudes and three site conditions were simulated using a proposed attenuation equation of response spectra. Nonlinear response analyses of six structures were conducted and the probability of damage of the structures in Tokyo and Osaka was evaluated.

2 SIMULATED GROUND MOTIONS

Kawashima and Aizawa (1984) proposed the following attenuation equation of earthquake acceleration response spectra based on 394 horizontal components of strong motions recorded in Japan.

$$\tilde{S}_a(T_k, M, \Delta, G_i) = a(T_k, G_i) \times 10^{b(T_k, G_i)M} \times (\Delta + 30)^c \quad (1)$$

where T_k, M, Δ G_i are the natural period, magnitude, epicentral distance and the soil type, respectively. There are three soil types according to the natural period of the ground, T_g, i.e., Type 1 ($T_g < 0.2$s), Type 2 ($0.2 < T_g < 0.6$s), and Type 3 ($T_g > 0.6$s). The coefficients a and b are given at 10 natural periods from 0.1 through 3 second for the three ground conditions. The coefficient c is constant so that the spectral shape does not change with respect to distance. Standard deviation of $\ln S_a$ is also given for each natural period and ground condition.

To consider the effects of variability of response spectra on nonlinear response, a group of response spectra that satisfy the standard deviation at each period and the correlation between periods of response spectra of the recorded motions used by Kawashima and Aizawa were simulated. The correlation coefficients between spectral values at two periods, T_1 and T_2, are plotted versus $|\ln T_1 - \ln T_2|$ in Fig. 1. The correlation coefficients decrease as the values of $|\ln T_1 - \ln T_2|$ increase, and the slope is steeper for the softer ground. Simulated ground motions fitting to the response spectra were generated by the sinusoidal wave superimposition method with random phase angles. The Jennings type envelope function is used to simulate the time history. Five ground motions were generated for each combination of four magnitudes ($M = 5.5, 6.5, 7.5, 8.5$) and three ground conditions. Acceleration response spectra for $M = 8.5$, $\Delta = 10$km, and the soil type 1 are shown in Fig. 2 with the mean spectrum.

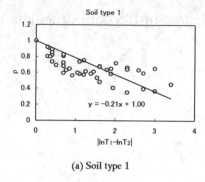

(a) Soil type 1

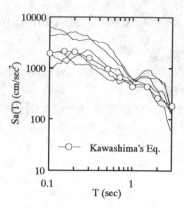

Fig. 2 Simulated acceleration response spectra
(M=8.5,$\varDelta$=10km, Soil type 1)

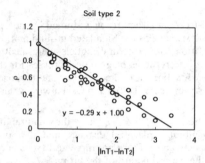

(b) Soil type 2

Table 1. Physical properties of RC 3 story

Story	w	h	K_1	Q_{y1}	K_2	Q_{y2}
	(t)	(m)	(tf/rad)	(tf)	(tf/rad)	(tf)
3	525	3.55	620	193	207	386
2	525	3.58	674	248	225	495
1	555	3.83	747	312	249	624

Table 2. Physical properties of RC 8 story

Story	w	h	K_1	Q_{y1}	K_2	Q_{y2}
8	152	3.50	86.50	48.5	28.8	97
7	111	3.50	102.3	56.0	34.1	112
6	111	3.50	139.0	84.5	46.3	169
5	111	3.50	157.5	88.5	52.5	177
4	121	3.50	195.9	109	65.3	218
3	121	3.50	247.6	118	82.5	236
2	128	3.60	306.9	143	102.3	286
1	152	4.30	303.8	159	101.3	318

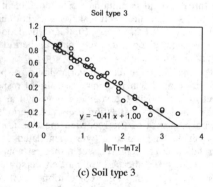

(c) Soil type 3

Fig. 1 The correlation coefficients between spectral values ;
two periods, T_1 and T_2

3 STRUCTURAL MODELS

Two reinforced concrete (RC), three steel (S), and one composite (SRC) structures are modeled as stick models (AIJ 1976, 1992, Kobayashi 1989). The ultimate limit states of stories are defined as the story drift angle of 1/50 for RC, ductility μ =8.0 from the first bending point for S, and the story drift angle of 1/30 for SRC. Takeda model for RC and the normal trilinear model for S and SRC

are used as the hysteretic relationship. Physical properties of six models are shown in Tables 1 through 6 where w, h, K_1, Q_{y1}, K_2, Q_{y2} are weight, height, initial stiffness, strength at the first bending point, secondary stiffness, strength at the second bending point, respectively.

Table 3. Physical properties of S 3 story

Story	w	h	K_1	Q_{y1}	K_2	Q_{y2}
3	89	3.00	67	70	44	97
2	126	3.00	81	107	53	184
1	126	3.00	116	143	75	245

Table 4. Physical properties of S 5 story

Story	w	h	K_1	Q_{y1}	K_2	Q_{y2}
5	265	3.50	144	186	0	186
4	309	3.50	158	280	79	316
3	305	3.50	164	321	82	412
2	306	3.50	175	349	88	484
1	308	3.80	219	385	110	532

Table 5. Physical properties of S 18 story

Story	w	h	K_1	Q_{v1}	K_2	Q_{v2}
18	190	4.10	100	194	99	199
17	771	5.50	170	726	141	827
16	669	4.10	362	1100	289	1262
15	666	3.85	474	1434	328	1620
14	668	3.85	512	1664	331	1888
13	668	3.85	541	1730	364	2127
12	671	3.85	577	1736	442	2296
11	674	3.85	593	1810	443	2399
10	674	3.85	615	1840	478	2531
9	677	3.85	652	1900	470	2611
8	680	3.85	683	1936	436	2772
7	680	3.85	714	2030	550	2913
6	682	3.85	765	2106	575	3026
5	685	3.85	807	2260	522	3119
4	685	3.85	870	2314	618	3178
3	688	3.95	1086	2534	773	3227
2	1341	4.00	4807	4765	3486	6068
1	1424	5.00	4746	5280	4392	6723

Table 6. Physical properties of SRC 14 story

Story	w	h	K_1	Q_{v1}	K_2	Q_{v2}
14	2700	3.45	5732	1095	1911	7851
13	2000	3.45	5963	1161	1988	7216
12	2000	3.45	6158	1210	2053	7280
11	2000	3.45	6324	1304	2108	7566
10	2000	3.45	6526	1241	2175	8112
9	2000	3.45	6564	1331	2188	8585
8	2000	3.45	6755	1343	2252	8893
7	2000	3.45	6854	1399	2285	9254
6	2000	3.45	7029	1375	2343	9503
5	2000	3.45	7082	1461	2361	9682
4	2000	3.45	7218	1704	2406	9923
3	3310	3.45	8976	1559	2992	9643
2	3210	3.45	10090	1542	3363	9323
1	3220	4.20	11686	1695	3895	12280

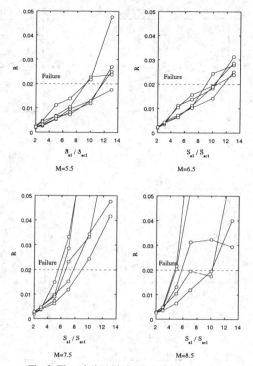

Fig. 3. The relationship between $Sa1/Sac1$ and R
(RC 3 story, soil type 1)

4 SPECTRAL REDUCTION FACTOR

In this study, the spectral reduction factor, F, is defined as au/ac, where au and ac are the peak ground acceleration when at least one story of a structure reaches the ultimate limit state and the elastic limit, respectively. F is the function of the ground motion, the structural model, and the ultimate limit state. If the level of the ground motion is represented by the value of acceleration response spectrum at the first natural period of the structure, $Sa1$, at least one story of the structure will fail when $Sa1 \geq FSac1$, where $Sac1$ is the value of $Sa1$ corresponding to ac. The maximum story drift angles, R, of RC 3 story are plotted versus $Sa1/Sac1$ in Fig. 3. The value of $Sa1/Sac1$ which corresponds to the ultimate limit state of $R=0.02$ is the F value. The values of F of structural models are plotted versus magnitude in Fig. 4. Linear regression equations of F on M are shown in Table 7. The values of F decrease as M increases except for the case of S 18 story on the soil type 1 and 2. As earthquakes of large magnitude generally contain longer period components more than small magnitude earthquakes do, nonlinear response of structures tends to be larger as the magnitude of earthquakes increases. In the case of S 18 story, the first natural period of the structure is longer than other models, and the nonlinear response does not increase for large magnitude earthquakes.

5 SEISMIC HAZARD OF MDOF STRUCTURES

At least one story of a structure exceeds the ultimate limit state when $Sa1/F \geq Sac1$. $Sa1$ is usually given by a spectral attenuation equation of M and Δ, and is assumed to be lognormally distributed. If we assume F and $Sac1$ are also lognormally distributed and express them as functions of M and Δ, $Sa1/F/Sac1$ is also lognormally distributed and a function of M and Δ. The function of $Sa1/F/Sac1$ is a kind of the limit state function. The annual rate of the failure of a structure is given by:

$$\lambda = \sum_{i=1}^{N} \nu_i \left\{ \iint_{\Delta \ M} P\left[\ln(S_{a1}/F/S_{ac1}) \geq 0 | m, \delta\right] f_{M,\Delta}(m,\delta) dm d\delta \right\}_i$$

(2)

1505

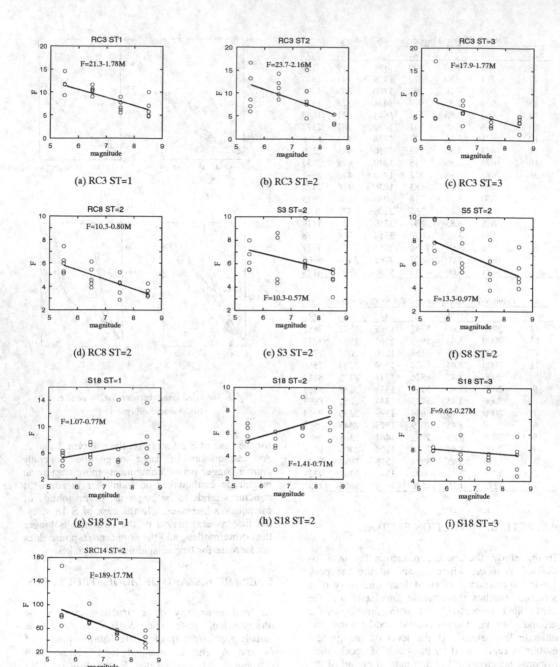

Fig. 4. The relationship between magnitude and F

where N is the number of seismic sources, v_i is the mean annual rate of occurrence of earthquakes in source i (Cornell 1968).

The standard deviations of $\ln(Sa1/F/Sac1)$ obtained by response analyses are almost the same as those of $\ln Sa1$, i.e., the standard deviations of Kawashima's attenuation equation. As Bazzurro and Cornell (1996) proposed, it can be conservative if we assume $\ln Sa1$, $\ln F$, and $\ln Sac1$ are mutually independent and use the following equation.

Table 7. Linear regression equations of F on M

Structural model	T_1(sec)	Soil type	Mean of F	C.O.V.	Regression equation	Conditional S.D.
RC 3	0.39	1	8.81	0.30	21.3-1.78M	1.77
RC 3	0.39	2	8.61	0.48	23.7-2.16M	3.44
RC 3	0.39	3	5.56	0.62	17.9-1.77M	2.83
RC 8	0.83	2	4.63	0.26	10.3-0.80M	0.79
S 3	0.47	2	6.27	0.31	10.3-0.57M	1.85
S 5	0.89	2	6.48	0.28	13.3-0.97M	1.50
S 18	2.02	1	6.49	0.44	1.07+0.77M	2.80
S 18	2.02	2	6.39	0.33	1.41+0.71M	1.97
S 18	2.02	3	7.72	0.33	9.62-0.27M	2.60
SRC 14	0.96	2	65.11	0.46	189-17.6M	22.3

Table 8. The means and standard deviations of $\ln(Sa1/F/Sac1)$ of structural models

Structural model	T_1(sec)	Soil type	Mean of $\ln(Sa1/F/Sac1)$	Standard deviation
RC 3	0.39	1	$-3.10 + 0.87\,M - 1.18\ln(\Delta+30)$	0.63
RC 3	0.39	2	$-4.38 + 1.15\,M - 1.18\ln(\Delta+30)$	0.73
RC 3	0.39	3	$-2.28 + 0.89\,M - 1.18\ln(\Delta+30)$	0.68
RC 8	0.83	2	$-4.65 + 1.25\,M - 1.18\ln(\Delta+30)$	0.66
S 3	0.47	2	$-3.56 + 0.97\,M - 1.18\ln(\Delta+30)$	0.65
S 5	0.89	2	$-6.15 + 1.34\,M - 1.18\ln(\Delta+30)$	0.70
S 18	2.02	1	$-4.18 + 0.83\,M - 1.18\ln(\Delta+30)$	0.75
S 18	2.02	2	$-5.53 + 1.15\,M - 1.18\ln(\Delta+30)$	0.74
S 18	2.02	3	$-6.95 + 1.38\,M - 1.18\ln(\Delta+30)$	0.74
SRC 14	0.96	2	$-8.02 + 1.47\,M - 1.18\ln(\Delta+30)$	0.73

Table 9. Annual probability of failure of structures in Tokyo and Osaka

Structural Model	Base shear coefficients	Soil Type	Tokyo		Osaka	
			Pf	β	Pf	β
RC 3	0.19	1	1.83E-04	3.56	7.00E-05	3.81
RC 3	0.19	2	4.34E-03	2.62	2.06E-03	2.87
RC 3	0.19	3	8.35E-03	2.39	3.28E-03	2.72
RC 8	0.16	2	1.14E-02	2.28	5.91E-03	2.52
S 3	0.42	2	6.07E-04	3.24	2.47E-04	3.48
S 5	0.26	2	1.15E-03	3.05	6.02E-04	3.24
S 18	0.40	1	1.37E-06	4.69	5.36E-07	4.92
S 18	0.40	2	1.13E-04	3.69	4.88E-05	3.90
S 18	0.40	3	3.10E-04	3.42	1.61E-04	3.60
SRC 14	0.05	2	7.42E-05	3.79	3.89E-05	3.95

$$\sigma_{\ln(S_{a1}/F/S_{ac1})} = \sqrt{\sigma^2_{\ln S_{a1}} + \sigma^2_{\ln F} + \sigma^2_{\ln S_{ac1}}} \qquad (3)$$

The means of $\ln(Sa1/F/Sac1)$ and the standard deviations obtained by the equation above are shown in Table 8.

6 FAILURE PROBABILITY OF STRUCTURES

The annual probability of failure of structural models when they are located at the center of Tokyo and Osaka was evaluated. Parameters of seismic source areas are same as those by Inoue and Kanda (1994). The program EQRISK (McGuire 1976) was used for the analyses. Base shear coefficients at the first bending point, annual probability of failure P_f, and the reliability indices $\beta = -\Phi^{-1}(P_f)$ are shown in Table 9. The reliability indices are also shown in Fig. 5.

The value of P_f increases as the ground becomes softer both in the cases of RC 3 story and S 18 story. For the same soil type, the value of P_f becomes larger for the smaller base shear coefficients. The value of P_f in Tokyo is greater than that in Osaka for all cases. The reasons for the small P_f values for RC structures seem to be the usage of weak structural models and the conservative limit state. Moreover, the value of P_f will decrease if more precise structural analysis model is used.

Table 10.50-year probability of failure of structures at Tokyo

Models	This study	The method of Kanda et al.
RC 3 story	0.86	2.19
S 3 story	1.88	3.06

The failure probability of the structural models in 50 years were evaluated by multiplying the annual rate of earthquake occurrence by 50, and the results were compared with those obtained by the method proposed by Kanda et al (1994). The input motions and the ultimate limit states used for the analyses are the same in both methods. The reliability indices in 50 years of RC 3 story and S 3 story in Tokyo are shown in Table 10. The values of β by this study are smaller than those by the method of Kanda et al. In the method of Kanda et al. C.O.V. of structural resistance and input motions are assumed as 0.2 and 0.6, respectively. Total C.O.V. assumed is about 0.6. In this study, as the standard deviations of $\ln(Sa_1/F/Sac_1)$ is about 0.6 and the variations of magnitude and epicentral distance are added to that. The difference in β seems to be caused by the difference of the variation used in the analyses.

7 CONCLUSIONS

The seismic hazard of nonlinear multi-degree-of-freedom structures was studied by incorporating nonlinear response factors in a conventional seismic hazard analysis equation.

Simulated ground motions for four magnitudes and three ground conditions were generated using a proposed response spectral attenuation equation. Response spectra that satisfy the standard deviation at each period and the correlation between periods of response spectra of recorded motions were simulated, and then ground motions that fit the response spectra were generated. The spectral reduction factors, F, of six structures were evaluated.

The values of F decrease as magnitude increases except for the case of the 18-story steel structure on the type 1 and 2 ground. The standard deviations of the seismic hazard evaluation function are almost the same as those of the attenuation equation.

The probability of failure of the structures in Tokyo and Osaka was evaluated. For the same structural model, the probability of failure increases as the natural period of the ground increases. For the same ground condition, the probability of failure increases as the base shear coefficient decreases.

A practical analysis method of nonlinear MDOF structures which can reflect the characteristics of earthquakes was proposed. As future studies, evaluation of the actual structural resistance, usage of physically clear attenuation equations, studies on various limit states, consideration of soil-structure interaction, and usage of more precise analysis models need to be conducted.

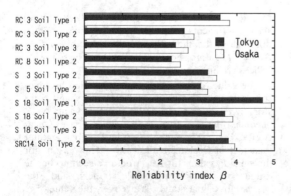

Fig. 5. Reliability indices of structures at Tokyo and Osaka

REFERENCES

Inoue, T. 1990. Seismic hazard analysis of multi-degree-of-freedom structures. Report No. RMS-8, Dept. of Civil Engineering, Stanford University.

Kawashima, K. and Aizawa, K. 1984. Attenuation of earthquake response spectra based on multiple regression analysis of Japanese strong motion data. Proc. of Japan Society of Civil Engineers, No.350/I-2 : 181-186.

Architectural Institute of Japan 1976. Seismic loading and the seismic response of structures.

Architectural Institute of Japan 1992. Standard for structural calculation of reinforced concrete structures.

Architectural Institute of Japan 1992. Seismic loading-strong motion prediction and building response.

Kobayashi, M. 1989, Feasibility of probability-based seismic margin index considering inelastic response, Master's degree thesis, Univ. of Tokyo.

Cornell, C.A. 1968. Engineering seismic risk

analysis. Bull. Seism. Soc. Am., Vol.58, No.5 : 1583-1606.

Bazzurro, P. and Cornell, C. A. 1994. Seismic hazard analysis of non-linear structures, I: Methodology, II: Applications, Journal of Structural Engineering, ASCE : 3320-3365.

Inoue, T. and Kanda, J. 1993. Seismic hazard analysis using source models for interplate earthquakes. Proc. of ICOSSAR '93 : 2125-2130.

McGuire, R.K. 1976. FORTRAN Computer program for seismic risk analysis, U.S. Geological Survey Open-File Report : 76-67.

Kanda, J., Iwasaki, R., Kobayashi, H., Ellingwood, B.R. 1994. Seismic safety evaluation of existing buildings in Japan, Structural Safety and Reliability, :.2147-2153.

Structural Safety and Reliability, Shiraishi, Shinozuka & Wen (eds) © 1998 Balkema, Rotterdam, ISBN 90 5410 978 5

Consistent ground motion at Tokyo based on 50-year magnitude and distance joint probability density function

Khaled A. Ahmed
GulfNet Communications Co. Ltd, Tokyo, Japan

Jun Kanda
Architecture Department, Tokyo University, Japan

ABSTRACT: In conventional seismic hazard analyses, peak ground acceleration *PGA* or velocity *PGV* is probabilistically estimated, then, magnitude *M* and distance *R* are assumed to obtain a normalized response spectrum *S(T)* and duration *(D)*. In this paper a hazard-consistent methodology is developed to estimate the ground motion parameters such as *M*, *R*, *S(T)*, and *D* in a probabilistic manner. Thus, consistency of the synthesized time history can be improved and the random uncertainty can be studied. Unlike the previous research, here, the consistent parameters are estimated based on 50-year joint probability function of *M* and *R*. Lifetime-hazard-consistent method is proposed based on a bivariate extreme value distribution of *M* and *R*. The 50-year joint probability function is estimated based on 50-year independent marginal distributions of *M* and *R* and a proposed dependence function. The proposed methodology is applied for a site in Tokyo.

1. INTRODUCTION

In conventional seismic hazard analyses, peak ground acceleration *PGA* or velocity *PGV* is probabilistically estimated, then, magnitude *M* and distance *R* are assumed to obtain a normalized response spectrum *S(T)*. This spectrum shape is then scaled to the estimated *PGA* or *PGV* or sometimes both. Time history is synthesized by assuming the duration *D*, as a function of the magnitude, and choosing an appropriate envelope function. Uncertainty in spectral shape and duration of ground motion at a certain site can be classified into modeling uncertainty and a random one. The first type of uncertainty comes from the difference between their given empirical mathematical forms and values estimated from recorded ground motion time histories. The random part of uncertainty comes from different possible combination of *M* and *R* at the concerned site. When parameters like *M, R, S(T)*, and *D* are also probabilistically estimated, then consistency of synthesized time history can be improved and the random uncertainty can be examined. In such case these parameters are called hazard-consistent parameters and resulted ground motion is called hazard-consistent ground motion. In this paper, a hazard-consistent ground motion model is proposed to improve the consistency of

earthquake load evaluation. Unlike the hazard-consistent model used in Japan [Itoh et al. 1987, Kameda et al. 1988], here, an alternative model is proposed based on bivariate extreme value distribution as a lifetime-exceedance probability.

2. PROBABILISTIC MAXIMUM EARTHQUAKE GROUND MOTION MODEL

Hazard-consistent analysis has been carried out in Japan based on annual joint probability function of *M* and *R* conditioned to *PGA* value that has a certain annual exceedance probability. Consistency is taken with respect to a confined range of *PGA* [Itoh et al. 1987] or with respect to all values larger than a certain *PGA* [Ishikawa et al. 1988, Nojima et al. 1988]. All previous studies are based on annual exceedance probability distribution *P1* estimated according to Cornell's method [Cornell 1968]. When only the value of *PGA* is needed, it can be estimated based on *P1* or based on 50-year exceedance probability *P50*. 50-year is chosen as a reference value for lifetime of ordinary structures and, thus, can be easily understood by engineers. When the mean of 50-year exceedance probability distribution is taken to represent the probabilistic value of *PGA*, it will be approximately equal to the

PGA of *P1*=0.01. The two *PGA* values are close when Gumbel distribution is adapted for the exceedance probability distribution, and slightly different when other distributions are used [Ahmed et al.1995].

Lifetime-hazard-consistent method is proposed here based on a bivariate extreme value distribution [Gumbel et al. 1967]. The 50-year joint probability function is estimated based on 50-y. independent marginal distributions of *M* and *R* and a proposed dependence function. Although such joint probability density function can be enhanced when longer data period is used, 100-y data period is used here to be consistent with the authors' previous research [Ahmed et al.1995].

3. CONSISTENT PARAMETERS

3.1. Definition of hazard-consistent parameters.

Hazard analysis is first carried out for a certain ground motion parameter *Y*. A value y_p is then selected based on a certain exceedance probability *P*. In this exceedance probability distribution, the joint probability function of *M* and *R*, $f_{MR}(m,r)$, is explicitly or implicitly used. For any other parameter *X* which is a function of *M* and *R*, i.e., *X=g(M,R)*, the consistent value of *x* is then estimated from the theory of total probability as [Nojima et al. 1988]:

$$\bar{X}_C = \iint_{r\ m} g(m,r) \bullet f_{M,R}(m,r \setminus [condition]) \bullet dmdr \quad (1)$$

or in discrete form as:

$$\bar{X}_C = \sum_r \sum_m g(m,r) \bullet p_{M,R}(m,r \setminus [condition]) \quad (2)$$

Where $p_{M,R}(m,r|[condition])$ is the conditional joint probability mass function of *M* and *R* given that a certain condition is true. Such condition can be $Y \geq y_p$ or $y_{p1} \geq Y \geq y_{p2}$. Where y_p, y_{p1} and y_{p2} are the values of ground motion parameter *Y* at certain exceedance probabilities *P*, *P1*, and *P2* respectively. Following equation 2, the mean values of consistent magnitude M_c and distance R_c can be expressed as [Ishikawa et al. 1988]:

$$\bar{M}_C = \sum_r \sum_m m \bullet p_{M,R}(m,r \setminus [condition]) \quad (3\text{-}a)$$

$$\bar{R}_C = \sum_r \sum_m r \bullet p_{M,R}(m,r \setminus [condition]) \quad (3\text{-}b)$$

As a first order approximation, the mean of the conditional parameter *x* can be expressed as [Nojima et al. 1988]:

$$\bar{X}_C \cong g(\bar{M}_C, \bar{R}_C) \quad (4)$$

Conditional variance *VAR* and conditional covariance *CVR* of *M* and *R* can be expressed as:

$$VAR[X_C] = E(X_C^2) - [E(X_C)]^2 \quad (5\text{-}a)$$

$$VAR(M_C) = \sum_r \sum_m m^2 \bullet p_{M,R}(m,r \setminus [condition])$$

$$- \left[\sum_r \sum_m m \bullet p_{M,R}(m,r \setminus [condition]) \right]^2 \quad (5\text{-}b)$$

$$VAR(R_C) = \sum_r \sum_m r^2 \bullet p_{M,R}(m,r \setminus [condition])$$

$$- \left[\sum_r \sum_m r \bullet p_{M,R}(m,r \setminus [condition]) \right]^2 \quad (5\text{-}c)$$

$$CVR(M_C, R_C) = E[MR \setminus [condition]] - \bar{M}_C \bar{R}_C \quad (5\text{-}d)$$

Correlation between *Mc* and *Rc* can be examined with the covariance or with the normalized covariance, i.e., coefficient of correlation.

3.2. Conventional conditional joint mass function based on Cornell's method

In Cornell's method, hazard curve (annual exceedance probability) is estimated from the total theory of probability as:

$$P_Y(Y \geq y_p) = \sum_r \sum_m P[Y \geq y_p \setminus m,r] \bullet p_{M,R}(m,r) \quad (6)$$

where $P[Y \geq y_p|m,r]$ is the conditional probability that *Y* exceeds y_p for a certain value of magnitude and distance. This conditional probability can account for the uncertainty in the attenuation equation. Magnitude and distance are usually assumed to be independent within a single homogeneous seismic source and so their joint probability mass function can be expressed as the product of their marginal probability mass functions as follows:

$$p_{M,R}(m,r) = p_M(m) \bullet p_R(r) \quad (7)$$

From Bay's theorem we can write

$$p_{M,R}(m,r \setminus [Y \geq y_p]) \bullet P_Y(Y \geq y_p)$$
$$= P_Y(Y \geq y_p \setminus m,r) \bullet p_{M,R}(m,r) \quad (8)$$

$$p_{M,R}(m,r \setminus [Y \geq y_p])$$
$$= \frac{P_Y(Y \geq y_p \setminus m,r) \bullet p_{M,R}(m,r)}{P_Y(Y \geq y_p)} \quad (9)$$

From equation 6 and 9, the conditional joint probability mass function can be expressed as:

$$p_{M,R}(m,r \setminus [Y \geq y_p])$$
$$= \frac{P_Y(Y \geq y_p \setminus m,r) \bullet p_{M,R}(m,r)}{\sum_m \sum_r P_Y(Y \geq y_p \setminus m,r) \bullet p_{M,R}(m,r)} \quad (10)$$

Equations 9 and 10 are also valid when other conditions are considered such as $y_{p1} \geq Y \geq y_{p2}$ instead of $Y \geq y_p$.

3.3. Proposed conditional joint probability mass function based on bivariate extreme theory

In Cornell's method, explicit assumptions for $f_M(m)$ and $f_R(r)$ are needed before the exceedance probability of ground motion parameter Y can be estimated. In extreme value analysis, no such assumption is needed since Y is firstly estimated from M and R by the attenuation model, then, the annual extreme values are directly picked up and plotted with Hazen method and fitted to an extreme value distribution. Thus, $f_M(m)$ and $f_R(r)$ are implicitly included in the analysis. An expression in which such probabilities explicitly appear can be written from the total probability theory as:

$$F_Y(y_p) = F_Y(Y \le y_p)$$
$$= \iint_{m\,r} P[Y \le y_p \setminus m, r] \bullet f_{M,R}(m,r) \bullet dm dr \quad (11)$$

which can be written in discrete form as:
$$P_Y(y_p) = P_Y(Y \le y_p)$$
$$= \sum_m \sum_r P[Y \le y_p \setminus m, r] \bullet p_{M,R}(m,r) \quad (12)$$

In equation 12, the joint probability function $f_{M,R}(m,r)$ is discritized and replaced with the joint probability mass function $p_{M,R}(m,r)$ such that:
$$p_{M,R}(m,r) \cong f_{M,R}(m,r) \bullet \Delta m \Delta r \quad (13)$$

The values of Δm and Δr are usually taken around the point (m,r) for numerical integration. The value of $p_{M,R}(m,r)$ is then calculated as the volume under the joint probability $f_{M,R}(m,r)$ defined with the four points; $f_{M,R}(m+\Delta m/2, r+\Delta r/2)$, $f_{M,R}(m+\Delta m/2, r-\Delta r/2)$, $f_{M,R}(m-\Delta m/2, r+\Delta r/2)$, and $f_{M,R}(m-\Delta m/2, r-\Delta r/2)$. From equations 12 and Bay's theory, the joint probability mass function of M and R conditioned with $[Y=y_p]$ can be written as:

$$p_{M,R}(m,r \setminus [Y = y_p])$$
$$= \frac{P_Y(Y = y_p \setminus m, r) \bullet p_{M,R}(m,r)}{\sum_m \sum_r P_Y(Y = y_p \setminus m, r) \bullet p_{M,R}(m,r)} \quad (14)$$

Since the integration is done within $m \pm \Delta m$ and $r \pm \Delta r$, the condition of $[Y=y_p]$ is actually $[y_{p1} < Y \le y_{p2}]$, where y_{p1} and y_{p2} are the values of Y that correspond to the points $(m-\Delta m/2, r+\Delta r/2)$ and $(m+\Delta m/2, r-\Delta r/2)$. For very small Δm and Δr, y_{p1}, y_{p2} and Y are almost equal and, thus, the condition is written as $[Y=y_p]$ hereafter. From equation 14 it can be seen that $p_{M,R}(m,r|[Y=y_p])$ of a certain m and r is the value of $p_{M,R}(m,r)$, if m and r fall on the $Y=y_p$ line plotted in the m-r space, normalized by the summation of all $p_{M,R}(m,r)$ values along that line. The advantages of using the condition $[Y=y_p]$ are:

1. Consistent M and R are linearly related with coefficient of correlation=1, and, thus, only one value is needed to define their hazard-consistent pair.
2. $p_{M,R}(m,r|[Y=yp])$ is defined only along the line $Y=y_p$ plotted in the m-r space and thus, it can be easily written for only one parameter with varying increment as:

$$p_M(m \setminus [Y = y_p]) = \sum_r p_{M,R}(m, r \setminus [Y = y_p])$$
$$= p_{M,R}(m, r \setminus [Y = y_p]) \quad (15\text{-a})$$
$$p_R(r \setminus [Y = y_p]) = \sum_m p_{M,R}(m, r \setminus [Y = y_p])$$
$$= p_{M,R}(m, r \setminus [Y = y_p]) \quad (15\text{-b})$$

Thus, we can write:
$$p_M(m \setminus [Y = y_p]) = p_R(r \setminus [Y = y_p])$$
$$= p_{M,R}(m, r \setminus [Y = y_p]) \quad (15\text{-c})$$

And the probability functions for any pair of m and r along the line $Y=y_p$ can be estimated as:

$$f_M(m \setminus [Y = y_p]) \cong p_M(m \setminus [Y = y_p]) / \Delta m \quad (16\text{-a})$$
$$f_R(r \setminus [Y = y_p]) \cong p_R(r \setminus [Y = y_p]) / \Delta r \quad (16\text{-b})$$
$$F_M(m \setminus [Y = y_p]) \cong \sum_m p_M(m \setminus [Y = y_p]) \quad (16\text{-c})$$
$$F_R(r \setminus [Y = y_p]) \cong \sum_r p_R(r \setminus [Y = y_p]) \quad (16\text{-d})$$

3. Since the estimated means of consistent M and R are linearly related, they give the value of y_p when used in the attenuation equation and, thus, the meaning of consistency is much clearer than in the conventional method.

Bivariate extreme theory is well developed for the estimation of bivariate extreme distribution [Sibuya 1960 and Oliveira et al. 1962]. In the literature, axioms, properties, necessary conditions and proposed forms of bivariate extreme theory are well-summarized [Jonson et al. 1972]. In general, if X and Y are two independent maximum values having marginal extreme distributions $F_X(x)$ and $F_Y(y)$ given by one of the three asymptotic distributions then:

$$F_{X,Y}(x,y) = F_X(x) \bullet F_Y(y) \quad (17)$$

is a stable bivariate probability distribution [Gumbel et al. 1967]. When X and Y are assumed to be independent, the bivariate joint probability function can be written as:

$$f_{X,Y}(x,y) = f_X(x) \bullet f_Y(y) \quad (18)$$

Since Kanda's empirical distribution [Kanda 1981] has similar properties of the three theoretical asymptotic distributions, equations 17 and 18 are considered to be applicable for such distribution which is expressed as:

$$F_X^n(x) = \exp\left[-n\left(\frac{w-x}{v(x-l)}\right)^k\right] \qquad (19)$$

Where n is the distribution power (1 for annual and 50 for lifetime probabilities), w and l are the upper and lower bounds of the random parameter X and v and k are location and shape parameters. The marginal distributions of M and R can be conveniently estimated by Kanda distribution of maximum values for M and of minimum values for R. To simplify the analysis, for R=-distance, Kanda distribution of maximum values can be used. The bounds w and l can be assumed based on physical evidences. Then, by using the non-linear least square fitting for the annual extremes of M and R plotted with Hazen method, the distributions remaining parameters can be estimated. The appropriateness of the proposed bivariate joint probability function can be judged by equation 12. Once $f_{M,R}(m,r)$ is verified, it can be directly used with equations 13 and 14 to provide the conditional joint probability mass function.

4. APPLICATION EXAMPLE FOR TOKYO

The previous formulation is applied for an example site at Tokyo. Since extreme value distributions are used for the probabilities, results are sensitive to the accuracy of numerical integration. Probability density functions have a sharp peak and thus a small integration step is required. It is found that results are relatively stable for $\Delta m < 0.05$ and $\Delta r < 0.5$. The results presented here are for $\Delta m = 0.025$ and $\Delta r = 0.25$.

4.1. Conditional joint mass function
100-y earthquake data are extracted from the catalogs. Annual extreme sets for bedrock velocity V, M, and R are independently picked up such that velocity is larger than $Vc=2.0$ cm/s. Kanda distributions for V, M, and R are estimated using fixed values for w and l as shown in table 1. Plots and fitted distributions for M, and R are shown in figures 1-a and 1-b. For V and M bounds are estimated from previous study [Ahmed et al.1995]. Upper bound of $-R$ is assumed as the minimum (-) distance used in Kanai's attenuation equation [Kanai 1968]. On the other hand, lower bound values are taken to be the limits of engineering interest for M and R. The 50-y joint probability function is based on 50-y. marginal distributions of M and R. Values of M and R from the parent distribution are not correlated as shown in figure 2-a. Once a condition is imposed such as picking up the values that resulted in annual extreme velocity, then a correlation exists between those annual extremes as shown in figure 2-b. If a further condition is imposed, such as $V \le Vc$, then an arbitrary higher correlation between extreme M and R exists due to the use of Vc as shown in figure 2-c. Since annual extreme values of M and R are independently picked up such that $V \le Vc$, a certain degree of dependence exists between them.

Table 1: Kanda distribution parameters and moments for V, M and $-R$.

Variable	w	v	k	l	50-y mean	50-y cov
V	11.2	113.2	0.77	0	7.42	0.35
M	9.0	8.89	1.72	5.5	7.56	0.06
$-R$	-30	95.82	0.58	-120	-38.9	0.40

In order to get a joint probability that satisfies equations 12 and 19, a certain part of the joint density function should be truncated and redistributed over the remaining part. The cut part should be the joint probability values that, when integrated in equation 12, give velocity larger than the velocity upper bound. When this part is homogeneously redistributed over the remaining joint probability values, the integration of such joint probability by equation 12 is found to be far from Kanda distribution of the velocity as shown by the dotted line in figure 3. This shows the need of a non-homogenous redistribution function. From equations 12 and 13, the probability mass function of ground motion parameter y between y_i and y_{i+1} can be written as:

$$P_Y(y_i < Y \le y_{i+1}) = F_Y(y_{i+1}) - F_Y(y_i)$$
$$\cong \sum_m \sum_r (P_Y[(y_i < Y \le y_{i+1}) \setminus m,r] \bullet$$
$$f_{M,R}(m,r) \bullet \Delta m \Delta r) \qquad (20)$$

If a redistribution function $D(Y)$ is defined as:
$$D(y_i < Y \le y_{i+1}) = [F_Y(y_{i+1}) - F_Y(y_i)]/$$
$$\sum_m \sum_r (P_Y[(y_i < Y \le y_{i+1}) \setminus m,r] \bullet \qquad (21)$$
$$f_M^{50}(m) \bullet f_R^{50}(r) \bullet \Delta m \Delta r)$$

for the values of Y between the minimum Y, given by lower bounds of M and R, and the upper bound of Y, and zero otherwise. Then the joint probability density function can be written as:

$$f_{M,R}(m,r) = f_R^{50}(r) \bullet f_M^{50}(m) \bullet D[Y(m,r)] \qquad (22)$$

As expected, this proposed joint density function is found appropriate since $F_V^{50}(v)$ values from equations 12 and 19 are identical at any checking points as shown in figure 3. 2-dimensional

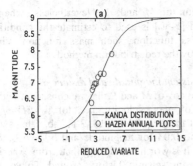

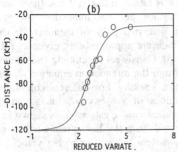

Figure 1: Hazen plots and fitted Kanda distribution for magnitude and (-)distance at Tokyo. (Vc=2.0 cm./sec. 100-year data)

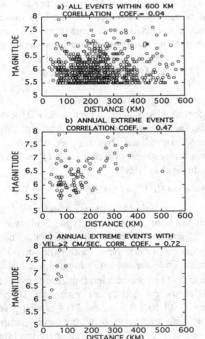

Figure 2: Magnitude and distance distribution for earthquakes around Tokyo (100-year).

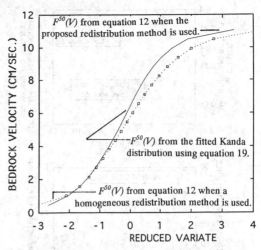

Figure 3: Comparison between $F^{50}(V)$ from Kanda distribution and the ones from integrations of truncated joint probability functions of M and R.

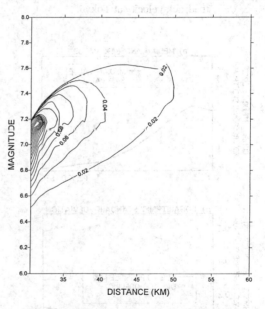

Figure 4: 2-D plot of the proposed 50-year joint probability function of M and R.

representation of such joint probability function is shown in figure 4 from which the correlation between M and R can be observed. Using such joint probability function resulted in a correlation coefficient 0.42 between M and R. Marginal mean and cov from this truncated function are 45.1, 0.34, 7.15, and 0.04 for M and R respectively.

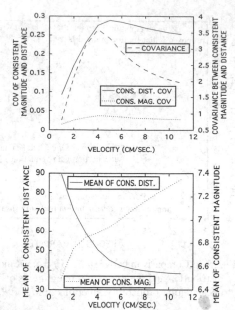

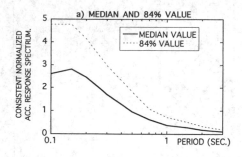

Figure 5: Consistent moments for different values of bedrock velocity at Tokyo.

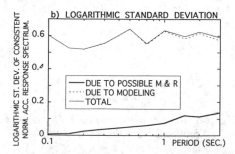

Figure 6: Median, 84% value and logarithmic standard deviation of consistent acceleration spectral shape at Tokyo using Kawashima's spectrum.

It is worth mentioning here that when the condition $[Y=y_p]$ is used to estimate the conditioned joint mass function given in equation 14, estimated consistent values depend only on the 50-y. marginal

distribution of M and R. Nevertheless, when the condition $[Y \geq y_p]$ is used to estimate the conditioned joint mass function, such mass function will be affected by the redistribution method.

4.2. Consistent magnitude and distance

Mean and cov of M and R that are consistent with 50-y mean of max. velocity, i.e., for $y_p=E[V_{50}]$, are estimated from equations 14, 3-a, 3-b, 5-b, and 5-c as 7.1 and 0.03 for magnitude and 39 and 0.28 for distance. It is worth mentioning that, from experience gained from seismic history around Tokyo, such combination is rather unlikely. Thus, the values with 84% probability are recommended for practical application. The two pairs of mean±σ for distance and magnitude are approximately given as (30,6.87) and (50,7.35). Consistent magnitude and distance are related through the attenuation equation at the 50-y mean of max. velocity. For different conditions, i.e., different values of velocity y_p, mean and cov of consistent values can be estimated as shown in figure 5. As expected from the linear relation between the mean of consistent values, for higher velocity, mean of the consistent magnitude is increased while that of consistent distance is decreased. On the other hand, covariance and cov values for both consistent magnitude and distance are increased with velocity until 4.0-5.0 cm/s. For the simulation of ground motion if only one pair of M and R is needed then the pair of consistent means can be used. If more than one pair are needed, other consistent pairs can be simulated from distribution functions such that the condition $y_p=E[V_{50}]$ remains true, i.e., the linear relation between M and R is maintained.

4.3. Consistent spectrum shape

The spectral shape $S(T)$, where T is the period in seconds, is defined as the acceleration response spectrum normalized by the PGA value. The acceleration response spectrum $S^o(T)$ is given as [Kawashima et al. 1984]:

$$S^o(T) = a_T \bullet 10^{b_T m} \bullet (\Delta + 30)^{c_T} \qquad (23)$$

Where Δ is the epicentral distance and a_T, b_T, and c_T are functions of T and soil type. Soil type 1 is selected here to represent the bedrock. The term $(\Delta+30)$ is replaced here with the hypocentral distance. The values of logarithmic standard deviation $\beta_s(T)$ of the acceleration response spectrum as well as a_T, b_T, and c_T are given for 10 periods between $T=0.1$ to 3.0 seconds. PGA is also give as a function with the same form but with parameters independent on T. The normalized spectrum (spectral shape $S(T)$) can be estimated from equation 23 divided by PGA when both are calculated for the

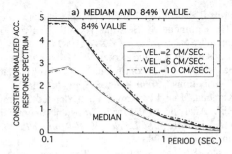

a) MEDIAM AND 84% VALUE.

84% VALUE

VEL.=2 CM/SEC.
VEL.=6 CM/SEC.
VEL.=10 CM/SEC.

MEDIAN

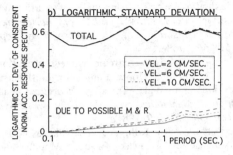

b) LOGARITHMIC STANDARD DEVIATION.

TOTAL

VEL.=2 CM/SEC.
VEL.=6 CM/SEC.
VEL.=10 CM/SEC.

DUE TO POSSIBLE M & R

Figure 7: Effect of conditioning velocity on median, 84% value and logarithmic standard deviation of consistent acceleration spectral shape at Tokyo using Kawashima's spectrum.

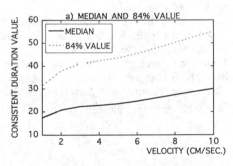

a) MEDIAN AND 84% VALUE

MEDIAN
84% VALUE

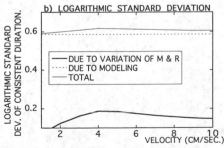

b) LOGARITHMIC STANDARD DEVIATION

DUE TO VARIATION OF M & R
DUE TO MODELING
TOTAL

Figure 8: Effect of conditioning velocity on median, 84% value and logarithmic standard deviation of consistent duration at Tokyo using Hisada's formula.

same values of M and R. If a lognormal distribution is assumed for $S(T)$ then the mean of consistent $ln[S(T)]$ is the median of consistent $S(T)$ and can be estimated from equation 2 or a first degree approximation can be estimated from equation 4. Mean and median values of consistent $S(T)$ are estimated for 10 values of T as shown in figure 6-a by using equation 2. Equation 4 gives values very close to the plotted ones and, thus, it can be used for practical application. The variance of consistent $ln[S(T)]$, $var(ln[S(T)]_c)$, which is due to the various possible combinations of M and R, is estimated with equation 5-a. In figure 6-b, the total logarithmic standard deviation values at different periods are also plotted. Such values resulted from the total logarithmic variance of spectral shape which can be estimated as:

$$var(\ln[S(T)]) = var(\ln[S(T)_c]) + \beta_\varepsilon^{2}(T) \qquad (24)$$

Modeling standard deviation values are given for $log(S(T))$ in Kawashima's study and thus they are transformed to be in terms of $ln(S(T))$ by multiplying in $ln(10)$. The median, 84% values and logarithmic standard deviation are shown in figure 7.

4.4. Consistent strong motion duration

A commonly used formula for the total duration in seconds is given as [Hisada et al. 1976]:

$$D = 10^{0.31M - 0.774} \qquad (25)$$

If this duration is assumed to have a lognormal distribution, then the median and logarithmic variance of consistent D can be estimated from equation 2 and 5-a as 26.6 and 0.026 seconds respectively, i.e., cov=0.16. Such variance is only due to the various possible combinations of M and R. It can be considered independent from modeling uncertainties due to equation 25 and can be combined as:

$$var(D) = var(D_c]) + 0.255^2 \qquad (26)$$

The median, 84% value and the logarithmic variance of D variations with the velocity used to condition them are shown in figure 8. All these values are increasing with larger velocities.

For the simulation of ground motion, pairs of consistent $S(T)$ and duration D are needed. If only one pair is needed then the pair of their consistent values means can be estimated from equation 2 or equation 4 and used in the simulation. If more than one pair are needed, other consistent pairs can be simulated from the probability distribution functions of $S(T)$ and D taking into account the correlation between both variables.

5. CONCLUSION

A method is proposed for the estimation of the consistent ground motion parameters such as magnitude, distance, spectral shape, and duration. In such method a bivariate extreme distribution with a dependent function is utilized to model the lifetime joint probability density function of magnitude and distance. Possible combination of magnitude and distance are discussed in light of this function. Results are presented in the form of the first and second order moments. The method has the following advantages over the conventional methods:

1. The 50-y. probability density functions are used so that the probabilities are clearly related to the maximum events in reference lifetime of ordinary structures.

2. The mean values of consistent magnitude and distance are linearly related so that any consistent pair results in the velocity used to condition their joint distribution. Thus, consistency with a certain velocity level is clearly modeled and mentioned.

3. Although the bounded distribution is used here due to its adequacy for modeling the physical parameter probability distribution, other distribution models can be used without any complications.

4. For a simplified hazard-consistent design, only the mean values of the consistent magnitude and distance are needed since the first order approximation of the mean of consistent spectrum shape and duration using such values gives good approximation.

REFERENCES

1. Ahmed, K.A. and J. Kanda, "Characteristics of Extreme Bedrock Velocity Estimated From Extreme Value Distributions," *Application of Statistics and Probability - ICASP 7, pp. 1287-1294,* Paris, France, 1995.

2. Cornell, C. A., "Engineering Seismic Risk Analysis", *BSSA, V. 58, No. 5, pp. 1503-1606,* 1968.

3. Gumbel, E. J., and Mustafi, C. K., "Some Analytical Properties of Bivariate Extremal Distributions", *Journal of the American Statistical Association, 62, pp. 569-588,* 1967.

4. Hisada, T., and Ando, H., "Relation between Duration of Earthquake Ground Motion and the Magnitude", *Kajima Institute of Construction Technology,* 1976.

5. Ishikawa, Y., and Kameda, H., "Hazard-Consistent Magnitude and Distance for Extended Seismic Risk Analysis", *Proceeding of Ninth World Conf. on Earthq. Engng. Vol. II, pp. 89-94,* 1988.

6. Itoh, T., Ishii, K., Okumura, T., and Ishikawa, Y., "Development of Seismic Hazard Analysis in Japan", *SMiRT., K1, pp. 69-74,* 1987.

7. Johnson, N. L., and Kotz, S., "Distributions in Statistics: Continuous Multivariate Distributions", *John Wiley & Sons, Inc.,* 1972

8. Kameda, H. and Ishikawa, Y., "Extended Seismic Risk Analysis by Hazard-Consistent Magnitude and Distance", *JSCE, No. 392/I-9, pp. 395-402,* (in Japanese), 1988.

9. Kanai, K., and Suzuki, T., "Expectancy of the Maximum Velocity Amplitude of Earthquake Motion at Bedrock", *Bull. of Earthquake Research Institute, Vol. 46, Univ. of Tokyo, pp. 663-666,* 1968.

10. Kanda, J., "A New Extreme Value Distribution with Lower and Upper Limits for Earthquake Motion and Wind Speed", *Theoretical and Applied Mechanics, Vol. 31, Univ. of Tokyo Press, pp. 351-360,* 1981.

11. Kawashima, K., Koh, A., and Takahashi, K., "Attenuation of Peak Ground Motion and Absolute Acceleration Response Spectra", 8th *WCEE., pp. 257-264,* 1984

12. Nojima, N., and Kameda, H., "Simulation of Risk-Consistent Earthquake Motion", *Proceeding of Ninth World Conf. on Earthq. Engng. Vol. II, pp. 95-100,* 1988

13. Sibuya, M., "Bivariate Extreme Statistics, I", *Annals of the Institute of Statistical Mathematics, Vol. XI, No. 3, pp. 195-210,* 1960.

14. Tiago de Oliveira, J., "Structure Theory of Bivariate Extremes", *Extensions, Estudos de Matematica, Estatistica e Econometria, Vol. 7, pp. 165-95,* Lisbon, 1962-1963.

Structural Safety and Reliability, Shiraishi, Shinozuka & Wen (eds) © 1998 Balkema, Rotterdam, ISBN 90 5410 978 5

Seismic hazard from low frequency-high impact fault activities using probabilistic scenario earthquakes

Y. Ishikawa & T. Okumura
Institute of Technology, Shimizu Corporation, Tokyo, Japan

H. Kameda
Disaster Prevention Research Institute, Kyoto University, Japan

ABSTRACT : The applicability of the probabilistic seismic hazard analysis to low frequency range is discussed through the results of a case study for Kobe by using the concept of probabilistic scenario earthquakes and contribution factors from corresponding seismic sources. On this basis, data and the conditions inevitable for such an application are summarized. In summary, the active fault data are indispensable to the future seismic hazard assessment because the Kobe Earthquake cannot be identified as an earthquake of precaution either in the deterministic or probabilistic manner when only the historical earthquake data are used. In addition, we should consider the return period in the order of 1,000 years, not in 100 years, for such a "low frequency-high impact seismic event."

1 INTRODUCTION

On January 17, 1995, an earthquake of magnitude 7.2 ("Kobe Earthquake") hit the city of Kobe and its surrounding area to cause more than 6,000 deaths and serious damage to various structures. The strongest earthquake ground motions ever observed in Japan were recorded in Kobe region located near the causative fault. Such strong earthquake motions have not been clearly defined either in the earthquake resistant design for structures or urban earthquake hazard mitigation planning in Japan. On the other hand, the average recurrence interval of the Rokko fault system that was the source of the Kobe Earthquake is estimated to be more than 1,000 years from the geological data. It has therefore become an urgent issue to establish the methodology of determining such low frequency- high impact earthquake ground motions.

In this study, the applicability of the probabilistic seismic hazard analysis considering the fault activities to low probability range is discussed through the results of the case study for Kobe. In particular, the concept of probabilistic scenario earthquakes proposed by Ishikawa and Kameda (1991, 1994) is examined to evaluate a low frequency- high impact seismic event. The regional differences of low frequency seismic hazard are also discussed through the case studies for eight major cities in Japan.

2 PROCEDURE OF SEISMIC HAZARD ASSESSMENT CONSIDERING FAULT ACTIVITIES

Fig.1 schematically shows the general flow to evaluate the seismic hazard. In the seismic hazard assessment, two typical ways are generally used in regard to the future earthquake occurrences. One is the probabilistic seismic hazard analysis (PSHA; left side of Fig.1) and the other is the use of deterministic scenario earthquakes (SE; right side of Fig.1). While

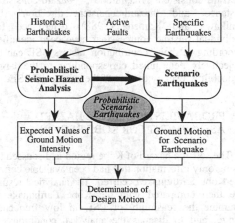

Fig. 1 Procedures of seismic hazard assessment

most of seismic hazard assessments in Japan were performed on the basis of the historical earthquake data before the Kobe Earthquake, in the future PSHA, we should consider the active fault data which may represent the low frequency seismic activities.

PSHA is useful as it is capable of determining the ground motion intensity corresponding to a target risk level such as annual probability of exceedance, and has been used as a major tool for the site ground motion estimation. However, they tend to eliminate the information on the physical characteristics of earthquakes such as their magnitude and epicentral locations. In a sense, this can be regarded as an advantage of PSHA, as it greatly simplifies the issue of design seismic load evaluation. With recent increasing demand for dynamic seismic design of structures, the time history of the earthquake ground motions should be determined in addition to the intensity parameter. It is therefore desirable to clarify the magnitude and epicentral location of the typical earthquakes under the specific risk level.

SE, on the other hand, has been used to estimate regional ground motion distributions for urban earthquake hazard mitigation planning as well as the site earthquake ground motion for design of important structures. In such a case, the physical characteristics of SE are unique and deterministic, then the time history of the earthquake ground motion can be readily estimated. SE is generally determined from the geological and seismo-tectonic considerations. However, the relationship between SE and a target risk level is not clear in most cases.

The concept of probabilistic scenario earthquakes (PSE ; horizontal bold arrow in Fig.1) proposed by Ishikawa and Kameda (1991, 1994) makes it possible to establish a logical link between PSHA and SE. It is characterized by using the "hazard-consistent magnitude", "hazard-consistent distance" and "hazard-consistent direction" (by Ishikawa and Kameda (1988)) determined for individual seismic sources that have been identified according to their "contribution factors". SE can be objectively determined corresponding to the target probability level by the use of the concept of PSE.

3 PROBABILISTIC SEISMIC HAZARD ASSESSMENT FOR KOBE REGION

The seismic hazard of Kobe region is discussed by using only information that had been available before the Kobe Earthquake occurred. The analytical results are then compared with the Kobe Earthquake to examine the feasibility of PSE in low frequency range, and to discuss the analytical conditions of being necessary to evaluate the low frequency- high impact seismic event.

3.1 Analytical model and conditions

(1) Active fault model for PSHA

The following issues regarding the active fault data largely influence the results of PSHA: i) modeling the earthquake faults based on the active fault data published by the Research Group for Active Faults of Japan (1991) (the issue of grouping and segmentation of the active faults); ii) treatment of uncertainties involved in various relationships for active faults; and iii) interpretation and combination of the historical earthquake data and active fault data.

These issues are treated in the following way in this study. i) The "seismogenic active fault (proposed by Matsuda (1990))", which can be responsible for the occurrence of individual great earthquake, is used as the active fault model in PSHA. However, there are seismological views that the Rokko fault system which is one of the seismogenic active faults, was not accurately consistent with the source of the Kobe Earthquake (Shimazaki (1995)). Therefore, in the future PSHA, the active fault model should reflect the up-to-date information obtained from the active fault surveys which are being actively exercised since the Kobe Earthquake. ii) The relationships between various active fault parameters will be described in the following paragraph (Table 1). iii) The historical earthquake data and the active fault data are assumed to be independent. The results from each of these data are combined on this basis. Generally, the active fault should be removed from the data when there is a clear evidence of recent energy release. However, in case of Kobe, there was no active fault in this category if the information prior to the Kobe Earthquake are taken into account.

(2) PSHA conditions

Table 1 shows the analytical conditions in PSHA. A polygon-shaped source-areas characterizing earthquakes occurring randomly in each area is used in historical earthquake-based PSHA. The b-value model is applied to each source-area, whereas the Nankai-type interplate earthquake with a characteristic magnitude is modeled separately. All the earthquakes including the interplate earthquake are assumed to occur according to the stationary Poisson process in the time domain. Fig.2 shows the detail of the source-area model for Kobe.

In PSHA based on the active fault data, it is assumed that an earthquake with a characteristic magnitude will occur randomly in time on each active fault model. The earthquake occurrence rate is evaluated from the annual slip rate and the displacement per seismic event. The annual slip rate of each active fault is assumed to be 5mm, 0.5mm,

Table 1 Earthquake occurrence and ground motion models in PSHA for Kobe

	PSHA by Historical Earthquake Data		PSHA by Active Fault Data
Seismic Source	Source-area (Modeling for Randomly Occurring Earthquake)	Interplate Earthquake (Nankai Earthquake)	Active Fault (Seismogenic Active Fault)
Occurrence Model	Stationary Poisson	Stationary Poisson	Stationary Poisson
Earthquake Occurrence Rate	Based on Historical Earthquake · Usami 1600~1884 ($M{\geq}7.5$) · Utsu 1885~1925 ($M{\geq}6.0$) · JMA 1926~1990 ($M{\geq}5.0$)	Based on Historical Earthquake · Nankai EQ : 1/117years	Based on Displacement per Event and Average Slip Rate
Probability of Magnitude	Exponential Distribution between Upper and Lower Magnitude (Gutenberg-Richter's Relationship)	Uniform Distribution between Upper and Lower Magnitude · Nankai EQ : 8.0~8.4	Characteristic Magnitude (Based on Fault Length)
Probability of Distance	Based on Earthquake Occurring Uniformly in each Source-area	Characteristic Distance (Fault Distance) · Nankai EQ : 130km	Characteristic Distance (Fault Distance)
Ground Motion Model	Attenuation Model by Fukushima and Tanaka (1991) $[\log_{10}A_{max} = 0.51M_J - \log_{10}(R+0.006 \cdot 10^{0.51M_J}) - 0.0034R + 0.59]$ Uncertainty : Logarithmic Normal Distribution with $\zeta = 0.5$		

Table 2 List of major earthquakes in the vicinity of Kobe

	Date (y.m.d)	M_J	Δ (km)	PGA (Gal)	Name of Earthquake (Damaged Region)
1	1596. 9.5	7.5	38	229	Keicho-fushimi Earthquake
2	868. 8. 3	7.0	37	174	(Harima/Yamashiro)
3	1916.11.26	6.1	19	156	(Kobe)
4	1510. 9.21	6.8	39	144	(Settsu/Kawachi)
5	1185. 8.13	7.4	67	131	(Ohmi/Yamashiro/Yamato)
	1854.12.24	8.4	187	55	Ansei-nankai Earthquake
	1995. 1.17	7.2	15	317 (632)*	Kobe Earthquake

* PGA when the fault distance instead of the hypocentral distance is used.
M_J : JMA Magnitude, Δ : Epicentral Distance,
PGA : Peak Ground Acceleration by Fukushima and Tanaka's Attenuation Model

Table 3 Parameters of major seismogenic active faults in the vicinity of Kobe

Name of Fault System	Class	T_R (years)	L (km)	M_J	R (km)	PGA (Gal)
Rokko	B	3,100*	31	7.3	0.6	633
Arima-takatsuki	B	8,200	52	7.7	10	498
East-coast of Awaji Island	B	3,500	22	7.1	16	342
West-coast of Awaji Island	B	2,200	14	6.7	19	256
MTL Izumi-kongo	A	840	53	7.7	42	255
MTL South of Awaji Island	A	700	44	7.6	52	198

* Average slip rate is assumed to be 0.8mm/year.
Class : Class of Fault Activity, T_R : Average Recurrence Time, L : Fault Length, M_J : JMA Magnitude, R : Fault Distance, PGA : Peak Ground Acceleration by Fukushima and Tanaka's Attenuation Model
MTL : Median Tectonic Line

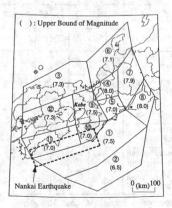

Fig. 2 Source-area model for Kobe

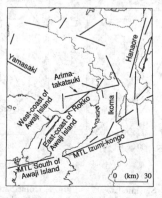

Fig. 3 Distribution of major seismogenic active faults in the vicinity of Kobe

and 0.05mm per year corresponding to activity class A, B, and C respectively. For the Rokko fault system, the annual slip rate is assumed to be 0.8 mm per year referring to Matsuda (1981). The magnitude and the displacement of earthquakes are obtained by using the Matsuda's relationships (1975). It is assumed that earthquake occurrence on the active faults also follows the stationary Poisson process, because there are very few active faults whose activity history was known before the Kobe Earthquake.

The peak ground acceleration attenuation model by Fukushima and Tanaka (1991) is used in this study. Attenuation uncertainty is assumed to follow the logarithmic normal distribution with logarithmic standard deviation of $\zeta=0.5$.

3.2 Historical earthquakes and active faults around Kobe

The seismic activity in Kobe is reviewed. Table 2 shows the major earthquakes around Kobe listed in the Japanese earthquake catalogs. From the earthquake catalog which covers more than 1,000 years, the peak ground acceleration in Kobe during the Kobe Earthquake is estimated to be the strongest in the time span looked at herein.

Fig.3 shows the distribution of major seismogenic active faults in the vicinity of Kobe, and Table 3 gives their specifications. It has been a known fact that not a few active faults are located around Kobe as shown in Fig.3. However, as listed in Table 3, the average recurrence interval of Rokko fault system is estimated to be about 3,100 years, which seems to keep this fault away from serious attention in engineering decision and regional disaster mitigation planning.

3.3 Seismic hazard curves for Kobe

Fig.4 shows the seismic hazard curves for Kobe. In Fig.4, the solid and dotted lines indicate the hazard curves based on the historical earthquake data and the active fault data respectively. The annual probability of exceedance derived from the historical earthquake data is larger than that from the active fault data up to 200 Gal of the peak acceleration. However, in higher acceleration range (i.e. low probability level), the annual probability of exceedance based on active fault data dominates.

The bold solid line in Fig.4 represents the results obtained by combining the historical earthquake data and the active fault data. Even when these combined values are used, only the peak acceleration of 190 Gal is expected at the return period of 100 years, and at the return period of 1,000 years, the peak acceleration of 460 Gal is expected. According to this result, the peak acceleration of 600 to 800 Gals, which were actually recorded in the Kobe region during the Kobe Earthquake, has a return period of more than 1,000 years (the order of 1,000 years).

3.4 Probabilistic scenario earthquakes for Kobe

Fig.5 shows the contribution factors of major seismic sources (i.e. source-area model, Nankai Earthquake and active fault model) for Kobe region. Table 4 shows the parameter values determined for

Table 4 Probabilistic scenario earthquakes for Kobe

Seismic Source	Annual Probability $p_0=10^{-2}$ PGA 189 (Gal)			Annual Probability $p_0=10^{-3}$ PGA 464 (Gal)			Annual Probability $p_0=10^{-4}$ PGA 959 (Gal)		
	c_k (%)	$\overline{M_j}$	$\frac{\overline{\Delta}}{R}$ (km)	c_k (%)	$\overline{M_j}$	$\frac{\overline{\Delta}}{R}$ (km)	c_k (%)	$\overline{M_j}$	$\frac{\overline{\Delta}}{R}$ (km)
Source-area No.9	43	6.5	29	25	6.9	25	7	7.1	22
Nankai Earthquake	7	8.2	130	<5	—	—	<5	—	—
Rokko Fault System	<5	—	—	24	7.3	0.6	65	7.3	0.6
MTL Izumi-kongo Fault System	9	7.7	42	14	7.7	42	5	7.7	42
East-coast of Awaji Island Fault System	<5	—	—	8	7.1	16	6	7.1	16
Arima-takatsuki Fault System	<5	—	—	7	7.7	10	11	7.7	10
MTL South of Awaji Island Fault System	8	7.6	52	6	7.6	52	<5	—	—
West-coast of Awaji Island Fault System	<5	—	—	5	6.7	19	<5	—	—

* c_k: Contribution Factor, M_j: JMA Magnitude,
Δ: Epicentral Distance, R: Fault Distance

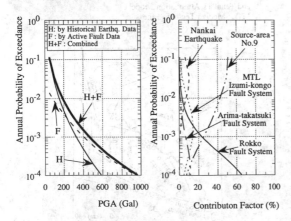

Fig. 4 Seismic hazard curves for Kobe

Fig. 5 Contribution factors for individual seismic sources

PSE that have contribution factors of more than 5% with annual probability of exceedance of 10^{-2}, 10^{-3}, and 10^{-4}.

When the return period is in the order of 100 years (i.e. annual probability of exceedance $=10^{-2}$ to 10^{-3}), the source-area No.9 which represents randomly occurring earthquakes with close distances has the largest contribution. On the other hand, the contribution factor of the Rokko fault system is less than 5%.

However, the contributions of most of active fault model are relatively large when the return period is in the order of 1,000 years (i.e. annual probability of exceedance $=$ 10^{-3} to 10^{-4}). In particular, the contribution of the Rokko fault system remarkably increase in this probability level, and it becomes dominant over all other seismic sources when the annual probability of exceedance reaches 10^{-4}.

From these results, the following views on the PSE for Kobe region may be established: i) It would be quite difficult to identify the Kobe Earthquake as a precaution earthquake by using only the historical earthquake data; and ii) Although an idea of PSE considering the active fault data would have selected the Rokko fault system as a scenario earthquake with a considerable contribution, the target return period would have to be more than 1,000 years (the order of 1,000 years).

In summary, the active fault data are indispensable to the future seismic hazard assessment because the Kobe Earthquake cannot be identified as an earthquake of precaution either in the deterministic or probabilistic manner when only the historical earthquake data are used. In addition, the concept of PSE can be applied to the evaluation of a low frequency-high impact seismic event by considering the return period in the order of 1,000 years, not in 100 years.

After the Kobe Earthquake, there are two opposite opinions regarding the consideration of the fault activities. i) The fault activities should be considered as deterministic earthquake sources in the ground motion estimation. ii) It is not realistic to unconditionally consider the fault activities in the absence of information on when they become active. The concept of PSE would be a rational means to fill a gap between these two extreme claims on low frequency seismic events, for the contribution factor of the PSE changes continuously according to the risk level. Thus, the contribution factor can be a useful index which represents the dominant earthquake at any specified probability levels of interest.

4. PSE FOR EIGHT MAJOR CITIES IN JAPAN

Since the applicability of the PSHA and PSE to the low frequency range has been examined through the case study for Kobe, the same procedure is applied to eight major cities in Japan to estimate the PSE for these cities, then the regional difference of the low frequency seismic hazard is discussed based on the results.

4.1 Analytical model and conditions

The eight major cities in Japan, i.e., Sapporo, Sendai, Tokyo, Nagoya, Osaka, Hiroshima, Takamatsu and Fukuoka are selected for the estimation of PSE. The analytical method and conditions used for Kobe are also applied to these cities. The return period of 1,000 years is considered as the target risk level of the low frequency seismic hazard.

4.2 PSE for eight major cities

Table 5 shows the results of PSE for eight cities corresponding to the return period of 1,000 years. The results of Kobe are also shown in the table. The selected PSE are: i) PSE with the maximum contribution; and ii) PSE with the maximum peak acceleration re-evaluated by Fukushima and Tanaka's attenuation model for those with more than 5% of the contribution factor. Also listed in the table are the maximum peak acceleration directly calculated from the historical earthquake data in the deterministic manner, that from the seismogenic active faults, and the expected peak acceleration for the return period of 1,000 years according to PSHA. From the table, the followings are observed.

The order of the peak accelerations by the three different methods differs from city to city. Therefore, in the evaluation of the low frequency seismic hazard, the comprehensive studies should be carried out following the flow chart in Fig.1.

For the cities except Tokyo, PSE with the maximum re-evaluated peak acceleration is identified based on the active faults. This means that, as was the case for Kobe, the active fault data are indispensable to the seismic hazard assessment especially in the low frequency range. It is also pointed out that further information on active faults such as their history of activities should be collected for the seismic hazard analyses, so as to make the results more precise.

Regional difference of the low frequency seismic hazard such as the expected peak acceleration for the return period of 1,000 years is very large. This regional difference observed here is greater than the difference of the regional coefficient of the seismic load used in the present earthquake resistant design in Japan. The issue on such a major regional difference should be discussed in the future studies.

Table 5 Probabilistic scenario earthquakes for eight major cities in Japan

City	Max.PGA by Historical Earthq. (Gal)	Max.PGA by Active Fault (Gal)	1,000 Years Expected PGA (Gal)	PSE for 1,000 Years Return Period $(c_k \geq 5\%)$									
				PSE with Maximum Contribution					PSE with Maximum Re-evaluated PGA				
				Seismic Sources	c_k (%)	$\overline{M_J}$	$\overline{R,\Delta}$ (km)	re-PGA (Gal)	Seismic Sources	c_k (%)	$\overline{M_J}$	$\overline{R,\Delta}$ (km)	re-PGA (Gal)
Sapporo	179	201	236	Earthquake with Close Distance	70	6.0	19	156	West of Umaoi-kyuryo Fault System	12	7.0	33	201
Sendai	334	616	432	Earthquake with Close Distance	51	6.5	19	273	Nagamachi-rifu Fault System	26	7.2	1.2	616
Tokyo	400	327	560	Kanto Earthquake	82	8.0	21	355	Kanto Earthquake	82	8.0	21	355
Nagoya	534	481	675	Tenpaku-kako Fault System	34	6.7	13	323	Gifu-ichinomiya Fault System	9	6.9	6	481
Osaka	406	559	527	MTL Izumi-kongo Fault System	22	7.8	28	357	Uemachi Fault System	12	7.3	3.9	559
Kobe	311	633	464	Earthquake with Close Distance	25	6.9	25	225	Rokko Fault System	24	7.3	0.6	633
Hiroshima	306	420	360	Earthquake with Close Distance	40	6.6	31	193	Itsukaichi Fault System	20	7.0	9.5	420
Takamatsu	393	423	392	Nankai Earthquake	24	8.2	94	149	MTL Shikoku Fault System	23	8.5	28	423
Fukuoka	172	325	297	Earthquake with Close Distance	73	6.5	26	188	Nishiyama Fault System	15	7.1	19	325

* c_k : Contribution Factor, M_J : JMA Magnitude, Δ : Epicentral Distance, R : Fault Distance
re-PGA : Peak Acceleration re-evaluated by Fukushima and Tanaka's Relationship, MTL : Median Tectonic Line

5. CONCLUSIONS

In this study, the evaluation of the low frequency seismic hazard is discussed through the case study for Kobe and eight major cities in Japan. The main results may be summarized as follows.

The results of the probabilistic seismic hazard analysis indicate that the return period of the peak ground acceleration recorded in Kobe during the Kobe Earthquake exceeds 1,000 years even when both the historical earthquake data and active fault data are used. Although the concept of probabilistic scenario earthquakes considering the active fault data would have identified the Rokko fault system as a scenario earthquake with a considerable contribution, the target return period would have to be more than 1,000 years.

Therefore, it is pointed out that the active fault data are indispensable to the future seismic hazard assessment. In addition, we should consider the return period in the order of 1,000 years, not in 100 years, for such a "low frequency- high impact seismic event."

REFERENCES

Fukushima, Y. and Tanaka, T. 1991. A new attenuation relation for peak horizontal acceleration of strong earthquake ground motion in Japan. Shimizu Technical Research Bulletin 10: 1-11.

Ishikawa, Y. and Kameda, H. 1988. Hazard-consistent magnitude and distance for extended seismic risk analysis. Proc. 9th WCEE, Vol.II : 89-94.

Ishikawa, Y. and Kameda, H. 1991. Probability-based determination of specific scenario earthquakes. Proc. 4th International Conference on Seismic Zonation, Vol.II : 3-10.

Ishikawa, Y. and Kameda, H. 1994. Scenario earthquakes vs probabilistic seismic hazard. Proceedings of the 6th International Conference on Structural Safety and Reliability (ICOSSAR'93), Vol.3: 2139-2146.

Matsuda, T. 1975. Magnitude and recurrence interval of earthquakes from a fault. Journal of the Seismological Society of Japan (Zisin) 2-28: 269-283 (in Japanese).

Matsuda, T. 1990. Seismic zoning map of Japanese islands, with maximum magnitudes derived from active fault data. Bulletin of the Earthquake Research Institute, University of Tokyo 65: 289-319 (in Japanese).

Matsuda, T. 1981. Active faults and damaging earthquakes in Japan — Macroseismic zoning and precaution fault zones. Maurice Ewing Ser., Vol.4, Am. Geophys. Union: 271-289.

Shimazaki, K. 1995. Long-term forecast of a large earthquake on the basis of active fault data. Proc. 23rd Symposium of Earthquake Ground Motion, Sponsored by Architectural Institute of Japan: 5-10 (in Japanese).

The research group for active faults of Japan, 1991. Maps of active faults in Japan with an explanatory text. University of Tokyo press (in Japanese).

Structural Safety and Reliability, Shiraishi, Shinozuka & Wen (eds) © 1998 Balkema, Rotterdam, ISBN 90 5410 978 5

Seismic hazard: Recurrence and attenuation of subcrustal (60-170 km) earthquakes

Dan Lungu & Anton Zaicenco
Technical University of Civil Engineering, Bucharest, Romania

Tiberiu Cornea
IPCT S.A., Bucharest, Romania

Pieter van Gelder
Delft University of Technology, Netherlands

ABSTRACT: The hazard analysis for the Vrancea subcrustal earthquakes in Carpathian Mountains, Romania, include relationships for the recurrence of magnitude and directional attenuation functions for the ground acceleration. Sensivity of results to the maximum credible magnitude of the source and to the maximum recorded ground acceleration is discussed.

1 RECURRENCE-MAGNITUDE RELATIONSHIPS

The major contribution to seismic hazard in Romania comes from Vrancea seismogenic zone, located where the Carpathian Mountains arc bends.

The both historical and instrumental Catalogues of Vrancea events use, the Gutenberg-Richter magnitude, M (Gutenberg - Richter, 1954).

As a systematization requirement, the Global Seismic Hazard Assessment Program in Europe (GSHAP, 1993) promoted at the GeoForschungsZentrum, Potsdam, Germany, recommends the use of the moment magnitude M_w.

For the subcrustal Vrancea earthquakes, the following magnitude conversion relationship may be obtained from the linear regression of available records during the 60yr.:

$$M_w = 1.09 \, M - 0.36 \qquad (1)$$

where: M is the Gutenberg-Richter magnitude and M_w is the moment magnitude.

The Gutenberg-Richter law for the recurrence of earthquakes with magnitude equal to and greater than M is determined from the Radu's catalogue of Vrancea intermediate depth magnitudes ($M \geq 5.0$) occurred during this century (1901-1994). It contains 103 seismic events.

The average number per year of Vrancea earthquakes with magnitude $\geq$ M, as resulting also from Fig.1, is (Lungu et al, 1995):

$$\log n(\geq M) = 3.49 - 0.72 \, M \qquad (2)$$

The Hwang and Huo (1994) modification of the Gutenberg-Richter relationship:

$$n(\geq M) = e^{\alpha - \beta M} \; \frac{1 - e^{-\beta(Mmax-M)}}{1 - e^{-\beta(Mmax-Mo)}} \qquad (3)$$

was determined for the Vrancea source as (Elnashai, Lungu, 1995):

$$n(\geq M) = e^{8.036-1.658M} \; \frac{1 - e^{-1.658\,(7.8 - M)}}{1 - e^{-1.658\,(7.8 - 6)}} \qquad (4)$$

where the threshold magnitude was selected as $M_0=6.0$,. the maximum credible magnitude of the source was selected as $M_{max}=7.8$, and $8.036 = 3.489$ ln10 and $1.658 = 0.720$ ln10. The magnitude recurrence relationship depend on the magnitude intervals it refers, such as, the threshold magnitude calibrates the coefficients of recurrence expression (2).

Although an exact estimation of the maximum credible magnitude of the source can not be done, even an approximate estimation of it has very important numerical consequences on the prediction of magnitude having large recurrence intervals. The maximum credible magnitude of the Vrancea source was estimated in the past to be at most M=8.0 and at least M=7.5.

Marza, Kijko and Mäntyniemi (1991) estimate as "reasonable and stable" a maximum magnitude of the source $M_{max} = 7.8$, (standard deviation) of 0.2. According to the same authors, the strongest experienced Vrancea earthquake is the 1802 event with a magnitude of M = 7.7 ± 0.3.

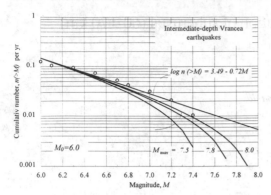

Fig.1 Magnitude-recurrence relation for the subcrustal Vrancea source (M≥6.0)

The strong correlation (r=0.84-0.96) between the source magnitude and the rupture parameters, given by regression equations developed (from a databank of 244 events in the period 1857-1993) by Wells and Coppersmith (1994), are used to establish confidently the maximum credible magnitude of the Vrancea source.

Firstly, the results obtained from Wells and Coppersmith equations are compared with the past experience of strongest Vrancea earthquakes duringthe last 60 years, Table 1.

Secondly, the validation of Wells and Coppersmith equations by the past experience of Vrancea events recommends the use of equations for the prediction of the rupture parameters for the maximum magnitude in the Vrancea region:

$$logRA=-3.49+0.91M_w \quad s=0.24 \quad 4.8<M_w<7.9 \quad (5)$$
$$logSRL=-3.22+0.69M_w \quad s=0.22 \quad 5.2<M_w<8.1 \quad (6)$$

The local geology combined with the mean and the mean plus one standard deviation values of rupture area (RA) and surface rupture length (SRL) from Wells and Coppersmith equations suggest as the (most probable) maximum credible Vrancea magnitude: $M_w=8.1$ (M=7.8).

Rupture parameters in Table 1 were excerpted from [1]Tavera (1991) and [2]Enescu (1985).

The sensitivity to M_{max} of the mean recurrence interval of the Vrancea magnitudes is presented in Table 2 and as well as in Fig.1.

The statistical counting procedure applied to Radu's historical catalogue of observed epicentral intensity during a millennium (threshold MSK intensity $I_0=6.0$; aftershocks not included; 182 events) yields the following intensity recurrence relation for subcrustal Vrancea events, (Lungu, Cornea, Coman, 1996):

$$log n(≥I_0) = 1.99 - 0.46 I_0 \quad (7)$$

where n (≥I_0) is the average number of events per year with an epicentral intensity ≥ I_0.

Based on the epicentral intensity-magnitude conversion relationship recommended by Radu (1974), for intermediate depth Vrancea earthquakes:

$$M = 0.56 I_0 + 2.18 \quad (8)$$

Eq.(7) combined with Eq.(8) lead to :

$$log n(≥M) = 3.78 - 0.82 M \quad (9)$$

The recurrence-magnitude relations determined for Radu's historical (984-1900) and XX century (1901-1994) catalogues of Vrancea events are compared in Fig.2.

Table 1 Application of the Wells and Coppersmith regression equations (1994) to the Vrancea source

Gutenberg-Richter magnitude M	Moment magnitude M_w	Event	Observed rupture area, km²	Wells and Coppersmith equations			
				Eq.(5) RA, km²		Eq.(6) SRL, km	
				mean	mean+1 st.dev.	mean	mean+1 st.dev.
6.7	7.0	May 30, 1990	1100[1]	646	1318	41	68
7.0	7.2	Aug.30, 1986	1400[1]	1153	2005	56	93
7.2	7.5	Mar.4, 1977	63x37=2331[2]	2163	3760	91	150
7.4	7.7	Nov. 10, 1940	-	3290	5715	124	206
7.8	8.1	Max. credible	-	4055	7046	145	240

Table 2   Mean recurrence interval of Vrancea magnitude, T(≥M) as function of the maximum credible magnitude of the source, in years

Gutenberg-Richter magnitude, M	From Eq.(4), for maximum credible magnitude, $M_{max}=$		From Eq.(2)
	7.8	8.0	
8.0	-	-	187
7.9	-	996	158
7.8	-	457	134
7.7	704	279	114
7.6	323	191	96
7.5	197	139	81
Nov.10,1940 7.4	135	105	69
7.3	98	82	58
Mar. 4, 1977 7.2	75	65	50
7.1	58	52	42
Aug 30, 1986 7.0	46	42	36
6.9	37	35	30
6.8	30	28	26
May 30, 1990 6.7	24	24	22
6.6	20	20	18
6.2	10	10	9

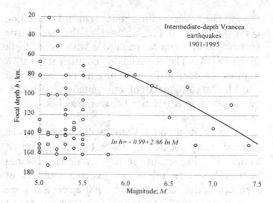

Fig.3 Vrancea source: magnitude (M≥6.0) versus focal depth

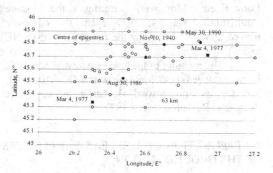

Fig.4 Vrancea source: location of epicentres in the period 1901-1995

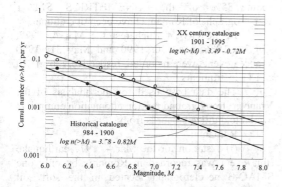

Fig.2 Comparison of magnitude-recurrence relations computed with the data from historical and instrumental catalogues of events

As generally is expected, the data collected during XX century are more severe than the historical data collected over a millennium. This is the result of the inherent inaccuracies of the historical catalogue data caused by many reasons such as: subjective interpretation of the damages done by the past seismic motions, general non-homogeneity of the macroseismic observations, etc.

2 LOCATION OF VRANCEA FOCUS

The recurrence interval of the intensity of the damage of a Vrancea earthquake is not the same as the recurrence interval of the corresponding magnitude.

The damage intensity of subcrustal Vrancea earthquakes is the combined result of: (i) magnitude and (ii) location of the focus inside the earth.

The focus depth and the position of the epicentre on the surface had a great influence on the experienced intensity of the past earthquakes.

Investigating the possible relationship between the magnitude of a destructive earthquake (M≥6.0) and the corresponding focal depth, the following dependence was found, Fig.3:

$$\ln h = - 0.77 + 2.86 \ln M - 0.18 P \qquad (10)$$

where P is a binary variable: P=0 for the mean relationship and P=1.0 for mean minus one standard deviation relationship.

The mean minus one standard deviation curve in Fig.4 should be used as the pessimistic correlation of Vrancea magnitude with focus depth in the PSHA. The correlation coefficient $\rho=0.78$ implies a moderate joint linear tendency between h and M. The earthquakes of a magnitude smaller than 6.0 display non-correlation between h and M.

A conventional Vrancea epicentre may be approximately located at 45.7° Lat. N and 26.6° Long. E, Fig.3. In reality, various Vrancea earthquakes have proved an extreme mobility of their epicentre: the 1940 and 1990 epicentres were located towards NE (Moldavia) i.e.: 45.8° Lat. N and ≈ 26.8 Lat. E, the 1986 epicentre was located towards SW (Bucharest) i.e.: 45.5 Lat. N and 26.5 Long. E, etc. Moreover, during the same (multishock) Mar. 4, 1977 event the epicentre moved about 61 km along the fracture line, from NE to SW.

The mobility of the epicentre toward Moldavia is more dangerous to Moldavian sites (Nov.10, 1940) and the mobility toward Bucharest induces more damage in Bucharest (Mar.4,1977).

3 ATTENUATION OF THE PEAK PARAMETERS OF THE GROUND MOTION

A Joyner and Boore model was selected for the analysis of the attenuation phenomenon:

$$\ln PGA = c_1 + c_2 M + c_3 \ln R + c_4 h + \varepsilon \qquad (11)$$

where:

PGA is the maximum peak ground acceleration at the site
M - magnitude
R - hypocentral distance to the site
h - focal depth
c_1, c_2, c_3, c_4 - data dependent coefficients.

ε is modeled as a random variable with zero mean and the standard deviation $\sigma_\varepsilon = \sigma_{\ln PGA}$ (standard deviation of ln PGA variable). From second order moment formats in the case of small coefficients of variation: $\sigma_{\ln PGA} \cong V_{PGA}$

If decimal logarithms are used instead of natural ones in Eq.(11) then:

$$\sigma_{\log PGA} = 0.434\,\sigma_{\ln PGA} \qquad (12)$$

Taking into account :
(a) The deep fracture structure in the Vrancea zone where three tectonic units come into contact;

(b) The stability of the angles characterizing the fault surface and the motion on this surface;
(c) The ellipse-shape of the macroseismic field produced by the Vrancea source;
the attenuation analysis was performed on two orthogonal directions corresponding to the average direction of the strike of the Vrancea fault plan ($\phi° = 225°$) and to the normal to this direction.

As a result 3 circular sectors (of 90° each) centred on these directions were established :
(a) The first sector contains stations in Bucharest area and in central Walachia, on the "young, thin and warm" (Oncescu, 1993) Moesian Platform;
(b) The second sector contains stations in Moldova, on "older, thicker and colder" (Oncescu, 1993) East European Platform;
(c) The third sector contains stations in Eastern part of Walachia and in Dobrogea, including Cernavoda Nuclear Power Plant site as well as the contact line between the East European and Moesian platforms.

During the 1986 and 1990 Vrancea events, about 85% of the KINEMETRICS SMA-1 accelerographs of Romania have been operational.

In the city of Bucharest the Mar 4, 1977, Aug.30, 1986, May 30, 1990 and May 31, 1990 Vrancea events were recorded, respectively, by 1, 10 and 11 instruments.

The data base used for the analysis of the Vrancea strong ground motion attenuation comprises available digitized records from:
Romania:
(i) 1 station for the Mar 4, 1977 earthquake (this event was recorded in Romania by only one SMAC-B accelerograph located in the soft soil condition of Bucharest;
(ii) 44 stations for the Aug 30, 1986 event;
(ii) 46 stations for the May 30, 1990 event;
Republic of Moldova:
(i) 2 stations for the Aug 30, 1986 event;
(ii) 4 stations for the May 30, 1990 event and
Bulgaria:
(i) 6 stations for the May 30, 1990 event.

The stations with available records from Romania belong to three seismic networks: INFP (National Institute for Earth Physics) - 10, INCERC (Building Research Institute of Bucharest) - 44, Bucharest, GEOTEC (Institute for Geophysical and Geotechnical Studies, Bucharest) - 3.

The INFP and GEOTEC seismic stations, as well as, 34 from 44 stations with records from INCERC seismic network are located in approximately "free field" conditions (basement and

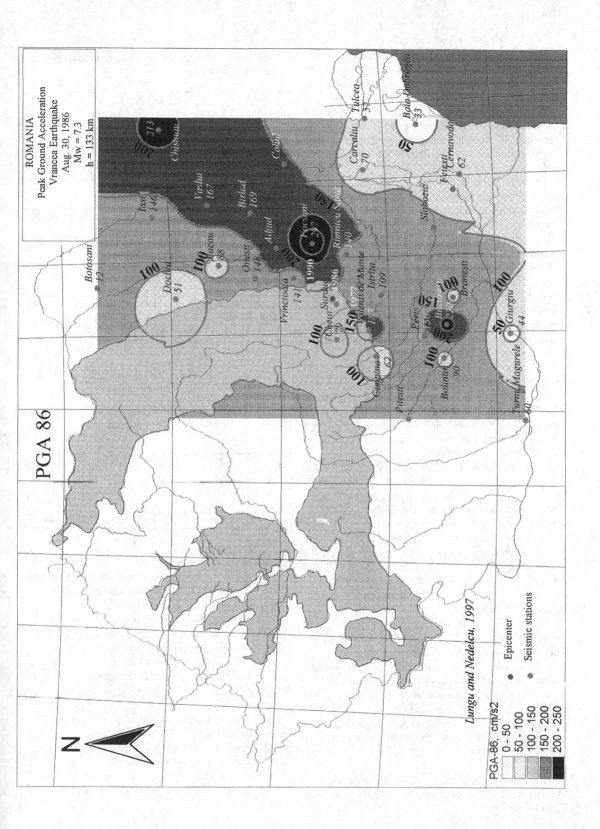

ROMANIA
Peak Ground Acceleration
Vrancea Earthquake
Aug. 30, 1986
Mw = 7.3
h = 133 km

PGA 86

Lungu and Nedelcu, 1997

Epicenter
Seismic stations

PGA-86, cm/s2
0 - 50
50 - 100
100 - 150
150 - 200
200 - 250

N

ground floor in one or max. two-stories buildings).

Other available records comes from the basement of 6, 8 or 10 stories buildings. They were not included in the present attenuation analysis.

The distribution on events and sectors of the maximum PGA at a station is given in Table 3. The recorded PGA field during the August 30, 1906 event is mapped with the ARCVIEW spatial analyst software of ESRI, Inc., USA.

The highest peak ground acceleration ever recorded in Romania was 297.1 cm/s^2 at the Focsani, INFP seismic station in the epicentral area during Aug 30, 1986 event.

The highest peak ground acceleration recorded in Bucharest was 207.6 cm/s^2 during the Mar 4, 1977 event at INCERC seismic station.

Mean and mean plus one standard deviation attenuation functions appropriate for the Vrancea subcrustal source were established through nonlinear multi-regression of the available sets of peak ground accelerations, as function of magnitude, hypocentral distance, focal depth and azimuth.

The data-dependent coefficients $c_1 \div c_4$ as well as the corresponding standard deviation of the lnPGA attenuation functions are found as given in Table 4. These attenuation functions can be used to predict 50 and 84 percentile of PGA, produced by a magnitude having a specified recurrence interval and a corresponding focal depth.

The influence of the data obtained for the largest ever recorded Vrancea event in Romania (Mar 4, 1977) is extremely strong resented in the multi-regression procedure, though these data come from a single station in Bucharest.

The regression results from Table 4, as well as the simple regression results for individual 1986 and 1990 events (Lungu et al, 1995) reveal the attenuation characteristics for the recorded PGA:

(i) The azimuthal dependence of the attenuation pattern i.e.:

- A slower attenuation along the direction of the fault plane (N45^{0}E) compared to the attenuation normal to this direction (E45^{0}S);

- A slower attenuation along the Bucharest sector compared to Cernavoda (NPP) sector;

- A slower attenuation along Moldova sector compared to the Bucharest sector;

(ii) A faster attenuation for greater magnitude and deeper focus (i.e. for the 1986 event compared to the 1990 event);

(iii) A relatively constant (0.35 ÷ 0.45) coefficient of variation of the attenuation function of the peak ground acceleration.

Table 3 Distribution of the free-field data set on events and sectors [2]

	Earthquake			All events
	Mar4 1977	Aug 30, 1980	May 30, 1990	
Epicentral area [2]	-	(4) 4	(4) 4	(8) 8
Bucharest sector	(1)	(16) 21	(18) 24	(35) 46
Moldova sector	-	(8) 11	(11) 13	(19) 24
Cernavoda sector	-	(6) 10	(10) 15	(16) 25
Complete data set	(1)	(34) 46	(43) 56	(78)103

[1] The numbers in parenthesis represents the free-field accelerograms used in the attenuation analysis
[2] Included in the data set for each sector

Table 4 Coefficients of the attenuation function for Vrancea subcrustal earthquakes, Eq.(11)

Coeff.	Complete data set	Bucharest sector	Cernavoda and Bucharest sectors	Moldova and Bucharest sectors
c_1	5.128	7.249	8.886	4.601
c_2	1.063	0.904	0.905	0.929
c_3	-1.297	-1.492	-1.786	-1.030
c_4	-0.009	-0.0081	-0.0096	-0.008
σ_{lnPGA}	0.449	0.358	0.349	0.465

The conclusion (iii) simply indicates that the mean plus one standard deviation attenuation for the PGA ordinates can be obtained by multiplying the mean attenuation relation by a factor of about 1.4.

For the Bucharest sector, the use of Eq.(11) is illustrated in Fig.5. The prediction of the PGA for the city of Bucharest is illustrated in Table 5.

The most unfavorable focus depth (h) corresponding to a specified magnitude (M) was estimated from Eq.(10) with P=1, indicated by x in table 5.

The epicentral distance for Bucharest is approximately Δ=135±35 km; of course, it depends on the location of the site within the city and on the location of the epicentre. Experienced epicentral distances for the city of Bucharest were about: 105km in 1977, 130 km in 1986, 170 km in 1990.

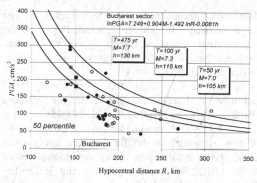
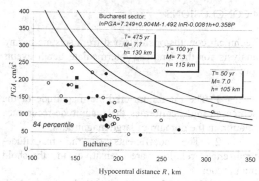

Fig.5   Bucharest sector: Attenuation found from three Vrancea events:
■ Mar 4, 1977 (M=7.2),   ● Aug 30, 1986 (M=7.0),   ○ May 30 1990 (M=6.7)

Table 5   Prediction of the peak ground acceleration in Bucharest

Δ=135 km: *Mean PGA, m/s²*

M \ h, km	7	7.1	7.2	7.3 (T=100yr)	7.4	7.5	7.6 (T=475 yr.)	7.7	7.8
80									
90									4.0
100				2.5				3.5	
110									
120					X				
130							X	3.0	
140		1.5							
150									

Δ=135 km: *Mean + 1 standard deviation PGA, m/s²*

M \ h, km	7	7.1	7.2	7.3 (T=100yr)	7.4	7.5	7.6 (T=475 yr.)	7.7	7.8
80									
90									
100							5.0		
110					3.5	4.5			
120					X				
130				2.5			X	4.0	
140	2.0								
150									

The results in Table 5 are for Δ=135km; for Δ=(135 - 35) km, the PGA values in Table 5 increase with 0.4 m/s² (mean values) and 0.6 m/s² (mean plus one standard deviation values).

The damage intensity of subcrustal earthquakes is the combined result of magnitude and location of the focus inside the earth. Since the marginal recurrence interval for magnitude T(M)=1/n(≥M) has less significance for subcrustal earthquakes than for shallow earthquakes, the bivariate extremes theory can be used to estimate the recurrence intervals of Vrancea events in terms of both magnitude and focus depth:

$$T(M,h)=1/(1-F(M,h)) \qquad (13)$$

where F(M,h) is the bivariate CDF. A forthcoming paper is under preparation with more details on a bivariate generalized extreme value distribution.

4 CONCLUSIONS

Technical conclusions obtained from seismic hazard analysis for the Vrancea intermediate depth events are:

1. The maximum credible magnitude of the source strongly calibrates the magnitude-recurrence relation in the domain of large magnitudes;
2. The coefficients of the magnitude-recurrence relation are sensitive to threshold magnitude;
3. The XX century (partially-instrumental) catalog of Vrancea earthquakes is clearly more severe than the historical catalogue (see also Van Gelder and Lungu, 1997).
4. The attenuation pattern of PGA from Vrancea subcrustal source is slower along the direction of the fault plan (Bucharest and Moldova), compared to the attenuation normal to this direction (Cernavoda NPP).
5. The Mar 4, 1977 data (M=7.2) strongly calibrates the PGA attenuation function.
6. The mean plus one standard deviation attenuation function can be obtained as 1.4 times the mean attenuation.
7. In the case of subcrustal earthquakes, the influence on PGA of the combination of focus depth and epicenter location seems to be more important than the influence of magnitude.
8. The differences between the random PGA field recorded in real events and resulted from the attenuation analysis seems to be quite unexpected (see the appended map). The site (soil) effects might partly explain the differences.

REFERENCES

Elnashai A., Lungu D., 1995. Zonation as a tool for retrofit and design of new facilities. Report of the Session A.1.2. 5th International Conference on Seismic Zonation. Nice, France, Oct. 16-19, Proceedings Vol.3, Quest Editions, Preses Academiques.

Hwang H.H.M., Hsu H-M., 1991. A study of reliability based criteria for seismic design of reinforced concrete frame buildings. Technical Report NCEER-91-0023. National Center for Earthquake Engineering Research. State University of New York at Buffalo, Aug.

Lungu D., Cornea T., Coman O., 1996. Probabilistic hazard analysis to the Vrancea earthquakes in Romania. Part I in "Experience database of Romanian facilities subjected to the last three Vrancea earthquakes, Research Report to the International Atomic Energy Agency, Vienna, Contract No. 8233/EN R1. Stevenson & Assoc. Office in Bucharest.

Marza V.I., Kijko A.P. Mantyniemi '(1991) Estimate of Earthquake hazard in the Vrancea (Romania) region, PAGEOPH 136: 143-154.

P.H.A.J.M. van Gelder, and D. Lungu, 1997, A new statistical model for Vrancea earthquakes using prior information from eartquakes before 1900, ESREL'97 European Safety and Reliability Conference, Lisbon, 1997.

Tavera J., 1991. Etude des mecanismes focaux de gros seismes et sismicite dans la region de Vrancea, Roumanie, Uniniversite de Paris 7

Wells, D.L., Coppersmith K.J., 1994. New empirical relations among magnitude rupture length, rupture width, rupture area, and surface displacement. Bulletin of the Seismological Society of America, Vol.84, No 4, pp.974-1002, Aug.

Structural Safety and Reliability, Shiraishi, Shinozuka & Wen (eds) © 1998 Balkema, Rotterdam, ISBN 90 5410 978 5

Earthquake safety of large panel buildings retrofitted with hysteretic devices

U. E. Dorka & A. Ji
University of Kaiserslautern, Germany

S. Dimova
Bulgarian Academy of Sciences, Sofia, Bulgaria

ABSTRACT: An earthquake retrofitting scheme for large panel buildings is presented that is based on the concept of hysteretic device systems. A 3D FEM model is developed that allows rapid non-linear Monte Carlo simulations to assess the safety of these buildings with great accuracy.

1 INTRODUCTION

Large panel buildings (LPBs) are made of standard prefabricated reinforced concrete panels. Because of standardized plans, they are inexpensive to build and therefore comprise a large part of the residential buildings in East and Central Europe and some regions in Asia.

They are also vulnerable to seismic forces, as recent earthquakes have demonstrated and many need retrofitting. During an earthquake, complete collapse can be initiated by failure of but a few of the brittle panel connections (Kossev 1982) causing a domino effect in the structure. Brittle failure modes in the panels themselves may trigger a similar collapse mechanism. To ensure the safety of these buildings therefore means to prevent those localized brittle failures.

With conventional retrofitting schemes failing to provide adequate solutions and in view of the strained economic situation in many regions, LPBs pose a substantial hazard and create a formidable problem that requires new approaches.

2 HYSTERETIC DEVICE SYSTEMS IN LPBS

Within the emerging field of structural control, a passive system has been proposed (Dorka 1994) that allows the designer to put a physical limit on the maximum forces transmitted into the structure during an earthquake by placing hysteretic devices (HYDEs) in seismic links. The structure is designed such that, forces and deformations are concentrated in the links. There, HYDEs are placed to (1) act "as structural fuses" by physically limiting the forces transmissible through the link and (2) dissipate large amounts of energy.

This requires elasto-plastic HYDEs and therefore, only devices based on a friction or yielding mechanism may be considered within this concept. Additionally, not only the devices but also the horizontal load resisting system containing the seismic links should be as stiff as possible to take full advantage of the HYDEs' energy dissipation capabilities already under small deformations.

A well designed HYDE system can have limit forces comparable to very ductile systems, deformations comparable to very stiff systems and dissipate up to 85% of an earthquake's input energy (Dechent, Dorka & Calderon 1995). The concept has been applied successfully in retrofitting brittle reinforced concrete frames (Dorka & Conversano 1995).

LPBs are very stiff by nature and by making horizontal cuts between walls and slabs, seismic links can be introduced quite easily. Putting the links only into the transverse basement walls allows this measure to be taken with no considerable disturbance to the residents. Thus, a "basement isolation system" is created (Fig.1) based on the concept of HYDE systems.

The maximum forces transmissible through the links in the basement by the HYDEs are dictated by the elastic limit state of the panels and their connections.

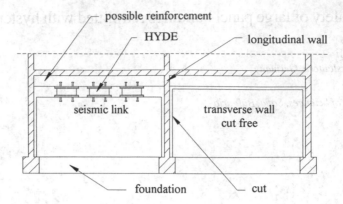

possible reinforcement
HYDE
longitudinal wall
seismic link
transverse wall cut free
foundation
cut

Figure 1: Basement Isolation. The HYDE system concept applied to a transverse basement wall of an LPB: HYDEs in a seismic link (left). Other transverse walls cut free (right). Longitudinal walls carry the vertical loads. Reinforcements help first floor walls to distribute vertical loading to longitudinal basement walls and concentrate horizontal (earthquake) loads and deformations in the HYDEs.

That way, the dangerous failure modes and subsequent collapse mechanisms are effectively prevented in the stories above the basement.

Since most horizontal deformations will now be concentrated in the basement, a deformation limit governs the design there and becomes a crucial factor in determining the feasibility of this structural concept. This limit state may be defined as the maximum horizontal drift at which the limit is reached for the integrity and vertical load bearing capacity of the remaining wall panels that support the load of the structure. For illustrative purposes, we assume this to be h/200, with h as the structural height of the basement. Whether this value is realistic needs further elaboration and experimental verification which is not the scope of this paper.

3 STRUCTURAL MODEL OF BASEMENT ISOLATED LPBS

With the limit states defined, a structural model is needed to assess the safety of the design. It must allow a detailed and accurate analysis of the structure considering the non-linear action of the HYDEs, yet be computationally efficient to carry out a safety analysis that, in its simplest form, may be based on 2nd order statistical moments (SORM).

For HYDE systems, it was suggested to perform 500 non-linear time history analyses under statistically equivalent earthquake records to be able to evaluate the standard deviations of the response, R_i^{STD} with a confidence of about 95% (Dorka & Pradlwarter 1993). This may be considered accurate enough to determine the safety index β_i for the i-th response value as the ratio of its limit state L_i over R_i^{STD}:

$$\beta_i = L_i/R_i^{STD} \qquad (3.1)$$

Acceptable minimum values for β_i may be based on typical safety margins (failure probabilities) for earthquake loading in modern building codes (e.g. Eurocode 8).

To develop modeling criteria for basement isolated LPBs, a detailed 3D FEM model was constructed for a typical LPB where actual test data were available (Tzenov 1968). Linear shell elements were used to model all panels. The soil structure interaction was modeled by springs. Their parameters were derived from the local soil conditions following the procedure used by Tzenov (Tzenov 1968). Stairs and strip foundations were modeled with 3D beam elements including normal force deformations. The masses were generated automatically by the program (ANSYS). 5% viscous damping was considered as Raleigh damping. The HYDEs were modeled with elasto-plastic spring elements. This refined model had about 4500 dynamic DOFs. Besides eigenfrequencies and mode shapes (Fig.2), the non-linear response to

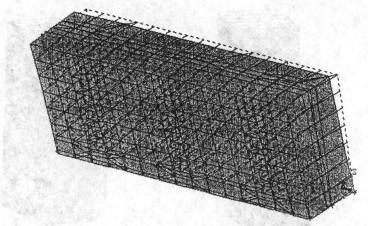

Figure 2   Element distribution and transverse eigenmode of elaborate model without basement isolation.

the WE component of the 1986 Kalamata townhall record earthquake (Greece) was computed (Fig.3). The earthquake was applied in the critical transverse direction only.

In a next step, a "reduced" dynamic FEM model was developed for the transverse direction. It comprises one standard 3D section of the building (around the stairs) that repeats itself in longitudinal direction. As in the elaborate model, shell, beam and spring elements were used to represent the panels, stairs, foundation beams and soil-structure interaction. In contrast to it, only 2 transverse dynamic DOFs were placed in the foundation and the slabs of every 2nd story, beginning with the ground floor slab. They

were vertically aligned with the locations of the seismic links in the basement. This reduced the number of dynamic DOFs from over 4500 to a mere 10! The matrices for the dynamic computation (mass and stiffness) were then generated using static condensation. These computations were performed using the SLANG software (Bucher 1996).

The non-linear action of the HYDEs in the basement was modeled by two elasto-plastic shear springs connecting the two dynamic DOFs of the foundation with the ones of the ground floor. The P-Δ effect was considered by reducing the dynamic stiffness matrix by the geometric terms. They turned out to be negligible.

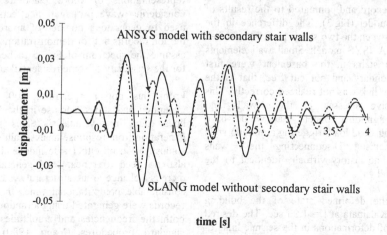

Figure 3   Comparison of time histories: Horizontal roof displacements of elaborate ANSYS model and "reduced" SLANG model under Kalamata.

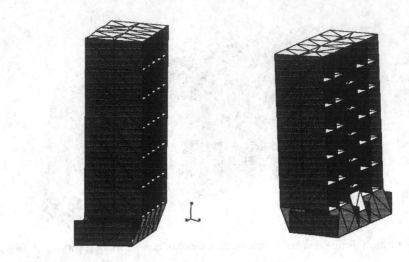

Figure 4   Deformed state of "reduced" model under Kalamata at t = 1.06 sec

The transverse eigenfrequency of this reduced model was computed without the seismic links and compared to the elaborate model and measured values (Tab.1). They show good agreement.

Table 1. Comparison of transverse eigenfrequencies of a LPB without seismic links.

	measured	ANSYS model	"reduced" model
frequency	3.03 HZ	3.15 HZ	3.20 HZ

The non-linear response of the reduced model including the seismic links was also computed using the Kalamata record and compared to the results of the elaborate model (Fig.3). The difference in the time history between the two stems from a "mistake" in the refined ANSYS model: Small wall elements supporting the stairs in the basement were first considered secondary and not cut free, that is the required seismic link was not realized correctly. This caused excessive stresses in these walls and neighboring longitudinal panels that would have failed under their dead load triggering a domino-style collapse mechanism! Disconnecting these walls resulted in a time history virtually identical to the "reduced" model.

Fig.4 shows the deformed state of the building module under Kalamata at t = 1.06 sec. The desired concentration of deformations in the seismic links of the basement is clearly visible.

The study shows that the "reduced" model accurately reproduces the behavior of the elaborate ANSYS model in detail and therefore can be used instead. It has also enough computational efficiency to be used in a safety analysis.

4   SAFETY   ANALYSIS   OF   BASEMENT ISOLATED LPBS

For such a safety analysis, a statistical load model must be provided. A convenient and simple way is to use a power spectrum for this purpose. Fig.5 shows a modified Kanai-Tajimi spectrum with similar statistical properties like the strong motion phase of the Kalamata record. Other smoothed spectral representations or more elaborate load models considering wave propagation effects may also be used to generate a number of appropriate ground motion records but for demonstrational purposes, we assume the spectrum of Fig. 5 to be representative for the seismicity of some residential area in Bulgaria.

From this power spectrum, 500 records were generated and stored for use in the following non-linear time history analysis. This separates load generation from response analysis allowing increased sophistication on either side independently. There is also no need to repeat load generation whenever there is a change in the structural system which saves considerable computational time. In this case, the records were generated using a random generator for both, the frequencies and amplitudes and following standard procedures (Yang 1980). This avoids possible bias that can occur when using equally spaced frequencies in Monte-Carlo simulations.

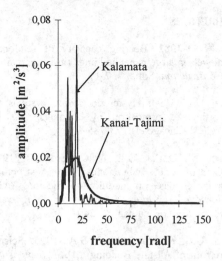

Figure 5   Modified Kanai-Tajimi spectrum with similar statistical properties like the strong motion phase of Kalamata.

The non-linear time history analysis was performed with a newly developed time stepping scheme that does not perform iterations in each time step. It is based on the fact that all time stepping schemes can be formalized as a linear control equation during the time step. It was developed for real-time substructure testing of building components under earthquakes (Dorka & Heiland 1991) and can also be used with advantage in analysis because it minimizes the equilibrium error and does not perform any matrix conversions and therefore is very fast.

Within the framework of structural control, the HYDEs can be seen as added control devices acting on a structural system through its feed back. In the analysis (and the computer code), they are therefore treated as separate (sub)systems communicating with the main structure via displacement and force links and each having its own particular characteristics described independently. They may be substituted by a description of any other structural control system, such as actively controlled hydraulic cylinders. Thus, the method of analysis presented here is not limited to HYDEs or other systems with passive devices but may be used for structural control systems in general.

During each time step, the standard deviations (STDs) were evaluated from all 500 solutions and stored. Fig.6 shows the development of the STDs over time. It is noticed that they stabilize after a few seconds. This means that the duration of the earthquake's strong motion phase has practically no effect on the STDs which reach a limiting value. It can also be seen that the deformations do concentrate in the basement where the jump in STD (from foundation to ground floor slab) is largest.

Fig. 7 shows the change of maximum STD of the ground floor displacement when the limit force of the HYDEs is changed. Considering the limit state given earlier with a safety index β of 3.5 (equivalent to about 99.97% survival probability), the "design point" gives a HYDE limit force of 380 kN in this illustrative example which is well below the limit dictated by the brittle failure modes of the panel connections (900 kN). This shows that basement isolation is a retrofitting concept that can drastically improve the safety of LPBs.

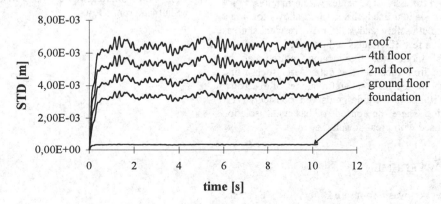

Figure 6   Standard deviations of transverse story displacements vs. time.

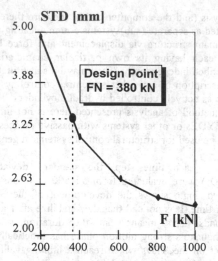

STD [mm]

Design Point
FN = 380 kN

F [kN]

Figure 7   Example for determining the optimum limit force for HYDEs.

5. SUMMARY AND CONCLUSIONS

A new retrofitting concept for LPBs is presented that is based on the concept of hysteretic device systems. By using HYDEs in seismic links in the basement of such buildings, their earthquake safety can be greatly improved.

A "reduced" 3D dynamic model is developed for LPBs that is computationally efficient enough to be used in extensive non-linear Monte-Carlo simulations to assess the safety of the design, yet sophisticated enough to provide detailed information on local stress conditions in the panels and their connections.

Using this model, the safety indices β can be computed for a set of variables within minutes. Since LPBs are standardized, this method allows for a fast and complete safety analysis of many residential areas using but a few 3D models and provided a reasonable statistical model for the ground motion can be estimated from local seismic data. After such a first step, only those LPBs that are in danger of exceeding their brittle failure modes must be considered for retrofitting where the concept of basement isolation may be used with great advantage.

ACKNOWLEDGMENT

This work was sponsored by the Deutsche Forschungsgemeinschaft (DFG).

REFERENCES

Kossev, S. 1982. Bearing capacity of reinforced dowels in large panel buildings (in Bulgarian). *J. Construction*. Sofia. 7: 7-11.

Dorka, U.E. 1994. Hysteretic device systems for earthquake protection of buildings. *5th US NCEE*. Chicago. 1: 775-785.

Dechent, P. Dorka, U.E. & Calderon, R. 1995. Control de vibraciones en estructuras amortiguadas con modulos de friccion. *XXVII Jornadas Sudamericanas de Ingenieria Estructural*. Tucuman,. 2: 249-260.

Dorka, U.E. &. Conversano, G.A. 1995. Seismic retrofit of Allstate Building. *IABSE Symposium*. San Francisco. 73/1: 145-150.

Dorka, U.E. &. Pradlwarter, H. 1993. Reliability based retrofitting of rc-frames with hysteretic devices. *ICOSSAR'93*. Innsbruck. 3: 1545-1552.

Tzenov, L. 1968. Study of vibrations of typical Bulgarian buildings in seismic regions (in Russian). *PH.D. Thesis CNIISK*. Moscow.

Bucher, C. & York, Y 1996. *SLANG the structural language*. Weimar: University of Architecture and Building Sciences Weimar (HAB).

Yang, C.Y. 1986. *Random vibrations of structures*. New York: John Wiley & Sons.

Dorka, U.E. & Heiland, D. 1991. Fast-online earthquake simulation utilizing a novel PC supported measurement and control concept. *4th Int. Conf. on Recent Advances in Struc. Dyn*. Southampton. 636-645.

Structural Safety and Reliability, Shiraishi, Shinozuka & Wen (eds) © 1998 Balkema, Rotterdam, ISBN 90 5410 978 5

Stochastic seismic responses of irregular topography for incident incoherent waves

Katsuhisa Kanda
Kobori Research Complex, Kajima Corporation, Tokyo, Japan

Masato Motosaka
Disaster Control Research Center, Tohoku University, Sendai, Japan

ABSTRACT: The effect of the spatial variation of earthquake ground motion is significant for local site response. The stochastic analyses with the boundary element method and finite element method have been performed to evaluate local site response considering the spatial variation of free-field motion. The incoherent wave is characterized by the exponential-decayed coherence function over spacing distance and frequency. The incoherence effect depends on frequency and the type of irregular topography, and tends to reduce focusing and shadowing effects of ground motion in topographic irregular sites compared to vertically propagating plane waves. The soil amplification characteristics derived from vertical array data of Kushiro Local Meteorological Observatory site are well simulated with the presented methods.

1.INTRODUCTION

The effect of spatial variation of earthquake ground motions, namely, the incoherence effect has been focused on the soil-structure interaction problem (Abrahamson 1991). The influence has been often discussed in terms of the response of elongated structures supported on extended foundations or on multiple supports in the structural engineering field.

Furthermore, the effect is significant for the local site response. As the spatial varying incident wave from bedrock propagates upward, the amplitude and frequency content are influenced due to the wave scattering and superposition (Der Kiureghian 1996). Especially, Local topographic irregularity increases scattering waves and affects the incoherence effect. If a structure is located on a topographic irregular site, the incoherence effect should be considered to explain the input earthquake to the structure in detail (Toki 1990).

It has been said that the incoherence effect is caused by the wave scattering in the heterogeneous medium from the source to the site. And it has been stochastically characterized by the coherence function, which has been investigated based on the ground motion data observed in dense strong-motion arrays (Harichandran 1986, Abrahamson 1991 and Toksöz 1992). Several different expressions have been proposed by decayed function over frequency and spacing distance (Hoshiya 1983 and Loco 1986).

This paper deals with the investigation of the local site response considering incoherence effect. The two types of stochastic approach using the boundary element method (BEM) and the finite element method (FEM) are employed for this purpose : (1) deterministic analyses are repeatedly performed using free-field motions generated with random phase angles as a random field, denoted herein as the simulation approach; and (2) the covariance of responses is uniquely evaluated by the analytical solution without simulation, denoted herein as the analytical approach. In these approaches, the free-field motions are modeled with a cross-spectral density matrix including the exponential-decayed coherence function.

The preliminary survey adopts cosine-shaped ridges and semi-ellipse alluvial valleys as typical topographic irregularity models. The amplification characteristics of surface layers are evaluated from the analytical approach of BEM and compared to the case of a vertically propagating coherent wave. The incoherent wave reduces the fluctuations of amplification characteristics caused by local topographic irregularity. The effect increases as frequency increases and shows some difference from the effect of material damping.

The spectral ratio derived from the observation data of vertical array at the site of Kushiro Local Meteorological Observatory (Kushiro JMA) is discussed as a simulation target of amplification characteristics for practical validation of the presented methods. According to the vertical array data, the spectral amplification of surface soil to bedrock cannot be simulated under the assumption of vertically propagating coherent waves with rational material damping. The amplification characteristics show high damping profile at low frequencies. Though the seismometer recorded 922cm/s^2 in PGA during Kushiro-oki Earthquake on January 15, 1993, the buildings in the site were quite slightly damaged. It is supposed that the incoherence effect including the local site effect might play an important role to reduce the responses of the buildings.

The soil profile of Kushiro JMA site is determined based on available geological data. The north-south cross section of surface soil is analyzed as a 2-dimensional anti-plane vibration problem using the analytical approach of BEM and the simulation approach of FEM. The comparison between the analytical results and the observation data indicates the influence of the incoherence effect and local site effect.

2. METHODOLOGY
2.1 Analytical approach

In this paper, the analytical approach is applied to BEM analysis only. The soil profile is model as depicted in Fig.1, in which zone II denotes topographic irregularities such as alluvial valley and ridge, and connects with half space zone I through the boundary Γ.

In order to analyze the local site response by the BEM, the boundary is divided into elements and then the element stresses $\{\tau\}$ can be given with element displacements $\{u\}$ and free-field motions $\{u_f\}$ as:

$$\{\tau_1\} = [G_1]^{-1}[H_1]\{u_1\} - [G_1]^{-1}\{u_f\} \quad (1a)$$

$$\{\tau_2\} = [G_2]^{-1}[H_2]\{u_2\} \quad (1b)$$

where $[G]$ and $[H]$ are Green's function matrices related to displacement and stress and the subscripts show the zone number involving its elements. The continuity and free-surface boundary conditions are imposed and Eq.(1) can be written as follows:

$$\{u\} = [K]^{-1}\{q\} \quad (2)$$

where $[K]$ is the impedance matrix obtained from the

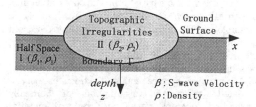

Fig. 1 Soil Profile Model of Topographic Irregularity Site

combination of $[G]^{-1}[H]$, and $\{q\}$ is a driving force vector given as follows:

$$\{q\} = \begin{bmatrix} [G_1]^{-1}\{u_f\} \\ 0 \end{bmatrix} \quad (3)$$

Using Eq.(3) substituted into Eq.(2), in the similar fashion of soil-structure interaction problem (Loco 1986), the covariance matrix $[U]$ of displacements on the boundary can be written as:

$$[U] = E\left[\{u\}\{\tilde{u}\}^T\right] = [K]^{-1} E\left[\{q\}\{\tilde{q}\}^T\right] \left[\tilde{K}\right]^{-1^T}$$

$$= [K]^{-1} \begin{bmatrix} [G_1]^{-1}[S_f]\left[\tilde{G}_1\right]^{-1^T} & 0 \\ 0 & 0 \end{bmatrix} \left[\tilde{K}\right]^{-1^T} \quad (4)$$

where $E[\cdot]$ = expectation and $\sim$ = conjugate complex. Note that $[S_f]$ =cross-spectral density matrix of free-field motion, which is a decayed function over frequency ω and horizontal spacing distance $|x_i-x_j|$ as:

$$s_{ij}(\mathbf{r}_i, \mathbf{r}_j) = \cos(\omega z_i / \beta_1)\cos(\omega z_j / \beta_1)\exp(-\gamma\omega|x_i - x_j| / \beta_1)s_0(\omega) \quad (5)$$

where β_1 is a shear wave velocity of half space and γ is a coefficient of decay factor of coherence.

The variance $|\hat{u}_2|^2$ of displacements at inner point of zone II can be also obtained as:

$$|\hat{u}_2|^2 = \{G_2\}^T[T_2]\{\tilde{G}_2\} + \{H_2\}^T[U_2]\{\tilde{H}_2\}$$

$$- \{G_2\}^T E\left[\{\tau_2\}\{\tilde{u}_2\}^T\right]\{\tilde{H}_2\} - \{H_2\}^T E\left[\{u_2\}\{\tilde{\tau}_2\}^T\right]\{\tilde{G}_2\} \quad (6)$$

Introducing covariance matrices in terms of stress and displacement on the boundary Γ of zone II:

$$[T_2] = E\left[\{\tau_2\}\{\tilde{\tau}_2\}^T\right] = [G_2]^{-1}[H_2]E\left[\{u_2\}\{\tilde{u}_2\}^T\right]\left[\tilde{H}_2\right]^T\left[\tilde{G}_2\right]^{-1^T} \quad (7a)$$

$$E\left[\{\tau_2\}\{\tilde{u}_2\}^T\right] = [G_2]^{-1}[H_2]E\left[\{u_2\}\{\tilde{u}_2\}^T\right] \quad (7b)$$

$$E\left[\{u_2\}\{\tilde{\tau}_2\}^T\right] = E\left[\{u_2\}\{\tilde{u}_2\}^T\right]\left[\tilde{H}_2\right]^T\left[\tilde{G}_2\right]^{-1^T} \quad (7c)$$

If Eq.(2) is also introduced in the case of FEM, it is possible to apply the same procedure, Eqs.(3)~(5).

2.2 Simulation approach

In the FEM analysis, there are artificial boundaries at the bottom and side of finite element region as shown in Fig.2. If the free-field motions along these boundaries are given, the responses of finite element region can be calculated.

1540

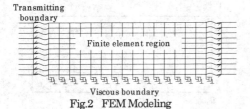

Fig.2 FEM Modeling

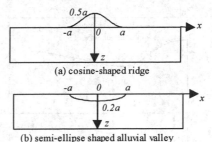

(a) cosine-shaped ridge

(b) semi-ellipse shaped alluvial valley

Fig.3 Models of topographically irregular site

If a cross-spectral density matrix of free-field motion is given according to Eq.(5), free-field motions are perfect-correlated along side boundary and incoherent along the bottom boundary. In the case of BEM, the free-filed motion is defined along the boundary of a half space in the same manner.

The free-field motions at the boundary are generated as a one-dimensional, multi-variate random process in the x direction (Shinozuka 1985). The cross-spectral density matrix $[S_f]$ of ith circular frequency ω_i is decomposed into a lower triangular matrix $F(\omega_i)$ which possesses an Fourier transform as follows:

$$\left[S_f(\omega_i)\right] = \left[F(\omega_i)\right]\left[F(\omega_i)\right]^T \qquad (8)$$

Once $[F(\omega_i)]$ is obtained, a set of n homogeneous processes of free-field motion $U_{fl}(\omega_i)$ can be simulated by following series:

$$U_{fl}(\omega_i) = \frac{\sum\limits_{k=1}^{l} F_{lk}(\omega_i)\cos(\phi_{ki})}{F_{11}(\omega_i)\cos(\phi_{1i})} U_{f1}(\omega_i) \qquad (9)$$

$$l=1,2,..n$$

where $\phi_1, \phi_2,...\phi_n$ are independent random phase angles distributed uniformly over the range $(0, 2\pi)$, $F_{lk}(\omega_i)$ is an element of matrix $[F(\omega_i)]$ and $U_{fl}(\omega_i)$ is a given free-field motion at an initial point.

3. FUNDAMNETAL EFFECTS OF INCOHERENT WAVE TO SITE-RESPONSE

In this section, typical topographically irregular models as shown in Fig.3 are considered to investigate fundamental incoherence effects to the response of local site, using the analytical approach of the two-dimensional (2-D) BEM described in section 2.1.

Numerical values for the square root of variance of the displacements on the ground surface are calculated versus the dimensionless frequency $\eta=2a/\lambda$, denoted herein as the 'displacements', in which λ is a wavelength. The incident waves are assumed to be spatially varying SH waves (anti-plane vibration problem). γ in Eq.(5) is estimated to be 0.11 hereafter so that the coherence decline to 0.5 with about a wavelength (Toksöz 1992). No material damping is assumed.

3.1 Verification with Monte Calro simulation

Let the results from the analytical approach of BEM compare to that from the simulation approach in order to verify its methodology. The both results should be equal, if the number of simulation is sufficiently large, namely, Monte Calro simulation.

Two cases of soil profile ratio between the zone I and II for the model (a) in Fig.3 is adopted i.e. $\rho_1/\rho_2=1.0, \beta_1/\beta_2=1.0$ (uniform) and $\rho_1/\rho_2=1.5, \beta_1/\beta_2=2.0$. The results shown in Fig.4 are resulting from 400 times simulation and the proposed analytical method. The displacements on the ground surface are normalized by free-field surface motion u_0. The excellent agreement between the results suggests that the proposed method is efficient to evaluate the displacements.

3.2 Comparison to vertically propagating coherent wave

In order to evaluate the incoherence effect on displacements on the ground surface, the results of the

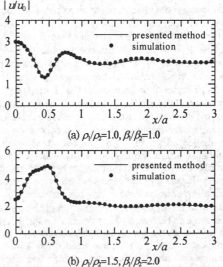

(a) $\rho_1/\rho_2=1.0, \beta_1/\beta_2=1.0$

(b) $\rho_1/\rho_2=1.5, \beta_1/\beta_2=2.0$

Fig.4 Verification with simulation (model(a), $\eta=1.5$)

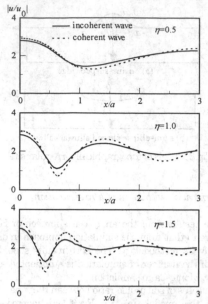

Fig.5 Displacement on the ground surface (Case 1)

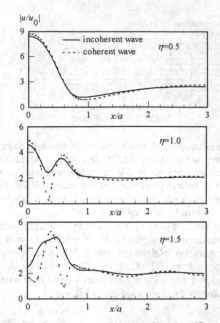

Fig.6 Displacements on the ground surface (Case 2)

case of incoherent wave input are compared to that of the case of vertically propagating coherent wave input. The analytical cases are as follows:

Case 1: model (a) of $\rho_1/\rho_2=1.0$, $\beta_1/\beta_2=1.0$
Case 2: model (a) of $\rho_1/\rho_2=1.5$, $\beta_1/\beta_2=2.0$
Case 3: model (b) of $\rho_1/\rho_2=1.5$, $\beta_1/\beta_2=2.0$

The results of above cases are depicted in Fig.5, 6, and 7, respectively. Each figure shows the displacements in terms of the location of ground surface at three different dimensionless frequencies η.

The incoherence effect tends to smooth displacement on the ground surface. Especially, dips of displacements are thoroughly disappeared for the case 2 at $\eta=1.5$. Therefore, it is supposed that the incoherent waves reduce the effect of wave focusing and shadowing caused by irregularities. As the frequency increases, there is indication of increasing the discrepancy of displacements between incoherent and coherent waves.

As for Case 2, displacements on the ground surface are plotted over frequency for three locations on the cosine-shaped ridge in Fig.8, besides. It is further comprehensive that the discrepancy between coherent and incoherent waves tends to increase as the frequency increases. Especially, incoherent waves raise up dips and the discrepancy is large at high frequencies.

The ratio of displacement on the top of the cosine-shaped ridge to that at $z=0$ are depicted in Fig.9. This figure represents the spectral amplification of the ridge. It is indicated that the resonant steep peaks lower at low frequencies and the dips raise at high frequencies

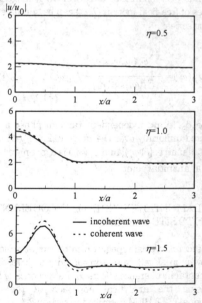

Fig.7 Displacement on the ground surface (Case.3)

due to the incoherent input wave. This effect corresponds to the displacement shown in Fig.8. The vibration nodes in which displacement is small, cause steep peaks and dips in the spectral amplification. Therefore, it is obvious that the incoherent waves erase the nodes.

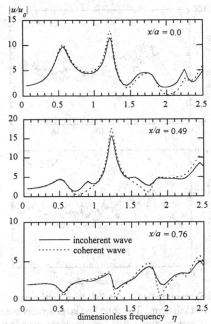

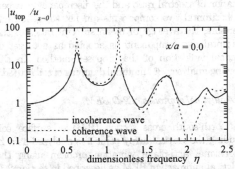

Fig.8 Displacements on the ground surface over
dimensionless frequency (Case 2)

Fig.9 Amplification of displacements over dimensionless
frequency at the top of cosine-shaped ridge (Case 2)

3.3 *Comparison to the effect of material damping*

If a material damping is appended to model, the
displacements on ground surface get smooth in the
same way. Though the material damping directly
absorbs wave energy in the medium, there is no energy
loss in the case of incoherent wave. There must be some
discrepancy of spectral amplification between the effects
of incoherent wave and material damping.

The comparison between no and 5% material
damping ratio is plotted in Fig.10 for the both cases of
incoherent wave and coherent wave. The result
indicates that appending of material damping only

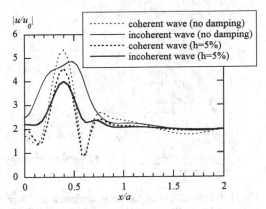

Fig.10 Displacements on ground surface (Case 2). The
thick lines are the case of appended damping.

lowers the resonant peaks, but incoherent incident
waves raise up dips, besides.

4. APPLICATION TO OBSERVED SEISMIC DATA

Though the seismometer at Kushiro JMA site recorded
922cm/s² in PGA during Kushiro-oki Earthquake on
January 15, 1993, the buildings in the site were quite
slightly damaged. The similar phenomena ware
observed in the vicinity of Kobe JMA site (818cm/s² in
PGA) during Hyogoken-Nanbu Earthquake on January
17, 1995. It might be considered that the incoherence
effect and local site effect played an important role to
reduce damages of buildings.

4.1 *Kushiro JMA site vertical seismic array*

Kushiro JMA site is located in the south of the
Kushiro River and on the top of a hill with a gentle slope
toward the river. The configuration of two free-field
vertical arrays in the site is shown in Fig.11 (Ishida
1996).

The soil profile of point 2 shown in Table 1 is
determined based on geological data such as the core
boring test and seismic refraction prospecting.

Each array consists of two triaxial accelerometers in
vertical direction. The horizontal components of the
accelerometer are oriented to the directions of buildings
in the site (N063E, N153E). The point 2 array has been
recording earthquake events since the end of 1993.
Table 2 shows selected events observed at the point 2.
Though there are no shallow and near-field events,
there is the variety of earthquake magnitude and PGA.
The ground motion amplification due to the local soil
can be evaluated from the ratio of peak acceleration
between GL-2m and GL-22m, whose averages are 5.2
for N063E and 3.9 for N153E.

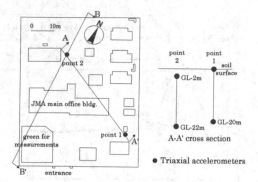

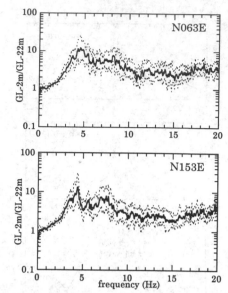

Fig.11 Kushiro JMA site and array configuration. Black circles are location of observed station. A-A' line shows a cross section line for analytical model

Table 1   Soil Profile (Point 2)

Depth(GL-) (m)	S-wave velocity (m/sec)	Poisson's Ratio	Density (g/cm³)
0.0 ~ 1.00	120	0.313	1.59
~ 5.50	140	0.206	
~ 6.80	220	0.425	1.65
~ 12.10	340	0.275	
~ 13.00	310	0.326	1.77
~ 15.30		0.480	
~ 18.40	340	0.476	
~ 21.00	510	0.480	1.82

Table 2   Selected observed events (Point 2)

Date	Dist.[*1] (km)	Depth (km)	Az.[*2]	M[*3]	Peak Accel.(cm/sec²)			
					GL-2m		GL-22m	
					N063 E	N153 E	N063 E	N153 E
94/2/18	187	107	254°	5.1	13.0	7.6	2.5	2.3
94/3/5	105	101	214°	4.0	11.1	5.5	1.9	1.9
94/4/12	266	134	53°	5.9	6.3	3.7	1.7	1.4
94/4/29	178	128	271°	5.0	10.4	5.5	1.3	1.4
94/5/5	103	70	66°	4.7	8.9	11.2	2.0	2.2
94/7/1	149	67	234°	5.3	10.1	9.0	2.0	2.0
94/7/6	115	107	234°	4.8	18.2	17.8	4.1	5.6
94/8/25	94	65	113°	5.3	67.0	58.3	7.5	8.2
94/8/31	169	84	67°	6.5	113.5	71.6	43.0	22.3
94/10/4	271	30	80°	8.1	402.6	258.3	119.0	95.4

[*1] Hypocentral distance [*2] Azimuth of hypocenter from the Kushiro JMA site [*3] JMA magnitude

The spectral ratio of the vertical array (GL-2m/GL-22m) is calculated for ten earthquake events shown in Table 2. The ratios represent the spectral amplification of local soil in the site. The mean and confidence bound of the ten events is plotted in Fig. 12.

Though 4Hz is considered to be a resonant peak, there are no remarkable peaks and dips in high frequency range. It shows high damping features. The

Fig.12 Spectral ratio (GL-2m/GL-22m) in the point 2 vertical array. The solid line is mean of selected 10 events, and dotted line shows the confidence bound of ± standard deviation

variation of spectral ratio and the discrepancy between the horizontal two components are not so significant. Therefore, the average of mean spectral ratios of the horizontal two components is adopted as a target of practical validation of the proposed method. In the following analyses, 3% material damping of soil is used.

4.2 Analytical approach of 2-D BEM

The north-south cross section (B-B') of surface soil including the vertical array point 2 is analyzed as a 2-dimensional anti-plane vibration problem using the analytical approach of BEM as described in section 2.1. The analyzed model is simplified so that all regions except the half space should be a closed space based on soil profile data of point 2 as shown in Fig.13. The analysis is employed from 1.0 through 10Hz in frequency due to the assurance of accuracy related to the boundary element length.

In order to clarify the effect of topographic irregularity and that of incoherent wave separately, the result obtained from the analytical approach of 2-D BEM with incoherent wave input is compared to that from the 1-D multiple reflection analysis and the 2-D BEM analysis with vertically propagating coherent wave input, as depicted in Fig.14.

Though the peak frequencies from all models are roughly corresponding to that of the observed data, the peak values of spectral ratio are quite different. The correlation coefficients of analytical results and observed

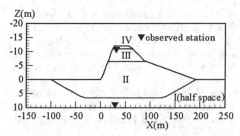

Soil Layer	S-wave Velocity (m/s)	density (g/cm³)
IV	120	1.56
III	140	1.56
II	310	1.77
I	510	1.82

Fig.13 Cross section model of Kushiro JMA site and its soil profiles for BEM covariance analysis (B-B' cross section in Fig.10)

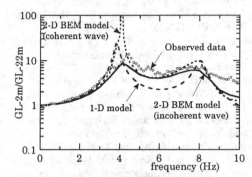

Fig.14 Comparison of spectral ratio (GL-2m/GL-22m) referred to the spectral amplification of surface layers of 20m in depth. Solid and broken lines are from analytical results and circles are from observed data.

data are estimated to be 0.50 for the 1-D model, 0.69 for the 2-D BEM model with coherent wave, and 0.88 for the 2-D BEM with incoherent wave. It suggests that the incoherence effect and local site effect are equivalently effective for this case. Though the proposed method results in a little underestimation of amplification, it shows the best fitness.

The correspondence between the 1-D model, the 2-D BEM model and observed data, suggests that the effect of modeling of topographic irregularity is significant for the frequency range from 4 to 8Hz, and the incoherence effect is significant for the peak around 4Hz.

4.3 Simulation approach of 2-D FEM

2-D FEM can model local topography down to smaller detail than 2-D BEM. Though the result of the analytical approach of 2-D BEM originally shows

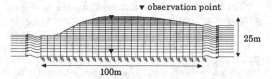

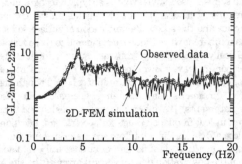

Fig.15 FEM model for Kushiro JMA site (B-B' cross section in Fig.11). The viscous boundary is adopted for the bottom of the model and the energy-transmitting boundary for the sides.

Fig. 16 Comparison of spectral ratio (GL-2m/GL-22m). Solid lines are from 2D-FEM simulation results and circles are from observed data.

ensemble average, each observed data is only one sample, besides. These factors might be possible to yield the discrepancy between the result of the analytical approach of BEM analysis and the observed data. In this section, the simulation approach of 2-D FEM as described in section 2.2 is employed. Fig.15 shows the 2-D FEM model whose soil properties are derived from point 2 data in Table 1.

The incident wave for this FEM model is given as free-field motions along the bottom and side boundary. The incoherent free-field motions are considered only for the bottom boundary, and are generated with random phase angles as a multi-variate random process as mentioned in section 2.2. The results of five simulations with different free-field motion are superimposed to consider the variation of wave number. Fig.16 shows the spectral ratio from the analysis compared to that from observed data. Though the result from the analysis is fluctuated over frequency due to used random phase angles, it is in the best agreement with the observed data.

5. CONCLUSIONS

The local site effect considering the incoherence effect of free-field motion has been investigated based on stochastic analyses and seismic observation data of a vertical array.

The analytical and simulation approaches have been developed to consider incoherent wave input using the 2-D BEM and the 2-D FEM. The analytical approach can uniquely compute the covariance of responses by the analytical solution without the Monte Carlo simulation. It is efficient to explain fundamental effects of incoherent wave input due to the simplicity of calculation. On the other hands, though the simulation approach needs several calculations to consider the variation of wave number, it can model surface irregularities and soil heterogeneity in detail.

The preliminary survey adopts cosine-shaped ridges and semi-ellipse alluvial valleys as typical topographical irregularity models. The displacements on the ground surface and the spectral amplification of surface soil for the incoherent wave input are compared to those for the vertically propagating coherent wave input. The incoherent waves lower peaks and raise dips of the displacements and spectral amplification. Though the effect increases as frequency increases for the displacements, the effect appears at peaks and dips even in low frequency range for spectral amplification. These effects are different from the material damping.

The spectral amplification of surface soil evaluated from the observation data of vertical array at the site of Kushiro JMA is adopted to validate the presented methods and to clarify the effect of incoherent wave and local site topography in actual data. The soil profile is determined based on available geological data. The north-south cross section of surface layers is analyzed as a two-dimensional anti-plane vibration model. The agreement between the results from the analyses and the observed data indicates that the incoherence effect and local site effect are equivalently significant for this case and the simulation approach of 2-D FEM can evaluate the most similar results to the observed data.

ACKNOWLEDGMENT

The earthquake data used in this study has been observed from a collaborative effort among Japan Meteorological Agency, Building Research Institute, and Kajima Technical Research Institute.

REFERENCES

Abrahamson, N. A., J.F.Schneider & J.C. Stepp 1991. Empirical spatial coherency functions for application to soil-structure interaction analyses. Earthquake Spectra 7(1): 1-27

Bolt, B. A., Y. B. Tsai, K. Yeh & M. K. Hsu 1982. Earthquake strong motions recorded by a large near-source array of digital seismographs, Earthquake Engrg. Struct. Dyn., 10: 561-573

Der Kiureghian, A. 1996. A coherency model for spatially varying ground motions, Earthquake Engrg. & Struct. Dyn. 25: 99-111

Harichandran, R.S. & E. H. Vanmarcke 1986. Stochastic variation of earthquake ground motion in space and time, J. Engrg. Mech., ASCE, 112: 154-174,

Hoshiya, M., & K. Ishii 1983. Evaluation of kinematic interaction of soil foundation system by stochastic model. J. Soil Dyn. & Earthquake Engrg.,2(3):128-134

Ishida, H., T. Sasaki, M. Niwa, Y. Kitagawa & T. Kashima 1996. Amplification characteristics of surface layers obtained from earthquake observation records of vertical instrument arrays at Kushiro local meteorological observatory, J. Struct. Constr. Engrg., AIJ 490: 91-100 (in Japanese)

Kitamura, E., M. Motosaka, K. Urao, M. Kamata, & T. Ohta 1987. Simulation analysis, using BEM-FEM hybrid model, of strong ground motion in Mexico City during Mexico Earthquake 1985, 10th Int. Conf. on B.E.M.,4: 195-206

Loh, C. H., J. Penzien & Y. B. Tsai 1982. Engineering analyses of SMART 1 array accelerograms, Earthquake Engrg. Struct. Dyn., 10, 575-591

Luco, J. E. & H. L. Wong 1986. Response of a rigid foundation to a spatially random ground motion, Earthquake Engrg. and Struct. Dyn., 14: 891-908

Shinozuka M. 1985. Stochastic fields and their digital simulation, Lecture notes for CISM course on Stochastic Methods in Struct. Mech., Udine, Italy

Toki, K., T. Sato and J. Kiyono 1990. Modeling of spatial variation of ground motion on irregular profile, 8th Japan Earthquake Engrg. Sympo. 1: 331-336

Toksöz, M. N., A. M. Dainty & R. Coates 1992. Effects of lateral heterogeneity on seismic motion, Int. Sympo., Effects of Surface Geology on Ground Motion, Odawara, Japan: 33-64

Veletsos, A. S. & A. M. Prasad 1989. Seismic interaction of structures and soil: stochastic approach, J. Struct. Engrg. 115(4): 935-956

Structural Safety and Reliability, Shiraishi, Shinozuka & Wen (eds) © 1998 Balkema, Rotterdam, ISBN 90 5410 978 5

Accuracy of seismic response prediction by SRSS (square-root-of-sum-of-squares) method

Masato Abé, Yozo Fujino & Masayuki Yoshimi
Department of Civil Engineering, The University of Tokyo, Japan

ABSTRACT: Accuracy of modal combination rules are studied, with emphasis on square-root-of-sum-of-squares (SRSS) method. SRSS method is commonly used and known to give accurate estimates of responses for structures with widely spaced natural frequencies provided that the excitations are stationary random processes and each modal response is considered to be uncorrelated. However, seismic ground motions are not stationary and can be impulsive especially in the case of near-field ground motions, which may induce simultaneous occurrence of maximum responses for multiple modes. The paper starts with construction of several combination rules which accommodate the effect of simultaneous occurrence of peaks. Then, their validity is discussed using several near-field and far-field observed ground motion records. SRSS method is found to be generally accurate with slight tendency of underestimation, which can be improved by employing proposed modal combination methods. The effects of near-field ground motions are also studied and found to be insignificant.

1. INTRODUCTION

To compute seismic responses of multiple degrees of freedom structures using response spectra, certain modal combination rule such as absolute sum method, square-root-of-sum-of-squares (SRSS) method, or complete quadratic combination (CQC) method is usually employed. Among them, SRSS method is the most commonly used method because it is known to give the ensemble mean of maximum response for structures with widely spaced natural frequencies provided that the excitations are stationary random processes and the peak factor for each modal response is approximately equal (Der Kiureghian, 1980, 1981). CQC method is the generalization of SRSS method which includes the effect of correlation among modal responses introduced by closely spaced natural frequencies (Igusa 1992). Although the excitation is assumed to be stationary in development of both methods, they are known to give good approximation of maximum structural responses subject to earthquake ground motions which are usually strongly non-stationary.

Near-field ground motion is known to have impulsive time history. One of the typical examples is 1966 Parkfield earthquake, whose ground velocity is shown in Figure 1. Several authors have studied this near-field effect on structural response and found that it requires higher ductility demand for short period structures and larger displacement for long period structures, which leads to increase of inter-story drift (Anderson and Bertero, 1987, Iwan, 1994, Hall, et. al., 1995). Because of the impulsive nature of excitation, several vibration modes in structures may take maximum responses simultaneously and increase response more than the expected values computed by SRSS method even when the natural periods are not closely spaced. In other words, certain correlation among modal responses can be introduced because of the strong non-stationary characteristics of excitation of near-field records. It should be noted that CQC method takes care of the effect of modal coupling induced by structural system parameters, but not the coupling introduced by the characteristics of excitation.

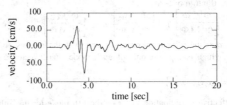

Figure 1. Ground velocity of 1966 Parkfield earthquake.

The purposes of this paper are as follows: (i) to evaluate the accuracy of SRSS method using a number of earthquake strong motion records which includes near-field records such as Northridge earthquake and Kobe earthquake; (ii) to construct several alternative methods which accommodate correlation of modal responses introduced by the characteristics of seismic excitation and compare their accuracy; (iii) to evaluate the effect of near-field earthquakes.

At the first part of the paper, modal combination rules are briefly summarized and two combination rules which accommodate the correlation of modal responses introduced by the characteristics of excitation are constructed. The first rule to be constructed uses autocorrelation of each modal response to estimate the time history before and after the maximum response. In this method, correlation among modes is explicitly treated by including the time lag among occurrence of maximum response in each mode. The second method is to use n-norm as modal combination. SRSS, which is the 2-norm of the modal responses, gives the mean value of response when all modes are uncorrelated, while the absolute sum, which is the 1-norm, gives the exact response value when all modal responses take their maxima simultaneously. The real seismic response, which is somewhere in-between, can be approximated by finding appropriate value of n between 1 and 2.

At the second part of the paper, accuracy of these modal combination rules is numerically studied using examples of an elastic 10 story shear building. The 10 story building example is so chosen that it does not have closely spaced natural frequencies and SRSS method is considered to be applicable according to the condition given by Der Kiureghian (1980). Sixteen ground motion records, which contain 10 near-field and 6 far-field/design earthquakes are employed. Response characteristics due to near-field and far-field/design earthquakes are also studied to clarify the effect of near-field motions.

2. MODAL COMBINATION RULES

In this section, several modal combination rules which can accommodate the effect of simultaneous occurrence of peaks in several vibration modes are developed along with brief review on SRSS method.

2.1. Equations of motion

Equations of motion of N-degree-of-freedom linear elastic structures are given by,

$$\mathbf{M}\ddot{\mathbf{x}} + \mathbf{C}\dot{\mathbf{x}} + \mathbf{K}\mathbf{x} = -\mathbf{M}\mathbf{r}\ddot{z}, \qquad (1)$$

where, $\mathbf{x}$ is the relative displacement to the ground, z is the ground motion, $\mathbf{r}$ is the influence vector, and $\mathbf{M}$, $\mathbf{C}$, and $\mathbf{K}$ are the mass, damping and stiffness matrices respectively. By assuming the structure is classically damped, Eq.(1) is decoupled into modes as,

$$\ddot{q}_i + \left[\frac{\Phi^T \mathbf{C} \Phi}{\Phi^T \mathbf{M} \Phi}\right]_i \dot{q}_i + \left[\frac{\Phi^T \mathbf{K} \Phi}{\Phi^T \mathbf{M} \Phi}\right]_i q_i = -\left[\frac{\Phi^T \mathbf{M} \mathbf{r}}{\Phi^T \mathbf{M} \Phi}\right]_i \ddot{z} \qquad (2)$$

where, q_i is the i-th modal response, and Φ is the mode shape matrix which is the assembly of each mode shape vector ϕ_i, i.e.,

$$\Phi = \left[\phi_1, \phi_2, ..., \phi_N\right]. \qquad (3)$$

Effective participation factor of the i-th mode for the j-th physical coordinate x_j is,

$$a_{ij} = -\left[\frac{\Phi^T \mathbf{M} \mathbf{r}}{\Phi^T \mathbf{M} \Phi}\right]_i [\Phi]_{ij}. \qquad (4)$$

Using this effective participation factor, the response x_j is expressed as,

$$x_j(t) = \sum_{i=1}^{N} a_{ij} q_i(t). \qquad (5)$$

2.2. Modal combination rules

Given the peak response of i-th mode as Q_i from response spectra, one can compute the peak response of j-th response coordinate R_j by appropriate combination of Q_i's. When the structure has no closely spaced natural frequencies, SRSS method is known to give the mean value of the peak response value if the excitation is stationary (Der Kiureghian, 1980, 1981). SRSS combination rule is given by

$$R_j^{SRSS} = \left\{\sum_{i=1}^{N} \left(a_{ij} Q_i\right)^2\right\}^{1/2}. \qquad (6)$$

When several modes take the maximum responses at the same time, Eq.(6) will underestimate the response. To include the effect of simultaneous occurrence of peaks explicitly, mean of response time history subject to stationary gaussian process, given by Vandiver, et. al (1982), is introduced:

$$\bar{q}_i(\tau) = \frac{C_{ii}(\tau)}{C_{ii}(0)} q_i(0), \qquad (7)$$

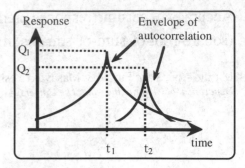

Figure 2. Correlation among peak responses of modes.

where $q_i(0)$ is the known response value at time 0, and C_{ii} is the autocorrelation function of the i-th mode, i.e.,

$$C_{ii}(\tau) = \frac{S_0}{4\zeta_i \omega_i^3} e^{-\zeta_i \omega_i |\tau|} \times$$
$$\left(\cos \omega_i \sqrt{1-\zeta_i^2}(\tau) + \frac{\zeta_i}{\sqrt{1-\zeta_i^2}} \sin \omega_i \sqrt{1-\zeta_i^2} |\tau|\right). \qquad (8)$$

Here, modal frequencies and damping ratios are denoted by ω_i and ζ_i respectively.

Figure 2 shows the conceptual schematics of the envelopes of modal responses for $i=1$ and 2. It can clearly be seen that the structural response, which is the weighted sum of modal responses, becomes larger when t_1 and t_2 are close to each other. To accommodate this effect, the following modal combination rule which explicitly includes the effect of occurrence time of peaks using the envelope of Eq.(7) is proposed here.

$$R_j^{AC} = \max_{\tau}\left\{\sum_{i=1}^{N} a_{ij} Q_i e^{-\zeta_i \omega_i |\tau - t_i|}\right\}. \qquad (9)$$

It should be noted that Eq.(7) gives mean response when the excitation is stationary gaussian process. Hence, seismic excitation before and after the occurrence of peak is assumed to to be stationary gaussian in Eq.(9).

To compute Eq.(9), peak occurrence time t_i, which is usually not available, needs to be obtained. It can be calculated through ordinary computation of response spectra by storing kthe occurrence time of peak responses, or directly from ground motion record using wavelet transform as shown in the Appendix.

The response value becomes the largest when the peaks of all modes occur simultaneously. This value is calculated simply by taking the absolute sum of the modal responses, as,

$$R_j^{ABS} = \sum_{i=1}^{N} |a_{ij} Q_i|. \qquad (10)$$

This combination rule assumes perfect correlation among modes, while SRSS assumes independence of peak occurrence. Because absolute sum is given in 1-norm and SRSS is given in 2-norm, a possible extension is to use n-norm where $1<n<2$ to express realistic correlation among modes.

$$R_j^{n-norm} = \left\{\sum_{i=1}^{N} |a_{ij} Q_i|^n\right\}^{1/n} \qquad (11)$$

This combination rule is much more convenient to implement than the previous rule of Eq.(9) which uses the autocorrelation. The value of n needs to be selected heuristically based on the results of numerical simulations.

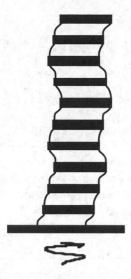

Figure 3. 10 degrees of freedom shear building.

Table 1. Near-field earthquake records

Near-field earthquakes	PGA [cm/s^2]	Duration [sec]
1966 Parkfield	479	12.1
1971 San Fernando (Pacoima Dam)	1148	9.5
1979 Coyote Lake	409	8.0
1979 Imperial Valley	454	10.6
1992 Landers	720	34.0
1994 Northridge Sylmar	827	10.0
1995 Kobe		
JMA Kobe	818	14.9
JR Takatori[Nakamura, et.al. 1996]	606	21.3
Fukikai	802	11.3
Higashi Kobe Bridge	325	18

3. NUMERICAL SIMULATION WITH 10 DEGREES OF FREEDOM STRUCTURES

In this section, accuracy of modal combination rules are studied numerically using the model structure of Figure 3. The structure has equal mass and stiffness for each floor, and damping is proportional to stiffness. The values of fundamental natural period are varied between 0.5[sec] and 1.5[sec] and two values of damping ratios (1%, 5%) for the fundamental mode are taken in simulation.

3.1. Ground motions

The following 16 earthquakes shown in Tables 1 and 2, which are categorized into near-field earthquakes and design/far-field earthquakes are employed for calculation. Ground motions which are known by its impulsive characteristics with relatively small epicentral distances are chosen as near-field strong motions. Although El Centro earthquake can be considered as a near-field record, it is included in far-field/design earthquakes, because El Centro record has been extensively used as an design ground motion and SRSS methods have been shown to be applicable.

The duration of ground motion is computed by taking the first and the last passage time of 10% of peak ground acceleration (PGA). Near-field motions are observed to generally have shorter duration.

3.2. Accuracy of modal combination rules

Figure 4 shows the ratio between the predicted response calculated by modal combination rules and the actual response values obtained by numerical integration. All 16 ground motions are used and their average response values are shown for each fundamental natural periods. SRSS is observed to give good approximation with slight tendency of under-estimation. The absolute sum gives conservative results with over-estimation around 20% in average. The modal combination of Eq.(9) which uses autocorrelation eliminates

Table 2. Far-field/design earthquake records

Far-field/design earthquakes	PGA [cm/s^2]	Duration [sec]
1940 El Centro	340	30.3
1952 Taft	176	37.4
1968 Tokachi Oki		
Aomori	210	72.4
Hachinohe	249	43.3
1985 Mexico	80	168.7
1993 Kushiro-Oki	919	50.1

under-estimation of SRSS and has the tendency of over-estimation of less than 10%. Combination by 1.2-norm is also shown in the same figure. This method gives similar values of autocorrelation method when the damping ratio is 1%, but more conservative for the case of 5%, which implies that this *n*-value may need to be adjusted according to the damping ratio.

SRSS gives better approximation for the case of 5% damping than the case of 1%. This can be explained by looking at the correlation between modes introduced by Eq.(9), which is exponentially decreasing with time difference and damping ratio. This fact implies that the modal coupling effect is decreasing with increase of damping ratio.

3.3. Near-field effects

Near-field earthquakes and far-field/design earthquakes are compared here. Figure 5 shows the accuracy of SRSS for average of responses of 10 near-field earthquakes and 6 far-field/design earthquakes. Both results show similar characteristics, with slight difference around fundamental period of 1[sec].

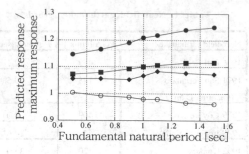

(a)Damping ratio of first mode = 1%

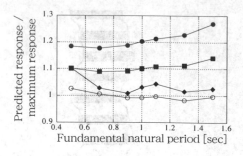

(b)Damping ratio of first mode = 5%

Figure 4. Accuracy of modal combination rules for the 10 degrees of freedom structure.

$\bigcirc$: SRSS, $\blacklozenge$: Autocorrelation, $\bullet$: Absolute sum, $\blacksquare$: 1.2-norm.

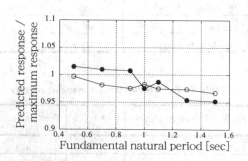

(a)Damping ratio of first mode = 1%

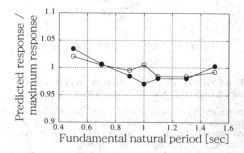

(b)Damping ratio of first mode = 5%

Figure 5. Accuracy of prediction by SRSS method for near-field earthquakes. $\bigcirc$: Near-field, $\bullet$: Far-field/design.

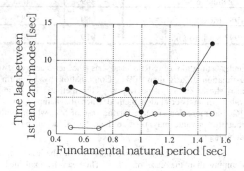

(a)Damping ratio of first mode = 1%

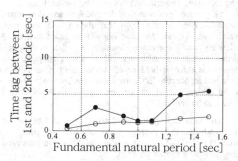

(b)Damping ratio of first mode = 5%

Figure 6. Time lag between occurrences of peak responses of first and second modes. $\bigcirc$: Near-field, $\bullet$: Far-field/design.

Figure 6 shows time lag between the occurrence time of peaks of the first mode and second mode $\Delta t = |\ t_1 - t_2\ |$. It can clearly be seen that near-field ground motions have smaller values which reflects the simultaneous occurrence of peaks due to the effect of impulsive excitation.

The results of Figure 5 and Figure 6 appear to be contradictory because the correlation should be larger for smaller values of Δt in regard to the expression of Eq. (9). This discrepancy can be explained by looking at the displacement response spectra. Figure 7 shows the ratio of average displacement response spectra of near-field and far-

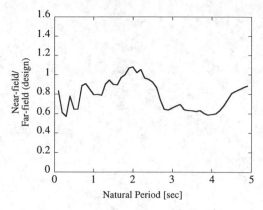

Figure 7. Ratio of response spectra of near-field and far-field/design earthquakes with damping ratio 5%.

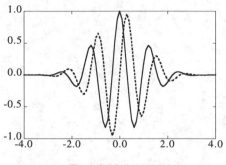

Figure 8. Morlet's wavelet:

————, Real part; - - - - - -, Imaginary part.

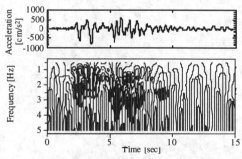

Figure 9. Accelerogram and contour plot of wavelet transform of 1995 Kobe earthquake (Kobe JMA, NS component)

field/design earthquakes. Because each record has different magnitude, all the records are normalized by maximum ground velocity by multiplying appropriate scaling factor. It can be seen that the near-field response is smaller for natural periods shorter than 1[sec], which corresponds to the natural frequencies of higher modes of the example 10 degrees of freedom structure. Therefore the possible increase in response due to shorter time lag Δt is reduced by the small values of response spectra for higher modes.

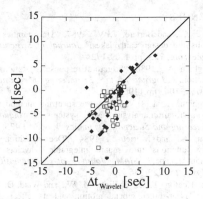

Figure 10. Time lag of peak occurrence of modal responses and time lag estimated by wavelet transform.

□ : Loma Prieta, ◆ : Kobe.

4. CONCLUSIONS

Accuracy of SRSS method is studied with emphasis on the investigation of the effect of near-field ground. Ten degrees of freedom structural model subject to 10 near-field and 6 far-field/design earthquakes are employed for numerical simulations. Major results are as follows:

1. SRSS method is shown to be accurate even for near-field seismic ground motions but gives slight underestimation of response values.
2. By approximating time history of modal response before and after the maximum response using the envelope of autocorrelation, alternative modal combination rule which includes not only modal response values but also the effect of closeness of occurrence time of peaks in several modes are constructed. This method eliminates the under-estimation of SRSS, and gives insight on the cause of error in SRSS method.
3. Simple combination rule which uses n-norm is also proposed and is shown to give good approximation by taking the value $n=1.2$ when damping ratio is 1%. The value of n needs to be adjusted appropriately for general application.
4. Although time lag between occurrence of peaks of modal responses is shorter for near-field earthquakes, SRSS method is shown to have almost the same accuracy for both near-field and far-field/design earthquakes. This is because response spectra for higher modes of 10 degrees of freedom structure was small.

ACKNOWLEDGMENT

The research work in this paper is partly supported by the Scientific Research Grant (Fundamental Research B, No. 08455209) of the Ministry of Education, Science and Culture of Japan. This support is gratefully acknowledged.

REFERENCES

Anderson, J. C., and Bertero, V. V., 1987. "Uncertainties in establishing design earthquakes," *Journal of Structural Engineering*, **113**, pp.1709-1724.

Der Kiureghian, A., 1980. "Structural response to stationary excitation," *Journal of the Engineering Mechanics Division*, **106**, pp.1195-1213.

Der Kiureghian, A., 1981. "A response spectrum method for random vibration analysis of MDF systems," *Earthquake Engineering and Structural Dynamics*, **9**, pp.419-435.

Grossmann, A., and Morlet, J., 1984. "Decomposition of Hardy functions into square integrable wavelets of constant shape," *SIAM Journal of Mathematical Analysis*, 15, 723-736.

Hall, J. F., Heaton, T. H., Halling, M. W., and Wald, D. J., 1995. "Near-source ground motion and its effects on flexible buildings," *Earthquake Spectra*, **11**, pp.569-605.

Igusa, T., 1992. "A unified mode combination theory for stationary response of structural systems," *Earthquake Engineering and Structural Dynamics*, **21**, pp.109-126.

Iwan, W. D., 1994. "Near-field considerations in specification of seismic design motions for structures," *10th European Conference on Earthquake Engineering*.

Nakamura, Y., Uehan, F. and Inoue, H, 1996. "Waveform and its analysis of the 1995 Hyogoken-Nanbu Earthquake (II)," *JR Earthquake Information* **23d**, Railway Technical Research Institute.

Vandiver, J. K., Dunwoody, A. B., Campbell, R. B., and Cook, M. F., 1982. "A mathematical basis for the random decrement vibration signature analysis technique," *Journal of Mechanical Design*, **104**, pp.307-313.

APPENDIX:

COMPUTATION OF OCCURRENCE TIME OF PEAK BY WAVELET TRANSFORMATION

Time lag of peak occurrence of modal responses can approximately be derived by looking at wavelet transform of accelerogram. By applying wavelet transform using Morlet's wavelet (Grossmann and Morlet, 1984), shown in Figure 8, accelerogram is transformed into time-frequency domain as shown in Figure 9. Then, by locking at the peak amplitude at specified modal frequencies, approximate occurrence time of peak responses can be identified.

The accuracy of this estimation is demonstrated by the example using ground motion records with various epicentral distances observed at Loma Prieta and Kobe earthquakes using the first two modes of the 10 degrees of freedom structure with fundamental period 1 [sec] and damping ratio of 1%.

Structural Safety and Reliability, Shiraishi, Shinozuka & Wen (eds) © 1998 Balkema, Rotterdam, ISBN 90 5410 978 5

Near-field earthquake motion simulation for risk assessment of large-scale infrastructures and lifeline systems

Ray Ruichong Zhang
Colorado School of Mines, Golden, Colo., USA

Masanobu Shinozuka
University of Southern California, Los Angeles, Calif., USA

ABSTRACT: In this study, near-field earthquake ground motion is simulated with the aid of computer code "SEISMO" that is developed on the basis of a stochastic computational mechanics model for earthquake wave motion in a realistic earth medium generated by a physically-consistent or seismologically-consistent seismic source. The effects of seismic source characteristics and local geological profile of the earth medium on near-field ground motion are also qualitatively and quantitatively estimated, which is fundamentally important for the risk assessment of large-scale infrastructures and lifeline systems under near-field earthquake motion.

1 INTRODUCTION

Recent large earthquakes, especially the 1994 Northridge and 1995 Hyogoken-nanbu (Kobe) earthquakes, have provided an extremely good lesson for both seismologists and engineers. Firstly, major structural damages and/or malfunction of large-scale infrastructures and lifeline systems (e.g. multi-supported highway structures and long-span bridges) caused by near-field ground motion are not evenly and proportionally distributed from earthquake epicenter, depending strongly on seismic source characteristics (e.g. rupture pattern and slip distribution) and local geological profile of the earth medium (e.g. irregular topography and laterally non-homogeneous earth medium properties). Secondly, the existing records associated with the near source quite often distort the nature of the shaking, especially for low-frequency components (see also Heaton, et al, 1995, Hall, et al, 1995). Since the occurrence of large earthquakes in urban areas is highly likely in the near future (see Working Group in California Earthquake, 1990), it becomes extremely important to know qualitatively and quantitatively the near-field ground motion effects on large-scale infrastructures and lifeline systems. To do so, realistic modeling, synthetics and simulation of strong earthquake ground motion play a crucial role, which cannot be well carried out without integrating the knowledge of state-of-the-art engineering seismology and earthquake-resistant structural design principles. The objective of this study is thus to numerically simulate near-field ground motion with consideration of both a realistic earth medium and seismic source, which is fundamentally important for the risk assessment of large-scale infrastructures and lifeline systems under near-field earthquake motion.

2 MODELING OF EARTHQUAKE MOTION

Since earthquake motion is the result of propagating seismic waves in the earth medium which are originally generated at a seismic source, appropriate modeling for earth medium and seismic source becomes crucially important for synthesizing the realistic earthquake wave motion. Equally important are the methodology used for the wave propagation analysis and corresponding numerical computation which are associated with an efficient computer code. All of these are described in the following subsections.

2.1 Seismic Source Modeling

Seismic source can be described as a slip or dislocation rupturing over a certain area of a fault. The slip pattern, mechanism and final amount can be either assumed appropriately (in terms of human's experience and understanding from past earthquakes and following certain physics rule) or obtained primarily on the basis of earthquake ground motion records (an inverse solution). The former is referred in this paper to as physically-consistent modeling of a seismic source while the latter as seismologically-consistent modeling.

Among various physically-consistent (kinetic) seismic source models, circular crack source mechanism is perhaps the best one from physics as well as mathematics viewpoint. However, most of seismic faults are usually very large in size and can not be represented by a single circular crack, especially when near-field ground motion is under investigation. Hence, Papageorgiou and Aki (1983) proposed a specific barrier model, in which a seismic fault is assumed to rupture consecutively in a series of circular sub-faults separated by unbroken barriers. This model was applied by Deodatis and Zhang (1993) to synthesize ground motion with earth modeled as a layered half-space. Recently, a stochastic barrier model was developed by Deodatis et al. (1996) to capture the nature of randomness of realistic source mechanism. Specifically, a barrier model with irregular boundaries has been utilized to calculate the distribution and the amount of final slip over a fault plane. The basic idea is that an underlying barrier model with regular circular boundaries is transformed into a corresponding one with irregular boundaries which are regarded as a stochastic field and simulated with the use of spectral representation method (Shinozuka and Deodatis, 1991 and 1996).

While barrier mechanism can be used as a general model for seismic source, a specific earthquake source model can also be established by solving inverse problem with the aid of earthquake ground motion records as well as wave propagation theory. For example, for the specific earthquake of Loma Prieta of magnitude 7.1 struck at the San Francisco Bay area on October 17, 1989, the seismic source modeling and ground motion prediction have been made. One of the best models was proposed by Zeng et al (1993) using ray method and near-field earthquake records (14 observation sites within 35 km around epicenter), in which the distribution of final slip on the fault plane is predicted. This model has been successfully applied by Zhang and Deodatis (1996) to synthesize both near- and far-field Loma Prieta earthquake in a layered half-space which is modeled on the basis of geological profiles of Santa Cruz mountain area.

Theoretically, a seismic source can be best described by either physically-consistent or seismologically-consistent model. However, since the detail of seismic source will greatly affect near-field motion from one location to another in comparison with far-field motion, judicial selection of seismic source model is still important particularly to the risk assessment of large-scale infrastructures and lifeline systems under near-field earthquake motion.

2.2 Earth Medium Modeling

In investigating seismic wave propagation and its correspondingly induced ground and/or underground motion responses, the earth is often modeled as a vertically non-homogeneous medium, idealized as a layered half-space with each layer being homogeneous. In reality, the earth medium can never be of perfectly lateral homogeneity and is always of stochastically lateral non-homogeneity to a certain extent (see e.g. Chu et al, 1981, Ishimaru, 1978 and Caviglia and Morro, 1992). It is apparent that not all of the lateral non-homogeneities are necessarily concerned in earthquake wave motion modeling from an engineering point of view. A fundamental issue is thus raised, i.e. what is the criterion for a real laterally non-homogeneous earth medium being or not being approximated as laterally homogeneous when seismic wave propagation in such a medium is under investigation?

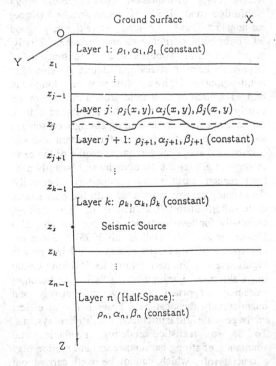

Figure 1: Earth medium modeling as a layered half-space with lateral non-homogeneities

Recently, Zhang (1994), Zhang and Shinozuka (1996b) and Zhang et al. (1997a,b) investigated qualitatively and quantitatively three-dimensional wave scattering phenomena in a layered half-space with lateral non-homogeneity under consideration (see *Fig.* 1). Their study shows that the introduction of lateral non-homogeneity into the earth medium model of a layered half-space results in the complexity of the problem not only mathematically but also physically. Specifically, when the irregular boundaries (surface and/or interfaces) and/or laterally non-homogeneous medium properties (wave speeds and density) are under consideration, wave scattering occurs due to these irregularities and/or lateral non-homogeneities, resulting in coupling between P-SV and SH waves, which happens neither in the case of a perfectly layered half-space (without presence of the lateral non-homogeneity) nor the case of a layered medium with two-dimensional lateral non-homogeneity. The existence of the lateral non-homogeneity in the earth medium not only affects seismogram envelops, response spectra, and power spectra of earthquake motion to a certain extent, but also is responsible for the generation of coda waves. The extent of these effects is primarily dependent on the dominant wavelength and the intensity of lateral non-homogeneities.

Therefore, when risk assessment of large-scale infrastructures and lifeline systems under near-field ground motion are carried out, the simulated ground motion with consideration of the aforementioned lateral non-homogeneities of earth medium becomes very important. This is particularly substantial when the dimension of the lateral non-homogeneities of the earth medium is comparable with that of structures.

2.3 Methodology for Wave Propagation Analysis

Among the techniques applied to analyze earthquake wave propagation, especially in a layered half-space, discrete wave number method is perhaps most convenient and applicable, which not only takes into account all kinds of travelling waves, i.e. body waves and surface waves, but also minimizes numerical computation problems. In particular, this methodology is developed on the basis of the work of Lamb (1904), Bouchon (1979), Chouet (1987), and Dunkin (1965). The discrete wave number technique is used to propagate waves due to the rupture of an extended seismic source through a 3-dimensional layered half-space.

For the analysis of wave propagation and scattering in a layered half-space with lateral non-homogeneities, a first order perturbation approach can be applied first with ease (see Zhang, 1994). Specifically, the total wave field, generated by a seismic dislocation source buried in the layered half-space, is decomposed into two wave fields. One is a mean wave field, which is a response field in a perfectly layered half-space subjected to a seismic dislocation source. This mean wave field can then be solved using the discrete wave number method. The other is a scattered wave field, which is due to the existence of lateral non-homogeneities. The effects of the non-homogeneities on the scattered wave field are equivalent to those of fictitious discontinuity sources acting on the perfectly plane boundaries in case of irregular boundaries or those of fictitious distributed body forces acting in the homogeneous medium in case of the laterally non-homogeneous medium properties. The intensity of the fictitious forces depends on both the mean wave response field and the lateral non-homogeneities. The solution for the scattered wave field is also obtained using the discrete wave number method.

2.4 Computer Code ``SEISMO"

Based on the aforementioned earthquake wave motion model accounting for realistic seismic source, earth medium and appropriate methodology used for the analysis of wave propagation and scattering, a computer code called "SEISMO" was developed primarily by Deodatis, Papageorgiou, Shinozuka, Theoharis, L. Zhang and R. Zhang. Its validity and accuracy were verified by comparing the results using "SEISMO" with corresponding results by Archuleta and Hartzell (1981). "SEISMO" has also been successfully used to synthesize both near- and far-field 1968 Tokachi-Oki and 1989 Loma Prieta earthquake in a layered half-space with seismologically-consistent source models (see, e.g. Zhang and Deodatis, 1996a). The synthesized Loma Prieta earthquake ground motion has been verified to be consistent with the actual records in terms of magnitude (intensity), wave form (frequency content) and time duration.

3 NUMERICAL EXAMPLES

Three numerical examples of synthesized ground motion are presented as follows for illustration of the use of the aforementioned earthquake wave motion models and corresponding "SEISMO" code, which can be used for risk assessment of large-scale infrastructure and lifeline systems under near-field earthquake motion.

3.1 Loma Prieta Earthquake Ground Motion

The 1989 Loma Prieta earthquake ground motion was synthesized with the use of seismologically-consistent source model and a layered half-space earth model. *Fig.* 2 presents the synthesized wave motion at a dense grid of observer locations at selected time instants. The generation and propagation of different kinds of seismic waves, the spatial and temporal variability of ground motion, as well as the development of the permanent (static) ground deformation, can be examined by carefully studying the plots in *Fig.* 2. It is of interest to note that the near-field motion around the epicenter changes dramatically from point to point largely due to the detail of seismic source such as fault directivity, rupture pattern and final slip distribution, implying the importance of near-field motion in the risk assessment of large-scale infrastructures and lifeline systems under near-field motion.

3.2 Effects of Lateral Non-Homogeneities on Ground Motion

While the previous example uses a perfectly layered half-space as the earth medium model, the effects of lateral non-homogeneities of the earth medium are examined in this one. In particular, the earth medium is modeled as two layers over a half-space with the top layer properties being laterally non-homogeneous. In other words, the wave speeds and density of the top layer are function of lateral coordinates. For comparison, two kinds of common factor $a(x,y)$, characterizing the perturbed parts of P and S wave speeds and density of the top layer, are shown in *Fig.* 3. The vertical ground accelerations to a point source (This is for simplicity and demonstration. It is straightforward to apply the case of the point source to that of the extended source) at selected observation sites with and without the presence of lateral non-homogeneities are depicted correspondingly in *Fig.* 3. It can be seen from *Fig.* 3 that the effects of "smooth" (long dominant wavelength) lateral non-homogeneities on the ground motion are primarily on the variation of peak acceleration, while the effects of "rough" (short dominant wavelength) lateral non-homogeneities on the ground motion are primarily on the broadening of the seismogram envelops. These phenomena are consistent with what Aki (1975) and Sato (1989) observed in their relatively simple models.

3.3 Near-Field Motion Effects on Long-Period Structures

Due to the high-pass filtering in processing the data obtained from the seismometers of earlier vintage, the observed ground motion can not always be adequately used to examine its effects on flexible structures. Recently, Zhang and Shinozuka (1996c) applied the aforementioned earthquake motion model and code "SEISMO" to show the extent of the underestimation of response spectra with the use of observed ground motion, effects of source information such as rupture pattern, slip distribution as well as directivity of the fault on the response spectra. Specifically, Loma Prieta earthquake is used as an example again, in which the simulated and observed ground motion at selected observation sites are compared and the corresponding response spectra to both simulated and observed ground motion are then calculated. Consequently, the low-frequency near-field motion effects on long-period structures can be analyzed.

In their study, the near-field ground motion is first simulated, which consists of two parts. The low-frequency part (up to 1 *Hz*) is synthesized using computer code "SEISMO". The high-frequency part is obtained by modifying real earthquake records by deleting the corresponding low-frequency part from the recorded data and adjusting peak magnitude on the basis of the relative distance away from the observation sites. The reasons why the synthetics and filtered observation data are combined to form the simulated ground motion are detailed as follows. (1) Many studies indicated that the synthetics of the ground motion by using theoretical models can successfully predict the ground motion in the low-frequency range (usually less than 1.5 *Hz*). However, the synthetics of higher frequency motion are either time-consuming using theoretical models or not as good as the prediction of low-frequency motion. (2) The existing records particularly at near field quite often distort the nature of the shaking, especially for low-frequency motion. For example, some accelerometers do not record very low frequency components (e.g. less than 0.1 *Hz*). In addition, the relatively low frequency components (e.g. less than 0.3 *Hz*) of the recorded data are underestimated (Iwan and Chen, 1995). (3) As far as the long-period structures are concerned, the high-frequency motion is not as important as the

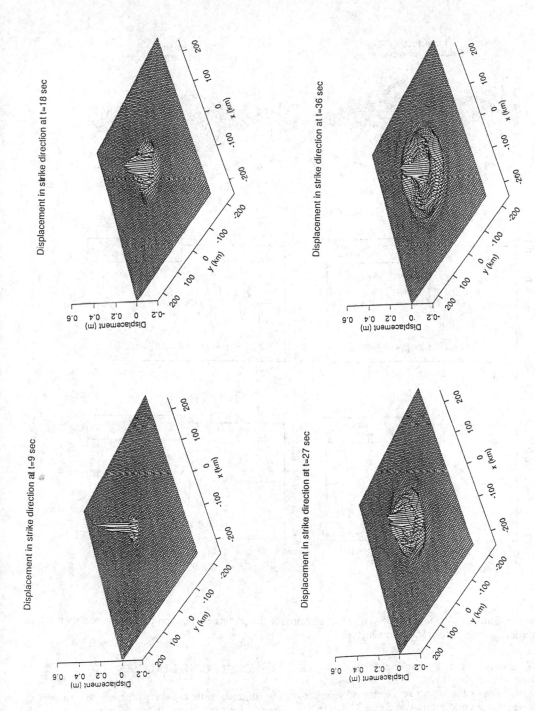

Figure 2: Synthesized Loma Prieta earthquake displacements in the strike direction at time instants of 9, 18, 27 and 36 seconds

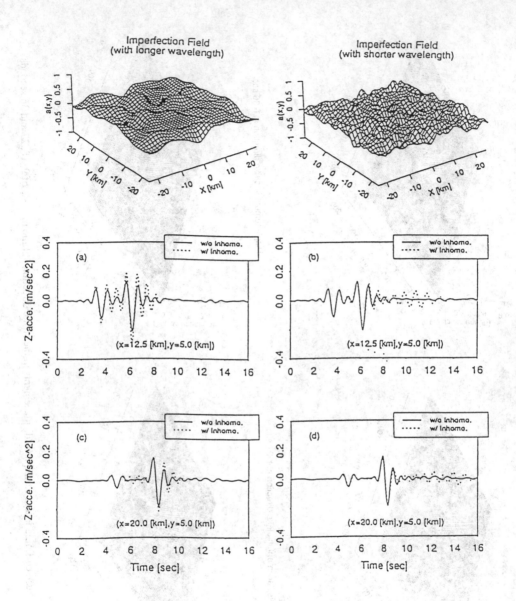

Figure 3: Simulated common factor $a(x,y)$, characterizing the perturbed medium properties, and their effects on vertical ground acceleration time histories

low-frequency motion, especially beyond the frequency larger than 1 *Hz*.

Fig. 4 shows the response spectra of simulated and observed ground motion at Santa Cruz (16 *km* away from the epicenter). As can be seen from the figure, larger acceleration responses at moderate to long period (1 to 6 *sec.*) under a simulated motion is observed than a recorded motion, implying that the use of recorded data underestimates the response of structures with a moderate to long period.

4   CONCLUDING REMARKS

In summary, this paper presents the modeling, synthetics, and simulation of strong earthquake wave motion, in which uncertainties in both the earth medium and seismic source are taken into consideration.

The simulated ground motion in this study can be used to develop a contour map of peak spectral responses (PSR) at several different periods

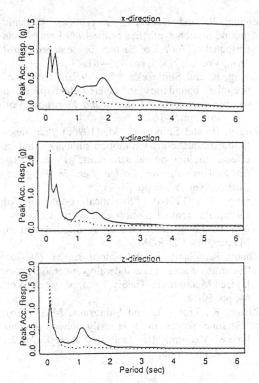

Figure 4: Comparison of acceleration response spectra with damping ratio being 5% at Santa Cruz (solid line is associated with simulated motion and the dotted line with recorded motion)

in the near field around the epicenter, taking into account site-specific effects on the structural seismic vulnerability. Such constructed PSR map provides better insight into the demands imposed by ground motion on structures than does peak ground motion. With the aid of geographic information systems, the contour map of PSR can be used for the further study with respect to planning, design, analysis, construction, retrofitting, maintenance, emergency repair and restoration of large-scale infrastructures and lifeline systems.

Statistics of a strong ground motion, such as frequency-wave number spectrum and coherence function which characterize the temporal and spatial variations of a strong ground motion, can also be estimated using the earthquake wave motion model presented in this study (Zhang, 1996d). These statistical properties can then be used in simulating spatially-correlated earthquake ground motion and consequently used for earthquake-resistant structural design, especially for elongated structures such as pipelines and long-span bridges. The other engineering applications of this study may be

mentioned of modeling and hazards mitigation of Tsunamis inundation, liquefaction phenomena investigation, interaction analysis in a seismic source-soil-structure system (e.g. Yong, et al. 1997a,b), effects on foundation and underground structures, and vertical component motion effects on earthquake-resistant structural design.

ACKNOWLEDGMENTS

This work was supported by the National Science Foundation with Grants # CMS 96-12127, # 94-3302A, by the Federal Highway Administration through the National Center for Earthquake Engineering Research under Contract # DTFH61-92-C-00106, and by Colorado School of Mines under Grant #CSM 2-30131.

REFERENCES

Aki, K.(1975). "Original of coda waves: source, attenuation, and scattering effects," *J. Geophys. Res.*, 80, pp. 3322-3342.

Archuleta, R.J. and Hartzell, S. (1981). "Effects of fault finiteness on near-source ground motion," *Bull. Seism. Soc. Am.*, Vol. 71, pp. 939-957.

Bouchon, M. (1979). "Discrete wave number representation of elastic wave fields in three-dimensional space," *J. Geophys. Res.*, Vol. 84, No. B7, pp.3609-3614.

Caviglia, G. and Morro, A., 1992. *Inhomogeneous waves in solids and fluids*, World Scientific.

Chouet, B. (1987). "Representation of an extended seismic source in a propagator-based formalism," *Bull. Seism. Soc. Am.*, Vol. 77, No. 1, pp. 14-27.

Chu, L., Askar, A. and Cakmak, S., (1981) "Earthquake waves in a random medium," *Int'l J. Num. & Analy. Meth. in Geomech.*, Vol. 5, pp. 79-96.

Deodatis, G. and Zhang, R. (1993). "Seismic ground motion generation using a specific barrier model description of the seismic source," *Princeton-Kajima Joint Research Report*.

Deodatis, G., Durukal, E., Papageorgiou, A.S. and Shinozuka, M. (1996). "Synthesis of ground motions of a Loma Prieta-type earthquake in the vicinity of the San Francisco metropolitan area," *Proc. 11th World Conf. on Earthq. Eng.*, Acapulco, Mexico, in 4 CD-ROM..

Dunkin, J.W. (1965). "Computation of modal solutions in layered, elastic media at high frequencies," *Bull. Seism. Soc. Am.*, Vol. 55, No. 2, pp. 335-358.

Hall, J.F., Heaton, T.H., Halling, M.W. and Wald, D.J. (1995). "Near-source ground motion and its effects on flexible buildings," *Earthquake Spectra*, Vol. 11, No. 4, pp. 569-605.

Heaton, T.H., Hall, J.F., Wald, D.J. and Halling, M.W. (1995). ``Response of high-rise and base-isolated buildings to a hypothetical *Mw* 7.0 blind thrust earthquake," *Science*, Vol. 267, pp. 206-211, Jan. 13.

Ishimaru, A., 1978. *Wave Propagation and Scattering in Random Media*, Vol. 1 and 2, Academic Press, New York, San Francisco, London.

Iwan, W. and Chen, X. (1995). "Important near-field ground motion data from the Landers earthquake," *Proc. of 10th European Conf. on Earthq. Eng.*, Vienna, Austria.

Lamb, H. (1904). "On the Propagation Tremors at the Surface of an Elastic Solid," *Phi. Trans. of Roy. Soc. of London*, Vol. A203, pp. 1-42.

Papageorgiou, A.S. and Aki, K. (1983). "A specific barrier model for the quantitative description of inhomogeneous faulting and the prediction of strong ground motion. I description of the model," *Bull. Seism. Soc. Am.*, Vol. 73, No. 3, pp. 693-722.

Sato, H. (1989). "Broadening of seismogram envelopes in the randomly inhomogeneous lithosphere based on the parabolic approximation: southeastern Honshu, Japan," *J. Geophys. Res.*, Vol. 94, No. B12, pp. 17735-17747.

Shinozuka, M. and Deodatis, G. (1991). "Simulation of Stochastic Processes by Spectral Representation," *Appl. Mech. Rev.*, ASME, Vol. 44, No. 4, pp. 191-204.

Shinozuka, M. and Deodatis, G. (1996). "Simulation of Multi-Dimensional Gaussian Stochastic Fields by Spectral Representation," *Appl. Mech. Rev.*, ASME, Vol. 49, No. 1, pp. 1-53.

Working Group on California Earthquake Probabilities, U.S. Geol. Surv. Circ., p.1053, 1990.

Yong, Y., Zhang, R. and Yu, J. (1997a). "Motion of foundation on a layered soil medium – I. Impedance characteristics," *Int'l J. of Soil Dyn. and Earthq. Eng.*, Vol. 16, pp. 295-306.

Yong, Y., Zhang, R. and Yu, J. (1997a). "Motion of foundation on a layered soil medium – II. Response analysis," *Int'l J. of Soil Dyn. and Earthq. Eng.*, Vol. 16, pp. 307-316.

Zeng, Y., Aki, K. and Teng, T.L. (1993). "Mapping of the high frequency source radiation for the Loma Prieta earthquake, California," *J. Geophys. Res.*, Vol. 98, No. B7, pp. 11981-11993.

Zhang, R. (1994). "Stochastic seismic ground motion modeling with imperfectly stratified earth mcdium," *J. Sound and Vibration*, Vol. 176, No. 1, pp. 69-92.

Zhang, R. and Deodatis, G. (1996a). "Seismic ground motion synthetics of the 1989 Loma Prieta earthquake," *Int'l J. of Earthq. Eng. and Structural Dyn.*, Vol. 25, No. 5, pp. 465-481.

Zhang, R. and Shinozuka, M. (1996b). "Effects of irregular boundaries in layered half-space on seismic waves," *J. of Sound and Vibration*, Vol. 195, No. 1, pp. 1-16.

Zhang, R. and Shinozuka, M. (1996c). "On near-field earthquake ground motion simulation and its effects on long-period structures," *Proc. of 4th Nat'l Workshop on Bridge Res. in Progress*, Buffalo, New York, pp. 71-76.

Zhang, R. (1996d). "Statistical estimation of earthquake ground motion characteristics," *Proc. of 11th World Conf. on Earthq. Eng.*, Acapulco, Mexico, in 4 CD-ROM.

Zhang, R., Zhang, L. and Shinozuka, M. (1997a). "Seismic waves in a laterally inhomogeneous layered Medium. I: Theory," *J. Appl. Mech.*, Vol. 64, pp. 50-58.

Zhang, R., Zhang, L. and Shinozuka, M. (1997b). ``Seismic waves in a laterally inhomogeneous layered Medium. II: Analysis," *J. Appl. Mech.*, Vol. 64, pp. 59-65.

Structural Safety and Reliability, Shiraishi, Shinozuka & Wen (eds) © 1998 Balkema, Rotterdam, ISBN 90 5410 978 5

Optimum subdivision control of an extended system under earthquake emergency

N. Nojima
Faculty of Engineering, Hiroshima Institute of Technology, Japan

H. Kameda
Disaster Prevention Research Institute, Kyoto University, Japan

ABSTRACT : A probabilistic method has been proposed to subdivide an extended system so that reliability of the system function is maximized in an earthquake emergency. On the basis of probability, reliability and optimization theory, optimum configuration of subdivision has been determined so as to localize the damage to the system and to minimize damage spread to the whole system by real-time isolation of damaged segments.

1. INTRODUCTION

Modern urban area is strongly dependent on utility lifelines and transportation facilities. Those systems are necessarily in the shape of extended systems to cover the wide-spread urbanized tract. In normal situation, network property of extended systems provide essential functions of supply, disposal, transmission, and transportation. In an earthquake disaster, however, the network property turns to be inherent defect, i.e., physical and/or functional damage spread.

Several recent earthquake disasters revealed high vulnerability of such extended systems. In the 1978 Miyagiken-oki Earthquake in Japan, city gas supply network including slightly- and non-damaged area was totally shut off because of partially heavy damage. Great lesson was derived that hard-hit area should have been isolated to localize the spatial extent of malfunction. In the 1989 Loma Prieta Earthquake in the U.S., high-pressure water supply system AWSS (Auxiliary Water Supply System) for fire-fighting failed to function because breaks in the network's southern section pipes could not be located and isolated before water pressure of the whole system was lost (Austin, 1990). The 1995 Hanshin-Awaji Earthquake Disaster in Japan also left similar examples. In Kobe City, many reservoirs were drained and most hydrants were out of order shortly after the earthquake, because excessive water leaks took place throughout the city, which significantly disabled fire-fighting performance (Nojima and Kameda 1996).

Earthquake disaster countermeasures in lifelines are categorized into: 1) physical improvement, 2) network organization, 3) system automation, and 4) operations by human-power , each of which has three phases: a) advance preparation, b) emergency operations, and c) recovery work (Nojima et al. 1990). Because of large number of existing components, uniform strengthening of the whole system is unreal; physical damage is inevitably accepted to some extent. Given the initial damage, second-best mitigation measure is emergency operation of the system to minimize the effect of damage. In fact, "real-time disaster prevention" is one of the most highlighted and promising concept in earthquake engineering, which includes real-time identification of seismic source, real-time seismic microzonation, real-time estimation and detection of damage, emergency control of facilities, recovery work support system, etc.

Among these facets, post-earthquake subdivision of an extended system is a direct measure to prevent secondary damage in lifeline systems. One can localize damage, prevent damage spread, and maintain service as far as possible by emergency isolation of affected part, thus the subsequent impact of an earthquake can be minimized. Subdivision control is particularly effective when contrast of damage distribution is prominent, which is general tendency in urban earthquake disaster.

Practically, several lifeline sectors took advantage of the concept of subdivision control in the 1995 Hanshin-Awaji Earthquake Disaster. Osaka Gas Co. successfully isolated five segmented areas called "middle block" including 834 thousand customers in the hardest-hit area and kept the remaining service area almost intact. Without this operation on the day of the earthquake, much wider area could have experienced cutoff of gas supply, requiring much longer restoration time. Kobe Waterworks Bureau owns 21 distribution basins equipped with emergency shutdown valves triggered by acceleration sensors in order to reserve water for emergency supply. Eighteen of them worked as designed and 42.2 thousand tons of water was successfully reserved.

In performing subdivision control, it is presumed

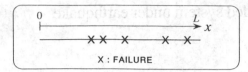

Fig.1 Location of failures on a link with length L

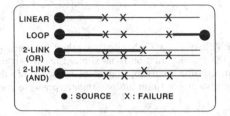

Fig.2 Conditional $(N \geq n)$ PDF of location of n th failure

that the extended system concerned is subdivided into appropriate number and size of segments so that the damaged segments can be isolated from the others without damage. Then, a question arises; how an extended system should be subdivided as a pre-quake strategic measure ? Only a few studies have been done attempting to answer this question : for example, the study on subdivision of urban space for reduction of conflagration hazard (Kobayashi 1993), and the study on subdivision of gas supply network for optimum restoration (Nojima and Kameda 1992). The reason is, conceivably, empirical judgment has been virtually the only resort to solve this kind of complicated problem without an analytical model.

In this view of the problem, this study presents an analytical method to subdivide an extended system so that reliability of the system function is maximized in an earthquake emergency. For simplicity, this study deals with only elementary systems composed of one or two link(s) with one or two source node(s). The reliability of the system function is measured in terms of the length connected to the source node (LC). However, since damage distribution is essentially unknown until damage actually occurs, probabilistic approach has been employed in this study; expected length connected to the source node (ELC) is used as a measure of reliability in the following sections.

In spite of the uncertainty in damage location, on the basis of probability theory, system reliability theory, and system optimization theory, the method proposed below determines optimum subdivision configuration with subdivision devices which are potentially activated according to the actual circumstances.

2. ELC OF NON-SEGMENTED LINK SYSTEMS

2.1 Damage distribution on a simple link

Consider a simple link of length L shown in Fig.1 where x denotes distance from the source on the left terminal. Assume uniform, random and independent occurrence of failure with failure rate (expected number of failure per unit length) λ. The probability $\mathrm{Po}(N)$ that N failures occur to the system is given by Poisson distribution.

$$\mathrm{Po}(N) = \frac{(\lambda L)^N e^{-\lambda L}}{N!} \qquad (1)$$

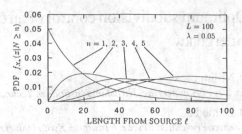

Fig.3 Location of failures and LC (length of connectivity) of non-segmented systems

Then, under the condition that at least $n(1 \leq n \leq N)$ failure(s) occur, the conditional probability density function (Papoulis 1965) of the location of n th failure from the source are obtained as gamma distribution defined for the interval $[0, L]$.

$$f_{X_n}(x; \lambda | N \geq n) = \frac{\lambda(\lambda x)^{n-1} e^{-\lambda x}}{(n-1)!} \cdot \frac{1}{\mathrm{Po}(N \geq n)} \qquad (2)$$

Figure 2 graphically shows the conditional PDF for $\lambda = 0.05$ and $L = 100$. The conditional expected location of n th failure is obtained as follows:

$$\overline{x_n(\lambda, L | N \geq n)} = \frac{n}{\lambda} \cdot \frac{\mathrm{Po}(N \geq n + 1)}{\mathrm{Po}(N \geq n)} \qquad (3)$$

The PDF of location of n th failure given by beta distribution if the number of failures N is known (Kawakami 1990).

2.2 Definition of LC and ELC of non-segmented systems

Consider four types of link systems with source node(s) at either or both terminals as shown in Fig.3. In this section, "Length of Connectivity" (LC) indicated by thick lines on each system in Fig.3 is defined by the length of link connected to the source node(s) without any failure. "Expected Length of Connectivity" (ELC) is given by the expected value of LC.

"Linear" system is a basic system with a single link and a single source node. ELC is defined by integration at the interval $[0, L]$ of the probability that infinitesimal dx at location x is connected to the source

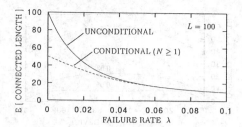

Fig.4　Conditional ($N \geq 1$) and unconditional ELC of "Linear" system

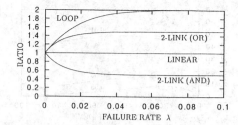

Fig.5　ELC of four types of systems (normalized to ELC of "Linear" system, See Fig.3 and Fig.4)

node:

$$\overline{x_{LIN}(\lambda)} = \int_0^L e^{-\lambda x} dx = \frac{1 - e^{-\lambda L}}{\lambda} \qquad (4)$$

The conditional ELC, given $N \geq 1$, is obtained by substituting $n = 1$ into Eq.(3).

$$\overline{x_1(\lambda, L | N \geq 1)} = \frac{1}{\lambda} \cdot \frac{1 - e^{-\lambda L} - \lambda L e^{-\lambda L}}{1 - e^{-\lambda L}} \qquad (5)$$

Figure 4 shows conditional/unconditional ELC where $L = 100$.

"Loop" system is a circumferential line with single source node, which is obviously equivalent to a single link with two source nodes at both terminals as shown in Figure 3. ELC is obtained by

$$\overline{x_{LOOP}(\lambda)} = \int_0^L \left\{ e^{-\lambda x} + e^{-\lambda(L-x)} - e^{-\lambda L} \right\} dx$$
$$= \frac{2(1 - e^{-\lambda L})}{\lambda} - L e^{-\lambda L} \qquad (6)$$

"2-link OR" and "2-link AND" systems consist of two links sharing single source node at one terminal, LC's being defined by longer and shorter length of two LC's of two links, respectively. ELC's of these two systems are obtained as following equations.

$$\overline{x_{OR}(\lambda)} = \int_0^L \left(2e^{-\lambda x} - e^{-2\lambda x} \right) dx$$
$$= \frac{3 - 4e^{-\lambda L} + e^{-2\lambda L}}{2\lambda} \qquad (7)$$

$$\overline{x_{AND}(\lambda)} = \int_0^L e^{-\lambda x} \cdot e^{-\lambda x} dx = \frac{1 - e^{-2\lambda L}}{2\lambda} \qquad (8)$$

Figure 5 shows ELC's for four types of systems normalized to ELC of "Linear" system for various value of failure rate λ. Redundant systems become more reliable than the simple "Linear" system with increasing λ.

3.　ELC OF SEGMENTED LINK SYSTEMS

3.1　Concept of subdivision

In the previous section, LC and ELC have been defined on the assumption that failures remain damage to the place where they occur and do not affect other part of the system. In reality, however, it may happen

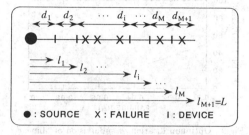

Fig.6　Location and length of segments of a link

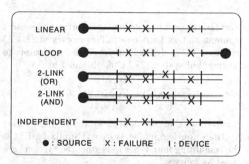

Fig.7　Location of failures and LC (length of connectivity) of segmented systems

that single failure leads to disruption of the whole system, as mentioned in Section 1. Therefore, discretized form of LC and ELC are defined below.

Suppose that the link system is composed of several segments divided by subdivision devices which can be put into function to isolate damaged segments according to actual situation. Figure 6 is graphical notations of a link system subdivided into $(M + 1)$ segments with M subdivision devices, where L, ℓ_i, and d_i are the length of the system, location of i th subdivision device, length of i th segment, respectively.

3.2　Definition of LC and ELC of segmented systems

Figure 7 shows illustrative examples of LC's for five types of segmented systems. In "Linear" system, given

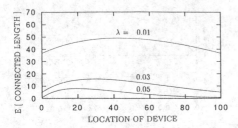

Fig.8 ELC of "Linear" system divided into two segments at various locations

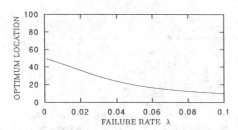

Fig.9 Optimum location of subdivision of "Linear" system

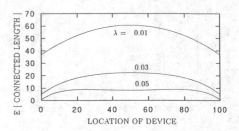

Fig.10 ELC of "Loop" and "Independent" system divided into two segments at various locations

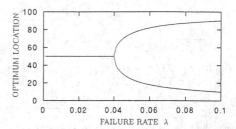

Fig.11 Optimum location of subdivision of "Loop" and "Independent" system

that no failure occurs between the source node and i th segment and at least one failure occurs at $(i+1)$ th segment, LC is defined by ℓ_i. Then, analogous to non-segmented systems, ELC is obtained by

$$\overline{x_{LIN}(\lambda, \boldsymbol{d})} = \sum_{i=1}^{M+1} e^{-\lambda \ell_i} \cdot d_i \qquad (9)$$

It is apparent that segmented systems give shorter ELC's than non-segmented systems. Similarly, ELC's for the remaining four types of segmented systems are obtained as follows.

$$\overline{x_{LOOP}(\lambda, \boldsymbol{d})} = \sum_{i=1}^{M+1} \left\{ e^{-\lambda \ell_i} + e^{-\lambda(L-\ell_{i-1})} \right\} \cdot d_i - L e^{-\lambda L} \qquad (10)$$

$$\overline{x_{OR}(\lambda, \boldsymbol{d})} = \sum_{i=1}^{M+1} \left(2e^{-\lambda \ell_i} - e^{-2\lambda \ell_i} \right) \cdot d_i \qquad (11)$$

$$\overline{x_{AND}(\lambda, \boldsymbol{d})} = \sum_{i=1}^{M+1} e^{-2\lambda \ell_i} \cdot d_i \qquad (12)$$

$$\overline{x_{IND}(\lambda, \boldsymbol{d})} = \sum_{i=1}^{M+1} e^{-\lambda d_i} \cdot d_i \qquad (13)$$

In "2-link OR" and "2-link AND" systems, for simplicity, it is assumed that two links are segmented at the same locations. "Independent" system is a system such that segments without failure are functional independently; elevated highway is one of these systems.

4. OPTIMUM SUBDIVISION OF LINK SYSTEMS

4.1 Formulation

While ELC of non-segmented system is a function of failure rate λ, ELC of segmented system is additionally dependent on the number and locations of subdivision devices. Therefore, there exists an optimum subdivision that maximizes ELC for given number of subdivision devices. Using notations in Fig.6, the optimization problem is formulated as follows:

$$\text{find} \quad \boldsymbol{d}^* = \{d_i^* | i = 1, \cdots, M+1\}$$
$$\text{which maximize} \quad G_M(\boldsymbol{d}, L) \qquad (14)$$
$$\text{subject to} \quad \sum_{i=1}^{M+1} d_i = L, \quad d_i \geq 0$$

where $G_M(\boldsymbol{d}, L)$ denotes an objective function in terms of configuration of subdivision determined by locations of M devices; specifically, ELC for each segmented systems defined by Eqs.(9)-(13).

4.2 Optimum subdivision into two segments

Given only one device for subdivision $(M=1)$, optimum subdivision is easily found by employing straightforward search method. ELC for "Linear" system with $L=100$ is shown in Fig.8 for arbitrary location of single subdivision device. Optimum subdivision is shown in Fig.9 for various failure rate λ. It is observed that the optimum location approaches the source node with increasing failure rate, and the location is in good agreement with conditional ELC for non-segmented "Linear" system shown in Fig.4. Figure 10 shows ELC for "Loop" and "Independent" systems, which are identical if $M = 1$. Figure 11 shows optimum subdivision. In case where λ is less than 0.04 ($\lambda L < 4$), even subdivision is be optimum. Elsewhere, uneven subdivision is optimum; shorter segment is expected to survive better than longer one. Because of symmetry, optimum location is twofold in Fig.11.

4.3 Optimum subdivision into arbitrary number of segments

Suppose that there are M' locations where M subdivision devices are potentially located. Straightforward search method is not applicable because as many as $\binom{M'}{M}$ cases must be searched. To avoid complication, in this study, one-dimensional allocation process of DP (Dynamic Programming) is modified to solve the optimization problem formulated in 4.1. DP is an optimization method based on a "principle of optimality," i.e., "*An optimal policy has the property that whatever the initial state and initial decision are, the remaining decisions must constitute an optimal policy with regard to the state resulting from the first decision*" (Bellman 1957). The principle of optimality in this study is :

$$G_M(\boldsymbol{d}, L) \tag{15}$$

$$= \max_{d_1 + \cdots + d_{M+1} = L, \ d_i \geq 0} \left[\sum_{i=1}^{M+1} g(d_i, \ell_i) \right]$$

$$= \max_{0 < d_{M+1} < L} [\max_{d_1 + \cdots + d_M = L - d_{M+1}, \ d_i \geq 0}$$

$$[g(d_1, \ell_1) + \cdots + g(d_{M+1}, \ell_{M+1})]]$$

$$= \max_{0 \leq d_{M+1} \leq L} [g(d_{M+1}, L) + \max_{d_1 + \cdots + d_M = L - d_{M+1}, \ d_i \geq 0}$$

$$[g(d_1, \ell_1) + \cdots + g(d_M, \ell_M)]]$$

$$= \max_{0 \leq d_{M+1} \leq L} [g(d_{M+1}, L) + G_{M-1}(\boldsymbol{d}, L - d_{M+1})]$$

where $g(d_i, \ell_i)$ denotes termwise contribution of i th segment to ELC. General expression of termwise contribution is $g_i(d_i)$, in which it is assumed that each term has its own gain function solely in terms of allocated resource d_i independent of the other terms. However, the principle of optimality holds even if this assumption does not apply as shown in Eq.(15).

4.4 Extension to non-uniform failure rate

In the previous sections, failure rate λ has been assumed to be uniform over the system length L. In general, however, failure rate is non-uniform, i.e., failure rate $\lambda(x)$ is a function of location x. Let

$$\Lambda(x) = \int_0^x \lambda(s)ds \tag{16}$$

denote an average function of number of failures. Number of failures at the interval $[x, x + s]$ is given

by Poisson distribution with average number of failures $\Lambda(x + s) - \Lambda(x)$, which implies that this case is appropriately modeled with non-homogeneous Poisson process (Fushimi 1987). By performing the following substitution into ELC's defined by Eqs.(9)-(13), optimization method proposed in this section can be extended to cases with non-uniform failure rate.

$$\lambda \ell_i \rightarrow \int_0^{\ell_i} \lambda(x)dx = \Lambda(\ell_i) \tag{17}$$

$$\lambda d_i \rightarrow \int_{\ell_{i-1}}^{\ell_i} \lambda(x)dx = \Lambda(\ell_i) - \Lambda(\ell_{i-1}) \tag{18}$$

5. NUMERICAL EXAMPLES

For illustrative demonstration, some numerical examples are shown below.

5.1 Uniform failure rate

Figure 12 shows optimum subdivision of "Linear" system with $L = 100$ for low ($\lambda = 0.01$), medium($\lambda = 0.05$), and high ($\lambda = 0.1$) failure rate. Expected number of failures given by λL are 1, 5 and 10, respectively. Results are shown for number of subdivision devices $1 \leq M \leq 10$. For low λ, optimum configuration is almost uniform subdivision. However, for high λ, small segments concentrate close to the source node for adaptive isolation, whereas distant segments are left undivided, accepting failure occurrence without hope of being connected to the source node. In "Loop" system, similar tendency can be observed for high λ that small segments concentrate close to the two source nodes at both terminals as shown in Fig.13. Optimum subdivision of "Independent" system is shown in Fig.14, where only the length of segments makes sense regardless of their locations. Rigorously uniform subdivision of the whole system is optimum for low λ. Given high λ and small M, however, uniform subdivision of a minor part of the system is optimum; for maximization of ELC, failure of major part must be accepted.

Figure 15 shows number of subdivision devices versus ELC as a result of optimum subdivision. Without question, larger number of subdivision gives larger ELC, up to that of non-segmented system for "Linear" and "Loop" systems, and total length L for "Independent" system. It is generally observed that a few number of subdivision devices, if appropriately allocated, substantially improve reliability of an extended system. Moreover, in "Independent" system with high λ, ELC becomes larger almost linearly with increasing number of devices up to 10. However, in "Linear" and "Loop" systems, it can be seen that large M, say more than five, is not significantly important.

5.2 Non-uniform failure rate

Consider the hypothetical underground pipeline system ($L = 100$) with a source node at the left ter-

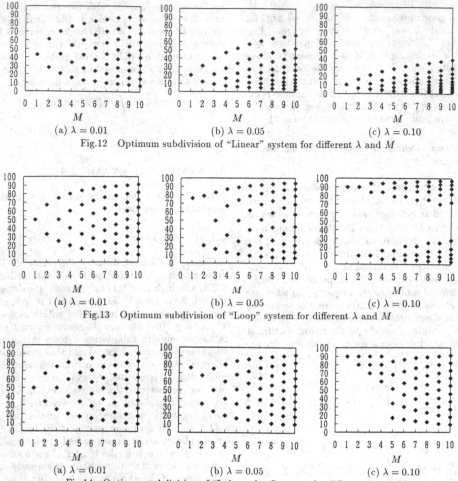

(a) $\lambda = 0.01$ (b) $\lambda = 0.05$ (c) $\lambda = 0.10$

Fig.12   Optimum subdivision of "Linear" system for different λ and M

(a) $\lambda = 0.01$ (b) $\lambda = 0.05$ (c) $\lambda = 0.10$

Fig.13   Optimum subdivision of "Loop" system for different λ and M

(a) $\lambda = 0.01$ (b) $\lambda = 0.05$ (c) $\lambda = 0.10$

Fig.14   Optimum subdivision of "Independent" system for different λ and M

minal as shown in Fig.16. Relative failure rate is assumed to be prescribed by pipe material (strong : 0.1, weak : 0.2), and ground condition (stiff : 0.5, soft : 1.0, stiff/soft boundary : 2.0) as denoted by "Factor(overall)" in Fig.16. The relative failure rate has been converted to failure rate function so that the average failure rate over the system

$$\overline{\lambda} = \frac{\Lambda(L)}{L} = \frac{\int_0^L \lambda(s)ds}{L} \tag{19}$$

is equal to 0.01, 0.05 and 0.10 in order to make a comparison to the results obtained in 5.1. Figure 17 shows conversion of length to equivalent length taking account of the non-uniformity of failure rate, which is used for Eqs.(17)-(18).

Optimum subdivisions for non-uniform failure rate are shown in Figs.18-20 corresponding to those for uniform failure rate in Figs.12-14. The configuration is characterized by distribution of failure rate $\lambda(x)$ as

well as type of systems and number of subdivision devices M. Generally, two contrary differences can be seen; a section with high failure rate is (1) densely subdivided for adaptable isolation, or (2) undivided. In "Linear" system with low average failure rate $\overline{\lambda}$, section [20, 80] including high failure rate section [20, 40] is subdivided into smaller segments than the other sections. For high $\overline{\lambda}$, section [0, 30] is subdivided into small segments. In "Loop" and "Independent" systems with low $\overline{\lambda}$, similar tendency can be observed as in "Linear" system. On the contrary, with high $\overline{\lambda}$, high failure rate section [20,40] remains undivided, because damage to this section does not necessarily affect the other section in these two systems.

These examples imply that disaster prevention strategy should be based on different concepts in different size of disaster: LFTS (local failure in total safety) and LSTF (local safety in total failure). If failure rate is low, failures remain local incident for the

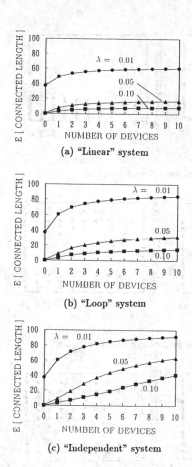

(a) "Linear" system

(b) "Loop" system

(c) "Independent" system

Fig.15 ELC with different λ and M

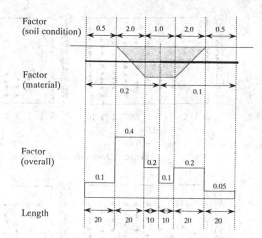

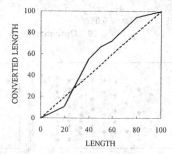

Fig.16 Relative failure rate in terms of pipe material and ground condition

Fig.17 Conversion of length to equivalent length

whole system, where the former concept is effective and the major part of the system is supposed to survive. On the other hand, if failure rate is very high, failures prevail on the whole system, where the latter concept replaces the former and only a piece of the system should be preserved in the "total-risk-minimum" scheme. To fight against both large and moderate size of disaster, which is inevitably unknown in advance, LFTS and LSTF are desired to be compatible in a hybrid strategy.

6. CONCLUSIONS

Major conclusions derived from this study is summarized as follows.

(1) PDF of location of failures on single link system has been derived as a gamma distribution defined at the entire length of the system.

(2) LC (length of connectivity) and ELC (expected length of connectivity) have been defined as measures of system reliability and obtained for several types of elementary systems composed of links (in both non-segmented and segmented form) and source nodes .

(3) An optimum subdivision problem of link systems has been formulated to maximize ELC for various number of subdivisions and various distribution of failure rate over the whole system.

(4) A method to solve the optimization problem has been proposed using a modified algorithm of dynamic programming and non-homogeneous Poisson process.

(5) As numerical examples, optimum subdivisions of "Linear", "Loop" and "Independent" systems have been demonstrated. It has been found out that the results are significantly dependent on system configuration, number of subdivisions, and relative failure rate and its distribution.

(6) The concepts of LFTS (local failure in total safety) and LSTF (local safety in total failure) have been presented as alternative (or compatible if possible) principles in disaster prevention strategy.

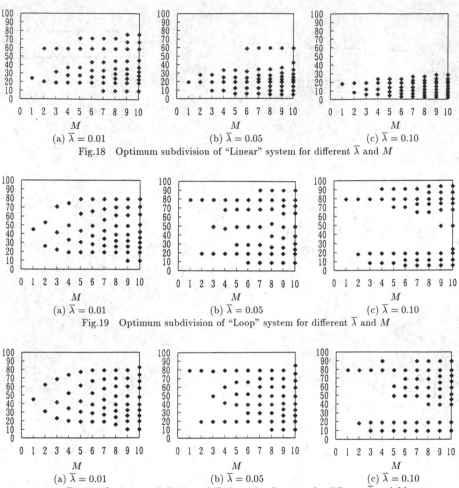

(a) $\bar{\lambda} = 0.01$ (b) $\bar{\lambda} = 0.05$ (c) $\bar{\lambda} = 0.10$

Fig.18   Optimum subdivision of "Linear" system for different $\bar{\lambda}$ and M

(a) $\bar{\lambda} = 0.01$ (b) $\bar{\lambda} = 0.05$ (c) $\bar{\lambda} = 0.10$

Fig.19   Optimum subdivision of "Loop" system for different $\bar{\lambda}$ and M

(a) $\bar{\lambda} = 0.01$ (b) $\bar{\lambda} = 0.05$ (c) $\bar{\lambda} = 0.10$

Fig.20   Optimum subdivision of "Independent" system for different $\bar{\lambda}$ and M

REFERENCES

Austin T. 1990. Keeping lifelines alive, *Civil Engineering*, ASCE : 58-59.

Bellman, R. 1957. *Dynamic programming*, Princeton University Press : 81-115.

Fushimi, M. 1987. *Probability and stochastic process*, Kodansha (in Japanese).

Kawakami, H. 1990. Earthquake physical damage and functional serviceability of lifeline network models, *Earthquake Engineering and Structural Dynamics*, Vol.19 : 1153-1165.

Kobayashi, M. 1993 Fail-safe design in urban disaster prevention, *Operations Research*, Vol.38, No.1 : 24-28 (in Japanese).

Nojima, N. and H. Kameda 1992. On algorithm for optimum post-earthquake restoration of hierarchically separated lifeline networks, *Proc. of JSCE*, No.450/I-20 : 171-180 (in Japanese).

Nojima, N. and H. Kameda 1996. Lifeline interactions in the Hanshin-Awaji Earthquake Disaster, *The 1995 Hyogoken-Nanbu Earthquake Investigation into Damage to Civil Engineering Structures*, Committee of Earthquake Engineering, JSCE : 253-264.

Nojima, N., H. Kameda and M. Shinozuka 1990. Fundamental structure of earthquake disaster countermeasures in lifelines, *Journal of Natural Disaster Science*, Vol.12, No.1 : 29-47.

Papoulis, A. 1965. *Probability, random variables, and stochastic process*, McGraw-Hill, New York.

Structural Safety and Reliability, Shiraishi, Shinozuka & Wen (eds) © 1998 Balkema, Rotterdam, ISBN 90 5410 978 5

Lifeline seismic performance of electric power systems during the Northridge earthquake

Satoshi Tanaka & Yoshiaki Kawata
Disaster Prevention Research Institute, Kyoto University, Japan

Masanobu Shinozuka
University of Southern California, Los Angeles, Calif., USA

Anshel Schiff
Precision Measurement Instruments, Los Altos Hills, USA

ABSTRACT : The seismic performance of an electric power system is evaluated under the Northridge earthquake. Utilizing GIS, numerical analysis is carried out on the electric power transmission network of Los Angeles Department of Water and Power with Monte Carlo technique. The simulation result shows a good agreement with the post-earthquake restoration process.

1. INTRODUCTION

The Northridge earthquake inflicted considerable physical damage and in many cases disastrous destruction upon the build environment in a large region of the San Fernando Valley and Los Angeles Basin. Many lifeline systems in the area including LADWP's (Los Angeles Department Water and Power's) electric power system did not escape the impact of the earthquake. Under the Northridge earthquake, high voltage power facilities of the LADWP's electric power system sustained extensive damage. Most of the damage was done to high voltage equipment within substations. Indeed, the physical damage sustained by these equipment produced corresponding system malfunctions that required concentrated repair and restoration effort to make them operational again.

The seismic performance of electric power systems has been studied by many researchers including Schiff (1978), Ando et al. (1987), and Ang et al. (1992). This paper further extends the scope of the earlier studies by these and other authors and presents an analysis of the seismic performance primarily of the LADWP's electric power network under the Northridge earthquake.

In the following, numerical results are obtained using analytical models developed for the corresponding LADWP's system. These are not exact models of the LADWP's system due to the unavailability of complete information, although they are expected to simulate approximately the physical and functional characteristics of the LADWP's system reasonably well. In this regard, caution must be exercised if the numerical results obtained are to be used for the purpose of deriving specific technical and operational recommendations for the LADWP's system.

2. ELECTRIC POWER SYSTEM

2.1 LADWP's System

LADWP's electric power transmission system is depicted in Fig. 1. There are two electric power networks in the Los Angels region operated by different organizations, Los Angels Department of Water and Power, and Southern California Edsion. Although, these networks are managed independently, they are integrated connected each other at the several substations. In addition, since the networks are a part of the very large electric power transmission network known as the Western Systems

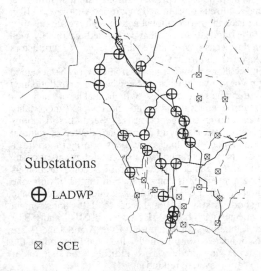

Substations

⊕ LADWP

⊠ SCE

Fig. 1 LADWP's Electric Power Transmission Network

Coordinating Council, which covers from British Columbia, Canada to the state of Colorado, the black out condition was observed over the several states at the Nothridge earthquake.

2.2 Conditions for System Failure

In analyzing the functional reliability of each substation, the following modes of failure are usually taken into consideration; (1) loss of connectivity, (2) failure of substation's critical components, and (3) power imbalance. Each of these failure modes is indeed considered in this paper. However, it is noted that most of the transmission lines of the LADWP's system are aerial supported by transmission towers. While by no means this implies that the transmission lines are completely free from seismic vulnerability, it is assumed in this study that they are, primarily for the purpose of analytical simplicity.

2.3 Substation Model

An electric substation consists of several electric nodes subjected to various values of voltage and connected each other through transformers in order to reduce the voltage and/or distribute the power to the service areas. Each electric node consists of various electric equipment such as buses, circuit breakers, and disconnect switches. Among the equipment, buses, circuit breakers and disconnect switches are seismically most vulnerable, as observed during the 1971 San Fernando, the 1989 Loma Prieta and the 1994 Northridge earthquake (Benuska 1990; Hall 1994; Schiff 1995).

The physical damage thus sustained by the system produced corresponding system malfunction that required concentrated repair and restoration effort to make them operational again. However, in spite of the damage, the system performed reasonably well on the occasions of these earthquakes. Two factors played a significant role in this respect. First, the high voltage power transmission network is designed topologically with a sufficient degree of redundancy in transmission circuits, which makes it easy for system operators to respond and restore functionality at least on an emergency basis. Second, substations are designed also with a sufficient degree of internal redundancy. Actual equipment configuration in a node is so complicated that it defies a rigorous modeling. Therefore, a simplified configuration as shown in Fig. 2 is employed. In Fig. 2, if only one circuit breaker CB11 is damaged due to an earthquake, the node is still functional because all the lines remain connected each other. However, if CB11 and CB13 are damaged simultaneously, Line A and Line B are disconnected from the node, thus the function of the node is impaired. This indicates the nature of substation system redundancy.

Utilizing the results of the previous studies by Shinozuka et al. (1989) and Ang et al. (1992) the

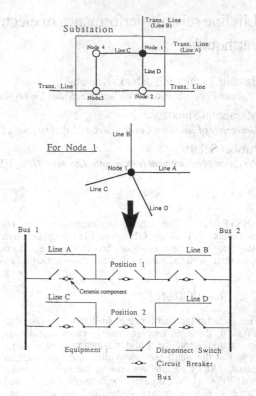

Fig. 2 Typical Node Configuration Model

fragility curve $F_c(a)$ for a circuit breaker is chosen to be a log-normal distribution function with the median and coefficient of variation equal to 0.45g and 0.38 respectively. This curve is assumed also applicable for the bus fragility for the purpose of simplicity.

3. MONTE CARLO SIMULATION

Utilizing the GIS (Geographical Information System) (ESRI, 1988; Tanaka et al., 1994) capability, the map of the electric transmission network is overlaid with the map of PGA in order to identify the PGA value associated with each substation under the Northridge earthquake. The fragility curve developed for the equipment (buses and circuit breakers) can then be used to simulate the state of equipment damage involving the equipment in all the nodes at all the substations of the transmission system. For each damage state, the connectivity and flow analyses are performed with the aid of an computer code IPFLOW developed and distributed by Electric Power Research Institute (EPRI) (1992).

The loss of connectivity occurs when the node of interest survives the corresponding PGA, but is isolated from all the generating nodes because of the malfunction of at least one of the nodes on each and every possible path between this node and any of the generating nodes. Hence, the loss of connectivity with respect to a particular node can be confirmed on each damage state by actually verifying the loss of connectivity with respect to all the paths that would otherwise establish the desired connectivity. The loss of connectivity is primarily due to the equipment failure not only at the node of interest but also all other nodes in the network.

As to the abnormal power flow, it is noted that the electric power transmission system is highly sensitive to the power balance and ordinarily some criteria are used to judge whether or not the node continues to function immediately after internal and external disturbances. Two kind of criteria are employed at each node for the abnormal power flow; (a) power imbalance and (b) abnormal voltage. When some nodes in the network are damaged due to an earthquake, the total generating power becomes greater or less than the total demanding power. Under a normal condition, the power balance between generating and demanding power is in a certain tolerance range. Actually, the total generating power must be between 1.0 and 1.05 times the total demanding power for normal operation even accounting for the power transmission loss.

If this condition is not satisfied, the operator of the electric system must either reduce or increase the generating power to keep the balance of power. However, in some cases, supply cannot catch up with the demand because the generating system is unable to respond quickly enough. In this case, it is assumed that the generating power of each power plant cannot be quickly increased or reduced by more than 20% of the current generating power. When the power balance cannot be maintained even after increasing or reducing the generating power, the system will be down and this kind of outage is defined as a power imbalance.

As for the abnormal voltage, voltage magnitude at each node can be obtained by power flow analysis. Then, if the ratio of the voltage of the damaged system to the intact system is out of a tolerable range (plus/minus 20% of the voltage for the intact system), it is assumed that a black out will occur in the area served by the substation.

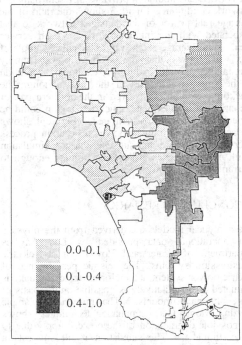

0.0-0.1

0.1-0.4

0.4-1.0

Fig. 3 Ratio of the Average Power Output under the Damaged Condition to the Intact Condition for Service Areas

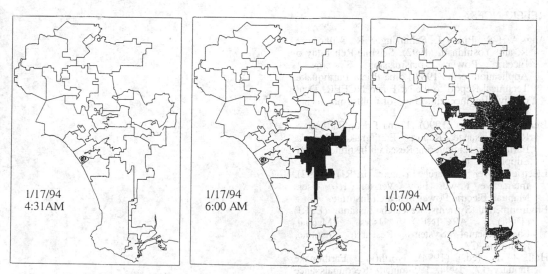

1/17/94
4:31AM

1/17/94
6:00 AM

1/17/94
10:00 AM

Fig. 4 Actual Electric Power Restoration Process at the Northridge Earthquake
(Shaded area indicates the power restored service area)

For the Monte Carlo simulation under the Northridge earthquake, each substation is examined with respect to its possible malfunction under these three modes of failure for each simulated damage state. Thus, each simulation identifies the substations that will become inoperational.

The simulation is repeated 15 times on the network. Each simulation provides different damaged network condition. Figure 3 shows the ratio of the average real power of the damaged network to that associated with the intact network for each service area. The average is taken over the entire sample of 15. It shows that the average power supply maintains at least 40% of the pre-earthquake condition in the south-eastern part of the city, although the blackout condition is observed in the northern part of the city. It implies that a quick restoration could be expected in the south-eastern area. Figure 4 shows the actual post-earthquake power restoration process after the earthquake and suggests that the simulation result in this paper is at least encouraging enough to warrant function study.

4. CONCLUDING REMARKS

The analytical models are derived from the physical and operational data provided by Los Angeles Department of Water and Power for its electric transmission systems. The seismic performance of electric power system at the Northridge earthquake is evaluated as quantitatively as possible on the basis of these analytical models. The numerical example utilizing Monte Carlo simulation techniques shows the possible degradation of the power supply due to the earthquake. The simulation result suggests a promising agreement of the actual power restoration process.

REFERENCES

Ang, A.H-S., Pires, J., Schinzinger, R., Villaverde, R. and Yoshida, I. (1992). Seismic Reliability of Electric Power Transmission Systems - Application to the 1989 Loma Prieta Earthquake. Technical Report to the NSF and NCEER, Dept. of Civil Engineering, Univ. of California, Irvine, CA.

Benuska, L. (ed.) (1990). Loma Prieta Earthquake Reconnaissance Report. Earthquake Spectra, Earthquake Engineering Research Institute (EERI), Supplement to Vol. 6.

Electric Power Research Institute (EPRI) (1992). Interactive Power Flow Version 1.0 Users Manual. Electric Power Research Institute.

Environmental Systems Research Institute (ESRI) (1988). ARC/INFO Users Manual. Environmental Systems Research Institute, Redlands, CA.

Hall, J. F. (ed.) (1994). Northridge Earthquake January 17, 1994. Preliminary Reconnaissance Report, Earthquake Engineering Research Institute (EERI).

Schiff, A., Tognazzini, R., and Ostrom, D. (1995). Power Systems After the Northridge Earthquake: Emergency Operations and Changes in Seismic Equipment Specifications, Practices, and System Configuration, Proc. of the 4th U.S. Conference Sponsored by the Technical Council on Lifeline Earthquake Engineering of the ASCE, pp. 549-556

Shinozuka, M., Mizutani, M., Takeda, M., and Kai, Y. (1989). A Seismic PRA Procedure in Japan and Its Application to a Building Performance Safety Estimation, Part 3 Estimation of Build and Equipment Performance Safety. Proc. of ICOSSAR '89, pp. 637-644.

Shinozuka, M., Shumuta, Y., Tanaka, S., and Koiwa, H. (1994). Interaction of Lifeline Systems under Earthquake Conditions. Proc. of the Second China-Japan-US Trilateral Symposium on Lifeline Earthquake Engineering, pp. 43-52.

Shinozuka, M., Tanaka, S. (1996). Effects of Lifeline Interaction under Seismic Conditions. Proc. of the 11th World Conference on Earthquake Engineering, CD-ROM.

Tanaka, S., Nishitani, A., and Shinozuka, M. (1994). Lifeline Seismic Reliability Analysis Utilizing Geographical Information System, J. of Struct. Constr. Eng., AIJ, No. 465, pp. 27-36.

Structural Safety and Reliability, Shiraishi, Shinozuka & Wen (eds) © 1998 Balkema, Rotterdam, ISBN 90 5410 978 5

Developments of early earthquake damage assessment systems in Japan

Fumio Yamazaki & Kimiro Meguro
Institute of Industrial Science, The University of Tokyo, Japan

Shigeru Noda
Department of Social Systems Engineering, Tottori University, Japan

ABSTRACT: This paper highlights recent developments of earthquake monitoring systems and early damage assessment systems in Japan. Recently, several earthquake monitoring networks have been established in order to use earthquake information for early warning or damage assessment of urban systems. UrEDAS of Japan Railway (JR) group and SIGNAL of Tokyo Gas Company are the pioneers of such systems. A few other early damage assessment systems were also developed by local government agencies. After the 1995 Hyogoken-Nanbu Earthquake, installation of seismometer networks and development of early damage assessment systems by national and local governments as well as utility companies in Japan boomed. Although some networks and systems are still under construction, this paper provides an overview of recent vintage and future directions of real-time earthquake hazard assessment are discussed.

1 INTRODUCTION

After the 1994 Northridge Earthquake, CUBE (The Caltech-USGS Broadcast of Earthquakes) system had drawn considerable attention in Japan as well as in the United States. The system determines earthquake locations and magnitudes soon after they occur using records from the Southern California Seismic Network and disseminates the information to CUBE subscribers via commercial radio pager service (Kanamori et al. 1991). It might be an innovative system in the United States.

However, in Japan, situation is different. The Japan Meteorological Agency (JMA) monitors the seismic intensity (JMA scale; calculated from accelerograms) at more than hundred locations throughout Japan and determines the hypocenter and magnitude within a few minutes after an event. The information from the JMA is broadcasted nationwide by public TVs and radios soon after an earthquake. Although CUBE has some novel functions such as the use of paging system and display of epicenters on computer, its basic function has been covered by the JMA for many years.

The first practical tool of real-time seismology may be the UrEDAS (Urgent Earthquake Detection and Alarm System) of the Railway Technical Research Institute (RTRI), which was proposed more than ten years ago (Nakamura 1986). Detecting the arrival of the P-wave by their own network at near source, the system estimates the location and magnitude of an earthquake very quickly. Then the system uses this information to stop high speed trains before the

arrival of S-wave. The first UrEDAS network started operation in 1989 in Tokyo Metropolitan area.

Using the geographic information system (GIS), EPEDAT (the Early Post-Earthquake Damage Assessment Tool) was developed to estimate building and lifeline damage in Southern California (Eguchi et al. 1994). During that period, similar real-time damage assessment systems were also developed in Japan. SIGNAL (the Seismic Information Gathering and Network Alert) system of Tokyo Gas Company performs damage estimation of a natural gas network based on extensive earthquake monitoring and GIS (Yamazaki et al. 1994). In the system, identification of the magnitude and location of an event is also conducted using data from their own accelerometers and radio network. Kawasaki City and Tokyo Fire Department also developed their own early damage assessment systems for emergency management. These systems in Japan have been functioning since early 1994, about a year before the Hyogoken-Nanbu (Kobe) Earthquake of January 17, 1995.

After the Hyogoken-Nanbu Earthquake, countermeasures against earthquakes have got higher priority than before. With good financing, thousands of strong motion seismometers will be installed within a few years. A number of damage assessment systems are also being developed by different organizations using the data from the JMA or their own seismometer networks. This paper provides a recent overview of seismometer networks and early damage assessment systems in Japan and their future directions are discussed.

2 PIONEER WORK

2.1 UrEDAS and HERAS

The first practical tool of real-time emergency countermeasures in the world may be UrEDAS of the RTRI mentioned above. The first UrEDAS network with five instruments was installed in the Tokyo Metropolitan area in 1989. Since then, several UrEDAS networks have been deployed for rapid railway systems in Japan as shown in Fig. 1. The first UrEDAS network for rapid railway systems began operation with 14 instruments in 1992 on the Tokaido (between Tokyo and Osaka) Shinkansen (bullet train). Triggered by the Kobe Earthquake, a UrEDAS network for the Sanyo (between Osaka and Fukuoka) Shinkansen was introduced. Other UrEDAS networks, e.g., Seikan (between Aomori and Hakodate) Tunnel, a test site in Pasadena, California, have also been in operation. If an earthquake occurs, trains should be stopped as soon as possible to avoid disasters. UrEDAS is considered to be one of the most important earthquake counter-measures for railway systems in Japan.

The RTRI also developed a system named HERAS (Hazards Estimation and Restoration Aid System), which estimates the degree of damage to railway systems caused by an earthquake based on the synthesized information from UrEDAS. Using the database on characteristics of ground and railway structures and damage experiences of past earthquakes, HERAS can provide damage estimation of railway systems within five minutes after an event (Nakamura 1996). A prototype of HERAS was completed in 1992. Information on UrEDAS and HERAS is available on the Internet.

2.2 SIGNAL

The first early damage assessment system actually introduced for lifeline systems may be SIGNAL of Tokyo Gas Company (Yamazaki et al. 1994). Since the service area of the natural gas system became very large (with 8.1 million metered customers), the earthquake monitoring and early warning system was introduced to avoid secondary disasters. The unique feature of SIGNAL is its extensive earthquake monitoring network, probably the largest in the world. The monitoring system measures the peak ground acceleration (PGA) and spectrum intensity (SI) at 331 locations in the service area by SI-sensors (Katayama et al. 1988) as shown in Fig. 2. Acceleration time histories at 5 locations and pore-water rises at 20 locations are also observed. Once an earthquake occurs, these values are sent to the supply control center of the headquarters by the company's radio and are used in decision making on the gas supply shut-off for medium-pressure trunk lines.

The early warning system consists of sub-systems for damage estimation, hypocenter estimation, spectrum evaluation, and decision. The monitored earthquake ground motion data are fully employed in these sub-systems. For the damage estimation, data on the service area, e.g. soil conditions, customers' buildings and pipelines, are stored on a workstation using GIS of 175 m × 250 m square mesh. The prototype of SIGNAL was completed in 1992 and the actual system has been operating since June, 1994. Information on SIGNAL and the recorded PGA and SI values from recent earthquakes are available at the homepage (*http://www.tokyo-gas.co.jp/signal*).

Legend

- ■ UrEDAS Center in Kunitachi
- ● Metropolitan UrEDAS Network
- ▲ Miyako City UrEDAS Test Site
- ● California UrEDAS
- ▲ Seikan Tunnel UrEDAS
- ■ Tokaido Shinkansen UrEDAS
- ■ Sanyo Shinkansen UrEDAS
  (Under Construction)

Fig. 1 UrEDAS network of RTRI in Japan
(after *http://www.rtri.or.jp*)

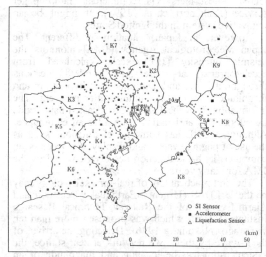

Fig. 2   Location of earthquake monitors of SIGNAL system of Tokyo Gas Company.

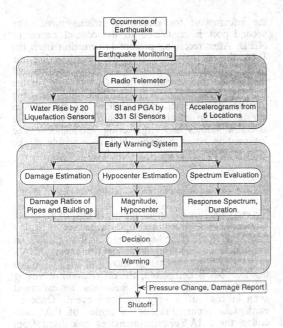

Fig. 3 Flowchart of SIGNAL.

2.3 Damage Assessment System of Kawasaki City

As a part of emergency management system, Kawasaki City has developed a damage assessment system (Mochida 1994) for the city with a population of about 1.2 million. The system consists of three modules: 1) estimation of the distribution of seismic intensity, 2) prediction of various hazards, structural damage and human casualties, 3) suggesting policy for crisis management. This system is unique in the sense that it not only predicts damage statistics but also serves as an emergency operation manual.

The earthquake information is collected through the city's radio system from seismometers placed on each ward office as well as from the JMA. The damage assessment system using GIS predicts hazards such as tsunami, liquefaction and landslide, damage of buildings, roads (Fig. 4), bridges, river embankments and lifeline systems (power, water, gas, telephone), and human casualties. A 500 m × 500 m square mesh, which is commonly used in damage assessment in Japan, is employed in the system. The system was installed at the Disaster Prevention Center in the city hall and a terminal system was installed at each of the seven ward offices. Test operation of the system started in April, 1994.

2.4 Damage Assessment System of Tokyo Fire Department

Tokyo Fire Department also developed an early damage assessment system for fire fighting and rescue operations. The system is basically a computer package of a damage assessment tool for scenario earthquakes. The system has a database for soil conditions, buildings, fire occurrence risk, and time-dependent population. If the magnitude and location of an earthquake are given, the system first estimates the distribution of PGA, seismic intensity and liquefaction hazard throughout Tokyo Metropolis by 500 m × 500 m square mesh using an attenuation relation of earthquake ground motion and soil classification. Then the number of collapsed buildings, fire breakouts (Fig. 5), and human casualties are estimated based on empirical formula for each mesh. The area which the fire might cover one hour after an event is also estimated. The results of the estimation will be used to prepare for fire-fighting and search-and-rescue in an early stage. The first version of the system was completed in 1994. Using data from the new seismometer network of the department, the system was upgraded recently.

Fig. 4 Damage assessment system of Kawasaki City - indicating the road damage ratio.

Fig. 5 Damage assessment system of Tokyo Fire Department - estimating the number of fire breakouts after an M=6.5 earthquake.

3 NEW SEISMOMETER NETWORKS IN JAPAN

There had been thousands of seismometers of various kinds deployed in Japan. The number of new digital accelerometers is increasing although seismometers of older types still remain. After the 1995 Kobe Earthquake, installation of new seismometers was highly accelerated. Following are some of the new seismometer networks introduced.

3.1 JMA's Network

The JMA is in charge of earthquake information in Japan. The JMA used mostly displacement-type seismographs before. Since 1987, the JMA has been deploying new JMA-87-type accelerometers in recording stations throughout Japan (Molas and Yamazaki 1995). These new accelerometers have a flat sensitivity from 0.05 to 10 Hz and can measure accelerations from 0.03 to 980 cm/s^2 for periods 1 sec to 10 min. The network started with 76 stations. The recorded accelerograms were available from the Japan Weather Association in magnetic tapes.

In 1993 and 1994, several damaging earthquakes occurred in northern Japan (Yamazaki et al. 1995). Hence, mainly for early tsunami warning, the number of accelerometer stations was increased to 268. After the Kobe Earthquake, in order not to miss localized heavily damaged areas, the number of stations was further increased to 574 as of April, 1996 (Fig. 6). Using time histories from several stations, the JMA determines the location and magnitude of an event within a few minutes. The JMA intensities at these 574 stations are also collected by JMA's telecommunication system at the headquarters and disseminated nationwide through mass media. Since a telecommunication line connected to Kobe Observatory had a trouble soon after the Kobe Earthquake, the JMA recently strengthened the communication network to have a backup system through satellites.

3.2 Kyoshin Net

After the Kobe Earthquake, the National Research Institute for Earth Science and Disaster Prevention (NIED) of the Science and Technology Agency deployed a total of 1,000 strong motion accelerometers throughout Japan (Fig. 7). This network is named "Kyoshin Net" or "K-NET" and the average distance between stations is 25 km. Each station has a digital accelerometer having a wide frequency band and wide dynamic range. The maximum acceleration which can be measured is 2.0 g. Instruments are placed on free field. At each site, P and S-wave velocities were measured by downhole PS-logging as well as SPT N-values.

Each instrument has two communication ports. The first one is directly connected to a modem belonging to a municipality. The municipality can use the information for emergency management. The second port is connected to the control center of NIED. After receiving prompt information from the JMA, the control center acquires records using this port. The control center compiles these records and then makes the compiled data set available on the Internet. The center will distribute the data file through the Internet. The center also maintains a strong motion database and site information for scientific studies and engineering applications. The information about Kyoshin Net is available at the homepage of NIED (*http://www.bosai.go.jp*).

3.3 Network of the Fire Defense Agency

Recently the Fire Defense Agency (FDA) of Japanese Government also ventured upon a project to deploy one accelerometer in each municipality (3,255 in total) in Japan excluding municipalities having JMA's or K-NET's instruments as shown in Fig. 8. When this network is completed, the distribution of strong ground motion for an earthquake can be estimated even in case of a very localized event. Once an earthquake occur, the control center of FDA will collect the JMA seismic intensities calculated from records through ISDN (Integrated Services Digital Network) of NTT (The Nippon Telegraph and Telephone Corporation). The FDA and the JMA will also exchange their collected data through private communication lines. The FDA will use the collected information for identifying affected areas and preparing for crisis management at a national level.

3.4 Other Networks

In addition to the three national networks described above, many public and private organizations have started or are planning to deploy seismometer networks within their territories.

Kanagawa Prefecture installed their own strong motion observation and telemeter system with 16 seismometers in 1994. The control center will collect the seismic intensities obtained by the network through NTT's private lines. The collected data will be used for crisis management after an earthquake.

Yokohama City started a project to deploy a very dense strong motion accelerometer network with as many as 150 instruments and three control centers (Fig. 9). In the fiscal year of 1995, the main control center was constructed and 18 instruments were placed. The remainder of the system was completed by the end of March, 1997. Once an earthquake occur, recorded data will be sent to the control centers through ISDN and digital private lines within three minutes. The collected data will be used for crisis management of the city. Yokohama city is now planning to develop an early damage estimation system using the strong motion data from the network and GIS data of the city.

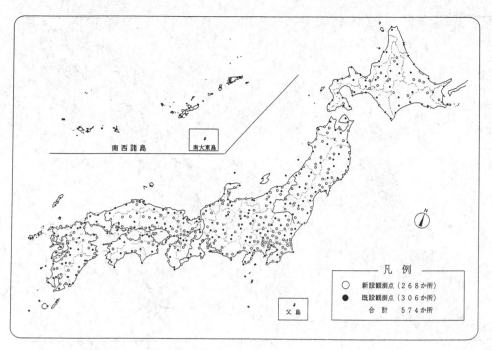

Fig. 6 Strong motion accelerometers of the JMA as of April, 1996 (574 sites in total).

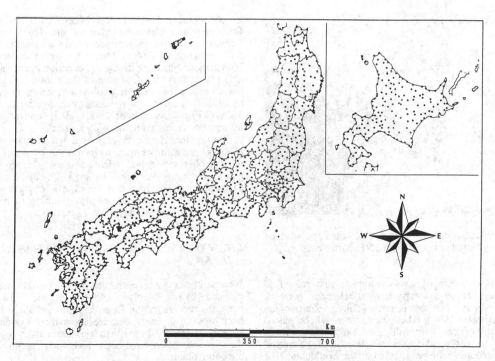

Fig. 7   Locations of 1,000 strong motion accelerometers of K-NET by NIED.

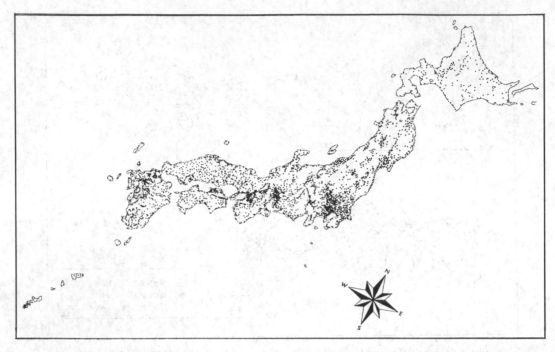

Fig. 8 New seismometer network for all the municipalities in Japan by the Fire Defense Agency.

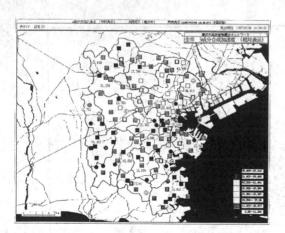

Fig. 9 Dense strong motion accelerometer network of
Yokohama City with 150 instruments.

Tokyo Metropolitan Government also started to
develop its own strong motion telemeter network
with about 100 instruments (Tokyo Metropolitan
Government 1996). These instruments will be placed
at ward offices, city halls, and fire stations. Soon
after an earthquake, seismic intensities calculated
from records will be gathered at the headquarters of
the Metropolitan Disaster Prevention Center and the
Command and Control Center of the Tokyo Fire
Department by the disaster prevention administrative
radio network of Tokyo. The exchange of collected
information with other disaster prevention agencies is
also planned. As the first step of the network, about
twenty seismometers were deployed in the fiscal year
of 1996. The early damage assessment system of the
Tokyo Fire Department will also utilize the
information from this monitoring system.

Some other large cities, such as Kyoto and
Nagoya, are also planning to have their own strong
motion observation and telemeter networks. Some
public corporations, e.g. Japan Highway Public
Corporation, and private companies, e.g. city gas and
electric power companies, are also planning to have
their own strong motion telemeter systems.

4 NEW DAMAGE ASSESSMENT SYSTEMS IN
JAPAN

New early damage assessment systems are also being
planned by a number of public and private
organizations. After the Kobe Earthquake, there has
been a boom on early damage assessment systems.
Hence, it may not be easy to get information on all
the systems which have been developed recently or
are being planned.

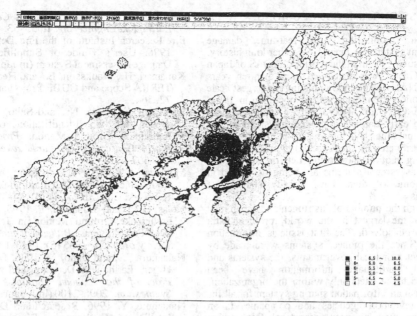

Fig. 10 Early damage assessment system of the National Land Agency. The figure shows estimated seismic intensity distribution during the Kobe Earthquake by interpolation of observed data.

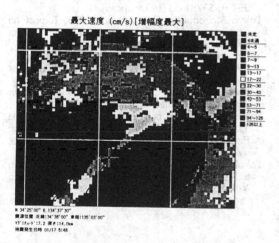

最大速度 (cm/s) [増幅度最大]

N 34°25'00" E 134°37'30"
震源位置 北緯:34°36'00" 東経:135°03'00"
マグニチュード:7.2 深さ:14.0km
地震発生日時 01/17 5:46

Fig. 11 Simplified damage assessment system for municipalities by the Fire Defense Agency.

As a typical example of such systems, the National Land Agency, which is in charge of disaster prevention administration in Japan, developed the first version of early damage assessment system (Fig. 10) and started its operation in April, 1996. Using the intensity and source information from the JMA and the GIS data of entire Japan by 1 km × 1 km square mesh, this system estimates the seismic intensity, the number of collapsed wooden houses, and the number of deaths due to collapse of houses in each mesh. Distribution of tsunami height and flooded area is also estimated by this system. In case of devastating disaster like the Kobe Earthquake, there is a delay in the flow of information on damage to the government. Hence, the result of damage estimation by the new system will be used in the crisis management by Japanese Government in an early stage. The National Land Agency is now developing a more integrated emergency management system called the Disaster Information System (DIS). The above mentioned damage assessment system will be a part of the integrated system.

The Fire Research Institute of the Fire Defense Agency developed a simplified earthquake damage assessment system in 1996. The system estimates the peak ground velocity and the number of collapsed wooden houses, fire breakouts, and deaths based on empirical relationships if the location and magnitude of an event are given. The system contains basic GIS data of Japan with a square mesh of 1 km × 1 km for strong motion and damage estimations as shown in Fig. 11. The system was distributed to all the municipalities in Japan by CD-ROM.

The National Land Agency is also developing a prototype damage assessment system for local municipalities. The use of microscopic GIS is considered in this system since a square mesh of 1 km × 1 km or 500 m × 500 m is too large to show local geographical data. When this system is completed, it will be used for both disaster planning and post-earthquake operations of municipalities.

5 DISCUSSIONS AND CONCLUSIONS

Earthquake monitoring and real-time damage assessment systems in Japan have rather long history. The first such system in the world, UrEDAS of Japan Railway Group, was developed more than ten years ago. SIGNAL of Tokyo Gas having the largest scale strong motion monitoring started operation in 1994. Kawasaki City and Tokyo Fire Department also developed early damage assessment systems almost at the same time. As introduced in the preceding sections, triggered by the Kobe Earthquake, so many new strong motion monitoring networks and early damage assessment systems are being developed in Japan. Some of them have already started test operations.

Although the number of instruments in Japan may be by far the largest in the world, problems still remain to be solved. The first issue is information sharing. Since the pioneer systems were made by private sector or local governments, the systems and associated earthquake information have been considered to be used only within the organization. To establish an information sharing system for all the disaster prevention agencies and companies in an early stage may be very important. Considering mutual aid in case of disaster, the coordination between neighboring cities and prefectures is also very important. Establishment of communication measures is necessary in order to realize such coordination. New communication tools such as ISDN, satellite communication and the Internet may be promising for the purpose.

Since Japan has a lot of experiences of scenario earthquake studies, damage assessment often means calculating damage statistics using empirical formulas. However, such estimated damage has a wide range of variability. To give a range of estimation may be better than to predict a single number. The use of story simulation (scenario) is also important since the feature of disaster is difficult to describe using only numbers. It is obviously very important to revise damage estimation functions by introducing recent experiences, especially those from the Kobe Earthquake.

Japan had been rather well prepared for earthquake disasters. However, the damage in the Kobe Earthquake was much more than expected and the weakness of crisis management in Japan was revealed. Lessons learned from the earthquake should be used in disaster mitigation. In order to avoid a lack of information just after an earthquake, early damage assessment systems with intensive earthquake monitoring are expected to play a vital role in the near future.

REFERENCES

Eguchi, R., Goltz, J.D., Seligson, H., and Heaton, T.H. 1994. Real-time Earthquake Hazard Assessment in California: the Early Post-earthquake Damage Assessment Tool and the Caltech-USGS Broadcast of Earthquakes, *Proc. of the 5th U.S. National Conference on Earthquake Engineering.* II: 55-63.

Fire Research Institute of the Fire Defense Agency. 1996. User's Guide of Simplified Earthquake Damage Assessment System (in Japanese).

Kanamari, H., Hauksson, E., and Heaton, T. 1991. TERRA Scope and CUBE Project at Caltech, *EOS.* 72: 564.

Katayama, T., Sato, N., and Saito, K. 1988. SI-sensor for the Identification of Destructive Earthquake Ground Motion, *Proc. of the 9th World Conference on Earthquake Engineering.* VII: 667-672.

Mochida, T. 1994. System to Support Countermeasures against Earthquake Disasters in Kawasaki City, *Kasai.* 44 (6): 44-49 (in Japanese).

Molas, G.L., and Yamazaki, F. 1995. Attenuation of Earthquake Ground Motion in Japan Including Deep Focus Events, *Bulletin of the Seismological Society of America.* 85 (5): 1343-1358.

Nakamura, Y., and Ueno, M. 1986. Development of Urgent Earthquake Detection and Alarm system, *Proc. of the 7 Japan Earthquake Engineering Symposium.* 2095-2100 (in Japanese).

Nakamura, Y. 1996. Research and Development of Intelligent Earthquake Disaster Prevention Systems UrEDAS and HERAS, *Journal of Structural Mechanics and Earthquake Engineering. JSCE.* 537: 1-33 (in Japanese).

Tokyo Metropolitan Government. 1996. Report on Seismometer Network by Research Committee on Disaster Information System (in Japanese).

Yamazaki, F., Katayama, T., and Yoshikawa, Y. 1994. On-line Damage Assessment of City Gas Networks based on Dense Earthquake Monitoring. *Proc. of the 5th U.S. National Conference on Earthquake Engineering.* IV: 829-837.

Yamazaki, F., Meguro, K., Tong, H., and Katayama, T. 1995. Review of Recent Five Damaging Earthquakes in Japan, *Proc. of Pacific Conference on Earthquake Engineering.* 2: 283-292.

Yokohama City. 1996. High-Concentration Seismograph Network - Seismometry System in Yokohama City.

Structural Safety and Reliability, Shiraishi, Shinozuka & Wen (eds) © 1998 Balkema, Rotterdam, ISBN 90 5410 978 5

Basic methodology of Seismic Risk Management (SRM) procedures

Mamoru Mizutani
Shinozuka Research Institute, Tokyo, Japan

ABSTRACT : In this paper, the basic methodology of a Seismic Risk Management (SRM) procedures is presented with a simple numerical example. The SRM is a tool to quantify the seismic risk of individual facility , which aimed to be used as an information for decision making on the risk mitigation of the facility. In the procedures risks are quantified by expected losses and event tree modeling of the seismic damages are adopted to deal with the multiple potential seismic damages. The seismic loss function that characterize the vulnerability of the facility and the expected annual loss that represent the magnitude of the seismic loss potential are introduced. With the example, it is revealed that the information generated by the SRM procedures is useful for studying seismic risk of the facility as well as the decision making on the risk reduction measures.

1. INTRODUCTION

Recently, three major damaging earthquakes, Loma Prietta 1989, Northridge 1994 and HyogoKen-Nanbu 1995, hit densely inhabited city areas, and we saw various kinds of earthquake damages that resulted in huge losses. The possibility of the most of these damages had been predicted by structural engineers, however it had been considered small enough to ignore or not to response urgently.

Now, after these events, the awareness of the seismic risks has arisen among societies; individuals, corporations and governments, and the seismic design codes for structures are being refined reflecting these experiences. However, it seems still difficult to have a general solution about the seismic risk since the risks are not the same to all the facilities with various functions and different values.

The major characteristics of seismic risk of individual facility are summarized:

1) Seismic design codes are only the minimum requirements and do not guarantee the structural safety against any earthquakes, then each facility owner should own its seismic risks.

2) Damaging earthquake is quite rare to happen and the occurrence may not be predicted.

3) There are plenty of damage modes induced by an earthquake and they show scattering nature.

4) An earthquake may damage all kinds of structures and facilities in a vast area simultaneously and those damages may form complicated secondly damages.

5) Seismic losses are results of the combination of the direct and secondary damages affecting on facilities, and are unique to individual facilities and subjective to the owners; individuals, corporations, organizations and governments.

6) The counter measures to the seismic risks such as strengthening structures will require additional expense to the facility owners.

To manage the seismic risk, which is the loss potential with above characteristics, we should first know the magnitude and content of the risk unique to the facility, then find out the cost effective counter measures. For this purpose, quantitative evaluation of the seismic risks is desirable

The probabilistic risk assessment (PRA) procedures[1] that quantify risks using probabilistic approach have been developed for nuclear power plants and as a part of them there already exists seismic PRA dealing with seismic events. For the development of the seismic PRA procedures, enormous kinds of study have been conducted and the procedures form a large scale systematic approach, however the application of the seismic PRA to a nuclear power plant requires too much efforts, which is not adequate for ordinary facilities.

We introduced many suggestions gained from studies for the development of the seismic PRA procedures to synthesize the seismic risk management (SRM) procedures that are practical and aimed to generate information for decision making on seismic risk mitigation for individual facilities by their owners. In this paper, the basic method and general procedures of the SRM are presented.

2. BASIC METHOD

The SRM procedures quantify the seismic risk for individual facility accounting for vulnerability of the structures, contents and functions, considering the earthquake circumstances of the site.

The flowchart of the SRM procedures is depicted in Figure 1. In the SRM, the earthquake damages are modeled as probabilistic phenomena in order to represent the scattering nature of their occurrence and the seismic risk is quantified as an expected loss.

Thus quantified risk is used to evaluate the magnitude of the seismic risk, to investigate significant contributors to the risk and also to examine the efficiency of potential counter measures.

The SRM procedures are practical tools and made not very complicated. One of the major features of the SRM is the use of event tree modeling that expresses the seismic risk clearly and enables simple quantification.

The procedures of the SRM are arranged to the seismic risk management but the basic concept of SRM may be adopted to any other kind of risk study so long as risks are considered coming with

uncertainty.

2.1 Seismic Risk Modeling

The damages induced by an earthquake may be appeared in various forms, and in the SRM, every possible damages are modeled as physical damage states. To enumerate the seismic damage states, consideration of the functions of the facility and their values is helpful, as the damage is the state that obstruct the normal functions of the facilities.

For the neat categorization of the physical damage states, the event tree modeling of the damage states is useful, where each physical damage state is represented as a sequence (combination) of several seismic events; ground failure, liquefaction, structural damage, vibratory damage, fire following earthquake damage etc.

The occurrence of these seismic events are modeled as probabilistic phenomena dependent on ground motion level and consequently, an occurrence probability conditional to the ground motion of each physical damage state is evaluated. Using event tree modeling, all the physical damage states are categorized into subsets mutually exclusive and totally exhaustive.

Event tree modeling that is unique to individual structure is carried out as the following manner:

1)List up every possible damage modes as physical states caused by earthquakes that arise losses to the facilities.

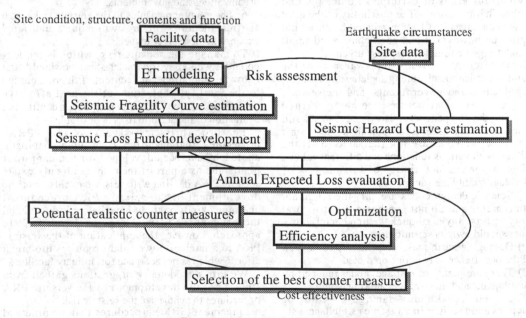

Figure 1. Flowchart of SRM procedures

2) List up seismic events related to the above damage modes.

3) Model each seismic event as binominal or multinominal event.

4) Line up the above seismic events in proper order and set up an event tree.

5) Eliminate unnecessary branches and obtain the event tree model.

2.2 Risk Quantification

For the quantification of an uncertain event, the expected value is one of the proper parameters especially when the occurrence of the event is characterized by a probability. In the SRM, the seismic risk is quantified as an expected loss that is the product of the state probability and loss amount associated with the state.

R(risk: expected loss)
  = P(probability)×C(loss amount)

These two parameters, P and C, are the two major aspects of the risk and according to this formulation the relation that the risk is larger when the probability and/or the loss amount is larger is properly expressed.

When there are multiple possible damage states, and these states are mutually exclusive and totally exhaustive, the risk is calculated by the below equation.

$$R = \sum_{i=1}^{n} (P_i \times C_i),$$
$$\sum_{i=1}^{n} P_i = 1,$$
$$\quad\quad\quad\quad\quad \ldots\ldots (1)$$

where, P_i is occurrence probability of state i and C_i is the loss amount associated with state i.

2.3 Loss Amount Evaluation

In the SRM, since the risk is quantified as the expected loss, the loss amount associated with each physical damage state should be evaluated properly. Referring the sequence of each damage state expressed in the event tree, one can easily imagine the meaning of the state. The loss amount should be evaluated for each state (no matter how likely it occurs) with the help of the facility owner since the value of the facility is subjective to the owner to some extent.

To assign the loss amount, the categorization of the type of the losses is useful: Direct losses that include substantial replacement expenses and functional (commercial) loss during a period until the facility recovered, and indirect losses such as

unfavorable reputation among public and clients and/or any other disadvantages.

2.4 Calculation of Seismic Risk

Given a ground motion level, the probabilities of branches of each seismic event in the event tree modeled as binominal or multinominal phenomenon are evaluated following the reliability method, and the conditional probability of each physical damage state is obtained by multiplying the branch probabilities in its sequence. The conditional risk to the ground motion level is calculated using equation (1). Repeating this procedure for all of ground motion levels, the seismic (expected) loss function (SLF) of the facility is generated.

The SLF is a conditional risk curve to the ground motion level that represent the seismic vulnerability of the facility. In other aspect, SLF is the summation of risk contribution of each physical damage state versus ground motion level. Looking into the SFL, we may see the change of the dominant damage states along with the ground motion level.

Given the probabilistic seismic hazard curve (PSHC) at the facility site, the annual expected loss (AEL) is obtained by convoluting SLF with PSHC. The PSHC represents the annual exceedance probability of ground motion at the site and it corresponds to the annual maximum ground motion.

The AEL is a single number that shows over all seismic risk magnitude of the facility settled at the site. The AEL of each physical damage state is also evaluated as the same manner and the contribution of each states to the total AEL is quantified.

Thus identified dominant damage states are not always severe damage states like total collapse of a building. In general occurrence probability of slight damage states are quite larger reflecting larger probability of smaller ground motion.

The AEL is a seismic risk index counting for not only the vulnerability of the facility itself but also the seismic circumstances around the site. For example, if there are two identical facilities in different places, their SLFs are the same but their AELs may be different reflecting the difference of their seismic hazards.

The AEL together with the SFL will provide wide spectrum of the seismic risk characteristics of individual facility and will help to manage the seismic risk.

2.5 Efficiency Analysis

The efficiency of the potential counter measure to the seismic risk reduction is evaluated by recalculating the AEL for the hypothetical facility assumed the counter measure to be undertaken. By replacing the branch probabilities of corresponding seismic events and/or changing loss amounts assigned for damage states in the original event tree, the AEL for the hypothetical facility is calculated. The reduced quantity from the original AEL is the quantified efficiency of the counter measure.

For this efficiency analysis several alternative counter measures should be prepared. The counter measures should have an effect to reduce the probability of damages and/or the loss amount. For the lining up the alternative counter measures, the information obtained from the SLF and AEL are quite useful.

After evaluating the quantitative efficiency of each alternative, judgment on the counter measures should be made by the owner of the facility considering the expenses and efforts needed for them.

2.6 Sensitivity Study

For the quantification of the risk, the loss amount of each physical damage state and branch probabilities of each seismic event are essential parameters to be estimated. In general, these values and PSHC have uncertainties of considerable magnitude. To deal with these uncertainties, several sensitivity studies should be done to examine the robustness of the relative relation of efficiencies of alternative counter measures. The SRM procedures are made to adopt this sensitivity study that the quantification procedures of the seismic risk are simple and straightforward, once the event tree proper to the facility has developed.

The sensitivity study is conducted by changing certain parameter; probability or loss amount, then calculating the efficiency of each counter measure and if the selected best alternative remain the same, the counter measure is truly effective. On the contrary, if the relative relation of efficiencies changes case by case basis, it is difficult to identify the best counter measure. However, even if such thing happens, the information gained from the SRM is still useful for the judgment. The effect of these uncertainties is refracting the lack of knowledge and/or data and it is difficult to resolve the problem right now, even though the judgment should be made knowing the uncertainty of the estimation.

2.7 Side Effects

There are significant side effects to conduct the SRM besides the selection of the best effective counter measures. In the event tree modeling, the possible physical damage states of the facility are clearly represented and the facility owners can recognize them together with their seriousness assigned as the loss amounts to them. This may help their crisis management when an earthquake occurs, even if any counter measure is not undertaken.

Another side effect is that the major source of uncertainty of the seismic risk is identified through the sensitivity analysis. If the vagueness of the loss amount of certain physical damage state is identified as a major source of the uncertainty, the facility owner should study more about the value of the facility. Also, if the branch probability of the seismic event is identified as the major contributor to the uncertainty, more consideration should be made by engineers. Thus the preciseness of the evaluation results may be improved efficiently.

3. GENERAL PROCEDURES

In this chapter, the SRM procedures are explained using a simple example facility, a hypothetical store house that is assumed to be a simple one story building and contains delicate electric devices placed in ordinary rack on the floor. All the parameters; branch probabilities and loss amount, are just given by the author's judgment.

3.1 Consideration of Damages

The consideration of earthquake damages is first to be performed. The damages correspond to the facility configuration and functions. For the example facility, the damage may be limited only to those of the contents and the building.

The next thing to do is the identification of seismic events that relate to the earthquake damages of the facility listed. The potential seismic events acting on damages are some relating on the siting; seismic wave amplification, land slide, liquefaction and seismically induced flood, some due to vibratory motion; structural failure, over turning of contents and malfunctions caused by the vibration, and some secondary damages; fire following earthquake and functional failure due to any lifeline services suspensions.

As for the example facility, about the siting, only the potential of large scale land slide is identified. The structural damages and overturning of the rack are found as major vibratory events. The damages of lifelines do not likely affect the facility.

3.2 Event Tree Modeling

To enumerate the physical damage states of the facility mutually exclusive and totally exhaustive, the sequences of the related seismic events are modeled in an event tree.

Figure 2 depicts the event tree for the example store house, in which three seismic events, land slide, structural damage and overturning of contents are considered and six physical damage states are obtained eliminating unnecessary branches. When an earthquake occurs, only one of these six physical damage states will appear. In the event tree, the seismic events are modeled as binominal (eg. Event 1 and 3 in figure 1) or multinominal (Event 2) phenomena. There must exist other intermediate states for each event, however, this simplification is introduced in order to avoid generating too much end branches. The choice of the number of branches of each event is arbitrary and is a matter of datelines required.

Meaning of each branch should be clearly defined and interpreted as a physical condition using proper parameters. For instance, Event 1 in the example is defined as a land slide larger than certain size and will happen when the ground motion exceeds certain value (capacity) represented by a probabilistic density function. Structural collapse of Event 2 corresponds the state that the seismic load exceeds the ultimate strength of the structure or that response drift become larger than a certain threshold level.

The advantages of the use of the event tree models are listed below:

1) Possible damages are modeled as a set of physical damage states that are mutually exclusive and totally exhaustive.

2) Each physical damage states is clearly expressed as a sequence of seismic events.

3) Dependency of the occurrence can be considered by assigning conditional probabilities at each branch of the event according to the sequence of pre-events: The branch probabilities P32 and P34 in figure1 is not necessary the same.

4) The quantification procedures are simple and straightforward.

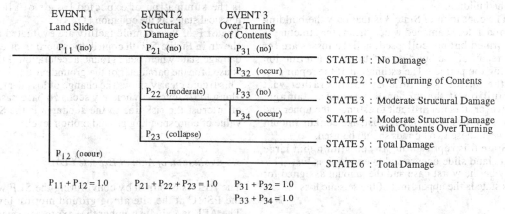

Figure 2. Example of Event Tree for a Store House

Table 1. Example of Loss Amount Evaluation

in 1000$

STATE	Direct				Indirect	Total
	Substantial		Commercial			
	Structure	Content	Period (month)	amount		
1	0	0	0	0	0	0
2	0	300	1	25	0	325
3	100	0	2	50	10	160
4	100	300	2	50	20	470
5	500	300	10	250	100	1150
6	700	300	12	300	100	1400

3.3 Assignment of Loss Amount

For each physical damage state, the corresponding loss amount should be assigned. For the example facility, a store house, direct losses are counted for the building and contents and the business interruption. It is assumed for the indirect losses that certain disadvantage may happen when the recovery of the business take too long time.

The feature of each damage state is easily recognized by looking into the event tree. Imagining the occurrence of the state, the amount of each type of losses are assigned

Table 1 shows the evaluation of the loss amounts for the physical damage states of the example facility.

Nothing happens for the state 1 and no losses are assigned for it.

State 2 is the condition that just the contents are damaged due to overturning of the rack then the losses are for the contents and also for business interruption during the period to clean up the inside of the building.

The condition of State 3 is that only the building is moderately damaged, which means the structure is deformed but not collapsed, and the losses are for the repair of the building and business interruption during the period. The estimation of the repair cost of the building is not easy for the rather vast definition of the moderate structural damage. However, it is not difficult to estimate the upper and lower bounds of the repair cost, and certain amount between these two bounds should be used.

State 6 is representing the condition that large scale land slide occurs and every thing is lost. This may be the worst case and the amount assigned for this state is the upper limit of the seismic loss.

3.4 Evaluation of Seismic Loss Function

The SLF is obtained by quantifying the event tree for each level of ground motion. The parameter of the ground motion should be identical for all the seismic events and also for the PSHC at the site.

The conditional branch probabilities may be evaluated applying conventional reliability method, which models the occurrence of failure as the state that the probabilistic response exceeds the probabilistic capacity and the failure probability is calculated by the equation shown in Figure 3. In case of multinominal events, the branch probabilities are evaluated according to dependencies between the branches. Figure 4 explains the relation of the seismic fragility curves and branch probabilities for the Event 2 of the example facility.

For each physical state, probability is calculated by multiplying the branch probabilities lying in the sequence, and the expected loss of the state is evaluated as the product of the probability and loss amount. The conditional loss to the ground motion is the summation of expected losses of all the physical states as the equation (1).

The SLF of the example facility are evaluated and shown in Figure 5 with contribution portion of each damage state where peak ground acceleration (PGA) is used for the parameter of the ground motion level. This figure clearly shows the change of loss contents along PGA level. When any scenario base case is of interest the risk due to the scenario is the SLF value of corresponding ground motion level.

3.5 Evaluation of Annual Expected Loss

The AEL is obtained by convoluting the SLF with the PSHC at the site along ground motion level. The AEL is a single number that expresses seismic risk magnitude of the facility.

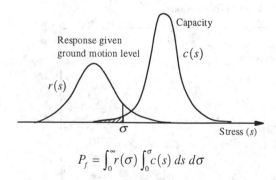

$$P_f = \int_0^\infty r(\sigma) \int_0^\sigma c(s)\, ds\, d\sigma$$

Figure 3. Evaluation of Failure Probability

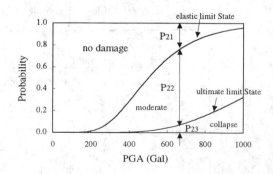

Figure 4. Evaluation of Branch Probability of Structural Damage

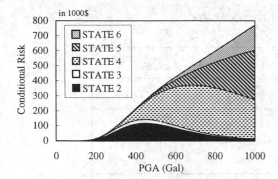

Figure 5. Seismic Loss Function of
Current State

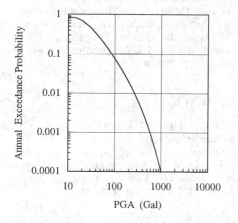

Figure 6. Probablistic Seismic Hazard Curve

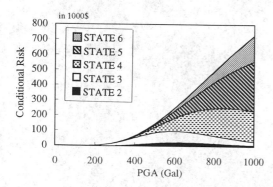

Figure 8. Seismic Loss Function in the Case
of Fixing Rack

Figure 6 is a hypothetical PSHC at the example
site and Figure 7 shows calculated AEL of the
facility together with the contribution of each

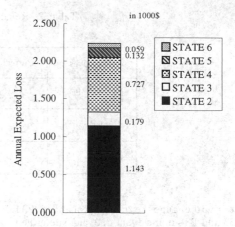

Figure 7. Annual Expected Loss of
Current State

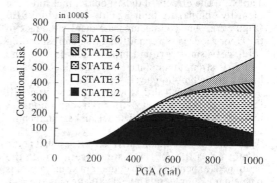

Figure 9. Seismic Loss Function in the Case
of Strengthening Structure

physical damage state. It is observed from Figure 7
that the major risk contributors are State 2 and State
4 for the example facility, and this insight is hardly
obtained only from the SLF.

3.6 Consideration of Counter Measures

To reduce the seismic risk, several counter measures
should be listed as alternatives by investigating the
risk characteristics, consulting with the SFL and the
AEL. As these counter measures require additional
expenses, the efficiency of them should be studied.
For the example facility it looks reasonable to fix the
rack to the floor and to strengthen the building,
which can be two alternative counter measures.

The effect of each alternative is represented by
changes of branch probabilities and/or loss amount
and the efficiency is quantified as the reduction of
AEL. For the example facility, fixing the rack to the

Table 2. Result of Efficiency Analyses

in 1000$

Alternatives	Current State	Fixing Rack	Strengthening Building
Annual Expected Loss	2.24	0.82	1.81
Efficiency		1.42	0.43
Expense		10	50

floor will change the branch probability P31, P32, P33 and P34 in the event tree, and strengthening of the building will affect P21, P22 and P23.

The result of the efficiency analyses for these two alternatives are summarized in Figures 8, 9 and Table 2. The effects of these counter measures are clear by comparing their SLF to the original SLF (Figure 5). The counter measure that fix the rack to the floor reduces the conditional risk corresponding relatively small ground motion levels. On the contrary, strengthening the building reduces risk on higher ground motion level.

It is noticed that this kind of consideration will lead to find out another alternatives; a counter measure with both fixing the rack and strengthening the building for example.

In Table 2, The quantitative efficiency that is the reduction of the AEL is listed together with the estimated expense of each counter measure. For this particular example, it is revealed that fixing the rack to the floor is a reasonable counter measure as it has large efficiency with small expense.

However, the choice and practice of the counter measures must be decided by the facility owner knowing the content and magnitude of the seismic risk and the efficiencies of potential counter measures.

4. CONCLUDING REMARKS

In this paper, the basic methodology of the seismic risk management (SRM) procedures are presented together with an example, and several applicability studies are also presented in the companion papers.

The SRM is a tool to quantify the seismic risk of individual facility. The information derived by the procedures is to be used for the decision making by the facility owners on the seismic risk reduction. The procedures are based on the seismic reliability analyses to count for the scattering nature of seismic events and they are synthesized in a rather simple systematic approach.

For the application, some difficulties still exist in the assignment of branch probabilities and loss amount in the event tree and they may affect on the decisions. However, the SRM is made adoptive to conduct sensitivity studies. Knowing the uncertainty of the results, the information gained by the SRM may be beneficial for the decision making on the seismic risk reduction.

REFERENCES

USNRC, 1983. PRA Procedures Guide. NUREG/CR-2300,

M. Mizutani, 1994. Procedures of Probabilistic Seismic Risk Assessment and Related Issues (in Japanese). The 43rd Nat. Cong. of Theoretical Applied Mechanics, pp189-190

Structural Safety and Reliability, Shiraishi, Shinozuka & Wen (eds) © 1998 Balkema, Rotterdam, ISBN 90 5410 978 5

Decision making model for post-disaster crisis management : Lessons learned from the great Hanshin-Awaji earthquake disaster

H. Hayashi

Research Center for Disaster Reduction Systems, DPRI, Kyoto University, Japan

ABSTRACT: Socictal reactions after the Hanshin-Awaji earthquake disaster of January 17, 1995 was reviewed from emergency management point of view. Based on the lessons we learned as to the post-disaster organizational reactions, we introduced a decision-making model for post-disaster crisis management, which consisted of emergency responses, relief activities, restoration activities, and logistics.

1. INTRODUCTION

At 5:46 am on January 17, 1995, an earthquake of a magnitude of 7.2 (JMA) hit the southern parts of Hyogo prefecture and Osaka prefecture, which resulted in the worst earthquake disaster occurred in Japan since 1923 Kanto earthquake. It was named as Hanshin-Awaji earthquake disaster.

The area around Kobe is one of the most densely populated and wealthy urban areas in Japan in which more than three million people live. It was the first earthquake disaster for post-war Japanese megalopolis and the resulting damages was so devastating that it was not but catastrophe. A total of 5,502 people were killed and still 2 persons were missing. More than 200,000 residential buildings were totally collapsed or severely damaged so that at most 320,000 earthquake homeless were created. Lifeline systems were also severely damaged and resulted in functional failure for more than one million households for very long period. 294 fires burned down more than 1,100 buildings, and the destroyed area exceeded 7,000 hectares. The total of direct loss for Hyogo Prefecture is estimated to be 100 billion US dollars. And it is also estimated the amount of indirect loss for Hyogo Prefecture for the first 10 years after the earthquake would be 200 billion US dollars.

Hanshin-Awaji Earthquake Disaster made us to critically review earthquake disaster management in Japan. Since the Kanto Earthquake of 1923, Japanese disaster management system. has been relied heavily upon structural mitigation measures and achieved first rate earthquake resisting performances. It was the fact that well designed structures survived the severe ground motion amounted. It was revealed that old and ill designed structures in urban areas outnumbers well designed structures and they performed poorly and resulted in great amount of damages. In other words, urban vulnerability was still high even though the long and continuous efforts for the promotion of structural mitigation. It was also revealed that Japanese preparedness for crisis management proved to be insufficient and not well practiced for mass disaster in particular and maybe for any disasters. We now need to have a more well-balanced disaster management system in which prepared measured should be incorporated as the fail-safe system for structural mitigation. The best mixture of both preparedness and mitigation should be our new goal to achieve.

2. THREE TASKS OF POST-DISASTER CRISIS MANAGEMENT

A new but undesirable reality was created in the impacted area by the earthquake. Everything in the impacted area has been changing rapidly and drastically ever since its onset. In a sense, the goal of societal reactions to the disaster is to construct and to maintain the new reality initiated by the disaster in such a way as to make the adaptation processes of local people in the impacted area to the new reality as free from stress as possible. As a result, many victims as well as researchers pointed out that different issues may become salient and critical depending on the following phases of chronological development of societal reactions to the disaster: response, relief, and reconstruction. At the same time, it should be noted that these three different reactions can be distinguished as follows in terms of the differences in the goals set by each task.

1)Response: Protection of human lives, provision of safety for the community, and prevention of secondary disasters.
2)Relief: Restoring social flow system (which me be symbolized by lifeline system) impaired by the disaster, and mass care during that period.
3)Reconstruction: Reconstruction of both community as well as people in order to adapt to new reality created by the disaster.

As a practice, both Hyogo prefectural government and Kobe city government in an ad hoc manner did set up three different task forces to handle each of these three tasks. From crisis management point of view, it was the lessons that there are at least three different goals to be set in disaster crisis management.

3. EMERGENCY RESPONSE ACTIVITIES

The purpose of emergency response activities is the minimization of casualties. It is time urgent task so that each society has already deployed such professional workers in the fields of fire suppression, law enforcement, search and rescue, ambulance, and medical services on 24 hours basis in our communities. At the time of disaster, those professionals are expected to take care of at least four tasks listed below. In order to achieve these tasks effective, it is quite important to mobilize all the available resources to those who need help as soon as possible, and as much as possible.

1) Search and rescue, and medical treatment
2) Prevention of secondary disasters caused by tusnami, fire, landslide, toxic substance spill, infectious disease, and so forth.
3) Law enforcement
4) Services for the mortalities and their families

3.1 Deaths and Injuries

There are six areas where showed high mortality rates. They are Suma Ward, Nagata Ward, Nada Ward, and Higashinada Ward of Kobe City, in addition to Ashiya City and Nishinomiya City. All of these areas are mostly residential areas. Fig.1 shows the spatial distribution of the mortalities. Fig.2 shows the spatial distribution of collapsed buildings. As the high correspondence between the spatial distribution of mortalities and collapsed buildings, over 95% of people have been killed because of the collapse of their residential building. This fact may reflect the effect of the time of day when the earthquake occurred: 0546.

According to the corner's office of Hyogo Prefecture, which examined 2,416 bodies, 92% of them were killed within the first 15 minutes after the earthquake, and 95% of them were killed by 2400 of January 17. The cause of death was also investigated based on the 3,651 examinations, 54% suffocation, 12% compression, and 12% burned to death by fires. It was also found the 44 % of them were senior citizens whose age were 65 years old or more.

Fig.1 Spatial Distribution of Mortalities

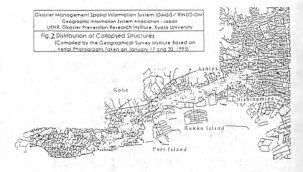

Fig.2 Spatial Distribution of Collapsed Buildings

3.2 Search and Rescue

Since the building collapse is the main cause for mortalities, many search and rescue operations were conducted in the severely impacted area. Fig.3 shows search and rescue operations done by Kobe City Fire Department between 17th and 31st of January. They saved a total of 1,891 persons and 724 of them were alive. It is obvious that search and rescue operations were virtually completed within the first four days. A total of 1,700 persons were save during that period, which amounted to be 90% of total rescue.

The statistics of people rescued alive, however, revealed the existence of critical period for rescue. For those who rescued on the Day 1, 80% of the stayed alive. On Day 2, the survival rate went down to 27%, Day 3 to 22%, and Day 4 further down to 6%, which proved the 'Golden 72 hours" theory.

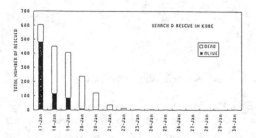

Fig.3 Search & Rescue Operations by Kobe City Fire Department between January 17 and 31, 1995

The capability to mobilize the necessary resources for search and rescue efforts within the first 72 hours after an earthquake therefore appears to be decisive factor for the success of search and rescue operations. In this respect, the majority of search and rescue operations were done spontaneously among disaster victims during the first few hours after the earthquake in every corner of the impacted area. This fact suggests that it is important to increase the preparedness of the local residents as single individuals and as community group members.

4. RELIEF ACTIVITIES

Because of earthquake, societal flow system may be disturbed in such way as the functional failure of utilities, telecommunication and transportation. Daily living under such circumstances may become more difficult and cumbersome for those live in such damaged area as compared with normal circumstances. The purpose of relief activities is to provide essential care for those disaster survivors who have difficulties for daily living. The relief activities can be divided into two tasks: 1) The restoration of normal social flow system, and 2) the provision of mass care by the creation of alternative temporary flow system. To be specific, at least the following tasks should be considered in relief activities:

1) The restoration of lifeline systems as soon as possible, especially the restoration of electricity system and road system should have highest priority.
2) The restoration of market system as soon as possible.
3) Mass feeding
4) Shelters
5) Distribution of Bulk supply and donation in kinds
6) Dissemination of information about post-disaster reality

In Hanshin-Awaji earthquake disaster, the focus of relief activity operation was shelters. A total of about 1,000 shelters were opened up using various types of public facilities to accommodate a maximum of about 320,000 disaster victims. Educational facilities such as primary schools and junior high schools were typical site for shelters. For example, about 150 schools (out of 345 in total) have been used as shelters in case of Kobe City. And in those schools, teachers have been actively involved in the operation of shelters as the operational managers. This created a severe conflicts in the minds of school teachers about their jobs. The more they have committed themselves to shelter management, they may result in the less time and efforts left for their job of teaching children. Even though school facilities are still used as shelters, all schools in Kobe City were reopened their education by February 24th.

Fig.4 shows the mass care at shelters operated by Kobe City Hall on a daily basis. Kobe city officially closed its shelters on August 20th, 1995, more than 7 months later from the earthquake. As you can see from the figure, there is big differences in number between mass feeding and homeless. By the end of March, the number of mass feeding tended to be double in number as compared with the number of homeless. It is also obvious that the number of mass feeding showed large daily changes by the end of March. These data suggested that shelter functioned as temporary alternative social flow service suppliers for both homeless people and for those who have daily suffering from the damage to

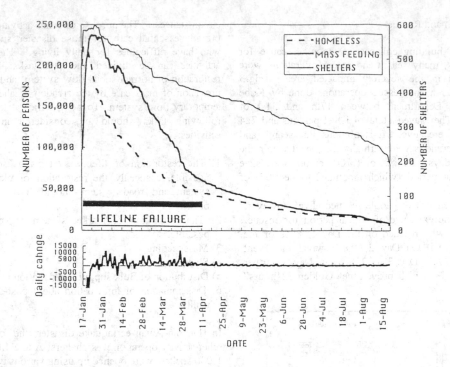

Fig.4 Mass Care Operations by Kobe City after Hanshin-Awaji Earthquake Disaster

lifeline systems. It is also suggested that the timing to close the shelter should take into consideration how lifeline services are restored in the surrounding communities.

5. RECONSTRUCTION ACTIVITIES

It may be too early to review the restoration processes because it has just begun and many of them are still under flux. It is clear that the reconstruction of the impacted areas due to Hanshin-Awaji earthquake is definitely a new and complex issues for the present Japanese disaster management system. The present system as mentioned earlier established based on our experiences and lessons taken from severe typhoon disasters, which is basically aiming at the restoration to the state of affairs before the disaster. It is partly because the typhoon disaster hampers societal flow system intensively but relatively small damages to societal stocks. In contrast, urban earthquake disaster destroys both societal flow systems and societal stocks. In other words, restoration from urban earthquake disaster should not return to the pre-disaster level but creating a new community. So it should be names as "creative restructuring of community".

Both Hyogo prefectural government and Kobe city submitted their restoration plan packages to the national government by the end of June, 1995 to apply for maximum financial support in the 1996 national budget. As a consequence, they listed the hundreds of programs consisting of the reconstruction of infrastructure and public facilities. In order to promote "creative restructuring of community", we need to achieve not only the reconstruction of community "hardware" but also to have "software" to help the disaster victims to be "self-empowered" to heal their psychological trauma due to the disaster and to adapt themselves to a new reality. In other words, there are at least two level of reconstruction: one at individual or family level, and the other would be community level.

Hanshin-Awaji earthquake disaster is the first disaster in the history of Japanese disaster management that the much attention was paid for the well-being of disaster victims in the reconstruction activities. For example, for the first time, the expenses for debris clearance for their residential building was covered by the national government. For the first time, a total of 48,000 units of temporary housing in about 700 locations were constructed to accommodate all of 50,000 victims who wished to move in free housing program for the next two years. For the first time, Psychological stress care program was initiated to prevent posttraumatic stress disorder(PTSD)[5]. For the first time, more than one million spontaneous volunteer participated to intend to help the reconstruction process of disaster victims at various phases. For the first time, a great deal of attention was paid to those vulnerable population with all kinds of handicaps and disabilities.

6. DISASTER MANAGEMENT AS DECISION-MAKING PROCESS

At performance level, three different time phase may be identified as the tasks of post-disaster crisis management: in the order of response, relief, then reconstruction. In addition, logistics operations for the coordination and the distribution of available resources should be the common basis for all of these three tasks. As discussed so far, however, all of these three tasks has independent and different goals to achieve. Thus, it may often result in a state of conflicts among three tasks in which every claims to be the number one priority of all the operations. Therefore, it is recommended to start these three tasks with three different work groups concurrently from the beginning of post-disaster crisis management as shown in Fig. 5. However, these three different efforts should be integrated through the logistics management system which functions as the common database for all resource tracking and operations.

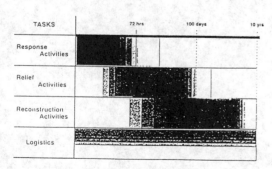

Fig.5 Concurrent Nature of Three Post-Disaster Crisis Management Tasks

In summary, it would become very important to have the commander of all the post-disaster crisis management operations so that he/she could decide or integrate which operations should be prioritized taking into account logistics information, both in terms of intelligence they acquired as well as the

resources they could mobilize. Fig.6 represents the basic model of decision making processes for disaster management.

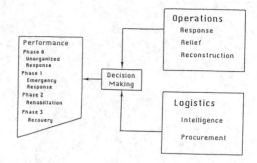

Fig. 6 A Decision Making Model of Post-Disaster Crisis Management

7. CONCLUSIONS

1) We learned a lesson from the Hanshin-Awaji earthquake disaster that Japanese engineering approach could not perform so well as we expected with two reasons: a) engineering mitigation could not reach the point to prevent a catastrophic disasters, and b) preparedness for post-disastrous crisis management was relatively inadequate.
2) As a result, the post-disaster crisis management was started in an ad hoc manner so that the relief activities and reconstruction activities were full of confusion and the lack of coherent policies.
3) In this paper, decision making model consisting of four components is introduced: responses, relief, reconstruction and logistics to develop a more well-balanced disaster management system in terms of mitigation and preparedness for the future disaster.

8. REFERENCES

H.Hayashi 1995 Psychological Stress Care After the Great Hanshin Earthquake, UNCRD Res. Series.

H.Hayashi & T.Katsumi, 1996 Generation and management of disaster waste. Soils and Foundations, Special Issue, 349-358.

H.Hayashi & Y.Kawata 1995 societal implications of great Hanshin-Awaji earthquake disaster of January 17, 1995, Natural Disaster Science, 16-3.

H.Kameda, S. Kakumoto, H.Hayashi, S.Iwai & T.Usui, 1995 DiMSIS- A GIS for Disaster Information Management of the Hyogoken-Nanbu Earthquake, Natural Disaster Science, 16-2.

Structural Safety and Reliability, Shiraishi, Shinozuka & Wen (eds) © 1998 Balkema, Rotterdam, ISBN 90 5410 978 5

Lessons of emergency management and its philosophy in urban earthquake disaster

Yoshiaki Kawata
Research Center for Disaster Reduction Systems, DPRI, Kyoto University, Japan

ABSTRACT: The outline of emergency management and their lessons were presented. The Great Hanshin-Awaji Earthquake Disaster gave us many lessons which will contribute to reduction of human and property damage due to coming urban disasters. Emergency management can be divided into risk management and crisis management. Disaster information management is the most important to reduce the damage. The disaster reduction systems with information management can be proposed with combination of pre-disaster risk management and post-disaster crisis management. In order to get good aftermath recovery, it is necessary to enlarge the concept of mitigation in disaster management. In this paper, social mitigation was defined as humane technology which includes ecological infrastracture and amenity infrastructure.

1 INTRODUCTION

The 1995 Great Hanshin-Awaji Earthquake Disaster (magnitude: M =7.2 on the JMA scale) came about on 5:46 of 17 January. The disaster was the worst after the world war II in our country. The destruction resulting from the earthquake included damage to, or the collapse of, some 200,000 buildings (mostly, old wooden houses and concrete buildings) and an estimated area of 90ha blackened by fires that erupted in more than 200 locations. Moreover, damage to highway, railway and waterway systems, which halted transport of people and logistics, along with disruption of utilities such as gas, electricity, water and sewage, produced a widespread and long-term cessation of lifeline functions. Reclaimed land along the coastline liquefied causing deformation and exacerbating damage. As a result of structural collapse and ensuing fires, the death toll was 6,308, the missing was two and the number of the injured was more than 38,000 and estimated direct property damage, and indirect and secondary one were about $100 and 200 billion respectively. At its peak, over 300,000 residents sought refuge in emergency shelters. The aftermath and the impact on the affected population and economics are expected to be a source of continued controversy. During this 30 years, we have never had the natural disaster with the death toll of more than 300. And also this is truly urban disasters which has never been experienced in our highly complicate and densely populated urban areas. Historically, our emergency management as disaster one was very poor in every local government level as well as Japanese government. After one and half year of the 1995 disaster, about 45,000 residents were still obliged to stay at temporal housing units. We would like to introduce characteristics of catastrophic urban disaster, its management systems and social mitigation as a key of urban environment improvement after urban disaster.

2 CATASTROPHIC NATURAL DISASTERS

2.1 *Characteristics of urban disasters*

In order to manage natural disasters, we have to understand revolution of the disasters. Damage processes have changed by social environment as well as natural one. The major factor of the revolution is urbanization in which vulnerability has increased due to imbalance between construction of infrastructures and increment of population. This imbalance is typically appeared at a cluster of tall intelligent buildings surrounded by slum in metropolitan areas in developing countries and those mixed with inner cities in developed countries. Under the large difference of vulnerability in every local area, the areas with the largest vulnerability are firstly damaged through collapsed of poorly-made houses, eruption of fires and troubles of old lifeline networks. The damage will be easily enlarged in neighboring areas.

The classification of natural disasters is shown in Table 1. Natural disasters are divided into four categories from the view points of population and infrastructures following as:

Table 1 Classification of natural disasters

	population density	population	infrastructure	kind of damage	damage enlargement process
rural disaster	average	independent	not constructed	classic	single · known
urbanizing disaster	annually increasing	$O(10^4)$	under construction	classic	single · known
urbanized disaster	more than several to 10 times	$O(10^5)$	completion	property damage	multi · known
urban disaster	more than 20	$O(10^6)$	imbalance	human and property damage	multi · unknown

1) Rural disasters: The largeness of hazard decides the scale of human and property damage.

2) Urbanizing disasters: At first stage of urbanization, population rapidly increases at newly developed areas such as flood-prone lowlands and foot of cliff and hill.

3) Urbanized disasters: The increase rate of population becomes small after rapid urbanization. The construction of countermeasures against natural disasters can contribute to reduction of human damage, but many infrastructures such as various lifelines were severely damaged.

4) Urban disasters: Even if hazard is not enough large, phase shift occurs under densely populated condition in metropolitan areas. Human and property damage become huge. Some characteristics of the disasters are summarized in Table 1. In urban disasters, the damage much depends on human factors so that characteristics of man-made disaster are included.

The revolution of natural disasters is shown in Fig. 1 in which the horizontal axis corresponds to length of affected time and the vertical one represents the largeness of damaged area. We defined that the secondary disaster has very long affected time and complex disaster has very wide damaged area. In this figure, some typical natural disasters are plotted. Disaster lessons are changed in every kind of natural disasters. If huge hazard will attack on metropolitan areas, we have all kinds of natural disasters because in the city center urban disasters occur and in the suburbs urbanizing or rural natural disasters may rise up. This situation depends on the locality and the history of formation of metropolitan areas.

2.2 Process of damage enlargement and its measures

Flow charts of required measures against various kind of themes are shown in Fig. 2 in which the horizontal axis represents a timeline divided into two sections, separated by the occurrence of the 1995 Great Hanshin-Awaji Earthquake Disaster. To the left of the occurrence of the earthquakes are the pre-disaster risk management and to the right are post-disaster crisis management. Depicted in the vertical axis are themes related to physical attributes

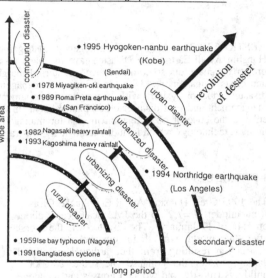

Fig. 1 Revolution of natural disasters

(Natural World) in the lower region and societal attributes (Social World) in the upper region. Acting as the combining agent for the two attributes, information is represented as having a role in every phase of disasters. Six zones, A through F, are defined in relation to periodic phases. Especially, topics important in understanding the socio-cultural setting and appropriate disaster-control philosophies are presented in zone G. A comprehensive and strategic approach to disaster-related topics is shown in zone H, whereby the lessons learned from the latest earthquake may be utilized. The holistic approach to disaster-control measures is the focus, in lieu of taking up each of the attributes individually. Each of zones is detailed below, sequenced in the order of relevance.

1) Zone A : We call this zone as Physical (Structural) Mitigation and Mitigation by Design and Planning. Earthquake reinforcement of existing structures is extremely important. Design standard with long return period of occurrence and including redundancy is also essential. Non-structural components such as urban grand design for

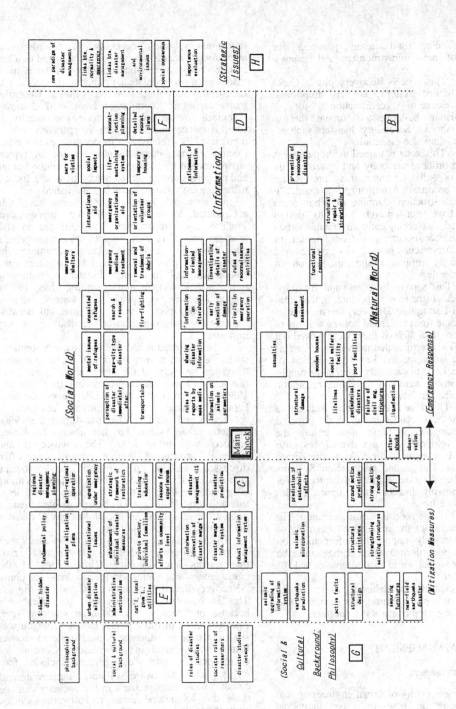

Fig. 2 Integrated research on urban disaster reduction

safe/security society and urban planning for arrangement of new infrastructures and renewal ones.

2) Zone *B* : This zone is Recovery phase. Quick recovery of lifeline systems is very important. Damage assessment (certification for earthquake-resistant buildings) is urgent due to following aftershocks. Secondary disasters such as fire and tsunamis are also essential.

3) Zone *E* : This zone is named as Preparedness and Tactics. In order to smoothly and systematically perform the post-disaster measures, pre-disaster preparedness becomes extremely important. It include the reconstruction planning of urban areas because we have not enough time to design amenity-oriented and ecologically sustainable urban areas after disaster occurrence. Coordination of activities by fire-rescue teams, riot police and self-defense army (military) and distribution of volunteers are needed.

4) Zone *F* : This zone is Response and Strategy. Search and rescue is the most important. In the Great Hanshin-Awaji Earthquake Disaster, the number of the rescued people from collapsed houses was about 18,000 and more than 80% of them were picked out by neighbors. This certifies that individual efforts as well as public ones are the key of reduction of human damage. Logistics are also essential to supply anything the victims want and to require resolution of disposal of disaster debris.

5) Zone *C* : This zone is Abundancy. Acting as a unifying agent between societal and physical attributes, information systems must ensure the harmonious development of the overall response operation as it evolves over time. As a core device for this systems, Geographic Information Systems (GIS) should be promoted. Educational software for training and knowing disaster plays important roles in disaster preparedness.

6) Zone *D* : This zone is Communication. The role of information in the immediate aftermath of disasters is extremely important. Information on seismic activity and information on damage must be conveyed to the social world in real-time or at least within a short period.

In catastrophic disaster, Zone *G* as socio-cultural and philosophical background and Zone *H* as strategic topics are also important.

3 DISASTER MANAGEMENT

3.1 Disaster management

Traditionally, view points of urban engineering and technology focus on how to solve individual problems so that mind of urban engineers is not always enough microscopically well-balanced with our society. At first, they usually think how to construct urban functions. On the contrary, urban residents think that what is the most important thing to support their urban life. Under this requirement design and planning assessment is more essential than construction assessment. In Japan,

unfortunately, such necessity of environmental assessment systems has not been recognized as a key of role to realize sustainable society. It takes more than 30 years to regulate the public nuisance such as industrial water pollution and air pollution. Recently, many Japanese companies have shift domestic manufacturing facilities to overseas especially in south Asian countries in which the pollution code of regulation is relatively moderate, even now. Occurrence of natural disasters is one of typical environmental problems. In order to reduce human and property damage due to natural disaster, disaster management systems should be established.

In Japan, no level of government has been accustomed to providing disaster management. Traditionally, importance has been put on risk management before disasters, but crisis management after disaster is equally important. For examples, the logistics of providing materials, workers and communications just after disaster is extremely important. Reconstruction planning has to be prepared before occurrence of disasters, because good planning takes a very long time and because accurate damage estimation before disaster is very important.

To have a good urban and regional environment, social mitigation is very important, social mitigation being the recovery of the urban environment lost due to rapid industrialization during the 1970s and 1980s in Japan. Previously public works had been kept in balance with such urban functions as economics and our life style, but during the 1990s the total urban system has not always been well balanced with urban life. The engineering and technical aspects of disaster measures are often discussed without the holistic and societal significance of the disaster-related subjects. Without clear understanding as to how to keep our society safe and comfortable, it will be impossible to realize good urban environment. The philosophy of disaster management is very important.

Disaster management has two components such as risk management before disaster and crisis management after disaster. Time series of the management are Mitigation-Preparedness-Response -Recovery-Social Mitigation as shown in Fig. 3. This is not circulation structure but spiral one because our society has advanced year by year. Reconstruction of old type infrastructure which was constructed before disaster is inadequate to recover better environments in our society. Contents of catastrophic disaster management include four wares, such as hardware, software, humanware and commandware management. In the ordinary damage scale due to natural disaster, software includes humanware and commandware, but in catastrophe, we recommend that the last two wares independently form the disaster management systems as shown in Table 2.

3.2 Crisis management

In order to reduce human and property damage due

Table 2 Disaster management and four wares

| | emergency management | |
	risk management	crisis management
hardware	**reduction or mitigation** return period, encounter probability, fail-safe, redundancy	**recovery** reinforced lifeline, temporal housing
software	**abundance** disaster information, training, planning, education, evacuation manual	**communication** recovery information of lifeline, provision of emergency necessities
humanware	**preparedness** search & rescue, volunteer, psychological counsellor	**response** care for PTSD, emergency medical care
commandware	**tactics** headquater of disaster measure, command system, management system	**strategy** logistics, long-term reconstruction

to unexpected large scale disaster, post-crisis management is very important. The final goal of crisis management is to get societal recovery and to create new urban environment. Crisis management consists of five stages as shown in Fig. 4.

1) Direct response (24 hour basis just after disaster): Search and rescue (security of life), disaster medical care, secondary disaster warning such as eruption of fire, toxic substance spill out and tsunamis, urgent attendance to the government office including fire station, police station and military base. Muster of central and local government officers is also very urgent. Search and rescue operations done by Kobe City Fire fighting Rescue Teams in the 1995 disaster is shown in Fig. 5. They saved a total of 1,888 from 17th to 23rd of January

and the survived was 733. On only first day, the number of the survived was larger than those of the dead. In the case of collapsed wooden houses, "golden 72 hours" is too late to reduce loss of human lives. Collection, analysis and share of information is the key of direct response and following management.

2) Urgent response (one to three days after): Shelter, control of traffic, information network, logistics and emergency of medical are included.

3) Emergent response: Temporal housing, share of information about life, lifeline and infrastructures, planning recovery, continued logistics, support of life by volunteer and NPO are very important.

4) Recovery: Care of PTSD, removal of debris, planning of enforcement of infrastructure are also included.

5) Social mitigation: Construction of amenity and ecological infrastructures will recover urban environment.

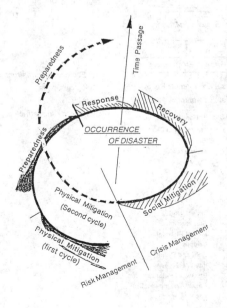

Fig. 3 Spiral structure of disaster management

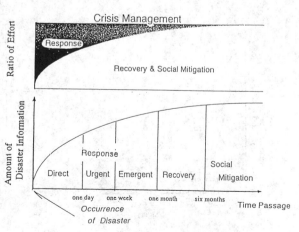

Fig. 4 Crisis management

4 SOCIAL MITIGATION

As already described here, social mitigation includes construction of amenity and ecological order to get good recovery after urban disasters such as the Great Hanshin-Awaji Earthquake disaster, it is necessary to enlarge the concept of mitigation in disaster management. Fig. 6 shows the frame work of mitigation and its classification. Social mitigation was defined as humane technology which includes combination of ecological infrastructure and amenity infrastructure.

The former focuses on cut-off of energy, circulation utility of water and other natural resources, reduction of public nuisance and recovery of green forest zone in urban environment. The latter has environmental efforts such as safety and security, convenient access for public sectors, economics, culture and information. Improvement recovery means not only enforcement of structural infrastructure such as lifeline systems and buildings but also natural and social environment recovery. The concept of " Nature has a will. " was proposed as a philosophy of creation of urban environment.

No exceptions to the rule, all major cities in Japan have painted a pretty picture in the city plans they have adopted. During the "bubble economy" (Japan's period of inflated prices), land prices rose quietly as time passed and land owners built high hopes of turning a profit. This put a halt to public land acquisition, and the failure to compromise broke off negotiations. The City of Kobe was perhaps the worst hit in the Hanshin area this time, but they cannot grieve about their misfortune forever. They have before them the opportunity to rebuild the city in greater consideration of Mother Nature. They should be taking advantage of this situation and doing everything possible to realize this vision. There are a mountain of issues to think about, including whether or not the city really needs an expressway down the middle of it, or whether there are ways to keep areas from becoming overpopulated. Both government and the people must cooperate in restoration planning so as to build a city where sustainable development can work. Restoration of a lost urban environment is the golden opportunity to reduce energy consumption, live in harmonious coexistence with Mother Nature, and preserve the diverse ecosystems that make up this part of the world. It has never been as important as now to bolster public consensus and support for this vision in which the task of restoration is taken on in full unison and cooperation. Always thinking about economic shortcomings in the near future and putting off important issues and the opportunity to set things right will place a tremendous burden on future generations.

Mitigation is a technology with which ecosystems are not destroyed or hurt by development such as filling-in low-lying coastal areas and wetlands to build a port. I want to define "social mitigation" as using this approach in rebuilding the urban environment. This also includes improvements to the disaster environment. Let us use this approach to build a society where the goal is sustainable development. The effort must start today to review our aging social infrastructure, to seek the wisdom of developing a city that is gentle on the environment, and to minimize the burden borne by future generations.

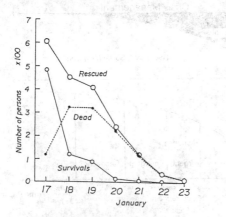

Fig. 5 Rescue activities done by Kobe Fire Fighters

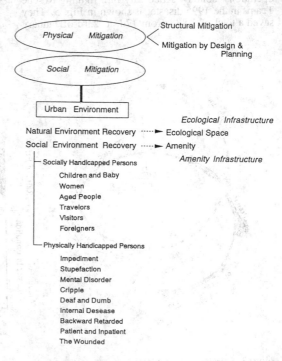

Fig. 6 Mitigation and its classification

5 DISASTER LESSONS

There are many lessons to be learned from the Great
Hanshin-Awaji earthquake disaster
in relation to emergency management:

1) Reinforcement of old buildings and infrastructures: As Japan has experienced many
earthquake disasters, the seismic code has been
revised The Great Hanshin-Awaji disaster showed
that buildings and infrastructures designed under the
new code which was issued in 1981 are mostly safe.
During the 1970s the economy developed and public
investments were many such as construction of the
Shinkansen railway, Meishin Expressway and urban
elevated highways as well as downtown high rise
office building in big cities. The 1968 Tokachi-Oki
and the 1978 Miyagiken-Oki earthquake disasters
came subsequent to the changes in building seismic
code, but construction management was not so
concrete and systematic at that time.

2) Revision of the Disaster Countermeasure Act:
This act was made law in 1961, after the Ise Bay
typhoon in which 5,101 people were killed. At that
time our country was very poor so that restoration of
original form of infrastructures before disaster was
fundamental policy of our government. Disaster
investment which respond to the changes of disaster
characteristics in accompany with the changes of
social environment has no financial support from
our government, but fortunately we have not major
disasters in our big cities for more than 30 years.
During these years, there has been large scale
urbanization, and many people have moved from
rural districts. Disaster investment, however, has
not been proportional to the increase in population.

3) Expensive land costs stop public works within
the inner city: During the bubble economics of late
1980s through early 1990s in our country, land costs
increased year by year. Every bank lent much money
to enterprises, land owners, and individuals. During
that stage, it was very difficult to buy land for
infrastructure construction or redevelopment of
urban area. No redundancy or fail-safe systems were
adopted. The explosion of urban area was so large.
The total balance of urban activity and life have never
discussed from the view point of macroscope.

4) Disaster reduction or mitigation must be adopted. : In Japan, no level of government has been
accustomed to providing disaster management.
Traditionally, importance has been put on risk
management before disasters, but crisis management
after disaster is equally important. For examples, the
logistics of providing materials, workers and
communications just after disaster is extremely
important, but in Kobe City there was no food,
water, or blankets stockpiled , nor any in Hyogo
Prefecture. I propose that reconstruction planning
has to be prepared before a disaster occurs, because
it takes a very long time and because accurate
damage estimation before disaster is important.

5) Emergency management should be based on
philosophy: To have a good urban environment,
social mitigation is very important, social mitigation
being the recovery of the urban environment lost
due to Japan's rapid industrialization during the
1970s and 1980s. Previously public works had been
kept in balance with such urban functions as
economics and our life style, but during the 1990s
the total urban system has not always been well
balanced with urban life. The engineering and
technical aspects of disaster measures are often
discussed without the holistic and social significance
of the disaster-related subjects. Without clear
understanding as to how our society values safety
and assurance, it will be impossible to realize good
urban environment. The philosophy of disaster
management is very important.

6) Management of information is the key to
disas-
ter reduction: In catastrophic disasters, both the
natural (physical processes of the generation and
enlargement of damage) as well as social (search
and rescue, psychological care for post traumatic
stress disorder, volunteers) factors are important.
Information systems harmonize them at the time of a
disaster. As yet there is no practical GIS (Geographical Information Systems), but the development of
such systems will help to reduce human and property
damage.

6 CONCLUSIONS

Urban disasters are one of environmental problems
which include global environmental problems.
Construction of infrastructures has supported rapid
industrialization, but by only hard countermeasures,
it is impossible to reduce human and property
damage. Soft countermeasures should be included
with disaster information systems. Post-disaster
crisis management is also essential. Especially,
social mitigation defined here play a important role to
get good urban environment.

Structural Safety and Reliability, Shiraishi, Shinozuka & Wen (eds) © 1998 Balkema, Rotterdam, ISBN 90 5410 978 5

Application of virtual reality to human evacuation behavior

Kimiro Meguro – *International Center for Disaster-Mitigation Engineering, Institute of Industrial Science, The University of Tokyo, Japan*

Yasunori Haga – *Tokyo Gas Co., Ltd, Japan*

Fumio Yamazaki – *Institute of Industrial Science, The University of Tokyo, Japan*

Tsuneo Katayama – *National Research Institute for Earth Science and Disaster Prevention, Science and Technology Agency*

ABSTRACT: A simulator using virtual reality (VR) is developed as a new tool to study human evacuation behavior. The system is then applied to study evacuation from a maze. Comparing the results of experiments using the real maze and VR maze, both of which have the same structure, applicability and potential of VR for evacuation behavior are examined. Although there are problems to be solved, it is found that evacuation behavior can be simulated by the VR system, and the training using VR helps smooth evacuation from the maze. Considering the issues related to education of disaster-prevention and disaster-fighting drills, such as human mannerism, decrease of participants and their low volition, and safety of the drill, the VR simulator developed here has high potential and can be a useful tool for disaster mitigation. This simulator can also be applied to study the safety of the structures in the planning and design stages as well as existing ones from the view point of human evacuation.

1 INTRODUCTION

Conventionally, three major ways have been used to understand human behavior; i) investigation of real accidents; ii) experiments using subjects; and iii) computer simulation. By the first method (Morita K. 1973, Osada K. 1980), we can obtain real data during accidents which is very important and significantly different from other two ways. However, the amount of data obtained from such situations is inadequate and it is practically impossible to get the data of the people who were killed during the accidents. Thus, sufficient analyses cannot be carried out based on only the data obtained by the first method. With the second way (Watabe, Y. 1982, Hokugo, A. 1985, Funahashi, K. 1991), because of the safety issues of the subjects, it is difficult to simulate the circumstances in actual disaster situations making it hard to obtain the data under such situations. It is also difficult to carry out the experiment when the objective space is very large or the number of subjects are numerous. The improvement of computer systems has made the third approach more attractive because the application potential has improved greatly during recent years (Ozaki, S. and Matsushita, S. 1992). However, there are many assumptions which define the model and/or estimating of parameters for the simulation model. Consequently, individual personal characteristics of users and detailed information relating to the objective space can not be taken into consideration.

Recently, the improvement of 3-dimensional (3-D) computer graphics, interactive-man-machine interface, and telepresense has caused virtual reality (VR) in which people can feel artificial and virtual worlds as a real world, to attract more interest (Tachi, S. et al. 1991, Yanagida, Y. and Tachi, S. 1993).

Under these situations, we have studied human behavior by both experimental and numerical methods to develop a new integrated model which can supplement the weak points of every method and combine their strong points (Yokoyama, H. et al. 1994, Meguro, K. et al. 1995). A new simulator using virtual reality (VR) technology which is introduced in this paper is one possible example.

The proposed approach is a combined model of the second and third ways, namely, it has a high potential to obtain personal characteristics in disaster and high applicability for disaster-education and disaster-fighting drills. In this paper, following the flow shown in Figure 1, we discuss the reality and reliability of VR simulator and its training effects by comparing the results of evacuation experiment using real and VR mazes both of which have the same scale and structure. And from these results, we

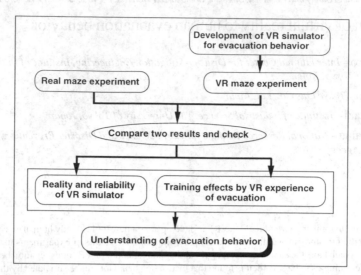

Figure 1 Flow of analysis

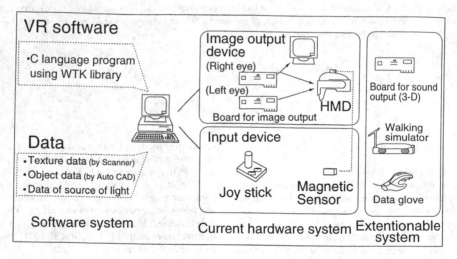

Figure 2 Components of VR system

analyze the human evacuation behavior characteristics from the maze.

2 VR EVACUATION SIMULATOR

The VR evacuation system used in this study is illustrated in Figure 2. We used DOS/V personal computer with image handling board and World Tool Kit (WTK) by W. Industry Co. Ltd. as a tool of VR development. WTK is a C language library composed of about 400 function commands. The VR program was created by selecting the required proper commands from WTK and compiling them using C language. Walls and doors in the VR maze were developed by an Auto-CAD system and some efforts such that photo image scanned were pasted, were

performed to raise the reality.

One joystick and a magnetic sensor, set on head mounted display (HMD) which monitors the movement of the head of the subject, are used as the image input devices. HMD is used as the image output device. HMD is the device which provides the subject with 3-dimensional moving images by providing sight angle differences to the image of both eyes. The monitoring data of the movement of the subject's head by a magnetic sensor set on HMD is used to perform coordinate transformation. Shade handling is performed and the image which agrees to the movement of the head is projected to the HMD screens (Figure 2).

The VR system introduced here was developed as the first step of the study for the purpose of simulating sight

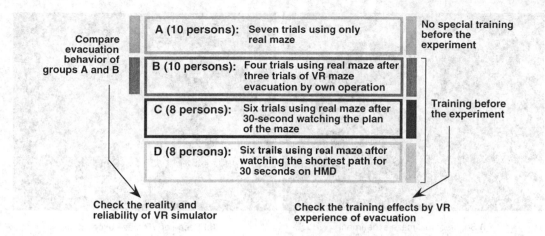

Compare evacuation behavior of groups A and B	A (10 persons):	Seven trials using only real maze	No special training before the experiment
	B (10 persons):	Four trials using real maze after three trials of VR maze evacuation by own operation	
	C (8 persons):	Six trials using real maze after 30-second watching the plan of the maze	Training before the experiment
	D (8 persons):	Six trails using real maze after watching the shortest path for 30 seconds on HMD	

Check the reality and reliability of VR simulator

Check the training effects by VR experience of evacuation

Figure 3 Experiment groups

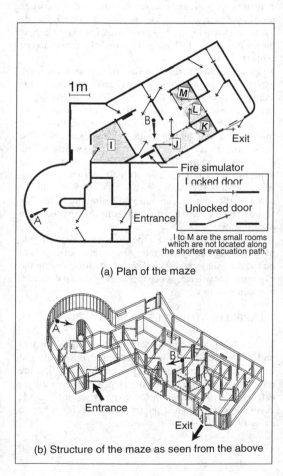

1m

Exit

Fire simulator

Locked door

Unlocked door

Entrance

I to M are the small rooms which are not located along the shortest evacuation path.

(a) Plan of the maze

Entrance

Exit

(b) Structure of the maze as seen from the above

Figure 4 The maze use for study

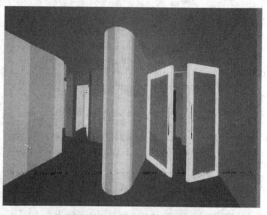

(a) VR scene from the view point of A

(b) VR scene from the view point of B (Simulated fire can be seen the right)

Figure 5 Scene inside VR maze

(a) Scene of real maze experiment   (b) Scene of VR maze experiment

Figure 6 Scene of real and VR maze experiment

which is thought to be the most important factor during evacuation of the people who are not physically handicapped.

With real evacuation behavior, of course, additional senses such as hearing, touch and smell, etc., are important, and they should be taken into account for more detailed evacuation analysis. The system will be extended to consider senses other than sight.

3 EXPERIMENT USING REAL AND VR MAZE

The experiments were carried out during December 19-20, 1994 and on January 9, 1995. To make the characteristics of the group of subjects homogenous, we used 36 male graduate students of Department of Civil Engineering and Architecture from the University of Tokyo as subjects of the maze experiment. We set up our VR simulator system beside the real maze at Ikebukro Disaster-Drill Center of Tokyo Fire Fighting Agency.

We divided 36 subjects into four groups with different conditions (A: 10, B: 10, C: 8, D: 8 persons) as shown in Figure 3, and measured evacuation time and path and compared them by changing conditions. Namely, A is the group in which no training was carried out before the real maze experiment. In group B, subjects had three VR maze evacuation trials by their own operation before the real maze experiment. Subjects in group C watched the plan of the maze structure for 30 seconds before the real maze experiment, and in group D, moving VR images of shortest evacuation path for 30 seconds were provided before the real maze experiment. Including the training before the real maze experiment, every subject of all the groups had seven trials in total. At the seventh trial, all the lights in the maze were switched off when the subjects entered the maze. The subjects were not aware that the light would be extinguished.

Before entering the real maze, we asked each subject to check the locations of entrance and exit and to evacuate along the center of the pass of the maze by walking at the normal speed. Figure 4 shows the structure of the maze used in the study and an image provided by HMD (for one eye) is shown in Figure 5. Rooms I to M in Figure 5 show the small spaces which are not located along the shortest route.

Figure 6 shows the snap shot of real and VR maze experiment. Because there is a large difference among the subjects in operational technique of VR simulator, we proposed two simple mazes and every subject was instructed by repeating evacuations using these two mazes. This training using simple mazes was completed before the subjects started the VR maze experiment with the same structure shown in Figure 4. By using the experimental trials for operational instruction before implementing the main experiments, we were able to examine the subjects' operational technique of the VR simulator and their learning capacity before the main experiment.

After finishing all the experimental trials, a simple questionnaire survey and interviews were carried out to understand subjects' psychological situation during the experiment which can not be captured by digital data such as evacuation time.

4 EXPERIMENT RESULTS AND CONSIDERATION

The results of the experiments by both real and VR mazes and responses from the questionnaire survey and interview are compared. Based on these results, the reliability of VR simulation developed, and the training effects of virtual evacuation experience by the VR simulator were examined and the characteristics of human evacuation behavior is discussed.

4.1 Training effects of virtual experience provided by VR simulator

Figures 7 and 8 show the average evacuation time and walking velocity of each trial. From these figures, it can

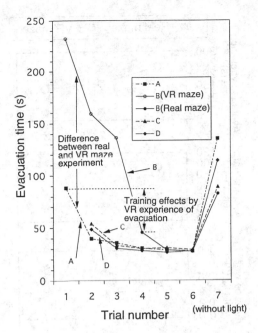

Figure 7 Average evacuation time of each group

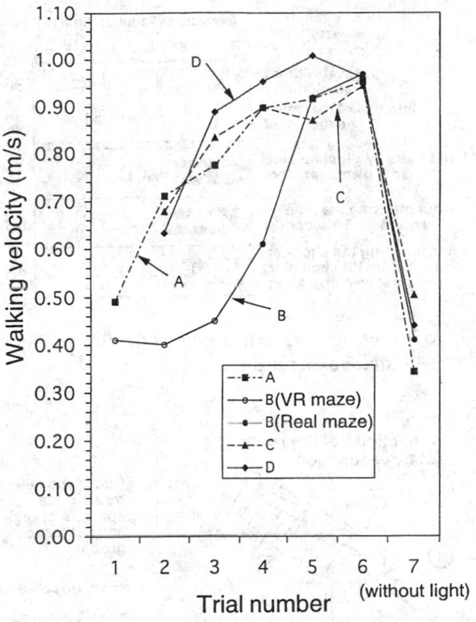

Figure 8 Average walking velocity of each group

be noted that with repeating trials evacuation time tends to be shorter and walking velocity becomes higher. Also, subjects who had some experience before the real maze experiment (2nd trial of group A, the first real maze trial of groups B, C and D) could evacuate from the maze in shorter time and with a faster velocity as compared with the first trial of group A who had no experience beforehand.

The first trial of group A had an average evacuation time of 88 seconds. Other groups including the second trial of group A, are shorter by 34 to 48 seconds (Figure 9). A similar trend can be seen from evacuation path length. The path of the first trial of group A was 41.8 m while the results of the others were 27.2 m (2nd of A), 26.8 m (B), 33.1 m (C) and 27.7 m (D). Therefore, to examine whether virtual experience by the VR simulator has training effects for the real maze evacuation behavior, we applied a statistical method, in which average evacuation time vs. number of trials is assumed to obey the t-type distribution. It was proved that subjects trained with VR could evacuate faster than those subjects who had no training beforehand.

Because group B's first trial had an evacuation time similar to the second trial of real maze experiment of group A, it can be noted that training effects of three trials of the VR experience correspond to that from one real experience in case of the maze used here. And since group D (who watched moving VR images of shortest path) was able to evacuate faster than group C, who studied the plan of maze structure, we can conclude that virtual experience by moving VR images has high training effects for real maze evacuation. Before the experiment, we thought that group C could evacuate most smoothly and the training effects of

watching plan was the best among B to D. However, the average evacuation time of group C is longer than those of groups B and D, and deviation of group C was large. From the questionnaire survey and interviews, we found that this result came from large ability difference of imaging 3-D space from 2-D plan. Considering the conditions that the subjects participated in this experiment were graduate students of departments of civil engineering or architecture, who took the courses of geometry and drawing, their capacity of imaging 3-D space from 2-D plan is certainly much higher than ordinary people. From this result, evacuation guidance for ordinary people should be carried out by moving image showing the route to exit in addition to the conventional 2-D plan illustrating the evacuation route. For example, hotels depict evacuation route on a 2-D plan, however, an alternative to show the evacuation route from the room to exit including surrounding 3-D circumstance by moving images on TV.

4.2 *Reality and reliability of VR simulator*

To examine the reality and reliability of the VR simulator developed, we investigated the route selection at three junctions in the maze of the subjects in the first trial using real maze experiment (Figure 10). At the first junction, subjects of both real and VR maze group tend to go straight when the right side is close to the exit. At the other two junctions, the same tendency can be observed. Based on these results, we can say that the VR simulator developed here can simulate the route selection in evacuation behavior qualitatively.

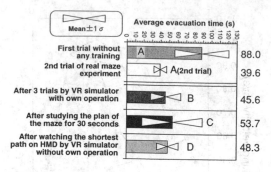

Figure 9 Average evacuation time of the first trial of real maze experiment

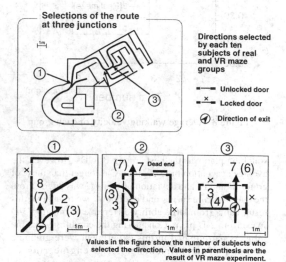

Figure 10 Comparison of route selection between real and VR maze experiment

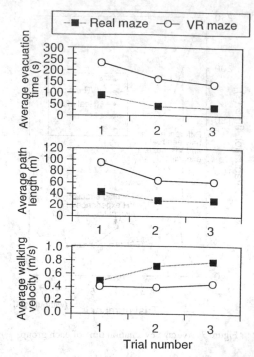

Figure 11 Comparison of average evacuation time, path length and walking velocity between real and VR maze experiment

4.3 Evacuation behavior in disaster

Next, we compared the experimental results (evacuation time, path and velocity) of groups A and B (Figure 11). From the figure, average evacuation time, path length and velocity of the VR maze experiment are respectively about 2 to 3 times, 1.5 to 2.5 times and 0.7 to 0.8 times as much as that of real maze experiment. As the trial number increase, evacuation time and path length shorten becoming more like the real experiment while the evacuation velocity does not have as good of a match. Although the difference at the first trial is small compared to the second and third trials, the velocity increases in the real maze experiment, but the increasing ratio of the VR maze experiment is small. Possible reasons for these differences are maximum velocity adopted in the experiment, operational difficulty of the VR simulator and the view angle of HMD, etc.

From Figures 7 and 8, we can conclude that every subject mastered the shortest route and that he could evacuate very smoothly due to training trials. At the seventh trial without light, however, it took several times longer time for evacuation. Therefore, we plot the relation between the evacuation time without light and the maximum evacuation time among the six trials (Figure 12). Figure 13 shows the relation between the number of small rooms (Nr=0-5) which the subject entered during experiments. We can assume that the subject whose maximum evacuation time or Nr is large was wandering in the maze to find the exit. During his search for the exit, he was able to learn the whole structure of the maze as well as the shortest path. This experience helps him to evacuate smoothly under the condition of no light. While the subject whose maximum evacuation time is short or Nr is small, could evacuate very smoothly with light, and it means that those subjects could not learn the whole structure of the maze excluding the shortest route as well. From the interview, we learned that the latter group was confused and lost direction under the condition of no light. Considering the purpose of evacuation drills, that is disaster mitigation, the important factor is not the number of trials, however, its content is much more important. We know that there is strict limitation of evacuation drills due to the safety issue of the subject, but this result pointed out

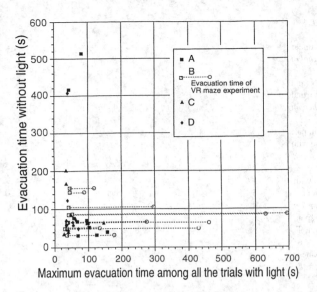

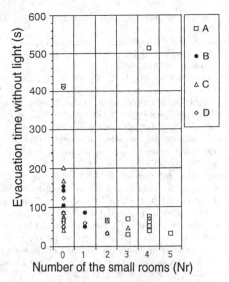

Figure 13 Relation between evacuation time without light and maximum evacuation time with light

Figure 14 Relation between evacuation time without light and the number of the small rooms which are not located along the shortest path length and walking velocity between real and VR maze experiment

that it is very important to carry out the drill based on the situations and conditions in case of disaster. We should recognize that we may face similar situations in our disaster drills or in daily life. For example, an evacuation drill for studying only the shortest path, routine use of a subway and the underground facilities, etc. may create trouble for users in disaster.

5 CONCLUSIONS

We can conclude that the urban space and the structure are safe only when the safety of the people using the facility is secured in both the usual and unusual use. In this paper, to study the human behavior which is indispensable for the above issue, we developed the virtual reality evacuation simulator and examine its usefulness and potential.

Evacuation experiment using real and VR maze both of which have the same structure were performed and the results were compared. From this study, it was recognized that the virtual experience obtained by the VR simulator can help people evacuate from the real maze. Although there are issues which need to be resolved such as defining up of maximum velocity and operational problems, it was proved that the VR simulator has applicability to human evacuation behavior.

The potentials of the VR simulator for disaster education or disaster fighting drill is very high because it is impossible for us to have experience of disaster in daily life and once a disaster occurs we will face a terrifying and risky situation. The experiment using VR simulator is very useful since it can be, also, a tool to obtain the

individual human characteristics which are very difficult to get and very important for computer simulation. Considering the issues related to education of disaster-prevention and disaster-fighting drills, such as human mannerisms, the decrease of participants and their low volition, and the safety of the drill, training using the VR simulator will become more popular. Moreover, the proposed model can be applied to the space and structure in the planning and design stages as well as to existing ones from the view point of human evacuation.

REFERENCES

Funahashi, K. 1991. Experimental study on route selection and understanding the space inside of the structure. *Journal of architecture, planning and environmental engineering, Architecture Institute of Japan (AIJ)*, 429: pp. 61-72.

Hokugo, A. 1985. An experimental study on evacuation ability in smoke (in Japanese with English abstract). *Journal of architecture, planning and environmental engineering, AIJ*, 353: 32-38.

Meguro, K., Haga, Y., Yamazaki, F. and Katayama, T. 1995. Comparison of evacuation behavior using a real and virtual reality mazes (in Japanese). *Proc. of 23rd Conference on earthquake engineering*: 719-722.

Morita, K. 1973. Record of 53 persons in the Playtown of Osaka Sen-nichi Department Store in fire (in Japanese). *Journal of Kasai (fires)*, 23-1: 28-34.

Okazaki, S. and Matsuhita, S. 1992. Model for walking simulation and evaluation of safety for a large group of people (in Japanese with English abstract). *Journal of architecture, planning and environmental engineering, AIJ,* 436: 49-58.

Osada, K. 1980. Report on the gas explosion accident in under ground facility, Jordan Town of Shizuoka Station. *Journal of Kasai (fires),* 30-6: 3-8.

Tachi, S., Arai, H., Maeda, T., Oyama, E., Tsunemoto, N. and Inoue, Y. 1991. Tele-existence in Real World and Virtual World. *Proceedings of the fifth International Conference on Advanced Robotics ('91 ICAR):* 193-198. Pisa, Italy.

Watabe, Y. 1982. Report on human evacuation experiment, part 1, Memory of the route selection of subjects (in Japanese with English abstract). *Journal of architecture, planning and environmental engineering, AIJ,* 322: 157-161.

Yanagida, Y. and Tachi, S. 1993. Virtual Reality System with Coherent Kinesthetic and Visual Sensation of Presence. *Proceedings of the 2nd International Conference on Advanced Mechatronics (ICAM '93):* 98-103. Tokyo, Japan.

Yokoyama, H., Meguro, K., Yamazaki, F. and Katayama, T. 1994. Computer simulation model for the analysis of evacuation in populous underground facilities (in Japanese with English abstract). *Proc. of 9th Japan Earthquake Engineering Symposium:* 2353-2358.

Structural Safety and Reliability, Shiraishi, Shinozuka & Wen (eds) © 1998 Balkema, Rotterdam, ISBN 90 5410 978 5

Seismic vulnerability assessment of building structures using microtremor measurements

Takuji Hamamoto, Jiadong Yu & Hiromichi Mori
Department of Architecture, Musashi Institute of Technology, Tokyo, Japan

ABSTRACT: A simplified method is presented to evaluate the seismic vulnerability of building structures using microtremor measurements. The seismic vulnerability is evaluated by a stochastic-fuzzy integrated method. Microtremor measurements are used to identity the fundamental periods and damping ratios of building structures and the underlying soil. Maximum inter-story drift is predicted by a random vibration theory, taking into account the inelastic response and variability of model parameters. Damage states are quantified in terms of a damage measure by using membership functions in a fuzzy set theory. Past seismic damage data are used to derive two earthquake damage functions which relate the maximum inter-story drift to the damage measure for off-shore and in-land earthquakes, respectively. To show the applicability of the method, future damage states of existing reinforced concrete buildings are predicted against assumed off-shore and in-land earthquakes at a specific area.

1 INTRODUCTION

Many severe earthquakes have attacked major cities in Japan so far. Among them, Hyougoken-nanbu earthquake (M=7.2, 1995) caused unprecedented damage on Kobe. More than 5,500 people were killed and a number of building structures suffered severe damage or collapse. Urban function had been inactivated for a long time due to destruction of infrastructures such as transportation and lifeline systems. To prevent and mitigate such a seismic disaster, it is useful and helpful to assess the seismic vulnerability of building structures at a specific area in advance.

A variety of seismic vulnerability assessments have been proposed, *ex.*, by Bouhafs(1986) and Scawthorn *et al.*(1981). In these studies, seismic damage is evaluated by using past damage data as well as empirical and theoretical models deterministically or probabilistically. Although it is easy to calculate structural response, it is not easy to evaluate structural damage quantatively. Yao(1985) has presented the way of evaluating the ambiguous damage state by a fuzzy set theory. It is well known that earthquake response and damage depend heavily on dynamic properties of structures and the underlying soil. Kanai and Tanaka(1954) have used microtremor measurements to estimate the predominant period of soil. Microtremor

measurements have been also applied to identify dynamic properties of different types of building structures. These properties can be used to construct the transfer functions of structures and soil. The reason why microtremor measurements are usefull is mainly due to the daily acquisition of measurement data, the easy installation of measurement device and the low cost compared to artificial excitations such as vibration generator and explosion tests. However, there are some problems to use microtremor measurements in the seismic vulnerability assessment. One of the problems is the translation from dynamic characteristics of structures and soil under microtremor to those under strong motion. Another problem is the possibility of reliable and accurate microtremor measurements in the noisy urban environments.

In this study, a simplified seismic vulnerability assessment of building structures is proposed by using microtremor measurements of both structures and soil. The vulnerability assessment is formulated by a stochastic-fuzzy integrated method. The stochastic responses are calculated by a stationary random vibration theory, taking account of structural and soil nonlinearities as well as statistical uncertainties. Seismic damage states are predicted by using earthquake damage functions which are derived for off-shore and in-land earthquakes by a fuzzy set theory. Application examples are presented

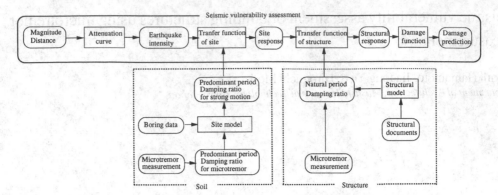

Fig.1 Seismic vulnerability assessment using microtremor measurements

to show the applicability of the proposed method.

2 FRAMEWORK OF METHODOLOGY

The overall framework for evaluating the seismic vulnerability of building structures using microtremor measurements is shown in Fig.1. Dynamic properties of buildings and soil are characterized by their predominant periods and damping ratios. These parameters are estimated by microtremor measurements and prior information such as soil boring data and structural documents. Soil proprieties under microtremor are translated to those under strong motion because of their strong strain dependent nature.

A source-path-site-structure system is considered in the seismic vulnerability assessment. Assuming the magnitude and fault distance of an off-shore or in-land earthquake, the earthquake intensity at bed rock is determined by an attenuation curve. Site response is calculated by multiplying the earthquake intensity by the site transfer function estimated by microtremor measurements. Structural response is calculated by multiplying the site response by the structural transfer function estimated by microtremor measurements, taking account of the inelastic response by an equivalent energy concept. Future seismic damage states of building structures are predicted by using earthquake damage functions which will be derived later for off-shore and in-land earthquakes, respectively.

3 PARAMETER ESTIMATION

An inference system is developed to estimate dynamic parameters in the transfer functions of buildings and the underlying soil by using

microtremor measurements as well as prior information as shown in Fig.2. Microtremor measurement is a powerful tool to estimate dynamic parameters of buildings and soil in an inductive way. Measurement data are recorded by locating a measurement device on different places in buildings and on ground. Parameter estimation is carried out by a random decrement method in the time domain and a spectral analysis in the frequency domain. An estimation in the time domain is usually more accurate than in the frequency domain, although the frequency domain technique is more tractable than the time domain technique. Measurement data are processed using different filtering and smoothing. Consequently, estimated parameters have random uncertainties.

Generally speaking, it is not an easy task to obtain the reliable and accurate results of microtremor measurements, because the meaningful information is easily disturbed by different sources of noise in urban areas. To overcome this problem, prior information such as structural documents and soil boring data are used to evaluate dynamic parameters of structures and soil in a deductive way through existing empirical equations and simplified theoretical models, taking into account statistical variability. In Fig.2, Inference 1 and 2 are used to update and improve each result of microtremor measurements and prior information, respectively, whereas Inference 3 is used to integrate both results of microtremor measurements and prior information. The final outputs are used as random parameters in the transfer functions of buildings and soil, respectively.

4 STOCHASTIC RESPONSES

The Fukushima-Tanaka (1991) attenuation equation

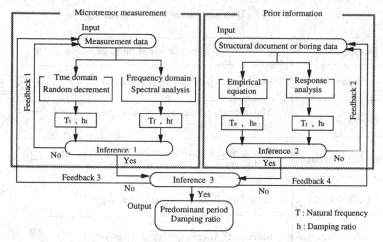

Fig. 2 Estimation of predominant periods and damping ratios

is used to relate the earthquake magnitude and fault distance of an off-shore or in-land earthquake to the earthquake intensity at a site. The maximum acceleration is given by

$$\log S_A = 0.51M - \log\left(X + 0.006 \cdot 10^{0.51M}\right)$$
$$-0.0034X + 0.59 , \qquad (1)$$

where S_A is the maximum acceleration, M is the earthquake magnitude and X is the fault distance. Figure 3 shows the attenuation curves together with recorded data on Hyogoken-nanbu (1995) and Miyagiken-oki (1978) earthquakes. The variability in attenuation curves is disregarded in this study. The spectral intensity G_0 at bed rock can be related to the maximum acceleration S_A through Kanai-Tajimi power spectral density function (Tajimi, 1960) as

$$G_0 = \frac{4h_G(S_A/g_G)^2}{\pi\omega_G(1+4h_G^2)} \qquad (2)$$

where ω_G and h_G are the circular frequency and damping ratio of soil, respectively, and g_G is the peak

factor. The mean and standard deviation of g_G are respectively given by

$$m_G = \sqrt{2\ln v_0^+ t_0} + \frac{0.557}{\sqrt{2\ln v_0^+ t_0}} ,$$

$$\sigma_G = \frac{\pi}{6\sqrt{2\ln v_0^+ t_0}} , \qquad (3)$$

where t_0 is the earthquake duration and v_0^+ is the zero-upcrossing rate approximated by $f_G = \omega_G/2\pi$.

Using dynamic parameters estimated by microtremor measurements, the transfer function of the underlying soil are given by

$$H_G(\omega) = \frac{2ih_G\omega_G\omega + \omega_G^2}{-\omega^2 + 2ih_G\omega_G\omega + \omega_G^2} , \qquad (4)$$

where ω_G and h_G are translated from those with small strains to those with large strains by a computer program SHAKE (Shnabel et al., 1972).

A building structure is idealized as a one-degree-of-

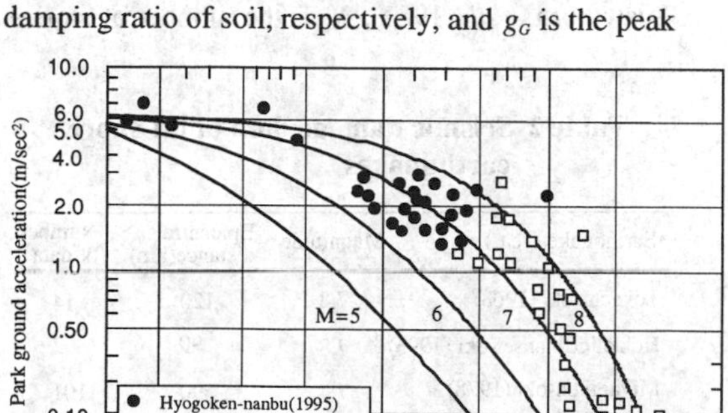

Park ground acceleration(m/sec²)

M=5   6   7   8

● Hyogoken-nanbu(1995)
□ Miyagiken-oki(1978)

Fault distance X(km)

Fig.3 Attenuation curves

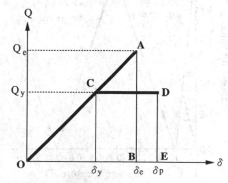

Fig.4 Relationship between elastic and inelastic responses

1613

Table 1 Damage states of RC buildings

Damage state	Description of damage	
Collapse	Building partially or totally collapsed	
Severe damage	Major structural damage; possibly total non-structural damage	
Moderate damage	Widespread, extensive non-structural damage; readily repairable structural damage	
Light damage	Minor, localized non-structural damage	
No damage	No or insignificant structural damage	

freedom system. The transfer function of the building is given by

$$H_S(\omega) = \frac{1}{-\omega^2 + 2ih_S\omega_S\omega + \omega_S^2} , \qquad (5)$$

where ω_S and h_S are the circular frequency and damping ratio of the building, respectively. Structural parameters estimated by microtremor measurements are directly used to construct the transfer function of the building.

If buildings behave elastically, the maximum displacement at the top of building, δ_e, can be calculated as

$$\delta_e = g_S\sqrt{G_0\int_0^\infty |H_G(\omega)H_S(\omega)|^2 d\omega} , \qquad (6)$$

where g_S is the peak factor. The mean and standard

deviation of g_S are given by Eq.(3) where v_0^+ is approximated by $f_S = \omega_S / 2\pi$. Buildings are damaged if structural response goes into the inelastic range, whereas they are not damaged if structural response remains within the elastic range. Assuming the inter-story drift at a yield point as $\Delta_y = 0.0044$ (Bouhafs, 1986), the linear response δ_e may be translated to the nonlinear response δ_p by using an equivalent energy concept ($\triangle$ AOB= $\square$ COED) as shown in Fig. 4. The inter-story drift of the 1st story is usually the largest for low-to-middle-rise reinforced concrete buildings. The inter-story displacement δ_1 of the 1st story may be evaluated by

$$\delta_1 = \left[\frac{1}{N}\right]^B \delta_P , \qquad (7)$$

where B is the coefficient which represents the shape of displacement distribution (B is selected as 0.5; Scawthorn et al., 1981), N is the number of stories.

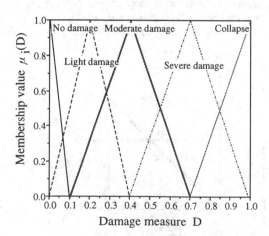

Fig. 5 Membership functions of damage state

Table 2 Seismic damage data of off-shore earthquakes

Earthquake (year)	Magnitude	Epicentral distance(km)	Number of data
Tokachi-oki (1968)	7.8	120	14
Hokkaido-nansei-oki (1993)	7.8	90	2
Miyagiken-oki (1978)	7.4	90	101
Uraga-oki (1982)	7.1	70	6
Kushiro-oki (1993)	7.8	85	3

Total 126

Table 3 Structural response and damage for off-shore earthquakes

| Damage state | Mean | | COV |
	Inter-story drift ($\triangle$)	Ductility ratio (μ)	
Collapse	0.0133	3.02	0.17
Severe damage	0.0120	2.73	0.20
Moderate damage	0.0095	2.16	0.24
Light damage	0.0060	1.36	0.20
No damage	0.0037	0.84	0.23

Table 4 Structural response and damage for in-land earthquakes

| Damage state | Mean | | COV |
	Inter-story drift ($\triangle$)	Ductility ratio (μ)	
Collapse	0.0110	2.50	0.17
Severe damage	0.0092	2.09	0.20
Moderate damage	0.0076	1.73	0.22
Light damage	0.0051	1.16	0.20
No damage	0.0031	0.71	0.21

The inter-story drift Δ_1 of the 1st story is calculated by

$$\Delta_1 = \delta_1 / H_1, \tag{8}$$

where H_1 is the height of the 1st story. Δ is the function of N, B, H_1, ω_G, h_G, ω_S, h_S, g_G, g_S and Δ_y. Among them, N, B, H_1 and Δ_y are deterministic variables and ω_G, h_G, ω_S, h_S, g_G and g_S are random variables in this study. The means and coefficients of variation of Δ_1 are calculated to evaluate parameter uncertainties.

5 FUZZY DAMAGE FUNCTION

Damage states of low-to-middle-rise reinforced concrete buildings are shown in Table 1. Damage states are classified into 5 stages: no damage, light damage, moderate damage, severe damage and collapse. The damage states are subjectively judged according to the most probable damage description. A damage measure D ($0 \leq D \leq 1$) is introduced to quantify the damage state. To describe the ambiguity of the definition and boundary of each damage state, membership functions are appropriately established for each damage state as shown in Fig.5. The mean value of each damage state is: 0.05 for no damage, 0.2 for light damage, 0.4 for moderate damage, 0.7 for severe damage and 0.85 for collapse, respectively.

To construct two earthquake damage functions which relate the maximum inter-story drift to the damage measure for off-shore and in-land earthquakes, more than 100 existing damage data of low-to-middle-rise reinforced concrete buildings are

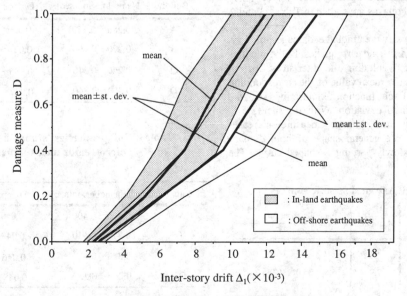

Fig. 6 Earthquake damage functions

1615

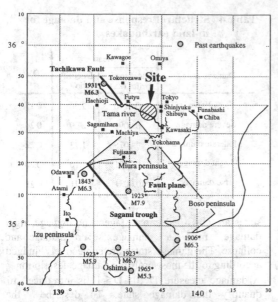

Fig. 7 Building sites and seismic sources

Fig. 8 Building sites and soil condition

used for both types of earthquake, respectively. Most of the damage data for off-shore earthquakes are those of Miyagiken-oki (1978) as shown in Table 2, whereas all of the damage data for in-land earthquakes are those of Hyogoken-nanbu (1995).

Site and structural responses are predicted by microtremor measurements. Structural damage is evaluated by real seismic damage data. For each damage state, the means and coefficients of variation of inter-story drift and ductility ratio for off-shore and in-land earthquakes are shown in Tables 3 and 4, respectively.

Figure 6 shows two earthquake damage functions for off-shore and in-land earthquakes. Both functions are constructed by plotting the inter-story drift of each building at the mean value of the corresponding damage state. Each function is described by the mean and standard deviation. With the increase of inter-story drift, the damage measure increases monotonically. The general shape of both damage functions is a slowly varying S-shaped curve. The

variability of damage functions is large for $D \geqq 0.4$. If the damage measure is the same value, the mean of the inter-story drift for in-land earthquakes is always less than that for off-shore earthquakes.

Table 6 Structural properties estimated by microtremor measurements

Building	Natural period(sec)	Damping ratio
A	0.280~0.350	0.030~0.035
B	0.270~0.290	0.032~0.040
C	0.260~0.310	0.035~0.045
D	0.300~0.340	0.037~0.044

Table 7 Soil properties estimated by microtremor measurements

Site	Predominant period(sec)	Damping ratio
A	0.360~0.400	0.049~0.053
B	0.370~0.410	0.049~0.054
C	0.340~0.400	0.046~0.052
D	0.290~0.350	0.048~0.054

Table 5 Assumed seismic sources

Seismic source	Magnitude	Fault distance(km)			
		A	B	C	D
Tachikawa fault	7.2	17.0	17.5	18.0	19.0
Sagami trough	7.9	35.5	35.0	36.0	34.5

Thus, the damage increases more rapidly with the inter-story drift for in-land earthquakes than for off-shore earthquakes. The difference between two damage functions may be related to large vertical ground motion as well as impulsive high-frequency nature of in-land earthquakes.

6 APPLICATION EXAMPLES

To show the applicability of the method, the future seismic damage of low-to-middle-rise reinforced concrete buildings which are located at the western part of Tokyo is predicted for assumed off-shore and in-land earthquakes. Figure 7 shows building sites and the location of assumed seismic faults. The rupture of Sagami trough is presumed for an off-shore earthquake, whereas the rapture of Tachikawa fault for an in-land earthquake. The magnitudes and fault distances of both earthquakes are shown in Table 5.

The seismic vulnerability assessment is performed

Table 8 Random parameters in structural transfer function

Building	Natural period		Damping ratio	
	Mean(sec)	COV	Mean	COV
A	0.32	0.14	0.032	0.14
B	0.28	0.05	0.035	0.12
C	0.29	0.07	0.040	0.17
D	0.32	0.09	0.040	0.13

Table 9 Random parameters in soil transfer function for off-shore and in-land earthquakes

Site	Off-shore earthquake				In-land earthquake			
	Predominant period		Damping ratio		Predominant period		Damping ratio	
	Mean(sec)	COV	Mean	COV	Mean(sec)	COV	Mean	COV
A	1.37	0.16	0.24	0.32	1.38	0.18	0.25	0.30
B	1.42	0.15	0.28	0.31	1.44	0.14	0.31	0.30
C	1.43	0.17	0.26	0.35	1.44	0.16	0.26	0.34
D	1.25	0.16	0.33	0.29	1.24	0.19	0.32	0.27

Table 10 Seismic damage prediction for different earthquake intensities

Earthquake	Building A				Building B			
	S_A (m/sec^2)	Δ ($\times 10^{-3}$) Mean (COV)	Damage measure Mean (COV)	Damage state	S_A (m/sec^2)	Δ ($\times 10^{-3}$) Mean (COV)	Damage measure Mean (COV)	Damage state
Off-shore	4.11	6.87 (0.26)	0.25 (0.20)	Light damage	4.11	5.71 (0.23)	0.18 (0.16)	Light damage
In-land	4.28	7.26(0.23)	0.41(0.42)	Moderate damage	4.28	6.06 (0.27)	0.28 (0.26)	Light damage

Earthquake	Building C				Building D			
	S_A (m/sec^2)	Δ ($\times 10^{-3}$) Mean (COV)	Damage measure Mean (COV)	Damage state	S_A (m/sec^2)	Δ ($\times 10^{-3}$) Mean (COV)	Damage measure Mean (COV)	Damage state
Off-shore	4.04	5.81 (0.25)	0.19 (0.19)	Light damage	4.18	7.41 (0.26)	0.30 (0.22)	Moderate damage
In-land	4.15	6.05 (0.27)	0.28 (0.26)	Light damage	4.04	7.38 (0.27)	0.42 (0.45)	Moderate damage

for four school buildings. All school buildings are 4 story reinforced concrete structures. Buildings A and B are located on the alluvial deposits of Tama river and Buildings C and D are located on the plateau of Kanto loam as shown in Fig.8. The predominant periods and damping ratios of buildings and the underlying soil are estimated by microtremor measurements as shown in Tables 6 and 7. The estimation range is described by mean value ± standard deviation. The natural periods of Buildings A to C are smaller than the predominant periods of the underlying soil, while the natural period of Building D is in the neighborhood of the predominant period of the underlying soil. The predominant periods at Sites A and B are larger than those at sites C and D.

The predominant period and damping ratio of soil are translated to those for strong ground motion. The means and coefficients of variation of predominant periods and damping ratios of four buildings and the underlying soil are shown in Tables 8 and 9. The predominant periods and damping ratios of soil increase significantly. These random parameters are used in the structural and soil transfer functions, respectively.

Table 10 shows the results of seismic vulnerability assessment of four buildings. The means and coefficients of variation of maximum inter-story drift are calculated. The corresponding damage measures are determined by two earthquake damage functions given by Fig.6. Then, damage states are represented verbaly by selecting the damage state with larger membership value for the damage measure shown in Fig.5. Ground accelerations are close for off-shore and in-land earthquakes at all sites. However, damage states of buildings are different because of the different nature of off-shore and in-land earthquakes. The structural damage of Buildings B and C is relatively small, while Building D suffers the largest damage. The difference in damage states is due to the proximity of structural and soil periods.

7 CONCLUSIONS

A simplified stochastic-fuzzy integrated method is presented for evaluating the seismic vulnerability of existing building structures using microtremor measurements. Two earthquake damage functions which relate maximum inter-story drift to damage measure are derived by using more than 100 damage data for off-shore and in-land earthquakes, respectively. It is found that buildings suffer more severe damage for in-land earthquakes than for off-shore earthquakes if the inter-story drift is the same value. To show the applicability of the method, future damage states of existing reinforced concrete buildings are predicted for assumed off-shore and in-land earthquakes. It is concluded that structural damage depends heavily on earthquake types, off-shore or in-land, as well as soil conditions.

REFERENCES

Architectural Institute of Japan. 1968. Report on damage investigation of the 1968 Tokachi-oki earthquake.

Architectural Institute of Japan. 1979. Report on damage investigation of the 1978 Miyagiken-oki earthquake.

Bouhafs, M. 1986. Evaluation of the seismic performance of buildings: Techniques for rapid assessment of seismic vulnerability, ASCE. 41-66.

Central Research Institute of Electric Power Industry. 1995. Preliminary report on characteristics and damages investigation of the 1995 Hyogoken-nanbu earthquake, Report No. U94042.

Fukushima, Y. Tanaka, T. 1990. A new attenuation relation for peak horizontal acceleration of strong earthquake ground motion in Japan, Bull. Seism. Soc. Amer. 80, 757-783.

Kanai, K., T. Tanaka. 1954. Measurement of the Microtremor I, Bull. Earthq. Res. Inst., 27, 199-209.

Scawthorn, C. et al. 1981. Seismic damage estimation for low-and mid-rise buildings in Japan, Earthq. Eng. Struct. Dyn. Vol.9: 93-115.

Schnabel., P. B., Lysmer, J., Seed, H. B. 1972. SHAKE-A computer program for earthquake response analysis of horizontally layered site, Univ. of California, Berkeley.

Tajimi, H. 1960. Statistical method of determining the maximum response of building structure during an earthquake, Proc. of the 2nd WCEE, Vol.2: 781-798.

Takenaka Corporation. 1995. 1st and 2nd reports on damages investigation of the Hyougoken-nanbu earthquake.

Yao, J. T. P. 1985. Safety and reliability of existing structures, Pitman Pub.

Structural Safety and Reliability, Shiraishi, Shinozuka & Wen (eds) © 1998 Balkema, Rotterdam, ISBN 90 5410 978 5

Evaluation of lifetime risk in reinforced concrete structure subjected to big earthquakes

Motoyuki Suzuki & Kou Ibayashi
Tohoku University, Sendai, Japan

Yoshio Ozaka
Tohoku Gakuin University, Tagajo, Japan

ABSTRACT: The evaluation method of lifetime risk in reinforced concrete structure is proposed. In the earthquake risk analysis, historical earthquake data are efficiently taken into account. A new damage index is defined in which accumulative damage is taken into consideration for RC member. Then new evaluation method of lifetime risk in RC member is proposed on the basis of damage probabililty matrix. As a result, it is clarified that current seismic design method does not necessarily provide sufficient safety during the lifetime of RC structure.

1 INTRODUCTION

In principle, current seismic design methods consider the effects of earthquakes based on the safety of a structure during a powerful earthquake that is likely to occur once during the lifetime of the structure at the location of the structure, and on its ability to continue to provide the required performance after such an earthquake. But considering the behavior of structures during their lifetimes, there are likely cases where members or a structure reach their ultimate limit state during one powerful earthquake motion and cases where a structure or members reach their ultimate limit state as a consequence of several medium strength earthquakes. In the latter case, it is appropriate to assume that repeated earthquake motions occurring during the lifetime of a structure causes an accumulation of damage to the structure, and that when this damage has reached a certain limit, the structure is in the ultimate state.

So the purpose of this research is to propose a method of evaluating the lifetime risk of reinforced concrete structures. The first step was a seismic risk analysis to find the annual average occurrence probabilities of earthquake motion intensities at an observed location. To do so, a method of effectively using historical earthquake data which were said to be a relatively imprecise was established, and seismic risk curves were calculated for ten principal Japanese cities.

The next step was the definition of a damage index that accounts for load hysteresis as seismic performance measure capable of expressing the accumulation of damage in a reinforced concrete member.

So the results of the seismic risk analysis and the accumulative damage index were used to hypothesize the change from "a certain state" to "new certain state" of the damage to a reinforced concrete structure at an observed location whenever earthquake motion occurs, and a damage probability matrix which expresses the probability of this change is used to evaluate the lifetime risk of the reinforced concrete structure. It is possible to define structural and ground conditions and vary the maximum acceleration of the model seismic waves to find the nature of changes in the state of the damage, and organize these findings in matrix form to find the damage probability matrix.

Fig.1 is a flow-chart of the lifetime risk evaluation method described above.

2 SEISMIC RISK ANALYSIS ACCOUNTING FOR HISTORICAL EARTHQUAKE

2.1 *Earthquake data*

In this research,the authors used the following categorization of usable earthquake data by historical period proposed by Katayama et. al (Katayama 1989).

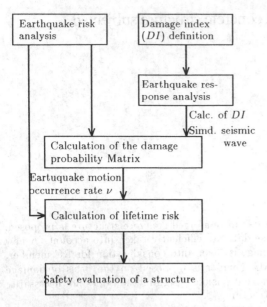

Fig. 1. Flow-chart of the method of evaluating the lifetime risk of a structure

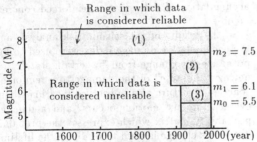

Fig. 2. Historical earthquake data usability categories proposed by Katayama.

$$
\begin{aligned}
5.5 &\leq M < 6.1 \quad \text{Since } 1926 \\
6.1 &\leq M < 7.5 \quad \text{Since } 1885 \\
7.5 &\leq M \qquad\quad\ \text{Since } 1600
\end{aligned} \tag{2.1}
$$

Fig.2 presents a summary of this categorization.

And the magnitudes in the Meteorological Agency documents containing earthquake data from 1885 until March 1988 has been corrected using the method shown below which was proposed by Hattori et. al (Hattori 1977).

$$
\begin{aligned}
M &= M'-0.5 \quad \text{(Data from 1885 until 1895)} \\
M &= M'-0.6 \quad \text{(Data from 1896 until 1915)} \\
M &= M'-0.5 \quad \text{(Data from 1916 until 1925)}
\end{aligned} \tag{2.2}
$$

Where: M :   Magnitude after correction
         M' :   Magnitude before correction

2.2 Calculation of earthquake occurrence probability

In order to calculate earthquake occurrence probability it is first necessary to establish the earthquake region. It was assumed that earthquake activity within each region is uniform. For this analysis, as in reference (Suzuki 1991), the region between north latitude 25 degrees and 50 degrees and between east longitude 125 degrees to 150 degrees was divided into square sections with sides of 0.5 degrees.

The points where earthquake motion strength was calculated were earthquake observation sites at meteorological observation stations in 10 major cities in Japan(See Table 1).

The attenuation formula is the formula for standard ground proposed by Hattori et. al.(Hattori 1977), shown below.

$$
Acc_{\max} = 18.4 \cdot 10^{0.382M} \cdot \Delta^{-0.8} \tag{2.3}
$$

Where, $Acc_{\max}$: Maximum acceleration (gal), M : Magnitude, Δ : Epicentral distance (km).

The following method is used to find the distribution of earthquake motion strength.

1) A certain mesh i is assumed to be the point epicenter, and the epicentral distance Δ from the center of the mesh to the city is calculated.

2) The magnitude M_i is found by solving the attenuation formula for the epicentral distance Δ and the acceleration $Acc_{\max}$.

$$
M_i = g(Acc_{\max}, \Delta) \tag{2.4}
$$

3) The probability of acceleration $Acc_{\max}$ in a certain city $\nu_i(Acc_{\max})$ when an earthquake occurs in mesh i.

4) As shown by the following formula, if the above series of operations are performed for all meshes for a certain acceleration, it is possible to find the occurrence probability of this acceleration $\nu(Acc_{\max})$ for a certain city.

$$
\nu(Acc_{\max}) = \sum_i \nu_i(Acc_{\max}) \tag{2.5}
$$

The results clearly demonstrate that the relationship between annual average occurrence probabilities and an acceleration is approximated by almost straight lines on a both logarithem graph. Hence this straight line is expressed by the following formula.

$$
\log \nu = a - b \log Acc_{\max} \tag{2.6}
$$

Table 1. Values of the parameters a and b of risk curves for major cities

Location	a	b	Location	a	b
Sapporo	4.599	2.992	Kyoto	4.664	2.825
Sendai	4.373	2.650	Osaka	4.157	2.566
Tokyo	4.023	2.401	Hiroshima	3.204	2.211
Niigata	1.379	1.311	Takamatsu	4.724	2.928
Nagoya	3.468	2.138	Fukuoka	4.068	2.771

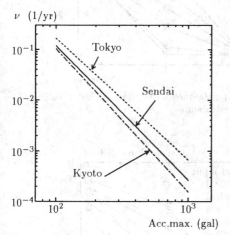

Fig. 3. Examples of earthquake risk curves for major cities

Table 2. Properties of the concrete and the reinforcement

Concrete	Compressive strength (kgf/cm^2)	240
	Tensile strength (kgf/cm^2)	32
	Strain at maximum compressive stress	0.002
	Ultimate strain	0.0035
Reinforcement	Yield strength (kgf/cm^2)	3500
	Tensile strength (kgf/cm^2)	5000
	Yield strain	0.002
	Strain when strain hardening begins	0.02
	Ultimate strain	0.1

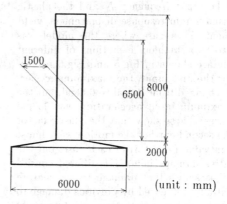

Fig. 4. Structure analyzed

Table 1 shows the values of a and b for 10 major cities. Fig.3 shows sample risk curves for three cities: Tokyo, Sendai, and Kyoto.

3 EVALUATIONS OF DAMAGE

3.1 Damage index

The authors (Suzuki 1994) defined the damage index DI of a reinforced concrete member that suffered bending failure after bending yielding as follows using hysteresis energy.

$$DI = \frac{W_{\text{acc}}}{W_{\text{max}}} \qquad (3.1)$$

Where, W_{max} is the maximum consumed energy of the member, in other words the amount of energy that the member could consume till the ultimate state, and has a unique value for each member.

And W_{acc} the accumulative consumed energy, is represented by the following formula

$$W_{\text{acc}} = W_u + 0.25 \cdot W_i \qquad (3.2)$$

Where: W_u: Amount of energy consumed by the virgin loading portion (area of the envelope of hysteresis loop) W_i: Amount of energy consumed by the repetitive loading portion (area obtained by deducting the initial loading portion from the total area of the hysteresis loop)

3.2 Elasto-plastic earthquake response analysis

The authors performed elasto-plastic analysis of single column type reinforced concrete bridge piers to obtain new information about their behavior during earthquakes and to simultaneously study the evaluation of damage to bridge piers. An outline of this bridge pier analyzed is shown in Fig.4. Table 2 shows the material properties of the concrete and steel reinforcement. Elasto-plastic response analysis of a single mass model was done based on the consecutive integration method using Newmark's β method ($\beta=1/4$). The damping coefficient was set at 0.02.

1621

The skeleton curve was the Takeda model (Takeda 1970). The input seismic wave form was El-Centro Earthquake Wave (NS component May 18, 1940).

Generally, a structure is effected by many earthquakes during its lifetime. The following hypothesis was established in order to evaluate the damage to a structure after it has been subjected to several earthquakes. "The behavior of a structure that has been effected by two earthquake motions is equivalent to the results of a response analysis which treats the two earthquake motions as a single continuous earthquake motion."

The relationship between the input frequency N and the damage index DI and the relationship between the input frequency N and the plastic factor μ (maximum response displacement/yield displacement) in a case where the model was exposed to two earthquake motions of different magnitude are shown in Fig.5 and Fig.6 respectively. For the first input, the maximum acceleration was changed from 100gal to 600gal, but the second maximum input acceleration was 600gal in both cases. These show that the plastic factor μ after the second earthquake motion was almost identical in value (about 3) in each case, but the accumulative damage index DI differed considerably. This shows that damage to a structure is substantially influenced by previous damage to the structure, and that past plastic factors could not demonstrate this effect.

4 EVALUATION OF LIFETIME RISK

4.1 Calculating earthquake motion strength

The probability density function of earthquake motion produced at a point being evaluated is found from the seismic risk function found in 2. above. When it is assumed that the strength of earthquake motion (ground motion force) is X(gal) and the average annual occurrence frequency is ν (times per year), it can be represented by the following formula from the parameters a and b (Table 1) found with equation (2.6) and 2.

$$\log \nu = a - b \log X \qquad (4.1)$$

If the lower limit value for ground motion strength is assumed to be x_0 and the average annual frequency of earthquake motion with strength of x_0 or greater is assumed to be ν_0;

$$\nu_0 = 10^{a - b \log x_0} \qquad (4.2)$$

And consequently,

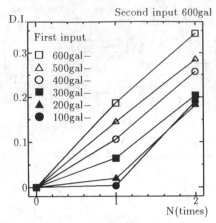

Fig. 5. Input frequency N - damage index value DI relationship

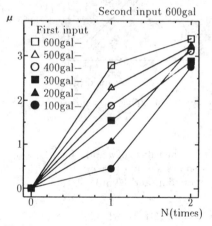

Fig. 6. Input frequency N - plastic factor μ relationship

$$\nu = \nu_0 10^{-b(\log x - \log x_0)} = \nu_0 \left(\frac{x}{x_0}\right)^{-b} \qquad (4.3)$$

Consequently, the probability distribution function F_X and the probability density function f_x of earthquake motion strength are:

$$F_X = 1 - 10^{-b(\log x - \log x_0)} = 1 - \left(\frac{x}{x_0}\right)^{-b} \qquad (4.4)$$

$$f_X = b10^{-b(\log x - \log x_0)} = b\left(\frac{x}{x_0}\right)^{-b} \qquad (4.5)$$

Geologically, there is an upper limit on actual earthquake motion. In order to account for this upper limit x_L, if the upper limit value x_L is such that the probability distribution function $F_X(x)$

is equal to 1, the probability distribution function of earthquake motion strength can be expressed as follows.

$$F_X(x) = \frac{1 - 10^{-b(\log x - \log x_0)}}{1 - 10^{-b(\log x - \log x_L)}}$$

$$= \frac{1 - \left(\frac{x}{x_0}\right)^{-b}}{1 - \left(\frac{x}{x_L}\right)^{-b}} \quad (4.6)$$

This shows that $F_X(x)$ is determined solely by the value of the constant b. If it is assumed that earthquake motion produced at the location to beassessed is continuous and that it is possible to evaluate its frequency distribution based on this distribution function, the value of x for a certain given accumulative probability $F_X(x) = u$ is provided by the following formula.

$$x = F_X^{-1}(u) \quad (4.7)$$

If u is now the standard uniform variable u which has a uniform probability density function between 0 and 1.0;

$$F_U(u) = u \quad (4.8)$$

In other words, accumulative probability where $U \le u$, is equivalent to u.

From this, if the value taken by U is assumed to be u, the accumulative probability of the value taken by x which corresponds to this and is obtained from formula (4.7) is:

$$\begin{aligned} P(X \le x) &= P[F_X^{-1}(U) \le x] \\ &= P[U \le F_X(x)] \\ &= F_U[F_X(x)] = F_X(x) \quad (4.9) \end{aligned}$$

Consequently, if $(u_1, u_2, ..., u_n)$ is assumed to be the set of values obtained from U, the set of values obtained from formula (4.7) for each of these values, in other words:

$$x_i = F_X^{-1}(u_i) \quad (i = 1, 2, ..., n) \quad (4.10)$$

has the target accumulative distribution function $F_X(x)$. From eq.(2.6), the following equation is obtained.

$$x = F_X^{-1}(u) = \frac{x_0}{\left\{1 - u \times \left(1 - \left(\frac{x_0}{x_L}\right)^b\right)\right\}^{1/b}} \quad (4.11)$$

This formula is set based on the values of x_0, x_L, and b.

Table 3. Relationship between damage index values and degree of damage

	Degree of damage	DI
1	Slight - Sporadic occurrence of cracking	$0 \sim 0.1$
2	Minor - Minor cracks	$0.1 \sim 0.2$
3	Moderate - Extensive large cracks	$0.2 \sim 0.4$
4	Severe - Extensive crasing of concrete	$0.4 \sim 1.0$
5	Collapse - Total or partial collapse	$1.0 \sim$

4.2 Selection of the seismic waves

This research project used a damage index that can explain how the damage suffered by a reinforced concrete structure can be influenced by its load history. So the form of seismic waves are important to the analysis. Earthquake wave forms expected to occur at a certain site were considered to be a sample function of a probabilistic process with certain spectrum characteristics that account for the ground characteristics, the hypocenter, and propagation properties, and so-called simulated earthquake motion were incorporated to use random numbers to produce a sufficient number of probabilistic equivalent model strong earthquake wave forms.

4.3 Damage categories

It is necessary to establish a correspondence between the degree of damage and damage to actual members for the damage index DI. Here it is categorized as shown in Table 3 based on the results of research on the quantitative evaluation of the degree of damage to reinforced concrete members reported by Park et. al (Park 1985)

4.4 Damage probability matrix

Based on the hypotheses and conditions described in previous sections of this paper, the following method was used to prepare a damage probability matrix which expresses the degree of probability that the damage to a structure will be transformed from a certain condition to another condition by earthquake motion with a certain band of strength.

1623

$$M(X;Y) = \begin{bmatrix} M_{11} & & & \\ & \ddots & & \\ & & M_{IJ}(X;Y) & \\ & & & \ddots & \\ & & & & M_{55} \end{bmatrix}$$

Here, the element M_{IJ} in this matrix represents the probability that an earthquake with strength between X and Y will transform damage condition I of a structure to damage condition J.

Various degrees of damage caused to structures by earthquakes are considered. It is assumed that if repair or retrofit work is not performed after an earthquake, the next earthquake will inflict further damage on the structure. So from the above transition probabilities, it is possible to determine the likelihood that a structure will be in a specified damage condition after a number of earthquakes or after a certain period of time has elapsed. In this case, because changes in state or the occurrence of earthquake motion can only occur at discrete point on a temporal axis, the process is thought of as the discrete parameter known as the Markov Process. If the damage probability matrix is considered to be independent of the state of the system (bridge pier or other structure), this process results in the Poisson Process.

The probability of the initial condition of a system can be expressed by the following line-vector. (Ang 1984)

$$M(0) = [m_1(0), m_2(0), \cdots, m_m(0)]$$

Here, $m_i(0)$ is the probability that the system will initially be in state i. So using the induction method, it can be proven that the state probability vector after n stages is provided by the following formula.

$$\begin{aligned} M(n) &= M(n-1)M = M(n-2)MM \\ &= \cdots = M(0)M^n \end{aligned} \quad (4.12)$$

Two probability matrices for two earthquake motions with different strengths are M_1, M_2. The state probability vectors when these have each occurred n times and m times are found as follows.

$$M(n;m) = M(0)M_1^n M_2^m \quad (4.13)$$

The probability $m_i(t)$ that the system is in state i at time t depends upon both the number of stage n and state probability after n stages.

Using the formula of total probability,

$$m_i(t) = \sum_{n=0}^{\infty} m_i(t)p_N(n;t) \quad (4.14)$$

Here, $m_i(n)$ is the probability that the system will be in state i after stage n, and $p_N(n;t)$ is the probability function for N stages during time period t.

The number of stages N exceeding n during time t is a event identical to total probabilities required for the change to occur in $(n+1)$ stages being t or less. So the accumulative distribution function of N is expressed by the following formula.

$$\begin{aligned} F_N(n) &= 1 - P(N > n) \\ &= 1 - P(T_1 + T_2 + \cdots \\ &\qquad \cdots + T_{n+1} \leq t) \end{aligned} \quad (4.15)$$

Here, $T_i(i = 1, \cdots, n+1)$ is the time required for the stage i change.

If the sum of the times required for S_{n+1} to change to $n+1$, in other words, $T_1 + T_2 + \cdots + T_{n+1}$ is expressed, equation (4.15) is as shown below.

$$F_N = 1 - F_{S_{n+1}}(t) \quad (4.16)$$

Here, $F_{S_{n+1}}(t)$ is the accumulative distribution function of S_{n+1}. The probability function of N is as shown below.

$$\begin{aligned} p_N(n;t) &= F_N(n) - F_N(n-1) \\ &= F_{S_n}(n) - F_{S_{n+1}}(n-1) \end{aligned} \quad (4.17)$$

If it is assumed that the change times T_j are now mutually independent and in accordance with the same normal distribution $N(\mu, \sigma)$, S_n also conforms to normal distribution, and its distribution is $N(n\mu, \sqrt{n}\sigma)$. Therefore:

$$p_N(n;t) = \Phi\left(\frac{t - n\mu}{\sqrt{n}\sigma}\right) - \Phi\left[\frac{t - (n+1)\mu}{\sqrt{n+1}\sigma}\right] \quad (4.18)$$

If the earthquake occurrence process is assumed to be a Poisson Process, the change time is in accordance with exponential distribution. Therefore, $p_N(n;t)$ in equation (4.14) is calculated using the following formula.

$$p_N(n;t) = \frac{e^{-\nu t}(\nu t)^n}{n!} \quad (4.19)$$

Where, ν is the average rate of occurrence of change.

And in a case where it is assumed that there are two transition matrices for the earthquake motion strength being considered, and there are two average occurrence rates ν_1, ν_2 for these, the probabilities of each occurring n times and m times are calculated using the following equation.

$$p_N(n, m; t) = \frac{e^{-\nu_1 t}(\nu_1 t)^n}{n!} \cdot \frac{e^{-\nu_2 t}(\nu_2 t)^m}{m!} \quad (4.20)$$

Therefore, the probability $p_i(t)$ of the system being in state i at time t can be expressed as follows based on formula (4.14).

$$p_i(t) = \sum_{n=0}^{\infty} \sum_{m=0}^{\infty} m_{1i} m_{2i} p_N(n, m; t) \quad (4.21)$$

Because earthquake strengths were categorized in four classes for this study, in this case, the state of the system after t years would be as follows.

$$p_i(t) = \sum_{k,l,m,n=0}^{\infty} m_{1i} m_{2i} m_{3i} m_{4i} p_N(k, l, m, n; t)$$

$$(4.22)$$

4.5 Analysis results

Table 4 shows an example of a the damage probability matrices obtained: a matrix for Sendai. And Table 5 shows an example of the final results of calculations performed using this matrix: a matrix showing the state of damage to a structure at the end of its lifetime when its lifetime is assumed to be 50 years, 100 years, and 200 years. The element $m(I, J)$ in row I, column J, represents the probability that the structure will be in damage condition J after T years if its initial condition was state I.

Fig.7 and Fig.8 represent the probability that structures in three major cities (Sendai, Tokyo, and Kyoto) will during their lifetime T, be in damage State 2 or reach damage State 5 respectively. The probability of reaching State 5, which signifies complete collapse, after a lifetime of T years is more than three times as high for Tokyo as it is for Kyoto and Sendai.

Fig.9 shows changes in the average values of the damage indices for the lifetime of structures in the three major cities. The average value of the damage indices refers to values obtained by increasing the median values of the damage indices for each damage state by the value of the product of these median values and the probability of reaching each damage state. This will allow designers to determine at a glance differences in

Table 4. Damage probability matirices for Sendai

$$M(100; 300) = \begin{bmatrix} 0.4908 & 0.4768 & 0.0306 & 0.0018 & 0.0000 \\ 0.0000 & 0.2850 & 0.7100 & 0.0050 & 0.0000 \\ 0.0000 & 0.0000 & 0.9481 & 0.0512 & 0.0007 \\ 0.0000 & 0.0000 & 0.0000 & 0.9950 & 0.0050 \\ 0.0000 & 0.0000 & 0.0000 & 0.0000 & 1.0000 \end{bmatrix}$$

$$M(300; 500) = \begin{bmatrix} 0.0000 & 0.5188 & 0.4628 & 0.0184 & 0.0000 \\ 0.0000 & 0.2020 & 0.7783 & 0.0148 & 0.0049 \\ 0.0000 & 0.0000 & 0.6154 & 0.3812 & 0.0034 \\ 0.0000 & 0.0000 & 0.0000 & 0.9925 & 0.0075 \\ 0.0000 & 0.0000 & 0.0000 & 0.0000 & 1.0000 \end{bmatrix}$$

$$M(700; 900) = \begin{bmatrix} 0.0000 & 0.0000 & 0.3012 & 0.6419 & 0.0569 \\ 0.0000 & 0.0000 & 0.0901 & 0.8531 & 0.0569 \\ 0.0000 & 0.0000 & 0.0000 & 0.9126 & 0.0874 \\ 0.0000 & 0.0000 & 0.0000 & 0.5306 & 0.4694 \\ 0.0000 & 0.0000 & 0.0000 & 0.0000 & 1.0000 \end{bmatrix}$$

Table 5. Damage state matrix for a structure after a lifetime of T years (Sendai)

T = 50 years

$$M = \begin{bmatrix} 0.6493 & 0.1967 & 0.1182 & 0.0358 & 0.0000 \\ 0.0000 & 0.4083 & 0.4397 & 0.1252 & 0.0000 \\ 0.0000 & 0.0000 & 0.6106 & 0.3893 & 0.0001 \\ 0.0000 & 0.0000 & 0.0000 & 0.9999 & 0.0001 \\ 0.0000 & 0.0000 & 0.0000 & 0.0000 & 1.0000 \end{bmatrix}$$

T = 100 years

$$M = \begin{bmatrix} 0.4216 & 0.2300 & 0.2352 & 0.1132 & 0.0000 \\ 0.0000 & 0.1667 & 0.4532 & 0.3801 & 0.0001 \\ 0.0000 & 0.0000 & 0.3729 & 0.6270 & 0.0001 \\ 0.0000 & 0.0000 & 0.0000 & 0.9997 & 0.0003 \\ 0.0000 & 0.0000 & 0.0000 & 0.0000 & 1.0000 \end{bmatrix}$$

T = 200 years

$$M = \begin{bmatrix} 0.1778 & 0.1652 & 0.3146 & 0.3423 & 0.0002 \\ 0.0000 & 0.0278 & 0.2496 & 0.7223 & 0.0004 \\ 0.0000 & 0.0000 & 0.1390 & 0.8605 & 0.0005 \\ 0.0000 & 0.0000 & 0.0000 & 0.9995 & 0.0006 \\ 0.0000 & 0.0000 & 0.0000 & 0.0000 & 1.0000 \end{bmatrix}$$

the risk during a structure's lifetime according to the city it is to be constructed. This process confirmed that, as expected, the value for Tokyo is the highest.

4.6 Commentary on the results

Table 6 shows the lifetime of a structure (T), the accumulative damage to the structure during this lifetime, the recurrence interval (R) of one earthquake motion that will inflict damage equal to this accumulative damage, and the recurrence interval/lifetime ratio (R/T). It reveals

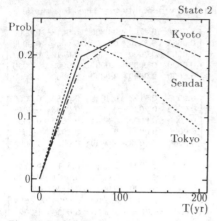

Fig. 7. Probability of reaching damage State 2 in a lifetime of T years

Table 6. Earthquake recurrence period and multiplier for various lifetimes

	Lifetime (yr) (T)	Accumulative damage DI	Recurrence period (yr) (R)	Multiplier (R/T)
Sendai	50	0.122	243	4.86
	100	0.205	425	4.25
	150	0.290	629	4.19
	200	0.368	839	4.20
Tokyo	50	0.180	189	3.78
	100	0.315	345	3.45
	150	0.431	491	3.27
	200	0.518	611	3.06
Kyoto	50	0.104	314	6.28
	100	0.168	527	5.27
	150	0.236	774	5.16
	200	0.303	1047	5.24

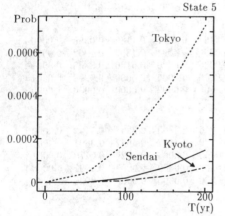

Fig. 8. Probability of reaching damage State 5 in a lifetime of T years

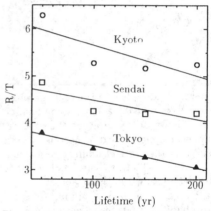

Fig. 10. Relationship between the lifetime and the multiplier in each city

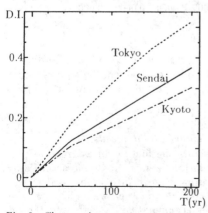

Fig. 9. Changes in average values of the damage indices

that when considering accumulative damage, designers must account for one earthquake motion with a recurrence period ranging from three times to five times the lifetime of the structure.

If, for example, the lifetime of a structure is assumed to equal 100 years, in these three major cities, it is essential to consider one earthquake motion with a recurrence period between 3.5 and 5.3 times that which is considered when designers do not account for the accumulative damage. Considering the size of the difference between a case where the accumulative damage is considered and a case where it is not, it is, as expected, essential to consider accumulative damage when designing a structure.

5 CONCLUSIONS

The following principal conclusions were obtained at the completion of the project.

1) Increased damage to a structure caused by earthquake motion is influenced by previous damage to the structure.

2) A damage probability matrix can be used to rationally evaluate the lifetime risk of a structure.

3) It was clearly shown that the concept "design for a single earthquake" stipulated in present earthquake resistant design guidelines might not provide sufficient safety of structures.

4) When consideration is not given to the accumulation of damage, it is necessary to design structures to withstand one earthquake motion with a recurrence period between three times and five times the lifetime of the structure depending on the city and the lifetime of the structure.

REFERENCES

Ang, A. H-S., & Tang, W.H. 1984. *Probability concepts in engineering planning and design. II. –desision, risk, and reliability –*. John Wiley and Sons, Inc,.

Hattori S. 1977. Studies of earthquake risk near japan. - Proposal for an earthquake risk map accounting for levels of earthquake activity and ground properties . *Building construction research reports*. 81 : 12 – 19.

Katayama Tsuneo & Japan Society of Civil Engineers 1989. *Dynamic analysis and earthquake resistant design (Volume I). Earthquake motion dynamic properties*. Gihodo : 36 – 39.

Park, Y. -J., Ang, A. H. -S. & Wen, Y. K. 1985. Seismic damage analysis of reinforced concrete buildings, *Journal of structural engineering. ASCE*. 111.4. : 740 – 757.

Suzuki, M., Chida, H., Kudou, M. & Ozaka, Y. 1991. Seismic risk analysis based on strain energy accumulation in focal region. *JSCE Structural Eng. / Earthquake Eng*. 8.3 : 143s – 152s.

Suzuki. M., Akakura, Y., Adachi H. & Ozaka, Y. 1994. Fundamental research on damage evaluation of reinforced concrete structures, *Proceedings of Japan Society of Civil Engineers*. 490/V-23 : 121 – 129.

Takeda, T., Sozen, M. A. & Nielsen, N. N. 1970. Reinforced concrete response to simulated earthquakes. *Journal of Structural Division, Proc. of ASCE*. 96. ST12. 2557-2573.

Structural Safety and Reliability, Shiraishi, Shinozuka & Wen (eds) © 1998 Balkema, Rotterdam, ISBN 90 5410 978 5

Seismic demand for SDOF system – In relating to seismic design

Wen-Yu Jean & Chin-Hsiung Loh
Department of Civil Engineering, National Taiwan University, Taipei, Taiwan

ABSTRACT: The evaluation of design parameters was performed, in this paper, for Elastic-Perfectly-Plastic- Single-Degree-Of-Freedom system. The Park & Ang's damage model was used as the "Structural Damage Control Model" and was implemented to discuss the seismic design parameters. Because of the implement of the specified damage model, the demand parameters include not only the effect of maximum displacement but also that of hysteretic energy dissipation. The seismic design parameters are, then, energy-based. The seismic records collected from different site conditions in Taiwan area were used as the analysis database and the presented results were discussed.

1. INTRODUCTION

Equivalent lateral force procedures are used in structural seismic design (e.g. Uniform Building Code). The design earthquake is described by a total design base shear, which is primarily relating to the peak ground acceleration (Z or PGA) of design earthquake, the smoothed elastic design response spectrum (C), and the reduction factor (R). Although all design parameters in this procedure are simple and meaningful in practice, more studies need to be conducted to ascertain the effects and relationships among these design parameters. These works need to predict the response of structure to the extreme ground motions and usually involve the definition of structural limit-state under cyclic actions.

The definition of structural damage or collapse is a complex problem in the estimation of seismic design parameters. The displacement ductility, defined by the maximum plastic excursion and the specified structural ultimate value, is the most commonly used damage criterion to date. It is used to estimate the inelastic design response spectra for the traditional earthquake-resistant structural design. However, the displacement ductility by itself can not properly define the degree of structural damage under earthquake ground motions that generally induce the structural low cycle fatigue failure. The energy-based design concepts, first proposed by Housner (1956), should be taken into consideration

in the definition of structural limit-state under critical earthquake loading.

The Park and Ang's damage model is widely used to predict the limit-state of structure under seismic actions. Cosenza, Manfredi and Ramasco (1993) examined various structural damage functionals under significant earthquake records. They concluded that the results of Park and Ang's damage functional are similar to those of the others (Banon and Veneziano's model and the linear cumulative law of plastic fatigue). It is noted that the energy design concept, on the other hand, can be automatically incorporated into the traditional structural seismic design procedure through the use of the Park and Ang's damage model.

The objective of this paper is to examine the seismic demands of Single-Degree-Of-Freedom (SDOF) system. These structural demands include the yield strength, reduction factor, and allowable displacement ductility. The Park & Ang's damage model is used as the *Structural Damage Control Model*. With the implementation of this damage model, the seismic design parameters can be estimated. A discussion on the reduction factor and the yield base shear coefficient were made. It is observed that an allowable ductility ratio that depends on the seismic energy should be used to reflect the effects of low-cycle fatigue failure of the structural system under seismic actions.

2. ENERGY EQUATION

It had been widely recognized by previous researchers that the level of structural damage due to earthquake depend on not only the displacement ductility but also the cumulative damage resulting from numerous inelastic cycles. The cumulative damage potential of ground motion is related to the input energy and/or hysteretic energy. The energy equation is, therefore, necessary to be derived to develop reliable design parameters.

The equation of motion of a viscous damped SDOF system subjected to a base excitation is given as

$$m\ddot{v}_t + c\dot{v} + f_s = 0 \tag{1}$$

where m = mass, c = viscous damping coefficient, f_s = restoring force, $v_t = v + v_g$ = absolute displacement of the mass, and, v_g = base (ground) displacement. Integrating equation (1) with respect to v, the energy equation can be obtained as

$$\frac{m\dot{v}_t^2}{2} + \int c\dot{v}\,dv + \int f_s\,dv = \int m\ddot{v}_t\,dv_g \tag{2a}$$

or in short form

$$E_k + E_d + (E_s + E_h) = E_i \tag{2b}$$

where the RHS term is the seismic input energy (E_i), the three terms of LHS are the kinetic energy (E_k), the damping energy (E_d), and recoverable elastic strain energy (E_s) and irrecoverable hysteretic energy (E_h), respectively. Equation (2) is the so-called absolute energy equation (Uang and Bertero, 1990).

Considering the energy-based design method, a satisfactory design of structure implies that the energy supply ($E_d + E_h$) should be larger than the energy demand (E_i). Neither the displacement ductility nor the energy demand spectrum alone is sufficient for conducting reliable design of structure. It is necessary to develop practical design methods that can take the displacement ductility as well as the energy demand into considerations.

3. DAMAGE PARAMETERS AND DAMAGE CRITERIA

Structures are designed to against the seismic actions. The collapse of structure under earthquake is not allowable. In design practices, there are many structural response quantities can be considered as the damage parameters. These parameters can be estimated from eqs. (1, 2), and then, be used to construct proper damage criteria for structure. Among these parameters, the displacement ductility μ_d and hysteresis ductility μ_e were frequently used and defined as

$$\mu_d = \frac{v_{max}}{v_y} \tag{3a}$$

$$\mu_e = \frac{E_h}{f_y \cdot v_y} + 1 \tag{3b}$$

where f_y = yield strength, v_y = yield displacement, and, v_{max} = maximum displacement under ground excitation. As noted by other researchers either the displacement ductility or the hysteresis ductility by itself can not properly predict the structural damage under seismic actions. A more reliable damage functional that could properly define the degree of structural damage should take the displacement ductility and hysteresis ductility (energy) into consideration.

One of the widely used damage models is the Park & Ang's model (1985) which was defined as

$$D_{PA} = \frac{v_{max}}{v_{utl}} + \beta \frac{E_h}{v_{utl}\, f_y} \tag{4a}$$

or

$$D_{PA} = \frac{\mu_d + \beta(\mu_e - 1)}{\mu_{d,utl}} \tag{4b}$$

where $\mu_{d,utl}$ = ultimate displacement ductility due to monotonic loading , v_{utl} = ultimate displacement due to monotonic loading, β = a structure relating parameter. The β-value, which depends on the post-yield behavior of structure, is assumed completely independent of the loading history. The better the behavior of post-yielding of structure the smaller the β-value. It is noted that the Park and Ang's model is a linear combination of displacement ductility and hysteresis ductility, and is not a normalized damage functional.

For a specified time history of ground motion, the structural response and the cumulative damage can be calculated by a step by step integration method. The time histories of D_{PA} with different β-value were quite similar to hysteretic energy (E_h) in shape (Jean, 1996) and were believed to be applicable for engineering practices. Furthermore, the definition of model parameters and the calculation of damage functional are easier for the Park and Ang's model. The Park and Ang's damage model was used to study the seismic design parameters (demands) in this paper.

4. SEISMIC DEMANDS BASED ON DAMAGE CONTROL

In practical procedure, the ultimate displacement ductility $\mu_{d,utl}$, the parameter β and the level of damage (D_{PA}) are assumed to be prescribed. For each record of earthquake, given a f_y-value, the maximum (allowable) displacement v_{max} (or v_a) and other response quantities can be calculated from eqs. (2, 4). As the damage parameters were calculated, the level of structural damage (e.g. D_{PA} could be obtained. By changing the f_y-value, the relationship between D_{PA} and seismic demand parameters can be constructed. The quantities of seismic demand can be obtained using damage functional. A schematic flow chart of this procedure is shown in Fig 1.

The process of determining the yield level for specified ductility ratio (or damage functional value) should be done very carefully because the relationship between yield level and ductility demand (f_y vs. μ_d) is not necessary a monotonic function. Most earthquake records result in a specified ductility demand (so as the damage functional) many yield levels. Figure 2 illustrated one specific case with structural period $T_s = 1.5$ second. The yield level was represent by the strength ratio, η, that is defined by

$$\eta = \frac{f_y}{f_e} \qquad (5)$$

where f_e is the maximum base shear of elastic response to the same seismic input.

It should be noted that the procedure used to find the strength demand for specified target ductility by iteration method is inadequate. As shown in Fig 2(a) for the η-μ_d relationship, there exist 3 yield-levels could result in a ductility demand for some ductility range. Clearly, it is only the highest one that defines the strength demand needed to limit the damage of

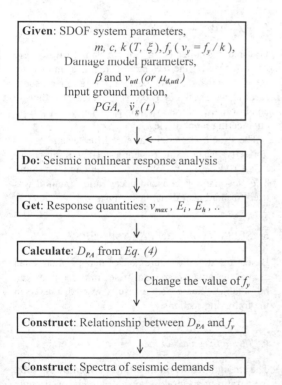

Fig. 1 A schematic flow chart for the calculation of $D_{PA} = D_{PA} (f_y, ...)$, and the estimation of design parameter

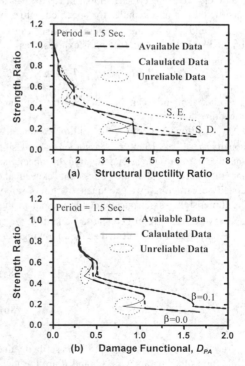

Fig. 2 Relationship between (a) strength ratio and structural ductility; (b) strength ratio and damage function D_{PA} for $\beta = 0.0$ and 0.1

Table 1. Primary database (recorded in Taipei basin) used in this study

Station Code	Recording Date	Peak Ground Acceleration	Predominate Frequency (Hz)	Earthquake Magnitude
CKS, 4010L	Nov. 15, 1986	96.304 (gal.)	1.392 Hz (Tp = 0.719 Sec.)	6.5
CKS, 4010T	Nov. 15, 1986	79.895 (gal.)	0.928 Hz (Tp = 1.078 Sec.)	6.5
TAP037E	Jun. 25, 1995	61.126 (gal.)	1.074 Hz (Tp = 0.931 Sec.)	6.1
TAP037N	Jun. 25, 1995	75.918 (gal.)	1.074 Hz (Tp = 0.931 Sec.)	6.1

structure to a specified level. The others are unreliable and should be ignored for design practices (Nassar and Krawinkler, 1991).

If the unreliable data were excluded, a monotonic relationship between damage functional and yield strength demand can be obtained as shown in Fig. 2(b) by dark-dash-dot line. The structural damage can be expressed as a function of seismic demand, for example, the yield strength

$$D_{PA} = D_{PA} (f_y , \mu_{d,utl} , T , \beta , ...) \qquad (6)$$

A relationship between any two of the parameters (the others were prescribed) shown in eq. (6) can be constructed. As an example, for specified values of $\mu_{d,utl}$, T and β, ..., the strength demand can be obtained by inverting eq. (6) and is expressed as

$$f_y = f_y (D_{PA} , \mu_{d,utl} , T , \beta , ...) \qquad (7)$$

The other demands can be obtained by the same procedure.

As mentioned above, the ultimate ductility capacity, $\mu_{d,utl}$, of structure is assumed. The design objective is to provide sufficient strength capacity so that the ductility demand does not exceed the capacity of structure by an adequate margin of safety. The dimensionless seismic demands present in this paper were for prescribed target ductility, $\mu_{d,utl}$. These parameters were defined as the followings

$$C_y = \frac{f_y (D_{PA} , ...)}{PGA \cdot m} \qquad (8a)$$

$$R = \frac{f_e}{f_y (D_{PA} , ...)} \qquad (8b)$$

where f_y is obtained from eq. (7) for prescribed value of D_{PA} and other parameters; C_y and R are the yield base-shear-coefficient (BSC) and the reduction factor, respectively; f_e is maximum base shear of elastic response to the same ground motion (PGA

was normalized to 1g).

The spectra of dimensionless design parameters, C_y and R, can be generated from eqs. (8) through statistical analysis. It should be emphasized that using Park and Ang's damage model, the energy design concept was automatically introduced into eqs. (8). Therefore, the energy demand (E_h) is implicitly included; the spectra calculated by the procedure mentioned above are more reliable and can be used in the traditional seismic design, straightforwardly. It is not necessary to change the procedure of the traditional seismic design.

5. DATABASE AND STRUCTURAL MODEL

Four records collected in Taipei basin, Taiwan, were used to study the effects of damage model on seismic demands. The basic information of these records was shown in Table 1. It is clear that the site condition of these stations is very soft from engineering point of view.

The structural model was simplified as an Elastic-Perfectly-Plastic Single-Degree-Of-Freedom (EPP-SDOF) system with 5% structural damping ratio. The Newmark -β constant acceleration method was used for nonlinear dynamic analysis.

6. SEISMIC DESIGN PARAMETERS

Based on the procedure and database mentioned above, the average spectra of seismic demands can be obtained. Some of the results were discussed in the following sections.

6.1 Strength reduction factor

The strength reduction factor, as defined by eq. (8b), is the ratio of spectral ordinate of the elastic strength demand and the inelastic strength demand. This factor shows how much the yield BSC demand of a given elastic SDOF system can be reduced, by allowing the system to behave inelastically, within the limit of a predefined damage level (also the ultimate ductility ratio).

Considering the structural damage at a level of limit-state of collapse ($D_{PA} = 1.0$) and the ultimate structural ductility $\mu_{d,utl} = 4.0$, the strength reduction factor was shown in Fig. 3 for cases of $\beta = 0.0, 0.1, 0.2,$ and 0.4, respectively. It somewhat followed the Newmark's format. The spectra of reduction factor with Newmark's format were also shown in the same figure for comparing (dashed lines, for $\mu = 4$ and 2.5, respectively). It is clear that the strength reduction factor depends strongly on the structural period and damage model (β-value), also on the ductility capacity (Jean, 1996).

Some results were observed. First, the increase of β-value in D_{PA} will reduce the value of reduction factor. Second, the spectrum of reduction factor is smoother for the case that β-value is lager or ductility capacity is smaller. Third, a reduced ductility (allowable ductility) should be used to estimated the ductility-dependent reduction factor for structure failed by low-cycle fatigue ($\beta > 0.0$). This observation of reduction factor will be discussed again.

6.2 Strength demand

The strength demand was expressed here as a base shear coefficient (eq. (8a)). The inelastic strength demand spectra represent the period dependent yield level of a structural system. As a matter of the fact from this study the yield BSC can be derived from the damage control model ($D_{PA} = 1.0$ with $\beta = 0.4 \sim$

0.1), as shown in Fig. 4. It should be noted that the values of BSC of the case with $\beta = 0.2$ were about 20% higher, for some period range, than those of the case with $\beta = 0.0$. The later case is used in traditional seismic design (no hysteretic energy (E_h) is considered). Neglect the low-cycle fatigue damage on the analysis of structural damage is inadequate.

The effect of ultimate ductility on the yield BSC was shown in Fig. 5 for cases of $D_{PA} = 1.0$ with $\beta = 0.2$ and $\mu_{d,utl} = 1, 2, 3, 4, 5$ and 6, respectively. The case of $\mu_{d,utl} = 1$ (the upper line in Fig. 5) is the elastic spectrum, which shows many peaks. In the inelastic spectra the peaks diminish and essentially disappear for larger ductility ratio or smaller β-value. The shape of the elastic and inelastic strength demand spectra are not necessarily similar, and are in fact rather dissimilar if the elastic spectrum has steep peaks.

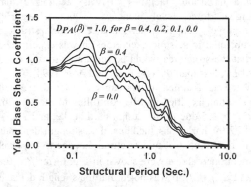

Fig. 4 Sprectral plot of yield base shear coefficient

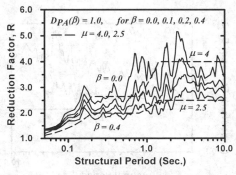

Fig. 3 Spectral plot of reduction factor for $\beta = 0.0, 0.1, 0.2,$ and 0.4, respectively ($\mu_{d,utl} = 4$ for damage model D_{PA})

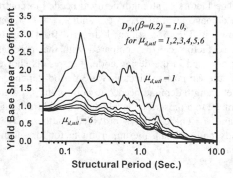

Fig. 5 Sprectral plot of yield base Shear coefficient for ultimate ductility from 1 through 6

Comparing to the spectra of reduction factor shown in Fig. 3, the peaks and valleys in the elastic strength demand spectrum usually coincided with those of the strength reduction factor spectrum. This is the reason why the inelastic strength demand spectrum is much smoother than the elastic one. Thus, the yield BSC developed from the elastic strength spectrum divided by the strength reduction factor, as adopted in many seismic-design codes, may be inadequate to the seismic design for the site condition similar to that of Taipei basin. A more reliable design yield BSC should be estimated directly from the inelastic strength demand spectrum as shown in Fig. 5(b) for different ductility ratio.

6.3 Important factor

The important factor is used in many seismic design codes to increase the design BSC level for essential and hazardous facilities. It was recognized that higher force level alone does not necessarily improve seismic performance. For structure subjected to seismic excitations, it was experienced that the structures would be repairable for the cases of D_{PA} less than 0.5 (De Leon and Ang, 1994).

It was assumed in this paper that the damage of essential facilities will be controlled to the level of $D_{PA} = 0.5$ due to the design earthquake, and $D_{PA} = 0.75$ for hazardous facilities. The strength demands needed to control the structural damage to the level mentioned above were shown in Fig. 6 (for $\beta = 0.2$ and $\mu_{d,utl} = 4$). It was noted that the strength demand for case of $D_{PA} = 0.5$ ws quite similar to that for case of $D_{PA}(\mu_{d,utl} = 2) = 1.0$ as shown in Fig. 5(b). It was similar, too, for case of $D_{PA} = 0.75$ and $D_{PA}(\mu_{d,utl} = 3) = 1.0$.

The factors of strength demand needed to control the damage level to $D_{PA} = 0.5$ and $D_{PA} = 0.75$ were shown in Fig. 7 (estimated directly from Fig. 6). These factors can be compared with the important factors used in the design code. The results showed that the (important) factors were period dependent. The strength demand needed to control the structural damage to a prescribed level can be found from Figs. 6 and 7. These figures provided another way to study and estimate the important factor for seismic design.

6.4 Allowable ductility

The allowable ductility μ_a is defined as the

maximum ductility that can be allowed to against the damage of structure due to design earthquakes. The form of μ_a is same as that defined in eq. (3a). For specified damage model and damage level, the allowable ductility can be obtained, again, through the procedure described in section 4. Figure 8 showed the relationship between allowable ductility and ultimate ductility for the Park and Ang's damage model with $\beta = 0.2$ and structural period $T_S = 0.2, 0.5, 1.0,$ and 1.5 second, respectively. It showed that the relationship between μ_a and $\mu_{d,utl}$ was almost linear for $\mu_{d,utl} \le 6.0$. (The relationship become unstable for cases with $\mu_{d,utl} > 8.0$).

Define a reduced-ductility factor Δ as

$$\Delta = \frac{D_{PA} \cdot \mu_{d,utl} - 1}{\mu_a - 1} \qquad (9)$$

Obviously, Δ can be a function of β if $D_{PA} = 1.0$ was assumed for the damage control model.

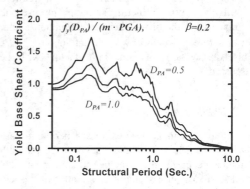

Fig. 6 Comparison of yield base shear coefficient for different damage levels (0.5, 0.75, 1.0)

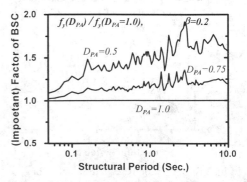

Fig. 7 Factors of base shear coefficient needed for different damage levels

The reduced-ductility factor, Δ, is a key-role in seismic design. As mentioned before, the energy design concept can take into account the effects of low-cycle fatigue failure of structure due to seismic loading. The implementation of energy design concept can be done through the used of factor Δ and, then, the energy-based design parameters can be obtained and applied to traditional seismic design.

The value of the damage-model-dependent factor Δ was shown in Fig. 9 for Taipei site, those of other site condition were shown in the same figure for comparison. It showed the following results. (1) The relationship between Δ and β was quite stable. (2) The value of Δ was higher for Taipei basin due to the effect of local site condition. However, (3) there was no significant difference for other site conditions (soft and hard site). For a typical structure system, the β-value in damage model D_{PA} could be obtained by experience. Thus, the Δ-value can be estimated from Fig. 9 for a prescribed damage level, D_{PA}. The allowable ductility can be obtained by inverting eq. (9)

$$\mu_a = 1.0 + \frac{\mu_{d,utl} - 1.0}{\Delta} \qquad (10)$$

It is necessary to use the allowable ductility μ_a-value instate of $\mu_{d,utl}$ in the calculation of strength reduction factor in traditional seismic design procedure.

According to the Taiwan seismic design code, eq. (10) is used to calculate the allowable ductility. This allowable ductility is applied in the calculation of strength reduction factor. The Δ-value is set as 2 for building design. In other words, the β-value is

assumed to be about 0.2 as shown in Fig. 9 for Taipei basin, and much higher for other sites. It seems that the Δ-value needed to be studied more carefully.

6.5 Energy demand

The design parameters estimated from the proposed procedure in this paper are energy-based. In order to explain how the energy demand was introduced into the design parameters, eq. (4) was substituted into eq. (9) to obtain the following equation

$$\Delta = 1.0 + \beta \cdot \lambda \qquad (11)$$

where

$$\lambda = \frac{E_h}{f_y(v_{max} - v_y)} \qquad (12)$$

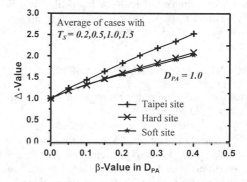

Fig. 9 Relationship between reduction of ductility Δ and β-value of Park and Ang's damage model (D_{PA}=1.0)

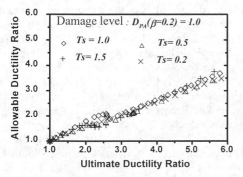

Fig. 8 Relationship between allowable ductility and ultimate ductility

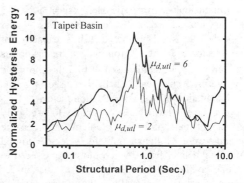

Fig. 10 Spectral plot of index of hystersis energy, λ

The parameter, λ, is a normalized-dimensionless index of hysteretic energy (E_h, the energy demand).

The value of λ controlled the relationship between allowable ductility and the ultimate ductility as shown in eqs. (11, 12). It can be estimated from hysteretic energy for every earthquake record. It should be noted that: (1) the λ-value can be directly estimated from Fig. 9 (the slope of Δ-β relationship curve); (2) the λ-value is damage model (β-value) independent by definition.

The average λ-spectra of Taipei basin were shown in Fig. 10 (for cases of $\mu_{d,utl} = 6$ and 2). Again, the λ-spectrum (also the E_h-spectra) was highly period-dependent. It showed a steep peak around structural period $T_S = 0.7$ second. This was due to the local site condition. The λ-value estimated from Fig. 9 was 3.83 for $\mu_{d,utl} = 4$. This value was reasonable for most period range, however, under estimated for period near 0.7 second. Consequently, if the λ-value was under estimated, the allowable ductility will be over estimated (eqs. (10, 11)) and the strength demand will be under estimated.

7. CONCLUSIONS AND DISCUSSIONS

Based on this study, there are some concluding remarks could be drawn:

(1) The damage functionals should be used to define the damage level of structure. The effects of low-cycle-fatigue due to design earthquake or the energy design concepts can be incorporated into the design parameters.

(2) An allowable ductility ratio should be introduced for the estimation of reduction factor in design practice. The allowable ductility can be obtained from the normalized-dimensionless hysteretic energy spectra λ.

(3) The normalized hysteretic energy was a good index to modify the ductility capacity of structure. The proposed dimensionless parameter, λ, can be used to find the allowable ductility that can, then, be used for the calculation of strength reduction factor.

It must be emphasized that this study focused only on a small part of a big problem. The seismic demands were evaluated only for selected ground motions in Taipei basin. Much more works need to be done in the context of demand evaluation for seismic design, especially, the definition of structural damage. If a proper damage model could

be found, the more reliable damage-control-based design parameters could be obtained by the procedures proposed in this paper.

8. ACKNOWLEDGMENT

The authors wish to express their thanks to the support from NSC (Taiwan, ROC) under Grant No. NSC86-2621-P-002-024.

REFERENCES

Cosenza, E., G. Manfredi and R. Ramasco, 1993, The Use of Damage Functionals in Earthquake Engineering: A Comparison Between Different Methods, *Earthquake eng. struct. dyn.* 22, pp. 855 – 868.

De Leon, D. and A.H-S. Ang, 1994, A Damage Model for Reinforced Concrete Buildings - Further Study with 1985 Mexico City, *Proc. Of 6th Int. Conf. On Struc. Safety and Reliab.*, Vol. 3, pp. 2801 – 2087.

Fajar, P.V. and T. Vidic, 1994, Consistent Inelastic Design Spectra : Hysteretic and Input Energy, *Earthquake eng. and Struct. dyn.*, 23, pp. 523 – 537.

Housner, G.W., 1956, Limit design of structures to resist earthquake, *Proc. 1st world conf. Earthquake eng.*, Berkeley, California, 5-1 – 5-13.

Jean, W.Y., 1996, A Study On Seismic Design Parameters and Structural Reliability Analysis, Ph.D. Thesis, Dept. of Civil Eng., National Taiwan University, Taipei, Taiwan.

Nassar, A.A. and H. Krawinkler, 1991, Seismic Demands for SDOF and MDOF System, The John A. Blume Earthquake Engineering Center, Department of Civil Engineering, Stanford University, Stanford, CA., EEC Report No. 95.

Park, Y.J. and A.H-S. Ang, 1985, Mechanistic Seismic Damage Model for Reinforced Concrete, *Journal of Structural Engineering, ASCE*, Vol. 111, No. 4, pp. 722 – 739.

Uang, C.H. and V.V. Bertero, 1990, Evaluation of Seismic Energy in Structures, *Earthquake eng. struct. dyn.* 19, 77 – 90.

Uniform Building Code, 1995, International Conference of Building Officials, Whittier, California.

Structural Safety and Reliability, Shiraishi, Shinozuka & Wen (eds) © 1998 Balkema, Rotterdam, ISBN 90 5410 978 5

Seismic damage and reliability analysis of uncertain structural systems

Yoshiyuki Suzuki
Disaster Prevention Research Institute, Kyoto University, Japan

Tokihiko Araki
Graduate School of Engineering, Kyoto University, Japan

ABSTRACT: Approximate and numerical methods for evaluating stochastic damage processes and computing the reliability of structural systems with uncertain parameters under seismic excitations are presented. An approximate method adopted here for simulations is based on the response surface methodology. The reliability functions of structural systems are determined analytically by introducing approximate probability density functions of damages. The simulation analysis verifies that the approximate probability density functions are applicable to the reliability analysis of uncertain structural systems.

1 INTRODUCTION

In the dynamic reliability problems of structural systems subjected to seismic excitations, it is important to consider uncertainties in both of structural systems and seismic excitations. In this study, the uncertainties in structural systems are mainly considered. As measures of structural damage states the maximum absolute displacement and cumulative plastic deformation are considered. The uncertain parameters within structures are modeled by random variables. As far as the time-dependent reliability problems for the uncertain structural systems, in particular, uncertain hysteretic systems are concerned, it is difficult to obtain the analytical solutions. Approximate numerical analyses based on response surface methodology are efficient to reduce computational efforts (Faravelli 1989, Yao & Wen 1993). In this study, a response surface method is used to evaluate the time-dependent statistics of structural damages.

Firstly, an analytical form of approximate probability density function of damage expressed by finite series expansions in terms of different sets of orthogonal polynomials is introduced (Suzuki &

Minai 1989, Suzuki & Yamagishi 1995). The system reliability function of the whole structural system as well as that of each structural component is directly obtained by integrating the probability density functions of damages. The Monte Carlo simulation analysis for single-degree-of-freedom linear structural systems with uncertain parameters under random excitations shows that the above approximate probability density function of damage is applicable to the uncertain structural systems.

Secondly, the reliability analysis is presented for hysteretic structures with uncertain parameters subjected to real seismic excitations. The response surface method is adopted as an approximate method. Here, the structural capacities related with the failure criterion as well as the structural parameters such as stiffnesses and damping coefficients are considered as uncertain parameters. Numerical examples are illustrated for two-degree-of-freedom uncertain hysteretic structures.

2 MODELING OF STRUCTURAL SYSTEM

The seismic responses including structural damage processes of multi-degree-of-freedom hysteretic structural systems are considered here. By making use of the differential forms of hysteretic characteristics and damage measures and by defining the state vector $Z(t)$ which describes the whole dynamic system consisting of the hysteretic structural system and damage measures, the state space equation of the whole dynamic system can be expressed in the following form:

$$\dot{Z}(t) = F(Z,t) + V(t)W(t) \tag{1}$$

where F is a vector-valued nonlinear function of Z and time t, V is a matrix-valued function of t and W is an input excitation vector.

2.1 Differential formulation of hysteresis

The hysteretic restoring force characteristic $\Phi(t)$ is described as follows:

$$\Phi_i = k_i \{ r_i x_i + (1 - r_i) z_i \} \tag{2}$$

where x_i and z_i are, respectively, the displacement and hysteretic component of the ith story, k_i is the initial rigidity, r_i is a weight of x_i to Φ_i. In this study, the hysteretic model is the bilinear hysteretic model. The differential representation of this model can be expressed as follows (Suzuki & Minai 1988a):

$$\dot{z}_i = \dot{x}_i \left[1 - U(\dot{x}_i)U(z_i - \delta_i) - U(-\dot{x}_i)U(-z_i - \delta_i) \right]$$

$$\equiv g_{z_i}(\dot{x}_i, z_i) \tag{3}$$

Here $U(\ )$ is the unit step function, and δ_i is the yielding deformation of hysteresis.

2.2 Differential formulation of damage measures

In the dynamic reliability analysis, it is necessary to define measures of damages. The maximum absolute displacement and the cumulative plastic deformation are considered here. The differential representations

of the maximum absolute displacement and the cumulative plastic deformation of ith story are, respectively, given as

$$\dot{\eta}_{mi} = |\dot{x}_i| U(x_i \dot{x}_i) U(|\dot{x}_i| - \eta_{mi}) \tag{4}$$

and

$$\dot{\eta}_{pi} = (1 - r_i) \text{sgn}(\dot{x}_i)(\dot{x}_i - g_{zi}) \tag{5}$$

where sgn( ) is the sign function and g_{z_i} denotes the differential representation of hysteretic component as shown in Eq. (3).

3 ANALYTICAL METHOD

In the case of deterministic hysteretic structural systems under random excitations, Eq. (1) can be rewritten to a form of the Ito vector stochastic differential equation. The moment equations are derived from Ito-Dynkin formula. In order to solve the moment equations, it is necessary to truncate the moment equations given a specified order by approximate the time-dependent joint probability density function of state vector. The truncated moment equations could be solved by introducing a finite mixed-type series expansion of the probability density function in terms of different sets of orthogonal polynomials depending on the range of each state variable (Suzuki & Minai 1988b).

It is difficult to extend the above-mentioned analytical method for the deterministic systems to uncertain systems. Therefore, the response surface methodology is adopted to solve the dynamic reliability problems of uncertain hysteretic structural systems.

3.1 Approximate probability density function

The joint probability density function concerning damages of the uncertain system is assumed to be expressed by the same analytical form as used in the analysis of the deterministic systems as follows:

$$p_\eta(\eta_1, \eta_2, \cdots, \eta_m; t) = \prod_{j=1}^{m} w_G(\eta_j)$$

$$\sum_{\sum q_j = 0}^{M} C_{q_1 q_2 \cdots q_m} \sum_{j=1}^{m} L_{q_i}^{(\beta_j - 1)}(\overline{\eta}_j) \tag{6}$$

where

$$C_{q_1 q_2 \cdots q_m} = E \left[\sum_{j=1}^{m} L_{q_i}^{(\beta_j - 1)}(\overline{\eta}_j) \right] \prod_{j=1}^{m} \frac{q_j! \Gamma(\beta_j)}{\Gamma(\beta_j + q_j)}$$

$$\overline{\eta}_j = v_j \eta_j$$

$$\beta_j = E^2[\eta_j] / \sigma_{\eta_j}^2$$

$$v_j = E[\eta_j] / \sigma_{\eta_j}^2$$

In the above equation, w_G denote the gamma density function, $L_{q_j}^{(\beta_j - 1)}$ is the Laguerre polynomials, m is the number of damages, M denotes the order of expansion, and $\Gamma(\bullet)$ is the gamma function.

3.2 Reliability function

The structural capacity of ith structural component represents the upper limit of the corresponding damage η_i. When the upper limit c_i is deterministically given, the safe domain $_M S(C)$ is also deterministically given by

$$_M S(C) = [0, c_1) \times [0, c_2) \times \cdots \times [0, c_m) \tag{7}$$

By making use of Eq. (6), the reliability function is written as follows:

$$R(t; {}_M S(C)) = \int_{_M S(C)} p_\eta(\eta_1, \eta_2, \cdots, \eta_m; t) d\eta$$

$$= \sum_{\sum q_j = 0}^{M} \sum_{s_1 = 0}^{q_1} \cdots \sum_{s_m = 0}^{q_m} (-1)^{\sum_{j=1}^{m} s_j} \prod_{j=1}^{m} \frac{\Gamma(\beta_j + q_j)}{q_j} \binom{q_j}{s_j} \frac{v_j^{s_j}}{\Gamma(\beta_j + s_j)}$$

$$\cdot M(s_1, \cdots, s_m; t) \sum_{r_1 = 0}^{q_1} \cdots \sum_{r_m = 0}^{q_m} (-1)^{\sum_{k=1}^{m} r_k}$$

$$\cdot \prod_{k=1}^{m} \binom{q_k}{r_k} \frac{\gamma(\beta_k + r_k, v_k c_k)}{\Gamma(\beta_k + r_k)} \tag{8}$$

where $\gamma(\cdot, \cdot)$ is the incomplete gamma function, and $M(\cdots; t)$ is the moment function concerning the damages.

Alternatively the safe domain is uncertain, the structural capacity C is treated as a random vector. When the structural capacity is independent of the structural damages, the reliability function $R(t)$ is evaluated by convoluting the probability function $p_\eta(\eta, ; t)$ and the probability density function $p_C(c)$ of the corresponding structural capacity as follows:

$$R(t) = \int_{R_C} p_\eta(c) dc \int_{_M S(C)} p_\eta(\eta; t) d\eta \tag{9}$$

Assuming that the probability density function concerning the vector C of the structural capacities can be expressed as the expansion by using the gamma density functions and Laguerre polynomials as similar to Eq. (6), the reliability function is obtained from Eq. (9) by (Suzuki & Minai 1989)

$$R(t) = \prod_{k=1}^{m} A_k + \sum_{i=1}^{m-1} \sum_{j=i+1}^{m} C_{\eta_{ij}} \prod_{k \neq i, j}^{m} A_k B_i B_j$$

$$+ \sum_{i'=1}^{m-1} \sum_{j'=i'+1}^{m} C_{c_{i'j'}} \prod_{k \neq i', j'}^{m} A_k C_{i'} C_{j'}$$

$$+ \sum_{i=1}^{m-1} \sum_{j=i+1}^{m} \sum_{i'=1}^{m-1} \sum_{j'=i'+1}^{m} C_{\eta_{ij}} C_{c_{i'j'}} \prod_{k \neq i, j}^{m} A_k$$

$$\cdot \left[\left\{ (1 - \delta_{ii'})(1 - \delta_{ij'}) B_i C_{i'} + \delta_{ii'} D_i \right\} \right.$$

$$\cdot \left\{ (1 - \delta_{jj'})(1 - \delta_{ji'}) B_j C_{j'} + \delta_{jj'} D_j \right\}$$

$$\left. + (1 - \delta_{ii'})(1 - \delta_{jj'})(\delta_{ij'} B_j C_{i'} D_i + \delta_{ji'} B_i C_{j'} Dj) \right] \tag{10}$$

In which δ_{ij} denotes the Kronecker delta, and

$$C_{\eta_{ij}} = E[\eta_{d_i} \eta_{d_j}] / (E[\eta_{d_i}] E[\eta_{d_j}])$$

$$C_{c_{i'j'}} = E[c_{d_{i'}} c_{d_{j'}}] / (E[c_{d_{i'}}] E[c_{d_{j'}}])$$

$$\eta_{d_i} = \eta_i - E[\eta_i]$$

$$c_{d_{i'}} = c_{i'} - E[c_{i'}]$$

$$A_k = I\left(\beta_{\eta_k}, \beta_{c_k}, v_{\eta_k} / v_{c_k}\right)$$

$$B_k = \beta_{\eta_k}\left[I\left(\beta_{\eta_k}, \beta_{c_k}, v_{\eta_k} / v_{c_k}\right)\right.$$
$$\left. -I\left(\beta_{\eta_k} +1, \beta_{c_k}, v_{\eta_k} / v_{c_k}\right)\right]$$

$$C_k = \beta_{c_k}\left[I\left(\beta_{\eta_k}, \beta_{c_k}, v_{\eta_k} / v_{c_k}\right)\right.$$
$$\left. -I\left(\beta_{\eta_k}, \beta_{c_k} +1, v_{\eta_k} / v_{c_k}\right)\right]$$

$$D_k = \beta_{\eta_k}\beta_{c_k}\left[I\left(\beta_{\eta_k}, \beta_{c_k}, v_{\eta_k} / v_{c_k}\right)\right.$$
$$-I\left(\beta_{\eta_k} +1, \beta_{c_k}, v_{\eta_k} / v_{c_k}\right) - I\left(\beta_{\eta_k}, \beta_{c_k} +1, v_{\eta_k} / v_{c_k}\right)$$
$$\left. +I\left(\beta_{\eta_k} +1, \beta_{c_k} +1, v_{\eta_k} / v_{c_k}\right)\right]$$

where

$$I\left(\beta_\eta, \beta_c, v_\eta / v_c\right) = \frac{1}{\Gamma(\beta_\eta)\Gamma(\beta_c)} \int_0^\infty \gamma\left(\beta_\eta, \bar{c}_\eta\right)$$
$$\cdot \bar{c}_c^{\beta_c -1} \exp(-\bar{c}_c) d\bar{c}_c$$

$$\bar{c}_\eta = v_\eta c, \quad \bar{c}_c = v_c c$$

As mentioned above, the time-dependent statistics concerning the structural damages are necessary in order to evaluate the reliability functions of the whole structural system and its structural components. For the case of uncertain systems the required time-dependent statistics are estimated as response variables. Suppose the uncertain parameters denoted as $\xi_i (i = 1, \cdots, k)$. A response variable $y(t)$ is approximately described by a second order polynomial model:

$$y(t) \approx \theta_0 + \xi^T \theta_1 + \xi^t \theta_2 \xi \tag{11}$$

In which, θ_0, θ_1 and θ_2 are the scalar-, vector-, and matrix-valued regression coefficients obtained by using the method of least squares. In this study, a central composite design is used to fit a second order

response surface (Myers 1971).

4 NUMERICAL EXAMPLES

The numerical examples are illustrated for a single-degree-of-freedom linear structural system and a two-degree-of-freedom hysteretic structural system subjected to real seismic excitations.

4.1 Verification of approximate probability density function

In order to verify the proposed approximate probability density function of damages, the numerical example based on the time-domain Monte Carlo simulation method for a simple single-degree-of-freedom linear system subjected to white noise excitations. The damage measure is the maximum absolute displacement.

The numerical results are shown in Fig.1 to Fig.4. The non-dimensional natural angular frequency and critical damping ratio of the deterministic system are, respectively, 1.0 and 0.05. In uncertain systems, the natural angular frequency and critical damping ratio are selected as uncertain parameters and they are assumed to be normal random variables. The mean values of the uncertain parameters are coincident with the deterministic values. Two values of the coefficients of variation (C.O.V) of both the uncertain parameters are assumed to be 0.05 and 0.15. The spectral intensity level of stationary white noise is 1.0. In the simulation analysis the sample size is 5000.

The time-dependent mean value and variance of maximum absolute displacement are shown, respectively, in Figs. 1 and 2 for three levels of uncertainty, namely, two values of the coefficients of variation, C.O.V = 0.05 and 0.15, and the deterministic system. The abscissas in these figures are normalized with reference to the natural period T of the deterministic system. The relative effect of each uncertainty on variances of maximum absolute displacement is shown in Fig. 2.

Fig. 3 shows the probability density function of

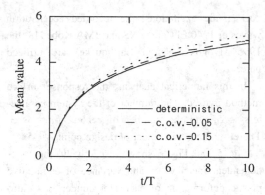

Fig.1 Mean value of maximum absolute
displacement.

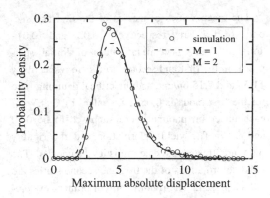

Fig.3 Probability density function of maximum
absolute displacement
(C.O.V = 0.15, t/T = 7.5).

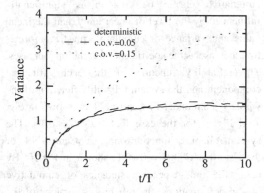

Fig.2 Variance of maximum absolute
displacement.

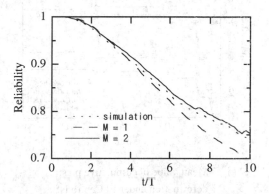

Fig.4 Reliability function for $C_F = 6.0$.

the maximum absolute displacement at $t/T = 7.5$ for the case that C.O.V = 0.15. This figure shows the comparison of the approximate probability density functions for $M = 1$ and $M = 2$ in Eq. (6) with simulation estimates. The approximation of probability density function for $M = 2$ appears to be more satisfactory than that for $M = 1$.

Fig. 4 illustrate the reliability function concerning the maximum absolute displacement for the case that C.O.V = 0.15 and the threshold level $C_F = 6.0$. The reliability functions for $M = 1$ and $M = 2$ in Eq. (8), and the simulation estimate are also shown in this figure. The reliability function for $M = 2$ fits to the simulation estimate better than that for $M = 1$.

4.2 Damage and reliability analysis of uncertain
systems

The numerical results for a two-degree-of-freedom bilinear hysteretic structural system subjected to real seismic excitations are illustrated in Fig. 5 to Fig. 12. The cumulative plastic deformation is considered as the damage measure. As uncertain parameters, the mass and initial stiffness of each story and critical damping ratio are selected, and have normal distributions. The structural capacities are also uncertain and their random variables belong to the gamma distribution. All the uncertain parameters are statistically independent.

The mean values of masses of the first and second stories are respectively 0.02 and 0.014 $ton \cdot sec^2 / cm$. The mean values of initial stiffnesses in the first and second stories are respectively 11.55 and 7.15ton/cm, and the critical damping ratio for the first mode is 0.05. Two values of C.O.V for each uncertain parameter are supposed to be 0.10 and 0.15. The yield deformation and the rigidity ratio are treated as deterministic parameters. The yield deformations of the first and second stories are 1.8 and 1.7cm. The rigidity ratio of bilinear hysteresis in each story is 0.1.

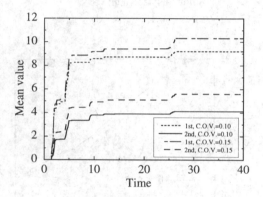

Fig.5 Mean value of cumulative plastic
deformation under El Centro NS.

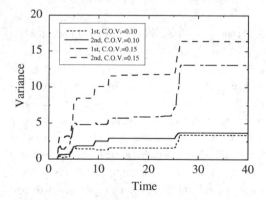

Fig.6 Variance of cumulative plastic
deformation under El Centro NS.

As seismic excitations, the recorded acceleration waves of 1940 El Centro NS and JMA Kobe NS (the 1995 Hyogoken-Nanbu Earthquake) are utilized here.

In this numerical analysis, the response surface method is used. The number of the system parameters is 5, and the number of center points is 3. Therefore the total number of design points is 45.

Fig. 5 and Fig. 6 show, respectively, the time-dependent mean value and variance of cumulative plastic deformation of each story under El Centro NS for two levels of uncertainty, namely C.O.V = 0.10 and 0.15. The dimension of abscissas in these figures is time (sec.). These figures indicate that the cumulative plastic deformation is significantly influenced by the level of uncertainty, and the mean value and variance of cumulative plastic deformation increase as the coefficient of variation increases. The reliability function of the each structural component and the system reliability function of the whole system under El Centro NS are shown in Fig. 7 to Fig. 9 for the case that C.O.V = 0.15. The system reliability function under El Centro NS for the case that C.O.V = 0.10 is shown in Fig.10. By using the time-dependent statistics of cumulative plastic deformations, the reliability functions of the structural components and the system reliability function of the whole structural system are evaluated from Eq. (10). Here, the mean values of the structural capacity C_F of each story are supposed to be 5, 10, 15 and 20. The value of the coefficient of variation of structural capacity $C.O.V(C_F)$ is assumed to be 0.20. As the mean value of the structural capacity decreases, the reliability function concerning the cumulative plastic deformation rapidly diminishes.

Fig.11 and Fig.12 show, respectively, the mean value of the cumulative plastic deformation of each story and the system reliability function under JMA Kobe NS. Since the earthquake excitation is extremely intense, the system reliability function decreases drastically during short time-duration.

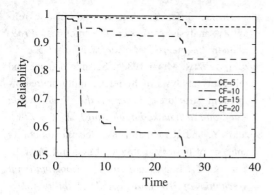

Fig.7 Reliability function of the first story
under El Centro NS (C.O.V = 0.15).

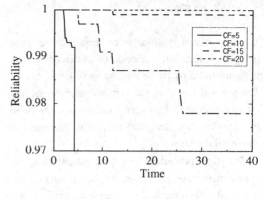

Fig.10 System reliability function under
El Centro NS (C.O.V = 0.10).

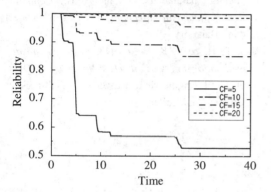

Fig.8 Reliability function of the second story
under El Centro NS (C.O.V = 0.15).

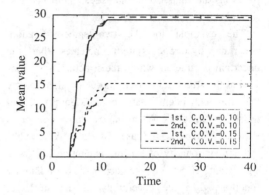

Fig.11 Mean value of cumulative plastic
deformation under JMA Kobe NS.

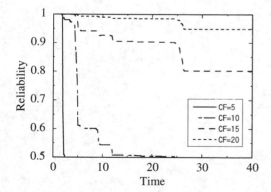

Fig.9 System reliability function under
El Centro NS (C.O.V = 0.15).

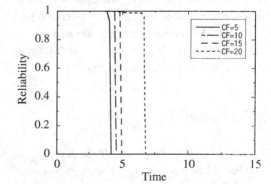

Fig.12 System reliability function under JMA
Kobe NS (C.O.V = 0.15).

5 CONCLUSIONS

The approximate method is presented for obtaining the system reliability function of hysteretic systems with uncertain parameters under seismic excitations. The method based on the response surface methodology makes use of the analytical forms of probability density function concerning the measures of structural damages.

The first numerical example indicates that the approximate probability density function introduced in the analytical method is applicable to the reliability analysis of uncertain systems. The approximation of probability density functions is more successful by using the higher-order statistical moments than second-order.

The example for the two-degree-of-freedom uncertain hysteretic system indicates that the uncertain parameters within the structural system as well as the structural capacity influence significantly the time-dependent statistics of damages and reliability functions. When the seismic excitation is extremely intense as the case of 1995 JMA Kobe NS, the non-stationarity of seismic excitation has more significant effect on the decrease of reliability functions than the uncertainty of the structural system.

The proposed method has the advantage that the system reliability of whole structural system as well as the reliability functions of structural components are directly evaluated from the time-dependent joint probability density function of damage measures by taking account of uncertainty in the hysteretic structural system and failure criterion.

REFERENCES

Faravelli, L. 1989. Response surface approach for reliability analysis. *J. of Engineering Mechanics*. 115 (12).

Myers, R. H. 1971. *Response Surface Methodology*. *Boston*: Allyn and Bacon.

Suzuki, Y. & R. Minai 1988a. Application of stochastic differential equation to seismic reliability analysis of hysteretic structures. *Probabilistic Engineering Mechanics*. 3(1): 43-52.

Suzuki, Y. & R. Minai 1988b. Seismic damage and reliability analysis of hysteretic multi-degree-of-freedom structures. *Proc. of the Ninth World Conf. on Earthquake Engineering*, VIII: 773-778.

Suzuki, Y. and R. Minai 1989. Seismic reliability analysis of hysteretic structural systems. In W.K. Liu & T. Belytschko (eds.), *Computational Mechanics of Probabilistic and Reliability Analysis*: 509-541. Lausanne: Elmepress International.

Suzuki, Y. & Y. Yamagishi 1995. Seismic reliability analysis of hysteretic structural systems with uncertain parameters. In Spanos (eds.), *Computational Stochastic Mechanics*: 259-266. Rotterdam: Balkema.

Yao, T. H. & Y. K. Wen 1993. *Response surface method for time-variant reliability analysis*. Dept. of Civil Engineering, University of Illinois at Urbana-Champaign.

Structural Safety and Reliability, Shiraishi, Shinozuka & Wen (eds) © 1998 Balkema, Rotterdam, ISBN 90 5410 978 5

Redundancy of steel frame buildings under seismic loads

C.-H. Wang & Y. K. Wen
Department of Civil Engineering, University of Illinois at Urbana-Champaign, Ill., USA

ABSTRACT: The recent Northridge and Hyogoken-Nanbu earthquakes revealed that the highly regarded ductile welded steel moment frame buildings for seismic forces are vulnerable to brittle connection fracture failures. The reliability and redundancy of a large number of such structures in the building stock against future earthquakes has become a legitimate concern to the profession and needs to be investigated. For this purpose, a 3-D dynamic structural analysis method is developed which is capable of accounting for biaxial and torsional effects of inelastic, degrading structures, brittle connection fracture, and member failure. It can be used for quantification of structural system redundancy in terms of reliability against limit state being exceeded. Numerical examples and results are given.

1 INTRODUCTION

The welded steel moment frame (WSMF) buildings had long been regarded as the best system against lateral loads such as those due to earthquakes because of its large ductility capacity. In the 1994 Northridge earthquake and the 1995 Hyogoken-Nanbu earthquake, however, there were many connection brittle fracture failures. The test results of steel connections in the recent SAC program in the US have verified the field observations and also shown a large variability in the load carrying capacity of these connections.

In view of the recent findings, an urgent question to answer is what is the reliability and redundancy of a large number of such structures in the building stock against future earthquakes. In other words, although very few steel structures collapsed in these two earthquakes, the influence of connection fracture on the performance of buildings against future earthquakes remains unclear at present, there is a need to investigate whether such structures have enough reserve strength to survive future earthquakes.

Under earthquake excitation, member failure or connection fracture may alter the dynamic properties of structures such as vibration periods and mode shapes. Furthermore, torsional motion may be significantly increased so that structural response may be considerably amplified. Therefore, a dynamic structural analysis that can account for such effects is necessary in order to fully understand structural behavior under seismic loads. Currently available computer programs such as DRAIN-2DX and IDARC, however, are primarily for analysis of plane frames, therefore can not be used for study of torsional effect and biaxial interaction. Also, new models are needed for brittle connection fracture.

A methodology for inelastic, dynamic three-dimensional analysis of multistory building structures is presented herein. This model can account for biaxial and torsional response, pinching and connection fracture, and member failure of inelastic, degrading structures. Therefore it can be employed for the study of structural system redundancy and gauging the adequacy of building performance under future earthquakes.

2 SMOOTH HYSTERESIS MODEL FOR RESTORING MOMENTS

In inelastic dynamic structural analysis, restoring force models are needed which can account for various degrees of non-linearity and yet are efficient in computation. A smooth hysteresis model proposed by Wen (1980), and Park, Wen and Ang (1986) can be used for this purpose.

For a single degree of freedom, orthotropic system

with different stiffness in the structural principal directions, the restoring moments can be expressed as

$$\begin{cases} H_x = \alpha k_x h_x + (1-\alpha) k_x z_x \\ H_y = \alpha k_y h_y + (1-\alpha) k_y \dfrac{\Delta_y}{\Delta_x} z_y \end{cases} \quad (2.1)$$

in which α is the post-to-pre-yielding stiffness ratio; k_x and k_y are the stiffness along X- and Y-axes, respectively; h_x, h_y and z_x, z_y are the elastic and hysteretic displacements, respectively; Δ_x and Δ_y are the yield rotations with respect to X- and Y-axes; z_x and z_y satisfy the following coupled differential equations:

$$\begin{cases} \dot{z}_x = \dfrac{1}{\eta}\{A\dot{h}_x - \nu[\beta(|\dot{h}_x z_x|z_x + \dfrac{\Delta_x}{\Delta_y}|\dot{h}_y z_y|z_x) + \\ \quad \gamma(\dot{h}_x z_x^2 + \dfrac{\Delta_x}{\Delta_y}\dot{h}_y z_x z_y)]\} \\ \dot{z}_y = \dfrac{1}{\eta}\{A\dfrac{\Delta_x}{\Delta_y}\dot{h}_y - \nu[\beta(\dfrac{\Delta_x}{\Delta_y}|\dot{h}_y z_y|z_y + |\dot{h}_x z_x|z_y) + \\ \quad \gamma(\dfrac{\Delta_x}{\Delta_y}\dot{h}_y z_y^2 + \dot{h}_x z_x z_y)]\} \end{cases}$$

$$(2.2)$$

in which A, β and γ are parameters controlling the shape of hysteresis; η and ν are parameters controlling the pre-yielding stiffness and ultimate strength, respectively. For deteriorating systems the parameters A, η and ν vary with time characterizing the extent of structural damage. In this study, they are assumed to be functions of dissipated hysteretic energy,

$$\begin{cases} A = A_0 - \delta_A E \\ \eta = \eta_0 + \delta_\eta E \\ \nu = \nu_0 + \delta_\nu E \end{cases} \quad (2.3)$$

where A_0, η_0 and ν_0 are initial values; δ_A, δ_η and δ_ν are the rate of degradation; E is the normalized dissipated hysteretic energy

$$E = \frac{(1-\alpha)}{F_x \Delta_x + F_y \Delta_y} \int_0^t \left(k_x z_x \dot{h}_x + k_y \frac{\Delta_x}{\Delta_y} z_y \dot{h}_y \right) dt$$

$$(2.4)$$

where F_x and F_y are the yield moments with respect to principal directions.

The above is for the modeling of restoring moments without fracture. Additional considerations for connections with fracture failure will be stated in Section 5.

3 EQUATIONS OF MOTION OF ASYMMETRIC MULTISTORY BUILDINGS

A two-story steel building with mass eccentricity is shown in Figure 1. Although the building is symmetric, the formulation given below applies also to buildings with asymmetry. Each floor diaphragm, of mass M_i and moment of inertia I_i, is assumed to be rigid in its own plane but flexible out-of-plane, which is reasonable for the floor system. By this assumption, the movement of the diaphragm at each floor level can be characterized by 3 rigid-body degrees of freedom in its own plane: translation in the X and Y directions, plus a rotation about the vertical axis.

In addition, because the floor diaphragms are flexible out-of-plane, the column ends are allowed to rotate with respect to X and Y axes. As a result, there are two rotational degrees of freedom at each column end. Therefore the vector of all structural degrees of freedom is

$$u = \left\langle \cdots u_x^i \; u_y^i \; u_\theta^i \; \cdots \middle| \cdots \theta_x^{ij} \; \theta_y^{ij} \; \cdots \right\rangle^T \quad (3.1)$$

in which u_x^i, u_y^i and u_θ^i are the 3 rigid-body displacements of the i-th floor; θ_x^{ij} and θ_y^{ij} are the column-end rotations of the j-th column at the i-th floor.

It is assumed that inertial resistance to rotation at column ends can be neglected, therefore, in dynamic analysis the rotational degrees of freedom of the columns can be eliminated by static condensation. After performing static condensation, the equations of motion, excluding damping term, can be expressed in matrix form

$$M \ddot{u}_a + T_s S = -M \ddot{u}_g \quad (3.2)$$

in which M is the lumped mass matrix including the moment of inertia of translation and rotation of diaphragms; $\ddot{u}_a$ is the relative acceleration vector of the mass center of diaphragms with respect to the ground; $\ddot{u}_g$ is the vector of ground acceleration; S is the vector of column-end shears; the matrix T_s adds the column-end shears acting at a particular floor diaphragm, as well as the torsion induced by those shears. Notice that the damping term has not been included in Eq. (3.2). but will be added in the next section.

4 MODELING OF THE ASYMMETRIC MULTISTORY BUILDINGS

The yielding of the buildings is assumed to be confined to discrete hinge regions, which is located at the member ends. For beams, because the biaxial interaction effect is negligible, the hinge yielding is restricted to happen only with respect to one principal axis of the beam cross section. For columns, in order to take into account the biaxial interaction, each column end is able to form two hinges with respect to the two principal axes of the column cross section; therefore there may be up to four plastic hinges formed on one column.

The displacement vector u can be partitioned into two vectors, u_a consisting of all the degrees of freedom with inertia, and u_c consisting of those without inertia. The member-end rotations at joint j are the joint rotation minus the deformations of the connecting plastic hinges. Thus the member-end moments can be expressed as

$$F = K_F u - K_H (h - z) \qquad (4.1)$$

in which F is the vector of column-end shears and member-end moments, h is the vector of plastic hinge rotation, z is the vector of the hysteretic components of hinge rotations. Partitioning F into three parts: S for column-end shears, R for member-end moments at ends without hinges, and H for member-end moments at ends with hinges, Eq. (4.1) can be partitioned into the following

$$\begin{Bmatrix} S \\ R \\ H \end{Bmatrix} = \begin{bmatrix} K_{SS} & K_{SC} \\ K_{RS} & K_{RC} \\ K_{CS} & K_{CC} \end{bmatrix} \begin{Bmatrix} u_a \\ u_c \end{Bmatrix} - \begin{bmatrix} K_{SH} \\ K_{RH} \\ K_{HH} \end{bmatrix} \{h - z\} \qquad (4.2)$$

The member-end moments H should be equal to the hinge element moments; therefore

$$H = K_e h + K_z z \qquad (4.3)$$

The vector z is determined by employing the smooth hysteresis model, written symbolically,

$$\dot{z} = g(\dot{h}, z) \qquad (4.4)$$

Considering the fact that rotational masses are not present at joints, the joint rotational equilibrium may be expressed in terms of only the member-end moments; i.e.,

$$T_R \begin{Bmatrix} R \\ H \end{Bmatrix} = \{0\} \qquad (4.5)$$

where the matrix T_R is for summing up the end moments at a particular joint.

Examining Eqs. (3.2) and (4.2)–(4.5), one can verify that the number of unknowns (which are u_a, u_c, h and z) equals the number of equations. Therefore the dynamic response of the building is completely described by these equations.

Defining the following variables

$$K_{ES} = \begin{bmatrix} K_{RS} \\ K_{CS} \end{bmatrix}, \quad K_{EC} = \begin{bmatrix} K_{RC} \\ K_{CC} \end{bmatrix}, \quad K_{EH} = \begin{bmatrix} K_{RH} \\ K_{HH} \end{bmatrix}$$

and substituting the 2nd and 3rd rows of Eq.(4.2) into Eq.(4.5), u_c can be solved as

$$u_c = -(T_R K_{EC})^{-1} (T_R K_{ES} u_a - T_R K_{EH} h + T_R K_{EH} z) \qquad (4.6)$$

Equating the right-hand side of the 3rd row of Eq. (4.2) to that of Eq. (4.3), and replacing u_c by Eq. (4.6), one has

$$Q_1 u_a + Q_2 h + (K_z + K_e - Q_2) z = 0 \qquad (4.7)$$

where

$$\begin{cases} Q_1 = K_{CC} (T_R K_{EC})^{-1} T_R K_{ES} - K_{CS} \\ Q_2 = K_e + K_{HH} - K_{CC} (T_R K_{EC})^{-1} T_R K_{EH} \end{cases}$$

Substituting Eq. (4.6) and the 1st row of Eq. (4.2) for S into Eq. (3.2), the equations of motion can be expressed as

$$M \ddot{u}_a + Q_3 u_a + Q_4 h = Q_4 z - M \ddot{u}_g \qquad (4.8)$$

where

$$\begin{cases} Q_3 = T_S \left[K_{SS} - K_{SC} (T_R K_{EC})^{-1} T_R K_{ES} \right] \\ Q_4 = T_S \left[K_{SC} (T_R K_{EC})^{-1} T_R K_{EH} - K_{SH} \right] \end{cases}$$

Combining Eqs. (4.7) and (4.8) into matrix form,

$$\begin{bmatrix} M & 0 \\ 0 & 0 \end{bmatrix} \begin{Bmatrix} \ddot{u}_a \\ \ddot{h} \end{Bmatrix} + \begin{bmatrix} Q_3 & Q_4 \\ Q_1 & Q_2 \end{bmatrix} \begin{Bmatrix} u_a \\ h \end{Bmatrix} = \begin{Bmatrix} Q_4 z - M \ddot{u}_g \\ (Q_2 - K_z - K_e) - K_z z \end{Bmatrix} \qquad (4.9)$$

which is a system of equations of motion without damping terms.

If Rayleigh damping is assumed and has the following form

$$C = a_0 \begin{bmatrix} M & 0 \\ 0 & 0 \end{bmatrix} + a_1 \begin{bmatrix} Q_3 & Q_4 \\ Q_1 & Q_2 \end{bmatrix} \qquad (4.10)$$

in which a_0 and a_1 are proportionality constants, then Eq. (4.9) becomes

$$\begin{bmatrix} M & 0 \\ 0 & 0 \end{bmatrix} \begin{Bmatrix} \ddot{u}_a \\ \ddot{h} \end{Bmatrix} + \left(a_0 \begin{bmatrix} M & 0 \\ 0 & 0 \end{bmatrix} + a_1 \begin{bmatrix} Q_3 & Q_4 \\ Q_1 & Q_2 \end{bmatrix} \right) \begin{Bmatrix} \dot{u}_a \\ \dot{h} \end{Bmatrix} +$$

$$\begin{bmatrix} Q_3 & Q_4 \\ Q_1 & Q_2 \end{bmatrix} \begin{Bmatrix} u_a \\ h \end{Bmatrix} = \begin{Bmatrix} Q_4 z - M \ddot{u}_g \\ (Q_2 - K_e - K_z) z \end{Bmatrix} \qquad (4.11)$$

Setting a state-variable vector y and its derivative as

$$y = \langle u_a \quad \dot{u}_a \quad h \quad z \rangle^T, \quad \dot{y} = \langle \dot{u}_a \quad \ddot{u}_a \quad \dot{h} \quad \dot{z} \rangle^T$$

one can solve Eqs. (4.4) and (4.11) for given initial conditions, and obtain the time history of the state variables.

5 BEHAVIOR OF BRITTLE CONNECTION FRACTURE

Since the biaxial interaction effects are small in beams, the uniaxial smooth hysteresis model is used. After beam fractures occur, however, the hysteresis loops usually are asymmetric. Therefore the restoring force model of Park, Wen and Ang (1986) is modified as follows

$$\dot{z} = \frac{\dot{u}_1}{\eta}\left\{A - \nu|z|^n\left[\beta\,\text{sgn}(\dot{u}_1\,z) + \gamma + \varphi\big(\text{sgn}(z) + \text{sgn}(\dot{u}_1)\big)\right]\right\}$$

(5.1)

in which φ is an additional parameter to model asymmetric yielding behavior after beam fractures; the symbol sgn$(\cdot)$ stands for the signum function. To model the slip and pinching behavior after fracture the slip-lock element (Baber and Noori, 1985) is used. The slip rates of slip-lock elements are given as

$$\dot{u}_2 = f(z)\,\dot{z}$$

(5.2)

in which $\dot{u}_2$ is the vector of slip rates of slip-lock elements. The velocity of plastic hinge rotations, $\dot{u}$, is $\dot{u}_1 + \dot{u}_2$. Therefore

$$\dot{u}_1 = \dot{u} - f(z)\,\dot{z}$$

(5.3)

Substituting Eq. (5.3) into Eq. (5.1) and noting the fact that $\text{sgn}(\dot{u}) = \text{sgn}(\dot{u}_1) = \text{sgn}(\dot{u}_2)$, $\dot{z}$ can be expressed as

$$\dot{z} = \frac{h(z)}{\eta}\left\{A - \nu|z|^n\left[\beta\,\text{sgn}(\dot{u}\,z) + \gamma + \varphi\big(\text{sgn}(\dot{u}) + \text{sgn}(z)\big)\right]\right\}\dot{u}$$

(5.4)

in which

$$h(z) = \frac{1}{1 + \frac{f(z)}{\eta}\left\{A - \nu|z|^n\left[\beta\,\text{sgn}(\dot{u}\,z) + \gamma + \varphi\big(\text{sgn}(\dot{u}) + \text{sgn}(z)\big)\right]\right\}}$$

is the so-called pinching function. $f(z)$ controls the spread and severity of pinching and is given by

$$f(z) = \sqrt{\frac{2}{\pi}}\,\frac{a}{\sigma}\exp\left\{-\frac{1}{2}\left[\frac{\text{sgn}(\dot{u})\dfrac{z}{z_u} - q}{\sigma}\right]^2\right\}$$

where a, q, σ are coefficients of the spread and severity of pinching, z_u is the ultimate value of z. Detailed discussion of those pinching parameters can be found in Baber and Noori(1985) and Foliente(1995).

Experimental results indicate that fracture mostly originated from the bottom side of beam flange (Kaufmann, et al, 1997). Furthermore, although extensive fracture sometimes propagated into beam web or even column flange and web, in many cases there remained some residual resistance at connections (SAC, 1995).

In this study, it is assumed that the occurrence of beam fracture is limited to the bottom side; i.e., the fracture occurs only when the beam segment is under positive moment. Results from SAC program indicate that the residual resisting moment after cracking is about 20–40% of the original strength. When the bending direction reverses, the crack is closed up and the fractured cross section regains 70–90% of its uncracked strength. As for columns, it is a reasonable assumption that once a column fracture occurs the damaged column has no resistance at all. In order to determine the occurrence of fracture, a damage index, proposed by Park, Ang and Wen (1984), which accounts for the effects of excessive displacement and cumulative damage, is used as a measure of the capacity against fracture failure.

For the analysis of structures with possible connection fracture failure, a threshold value of damage index is assigned to each structural member-end with plastic hinges. It is assumed that the fracture at a connection will occur at a particular time instant if the threshold value of the connection is exceeded. The residual resistance of the fractured connection to positive moment is then reduced to a fraction, e.g., 25% of the original strength. An example of the resultant hysteresis loops at fractured connections is shown in Figure 6.

6 STRUCTURAL SYSTEM REDUNDANCY

As mentioned before, structural redundancy plays an important role in response behavior beyond first yielding or brittle connection fracture failures. However, it has not been rationally quantified in the past. In view of the recent connection failures, there is a need for quantifying redundancy from a system perspective.

Factors affecting system redundancy are complicated, such as configuration of structure, number of members, connection behavior, material properties, and the variability of loads and resisting capacity, etc., therefore a rational measure has been difficult to obtain. Since many of the above factors are random in nature, a realistic quantification of redundancy needs to be stated in terms of system reliability.

In view of the large number of factors and the complicated restoring force behavior such as those due to brittle connection failures, simulation techniques may be the most appropriate method for dynamic system reliability evaluation. With given probability distributions for the system variables, the simulation may be used to yield useful probability information for evaluation of structural performance.

7 NUMERICAL STUDIES

7.1 Effect of connection failure

Consider a two-story building as shown in Figure 1. The mass centers of floor slabs have an eccentricity of *2.5 ft* and *3.75 ft* in X- and Y- directions, respectively, with respect to the center of geometry. The first three vibration periods of the structure with rigid floor diaphragms are *.396* (Y-direction), *.338* (X-direction), and *.207* (torsion) seconds, while they are *.616*, *.499* and *.310* seconds, respectively, with a flexible diaphragm assumption.

A pair of earthquake records generated in Phase II of SAC project (SAC, 1997) for Los Angeles, California, is used as the ground motion; namely, LA27 (fault-normal) and LA28 (fault-parallel), shown in Figure 2. The La27 and LA28 records are applied concurrently to the Y- and X-directions, respectively.

In the following computation, the damping ratios for the first two modes are assumed to be *2%*; the rate of degradation for *A*, *v*, and *η* are *0.*, *.02*, and *.1*, respectively. The P-Δ effect is taken into consideration. The residual strength of connections after cracking is assumed to be *30%* of that before cracking on the cracked side and *90%* on the uncracked side (SAC, 1996).

Six cases are investigated:

1. Floor diaphragms are rigid; structural members and connections are perfectly ductile.
2. Floor diaphragms are flexible; structural members and connections are perfectly ductile.
3. Same as in Case 2 except that beams *1–3* have a threshold value of damage capacity index of *0.1* for connection fractures, i.e., if the value is exceeded, connection fracture will occur.
4. Same assumptions as in Case 2 except that beams *1–6* have a threshold value of damage capacity index of *0.1* for connection fractures.
5. Same assumptions as in Case 2 except that beams *1* and *3* will fail completely once a damage index threshold value of *0.1* is reached.
6. Same assumptions as in Case 2 except that column *4* will fail completely once a damage index threshold value of *0.5* is reached.

Tables 1–3 list the maximum values of interested response quantities for the considered cases. Figure 3 shows the displacements of the 1st-floor mass center for cases 1 and 6. Figure 4 shows the hysteresis loops illustrating biaxial interaction effect of column *1*. Figure 6 and Figure 5 show the hysteresis loops for beams *1* with and without fracture failure. The effects of connection fracture, member failure, biaxial interaction and torsion are clearly shown in the Tables 1–3 and Figures 3–6. The pinching and degradation of connection moment-rotation behavior compare favorably with test results (SAC, 1995).

Examining the results, the following can be inferred:

a. The flexible diaphragm assumption causes apparently the effects of period elongation and, in this case, response amplification.
b. Comparing Case 2 to 3, as expected the torsion is significantly amplified. However the displacements of floor mass centers in Case 3 increase only moderately, while the maximum column drift is even less than that in Case 2.
c. Comparison of Case 3 to 4 shows a somewhat unexpected result — the response with more fractured connections increases only moderately. This may be attributed to that (1) the fracturing of all 6 first-story beams are more symmetric compared to the fracturing of beams *1–3* only, (2) if fractured connections possess some residual strength, even as low as *30%* of uncracked strength, it can have remarkable beneficial effects.
d. The comparison of Case 3 (or 4) and 5 again supports the finding in c. — total (unsymmetric) failures of beams *1–3* considerably amplify the response of the structure.
e. In Case 6, the response as well as permanent displacements increase drastically, confirming the expectation that any column failure can lead to serious consequences such as collapse.

7.2 Structural reliability and redundancy

The suites of ground motions in Phase II of SAC program are used as earthquake excitations. This program generated three suites of time histories corresponding to the probability of occurrence of 50%, 10% and 2% in 50 years. Each suite has 10 pairs of time histories. Each pair consists of a fault-normal and a fault-parallel time histories.

In order to examine the influences of biaxial excitation and possible connection fracture on structural response, three cases are investigated: (1) only fault-normal component of time histories is applied along the Y-direction, which is the weak direction, of buildings with ductile connections (no fracture); (2) fault-parallel and fault normal components are applied along X- and Y- directions respectively, of buildings with ductile connections; (3) fault-parallel and fault-normal components are applied along X- and Y-directions respectively, of buildings with pos-

Table 1. Maximum column drift ratios.

CASE	X (%)	Y (%)	D* (%)
1	3.012	1.125	3.106
2	4.664	4.023	4.936
3	4.645	4.560	4.806
4	4.907	4.807	5.089
5	4.929	5.186	5.483
6	4.664	5.831	6.019

* D denotes the maximum value of the absolute column drift ratios.

Table 2. Maximum displacements of 1st-floor mass center.

CASE	X (in)	Y (in)	R (rad), $\times 10^{-3}$
1	4.618	1.883	2.046
2	4.333	5.044	1.704
3	4.531	5.649	2.498
4	4.553	6.322	1.210
5	5.189	6.638	4.291
6	4.333	7.642	2.955

Table 3. Maximum displacements of 2nd-floor mass center.

CASE	X (in)	Y (in)	R (rad), $\times 10^{-3}$
1	6.235	2.698	2.467
2	10.47	10.85	4.097
3	11.11	12.08	6.037
4	11.44	13.63	2.922
5	10.43	14.52	8.907
6	10.47	16.16	6.132

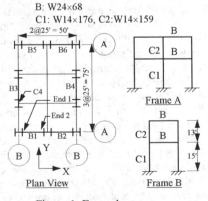

Figure 1. Example structure.

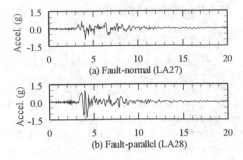

Figure 2. Time histories of a SAC-2 earthquake.

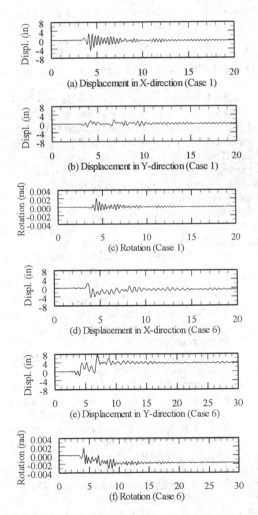

Figure 3. Displacements of 1st-floor mass center for Cases 1 and 6.

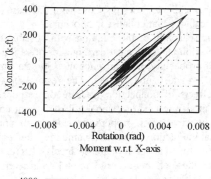

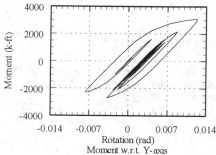

Figure 4. Hysteresis loops at base of column 1
(Case 1).

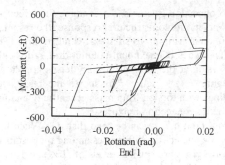

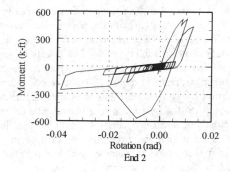

Figure 6. Hysteresis loops of beam 1 (Case 4).

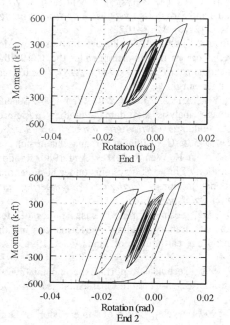

Figure 5. Hysteresis loops of beam 1 (Case 2).

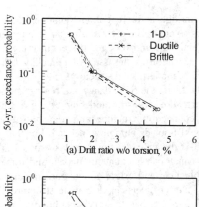

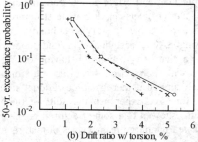

Figure 7. Maximum column drift ratio vs. 50-year
probability of exceedance.

sible connection fractures. To examine the effects of torsional motion on structural response, the response of building without torsion was studied first. The median values of maximum column drift ratio without torsion at the three probability levels are shown in Figure 7 (a). Figure 7(b) shows the results for buildings with torsion from mass eccentricity and unsymmetric connection fractures.

From Figure 7, it can be seen that: (1) When torsion is neglected, the differences among the results of the three cases are small at levels of 50% and 10% in 50 years. They become notable, however, at level of 2% in 50 years when biaxial excitation becomes important. (2) Contrasting with the above observation, when torsion is included, the responses increase significantly at all probability levels. The effects of torsion and biaxial interaction, therefore, play an essential role in structural response. (3) The response amplification by connection fracture is only moderate compared to that by torsion and biaxial interaction, particularly at small probability levels. One contributing factor is that fractures may increase damping and shift the natural frequencies which compensate the effect of the loss of strength after fracture.

8 CONCLUSIONS

The Northridge and Hyogoken-Nanbu earthquakes provided severe seismic tests of a large number of WSMF buildings and brought the engineering community's attention to the issue of reliability and redundancy of modern steel structures.

To investigate the redundancy and reserve strength of the structure, realistic modeling of the beam-to-column connection fracture and the out-of-plane flexibility of floor diaphragm is needed. For this purpose, a 3-D dynamic structural analysis model is developed which can account for biaxial and torsional effects, pinching and brittle connection fracture, and member failure of inelastic, degrading structures. For verification, a 2×3 bay, 2-story steel building is analyzed using SAC-2 earthquake ground motions. It was found that the response behavior of WSMF buildings with connection fractures may only be moderately altered if there is some residual strength after the fracture. Experimental results of the SAC project also showed that some fractured connections are still able to undergo many cycles of load reversal; therefore such connections may act as energy dissipators, and to some extent are "beneficial" in reducing structural response. On the other hand, once connecting fracture results in complete structural

member failures, the response will increase more drastically so that collapse may occur.

The reliability of the building with possible brittle connection failure against earthquakes of various levels of probability of occurrence in a 50 year time interval was also investigated. The results show that the effects of connection fracture on response are only moderate when torsional effects are not considered, whereas when properly considered, torsion and biaxial interaction significantly amplifies the response of structures at all probability levels. Therefore in design these effects deserve careful consideration to ensure safety and reliability.

ACKNOWLEDGMENTS

This study is supported by the National Science Foundation under grants NSF CMS-95-10243 and SBC-SUNY 95-4102C.

REFERENCES

Baber, T. T., and M. N. Noori 1985. Random Vibration of Degrading, Pinching Systems. *J. of Engng. Mech., ASCE* 111(8): 1010–1026.

Foliente, G. C. 1995. Hysteresis Modeling of Wood Joints and Structural Systems. *J. of Struct. Engng., ASCE* 121(6): 1013–1022.

Kaufmann, E. et al. 1997. Failure analysis of welded steel moment frames damaged in the Northridge earthquake. *NISTIR 5944, NIST.* Maryland: Gaithersburg.

Park, Y.J., A.H-S. Ang & Y.K. Wen 1984. Seismic damage analysis and damage-limiting design of R.C. buildings. *Civil engng studies, structural series no. 516.* U. of Illinois, Urbana-Champaign.

Park, Y.J., Y.K. Wen & A.H-S. Ang 1986. Random vibration of hysteretic systems under bi-directional ground motions. *Earthquake engineering and structural dynamics.* 14: 543–557.

SAC 1995. Technical report: case studies of steel moment frame building performance in the Northridge earthquake of January 17, 1994. SAC 95-07.

SAC 1996. Technical Report: Experimental Investigation of Beam-Column Subassemblages. SAC 96-01, Part 1.

SAC 1997. Develop Suites of Time Histories. Draft Report.

Wen, Y.K. 1980. Equivalent linearization for hysteretic system under random excitation. *J.Applied Mechanics, ASME.* 47: 150–154.

Structural Safety and Reliability, Shiraishi, Shinozuka & Wen (eds) © 1998 Balkema, Rotterdam, ISBN 90 5410 978 5

Proposal of a methodology to correlate seismic damage analyses, vulnerability sources, construction praxes

G. Sarà & R. Nudo
Department of Constructions, University of Florence, Italy

ABSTRACT: Evolutionary process relating to aseismic forecasting and prevention techniques is pointed out connecting it to experiences derived from damage analysis on the occasion of seismic events. A suitable methodology and relative procedures are illustrated, the purpose of which is to go back from damage analysis to detection of forecast errors as sources of seismic hazard and vulnerability. With reference to R.C. buildings, current design procedures, including seismic codes, are critically discussed on the basis of damage analyses relating to recent seismic events. It is finally proposed that international organizations for seismic prevention recommend standard procedures as regards both damage analysis of future seismic events and elaboration of obtained data, in order to achieve, through experimental knowledge, useful directions to remove remaining causes of seismic vulnerability of constructions.

1 INTRODUCTION

Seismic events that recently hit several countries in different places of the world have pointed out, through their heavy amount of damages, as today, at the end of the twentieth century, earthquake is still, among natural disasters, one of the most active and dangerous.

Despite the considerable developments of scientific and technological knowledges which have had a great growth in the last decades, the seismic hazard of built-up areas and relative service infrastructures is still high for all the countries, both those more advanced technically and the less developed ones.

Activation of a policy aimed at the reduction of seismic risk for the future needs the awareness, from the technical-scientific community, of persistence of such risk and consequently a serious analysis of generating causes.

In such context experience and learning drawn from the past seismic events play a fundamental role.

Analysis of damages, due to recent seismic events, of nominally earthquake-resistant constructions, shows as such damages are mainly due to forecast faults in determination of the response process and, consequently, of its outcome.

Such forecast faults are mostly caused either by overestimation of "capacity" or by underestimation of "demand", and also by oversight in accounting for various factors conditioning seismic response and by omissions in quality controls relating to the overall realization process.

In substance, forecast errors give the construction anomalous characteristics, that is pathological, of vulnerability. It is important to go back, through a procedure which allows to establish relationships between effects (anomalous damages) and causes that produced them, up to the origins or sources of such pathological vulnerability. The procedure has to be conducted having a clear vision of the process of absorption of seismic action, as well as of the overall realization process so as structured into different phases. By this way it is possible to go back, starting from various damage episodes, to the chrisis mechanisms that generated them, to related physical phenomena of activation, to geometrical and mechanical characteristics of the architectonic-structural system (architectonic morphology, structure, materials) triggering such activation and, finally, to the origins and responsibilities of forecast deficiencies which are at the basis of such damage phenomena. These origins are referable in any case to one, or more, of the "realization" phases of construction, namely the normative, design and execution phases (Sarà 1992, 1993, 1994).

2 PROCEDURE FOR ASCERTAINMENT OF VULNERABILITY SOURCES BY MEANS OF DAMAGE ANALYSIS

The proposed procedure, aimed at going back from

the analysis of damage (Folić 1991) to ascertainment of the relating sources of vulnerability and then to ascertainment of primary causes, or origins, of structural failures (Sarà 1987b, 1991), is structured according to a chain of "effect-cause" relationships, as indicated in table 1 (Sarà 1994).

Table 1. Procedure for ascertainment of vulnerability sources by means of damage analysis.

---

(1) analysis of damage:
  a) identification of location and characteristics (type and amount) of damage;
  b) ascertainment of damage mechanism;
(2) analysis of vulnerability:
  c) ascertainment of phenomenon activating damage mechanism;
  d) ascertainment of construction characteristics recognizable as sources of vulnerability connected to the specific considered damage;
(3) analysis of failure origins (and then of responsibilities):
  e) ascertainment of the cause of the specific seismic vulnerability, meant as the factor of the "demand-capacity" or "stress-strength" balance that, presumably, did not agree to design expectations. As regards the definition of "stress", the aspect of "action", connected to the seismic energy absorbed by the structure, has been differentiated from the aspect of "stress" in the proper sense, that is the state of internal forces depending on the above mentioned action and its distribution among structural elements; as regards meaning of "strength", it is referred to the resistant capabilities including ductile capacities;
  f) ascertainment of the origin of the specific seismic vulnerability, where "origin" is meant as the regulation, realization (design-execution) or utilization phase to which the primary cause, or "responsibility", of the structural failure can be related; that is the phase which mainly has contributed to determine a distortion in the preventive evaluation about construction outcome. Consequently we can refer to deficiencies concerning regulations (codes in force at the time of the building realization), design, execution or utilization.

The methodology has been applied, with reference to damage suffered by R.C. civil buildings as documented by available technical literature, to the analysis of sets of failures occurred in a series of places which have been hit by recent seismic events.

The results of the survey are reported below with reference to some analyzed earthquakes and localities:

I) S. Angelo dei Lombardi (Italy). Irpinia earthquake, 23rd November 1980, IX-X MCS degree. Locality subjected to seismic protection rules at the time. References concerning examined technical documents: Parducci 1981, Cestelli Guidi 1981, Gavarini 1981, Aristodemo 1985, Sarà 1987b.

II) Mexico City, zone C (soft lake sediments) (Mexico). Mexican earthquake, 19th September 1985, IX MCS degree. Locality subjected to seismic protection rules at the time. References concerning examined technical documents: Angeletti 1985, Munich Reinsurance Company Report 1986, EEFIT Report 1986, Mitchell 1987.

The results of the developed analyses are shown in tables 2 and 3.

Table 2. Concatenation patterns "damage - source of vulnerability - origin of failure". Irpinia earthquake of 23/11/1980. Locality: S. Angelo dei Lombardi.

---

(1) Activation of critical states for combined bending and axial forces in columns, due to lack of connecting beams. Recurrence degree: medium.
Analysis of damage
(a) Damage located at the end zones of columns or partial collapse.
(b) Failure of columns for combined bending and axial forces because of the overall interstorey shear.
Analysis of vulnerability
(c) Activation of critical states for combined bending and axial forces in columns.
(d) Lack of connecting beams among columns.
Analysis of failure origins
(e) Excess of stress in columns for bending due to earthquake.
(f) Design fault ([1]).

(2) Activation of critical states for combined bending and axial forces, due to the presence of frames having a curvilinear shape in plan. Recurrence degree: low ([2]).
Analysis of damage
(a) Damage located at the end zones of columns.
(b) Failure of columns for combined bending and axial forces because of the overall interstorey shear.
Analysis of vulnerability
(c) Activation of critical states for combined bending and axial forces in columns.
(d) Presence of frames having a curvilinear shape in plan.
Analysis of failure origins
(e) Excess of stress in columns for bending due to earthquake.
(f) Design fault ([1]).

(3) Critical activation of torsional motions, due to the building asymmetry. Recurrence degree: medium.
Analysis of damage
(a) Damage located at the end zones of columns belonging to perimetric frames.
(b) Failure of columns for combined bending and axial forces because of the overall interstorey torsion.
Analysis of vulnerability
(c) Critical activation of torsional motions.
(d) Building asymmetry.
Analysis of failure origins
(e) Excess of stress in columns for bending due to earthquake.
(f) Regulation-design fault ([3]).

(4) Activation of critical states for combined bending and axial forces in columns, due to the presence of staircase frames stiffened by flight beams. Recurrence degree: high.
Analysis of damage
(a) Damage located at the end zones of columns belonging to staircase frames with flight beams.
(b) Failure of columns for combined bending and axial forces because of the overall bending and interstorey shear.
Analysis of vulnerability
(c) Activation of critical states for combined bending and axial forces in columns.
(d) Presence of staircase frames, with flight beams, characterized by high flexural and transversal stiffness.
Analysis of failure origins
(e) Excess of stress in columns for combined bending and axial forces due to earthquake.
(f) Regulation-design fault (^{3}).

(5) Activation of critical states for shear forces in squat columns belonging to staircase frames with flight beams. Recurrence degree: high.
Analysis of damage
(a) Damage located (inclined cracks) at the squat columns of staircase frames with flight beams.
(b) Cracking of columns for shear forces because of the overall interstorey shear.
Analysis of vulnerability
(c) Activation of critical states for shear forces in columns.
(d) Presence of squat columns, characterized by high shear stiffness, in staircase frames with flight beams.
Analysis of failure origins
(e) Excess of stress for shear in squat columns of staircase frames.
(f) Regulation-design fault (^{3}).

(6) Activation of critical states for combined bending and axial forces in columns, due to shortage of stirrups. Recurrence degree: medium.
Analysis of damage
(a) Damage located at the end zones of columns.
(b) Failure of columns for combined bending and axial forces because of the overall interstorey shear.
Analysis of vulnerability
(c) Activation of critical states for combined bending and axial forces in columns.
(d) Shortage of stirrups at the end zones of columns.
Analysis of failure origins
(e) Deficiency in ductility capacities at the end zones of columns.
(f) Regulation-design fault (^{3}).

(7) Activation of critical states for combined bending and axial forces in shear walls, due to their high stiffness (frames-shear walls dual systems). Recurrence degree: low (^{2}).
Analysis of damage
(a) Damage located (horizontal cracks) at the foot of shear walls.
(b) Cracking of shear walls for combined bending and axial forces because of the overall bending.

Analysis of vulnerability
(c) Activation of critical states for combined bending and axial forces in shear walls.
(d) Presence of shear walls, characterized by high flexural and transversal stiffness.
Analysis of failure origins
(e) Excess of stress for bending in shear walls.
(f) Regulation-design fault (^{3}).

(8) Activation of critical states for shear forces in coupling beams of shear walls, due to their high stiffness (frames-shear walls dual systems). Recurrence degree: low (^{2}).
Analysis of damage
(a) Damage located (inclined cracks) at coupling beams of shear walls.
(b) Cracking of coupling beams for shear forces because of the sliding between the connected walls.
Analysis of vulnerability
(c) Activation of critical states for shear forces in coupling beams of shear walls.
(d) Presence of coupled shear walls, characterized by high flexural stiffness.
Analysis of failure origins
(e) Excess of stress for shear in coupling beams of shear walls.
(f) Regulation-design fault (^{3}).

(^{1}) Fault in the calculation modelling.
(^{2}) Low degree also due to the small number of buildings having constructive characteristics of the indicated type, in the surveyed locality.
(^{3}) Seismic code lacking in specific prescriptions concerning ductility requirements at the critical zones of structures.

Table 3. Concatenation patterns "damage - source of vulnerability - origin of failure". Mexican earthquake of 19/09/1985. Locality: Mexico City, zone C.

---

(1) Critical activation of translational vibration modes higher than the first one, due to great "seismic flexibility" (^{1}) of the building. Recurrence degree: high.
Analysis of damage
(a) Partial collapse owing to the failure of the set of columns belonging to an upper storey.
(b) Failure of columns for combined bending and axial forces because of the overall interstorey shear.
Analysis of vulnerability
(c) Critical activation of translational vibration modes higher than the first one.
(d) Building characterized by great "seismic flexibility" (^{1}).
Analysis of failure origins
(e) Excess of action (double resonance: seismic wave-soil, soil-building).
(f) Regulation fault (^{2}).

(2) Critical activation of translational vibration modes and hammering on adjacent buildings, due to great "seismic flexibility" (^{1}) of the building. Recurrence degree: medium.

1655

Analysis of damage
(a) Partial collapse owing to the failure of the set of columns belonging to an upper storey.
(b) Failure of columns for combined bending and axial forces because of the overall interstorey shear.
Analysis of vulnerability
(c) Critical activation of translational vibration modes and consequent hammering on adjacent buildings.
(d) Building characterized by great "seismic flexibility" (^{1}) and adjacency of other constructions.
Analysis of failure origins
(e) Excess of action (double resonance).
(f) Regulation fault (^{2}).

(3) Critical activation of translational modes, due to the presence of a "soft" ground storey. Recurrence degree: low.
Analysis of damage
(a) Partial collapse owing to the failure of the set of columns belonging to the ground storey.
(b) Failure of columns for combined bending and axial forces because of the overall interstorey shear.
Analysis of vulnerability
(c) Critical activation of translational vibration modes.
(d) Presence of a "soft" ground storey (lacking or poor in infilling walls).
Analysis of failure origins
(e) Shortage of "strength" capability (shortage of ductility capacities).
(f) Regulation-design fault (^{3}).

(4) Activation of critical states for shear forces in sets of interstorey columns. Recurrence degree: low (^{4}).
Analysis of damage
(a) Cracking (inclined cracks) in a set of interstorey columns.
(b) Failure of columns for shear forces because of the overall interstorey shear.
Analysis of vulnerability
(c) Activation of critical states for shear forces in a set of interstorey columns.
(d) Presence of storeys with squat columns, characterized by high shear stiffness, owing to deep beams or rigid infilling walls with limited rise.
Analysis of failure origins
(e) Excess of stress.
(f) Regulation-design fault (^{5}).

(5) Critical activation of torsional motions, due to in plan asymmetry of the building. Recurrence degree: medium.
Analysis of damage
(a) Partial collapse owing to the failure of perimetric columns.
(b) Failure of interstorey columns for combined bending and axial forces because of the overall interstorey torsion.
Analysis of vulnerability
(c) Critical activation of torsional motions.
(d) In plan asymmetry of the building (^{6}).
Analysis of failure origins
(e) Excess of stress in columns for bending due to earthquake.
(f) Regulation-design fault (^{5}).

(6) Activation of critical states of stress in the ground due to yielding soil. Recurrence degree: medium.
Analysis of damage
(a) Sinking or overturning, complete or partial, of the building.
(b) Soil settlement owing to compression.
Analysis of vulnerability
(c) Activation of critical states of stress in the ground , with consequent settlement, under the seimic action.
(d) Yielding foundation soil (may be for presence of water).
Analysis of failure origins
(e) Shortage of strength capacity (in foundation).
(f) Design fault (^{7}).

(7) Activation of critical states for combined bending and axial forces in shear walls, due to their high stiffness (frames-shear walls dual systems). Recurrence degree: low (^{4}).
Analysis of damage
(a) Damage located (horizontal cracks) at the foot of shear walls.
(b) Cracking of shear walls for combined bending and axial forces because of the overall bending.
Analysis of vulnerability
(c) Activation of critical states for combined bending and axial forces in shear walls.
(d) Presence of shear walls characterized by high flexural and transversal stiffness.
Analysis of failure origins
(e) Excess of stress for bending in shear walls.
(f) Regulation-design fault (^{3}).

(8) Activation of critical states for bending forces in transversal braced frames. Recurrence degree: low (^{4}).
Analysis of damage
(a) Total collapse owing to the failure of columns of the ground storey.
(b) Failure of columns of the ground storey for combined bending and axial forces and interstorey shear.
Analysis of vulnerability
(c) Activation of critical states for bending forces in braced frames.
(d) Presence of transversal braced frames characterized by high flexural and transversal stiffness.
Analysis of failure origins
(e) Excess of stress for axial forces in columns belonging to braced frames
(f) Regulation-design fault (^{5}).

(9) Activation of critical states for shear, bending and axial forces in joints of frames, due to shortage of stirrups and anchorage of bars. Recurrence degree: low.
Analysis of damage
(a) Damage located at joint zones.
(b) Cracking of joints for shear, bending and axial forces.
Analysis of vulnerability
(c) Activation of critical states for shear, bending and axial forces in joints.
(d) Presence of joints of frames characterized by shortage of stirrups and anchorage of the beam bars.

Analysis of failure origins
(e) Deficiency in "strength" (strength capability and ductility capacities) of joints.
(f) Regulation-design fault ([5]).

([1]) Flexibility inclusive of the "mass effect" on oscillation characteristics: tall buildings having a framed structure with great bays, massive floors, light face panels.

([2]) Fault in modelling the placing site and then in estimating response to seismic waves.

([3]) Seismic code lacking in adequate specific prescriptions concerning ductility requirements in critical zones of the structure.

([4]) Low degree also due to the small number of buildings having constructive characteristics of the indicated type, in the surveyed locality.

([5]) Shortage of "strength" capability (strength and ductility capacities) in critical zones of the structure.

([6]) Corner building or, in general, building with asymmetry in plan.

([7]) Fault in estimating soil characteristics.

---

3 THE ROLE OF CODES IN REMOVAL OF CAUSES OF SEISMIC VULNERABILITY

A comprehensive examination of damages in earthquake-resistant constructions, caused by the recent seismic events, shows that they, and so the corresponding sources of anomalous vulnerability, are principally imputable to an inadequate forecast (owing to deficiencies in structural modelling) of response with reference to the following aspects:
- effects due to the real properties of the soil (alteration in characteristics of seismic input);
- effects due to structural non-regularity (in particular the activation of torsional motions);
- influence of real ductile capacity of the structure (in construction systems characterized by hysteretic dissipation);
- effects due to the presence or absence of infill elements (in systems with framed structure).

Removal of recognized causes of seismic vulnerability is, first of all, a task of codes for earthquake-resistant constructions, codes which in the past have often revealed their inadequacy even though they experienced a considerable evolution, particularly starting from the seventies (Sarà 1987a, 1988).

The recent european code for aseismic design (Eurocode 8) rightly devotes particular attention to the above mentioned causes of vulnerability, furnishing indications relating both to calculation models and execution techniques. It has to underline, above all, for their innovative character with respect to the preceding national rules and particularly to the italian ones, the provisions aimed at defining response spectra differentiated on the basis of the type of soil, the instructions directed to the definition of structural non-regularity degrees as well as ductility levels (degrees and levels which have to be taken into account in choosing calculation models) and, finally, the indications specifying how to include effects due to infills in computational procedures.

It is advisable that the new generation of seismic codes, which will be issued in different countries in the next future, will be able to remove radically, through innovations suggested mainly by observation of damages caused by the latest earthquakes, the remaining, but still conspicuous, sources of vulnerability present in constructions nominally defined as aseismic. Attention of operators, and so of codes, by this way can shift, as already it is occurring, towards problems of micro-damaging, i.e. damaging of extra-structural elements, which has to be absolutely avoided on the occasion of medium-weak earthquakes so as to save heavy economic burdens for repairing.

On the other hand it is necessary to consider that advance of construction technologies and techniques is going to introduce a set of new problems (let us consider, for instance, the problem of high-strength materials and their reduced possibilities to take advantage of ductility characteristics, as well as the problem of the real behaviour of constructions realized through modern structural systems) which will be settled in a satisfactory and reliable way only after "testing" exerted by future earthquakes.

At the moment possibilities to reduce drastically seismic risk, which is still seriously impending on building inheritance of several countries, seem to be substantially linked to further advances in evolutionary process of aseismic forecast and prevention tools, advances which have to develop mainly in the following directions:
- refining of forecasting tools aimed at defining seismicity of various areas: more accurate macro-zonations and micro-zonations for a more correct forecast of the seismic input;
- better control of the real "aseismic quality" of constructions, both new and old, so as to improve forecasting levels with reference to the process of structural response towards seismic actions; that also through creation of normative tools more efficacious and consistent with construction reality;
- greater attention, supported by adequate econo-mical resources, towards more intrinsically aseismic construction techniques, such as modern systems provided with special dissipation or isolation devices; in this case also it is necessary an adequate development of specific normative tools which may encourage diffusion of the new construction techniques;
- working out of plans, supported by suitable funds, aimed at an efficacious intervention on the existing buildings not provided with aseismic characteristics

or provided with not adequate aseismic characteristics owing to updating in zonation or, in general, in aseismic regulation;
- careful assimilation, at every level of the realization process of constructions (normative, design and execution level), of learning drawn through systematic analyses of the outcome of constructions on the occasion of recent seismic events and of the future ones, particularly as regards earthquake "testing" of models for computational procedures and, moreover, earthquake "testing" both of new construction techniques and of the refitting ones.

4 PROPOSAL OF A STANDARDIZATION OF DAMAGE SURVEY MODALITIES

With reference to the last of the above listed points, concerning teachings drawn from earthquakes, it seems opportune to propose to the attention of the national and over-national organizations devoted to aseismic prevention the suitability of standardization in damage survey modalities referred to future seismic events. That should facilitate the subsequent analysis procedure for the ascertainment of connections of damages with sources of seismic vulnerability associated to faults in codes, design or execution.

In the opinion of the Authors, the survey of damages ought be conducted through a systematic procedure like that suggested in the present work so as to allow to establish easily, with reference to the single seismic event, the above-mentioned relations with the sources of vulnerability. It is also important, for the significance of the survey, that the ascertainment procedure should be conducted, as far as possible, by a statistical approach, so as to have available a set of documents sufficiently complete and reliable containing both success and failure situations of the whole of constructions.

The Authors, therefore, urge the promulgation, from international organizations, of instructions and recommendations on modalities to carry out post-earthquakes structural performance surveys as well as on criteria to elaborate the collected data.

Compilation of suitable reports uniformly structured and aimed at the individuation of various sources of vulnerability as well as at the evaluation of relating incidence on the overall damage should allow a more incisive utilization of valuable and fundamental teaching deriving from observation of structural response of building inheritance in case of severe earthquakes. All that may also allow to quicken evolution of tools and techniques capable to control normative, design and execution quality in building realization and then the construction process on the whole.

REFERENCES

Angeletti, P., Benedetti, D., Carpinteri, A. et al. 1985. Osservazioni preliminari sul comportamento delle costruzioni e sui danni. *Ingegneria Sismica* 3: 52-63.

Aristodemo, M., Sarà, G. & Vulcano, A. 1985. Esperienze relative al comportamento sotto sisma delle costruzioni: sisma in Campania e Basilicata del 23/11/1980. In: Sarà, G. (ed.), *Ingegneria Antisismica*: chapter XIII, 415-485. Napoli: Liguori.

Blockley, D.I. 1985. Reliability or responsibility. *Structural Safety* 2: 273-280.

Cestelli Guidi, C. 1981. Aspetti salienti del comportamento dei fabbricati allo scuotimento sismico. *L'Industria Italiana del Cemento* 10: 653-672.

Comerford, J.B. & Blockley, D.I. 1993. Managing safety and hazard through dependability. *Structural Safety* 12: 21-33.

EEFIT Report 1986. *The Mexican earthquake of 19th September 1985*. London: SECED.

Folić, R.J. 1991. A classification of damage to concrete buildings in earthquakes, illustrated by examples. *Materials and Structures* 24: 286-292.

Gavarini, C. 1981. Dopo il terremoto del 23/11/1980. *L'Industria Italiana del Cemento* 10: 631-652.

Mitchell, D. 1987. Structural damage due to the 1985 Mexican earthquake. *Proc. 5th Canadian Conference on Earthquake Engineering*: 87-109. Ottawa.

Munich Reinsurance Company Report 1986. *Earthquake Mexico '85*. Munchen.

Parducci, A. 1981. Considerazioni sul comportamento delle costruzioni in c.a. durante il terremoto del 23/11/1980. *L'Industria Italiana del Cemento* 1: 45-56.

Sarà, G. 1987a. Genesi ed evoluzione delle norme italiane per le costruzioni in muratura in zona sismica. *Proc. Seminario Tecnologia, Scienza e Storia per la conservazione del costruito. Annali Fondazione Pontello*: 41-58. Firenze.

Sarà, G. 1987b. Valutazione della vulnerabilità sismica degli edifici. *Proc. Specialization Course on Static Refitting*: 1-39. Catania: Engineer Association.

Sarà, G. 1988. Evoluzione delle norme italiane per le costruzioni in muratura in zona sismica. *Proc. Celebrazioni Cinquantenario Facoltà di Architettura di Napoli e Prof. Franco Jossa*: 631-667. University of Napoli.

Sarà, G. 1991. Fonti di vulnerabilità e criteri di progetazione per le costruzioni in c.a. in zona sismica. *Proc. Specialization Course on Seismic Engineering*: 397-407. Augusta.

Sarà, G. & Nudo, R. 1992. Meaning and evolution of building codes: Eurocode 8 and reinforced concrete constructions in seismic zones. *Proc. 10th WCEE*: 5661-5666. Madrid.

Sarà, G. & Nudo, R. 1993. Codes and reliability of reinforced concrete buildings in seismic zones. *Proc. 6th ICOSSAR*: 2281-2284. Innsbruck.

Sarà, G. & Nudo, R. 1994. Analysis of damage mechanisms: codes and seismic vulnerability of buildings. *Proc. 10th ECEE*: 1035-1040. Vienna.

Turner, B.A. 1978. *Man-made disasters*. London: Wykeham Press.

Structural Safety and Reliability, Shiraishi, Shinozuka & Wen (eds) © 1998 Balkema, Rotterdam, ISBN 90 5410 978 5

A simplified procedure to estimate liquefaction-induced large ground displacement using spatial liquefaction potential

M. Yoshida
Fukui National College of Technology, Sabae, Japan

M. Miyajima & M. Kitaura
Kanazawa University, Japan

ABSTRACT: The present paper deals with a simplified procedure to predict the magnitude and direction of liquefied ground flow. The procedure proposed here was applied to the liqufied sites after the 1964 Niigata earthquake. The relation between the estimated spatial liquefiable area and permanent ground displacements induced by liquefied ground flow was investigated. Furthermore the relation between the correlation distance of SPT N-values and direction of liquefied ground flow was studied.

1 INTRODUCTION

Horizontal and vertical ground displacements induced by soil liquefaction caused severe and extensive damage to many structures such as underground foundations and buried pipelines during the past earthquakes. During the 1995 Hyogoken-nambu earthquake in Japan, extreme liquefaction occurred at the coastal reclaimed lands of Hanshin area and the liquefaction-induced large ground displacements were also caused there. The large ground displacements seem to be one of the most influential factors of the damage to underground structures. It is important in seismic design to evaluate the displacement, force and direction acting on structures induced by movements of liquefied ground. This study deals with the horizontal displacement induced by liquefied ground flow.

The two approaches are proposed here to predict the magnitude and/or direction of liquefied ground flow. One is to estimate the spatial liquefiable area. The spatial liquefiable area estimated is very useful for prediction of the magnitude and direction of liquefied ground flow. The authors have proposed a method to estimate the spatial liquefaction potential which is based upon a geostatistical procedure which is called as the Kriging technique using the variogram (Yoshida et al. 1995). This method can estimate the three-dimensional liquefaction potential using limited borehole data. This method was applied to the

liquefied sites during the 1964 Niigata earthquake in Japan. The relation between the estimated spatial liquefiable area and observed ground flow after the earthquake was investigated.

The other is to estimate the spatial continuity of soil parameters such as SPT N-value, underground water level and so on. The spatial continuity of SPT N-values was estimated by using anisotropy axes of the variogram to predict the direction of liquefied ground flow. The relation between the correlation distance of SPT N-values and direction of liquefied ground flow was investigated.

2 KRIGING AND VARIOGRAM

The Kriging is a geostatistical procedure which predicts a sample field at non-observation points on condition that an estimated field coincides with the sample values at observation points. It is often associated with the acronym B.L.U.E. for "best linear unbiased estimater". An unknown value is estimated by the weighted linear combination of known values that exist in the area close to the unknown value. The weighted linear combinations is expressed as follows:

$$\hat{V}(x_0) = \sum_{i=1}^{n} w_i \cdot V(x_i) \qquad (1)$$

in which $\hat{V}(x_0)$ is a value estimated at x_0, $V(x_i)$ is an observed value at x_i, n is a number of observed samples, w_i is a weight for $V(x_i)$, respectively. The weight w_i is determined by two conditions using the technique of Lagrange parameters as follows.

$$\sum_{i=1}^{n} w_i = 1 \qquad (2)$$

$$\tilde{\sigma}_R^2 = E\left[\left\{\hat{V}(x_0) - V(x_0)\right\}^2\right] \to \text{minimum} \qquad (3)$$

Eq.2 means the unbiasedness condition of the estimated value and Eq.3 indicates minimization of the error variance. The optimum estimated value can be obtained by substitution of the weight to Eq.1. The modeled error variance is given by following equation.

$$\tilde{\sigma}_R^2 = \sum_{i=1}^{n} w_i \cdot \tilde{\gamma}_{i0} + \mu \qquad (4)$$

where, $\tilde{\gamma}$ is the variogram and μ is the Lagrange parameter.

The variogram is evaluated in consideration of disposition and value of samples to understand the characteristics of sample distribution. Let V be a sample value observed at a point of a geometrical field, the theoretical variogram γ_i is as follows:

$$\gamma_i = \frac{1}{2} E\left\{\left[V_i - V_i\right]^2\right\} \qquad (5)$$

This equation represents characteristics of distribution of sample values. $\gamma^*(h)$ which is called as an model variogram is actually used in calculation as follows:

$$\gamma^*(h) = \frac{1}{2N(h)} \sum_{i=1}^{N(h)} \left\{V(x_i) - V(y_i)\right\}^2 \qquad (6)$$

where, $N(h)$ is number of pairs of samples relative to the separation vector h. In this study, the experimental variogram $\gamma^*(h)$ is assumed as the following equation by using an exponential function:

$$\tilde{\gamma}(h) = a \cdot (1 - e^{-b \cdot h}) \qquad (7)$$

where, a and b mean coefficients of variogram value and correlation distance between sample values, respectively.

3 TARGET AREA OF ANALYSIS

The Niigata earthquake, with a magnitude of 7.5, occurred under the Japan sea about 50km north off Niigata city at Niigata prefecture on June 16, 1964, causing severe damage to structures such as buildings, bridges, oil storage tanks and lifeline facilities due to soil liquefaction. A central part of Niigata city located between the Shinano river and the Niigata railway station was focused in this study as shown in Fig.1. The Shinano river is shown at the left-upper side in Fig.1 and it flows from southwest

to northeast. The target area is 0.6 km long in east-west direction and 1.1 km long in north-south direction. Most of this area has no gradient of the ground surface. Twenty six borehole data were obtained in and around here. The data within an altitude of 3m to -16m were used. The water level in this area was supposed to be at the ground surface. The maximum horizontal acceleration of this earthquake in Niigata city was about 0.16g (Hamada 1992). This acceleration was used to calculate the factor of liquefaction resistance F_L-value (J.R.A. 1991) in the study.

Fig.2 shows the horizontal and vertical ground displacements after the earthquake. The data were transformed from the actual displacements which were measured by pre- and post-earthquake aerial surveys (Hamada 1992) to raster data. The maximum permanent ground displacements measured in this area were about 4.0 m of lateral flow, 3.0 m of settlement and 1.4 m of upheaval. Fig. 3 illustrates the magnitude and direction of the liquefied ground flow using a polar coordinate. It can be seen from this figure that the southeast direction of the displacements are predominant.

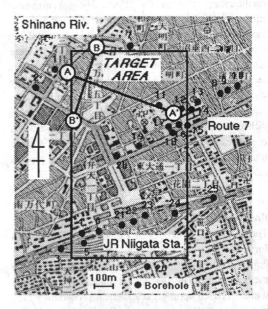

Fig.1 Map of Niigata city and distribution of boreholes.

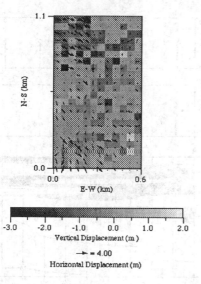

Vertical Displacement (m)

→ = 4.00

Horizontal Displacement (m)

Fig.2 Horizontal and vertical permanent ground displacements.

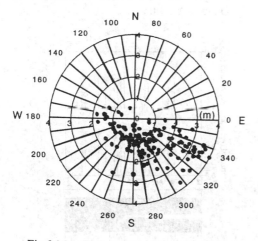

Fig.3 Magnitude and direction of horizontal displacements.

4 ESTIMATION OF SPATIAL LIQUEFACTION POTENTIAL WITH F_L AND N-VALUE

Fig.4 shows the three-dimensional view of liquefiable portion made by superposing some two-dimensional planes of the factor of liquefaction resistance F_L-value estimated here. The two-dimensional planes were calculated at interval of 50 m along north-south and east-west directions, and at

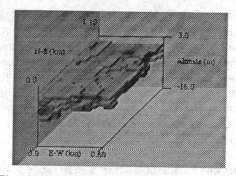

Fig.4 Three-dimensional view of F_L-value of less than or equal 1.0.

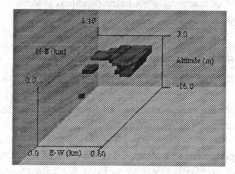

Fig.5 Three-dimensional view of N-value of less than or equal 5.

interval of 0.5 m vertically. The opaque area expresses that F_L-values are less than or equal to 1.0, that is, liquefiable area. The thickness and inclination of liquefied layer can be obtained from this figure roughly. Although the liquefiable layer exists above 10 m in depth, liquefaction does not occur at very shallow layer because of soil type. The thickest liquefiable layer exists on the northwest area along the right bank of the Shinano river, and its thickness gradually decreases towards the southeast. The boundary between the liquefied layer and the upper non-liquefied layer is inclined from the northwest area toward the northeast with the maximum gradient of about 3 %. This direction corresponds with the large vectors of horizontal displacement at the northwest area as shown in Fig.2.

The boundary conditions between liquefied and non-liquefied area seem to be one of the crucial factors to predict the liquefaction-induced ground movements. Although F_L-value can give the information of liquefaction potential, the information of non-liquefiable area can not be obtained. The distribution of SPT N-value was, therefore, investigated because N-value expresses the stiffness of soil and affects the deformation of ground. The distribution of N-value was estimated in much the same way as that of F_L-value. In this case, two-dimensional planes were calculated at interval of 1 m vertically. Fig.5 shows the three-dimensional view of N-value of less than or equal to 5. The loose soil layer with N-value of less than or equal to 5, exists in a part of the surface layer. The three-dimensional view of ground softness in an area evaluated by N-value can give the important information of non-liquefiable area as a boundary condition of deformed ground.

5 EVALUATION OF MAGNITUDE AND DIRECTION OF LIQUEFIED GROUND FLOW

According to Fig.3, almost all liquefied ground flow from northwest to southeast. The large vectors were distributed at the northwest area and the maximum displacement was about 4.0 m. Two sections along A-A' and B-B' as shown in Fig.1 were investigated here. These two lines are mutually perpendicular. The ground adjacent the right bank of the Shinano river moved toward the river in the northwest direction. However, the area along A-A' moved to the southeast, almost opposite that on the river bank.

Fig.6 shows the distribution of the estimated F_L-value and the observed permanent ground displacements along A-A' section. Those, along B-B' section, are also shown in Fig.7.

These figures of estimated F_L-value along any section were obtained from Fig.4. The dark portion shows the liquefiable layer where F_L-values are less than or equal to 1.0. The thickest liquefiable layer of about 10 m exists on the left side in Fig.6. The upper and lower boundary of liquefiable layer was inclined down from A to A'. It seems that the large horizontal displacements occurred on the left side and the ground moved from A to A' corresponding to thickness and inclination of liquefied layer. Along B-B' section, there are no particular change of thickness and inclination of liquefied layer. Therefore, there is no horizontal displacements in direction along B-B' according to Fig.2. Consequently, the direction of lateral liquefied ground flow is influenced by

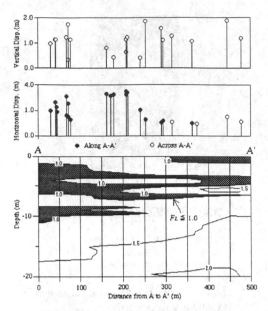

Fig.6 Distribution of estimated F_L-values and permanent ground displacements along A-A' section.

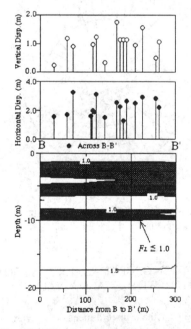

Fig.7 Distribution of estimated F_L-values and permanent ground displacements along B-B' section.

thickness and inclination of liquefied layer.

Next, the spatial continuity of soil parameters is focused here to predict the direction of liquefied ground flow. The relation between the spatial continuity of soil parameters and the direction of liquefied ground flow was investigated. The present study estimated the spatial continuity of soil parameters by using anisotropy axes of a variogram (Isaaks et al. 1989). Although the omnidirectional variogram was evaluated in the estimation mentioned above, the directional variogram was adopted here to investigate the anisotropy axes. Fig.8 illustrates the tolerance of the distance of data pairs h. A tolerance

Δh of ± 0.05 km on the magnitude of h and a tolerance θ of ± 20 degrees was allowed on the direction in this study. The interval of distance was 0.1 km and the interval of direction from east direction α was 20 degree in the calculation.

The N-value from surface to 5 m in depth was used to evaluate the spatial continuity of soil parameters. The directional variograms of the average N-value from surface to 5 m in depth were calculated. Fig.9 shows the examples of directional variograms of 0 degree and 100 degree from east

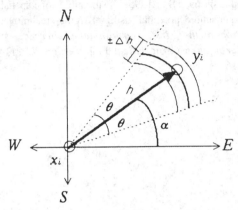

Fig.8 Illustration of tolerance of distance and direction for anisotropy axes.

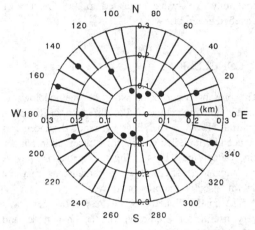

Fig.10 Rose diagram of correlation distance of N-value.

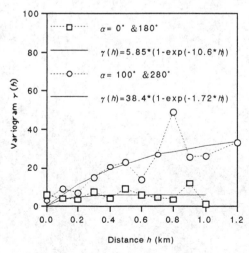

Fig.9 Variograms of 0 and 100 degree from east direction.

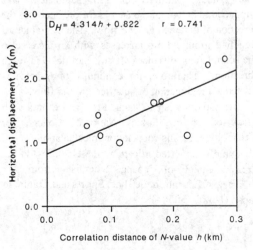

Fig.11 Relation between correlation distance of N-value and horizontal displacements.

direction. The shape of variograms are different in each direction. The regression curves obtained from an exponential function described in Eq.7 are also shown in this figure. The distance at which the variogram reached 5 by the regression curves was estimated as a correlation distance. Fig.10 illustrates a rose diagram of the correlation distance. According to this figure, the correlation distance is large in the northwest to southeast direction. Fig.11 shows the relation between the average horizontal displacement and correlation distance in each direction. The horizontal displacement increases with an increase in the correlation distance. This suggests that the continuity of N-value is related to the direction of liquefied ground flow.

6 CONCLUSIONS

The present paper deals with the methodology to predict the magnitude and/or direction of liquefied ground flow. The large ground displacements induced by liquefied ground flow observed in Niigata city after the 1964 Niigata earthquake were investigated. The following conclusions may be drawn based on the present study.

The spatial liquefiable area estimated here was very useful for prediction of the magnitude and direction of liquefied ground flow. The direction and magnitude of liquefied ground flow were influenced by the thickness and inclination of liquefied layer. The spatial continuity of soil parameters was supposed to be one of the factors for prediction of the direction of liquefied ground flow. The magnitude of liquefied ground flow increases with an increase in the correlation distance of soil softness in each direction. Therefore, the continuity of N-value is related to the direction of liquefied ground flow.

The authors wish to thank Mr. H. Ueyama who graduated from Fukui National College of Technology, for his cooperation in calculation.
This study supported in part by the Grant-in-Aid for Encouragement of Young Scientists from the Ministry of Education, Science, Sports and Culture in Japan (No.09750584).

REFERENCES

Isaaks, E.H. & Srivastava, R.M. 1989. *An Introduction to applied geostatistics*. Oxford University Press.

Hamada, M. 1992. Large ground deformations and their effects on lifelines: 1964 Niigata earthquake. *Case Studies of Liquefaction and Lifeline Performance During Past Earthquakes*. 1. NCEER: 3.1-3.123.

Japan Road Association 1991. *Earthquake resistant design of specifications for highway bridges*. Part 5.

Yoshida, M., Miyajima, M., Kitaura, M. and Fukushima, S. 1995. Estimation of spatial liquefaction potential using Kriging technique. *Proc. of the First International Conference on Earthquake Geotechnical Engineering*. 2: 911-916.

Earthquake engineering (ongoing research)

Structural Safety and Reliability, Shiraishi, Shinozuka & Wen (eds) © 1998 Balkema, Rotterdam, ISBN 90 5410 978 5

Design target reliability of reinforced concrete buildings under earthquake loads

T. Saito
Building Research Institute, Ministry of Construction, Tsukuba, Japan

ABSTRACT: The purpose of this study is to quantify the uncertainty of seismic loads and to evaluate the seismic reliability of reinforced concrete buildings designed according to the recently proposed design guideline in Japan. The obtained reliability levels provide basic information on determining the target reliability levels in the performance based design procedures, where the building performances are described explicitly.

1 OBJECTIVE

In the developing performance based design procedures, it is an important task to identify the uncertainties in design parameters and to establish the reliability levels associated with design performance objectives. Particularly in Japan, the treatment of the large uncertainty of seismic loads is quite important since the seismic design procedures usually dominate the design processes. The purpose of this study is to quantify the uncertainty of seismic loads and to evaluate the seismic reliability of the reinforced concrete buildings designed according to the recently proposed design guidelines in Japan.

In the references (Saito and Wen 1992, Saito et al. 1996), the author studied the seismic reliability of reinforced concrete moment-resisting-frames at the several construction sites in Japan. This study extends the previous study by increasing the number of construction sites and structural types.

The obtained seismic reliability levels are presented in terms of safety indices β for several design criteria, such as the limitations of story drift at the serviceability limit state and the ultimate limit state.

2 MODEL OF EARTHQUAKE GROUND MOTION

The sites of buildings are assumed to be in six major cities at various areas in Japan as shown in Figure 1. The historical earthquake data available at the sites are selected under the following conditions:
1) recorded between 1885 to 1995
2) epicentral distance R is less than 350km
3) magnitude M is greater than 5.5
4) focal depth is less than 100km.

To obtain the statistics of earthquake acceleration response spectrum at each site, the selected seismicity data are substituted into the following attenuation formula proposed by Kawashima et al. (1985):

Figure 1. Selected sites in Japan

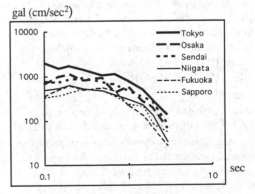

Figure 2. The mean maximum response spectrum in 100 years

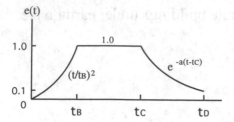

Figure 3. Jennings type envelope

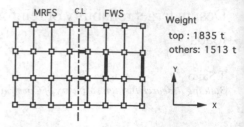

Weight
top : 1835 t
others: 1513 t

Figure 4. Plan view of RC building frames

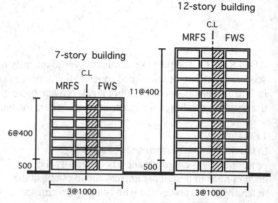

Figure 5. Elevation of RC buildings (Y-direction)

$$S_A(T,M,R,GC)=a\,(T,GC)\times10^{b(T,GC)M}\times(R+30)^c \qquad (1)$$

where $S_A(T,M,R,GC)$ is an earthquake response spectra, $a(T,GC)$, $b(T,GC)$ and c are the factors tabulated in the reference for several values of natural period, T, and ground condition, GC. The ground condition GC is assumed to be stiff condition for all the sites. Substituting the data of magnitude M and distance R into the above equation, the probability distribution function (p.d.f) of $S_A(T)$ is evaluated for each site as a log-normal distribution. Furthermore, assuming the Poisson process for the occurrence model of earthquakes, the p.d.f of "maximum acceleration spectrum $S_{A,max}(T)$ in t years" is obtained as the Type 2 extreme distribution (Saito et al. 1996). The mean values of the maximum spectrum in 100 years for the six sites are plotted in Figure 2.

The following nonstationary stochastic process is used for the model of input ground motions:

$$a(t)=e(t)s(t) \qquad (2)$$

where $e(t)$ is an envelope function and $s(t)$ is a stationary stochastic process having a certain power spectrum, $PS(\omega)$. The power spectrum $PS(\omega)$ is determined to be compatible with the sample value of maximum acceleration response spectrum $S_{A,max}(T)$ which is generated from the estimated probability distribution (Saito et al. 1996). The envelope function $e(t)$ is assumed to be a Jennings type envelope (Jennings et al. 1968) as shown in Figure 3, where the time parameters t_B, t_C, and t_D are determined by the following formula (Hisada and Ando 1976) :

$$t_B = \{0.16-0.04(M-6)\}t_D \qquad (3-1)$$
$$t_C = \{0.54-0.04(M-6)\}t_D \qquad (3-2)$$
$$t_D = 10^{\,0.31M-0.774} \qquad (3-3)$$

Substituting the data of magnitude M into Eq.(3-3), the p.d.f of t_D is modeled as a log-normal distribution and its mean value, μ_{tD}, considering the correlation to the spectral intensity $S_A(T)$, is adopted for the duration of input ground motions (Saito et al. 1996). Once the duration t_D is obtained, other parameters, t_B and t_C, are easily calculated from the above equations.

3 MODEL OF R.C. BUILDING

Four different reinforced concrete buildings are designed in accordance with a new design guideline which was presented by the Japan PRESSS (PREcast Seismic Structural System) working group in 1993. Two of the buildings are the 7-story and 12-story moment-resisting frame systems (MRFS), and others are the frame wall systems (FWS) with shear walls in the middle spans. The plan view and the elevation views of the buildings are shown in Figures 4 and 5, respectively. This study uses the Y-directional frames for the analysis. The structural dimension and the design of reinforcement steels are presented in Table 1 and Table 2, in the case of Tokyo site. The concrete is assumed to have nominal strength $Fc=360kg/cm^2$, and the reinforcement consists of Grade SD395 steel. The only difference among the design parameters of the six sites is the "seismic zone factor Z"; Z=1.0 for Sendai, Tokyo, and Osaka, Z=0.9 for Sapporo and Niigata, and Z=0.8 for Fukuoka site. So, the buildings designed for Tokyo site are modified for the buildings of other sites by multiplying the seismic zone factor, Z, to the strength of every member. The uncertainties associated with structural properties are assumed to be negligible comparing the uncertainties of earthquake loads, and not considered in this study.

Table 1. Dimension of structural members

7-story build.	1	2-7	Roof
column (b×D)	85×85	85×85	
beam (b×D)	55×200	40×90	40×90
wall (t)	15	15	
12-story build.	1	2-12	Roof
column (b×D)	90×90	90×90	
beam (b×D)	55×200	55×90	55×90
wall (t)	15	15	

b:width, D:height, t:depth　　　　　(unit: cm)

Table 2. Reinforcement steels (JIS standard)

7-story build.	1T	1B	2,3	4,5	6	7	R
column	12-D38	10-D38					
beam	8-D35		6-D38	5-D35		4-D29	
wall	2-D16@200 Double						
12-story build.	1T	1B	2,3,4	5,6,7	8,9,10	11,12	R
column	16-D41	12-D41			12-D38		
beam	10-D35		7-D41		5-D41	5-D32	
wall	2-D16@200 Double						

The main feature of the PRESSS guideline is to examine the performance of the buildings under both the serviceability limit state and the ultimate limit state by conducting a nonlinear static analysis under static lateral incremental loading. The design criterion on each design limit state is defined in terms of story drift ratio (inter-story drift divided by story height) as follows: 1) At the serviceability limit state with standard base shear coefficient C_B=0.2, no member is allowed to yield, and the story drift ratio must be less than 1/200 rad. 2) At the ultimate limit state, the story shear resistance at the design limit deformation R_{u1} shall be greater than 90 percent of the required lateral load resisting capacity C_{unB}. And the story shear at the design proof deformation R_{u2} shall be greater than the required resistance C_{unB}. In Table 3, the values of design deformations, R_{u1} and R_{u2}, and the required lateral load resistance C_{unB} are specified, and the performances of the designed buildings are examined to satisfy the design criteria.

Table 3. Check of design criteria

Limit State	Serviceability	Ultimate	
MRFS	C_B=0.2	R_{u1}=1/100	R_{u2}=1/50
Criteria	R<1/200	C_B>0.27	C_B>0.3(=C_{unB})
7-story	1/333	0.34	0.35
12-story	1/200	0.29	0.31
WFS	C_B=0.2	R_{u1}=1/120	R_{u2}=1/60
Criteria	R<1/200	C_B>0.315	C_B>0.35(=C_{unB})
7-story	1/800	0.48	0.54
12-story	1/360	0.34	0.39

4 SEISMIC RELIABILITY ESTIMATE

According to the same procedures described in the reference (Saito et al. 1996), the conditional distribution of the maximum response Y is modeled as a Type 1 extreme distribution as follows:

$$F_{Y|X}(y|x)=\exp[-\exp\{-\alpha(y-u)\}] \qquad (4)$$

$$\alpha=f_1(X), \quad u=f_2(X) \quad , X=S_{A,max}(T) \qquad (5)$$

The parameters, α and u, are modeled as the second order polynomial functions, $f_1(X)$ and $f_2(X)$, using the response surface method, where X is the random variable, $X=S_{A,max}(T)$. The simple way to calculate the "unconditional" failure probability is to apply the Monte-Carlo Method as follows:

$$p_f(y)\approx\frac{1}{N}\sum_{i=1}^{N}p_f(y|x_i) \qquad (6)$$

where, $p_f(y|x) = 1-F_{Y|X}(y|x)$: the conditional failure probability of Y giving the value of $X=S_{A,max}(T)$, N : the number of sample sets X_i (i=1,2,...,N). Since the parameters of the conditional failure probability $p_f(y|x)$ are already given as the functions of the random variable X (as in Eq.(4)), the failure probability $p_f(y)$ can be calculated by simply substituting the random samples of X into Eq. (6). All of the estimated reliability levels are standardized to be the annual safety index β using the following relation:

$$\beta=\Phi^{-1}(1-p_{f,annual}) \qquad (7)$$

where, Φ is the standard normal distribution function and $p_{f,annual}$ is the annual failure probability. Note that the probability $p_{f,annual}$ =10^{-3},10^{-4} and 10^{-5} correspond to β =3.09, 3.71 and 4.26, respectively.

Figures 6-(a) and 6-(b) show the relation between the maximum drift ratio R and the safety indices β for the 7-story and 12-story MRFS buildings . The drift ratio R is calculated using the maximum displacement at the particular story (4th story of 7 story building, 7th story of 12 story building) divided by its height. As shown in the figures, the safety index β of Tokyo site is generally smaller than those of other sites, on the contrary, the index β of Fukuoka site is generally larger than those of other sites. The difference of the safety indices between the 7-story and 12-story MRFS buildings in the same site is not so large. Figures 7-(a) and 7-(b) show the safety indices β for the 7-story and 12-story (MRFS and FWS) buildings. The results are presented only for the three sites, Sendai, Tokyo and Osaka. The safety indices β of FWS buildings (indicated by Sendai-w, Tokyo-w, Osaka-w) are generally larger than those of MRFS buildings in the both cases of 7-story and 12-story buildings.

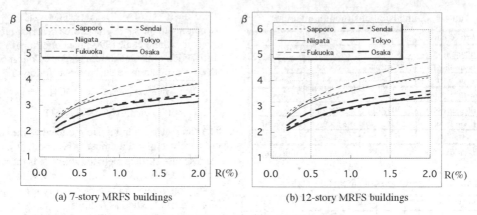

(a) 7-story MRFS buildings   (b) 12-story MRFS buildings

Figure 6. Annual reailability index β for MRFS buildings

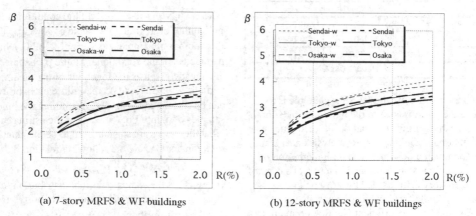

(a) 7-story MRFS & WF buildings   (b) 12-story MRFS & WF buildings

Figure 7. Annual reailability index β for MRFS & WF buildings

5 CONCLUSIONS

Seismic reliability levels of reinforced concrete buildings designed according to the recently proposed Japanese design guideline are evaluated in terms of safety indices β, and are compared among different construction sites as well as different building systems. Those results should be helpful in formulating reliability-based design guidelines of reinforced concrete buildings in Japan.

ACKNOWLEDGEMENT

The author would like to thank Prof.A.Shibata for his suggestions and Mr. S.Abe for his contribution to this study.

REFERENCES

Kawashima, K. et al. 1985, Attenuation of Peak Ground Motions and Absolute Acceleration Response Spectra, *Report of the Public Works Research Institute*, 166.

Hisada, T. and H.Ando 1976, Relation Between Duration of Earthquake Ground Motion and the Magnitude, *Kajima Institute of Construction Technology*, 19-1.

Japan PRESSS Guidelines Working Group 1992, Ultimate Strength Design Guidelines for Reinforced Concrete Buildings, *The U.S.-Japan Meeting on Precast Seismic Structural Systems*, San Diego.

Jennings, P.C. et al. 1968, Simulated Earthquake Motions, *Earthq. Eng. Res. Lab*, California Institute of Technology, Pasadena.

Saito, T. and Y.K.Wen 1994, Seismic Risk Evaluation of R.C. Buildings in Japan Designed in Accordance with the 1990 AIJ Guidelines, *Civil Engineering Studies*, SRS No.587, University of Illinois at Urbana-Champaign, Urbana, Illinois.

Saito, T., S. Abe and A. Shibata 1996, Reliability Based Seismic Design Criteria of Reinforced Concrete Buildings in Japan, the Proceedings of 11th WCEE, Mexico.

Structural Safety and Reliability, Shiraishi, Shinozuka & Wen (eds) © 1998 Balkema, Rotterdam, ISBN 90 5410 978 5

Evaluation of lateral force distributions used in static push-over analyses

Brandi Outwin, Po-Tuan Chen & Kevin R. Collins
Department of Civil and Environmental Engineering, University of Michigan, Mich., USA

ABSTRACT: Due to the complexity of dynamic time history analyses, many engineers and researchers have advocated the use of linear and nonlinear static push-over analyses for seismic design. The choice of the lateral force distribution is one of the most important aspects of such analyses since any single lateral force pattern may not capture all deformation characteristics. This paper summarizes the results of a study to evaluate several possible force distributions in the context of a performance-based seismic design procedure proposed by the third author and others.

INTRODUCTION

In recent years, engineers and researchers have focused attention on the development of "performance-based" seismic design procedures. A basic framework for such a procedure has been developed by the third author and others (Collins *et al.*, 1996). The design procedure uses static push-over analyses as an alternative to dynamic analyses. The appropriate lateral force distribution to use in the push-over analyses is a key piece of information for these analyses.

This paper summarizes the results of a study to investigate several possible distributions in the context of the performance-based design procedure presented by Collins *et al.* (1996). The procedure uses uniform hazard spectra and "equivalent" single-degree-of-freedom (SDOF) models to evaluate the performance of a multi-degree-of-freedom (MDOF) structure. Performance is measured in terms of the probability of exceeding displacement-based limit state criteria. The parameters for the equivalent SDOF models are derived from the results of linear and nonlinear push-over analyses of the structure. These parameters are then used in deterministic design-checking equations to determine if the structure satisfies the target performance criteria.

EQUIVALENT SDOF MODELS

An equivalent system methodology is used to apply the equations for SDOF displacement response to MDOF structures. The starting point is the equation of motion of a two-dimensional MDOF cantilever type structure subjected to horizontal base motion:

$$[M]\{\ddot{u}\} + [C]\{\dot{u}\} + \{R\} = -[M]\{1\}\ddot{u}_g \quad (1)$$

where [M] is the mass matrix, {u} is the vector of lateral displacements at each floor, [C] is the damping matrix, {R} is the restoring force vector, {1} is the unity vector, and $\ddot{u}_g$ is the ground acceleration. Using the results of static push-over analyses, the above equation can be reduced to a single equation describing the displacement response of the roof relative to the base. The resulting equation is

$$\ddot{D} + 2\xi\omega^*\dot{D} + (\omega^*)^2 G(D) = -P^*\ddot{u}_g \quad (2)$$

where D is the roof displacement, P* is analogous to a participation factor, ω^* is the effective frequency of the "equivalent" system, ξ is the equivalent damping ratio, and G(D) is a function describing the relationship between base shear and roof displacement during the push-over analysis. Since the interstory drift, not roof displacement, is the key displacement parameter considered in seismic design, the maximum roof displacement from equation (2) is converted to a maximum interstory drift ratio using

$$(\Delta_L)_{max} = \beta_{LG} \frac{D_{max}}{H} \quad (3)$$

where Δ_L is the maximum interstory drift ratio, β_{LG} is a conversion factor, H is the building height, and D_{max} is the maximum roof displacement. Additional details are provided in Collins et al. (1996).

LATERAL FORCE DISTRIBUTION

There has been much debate concerning which lateral force distribution is most appropriate to use in static push-over analyses. A profile which is reasonably accurate for linear elastic push-over analyses may not be appropriate for nonlinear inelastic analyses. This paper outlines the observations and conclusions found by the application of four different lateral force distributions to six two-dimensional structural frames: two-story moment-resisting frame (MRF), nine-story MRF, twelve-story MRF, eight-story MRF with irregular mass and stiffness distributions, five-story concentrically braced frame (CBF), and five-story dual system considering both MRF and CBF. Detailed descriptions of the models are provided by Collins et al. (1996).

The four lateral force distributions considered in this study were as follows:
1. UBC (1994) Distribution: This is one variation of the triangular distribution used in many codes.
2. Mass-Proportional Uniform Distribution: Lawson (1994) has suggested the use of a uniform force distribution based on the masses of each floor. In order to calculate a uniform mass distribution, the mass of each floor "i" is divided by the total mass of the frame. This ratio of masses is numerically equal to the magnitude of the force applied at floor level "i".
3. "True" Uniform Distribution: This distribution is considered simply for general interest. In this distribution, the force at each floor is the same. Thus, it is identical to the mass-proportional distribution when all floors have the same mass.
4. Distribution Based on Building Aspect Ratio: Anderson (1989) presents various displacement profiles dependent on the ratio of the total height (H) of a frame divided by the total width (B) of a frame. Three specific cases are considered:
   a) for low-rise structures (H/B less than 1.5)

$$\Psi_1(x) = \sin\frac{\pi x}{2H} \qquad (4)$$

   b) for mid-rise structures (H/B between 1.3 and 3.0)

$$\Psi_1(x) = \frac{x}{H} \qquad (5)$$

   c) for high-rise structures (H/B greater than 3.0)

$$\Psi_1(x) = 1 - \cos\frac{\pi x}{2H} \qquad (6)$$

The function $\Psi_1(x)$ is the normalized lateral displacement at height x above the base. The displacement at each floor was calculated using the appropriate formula to determine a vector of floor displacements $\{\Psi_1\}$. The lateral force distribution was obtained by post-multiplying the mass matrix [M] by $\{\Psi_1\}$ and then normalizing the result by the corresponding base shear.

ANALYSES AND RESULTS

For each of the six frame MDOF models, linear elastic and nonlinear inelastic push-over analyses were performed using each of the four force distributions discussed above. The results of these analyses were used to calibrate the parameters for equivalent SDOF models of the frames. Both the virtual work formulation and the base shear formulation of the equivalent SDOF models, as discussed by Collins et al. (1996), were considered. These models were then analyzed for a small set of ground motion records, and the predicted responses from these equivalent models were compared to the responses determined from dynamic analyses of the MDOF models of the frames. Both linear and nonlinear dynamic analyses of the SDOF and MDOF models were performed. The nonlinear restoring force for the SDOF model was chosen as a bilinear restoring force. The nonlinear dynamic analyses of the MDOF models were carried out using the DRAIN-2DX computer program (Prakash et al., 1993).

To facilitate comparisons of the SDOF and MDOF dynamic analysis results, a bias factor, defined as the ratio of the maximum MDOF interstory drift ratio to the maximum drift ratio predicted by the equivalent SDOF model, was calculated for each earthquake record. Tables 1 through 4 present the mean and standard deviation of the bias factor for each frame and force distribution. Figures 1 through 4 represent graphical comparisons of the bias factor data shown in the tables.

The results of the analyses are somewhat surprising. For the purposes of calculating interstory drift using the equivalent system methodology, the choice of the lateral force distribution does not have a significant impact on the final results. Although one force distribution may be better than another when making a comparison for one particular record, there appears to be no clear preference when considering averages over many records.

It should also be noted that there is a significant amount of scatter in the drift bias factor as indicated by the values of standard deviation in Tables 1-4. Whenever simplified analysis techniques such as the equivalent system methodology are used in seismic design, such scatter should be considered if a true reliability-based, performance-based design is to result.

Finally, it should be noted that the conclusions reached in this study pertain to predicting displacement response (interstory drift ratio) and not force response (such as base shear or story shear). The choice of the force distribution could have a significant impact on the results when considering forces developed in the structure. This warrants further study.

Table 1. Bias factor for estimates of the maximum interstory drift ratio for linear elastic response and virtual work formulation

	UBC		Mass		Uniform		H/B Ratio	
	mean	s.d.	mean	s.d.	mean	s.d.	mean	s.d.
2-MRF	1.106	0.115	1.035	0.116	1.061	0.114	1.068	0.114
5-CBF	1.191	0.229	1.352	0.246	1.334	0.245	1.273	0.242
5-Dual	1.177	0.222	1.284	0.239	1.299	0.242	1.245	0.235
8-IRREG	1.211	0.179	1.148	0.170	1.138	0.168	1.168	0.173
9-MRF	1.297	0.349	1.143	0.305	1.155	0.310	1.238	0.337
12-MRF	1.441	0.372	1.260	0.325	1.277	0.33	1.427	0.369

Table 2. Bias factor for estimates of the maximum interstory drift ratio for linear elastic response and base shear formulation

	UBC		Mass		Uniform		H/B Ratio	
	mean	s.d.	mean	s.d.	mean	s.d.	mean	s.d.
2-MRF	0.995	0.096	1.015	0.149	1.010	0.130	1.010	0.127
5-CBF	0.895	0.164	1.268	0.289	1.216	0.28	1.025	0.194
5-Dual	0.904	0.166	1.194	0.281	1.183	0.278	1.011	0.189
8-IRREG	0.876	0.135	0.896	0.219	0.885	0.185	0.858	0.131
9-MRF	0.965	0.270	1.089	0.263	1.086	0.263	0.960	0.262
12-MRF	1.060	0.285	1.068	0.280	1.073	0.282	1.097	0.285

Table 3. Bias factor for estimates of the maximum interstory drift ratio for nonlinear inelastic response and virtual work formulation

	UBC		Mass		Uniform		H/B Ratio	
	mean	s.d.	mean	s.d.	mean	s.d.	mean	s.d.
2-MRF	1.035	0.140	0.949	0.120	0.975	0.128	0.980	0.130
5-CBF	1.210	0.259	1.100	0.218	1.119	0.226	1.185	0.254
5-Dual	1.105	0.199	1.057	0.170	1.051	0.173	1.039	0.180
8-IRREG	0.878	0.172	0.868	0.172	0.863	0.170	0.868	0.169
9-MRF	1.051	0.208	0.805	0.182	0.811	0.177	0.973	0.182
12-MRF	1.083	0.203	0.803	0.135	0.815	0.137	1.013	0.186

Table 4. Bias factor for estimates of the maximum interstory drift ratio for nonlinear inelastic response and base shear formulation

	UBC		Mass		Uniform		H/B Ratio	
	mean	s.d.	mean	s.d.	mean	s.d.	mean	s.d.
2-MRF	0.958	0.139	0.939	0.110	0.949	0.119	0.949	0.122
5-CBF	0.992	0.204	1.081	0.191	1.089	0.195	1.049	0.209
5-Dual	0.920	0.156	1.032	0.165	1.021	0.162	0.923	0.148
8-IRREG	0.644	0.133	0.695	0.152	0.677	0.130	0.637	0.132
9-MRF	0.884	0.180	0.782	0.234	0.782	0.235	0.828	0.170
12-MRF	0.899	0.164	0.720	0.120	0.735	0.127	0.867	0.167

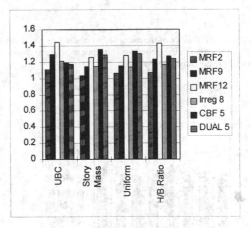

Figure 1. Comparison of the mean values of the bias factor for interstory drift ratio. (Linear elastic response, virtual work formulation of equivalent systems)

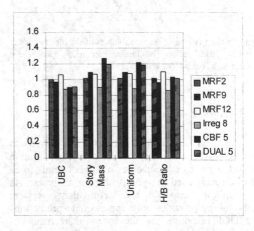

Figure 2. Comparison of the mean values of the bias factor for interstory drift ratio. (Linear elastic response, base shear formulation of equivalent systems)

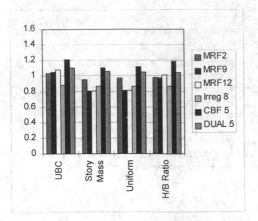

Figure 3. Comparison of the mean values of the bias factor for interstory drift ratio. (Nonlinear response, virtual work formulation of equivalent systems)

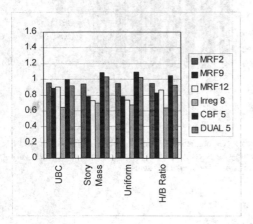

Figure 4. Comparison of the mean values of the bias factor for interstory drift ratio. (Nonlinear response, base shear formulation of equivalent systems)

SUMMARY & CONCLUSIONS

This paper has summarized the results of a study to investigate the sensitivity of the equivalent system methodology to the choice of the lateral force distribution(s) used in static push-over analyses. As one might expect, the equivalent system methodology provides only approximate predictions of MDOF response, and the approximate nature of such simplistic analysis models must be considered when developing reliability-based, performance-based design procedures.

ACKNOWLEDGMENTS

Support for this research has been provided by the University of Michigan and the Marion Sarah Parker Scholars Program. This support is gratefully acknowledged.

REFERENCES

Anderson, J.C. 1989. Dynamic Response of Buildings, Chapter 3 in *Seismic Design Handbook*, edited by Farzad Naeim. New York: Van Nostrand Reinhold.

Collins, K. R., Y. K. Wen, D. A. Foutch 1996. Dual-Level Seismic Design: A Reliability-Based Methodology. *Earthquake Engineering and Structural Dynamics.* 25:1433-1467.

International Conference of Building Officials (ICBO), *Uniform Building Code, 1994 Edition.*

Lawson, R. S., V. Vance, H. Krawinkler 1994. Nonlinear static push-over analysis- why, when, and how?, *Proceedings, Fifth US National Conference on Earthquake Engineering.* 1:283-292.

Prakash, V., G.H. Powell, and S. Campbell 1993, *DRAIN-2DX Base Program Description and User Guide*, Department of Civil Engineering, University of California - Berkeley, Report UCB/SEMM-93/17.

Structural Safety and Reliability, Shiraishi, Shinozuka & Wen (eds) © 1998 Balkema, Rotterdam, ISBN 90 5410 978 5

Study on structural seismic performance based on risk analysis

Itaru Kurosawa, Masatoshi Takeda & Yoshiro Kai
Power and Energy Project Division, Shimizu Corporation, Tokyo, Japan

ABSTRACT: Recently the seismic risk analysis can be proceeded with adequate accuracy. In this paper, using the result of the risk analysis, the expected total seismic cost of the structure is estimated during its life time. The total seismic cost includes the initial cost, restoring cost, missed benefit and so on. The expected total seismic cost can be the indicator of the structural seismic performance.

1 THE TOTAL SEISMIC COST

Once the hazardous earthquake occurred, the expense for the damage is huge. It is needed to recognize this expense even in the structural design of buildings. Here the total seismic cost is proposed as shown in Fig. 1. It includes the initial cost, reinforcing cost, missed loss and restoring cost. These cost can be definitely calculated after the disaster. To estimate the future expense for the hazardous earthquake, the probabilistic technique can be applied.

2 EXPECTATION OF THE TOTAL SEISMIC COST

Fig. 2 shows the flaw chart of the proposed expectation method of the total seismic cost. It consists of the seismic hazard analysis, fragility analysis, conditional risk analysis and the estimation of the total seismic cost.

In the hazard analysis, the database of active fault and the historical earthquake database are utilized. With these database, the seismic hazard curve and the expected earthquake motion is established. The detail of the hazard analysis is explained in the ref. (1).

In the fragility analysis, the failure criteria is estimated. The fragility curves are estimated using the non-linear dynamic response analysis with the expected input motion. The detail of the fragility analysis is explained in the ref. (2).

In the conditional risk analysis, the cost according to the each failure criteria is estimated. In the assumption of the cost, the database of the past earthquake damage and the opinion of the building owner is utilized. The conditional risk can be calculated as the product of the cost and the fragility curve. As each criteria is defined as a mutually exclusive event, the conditional risk for each failure criteria can be summed up.

The annual seismic risk can be estimated from the hazard curve and the conditional risk. The total seismic cost is the sum of the initial cost and the accumulation of the seismic risk during the expected life time of the building.

As the seismic performance of the building is expressed with the total seismic cost, the optimization of the seismic design can be achieved by minimizing the total seismic cost.

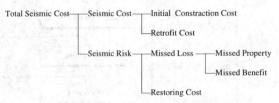

Fig.1 Total Seismic Cost

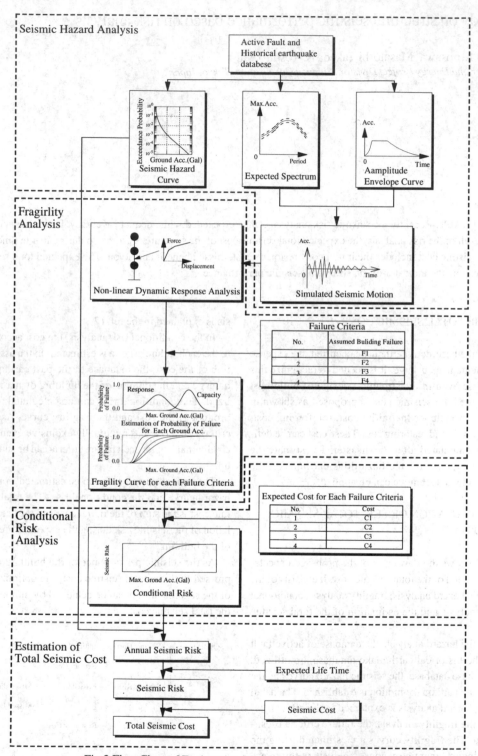

Fig.2 Flaw Chart of Expectation Method of Seismic Total Cost

3 EXAMPLE OF THE TOTAL SEISMIC COST

The utilization of the total seismic cost is demonstrated with a hypothetical building. The building is rather old and needs reinforcing. The total seismic cost is used to select the reinforcing method. Here three kind of reinforcing method is studied as shown on Table 1.

The failure criteria is assumed as table 2. The fragility curve is calculated according to the retrofit method as shown in Fig. 3.

The three case of the building occupancy type is studied, that is office, industrial and refrigerating storage. The expected expense due to the each failure criteria is summed up for each occupancy type. From this expected expense and the fragility curve, the conditional risk is calculated as shown in Fig. 4.

The seismic hazard curve for the building is assumed as Fig. 5. The annual risk is calculated from the conditional risk and the hazard curve.

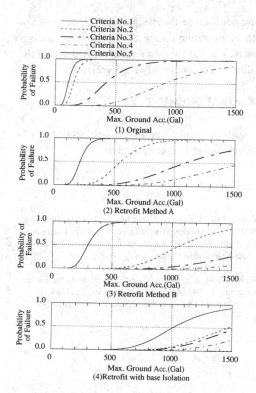

Fig.3 Fragility Curve

Finally the expected total seismic cost is estimated as shown in Fig. 6. It can be seen from the figures that the original is needed for the office building if the building will be in use only for 5 years. After 10 years, the retrofit method A become cheaper even for office building. For the office and the industrial, retrofit with base isolation

Table.1 Outline of Seismic Retrofit
(Retrofit cost is expresse as the ratio to the intial cost)

Model	Reinforcing Method	Retrofit Cost
Original	half as much as capacity of the present structure code	
Retrofit Method A	earthquake resisiting wall and brace	30%
Retrofit Method B	more earthquake resisiting wall and brace than Method A	35%
Base isolation	upper structure is as same as Non-reinforcing high damping laminated rubber is used	40%

Note: Maintenance cost (0.5% per year) for base isolation system is considered

Table.2 Assumed Damage Description

Assumed Damage Description	Criteria No.
Minor cracking / yielding of structural elements	1
Reduced residual strength and stiffness but lateral sysetm remains functional	2
No story collapse mechanism but large permanent drift	3
Partial or total collapse	4
Failure of isolated layer (Base-isolation)	5

Table.3 Assumed Seismic Loss
(Cost is expressed as the ratio to the intial cost, unit:%)

Criteria No.	Case1 Office			Case2 Industrial			Case3 Refrigerating Storage		
	A	B	A+B	A	B	A+B	A	B	A+B
1	15	0	15	15	0	15	15	150	165
2	30	0	30	30	0	300	30	300	330
3	100	0	100	100	300	400	100	500	600
4	100	0	100	100	1000	1100	100	1000	1100
5 *	100	0	100	100	1000	1100	100	1000	1100

A=Restoring Cost
B=Missed Loss
* Criteria No.5 is considered at the case of Base isolation

would not become the cheapest retrofit method, but for the refrigerating storage, the retrofit with base isolation may be the cheapest retrofit method even if the building will be in use only for 5 years.

ACKNOWLEDGEMENT

The authors would like to acknowledge Mr. M. Matubara for his kind cooperation.

REFERENCES

(1) Y. Ishikawa, H. Kameda: Hazard-Consistent Magnitude and Distance for Extended Seismic Hazard Analysis, Proceedings of the 9the World Conference on Earthquake Engineering, Tokyo-Kyoto, 1988

(2) M. Matubara, M. Takeda, Y. Kai: Estimation of the Failure Probability of Building Based Observed Earthquake Records, Reliability and Optimization of Structure System V(B-12), pp.157-164, 1993

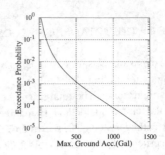

Fig.5 Seismic Hazard Curve

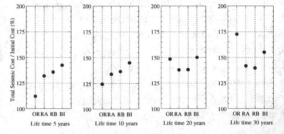

(1)Case1:Original

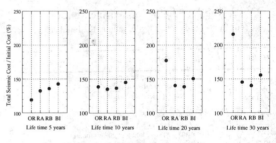

(2)Case2:Industrial

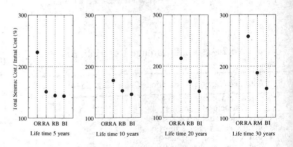

(3)Case3:Refrigerating Storage

Fig.6 Expected Seismic Total Cost
(Seismic cost is expressed as the ratio to the intial cost, unit:%)
OR : Original
RA : Retrofit Method A
RB : Retrofit Method B
B I : Retrofit with Base Isolation

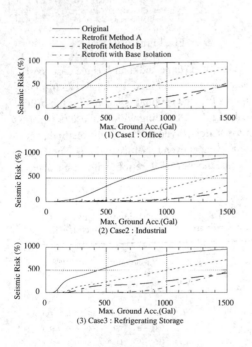

Fig.4 Conditional Risk
(Risk is expressed as the ratio to the intial cost, unit:%)

Structural Safety and Reliability, Shiraishi, Shinozuka & Wen (eds) © 1998 Balkema, Rotterdam, ISBN 90 5410 978 5

Dynamic response of a hemispherical canyon subjected to a buried-couple source

C.S.Yeh & T.J.Teng
National Center for Research on Earthquake Engineering, Taipei, Taiwan

W.I.Liao
National Taiwan University, Taipei, Taiwan

ABSTRACT: This paper presents the analysis of three-dimensional response of a hemispherical canyon subjected to a buried-couple source. The diffracted wave fields are constructed with linear combinations of three independent sets of Lamb's singular solutions which satisfy the traction free conditions on ground surface and radiation conditions at infinity, automatically, and their coefficients are determined by the traction free conditions along the canyon surface in the least square sense. Numerical results for the displacements on and near the canyon for various focal distances and source incident angles are presented.

1 INTRODUCTION

It has long been recongnized that the effect of scattering due to topographic irregularities may cause large amplification during earthquake. As this effect is an important factor for the aseismic design of structure systems, it has recently become an interesting problem for both seismologists and earthquake engineers to study such an effect on earthquake ground motions. Lee (1982) has used the method of wave function series expansion to analyze scattering of plane waves by a hemispherical canyon. Sañchez-Sesma (1983) has considered diffraction of a vertical incident P wave by canyon and alluvial basin using the c-complete wave functions. Mossessian and Dravinski (1989) have adopted the indirect boundary integral equation method to study the amplification of elastic waves by three-dimensional canyon of arbitrary shape. However, the plane incidence is inadequate to give a reasonable estimation of ground motion to seismic events from the near focal distance. Therefore, a three-dimensional geometry of irregularities under more realistic incidence of seismic wave is necessary.

In this work, we study the response of a hemispherical canyon model under the more realistic type of incident wave field. The incident wave field radiates from a point source which situates at the near focal distance or the far focal distance. The source corresponding to a strike-slip fault which is equivalent to a buried double-couple without moment is considered. For the hemispherical canyon subjected to the incident wave radiates from a strike-slip fault, three linear independent sets of basis functions which consist of higher order Lamb's singular solutions automatically satisfying traction free conditions on the ground surface and radiation conditions at infinity are developed to represent the scattered wave field, and the traction free conditions along the canyon surface are served to determine their coefficients in the least square sense. This method is motivated from Maunsell's earlier work (1936) in elastostatics. Yeh *et al.*(1995, 1997a, 1997b) have extended this method to study the two dimensional and three-dimensional problems of scattering of plane waves by surface irregularities and the dynamic analysis of a hemispherical foundation embedded in an elastic half-space. The surface displacements on and near the canyon for the problem considered here are computed for various focal distances and source incident angles and discussed in detail.

2. STATEMENT OF THE PROBLEM

The geometry of the problem is depicted in Figure 1, in which the half-space D composes of the flat surface S_f and the surface of the hemispherical canyon S_c. The material of the half-space is assumed to be linearly elastic, homogeneous and isotropic. Its material property is specified by Lamé constants λ and μ, and mass density ρ. The half-space is excited by a buried source with harmonic dependence $e^{i\omega t}$ at the point $\mathbf{x}_o = (R_o, \theta_o, \varphi_o)$, where ω is the circular frequency. For simplicity, the factor $e^{i\omega t}$ will be dropped from all expressions. In this three-dimensional model, the displacement field $\mathbf{u}$ is related to the displacement potentials according to

$$\mathbf{u} = \nabla\phi + \nabla \times (0,0,\psi) + \nabla \times \nabla \times (0,0,\chi) \quad (1)$$

where ϕ is the longitudinal wave potential, ψ and χ are the transverse wave potentials, respectively, which are governed by

$$\nabla^2\phi + k_p^2\phi = 0 \quad (2)$$
$$\nabla^2\psi + k_s^2\psi = 0 \quad (3)$$
$$\nabla^2\chi + k_s^2\chi = 0 \quad (4)$$

where $k_p = \omega/c_p$ and $k_s = \omega/c_s$ denote the longitudinal and transverse wave numbers, respectively. while $c_p = \sqrt{(\lambda + 2\mu)/\rho}$ and $c_s = \sqrt{\mu/\rho}$ denote the longitudinal and the transverse wave speeds, respectively. The traction free boundary conditions along the flat surface S_f are specified by

$$\sigma_{zx}|_{z=0} = 0$$
$$\sigma_{zy}|_{z=0} = 0$$
$$\sigma_{zz}|_{z=0} = 0, \quad \mathbf{x} \in S_f \quad (5)$$

On the surface of the hemispherical canyon S_c, the boundary conditions are of the form

$$\sigma_{RR}|_{R=a} = 0$$
$$\sigma_{R\theta}|_{R=a} = 0$$
$$\sigma_{R\varphi}|_{R=a} = 0, \quad \mathbf{x} \in S_c \quad (6)$$

where a is the radius of the hemispherical canyon. The source type considered here is a double couple without moment with magnitude F_o, which is situated at point $\mathbf{x}_o = (R_o, \theta_o, \varphi_o)$ and expressed as the following form

$$\rho\mathbf{F} = F_o\frac{\partial}{\partial y}\delta(\mathbf{x} - \mathbf{x}_o)\mathbf{e}_x + F_o\frac{\partial}{\partial x}\delta(\mathbf{x} - \mathbf{x}_o)\mathbf{e}_y \quad (7)$$

where $\mathbf{F}$ represent the body force of the elastic half-space, $\delta(\ )$ is the three-dimensional Dirac delta function, $\mathbf{e}_x$ and $\mathbf{e}_y$ denotes the unit vectors along x- and y-axes, respectively.

3. METHOD OF SOLUTION

The wave field consists of three parts : $\mathbf{u}^i$, the direct wave radiating from $\mathbf{x}_o$, $\mathbf{u}^r$, the reflected

wave by the flat ground surface S_f and $\mathbf{u}^s$, the scattered wave by the hemi-spherical surface S_c, thus

$$\mathbf{u} = \mathbf{u}^i + \mathbf{u}^r + \mathbf{u}^s \quad (8)$$

The solution for the direct wave field plus the reflected wave field $\mathbf{u}^i + \mathbf{u}^r$ can be obtained by solving eqn(2)-(4) with the action of body force $\mathbf{F}$ shown in eqn(7) and satisfy the free surface conditions eqn(5). The scattered wave field can be represented by three independent sets of higher order Lamb's singular solutions which satisfy the free surface conditions eqn(5) and radiation conditions at infinity. Then the scattered wave field can be written as

$$\mathbf{u}^s = \sum_{m=0}^{N}\sum_{n=0}^{m} P_{mn}^x \mathbf{u}_{mn}^x$$

$$+ \sum_{m=0}^{N}\sum_{n=0}^{m} P_{mn}^y \mathbf{u}_{mn}^y + \sum_{m=0}^{N}\sum_{n=0}^{m} P_{mn}^z \mathbf{u}_{mn}^z \quad (9)$$

where P_{mn}^x, P_{mn}^y, and P_{mn}^z are the unknown coefficients, N is the order of approximation. $\mathbf{u}_{mn}^x$, $\mathbf{u}_{mn}^y$ and $\mathbf{u}_{mn}^z$ are obtained by taking the (m-n)-th order derivatives with respect to x and n-th order derivatives with respect to y of Lamb's singular solutions due to surface point loads in x, y, z direction, respectively. The integral representations of the displacements and corresponding stresses of

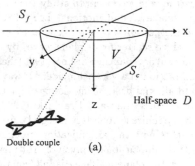

(a)

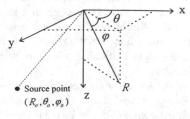

(b)

Figure 1. (a)Geometry of the model (b)coordinate system.

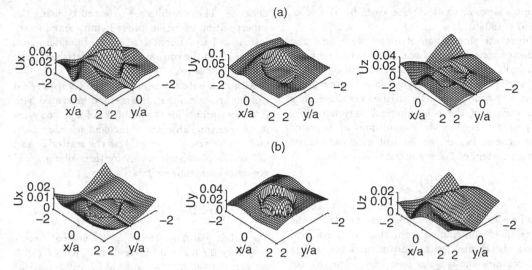

Figure 2. Surface displacement amplitudes for dimensionless frequency $\eta = 1.0$ when a double couple applied at $R_o/a = 8$. Source incidence angles are $\varphi_o = 30^o$(a) and 60^o(b), respectively.

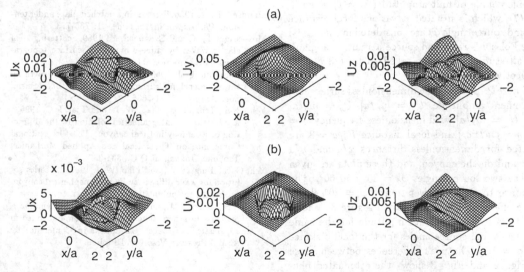

Figure 3. Surface displacement amplitudes for dimensionless frequency $\eta = 1.0$ when a double couple applied at $R_o/a = 16$. Source incidence angles are $\varphi_o = 30^o$(a) and 60^o(b), respectively.

Lamb's singular solutions are given by Yeh *et al.* (1997a, 1997b).

Since the summation of direct wave field and reflected wave field, and scattered wave field automatically satisfy the traction free conditions on the flat surface of half-space. Therefore, the remaining boundary conditions to be satisfied are those along the surface of the hemispherical canyon eqn(6). Imposing these boundary conditions at L points along the surface of the hemispherical canyon, we have a system of linear equations of the form

$$[G]\{c\} = \{f\} \qquad (10)$$

where vector $\{c\}$ contains the complex unknown coefficients, the vector $\{f\}$ corresponds to the stress field contributed from the free wave field along the hemispherical canyon, and the matrix $[G]$ contains the singular solutions. Eqn(10) can be solved in the least square sense.

4. NUMERICAL RESULTS

Responses of a hemispherical canyon subjected to the incident wave motion radiated from a buried double couple of unit amplitude($F_o = 1$) given in eqn(7), which is situated at various focal distance R_o and source angle φ_o are considered in this study. The Poisson's ratio and source azimuthal angle θ_o for all studied cases are taken to be $1/3$ and π, respectively.

Figure 2. presents the dimensionless surface displacement amplitudes $U_x = |u_x/a|$, $U_y = |u_y/a|$ and $U_z = |u_z/a|$ vs dimensionless frequency $\eta = 1.0(\eta = \omega a/\pi c_s)$ and focal distance $R_o/a = 8$ are plotted for dimensionless distances x/a and y/a near and on the canyon, and these plots are given for the two source angles $\varphi_o = 30°$ and $60°$. The response to the shallower source $\varphi_o = 30°$ shows more effect from surface wave. Figure 3. shows the surface displacement amplitude for the same frequency and source angles for the focal distance $R_o/a = 16$. The peak differences between those in Fig. 2 and Fig. 3 show the attenuated phenomena due to focal distances.

5. CONCLUSIONS

Some results are presented for the responses of a hemispherical canyon subjected to a buried-couple source, it is more realistic to represents the incident wave field to seismic events from near focal distance. These results are obtained by using the superposition of higher order Lamb's singular solutions as basis functions of series. Boundary conditions along the conyon surface are satisfied in the least square sense.

Although only the results for the hemispherical canyon are calculated, the method presented here is truely suitable for the problems of non-axis symmetric canyon subjected to incident seismic waves, and can be extended to analyze the scattering and diffraction of seismic waves by three-dimensional geological inhomogeneities.

ACKNOWLEDGEMENT

The authors gratefully acknowledge the financial support granted by the National Science Council, R.O.C., (NSC-085-2621-P-319-002). The facility of calculation provided bt National Taiwan University is also highly appreciated.

REFERENCES

Lee, V. W. 1982. A note on the scattering of elastic plane waves by a hemispherical canyon. *Soil Dynam. Earthq. Engng.*, 1: 122-129.

Maunsell, F. G. 1936. Stresses in a notched plate under tension. *Philosophical Magazine*, 21: 765-773.

Mossessian, T. K. and Dravinski, M. 1989. Scattering of elastic waves by three-dimensional surface topographies. *Wave motion*, 11: 579-592.

Sanchez-Sesma, F. J. 1983. Diffraction of elastic waves by three-dimensional surface irregularities. *Bull. Seism. Soc. Am.*, 73: 1621-1636.

Yeh, C. S., Teng, T. J., Liao, W. I., and Tsai, I. C. 1995. Application of integral series solution to the diffraction of a semi-sylindrical canyon. The 19th National Conference on Theoretical and Applied Mechanics, Taoyuan, Taiwan, R.O.C., 331-337.

Yeh, C. S., Teng, T. J., and Liao, W. I. 1997a. A series solution for wave diffraction by a hemispherical canyon. submitted for publication.

Yeh, C. S., Teng, T. J., and Liao, W. I. 1997b. Dynamic response of a hemispherical foundation embedded in an elastic half-space. To appear in Conference by ASME Pressure Vessel and Pipline.

Structural Safety and Reliability, Shiraishi, Shinozuka & Wen (eds) © 1998 Balkema, Rotterdam, ISBN 90 5410 978 5

Uncertainty of ground motion shape on building damage reflected by recent near-field earthquakes

Hitoshi Seya, Michio Sugimoto & Hideo Nanba
Takenaka R&D Institute, Chiba, Japan

ABSTRACT: The extent of seismic damage to typical buildings is determined for three types of ground motion shape: recent near-field earthquakes, standard earthquakes and simulated earthquakes. Two building systems, namely reinforced concrete and steel moment frames, which are consistent with the current code in Japan, are examined at three different heights. Uncertainty in ground motion shape is discussed by comparing the peak values of ground velocity, which determine the extent of damage to buildings.

1 INTRODUCTION

To develop reliability-based design in the seismic design of buildings, it is recognized that consideration of uncertainties in seismic loads is essential. Major uncertainties of seismic loads are the occurrence rates of large earthquakes and their dynamic characteristics. Seismic hazard curves and corresponding response spectra, which are based on statistical data of past earthquakes, provide design loads for general buildings. However, designing important buildings, such as tall structures and power plants, a design procedure based on dynamic analysis is dually performed together with the static design procedure. Dynamic analysis requires sufficient ground motion data. Long-term observation of earthquakes at the site can provide the data but this is not always possible.

In this paper, the uncertainties of ground motion shape are discussed in terms of building damage, using three types of ground motion: namely, recent near-field earthquakes, standard earthquakes and simulated ones, of which the latter two types are in conventional use in design.

The recent earthquakes at Northridge in 1994 and Kobe in 1995 resulted in major disasters. Observed records very close to the faults exhibited pulse waves that were predominantly one second in duration. The characteristic pulse waves raised the question of whether the recent near-field records might cause more damage to buildings than the conventionally used ground motion of the same intensity. Therefore, sensitivity analysis of building damage against different types of ground motion shape is carried out by means of non-linear dynamic response analysis.

The typical building models are assumed to be designed according to the current Japanese code enacted in 1982.

Reinforced concrete and steel moment resisting frames, are examined by varying their heights. These buildings are modeled by equivalent lumped-masses and non-linear springs. Varying the peak velocity of each ground motion, maximum responses are evaluated by the ratio of lateral drift to story height, which is related to the extent of building damage. Relations between the peak velocity of the different ground motion and the extent of damage provide useful information for deciding the design ground motion.

2 EARTHQUAKE GROUND MOTION

Uncertainties in ground motion shape are examined by three types of earthquake ground motion: recent near-field earthquakes, standard earthquakes and simulated earthquakes. Standard and simulated ground motion are often used for the design of important structures in Japan. Peak ground velocity is used as a parameter to express the intensity of earthquakes because peak velocity is a more stable descriptor than peak ground acceleration in terms of building damage (Seya 1994).

2.1 Recent near field earthquakes

Five records taken from the earthquakes at Northridge in 1994 and Kobe in 1995 are used. The distance from the fault is less than 7 km. The ground motion component of each fault's normal direction is used. A list of the recent near field earthquakes is shown in Table1.

2.2 Standard earthquakes

Five of the standard earthquakes (Table 2) which are conventionally used as a measure for tall structure design in Japan are compared.

Table 1 Data of recent near-field earthquakes

	Station	Magnitude	Fault distance (km)	Peak acceleration (m/sec^2)	Peak velocity (cm/sec)
Kobe 1995	JMA		3.4	8.48	105.5
	Fukiai	7.2	6.2	8.11	124.5
	Takatori		4.3	7.76	163.3
Northridge 1994	Newhall	6.7	6.7	7.25	118.9
	Sylmar		6.2	6.66	88.3

Table 2 Data of standard earthquakes

	Magnitude	Epicenter distance (km)	Peak acceleration (m/sec^2)	Peak velocity (cm/sec)
El Centro 1940	7.1	12	3.42	34.1
Taft 1950	7.7	42	1.76	17.8
Tokyo 101 1956	6.0	10	0.74	7.9
Hachinohe 1968	7.9	180	2.25	34.1
TH030 1978	7.4	94	2.03	26.7

Table 3 Data of simulated earthquakes

	Magnitude	Epicenter distance (km)	Peak acceleration (m/sec^2)	Peak velocity (cm/sec)	Phase angles
Sim1	7.5	5.0	4.74	43.6	JMA
Sim2	7.5	5.0	3.88	45.5	Fukiai
Sim3	7.5	5.0	3.96	40.6	Takatori
Sim4	7.5	5.0	3.31	35.3	Random
Sim5	7.5	5.0	3.50	37.5	Random

Table 4 Relations between extent of building damage and ratio of lateral   drift to story height

	Reinforced Concrete	Steel
Slight	$\frac{1}{200}$	$\frac{1}{125}$
Moderate	$\frac{1}{125}$	$\frac{1}{75}$
Severe	$\frac{1}{100}$	$\frac{1}{50}$

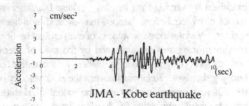
JMA - Kobe earthquake

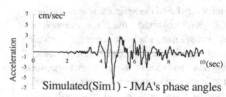
Simulated(Sim1) - JMA's phase angles

Fig.1 Acceleration time histories - JMA in Kobe and Simulated (Vmax=50cm/sec)

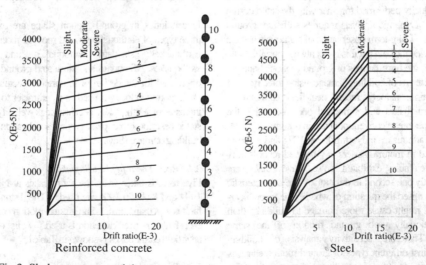

Reinforced concrete

Steel

Fig.2 Skeleton curves and damage extent of ten story reinforced concrete and steel buildings

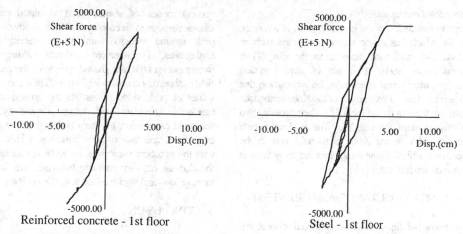

Fig.3 Hystersis loops of ten-story reinforced concrete and steel buildings
(Fukiai, Vmax=125cm/sec)

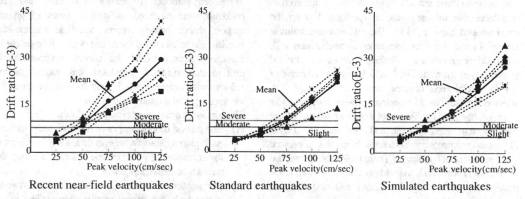

Recent near-field earthquakes   Standard earthquakes   Simulated earthquakes

Fig.4 Maximum drift ratio vs. peak ground velocity for ten-story reinforced concrete building

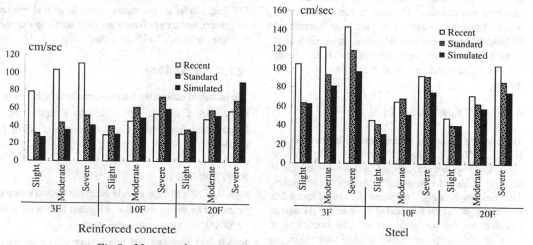

Reinforced concrete   Steel

Fig.5   Mean peak ground velocity vs. each extent of damage

2.3 Simulated earthquakes

A computer simulation of the ground motion of a specific earthquake which has major source parameters such as magnitude (M) and fault distance to the site (R) is performed (Seya 1994). Five sets of ground motion simulate empirical target spectra on the assumption that M=7.5 and R=5km. Phase angles of the Kobe earthquake are applied to three of them (Table 3). The remaining two records have random phase angles. The acceleration time histories at JMA in the Kobe earthquake and in the simulated one, which has the same phase angles as those at JMA records, are illustrated in Fig. 1.

3 BUILDING MODELS AND DAMAGE EXTENT

Moment frame building systems of reinforced concrete and steel are considered. The buildings are designed according to the current code in Japan and their heights vary between three, ten and twenty stories. Time domain non-linear dynamic analyses are performed using the multi-lumped mass model. The stiffness and ultimate strength of each story are determined to be consistent with the code requirements. Skeleton curves are decided empirically as shown in Fig. 2, which represents the case of ten-story reinforced concrete and steel buildings. In addition to structural damping caused by non-linear response, damping coefficients of three and two percent are used for reinforced concrete and steel models. Fig. 3 illustrates examples of hysteresis loops for reinforced concrete and steel buildings. These buildings are assumed to be built on firm soil, so that boundary conditions at the bottom are completely fixed, and soil and structure interaction effects are neglected.

The extent of building damage, identified as slight, moderate or severe, corresponds to observations in disastrous earthquakes. The ratio of lateral drift to story height during an earthquake is used as a measure of building damage. The overall building damage is defined by the largest value among all the peak story drifts. Table 4 shows the mean values of the drift ratio for each extent of damage.

4 ANALYTICAL RESULTS

The intensity of ground motion velocity increased in five levels; 25, 50, 75, 100 and 125 cm/sec. Fig. 4 shows calculated response in case of a ten-story reinforced concrete building for three different types of earthquakes. The vertical axis in Fig. 4 represents the ratio of lateral drift to story height, which is related to the extent of damage as indicated by the horizontal lines. The coefficient of variation of the response to each level of peak velocity is between 0.12 and 0.52. The mean values of peak velocity against each extent of damage are shown in Fig. 5. The

ground motion of standard and simulated earthquakes causes damage to three-story buildings at lower values of peak ground velocity than do the recent near-field earthquakes. For reinforced concrete buildings ten and twenty stories high, the ground motion of the recent near-field earthquakes causes any given level of damage at lower values of peak velocity than do the ground motion of standard and simulated earthquakes. Particularly, in recent near-field earthquakes ten-story buildings are more fragile than three- and twenty-story buildings. This coincides with the statistical surveys of the Kobe earthquake, where the damage ratio for mid-rise buildings was larger than those of low- and high-rise buildings (Seya 1996).

5 CONCLUSIONS

The recent near-field earthquakes caused great damage to buildings and significant pulse waves were observed. Three height models of reinforced concrete and steel buildings were analyzed using three types of ground motion shape: namely, recent near-field earthquakes, standard earthquakes and simulated ones. The extent of damage is measured using the ratio of maximum lateral drift to story height. Calculated peak ground motion velocity which causes each damage level is compared for the three types of ground motion shape.

The conclusions are summarized as follows:

(1) The ground motion shapes of standard and simulated earthquakes cause damage to three-story buildings at lower values of peak ground velocity than do the recent near-field earthquakes.

(2) For reinforced concrete buildings ten and twenty stories high, the ground motion shape of the recent near-field earthquakes is most severe among the three different earthquake types studied.

(3) Particularly, for the recent near-field ground motion shape, ten-story buildings are most fragile among the three heights of buildings studied.

ACKNOWLEDGEMENTS

The near-field earthquake data were made available by the Osaka Gas Co. Ltd, Japan Railway Company, Japan Meteorological Agency and California Division of Mines & Geology.

REFERENCES

Seya, H. Y. Abe, M. Ishiguro & H. Nanba 1994. Ground motion parameter for damage estimation of high and low-rise buildings. *ICOSSAR'93*: 2209-2215. Rotterdam: Balkema.

Seya, H & M. Sugimoto 1996. Statistical aspects of damage due to the Great Hanshin Earthquake. *Probabilistic mechanics & structural reliability*: 186-189. New York: ASCE

Structural Safety and Reliability, Shiraishi, Shinozuka & Wen (eds) © 1998 Balkema, Rotterdam, ISBN 90 5410 978 5

Use of automata network for estimation of seismic site hazard from different faults

Maya E. Belubekian & Anne S. Kiremidjian
Stanford University, Calif., USA

ABSTRACT: An asynchronous stochastic automata network is developed to model the seismic processes on a fault, divided into cells. The network is used to simulate earthquake occurrences on several faults in the vicinity of the site of interest for the site hazard evaluation. The network is operated in an adjustment mode to obtain model parameters. These parameters are used at the forecast mode of the network operation to arrive at the estimation of the site hazard.

INTRODUCTION

The automata theory represents a mathematical description of the structure and behavior of an information-processing system, called an automaton. In this paper, an automata network is used to represent a seismic fault, divided into cells. Each fault cell is treated as a separate automaton, a mathematical device that can perform any defined function depending on the information on its inputs and its current state; and give the resulting information on its output. The interaction among the cells is achieved by a certain connection of their inputs and outputs into a network. Automata framework allows to capture the evolution of the earthquake occurrence process on a fault.

The behavior of the fault automata network depends on the assumed mechanisms for slip accumulation and release on the individual cells (automata) and the scheduling of event occurrences on different cells. The interaction or information exchange between the cells takes place in large events (magnitude 6 or greater) when the rupture spans to several cells. Events of smaller magnitudes occur within a single cell and do not affect the slip state on the other cells. This mechanism allows to simulate the small to moderate events as a Poissonian sequence and incorporate time- and space-dependence into the process of large event occurrence.

The parameters of the network are adjusted to a "target" sample of events constructed using bootstrap statistical technique. The use of bootstrap provides an ability to construct confidence bounds on the estimated parameters as well as the forecast hazard.

1 AUTOMATA NETWORK FOR A SEISMIC FAULT

The states of an automaton can be represented by a single variable or can include several variables. An elementary *automaton* is defined by the following sextuple:

- *set of states;*
- *set of inputs;*
- *set of outputs;*
- *initial state;*
- *state transition function;*
- *output function.*

An automaton is moving from one state to another according to the state transition function at certain time increments, Δt, also called transition times. If $\Delta t = $ constant, then an automaton is called *synchronous*; otherwise it is called *asynchronous*. If the automaton state variable or/and the transition time are random variables, then the automaton is *stochastic*.

An *automata network* is developed by means of inter-connection of inputs and outputs of several automata. In general, automata, constituting the network (also called *nodes*), do not have to be of the same type: they may have different state variables, transition functions, inputs and outputs. The only requirement of the network is that the connected inputs and outputs exchange the same type of information. The transition times of an automata network are either constant (*synchronous network*) or can depend in a more or less complicated way on time increments of automata, constituting the network and their states (*asynchronous network*).

A seismic fault divided into N cells is represented by an $(N+1)$-node automata network. Each fault cell is formulated as an asynchronous stochastic automaton. Physically, a fault cell is defined as a dislocation surface used to calculate the slip distribution in a large event. The $(N+1)$-st cell, called the *resulting cell*, is also represented by an asynchronous stochastic automaton, but with different inputs, outputs and transition function. This cell is used only to store summary information. The fault behavior is simulated by connecting N fault cells and the resulting cell into an automata network. The network can be activated by a fault cell, which initiates an earthquake, called the *triggering cell*. The transition times of this network depend on the transition times scheduled for all fault cells.

1.1 Definition of a fault cell

Each i-th fault cell is defined by the following automaton at time t :
• A two-variable state: $q_i(t) = \{ SA_i(t),\ TN_i(t) \}$, where SA_i is the amount of slip accumulated on the cell, and TN_i is the *time to next event* scheduled on that cell. Time to next event is a lognormally distributed random variable with parameters estimated from the target event sample.
• N inputs: $SR_i^j(t);\ j = 1, 2, ..., N$,
where SR_i^j is the amount of slip which would have been released on the i-th cell due to an event triggered on the j-th cell, provided that the mentioned amount of slip has been already accumulated on the i-th cell. At any time t only one input can have a non-zero value, since only one earthquake at a time can be triggered.
• $(N+1)$ outputs: $SR_j^i(t);\ j = 1, 2, ..., N$,
where $SR_j^i(t)$ is the amount of slip which would have been released on the j-th cell due to an event triggered on the i-th cell, provided that the mentioned amount of slip has been already accumulated on the j-th cell, and the $(N+1)$-st output is $SR_i(t)$ which represents the actual amount of slip released on the i-th cell;
• Initial state: $q_i(0) = \{ SA_i(0),\ TN_i(0) \}$,

where $SA_i(0)$ is the amount of the accumulated slip on the cell at the beginning of simulation, and $TN_i(0)$ is the time of the first event scheduled on that cell.
• State transition function:

$$SA_i(t+\Delta t) = max\{0, min([(SA_i(t) + V_i \Delta t),\ SA_i^{st}] - \sum_{j=1}^{N} SR_i^j(t))\} \qquad (1.1)$$

where Δt is the time increment until the next event, V_i is the *slip accumulation rate* on the cell, SA_i^{st} is the maximum amount of slip that can be accumulated on the cell, the *steady-state slip*. Slip accumulation rate and steady-state slip are model parameters, adjusted to the target sample of events. The level of steady-state slip is equal to the maximum slip that can be released in an earthquake on a single cell in case of the largest earthquake. Note that such a state transition function assumes a *bi-linear slip accumulation*, when the slip on a cell accumulates linearly with a rate V_i and stays constant after it reaches the level of steady-state slip, SA_i^{st}.
• The j-th output function ($j = 1, 2, ..., N$):

$$SR_j^i(t) = \begin{cases} RC_i(t) \cdot SA_i(t), & \text{if } i \text{ is } TC \text{ and } i = j \\ f(SR_i^i, d_{ij}), & \text{if } i \text{ is } TC \text{ and } i \neq j \\ 0, & \text{if } i \text{ is not } TC \end{cases} \qquad (1.2)$$

where TC denotes the triggering cell, $f(SR_i^i, d_{ij})$ is a slip distribution function, whose values are calculated prior to the beginning of the simulation using a dislocation model, d_{ij} is the distance between the i-th and j-th cells and RC_i is the *release coefficient*. Release coefficient defines the proportion of the accumulated slip on a cell that has to be released in an earthquake and is a random variable. The probability distribution of the release coefficient is derived in such a way that the number of small to moderate events (occurring within a single cell) agree with the Guttenberg-Richter magnitude-frequency relationship. The parameters of this distribution are also estimated from the target sample of events.

The $(N+1)$-st output function:

$$SR_i(t) = min\left\{ SA_i(t), \sum_{j=1}^{N} SR_i^j(t) \right\} \qquad (1.3)$$

1.2 *Definition of the resulting cell*

The resulting cell is defined by the following automaton at time t :
- An empty state: $q = \{\varnothing\}$.
- N inputs: $SR_i(t)$; $i = 1, 2, ..., N$,

where SR_i is the amount of slip released on the i-th cell in an earthquake.
- Single output: $SR(t)$, the total slip released in an earthquake on all ruptured cells;
- Initial state: $q(0) = SR(0) = \{\varnothing\}$.
- State transition function: any function that maps an empty set onto itself.
- Output function:

$$SR(t) = \sum_{i=1}^{N} SR_i(t) \qquad (1.4)$$

From the above definition it can be observed that the resulting cell is an elementary summator. This cell does not have any meaningful state variable and its output depends only on the inputs.

1.3 *Connection of cells into automata network*

The $(N+1)$-node automata network is formed by the interconnection of the fault cells and the resulting cell. These connections are established by the following simple rules. Each j-th output of the i-th cell, SR_j^i, is connected to the i-th input of the j-th cell, SR_i^j. According to the definition of a fault automaton, only the triggering cell has non-zero outputs, which correspond to all the cells that have to rupture in the triggered earthquake. If only one output of the triggering i-th cell has a non-zero value, SR_i^i, then only that cell ruptures and no interaction takes place between the fault cells in such an event. If more than one output of the triggering i-th cell have non-zero values, then a number of rupturing cells (equal to the number of the non-zero outputs of the triggering cell) have a non-zero i-th input, SR_j^i, where j is the number of the rupturing cell. The fault cell interaction, in this case, occurs through the information exchange between the triggering cell and the other cells which rupture in the earthquake. Here the information is represented by the released slip. The $(N+1)$-st output of each i-th fault cell is connected to the i-th input of the resulting cell.

The network is activated at a transition time, Δt, which depends on the current states of all fault cells, namely on the time to next event, TN, scheduled for

the cells. The minimum among the times to next event on all cells is chosen as Δt. The cell which corresponds to this time is the triggering cell, it initiates a network activation (earthquake).

1.4 *An illustrative example*

A five-cell fault is considered here to describe the algorithm of functioning of the introduced automata network. In this example, it is assumed that it has already been determined that the third cell is triggering an earthquake and the time increment, Δt, until the next network activation has been calculated. The following variables are also assumed to be known at the considered time t : the accumulated slip, the slip accumulation rate and the level of steady-state slip on each fault cell; and the release coefficient for the triggering cell. The pre-calculated slip distribution function for the triggering cell, $f(SR_3^3, d_{3j})$, where $j = 1, 2, 4, 5$, presumably, gives non-zero values for the slip released on the first, second and fourth fault cells. Only the fifth fault cell is not rupturing in the considered earthquake. The sixth cell adds up the amounts of slip released on the ruptured cells, and its output shows the total slip released in the earthquake, triggered at time t .

This six-node automata network is shown on Figure 1. Each node is shown as a box with node number in a circle near its upper left corner. The resulting cell is denoted by the Σ-sign to emphasize its role as a summator. For clarity only the non-zero inputs and outputs, which represent the levels of released slip, are shown.

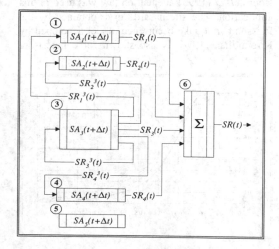

Figure 1. Six-node automata network

2 SITE HAZARD ESTIMATION

In order to estimate the earthquake site hazard, the closely located faults are formulated in terms of the described automata networks. The parameters of each fault network, such as the slip accumulation rate, steady-state slip, parameters of distribution of the time to the next event and the release coefficient, are estimated at the adjustment operation mode of the network in an iterative manner. The target samples for the adjustment are obtained using *bootstrap*. The bootstrap statistical technique represents sampling with replacement from the original sample of data (earthquake catalog). After obtaining several bootstrap samples the mean and the confidence bounds on the parameters of interest are estimated.

The network is operated in the forecast mode to estimate the hazard in the form of a *site hazard curve*. The site hazard curve is defined as the relationship between a ground motion parameter and the probability of exceeding this parameter at least once in T years. A ground motion parameter can be represented by the peak ground acceleration (PGA), peak ground displacement (PGD) or peak ground velocity (PGV). These parameters are obtained for each simulated event by using an attenuation law and depend on the magnitude, distance from the site to the rupture zone and the soil type at the site.

An example of PGA site hazard curve is shown on Figure 2. in terms of the mean and 95% confidence bounds. This curve was obtained for the city of Palo Alto by considering the Northern part of San Andreas, Hayward and Calaveras faults. The Boore *et. al* (1993) attenuation law was used in this application. The site hazard curve obtained by the Poisson earthquake occurrence model developed by Kiremidjian (1976) is also shown for comparison.

The latter tends to over-estimate the hazard because the Poisson process assumed for events of all sizes implies time- and space-independence of these events, which is not realistic for the large earthquakes.

3 CONCLUSIONS

The automata network is a convenient tool for formulation of a complicated information-processing system, such as a seismic fault, in a mathematically elegant way. It makes the dynamics of the system's evolution relatively simple to follow.

The presented automata network of seismic activity on a fault allows to simulate small and moderate events as a Poisson process. These events release a small amount of accumulated slip, occur within a single cell and do not affect other fault cells and, hence, they are time- and space-independent. In contrast, a large event releases a large proportion of the accumulated slip not only on the triggering cell but also on several neighboring cells, which prevents another large event from rupturing the same cells in a short time increment. This is consistent with the seismic gap hypothesis, which states that on a particular fault seismic hazard increases with time elapsed since the last large earthquake.

The earthquake occurrence model formulated as an automata network estimates the site hazard from several faults. The use of the bootstrap provides the estimation of the confidence bounds on the obtained mean site hazard curve.

REFERENCES

Bavel, Z. 1983. Introduction to theory of automata. *Reston Publishing Company, Inc.*

Belubekian, M. E. & A. S. Kiremidjian 1996. Magnitude-pattern adaptive earthquake occurrence model for a fault. *Proceedings of the 11th World Conference on Earthquake Engineering*, Mexico.

Boore, D. M., W. B. Joyner & E. Fumal 1993. Estimation of response spectra and peak accelerations from Western North American earthquakes: an interim report. *USGS survey open file report 93-509.*

Efron, B. & R. J. Tibshirani 1993. An introduction to the bootstrap. *Chapman & Hall.*

Kiremidjian, A. S. 1976. Probabilistic hazard mapping: development of site dependent seismic load parameters. *Ph.D. Dissertation submitted to the Dept. of Civil Engineering, Stanford University.*

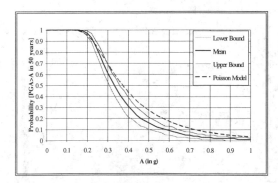

Figure 2. Site hazard curve for Palo Alto

Structural Safety and Reliability, Shiraishi, Shinozuka & Wen (eds) © 1998 Balkema, Rotterdam, ISBN 90 5410 978 5

Seismic risk analysis using equivalent nonlinear systems

Sang Whan Han
Department of Architectural Engineering, Hanyang University, Seoul, Korea

ABSTRACT: In reliability analysis and reliability-based design under seismic excitations, repeated time-history solutions of multi-degree-of-freedom (MDOF) inelastic structures are often required, which can become computationally expensive. To alleviate this difficulty, a simple equivalent nonlinear system (ENS) is developed which retains the dynamic characteristics of the first two modes and the global yielding behavior of the system. The computational advantage and accuracy of the method are demonstrated.

1.INTRODUCTION

In reliability evaluation of build- ings and structures under seismic excitation, repeated solutions of the response of MDOF systems in the inelastic range are often required and the computation can become excessive. The purpose of the present study is to develop an alternative procedure of approximating the original MDOF systems, which may improve the accuracy while keeping the computation within a reasonable limit. The idea is to replace the original structure by a simple equivalent nonlinear system (ENS) that retains the most important properties of the original system, i. e., the dynamic characteristics of the two modes and local and global yielding behavior of the MDOF system. The equivalency is achieved by the use of two empirical modification factors, a global response factor R_G and a local response factor R_L, applied to the responses of ENS to match those of the original MDOF system. More details can be found in Han and Wen (1994).

2. EQUIVALENT NONLINEAR SYSTEM

ENS is defined as a system consisting of two SDOF systems whose dynamic properties (natural frequency, mode shape, and modal participation factor) are the same as those of the first two modes of the original system. It is assumed that both SDOF systems have an yield displacement equal to the global yield displacement associated with the MDOF structure. The global yield displacement is

determined by a static pushover analysis in which a linear vertical distribution of the lateral force is assumed and applied proportionally on the building. To obtain the maximum overall (top) response and the interstory drift of the original system for reliability analysis, the responses of the equivalent system are multi-plied by a global and a local response modification factor, R_G and R_L and, respectively.

3. DETERMINATION OF RESPONSE MODIFI-CATION FACTORS

3.1 Selection and Design of Representative Structures

This study concentrates on low to mid-rise structures. Seven office buildings from one to 12 stories and one to four bays are selected. The structures are assumed to be located in zone 4 of UBC.

3.2 Selection of Historical Earth-quake Records

A suite of 88 real earthquake records are used in the dynamic-response time-history response analyses for the calibration of R_G and R_L. The records consist of moderate to severe ground-acceleration time histories in North America since 1933, including those of the recent North Ridge earthquake.

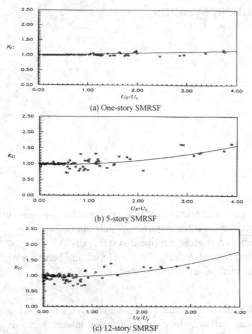

(a) One-story SMRSF

(b) 5-story SMRSF

(c) 12-story SMRSF

Fig. 1 Global Response Factor R_G: (a) One-story SMRSF; (b)5-story SMRSF; (c)12-story SMRSF

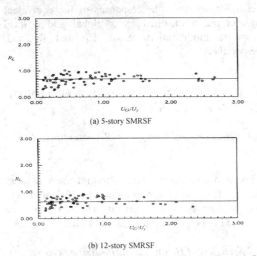

(a) 5-story SMRSF

(b) 12-story SMRSF

Fig.2 Local Response Modification Factor R_L: (a) 5-story SMRSF; (b) 12-story SMRSF

3.3 Regression Analysis of R_G and R_L

The global response modification factor, R_G, is defined as the ratio of the maximum displacement at the top of ENS (Ge) to that of the original MDOF structure (Gm) as follows:

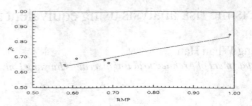

Fig.3 Regression of R_L on Modal Participation factor Ratio (γ)

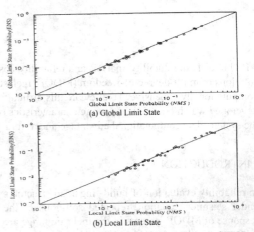

(a) Global Limit State

(b) Local Limit State

Fig.4 Comparison of Failure Probabilities of ENS and Nonlinear MDOF Systems at L.A.:(a) Global Limit State; (b)Local Limit State

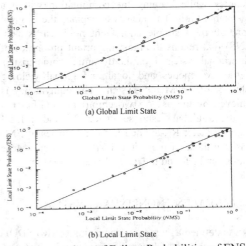

(a) Global Limit State

(b) Local Limit State

Fig.5 Comparison of Failure Probabilities of ENS and Nonlinear MDOF Systems at Imperial (a) Global Limit State;(b)Local Limit State

$$R_G = G_e / G_m \tag{1}$$

The local response modification factor, R_L, is defined as the ratio of the maximum global ductility to the local (interstory drift) ductility of the original MDOF structures as follows:

$$R_L = \frac{G_m / Y}{\max(d^i / y^i)} \tag{2}$$

where d^i = interstory drift at the ith story; y^i = ith story yield displacement; and Y = global yield displacement. The local yield displacement is obtained by the same procedure used for the global yield displacement.

Two stage regression analysis is carried out to obtain the functional relationship between R_G and system parameters, μ and γ, which is shown as follows:

$$R_G = C_0(\gamma) + C_1(\gamma)\,\mu + C_2(\gamma)\,\mu^2 \tag{3}$$

where C_0, C_1, and C_2 are assumed to be linear functions of the modal participation factor ratio defined as

$$\gamma = \frac{|P_1| + |P_2|}{\sum\limits_{i=1}^{n} |P_i|} \tag{4}$$

where P_i = ith modal participation factor; and n = number of modes considered. A two-stage regression analysis is then performed to determine the preceding coefficients. The results of the two-stage regression analysis are.

$$C_0 = 0.9695 + 0.0178\gamma \tag{5}$$
$$C_1 = -0.1664 + 0.2016\gamma \tag{6}$$
$$C_2 = 0.1473 - 0.1467\gamma \tag{7}$$

Fig. 1 shows the comparison of the data points with the regression results given by (3)-(7).

A similar two-stage regression analysis is carried out to calibrate the local response modification factor R_L. It is found that the variation of R_L is given by linear function of γ:

$$R_L = 0.3627 + 0.4774\gamma \tag{8}$$

Fig. 2 shows the comparison of regression equation of R_L with data points. Fig. 3 shows the regression equation of R_L as a function of γ.

4.RELIABILITY EVALUATION USING ENS

The performance of the building can be described in terms of drift limits being exceeded. To take the uncert-ainties on the problem into the consi- deration, the performance can be described in terms of the probability of certain drift limits being exceeded over a given time period as follows.

$$P_G = P\left(\frac{G_m}{H} > G_0\right) \tag{9}$$

$$P_L = P\left[\max\left(\frac{d^i}{h^i}\right) > L_0\right] \tag{10}$$

where H and h^i = height of the building and the story height, respectively; and G_0 and L_0 = limits for global and local drifts. The global limit-state probability can be expressed in terms of the response of ENS as follows:

$$P_G = P\left(\frac{G_e}{R_G H} > G_0\right) \tag{11}$$

Similarly, with aid of (2) and (11), the local limit-state probability can be expressed as

$$P_L = P\left(\frac{G_e}{R_G R_L H} > L_0\right) \tag{12}$$

where the following is assumed:

$$\frac{y^i}{Y} \approx \frac{h^i}{H} \tag{13}$$

Eq.(13) is an approximate relat-ionship that simplifies the calcul-ation since the story yield and story height need not be considered.

5.NUMERICAL RESULTS

The accuracy of the proposed method is verified by comparison of the limit-state probabilities for ENS with those for the original nonlinear MDOF systems, hereafter referred to as NMS. The seven steel SMRSFs on the foregoing are used for this purpose. The sites chosen are downtown Los Angeles (Santa Monica Boulevard) and Imperial Valley as in the previous study of reliability evaluation of steel buildings (Wen et al. 1994). The Santa Monica Boulevard site is 60 km from the Mojave segment of the Southern San Andrea fault, and the Imperial Valley site is 5 km from the Imperial fault. The drift limit covers a range of 0.5-3% of building or story height, which corresponds to levels from serviceability to ultimate limit. For a steel frame building, at 3% drift level it will probably suffer severe nonstructural or even structural damages. The probabilities are also compared in Fig.4 and 5.

The procedure for calculating the 50-year limit-state probabilities is the same as for the Los Angeles site. Tables 1 and 4 show the limit-state probabilities. It is seen that the agreements are still good though the scatters are larger.

Table 1. Global Limit State Probability (L.A.)

Structure No.	Used System	0.5% of height	1.0% of height	1.5% of height	2.0% of height	2.5% of height	3.0% of height
1	NMS	0.2415	0.0749	0.0387	0.0241	0.0167	0.0123
1	ENSS	0.2443	0.0741	0.0381	0.0237	0.0163	0.0120
2	NMS	0.3021	0.0906	0.0476	0.0300	0.0210	0.0156
2	ENSS	0.3050	0.0898	0.0468	0.0294	0.0205	0.0152
2	ELSS	0.3165	0.0804	0.0429	0.0259	0.0178	0.0140
3	ENSS	0.2459	0.0708	0.0368	0.0231	0.0161	0.0120
4	NMS	0.2477	0.0760	0.0403	0.0256	0.0180	0.0135
4	ENSS	0.2356	0.0692	0.0361	0.0227	0.0158	0.0112
5	NMS	0.2334	0.0695	0.0364	0.0230	0.0161	0.0120
5	ENSS	0.2513	0.0748	0.0392	0.0247	0.0172	0.0128
6	NMS	0.1650	0.0475	0.0233	0.0140	0.0094	0.0068
6	ENSS	0.1495	0.0422	0.0202	0.0119	0.0079	0.0056
7	NMS	0.1286	0.0375	0.0182	0.0108	0.0072	0.0052
7	ENSS	0.1212	0.0340	0.0161	0.0094	0.0062	0.0044

Table 2. Local Limit State Probability (L.A.)

Structure No.	Used System	0.5% of height	1.0% of height	1.5% of height	2.0% of height	2.5% of height	3.0% of height
2	NMS	0.3588	0.1153	0.0621	0.0399	0.0282	0.0212
2	ENSS	0.4229	0.1235	0.0637	0.0401	0.0280	0.0208
2	ELSS	0.3658	0.0869	0.0515	0.0303	0.0243	0.0165
3	NMS	0.4282	0.1345	0.0717	0.0460	0.0324	0.0243
3	ENSS	0.4367	0.1278	0.0639	0.0402	0.0281	0.0209
4	NMS	0.4676	0.1536	0.0831	0.0538	0.0382	0.0289
4	ENSS	0.4335	0.1268	0.0641	0.0404	0.0282	0.0210
5	NMS	0.3986	0.1224	0.0646	0.0412	0.0289	0.0216
5	ENSS	0.4615	0.1384	0.0703	0.0444	0.0311	0.0232
6	NMS	0.2990	0.0917	0.0468	0.0289	0.0198	0.0145
6	ENSS	0.3403	0.0917	0.0441	0.0262	0.0174	0.0125
7	NMS	0.2401	0.0748	0.0377	0.0230	0.0156	0.0113
7	ENSS	0.2914	0.0789	0.0377	0.0222	0.0147	0.0105

Table 3. Global Limit State Probability (Imperial)

Structure No.	Used System	0.5% of height	1.0% of height	1.5% of height	2.0% of height	2.5% of height	3.0% of height
1	NMS	0.8264	0.7045	0.2956	0.1155	0.0383	0.0109
1	ENSS	0.8264	0.6902	0.2879	0.0916	0.0245	0.0062
2	NMS	0.8258	0.5519	0.1930	0.0589	0.0166	0.0045
2	ENSS	0.8230	0.5595	0.2154	0.0568	0.0140	0.0051
2	ELSS	0.8218	0.4835	0.1652	0.0421	0.0110	0.0029
3	NMS	0.8253	0.4241	0.0886	0.0147	0.0023	0.0003
3	ENSS	0.7942	0.4551	0.1020	0.0154	0.0021	0.0003
4	NMS	0.8252	0.4607	0.1209	0.0255	0.0051	0.0001
4	ENSS	0.7927	0.4495	0.1023	0.0160	0.0023	0.0003
5	NMS	0.8247	0.4282	0.0923	0.0157	0.0026	0.0004
5	ENSS	0.8026	0.4859	0.1192	0.0193	0.0028	0.0004
6	NMS	0.8178	0.1820	0.0152	0.0012	0.0001	0.7e-4
6	ENSS	0.7676	0.1506	0.0111	0.0008	0.0001	0.4e-4
7	NMS	0.7676	0.0821	0.0054	0.0004	0.3e-4	0.2e-5
7	ENSS	0.6702	0.0824	0.0065	0.0005	0.4e-4	0.3e-5

Table 4. Local Limit State Probability (Imperial)

Structure No.	Used System	0.5% of height	1.0% of height	1.5% of height	2.0% of height	2.5% of height	3.0% of height
2	NMS	0.8245	0.6632	0.3522	0.1718	0.0792	0.0350
2	ENSS	0.8257	0.7000	0.3798	0.1761	0.0759	0.0313
2	ELSS	0.8256	0.6083	0.3298	0.1009	0.0500	0.0179
3	NMS	0.8264	0.8237	0.4890	0.1695	0.0494	0.0133
3	ENSS	0.8213	0.6951	0.3931	0.1352	0.0367	0.0093
4	NMS	0.8264	0.8246	0.6529	0.3364	0.1428	0.0549
4	ENSS	0.8212	0.6987	0.4034	0.1453	0.0415	0.0109
5	NMS	0.8264	0.8178	0.4769	0.1634	0.0441	0.0110
5	ENSS	0.8237	0.7235	0.4480	0.1738	0.0520	0.0142
6	NMS	0.8264	0.6832	0.2281	0.0416	0.0065	0.0010
6	ENSS	0.8254	0.5865	0.1688	0.0321	0.0056	0.0010
7	NMS	0.8264	0.5596	0.1381	0.0236	0.0038	0.0006
7	ENSS	0.8222	0.4473	0.1081	0.0219	0.0044	0.0009

6. SUMMARY AND CONCLUSIONS

The equivalence is achieved by using two empirical response-modification factors for local (interstory drift) and global (structural drift) responses based on extensive regression analyses of the responses of the two systems to ground accelerations recorded in past earthquakes. Comparison of 50-year global and local limit-state probabilities of SMRSF buildings of one to 12 stories at two sites in Southern California indicate that the method gives satisfactory predictions. It is therefore a useful tool in reliability evaluation and calibration of design parameters based on reliability as shown in the companion paper.

7. ACKNOWLEDGMENTS

The support of STRESS is gratefully acknowledged.

REFERENCES

Han, S. W., and Wen, Y. K (1994). "Method of reliability-based calibration of seismic design parameters." *Struct. Res. Ser. No. 595,* Dept. of Civ. Engrg., Univ. of Illinois at Urbana-Champaign, Urbana, Ill.

Inoue, T., and Cornell, C. A. (1991). " Seismic hazard analysis of MDOF structures." *Proc., of ICASP,* Mexico City, Mexico.

Ostweaas, J. D., and Krawinkler, H. (1990). " Strength and ductility consideration in seismic design." *Rep. No. 90,* Dept. of Civ. Engrg., Stanford Univ., Stanford, Calif.

Uniform building code. (1991). International Conference of Building Officials, Whittier, Calif.

Han, S. W., and Wen, Y. K. (1994). "Method of reliability-based calibration of seismic design parameters." *Struct. Res. Ser. No. 595,* Dept. of Civ. Engrg., Univ. of Illinois at Urbana-Champaign, Urbana, Ill.

Structural Safety and Reliability, Shiraishi, Shinozuka & Wen (eds) © 1998 Balkema, Rotterdam, ISBN 90 5410 978 5

Seismic hazard assessment for a site in Western Ukraine considering the effect of Vranchea source

P. Varpasuo
IVO Power Engineering Ltd, Vantaa, Finland

ABSTRACT: The Vranchea source is one of the most important subcrustal sources in the world. The estimation of the seismic hazard on the site in western Ukraine has been made with the aid of standard hazard estimation methods using the USGS computer program SEISRISK III. The seismic hazard curve for the investigated site was developed for mean return periods of thousand, ten thousand, one hundred thousand and one million years. In addition to the seismic hazard curve also the uniform hazard spectra and the compatible ground motion in horizontal direction for the mean return period of ten thousand years were developed for the site.

1. INTRODUCTION

The Vranchea region is situated in the Carpathian Arc. It is the source of subcrustal seismic activity. The hypocentral depths vary from 60 to 200 kilometers.

The Vranchea region is the transfer region between the layered structures of Eastern Carpats and the Carpathian Bend. The hypocentral depth in this region decreases in eastern-south-eastern direction, where the subcrustal sources change to crustal. In terms of global plate tectonics in Vranchea region two lithospheric plates collide.

Vranchea earthquakes are very localized and they have very high seismic energy compared to other Carpathian earthquakes. The diameter of the Vranchea source area is about 100 km.

Vranchea events are felt in enormous area including Romania, Ukraine, Belorussia, the European part of Russian Federation, Bulgaria, Turkey, Yugoslavia, Slovakia, Czech Republic and Poland. The felt area of Vranchea earthquakes exceeds a couple of times the felt area of crustal earthquakes of the same size.

In the time frame from 1091 to 1990 there has been 56 events greater than 6 in magnitude in Vranchea source area. The seismicity of the Vranchea source and Western Ukraine has been presented in the following references (1 Shebalin 1995), (2 Bune 1980) and (3 Riznichenko).

2. EPICENTRAL MAP

Using Shebalin catalog the earthquakes greater than 3 in magnitude inside the window 20° E-31 ° E and 44 ° N - 52 ° N and between the years of 1091 and 1990 were plotted on map. The resulting epicentral map is depicted in Figure 1.

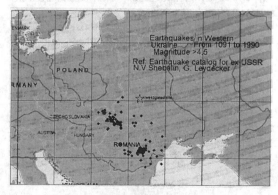

Figure 1 Epicentral map for Western Ukraine

The zoom-in for the investigated window has been presented in Figure 2.

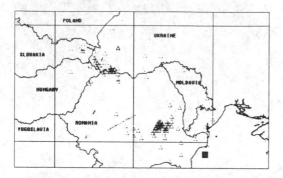

Figure 2 The zoom-in for investigated window

3. SOURCE AREA DELINEATION

When the seismicity of the investigated window is studied three source areas can be distinguished. The obvious one is the Vranchea source about 500 km due south from the site. In addition to Vranchea the clear cluster of epicenters can be seen in the junction of Romanian, Hungarian, Slovakian and Ukrainian borders near the town Uzhgorod. The third type of source is background seismicity for which the characteristics of Russian plain seismicity were adopted. The size of Vranchea source was taken as a square with 100 km side length and the Uzhgorod source area was taken in the shape of an rectangle with north-south side length of 200 km and east-west side length of 400 km. The background seismicity was assumed to be present in the area of whole investigated window. The Gutenberg-Richter type recurrence relationships for the source areas are presented in Figure 3.

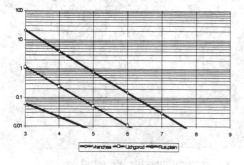

Figure 3 The magnitude-recurrence relationships

The ordinate axis in Figure 3 shows the annual number of earthquakes greater than the given magnitude value depicted in abscissa. The curves are given for the three sources described in Section 3.

4. ATTENUATION EQUATION

Two types of attenuation equations were used in this study. For the Vranchea source the pga attenuation developed by Lungu and coworkers was used. It is based on a database of digitized triaxial strong motion records of Vranchea events in Mar 04, 1977, Aug. 30, 1986, May 30, 1990 and May 31, 1990. The number of records available in the database are. 1 record for Mar 04, 1977 event ; 42 records for Aug. 30 1986 event; 54 records for May 30 1990 event and 40 records for May 31 1990 event. All these recording stations were located in Romania. The database was appended with 3 Moldavian and 8 Bulgarian recordings (4 Lungu 1995). The Lungu attenuation equation for pga for magnitude 8 has been depicted in Figure 4.

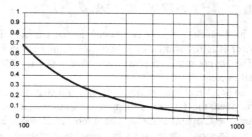

Figure 4 The Lungu attenuation equation. The distance from epicenter in km and acceleration in g's. The magnitude value for the curve is 8.

In addition, for Uzhgorod and Russian plain earthquakes the second attenuation relationship was used. It has been developed by Dahle (5 Dahle 1990) and coworkers. It gives the pga attenuation and the attenuation for spectral ordinates for frequencies from 0.25 Hz up to 10 Hz. In order to develop the uniform hazard spectra for higher frequencies the Dahle equations were appended with EPRI (6 EPRI 1993) equations for frequencies between 10 Hz and 35 Hz. The EPRI equations were so calibrated that they gave the same attenuation at 10 Hz than the Dahle equations. The Dahle and EPRI attenuation equations have been depicted in Figures 5 and 6.

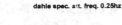

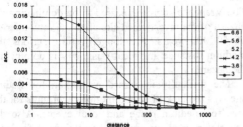

Figure 5 Dahle spectral attenuation for 0.25 Hz.

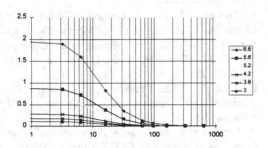

Figure 6 EPRI spectral attenuation for 25 Hz.
Acceleration in g's ,distance in kilometers

The standard deviation for logarithm of acceleration
in Lungu attenuation was 0.397 and in case of Dahle
and EPRI attenuation's 0.7, respectively.

5.   MAXIMUM MAGNITUDES

Maximum magnitudes and magnitude interval to be
taken into account in hazard evaluation were
selected as follows: (1) For Vranchea source the
maximum magnitude was 7.5 and the lower limit of
the integrated magnitude interval was 6; (2) for
Uzhgorod source the maximum magnitude was 6.5
and the lower limit was 4; (3) for Russian plain
background source the maximum magnitude was 5.2
and the lower limit was 3. These values were
selected on the basis of reference (2 Bune 1980). It
is to be mentioned that for maximum magnitudes the
values actually observed were adopted and this is a
source of non-conservatism in the subsequent hazard
analyses. This has to kept in mind when the obtained
results are assessed.

6.   DEVELOPMENT OF SITE HAZARD

The investigated site is the Khmelnitsky NPP in
vicinity of town Netishin in western Ukraine. The
site is depicted with asterisk in the Figure 1.

The methodology used for the hazard evaluation
was the standard procedure described in reference (7
Bender 1987). The input procedure for both
attenuation and recurrence description is tabular
facilitating the use various formulations for
attenuation and recurrence relationships.

7.   RESULTS

The results of the performed work are given in the
form of hazard curve, uniform hazard spectra and
simulated ground motion for the prospective site.

The ground motion describes the horizontal
component and is fitted with the uniform hazard
spectrum corresponding to the mean return period of
10 000 years.

The obtained results are depicted in Figures 7, 8,
9 and 10.

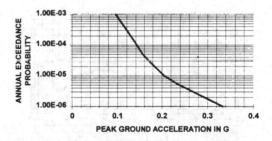

Figure 7 The hazard curve of site

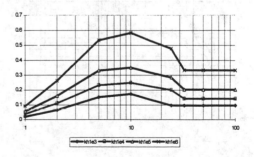

Figure 8 The uniform hazard spectra of the site

In Figure 8 the spectral ordinates for acceleration are in g's and the frequency in Hz. The uniform hazard spectra correspond to the mean return periods of 1000, 10 000, 100 000 and 1 000 000 years.

For the 10 000 year spectrum an acceleration time history was simulated using the methodology described by Vanmarcke (8 Vanmarcke 1976).

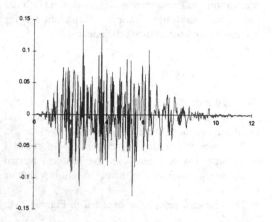

Figure 9 Simulated acceleration time-history

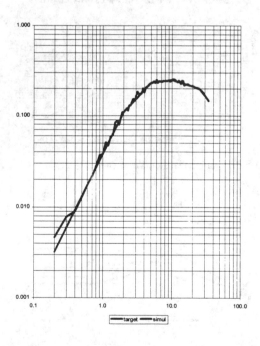

Figure 10 Target spectrum and spectrum of simulated motion

8. CONCLUSION

The Vranchea source appeared to be dominating the hazard of the investigated site up to the return period of 50 000 years. For longer return periods the medium distance and local seismicity is dominating the hazard.

The difficulty in hazard estimation for studied site was the lack of strong motion recordings for the area for medium range and local events. Also the completeness of the earthquake catalogs is for local seismicity is difficult to assess.

REFERENCES

1 Shebalin N.V. & Leydecker (eds) 1996. Earthquake Catalogue for the former USSR and borders up to 1988. *Final Report to EC Contracts No. ETNU-CT91-0041(DOEO) and No COSU-CT92-00123*

2 Bune V. I & Gorskov G. P. (eds) 1980. *Seismicheskoye raionirovanie territorii CCCP.* Moscow: Nauka.

3 Riznichenko Yu. V. (ed) 1979. *Seismicheskaya sotryasayemost territorii CCCP.* Moscow: Nauka.

4 Lungu D. & al. 1995. Hazard analysis for Vranchea earthquakes. Application to Cernavoda NPP site in Romania. *Trans. of SMiRT- 13,vol III:289-294.* Porto Alegre:Universidade Federal do Rio Grande do Sul.

5 Dahle A. & al. 1990. Attenuation Models Inferred from Intraplate Earthquake Recordings. *Earthquake Engineering and Structural Dynamics, vol 19: 1125-1141.*

6 Electric Power Research Institute, EPRI TR-102293. 1993. Guidelines for Determining Design Basis Ground Motions. Volume 1: Method and Guidelines for Estimating Earthquake Ground Motion in Eastern North America.

7 Bender B. & Perkins D. M. 1987. SEISRISK III: A Computer Program for Seismic Hazard Estimation. U. S. Geological Survey Bulletin 1772. Denver, U. S. Department of the Interior.

8 Vanmarcke E. 1976. Simulated Earthquake Motions Compatible with Prescribed Response Spectra. MIT Report R76-4, Order No. 527.

Structural Safety and Reliability, Shiraishi, Shinozuka & Wen (eds) © 1998 Balkema, Rotterdam, ISBN 90 5410 978 5

Damage spectra of ground accelerations during earthquakes

Yoshio Sunasaka
Civil Engineering Design Division, Kajima Corporation, Tokyo, Japan

ABSTRACT: Linear or non-linear response spectra are frequently used to estimate the intensity or potential of ground accelerations during earthquakes. However, the correlation between the response spectra and structural damage is not clear. This paper introduces the damage spectrum of ground acceleration during an earthquake to estimate its intensity or potential. The damage spectrum is defined here as damage indexes of single degree of freedom systems with natural periods ranging from 0.05 to 5.0 sec. The damage index proposed by Park and Ang(1985) and the bilinear model are used to calculate the damage spectrum.
Structural damage in Kobe during the 1995 Hyogoken Nanbu earthquake was concentrated in a belt 0.7 to 1.2 km wide stretching from southwest to northeast along the foot of the Rokko Mountains. This is mainly explained by the geological ground conditions of Kobe. According to the dynamic 2D analysis of the Kobe ground model, ground motions are especially large at the belt. This paper studies the damage spectra of the recorded ground accelerations and the analytical ground accelerations during the 1995 Hyogoken Nanbu earthquake. The results show that the damage spectra correlate well with damage to structures in Kobe.

1 INTRODUCTION

Linear or non-linear response spectra are frequently used to estimate the intensity or potential of ground accelerations during earthquakes. However, the correlation between the response spectra and structural damage is not clear. This paper introduces the damage spectrum of ground acceleration during an earthquake to estimate its intensity or potential. The damage spectrum is defined here as damage indexes of single degree of freedom systems with natural periods ranging from 0.05 to 5.0 sec. The damage index proposed by Park and Ang(1985) [1],[2] and bilinear model are used to calculate the damage spectrum.

2 DAMAGE SPECTRA

2.1 STRUCTURAL DAMAGE

Researchers have proposed damage indexes to represent structural damage levels. These indexes describe the state of the structure from slight damage to severe damage or collapse. They can be calculated by non-linear analysis of structural response during earthquakes.

Structural damage depends on the characteristics of the structure as well as the ground motions. Thus, we must select an appropriate damage measure that reflects the characteristics of a structure. The damage index proposed by Park and Ang(1985)[1],[2] is appropriate to evaluate the damage to concrete structures during earthquakes.

This index is expressed as a linear combination of the maximum deformation and the hysteretic energy as follows:

$$D = \frac{\delta_m}{\delta_u} + \beta \int \frac{dE}{(Q_y \delta_u)} \qquad (2.1)$$

where D is the damage index, an empirical measure of damage (D>1 indicates total damage or collapse); δ_m is the maximum response deformation; δ_u is the ultimate deformation capacity under static loading; Q_y is the calculated yield strength; dE is the incremental dissipated hysteretic energy; and β is the coefficient for cyclic loading effect. The limiting value of D (i.e., damage capacity of a member) is log normally distributed with a mean of approximately 1.0 and a standard deviation of 0.54.

2.2 DAMAGE SPECTRA

This paper introduces the damage spectrum of ground motion during an earthquake to estimate its intensity or potential. The damage spectrum is defined here as damage indexes of single degree of freedom(SDOF) systems with natural periods ranging from 0.05 to 5.0 sec. To calculate the damage index by Park and Ang(1985), a non-linear force-displacement relationship is needed. For simplicity, this paper uses a bilinear force-displacement relationship.

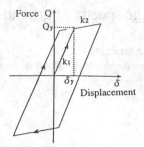

Figure 1 Bilinear force-displacement relationship

3 CHARACTERISTICS OF DAMAGE SPECTRA

The damage index proposed by Park and Ang(1985) is calculated by non-linear response analysis of the SDOF system, which has the bilinear force-displacement relationship shown in Figure 1. The parameters of the SDOF system and the damage index are shown in Table 1. Since the force-displacement relationship is bilinear, it is appropriate to assume that the value of parameter β in equation (2.1) is 0.05 in the analysis.

3.1 Basic characteristics of the damage spectra

This section describes parametric studies. The selected ground motion is the acceleration recorded at JMA Kobe during the 1995 Hyogoken Nanbu earthquake. The ground motion is shown in Figure 6 and the location of JMA Kobe is shown in Figure 3. The results of parametric studies on the damage spectra are shown in Figure 2. The basic parameters for this analysis are the same as those shown in Table 1. Figure 2(a) shows the damage spectra for cases of yield strength Qy=0.3W,0.4W and 0.5W, where W is the weight of the SDOF system. Figure 2(b) shows the damage spectra for cases of damping ratio h=0.02,0.05 and 0.1. Figure 2(c) shows the damage spectra for cases of ultimate deformation capacity $\delta_u=2\delta_y$, $4\delta_y$ and $6\delta_y$, where δ_y is the yield deformation of the SDOF system. According to Figure 2, the damage spectra of ground acceleration

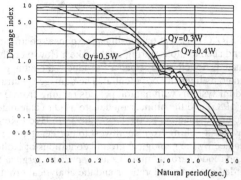

(a) Damage spectra for Qy=0.3W,0.4W and 0.5W

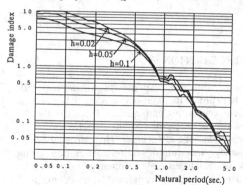

(b) Damage spectra for h=0.02,0.05 and 0.1

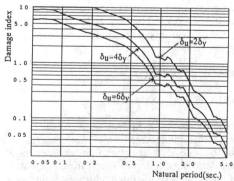

(c) Damage spectra for $\delta_u=2\delta_y$, $4\delta_y$ and $6\delta_y$

Figure 2 Results of parametric studies on damage spectra

Table 1 Basic parameters for analysis

SDOF Model	damping ratio h	0.05
	second stiffness k_2	$0.05k_1$
	yield strength Q_y	0.4W
Damage Index	coefficient β	0.05
	ultimate deformation capacity δ_u	$4\delta_y$

where W: weight of SDOF, δ_y: yield deformation
k_1: initial stiffness

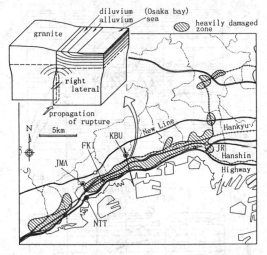

Figure 3 Heavily damaged zone in Kobe City and schematic diagram of underground structure near Rokko fault zone[3]

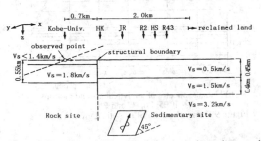

Figure 4 Two dimensional model of deep irregular underground structure orthogonal to Rokko fault plane[3]

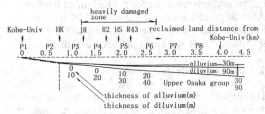

Figure 5 Configuration of shallow surface layers[3]

at JMA Kobe are scattered by these parameters, but they are larger than 1.0 at natural periods ranging less than around 0.8 sec.

3.2 Application to ground motions during the Hyogoken Nanbu earthquake

Structural damage in Kobe during the 1995 Hyogoken Nanbu earthquake was concentrated in a belt 0.7 to 1.2 km wide stretching from southwest to northeast along the foot of the Rokko Mountains as

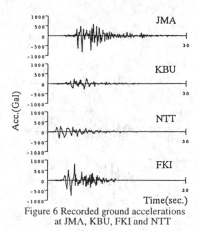

Figure 6 Recorded ground accelerations at JMA, KBU, FKI and NTT

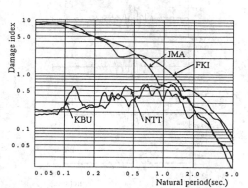

Figure 7 Damage spectra of recorded ground motions at JMA, KBU, FKI and NTT

shown in Figure 3. Figure 6 shows the recorded ground motions during the Hyogoken Nanbu earthquake in or around the heavily damaged zone shown in Figure 3. Figure 7 shows the damage spectra of the ground motions shown in Figure 6. The damage spectrum of ground motion record at Fukiai(FKI) in the heavily damaged zone is larger than that at JMA Kobe in almost all natural period ranges and larger than 1.0 at natural periods smaller than 1.2 sec. However, the damage spectra of ground motion records at Kobe University(KBU) and NTT around the zone are smaller than 1.0 in all natural period ranges.

Analytical results conducted by M. Motosaka and M. Nagano(1996)[3] have demonstrated that the concentration of structural damage in the shallow zone stretching from southwest to northeast along the foot of the Rokko Mountains is mainly explained by the geological ground conditions of Kobe. To estimate the amplification characteristics of the ground motions in the heavily damaged zone, M. Motosaka and M. Nagano(1996)[3] performed 3-D wave-propagation

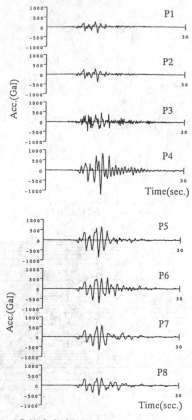

Figure 8 Analytical ground accelerations from P1 to P8[3]

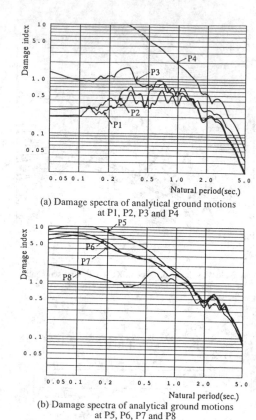

(a) Damage spectra of analytical ground motions
at P1, P2, P3 and P4

(b) Damage spectra of analytical ground motions
at P5, P6, P7 and P8
Figure 9 Damage spectra of analytical ground motions

analyses of a 2-D deep irregular underground structure model with vertical discontinuity for incident plane waves. Figure 4 shows the two-dimensional model of the underground structure orthogonal to the Rokko fault plane, and Figure 5 shows the configuration of shallow surface layers[3]. The analytical results show that the ground motions in the heavily damaged zone were amplified due to the focusing effect in the deep irregular underground structure as well as in the shallow surface layers. Figure 8 shows the analytical ground motions by M. Motosaka and M. Nagano(1996)[3] at ground surface points P1 to P8 shown in Figure 5. Ground surface points P4 to P6 are located in the heavily damaged zone, and P4 among them is located in the most heavily damaged zone between JR and the Hanshin Railway Line(HS)[4]. Figure 9 shows the damage spectra of the analytical ground motions. According to Figure 9, the damage spectrum of ground acceleration at P4 has the greatest intensity. The damage spectra of ground accelerations at P1 to P3 are smaller than 1.0, and the intensity of the damage spectra of ground accelerations decreases with distance from P4 to the ground surface point for the Rokko Mountains. The

intensity of the damage spectra of ground accelerations at P5 to P8 decreases with distance from P4 to the ground surface point for the reclaimed land, but those of ground accelerations at P5 to P7 have great intensity. These results demonstrate that the damage spectra correlate well with the structural damage.

4. CONCLUSIONS

This paper introduces the damage spectrum of ground motion during an earthquake to estimate its intensity or potential. This spectrum is applied to the recorded and analytical ground accelerations in Kobe during the 1995 Hyogoken Nanbu earthquake. These results demonstrate that the damage spectra correlate well with the structural damage.

ACKNOWLEDGMENTS

It is gratefully acknowledged that the recorded ground accelerations analyzed in this paper, JMA, KBU, FKI and NTT, were made available by the Japan Meteorological Agency, Kansai Earthquake Motion Observation and Research Committee, Osaka Gas Co., and NTT, respectively.

REFERENCES

[1] Park Y. J., Ang A. H-S., Wen Y. K.,:"Seismic
    Damage Analysis of Reinforced Concrete
    Buildings", *Journal of Structural Engineering,
    ASCE,* Vol.111, No.4, pp.722-739, 1985.4.
[2] Park Y. J., Ang A. H-S.,:"Mechanistic Seismic
    Damage Model for Reinforced Concrete", *Journal
    of Structural Engineering, ASCE*, Vol.111, No.4,
    pp.740-754, 1985.4.
[3] Motosaka M., Nagano M.,:"Analysis on
    Amplification Characteristics of Ground Motions
    in Kobe City Taking Account of Deep Irregular
    Underground Structure - Interpretation of Heavily
    Damaged Belt Zone During the 1995 Hyogoken
    Nanbu Earthquake -", *Journal of Structural and
    Construction Engineering, AIJ*, No.488, pp.39-
    48, October, 1996.
[4] Japan Society of Civil Engineers,:"Preliminary
    Report on the Great Hanshin Earthquake January
    17, 1995", Japan Society of Civil Engineers,
    1995.

Structural Safety and Reliability, Shiraishi, Shinozuka & Wen (eds) © 1998 Balkema, Rotterdam, ISBN 90 5410 978 5

Ductility and strength demand for near field earthquake ground motion: Comparative study on the Hyogo-ken Nanbu and the Northridge earthquakes

Hirokazu Iemura, Akira Igarashi & Yoshikazu Takahashi
Graduate School of Civil Engineering, Kyoto University, Japan

ABSTRACT: The Hyogo-ken Nanbu Earthquake of January 17, 1995 caused severe damage to buildings, highway bridges, railways, lifeline systems, port facilities, and so on. This event is the first instance in which engineering structures which were designed for the highest seismic forces in the world have been subjected to such destructive ground motions. This paper shows several calculated response spectra for the Kobe record together with the Sylmar record obtained during the Northridge Earthquake, which occurred on exactly the same day of 1994. Comparing these response spectra with those for previously obtained historical earthquake records, extremely high damage potential is revealed for near field earthquake ground motion. Urgent retrofit of old structures and re-examination of present seismic design codes are essential.

1 Outline of the Hyogo-ken Nanbu Earthquake

The Hyogo-ken Nanbu earthquake (the name officially given by the Japanese Meteorological Agency (JMA), indicating the location of the epicenter and the fault zone) was of magnitude 7.2 and occurred at 5:46 a.m. on January 17, 1995 in the Hanshin area, one of the most densely populated areas in Japan. The shaking intensity on the JMA scale at several regions in the Awaji-shima island, and areas extending from Suma-ku of Kobe to Nishinomiya, was announced to be 7; that roughly corresponds to a shaking intensity of X or more on the Modified Mercalli Intensity (MMI) scale. The distribution of damage to traditional Japanese houses is concentrated in these areas, which as shown in Fig. 1[2] encompasses a region with a length of about 20km and a width of 1km. The extent of the fault zone, as well as the specific soil conditions and topography of the area (narrowed by mountains in the north and by coastline in the south), played a very strong role in the regional damage distribution for this earthquake.

Peak horizontal accelerations of the ground exceeded 0.8g in Kobe and were as high as 0.23g at a distance of 50km in Osaka. One of the measured ground accelerations, recorded at Kobe Marine Meteorological Observatory in Chuo-ku, is shown in Fig. 2. This record also shows a peak acceleration over 0.8g, and strong shaking lasted only 10 seconds.

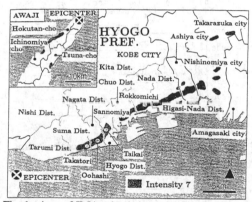

Fig. 1. Area of JMA seismic intensity 7 in the Hyoto prefecture and Awaji island (after Ref. 2).

2 Comparison of the Recorded Accelerograms

In Fig. 2, the N-S components of recorded earthquake ground motion are compared for the Kobe record of the Hyogo-ken Nanbu Earthquake, the Sylmar record of the Northridge Earthquake, the El Centro record of the Imperial Earthquake in 1940, and the Hachinohe record of the Tokachi-oki Earthquake in 1968. The latter two records have been used for earthquake resistant design of critical structures in Japan.

It is clear that the Kobe and Sylmar records obtained very close to the faults have high intensity

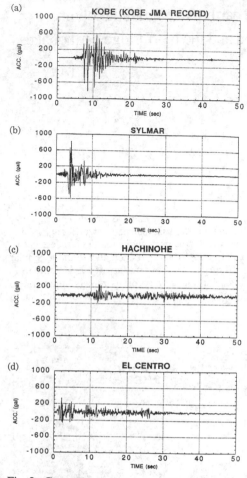

(a)

KOBE (KOBE JMA RECORD)

(b)

SYLMAR

(c)

HACHINOHE

(d)

EL CENTRO

Fig. 2. Comparison of the recorded accelerograms.

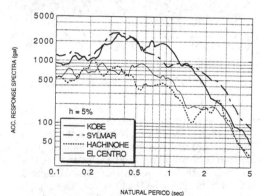

h = 5%

KOBE
SYLMAR
HACHINOHE
EL CENTRO

NATURAL PERIOD (sec)

Fig. 3. Absolute acceleration response spectra.

but short duration, which are quite unique features of near field earthquake ground motion.

3 Comparison of Acceleration Response Spectra

As can be seen in Fig. 3, the absolute acceleration response spectra for the Kobe and Sylmar records show higher acceleration response than the El Centro and Hachinohe records in all period ranges. The response of Kobe shows more than 1g in the period range from 0.15 to 1.2 seconds. Especially in the 0.3 to 0.5 range, the response even exceeds 2g. It is interesting to see that the Kobe and the Sylmar records show similar acceleration responses in almost all period ranges.

4 Evolutionary Power Spectra

To examine the nonstationary power imported to structures with different natural periods, evolutionary power spectra for the four earthquake ground motion records are calculated and compared in Figs. 4(a)-(d). The evolutionary power spectra is the power of a simple structure with natural period $T_0 = 2\pi/\omega_0$ and damping ratio $h_0 = 0.05$, as given by following equation[4]:

$$G(t, \omega_0) = \frac{2h_0\omega_0^3}{\pi}\left\{x^2(t) + \frac{\dot{x}^2(t)}{\omega_0^2}\right\} \tag{1}$$

where, $x(t)$ and $\dot{x}(t)$ are displacement and velocity time history responses. The Kobe record in Fig.4(a) shows a very high and sharp peak in power around 1.0 second after the beginning of the earthquake motion. This peak was felt as an extremely strong shock by local residents. Two strong peaks of the power are observed in the first several seconds, which could have contributed to the serious damage of structures.

The Sylmar record in Fig. 4(b) also shows sharp peaks, but the level of the power is not as high as the Kobe record. Instead, in the longer period range (larger than 1.5 seconds), moderate but relatively high peaks of the power are seen, which could have contributed to the observed damage of flexible steel frame buildings. Compared to the Kobe and the Sylmar records which were measured very near the faults, the Hachinohe and El Centro records in Figs. 4(c) and (d) show a very low level of the power, even though the duration of strong motion is about 30 seconds long.

5 Inelastic Displacement Response Spectra

The structural damage we observe at the local site just after the earthquake may be highly correlated with the experienced maximum displacement response relative to the yielding displacement.

(a) Kobe JMA record.   (b) Sylmer record.

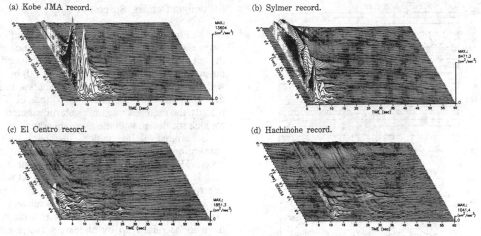

(c) El Centro record.   (d) Hachinohe record.

Fig. 4. Comparison of the evolutionary power spectra.

(a) Perfectly elasto-plastic hysteresis loop.

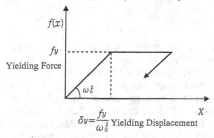

$$\delta y = \frac{f y}{\omega_0^2} \text{ Yielding Displacement}$$

(b) Yielding force of the elastic seismic design.

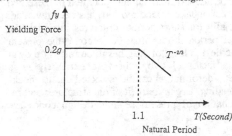

Fig. 5. Calculation of inelastic displ. spectra.

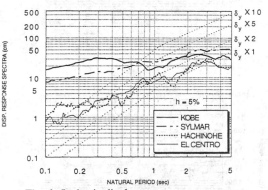

Fig. 6. Inelastic displacement response spectra.

Hence, in this section, inelastic displacement response spectra of a single degree of freedom structure with a perfect elasto-plastic bilinear hysteretic restoring force shown in Fig. 5(a) is calculated. The yielding level, set as shown in Fig. 5(b), was used for most of the damaged old structures.

The calculated inelastic displacement response spectra are shown in Fig. 6. the Kobe and Sylmar records give very large displacements in the short period range (0.1-0.7 seconds). This effect is

due to the large plastic deformation caused by the high intensity, shock-type loading. The yielding displacement δ_y corresponding to a yielding acceleration and natural period of the structures ($\delta_y = f_y / \omega_0^2$) is plotted by the dashed line. Also plotted are 2, 5, and 10 times δ_y. In the short period range, the inelastic displacement response exceeds the allowable ductility level, thus the yielding level of adequately designed structures, needs to be increased.

On the contrary, in the medium period range (0.7-3.0 seconds), the inelastic displacement response shows lower values than those of linear structures. The reason is that hysteretic energy dissipation suppresses the displacement response.

For long period structures (over 3 seconds), the inelastic displacement becomes smaller than 2 δ_y, and not much difference is found between the linear and nonlinear response spectra.

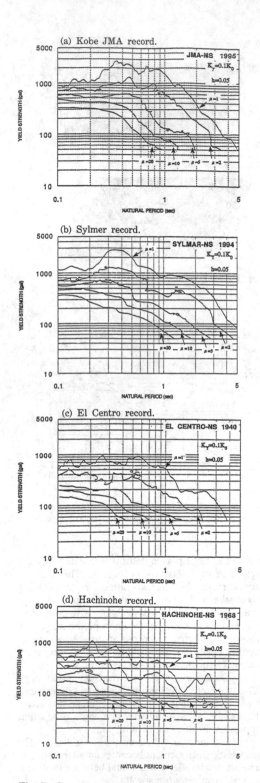

Fig. 7. Comparison of the strength demand spectra

6 Strength Demand Spectra

For structures with the higher ductility, the lower elastic strength is required for inelastic seismic design. The required elastic strength is plotted with the given ductility factor (μ=1, 2, 5, 10, 20) in Fig. 7, which is called as the strength demand spectra. For the conventional Hachinohe and the El Centro records, the required maximum elastic strength level for inelastic design with the allowable ductility factor 5 is around 0.2g, which matches with the conventional earthquake design of buildings and bridges. However, for the Kobe and Sylmar records, 0.5g is required as the elastic strength even with the allowable ductility factor 10, for the short period range (0.1-0.4 seconds). Hence, in this range, present elastic design level and allowable ductility factor both have to be raised up by at least a factor of two, otherwise extremely large damage can be expected due to the shock-type loading of the near-field earthquake ground motion.

7 Conclusions

The recently obtained Sylmar records from the Northridge Earthquake (Jan. 17, 1994) and Kobe records from the Hyogo-ken Nanbu Earthquake (Jan. 17, 1995) have been analyzed based on different types of response spectra. Compared with the El Centro records obtained during the Imperial Valley Earthquake (May 18, 1940) and the Hachinohe record obtained during the Tokachi-oki Earthquake (May 16, 1968). Extremely high damage potential of these two recent earthquake ground motions has been revealed. Especially for short period structures in which the natural period is less than 0.7 second, the present elastic design level of 0.2g has to be raised up by at least a factor of two, otherwise extremely large inelastic deformation can be expected due to shock-type loading. Urgent retrofit of old structures and re-examination of present seismic design codes are essential.

References

1) Japan Society of Civil Engineers (1995), The First and the Second Reconnaissance Report of the Great Hanshin Earthquake Disaster (in Japanese).
2) F. Oka, M. Sugito, A. Yashima and J.P. Bardet (1995), Preliminary Investigation Report of the Great Hanshin Earthquake Disaster.
3) CSMIP Strong-Motion Records from the Northridge, California Earthquake of January 17, 1994 (1994).
4) H. Kameda (1975), Proc. of the Japan Society of Civil Engineers, No. 235, 55-62.
5) Japan Road Association (1990), Part V Seismic Design Specifications of Highway Bridges.

Structural Safety and Reliability, Shiraishi, Shinozuka & Wen (eds) © 1998 Balkema, Rotterdam, ISBN 90 5410 978 5

Interstory drift and damage of steel buildings in 1995 Kobe earthquake

M. Kohno & M. Hattori
Nagoya University, Japan

ABSTRACT: In the Great Hanshin earthquake 1995, many steel structured buildings were partially damaged and/or forced to lose some of building service performance though they did not completely collapse. Thus the earthquake gave us a good opportunity to reconsider relation between the building design and the actual performance of the designed building. Actual behavior of a building in an earthquake is not easy to measure and there are few such data. Non-linear structural analyses are performed using actual earthquake records as an input to estimate accelerations, shearing forces and interstory drifts of each story during the 1995 Hyogo-ken nanbu earthquake. On the other hand, accommodable deformation of a PCa panel is estimated from the design details of the panel. Combining the estimated structural behaviors and accommodable deformations of curtain wall together with damage survey data, relation between the design values and performance levels of steel structured buildings in earthquake occasions is discussed.

1 METHODS OF ANALYSIS

Eighteen steel structured buildings had been selected and three types of data for each building were collected. The data consist of (1) structural characteristics as weigh of floors and restoring force characteristics which were assumed at the structural design stage of each building, (2) design details of pre-cast concrete (PCa) curtain wall which covered the building, and (3) damage survey data of the PCa curtain walls after the earthquake. Structural behavior of a building in the 1995 Hyogo-ken nanbu earthquake is estimated by a non-linear dynamic analysis. Accommodable deformation of a PCa panel is estimated from the design details of the panel. Combining these results together with damage survey data, correspondence of structural response and PCa curtain wall damage is discussed.

1.1 *Selection of buildings*

Eighteen existing buildings in Hanshin area was selected to analyze the relation between structural response and pre-cast curtain wall damages in the earthquake. These buildings include 8-story medium height buildings to a 40-story tall building. These buildings were selected to satisfy the following conditions.

- Main structural members were steel and exterior wall was covered with PCa curtain walls.

- Building were designed in accordance with the New Seismic Design Standard effective from 1981.

- Damage data of PCa curtain walls were available.

- Structural design documents were available.

- Design details of PCa curtain walls were available.

Type of structure, number of story and design class of the buildings thus selected are summarized in Table 1. In Japan buildings taller than 45 (m) are required to perform non-linear dynamic analysis with bi-level inputs to confirm the serviceability in moderate earthquakes and the safety against severe earthquakes. For buildings in this category (bldg.A to J) dynamic characteristics are available in their structural design documents. Yet for the other buildings (bldg.K to R) information is limited to story mass and elastic stiffness. For these buildings a simplified story restoring force model is applied to estimate the story restoring force characteristics based on the limited information.

1.2 *Estimation of ground motion*

To analyze numerically how a building responded to the earthquake, acceleration record at the building site is imperative. Unfortunately there were few reliable earthquake records for the earthquake and no site specific records are available for the selected buildings. Many research have been reported to estimate the ground motion in the earthquake [1, 2, 3, 4]. Referring to the literature the maximum velocity of ground motion is estimated and is listed in Table 2. Three earthquake records taken at Kobe meteorological station (JMA), Kobe Port island (POI) and Kobe University (KBU) are used as inputs for dynamic analysis

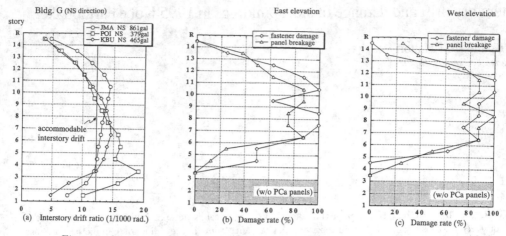

Figure 1: Structural response and PCa curtain wall damage correspondence(1)

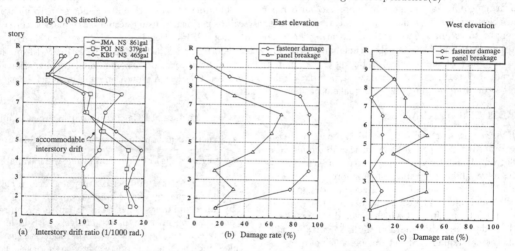

Figure 2: Structural response and PCa curtain wall damage correspondence(2)

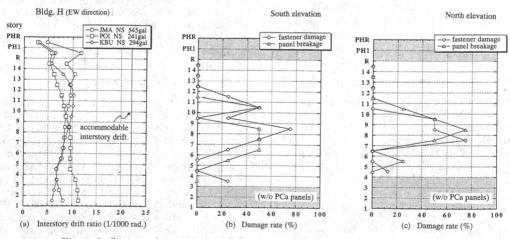

Figure 3: Structural response and PCa curtain wall damage correspondence(3)

Table 1: Selected 18 buildings

Bldg.	structure	story	dynamic analysis
A	S	40	yes
B	S*	21	yes
C	S	18	yes
D	S	18	yes
E	S*	16	yes
F	S	14	yes
G	S*	14	yes
H	S*	14	yes
I	S	13	yes
J	S	12	yes
K	S*	12	no
L	S*	12	no
M	S*	12	no
N	S*	10	no
O	S*	8	no
P	S*	8	no
Q	S	8	no
R	S*	8	no

S*: partially SRC

Table 2: Maximum velocity of input ground motion

place	direction	max. vel. (cm/s)
Hyogo ward	NS	80
	EW	46
Chuo ward	NS	95
(exclusive of Port island)	EW	55
Port island	NS	85
	EW	85
Higashinada ward	NS	95
(exclusive of Rokko island)	EW	55
Rokko island	NS	120
	EW	120
Nishinomiya city	NS	60
	EW	60

and the maximum velocity is modified to the value in Table 2 depending on the building site.

2 CURTAIN WALL DAMAGE

PCa curtain walls are designed and fabricated to accommodate interstory drift either by rocking-type or sway-type fasteners. An accommodable interstory drift ratio of a panel, or the maximum interstory drift ratio to which a PCa panel can follow is determined by surveying design details of the fastener. The accommodable interstory drift of the standard panel, or the most common panel of each building is listed in Table 3.

PCa curtain walls encounter several types of damage in earthquake occasions. From detailed damage survey data the damage are categorized in two types. The one is damage of fastener and the other is breakage of panel. In either type, damage is express in terms of damage rate or the number of damaged panels divided by the total number of panels in a story as in Figures 1 to 3.

3 STRUCTURAL RESPONSE AND DAMAGE

Displacement, velocity, acceleration, and story force of each building are calculated by the nonlinear dynamic analysis of the building to modified input ground motions. It was found that maximum interstory drift ratio, or the ratio of the maximum interstory drift to story height, is the most appropriate parameter to analyze the relation between structural response and damage of PCa curtain walls.

Typical examples of the results are shown in Figures. In each figure the maximum interstory drift ratio distributions to the 3 input ground motions are plotted in (a). Damage distribution of PCa curtain wall for two parallel sides (north/south or east/west sides) are given in (b) and (c), respectively.

In most cases distributions of the maximum interstory drift ratio among the results for 3 input ground motions resemble and which are analogous with the distribution of PCa curtain wall damage. Figures 1 and 2 show this type of result. The vertical line in the figure (a) indicates the accommodable interstory drift of the PCa panel. As in Figure 1, curtain wall damage becomes prominent if the interstory drift exceeds the panel's accommodable drift.

Yet in some cases structural response and damage patterns do not correspond well. Figure 3 illustrates this type of result. Careful consideration shows that this discrepancy is attributed to the following causes;

- irregularity of the building
- a balcony attached to a panel
- up/down vibration at the end of a cantilevered beam or at the middle of long-span beam
- phase lag between the above and the below beam displacements
- vertical discontinuity of curtain wall

Table 3 summarizes the maximum interstory drifts for 3 input ground motions and correspondence between structural response and the damage of PCa curtain walls of all 18 buildings.

4 CONCLUSIONS

For the selected 18 exiting buildings in Hanshin area pre-cast concrete curtain wall damage and the estimated structural response in 1995 Hyogo-ken nanbu earthquake was compared. In most cases damage was

Table 3: Correspondence of structural response and PCa curtain wall damage

Bldg.	accommodable interstory drift	input direction	JMA NS	story	POI NS	story	KBU NS	story	response/damage correspondence
A	1/97	NS	1/93	28	1/39	M3	1/85	28	good
		EW	1/99	30	1/38	3	1/84	3	
B	(EW elev.) 1/84	NS	1/51	11	1/30	8	1/40	12	good
	(NS elev.) 1/99	EW	1/53	10	1/39	6	1/37	11	
C	1/61	NS	1/34	11	1/31	12	1/48	6	good
		EW	1/34	11	1/36	9	1/45	6	
D	1/51	NS	1/103	16	1/98	9	1/89	9	good
		EW	1/66	16	1/60	10	1/60	12	
E	(EW elev.) 1/87	NS	1/34	11	1/36	11	1/29	11	good
	(NS elev.) 1/91	EW	1/40	16	1/39	8	1/38	8	
F	1/78	NS	1/70	14	1/72	4	1/78	4	poor
		EW	1/46	9	1/51	5	1/45	9	
G	1/81	NS	1/69	10	1/52	3	1/69	6	very good
		EW	1/106	6	1/91	5	1/100	7	
H	1/45	NS	1/89	PH1	1/88	2	1/100	12	poor
		EW	1/85	PH1	1/88	2	1/100	12	
I	1/69	NS	1/70	3	1/63	4	1/79	5	partially
		EW	1/71	3	1/57	5	1/70	5	
J	1/38	NS	1/51	9	1/50	3	1/70	5	good
		EW	1/103	7	1/97	5	1/93	5	
K	1/87	NS	1/51	4	1/37	4	1/57	6	good
		EW	1/89	8	1/74	2	1/114	4	
L	1/85	NS	1/40	1	1/36	2	1/44	2	partially
		EW	1/82	1	1/52	1	1/99	2	
M	1/85	NS	1/42	1	1/32	1	1/42	1	partially
		EW	1/64	1	1/42	1	1/76	1	
N	(EW elev.) 1/60	NS	1/46	2	1/35	3	1/37	3	poor
	(mullion) 1/32	EW	1/74	2	1/49	3	1/50	3	
O	1/83	NS	1/61	7	1/56	1	1/51	4	good
		EW	1/108	2	1/97	2	1/92	2	
P	1/57	NS	1/44	2	1/25	2	1/25	2	very good
		EW	1/73	3	1/55	3	1/56	2	
Q	1/117	NS	1/39	6	1/40	4	1/42	4	very good
		EW	1/54	6	1/110	3	1/118	5	
R	1/78	NS	1/48	1	1/35	1	1/33	1	partially
		EW	1/82	4	1/86	1	1/80	1	

prominent if the maximum interstory drift of a story exceeded the accommodable interstory drift of the PCa panel. Yet in some cases curtain wall damage occurred even for a small interstory drift. Irregularity of building, effect of a attached balcony, excessive up/down movement of beam was found to cause the discrepancy between response and damage.

To give high seismic performance to PCa curtain wall, it is recommended that the accommodable interstory drift of a panel is to be designed to exceed the target maximum interstory drift of the structure.

ACKNOWLEDGMENT

This study is partially supported by the Kozai-Kurabu. The support is gratefully acknowledged.

REFERENCES

[1] Kawase, H., Satoh T., Matsushima, S. & K. Irikura 1995. Ground motion estimation in the Higashinada ward in Kobe during the Hyogo-ken Nambu earthquake of 1995 based on aftershock records, J.Struct.Constr.Eng. 476:103–112

[2] Motosaka, M. 1996. Disaster caused by earthquakes, Proceeding of 1996 AIJ annual meeting (panel discussion of disaster div.):1–6

[3] Motosaka, M. & M.Nagano 1996. Analysis on amplification characteristics of ground motions in Kobe city taking account of deep irregular underground structure, — impression of heavily damaged belt zone during the 1995 Hyogo-ken Nanbu Earthquake, J.Struct.Constr.Eng. 488:39–48

[4] Survey report on the Great Hanshin Earthquake (Hyogo-ken Nanbu earthquake) Part.4 1995. Takenaka Co.

Structural Safety and Reliability, Shiraishi, Shinozuka & Wen (eds) © 1998 Balkema, Rotterdam, ISBN 90 5410 978 5

Estimation of cumulative damage of building using wavelet analysis of strong response records

Akira Sone, Shizuo Yamamoto & Arata Masuda
Kyoto Institute of Technology, Japan

ABSTRACT: In this study, in order to estimate the cumulative damage of building with hysteretic restoring force, the wavelet analysis is applied to the strong acceleration response. The discontinuity which should be produced at the point changing from the elastic limit to the plastic limit in restoring force is detected by wavelet analysis using three wavelets; Mexican hat, Daubechies' wavelet and Meyer's wavelet.

1 INTRODUCTION

The cumulative damage of building in a strong ground motion is the low cycle fatigue with large amplitude and small number of cycle, which occurs during time interval of 20 or 30 second. The authors have proposed a health monitoring system using wavelet transform of response as a method for the quatitative evaluation of the safety of a given structure (Sone et al. 1995). This system can detect the abnormal signals which occur in process of the low-cycle structural fatigue under noisy conditions.

In this paper, the estimation of cumulative damage of a single degree of freedom system with hysteretic restoring force using wavelet analysis of strong response is proposed. Firstly, it was assumed that the abnormal signals might be contained in the observed acceleration records, which should be produced at the point changing from the elastic region to the plastic region and might be detected by wavelet analysis. Through the numerical evaluation using the model, it is proven that this assumption is correct and it is confirmed that the wavelet analysis will be used to estimate the cumulative damage of buildings by earthquake, effectively.

2 DISCRETE WAVELET TRANSFORM

In the wavelet transform, the singularity of a function or signal is analyzed on the basis of compactly supported time and frequency domains. However, this is an oblique and over-complete system. Therefore, for the actual computation of wavelet transform, the dilation parameter and translation parameter should be made discrete. This is called the discrete wavelet transform. For some very special choices of analyzing wavelet ψ, the discretized wavelets $\{\psi_{j,k}\}$ constitute an orthonormal basis. By using the orthonormal bases, the wavelet expansion of a function $x(t)$ and the coefficients of wavelet expansion are defined as follows (Daubechies 1992, Yamada and Ohkitani 1991 and Sasaki and Maeda 1993).

$$x(t) = \sum_j \sum_k \alpha_{j,k} \psi_{j,k}(t) \tag{1}$$

$$\alpha_{j,k} = \int_{-\infty}^{\infty} x(t) \overline{\psi_{j,k}(t)} \, dt = \left\langle x(t), \psi_{j,k}(t) \right\rangle \tag{2}$$

where $\alpha_{j,k}$ is the coefficients of wavelet expansion and $\psi_{j,k}$ is the discrete basis generated by dilating and translating an analyzing wavelet ψ. The symbol of < , > signifies the inner product. Integers j and k denote the dilation parameter and the translation

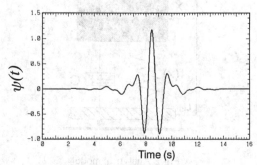

Fig. 1 Meyer's analyzing wavelet

parameter, respectively. Generally, by choosing the dilation parameter a to be $a_j = 2^j$, $\psi_{j,k}$ is expressed by

$$\psi_{j,k}(t) = 2^{j/2} \psi(2^j t - k) \qquad (3)$$

In this study, three types of analyzing wavelets; Mexican hat, Daubechies' wavelet and Meyer's wavelet, are introduced for numerical simulations. Figure 3 shows the Meyer's analyzing wavelet.

3 WAVELET ANALYSIS OF RESPONSE OF BILINEAR SYSTEM

As the analytical model for buildings, a single degree of freedom (SDOF) system with bilinear restoring force as shown in Fig. 2 is considered. m and c are mass and damping coefficient of system, respectively. $f(x)$ is the hysteretic restoring force. Input acceleration $\ddot{u}_g$ is assumed to be white noise.

In the numerical simulations, the parameters of SDOF system for the elastic deflection range are assumed to be the natural period T_0=1.0s, damping ratio ζ=0.01 and yield relative displacement response x_y=2.7cm. Also, five values are chosen for maximum input acceleration $\ddot{u}_{gmax}$ among the values of 250 cm/s^2 through 350 cm/s^2. In order to determine the characteristic of bilinear restoring force, the parameter of α =1-k_2/k_1 is introduced. k_1 and k_2 are the preyield stiffness and postyield stiffness, respectively. Four values are chosen for this parameter α among the values of 0.25 through 1.0. α=0 and α=1.0 correspond to the elastic system and perfectly elastoplastic system, respectively.

First, the input acceleration, absolute acceleration response and relative displacement response of system for case of α=0.5 and maximum input acceleration $\ddot{u}_{gmax}$ = 300cm/s^2 are shown in Fig.3(a), (b) and (c). The dashed line denotes the elastic limit of relative displacement response. When the relative displacement response of system is larger than x_y

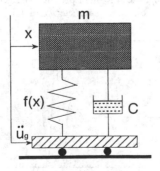

Fig.2 Analytical model

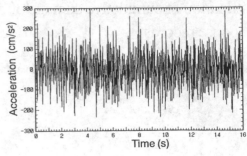

(a) Input acceleration

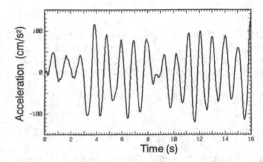

(b) Absolute acceleration response

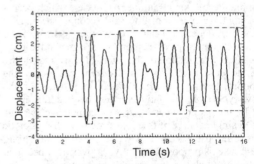

(c) Relative displacement response
Fig.3 Input acceleration and responses
($\ddot{u}_{gmax}$ =300cm/s^2 and α=0.5)

=2.7cm, the plastic deformation occurs. From this figure, it is shown that small plastic deformations occur at time of about t = 4s and 6.5s, while large plastic deformations occur at time of about t = 11.5s and 16s. This example shows the analytical results of relative displacement response of a SDOF system. Generally, the relative displacement response is not recorded and the absolute acceleration response is recorded. On the other hand, we can not identify the occurrence time of plastic deformation by inspecting only this acceleration response. However, the singularities in the acceleration response mayoccur as shown in the displacement response.

Next, applying the wavelet transform to this

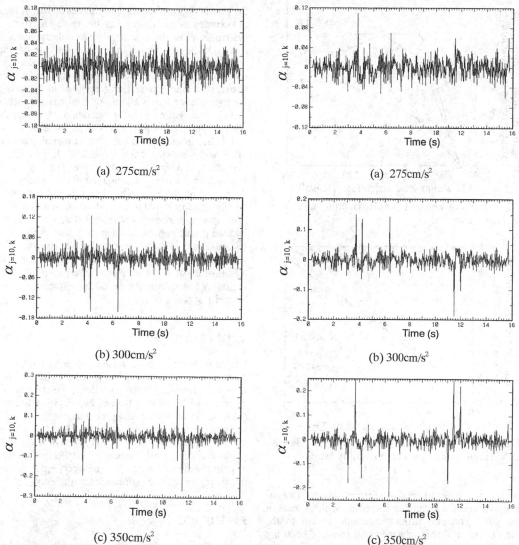

(a) 275cm/s^2 (a) 275cm/s^2

(b) 300cm/s^2 (b) 300cm/s^2

(c) 350cm/s^2 (c) 350cm/s^2

Fig.4 Coefficient of wavelet expansion of acceleration (Daubechies' wavelet with N=8 and α=0.5)

Fig.5 Coefficient of wavelet expansion of acceleration (Meyer's wavelet and α=0.5)

absolute response, its singularities which can not be observed by visual inspection are detected and number entering into the plastic region and cumulative plastic deformation is estimated. To apply wavelet transform for this purpose means that we choose the most appropriate filter based on the multi-resolution analysis. However, there are many choise of wavelet. Therefore, we intend to choose the most appropriate wavelet among various types of wavelets for our analysis. In this study, three types of wavelets; Mexican hat, Daubechies' wavelet and Meyer's wavelet, are used for the wavelet transform and their results are investigated.

Using Daubechies' wavele and Meyer's wavelet, the coefficients of wavelet expansion of acceleration response are shown in Figs. 4 and 5, respectively. These coefficients $\alpha_{j=10,k}$ are obtained from the wavelet with the highest scale for detecting the singularities in acceleration response. Because the singularities have high frequency component. These example are for cases of α=0.5, and maximum input acceleration $\ddot{u}_{gmax}$ =275cm/s^2, 300cm/s^2 and 350cm/s^2. From these figures, it is clear that the pulsive peaks are observed in coefficients of wavelet expansion. The

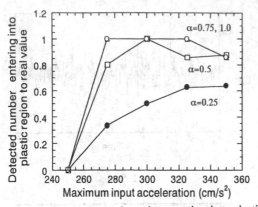

Fig. 6 Ratio of detected number entering into plastic region to real value

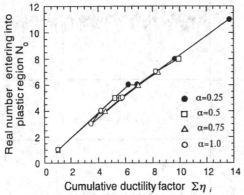

Fig. 7 Relation between real number entering into plastic region and cumulative ductility factor

occurrence time of peaks corresponds to that of singularities in acceleration response, which occurs at the point changing from the elastic region to the plastic region; that is change in stiffness of restoring force. In other words, the occurrence time of peaks in coefficients of wavelet expansion shows the point passing the corner of bilinear restoring force. It is natural from these figures that the number of peaks, namely number entering into plastic region, increases as the maximum input acceleration becomes large. The results obtained by three types of analyzing wavelets show a similar tendency.

Using Meyer's wavelets which can clearly detect the sigularities in acceleration response, the relationship between detected number entering into the plastic region and maximum input acceleration is obtained and discussed. The ratio of detected number entering into the plastic region by wavelet analysis to its real value is shown in Fig. 6. In this figure, x-axis denotes the maximum input acceleration. It is clear from this figure that the detected number entering into

the plastic region almost approximates its real value as α becomes large, namely as the restoring force of system is close to a perfectly elastoplastic restoring force. On the other hand, the error in the case of small input acceleration becomes large. These results agree with our physical intuition. Applying the wavelet transform to the acceleration response, in the case of the hyteretic system with strong nonlinearity such as $\alpha > 0.5$ and large input acceleration, the number entering into the plastic region can be estimated.

Finally, in order to predict the cumulative damage of system, the estimation of plastic deformation is important. Therefore, in this study, the relationship between detected number entering into the plastic region by wavelet analysis and cumulative ductility factor is obtained and discussed. Figure 7 shows the relationship between real number entering into the plastic region obtained from the displacement response and cumulative ductility factor for four values of α. It is clear from this figure that the relationship of real number entering into plastic region N_0 and cumulative ductility factor almost linear irrespective of α.

4 CONCLUSIONS

In this study, the fundamental investigation to estimate cumulative damage of building with hysteretic restoring force by using vavelet analysis is carried out. The results obtained herein are as follows.
(1) In the case of estimating the number entering into plastic region by wavelet analysis, Meyer's wavelets are most reasonable among three types of wavelets.
(2) As the change of hysteretic restoring force of system becomes large, the number entering into plastic region can be estimated remarkablely.

REFERENCES

Daubechies, I. 1992. *Ten lectures on wavelets.* CBMS-NSF series in applied mathematics. SIAM publ.
Daubechies, I. 1988. Orthonormal bases of compactly supported wavelets. *Comm. on pure and applied mathematics.* 41-7: 909-996.
Sasaki, F. and Maeda, T. 1993. Study of fundamental characteristics of the wavelet transform for data analysis. (in Japanese). *J. Struc.Constr. Engn.* AIJ. 453: 197-206.
Sone, A. et al. 1995. Health monitoring system of structures based on orthonormal wavelet transform. *Proc. the 1995 joint ASME/JSME PVP conf.* PVP.Vol. 312: 161-167.
Yamada, M. and Ohkitani, K. 1991. Orthonormal wavelet analysis of turbulence. *Fluid dynamics research.* 8: 101-115.

Structural Safety and Reliability, Shiraishi, Shinozuka & Wen (eds) © 1998 Balkema, Rotterdam, ISBN 90 5410 978 5

Bayesian method for updating building seismic fragilities

Ajay Singhal & Anne S. Kiremidjian
The John A. Blume Earthquake Engineering Center, Department of Civil Engineering, Stanford University, Calif., USA

ABSTRACT: As building damage data from past earthquakes become increasingly available, these data need to be combined with the existing fragility curves to arrive at the updated fragility curves. The Bayesian method provides a technique for updating these curves. Data on reinforced concrete frame buildings from the January 17, 1994 Northridge, California earthquake are used to illustrate the Bayesian method presented in this paper.

1 INTRODUCTION

Earthquake ground motion versus structural damage relationships are often used to characterize regional damage distribution. These relationships are frequently expressed as fragility curves or damage probability matrices (DPMs) which describe the conditional probability of structures sustaining different degrees of damage at specified levels of ground motion. An analytical method for developing building fragility curves and DPMs was presented by Singhal and Kiremidjian (1996). The major components of their methodology consist of the characterization of (1) the structure when subjected to extreme dynamic loads; (2) the potential ground motions; and (3) the structural response that includes the variability in the ground motion as well as the structural parameters.

This paper presents a method for combining the analytical fragility curves with observed building damage data from earthquakes using Bayesian statistical analysis. Bayes' theorem provides an approach for updating subjective knowledge with experimental results or observations. If the experimental outcome is a set of independent observed values $\{x_1, x_2, \ldots, x_n\}$ from a population X with underlying probability density function $f_{X|\Theta}(x|\theta)$, the parameters of the distribution, represented by the vector Θ, are revised in light of the experimental results by the following expression:

$$f_{\Theta}''(\Theta) = \frac{\left[\prod_{i=1}^{n} f_X(x_i \mid \Theta)\right] f_{\Theta}'(\Theta)}{\int_{\Theta} \left[\prod_{i=1}^{n} f_X(x_i \mid \Theta)\right] f_{\Theta}'(\Theta)\, d\Theta} \quad (1)$$

where:

$f_{\Theta}'(\theta)$ = prior density function of the parameters Θ,

$f_{\Theta}''(\theta)$ = posterior density function of Θ, and

$f_{X|\Theta}(x|\theta)$ = probability distribution function of the basic random variable X.

2 METHOD FOR BAYESIAN UPDATING

Damage to a structure is a function of structural capacity and environmental demands placed on the structure. The relationship between structural capacity and demand is expressed as:

$$g(\tilde{X}) = L(\tilde{X}_1) - R(\tilde{X}_2) \quad (2)$$

where:

$L(\tilde{X}_1)$ = demand as a function of the environmental variables, $\tilde{X}_1$, and

$R(\tilde{X}_2)$ = structural resistance as a function of the capacity variables, $\tilde{X}_2$.

The probability of damage to a structure exceeding certain damage thresholds at specified levels of ground motion can be expressed as follows:

$$P_{ik} = P\left[D \geq d_i | Y = y_k\right] = P\left[g(\tilde{X}) \geq d_i | Y = y_k\right] \quad (3)$$

where:

P_{ik} = probability of reaching or exceeding damage state d_i given the ground motion is y_k,

D = damage random variable defined on the damage state vector $\mathbf{D} = \{d_0, d_1, ..., d_n\}$, and

Y = ground motion random variable.

The conditional probabilities in Equation 3 describe the fragility curve for damage state d_i. The five discrete damage states used by Singhal and Kiremidjian (1996) are: *none*, *minor*, *moderate*, *severe*, and *collapse*.

The relationship between structural capacity and seismic demands is often expressed by means of damage indices. Thus, the damage function $g(\tilde{X})$ can be represented in terms of a damage index $I(\tilde{X})$, where $\tilde{X}$ is a set of random variables. For reinforced concrete structures, the Park and Ang (1985) model has been used widely in recent years. Singhal and Kiremidjian (1996) showed that the randomness in the Park and Ang damage index $I(\tilde{X})$ at a specified ground motion level can be represented by the lognormal probability distribution.

2.1 *Posterior distribution of the mean damage index*

The parameters of the prior distribution of $I(\tilde{X})$ are obtained from the analysis of the model structural frame (Singhal and Kiremidjian, 1996) subjected to an ensemble of simulated earthquake time histories. These parameters are used as the prior estimates of the lognormal distribution of the damage index and, in general, will be different at different ground motion values. Thus, the Bayesian updating needs to be repeated at each ground motion level. Data from past earthquakes are used to modify the parameters of the lognormally distributed damage index.

The mean damage index is considered to be a random variable since it is based on a limited number of simulations and represents the behavior of a model RC frame, rather than the ensemble of frames that belong to that structural class. The standard deviation of the damage index is assumed to be constant for simplicity as it was found that the coefficient of variation converges to a constant value.

For simplicity, conjugate distributions are used in the development of the posterior parameter densities. If the parent distribution is normal, the conjugate distribution of the mean, μ, will be also normal (Raiffa and Schlaifer, 1961). Multiplying the prior distribution by the likelihood function and normalizing the product, the posterior distribution of μ also is a normal density function given by:

$$f''_{M|X}(\mu|x) = \frac{1}{\sqrt{2\pi\sigma''^2}} e^{-\left[\frac{(\mu-m'')^2}{2\sigma''^2}\right]} \quad (4)$$

where the posterior mean and variance are expressed by the following two equations, respectively,

$$m'' = \frac{\left(1/\sigma'^2\right)m' + \left(n/\sigma^2\right)m}{\left(1/\sigma'^2\right) + \left(n/\sigma^2\right)} \quad (5)$$

and

$$\frac{1}{\sigma''^2} = \frac{1}{\sigma'^2} + \frac{n}{\sigma^2} \quad (6)$$

where:

$\dfrac{\sigma^2}{n}$ = variance of the sample mean, and

n = number of observations in the sample.

The randomness in the Park and Ang (1985) damage index was obtained through simulation of the model structural frame. The uncertainty in the index that arises from structural response parameters is determined from the results of Park et al. (1984). They conclude that the total variability associated with the mean of their damage index has a coefficient of variation equal to 0.6, whereas the inherent randomness in their damage index has a coefficient of variation of 0.5. Thus, the estimated coefficient of variation due to uncertainty in the median damage index is equal to $\sqrt{0.6^2 - 0.5^2} = 0.33$. This value is assumed to remain constant over all spectral acceleration values.

2.2 Damage data for Bayesian analysis

The January 17, 1994 Northridge, California earthquake is currently the best documented disaster in the history of the United States (OES, 1995). The *Governor's Office of Emergency Services for the State of California* (OES, 1995) provided the inventory of RC frame buildings in the city of Los Angeles which included the estimated dollar loss for the damaged buildings. Bayesian analysis is presented only for low rise frames because the number of mid rise and high rise RC frame buildings is very small. Low rise frames constructed after 1976 are treated in this study as ductile moment resisting frames and are used to update the fragility curves presented by Singhal and Kiremidjian (1996).

2.3 Posterior fragility curves

In order to evaluate the posterior distribution of the Park-Ang damage index at a specified level of ground motion, one must estimate the level of seismic excitation as well as the corresponding Park-Ang damage index of all the RC frame buildings in the OES database. The level of seismic excitation is measured in terms of spectral acceleration in the relevant period band (Singhal and Kiremidjian, 1996). The ground motion levels at the building sites are obtained by overlaying the buildings on the spectral acceleration contours, developed by Somerville et al. (1995), within a geographic information system. Figures 1 and 2 respectively present all the low rise RC frames, and those low rise RC frames for which damage was observed. These figures also present the average spectral acceleration contours.

The extent of damage is inferred from the damage factor data for the buildings provided in the OES database, where the damage factor is defined as the ratio between estimated loss and replacement value. The Park-Ang (1985) damage index for the damaged buildings is determined from their damage factors. De Leon and Ang (1993) arrived at a linear relationship between the damage factor and the Park-Ang global damage index for buildings damaged during the Mexico City earthquake. In this study, a piecewise linear relationship is assumed between the damage factor and the Park-Ang damage index, the relationship being linear for each damage state.

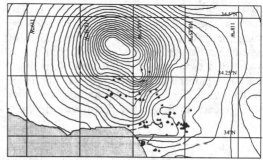

Figure 1: 184 low rise, ductile RC frame buildings and the average spectral acceleration contours from the Northridge earthquake at T = 0.3 s.

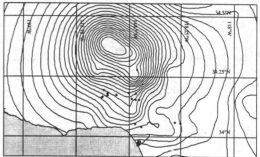

Figure 2: Seventeen low rise, ductile RC frame buildings for which damage was observed and the average spectral acceleration contours at T = 0.3 s.

The posterior parameters are used to obtain the probabilities of the different damage states. Figure 3 presents the probabilities of the damage states at the six levels of ground motion for which observed damage data were available, along with the prior probabilities of the damage states at other levels of ground motion obtained from the Monte Carlo simulation. The smooth fragility curves also shown on this figure are the analytical fragility curves as presented by Singhal and Kiremidjian (1996).

The analytical fragility curves in Figure 3 provide the best estimates of the posterior fragility curves based on the posterior probabilities of damage at the six levels of ground motion. Although the differences between the fragility curves in Figure 3 and the updated probabilities may seem significant at some levels of ground motion, the curves still represent the median values of the updated probabilities very well. For cases where large differences may be observed between the analytical fragility curves and the posterior probabilities, posterior fragility curves should be obtained by fitting curves through the posterior probabilities of the different damage states. For the limited sample of observed damage used in this study, it is found that the probabilities based on the posterior distributions of the damage index are consistent with those presented by Singhal and Kiremidjian (1996).

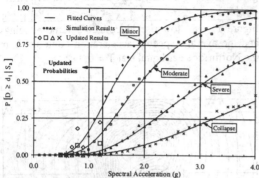

Figure 3: Updated fragility curves.

3 SUMMARY AND CONCLUSIONS

This paper presents a systematic approach for incorporating damage data with analytical earthquake ground motion vs. damage relationships. Such relationships cannot be obtained from existing data because such data are very limited. However, damage data can be effectively used to verify and update analytical motion-damage relationships. The Bayesian technique provides a formal approach for updating these relationships on the basis of observed damage. This technique will enable periodic modification of fragilities as damage data become available from future earthquake events.

The Bayesian technique was illustrated for low rise RC frames in the city of Los Angeles subjected to ground shaking during the January 17, 1994 Northridge, California earthquake. The limited data on low rise frames were combined with the analytical fragility curves and the updated curves were found to be consistent with the analytical fragility curves presented by Singhal and Kiremidjian (1996). In principle, a much larger sample is needed in order to develop more robust fragility curves.

ACKNOWLEDGMENTS

The authors gratefully acknowledge the support provided by NCEER under Contract 92-4101. The authors also express their gratitude to Governor's Office of Emergency Services of the State of California for providing the data.

REFERENCES

De Leon, D., and Ang, A.H-S. (1993), "A damage model for reinforced concrete buildings: Further study with the 1985 Mexico City earthquake", *Proceedings 6th International Conference on Structural Safety and Reliability*, Innsbruck, Austria, Vol. 3, pp. 2081-2087.

OES, (1995), "The Northridge earthquake of January 17, 1994: Report of data collection and analysis, Part A: Damage and inventory data", Prepared by EQE International, Inc., and the Geographic Information Systems Group of the Governor's Office of Emergency Services for the Governor's Office of Emergency Services of the State of California.

Park, Y-J., Ang, A.H-S., and Wen, Y.K., (1984), "Seismic damage analysis and damage-limiting design of RC buildings", *Structural Research Series, Report No. UILU-ENG-84-2007*, University of Illinois at Urbana-Champaign, Urbana, Illinois, Oct.

Park, Y-J. and Ang, A.H-S. (1985). "Mechanistic seismic damage model for reinforced concrete", *Journal of Structural Engineering*, ASCE, Vol. 111, No. ST4, pp. 722-739.

Raiffa, H., and Schlaifer, R., (1961), "Applied statistical decision theory", Division of Research, Graduate School of Business and Administration, Harvard University.

Singhal, A., and Kiremidjian, A.S., (1996), "A method for probabilistic evaluation of seismic structural damage", *Journal of Structural Engineering*, ASCE, Vol. 122, No. 12, pp. 1459-1467.

Somerville, P.G., Graves, R.W., and Saikia, C.K., (1995), "Characterization of ground motions at the sites of subject buildings", Report on Task 4 of the SAC Joint Venture Program for the Reduction of Earthquake Hazards in Steel Moment Frame Buildings.

Structural Safety and Reliability, Shiraishi, Shinozuka & Wen (eds) © 1998 Balkema, Rotterdam, ISBN 90 5410 978 5

Modeling uncertainty on seismic fragility of structures

Howard H.M. Hwang & Jun-Rong Huo
Center for Earthquake Research and Information, The University of Memphis, Tenn., USA

ABSTRACT: To consider modeling uncertainties in seismic fragility analysis of structures, two models for structures and two models for ground motion are used to generate four sets of seismic fragility curves. By comparing these fragility curves, modeling uncertainties are quantified. It is concluded that the modeling uncertainty needs to be included in the seismic loss assessment studies.

1 INTRODUCTION

In the event of an earthquake, a building may sustain no damage at a low level of ground shaking, while it may collapse at an extremely high level of ground shaking. The likelihood of structural damage caused by various levels of ground shaking is usually expressed as a set of fragility curves or a damage probability matrix. In general, fragility data can be established using earthquake experience data or analytical approaches. Earthquake-induced data in most earthquake-prone regions are too scarce to provide sufficient statistical information; thus, fragility data generated from analytical approaches and calibrated with available earthquake damage data may be an appropriate alternative.

Using an analytical method to generate fragility data, a structure needs to be represented by an appropriate model and the hysteretic relationship between restoring force and interstory displacement also needs to be described. Furthermore, synthetic earthquake ground motions exciting the structure are generated from a seismological model. In most studies, however, modeling uncertainties in these aspects are usually not included in the seismic fragility analysis. In this paper, we use two models for structures and two models for ground motion to include modeling uncertainties in the seismic fragility analysis of structures.

2 PROPOSED METHODOLOGY

In this study, the seismic fragility analysis of structures is performed using the approach proposed by Hwang and Huo (1994a) with the modification to include modeling uncertainties. First, two sets of synthetic acceleration time histories at the ground surface corresponding to various levels of ground shaking are generated with two seismologically based models. Second, the structures are modeled as a frame-wall model and a stick model. For each model, uncertainties in structural parameters are quantified. Third, inelastic seismic response analyses are performed for each combination of structural model and ground motion model at various levels of ground shaking. Regression analyses are then performed to determine the relationships between the structural response and ground shaking parameters. Fourth, several damage states of structures are established based on earthquake experience data and experimental data. Finally, seismic reliability analyses are performed to determine the damage probabilities of buildings subject to various levels of ground shaking and the results are displayed as fragility curves. The proposed approach is demonstrated through the fragility analysis of a typical Memphis building as described in the following sections.

3 DESCRIPTION OF BUILDING

The building selected for this study is a typical low-rise RC shear wall building in Memphis. The shear walls around two stairs provide the only seismic resistance for the building. The shear walls are 12 inches thick throughout the height of the building, which has a story height of 12 ft. The horizontal and vertical reinforcements in shear walls are No. 4 steel bars in two layers with a spacing of 12 and 18 inches, respectively. The walls are made of Grade 60 reinforcement and concrete with a specified compressive strength of 3000 psi.

4 STRUCTURAL MODELING

To incorporate uncertainty in modeling of structure, the building is modeled as a frame-wall model described in the IDARC program (referred to as IDARC Model) and also modeled as a stick model (Hwang et al., 1988).

4.1 IDARC Model

In the IDARC program (Kunnath et al., 1992), inelastic behavior of RC members (beam, column, and shear wall) is simulated using a trilinear skeleton curve and four model parameters (α, β_D, β_E, and γ). The trilinear skeleton curve is governed by the cracking point, yielding point, and post-yielding stiffness ratio α_S. These quantities are determined by the IDARC program from member properties such as dimension and reinforcement. The post-yielding stiffness ratio α_S is restricted in the range of 0.002-0.05. In the hysteretic model for RC shear walls, both flexural and shear behavior are considered. The parameter α is used for modeling stiffness degrading, β_D for ductility-controlled strength deterioration, β_E for hysteretic energy-controlled strength deterioration, and γ for pinching effect. The values of these structural model parameters are controlled by the amount of reinforcement and material properties.

4.2 Stick Model

In the stick model, inelastic behavior of buildings is simulated by a modified Takeda model with a bilinear skeleton curve (Hwang et al., 1988). The skeleton curve is governed by the yielding point (Q_Y, U_Y) and post-yielding stiffness ratio α_S. The hysteretic rules include the stiffness degrading which is described by a peak-oriented model, and the pinching effect represented by a pinching factor α_p. The yielding point is determined based on the properties of the RC members.

5 GENERATION OF GROUND MOTION

The strong ground motion data in the Memphis area are scarce, and thus the ground acceleration time histories are generated using seismologically based models. To incorporate uncertainty in synthesizing ground motions, two sets of synthetic ground motions are used. The first set, denoted as "HH", is generated by Hwang and Huo (1994b), while the second, denoted as "HB", is generated by Horton et al. (1996).

5.1 Approach by Hwang and Huo

In the approach by Hwang and Huo (1994b), a deep profile overlaying the bedrock is divided into rock layers and soil layers. For a given magnitude, distance, the Fourier acceleration amplitude spectrum at the base of the soil layers is established using the approach proposed by Boore (1983). From the Fourier spectrum, the corresponding power density function can be derived and used to generate the accelerograms at the base of the soil layers. Then, a nonlinear site response analysis is performed to generate the accelerograms at the ground surface.

5.2 Approach by Horton and Others

Given a moment magnitude and epicentral distance, Horton et al. (1996) generate rock accelerograms by convolving the scattering function with the primary arrivals propagating from an earthquake represented by an ω^{-2} model. The scattering functions account for all possible phases including super-critically reflected S-waves and surface waves. Then, rock motions are modified to account for the nonlinear response of uppermost soils at the study site.

6 PROBABILISTIC SEISMIC RESPONSE

In the simulation of ground motion, uncertainties in many seismic parameters and site parameters are considered. These seismic parameters include stress parameter, high-cut frequency, radiation coefficient, focal depth, phase angle, quality factor, and strong motion duration. The site parameters include static and dynamic soil properties. Furthermore, uncertainties in concrete strength f_c', strain ε_o corresponding to f_c', steel yield stress f_y, and structural viscal damping are considered in the constructions of structural models. Then, a set of earthquake-structure samples is established from the combination of structural models and accelerograms using the Latin Hypercube sampling technique (Iman and Conover, 1980). The detail of quantifying the uncertainties in ground motions and structural models can be found in Hwang and Huo (1994a).

For each sample of earthquake-structure system, an inelastic seismic response analysis is performed to determine the structural response, such as the interstory drift ratio. The seismic response analysis is carried out for a combination of magnitudes and distances. From a regression analysis of the structural responses, the relation of the maximum story drift ratio δ and the spectral acceleration (SA) corresponding to the structural fundamental period can be determined as follows:

$$Ln(\overline{\delta}) = a + b \cdot Ln(SA) \qquad (1)$$

$$\sigma_{Ln(\delta)} = c + d \cdot SA \qquad (2)$$

The regression coefficients for each combination of structural model and ground motion model are listed in Table 1.

Table 1. Regression Coefficients

Structural Model	Ground Motion	Coefficient			
		a	b	c	d
IDARC	HH	0.25	1.27	0.47	0.09
IDARC	HB	1.28	2.00	0.51	0.23
STICK	HH	0.26	1.43	0.30	0.21
STICK	HB	0.66	1.65	0.35	0.15

7 DAMAGE STATES

In this study, four damage states are considered: no damage, insignificant damage, moderate damage, and heavy damage. On the basis of the experimental results (Aktan and Bertero, 1985; Aoyama, 1981; Vallenas et al., 1979), the ranges of the story drift ratio for these damage states are determined and summarized in Table 2.

Table 2. Damage States

	Damage State	Max. Interstory Drift Ratio δ (%)
N	None	< 0.2
I	Insignificant	0.2 - 0.5
M	Moderate	0.5 - 1.0
H	Heavy	>1.0

8 FRAGILITY ANALYSIS

The structural fragility with respect to a damage state is defined as the probability that the structural response exceeds the structural capacity defined by the damage state. The probability PF_{ij} that the damage exceeds the ith damage state given the jth level of ground shaking SA_j can be determined as

$$PF_{ij} = Prob(\delta \geq \delta_i \mid SA = SA_j) \ (i=1,...,4) \qquad (3)$$

where δ is the maximum story drift ratio resulting from SA_j, δ_i is the low bound of the story drift ratio for the ith damage state. The fragility curve with respect to the ith damage state can then be constructed using the PF_{ij} values at various levels of ground shaking. Figure 1 shows the fragility curves from different ground motions with the same structural model, while Figure 2 shows the fragility curves from the different structural models with the same ground motions.

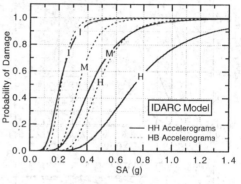

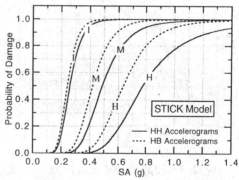

Fig. 1. Fragility Curves from Different Ground Motions

9 DISCUSSION AND CONCLUSIONS

Given the same structural model (Figure 1), the fragility curves using the HB accelerograms are significantly different from those generated using the HH accelerograms. The difference is particularly large at the high levels of ground shaking, especially using the IDARC model. At the high level of ground shaking, inelastic structural behavior is significant, and the difference in ground motion characteristics will have tremendous effects on the structural response.

The difference in fragility curves from different structural models (Figure 2) is smaller than that from different ground motion models (Figure 1). However, in some cases, the difference from different structural models is still large and cannot be ignored. For example, in Figure 2, the fragility curves from the IDARC model and HB accelerograms are much higher than those from the stick model and HB accelerograms.

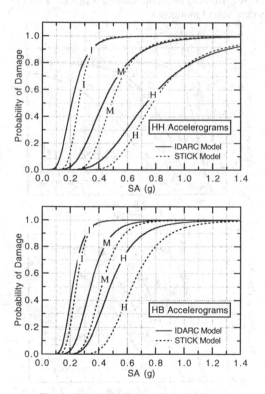

Fig. 2. Fragility Curves from Different Structural Models

In conclusion, this paper presents an investigation on the effect of modeling uncertainties in the seismic fragility analysis of structures. The results show that the difference in fragility curves may come not only from different ground motion models but also from different structural models. It is concluded that the modeling uncertainty should be included in the seismic loss assessment studies.

ACKNOWLEDGMENTS

This paper is based on research supported by the National Center for Earthquake Engineering Research under Project No. NCEER 954102B (NSF Grant No. BCS-9025010).

REFERENCES

Aktan, A.M. & V.V. Bertero, 1985. RC Structural Walls: Seismic Design for Shear, *Journal of Structural Engineering*, ASCE, **111**(8), 1775-1791.

Aoyama, H., 1981. A Method for the Evaluation of the Seismic Capacity of Existing Reinforced Concrete Buildings in Japan, *Bulletin of the New Zealand National Society of for Earthquake Engineering*, **14**(3), 105-129.

Horton, S.P., N. Barstow & K. Jacob, 1996. Simulation of Strong Ground Motion in Memphis, Tennessee, *Proceedings of 11th World Conference on Earthquake Engineering*, June 23-28, 1996, Acapulco, Mexico, Paper No. 1302.

Hwang, H. & J.-R. Huo, 1994a. Generation of Hazard-Consistent Fragility Curves, *Soil Dynamics and Earthquake Engineering*, **13**(5), 345-354.

Hwang, H. & J.-R. Huo, 1994b. Generation of Hazard-Consistent Ground Motions. *Soil Dynamics and Earthquake Engineering*, **13**(6), 377-386.

Hwang, H., J.-W, Jaw & H.-J. Shau, 1988. Seismic Performance Assessment of Code-Designed Structures, Technical Report NCEER-88-0007, National Center for Earthquake Engineering Research, State University of New York at Buffalo, Buffalo, New York.

Iman, R.L. & W.J. Conover, 1980. Small Sample Sensitivity Analysis Techniques for Computer Models, With an Application to Risk Assessment, *Communications in Statistics*, **A9**(17), 1749-1842.

Kunnath, S.K., A.M. Reinhorn & R.F. Lobo, 1992. IDARC Version 3.0: A Program for the Inelastic Damage Analysis of Reinforced Concrete Frame-Wall Structures, Technical Report NCEER-92-0022, National Center for Earthquake Engineering Research, State University of New York at Buffalo, Buffalo, New York.

Vallenas, J.M., V.V. Bertero & E.P. Popov, 1979. Hysteretic Behavior of Reinforced Concrete Structural Walls, Report No. UCB/EERC-79/20, University of California, Berkeley, California.

Structural Safety and Reliability, Shiraishi, Shinozuka & Wen (eds) © 1998 Balkema, Rotterdam, ISBN 90 5410 978 5

A study on efficiency of earthquake disaster response team in a private company

Hiroyasu Ohtsu
School of Civil Engineering, Kyoto University, Japan

Katsumi Kamemura
Taisei Corporation, Tokyo, Japan

Mamoru Mizutani & Tetsushi Uzawa
Shinozuka Research Institute, Tokyo, Japan

ABSTRACT: This paper deals with efficiency of the current response team in a private company as an application of SRM (Seismic Risk Management) method. In this paper, among various requirements that one must consider to fulfill the task under an emergent circumstance, the following matters, which are the reliability of communication tools and the feasibility of decision-making system, are focused on as key issues to recover the function of a private company. The reliability of communication tools is evaluated based on an event tree analysis. The feasibility of decision-making system is evaluated by the conditional expected numbers of executive directors who will be able to take part in a response team. As a conclusion, the results make it obvious that re-construction of current disaster response system in a private company is necessary to strengthen its reliability and its feasibility.

1. INTRODUCTION

Based on our Japanese bitter experience through the 1995 Hyougoken-Nanbu Earthquake, investigation on how soon a private company recovers its own function just after earthquake has become one of the urgent issues from a viewpoint of crisis management. In general, each private company has the pre-determined plan that an earthquake disaster response team is established to cope with damage suffered by disaster. However, the findings that one obtained in the 1995 Hyougoken-Nanbu Earthquake showed that it is uncertain whether a response team operates as efficiently as expected in prescribed scenario.

From these viewpoints, this paper deals with efficiency of the current response team in a private company as an application of SRM (Seismic Risk Management) method proposed by Mizutani (1997). It is predictable that one must consider various requirements to fulfill the task under an emergent circumstance. In this paper, the following matters, which are the reliability of communication tools and the feasibility of decision-making system, are focused on as key issues to recover the function of a private company. As for the reliability of communication tools, a model associated with a telecommunication network formed among headquarters and several branch offices are generated. On the other hand, as for decision-making system, it is assumed that executive directors only make important decision under an emergent circumstance.

In detail, the probability that how many branches will be able to communicate with headquarters is estimated based on predicted damage to each facility due to earthquake. Also, the feasibility of decision-making system is estimated by calculating the probability that how many executive directors of a private company will be able to take part in a current response team after earthquake based on the distance from their housings and their nearest office among telecommunication network.

Finally, as a conclusion, the results make it obvious that re-construction of current disaster response system in a private company is necessary to strengthen its reliability and its feasibility.

2. THE RELIABILITY OF COMMUNICATION TOOLS

As an example to investigate the reliability of communication tools in a private company, we focus on a telecommunication network model, which is generated among headquarters, computer center and six branch offices. The probability how many branches will be able to communicate with headquarters is estimated based on predicted damage to each facility due to earthquake.

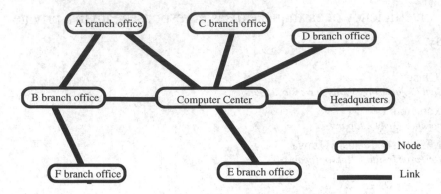

Fig.1   Tele-communication network model

2.1 Network model

Fig.1 shows the telecommunication network model that we focus on in this study. As shown in Fig.1, the network consists of headquarters, computer center and six branch offices. Here, among six branch offices, it is assumed that A-branch office is apart from the area where the damages due to the given earthquake may occur.

Also, we call each office such as headquarters and branch offices a node, and call the path connecting between two nodes a link. Therefore, the telecommunication network model is called node-link model.

According to pre-determined scenario to cope with the earthquake damage under an emergent circumstance, it is assumed that an earthquake disaster response team to cope with damage suffered by disaster is usually established in headquarters office, and that branch offices inform their own damage suffered by earthquake to headquarters, and accept the indication decided by an earthquake disaster response team through the tele-communication network.

2.2 Damage scenarios of each node due to earthquake

To investigate whether the tele-communication network really functions just after the occurrence of earthquake, it is essentially necessary to evaluate the reliability of nodes and links generating network shown in Fig.1. Here, generally speaking, it is assumed that the durability against earthquake of links generated by tele-communication companies is much superior to that of nodes. Therefore, in this study, we focus on the reliability of nodes alone.

In general, when one considers the damage scenarios due to the occurrence of earthquake, the modeling by means of an event tree (ET), which is adopted in Seismic Risk Management (SRM), is very effective. Here, to describe the scenarios associated with how nodes are damaged, we consider the following damage causes:

    (a) the damage due to large-scale liquefaction
    (b) the structural damage due to ground motion
    (c) the loss of tele-communication function

Fig.2 shows the ET that associates the above damage causes with the spread of damages at each node due to earthquake. Here, we describe below the basic concept to generate the ET shown in Fig.2.

(1) The scenarios associated with damage due to large-scale liquefaction

The scenarios associated with the damage due to large-scale liquefaction are assumed as follows:

1) Once large-scale liquefaction occurs, a node suffers from serious damages by large displacements such as settlement and lateral spreading of liquefied soil. Consequently, it is assumed that a node loses all functions as an office building.

2) Otherwise, a node is assumed to be an active state as an office building. Also, in this state, the possibility that a node becomes inactive as tele-communication facility is dependent on the probabilities of the two damage causes, which are following to liquefaction in Fig.2.

(2) The scenarios associated with structural damage due to ground motion

The scenarios associated with structural damage due to ground motion are assumed as follows:

1) When no structural damage due to ground motion occurs, a node is assumed to be an active state as an office building. In this state, the possibility that a node becomes inactive as tele-communication facility is dependent on the probabilities of the damage causes, which are following to the structural damage in Fig.2.

2) The structural damage due to ground motion is divided into two states dependent on damage level.

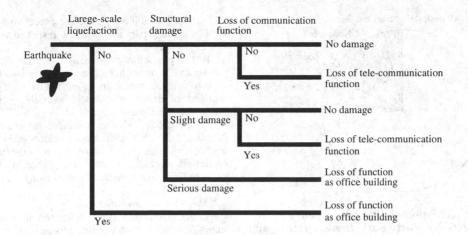

Fig.2   ET associated with damage scenarios of each node

3) The first state is defined as slightly damaged condition, which means that response stresses of members generating facilities due to ground motion exceed their allowable strength.   In this state, a node is assumed to be still an active state as an office building.   Also, the possibility that a node becomes inactive as tele-communication facility is dependent on the probabilities of the damage causes, which are following to the structural damage in Fig.2.

4) The second state is defined as seriously damaged condition, which means that response stresses of members generating facilities due to ground motion exceed their ultimate strength.   In this state, consequently, it is assumed that a node loses all functions as an office building.

(3) The damage scenarios due to the loss of tele-communication function
Here, we assume that the loss of tele-communication function is caused by the following factors:

(a) the damage due to slide and/or over-turning of tele-communication tools generating network.

(b) the damage of a computer room where tele-communication equipment are installed

Also, the damage scenarios associated with the loss of tele-communication function are assumed as follows:

1) A node is active as tele-communication facility is active without the loss of tele-communication function.

2) A node is inactive as tele-communication facility is active due to the loss of tele-communication function.

Therefore, as shown in Fig.2, the damage scenarios of each node due to earthquake are summarized as followed:

a) consequence-1: no damage associated with tele-communication function

b) consequence-2: the loss of tele-communication function

c) consequence-3: the loss of functions as an office building

2.3 *The results of investigation*
At present, we are going to investigate the probabilities associated with the occurrence of damage causes shown in Fig.2, in order to evaluate the reliability of the tele-communication network.

Therefore, in this study, we present the results of investigation to evaluate the strength of the tele-communication network shown in Fig.1 under a specific condition that probabilities of several consequences mentioned in 2.2 is assumed as follows:

1) The probability P_1 of consequence-1, which means no damage associated with tele-communication function, is 0.50.

2) The probability P_2 of consequence-2, which means the loss of tele-communication function is 0.25

3) The probability P_3 of consequence-3, which means the loss of functions as an office building is 0.25.

Under these assumptions, the probability how many branches are able to communicate with headquarters is estimated.

Fig.3 shows the numbers of nodes, which will be able to communicate with headquarters.   As shown in Fig.3, the possibility that all nodes are able to communicate with headquarters as expected in prescribed scenario is less than 1 %.   On the other hand, the possibility that no nodes are able to communicate with headquarters is 75 %.

Therefore, the results of this investigation obviously show that re-construction of current tele-communication network in a private company is

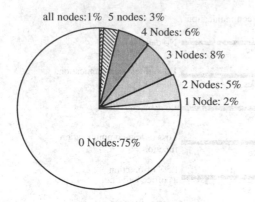

all nodes:1% 5 nodes: 3%

4 Nodes: 6%

3 Nodes: 8%

2 Nodes: 5%

1 Node: 2%

0 Nodes:75%

Fig. 3   The probability associated with the connectivity between headquarters and nodes

necessary to strengthen its reliability.

3. THE FEASIBILITY OF DECISION-MAKING SYSTEM

As mentioned in INTRODUCTION, we assume that executive directors only make important decision under an emergent circumstance. Therefore, the feasibility of decision-making system prescribed in this study is heavily dependent on whether executive directors of a private company will be able to take part in a current response team established in their nearest office among telecommunication network from their housings.

From these viewpoints, this study presents the result of investigation associated with how many executive directors will be able to arrive in each node quantitatively under a specific assumption.

3.1 *The assumption of investigation*
As for the investigation of the possibility whether executive directors of a private company are able to take part in a current response team established in their nearest node among telecommunication network from their housings, we make the following assumption:

1) The probability whether executive directors of a private company are able to take part in a current response team is dependent on the distance from their housings and their nearest node among telecommunication network.

2) When the distance from a housing of an executive director and his nearest office is less than 10 km, the probability P_{10} that the executive director is able to take part in a current response team is assumed to be 0.50.

3) When the distance from a housing of an executive director and his nearest office is less than 20 km, the probability P_{20} that the executive director is able to take part in a current response team is assumed to be 0.25.

4) The possibility how many executive directors will be able to arrive in each node is estimated by the expected values, which are calculated by multiplying numbers of executive directors with the gathering probability mentioned in 2) and 3).

5) The criteria whether a current response team established in each node among telecommunication network operates as effectively as expected in prescribed scenario is that the expected values evaluated in 4) are more than three persons.

3.2 *The results of investigation*
Under the assumption above mentioned, the expected values how many executive directors are able to arrive in each node is estimated. Here, the distance from the housings of executive directors and their nearest node among telecommunication network is estimated on the basis of the address book published by a private company.

As a result, the expected values of all branch offices are less than three persons. Consequently, it is revealed that executive directors of a private company are able to take part in a current response team established in headquarters and computer center. Also, as for decision-making system, the probability that a response team operates as efficiently as expected in prescribed scenario is very low.

Therefore, the results make it obvious that re-construction of decision-making system in a private company is necessary to strengthen its feasibility.

4. CONCLUDING REMARKS

In this paper, the investigations whether a response team operates as efficiently as expected in prescribed scenario are carried out by adapting Seismic Risk Management method.   Through the investigation, the following conclusion remarks are derived.

1) The reliability of current tele-communication network in a private company is very low.

2) The feasibility of decision-making system prescribed in prescribed scenario is very low.

3) From 1) and 2), re-construction of current disaster response system in a private company is necessary to strengthen its reliability and its feasibility.

REFERENCES

Mizutani, M., "Basic Methodology of a Seismic Risk Management (SRM) Procedures", ICOSSAR'97, 1997.

Structural Safety and Reliability, Shiraishi, Shinozuka & Wen (eds) © 1998 Balkema, Rotterdam, ISBN 90 5410 978 5

A study of the influence of energy input rate on inelastic response

Hitoshi Suwa, Arihide Nobata & Tetsuo Suzuki
Obayashi Corporation Technical Research Institute, Tokyo, Japan

ABSTRACT : Based on the concept of energy input rate, a simplified equivalent linearization method is proposed. The energy equivalent factor is defined by making 'ordinary' energy input and absorbed energy of system equal. It is found this factor is almost independent of allowable ductility factor in wide range of equivalent period. As a result, conservative demand resistance can be easily estimated by using the energy input rate to elastic system.

1. INTRODUCTION

The serious structural damage in the 1995 Hyogo-Ken-Nanbu earthquake in Japan was attributed to the high instantaneous energy input as well as the large total energy input by many researchers. In this study, based on the concept of energy input rate, a simplified equivalent linearization method is proposed from statistical point of view. The proposal method has the advantage of being easily able to estimate conservative demand resistance.

2. CHARACTERISTIC OF ENERGY INPUT RATE

2.1 Definition of Energy Input Rate

The equilibrium of energy input on a single-degree-of-freedom (SDOF) system subjected to an earthquake is defined as follows [1] :

$$\int_0^t m\ddot{X}\dot{X}dt + \int_0^t C\dot{X}^2 dt + \int_0^t Q(X)\dot{X}dt = -\int_0^t m\ddot{Z}\dot{X}dt \quad (1)$$

in which m is the mass of system, C is the coefficient of viscous damping, Q(X) is restoring force, X is relative displacement. From eq.(1), the seismic total energy input E_T is obtained as follows :

$$E_T = -\int_0^{t_0} m\ddot{Z}\dot{X}\,dt \quad (2)$$

in which t_0 is duration time of earthquake ground motion. The seismic total energy input to an elasto-plastic system can be approximately evaluated by an elastic system with viscous damping factor h=0.1 [1].

Energy input rate EIR(t), namely instantaneous energy input at time t, is defined by derivative of energy input with respect to time as follows [2].

$$EIR(t) = -m\ddot{Z}(t)\dot{X}(t) \quad (3)$$

The maximum value of energy input rate during duration time of earthquake ground motion is again defined as follows [3] and used in this study.

$$V_T = \max\{ EIR(t) \} \quad (0 \le t \le t_0) \quad (4)$$

2.2 Earthquake Records

Ten earthquake ground motions are selected for dynamic analysis from representative earthquakes as shown in table 1. From earthquake number one through three has been conventionally used in designing tall buildings in Japan, of which peak ground velocity (PGV) is normalized to 50(cm/s). From earthquake number six through eight was observed in the 1995 Hyogo-Ken-Nanbu earthquake.

2.3 Energy Input Rate to Elastic System

The energy input rate spectra V_{T0} to the elastic SDOF system, in which weight of mass W=1 (ton) and viscous damping factor h=0.1, are shown in Fig.1. The earthquakes that caused serious structural damage, such as Hyogo-Ken-Nanbu earthquake and Northridge earthquake, tend to show much larger energy input rate than the other earthquakes regardless of difference of elastic period. Since it seems that the high energy input rate is strongly correlated with the serious structural damage, energy input rate is considered to be the important damage index for

Table 1 Earthquake List

No.	Name	Year	Velocity (cm/s)	Acceleration (cm/s²)
1	EL-CENTRO	1940	50.0	482.2
2	HACHINOHE	1968	50.0	354.4
3	TOHOKU-1FL	1978	50.0	376.3
4	KUSHIRO	1993	67.7	817.4
5	SANRIKU	1994	26.7	604.2
6	KOBE-JMA	1995	90.7	818.0
7	KOBE-KOBEDAI	1995	54.8	270.3
8	KOBE-TAKATORI [4]	1995	120.7	605.6
9	CORRALITS	1989	54.9	617.7
10	SYLMAR	1994	127.4	826.8

earthquake resistant design.

2.4 Comparison of Energy Input Rate with Maximum Velocity Response

The characteristic of energy input rate was pointed out to be very similar to maximum velocity response V_{max}. The ratio ξ is defined in order to examine the difference of these quantity as follows :

$$\xi = \left| \frac{V_{T0}}{m\, \ddot{Z}_{max}\, V_{max}} \right| \qquad (5)$$

in which $\ddot{Z}_{max}$ is peak ground acceleration (PGA). Calculating the ratio ξ as shown in Fig.2, it seems that there is no constant relationship between the elastic period T_0 and the ratio ξ with any input ground motion.

3. EQUIVALENT LINEARIZATION BASED ON ENERGY INPUT RATE

3.1 Analytical Procedures

Demand resistance Q_{yn}, that is the shear force to keep deformation within allowable ductility factor μ_a, is calculated by convergence response analysis. The energy input rate V_{TN} to this elasto-plastic SDOF system is investigated in detail. Demand resistance is estimated through the energy input rate to elastic system.

3.2 Analytical Model

Takeda model is used as hysteresis restoring force characteristic as shown in Fig.3. K_0 is elastic stiffness, cracking strength $Q_C = 1/3\, Q_y$, yield stiffness $K_y = 0.3\, K_0$, $\kappa_2 = 0.01$ and K_r is stiffness at unloading given by the following equation.

$$K_r = \frac{Q_C + Q_y}{\delta_C + \delta_y} \times \left| \frac{\delta_y}{\delta_m} \right|^{0.4} \qquad (6)$$

Viscous damping factor of system is assumed to be 0.

3.3 Definition of Equivalent Period

The equivalent period of the elasto-plastic system is derived so that the shape of energy input rate spectrum to elasto-plastic system matches well with that to elastic system. Through many numerical simulations, equivalent ductility factor μ_e is obtained as shown in Fig.4.

$$\mu_e = \frac{1}{4} \times (\mu_a + 3) \qquad (7)$$

By using the equivalent ductility factor, the relationship between elastic period T_0 and equivalent period T_e is expressed as follows :

$$T_e = \frac{1}{\sqrt{\gamma_y \times \gamma_e}}\, T_0 \qquad (8)$$

in which $\gamma_e = \{1 + \kappa_2 (\mu_e - 1)\} / \mu_e$ and $\gamma_y = 0.3$.

3.4 Estimation of Energy Input Rate to Elasto-Plastic System

In order to evaluate the relationship between energy input rate to elastic system V_{T0} with viscous damping factor h=0.1 and that to elasto-plastic system V_{TN}, adjustment factor $\alpha(\mu_a)$, that is defined by V_{TN} divided by V_{T0}, is calculated for each allowable ductility factor. The result is shown in Fig.5. It is found that the adjustment factor tends to depend on input

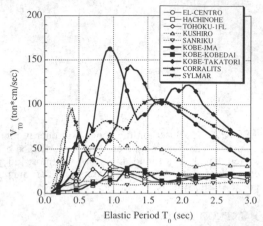

Fig.1 Energy Input Rate Spectra to Elastic System with Weight of Mass W=1(ton) and Viscous Damping Factor h=0.1

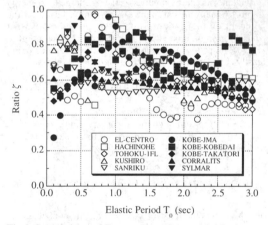

Fig.2 Comparison of Energy Input Rate with Maximum Velocity Response

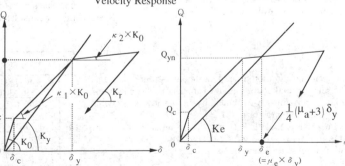

Fig.3 Hysteresis Model   Fig.4 Definition of Equivalent Period

ground motion for a constant allowable ductility factor, and as the allowable ductility factor increases, the adjustment factor decreases gradually for each input ground motion. Expectation $E[\alpha(\mu_a)]$ and coefficient of variation (C.O.V.) $V[\alpha(\mu_a)]$ are calculated with ten input ground motions in terms of each allowable ductility factor as shown in Fig.6. Carrying out the regression analysis, the following equations are obtained.

$$E[\alpha(\mu_a)] \approx 1.04 - 0.22 \times \log_{10}(\mu_a) \qquad (9.1)$$

$$V[\alpha(\mu_a)] \approx 0.15 + 0.03 \times \mu_a \qquad (9.2)$$

3.5 Definition of Energy Equivalent Factor

The property of energy input rate is investigated in detail by using 'ordinary' energy input E_V, that is defined by multiplying V_{TN} by appropriate time as the following equation.

$$E_V = V_{TN} \times (n \times T_e) \qquad (10)$$

On the other hand, absorbed energy of system E_R is assumed to be plastic potential energy as shown in Fig.7. Energy equivalent factor n_e is defined by making E_V and E_R equal as the following equation.

$$n_e = \frac{E_R}{V_{TN} \times T_e} \qquad (11)$$

The energy equivalent factor $n_e(T_e)$ is calculated for each allowable ductility factor as shown in Fig.8. From this figure, the energy equivalent factor is almost independent of difference of allowable ductility factor in wide range of equivalent period. This indicates that the relationship between energy equivalent factor and equivalent period can be evaluated regardless of allowable ductility factor. Therefore, the energy input rate strongly correlates to the plastic potential energy of system. Expectation $E[n_e(T_e)]$ and C.O.V. $V[n_e(T_e)]$ are calculated for several allowable ductility factors in terms of each equivalent period as shown in Fig.9. Carrying out the regression analysis, the following equations are obtained :

$$E[n_e(T_e)] \approx a_0 + a_1 T_e + a_2 T_e^2 + a_3 T_e^3 + a_4 T_e^4 \quad (12.1)$$

$$V[n_e(T_e)] \approx 0.41 + 0.13 \times T_e \qquad (12.2)$$

in which a_0=0.6874, a_1=-1.1147, a_2=0.8104, a_3=-0.2700 and a_4=0.0332. It should be noted that these equations are valid only for equivalent period from 0.1 through 3.0 (sec).

Equivalent energy input $E_{V0}(T_e,\mu_a)$ to elasto-plastic system can be obtained by using V_{T0}.

$$E_{V0}(T_e,\mu_a) = \{\alpha(\mu_a) \times V_{T0}\} \times \{n_e(T_e) \times T_e\} \qquad (13)$$

4. ESTIMATION OF DEMAND RESISTANCE

4.1 Formulation of Demand Resistance

Demand resistance $Q_{yn}(T_e,\mu_a)$ is formulated by equalizing $E_{V0}(T_e,\mu_a)$ with E_R as follows [5] :

$$Q_{yn}(T_e,\mu_a) = \sqrt{\frac{2 K_0 E_{V0}(T_e,\mu_a)}{b_0+b_1+b_2}} \qquad (14)$$

and $b_0 = \chi^2$,

$$b_1 = \{(1+\chi) \times (1-\chi)\} / \kappa_1 ,$$

$$b_2 = \{2+\kappa_2 \times (\mu_a-1)\} \times (\mu_a-1) / \chi_y$$

in which χ is 1/3 and κ_1 is 2/9. Assuming that random variables of $\alpha(\mu_a)$ and $n_e(T_e)$ are statistically independent each other, from eq.(14), expectation $E[Q_{yn}(T_e,\mu_a)]$ and

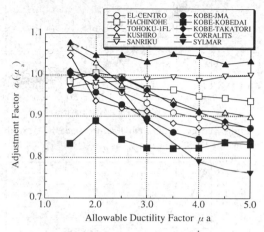

Fig.5 Adjustment Factor for each Input Ground Motion

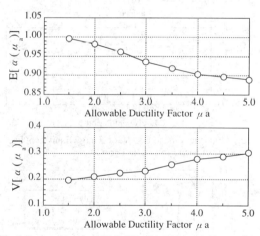

Fig.6 Expectation and C.O.V. of Adjustment Factor in terms of each Allowable Ductility Factor

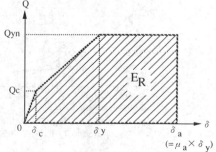

Fig.7 Assumption of Absorbed Energy of Structure

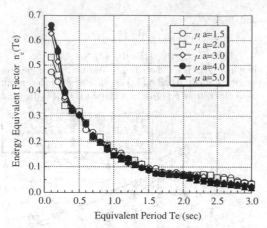

Fig.8 Energy Equivalent Factor for each Allowable Ductility Factor

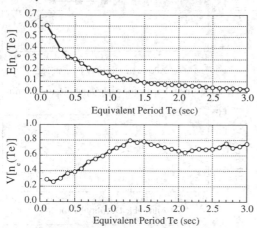

Fig.9 Expectation and C.O.V. of Energy Equivalent Factor in terms of each Equivalent Period

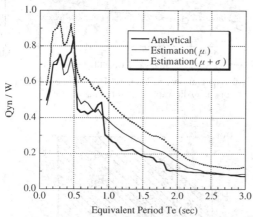

Fig.10 Demand Base Shear Coefficient with Allowable Ductility Factor μ_a=2.0 Subjected to TAFT-EW(1952)

standard deviation $\sigma[Q_{yn}(T_e,\mu_a)]$ are approximately obtained by the first-order second-moment method as follows :

$$E[Q_{yn}(T_e,\mu_a)] \approx \sqrt{\eta \times E[\alpha] \times E[n_e]} \qquad (15.1)$$

$$\sigma[Q_{yn}(T_e,\mu_a)] \approx \sqrt{\frac{1}{4} \times \eta \times \left(\frac{E[n_e]}{E[\alpha]}Var[\alpha] + \frac{E[\alpha]}{E[n_e]}Var[n_e]\right)}$$
$$(15.2)$$

in which $\eta = (2K_0 V_{T0} T_e)/(b_0+b_1+b_2)$ and $Var[\cdot]$ denotes variance.

4.2 Verification of the Proposal Method

In order to verify accuracy of the proposal method, demand base shear coefficient (Q_{yn}/W) with μ_a=2.0 is calculated. TAFT-EW(1952), that is not used in the regression analysis, is selected, of which PGV is normalized to 50(cm/s). The result is shown in Fig.10. It is found that the value of expectation is almost in agreement with the analytical value in wide range of equivalent period, and the value of expectation plus one standard deviation almost covers the analytical value. Therefore, by using this value, conservative demand resistance can be easily estimated without convergence response analysis.

5. CONCLUSIONS

The energy equivalent factor is defined under the condition of making 'ordinary' energy input and absorbed energy of system equal. It is found this factor is almost independent of allowable ductility factor in wide range of equivalent period. The proposal equivalent linearization method makes it easy to estimate conservative demand resistance, because equivalent energy input to elasto-plastic system can be easily obtained through the energy input rate to elastic system with viscous damping factor h=0.1.

ACKNOWLEDGMENT

The authors thankfully acknowledge the advice of Mr. M.Nakamura of my colleague.

REFERENCES

[1] H.Akiyama, Earthquake-Resistant Limit-State Design for Buildings, Univ. of Tokyo Press, 1985.
[2] K.Ohi et al. , Energy Input Rate Spectra of Earthquake Ground Motions, J. Struct. Constr. Eng. , AIJ, No.420, pp.1-7, Feb. ,1991.
[3] H.Suwa et al. , Phase Angle Influence of Earthquake Ground Motion on Energy Input Rate, Summaries of Technical Papers of Annual Meeting of AIJ, B-2, pp.583-584, Sep. ,1996.
[4] Y.Nakamura, F.Uehan and H.Inoue, Waveform and its Analysis of the 1995 Hyogo-Ken-Nanbu Earthquake (II), JR Earthquake Information No. 23d, Railway Technical Research Institute, Mar. 1996 (in Japanese). (Takatori Records from JR FD Serial No. R-008)
[5] H.Suwa et al. , A Method on Estimation of Demand Resistance Based on Energy Input Rate, J. of Struct. Eng. , AIJ, Vol.43B, pp.523-530, Mar. ,1997.

Structural Safety and Reliability, Shiraishi, Shinozuka & Wen (eds) © 1998 Balkema, Rotterdam, ISBN 90 5410 978 5

Mechanism of collapsed structures induced by impulsive action of vertical ground motions in the 1995 great Hanshin-Awaji earthquake

Seiichiro Natani

Department of Architectural Engineering, Osaka City University, Japan

ABSTRACT: This paper shows that the mechanism of story failure of reinforced concrete buildings destroyed by quake shocks during the Hanshin-Awaji (Hyogo-ken Nanbu) earthquake in Japan was caused by impulsive propagation of vertical ground motion. The various patterns of story failures are found to be dependent on distribution of proposed story impedance for impulsive stress wave propagation.

1 INTRODUCTION

The great Hanshin-Awaji earthquake struck the Hanshin district in Japan on Jan. 17th 1995 and caused serious disasters. In the region of the then JMA Scale VII which indicates severe shock, there were a great many story failures in reinforced concrete structures. In common failure patterns, X-shaped fractures occurred at midpoint of long columns of the mid story or piloti without large relative story displacement, and the same fracture in walls (Natani,1996b). The patterns were similar to the ones in the disaster of Northridge earthquake in Jan. 1994. They were entirely different from the fracture patterns in bend of long columns or in shearing of short columns destroyed by the horizontal ground motions of the past earthquakes. The author pointed out that they suddenly were caused by the impulsive vertical ground motion with characteristics of the severe earthquake of "directly-below-urban type" (Natani,1995).

The purpose of this paper is twofold. First, it is to state feasibility of impulse in existing quake records. Second, it is to apply the new quake-proof measure to specification of collapsed story. This measure is impulsive story impedance of stress wave propagation proposed by the author. As to its new impedance, it is easy to calculate and apply to the various multi-storied concrete structures as well as walled structures designed with the current or old quake-proof standards. Furthermore, it will be stated that these failures do not necessarily occur at

a mid story and that the occurrences at any story are possible according to the suggested impedance.

2 IMPULSIVE DYNAMICS

2.1 *Impulse*

Force (strain), density and velocity are related to an impulsive dynamic system and are basically restricted to have a finite magnitude. An impulsive wave constitutes a discontinuity wave plane in a propagated direction in elastic medium. This differs from elastic stress wave motion propagated in the same medium regard of multi-reflection theory. In the application of an impulsive system to structure, it is constituted that a preceding compressive stress wave with a very large finite magnitude propagates in only one direction between the media under the law of momentum conservation. In the original meaning of the Newton's second law and the demonstration of its proposition, it is stated that velocity is proportional to force and time. The differentiation of velocity with respect to time, introduced by L. Euler later, is suitable for the application to differentiable particle motion such as vibration without a sudden change. Therefore, it is intrinsic to consider the application of those laws.

2.2 *Non-manifestation of high-frequency band in ground motions*

If the failure of structures was caused by impulse,

the question whether there were high frequencies in the ground motion records is interesting. Most of the seismometers in that district were servo-type with feed-back circuit in amplifier having good advantages in linearity and resolution. However, there was the problem that electrical impedance had an effect of holding of high-frequency currents by necessary capacitance and inductance in that circuit. Its holding changes in accordance with a time constant in the circuit and has a filtering in that band. Input signals within that band cannot be distinguished from noises with the same band and cannot be amplified on the output side. In servo-accelerometers, several theorems including the generalized Gershgorin disk theory in the Nyquist diagram apply to stabilization of these transitional feed-back systems (Araki,1975). In this theory, if the natural frequency of that circuit tends to infinity, each radius of the disk which is the set of characteristic roots of that system approaches zero.

Moreover, digital recording from ground motion with analog signals eliminates higher frequency zone on the basis of the sampling theorem. Cut-off frequencies of almost all the records were set up at about 100 Hz. They are effective for only vibration system with 50 Hz sampling under aliasing effect.

Therefore, gain in the higher frequency band is reduced. It is too difficult to detect information on impulsive motions from the existing records.

2.3 *Stress wave propagation in ground-structure*

An incidence stress wave $_I\sigma$ soil in the ground is given for an upper structure, as shown in Fig.1. The contact surface is discontinuous interface. In a transmission at this interface, two conditions are given. The one, both forces at the interface are equal reciprocally. The other, both particle velocities are equal there. Under these conditions,

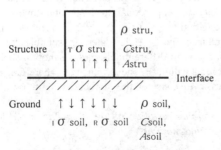

Fig. 1   Stress wave propagation system

a transmitted wave $_T\sigma$ stru and a reflected wave $_R\sigma$ soil are obtained. If a momentary match occurs through mediation of both characteristic impedance in each medium, ρ stru$C$stru and ρ soil$C$soil, then $_R\sigma$ soil becomes zero and $_T\sigma$ stru will reach at the maximum. This match have no relation with the multi-reflection theory. In this stress transmission at the interface, Eq. (1) is obtained from the momentary equilibrium of force.

$$A\text{stru}\ \rho\ \text{stru}C\text{stru} = A\text{soil}\ \rho\ \text{soil}C\text{soil} \quad \cdots (1)$$

A ratio of the transmission areas at the interface are obtained by Eq. (1).

2.4 *Axial and lateral rigidity of column or wall*

In such structural members as elastic columns or bearing-walls, vertical rigidity per story height is several times larger than lateral one. Under sudden vertical ground motion and inertia of the structure, they will bring instantaneously and progressively impulsive stress wave into the members without vertical relative displacement between floor levels.

3 STORY FAILURE

3.1 *Impulsive effect*

In a destroyed mid story, this story rigidity is reduced. This reduction makes a great difference in rigidity between the destroyed story and adjacent stories. If impulse acts from one medium to others, sudden motion has an analogy with elastic ball collision. If a mid ball is plastic, the impulse is reduced to about half, a reduction of 6 dB on the basis of the collision ball theory. If a certain story of multi-floored concrete structure is destroyed by the impulse, the story yields relatively a buffer. If upper stories subjected to half of the impulse have all the same sufficient vertical strength ratio, the number of story to be destroyed is only one.

3.2 *Impulsive story impedance of stress wave propagation and its distribution*

For the specification of story to be destroyed, the author obtained a new measure. This is the story impedance distribution of impulsive stress wave propagation determined at each story of a structure irrespective of the selfsame mechanical media in the wave propagation theory (Natani,1995). The story impedance is defined as the stress resistance to the stress propagation velocity. Each non-dimensional value is decided by a ratio of the sum of all weight from the upper story to the top to the sum of axial rigidity of all the members in that story. In dynamics including the vertical impulse, inertia force and restoring force of the imaginary part in the Gauss plane of the complex impedance are eliminated and vertical vibration is not occurred at the same time. The impedance of the real part faces the impulsive stress wave propagated with the same phase. Moreover it is necessary to decide the distribution of ratios of the story impedance at each story to the one at the top in order to specify a failure story.

3.3 Detection of story to be destroyed

In order to detect a story which could be destroyed, several examples are listed in Table 1. Type 1 gives an example of rigid framed concrete structures. Its columns become slender upward at each floor. This type was designed for old quake-proof standards and many were destroyed at the mid story. Type 3 gives an example of walled concrete structures having the same vertical rigidity

Table 1 The representative distribution ratios of the impulsive story impedance of stress wave propagation for various types of structures

Type	Fl. No.	Column or wall member size (cm · cm)	Column or wall profile	Impulsive impedance ratios
1	10	35 · 35		1.0
	9	40 · 40		1.54
	8	45 · 45		1.82
	7	50 · 50		1.97
	6	55 · 55		2.03
	5	60 · 60		2.05
	4	65 · 65		2.04
	3	70 · 70		2.01
	2	75 · 75		1.73
	1	80 · 80		1.52
2	8	45 · 45		1.0
	7	50 · 50		1.62
	6	50 · 50		2.43
	5	60 · 60		2.25
	4	70 · 70		2.07
	3	70 · 70		2.48
	2	75 · 75		2.52
	1	80 · 80		2.53
3	5	20 · 800		1.0
	4	*		2.0
	3	(ditto)		3.0
	2	*		4.0
	1	*		5.0

at each floor. Rigid frames designed by the current new standards have almost the same rigidity at each story and are included in Type 3. Several of this type were destroyed at the 1st floor. These stories in Types 1 and 3 were consistent with the ones having the maximum listed in Table 1. However, in Type 2 the vertical frame rigidity does not necessarily vary at each story subjected to the same weight. This type has a collapsed story different from the story with the maximum ratio. An example of Type 2 is shown in Photo.1.

Photo. 1 The outer view of a story failure at the 5th floor of the 8-storied municipal hospital building in Kobe

4 DISCUSSION

In the story failure of concrete structures, there were the vertically aligned X-shaped quadrangular pyramids destroyed at a midpoint of long column and X-shaped wedges in walls, as illustrated in Fig.2. They were caused by the compressive stress. X-shaped collapsed column and wall are shown in Photographs 2 and 3, respectively. Their fracture angles are subjected to material strength, constraint at the top/bottom and loading velocity, and range between 37 and 45 degrees under compression. Column fracture in that story above (Photo.1) is shown in Photo.4. Also, there were the frustums changed from the pyramids because of the after-shocks with slides and stress concentration.

These facts indicate that a destroyed story has a

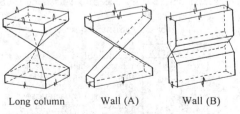

Long column   Wall (A)   Wall (B)

Fig. 2 The X-shaped concrete fractures of a destroyed midpoint of long column and walls

Photo.2 The destroyed long column in piloti designed with the current quake-proof standard

Photo.3 The destroyed support wall of highway

Photo. 4 The inner view collapsed at the 5th floor of building shown in Photo.1, taken by the NHK-TV and televised on Jan.17th 1995

near maximum impedance ratio distribution.
An inspection result of Type 2 is listed in Table 2. In Type 2, the data in Table 1 give 9 as the ratio of transmission area between soil and structure. The actual failure story was 5th. This failure mode

Table.2   Structural quantity

Fl	Stress ratio
8	0.89 *
7	0.72 *
6	0.72 *
5	1.0
4	0.74
3	0.74
2	0.64
1	0.56

The note of * is a stress ratio reduced to half in each floor of 6th, 7th or 8th under the law of momentum conservation. The allowable compressive concrete strength for impulse is 324 kgf/cm² which has already a magnification facter of 1.8.

is composed of both of Types 1 and 3. The stress of columns at each floor is obtained by a swelling effect of varied sectional areas regardless of the multi-reflection wave theory (Bridgman,1950; Natani,1996a). In this static calculated conversion, the ground acceleration to collapse only the 5th floor amounts to 613 gal. As to the others in Table 1, it is ascertained that necessary ground ones are not entirely more than the acceleration of gravity.

5 CONCLUSION

In this paper, it was stated that the story failure at any story of multi-storied structures was subjected to impulsive vertical motions of the Hanshin-Awaji earthquake. It is easy to specify the story failure from both the story impedance distribution of impulsive stress wave propagation and the strength ratio of vertical members. In estimation of the story impedance, the weight and vertical rigidity at each story are the required factors. Moreover, the arrangement of story impedance is very important. The author proposes that the story impedance for impulsive propagation will be an effective quake-proof measure against severe vertical earthquakes of "directly-below-urban type".

ACKNOWLEDGEMENT

A part of this work was supported by a subsidy of Ministry of Education, Science and Culture of Japan for promoting scientific researches (No. B2-08458104). The author would like to thank the authorities concerned.

REFERENCES

Araki, M & Nwokah, O.I. 1975. Bounds for Closed-Loop Transfer Functions of Multivariable Systems.
    IEEE Trans. on Autom. Control. AC-20. :666-670.
Bridgman,P.W. 1950. Physics above 20,000 kg/cm².
    Proc.Royal Soc. of London.A203:1-17.
Natani, S 1995. Story Collapses Mechanism of Structure in Hanshin Serious Disaster-Suggestion of Axial Impact Propagation Impedance for Vertical Motion.
    Proc. Ann. Conf. of Kinki B. of AIJ..33:245-248.
Natani, S 1996a. Shock Compression Collapse of Structures in Hanshin-Awaji Earthquake (Kobe 1995).
    Asia-Pacific Conference on Shock & Impact Loads on Structures. Singapore:339-346.
Natani, S 1996b. Distinguishing Features of Vertical Impulsive Collapses of Destroyed Structures in Sever Disaster Belt of the Hanshin-Awaji Earthquake.
    Disaster Prevention Institute.Kyoto Univ.UEHR Report E18:185-211.

Geotechnical engineering

Structural Safety and Reliability, Shiraishi, Shinozuka & Wen (eds) © 1998 Balkema, Rotterdam, ISBN 90 5410 978 5

Dynamic response variability of near-surface soil layer due to stochastic material properties

Hirokazu Nakamura
Japan Engineering Consultants Co. Ltd, Tokyo, Japan

Takanori Harada
Miyazaki University, Japan

Fumio Yamazaki
University of Tokyo, Japan

ABSTRACT: The spatially dynamic response variability of near-surface soil layer during earthquake has been so far inferred mainly from the observation records of closely spaced seismic arrays. On the dynamic response variability, this study investigates the influence of laterally heterogeneous soil properties by means of first-order perturbation (FOP) and stochastic finite element (SFE) techniques. The theoretical FOP solution is derived first as a frequency-wave number power spectrum. The SFE analysis is then conducted much more effectively by proposing the assumption of the spatial ergodicity. Then, this study shows that the response variability due to the soil heterogeneity is significant over the first predominant frequency of a building site. By using the frequency-dependent correlation distance proposed as a simple measure characterizing the response variability, this study also demonstrates that, within the extent of the heterogeneity published, the FOP analysis is practically available for the site approximated well as a single soil layer.

1 INTRODUCTION

Local site effects have a significant influence on the various characters of earthquake ground motion, especially on the spatial response variabilities of near-surface soil layer. The stochastic analysis is in course of accounting for the significance of the local site effects pertaining the total wave propagation problem from seismic source to site of interest (Wu & Aki, 1988). Since we can not determine uncertain material properties, the stochastic analysis becomes more important when we understand the spatial statistics of the uncertainties related to such things as the seismic source, traveling path of seismic waves, and near-surface local site.

As far as the ground response at near-surface local site during earthquake is concerned, the spatial response variability so far has been inferred mainly from the observation records of closely spaced seismic arrays (Kataoka et al., 1990; Schneider et al.,

1992; Nakamura, 1996). Some numerical analyses also have been made for the response variabilities. The stochastic analyses have been made for local site effects classified as the irregularities of free-surface and interface between soil layers (Harada, 1994), and the heterogeneity of soil properties (Frankel & Clayton, 1986; Harada & Fugasa, 1990; Fenton & Vanmarcke, 1991; Sato & Kawase, 1992). Deterministic analyses also emphasize the significance of surficial soil layer using the one dimensional multi-layer model (Anderson et al., 1996).

As an extension of those stochastic analyses mentioned above, this study is also aimed at investigating the spatial response variability of surficial soil layer which has laterally heterogeneous soil properties, as shown in Fig. 1. While we have to consider the indeterministic soil properties by some way, it is common in the stochastic analyses to treat the indeterministic nature of structural systems as a stochasticity. Then, the response variability mentioned in this study is a

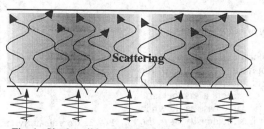

Fig. 1. Single soil layer model resting on rigid base.

Ground Surface

Heterogeneous
Soil Layer

Rigid Basement
Vertically
Incident Wave

Table 1. Parameters for laterally heterogeneous single soil layer model ($H = 30$ m).

Parameters	Symbols	Values
Density (t/m³)	ρ	1.8
Mean P-wave velocity (m/s)	c_{P0}	1530
Mean S-wave velocity (m/s)	c_{S0}	300
Poisson's ratio	v	0.48
Correlation function	S_{xx}^{Δ}	Gaussian
Correlation length (m)	a	25 to 100
Coefficient of variation	σ_0	0.00 to 0.25
Intrinsic damping ratio	D	0.05

seismic version of the response variability since we adopt the same way that has been extensively studied in engineering mechanics field for structural systems with stochastic material properties (e.g., Nakagiri & Hisada, 1985).

This study analyzes the response variability of the ground by using an analytical approximation and a numerical discretization, which are first-order perturbation and stochastic finite element techniques, respectively. After each analysis is done for the seismic response variability, the comparison as well as discussion is made for those obtained from both analyses. Then, this study shows the practical availability of the perturbation analysis.

2 EVALUATION OF STOCHASTIC GROUND RESPONSE

This study analyzes the surficial ground motion that is the stochastic response of heterogeneous single soil layer induced by the coherent base motion. That is, this is an analysis to obtain the practical and hence simple solution of the ground response with laterally heterogeneous soil properties. Then, this study presents two efficient methodologies using a first-order perturbation method and a stochastic finite element method to obtain the power spectrum in frequency and wave number domains, since the space-time stochastic ground response can be represented by the frequency-wave number power spectrum. As well as the frequency-wave number response, the space-time response can be obtained in both analyses once the space-time incident wave is decided at the rigid base.

2.1 First-order Perturbation Method

A first-order perturbation technique is adopted so as to derive the analytically approximate solution of the problem involving material stochasticities of small lateral extent. This study considers a viscoelastic single soil layer overlying a flat rigid base as shown in Fig. 2. The single soil layer has the density of ρ, the

complex elastic wave velocity of $c_J = c_J^0 (1 + iD)$ ($J = P, S$) where c_J^0 is the elastic P- and S-wave velocity, D is the linear hysteretic damping ratio, and $i = \sqrt{-1}$. The values of soil parameters used in this study are shown in Table 1. Since the constant thickness is supposed to be $H = 30$ m (= $z_1 - z_0$), the mean predominant frequency is 2.5Hz for the soil layer model. Such mean values of soil parameters are determined under the consideration of the Chiba site in Japan where the seismic array observation is performed since 1982 (Lu et al., 1990; Nakamura, 1996).

This study considers the P-SV waves subjected to a near-surface single soil layer. Following the Born-type approximation, the perturbation of elastic wave velocities is assigned in the single soil layer whose material properties vary laterally. The P-SV wave equation is solved theoretically by using an integral equation formulation (Kennett, 1972; Harada & Fugasa, 1990) on the Cartesian coordinate and corresponding displacement vector systems as shown in Fig. 2. Then, a closed-form analytic expression is obtained based on the propagator matrix method (Gilbert & Backus, 1966) for the laterally two dimensional single soil layer.

To obtain the perturbation solution, we utilize the condition that the vertical displacement is confined to zero to make the solution simple for practice. While the derivation of the perturbation solution is abbreviated, this paper shows a resultant solution of the frequency-wave number power spectrum describing the

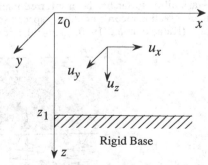

Fig. 2. Coordinate system in the perturbation analysis.

response variability due to laterally heterogeneous soil layer as mentioned above. The frequency-wave number power spectrum as functions of frequency, ω, in rad/sec and wave number vector, κ, in rad/m is given by:

$$S_{xx}^S(\kappa, \omega)$$

$$= \left| K_{AP}^\delta \, \delta(\kappa - \kappa_0) - 2K_{AP}^{\Delta_S} \, \overline{\Delta}_S(\kappa - \kappa_0) \right|^2 S_{xx}^B(\omega) \tag{1}$$

where δ = the Dirac's delta function and $\overline{\Delta}_S$ is the wave number spectrum describing the lateral heterogeneity of soil properties. Note that the heterogeneity of soil properties is not required to be isotropic in (1). κ_0 and $S_{xx}^B(\omega)$ in (1) are the apparent wave number vector and the wave number power spectrum of the incident SV base motion, respectively. By using v_{AP} and v_{AP0} standing for vertical wave number corresponding to horizontal wave number, κ and κ_0, respectively, K_{AP}^δ and $K_{AP}^{\Delta_S}$ in (1) are as follow:

$$K_{AP}^\delta = 1 \bigg/ \cos\left(\frac{c_P}{c_S} v_{AP} H\right) \tag{2a}$$

$$K_{AP}^{\Delta_S} = \frac{v_{AP0}^2 + \kappa\kappa_0}{v_{AP}^2 - v_{AP0}^2}\left\{ K_{AP}^\delta - 1 \bigg/ \cos\left(\frac{c_P}{c_S} v_{AP0} H\right)\right\} \tag{2b}$$

especially when vertically incident wave is considered, i.e., $\kappa_0 = 0$, K_{AP}^δ and $K_{AP}^{\Delta_S}$ at $\kappa = 0$ are given by:

$$K_{AP}^\delta = 1 \bigg/ \cos\left(\frac{\omega}{c_S} H\right) \tag{3a}$$

$$K_{AP}^{\Delta_S} = \frac{1}{2}\frac{\omega}{c_S} H \sin\left(\frac{\omega}{c_S} H\right) \bigg/ \cos^2\left(\frac{\omega}{c_S} H\right) \tag{3b}$$

In this case that $\kappa_0 = 0$ and $\kappa = 0$, K_{AP}^δ and $K_{AP}^{\Delta_S}$ for confined P-SV wave correspond those for SH and SV wave. Note that the homogeneous and heterogeneous parts in (1) are coupled since $\overline{\Delta}_S$ is not zero at $\kappa = \kappa_0$ except special case. Considering this coupling is an amelioration of the solution proposed by Harada & Fugasa (1990).

If the heterogeneous part in (1) is neglected, this two dimensional perturbation solution, in fact, gives the same solution for one dimensional soil layer. While the perturbation solution expressed by (1) is derived for the confined P-SV wave, the perturbation solution for SV and SH waves is also derived in the same way (Harada & Fugasa, 1990). We suppose the case hereafter that S_{xx}^B is unity since this study is aimed at evaluating the response variability of single soil layer with stochastic material properties.

2.2 Lateral Heterogeneous elastic wave velocity

It is assumed in stochastic analyses that the spatial correlation at different locations in random field decreases with increase of the distance between two locations. To deal with the lateral heterogeneity of elastic wave velocities in single soil layer, this study supposes this assumption as well as many other researches (e.g., Frankel & Clayton, 1986; Fenton & Vanmarcke, 1991; Sato & Kawase, 1992) which have been done under this assumption to the correlation structure. Then, this study adopts the Gaussian correlation function, R_{xx}^Δ, and its corresponding wave number power spectrum, S_{xx}^Δ, as follow:

$$R_{xx}^\Delta(\xi) = \sigma_0^2 \exp\left(-\frac{\xi^2}{a^2}\right) \tag{4a}$$

$$S_{xx}^\Delta(\kappa) = \sigma_0^2 \frac{a}{2\sqrt{\pi}} \exp\left(-\frac{a^2\kappa^2}{4}\right) \tag{4b}$$

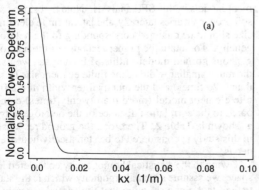

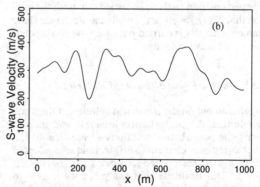

Fig. 3. (a) Wave number power spectrum describing laterally heterogeneous elastic wave velocity (correlation distance: $a = 50$ m; C.O.V.: $\sigma_0 = 15$ %), and (b) the realization of the corresponding elastic wave velocity for S-wave with mean velocity of 300 m/s.

Table 2. Correlation distances of the lateral heterogeneities and sizes of finite element models.

Parameters		FEM models			
		(1)	(2)	(3)	(4)
Correlation length (m)	a	25.0	50.0	75.0	100.0
Element width (m)	B_e	5.0	5.0	10.0	10.0
Total width (km)	B	1.0	1.0	2.0	2.0
Ratio of a and B_e	B_e/a	0.20	0.10	0.13	0.10
Ratio of a and B	B/a	40.0	20.0	26.7	20.0

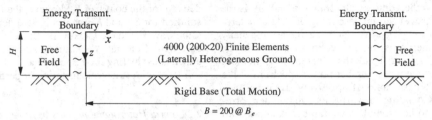

Fig. 4. Finite element model used in the response analysis of laterally heterogeneous soil layer.

where σ_0 and a indicate, respectively, the coefficient of variation (C.O.V.) and the correlation distance of laterally heterogeneous elastic wave velocity field. The extents of the C.O.V. and the correlation distance are determined based on the previous works (e.g., Fenton & Vanmarcke, 1991) as shown in Table 1. This Gaussian correlation function (4) is used in many other stochastic problems.

By using the Gaussian correlation function describing the stochastic elastic wave velocity, Fig. 3 (a) shows the example of wave number power spectrum in which the correlation distance, a, is 50 m and the C.O.V., σ_0, is 15 %, and Fig. 3 (b) shows the realization of the corresponding elastic wave velocity for S-wave with the mean velocity of 300 m/s. The correlation distance of 50 m and the C.O.V. of 15 % describing the stochasticity of the ground are used hereafter to show the response variability as a typical example. The perturbation analysis is carried out using the relation that $S_{xx}^{\Delta}(\kappa) = |\overline{\Delta}_S(\kappa)|^2$, while the stochastic finite element analysis is carried out using the corresponding elastic wave velocity.

2.3 Stochastic Finite Element (SFE) Method

In order to obtain the numerical solution of the same problem in the perturbation analysis and then to verify the perturbation solutions as shown above, a stochastic finite element (SFE) technique is adopted using a well-tested code, *super FLUSH* (KKEI, 1988). This finite element analysis code is used to compute the complex transfer functions at the surface of laterally heterogeneous single soil layer modeled as finite elements. This SFE analysis is conducted

considering that the vertical displacement is confined to make the same condition as the perturbation analysis mentioned above.

As shown in Fig. 4, the finite element model consists of 200 by 20 plane strain elements laterally and vertically, respectively. The boundaries are modeled as the fixed boundary for the bottom and the energy transmitting boundary for the left and right sides. This boundary conditions give the same condition used in the perturbation analysis. Note that in this SFE analysis each soil column with same soil properties is also divided (30m = 10 @ 1 m + 10 @ 2 m) to obtain the better estimate of the surficial response. The free-field is also modeled using mean soil property of the finite elements, so that 2.5 Hz is the mean of the first predominant frequency at each location.

Table 2 shows the correlation distances of laterally heterogeneous soil layer and the sizes of finite element models in this SFE analysis. Note that since the soil property varies laterally, the lateral finite element size should be changed corresponding to the heterogeneity. To obtain the proper response of the heterogeneous ground model in this SFE analysis, we use the much smaller width of the finite element size (less than 0.20 times) and the much larger width of the finite element model (more than twenty times) compared to the correlation distance of the heterogeneity, as shown in Table 2. Therefore, the ground response in this study is considered to be statistically homogeneous.

Owing to the statistical homogeneity considered in space, we assume a spatial ergodicity which is the statistical technique showing that the spatial ensemble mean is independent of the spatial sampling. By using this spatial ergodicity assumption, the computa-

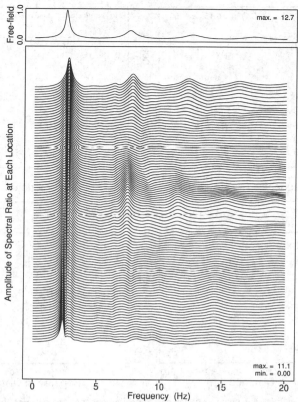

Fig. 5. Amplitude of complex transfer function estimated by the stochastic finite element analysis for laterally heterogeneous soil layer (a = 50 m, σ_0 = 15 %; upper: for 1-D response, lower: for 2-D response).

tional efficacy is enhanced for the evaluation of the statistically homogeneous response variability, while the ordinary finite element analysis gives a deterministic result per computation once the material properties are specified in the finite element model.

The statistically homogeneous and stationary transfer function between ground surface and rigid base is obtained for the *P-SV* waves propagating in stochastic soil layer. Then, the amplitude of the complex transfer function is estimated for the laterally heterogeneous soil layer in which a = 50 m and σ_0 = 15 %, as shown in Fig. 5. The upper figure shows the response of the one dimensional soil column and the lower figure shows the response of the two dimensional soil layer ranging over 500 m at intervals of 5 m. As this study assumes that the base motion is unity, it is found in Fig. 5 that the ground response is affected over the first predominant frequency, especially at each predominant frequencies. Note that the result obtained from the assembly of one dimensional analysis should be different from this *P-SV* wave propagation analysis in which the responses of each soil column are affected each other.

3 RESPONSE VARIABILITY DUE TO STOCHASTIC GROUND MODELS

The stochastic ground response is computed by means of the perturbation analysis and the stochastic finite element analysis. As a result, it is found in both analyses that while the C.O.V. of the ground response shows the increasing trend with increase of frequency, the mean ground response shows good agreement each other and with that of the one dimensional analysis. Then, we pay attention to the response variability which is evaluated in terms of the coherence function and then the frequency-dependent correlation distance of the ground response which is pertaining to spatially varying earthquake ground motion.

3.1 *Coherence Function Describing Spatial Response Variability of Stochastic Ground*

The coherence functions are computed analytically in space and frequency domains to describe the spatial response variability of laterally heterogeneous

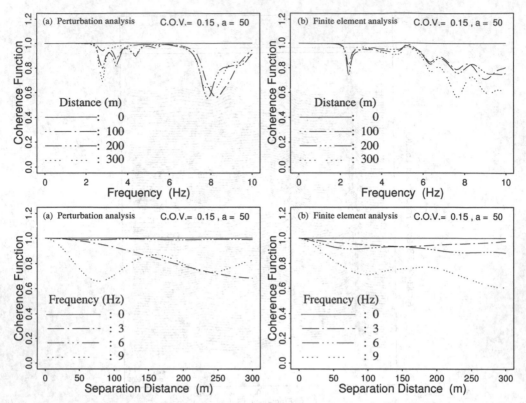

Fig. 6. Coherence function estimated from perturbation and finite element analyses for laterally heterogeneous soil layer ($a = 50$ m, $\sigma_0 = 15$ %; upper: frequency in Hz, lower: separation distance in meter).

ground models, since the frequency-wave number power spectrum is obtained from the first-order perturbation method and since the ground responses on surficial equidistant grid are obtained from the stochastic finite element method. Figure 6 shows the coherence functions representing the response variability of the ground model in which $a = 50$ m and $\sigma_0 = 15$ % as a typical example as mentioned above. The upper and lower figures indicate the coherence function with respect to frequency in Hz and separation distance in meter, respectively.

The coherence functions estimated from the both analytical and numerical analyses show the similar trend each other as shown in Fig. 6. It is found in this study that the coherence functions show the relatively monotonous decrease with increase of separation distance, while as frequency increases coherence function shows several decays especially around the dominant frequencies of the ground models. Furthermore, the coherence functions computed from both analyses are almost consistent with those obtained from the seismic array records which provides a useful information currently available (Kataoka et al., 1990; Lu et al., 1990; Nakamura, 1996). Then, the

frequency-dependent correlation distance obtained from the coherence function is adopted to evaluate the spatial response variability of laterally heterogeneous ground models.

3.2 Frequency-dependent Correlation Distance of Stochastic Ground Response

Suppose the coherence function decreases monotonously with respect to the separation distance. Then, the seismic response variability is efficiently evaluated by the frequency-dependent correlation distance of the ground response. For that reason, this study adopts a Gaussian-type coherence function model as follows:

$$\gamma_{xx}(\xi, f) = \exp\left\{-\xi^2 / q^2(f)\right\} \qquad (5)$$

where q indicates a frequency-dependent correlation distance of the ground response estimated by the regression analysis. Note that the maximum separation distance in this study is considered up to 300 m which is the same order in the analysis of the Chiba array

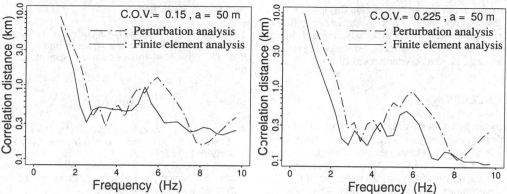

Fig. 7. Comparison of frequency-dependent correlation distances, q's in (1), estimated from perturbation (broken line) and finite element (solid line) analyses for laterally heterogeneous soil layer (left: case of $\sigma_0 = 15$ % and $a = 50$ m, right: case of $\sigma_0 = 22.5$ % and $a = 50$ m).

records (Nakamura, 1996).

It is demonstrated in this study that as the correlation distance (a) and C.O.V. (σ_0) of material properties increase, the spatial response variability shows the decreasing trend. Figure 7 shows the examples of the frequency-dependent correlation distance. The left and right show, respectively, the case that $\sigma_0 = 15$ % and $a = 50$ m and the case that $\sigma_0 = 22.5$ % and $a = 50$ m. Figure 7 also compares the frequency-dependent correlation distances q_P and q_F which are estimated from perturbation and stochastic finite element analyses, respectively.

To compare the both results, the L_2 norm difference between q_P and q_F is defined:

$$D_{PF}(\sigma_0; a) = \sqrt{\frac{\int_f \log^2\{q_P(f, \sigma_0)/q_F(f, \sigma_0)\}\, df}{\int_f \log^2\{q_F(f, \sigma_0)\}\, df}}$$

(6)

The L_2 norm difference indicates the difference of the results between perturbation and finite element analyses. That is, the results of both analyses become different from each other as the L_2 norm difference increases. Figure 8 shows the L_2 norm difference for laterally heterogeneous soil layer. The left and right figures indicate the cases of $a = 50$ m and the cases of $\sigma_0 = 15$ %, respectively. Note that, in both analyses, the frequency range of 2.5 to 10.0 Hz is used in the integration of above equations, since the ground responses of lower frequency components are coherent in this study, the frequency at least less than the predominant frequency of the ground, as can be seen in Figures 5, 6, and 7.

By comparing the results from perturbation analysis with those from stochastic finite element analysis, the largest L_2 norm difference is obtained in the case that $\sigma_0 = 22.5$ % and $a = 50$ m as shown in Fig. 8. It is found in Fig. 7 that even in the case of the largest L_2 norm difference, both results are allowable within the

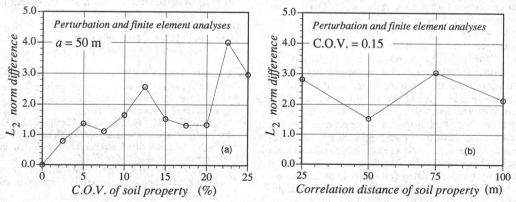

Fig. 8. L_2 norm difference between frequency-dependent correlation distances q_P and q_F, estimated from perturbation and finite element analyses, for laterally heterogeneous soil layer (left: $a = 50$ m, right: $\sigma_0 = 15$ %).

extent for frequency and separation distance of interest. Note again that the values of stochasticity for the material properties used in this study are carefully selected within the range properly estimated in previous works (e.g., Fenton & Vanmarcke, 1991).

4 CONCLUSIONS

Considering a stochastic approach to spatially dynamic response analysis, we have investigated the influence of the lateral heterogeneity of single soil layer on the response variability. The spatially dynamic response variability was examined by means of first-order perturbation and stochastic finite element techniques in this study. While the application treated is still simple, we hope that this study provides insight into the underlying mechanisms for further research to recognize the seismic response variabilities.

(1)   The perturbation solution of frequency-wave number power spectrum has been derived theoretically using an integral equation formulation with the Born-type approximation. The perturbation analysis presented in this study is applicable to the laterally two-dimensional stochastic problem, while the effort at present has been concentrated on the laterally one-dimensional stochastic problem.

(2)   By proposing the assumption of the spatial ergodicity, the stochastic finite element analysis has been conducted much more effectively, even though this analysis is still time consuming. Though used only for the single soil layer model, the finite element analysis is applicable for more complex heterogeneous ground model of interest.

(3)   To verify the result of the perturbation analysis, we have proposed the simple measure which is the frequency-dependent correlation distance of the ground response. By using this simple measure, this analysis has demonstrated that the perturbation analysis is practically useful for the building site which is approximated well as a single soil layer. Both analyses can be used for the inversion analysis to estimate the heterogeneity of soil properties, if the major cause of the spatial variability is considered to be local soil heterogeneities at the site of interest.

(4)   While the spatial response variability of the near-surface soil layer during earthquake has been so far inferred mainly from the observation records of closely spaced seismic arrays, this study also has demonstrated that the response variability due to the heterogeneous soil properties is significant over the first predominant frequency, especially at each predominant frequency. As a result, it is considered that the response variability of earthquake ground motion also may be manipulated considerably by the heterogeneity of the near-surface soil properties especially over the predominant frequency of the site.

ACKNOWLEDGMENT

This research was financially supported by the Grant-in-Aid for Scientific Research for Japanese Junior Scientists (No. 2827), the Ministry of Education, Science, and Culture.

REFERENCES

Anderson, J. G., Y. Lee, Y. Zeng, & S. Day 1996. Control of Strong Motion by the Upper 30 Meters. *Bull. Seism. Soc. Am.* 86: 1749-1759.

Fenton, G. A. & E. H. Vanmarcke 1991. Liquefaction Risk Assessment: 3-D Modeling. *Proc. 4th Int. Conf. Seismic Zonation, EERI* II: 669-676.

Frankel, A. & R. W. Clayton 1986. Finite Difference Simulations of Seismic Scattering: Implications for the Propagation of Short-Period Seismic Waves in the Crust and Models of Crustal Heterogeneity. *J. Geophys. Res.* 91: 6465-6489.

Gilbert, F. & G. E. Backus 1966. Propagator Matrices in Elastic Wave and Vibration Problems. *Geophysics* XXXI: 326-332.

Harada, T. & T. Fugasa 1990. Characteristics of Seismic Responses of 3-Dimensional Ground with Stochastic Soil Properties (in Japanese). *Memoirs of the Faculty of Engineering, Miyazaki University* 36: 31-39.

Harada, T. 1994. A Stochastic SH Wave Model of Earthquake Ground Motion. *J. Mech. Eng. Earthquake Eng., JSCE* I-28: 43-50.

Kataoka, N., H. Morishita & A. Mita 1990. Spatial Variation of Seismic Ground Motion at Lotung Soil-Structure Interaction Experiment Site. *Proc. 8th Japan Earthquake Eng. Symposium* 1: 607-612.

Kennett, B. L. N. 1972. Seismic Waves in Laterally Inhomogeneous Media. *Geophys. J. R. astr. Soc.* 27: 301-325.

KKEI 1988. *Super FLUSH*, Reference Manual. Kozo Keikaku Eng. Inc.: Tokyo, Japan.

Lu, L., F. Yamazaki & T. Katayama 1990. Soil Amplification Based on the Chiba Array Database. *Proc. 8th Japan Earthquake Eng. Symposium* 1: 511-516.

Nakagiri, S. & T. Hisada 1985. *Stochastic Finite Element Method, An Introduction* (in Japanese). Baifu-kan: Tokyo, Japan.

Nakamura, H. 1996. Depth-dependent Spatial Variation of Ground Motion Based on Seismic Array Records. *Proc. 11th World Conf. Earthquake Eng.*: Paper No. 731.

Sato, T. & H. Kawase 1992. Finite Element Simulation of Seismic Wave Propagation in Near-surface Random Media. *Proc. Int. Symposium Effects of Surface Geology on Seismic Motion* I: 257-262.

Schneider, J. F., J. C. Stepp & N. A. Abrahamson 1992. The Spatial Variation of Earthquake Ground Motion and Effects of Local Site Conditions. *Proc. 10th World Conf. Earthquake Eng.* 2: 967-972.

Wu, R.-S. & K. Aki 1988. Introduction: Seismic Wave Scattering in Three-dimensionally Heterogeneous Earth. *Pure Appl. Geophys.* 128: 1-6.

Structural Safety and Reliability, Shiraishi, Shinozuka & Wen (eds) © 1998 Balkema, Rotterdam, ISBN 90 5410 978 5

A proposal of probabilistic simulation by using point estimates method and its application to soil structure

Toshikazu Ikemoto
Department of Civil Engineering, Kanazawa University, Japan

Takayuki Fujino
Tokyo Metropolitan Government, Japan

ABSTRACT: The present study is to propose a new sampling technique to estimate reliability to loads of soil structure. This method is based on the efficient sampling technique using the point estimates for probability moment method proposed by Rosenblueth. The new probabilistic simulation method is applied to a finite element model of soil structure. The new proposed method was compared with the Monte Carlo simulation method. As a result, we obtained that the new method provides sufficiently accurate results, and is generally very useful, efficient and superior.

1. INTRODUCTION

In reliability analyses, the exact methods to determine probabilities become increasingly attractive. This is mainly due to the remarkable development of computational facilities. The Monte Carlo simulation method is one of the most powerful methods for calculating structural reliability. In order to obtain these results, the simulation has been frequently used. However in the simulation, the greater the number of parameters involved, the more the CPU time is needed. Therefore, the Monte Carlo method may be limited by computer capability. Recently, several efficient sampling techniques were developed to reduce the computational effort in the method, e.g. Importance sampling, Updated Latin hypercube sampling and so on[1]-[5]. These methods presented an accurate solution under short CPU time in engineering practices.

Soil parameters disperse in a great range so that they are in general treated as random variables. The coefficient of variation of soil strength influences on the estimated solutions of soil behavior. Monte Carlo simulation method predicts solutions for random problems based on more realistic analysis than the current techniques introducing the variability of soil properties.

For geotechnical problems, the stochastic finite element method for two dimensional soil behavior was suggested by Cornell[6]. In the method, the applicability of the second-moment approximation to the linear system was discussed. Applications of the stochastic finite element methods to rock and soil mechanics have been proposed by Su, et al.[7] and Cambou[8].

The present study is to propose a new sampling technique to estimate reliability of soil structures. This method is based on an efficient sampling technique by using the point estimates for the probability moment method(the point estimates method) proposed by Rosenblueth[9]. The new probabilistic simulation technique is applied to the linear problem for the finite element model of soil structures. One of the purpose is to compare the results of statistical estimations using the proposed method with the results by the Monte Carlo simulation method.

2. PROBABILISTIC APPROACH

2.1 Point estimates method

Several methods have been developed to estimate the moments of a function $y(x)$. These methods are used in the case that only the moments of $y(x)$ are needed or transformation of variables is mathematically impossible. The Monte Carlo simulation method is also involved in these approximate methods.

Although the Monte Carlo simulation technique provides a straightforward means of analyzing the complex mathematical models, it has still disadvantages such as a large number of trials required. The point estimates method, however, requires only two or three evaluations of a function for each variable considered. The method gives the accuracy comparable to a second order Taylor's series analysis, and is also applicable to non-analytical functions.

Figure 1 shows the shape of probability density and cumulative distribution functions of a soil parameter which is approximately normally distributed. A probability mass and its cumulative distribution function for three point estimates are also shown.

This method presented by Rosenblueth[9] is based on simple point evaluation of the function $y(x)$. The derivation of this method for a function of one variable $y(x)$ involves replacing a continuous density function of the independent variable $f(x)$ with a discrete mass function $p(x)$. The points x and their associated probabilities $p(x)$ are defined by matching the moments of the discrete mass function to the continuous density function $f(x)$.

2.2 Proposed sampling method

The transformation of variables for discrete distributions may be used to calculate the moments of $y(x)$. In the case of n independent variables, the general form is

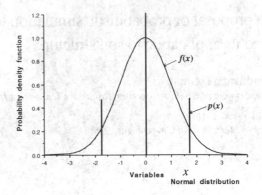

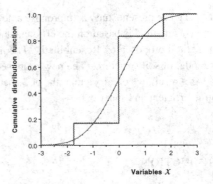

Fig.1 Probability density and cumulative distribution functions, and their corresponding three point estimations.

$$E[y^m] = \sum_{i_n}^{N} \cdots \sum_{i_2}^{N} \sum_{i_1}^{N} \underbrace{\left\{ p_{1,i_1}, p_{2,i_2}, \cdots, p_{n,i_n} \right\}}_{(a)} \times \underbrace{y^m \left(x_{1,i_1}, x_{2,i_2}, \cdots x_{n,i_n} \right)}_{(b)}$$

$$(1)$$

$x_{j,ij}$ is the ith variable evaluated at its i_jth point, i varies from 1 to the number of variables, n and i_j varies from 1 to the number of points used in the discrete approximation of x_i.

The discrete probability density is assumed to concentrate at points in the N^n hyperquadrants of the space defined by the n random variables. It is noted that the group(a) in eq.(1) is classified as the variable set when the probability is the same. The number of variable set, the probability and the weight for variable set in each group are shown in Fig.2.

The number of the variable sets as shown in Fig.(1) is smaller than the number of trials used in the simulation. We treat the variable sets as one group. We choose a random variable in a set. More generally, for the nth moment of X, the following important equation is obtained from the equation(1).

$$E[y^m] = \frac{1}{n_c}\left[\sum_{s=1}^{s}\left\{P_s \times y^m(\mathbf{v}_{s,r})\right\}\right] \quad (2)$$

v_s is variable sets which are picked up in the group randomly. n_c is the number of trials divided by the number of the variable set group.

3. APPLICATION AND RESULTS

3.1 Numerical model

The data of soil properties are estimated as the Young's modulus E, Poisson's ratio v and unit weigth γ. As for a probabilistic analysis, these variables are assumed to be normal distribution, and the other parameters are assumed to be deterministic. The coefficients of variations of soil properties are the statistical parameters, which are assumed to be 0.05, 0.1 and 0.3. The mean values of soil properties are listed in Table 1. The finite elements mesh is constructed as shown in Fig.3.

The model consists of 10 plane isoparametric elements with 18 nodes. The nodes at the lower edge of the model and at the right side are fixed. Static load acts

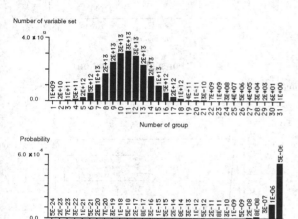

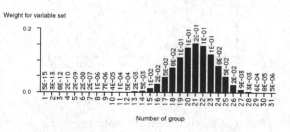

Fig.2 The number of variable set, the probability and the weight for variable set in each group.

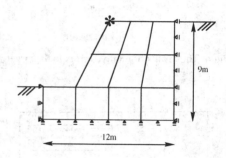

Fig.3 The finite elements mesh in the study.

Table 1 The mean values of soil properties.

Young's modulus E	55,000tf/m^2
Poisson's ratio v	0.3
Unit weight γ	2.3 tf/m^3

1 tf/m^2 = 9.8 kPa   1 tf/m^3 = 9.8 kN/m^3

on the nodes in the horizontal direction. The displacement field is defined in terms of two components u_x and u_y in this example. The field is subjected to the body forces of gravity and the external boundary force which is composed of earth pressure from the backfill soil. The result for the model with 28 elements and nodes was obtained. We do not have enough space to describe every thing about the accuracy of this method, and discuss a typical example.

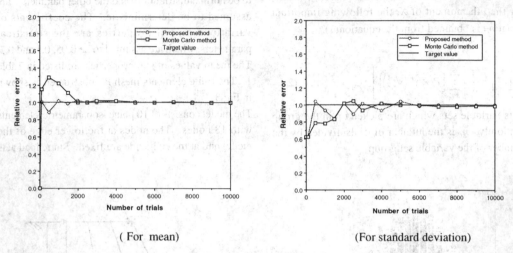

(For mean)   (For standard deviation)

Fig.4 The results of relative errors to the target value for 0.05 of the coefficient of variation of variables.

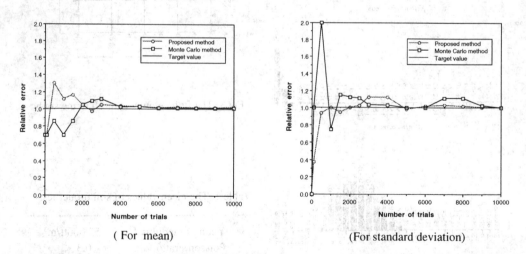

(For mean)   (For standard deviation)

Fig.5 The results of relative errors to the target value for 0.1 of the coefficient of variation of variables.

3.2 Results and discussion

The results calculated by the proposed method are compared with the results by the Monte Carlo method to discuss the accuracy of the proposed method. Calculation of the mean values of nodal displacement is the same as in the deterministic case.

The result shows the mean value and standard deviation of the nodal displacement at the * point as shown in Fig.3.

To compare the proposed method with the Monte Carlo method, the relative errors to the target value for mean and the standard deviation are plotted in Fig.4. The target values in this study are to be 1. Fig.5 is the result for 0.1 of the coefficient of variation of variables and Fig.6 for 0.3, respectively.

The results show the relative error of the ratio of the proposed method versus the 30,000-trial Monte Carlo method, and another relative error of the ratio of the Monte Carlo method versus 30,000-trial Monte Carlo method.

It can be observed from Figs.4-6 that: when the number of trials used in the simulation is larger than 2,000, the relative error by the proposed method is in good agreement with that by the Monte Carlo method. If the number of trials is smaller than 2,000 and the coefficient of variation of variables is 0.05, the results by the proposed method is also in better agreement with the target value. Fig.4 shows that the relative error of mean value calculated by the proposed method is close to the Monte Carlo method at a large number of trial. However, the two methods differ from each other in the errors of the sandard deviation, especially at high values of coefficient of variation of the random variables.

The relative errors of mean values of the displacement do not exceed the 0.6-1.4 range when the statistical parameter is assumed to be 0.05, or to be 0.1. The relative errors of mean values for most of results are smaller than those for the standard deviations.

It can be also concluded that the coefficient of variation of the displacement is larger than the

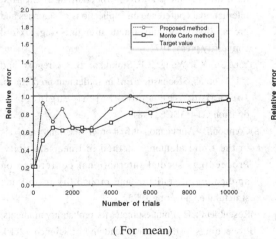

(For mean)

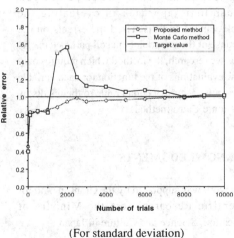

(For standard deviation)

Fig.6 The results of relative errors to the target value for 0.3 of the coefficient of variation of variables.

ordinary coefficient of variation values on soil properties in the Monte Calro method.

The caluculating time in the proposed method is remarkably shorter than that in the Monte Carlo method. These results suggest that the new method proposed here is very efficient and powerful in analyzing the displacement of the soil structure with uncertainty in soil parameters.

It seems that the relative errors become greater for the force level. This tendency is explained by the facts that softening of the soil modulus of elasticity makes the stiffness decrease, and that even small difference between the displacemnet obtained by the point estimates method and that obtained by the Monte Carlo method influences the relative error directly .

4. CONCLUSION

This study deals with the behavior of the displacement of soil structures, and points out the importance of considering the uncertainty in soil properties of the ground. We proposed a new probabilistic approach in evaluating the displacement and discussed the effects on the response of the uncertainty in soil parameters. As far as we research, the method which requires only a few evaluations of the function for each variable gives good accuracy comparable to the results by the Monte Calro method.

ACKNOWLEDGMENTS

This work was supported by the Grant-in Aid for Scientific Research from the Ministry of Education, Science and Culture in Japan.

REFERENCES

1) D. Novak and W. Kijawatworawet, A comparison of accurate advanced simulation methods and Latin hypercube sampling method with approximate curve fitting to solve reliability problems, Internal working report No.34-90, Innsbruck, pp.1-40, 1990.

2) A. Florian and D. Novak, The statistical model selection for random variables, Software for engineering workstations, pp.158-162,1988.

3) G.I. Schueller and M. Shinozuka, Stochastic methods in structural dynamics, Martinus nijhoff publishers, pp.1-80, 1987.

4) W. Shiraki and G.I. Schueller, An iterative fast Monte-Carlo procedure using conditional failure probability and its application to time-variant structural reliability analyses, Journal of structural engineering, JSCE, Vol.35A, pp.467-477,1989.

5) M. Hoshiya and Y. Kutsuna, Reliability analysis to importance sampling and Kalman filter, Journal of structural engineering, JSCE, No.437/I-17, pp.183-192,1991.

6) C.A. Cornell, First order uncertainty analysis in soils deformation and stability, Proceedings of the first international conference on applications of statistics and probability in soil and structural engineering, Oxford University press, 1971.

7) Y.L. Su, Y.J. Wang, R.F. Stefanko, B.B. Gregory and S.I. Thomas, Stochastic FEM in settlement predictions, Journal of the geotechnical engineering division,GT4,ASCE, 1981.

8) Combou,B., Application of first order uncertainty analysis in the finite elements method in linear elasticity, Proceedings second international conference on application of statistics and probability in soil and structural engineering,1975.

9) Rosenbleuth, E., Point estimates for probability moments, Proceedings of the natural academy of science 72-10, pp.3812-3814.1977.

Structural Safety and Reliability, Shiraishi, Shinozuka & Wen (eds) © 1998 Balkema, Rotterdam, ISBN 90 5410 978 5

Micromechanical analysis of randomly packed disks under cyclic shear loading

R. Ghanem
Civil Engineering Department, The Johns Hopkins University, Baltimore, Md., USA

M. El-Mestkawy
Civil Engineering Department, SUNY, Buffalo, N.Y., USA

ABSTRACT: A statistical model for soil compaction under cyclic shear strain loading is developed through a micromechanical analysis of soil fabric variation. The build up of the pore water pressure and the associated soil shear resistance reduction are examined. The sand particles are modeled as a two-dimensional random array of elastic, rough, quartz discs reconstituting the standard Ottawa sand grain size distribution. Deviations of the simulated disc arrangements from the stipulated grain size distribution are examined. Linear spring-dashpot contact between soil particles is used. The random packing of soil grain is done using the falling particle method. Desired void ratios are achieved by pre-applying monotonic compaction. The soil behavior under cyclic strain loading, at the micro-scale level, is calculated using the discrete element method. The outcome of these numerical experiments is used to define the statistical model at the macro-scale level. Control volumes of various sizes are used for that purpose, and the sensitivity of constitutive models, and statistical descriptors, to the size of the control volume is addressed.

1 INTRODUCTION

Mechanical soils behavior is very complicated and shows a great variety of behavior when subjected to different conditions. Drastic idealizations are therefore essential in order to develop simple constitutive models for practical applications. No mathematical model can completely describe the complex behavior of real soils under all conditions. Each soil model aims at a certain class of phenomena, captures its essential features, and disregards what is considered to be of minor importance in that class of applications. Thus, the soil's constitutive model meets its limits of applicability where a disregarded influence becomes important (Chen, 1990).

Since soils are multi-phase materials consisting of mineral grains, air voids and water, their mathematical models should be ideally based on a consideration of the behavior of individual constituents and their interaction. The distinct deformable solid particles interact only at contact points when loaded. Particles behave independently while interacting with each other. The Discrete Element Method (DEM) first introduced by Cundall(1971), to simulate the progressive failure of rock slopes provides a powerful tool in studying granular material. The technique was expanded further to analyze discrete numerical model for granular assemblies (Strak and Cundall, 1978; Cundall and Strak, 1979a, 1979b.1979c). The

program BALL written by Cundall(1979a) has been steadily expanding and modified to help understand the behavior of particulate soil media(Thornton, and Randall, 1988; Ng, 1989; Ting et al., 1989). Other DEM codes have been developed to fit a specific needs (e.g. Walton 1982; Kuhn1 989; Bathurst and Rothenburg 1989 ; Ng and Dobry 1991). In TRUBALL (Cundall and Strak, 1979c) the DEM model is a dynamic transient mechanical system, the transient state approaches a static equilibrium condition if loading rates are kept low enough that inertial particle forces are always a small fraction of average force acting through the assembly. Kinetic energy is dissipated through the introduction of artificial damping, without which, the approximation to a static equilibrium condition would not be achieved.

Seismically-induced soil liquefaction assessment is a complicated task. The occurrence of liquefaction at a specific site depends on many parameters some of which are a function of the soil fabric while others are function of the site profile. The many random parameters and uncertainty surrounding soil behavior and the likelihood of occurrence of soil liquefaction calls for a probabilistic approach for risk assessment.

Popescu (1995) compared the numerical simulation results (predicting excess pore-pressure build-up, liquefaction index, and liquefaction induced deformations) obtained using stochastic input constitutive parameters to deterministic input simulation results. The study concluded that for the case of dynamically induced pore water pressure build-up, the results of classical deterministic analyses are on the unconservative side.

The build up of pore water pressure and soil liquefaction was previously investigated using DEM. Ng and Dobry (1991) studied the cyclic loading of granular material for 2-D and 3-D simulations. The two dimensional model consisted of 240 circular discs of three sizes. The 2-D model was tested to study the effect of particles rotation on the analysis by comparing the results of shear tests between rotation-constrained and rotation-free particles. Two 3-D samples each consisting of 398 spheres of three different sizes were tested. The shear tests were similar to that of cyclic triaxial tests. The study concluded that damping is mostly associated with particles sliding and rearrangement. Pradhan and Sawada (1992) studied the effect of particle shape on soil liquefaction. The mechanical behavior of two disc assemblies consisting of 1000 elements is studied. One sample consisting of circular discs with mean diameters of $3mm$. The other sample consists of oval elements of flatness ratio fixed at 0.5. The two samples were subjected to approximately %6 cyclic strain amplitude. The study concluded that liquefaction potential of oval granular assemblies is higher than for rounded assemblies. Hakuno and Turami (1988) studied sand liquefaction using modified DEM that took into account pore water pressure build up through assembly void based on Darcy's law. Excess pore water pressure in the numerical results rose gradually due to the effect of shaking.

2 DISCRETE ELEMENT METHOD

The Discrete Element numerical technique has been developed specifically to model the behavior of discontinuous systems such as granular media. Each grain of material is modeled as a discrete object with geometric representation of its surface topology and description of its physical state (position, orientation, body forces, etc.). The fundamental component of DEM simulation is the contact detection which takes about 70% of the computing time. There are few different techniques for objects sorting and contact detection. O'Connor (1995) covers these techniques in details and discusses the limitations and the advantages of each one.

The DEM program developed in this study is based on a dynamic algorithm that solves the equations of motions of an assembly of disks by an explicit finite-difference scheme. Newton's second law of motion can be written for each particle as,

$$m_i \ddot{\mathbf{u}}_i + c_m m_i \dot{\mathbf{u}}_i = \mathbf{F}i + m_i \mathbf{g} \qquad (1)$$

Where $\ddot{\mathbf{u}}_i$ denotes the acceleration of the centroid of particle i, c denotes the mass proportional viscous damping constant, $\mathbf{F}_i$ is the sum of contact forces acting on the particle, m_i is the mass of the particle, and g is the gravity acceleration vector. The angular motion is governed by a similar equation,

$$I_i \ddot{\theta}_i + c_m I_i \dot{\theta}_i = \mathbf{M}_i \qquad (2)$$

where $\ddot{\theta}_i$ is the angular acceleration and $\mathbf{M}_i$ is the total moment acting on the particles. The contact forces are calculated from the current deformation of the contact springs in the local contact axis $\mathbf{n}$ and $\mathbf{S}$. The two disks are considered to be in contact only if the distance $d = |\,\boldsymbol{x}_i - \boldsymbol{x}_j|$ between their centers is less than the sum of their radii. Figure (1) shows a schematic drawing of springs and dashpots used to model soil particles. The contact forces in the normal and tangential direction are given respectively by,

$$F_n^N = \mathbf{d}_n^{N-1/2} k_n + \mathbf{D}_n$$
$$F_s^N = F_s^{N-1} + \mathbf{v}_s \Delta t k_s + \mathbf{D}_s \qquad (3)$$

where, k_n and k_s are the springs stiffnesses in the normal and tangent to contact directions, respectively, $\mathbf{d}$ is the contact spring deformation in a direction normal to the contact, calculated from the overlap of the elements, $\mathbf{D}_n$ and $\mathbf{D}_s$ are the contact stiffness damping forces evaluated as

$$\mathbf{D}_n = 2\zeta_n \mathbf{v}_n (mk_n)^{1/2};$$
$$\mathbf{D}_s = 2\zeta_s \mathbf{v}_s (mk_s)^{1/2} \qquad (4)$$

where m is the equivalent reduced mass given by,

$$m = \frac{m_i m_j}{m_i + m_j} \qquad (5)$$

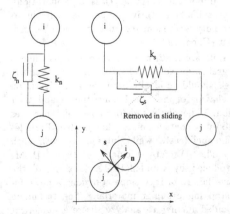

Figure 1: Contact springs and viscous dashpots between particles.

and m_i and m_j are the mass of particles i and j in contact. Global damping, proportional to the absolute velocity of particles, was added to the dynamics of the particles assembly during the compaction stage in order to enhance the numerical stability of the algorithms. Global damping is given by the equation,

$$\mathbf{D}^m = c_m \, m_i \, \dot{\mathbf{x}} \qquad (6)$$

A centered finite-difference procedure is used to integrate the equations of motion. The integration of the particle accelerations provides the new disk position and, therefore, the contact points displacement and velocities. The contact force-displacement law is then used to obtain the new contact forces.

The time-step Δt should be small enough so that within such a time step, the disturbances cannot propagate from any disk further than its immediate neighbors. The particles accelerations and velocities calculated from Newton's Second Law are assumed to be constant over each time step Δt and the resultant forces and moments acting on each particle are updated based on force-displacement laws applied at the contacts with neighboring particle.

Random Packing of Spheres

The random packing algorithm or procedure plays an important role in the study of particulate media. The randomness of the soil fabric comes from two sources: the size of the particle and the particle spatial location. Many studies have concluded that different procedures for packing granular particles give different cavity shapes and different behavior. In this study, the variation of the soil fabric in response to different compaction methods is investigated along with the corresponding effect on the behavior of the material. The creation of the random array of particles is an extension of the model proposed by Hakuno (1973). Hakuno used Mont-Carlo simulation analysis to create two dimensional packing of sand particles. The grain size distribution was one of three predefined curves.

In this work for any given grain size distribution curve a random array of disks or sphere is generated to reconstitute the soil particle size distribution. Different grain size distributions were tried as targets and recovered.

To simulate the random array of particles as a homogeneous medium, the sample dimension D should be big enough to have several load paths in each directions and to minimize the effect of the boundary conditions. A sample dimension

$$D > c \, d_{max} \qquad (7)$$

where D is the least dimension of a sample, d_{max} is the maximum particle diameter, and c is a constant value in the range 10 to 20, depending on particle

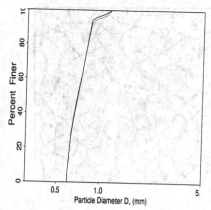

Figure 2: Samples grain size distribution
a)Sample A of 2000 particles
b)Sample B of 2003 particles

shape. These value of c have been found to allow for the modeling of particulate medium as a quantum. representation of the particulate medium.

Sand particles diameters lie in the range of 0.062 to 2.0 mm. A soil sample of a dimension 2.0 centimeter square is therefore enough to reduce the effect of the boundary condition on the soil behavior. In this study, the sample dimensions range from 1 cm for the 200 particle sample and 4.4 cm for the 2000 particles of uniform radii of 1 mm. Knowing the target void ratio and the specific gravity of the solids, the sample dimensions could be calculated.

Undrained Loading Conditions

The undrained loading condition is simulated by keeping the sample volume constant while applying simple shear strain loading. The stress tensor is calculated during the numerical experiment using a micromechanical average over the sample. The effective hydrostatic pressure is calculated as

$$p_o = \frac{\sigma_x + \sigma_y}{2} \qquad (8)$$

The shear stress is defined as τ_{xy} or as the deviatoric stress q calculated from

$$q = \sqrt{\left(\frac{\sigma_x - \sigma_y}{2}\right)^2 + (\tau_{xy})^2} \qquad (9)$$

The reduction which would be carried by the water in an actual physical model is calculated here by subtracting the current hydrostatic pressure from the initial one according to,

$$u_{(t=t_1)} = p_{o_{(t=0)}} - p_{o_{(t=t_1)}} \qquad (10)$$

Where $u_{(t=t1)}$ is the pore water pressure at time t_1,

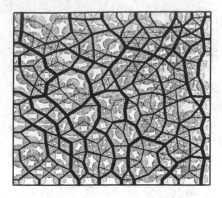

a)

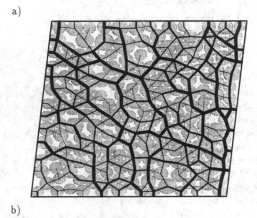

b)

Figure 3: Normal contact forces of a 200 particles sample subjected to monotonic shear strain, (a) Before Shearing, (b) After 10% Shear strain

$p_{o(t=0)}$ is the initial hydrostatic pressure, and $p_{o(t=t1)}$ is the hydrostatic pressure at time t_1.

3 NUMERICAL SIMULATION

To study the cyclic shear loading, three samples consisting each of about 2000 circular discs are used in this study. The first two samples A and B have a grain size distribution similar to that of regular Ottawa sand. Sample C has a uniform size. A random array of particle sizes is created using Monte Carlo method, then particles are randomly located in a box without touching each other. The assembly is compacted by three different methods. The first method consists of numerically arranging the particles by moving the lowest particle downward until it reaches a stable position. The stable position is defined as having two contacts or resting on the bottom of the box. The second method of compaction is achieved by moving

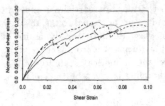

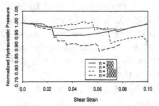

Figure 4: Effect of sample size on monotonic shear test results

the upped and lower walls until the assembly reaches the target void ratio. The third method consists of simply letting all the particles move under their own weight until they reach a static equilibrium which is defined by zero inertial forces. Samples compacted using the first and the third methods need further consolidation to reach the target void ratio. This is achieved by moving the upper wall. Figure (2) shows the grain size distribution of 2 samples, A and B, that have been compacted according to the first compaction method described above.

To study the effect of sample size on the analysis, four samples of different sizes were generated. The grain size distribution is similar to that of regular Ottawa sand. For monotonic shear loading, all samples were compacted to a void ratio $e = 0.22$.

The contact stiffness k_n is assumed constant with a value equal to $1.45 \ 10^3 \ N/mm$. The particles mass density is equal to $2.65 \ 10^{-3} \ kg/mm^3$, and the friction coefficient $\mu_s = \tan \phi_u = 0.5$

Before applying the shear loading, the samples are left until they have reached static equilibrium, which is attained when the inertial forces become zero. Following that, a sinusoidal strain load of amplitude 0.4% is applied. The strain is applied as a rotation of the rigid boundaries walls as shown in Figure (3). All experiments are strain controlled. During the experiment the stress tensor, coordination number and void ratio are calculated. Figure (3) presents the load paths before and after applying 10% monotonic shear strain on a 200 particle sample. The thicker lines indicate higher contact forces being transmitted.

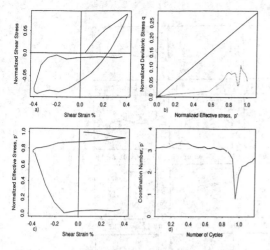

Figure 5: Cyclic strain controlled simple shear test, sample C compacted by moving boundaries.

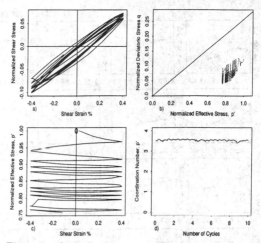

Figure 7: Cyclic strain controlled simple shear test, sample C compacted numerically

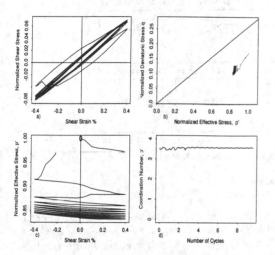

Figure 6: Cyclic strain controlled simple shear test, sample C compacted by free falling of particles

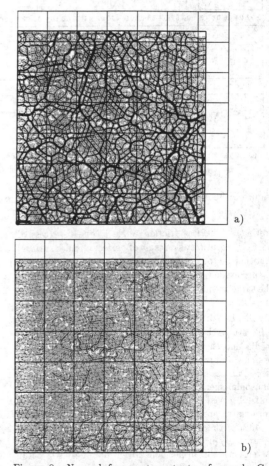

Figure 8: Normal forces at contacts of sample C, compacted by moving boundaries, (a)Initial condition, (b)After liquefaction.

4   RESULTS

Effect of sample size of particles

A monotonic shear test was performed on samples with different sizes. All samples were generated using the same procedures and parameters using numerical packing and compacting to 0.22% void ratio. The results are shown in Figure (4). From the monotonic results the sample friction angle $\phi = 14.5$ which compares well with the results of Ng and Dobry (1994) performed by applying axial strain (similar to triaxial

Hydrostatic Pressure

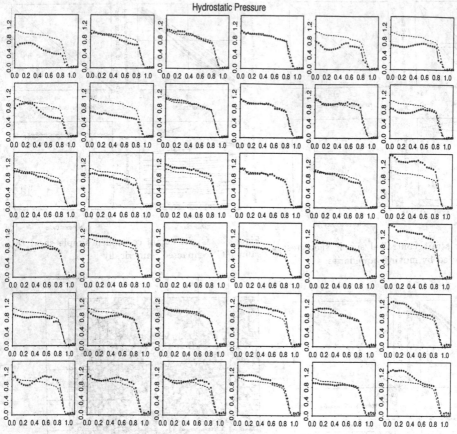

Regular Size Packing of 2000 Discs, Packed by Moving Boundaries, e = 0.24, Strain Amplitude = 0.4%

Figure 9: Spatial variation of the effective hydrostatic pressure

testing). The low friction angle is due to excessive particles rotation as a result of perfect circular surface. Another factor is that an angular sand has a higher ϕ than rounded sand. It is reasonable to assume that the same trends should be observed in rounded sand.

Cyclic Loading

To study the undrained shear behavior of granular media and the associated build up of the pore water pressure in granular soil under cyclic undrained shear stress, all samples are subjected to 10 cycles of 0.4% sinusoidal shear strain. The pore water pressure build up is observed in all samples. The typical value of the pore water pressure after ten cycles ranges from 15% to 40% of the initial hydrostatic stress. Liquefaction occurs only in one of th C samples which is packed by moving the upper and lower boundaries. Total loss of confining effective stress happens within the first cycle as shown in Figure (5). Figure (5.a)presents

the shear stress τ_{xy} versus shear strain. Figure (5.b) shows the state of stress in $p - q$ space and shows that failure happen at the origin of the failure envelope. The hydrostatic pressure versus shear strain is drawn in Figure(5.c). The coordination number variation is small for all experiment except the case that has reached liquefaction, see Figure (5.d). The increase of the coordination number after failure is due to the new contacts formed under the gravity forces.

Different behavior is observed for the other simulations which compare well with experimental results. Sample C which is compacted by free falling as defined above experiences about 15% reduction in the effective stress as shown in Figures (6). Figure (7) shows the same results for sample C which has been compacted according to the first method described above. The effective shear stress loss is about 25%. Samples A and B featuring Ottaw regular sand show similar response for their respective compaction procedures.

To study the spatial variation of the parameters within a sample, the sample is divided into sub-domains and the stress tensor of each sub-domain is plotted and compared to the average sample response. Figure (8.a) presents the initial load paths before cycling. The final load paths after the shear resistance loss is shown in Figure (8.b)

The spatial variation of the effective hydrostatic pressure is drawn for each sub-domain and compared to the average values plotted as dotted lines in Figure (9). The arrangement of the sub-domain in this figure reflects the spatial location in the overall sample.

5 CONCLUSION

The discrete element method (DEM) is applied to two-dimensional assemblies of granular particles. The paper investigates specifically the effect of fabric variability characterized by a grain size distribution function and compaction procedure as well as the effect of the number of particles used in the simulations. The study shows that granular materials having the same grain size distribution and void ratio could show different response. The random nature of the response requires further study to characterize the spatial variation of the soil fabric.

REFERENCES

Bathurst, R., and L., Rothenburg 1989. "Investigation of Micromechanical features of idealized granular assemblies Using DEM," Proc. 1st. U.S. Conf. on Discrete Element Methods, Golden, Colorado.

Chen, W.F., and Mizuno E. 1990. "Nonlinear Analysis in Soil Mechanics," Elsevier, Amsterdam, The Netherlands, 661pp.

Cundall, P.A. 1971. " A Computer model simulating progressive large-scale movements in bulky rock systems," Symposium Soc. Internat. Mechanique de Roches, Nancy, II-8

Cundall, P.A. 1978) " BALL - A computer program to model granular media using the Distinct Element Method," Technical Note TH-LN-13, Advance Technology Group, Dams and Moore, London, 74 pp.

Cundall, P.A., and O.D.L. Strack 1979a. " The Discrete Element Method as a tool for research in granular media, Part II," Report to National science Foundation, Department of Civil and

Mineral Engineering, University of Minnesota, Minneapolis, Minnesota, 204 pp.

Cundall, P.A., and O.D.L. Strack 1979b. " A Discrete Numerical model for granular assemblies," Geotechnique 29, 1, 47-65

Cundall, P.A., and O.D.L Strak 1979c. " The development of constitutive laws for soil using Discrete Element Method," Proceedings of Third International Conference, Numerical Methods in Geomechanics, Aachen, W.Witke(ed.) , 1, 289-298

Hakuno, M., and T. Hirao(1973). " Monte Carlo simulation analysis of two dimensional random packing of sand particle," Transaction of Japanese Society of Civil Engineers, 5, 160-151

Hakuno, M., and Tarumi, Y. 1988 . " A Granular assembly simulation for the seismic liquefaction of sand," Structural Eng. Earthquake Eng., 5, 2, 333s-342s.

Kuhn, M. 1989. " A relaxation algorithm for use with discrete elements," Proc. 1st. U.S. Conf. on Discrete Element Methods, Golden, Colorado.

Ng, T.-T. 1989. "Numerical Simulation of Granular Soils under Monotonic and Cyclic Loading: a Particulate mechanics approach," PhD Thesis, Rensselaer Polytechnic Institute, Troy, N.Y.

Ng, T.-T., and Dobry R. 1991. " CONBAL-Simulated granular material using quartz spheres with the Discrete Element Method," Rensselaer Polytechnic Institute, Troy, N.Y.

Ng, T-T, and R. Dobry 1994. "Numerical simulation of monotonic and cyclic loading of granular soils," Journal of Geotechnical Engineering, ASCE, 120, 2,388-403

O'Conner, R.(1995)." A Distributed Discrete Element Modeling Environment-Algorithms, Implementation and Applications,"Ph.D. Dissertation, Massachusetts Institute of Technology.

Papescu, R. 1995. "Stochastic variability of soil properties: Data analysis, digital Simulation, effect of System Behavior," Ph.D. Dissertation, Princeton University.

Pradhan, B.S.T., and Sawada, S. 1992. "Distinct Element analysis of sand under cyclic loading using oval elements," Earthquake Engineering Tenth World Conference, Balkema, Rotterd, 1163-1168.

Strak, O., and Cundall, P. 1978. " The Discrete Element Method as a tool for research in granular media," Part I," Report to National Science Foundation, Department of Civil Engineering, University of Minnesota, Minneapolis, Minnesota, 97pp.

Thornton, C., and Randall, C.W. 1988."Applications of theoretical contact mechanics to solid particle system simulation." Mechanics of Granular Materials, Satake and Jenkins, Elsevier Science Publishing, Amsterdam, Netherlands, 133-142

Ting, J.M., B.T. Corkum, C.R. Kauffman, and C. Greeco 1989."Discrete numerical model for soil mechanics." Journal of Geotechnical Engineering, ASCE3,379-398.

Walton, O.R. 1982."Explicit particle dynamics model for granular materials," 4Th International Conference on Numerical Methods in Geotechnics, 1261-1268.

Structural Safety and Reliability, Shiraishi, Shinozuka & Wen (eds) © 1998 Balkema, Rotterdam, ISBN 90 5410 978 5

Estimation of spatial distribution of soil properties using kriging with linear regression

W. Shiraki
Tottori University, Japan

M. Tsunekuni & M. Matsushima
Tokyo Electric Power Services Co., Japan

N. Yasuda
Tokyo Electric Power Co., Japan

ABSTRACT: In design and construction of foundation structures, strength parameters such as cohesion and internal friction angle are needed, however, may not have been sampled efficiently. This paper presents a method to improve the precision of the estimation using kriging combined with linear regression between better-sampled parameter, i.e. N-value, and less-sampled parameter, i.e. cohesion or internal friction angle. In numerical examples, the uplift capacity of a transmission tower foundation is evaluated using cohesion and internal friction angle estimated by the proposed method. Finally, the availability of the method is discussed.

1. INTRODUCTION

In design and construction of foundation structures, it is very important to get sufficient samples of soil properties such as N-value, internal friction angle, cohesion and so on. N-value is generally easy to obtain and is better-sampled datum, but internal friction angle and cohesion sometimes may not be sampled efficiently because of difficulty of the laboratory test, that is less-sampled.

Recently, some works have been treated problems of estimation by kriging technique for supporting the shortage of data. Assuming samples obtained from the survey in situ as realizations of random fields, kriging technique is utilized to estimate soil properties at the point where data are not available.

This paper presents a procedure to improve the precision of the estimation using kriging combined with linear regression between better-sampled variable, i.e. N-value, and less-sampled variable, i.e. cohesion C or internal friction angle ϕ. The modeling of the spatial distribution of N-value based on its sample data in situ is developed. Then, assuming the relationship between N-value and C or N-value and ϕ, the spatial distribution of ϕ and C are estimated using kriging technique on the basis of spatial distribution of N-value.

In numerical examples, the uplift capacity of transmission tower foundation is obtained form the estimation results. Then the availability of the estimation method using the linear relationship between correlated soil properties based on kriging technique is discussed in this paper.

2. ESTIMATION OF SPATIAL DISTRIBUTION OF SOIL PROPERTIES WITH CORRELATION

Considering correlation between N-values which we can easily obtain in situ and cohesion or internal friction angle, the spatial distribution of cohesion and internal friction angle are estimated from the spatial distribution of N-values using the estimation method of spatial correlation between two soil properties with correlation based on kriging theory in this chapter. Since the same method is used in the estimation of spatial distribution of cohesion and friction angle, in case of cohesion is only introduced bellows.

Relationship between N-values and cohesion in a layer assumes to be described as following linear equation.

$$C^{*}(z) = a \cdot N^{*}(z) + b \qquad (1)$$

Eq.(1) is rewritten as Eq.(2) by assuming that the linear equation between N-values and cohesion contains random errors ε with mean value zero.

$$C^{*}(z) = a \cdot N^{*}(z) + b + \varepsilon \qquad (2)$$

where, a, b are coefficients obtained from the linear regression analysis.

Random error ε indicates variable parameter with expected value zero. Random field $N^*(z)$ and $C^*(z)$ are independent respectively. $N^*(z)$ and $C^*(z)$ are assumed to be described as Eqs.(3) and (4) by assuming homogeneous lognormal random fields.

$$N^*(z) = \ln N(z) \tag{3}$$

$$C^*(z) = \ln C(z) \tag{4}$$

where, $N(z)$, $C(z)$ mean lognormal random fields. Expected value and variance of lognormal random field $C(z)$ are described as follows:

$$m_c(z) = E[C(z)] = E\left[\exp\{C^*(z)\}\right]$$

$$= \exp\left\{m_c^*(z) + \frac{1}{2}\sigma_c^{*2}(z)\right\} \tag{5}$$

$$\sigma_c^2(z) = m_c^2(z)\left[\exp\{\sigma_c^{*2}(z) - 1\}\right] \tag{6}$$

where, $m_c^*(z)$ and $\sigma_c^{*2}(z)$ indicate expected value and variance respectively.

$N^*(z)$ is obtained as following equation to describe by the spatial distribution of Type III (White, W. 1993.) as shown in Fig.1.

$$N^*(z) = m_N^*(z) + m_N^*(z) \cdot \xi_N^*(z) \tag{7}$$

where, $m_N^*(z)$ and $\xi_N^*(z)$ indicate the trend component and the random component of $N^*(z)$, respectively.

Assuming the relationship between Eqs.(1) and (2) at every points in the same layer, random field of cohesion is obtained as Eq.(8).

$$C^*(z) = a\left\{m_N^*(z) + m_N^*(z) \cdot \xi_N^*(z)\right\} + b$$

$$= \left\{a \cdot m_N^*(z) + b\right\} + a \cdot m_N^*(z) \cdot \xi_N^*(z)$$

$$= m_c^*(z) + m_c^*(z) \cdot \xi_c^*(z) \tag{8}$$

In case of considering random error, Eq.(8) is rewritten as Eq.(9).

$$C^*(z) = a\left\{m_N^*(z) + m_N^*(z) \cdot \xi_N^*(z)\right\} + b + \varepsilon$$

$$= \left\{a \cdot m_N^*(z) + b\right\} + a \cdot m_N^*(z) \cdot \xi_N^*(z) + \varepsilon$$

$$= m_c^*(z) + m_c^*(z) \cdot \xi_c^*(z) \tag{9}$$

The trend component $m_c^*(z)$ of $C^*(z)$, the random component $\xi_c^*(z)$, covariance function $\text{Cov.}\left\{\xi_c^*(z_1), \xi_c^*(z_2)\right\}$ and covariance function $\text{Cov.}\left\{\xi_N^*(z_1), \xi_c^*(z_2)\right\}$ are described Eqs.(10) $\sim$ (13) as the trend component $m_N^*(z)$ of N-value, the random component $\xi_N^*(z)$ and auto-covariance $\text{Cov.}\left\{\xi_N^*(z_1), \xi_N^*(z_2)\right\}$ are obtained from boring survey at a construction site.

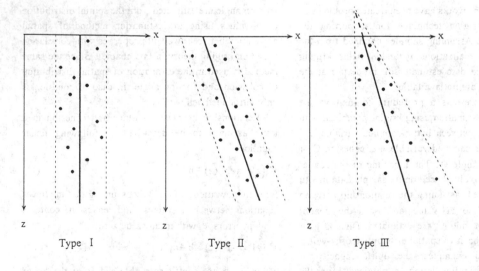

Type I   Type II   Type III

Fig.1 Random field models of soil properties

$$m_C^*(z) = a m_N^*(z) + b \tag{10}$$

$$\xi_C^*(z) = \frac{a m_N^*(z)}{a m_N^*(z) + b} \xi_N^*(z) \tag{11.a}$$

$$\xi_C^*(z) = \frac{a m_N^*(z)\xi_N^*(z) + \varepsilon}{a m_N^*(z) + b} \tag{11.b}$$

$$\mathrm{Cov}\{\xi_C^*(z_1), \xi_C^*(z_2)\} = K_1 K_2 \mathrm{Cov}\{\xi_N^*(z_1), \xi_N^*(z_2)\} \tag{12.a}$$

$$\mathrm{Cov}\{\xi_C^*(z_1), \xi_C^*(z_2)\} = K_1 K_2 \mathrm{Cov}\{\xi_N^*(z_1), \xi_N^*(z_2)\}$$
$$+ \left\{\frac{1}{a m_N^*(z_1) + b}\right\}\left\{\frac{1}{a m_N^*(z_2) + b}\right\} \mathrm{Var}(\varepsilon) \tag{12.b}$$

$$\mathrm{Cov}\{\xi_N^*(z_1), \xi_C^*(z_2)\} = K_2 \mathrm{Cov}\{\xi_N^*(z_1), \xi_N^*(z_2)\} \tag{13}$$

where,

$$K_1 = \frac{a m_N^*(z_1)}{a m_N^*(z_1) + b}, K_2 = \frac{a m_N^*(z_2)}{a m_N^*(z_2) + b}$$

The estimation of random components $\xi_C^*(x_r)$ at any points x_r can be expressed by a linear combination as follows:

$$\hat{\xi}_B(x_r) = \sum_{i=1}^{N} \lambda_i(x_r)\xi_A(x_i) + \sum_{i=N+1}^{N+M} \lambda_i(x_r)\xi_B(x_i) \tag{14}$$

where, λ_i are weight coefficients, N is the number of points where N-values are sampled and M is the number of points where C are sampled. Using the statistical properties of C given by Eqs.(10)~(13), N+M weights are calculated to ensure the conditions that are the unbiased estimation and the minimal variance of the estimation error(Shiraki,W., et.al. 1997). Assuming the spatial distribution of the logarithm of cohesion is same as N-value, i.e., Type III as shown in Fig.1, estimation value $\hat{C}^*(z_r)$ of the logarithm $C^*(z_r)$ of cohesion can be obtained. Furthermore, the estimation value $\hat{C}(z_r)$ of the logarithm $C^*(z_r)$ of cohesion is obtained using Eq.(11). Error covariance in $\hat{C}(z_r)$ is given as Eq.(15).

$$\sigma_{EC}(z_r) = E\left[\{C(z_r) - \hat{C}(z_r)\}^2\right]$$

$$= \sigma_C^2(z_r) + \{m_C(z_r) - \hat{C}(z_r)\}^2$$

$$= m_C^2(z_r)\{\exp(\sigma_C^{*2}) - 1\} \tag{15}$$

In this chapter, the method to estimate cohesion C(z) using kriging technique is presented using linear relationship between the logarithm $N^*(z)$ of N-values and the logarithm $C^*(z_r)$ of cohesion. And estimation of internal friction angle can be also carried out in same manner.

3. ESTIMATION OF UPLIFT CAPACITY OF TRANSMISSION TOWER FOUNDATION

The uplift capacity R_V of transmission tower foundation as shown in Fig.2 is obtained by Eq.(16) using the shear resistance method (TEPCO, 1988).

$$R_V = W_c + W_S + T \tag{16}$$

where,
  W_C: Weight of pile (tf) (=256.5 tf)
  W_S: Weight of filling soil (tf) (=19.2 tf)
  T: Shear resistance between pile and soil (tf).

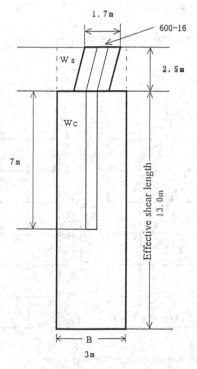

Fig.2 Outline of analytical model

Shear resistance T is given as Eq.(17).

$$T = \sum_{i=1}^{n} \ell_i \pi B \left(C_i + K_0 \sigma_i \tan \phi_i \right) \qquad (17)$$

where,

C_i: cohesion in i-th layer (tf/m^2)

ϕ_i: Internal friction angle in i-th layer ($°$)

σ_i: overburden pressure at center of i-th layer measured from design ground level

K_0: Coefficient of earth pressure at rest

B : Width of pile

l_i: thickness of i-th layer

n : number of layer

Eq.(17) is rewritten as Eq.(18) in order to estimate cohesion and internal friction angle predicted by kriging technique mentioned above.

$$\overline{R}_V = W_c + W_s + \overline{T} \qquad (18)$$

where,

$\overline{R}_V$:estimation value of uplift capacity.

$\overline{T}$ is the estimation value of shear resistance and described as:

$$\overline{T} = \sum_{i=1}^{n} \ell_i \pi B \left(\overline{C}_i + K_0 \sigma_i \tan \overline{\phi}_i \right) \qquad (19)$$

The spatial distribution of cohesion and internal friction

angle are estimated from one of N-values. Finally, the uplift capacity of transmission tower foundation can be evaluated by Eq.(17) and Eq.(18) using the estimation values.

4. NUMERICAL EXAMPLE

In order to evaluate availability of the method to predict the uplift capacity of transmission tower foundation as shown in Chapter 3, cohesion and internal friction angle is estimated using N-values obtained from actual survey data at site A. Using estimated cohesion and internal friction angle, the uplift capacity of transmission tower foundation is obtained in this paper.

(1) Estimation of cohesion and internal friction angle

The modeling of the spatial distribution of N-value at a leg of the transmission tower considered is shown in Fig.3 as an example. On the assumption that the random component at each leg is the ergodic random field with mean value zero, the statistical characteristic of the random component ξ_{lnN} at the construction site of the tower is calculated using all of random component at four legs in this paper. In the calculation of the auto-correlation coefficient, the difference in elevation at each leg is considered. The modeling characteristics of the spatial distribution of N-value at the tower considered is listed on Table 1.

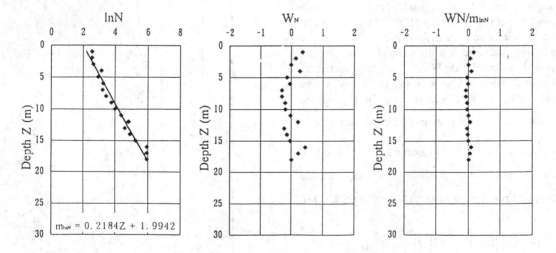

Fig.3 Modeling of spatial distribution of N-value

Table 1 Characteristics of spatial distribution of N-value

	Trend	Mean	Variance	Auto-correlation function
Leg-A	$m_{lnN}=0.2184z+1.994$			
Leg-B	$m_{lnN}=0.2112z+2.232$	0	0.0971	$\rho(\Delta z)=\exp\left(-\dfrac{z}{1.57}\right)$
Leg-C	$m_{lnN}=0.1905z+1.888$			
Leg-D	$m_{lnN}=0.1556z+2.431$			

Linear relationship between N-value and cohesion or N-value and internal friction angle using survey data sampled concentrately is obtained as Eqs.(20) and (21).

$$\ln C = 0.3296 \ln N - 1.6359 \qquad (20)$$

Correlation coefficient 0.55   Standard Deviation 0.61

$$\ln \phi = 5.4992 \ln N + 6.9778 \qquad (21)$$

Correlation coefficient 0.70   Standard Deviation 7.22

Correlation coefficient between ln C and ln N indicates 0.55 and varies in wide. Therefor, the linear relationship between both seems to be weak. Contrary to above results, Correlation coefficient between ln ϕ and ln N indicates 0.70 and the relationship seems to be strong.

Profile of cohesion is obtained using Eq.(11.b) as shown in Fig.4. Fig.4 shows estimation value (solid line) and estimation error (broken line). In addition, six sampling data of cohesion also indicates in the figure for comparison. Random error is contained in linear equation between N-value and cohesion in calculation. Normal distribution is assumed for random error ε with a mean of zero and standard deviation as shown in Eq.(19). In the case of estimating cohesion at the depth obtaining N-value, estimation error by kriging does not occur but error related to ε in Eq.(2) occurs. Estimation error increases with depth. Cohesion estimated using only N-values approximately agree with sampling data of one.

This results is obtained in case that correlation coefficient between ln C and ln N indicates 0.55, in other words, deviation error is large. Accuracy of the estimation more increases if correlation coefficient increases or approximately equal to 1.0. Estimation of cohesion only for soil profile of one leg is introduced above. Cohesion and internal friction angle in one meter interval at depth direction against all legs at site A are obtained in actual computation. Then, correlation coefficient of internal friction angle indicates 0.8 and estimation error is smaller than one of cohesion.

(2) Estimation of uplift capacity

The uplift capacity of transmission tower foundation as shown in chapter 3 is estimated using cohesion and internal friction angle in one meter interval along depth direction. Assuming estimation value of cohesion and internal friction angle obtained by kriging technique as mean value, the variable of normal distribution of C and ϕ are modeled by presuming error variance as variance. For sakes of simplicity in computation, C and ϕ assumes to be independence respectively. C and ϕ are generalized by a Monte Carlo simulation and the uplift capacity is obtained using

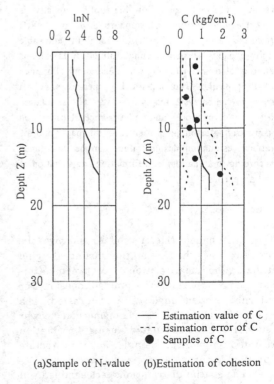

—— Estimation value of C
--- Esimation error of C
● Samples of C

(a)Sample of N-value   (b)Estimation of cohesion

Fig.4 Results of estimation of cohesion

Table 2 Results of calculation of uplift capacity of transmission tower foundation

	Estimated Values	Monte Calro Simulation		Comparison With Design Value
		Mena	Standard deviation	
Leg-A	2508.3	2600.7	339.9	2308.7
Leg-B	2643.8	2740.9	354.0	2308.0
Leg-C	2369.8	2454.3	308.2	2160.5
Leg-D	2178.3	2254.6	283.5	1990.3

(unit : tf)

Eqs.(18) and (19). Random numbers are 10000 for simulation. Estimation capacity obtained by substituting estimation values of C and ϕ into Eqs.(18) and (19) and the statistical properties of capacity obtained using a Monte Calro simulation are listed on Table 2.

Design capacity in the table indicates the uplift capacity calculated using estimation of C and ϕ from N-value in design code on transmission tower foundation. Allowable uplift capacity divided by safety factor 3 is adopted in design. Allowable uplift capacity for legs shown in Tab.3 indicates 770(tf). According to results of simulation, allowable uplift capacity is distance more 5 times of standard deviation 340(tf) from the mean value 2600(tf). Although the allowable uplift capacity seems to be underestimated, its value is appropriated in considering with uncertainty of applied load in design. The statistical properties of uplift capacity can be evaluated by a Monte Calro simulation based on estimation value and variance of estimation using kriging technique presented in this paper and the rational estimation design values can be determined according to a quantity of information and variation of soil properties.

5. Conclusion

In this paper, the method to improve the precision of the estimation using kriging utilizing the linear relationship between better-sampled N-value and less-sampled cohesion C or internal friction angle ϕ is suggested. The uplift capacity of a transmission tower foundation is calculated using estimation results in numerical example. The main results obtained in this paper are as follows:

(1) The spatial distributions less-sampled soil properties such as ϕ and C were estimated with acceptable precision by the use of the spatial distribution of better-sampled N-value and the linear regression of N-value and C or N-value and ϕ.

(2) The precision of estimation become higher depending on the number of data and height of correlation between N-value and ϕ or N-value and C.

(3) The uplift capacities of a transmission tower foundation were estimated using the estimations of ϕ and C with acceptable precision. And it is clarified that the proposed method can be applied to the rational design according to a quantity of information for design parameters or uncertainty in the parameters.

REFERENCES

Shiraki,W., Tsunekuni,M., Matsushima,M., & Yasuda,N. Estimation of bearing capacity of foundation of transmission tower using kriging with linear regression. Proc. of JSCE (in Japanese). (printing).

White,W. 1993. Soil variability: characterisation and modeling. Probabilistic Methods in Geotechnical Engineering, Li & Lo (des): 111-120. Balkema, Rotterdam.

Tokyo Electric Power Co.. 1988. Design Code of UHV transmission tower foundation (draft) (in Japanese).

Structural Safety and Reliability, Shiraishi, Shinozuka & Wen (eds) © 1998 Balkema, Rotterdam, ISBN 90 5410 978 5

Probability of liquefaction and reliability design for ground improvement

S. Nishimura, H. Fujii & K. Shimada
Okayama University, Japan

H. Shimizu
Gifu University, Japan

ABSTRACT: The calculation method of the probability of liquefaction is clarified in this paper. The spatial variability of soil parameters for the dynamic shear strength and the statistical characteristics of the earthquake occurrence are considered in the analysis. Secondly, the reliability design of the sand compaction piles for the ground improvement is discussed.

1 INTRODUCTION

In this research, the calculation method for the probability of liquefaction in a sandy ground and the reliability design method for liquefaction are discussed.

As previous work on this topic, Halder and Tang (1979), Fadris and Veneziano (1981) and Liao, et al. (1988) conducted the statistical analysis of liquefaction considering the variability of soil parameters and uncertainty of the evaluation equations for liquefaction. More references, Shimizu, et al. (1994) carried out the liquefaction analysis based on the statistical model of the historical earthquake occurrences.

The main purpose of our study is further development of the evaluation method of probability of liquefaction, considering the spatial variability of soil parameters and the statistical characteristics of earthquake occurrences based on the historical data recorded after the year 1600. Furthermore, the method is extended to the reliability design method for ground improvement. As a basic evaluation method of liquefaction, the safety factor of liquefaction and liquefaction index method (Iwasaki, et al. 1980, 1982) are applied.

Usually, the dynamic shear strength R is simply determined by the empirical equation based on the effective vertical stress $\sigma_v{}'$, the SPT blow count N, the median grain size D_{50}, and the fines content F_c. The last three parameters generally have great spatial variability, and appropriate statistical models of these parameters are required for the liquefaction analysis. The models are determined by minimizing AIC (Akaike's Information Criterion).

The dynamic shear strength used in this study is determined from the relationship between the empirical equation and the result of cyclic undrained triaxial tests. The error of this relationship is also taken into consideration.

The dynamic load L caused on earthquake is determined based on 1) the deterministic design maximum acceleration, or 2) the statistical model of earthquake occurrences. In the case 2), the statistical model of earthquake occurrences is decided from the maximum annual acceleration of the historical earthquakes data records. The annual maximum acceleration is drawn via the attenuation equation and the error of the attenuation equation is also considered in the analysis. This study is based on the case 2) model.

When the earthquake risk predicted from the historical earthquake is low, however, the probability of liquefaction is possibly underestimated, because the period of earthquake data record is very short for the great earthquakes. For important structures, case 1) analysis should be carried out for this reason. For case 1), the great value of the deterministic acceleration having low possibility of occurrence is used.

The Monte Carlo method is applied for all probabilistic parameters and probability of liquefaction in a sandy ground is evaluated. Finally, the optimum ground improvement is discussed based on minimization of the total cost. Particularly here, the sand compaction pile (SCP) method is picked up as a ground improvement method. The relationship between the optimum sand replacement ration and the importance index of the structures is clarified

2 PROBABILITY OF LIQUEFACTION

The safety factor of liquefaction is defined as follows.

$$F_L = \frac{R}{L} \tag{1}$$

in which R is the dynamic shear strength and L is the dynamic load.

Iwasaki et al.(1980, 1982) defined the liquefaction index P_L and proved this index explains the actual liquefaction phenomena well.

$$P_L = \int_0^{20} F \cdot w(z)dz \tag{2}$$

$$\begin{cases} F = 1 - F_L & (F_L < 1.0) \\ F = 0 & (F_L \geq 1.0) \end{cases}$$

$$w(Z) = 10 - 0.5Z$$

Z: Depth(m)

According to Iwasaki's investigation, the probability of liquefaction increases when P_L exceeds 5.0.

In this research, the probability of liquefaction is evaluated by

$$P_f = P\left(P_L \geq 5\right) \tag{3}$$

in which $P(\ )$ denotes the probability.

In this study, one-dimensional liquefaction analysis is conducted and the spatial variability of soil parameters is modeled one-dimensionally in the vertical direction to simplify the problem. Usually, the ground has relatively great correlation horizontally compared with vertically, therefore, the one-dimensional analysis is still meaningful as a simple approximation method.

3 DYNAMIC SHEAR STRENGTH

The next equation is proposed for R in Eq.(1)

$$R = a \cdot R_l + b + \varepsilon_R \tag{4}$$

where R_l is the dynamic shear strength based on the empirical equation. The parameters a and b denote the coefficients of conversion of dynamic shear strength from the empirical equation to the cyclic triaxial test results. ε_R is the error of the conversion and assumed to be a zero-mean normal variable. The parameters a, b, and ε_R are determined by comparison

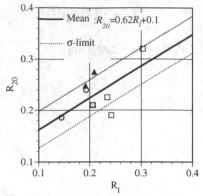

Fig.1 Relationship between R_{20} and R_l.

of the triaxial test results of the undisturbed soil samples with the empirical equation.

R_l is given by the next empirical equation (Japan road association 1990).

$$R_l = R_1 + R_2 + R_3 \tag{5}$$

$$R_1 = 0.0882 \sqrt{\frac{N}{\sigma_v' + 0.7}}$$

$$R_2 = \begin{cases} 0.19 & (0.02\text{mm} \leq D_{50} \leq 0.05\text{mm}) \\ 0.225\log_{10}(0.35/D_{50}) & \\ & (0.05\text{mm} \leq D_{50} \leq 0.60\text{mm}) \\ -0.05 & (0.60\text{mm} \leq D_{50} 2.00\text{mm}) \end{cases}$$

$$R_3 = \begin{cases} 0.00 & (0\% \leq F_c \leq 40\%) \\ 0.004F_c - 0.16 & (40\% \leq F_c \leq 100\%) \end{cases}$$

Here, F_c is the fines content(%), D_{50} is the median grain size (mm) and σ_v' is the effective vertical stress (kgf/cm²).

Fig.1 shows the regression line of R_{20} and R_l, and σ-limits of the regression line in the objective ground for analysis. R_{20} denotes the dynamic shear strength from the cyclic undrained triaxial test here. ε_R is found to be a N(0, 0.036) type normal variable from the standard deviation of the regression line.

By using the conversion of Eq.(4), the locality of the objective ground is added to the empirical result of Eq.(5) in evaluation of the dynamic shear strength.

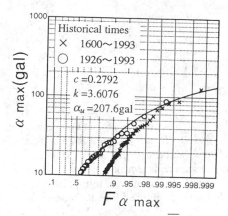

Fig.2 Cumulative distribution of $\overline{\alpha}_{max}$.

4 DYNAMIC LOAD

The dynamic load is given by the next equation.

$$L = \frac{\alpha_{max}\sigma_v}{980\sigma_v'} r_d \qquad (6)$$

in which α_{max} stands for the maximum ground surface acceleration, σ_v is the total vertical stress (kgf/cm^2), σ_v' is the effective vertical stress (kgf/cm^2) and $r_d = 1 - 0.015Z$, where Z is the depth (m) from the surface. The expected value of α_{max} is given by the next attenuation equation (7) (Fukushima and Tanaka 1990).

$$\log_{10}\overline{\alpha}_{max} = 0.52M - 1.87\log_{10}(\Delta + 30) + 2.09 \qquad (7)$$

Here, $\overline{\alpha}_{max}$ is the expected value of α_{max}, M is the magnitude of the earthquake, Δ is the epicentral distance from the source of the earthquake. $\ln\overline{\alpha}_{max}$ is defined as a probabilistic parameter following the extreme value distribution III.

$$F_{\overline{a}_{max}}(\alpha) = \exp\left[-\left\{c\ln(\alpha_u/\alpha)\right\}^k\right] \qquad (8)$$

$$\alpha \leq \alpha_u$$

in which α_u is the upper limit of the acceleration and c, k are constant coefficients.

The cumulative distribution of $\overline{\alpha}_{max}$ in South Okayama (Japan) is given in Fig.2. In this figure, $\overline{\alpha}_{max}$ is based on the annual maximum acceleration determined from the historical earthquakes data record. α_u, c and k are determined from the data of the years 1600-

1993. Firstly, the parameter c and k are identified by the data of the year 1926-1993. Secondly, α_u is determined from the data of the years 1600-1993 (Japan Meteorological Agency 1961-1993, National Astronomical Observatory 1997, Utsu, T. 1982). Historical earthquake data have been recorded well from the year 1600 in Japan. However, old data is not sufficient in quality and quantity. After 1926, the modern earthquake recording system was established. Because the parameters c and k contribute to the shape of the distribution, usage of data after 1926 is reasonable for determination of these two parameters. Determination of the upper limit acceleration α_u requires a long term data record and all data after 1600 are used for this purpose. Considering the error of the attenuation equation, α_{max} is determined from Eq.(9).

$$\alpha_{max} = 10^{\varepsilon_\alpha}\overline{\alpha}_{max} \qquad (9)$$

The error term ε_α is a N(0, 0.30) type normal variable here.

5 STATISTICAL MODEL OF GROUND IMPROVEMENT EFFECT

The sand compaction pile method is considered here as a ground improvement method. The effect of SCP is introduced by the following equations (Mizuno et al. 1987). In these formulations, the effect of the fines content in the ground is considered.

$$\hat{N}_1 = N_0 + \beta\left(\tilde{N}_1 - N_0\right) \qquad (10)$$

$$\beta = 1.05 - 0.51\log_{10}F_c \qquad (11)$$

in which $\hat{N}_1$ is the predicted N-value after SCP improvement, N_0 is the N-value before ground improvement, $\tilde{N}_1$ is the predicted N-value after improvement without consideration of fines content, and β is the reduction ratio of improvement. $\tilde{N}_1$ is described as follows.

$$\tilde{N}_1 = \left(\sigma_v' + 0.7\right)\left(D_{r1}/21\right)^2 \qquad (12)$$

$$D_{r1}(\%) = \frac{e_{max} - e_1}{e_{max} - e_{min}} \times 100 \qquad (13)$$

$$e_1 = e_0 - A_s\left(1 + e_0\right) \qquad (14)$$

$$e_0 = e_{max} - D_{r0}\left(e_{max} - e_{min}\right)/100 \qquad (15)$$

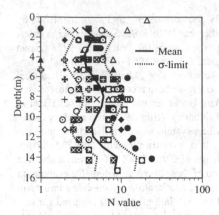

Fig.3 Distribution of N-value.

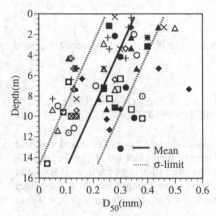

Fig.4 Distribution of median grain size.

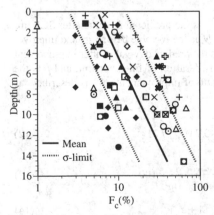

Fig.5 Distribution of fines content.

$$D_{r0}(\%) = 21\sqrt{\frac{N_0}{0.7 + \sigma_v'}} \qquad (16)$$

$$e_{max} = 0.02F_c + 1.0 \qquad (17)$$

$$e_{min} = 0.012F_c + 0.6 \qquad (18)$$

in which e_{max}, e_{min} are maximum and minimum void ratio, e_0, e_i and D_{r0}, D_{r1} are void ratio and relative density respectively before and after improvement, and A_s is the ratio of sand replacement.

Considering estimation error in Eq.(10), the improved N-value is determined from the next equation.

$$N_1 = \hat{N}_1(1 + \varepsilon_N) \qquad (19)$$

The error term ε_N is a N(0,0.248) type normal random variable based on Mizuno's data.

6 STATISTICAL MODEL OF SOIL PARAMETERS

The statistical models of soil parameters in the vertical direction are defined by the next equation.

$$Y_i = \sum_{j=0}^{n} a_{ij}Z^j + \varepsilon_i \qquad (20)$$

where Y_i stands for the value of random parameter i at the depth Z, $a_{ij}(j=0,1,2,..,n)$ are regression coefficients, and ε_i is a zero-mean normal random variable of the parameter i, which has the auto-correlation and the cross-correlation between two parameters. The auto- and cross correlation function is defined by the next equation.

$$r_{ij}(\Delta Z) = B_{ij}\exp(-\Delta Z/\delta_{ij}) \qquad (21)$$

in which B_{ij} is the correlation coefficient and δ_{ij} is the correlation distance between two parameters i and j, ΔZ is the distance between two points along the vertical direction. Minimizing AIC method is applied for the determination of optimum order of mean function n, regression coefficients $a_{ij}(j=0,1,2,..,n)$, standard deviation, and auto- and cross -correlation functions of ε_i.

The one-dimensional spatial distributions of N-value, D_{50}, and F_c are given in Figs.3- 5. The normal distribution is applied to $\log_{10} N$, D_{50} and $\log_{10}F_c$, judging from the spatial variability of parameters. In the Figs.3-5, solid and broken lines stand for the mean functions and σ-limits respectively. Table 1 shows the

Table1 Means and standard deviations of soil parameters.

Parameters	Means	Standard deviations
$\log_{10}N$	$-2.895136 \times 10^{-1} + 1.382580Z - 7.190219 \times 10^{-1}Z^2 + 1.670053 \times 10^{-1}Z^3 - 1.891469 \times 10^{-2}Z^4 + 1.023769 \times 10^{-3}Z^5 - 2.117457 \times 10^{-5}Z^6$	0.244
D_{50}	$0.3569298 - 0.01693042Z$	0.107
$\log_{10}F_c$	$0.7475127 + 0.05834805Z$	0.345

mean functions and standard deviations. AIC selects the 6th order regression line for $\log_{10}N$ and linear lines for D_{50} and $\log_{10}F_c$. In the upper and lower outside of sampling range, the parameter keeps the same value at the highest and lowest sampling points to prevent extrapolation by the high order regression line.

Table 2 shows auto- and cross- correlation parameters. These three parameters have relatively high correlation with one another. $\log_{10}N$ has high positive correlation with D_{50} and high negative correlation with $\log_{10}F_c$. D_{50} and $\log_{10}F_c$ have very high negative correlation. This means these two parameters give similar information. Auto-correlation distances of $\log_{10}N$ and $\log_{10}F_c$ are determined to be 1.1m and 1.3m respectively. These values are very reasonable for the correlation distances of the vertical direction for soil parameters. The correlation distance of D_{50} is not determined easily, and it is assumed to be 1.0m, considering the high correlation of D_{50} with $\log_{10}F_c$ and $\log_{10}N$, which is close and a little smaller value compared with the correlation distances of $\log_{10}F_c$ and $\log_{10}N$. It is difficult to determine the cross-correlation distance. δ_{ij} is assumed here to be the value between auto-correlation distances of the parameter i and j.

In the objective ground, the sand layer exists in the depth 0.0-15m and this layer is the object of liquefaction analysis. Below the depth 15m, the alluvial clay layer exists.

Table 2 Auto- and cross correlation parameters.

Parameter i, j	B_{ij}	δ_{ij} (m)
$\log_{10}N$, $\log_{10}N$	1.0	1.1
D_{50}, D_{50}	1.0	1.0*
$\log_{10}F_c$, $\log_{10}F_c$	1.0	1.3
$\log_{10}N$, D_{50}	0.70	1.0*
$\log_{10}N$, $\log_{10}F_c$	-0.68	1.1*
D_{50}, $\log_{10}F_c$	-0.81	1.0*

* Assumed values

7 MONTE CARLO SIMULATION METHOD

The Monte Carlo simulation method is applied to calculate probability of liquefaction. The normal distribution is applied to the next parameters. $\log_{10}N$, $\log_{10}F_c$, D_{50}, ε_R, ε_α, ε_N

The parameters, $\log_{10}N$, $\log_{10}F_c$ and D_{50} have to satisfy the auto- and cross- correlation characteristics, and the covariance matrix decomposition method is applied for this purpose. The extreme value III distribution is applied to $\ln \overline{\alpha}_{max}$. Number of iteration is 20000 in the minimum case and 100000 in the maximum. The total and effective overburden stresses σ_v, σ_v' are deterministic parameters here, because the variability of the unit weight of the ground is very small. The mean value of the unit weight is 1.853tf/m³.

Some simulated values of F_c are greater than 100% and some values of D_{50} are negative at the deep ground, which is attributed to the error of the normal distribution assumption. Because the layer including a very large amount of fines content is safe against liquefaction, it can be assumed the liquefaction never occurs in the layer. As a result, the effect of the error is not significant for evaluation of the liquefaction probability.

8 OPTIMUM DESIGN METHOD FOR GROUND IMPROVEMENT

In the case where the maximum horizontal acceleration is deterministic, the total cost of the design C_T is evaluated as:

$$C_T = C_I + P_f C_F = C_I \left(1 + \lambda \cdot P_f\right)$$
$$= C_0 \left(1 + \mu_s A_s\right)\left(1 + \lambda \cdot P_f\right) \qquad (22)$$

in which C_I is the initial cost including ground improvement cost, P_f is the probability of liquefaction, C_F is the cost of failure and C_0 is initial construction cost. The parameter λ is the importance index, which means the ratio of failure and initial cost.

$$\lambda = \frac{C_F}{C_I} \qquad (23)$$

The coefficient μ_s is defined as:

$$\mu_s = C_r \frac{4}{\pi d_s^2} \qquad (24)$$

Here, d_s is diameter of a SCP which is 70cm here, and C_r is the ratio of the cost for the unit length of SCP and unit volume of embankment, which is determined to be 1.38 here (Matsuo 1985). The length of SCP is assumed to coincide with height of the embankment in the analysis as shown in Fig.6.

In the case of considering that the occurrences of earthquakes are probabilistic, then the total cost is as follows.

$$C_T = C_I + P_{fa} \bullet t \bullet C_F$$
$$= C_0 \left(1 + \mu_s A_s\right)\left(1 + \lambda \bullet P_{fa} \bullet t\right) \qquad (25)$$

in which t is the lifetime span and P_{fa} is the annual probability of liquefaction.

The optimum improvement design and the optimum probability of liquefaction are determined by minimizing the total cost.

9 RESULT OF ANALYSIS

9.1 Outline of ground for analysis

An embankment constructed by sandy material is the objective of our analysis. The embankment has a relatively flat and very long shape, therefore it can be identified with a part of the original ground for simplicity in the analysis. It was constructed in the sea and the water table exists at 2.4m depth from the surface. Whole area of the embankment is assumed to be improved by sand compaction piles. The length of the SCP is equal to the embankment height in the analysis. The image of the ground improvement is shown in Fig.6. The ratio of sand replacement A_s is considered within the range 0.0-0.2 in this study.

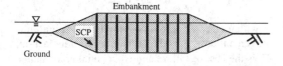

Fig.6 Image of SCP construction.

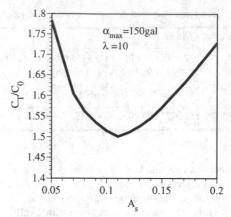

Fig.7 Minimization of total cost.

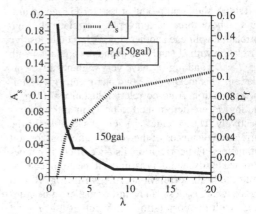

Fig.8 Optimum sand replacement rate and probability of liquefaction (α_{max}=150gal).

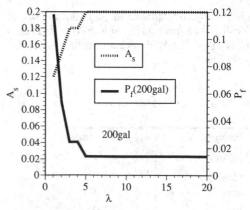

Fig.9 Optimum sand replacement rate and probability of liquefaction (α_{max}=200gal).

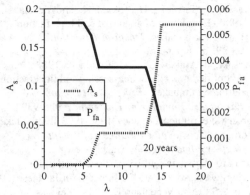

Fig.10 Optimum sand replacement rate and probability of liquefaction (life time = 20 years).

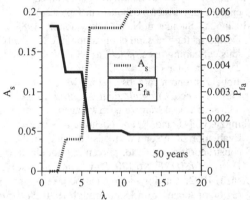

Fig.11 Optimum sand replacement rate and probability of liquefaction (life time = 50 years).

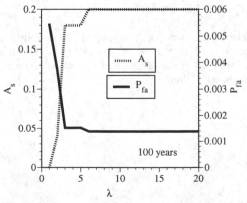

Fig.12 Optimum sand replacement rate and probability of liquefaction (life time = 100 years).

9.2 Case of deterministic maximum acceleration

The case that the maximum acceleration is deterministic is discussed here. The design acceleration values of the river embankment or road embankment can be used as an example of the deterministic acceleration. As maximum acceleration values, 150gal and 200gal are chosen. According to Fig.2, 150gal is a very high level acceleration in Okayama. Figs.7-9 presents the results of this analysis.

Fig.7 shows the example of optimization of the total cost in the case that α_{max}=150gal and λ=10. In the figure, the minimum total cost and optimum sand replacement ratio are determined well. Figs.8 and 9 are for the cases with the optimum replacement ratios, and the probability of liquefaction with the change of the importance index λ for 150gal and 200gal acceleration, respectively. According to the result, the replacement ratio A_s and probability of liquefaction P_f indicate an anti-proportional relationship with each other. Within the range $\lambda \leq 5$, the optimum A_s and P_f change drastically. In the case that λ=1.0, i.e. the initial cost is equal to the failure cost, the optimum probability of liquefaction is very great. In Fig.8, the value is 0.15 and in Fig.9 it is 0.12, while λ=20, the value is 0.004 and 0.014, which is relatively low.

9.3 Case of probabilistic maximum acceleration

In fact, the occurrence of earthquakes is probabilistic, and the optimum design considering the probabilistic characteristics of earthquakes is more reasonable. The optimum design of SCP is discussed here in the case that the dynamic load is a probabilistic variable as described in Section 4.

Figs.10-12 show the relationship of optimum A_s and P_{fa} with the importance index λ, and they correspond to the lifetimes 20, 50, and 100 years. The annual probability of liquefaction in Figs.10-12 is for an arbitrary year. The optimum A_s and P_{fa} roughly indicate an anti-proportional relationship with each other. In all cases, with increase of λ, A_s approaches 0.2. When the lifetime is longer, the speed of A_s approaching 0.2 is faster. In all cases, at λ=1.0, the optimum A_s is 0.0. This means no ground improvement is the best selection, when the initial cost is equal to the failure cost.

The probabilities that the liquefaction occurs at least once in the lifetime are 0.1, 0.24, 0.42 at A_s=0.0 and 0.027, 0.067, 0.129 at A_s=0.2 for the lifetime 20, 50 and 100years respectively. If no SCP is constructed, the probability of liquefaction in 100years is close to 50%. While the sand replacement ratio is 0.2, even in 100years, the probability of liquefaction is relatively low.

1773

10 CONCLUSIONS

(1) One-dimensional statistical models of soil parameters $\log_{10}N$, D_{50} and $\log_{10}F_c$ are determined well by minimizing AIC. The statistical models are characterized by mean functions, standard deviations and auto- and cross- correlation functions of the parameters.
(2) The dynamic shear strength is determined from the empirical equation Eq.(5) and the cyclic undrained triaxial test result. From the relationship of two kinds of dynamic shear strength, the conversion equation from R_l to R_{20} in the objective ground is established. By this conversion, the locality of the ground is added to the empirical equation.
(3) Distribution of the annual maximum horizontal acceleration is determined based on the historical earthquakes data record. The extreme value III distribution is applied to the distribution type of the $\log_{10}\overline{\alpha}_{max}$.
(4) Probability of liquefaction is calculated by the Monte Carlo method. N-value, D_{50}, F_c, the expected value of horizontal maximum acceleration $\overline{\alpha}_{max}$ and the error factors, ε_α, ε_R, ε_N are dealt with as probabilistic parameters in the analysis. Two types of calculation are tried. In one case, α_{max} is deterministic design value. In the other case, it is probabilistic parameter based on the statistical model of the earthquake occurrences.
(5) The statistical model of the SCP ground improvement effect is formulated. This statistical model also evaluates the effect of the fine content in the ground.
(6) The optimum design of SCP is clarified by the minimization of total cost. The optimum sand replacement ratio and probability of liquefaction are evaluated well in the two cases. In one case, α_{max} is the deterministic design value, and in the other case, it is probabilistic.

REFERENCES

Fadris, M.N. and Veneziano D. 1981 Statistical analysis of sand liquefaction, *Journal of the Geotechnical Engineering*, ASCE. Vol.107, No.GT10: 1361-1377.
Fukushima, Y. And Tanaka,T. 1990. A new attenuation relation for peak horizontal acceleration of strong earthquake ground motion. *Bulletin of the Seismological Society of America*. Vol.80, No.4.: 757-783.
Halder, A. and Tang,W. H. 1979. Probabilistic Evaluation of liquefaction potential, *Journal of the Geotechnical Engineering*, ASCE. Vol.105, No.GT2: 145-163.

Iwasaki, T., Tatsuoka, H., Tokida, K., and Yasuda, H. 1980. Estimation of degree of soil liquefaction during earthquakes. *Tsuchi-to-Kiso*. Vol.27, No.4: 23-29. (in Japanese)
Iwasaki, T., Arakawa,A. and Tokida, K. 1982. Simplified procedure for assessing soil liquefaction during earthquakes. *Proc. of Soil Dynamics & Earthquake Engineering Conference*: 925-939.
Japan Meteorological Agency 1961-1993. Earthquake origins. *Seismological Bulletin of the Japan Meteorological Agency.* (in Japanese)
Japan road association., 1990. Specification for highway bridge, Part V. Maruzen. (in Japanese)
Liao, S.S.C. and Veneziano D. 1988. Regression models for evaluating liquefaction probability. *Journal of the Geotechnical Engineering*, ASCE. Vol.114, No.GT4: 389-411.
Matsuo, M. 1985. Reliability in geotechnical engineering design. Gihodo. (in Japanese)
Mizuno, Y., Suematsu, N. and Okuyama, K. 1987. Design method of sand compaction pile for sandy soils containing fines. *Tsuchi-to-Kiso*. Vol.35, No.5: 21-26. (in Japanese)
National Astronomical Observatory 1997. Earth Science. *Chronological Scientific Tables*: 832-863: Tokyo Maruzen. (in Japanese)
Shimizu, H. Nakano, R. and Nishimura, S. 1994. Evaluation of the optimum design values in the construction methods for preventing liquefaction. *Trans. of JSIDRE*. No.170: 55-61. (in Japanese)
Utsu, T. 1982. Catalog of large earthquakes in the region of Japan from 1885 through 1980. *Bulletin of the Earthquake Research Institute*. 57: 401-463. (in Japanese)

ACKNOWLEDGMENT

This research was partly supported by Grant-in-Aid for Scientific Research (B) (Project Number 065566037) of the Ministry of Education, Science, Sports and Culture.

Structural Safety and Reliability, Shiraishi, Shinozuka & Wen (eds) © 1998 Balkema, Rotterdam, ISBN 90 5410 978 5

The effect of soil-structure interaction on damping of structures

M. Ali Ghannad
Graduate School of Engineering, Nagoya University, Japan

N. Fukuwa
Center for Cooperative Research in Advanced Science and Technology, Nagoya University, Japan

J. Tobita
School of Engineering, Nagoya University, Japan

ABSTRACT: The effect of Soil-Structure Interaction (SSI) on the dynamic properties of structure is investigated analytically and experimentally and the results are compared. In the analytical approach, the eigenvalues of the soil-structure system are evaluated through the complex eigenvalue analysis where the soil under the structure is replaced by frequency dependent springs and dashpots using cone models. As the experimental study, the microtremor measurements are conducted on fourteen buildings located in the Higashiyama campus of Nagoya University and their natural frequencies and damping ratios are estimated by employing the transfer function fitting and Random Decrement (RD) techniques. It is concluded that the dynamic characteristics of soil-structure systems, and especially the damping ratios, can be considerably different from those of structure itself. The SSI effect is more dramatic for the case of short buildings with large foundations located on soft soils.

1 INTRODUCTION

It is well known that the natural periods and damping ratios are the key parameters in the seismic design of structures. However, these dynamic characteristics of structure will be influenced by the flexibility of soil under the structure due to the soil-structure interaction. As a result, the soil-structure system usually has a longer natural period than the fixed-base structure model. It also has a higher damping ratio, due to the radiation damping in the soil which can drastically influence the response of the structure. The subject has been studied by many researchers during the years, analytically[1-5], and experimentally[6-8] and even has found its way into some seismic codes and provisions as simplified approximations.[9,10] Modal damping ratios of soil-structure systems have been evaluated by some researchers through the use of energy methods which are based on the assumption of equal damped and undamped mode shapes.[11-13] However, application of complex eigenvalue analysis is rare[1,3] and it is almost limited to the case of structure located on the surface of soil half-space with frequency independent impedance functions. The complex eigenvalue analysis was used by the first two authors[14] for the case of structure located on the surface of a homogeneous half-space where the soil is replaced by the frequency dependent springs and dashpots using cone models.

Some parts of the results of their study are presented here. As the experimental study, the ambient vibration measurements have always been a fast and efficient way of determining the dynamic properties of buildings. In this regard, the microtremor measurements are conducted on fourteen buildings located in the Higashiyama campus of Nagoya University. It should be mentioned that because of heavy earthworks during the years, the topography of the campus has been drastically changed from the original one. Therefore, the different parts of the campus have different soil conditions. On the other hand, most of the selected buildings have almost a typical plan of educational type buildings, i.e., a slender rectangular with almost the same width. So, the effect of soil condition on the eigenproperties of buildings can be studied well. The effect of different parameters on the severity of the interaction are then discussed and compared with the results of the analytical study.

2 ANALYTICAL STUDY

Figure 1 shows the uniform distributed mass and stiffness shear building model which is chosen as the basic model in this research. The soil under the structure is replaced with frequency dependent springs and dashpots using cone models.[15] Cone models based on the one dimensional wave propagation theory lead to simple formulations for spring and dashpot coefficients with sufficient accuracy for engineering practice. The concept can also be extended for the cases of layered site with or without foundation embedment.[15] The material damping in the soil isn't addressed. However, the hysteresis damping type of 1% is considered in the structure.

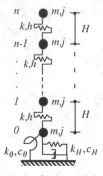

Fig.1. Analysis model

The uniform distribution of mass and stiffness in the structural model leads to a special form of stiffness matrix whose determinant can be expressed by a polynomial explicitly.[5] Therefore, the eigenvalues of the system can be calculated by solving the polynomial in the complex plane readily.

2.1 Results for a typical example

The results for an ordinary reinforced concrete (RC) rigid framed structure with square plan are presented in this section as a typical example. The number of stories, n, the number of spans, n_s (which is related to size of the foundation directly) and the shear wave velocity in the soil, V_s, are selected as key parameters while the other parameters are fixed to some typical values. Figures 2 and 3 show the dependency of the natural frequencies and damping ratios on the selected key parameters, respectively. In each figure, the results of the fixed base, the sway permitted and the sway & rocking permitted (SR) cases are shown together. Natural frequencies are scaled by the frequency of the single degree of freedom system, $\omega_0 = \sqrt{k/m}$. Figure 2 shows that the difference among the different models is practically seen only in the first mode of vibration. In this regard, the variation of the first natural periods with the selected key parameters are presented in Fig. 4. Again, the results for periods are scaled by the period of a single degree of freedom system, $T_0 = 2\pi/\omega_0$. Fig. 4-a shows almost a linear relationship between the first natural period of the system and the number of stories for the fixed-base and the sway-permitted models. On the other hand, the relationship for the SR model is not linear and the higher number of stories, the more necessity to consider the SSI effect. Figure 4-b is compatible with the fact that the sway-permitted and SR models converge to the fixed-base model for stiff subsoils. Also, a sudden change for the case of

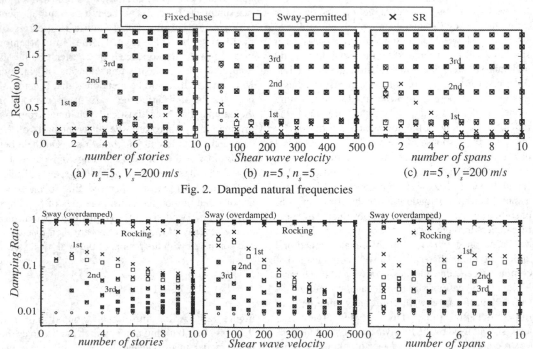

Fig. 2. Damped natural frequencies

Fig. 3. Modal damping ratios

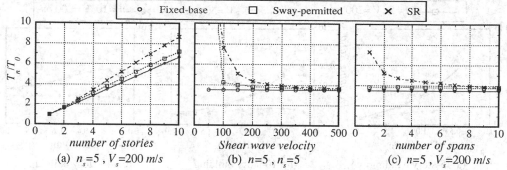

Fixed-base ○   Sway-permitted □   SR ✕

(a) $n_s=5$, $V_s=200$ m/s   (b) $n=5$, $n_s=5$ (c) $n=5$, $V_s=200$ m/s

Fig. 4. The first damped periods

very loose soils is observed. The results for the sway permitted case in Fig. 4-c show no special effect for the size of foundation. However, more drastic SSI effect for smaller foundations is seen for SR model. In relation to damping ratios, Fig. 3 shows very high values for the first structural mode which decrease for the higher modes and finally converge to the material damping in the structure. This tendency is seen more clearly for systems with lower shear wave velocities in soil, shorter buildings and higher number of spans. The results are compatible with the fact that the radiation damping is higher for softer soils, stiffer buildings and larger foundations. The structure-soil stiffness ratio is one of the key parameters in the SSI phenomenon and the higher the ratio, the stronger the SSI effect. However, attention should be paid to stiff structures located on very soft soils where the sway mode is not overdamped any longer. For example, table 1 shows the natural frequencies and modal damping ratios for the first four modes of a 5-story building located on the surface of a homogeneous half-space with different shear wave velocities. The results are related to the sway-permitted case. As shown, in the first three columns of the table the first mode related to the sway degree of freedom is overdamped and practically only the structural modes exist. In this situation, the modal damping ratios increase by softening the subsoil. However, for the next three columns, the sway mode is not overdamped any longer and the order of modes are changed. The sudden

change in the first natural periods for very loose soils in Fig. 4 can also be explained by this phenomenon. The complex mode shapes of some selected cases are

- - - Initial state   ——Real Part   ——Imag. Part

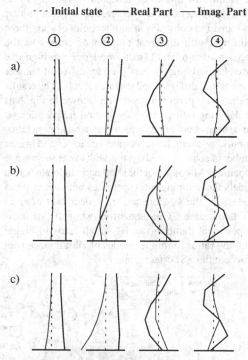

Fig. 5. The first four mode shapes for a 5-story building
a) $V_s=200$ m/s b) $V_s=40$ m/s c) $V_s=70$ m/s

Table 1 - The natural frequencies* and modal damping ratios for the building located on the surface of a homogeneous half-space with different shear wave velocities.

Order of Modes	Vs = 200		Vs = 100		Vs = 85		Vs = 70		Vs = 50		Vs = 40	
	ω	ξ	ω	ξ	ω	ξ	ω	ξ	ω	ξ	ω	ξ
1	Overdamped		Overdamped		Overdamped		0.095	0.914	0.053	0.880	0.041	0.877
2	0.261	0.097	0.237	0.355	0.224	0.489	0.210	0.828	0.468	0.408	0.496	0.293
3	0.825	0.044	0.840	0.094	0.850	0.110	0.872	0.127	0.928	0.126	0.958	0.106
4	1.310	0.019	1.324	0.036	1.330	0.041	1.343	0.045	1.368	0.045	1.382	0.041

* Frequencies are scaled by the natural frequency of the single degree of freedom system.

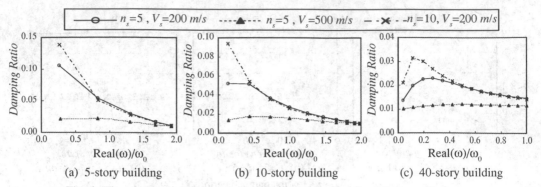

Fig. 6. The modal dampings versus the natural frequencies for sway-permitted case

drawn in Fig. 5. As it can be seen, it is difficult to distinguish between the sway and structural modes in the vicinity of this transition point (Fig. 5-c). The modal damping ratios also decrease for softer soils after this transition point. From another point of view, three buildings with different number of stories as the representative of short (stiff), moderate and high-rise (flexible) buildings are analyzed for different number of spans and different soil stiffness levels. The results for the sway-permitted model are shown in Fig. 6 as the damping ratios versus the natural frequencies. It can be seen clearly that there are higher damping ratios for buildings with lower number of stories and higher number of spans located on soils with lower shear wave velocities. Although for the short and moderate height models the damping ratio decreases with the order of modes, for the 40-story model, it decreases after an initial increase. Consequently, using the stiffness proportional damping model which leads to higher damping ratios for higher modes of vibration, can not represent the SSI effect properly.

3 EXPERIMENTAL STUDY

As the experimental study, the microtremor measurements were conducted on fourteen buildings located in the Higashiyama campus of Nagoya University. Also, for one of the buildings, which is a 10-story SRC building, the measurements were repeated for different stages of construction. Figure 7 shows the campus and the location of the selected buildings. The numbers on the figure refer to the order number of buildings in the first column of table 2. The groundfilled parts of the campus due to heavy earthworks from 1936 to 1991 is shown in the background. Darker shades indicate an increase in filling depth which even reaches up to 20 meters in some areas. The buildings were selected among the existing buildings considering some parameters which are of interest, e.g. the number of stories, plan's shape and size, soil condition and also the availability of boring data. It should be mentioned that totally, there are 202 boring data available in the campus which are

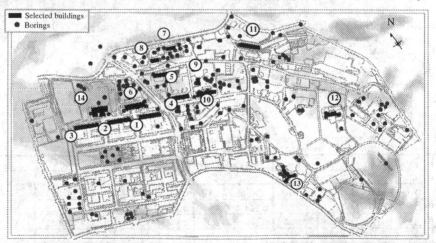

Fig.7. The location of the borings and selected buildings and the groundfilled area in the campus

Table 2 - Selected buildings' information

No.	Building	Ref. name	No. of Stories	Height (m)	Struc. System	Pile length (m)	Embedment (m)	Construc. Year	Average N-value
1	Faculty of Eng. No.1	Eng1	3+1	15.3	RC	-	1.2	1951-70	14.6
2	Faculty of Eng. No.2	Eng2	3+1	15	RC	-	1.1	1954-65	10.8
3	Faculty of Eng. No.3	Eng3	4	15.8	RC	5 - 16	1.5	1962-70	12.5
4	Faculty of Eng. No.4	Eng4	4	14.75	RC	6	1.25	1964-70	17.2
5	Faculty of Eng. No.5	Eng5	6	22.17	RC	5 - 33	1.7	1967-69	14.4
6	Faculty of Eng. No.7	Eng7	4	15.2	RC	20	1.2	1971-89	16
7	Faculty of Eng. No.8	Eng8	4	16	RC	9 - 10	2.8	1987	28.9
8	Faculty of Eng. No.9	Eng9	6	22.2	SRC	12	2.3	1982-93	22.9
9	Faculty of Science_A2	Sc.A2	5	18.1	RC	9	1.5	1979	17.2
10	Faculty of Science_E	Sc.E	5+1	19.7	RC	8	1.7	1967-85	21.6
11	Faculty of Agriculture	Agr.	6	21	RC	-	2	1966	23.1
12	Inst. for Hydrospher.	Hyd.	5	18.8	RC	9	1.6	1971	30.2
13	International Residence	Res.	8	33.2	RC	15	2	1981-88	27.8
14	Faculty of Eng. No.1(new)	Eng1_N	10	39.3	SRC	45	8.05	1995	11.6

mainly related to the northern and central parts of the campus as shown in Fig. 7. The information related to each of the selected buildings are summarized in table 2. As the criteria for the soil stiffness, the average of N-values over the first 10 meters from the ground surface are used. The reasons for this selection can be found in reference 8. Also, for the case of pile foundations with piles shorter than 10 meters, the average value over the length of piles is used in order to avoid the distortion of data due to significant difference between soil layers.[6]

Table 3 - The estimated parameters for NS direction

Ref. name	Average rms (m.kine)		Transfer Function Fitting Method								RD Method	
			Top / 1st floor				Top / Ground					
	@ ground	@ top	freq (Hz)	ξ	ξ/β	Error	freq (Hz)	ξ	ξ/β	Error	freq (Hz)	ξ
Eng1	0.213	0.397	5.13	0.134	0.102	1.82%	4.82	0.146	0.081	2.57%	5.08	0.117
Eng2	0.170	0.244	5.82	0.137	0.094	0.67%	5.51	0.134	0.093	0.86%	5.47	0.128
Eng3	0.098	0.196	-	-	-	-	5.25	0.310	0.142	2.29%	5.08	0.137
Eng4	0.380	0.486	6.93	0.243	0.113	3.42%	6.34	0.113	0.115	1.02%	6.64	0.132
Eng5	0.638	1.347	3.30	0.119	0.089	0.85%	3.06	0.057	0.048	1.50%	2.93	0.075
Eng7	0.374	0.273	6.64	0.184	0.115	0.45%	5.22	0.204	0.225	2.49%	5.08	0.161
Eng8	0.264	0.278	5.54	0.107	0.061	0.86%	5.16	0.003	0.067	1.46%	5.08	0.095
Eng9	0.277	0.406	4.72	0.156	0.076	1.43%	4.05	0.103	0.066	1.37%	3.71	0.089
Sc.A2	0.339	0.897	5.04	0.220	0.068	0.80%	4.48	0.096	0.040	2.70%	4.49	0.088
Sc.E	0.212	0.697	4.08	0.272	0.158	0.27%	3.48	0.055	0.031	1.43%	3.52	0.096
Hyd.	0.362	0.814	5.93	0.177	0.077	0.87%	5.36	0.122	0.060	3.57%	5.47	0.093
Agr.	0.152	0.251	3.70	0.189	0.080	3.70%	3.59	0.117	0.038	5.22%	3.32	0.114
Res.	0.235	0.809	3.37	0.054	0.018	1.41%	3.33	0.022	0.021	3.08%	3.32	0.056
Eng_N (3)	0.190	0.240	7.56	0.224	0.137	0.94%	9.10	0.150	0.261	0.96%	9.38	0.120
Eng_N (4)	0.196	0.305	5.67	0.194	0.093	0.66%	5.71	0.450	0.270	0.93%	4.30	0.203
Eng_N (5)	0.200	0.414	4.78	0.126	0.074	2.30%	4.60	0.217	0.177	1.61%	5.08	0.084
Eng_N (6)	0.208	0.483	3.05	0.086	0.076	5.55%	2.90	0.107	0.097	4.64%	2.73	0.101
Eng_N (7)	0.166	0.484	2.93	0.070	0.045	0.98%	2.74	0.065	0.056	11.60%	2.73	0.079
Eng_N (8)	0.167	0.528	2.67	0.071	0.039	0.56%	2.46	0.072	0.053	1.72%	2.54	0.104
Eng_N (9)	0.190	0.628	2.35	0.057	0.034	0.71%	2.23	0.059	0.043	1.00%	2.15	0.079
Eng_N (10)	0.204	0.715	2.09	0.051	0.030	0.54%	2.00	0.031	0.018	1.82%	2.06	0.042
Eng1	0.219	0.260	6.25	0.130	0.098	0.53%	6.12	0.121	0.130	1.99%	5.47	0.103
Eng2	0.256	0.196	5.95	0.118	0.102	0.58%	5.46	0.180	0.208	1.16%	5.08	0.140
Eng3	0.099	0.147	5.41	0.242	0.301	1.24%	5.99	0.216	0.229	2.50%	5.08	0.167
Eng4	0.280	0.460	4.81	0.114	0.080	0.54%	4.76	0.105	0.085	0.96%	4.69	0.101
Eng5	0.694	0.691	3.84	0.102	0.085	0.32%	3.42	0.117	0.127	1.14%	3.13	0.135
Eng7	0.367	0.251	5.55	0.060	0.049	1.22%	5.22	0.155	0.196	5.08%	5.47	0.107
Eng8	0.218	0.228	6.95	0.098	0.054	1.81%	6.03	0.085	0.049	1.29%	5.86	0.083
Eng9	0.261	0.393	5.06	0.207	0.097	2.25%	4.63	0.155	0.109	0.66%	4.10	0.152
Sc.A2	0.502	0.616	5.00	0.151	0.078	1.52%	4.67	0.104	0.046	2.45%	4.49	0.075
Sc.E	0.994	0.568	3.96	0.156	0.125	1.12%	3.66	0.083	0.067	1.77%	3.52	0.113
Hyd.	0.229	0.938	4.98	0.113	0.066	0.58%	4.57	0.084	0.050	2.03%	4.69	0.133
Agr.	0.175	0.242	3.85	0.119	0.041	2.93%	3.97	0.043	0.029	2.32%	4.10	0.047
Res.	0.828	0.719	3.17	0.036	0.029	1.11%	3.10	0.019	0.037	0.73%	3.13	0.030
Eng_N (3)	0.201	0.204	9.19	0.104	0.093	1.30%	11.62	0.153	0.421	1.08%	12.11	0.134
Eng_N (4)	0.200	0.231	7.17	0.175	0.080	1.32%	7.58	0.136	0.440	0.96%	7.42	0.121
Eng_N (5)	0.203	0.311	5.37	0.148	0.101	1.13%	5.17	0.244	0.263	6.57%	4.10	0.133
Eng_N (6)	0.231	0.414	4.55	0.138	0.082	3.58%	3.93	0.322	0.248	1.45%	-	-
Eng_N (7)	0.192	0.393	3.32	0.098	0.067	1.15%	2.90	0.100	0.098	1.26%	2.93	0.131
Eng_N (8)	0.198	0.494	3.01	0.111	0.059	1.05%	2.62	0.072	0.064	1.72%	2.54	0.095
Eng_N (9)	0.213	0.558	2.63	0.066	0.048	0.45%	2.42	0.076	0.061	1.09%	2.54	0.100
Eng_N (10)	0.221	0.685	2.32	0.070	0.039	0.75%	2.13	0.040	0.032	0.78%	2.15	0.067

β : Participation factor

3.1 *Microtremor tests and the parameter estimation methods*

The microtremor measurements were performed for NS and EW directions which are related to the transverse and longitudinal dimensions of buildings, respectively. The responses were measured at the first floor and top of the buildings as well as on the ground surface. The measurements on the ground surface were done at a distance from the building which are not affected by the building's vibration. In the case of the Eng1_N building, the test was repeated for different stages of construction, i.e. after completion of each story.

The moving coil type seismometers with natural period of 1.0 second were used to measure the responses simultaneously at the above mentioned locations and the velocity was measured in all cases. The signals, after amplification and low pass filtering (f_c =30 Hz) are digitized at the rate of 100 samples per second. In all cases, the measurements were conducted three times in ten-minute intervals, providing the total length of 30 minutes. The Fast Fourier Transform was computed for every 2048 points leading to a total of 87 specimens which were used for ensemble averaging.

For the parameter estimation methods, two techniques are used: 1) Transfer function fitting method by using the Hv estimation for the observed transfer function and the first vibration mode of a multi degree of freedom system as the fitting function[16]; and 2) Random Decrement (RD) technique.[17,18] Table 3 shows the estimated values for the natural periods and damping ratios for all the buildings. Three sets of results presented for each building are related to the following cases respectively: 1) Using the transfer function fitting method by considering the responses

at the ground as the input for calculating the observed transfer functions, 2) The same as case #1 but using the responses of the first floor as input, 3) Using the RD method. Also shown are the root mean square (rms) values of responses at the ground and top of the buildings. It is believed that the results of the second case can be considered as a quasi-fixed base model because the sway effect is not included. Although the results are not generally compatible with this quasi-fixed base idea, there are some cases where this idea works well. For example, the effect of SSI can be studied well in the case of Eng1_N building by comparing the 6th and 10th columns of table 3. The higher effect for the lower number of stories can be seen clearly. Also, the results show higher damping ratios for the longitudinal direction (EW). These results are compatible with the results of analytical study as well as the experimental results in the next sections. In the following sections only the results of the case #1 are presented and discussed.

3.2 *The effect of height of building on the results*

All the resulted natural periods for the curve fitting method, including the results of the different stages of the Eng1_N building are plotted in Fig. 8. A linear regression for the results leads to the following relationships for the NS and EW directions, respectively:

NS : $\quad T = 0.01233\,H - 0.0037$ \hfill (1)

EW : $\quad T = 0.01166\,H - 0.0074$ \hfill (2)

where T is the natural period of the building and H shows its height. Also, the resulted damping ratios for the transfer function fitting method are drawn versus

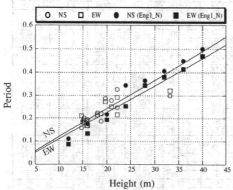

Fig.8. Distribution of period with the height of buildings (Trans. func. fit.)

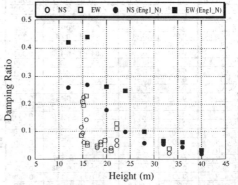

Fig.9. Distribution of the damping ratio with the height of buildings (Trans. func. fit.)

the height of the buildings in Fig. 9. It represents a general tendency of lower damping ratios for taller buildings which may be interpreted as the effect of SSI. Although the site's soil condition is not the same for all buildings, generally one may conclude that the SSI effect is higher for short buildings. More specifically, the results of the Eng1_N building, which are related to the different number of stories but the same soil condition, clearly lead to the same conclusion. There is an apparent difference between the results of the Eng1_N building and the other buildings. This difference also may be explained by the effect of SSI because the Eng1_N building has been located in the worst soil condition area in the campus where higher damping ratios can be expected. The results of the RD method show the same tendency and not presented here graphically.

3.3 *The effect of soil condition on the results*

For evaluation of the effect of soil condition on the dynamic properties of the building, the natural periods and damping ratios are plotted versus the average N-value of the soil. Since the height of the building affects the SSI effect, the buildings are divided into two categories according to their height: 1) Short buildings including 3 and 4-story buildings 2) Moderate height buildings including 5 and 6-story buildings. The results of the transfer function fitting method for these two categories are shown in Figs. 10 and 11, respectively. The results of the 6-story stage of the Eng1_N building is also included. A clear tendency of lower periods for stiffer soils can be seen for both NS and EW directions of moderate height buildings (Fig. 11-a). However, no specific conclusion can be reached from the results for the case of short buildings (Fig. 10-a). The effect of SSI on the damping of buildings can be studied by Figs. 10-b and 11-b. A general tendency of lower damping ratios for stiffer soils can be concluded for both directions of moderate height buildings and EW direction of short buildings. However, the data concerning the NS direction of short buildings is inconclusive. Two other general conclusions can be reached from Figs. 10-b and 11-b. First, the effect of SSI can be seen more clearly in the EW direction, i.e. the longitudinal direction. Secondly, the short buildings generally show higher damping ratios and

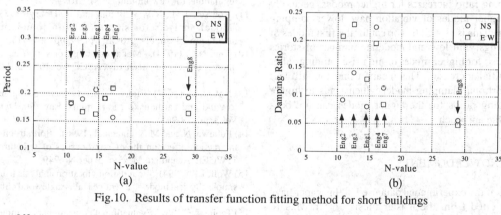

Fig.10. Results of transfer function fitting method for short buildings

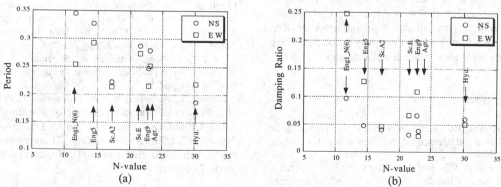

Fig.11. Results of transfer function fitting method for moderate height buildings

1781

the rate of change of damping ratio with the change in the N-values is faster for them. It means that buildings with lower aspect ratios (squat buildings) are affected by SSI more than slender buildings. All these conclusions are consistent with the results of the analytical study.

4 CONCLUSION

The effect of Soil-Structure Interaction on the dynamic properties of structure is investigated analytically and experimentally. The analytical results show that the SSI affects the modal damping ratios of structure significantly and very high damping ratios can be expected for soil-structure systems. This effect is even seen in higher modes of vibration. However, the effect of SSI on natural frequencies of structure is practically seen only in the first mode. It is concluded that the SSI effect is more drastic for buildings with lower number of stories and larger foundations located on softer soils. The conclusions were also confirmed by the results of the experimental study. Also found is although for the first modes of flexible structures the damping ratio increases for higher modes, generally the higher modes of vibration have lower damping ratios. This is especially correct for the first modes of buildings with low and moderate number of stories and also for higher modes of high-rise buildings after an initial increase. This means using the stiffness proportional damping model which leads to higher damping ratios for the higher modes can not be a suitable approach.

ACKNOWLEDGMENT

Most of the experimental data used in this paper have been cited from the master thesis of Mr. Masaru Nakagawa, department of Architecture of Nagoya University. The valuable cooperation of Dr. Riei Nishizaka from Nagoya University in the processing of the data is also gratefully acknowledged.

REFERENCES

1) Jennings, P.C. and J. Bielak (1973), "Dynamics of building-soil interaction", Bull. Seism. Soc. Am., Vol.63, pp. 9-48
2) Veletsos, A.S. and J.W. Meek (1974), "Dynamic behaviour of building-foundation systems", Earthquake Eng. Str. Dyn., Vol.3, pp. 121-138
3) Novak, M. and L. El Hifnawy (1983), "Effect of soil-structure interaction on damping of structures", Earthquake Eng. Str. Dyn., Vol.11, pp. 595-621
4) Aviles, J. and L.E. Perez-Rocha (1996), "Evaluaton of interaction effects on the system period and the system damping due to foundation embedment and layer depth", Soil Dyn. Earthquake Eng., Vol.15, pp. 11-27
5) Fukuwa, N., M.A. Ghannad and S. Yagi (1995), "A study on the effect of soil-structure interaction on the eigenproperty of structure", J. Str. Const. Eng., AIJ, No.475, pp. 35-44 (In Japanese)
6) Ohba, S. (1983), "A Study on the Effects of the Soil condition on the Dynamic Properties of structure", Ph.D. Thesis, Osaka Univ. (In Japanese)
7) Safak, E. (1992), "On Identification of Soil-Structure Interaction from Recorded Motions of Buildings", 10WCEE, Balkema, Rotterdam, Vol.3 , pp.1885-1890
8) Ghannad, M.A., J. Tobita, N. Fukuwa, M. Nakagawa, R. Nishizaka and E. Koide (1997), "A study on the effect of soil-structure interaction on the dynamic properties of RC structures based on the microtremor records", J. Structural Engineering, Vol. 43B, pp.441-450
9) Applied Technology Council (ATC) (1978), "Tentative provisions for the development of seismic regulations for buildings", ATC publication ATC-06
10) NEHRP recommended provisions for seismic regulations for new buildings (NEHRP-1994)
11) Roesset, J.M., R.V. Whitman and R. Dobry (1973), "Modal analysis for structures with foundation interaction", J. str. div., ASCE, Vol.99, pp. 399-415
12) Tsai, N.C. (1974), "Modal damping for soil-structure interaction", J. eng. mech. div., ASCE, Vol.100, pp. 323-341
13) Novak, M. (1974) "Effect of soil on structural response to wind and earthquake", Earthquake Eng. Str. Dyn., Vol.3, pp. 79-96
14) Fukuwa, N. and M.A. Ghannad (1996), "Soil-structure interaction effect on the eigenproperties of structure", 11WCEE, Acapulco, Mexico, paper No.949
15) Wolf, J.P. (1994), "Foundation vibration analysis using simple physical models", Prentice Hall, Englewood cliffs, N.J.
16) Tobita, J. (1996), "Evaluation of nonstationary damping characteristics of structures under earthquake excitations", J. of Wind Eng. and Industrial Aerodynamics, Vol.59, Nos.2,3, pp.283-298.
17) Jeary, A.P. (1986), "Damping in Tall Buildings - A Mechanism and A Predictor", Earthquake Eng. and Struc. Dyn., Vol.14, pp.733-750
18) Tamura, Y., A. Sasaki and H. Tsukagoshi (1993), "Evaluation of Damping Ratios of Randomly Excited Buildings Using the Random Decrement Technique", J. Struct. Constr. Eng., Transaction of Architectural Inst. of Japan (AIJ), No.454, pp.29-38 (In Japanese)

Structural Safety and Reliability, Shiraishi, Shinozuka & Wen (eds) © 1998 Balkema, Rotterdam, ISBN 90 5410 978 5

Reliability assessment of check dam subjected to impact load

Kazuo Itoh, Satoshi Katsuki & Nobutaka Ishikawa
Department of Civil Engineering, National Defense Academy, Yokosuka, Japan

Gakuto Fukawa
Defense Facility Administration Agency, Tokyo, Japan

ABSTRACT: The effect of the uncertainty of both the impact load and the resistance of the dam on the reliability assessment of a check dam subjected to impact load is examined using the hyperspace division method. This study deals with the inelastic deformation limit states in the dynamic behavior of a gravity dam which is constructed of gravel fill covered with a steel plate wall, subjected to the collision of a huge rock contained in the debris flow. First, a dynamic analysis with the two lumped masses system model is proposed for the impact analysis of this structure. Both the excessive local deformation at the impact point and the shear deformation of the dam are considered to be the dominant limit states of this structure. The hyperspace division method is developed as the system reliability analysis method and the Monte Carlo simulation method is used to verify this. Form the computational results of the sensitivity analysis, it is found that the mass and the collision velocity of rock, which govern the uncertainty in the kinetic energy of the rock, are very important factors for the safety assessment of this structure.

1. INTRODUCTION

Many accidents, including structural damage, injuries and loss of human life have occurred because of debris flow disasters, due to the large precipitation and the high rain fall density in Japan. Many check dam structures have been constructed in the mountainous areas of Japan, mostly to control the sediment in the rivers. Recently, however, some check dams have been constructed as a countermeasure to debris flow disasters. According to some investigations, it is considered that one of the most dangerous destructive powers of debris flow is induced by the impact load from the collision of huge rocks contained in high velocity floods. There are many structural types of check dams. The cellular check dam shown in Photo 1 and Fig. 1 is constructed to screen the huge rock contained in debris flow. This structure is a kind of gravity dam which is made of in-situ rocks and/or gravel, and covered with a steel cell wall. The large energy absorption capacity of both the gravel fill and the flexible cover steel under impact loading is expected. Actually, when a debris flow including nearly 6 m diameter rocks hit this type of structure in 1993(see Photo 1), the structure screened the numerous rocks and worked as expected (Nakayasu et al., 1994).

Evaluating the survivability of this structure, many uncertainties, i.e., the resistance of gravel fill, the kinetic energy of the impacting rock and/or its impacting location have to be considered. There is

Photo 1   Cellular check dam hit by debris flow

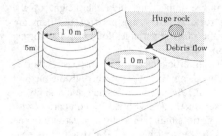

Fig.1   Cellular check dam and debris flow

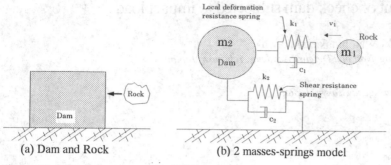

(a) Dam and Rock   (b) 2 masses-springs model

Fig.2   Modeling impact response of Cellular check dam

need of a stochastic approach to this problem, but, it is very difficult to compute the reliability and/or the probability, because the impact analysis involves a complex nonlinear dynamic analysis, and the limit states of this structure tentatively defined at this moment are associated with the nonlinear limit state in the system reliability problem.

This study presents a reliability assessment method for a check dam structure subjected to impact load due to the collision of a rock contained in the debris flow. First, the two masses - springs dynamic analysis model is proposed to simulate the response of the check dam under impact loading. Because of its reduced computation effort, it is possible to combine this dynamic analysis procedure with the system reliability analysis procedure. The verification of the proposed method in the deterministic analysis field is carried out by comparison with the experimental results obtained by authors (Itoh et. al, 1996). Second, a Monte Carlo simulation is carried out to obtain the fundamental knowledge of this problem, or the characteristics of the limit state functions from the view point of the system reliability analysis. Two limit states are treated to evaluate the survivability of this structure, i.e., the excess inelastic shear deformation of the dam over the allowable shear deformation, and the excess inelastic local deformation of the dam at the impact point over an allowable value. The mass of impacting rock, the velocity of the impacting rock, the height of the impacting rock and the resistance of the dam are treated as the random variables following the normal distribution.

Finally, an efficient reliability analysis method is proposed by using the hyperspace division method (Katsuki et. al,1994). The efficiency and validity of the proposed method is verified by comparing with the Monte Carlo simulation and the sensitivity of the uncertainty to the reliability of the structure is also discussed.

2. IMPACT ANALYSIS MODEL

The actual collision phenomenon between the dam and the huge rock shown in Fig. 2 (a) is simplified as shown in Fig. 2 (b) to analyze both the local deformation occurring at the impact point of the vertical wall and the shear deformation of the dam. The dynamic equation of this model is given as follows.

$$m_1\ddot{u}_1 + c_1(\dot{u}_1 - \dot{u}_2) + k_1(u_1 - u_2) = 0 \qquad (1)$$

$$m_2\ddot{u}_2 + c_2\dot{u}_2 - c_1(\dot{u}_1 - \dot{u}_2) + k_2u_2 - k_1(u_1 - u_2) = F_2 \qquad (2)$$

where, m_1: mass of impacting rock contained in debris flow, c_1: damping coefficient of the local resistance, k_1:stiffness of the local resistance spring, m_2: modeled mass of dam resisting the shear deformation, c_2: damping coefficient of the shear resistance of the dam, k_2:stiffness of the shear resistance dam spring, u_1, u_2: displacement of rock and dam, respectively, F_2: flood pressure load of debris flow; the symbol (˙) expresses the time differential.

According to the authors' previous study (Itoh et. al, 1997), the modeled mass of the dam, m_2, is obtained by using the actual mass of dam, m_B, as follows.

$$m_2 = \frac{1}{3}m_B \qquad (3)$$

where, m_B: total mass of actual dam.

The stiffness of the local deformation is given by regression analysis based on the experimental results as follows.

$$k_1 = C_L(C_S k_v)^{0.75}(EI)^{0.25} \qquad (4)$$

where, C_L: regression coefficient for total system $(2\sqrt{2})$, C_S: regression coefficient with respect to the fill material resistance, k_v: stiffness coefficient of fill material obtained by the plate bearing test at the upper surface, E:young's modulus of steel plate, I:

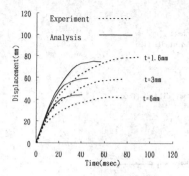

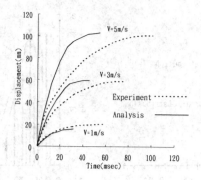

(a) Effect of steel plate thickness

(b) Effect of impact velocity

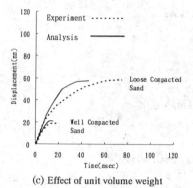

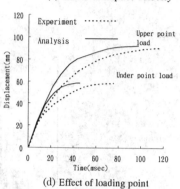

(c) Effect of unit volume weight

(d) Effect of loading point

Fig.3   Displacement ～ time relation

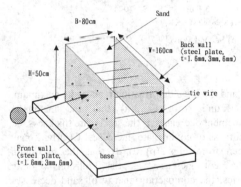

Fig.4   Test model of check dam

Table 1 Parameters for simulation for experiment

m_1	100kg		B	80cm
m_2	283kg		W	160cm
I	$B_t * t^3 /12$		γ_{hv}	2.3×10^{-3}/cm
t	1.6, 3.0, 6.0mm		H	50cm
ρ_s	loose	1.33gf/cm³	ϕ	loose	30°
	dense	1.53gf/cm³		dense	40°
h	15, 35cm		v	1.6
h_1	0.1		h_2	0.1
k_v	loose	0.7kgf/cm³	B_t	50cm
	dense	4.8kgf/cm³		

geometrical moment of inertia of steel plate section area.

The regression coefficient with respect to the fill material resistance is given by

$$C_S = B_t \times \gamma_{hv} \times (H - h) \tag{5}$$

where, B_t: effective length of local resistance of dam, γ_{hv}: transform coefficient from vertical resistance to horizontal resistance, H: height of dam, h: height of collision point.

The stiffness of the shear resistance dam spring, k_2,

is also given by using an empirical equation (Itoh et. al, 1997) as follows.

$$k_2 = \frac{dR_s}{du_2} \tag{6}$$

$$R_s = C_{SH}\left(4.44 \frac{u_2}{h} + 0.169 \left(\frac{u_2}{h} \right)^{0.2} \right) \tag{7}$$

$$C_{SH} = \left(\frac{2}{3}(1 + 0.5v) \right) \frac{\rho_s H^3 w \tan(\phi)}{h} \tag{8}$$

where, R_s: shear deformation resistance of dam,

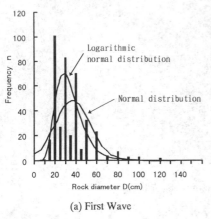
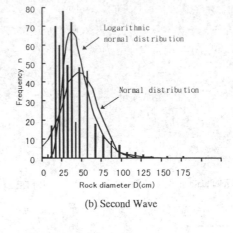

(a) First Wave

(b) Second Wave

Fig.5　Distribution of rock diameter

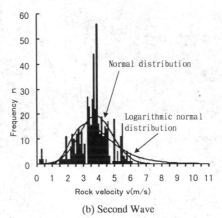

(a) First Wave

(b) Second Wave

Fig.6　Distribution of rock velocity

C_{SH}: transform coefficient from non-dimensional resistance to dimensional resistance, ν : height vs. width ratio of dam (B / H), B : width of dam, w : effective length of dam resisting the impact force, ϕ : angle of internal friction of fill material.

The damping coefficients, c_1 and c_2 are given as follows.

$$c_1 = h_1 \sqrt{m_1 k_1}, \quad c_2 = h_2 \sqrt{m_2 k_2} \qquad (9a , 9b)$$

where, h_1, h_2 : damping moduli (=0.1).

Fig. 3 illustrates the time history of the displacement (u_1) for both the computational results of Eqs. (1),(2) and the experimental results which where carried out by using the test model shown in Fig. 4 (Itoh et. al, 1996).

The analytical parameters shown in Table 1 are used in this simulation. The solid lines in Fig.3(a) are associated with the experimental results. All displacements increase monotonically, and reach a maximum displacement at which the collision weight

stops and the local deformation reaches its maximum. It is found from Fig.3(a) that the maximum displacement decreases as the steel plate thickness, i.e. the stiffness of cover plate, increases. Clearly, it may be seen from Figs.3(b),(c),(d) that the maximum displacement increases as the collision velocity increases, the compaction energy of sand decreases and/or the height of the collision location increases. The simulated results symbolized by broken line, especially with respect to the maximum displacement, are in good agreement with the experimental results for all cases, i.e., parameters of steel stiffness, collision velocity, density of fill material and collision height.

3.　STATISTICAL CHARACTERISTICS OF COLLISION PARAMETERS

The study of the destructive power or potential of debris flow is still ongoing. This study attempts to

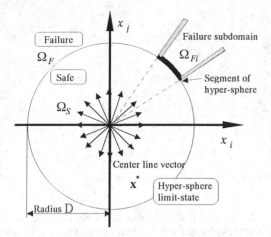

Fig. 7 Radial division and hyper-sphere limit state

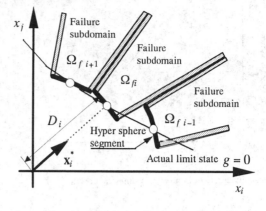

Fig. 8 Approximation of actual limit state function

Table.2 Mean and standard deviation values of each random parameters

	Diameter of rock D(cm)	Collision velocity v(cm)	Collision height h(cm)	Multiplier of local resistance a	Multiplier of shear resistance b
Mean value	300	500	500	1.0	1.0
Standard deviation	90	150	150	0.3	0.3

analyze the statistical characteristics of the diameter and the velocity of rocks contained in debris flow, based on the video record of debris flow in 1988 which was observed in Yake-dake mountain river, where the observation facilities of Kyoto University and Public Work are situated.

Two major waves of debris flow in the record are analyzed. Fig. 5 shows the diameter frequency distribution of rocks in the flow. It is found that the largest diameter in this record reaches 1.75m and a logarithmic distribution fits the observed results better than a normal distribution. Fig. 6 shows the velocity distribution of rocks in this record. Some of them exceed 5 m/s, and both the normal and the logarithmic distribution provide a good fit to the observed results. The coefficients of variation are almost 30%. It can be considered that these results, i.e., normally distributed velocities and a relatively small coefficient of variation are due to the fact that these rocks were part of the same wave, i.e, randomness under the same field conditions.

4. RELIABILITY ANALYSIS OF CHECK DAM BASED ON HYPER SPACE DIVISION METHOD

The hyperspace division method is adopted to analyze the reliability or safety assessment of the check dam. The hyperspace division method (Katsuki and Frangopol, 1994) divides the standard normal random variable space radially and equally into m subdomains as shown in Fig. 7. This method approximates the actual limit state function using hypersphere segment limit states as shown in Fig. 8.

By using this approximation, the probability of failure is computed as follows.

$$P_f \cong \sum_{i=1}^{m} P_{fi} = \sum_{i=1}^{m} [1 - \chi_n^2(D_i^2)]/m \qquad (10)$$

where, P_f = total probability of failure, P_{fi} = contribution of subdomain i to the total probability of failure, m = total number of subdomains, χ_n^2 = cumulative distribution function of the chi-square distribution with n degrees of freedom, D_i = radius of the hyper-sphere segment of the subdomain i.

In the case of a single limit state function, the radius D_i can be computed easily to solve following equation.

$$g(D_i \mathbf{x}_i^*) = 0 \qquad (11)$$

where, $g(\mathbf{x})$ = limit state function, $\mathbf{x}_i^*$ = unit center line vector associated with subdomain i which is given automatically by the unit centerline vector generation method.

In the case of multiple limit states and a series system problem, radius D_i is given by selecting the minimum one as follows.

$$D_i = \min_j D_{i,j} \qquad (12)$$

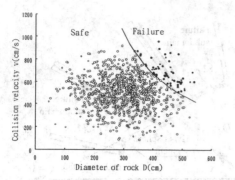

Fig. 9 Examples of Monte Carlo simulation result

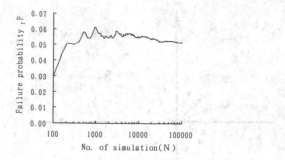

Fig. 10   Convergence process of Monte Carlo simulation

Table.3   Comparison of two simulation methods

Random parameters combination	P_f Monte Carlo simulation (10^5 samples)	P_f Hyper space division method (64 division)
D-v	5.171×10^{-2}	5.41340×10^{-2}
D-h	3.557×10^{-2}	3.65450×10^{-2}
D-a	4.501×10^{-2}	4.66680×10^{-2}
D-b	2.080×10^{-2}	2.19619×10^{-2}
v-h	8.51×10^{-3}	7.46452×10^{-3}
v-a	1.491×10^{-2}	1.45707×10^{-2}
v-b	6.6×10^{-4}	6.42119×10^{-4}
h-a	1.084×10^{-2}	1.07301×10^{-2}
h-b	2.61×10^{-3}	2.87202×10^{-3}
a-b	5.94×10^{-3}	5.86488×10^{-3}

where, $D_{i,j}$ satisfies each limit state function g_j as follows.

$$g_j(D_{i,j}\mathbf{x}_i^*) = 0 \tag{13}$$

5. NUMERICAL EXAMPLE

Five random parameters shown in Table 2, i.e., diameter of rock, collision velocity of rock, height of impact point, multiplier of local deformation resistance and multiplier of shear resistance, are considered as the dominant random variables in this study. It is also assumed that these are based on a normal distribution whose mean and standard deviation values are shown in Table 2.

Two limit states given by the following equations are used in this study.

$$g_{local} = \delta_{La} - \delta_L \tag{14}$$

$$g_{shear} = \delta_{Sa} - \delta_S \tag{15}$$

where, g_{local} : limit state function associated with the local deformation, δ_L : local deformation ($= u_1 - u_2$), δ_{La} : allowable local deformation, g_{shear} : limit state function associated with shear deformation of dam, δ_S : shear deformation of dam ($= u_2 / h$), δ_{Sa} : allowable shear deformation.

Before using the hyperspace division method, some examples are solved by using the Monte Carlo simulation. Fig. 9 shows the Monte Carlo simulation results. In this simulation the collision velocity and the diameter of the rock are treated as the random variables having the characteristics given in Table 2, whole the others are assumed to have the deterministic values given by the mean values in Table 2. The open circles (○) are associated with the survival simulation results and the solid circles (●) are associated with the failures exceeding the local deformation limit states. Therefore, the line in this figure is associated with the local deformation limit states. Increasing the collision velocity and/or the diameter of the rock makes the kinetic energy of rock at impact increase; therefore, the local deformation response, δ_L exceeds the allowable deformation δ_{La}. However, the shear deformation response doesn't exceed its allowable deformation in this simulation.

Fig.10 shows the convergence process of the Monte Carlo simulation. The simulation result with sample size of $n = 10^5$ converge sufficiently. The probability of failure obtained by this simulation is $P_f = 5.171 \times 10^{-2}$.

Using the hyperspace division method with 64 division, the probability of failure becomes $P_f = 5.413 \times 10^{-2}$.   This results is in very good agreement with the Monte Carlo simulation, though only 64 divisions are used.   Table 3 shows the comparison between the Monte Carlo simulation and the hyperspace division method for 11 combinations of two random variables. In all cases, the results of both simulations are in very good agreement.

As mentioned previously, the hyperspace division method needs relative less simulation effort. That is, the computational time decreases from 24 hours of Monte Carlo simulation to 10 minutes of the hyperspace division method.

Using the hyperspace division method, the

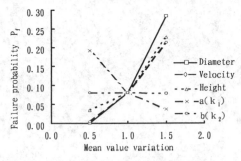

Fig. 11　Relationship between failure probability
and mean value variation

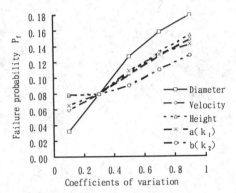

Fig. 12　Relationship between failure probability
and coefficients of variation

sensitivity analysis of the failure probability with respect to changes of both the mean value and the standard deviation are carried out.

Fig. 11 shows the relationship between the failure probability and the mean value variation. The horizontal axis in this figure indicates the multiplier to the mean value in Table 2. The positive sensitivity to the increment is very clear for the mean value of the diameter of rock, the collision velocity, and the collision height. On the other hand, a negative sensitivity is found for the increment of the local resistance multiplier(a). It is very important to note that little sensitivity is found with respect to the variation of the shear deformation resistance multiplier(b). This fact indicates that the limit state associated with local deformation is more dominant than that of shear deformation.

Fig. 12 also shows the sensitivity of the failure probability with respect to changes of the coefficients of variation. In this case a positive sensitivity is found in all cases; the sensitivity of the rock diameter is also the largest in all cases.

It is found from Figs.11,12 that the diameter of

rock and the collision velocity, i.e., the uncertainty in the kinetic energy of the collision rock are very important factors for the safety assessment of this structure.

6. SUMMARY

The safety assessment of check dam structures subjected to impact load has been carried out by using the hyperspace division method. The proposed method can solve the series system reliability problem based on an inelastic dynamic analysis with relatively less computational effort. The safety assessment of the check dam is very sensitive to the uncertainty factors of the kinetic energy of the rock, i.e., the rock diameter and its collision velocity.

REFERENCE

Itoh,K., Katsuki,S., Ishikawa,N., Abe,S. (1996) "Impact Resistance of Double Wall Check Dam", *Proceedings of the Asia-Pacific conference on shock & impact loads on structures.*,153-160.

Itoh,K., Katsuki,S., Ishikawa,N., Abe,S. (1997) "A study on impact test and shear resistance model of filled sand in cellular check dam", *Journal of Structural Engrg.*

Katsuki,S. and Frangopol, D. M.(1994) "Hyperspace Division Method for Structural Reliability", *Journal of Engrg. Mech.*, ASCE,120(11),2405-2427.

Nakayasu,M., Sirae,K., Sato,T.(1994) "The Effect of Steel Shell Dam on Debris Flow of August 1993", *Journal of the Japan Society of Erosion Control Engineering ,Vol.46 No.5(190). Jan.*,33-37.

"Design Manual for Steel Made Sabo Structure", Sabo and Land Sliding Technical Center, Japan, 1993(in Japanese).

Structural Safety and Reliability, Shiraishi, Shinozuka & Wen (eds) © 1998 Balkema, Rotterdam, ISBN 90 5410 978 5

Safety indices of breakwaters against sliding and foundation failure

Takashi Nagao
Port and Harbour Research Institute, Ministry of Transport, Yokosuka, Japan

Yasuyuki Yoshinami
Fukken Co. Ltd, Hiroshima, Japan

ABSTRACT: Safety indices of the whole system of caisson-type breakwaters were calculated and discussed using 76 cases of existing breakwaters in Japan. The mean values of safety indices against sliding and against foundation failure were 2.4 and 2.1 respectively. These calculation results were found to be consistent with those of past failure cases, and some considerations about soil properties of foundation were made with regard to this point.

1. INTRODUCTION

Until recently, in designing port structures, external forces and resisting forces were treated as deterministic parameters, and the effects of the deviations of design parameters from actual values, the errors in the structural-analysis formulae, and so on were usually considered in terms of a single factor, called the safety factor.

In the present design method of breakwaters, for instance, three failure modes of sliding, overturning, and foundation failure are considered. As for the safety against sliding, the equilibrium condition of horizontal forces is considered. And for the safety against foundation failure, Bishop's slice method is applied for circular failure with the equilibrium of moments taken into consideration. The judgement of the safety is made by using the safety factor, and the allowable safety factor for sliding is 1.2; that for foundation failure, 1.0. Usually, in most cases, the sections of the breakwaters are governed by either the sliding failure or the foundation failure under wave pressure.

Although such external forces and resisting forces and so on are, as a matter of fact, random variables subject to certain probability distributions, all factors were treated as deterministic values and the possibility of the actual values deviating from the design values toward the danger side has been dealt with by a margin given to the safety factor. This design method has been built based on the long-time experiences, but the safety of structures designed by this method and its rationality cannot be explained sufficiently.

Introducing a probability concept to the design of structures is, recently, increasingly popular. Such design method is called a reliability based design method or limit state design method, and the probabilities of the failure, not the safety factors, are kept less than a certain allowable value by this method.

The final purpose of this study is to apply the reliability based design method to the safety problems of the whole system of breakwaters. Accordingly, 76 cases of breakwaters are picked up from caisson-type breakwaters, designed in Japan, where the sliding or foundation failures are dominant, and the safety of these breakwaters is discussed by using the safety indices.

2. UNCERTAINTY IN DESIGN FACTORS

2.1 *Flow of present design*

As to the design conditions of breakwaters, the design parameters such as wind, wave, tide level, soil properties, body weight of breakwater, and so on are to be considered. In designing the basic section of a breakwater, its structural form is determined in the first instance, and then the crown height, the thickness of its upper structure, the thickness and width of its rubble mound, the sectional shape of its wave-dissipation structure, and so on are determined. In general, the breakwater sections are determined under the case of the maximum wave pressures acting on them. It is also common in Japan to use the Goda formula for calculating wave forces.

2.2 Extraction of uncertain factors

Uncertain factors involved in the safety of breakwaters are described as follows.

(1) Designed waves

The deepwater wave heights considered in the design of port structures are determined based on the values derived from a proper statistical processing of measured values, or determined based on estimated wave height under the conditions of virtual typhoons. Then, the effects of refraction, diffraction, shallow water, wave breaking, etc. are added to determine the standards of the design wave. Uncertain factors for the design wave are involved in every step of the above process.

(2) Horizontal wave pressure and uplift

The horizontal pressure and the uplift are calculated by the Goda formula. The formula was developed by using the experimental results from wave pressures and application results from the field. At present, Goda formula is considered as the most reliable. However, calculated results using the formulae are, of course, likely to contain certain errors.

(3) Designed tide-level

The mean high water levels (HWL) or the highest high water level (HHWL) is usually used as the designed tide-level. The HWL is the mean of the high water levels of each month. In abnormal weather such as typhoon, the tide level goes beyond the HWL as a matter of course.

(4) Buoyancy

For the portion of a breakwater body below the still water surface, its buoyancy has to be taken into account. Uncertain factors are involved in the establishment of the still water surface level and the unit weight of the seawater in this case.

(5) Weight of breakwater

The unit weights of plain concrete, reinforced concrete, and filling sand are necessary for the calculation of the weight of a breakwater body. Their actual values also vary from the design values.

(6) Coefficient of friction

To calculate the safety of breakwaters against sliding, it is necessary to use proper values of coefficients of friction. Although the coefficient of friction between concrete and rubble is usually taken as 0.6, its actual

value varies considerably. Besides, the case where asphalt mats are used to increase frictional resistance is very popular. In such cases, the designed coefficient of friction is taken 0.7 or so, but the actual value also varies in this case.

(7) Unit weights of rubble mound and foundation soil

As the rubble mound is built by throwing rubbles into the sea and the foundation ground has been formed by long-term sedimentation, the dispersion of unit weights of these materials is greater than that of the breakwater body. And it is to be noted that the weights of the rubble mound and the foundation soil act not only as loads but also as resisting forces.

(8) Strength of rubble mound

In the present design method, the strengths c and ϕ of rubble mounds are determined based on the results of triaxial compression test on crushed stones. In the test, the grain diameter of rubble was taken as an equivalent diameter, converted in accordance with the similitude theory.

(9) Strength of foundation soil

In the present design method, the strength of the foundation soil is estimated basically in terms of only either its angle of internal friction ϕ or cohesion c. And regarding the strength of the foundation soil, the errors in collecting test samples and soil testing as well as the dispersion of foundation soil characteristics in both the horizontal and vertical directions have to be taken into account.

2.3 Degrees of dispersion of uncertain factors

In this study, all the dispersions of the above design factors are assumed to be taking place in accordance with the normal distribution. The authors compiled the results of numerous past studies (refer to bibliography) as in Table 1, which shows the mean values and the degrees of dispersion.

$$X_{om} / X_0 = \alpha, \qquad \sigma_0 = \beta \cdot X_0 \qquad (1)$$

where:

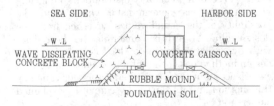

Fig-1 Standard section of caisson-type breakwater

X_0 = estimated value of factor X (usually used in designing)

X_{om} = mean of actual values of factor X

σ_0 = standard deviation of actual values of factor X

Uncertain factors other than those mentioned above are not considered in this study because of the insufficient data and so on.

3. SAFETY INDICES AGAINST SLIDING

3.1 *Performance function*

In the present design method, the safety is judged by the following equation. (Refer to Fig. 2)

$$F = \mu \cdot W / P \qquad (2)$$

where:

W = total weight of the breakwater (kN/m)

P = total horizontal force acting on the wall of breakwater (kN/m)

μ = coefficient of friction between the breakwater and foundation (rubble mound)

F = safety factor

tabel-1   Degree of dispersion of uncertainty

uncertainty	α	β
Wave		
deepwater wave height	1.00	0.10
wave deformation [1]	0.97	0.04
wave deformation [2]	1.06	0.09
breaking wave deformation	0.87	0.09
wave pressure [3]	0.91	0.17
wave pressure [4]	0.84	0.10
Unit weight		
reinforced concrete	0.98	0.02
plain concrete	1.02	0.02
filling sand	1.02	0.04
rubble mound	1.00	0.03
foundation soil	1.00	0.03
tide level		
H.H.W.L	1.0	0.0
H.W.L	1.5 ~ 2.5	0.0
coefficient of friction	1.06	0.16
strength of foundation		
rubble mound	1.0	0.1
foundation soil	1.0	0.1

1) slow changes of water-depth
2) rapid changes of water-depth
3) composite type
4) armored type

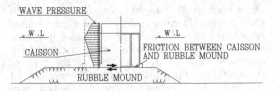

Fig-2   Failure mode of sliding

According to the present design specifications, the safety factor is taken 1.2 or higher than 1.2, and the section of breakwater is usually determined by the maximum wave pressure.

The equation (2) expresses concisely the sliding failure mode and this concept will be adopted as a performance factor in this study and it is defined by the following equation.

$$Z = R - S \qquad (3)$$

where:

$R = \mu \cdot W$

$S = P$

Accordingly, the safety index β is found by the following equation.

$$\beta = (Rm - Sm) / \sqrt{\sigma_R^2 + \sigma_S^2} \qquad (4)$$

where:

β = safety index

Rm = mean of resisting forces

Sm = mean of acting forces

σ_R = standard deviation of resisting forces

σ_S = standard deviation of acting forces

3.2 *Extraction of design cases*

The section of breakwater is designed not only to satisfy merely the prescribed safety factors but also designed with several alternative plans considering the applicabilities to the construction site such as relative difficulty of construction works, construction cost, construction time, etc.

To evaluate the safety of existing breakwaters designed and constructed in Japan, 76 cases of breakwaters were collected. The conditions for collecting such cases are described below:

(1) Collect the design cases from a wide range of areas to avoid one-sidedness in regions or design conditions.

(2) As to the structural type, the study is focussed on both the caisson-type composite breakwaters and the breakwaters armored with wave dissipating concrete blocks, which are the most common types in Japan.

(3) Exclude the cases under construction or the cases where the wave is assumed to be of a 10-year's probability.

(4) Also exclude the cases where the determining process of the design wave was unknown or ambiguous.

Out of above 76 cases, 59 cases were selected with the condition of having a safety factor, approximately close to the allowable value (F = 1.2 to 1.3) against sliding. In these 59 cases, when viewed from structural aspects, 31 cases are of the type of caisson-type composite breakwater; 28 cases are of the type of breakwater armored with wave dissipating concrete blocks.

3.3 *Safety indices*

Fig. 3 shows the safety indices against sliding for the above 59 cases.

Although all the breakwaters described in this chapter are of cases where sliding is dominant (Fs = 1.2 to 1.3), the safety indices of these 59 cases are scattered in the range from 2.0 to 2.9. Their mean is found to be 2.4; their standard deviation, 0.25. The range of the safety indices, converted into failure probability, turned out to be of the order of 10^{-2}.

This calculation result mentioned above will be discussed comparing with the past sliding failure cases occurred in Japan. At present approximately 15,000 caisson type breakwaters are constructed in Japan, and during the last 5 years 30 sliding failures are reported except for the failures caused by the deformation of wave dissipating concrete block and the scour of rubble mound. This means that 5 to 6 sliding failures occurred in a year. Taking the breakwaters' life span of 50 years, the probability of

sliding failure that may occur during the life span is of the order of 10^{-2}. It is considered that the failure probability obtained theoretically is in conformity with one obtained from the past sliding failure cases occured in Japan.

4. SAFETY INDICES AGAINST FOUNDATION FAILURE

4.1 *Present design method*

In the present design method, the foundation failure is analyzed by the Bishop's slice method that assumes the circular slip surface. The load conditions for using the Bishop's slice method are shown in Fig.4 and the salient features include the method of converting surcharges, the method of setting the starting point of circular sliding, the method of determining the soil properties and so on. The equation to examine safety is as shown below, and the allowable safety factor is set at 1.0 empirically.

$$F = \frac{\Sigma \left\{ \dfrac{[c'b + tan\phi'(w'+q)] \cdot sec\alpha}{1 + (tan\alpha \, tan\phi') / F} \right\}}{\Sigma(w'+q) \cdot sin\alpha + 1/r \cdot \Sigma H \, a} \quad (5)$$

where:

c' = apparent cohesion based on effective stress (kN/m²)

b = width of slices (m)

ϕ = angle of internal friction based on effective stress (rad)

w' = weight of slice (kN/m)

q = surcharge acting on slice (kN/m)

α = angle between slice and its bottom (rad)

H = horizontal load (kN/m)

a = arm length of horizontal load (m)

r = radius of sliding circular arc (m)

The feature of the Bishop's slice method is that its equation has an F in the right side, too. In designing, the values of the Fs are equated and the convergence calculation is made.

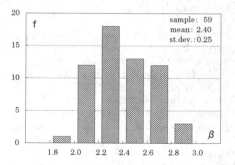

Fig-3   Safety indices against sliding

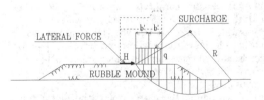

Fig-4   Failure mechanism by bishop's method

4.2 *Failure modes*

According to the centrifuge model test results under eccentric, inclined loads, the displacement of the mode close to sliding dominates if the effect of the horizontal load is comparatively larger than that of the vertical load, and conversely a vertical-displacement mode dominates if the effect of the vertical load is larger than that of the horizontal load. This does not necessarily agree with the circular slip surface. Besides, since the centrifuge model tests were conducted by applying loads statically, the foundation failure modes reproduced in the tests might be somewhat different from those of actual breakwaters under dynamic loads. In the case of the actual failure cases in the field, the foundation failures are very few compared to the sliding failure, and many unexplained problems remain in the mechanism of foundation failure.

Many problems in the foundation failure have not yet been elucidated: However, in accordance with the present design method, the same failure mechanism as of the Bishop's slice method is adopted in this study. Namely, the resisting force R is treated as the moment of resistance for the sliding circular arc, the load S is treated as the moment for sliding circular arc, and assume the sliding circular arc as to give the minimum safety factor under the present design method. Although the nonlinearity of the performance function should be taken into account for the exact calculation of the means and standard deviations of R and S, the first-order and second-moment method are used employing the Taylor expansion around the mean in this study.

4.3 Safety indices

Out of 76 cases of breakwaters described before, 35 cases were selected with the condition of having a safety factor, approximately close to the allowable value (F = 1.0 to 1.1) against foundation failure.

Fig. 5 shows the safety indices of these 35 cases. Safety indices are found to have the range from 1.2 to 3.0, and the mean of these is 2.1. This value of failure probability is considered to be relatively high compared with the case of sliding. Fig. 6 shows the relation between the safety indices against sliding and ones against foundation failure. In this Figure, 34 cases of breakwaters are selected whose safety factors are close to the allowable value in both cases of sliding and foundation failure.

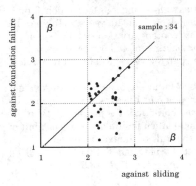

Fig-6   Relations of safety indices

4.4 Comparison of safety indices against sliding

In most failure cases of breakwaters, it is difficult to identify exactly the type of failure. As far as the present study is concerned, there are only two cases of breakwater failure due to the shortage of the bearing capacity of rubble-mound. On the other hand, sliding failure is reported 5 to 6 cases in a year. This fact in practice contradicts the analytical result, which shows that the safety indices against foundation failure are smaller than those against sliding. The reasons might be considered as follows.

The allowable safety factor against the foundation failure is lower than that against sliding in the present design method and the same failure mechanisms and soil properties are assumed as those of the present design method in the case of the safety indices. It means that, during the calculation of the safety indices, the ratio of resisting force to external acting force for the foundation failure has been kept lower than that for sliding failure. So, it is presumed that the safety indices against the foundation failure had become smaller than that against the sliding. With regard to the foundation failure, the present design method includes numerous empirical elements, and the failure modes as well as the soil properties seem not to agree with those of actual cases of failure.

5.   CONSIDERATION ON FOUNDATION FAILURE

5.1 The probability of failure from the past events

The lower limit of probability of foundation failure will be determined by a simplified calculation method.

First of all, the assumption will be made from the past events of foundation failures that one or two

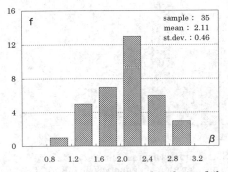

Fig-5   Safety indices against foundation failure

number of breakwaters undergo foundation failure during the period of 5 to 10 years. Taking the number of breakwaters, constructed in Japan as 15,000, the probability of failure that may occur during the life span (50 years) will be approximately 5.0×10^{-4}.

The foundation failure of one or two breakwaters during the period of 5 to 10 years is considered to be roughly an lower limit, and it is justified to take the probability of foundation failure as the lower limit of 5×10^{-4} for the rule-of-thumb calculation. When converted into the safety index, this figure will be approximately of the order of $\beta = 3.5$.

5.2 Consideration on Bishop's method

The cases of foundation failure are extremely few in Japan. According to the author's collected data on two cases of foundation failure, the safety factors are 0.68 and 0.73, when computed by Bishop's method. Furthermore, from other several collected data, it is found that there has not been any foundation failure for the cases where the safety factors are round about 0.9. From the foregoing facts, it is to be considered that there exists a kind of latent safety allowance in the present design method of foundation failure.

The cases with such a latent safety allowance are considered. In the previous chapter, the wave pressure, caisson's weight, etc. are clearly defined and used in the sliding failure analysis without any major problems. On the other hand, the Bishop's method used for the foundation failure analysis is considered as appropriate to the actual behaviors and its results are in conformity with those of the experiments. However, when the experimental data are observed, there is a time lag between the failure and the application of horizontal forces, introduced after the application of vertical loads. The strength of the rubble mound and the foundation soil depends upon the time of loading. It is suggested that, in the case of the short duration loads such as wave pressures, the strengths could be taken higher than that of static loading. Such an idea is also warranted in this regard. Hence the analysis will be carried out, with this point in mind, giving due consideration to the rate of strength increase in the dynamic load cases.

5.3 Analysis with consideration of dynamic load

Taking into accounts the effect of dynamic loads, the analysis is performed with the strength increase, and the results of the analysis are tabulated as in Table-2. The calculation for safety indices is conducted similarly with that of the previous chapter,

Table-2 Safety indices against foundation failure
(with consideration of dynamic load effect)

	strength increase of foundation	safety indices	
		mean	std.dev.
case-1	5 %	2.49	0.47
case-2	10 %	2.86	0.49
case-3	15 %	3.21	0.51
case-4	20 %	3.56	0.53
case-5	25 %	3.88	0.55
case-6	30 %	4.20	0.58

for the 35 cross-sections, the safety factors of which are in the range of 1.0 to 1.1. The safety indices are roughly directly proportional to the strength increase and the case 4 is calculated with 20% strength increase which is equivalent to the case with the failure probability $Pf = 5.0 \times 10^{-4}$, which is estimated from the past failure cases. And for this case 4, the distribution of safety indices is shown in Fig. 7.

Furthermore, when the safety factors are calculated with the 20% increase of the foundation strength for the above mentioned 2 cases of failure, the safety factors are still less than 1.0. From the above facts, it is to be concluded that the assumption of the 20% strength increase for rubble mound and foundation soil is not so much an over estimate.

6. CONCLUSIONS

Safety indices of caisson-type breakwaters against sliding and foundation failure are calculated and discussed using 76 cases of existing breakwaters in Japan. Concluding remarks are as follows.

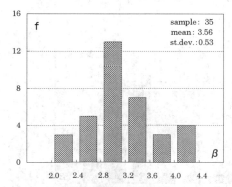

Fig-7 Safety indices against foundation failure
(with consideration of dynamic load effect)

1. Safety indices against sliding for the breakwaters whose safety factors are close to the allowable safety factor were found to have the range from 2.0 to 2.9, of which the average was approximately 2.4. This failure probability obtained theoretically is in conformity with one obtained from the past sliding failure cases occured in Japan.

2. Safety indices against foundation failure were found to have the range from 1.2 to 3.0, of which the average was approximately 2.1. Compared with the case of sliding, this value of failure probability is considered to be relatively high.

3. Although, in field, the failures of foundation are by far fewer than those of the sliding, the analytical result is inconsistent. Its reasons might be considered as follows: the allowable safety factor against the foundation failure is lower than that against sliding in the present design method, and the failure mechanisms were assumed to be same as that of the present design method in case of the calculation of safety indices.

4. Taking into account the effect of dynamic loads, case studies were performed with the strength increases of rubble mound and foundation soil. From these studies it was found that the failure probability of the 20% strength increase case was approximately equal to that obtained from past failure cases.

5. With regard to the foundation failure, the present design method includes many empirical elements, and the failure modes as well as the soil properties seem not to agree with those of actual cases of failures. There would be the possibility that we may, in near future, need to develop some other method regarding the reliability based design method for the foundation failure.

REFERENCES

Technical standards for port and harbour facilities in Japan: The overseas coastal area development Institute of Japan, 1991.

Horikawa, H. et al.: Statistical data analysis on caisson composite type breakwater, Technical note of port and harbour res. inst., No.644, 1989 (in Japanese).

Mizukami, J., Kobayashi, M. : Strength characteristics by large scale triaxial compression test, Technical note of port and harbour res. inst., No.699, 1991 (in Japanese).

Kobayashi, M., Terashi, M., Takahashi, K. et al.: A new method for calculating the bearing capacityof rubble mounds, Rept. port and harbour res.inst., Vol. 26, No.2, 1987, pp. 371 ～ 412 (in Japanese).

Terashi, M., Kitazume, M. : Bearing capacity of a foundation on top of high mound subjected to eccentric and inclined load, Rept. port and harbour res. inst., Vol. 26, No.2, 1987, pp. 3 ～ 24.

Takayama, T. and Ikeda, N.: Estimation of sliding failure probability of present breakwaters for probablistic design, Rept. port and harbour res. inst., Vol.31, No.5, 1993, pp. 3 ～ 32.

Nagao, T., Kadowaki, Y. and Terauchi, K. : Evaluation of safety of breakwaters by the reliability based design method (1st report: Study on the safety against sliding), Rept. port and harbour res. inst., Vol.34, No.1, 1995, pp. 39 ～ 70 (in Japanese).

Nagao, T., Kadowaki, Y., Tsuchida, T. and Terauchi, K. : Evaluation of safety of breakwaters by the reliability based design method (2nd report: Study on the safety against foundation failure), Rept. port and harbour res. inst., Vol. 36, No.1, 1997 (in Japanese).

Structural Safety and Reliability, Shiraishi, Shinozuka & Wen (eds) © 1998 Balkema, Rotterdam, ISBN 90 5410 978 5

Practical application of probability-based prediction of differential settlements to a pile foundation

Hideaki Tanahashi

University of Delaware, Del., USA (Formerly: Nikken Sekkei Ltd & Nikken Sekkei Nakase Geotechnical Institute, Osaka, Japan)

ABSTRACT: This paper presents a practical application of probability-based prediction of differential settlements of a warehouse supported by pile groups that reach a thin gravelly sand layer. Consolidation settlements of the clay layer, beneath the gravelly sand layer, were supposed to take place due to the stresses induced by live loads. Standard deviations of stresses and rotations of differential settlements on foundation girders are predicted. A vertical pile load test and strain measurements of the working pile shafts were carried out based on which the consolidation settlements are discussed. The serviceability and structural safety of the building are confirmed.

1 INTRODUCTION

The author has proposed a prediction method for estimating differential settlements of structures due to non-homogeneity of soil properties and loads (Tanahashi, 1994a, b). This method was applied actually to the design of Rinku International Logistics Center in Rinku Town, Osaka, Japan. The Rinku Town was developed on the reclaimed coast facing the Kansai International Airport in the southeastern part of Osaka Bay. This building consists of steel encased reinforced concrete structures including a large warehouse with ramps of four stories and an office

building of six stories.

The ground consists of a sandy reclaimed layer on the diluvial (Pleistocene) alternate layers of both sandy and clayey layers. It is different from other typical reclaimed land, for example, Port Island, Kobe and Kansai International Airport Island. Therefore, the consolidation settlement of clay layer due to the weight of reclaimed soils is expected not to take place, because the consolidation yield stress is large enough to sustain the overburden stresses of reclaimed soils.

The major problem of this ground is that the bearing layer of sufficient thickness can not be found down to very deep levels for the design of end bearing piles.

Thus, the building was designed to be supported by bored pile groups of prestressed high strength concrete (PHC) piles whose tips reach the thin gravelly sand layer to about 20m below the ground surface. The effective stresses of the clay layer beneath the gravelly sand layer may exceed the consolidation yield stress partially and result in some consolidation settlements when the design live loads of each floor act fully in the warehouse.

On the other hand, no consolidation settlements are supposed to occur when the live loads are small. Differential settlements, therefore, take place according to the load concentration, because the actual live load intensity and spatial distribution vary frequently in the warehouse. However, it is very difficult to assume the distribution characteristics of live loads in order to predict the differential settlements of the pile foundation, although the maximum floor live loads of the warehouse are

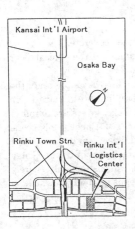

Fig.1 Location of the Building

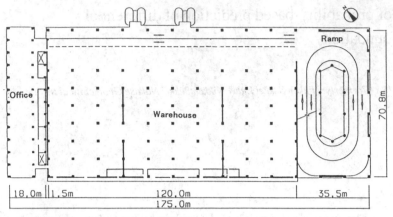

Fig.2 Typical Floor Plan of the Building

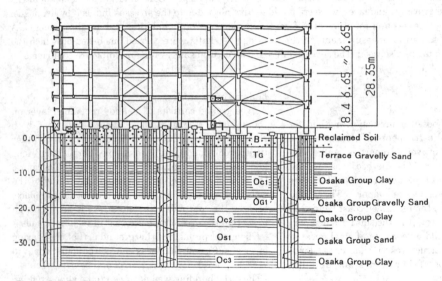

Fig.3 Soil Profile and Section of the Building

determined as 18~25 kPa. Thus, the probability-based prediction method of differential settlements was applied to the building with a pile foundation in order to confirm the serviceability and structural safety of the building. During construction, a vertical pile load test and strain measurements of the working pile shafts were carried out based on which consolidation settlements are discussed.

2 SOIL PROFILE AND OUTLINE OF THE BUILDING

The building consists of a large warehouse with ramps of four stories and an office building of six stories that made of steel encased reinforced concrete.

The location of this building and the typical floor plan are shown in Figs.1 and 2 respectively.

The geotechnical profile of the site and the transversal section of the building are illustrated in Fig.3. In this area, no alluvial clay layers are found. A terrace gravelly sand layer T_G (Upper Pleistocene Deposit) underlies the reclaimed sandy layer of a depth 6~8m. Sandy and clayey layers of Osaka Group (Pleistocene Deposit) are deposited alternately beneath T_G. Each layer descends gradually toward the north-north-west direction. The major soil properties of the layers are shown in Table 1.

Table 1 Major Soil Properties

Soil Layer	Depth	Soil Properties
Reclaimed Soil B	6~8m	N=20~60 : upper part N=10~15 : lower part
Terrace Gravelly Sand TG	2~6m	N=10~30 locally N=60
Clay Layer Oc1	9~11m	q_u=114~182kPa p_c=230~485kPa E_{50}=4.45~25.3MPa
Gravelly Sand OG1	3~6m	N=30~60 thin clay layers involve in lower portion.
Clay Layer Oc2	4~6m	q_u=178~290kPa p_c=510~620kPa E_{50}=14.46~28.21MPa
Sand Layer Os1	6~7m	N=40~60 : upper part N=10~30 : clay layers exisit alternatively
Clay Layer Oc3	9m or more	q_u=312~411kPa p_c=580~620kPa E_{50}=20.45~28.0MPa

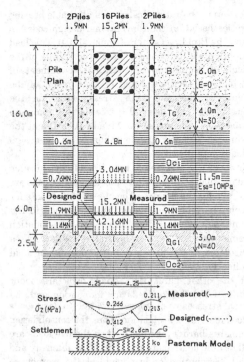

Fig.4   Vertical Stress Distribution of the Clay Layer Oc2 and Settlements

3 FOUNDATION DESIGN

The foundation of this building should be supported by a pile foundation, because the weight of the building is large (average weight 140kPa). However, it is difficult to select the kind of the piles and their bearing layer appropriately, because the sandy layers are rather thin and not so stiff enough to support the piles. Many case studies on pile foundations were carried out, considering both vertical and horizontal resistance of piles, settlements, construction costs, pile installation methods and so on.

The sand layer Os1 is thicker than the gravelly sand layer OG1, but rather loose in lower portion and it involves a thin clayey layer inside. If the piles are designed to be supported on this sand layer, the pile length is around 30m. On the other hand, the pile length is 18~22m in case of OG1. The vertical resistance of the longer pile is larger than that supported by OG1. On the contrary, horizontal resistance of each pile needs to be larger. As for the estimation of construction costs, the longer piles are more expensive than the shorter ones.

However, some problems remain in the shorter piles; consolidation settlements of the clay layer Oc2 may cause differential settlements of the foundation because of the concentrated stresses beneath the pile groups. Therefore, analytical study for consolidation settlements was carried out using the Boussinesq's solution and probability-based prediction of differential settlements of the pile foundation was conducted. Another problem is on the estimation of

the bearing capacity of the pile supported by a thin sand layer on a clay layer.

As the best solution, the author has chosen the bored PHC pile and decided the gravelly sand layer OG1 as the bearing layer. As for the installation method, a preboring method with forming of an enlarged pedestal was selected. The method has been authorized by the Japanese Government and been widely used recently in Japan.

At the same time, a vertical pile load test and field measurements of strains of the working pile shafts during construction were planned in order to confirm the serviceability and structural safety of the pile foundation.

4 CONSOLIDATION SETTLEMENTS

At first the vertical stress distribution in the clay layer Oc2 due to the pile loads in typical areas of the warehouse were analyzed using the Boussinesq's solution. One of the solutions is shown by broken lines in Fig.4. In this analysis, the friction loads are acted at the middle level of Oc1 and the end bearing loads of pile tips were acted at the pile bottom. Friction loads and end bearing loads are distributed respectively in proportion to the ratio of calculated allowable bearing capacities based on the conventional design codes in Japan (The Building Center of Japan, 1994). This load distribution will be compared with the results of the vertical pile load test and the strain measurements of pile shafts in sections 7 and 8. As a result of the calculations, the maximum stress acting on the surface of the clay layer O_{C2} exceeds the minimum consolidation yield stress 0.51MPa by 0.11MPa at the central area beneath the pile groups when the design live loads act fully.

However, the stresses do not exceed the yield value in the peripheral area. Here, the design live loads are 18~25 kPa for the floors and beams and 12~18 kPa for the columns and foundations, as determined in the conventional way. The maximum consolidation settlement of the clay layer due to the excess stresses is calculated as 2.6cm based on the one-dimensional consolidation theory.

On the other hand, the dead loads are about 57~79% of the design loads for foundation and the effective stresses of clay layer O_{C2} due to dead loads are too small for consolidation. Thus the consolidation settlements hardly take place when the live loads are small or only dead loads act. Since the intensity and spatial distribution of live loads of the warehouse depend on the service conditions and are supposed to vary frequently, consolidation settlements of pile groups may vary from 2.6 cm to 0 cm due to the variable live loads.

However, differential settlements are expected to be reduced by the rigidity of the soil and the foundation. The responses of the beam to differential settlements have been formulated as reduction coefficients of differential settlements by the author (Tanahashi 1994a) ; they are expressed generally in the form of wave number response function for a Timoshenko Beam resting on a Pasternak Model. The consolidation differential settlements of each foundation is reduced to be 4.5% approximately by the shear rigidity of the soils alone according to the reduction coefficients of differential settlements. This calculation is on the basis of deterministic treatment of two-dimensional Pasternak Model which consists of a shear layer on a Winkler Model. It is carried out using the following parameters as:

Reduction coefficient of differential settlements:

$$\alpha_s(\omega) = \frac{1}{1 + \omega^2/\gamma_s^2} = 0.045 \qquad (1)$$

where,

$$\gamma_s = \sqrt{k_o/G} = 0.16 \, \text{m}^{-1} \qquad (2)$$

: characteristic value of Pasternak Model.

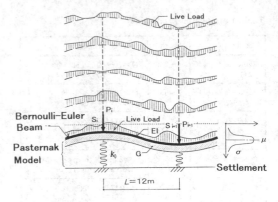

Fig.5 Mechanical Model of Analysis

$$\omega = 2\pi/L = 0.739 \, \text{m}^{-1} \qquad (3)$$

: wave number (L : wave length of differential settlement curve assumed approximately as a trigonometric function: in this case a spacing 8.5m of foundations is assumed).

$$k_0 = q/\mu = 7.69 \, \text{MPa/m} \qquad (4)$$

: subgrade reaction coefficient which is calculated from an average equivalent elastic settlement of the foundation $\mu = 0.013$m due to vertical average load $q = 0.1$MPa.

$$G = \sum \frac{EH}{2(1+\nu)} = 296.7 \, \text{MPa·m} \qquad (5)$$

: shear rigidity of the upper soil layers T_G, O_{C1} and O_{G1} on clay layer O_{C2} in the vertical direction.

$E = E_{50}$: modulus of elasticity for clay

$E = 2.8N$ (MPa) : that for sand. N is a blow count of SPT (Standard Penetration Test) .

H: depth of the layer

ν: Poisson's ratio : 0.5 for clay and 0.3 for sand. These values are shown in Fig.4.

Of course, the reduction effects of rigidity of the foundation itself and shear rigidity along the orthogonal axis of the direction considered can be expected. Any way, the differential settlements are small. The average settlement is not reduced and it is calculated as 1.3 cm which is around half of the maximum settlement.

Thus, the settlements {S_i} of the foundations can be assumed as discrete random variables distributing spatially from 0~1.3 cm, which are caused by live load concentration. Theoretically, these distribution can be treated as a local integral process (Vanmarcke, 1983) of a live load process with spatial distribution over five floors, including the roof for car park. However, there

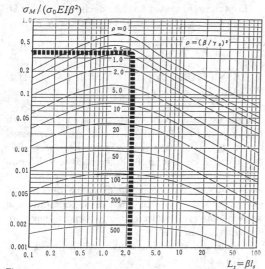

Fig. 6   Standard Deviations of Bending Moments
(Bernoulli–Euler Beam on Pasternak Model)

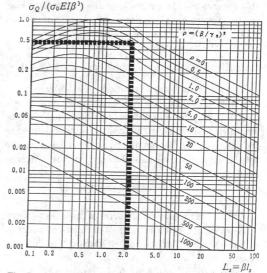

Fig. 7   Standard Deviations of Shear Forces
(Bernoulli–Euler Beam on Pasternak Model)

are little survey data available of live load spatial distribution of warehouses in recent service conditions as far as the author knows.

Consequently it is difficult to assume the type of the random process beforehand exactly. However, it might be reasonable to assume a Gaussian white noise process for such a random process in the practical design. Survey data are expected to be accumulated in future.

5 PROBABILITY-BASED PREDICTION OF STRESSES AND ROTATIONS DUE TO DIFFERENTIAL SETTLEMENTS

According to the probability-based prediction method for differential settlements proposed by the author, the standard deviations of displacements and stresses on the structure can readily be worked out using the calculation diagram if only four values are assumed; they are a standard deviation of settlements and a scale of fluctuation of the settlement curves and characteristic values in the case where the whole rigidity is ignored (Tanahashi 1994a,b).

A Bernoulli-Euler Beam on a Pasternak Model is suitable for the prediction of differential settlements in this case, because the reduction effects of the shear rigidity of the soil and the superstructure can be taken into account. The mechanical model of the structure and the foundation is assumed as shown in Fig. 5. Here, the superstructure is reduced to a Bernoulli-Euler Beam of foundation girders for the sake of

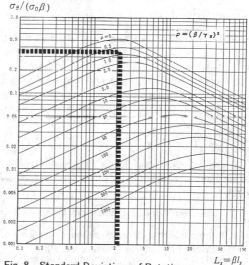

Fig. 8   Standard Deviations of Rotations
(Bernoulli–Euler Beam on Pasternak Model)

simplicity, neglecting the girders of upper floors which are flexible compared to the foundation girders. Of course, the whole structural frame can be modeled as a equivalent horizontal shear beam which is assumed as a Shear Beam on a Pasternak Model.

However, it is noted that this prediction is on the basis of an infinite homogeneous beam on a Pasternak Model. If it is applied to a finite beam, there may be some errors in the solutions due to the boundary conditions of the beam end. The bending moments and shear forces may be overestimated and rotations may be underestimated. However, accurate values are supposed to be of the same order.

Henceforth, assuming the standard deviation σ_0, the scale of fluctuation l_s and characteristic values (γ_s, β), the standard deviations of bending moment σ_M and shear forces σ_Q of foundation girders are obtained by the diagrams of Figs.6 and 7. The standard deviation of rotations σ_θ, which is defined as the gradient of a line joining two column bases on the foundation girder is also obtained by the diagram Fig.8.

Foundation girder of reinforced concrete :
$B \times D = 1.1m \times 1.8m$

$I = 0.535m^4$: moment of inertia of the cross section.
$E = 2.1 \times 10^4$ kPa : modulus of elasticity of concrete where, the creep effect and rigidity of the slab are offset.

$\sigma_0 = 0.002m$: standard deviations of settlements which is assumed as about 1/3 of $\mu = 0.007m$ approximately.

$B = 3 \sim 5m$: effective breadth of the foundation

$\beta = \sqrt[4]{k_0 B / 4EI} = 0.18 \sim 0.19 m^{-1}$: characteristic value of the foundation girder on the Pasternak Model.

$$k_0 = q/\mu = 17.38 \, \text{MPa/m} \qquad (6)$$

: subgrade reaction coefficient which is calculated from an average equivalent elastic settlement of the foundation $\mu = 0.007m$ due to the vertical average load $q = 0.1$MPa.

$$\gamma_s = \sqrt{k_o/G} = 0.23 \, \text{m}^{-1} \qquad (7)$$

: characteristic value of the Pasternak Model in the mechanical model in Fig.5, where G is the same as Eq.(5).

$l_s = 12m$: scale of fluctuation which is assumed as the minimum discrete distance, although the scale of fluctuation of white noise is zero theoretically.

$L_s = \beta \, l_s = 0.18 \sim 0.19 \times 12 = 2.16 \sim 2.28$: non-dimensional scale of fluctuation.

$\rho = (\beta/\gamma_s)^2 = 0.61 \sim 0.68$

Thus,

$\sigma_M/(\sigma_0 EI \beta^2) = 0.38 \sim 0.33$
$\sigma_Q/(\sigma_0 EI \beta^3) = 0.52 \sim 0.45$
$\sigma_\theta/(\sigma_0 \beta) = 0.38 \sim 0.33$

Then, standard deviations are as :
$\sigma_M = 0.38 \sim 0.33 \, \sigma_0 EI \beta^2 = 0.28 \sim 0.24$MN·m
$\sigma_Q = 0.52 \sim 0.45 \, \sigma_0 EI \beta^3 = 0.073 \sim 0.068$MN
$\sigma_\theta = 0.38 \sim 0.33 \, \sigma_0 \beta = 0.14 \sim 0.13 \times 10^{-3}$ rad.

Three times of these standard deviations should be combined with other loads for 99.9 percent non-exceedance probability.

6 SERVICEABILITY AND SAFETY OF THE BUILDING

The stresses and rotations should be combined with those due to other loads. Other loads are not accessed by probabilistic approach here. However, this discussion is focused on the differential consolidation settlements due to large live loads. Thus, vertical loads and horizontal seismic loads for the conventional allowable stress design are used. Simultaneous settlements are neglected here since they are negligible.

Stresses due to vertical loads including dead loads and live loads:

$Mv = 1.33$MN·m
$Qv = 0.48$MN

Stresses due to horizontal seismic loads including the those of horizontal displacements of piles, which are based on seismic codes of the Building Standard Law of Japan (The Building Center of Japan, 1994) for moderate earthquakes:

$Ms = 3.13$MN·m
$Qs = 0.53$MN

Then, total stresses are summed up as,

$\Sigma M = 3\sigma_M + Mv + Ms = 5.30$MN·m $< Ma = 6.45$MN·m
$\Sigma Q = 3\sigma_Q + Qv + Qs = 1.23$MN $< Qa = 1.77$MN

where, Ma and Qa are elastic limit stresses respectively.

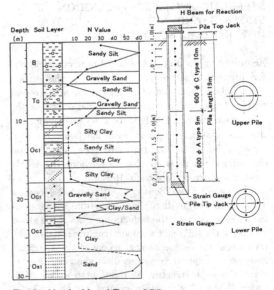

Fig. 9   Vertical Load Test of Pile

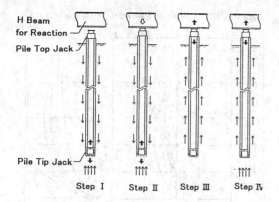

Fig.10 Loading Concept of Four Steps

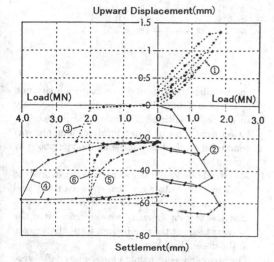

Step I ① : Pile Tip Load - Pile Tip Upward Displ.
  〃 ② : Pile Tip Load - Pile Tip Settlement
Step III ③ : Pile Top Load - Pile Top Settlement
Step IV ④ : Pile Top Load - Pile Top Settlement
  〃 ⑤ : Pile Tip Resistance - Pile Top Settlement
  〃 ⑥ : Pile Shaft Resistance -Pile Top Settlement

Fig.11 Load - Settlement Relationship of Test Pile

The rotation is as:
$\Sigma \theta = 3\sigma_\theta = 0.42 \times 10^{-3}$ rad. $< \theta_a = 4.0 \sim 3.3 \times 10^{-3}$ rad.
where, θ_a is serviceability limit of rotation (Tanahashi 1995). The rotations due to vertical loads are negligible and omitted here and those due to seismic loads have little influence on the serviceability.

As a result, these values are small enough for the serviceability and structural safety of the building, even if the stresses and rotations due to differential settlements may involve some errors in above prediction.

7 VERTICAL PILE LOAD TEST

A vertical pile load test was carried out in the site. Hydraulic jacks were set independently both at the tip and the top of the pile in order to obtain the ultimate base resistance of the pile and its shaft resistance separately as shown in Fig.9.

The load was charged at four steps as shown conceptually in Fig.10 as:

Step I : to get the ultimate base resistance by the pile tip jack.
Step II : ditto with the help of the pile top jack. This step was omitted because of enough shaft resistance.
Step III: to get the maximum shaft resistance of pile.
Step IV: to get the ultimate capacity of the pile totally.

The load-settlement relationships is shown in Fig.11. The ultimate base resistance of the pile was 1.7MN and the maximum shaft resistance was 2.4MN. The residual shaft resistance after its full mobilized friction was 2.0MN.

Therefore, the vertical allowable bearing capacity 0.95MN of a single pile was large enough for long term loading design. The distributions of friction resistance and transmission of pile top loads to the surrounding soils are shown in Fig.12. It shows that the pile behaves as a friction pile within the load level of 1.0MN.

8 STRAIN MEASUREMENTS OF PILE SHAFTS

Field measurements of pile strains were conducted at four working piles eight times during construction process of 15 months : inner pile **P1**, midside pile **P2** and corner pile **P3** of 4×4=16 pile group and a single pile **P4** were selected. Strain gauges were set at five

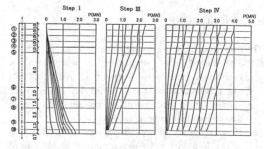

Fig. 12   Vertical Load Distribution of Test Pile

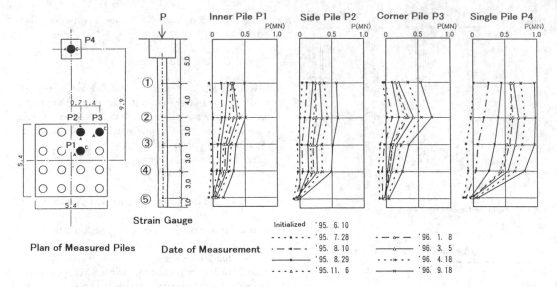

Fig. 13 Vertical Load Distribution of Measured Piles

levels ①∼⑤ of each pile as shown in Fig. 13.

The axial forces in Fig.13 are converted from measured strains using a modulus of elasticity of pile concrete 4.1×10^4 MPa which is reduced considering the creep effects for a long term loading.

The differences among sharing loads of pile groups are rather small. The axial loads at the pile bottom are almost zero. This fact reveals that the pile groups behave as friction piles within the load level of 1.0MN.

According to this distribution, the equivalent load level can be assumed at the level of 2.5m above the pile bottom and the stress distribution was analyzed again. The result is added to Fig.4 by solid lines showing the previous results analyzed at the design phase. The maximum stress of the surface of the clay layer Oc_2 decreased within the consolidation yield stress.

This result means that differential settlements of foundations due to consolidation of clay layer Oc_2 are confirmed not to occur and also the serviceability and safety of the building was confirmed to be sufficient.

9 CONCLUSIONS

The major conclusions are summarized as:

(1) The bored piles supporting a warehouse on reclaimed land was designed to reach a thin gravelly sand layer on a diluvial clay layer, where consolidation settlements were supposed to occur due to live load concentration.

(2) It is necessary to predict differential settlements of the foundation for serviceability and safety of the building, because the live load intensity and spatial distribution of pile groups vary frequently in service conditions. Therefore the probability-based prediction of differential settlements was conducted on the basis of the method proposed by the author.

(3) A vertical pile load test was carried out in order to confirm the ultimate base resistance and maximum shaft resistance. The results showed that the bearing capacity was sufficient and the bearing loads at the pile bottom were almost zero at the design load level.

(4) The strain measurements of four pile shafts were conducted during 15 months of construction. According to the results of load distributions, the group piles behaved as friction piles within the load level of 1MN. The stresses in the clay layer beneath the group piles were analyzed and resulted in no consolidation settlements.

(5) Finally, the serviceability and structural safety of the building were confirmed to be sufficient.

10 ACKNOWLEDGEMENT

The Rinku International Logistics Co. Ltd. is gratefully acknowledged for their generous permission to present the data.

REFERENCES

Tanahashi, H. 1994a : Probability-based prediction of differential settlements of structures using Timoshenko Beam on Pasternak Model. *Soils and Foundations*, Vol.34, No. 1, 77-89.

Tanahashi, H. 1994b : Probability-based prediction of rotations of structures due to differential settlements, *Soils and Foundations*, Vol.34, No. 4, 85-90.

Tanahashi, H. 1995 : Limit state design of differential settlements, *Proceedings of the symposium on limit state design of foundation structures*, Japanese Geotechnical Society.

The Building Center of Japan 1994: *The Building Standard Law of Japan and its Enforcement Order and Regulations*.

Vanmarcke, E. 1983 : *Random Fields : Analysis and Synthesis*, The MIT Press.

Structural Safety and Reliability, Shiraishi, Shinozuka & Wen (eds) © 1998 Balkema, Rotterdam, ISBN 90 5410 978 5

Stochastic modeling and its estimation of pile tip level using topographical information

Makoto Suzuki & Makoto Honda
Izumi Research Institute, Shimizu Co., Tokyo, Japan

Minoru Ueda
Chubu Electric Power Co., Inc., Nagoya, Japan

ABSRACT: Estimates of pile tip levels are very important in the design of piled structures. Detail estimation is, however, not feasible in mountain areas where the ground level is steeply undulating. Cokriging, which is one of the geostatistical methods, is a local estimation technique to simultaneous use of two or more correlated random fields. This paper describes that the estimation procedure using the topographical information is proposed and is applied to the design of piled structures such as electric substations.

1 INTRODUCTION

Pile foundations are often used when structures are constructed on the thick soft layer. It is frequently used to estimate the pile tip level based on limited boring data. Detailed estimation is not, however, feasible in mountain areas where the ground level is steeply undulating. In such as this, experts like geologists subjectively estimate the pile tip level fully relying on the limited results from the geological surveys and seismic prospecting.

Kriging, which is one of the geostatistical methods (Journel and Huijbregts 1978) is a local estimation technique which provides the best linear unbiased estimator of the unknown physical quantity. It is necessary to have enough data to estimate the steeply undulating level. This technique is extended to the simultaneous use of two or more correlated random fields, which is called "Cokriging". The accuracy of this estimation technique can then be improved by considering the spatial correlation between the random field of interest and other better-sampled fields. Since the correlation between the pile tip level and the ground level is strong, Cokriging is efficiently used where the ground investigation may not be performed intensively due to the investigation cost and/or physical difficulty.

In this study, the estimation procedure using the topographical information is proposed and is applied to the design of piled structures such as electric substations. Applicability of the procedure is verified comparing the estimation results of the pile tip level with those from seismic prospecting.

2 MODELING OF BI-VARIATE RANDOM FIELDS AND FORMULATION OF COKRIGING

Let Z_1 and Z_2 be the ground surface level and pile tip level as random fields, respectively. These random fields are assumed to be divided into trend components μ and stationary random components ε as

$$Z_1(\mathbf{x}) = \mu_1(\mathbf{x}) + \varepsilon_1(\mathbf{x}), \qquad \mathbf{x} \in S \qquad (1)$$

$$Z_2(\mathbf{x}) = \mu_2(\mathbf{x}) + \varepsilon_2(\mathbf{x}), \qquad \mathbf{x} \in S \qquad (2)$$

where $\mathbf{x}$ is a known vector of the spatial coordinates. The trend and random components are represented by statistical models (Vanmarke 1977). The two dimensional trend components are represented using orthogonal-polynomial technique. The covariance and the cross covariance of random components are assumed to have the same spatial correlation parameters since the two components possess similar correlation structures. For instance, these components are represented as

$$\begin{Bmatrix} \mu_1(\mathbf{x}) \\ \mu_2(\mathbf{x}) \end{Bmatrix} = \begin{Bmatrix} b_0^1 + b_1^1 x + b_2^1 y \\ b_0^2 + b_1^2 x + b_2^2 y \end{Bmatrix} \qquad (3)$$

$$\begin{cases} C_{11}(\mathbf{h}) = \sigma_1^2 \, exp\left\{-\left(\dfrac{\Delta x^2}{a_1^2} + \dfrac{\Delta y^2}{a_2^2}\right)^{1/2}\right\} \\[4mm] C_{22}(\mathbf{h}) = \sigma_2^2 \, exp\left\{-\left(\dfrac{\Delta x^2}{a_1^2} + \dfrac{\Delta y^2}{a_2^2}\right)^{1/2}\right\} \\[4mm] C_{12}(\mathbf{h}) = C_{21}(\mathbf{h}) = \rho \cdot \sigma_1 \cdot \sigma_2 \, exp\left\{-\left(\dfrac{\Delta x^2}{a_1^2} + \dfrac{\Delta y^2}{a_2^2}\right)^{1/2}\right\} \end{cases} \qquad (4)$$

where $\mathbf{h} = \{\Delta x\ \Delta y\}^T$ and $\boldsymbol{\theta} = \{a_1\ a_2\ \sigma_1^2\ \sigma_2^2\}^T$.

The spatial structures of both Z_1 and Z_2 can be obtained by maximum likelihood estimator (Suzuki 1991). Correlation between Z_1 and Z_2 can be estimated using N sampled data which is investigated in the same locations. To maximize the following likelihood, the spatial parameters are given:

$$p(\mathbf{z}|\boldsymbol{\theta}) = (2\pi)^{-2N/2} |\mathbf{Q}|^{-1/2} exp\left\{-\frac{1}{2}(\mathbf{z}-\boldsymbol{\mu})^T \mathbf{Q}^{-1}(\mathbf{z}-\boldsymbol{\mu})\right\}$$
(5)

where $\mathbf{Q}$ indicates the matrix represented by covariance and cross covariance associated with $\boldsymbol{\theta}$. $\mathbf{z}$ is an N vector of the sampled data. Practically, a negative log-likelihood can be minimized using the iteration algorithm, such as a Gauss-Newton method. Furthermore, the following least square method can be utilized to estimate the trend coefficients

$$\hat{\mathbf{b}} = (\mathbf{X}^T \mathbf{Q}^{-1} \mathbf{X})^{-1} \mathbf{X}^T \mathbf{Q}^{-1} \mathbf{z}$$
(6)

where $\mathbf{X}$ indicates the spatial matrix represented by the polynomial equations of spatial coordinates $\mathbf{x}$. The best model of the spatial structures can be selected from some model candidates based upon Akaike's Information Criteria (AIC) (Akaike 1974).

The estimator $\hat{Z}_2$ at the point $\mathbf{x}_0$ is assumed to be expressed in terms of a linear combination of all the available data from the topographical map, borings and outcrop as follows:

$$\hat{Z}_2(\mathbf{x}_0) = \sum_{i=1}^{N_1} \lambda_{1i} Z_1(\mathbf{x}_{1i}) + \sum_{i=1}^{N_2} \lambda_{2i} Z_2(\mathbf{x}_{2i})$$
(7)

where N_1 and N_2 are the number of the data from the topographical map and that of the borings and outcrop data, respectively. λ_{1i} and λ_{2i} are weight coefficients determined from non-biased estimator and minimized estimation variance as in the following:

$$E\left\{\hat{Z}_2(\mathbf{x}_0) - Z_2(\mathbf{x}_0)\right\} = 0$$
(8)

$$\sigma_E^2(\mathbf{x}_0) = E\left\{\left[\hat{Z}_2(\mathbf{x}_0) - Z_2(\mathbf{x}_0)\right]^2\right\}$$
to be minimized (9)

3 ESTIMATION OF PILE TIP LEVEL

3.1 Construction site

A piled foundation of an electric substation is planned to be constructed on the cutting ground in the mountain. The site is covered with the tuff, tuff breccia and andesite of Neogene period and is located in the west of Toyama prefecture, Japan. A contour map and a bird's-eye view of the topography are shown in Figs. 1 and 2, respectively. The site inclines in the north-

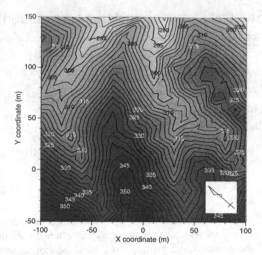

Fig.1 Topography (contour map)

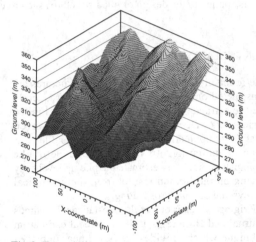

Fig.2 Topography (bird's-eye view)

east direction and has two major creeks from south to north. There is steep undulation where the elevation gap between ridge and creek is more than 20 meters.

Twenty-seven borings and seismic prospecting have been done. The locations of borings and seismic prospecting lines are shown in Fig.3. The ground is made of well-weathering layer with its bed thickness of 6-10 meters and the value in the standard penetration test (SPT) is less than 50. On the other hand, the SPT value in the deeper layer is over 50. Here, the pile tip level is defined in such a way that the value in SPT is over 50. Since the layer with the seismic wave velocity of 1.2-1.7 km/sec corresponds to the deeper layer, the upper level of the layer is defined as the pile tip level. Applicability of the proposed procedure is verified by comparing the estimation results of the pile tip level

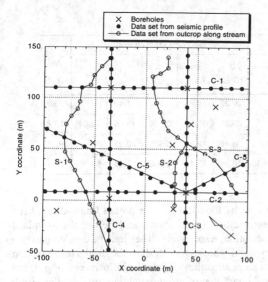

Fig.3 Boring, creeks and seismic prospecting

and those from seismic prospecting. Figure 3 also shows that the evaluation points marked by solid circle denote the estimation results in the site area at 200 meter by 200 meter. It also shows that the circle marks denote the sampled points of the outcrop along the creeks treated as pile tip level.

3.2 *Model of pile tip level*

Since the pile tip level is defined as the boundary between weathering layer and hard rock layer, it is strongly correlated with the steep undulation of the

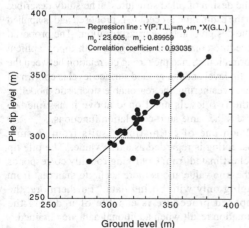

Fig.4 Relationship between pile tip level and ground level

ground surface level. Figure 4 shows the relationship between the pile tip level and the ground surface level at the boring points. The strong positive correlation is observed because the correlation coefficient of the two data is apparently more than 0.9.

If the spatial correlation structures of the two random fields are assumed to be statistically independent, it means the constraint that the correlation between the two random fields is weak. When the strong correlation is recognized, the same spatial correlation parameters associated with the random fields should be used. The parameters of the statistical models can be obtained from the maximum likelihood estimation. The best models are selected based upon the minimum AIC. Table 1 shows the estimated parameters of the best models in the case where the two random fields are assumed to be independent. The trend components are adopted to be linear functions and the covariance functions of the random components are adopted to be the one dimension exponential types. The spatial correlation parameters called "correlation distance" are given 38.55 meter for the ground level and 46.69 meter for the pile tip level, and both are not very different. The result that the same correlation distances is adopted to two covariance and cross-covariance functions is appropriate.

Table 2 shows the estimated parameters and AIC in the case of the same correlation distance using the sampled data at the 27 boring locations. In this case, the trend components are adopted to be linear functions, and the covariance functions of the random components are adopted to be the one dimension exponential types. The linear trend component is necessary for the purpose of the north-east slope because the difference of AIC between constant (0-th order) trend model and linear (first order) trend model indicate about 30. Comparing with covariance, the difference of AIC between one dimension exponential model and two dimension exponential model indicates about 1.5-2.0 and means isotropic spatial correlation of both of the random fields. The correlation coefficient ρ between the two random fields is as large as 0.89.

Table 1 Estimated parameters of two random fileds

Data set	Minimum AIC model	Trend components			Random components	
		b_0	b_1	b_2	σ	a
Ground level	Linear Trend 1-D Exp.	332.62	0.0102	-0.177	10.77	38.55
Pile tip level	Linear Trend 1-D Exp.	321.89	-0.0253	-0.164	10.02	46.69

Table 2 Estimated parameters of combined random filed

Model		Trend components						Random components					AIC
		Ground level			Pile tip level			σ_1 (G.L.)	σ_2 (P.T.L.)	ρ	a_1	a_2	
		b_0^1	b_1^1	b_2^1	b_0^2	b_1^2	b_2^2						
Constant Trend	1-D Exp.	326.18	-	-	316.85	-	-	20.22	19.55	0.942	21.41	-	426.78
	2-D Exp.	326.20	-	-	316.84	-	-	20.21	19.55	0.942	15.65	32.04	427.84
Linear Trend	1-D Exp.	332.63	0.0104	-0.1773	322.07	-0.0261	-0.1652	13.16	12.32	0.889	40.01	-	392.67
	2-D Exp.	332.63	0.0106	-0.1752	322.12	-0.0256	-0.1636	12.95	12.12	0.888	27.64	55.11	394.14

3.3 Estimation of pile tip level

Although the statistical estimation needs a pair of data from the same boring locations, it is not necessary to the spatial estimation by Cokriging that the sampled points of ground surface level coincide with those of the pile tip level. The ground levels of the 441 points at the 21 by 21 lattice location is digitized from the topographical map. The information of the pile tip level is based upon the borings and the outcrop along creeks.

First, the estimation of pile tip level by Kriging (Nishi and Suzuki 1994) is performed to compare with that by Cokriging. Statistical parameters are used in Table 1. Figure 5 shows the contour maps of estimation value (left) and estimation error (right). Although the slant in the north-east direction is described, the estimation value is all over flatly undulating with disregard to topography. The estimation error near boring points is 4-5 meters and the one which is more than 30 meters away from the boring points is 8 meters.

Figure 6 shows the results of estimation value (left) and estimation error (right) by Cokriging. The contour map of estimation value is similar to that of surface topography. The depth of the pile tip level is 10 meters in the south of the site and is 5 meters in the north. The contour of estimation error is similar to that by Kriging. The estimation error near the boring points is 2-4 meters and that of the whole area is less than 5 meters. It is approximately 60-70 percents of the error by Kriging.

3.4 Verification of estimation error

To verify the estimation results of the proposed procedure, it is compared with those from seismic prospecting in five sections where the seismic prospecting was conducted (C-1- C-5). Figures 7-11 show the results along the sections. The left figures show the results by Kriging, and the right ones show those by Cokriging. The dotted line indicates the estimation value above and below the standard deviation, respectively. They may be divided into two types. Figures 9 and 10 show the results in the section at slope direction. While the influence of slope trend is bigger, that of ground undulation is smaller. Both results are well estimated. The other figures show the results in the section across the creeks. In spite of ground undulation, the estimation values by Kriging are smoothly interpolated and the estimation errors are more than 15 meters. The estimation values by Cokriging illustrate undulation well and the estimation errors are less than 5 meters. The results by Cokriging are confirmed to be more accurate than those by Kriging in all sections. It is clear that the Cokriging technique incorporated with topography is useful for estimating the pile tip level based upon a limited number of boring data.

4 CONCLUSION

It is important to estimate the pile tip level accurately in the design of piled structures. The study describes that the estimation procedure is proposed and is applied to the design of the electric substation. The proposed procedure consists of Cokriging with topographical information. Since the strong correlation between the pile tip level and the ground surface level is confirmed due to weathering, the reasonable stochastic modeling of the two levels mentioned above is assumed to possess the same auto-correlation functions.

Each one of estimation results from seismic prospecting is regarded as a true value. The pile tip level estimated from Cokriging roughly corresponds to the true value and is more accurate than that from Kriging only with boring data. Furthermore, the proposed procedure is capable of updating the estimation result when additional data are obtained.

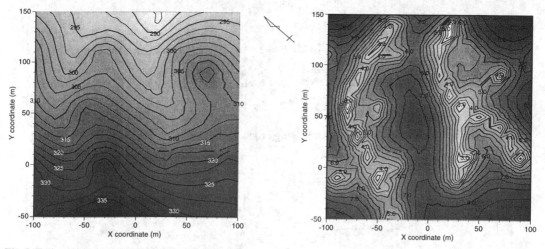

Fig.5 Estimation results by Kriging (left: estimation value / right: estimation error)

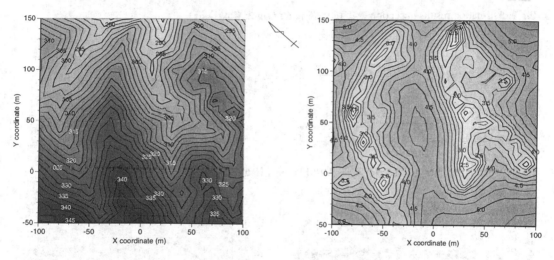

Fig.6 Estimation results by Coklriging (left: estimation value / right: estimation error)

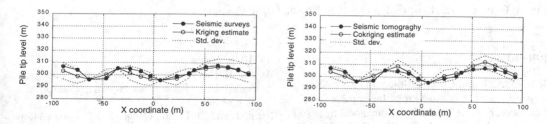

Fig.7 Estimation results in section C-1 (left: Kriging / right: Cokriging)

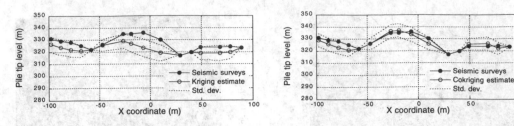

Fig.8 Estimation results in section C-2 (left: Kriging / right: Cokriging)

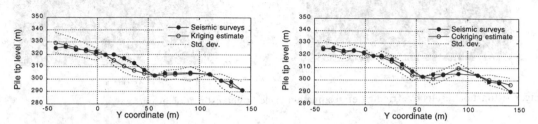

Fig.9 Estimation results in section C-3 (left: Kriging / right: Cokriging)

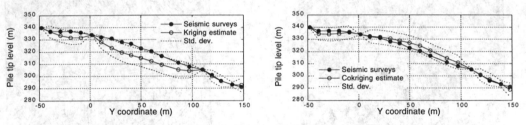

Fig.10 Estimation results in section C-4 (left: Kriging / right: Cokriging)

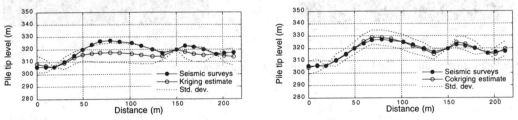

Fig.11 Estimation results in section C-5 (left: Kriging / right: Cokriging)

REFERENCES

Journel, A.G. and Ch.J. Huijbregts (1978). Mining geostatistics, Academic Press, Inc., pp.324-343.

Vanmarke, E.H. (1977). Probabilistic modeling of soil profiles, Jour. Geotech. Eng. Div., ASCE, Vol.103, No.11, pp.1227-1246.

Suzuki, M. (1991). Statistical estimation of spacially distributed soil properties, Proc. JCOSSAR, pp.707-710 (in Japanese).

Akaike, H. (1974). A new look at the statistical model identification, IEEE Trans. Automat. Control, AC-19, pp.716-723.

Nishi, T. and M. Suzuki (1994). A 3-D visualization system for geological modeling integrated with a GIS, Proc. 7th Int. IAEG Congress, pp.4501-4506.

Structural Safety and Reliability, Shiraishi, Shinozuka & Wen (eds) © 1998 Balkema, Rotterdam, ISBN 90 5410 978 5

Response of pile embedded in stochastic ground media

Makoto Suzuki & Tuyoshi Takada

Izumi Research Institute, Shimizu Co., Tokyo, Japan

ABSRACT: This paper reports a study on the response variability of piles in ground media which is uncertain and is assumed to be one-dimensional stochastic field along the depth. For such problems, no general solutions can be obtained in an analytical form. Accordingly, approximations need to be introduced. In this study, a stochastic analysis based on the Galerkin method (Takada 1991) and the first-order approximation is proposed for estimating the response variability of a single pile embedded in stochastic ground media. The horizontal force is assumed to be applied from a superstructure in a deterministic manner. Numerical examples are presented to show the usefulness of this method with regard to the spatial correlation property of the ground media. In addition, comparison is made using two different modelings, random variable modeling and stochastic field modeling for the stochastic ground media. Finally, the correlation-free upper bounds of response variation are proposed for the practical purpose.

1 INTRODUCTION

Ground behavior during big earthquakes is important for the seismic safety of structures supported by piles and foundations. It is obvious that rational treatment of the ground soil is essential for a limit state design of structures. It is, however, costly to accurately investigate the ground soil in site and it is even difficult to exactly identify the ground characteristics since they are significantly heterogeneous. Therefore, stochastic treatment of them is necessary.

This paper studies the response variability of piles in uncertain ground media which is assumed to be modeled as a one-dimensional stochastic field along the pile depth. For such problems, no general solutions can be obtained in an analytical form. Approximation need to be introduced. In this study, a stochastic analysis based on the Galerkin method (Takada 1991) and the first-order approximation is proposed for estimating the response variability of piles embedded in the stochastic ground media. The horizontal force is assumed to be applied from the superstructure in a deterministic manner. Numerical examples are presented to show the usefulness of this method with regard to the correlation property of the ground media. Finally, it is shown that this method can readily be used for practical application.

2 METHODS

A single pile subject to a lateral force is modeled as a simple beam on an elastic foundation as shown in Fig. 1. The fundamental equilibrium equation associated with the pile section can be described by the fourth order differential equation of displacement w with respect to the spatial coordinate x as follows:

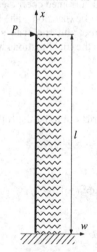

Fig.1 Analytical model

$$EI\frac{d^4w}{dx^4} + k(x)w - p = 0 \tag{1}$$

where p is a distributed lateral load, $k(x)$ is the coefficient of lateral subgrade reaction and EI indicates the uniform flexural rigidity of the pile.

In the formulation of the Galerkin method, a set of deterministic trial functions are introduced in such a way that boundary conditions can be satisfied by the trial functions. The problem to be solved here is to find an approximate solution $w(x)$ to a true displacement that must completely satisfy the following two equations, i.e., the fundamental equilibrium equation defined within a domain V and the boundary conditions at boundaries S:

$$\begin{aligned} L(w) - p &= 0 \quad x \in V \\ G(w) - q &= 0 \quad x \in S \end{aligned} \tag{2}$$

in which $L()$ is a differential operator, which is linear with respect to the displacement, and $G()$ is assumed to be an operator associated with boundary conditions. p and q are quantities that imply respectively load and boundary conditions. Considering the ground media as elastic, $L(w)$ becomes

$$L(w) = \left[EI\frac{d^4}{dx^4} + k(x)\right]w \tag{3}$$

Using the trial functions, the approximate displacement $w(x)$ can be expressed in terms of a linear summation with a trial function vector

$$w(x) = \sum_{i=1}^{n} a_i \phi_i(x) = \Phi^T(x)\mathbf{a} \tag{4}$$

where $\mathbf{a}$ is an undetermined coefficient vector and n is the total number of expansion. The residual between the approximated and the true solution is then orthogonalized to the trial functions within the domain V:

$$\int_V \{L(w) - p\}\Phi(x)\,dx = \mathbf{0} \tag{5}$$

This equation turns out to be the following algebraic equation

$$\mathbf{Ka} = \mathbf{P} \tag{6}$$

where

$$\mathbf{K} = \int_V \Phi(x)L\big(\Phi^T(x)\big)\,dx \tag{7}$$

$$\mathbf{P} = \int_V p\Phi(x)\,dx \tag{8}$$

Equation (6) yields the solution for an undetermined coefficient vector $\mathbf{a}$. Furthermore, the bending moment can be evaluated using $\mathbf{a}$:

$$M(x) = EI \cdot \Phi''^T(x) \cdot \mathbf{a} \tag{9}$$

in which the double prime denotes the second derivative with respect to the spatial coordinate x.

Now, the above-mentioned method is applied to stochastic problems. Let the coefficient of subgrade reaction be idealized as a statistically homogeneous and spatially continuous stochastic field (Vanmarke 1983). Other parameters are assumed deterministic. For the stochastic problem, it is almost impossible to find stochastic trial functions compatible with the deterministic boundary conditions. Therefore, the Galerkin solution is approximate both in a deterministic and stochastic sense. Since the matrix $\mathbf{K}$ includes stochastic components, the undetermined random vector $\mathbf{a}$ can also be evaluated as a vector of stochastic values. The expectation and auto-correlation function of the displacement response can be written formally as:

$$E[w(x)] = \Phi^T(x) \cdot E[\mathbf{a}] \tag{10}$$

$$R_{ww}(x,y) = \Phi^T(x) \cdot E[\mathbf{a}\mathbf{a}^T] \cdot \Phi(y) \tag{11}$$

where $E[]$ denotes the mathematical expectation.

It is difficult to rigorously evaluate the statistical moments of the random vector $\mathbf{a}$ from the statistical nature of $k(x)$ because of a nonlinear relationship between $k(x)$ and $\mathbf{a}$ as seen in Eq. (6). To overcome this difficulty, a first-order approximation can be used as has been done in most stochastic analyses (Ang and Tang 1984).

Employing the Taylor expansion of $\mathbf{a}$ in Eq. (6) with respect to the basic random variable k_{ij} at their expected values and taken up to the first-order term, $\mathbf{a}$ is given as:

$$\mathbf{a} \approx \mathbf{a}^0 + \sum_{i}^{n}\sum_{j}^{n} \mathbf{a}_{ij}^1 \Delta k_{ij} \tag{12}$$

with

$$\Delta k_{ij} = k_{ij} - E[k_{ij}] \tag{13}$$

where $\mathbf{a}^0$ and $\mathbf{a}^1_{ij}$ are

$$\mathbf{a}^0 = E[\mathbf{K}]^{-1}\mathbf{P} \tag{14}$$

$$\mathbf{a}_{ij}^1 = -E[\mathbf{K}]^{-1}\frac{\partial \mathbf{K}}{\partial k_{ij}}\bigg|_{k_{ij}=E[k_{ij}]} \cdot E[\mathbf{K}]^{-1}\mathbf{P} \tag{15}$$

Using Eqs. (12) and (13), the expectations in Eqs. (10) and (11) are approximated as

$$E[\mathbf{a}] = \mathbf{a}^0 \tag{16}$$

$$E[\mathbf{a}\mathbf{a}^T] = \mathbf{a}^0(\mathbf{a}^0)^T$$
$$+ \sum_i^n \sum_j^n \sum_k^n \sum_l^n \mathbf{a}_{ij}^1(\mathbf{a}_{kl}^1)^T E[\Delta k_{ij} \Delta k_{kl}] \quad (17)$$

$$E[\Delta k_{ij} \Delta k_{kl}]$$
$$= \int_V \int_V \phi_i(x)\phi_j(x)\phi_k(y)\phi_l(y)R_{ff}(x,y)dxdy \quad (18)$$

In a similar way, the expectation and auto-correlation function of the bending moment can be written as :

$$E[M(x)] = EI \cdot \Phi''^T(x) \cdot E[\mathbf{a}] \quad (19)$$

$$R_{MM}(x,y) = (EI)^2 \cdot \Phi''^T(x) \cdot E[\mathbf{a}\mathbf{a}^T] \cdot \Phi''(y) \quad (20)$$

3 EXAMPLES

3.1 Analytical model

Let the embedded length l be ten meters and the flexural rigidity EI be 11.386 MN-m² per pile diameter. Also, it is assumed that the coefficient of lateral subgrade reaction denoted by $k(x)$ is idealized as a one-dimensional stochastic field as in the following.

$$k(x) = k_0(1 + f(x)) \quad (21)$$

where k_0 is an expected value, and $f(x)$ is a fluctuating part which is assumed to constitute a homogeneous stochastic field. Without lack of generality, $f(x)$ has zero expectation. The auto-correlation function of $f(x)$ is now taken as

$$R_{ff}(\Delta x) = \sigma^2 \exp(-|\Delta x|/b) \quad (22)$$

where σ is a standard deviation associated with $f(x)$

and b is "a correlation distance (Vanmarke 1983)" that implies how fast the correlation decays along the depth. In this study, k_0 is set to 294 kN/m per pile diameter and σ is assumed to be 1/3.

Two types of boundary condition at the pile top are considered. One is assumed to be free and the other is fixed in a rotational component. The boundary condition at the bottom end is fixed in both types. These types of piles are referred to as, respectively, case 1 and case 2 throughout this paper. The following trial functions in case 1 and case2 are intuitively selected respectively:

$$\phi_i(x) = \frac{1}{2}\left(1 - \cos\frac{(2i-1)\pi}{2l}x\right)$$
$$(i = 1, 2, \cdots) \qquad 0 \le x \le l \quad (23)$$

$$\phi_i(x) = \frac{x}{l}\left(2 - \frac{x}{l}\right)\sin\frac{(2i-1)\pi}{2l}x$$
$$(i = 1, 2, \cdots) \qquad 0 \le x \le l \quad (24)$$

where l is the pile length.

Figures 2 and 3 show mode shapes of the trial functions respectively. The boundary conditions at both ends can be easily found to be satisfied by the trial functions above.

Two types of numerical examples are analyzed to evaluate the influence of the correlation distance. The lateral concentrated load P at the pile top is deterministic and is taken as 9.8 kN.

The influence that the total number of expansions taken in the proposed method gives to the accuracy of the pile response were clarified (Suzuki and Takada

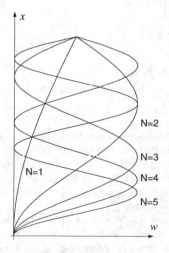

Fig. 2   Trial functions   (case 1)

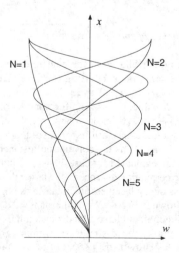

Fig. 3   Trial functions   (case 2)

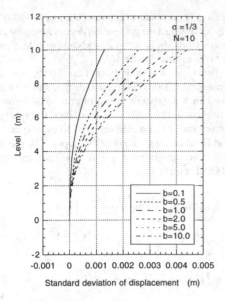

Fig. 4 Influence of correlation distance on the standard deviations of diplacements (case 1)

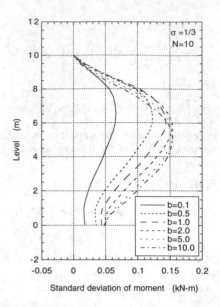

Fig. 5 Influence of correlation distance on the standard deviations of bending moments (case 1)

1996). The results are following: 1) The expectations of displacement roughly corresponds with the exact solution when up to the third-term expansion is used. 2) The expectations of bending moments needs the expansion higher than the fifth term, because the pile displacements rather than bending moment is defined as the trial functions. 3) While the standard deviations have a tendency similar to the expectations of both responses, those of the bending moments need expansions as high as the tenth term.

3.2 Influence of spatial correlation

The spatial correlation of the coefficients of lateral subgrade reaction $k(x)$ along the pile affects the response variability of the pile. The correlation distance, b-value, controlling the spatial correlation characteristic of $k(x)$ is a key parameter herein.

The standard deviations of displacements and bending moments as the correlation distance of $k(x)$ changes are evaluated for case 1. It is found that the larger the correlation distance is, the larger the standard deviations of displacement are obtained throughout the pile as shown in Fig. 4. While the standard deviations of bending moment have a tendency similar to that of displacement, the distribution shape gradually changes, as shown in Fig. 5. Figure 6 shows the coefficients of variation of displacements and bending

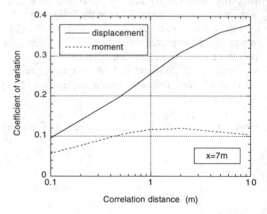

Fig. 6 Influence of correlation distance on the coefficients of variation (case 1)

moments versus the correlation distance at $x=7$m. It is observed that the mode of the trial function which most contributes to the response variation may change as the correlation pattern of fluctuating $k(x)$ changes. This cannot be taken account of by using the random variable modeling.

The standard deviations of displacements and bending moments for case 2 are also shown in Figs. 7 and 8. It is also observed that the larger the correlation distance is, the larger the standard deviations of

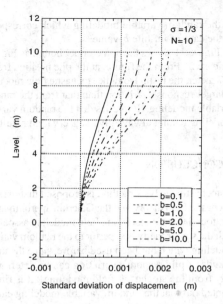

Fig. 7 Influence of correlation distance on the standard deviations of displacements (case 2)

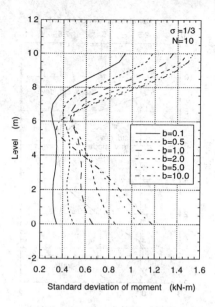

Fig. 8 Influence of correlation distance on the standard deviations of bending moments (case 2)

displacement are obtained in Fig. 7. Carefully observing Figs. 8 and 9, the standard deviations of bending moments at the center of pile tend to decrease in proportion to the correlation distance greater than around 2.0 meter, but they tend to increase at the both ends of pile. The distribution shape gradually changes, as shown in Fig. 8. The modes of the trial function and the correlation distance of $k(x)$ do not affect the standard deviations of the displacements, but affect more the standard deviations of the bending moments at the middle part of the pile.

3.3 Correlation free upper bounds of pile response

From the numerical result of the two above cases, there might be some upper bounds associated with the variation of pile responses. So, in this subsection proposed is the upper bounds of response variation. These bounds are defined in such a way that the variation of the pile response takes maximum value when the correlation distance, b-value, associated with the lateral subgrade reaction is changed from 0.1 meter to infinity (very large). These bounds can be called "correlation free upper bounds" and be useful for a practical purpose since it is very difficult to identify the auto-correlation function associated with $k(x)$ in reality. Note that these upper bounds can be derived not from the random variable modeling but from the

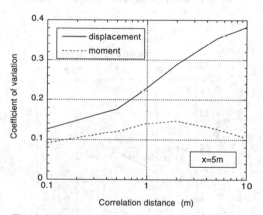

Fig. 9 Influence of correlation distance on the coefficients of variation

stochastic field modeling associated with $k(x)$. Of course, the upper bounds are computed at each pile location and are derived through numerical computations.

Figure 10 shows the upper bounds associated with the standard deviation of the bending moment response in arbitrary pile levels. The set of b-values, in which the maximum standard deviations are obtained, is also shown in this figure. In case 1, it is found that the upper bound of the standard deviation is equal to those

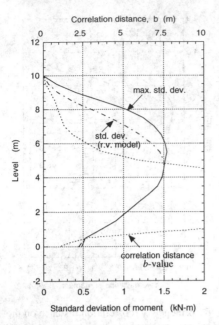

Fig. 10 Maximum standard deviation of moment in terms of different correlation distance (case 1)

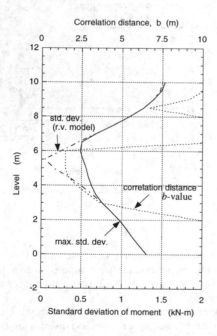

Fig. 11 Maximum standard deviation of moment in terms of different correlation distance (case 2)

of the random variable modeling which corresponds to the case of infinite *b*-value.

Figure 11 shows the some upper bound as Figs. 10 for case 2. From the figure, at the pile position from 3 to 7 meter, the result from the stochastic field modeling is larger response variation than that from the random variable modeling. It implies that the random variable modeling cannot always give conservation results.

4 CONCLUSION

A stochastic analysis method is proposed that uses the stochastic field theory and the Galerkin approximation. It is found that the stochastic field modeling associated with the soil property is superior to the random variable modeling which has been used before, since the upper bounds of pile response variation can be determined only from the stochastic field modeling. It is finally pointed out that the random variable modeling cannot always give conservation results.

REFERENCES

Takada, T. (1991). Galerkin method to analyze systems with stochastic flexural rigidity, Computational Stochastic Mechanics, edited by Spanos, P.D. and Brebbia, C.A., Computational Mechanics Publications, pp.511-522.

Vanmarke, E. (1983). Random field, MIT Press, Cambridge.

Ang, A. H-S. and W.H. Tang (1984). Probability Concept in Engineering Planning and Design, Vol. II, John Wiley and Sons.

Suzuki, M. and T. Takada (1996). Response of pile embedded in stochastic ground media, Probabilistic Mechanics and Structural Reliability, Proc. of the 7th Specialty Conference, ASCE, pp.612-615.

Geotechnical engineering (ongoing research)

Structural Safety and Reliability, Shiraishi, Shinozuka & Wen (eds) © 1998 Balkema, Rotterdam, ISBN 90 5410 978 5

Influence of frequency content of ground motion on seismically induced soil liquefaction

Jean H. Prevost, Radu Popescu & George Deodatis
Department of Civil Engineering and Operations Research, Princeton University, N.J., USA

ABSTRACT: The influence of frequency content of seismic excitation on the extent and pattern of pore water pressure build–up in saturated soil deposits is addressed. Seismic acceleration time histories are generated as uniformly modulated non–stationary stochastic processes, in accordance with prescribed response spectra and prescribed modulating functions. The influence of the inherent variability of soil properties on dynamic behavior is accounted for by performing Monte Carlo simulations which combine digital generation of non–Gaussian stochastic vector fields modeling soil properties with dynamic, non–linear finite element analyses. Results of a numerical example based on real field data show that the interplay between the frequency content of seismic excitation and the dynamic characteristics of the soil deposit have important implications on the dynamic response.

1 INTRODUCTION

Input ground motion and mechanical properties are the two main categories of data required for dynamic structural analysis and, as shown hereafter, are both probabilistic entities.

The characteristics of seismic ground motion at a specific location (e.g. frequency content, amplitude) are mainly governed by (1) distance from the seismic source, (2) local soil conditions, and (3) magnitude of the event. As a consequence of wave propagation and loss of coherence, there is a certain spatial variation of seismic ground motion from one location to another. To this end, the earthquake ground motion over the domain of interest can be described by a non–stationary stochastic vector process with evolutionary power, each component of the vector process representing the motion at a certain spatial location (e.g. Deodatis, 1996).

Many physical systems in general and soil materials in particular exhibit relatively large variability in their properties, even within so called homogeneous zones. Deterministic descriptions of this spatial variability are not feasible due to prohibitive cost of sampling and to uncertainties induced by measurement errors. A more rational approach to geotechnical design is made possible by use of stochastic field based techniques of data analysis, which rely more on analytical methods when dealing with various uncertainties related to soil properties.

Soil liquefaction seems to be particularly sensitive to spatial soil variability. Previous studies (e.g. Popescu, 1995) have shown that both the extent and the pattern of pore water pressure build–up in saturated soil deposits subjected to seismic excitation are different when computed accounting for the random spatial variability of soil properties, compared to numerical analyses which are using average values. An explanation is that liquefaction is triggered by the presence of loose pockets in the soil mass, which can only be accounted for by considering the stochastic nature of spatial variability of soil properties (e.g. Popescu et al, 1997b, 1997c).

2 REPRESENTING THE VARIABILITY OF SOIL PROPERTIES

The natural heterogeneity in a supposedly homogeneous layer may be due to: small scale variations in mineral composition, environmental conditions during deposition, past stress history, variations in moisture content, etc. In general soil properties follow non–Gaussian marginal probability distributions (e.g. they do not assume negative values). Consequently, the relevant material properties over the analysis domain can be modeled as a multi–variate, multi–dimensional (mV-nD), non–Gaussian stochastic field (e.g. Popescu 1995, Popescu et al. 1997b).

Several methods to estimate the correlation structure of spatial variability from results of in-situ soil tests are described in the literature. A comprehensive review is presented by DeGroot and Baecher (1993). For a detailed description of the stochastic data analysis methods used in this study, the reader is referred to Popescu et al. (1997c). The field data consists of results of an extended program of piezocone tests (in terms of cone tip resistance, sleeve friction and dynamic pore pressure), performed for the hydraulically placed sand core of an artificial island in the Canadian Beaufort Sea (Gulf, 1984).

Once the probabilistic characteristics of the spatial variation of soil properties are known, sample functions of the underlying stochastic field can be digitally simulated using the spectral representation method, ARMA models, Kriging, conditional probability, etc. (For a literature review the reader is referred to Soong and Grigoriu, 1993). Unlike Gaussian fields where the first two moments provide complete probabilistic information, non–Gaussian fields require knowledge of moments of all orders (to be precise, in the increasing order of completeness, the probability structure of a non–Gaussian stochastic field is described by the probability density functions of all orders). Unfortunately it is practically impossible to estimate moments higher than order two from actual (non–Gaussian) data. Therefore, the simulation of soil properties, that are represented as non–Gaussian stochastic vector fields, is done in practice using the cross–spectral density matrix and the marginal probability distribution functions. In this study, sample functions of a 2D–2V non–Gaussian stochastic field, modeling two soil properties over the domain of interest, are digitally generated using an extension of the spectral representation method described by Popescu et al. (1997a).

3 SEISMIC GROUND MOTION

Design codes provide response spectra to be used in structural seismic analyses. Different response spectra are prescribed for various locations, corresponding to the local soil conditions. An example is provided in Fig. 1a, where the first three types of response spectra correspond to the Uniform Building Code (Uniform, 1994), with type 1 for rock and stiff soils, type 2 for deep cohesionless or stiff clay soils, and type 3 for soft to medium clays and sands. The fourth response spectrum, with a range of maximum spectral values corresponding to frequencies that are lower than for types 1,2 and 3, is believed to be representative for locations very close to the epicenter.

A procedure for digital generation of non–stationary time histories (Deodatis, 1996) capable of simulating seismic ground motion time histories that: (1) are compatible with prescribed response spectra, (2) have prescribed modulating functions to control the duration of the strong motion, and

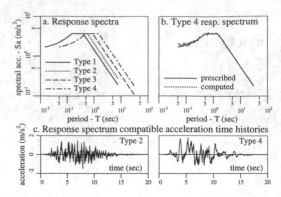

Figure 1: Response spectrum compatible acceleration time histories: a. prescribed response spectra; b. prescribed and computed values for the type 4 response spectrum; c. generated sample functions.

(3) are correlated according to a given coherence function, including the wave propagation effect, is used to generate the acceleration time histories. The effectiveness of the algorithm is illustrated in Figure 1b, where the prescribed type 4 response spectrum (continuous line) is compared to the response spectrum (dotted line) computed from the corresponding simulated acceleration time history. Two generated sample functions, compatible with type 2 and type 4 response spectra, respectively, are plotted in Fig. 1c.

4 MONTE CARLO SIMULATIONS OF SOIL LIQUEFACTION

Characteristic for the behavior of saturated soil deposits subjected to dynamic excitation is the phenomenon of pore water pressure build–up. Increases in pore pressure lead to reduction of effective normal stress and therefore of soil shear strength, with effect on the overall behavior and stability of the soil deposit. Consequently, the following results of Monte Carlo simulations of soil liquefaction are mainly presented in terms of predicted excess pore pressure ratio with respect to the initial effective vertical stress (u/σ_{v0}).

4.1 Influence of Spatial Variability of Soil Properties

A Monte Carlo simulation methodology, combining digital generation of non–Gaussian stochastic vector fields with dynamic, nonlinear finite element analyses is used to investigate the effects of spatial variability of soil properties on the pattern and amount of seismically induced soil liquefaction. The method is described in details by Popescu (1995) and Popescu et al. (1997b).

A loose to medium dense soil deposit, with geomechanical properties as well as spatial variability characteristics corresponding to a hydraulically placed sand deposit (Gulf, 1984), is selected for this numerical example (Fig. 4a). The multi–yield plasticity model (Prevost 1985) implemented in the computer code DYNAFLOW (Prevost 1995) is used for the finite element analyses. Fig. 2 compares the results of Monte Carlo simulations, performed for six different realizations of the spatial variation of soil properties, with those of a deterministic finite element analysis. The soil constitutive parameters for the deterministic analysis have the same values as the average values in the six stochastic input cases. From the results shown in Fig. 2, it can be concluded that (1) more pore pressure build–up is predicted by the stochastic input model than by the deterministic model; and (2) in the case of stochastic input, there are patches with large excess pore pressure, corresponding to the presence of loose pockets in the material (this predicted pattern explains better the phenomenon of sand boils observed in areas affected by soil liquefaction).

4.2 Influence of Frequency Content of the Ground Motion

As a dynamical system, a soil deposit has its own characteristic frequency (or lower eigenfrequency

value), which depends on soil properties (especially on shear modulus), soil deposit geometry, and degree of saturation. This characteristic frequency may decrease during dynamic excitation, due to the decrease in effective shear moduli as a result of pore pressure build–up and/or large shear strains. Any mechanical system is more sensitive to dynamic loading as its characteristic frequency is closer to the frequency range corresponding to the maximum spectral values of the excitation. Consequently, the frequency content of the seismic excitation can make a significant difference in the dynamic response of saturated soil deposits. This is illustrated in Figure 3, where contours of excess pore pressure ratio predicted for the same soil deposit, using input motions with the same energy but different frequency content, are compared.

Results of an extensive parametric study on the influence of frequency content of the ground motion on soil liquefaction (Popescu et al. 1997b) are summarized in Fig. 4. The predictions of the Monte Carlo simulations are represented as ranges of results obtained from six sample functions. For comparison purposes, the predicted excess pore pressure ratio is synthesized into the following comparison indices: (1) liquefaction index, Q, computed by averaging the excess pore pressure ratio in horizontal direction (Fig. 4b), and (2) area of liquefied zone, or A_{80} index, representing the proportion of the saturated soil deposit for which the excess pore pressure ratio exceeds 80% (Fig. 4c). Comparisons in terms of predicted horizontal displacements at the ground level are also provided in Fig. 4d.

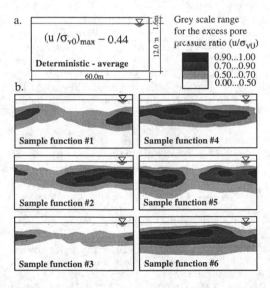

Figure 2: Comparisons between results of Monte Carlo (b.) and deterministic (a.) computations in terms of excess pore pressure ratio with respect to the initial effective vertical stress, at the onset of liquefaction (time $T = 8$ sec, input acceleration compatible with the type 2 response spectrum).

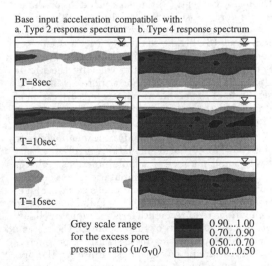

Figure 3: Excess pore pressure ratio predicted using base input accelerations with different frequency contents (the material properties are computed according to stochastic field #3 in Fig. 2).

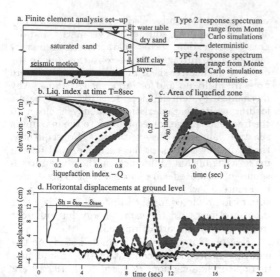

Figure 4: Liquefaction strength assessment of a soil deposit.

5 CONCLUSIONS

The following conclusions result from Figure 4, regarding the influence of frequency content of the seismic motion on predicted pore pressure build-up, for the type of soil deposit and the frequency ranges of input motion employed in the study: (1) larger pore pressures and horizontal displacements are predicted for input motions with lower frequency content, (2) the peak values of predicted excess pore pressure ratio are situated at lower elevations for input motions with lower frequency content, and (3) higher sensitivity to the frequency content of the input motion is exhibited by the deterministic analysis results than by the Monte Carlo simulation results. For a more detailed presentation of the parametric study and discussion of its results, the reader is referred to Popescu et al. (1997b).

As a limitation of the study, it is mentioned here that the Monte Carlo simulations involved a relatively small number of sample functions. This is due to the considerable computational burden imposed by nonlinear dynamic analyses in conjunction with parametric studies. Full Monte Carlo simulations require a much larger sample to reliably predict the statistics of the response. The present study is not computing these statistics, but merely a range of predicted responses. However, the predicted range might become wider if more than six sample functions were generated.

It should also be mentioned that the effects of stochastic variability of soil properties on seismi-

cally induced liquefaction are strongly dependent on the degree of variability and the marginal probability distributions of different soil properties (for more details on the effects of marginal probability distribution functions, the reader is referred to Popescu, 1995, and Popescu et al, 1997c). Therefore caution should be used if extrapolations of the results of this study are to be used for other types of soil deposits.

ACKNOWLEDGEMENTS

This work was supported in part by a collaborative research agreement between Kajima Corporation, Japan and Princeton University, and by the National Science Foundation under Grant #CMS-9523092 (Program Director, Dr. Clifford J. Astill).

REFERENCES

DeGroot, D.J. and Baecher, G.B., (1993). Estimating autocovariance of in–situ soil properties. *Journ. Geotechnical Engnrg.*, ASCE, 119(1):147–166.

Deodatis, G., (1996). Nonstationary stochastic vector processes: Seismic ground motion applications. *Probab. Engnrg. Mech.*

Gulf Canada Resources Inc, (1984). Frontier development – Molikpaq, Tarsiut delineation – 1984/85 season. Technical Report 84F012, Gulf Canada Resources Inc.

Uniform Building Code, (1994). International Conference of Building Officials.

Popescu, R., (1995). *Stochastic Variability of Soil Properties: Data Analysis, Digital Simulation, Effects on System Behavior.* PhD thesis, Princeton University, Princeton, NJ.

Popescu, R., Deodatis, G., and Prevost, J.H., (1997a). Simulation of non–Gaussian homogeneous stochastic vector fields. *Probabilistic Engnrg. Mechanics.*

Popescu, R., Prevost, J.H., and Deodatis, G., (1997b). Effects of spatial variability on soil liquefaction: Some design recommendations. *Géotechnique.*

Popescu, R., Prevost, J.H., and Deodatis, G., (1997c). Stochastic variability of soil properties: Field data analysis. *Journ. Geotech. Engnrg., ASCE.*

Prevost, J.H., (1985). A simple plasticity theory for frictional cohesionless soils. *Soil Dynamics and Earthquake Engrg.*, 4:9–17.

Prevost, J.H., (1995). DYNAFLOW: A nonlinear transient finite element analysis program. Technical Report, Princeton University.

Soong, T.T. and Grigoriu, M., (1993). *Random Vibrations of Mechanical and Structural Systems.* Prentice Hall.

Structural Safety and Reliability, Shiraishi, Shinozuka & Wen (eds) © 1998 Balkema, Rotterdam, ISBN 90 5410 978 5

Preliminary study on observation scheme evaluation for inverse analysis of ground deformation analysis

Yusuke Honjo & Nobuaki Kudo
Gifu University, Japan

ABSTRACT: The inverse analysis is actively under research in geotechnical engineering. One of the important problems in inverse analyses is to design an observation scheme that are most suited for the purpose under given restrictions. Since the sensitivity matrix (or the observation matrix) plays the essential role in the observation scheme evaluation, the bootstrap method is employed first to examine the accuracy of the sensitivity matrix obtained by the linearization using Taylor expansion at the prior mean value of the model parameters. Furthermore, several criteria for the observation scheme, such as E-opt, E-opt. and A-opt, are calculated for several alternative observation schemes taking an embankment of soft ground as an example. In this study, linear elastic constitutive relationship is assumed for the soil skeleton.

1. INTRODUCTION

Inverse analysis is under active research in geotechnical engineering. A study on observation scheme in order to obtain observation data that are most suitable for the inverse analysis under given time and budget restriction is one of the significant issues in this area.

This paper consists of two parts. The first part is to examine the accuracy of the linearization method that is used to evaluate the observation matrix (or the sensitivity matrix) by the bootstrap method. The linearization method in this paper is defined as a method to obtain approximated observation matrix by linearizing the nonlinear observation equations at prior mean values using Taylor expansion.

The second part consist of the evaluation of several criteria that are used in evaluating various observation schemes. All the criteria tested in this study is based on the observation matrix. Thus, the accuracy of the observation matrix is essential issue in evaluating observation scheme.

An embankment load applied on the ground model is studied in this paper. For simplicity, only the linear elastic constitutive model is considered for the soil skeleton, and water that saturates the soil void is controlled by Darcy's low. The finite element procedure is employed to solve the system under given boundary conditions.

2. ACCURACY OF THE APPROXIMATED OBSERVATION MATRIX

2.1 *The linearization method*

Observation equation for a non-linear problem is given as:

$$y = f(\theta) + \varepsilon \qquad (1)$$

where y: observation vector
    f : observation function(vector)
    θ : model parameter vector

ε : total error which is assumed to follow $N(0, V_\varepsilon)$

When the maximum likelihood method is introduced, the model parameter to be estimated is the θ which minimizes the following evaluation function:

$$\text{min.} \quad J(\theta) = (y - f(\theta))^T V_\varepsilon^{-1} (y - f(\theta)) \qquad (2)$$

The uncertainty of the estimated parameter, i.e. the covariance matrix of θ, can be obtained strictly for a case where the given observation equation is linear with respect to θ, and thus the multiple regression theory is directory applicable. For a case given, the observation equation is nonlinear, the observation matrix need to be evaluated by the linearization method:

$$V_\theta = (X^T V_\varepsilon^{-1} X)^{-1} \qquad (3)$$

where each component of X is given as

$$\{X_{ij}\} = \{\frac{\partial f_i}{\partial \theta_j}\}_{\theta = \hat{\theta}} \qquad (4)$$

The matrix X thus has m rows and n columns, where m is the number of parameters and n is the observation number.

2.2 *Accuracy evaluation by the bootstrap method*

The bootstrap method is a methodology to evaluate uncertainty of the statistical estimations (Efron, 1982). The principle idea of this method is to obtain many possible samples from given sample by using MonteCarlo simulation, and then use these samples to evaluate the estimation uncertainty.

The procedure of the parametric bootstrap method, one employed in the present study, is as follows:

Table 1 Conditions of cases for bootstrap sampling

		Estimates and Variance				Correlation Matrices by B.S.method					Correlation Matrices by Lin.method			
		①	②	③	④		①	②	③	④	①	②	③	④
Case A-1	True value	100.00	0.300	0.0086	0.0086	①	1.000	-0.851	-0.047	-0.061	1.000	-0.902	-0.005	0.091
	Estimates by B.S.method	100.04	0.301	0.0070	0.0089	②	-0.851	1.000	-0.171	-0.061	-0.902	1.000	-0.171	-0.061
	s.d. by B.S. method	0.82	1.43E-5	1.64E-5	2.12E-8	③	-0.047	-0.171	1.000	-0.861	-0.005	-0.171	1.000	-0.861
	s.d. by Lin. method	1.18	1.51E-5	1.94E-5	2.49E-8	④	-0.061	-0.061	-0.861	1.000	0.091	-0.061	-0.861	1.000
Case A-2	True value	100.00	0.300	0.0086	0.0086	①	1.000	-0.874	0.075	0.130	1.000	-0.903	-0.034	0.162
	Estimates by B.S.method	101.20	0.293	0.0068	0.0089	②	-0.874	1.000	0.107	-0.443	-0.903	1.000	0.107	-0.276
	s.d. by B.S. method	17.74	4.51E-4	4.39E-6	2.12E-7	③	0.075	0.107	1.000	-0.376	-0.034	0.107	1.000	-0.882
	s.d. by Lin. method	25.26	4.10E-4	4.87E-5	1.31E-6	④	0.130	-0.443	-0.376	1.000	0.162	-0.276	-0.882	1.000
Case A-3	True value	100.00	0.300	0.0086	0.0086	①	1.000	-0.882	0.003	0.056	1.000	-0.897	-0.003	0.087
	Estimates by B.S.method	100.10	0.301	0.0071	0.0088	②	-0.882	1.000	0.082	-0.113	-0.897	1.000	0.055	-0.089
	s.d. by B.S. method	1.65	2.89E-5	3.00E-5	6.70E-8	③	0.003	0.082	1.000	-0.871	-0.003	0.055	1.000	-0.918
	s.d. by Lin. method	1.94	2.98E-5	4.92E-5	6.37E-7	④	0.056	-0.113	-0.871	1.000	0.087	-0.089	-0.918	1.000
Case B-1	True value	100.00	0.300	0.0086	0.0086	①	1.000	0.515	—	0.306				
	Estimates by B.S.method	86.54	0.136	0.0000	0.0033	②	0.515	1.000	—	-0.161		Calculation not possible		
	s.d. by B.S. method	8.64	1.13E-5	0.00E-0	8.71E-9	③	—	—	—	—				
	s.d. by Lin. method	Calculation not possible				④	0.306	-0.161	—	1.000				
Case C-1	True value	100.00	0.300	0.0086	0.0086	①	1.000	—	-0.334	-0.553	1.000	—	-0.119	0.017
	Estimates by B.S.method	100.04	Given	0.0070	0.0089	②	—	—	—	—	—	—	—	—
	s.d. by B.S. method	2.53	Given	1.35E-6	2.39E-8	③	-0.334	—	1.000	-0.522	-0.119	—	1.000	-0.924
	s.d. by Lin. method	0.18	Given	1.57E-6	2.45E-8	④	-0.553	—	-0.522	1.000	0.017	—	-0.924	1.000

①Young's modulus(t/m²) ②Poasson's ratio ③Horizontal Petrmeability(m/day) ④Vertical Petrmeability(m/day)

B.S.method : Bootstrap method   Lin.method : Linearization method

Table 2 Results of the bootstrap method

	Horizontal direction (m)	Vertical direction (m)	Pore pressure(t/m²)	Number of observation	Observation item
Case A-1	0.010	0.005	0.100	20	Horizontal and Vertical displacement · Pore pressure
Case A-2	0.010	0.025	0.500	20	Horizontal and Vertical displacement · Pore pressure
Case A-3	0.010	0.005	0.100	10	Horizontal and Vertical displacement · Pore pressure
Case B-1	0.010	0.005	0.100	20	Horizontal and Vertical displacement
Case C-1	0.010	0.005	0.100	20	Vertical displacement · Pore pressure (Poasson's ratio = 0.03)

Step 1: Assume the form of the probability distribution of the observation noise, and estimates its parameter values from the residuals.

Step 2: Generate numbers of sets of observation data by MonteCarlo simulation method based on the parameter values obtained in Step 1.

Step 3: Estimate the model parameter values from the many sets of observation data generated in step 2 by the inverse analysis procedure.

Step 4: Evaluate the estimation uncertainty based on the inverse analysis results obtained in step 3.

2.3 Numerical example

(a) Description of the example

The model employed in this study is presented in Fig.1. The thickness of the homogeneous layer is 4m, Young's modulus E = 1MPa, Poison's ratio ν = 0.30, vertical and horizontal permeability $k_y = k_x$ = 0.0086 m/day. 60 kPa of load is applied for 6m length. The boundary conditions and the observation points are presented in Fig.1 also.

Presented in Table 1 are the observation items and their observation uncertainties given by the standard deviations for various cases compared in this study. It is assumed that all observation errors follows normal distribution with 0 mean and given standard deviations.

In case A, all items, namely vertical and horizontal displacement and pore pressure, are used in the inverse analysis. The differences between case A-1 and A-2 are standard deviations of vertical displacement and pore pressure: Those of A-2 is 5 times of those of A-1. The observation frequency in Case A-3 is 10 and is half of that of case A-1, otherwise these two cases are the same.

In case B-1, only vertical and horizontal measurements are introduced, and no observation data for the pore pressure.

Finally, in case C-1, only vertical displacement and pore pressure measurements are introduced; Poison's ratio is assumed to be known in this case, otherwise the inverse analysis becomes unstable.

(b) Results and discussions

All the calculated results are summarized in Table 2

For case A-1, unbiased estimated values are obtained for all 4 parameters. Also s.d.'s estimated by the linealization method are almost equal or slightly larger than those obtained by the bootstrap method. Furthermore, estimated correlation matrices by the two methods are surprisingly similar: high negative correlations exist between E and ν, and k_y and k_x, otherwise the correlation is negligible.

Case A-2 naturally gives larger s.d. values compared to case A-1 because of the larger observation error introduced. The correlation between k_y and k_x has become smaller, but other parts are very similar to case A-1.

The result of Case A-3 is very similar to that of A-1, thus it is considered that the influences of observation frequency in the present condition have little effect on the inverse analysis results.

The result of case B-1 has considerable biases. k_x is estimated to be 0.0 for all cases. It is speculated that without observed pore pressure measurement, the inverse analysis becomes illposed. Furthermore, the matrix given in Eq.(3) seems to deteriorates, thus the covariance matrix was not obtained by the linearization method.

In case C-1, it was impossible to simultaneously estimate four parameters based solely on vertical displacement and pressure observation. Thus, Poison's ratio was discarded from the inverse analysis, and fixed to 0.3. The result exhibits that the other three parameters are estimated very accurately and without bias. Furthermore, the estimated variances and correlation matrix show very similar properties to those of Case A-1.

3. CRITERIA TO EVALUATE OBSERVATION SCHEME

3.1 Criteria

Several parameters have been proposed to evaluate the properties of the observation matrix for linear observation equations. These criteria can be applied to nonlinear observation equations by employing the linear approximation given in Eq.(4):

$$D\text{-}opt: \quad \min \det[(X^T V_e^{-1} X)^{-1}]$$
$$E\text{-}opt: \quad \min \lambda_{max}$$
$$A\text{-}opt: \quad \min trace(X^T V_e^{-1} X)^{-1} \tag{5}$$
$$\min. \ conditional \ number: \quad \min \sqrt{\lambda_{max}/\lambda_{min}}$$

where λ_{max} and λ_{min} are the maximum and the minimum of the eigne values of Eq.(3).

The criteria presented in Eq.(5) are all comprehensive scaler values to evaluate the property of the observation matrix. However, one may be more interested in reliability of the value actually predicted based on the inverse analysis results.

A representative criterion for such evaluation is G-opt as follows:

$$G\text{-}opt: \quad \min \ [\max \ \{diag \ G(X^T V_e^{-1} X) \ G^T\}] \tag{6}$$

where G is a sensitivity matrix relating prediction value y_p and parameter values.

It goes without saying that all the criteria introduced in Eqs.

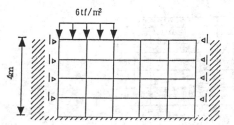

Fig. 1 Model employed in the analysis

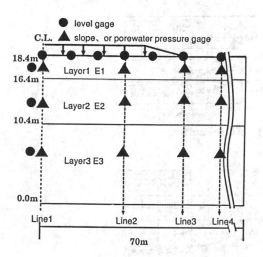

Fig.2 Observation points

Table 3 Analuzed cases in Case 2

	Hori. disp.	Verti. disp.	Pore press.
Line 1			Case 2-1p
Line 2	Case 2-2x	Case 2-2y	Case 2-2p
Line 3	Case 2-3x	Case 2-3y	Case 2-3p
Line 4	Case 2-4x	Case 2-4y	Case 2-4p

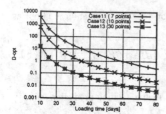

Fig.3 Results of Case 1 (D-opt)

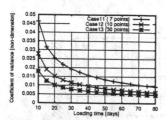

(a) E of the first layer

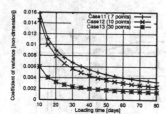

(b) E of the second layer

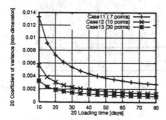

(c) E of the third layer

Fig.4 Variancec of E in Case 1

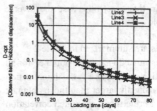

(a) vertical displacement

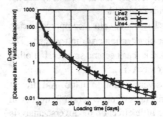

(b) horizontal displacement

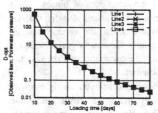

(c) pore pressure

Fig.5 Result of Case 2 (D-opt)

3.2 Numerical example

(a) Description of the example

A ground consists of 3 layers are considered as Fig.2. Young's modulus need to be evaluated, and settlement at the center after 100 days after construction of embankment is to be predicted. Poison's ratio and permeability are assumed to be known. 54kPa load is applied gradually in 10 days, and then kept constant. It is expected about 90% of primary consolidation takes place within 100days. The observations are made in 5 days interval for 15 times (i.e... 80 days from the start of loading), at vertical and horizontal displacement as well as pore pressure are measured at specified points.

The calculation of the various criteria are made for following cases:

Case 1: comparison of different observation items:

    Case 1-1 surface settlements

    Case 1-2 surface settlements and vertical displacements along the central line.

    Case 1-3 surface settlements, vertical displacement along the central line and horizontal displacement along the toe line.

Case 2:

    4 different observation lines combined with the different observation items are compared. These observation are taken in addition to the items observed in Case 1-2. The added items are shown in Table 3 together with the notations.

(5) and (6) are exact for linear observation equations, but only approximation in nonlinear cases, and their values are different depending on the point where Taylor expansion is taken.

The interpretations of these criterion based on information entropy is given in Honjo and Kudo (1998).

(b) Results and discussion

Presented in Fig.3 are D-opt values calculated for Case 1-1, 2 and 3 respectively. As the information increases, the values decrease. The coefficient of variation for each E for 3 cases are also presented in Fig.4. The values gets smaller as the information increases. Also, threshold values exist for each case.

D-opt values are presented in Fig.5 (a), (b) and (c) separately for different observation items. D-0pt values for horizontal displacement is one order smaller than for vertical displacement and pore pressure measurements. As far as observation location is concerned, line-3 exhibited the minimum D-opt for horizontal displacement, line-2 for the vertical displacement and no difference for the locations for the pore pressure measurement.

Other criteria, including G-opt, exhibit similar behavior as that of D-opt.

4. CONCLUDING REMARKS

The result presented are for the linear elastic ground. Further investigation is necessary for ground with nonlinear constitutive relation, and actual observation data.

REFERENCE
Efron, B.(1982) The Jackknife, the Bootstrap and other resampling plans, Society for Industrial and Applied Mathematics
Steinberg, D.M. and W.G. Hunter (1984) Experimental design: review and comment, Technometorics .26- 2
Honjo, Y. and Kudo, N. (1998) Proc. JSCE No.585/III-42

Structural Safety and Reliability, Shiraishi, Shinozuka & Wen (eds) © 1998 Balkema, Rotterdam, ISBN 90 5410 978 5

Evaluation of breakwater stability by probabilistic model

Hiroyasu Kawai & Tetsuya Hiraishi
Port and Harbour Research Institute, Ministry of Transport, Yokosuka, Japan

ABSTRACT: The encounter probabilities of sliding and overturning failures, and expected sliding distances of present breakwater caissons are computed in probabilistic design theory, assuming that the durable period of the breakwater is 50 years. The encounter probabilities and sliding distance are inversely proportional to the safety factors for sliding and overturning.

1 BACKGROUND OF THIS STUDY

The stability of breakwater caisson is evaluated by safety factors for sliding and overturning in the present design method in Japan. The safety factors are calculated with the deterministic deep water wave height and the highest tidal level.

The occurrence probability distributions of deep water wave height and tidal elevation are not considered in the present design method. Additionally, the estimation errors included in 1) deep water wave height hindcasting, 2) wave transformation computation, 3) calculation of wave force on breakwater caisson, 4) dead weight of the caisson, and 5) friction between the concrete caisson and rubble mound are not considered.

The degree of the stability of the designed breakwater cannot be evaluated quantitatively by using the safety factors. It should be evaluated in the probabilistic design method.

2 UNCERTAIN FACTORS AND THEIR ERROR CHARACTERISTIC

2.1 *Deep water wave*

In the present breakwater design method, the parameters of the design deep water wave is derived from the continuous data of annual maximum wave heights obtained in the field observation and numerically hindcasted. The occurrence probability density distributions of the deep water wave heights at almost all the ports in Japan fit the Weibull distribution ($k=0.75$, 1.0, 1.5, 2.0) and those at the others the FT−I (Gumbel) (Goda and Kobune 1990).

However, there is a difference between the extreme distribution function derived from wave data and the real function, because the number of adopted wave data is limited. Such an error gives the variation of the estimated probabilistic wave height H_0 around the real wave height H_R.

In this paper, the normal distribution $p_R(H_R)$ is applied to the probability density distribution of estimation error in the extreme wave height. The mean value and standard deviation of the normal distribution is $1.00H_0$ and $0.10H_0$ (Takayama et al. 1991). The duration time of a storm effective to the breakwater stability is assumed to be 2 hours in a year.

2.2 *Tidal level*

The high water level (H.W.L.) is used as a design tidal level at almost all the ports in Japan. The storm surge is considered at ports in the area suffered from typhoon attacks.

In the probabilistic design, the variable tidal level is employed. The tidal level can be calculated with four major tidal constituents, of which values are known at almost all the ports in Japan.

Figure 1 shows the distributions of the astronomical tidal elevation at the principal ports in the Pacific Ocean and the Sea of Japan (Kawai et al. 1996). The non−dimensional tidal level $\zeta *$ is defined as the ratio of the dimensional tidal level to the total amplitude of four major tidal constituents. The occurrence probability density of the tidal elevation around the high water level (H.W.L.) is much smaller than the density around the mean sea level (M.S.L.). The profile of the probability density distribution mainly varies with the port location.

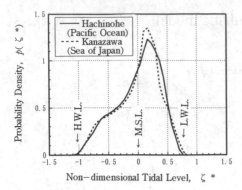

Figure 1. Occurrence probability distribution of astronomical tidal elevation

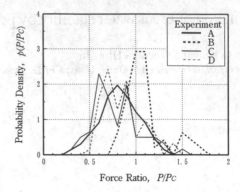

Figure 2. Probability density distribution of estimation error of wave force

2.3 Wave transformation in shallow water

The wave is transformed by the influence of the sea bottom topography in the area where the water depth is smaller than the half of wave length. The wave height at breakwater site is estimated by numerical models such as wave energy balance equation and mild slope equation.

The computed wave height H_m usually does not agree with the real wave height H_M, because the hydraulic phenomena in wave transformation are complicated. The probability density distribution of the real wave height $p_M(H_M)$ fits the normal distribution with a mean value of $0.87H_m$ and standard deviation of $0.09H_m$ (Takayama et al. 1991).

The Goda's simplified wave breaking model (Goda 1975) is applied to estimate the effects of wave breaking in this paper.

2.4 Wave force on breakwater caisson

The wave force on breakwater caisson is estimated by an experimental formula (Goda 1973), because the hydraulic phenomena is so complex that no computer models have been established. Therefore the calculated force P_C sometimes differs from the real force P. The probability density distribution $p_P(P)$ for breakwater covered with wave–dissipating blocks fits the normal distribution with a mean value of $0.84P_C$ and standard deviation of $0.10P_C$, and the distribution for breakwater without blocks fits the normal distribution with a mean value of $0.91P_C$ and standard deviation of $0.17P_C$ (Takayama et al. 1991).

In this paper, the modification formula (Takahashi et al. 1993) for estimating impulsive breaking force with wave accuracy is applied. **Figure 2** shows the distribution of the ratio of the experimental wave force on breakwater P to the wave force calculated by the Takahashi's formula

P_C for the case without blocks. The distribution of the ratio fits the normal distribution with a mean value of 0.88 and standard deviation of 0.22.

2.5 Dead weight of breakwater caisson

Breakwater caisson consists of reinforced concrete box filled with sand. The deviation range of the dead weight is smaller than that of the other uncertain factors, therefore it gives a slight influence to the encounter probabilities of sliding and overturning, and expected sliding distance. We have assumed that the actual weight is equal to the design weight.

2.6 Friction between concrete caisson and rubble mound

In the present breakwater design, the design friction coefficient between concrete caisson and rubble mound f_D is 0.6. However, the actual coefficient f is influenced by the roughness of the mound surface and another factors. According to the results of large scale model tests, the probability density distribution of the actual friction coefficient $p_f(f)$ fits the normal distribution with a mean value of $1.06f_D$ and standard deviation of $0.16f_D$ (Takayama et al. 1991).

3 ENCOUNTER PROBABILITY OF FAILURE AND SLIDING DISTANCE

3.1 Criteria of breakwater

Nineteen breakwaters covered with wave–dissipating blocks and thirty breakwaters without blocks are investigated in this paper. These breakwaters are located in the Pacific Ocean and the Sea of Japan. The occurrence distribution of deep water wave heights fits the Weibull distribution at almost all the ports, and the FT−I (Gumbel) distribution at the others. Assuming that the return period is 50 years, the design deep water wave heights for the breakwaters are between 2.4 and 14.0m, and the wave periods between 4.9 and 16.0s. The mean water depths at the breakwater sites are between 5.3 and 26.1m, the slope gradients between 0.001 and 0.014, and the amplitudes of astronomical tide from high water level to low water level between 0.6 and 2.4m. The widths of the breakwater caissons are between 4.5 and 25.0m.

3.2 Encounter probability of sliding failure

The safety factor for sliding Fs is defined as

$$Fs = f_D(W_D - U)/P_H \tag{3.1}$$

where f_D and W_D represents the design friction coefficient and the design weight of the caisson respectively, and U and P_H indicates the uplift and horizontal forces on the caisson respectively. The present design standard demands that the safety factor should be more than 1.2.

The encounter probability of sliding failure during 50 years Ps is given by

$$P_S = 1 - (1 - p_s)^{50} \tag{3.2a}$$

$$p_s = \int_{-\infty}^{\infty}\int_{0}^{\infty}\int_{0}^{\infty}\int_{0}^{\infty}\int_{0}^{\infty}\int_{0}^{f_0} \{p_f(f)p_P(P)$$
$$\cdot p_M(H_M)p_R(H_R)p_0(H_0)p_\zeta(\zeta)\}$$
$$dfdPdH_MdH_RdH_0d\zeta \tag{3.2b}$$

where, $p_f(f)$ is the distribution of estimation error in friction factor, $p_P(P)$ is that in wave force on caisson, $p_M(H_M)$ is that in wave height at breakwater site, and $p_R(H_R)$ is that in deep water wave height. Additionally, $p_0(H_0)$ is the occurrence distribution of deep water wave height, and $p_\zeta(\zeta)$ is that of water level due to astronomical tide. In this study, it is assumed that the sliding failure occurs under the condition of $Fs < 1$, and that the durable period is 50 years.

Figure 3 shows the relation between the safety factor Fs and encounter probability of sliding failure Ps. The relation is regressed as
i) breakwater covered with blocks:

$$P_S = 10^{(3.08 - 4.18Fs)} \tag{3.3a}$$

ii) breakwater without blocks:

$$P_S = 10^{(1.45 - 2.05Fs)} \tag{3.3b}$$

The encounter probability is inversely proportional to the safety factor, and depends on the structure type and design condition. The values of $Ps = 0.099$ and 0.012 is obtained for breakwater covered with wave−dissipating blocks and breakwater without blocks for the case of $Fs = 1.2$ respectively.

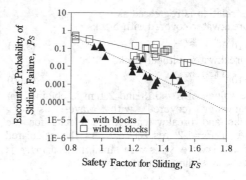

Figure 3. Relation between safety factor and encounter probability of sliding failure

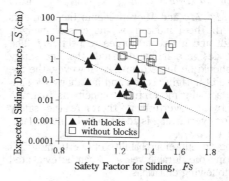

Figure 4. Relation between safety factor for sliding and expected sliding distance

3.3 Expected sliding distance

The sliding distance of breakwater caisson by a single wave S is calculated by the following equation (Shimosako et al. 1994).

$$S = \frac{g\tau_0^2(P' - fW')^3(P' + fW')}{8fWW'P'^2} \tag{3.4}$$

where, g is the gravity acceleration, τ_0 the duration time of wave force, and P' the equivalent sliding wave force. W and W' is the caisson weight in the air and water respectively.

The expected sliding distance during the durable years $\bar{S}$ can be evaluated as

$$\bar{S} = \int_{-\infty}^{\infty}\int_{0}^{\infty}\int_{0}^{\infty}\int_{0}^{\infty}\int_{0}^{\infty}\int_{0}^{f_0} \{S \cdot p_f(f)p_P(P)$$
$$\cdot p_M(H_M)p_R(H_R)p_0(H_0)p_\zeta(\zeta)\}$$
$$dfdPdH_MdH_RdH_0d\zeta \tag{3.5}$$

Figure 4 shows the relation between the safety factor Fs and expected sliding distance.

The relation is regressed as
i) breakwater covered with blocks :

$$\bar{S} = 10^{(3.04-3.25Fs)} \tag{3.6a}$$

ii) breakwater without blocks :

$$\bar{S} = 10^{(3.52-2.67Fs)} \tag{3.6b}$$

The values of $\bar{S}$ =0.13 and 2.1cm is obtained for breakwater covered with wave-dissipating blocks and breakwater without blocks for the case of Fs=1.2 respectively. As the calculated sliding distance $\bar{S}$ is very small, little damage is caused by sliding for port activities.

3.4 Encounter probability of overturning failure

The safety factor for overturning Fo is defined as

$$Fo = (Mw - Mu)/Mp \tag{3.7}$$

where Mw, Mu and Mp represents the moments around the heel induced by the caisson weight, the uplift and horizontal forces respectively. The present design standard demands that the safety factor should be more than 1.2. However, the toe pressure of upright section and instability for sliding are actually more critical conditions than the instability for overturning, therefore the safety factor for overturning is adopted to be much larger than 1.2.

The encounter probability of overturning failure during the durable years Po can be evaluated by the following equations.

$$Po = 1 - (1-po)^{50} \tag{3.8a}$$

$$p_o = \int_{-\infty}^{\infty} \int_{0}^{\infty} \int_{0}^{\infty} \int_{0}^{\infty} \int_{0}^{\infty} \int_{0}^{t_0} \{p_f(f)p_P(P)$$
$$\cdot p_M(H_M)p_R(H_R)p_0(H_0)p_\zeta(\zeta)\}$$
$$df dP dH_M dH_R dH_0 d\zeta \tag{3.8b}$$

Figure 5 shows the relation between the safety factor for overturning Fo and encounter probability of overturning failure Po. The relation for composite breakwater without blocks is regressed as

$$Po = 10^{(1.16-2.79Fo)} \tag{3.9}$$

The value of Po=0.0064 is obtained for the case of Fo=1.2. The encounter probability of overturning failure for the case of Fo=1.2 is smaller than that of sliding.

4 CONCLUSION

The encounter probabilities of sliding and overturning failure, and expected sliding distance of 49 breakwaters are evaluated. These values are inversely proportional to the safety factors, and are influenced by the structure type and design

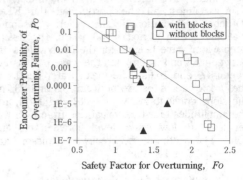

Figure 5. Relation between safety factor for overturning and encounter probability of overturning failure

condition. The probability of sliding becomes slightly larger than that of overturning at almost all the breakwaters.

REFERENCES

Kawai,H., H.Fujisaku and Y.Suzuki 1996. Occurrence probability of tidal level and its effect on stability of breakwater. *Proc. of Civil Eng. in the Ocean* 12: 261–266.

Kawai,H., T.Hiraishi, and T.Sekimoto 1997. Influence of uncertain factor in breakwater design to encounter probability of failure. *Proc. of Civil Eng. in the Ocean* 13: 579–584.

Goda,Y. 1973. A new method of wave pressure calculation for the design of composite breakwater. *Rept. of Port and Harbour Res. Inst.* 12–3: 31–70.

Goda,Y. 1975. Deformation of irregular waves due to depth-controlled wave breaking. *Rept. of Port and Harbour Res. Inst.* 14–3: 59–106.

Goda,Y. and K.Kobune 1990. Distribution function fitting storm wave data. *Proc. of 22nd Int. Conf. on Coastal Eng.* : 18–31.

Shimosako,K., S.Takahashi, and K.Tanimoto 1994. Estimating the sliding distance of composite breakwaters due to wave forces inclusive of impulsive breaking wave forces. *Proc. of 24th Conf. on Coastal Eng.* : 1580–1594.

Takahashi,S., K.Tanimoto, and K.Shimosako 1993. Experimental study of impulsive pressures on composite breakwater. *Rept. of Port and Harbour Res. Inst.* 31–5: 33–72.

Takayama,T. and H.Fujii 1991. Probabilistic estimation of stability of slide for caisson type breakwater. *Rept. of Port and Harbour Res. Inst.* 30–4: 35–64.

Structural Safety and Reliability, Shiraishi, Shinozuka & Wen (eds) © 1998 Balkema, Rotterdam, ISBN 90 5410 978 5

Automated reliability based design of footing foundations

B.K. Low
School of Civil and Structural Engineering, Nanyang Technological University, Singapore

Wilson H. Tang
Department of Civil and Structural Engineering, Hong Kong University of Science and Technology, People's Republic of China

ABSTRACT: First order reliability method can be implemented efficiently using an optimization tool that resides in most spreadsheet software. Correlated random variables and complicated non-explicit performance functions are dealt with easily. As illustrations, design examples are given to dimension footing foundation for a desired reliability. The reliability for multiple failure modes are also evaluated, and compared with Monte Carlo simulation using spreadsheet.

1 INTRODUCTION

This paper presents a practical reliability-based design procedure using a widely available spreadsheet optimization tool. As example, the bearing capacity of shallow foundations is considered. The results obtained are the same as the first order reliability method (FORM). The conceptual simplicity, ease of implementation, and versatility of the spreadsheet approach are stressed.

The matrix formulation (Veneziano 1974) of the reliability index as defined by Hasofer-Lind (1974) is:

$$\beta = \min_{\underline{x} \in F} \sqrt{(\underline{x} - \underline{m})^T \underline{C}^{-1} (\underline{x} - \underline{m})} \qquad (1)$$

where $\underline{x}$ is a vector representing the set of random variables, $\underline{m}$ their mean values, $\underline{C}$ the covariance matrix, and F the failure region. An established elegant approach exists that transforms the limit state surface into the space of standard normal uncorrelated variates, whereby the shortest distance from the transformed failure surface to the origin of the reduced variates is the reliability index β. The procedure is explained in Haldar and Mahadevan (1995), for example.

In the following sections a spreadsheet reliability evaluation method is proposed that literally sets up a tilted ellipsoid in the spreadsheet and minimizes the ellipsoid subject to the constraint that it be tangent to the failure surface. For this purpose Eq. 1 is rewritten as:

$$\beta = \min_{\underline{x} \in F} \sqrt{\left[\frac{x_i - m_i}{\sigma_i}\right]^T [R]^{-1} \left[\frac{x_i - m_i}{\sigma_i}\right]} \qquad (2)$$

in which $[R]^{-1}$ is the inverse of the correlation matrix, and σ_i the standard deviations. This equation will be used since the correlation matrix R displays the correlation structure explicitly. The proposed spreadsheet method does not require concepts of transformed space and diagonalization of correlation matrix, and can deal with correlated nonnormals or highly implicit performance functions.

2 A SIMPLE EXAMPLE OF PROPOSED APPROACH

The proposed spreadsheet reliability evaluation approach will be illustrated first for a case with two random variables. The problem concerns the bearing capacity of a strip footing sustaining non-eccentric vertical load. Extensions to higher dimensions and more complicated scenarios are given later.

With respect to bearing capacity failure, the performance function (*PerFunc*) for a strip footing, in its simplest form, is:

$$PerFunc = q_u - q \qquad (3a)$$

$$\text{where} \quad q_u = cN_c + p_o N_q + \frac{B}{2}\gamma N_\gamma \qquad (3b)$$

in which q_u is the ultimate bearing capacity, q the applied bearing pressure, c the cohesion of soil, p_o the effective overburden pressure at foundation level, B the width of foundation, γ the unit weight of soil below the base of foundation, and N_c, N_q, and N_γ are bearing capacity factors, which are functions of the friction angle (ϕ) of soil:

$$N_q = e^{\pi \tan\phi} \tan^2\left(45 + \frac{\phi}{2}\right) \qquad (4a)$$

$$N_c = \left(N_q - 1\right)\cot(\phi) \qquad (4b)$$

$$N_\gamma = 1.75\left(N_q - 1\right)\tan\phi \qquad (4c)$$

The N_γ given by Eq. 4c corresponds well with that of the chart in Fig. 2.8 of Tomlinson (1995). The coefficient 1.75 is the average between the 1.5 in Hansen (1970)'s equation—as cited in Bowles 1996—and the 2.0 in German code DIN 4017, as cited in Eq. 114 of Hansbo 1994.

The statistical parameters and correlation matrix of c and ϕ are shown in Fig. 1. The other parameters in Eqs. 3a and 3b are assumed known with values q = 230 kPa, p_o = 24 kPa, B = 1.2 m, and γ = 20 kN/m^3. The formulas for N_q, N_c, and N_γ and for the column vector $(x_i - m_i) / \sigma_i$ are entered based on the "xvalues", which are intially set equal to the mean values. Subsequent steps are:

1. Define a name for the correlation matrix, say "rmat", and for the column vector $[(x_i-m_i)/\sigma_i]$, say "nvect".

2. The formula of β is: "=sqrt(mmult(transpose(nvect), mmult(minverse(rmat), nvect)))", followed by pressing "Enter" while holding down the "Ctrl"and "Shift" keys. (mmult, transpose, and minverse are Microsoft Excel's built-in matrix functions.)

3. The formula of the performance function, $g(\underline{x})$ = q_u - q, is entered based on *xvalues*.

4. Solver is invoked, to Minimize β, By Changing the *xvalues*, Subject To *PerFunc* $\le$ 0, and *xvalues* $\ge$ 0.

The β value obtained is 2.065. The spreadsheet approach is simple and intuitive because it works in the original space of the variables; it does not involve orthogonal transformation of matrix or user-input partial derivatives.

The next section provides insights on the meaning of reliability index in the original space of the basic random variables. More details can be found in Low (1996) and Low and Tang (1997a).

3. DISPERSION ELLIPSOIDS IN ORIGINAL SPACE

The case in Fig. 1 is portrayed graphically in Fig. 2. Correlated random variables can be viewed as forming a tilted ellipsoid centered at the mean in original space. The 1-σ dispersion ellipse in Fig. 2 corresponds to β = 1 in Eq. 1 or Eq. 2, and the ellipse that touches the failure surface corresponds to β = 2.065.

The quadratic form $(x - \underline{m})^T C^{-1}(x - \underline{m})$ in Eq. 1 appears also in the negative exponent of the multivariate normal distribution. One may regard the gradually expanding ellipsoidal surfaces as representing the contours of decreasing probability density. Therefore, for normally distributed variables, to minimize β in Eq. 1 (or β^2 in the multivariate normal distribution) is to maximize the value of the multivariate normal probability density function; and to find the smallest ellipsoid that is tangent to the failure surface is equivalent to finding the *most probable failure point*. This perspective is consistent with Shinozuka (1983) that *"the design point $\underline{x}^*$ is the point of maximum likelihood if $\underline{x}$ is Gaussian, whether or not its components are uncorrelated."*

4. RELIABILITY-BASED DESIGN OF WIDTH OF RETAINING WALL FOUNDATION

Tomlinson (1995)'s Example 2.2 determines the factor of safety against bearing capacity failure for a retaining wall that carries a horizontal load (Q_h) of 300 kN/m run at a point 2.5 m above the base and a centrally applied vertical load (Q_v) of 1100 kN/m run. The base (5 m × 25 m) of the retaining wall is founded at a depth of 1.8 m in a silty sand with friction angle ϕ = 25°, cohesion c = 15 kN/m^2, and unit weight γ = 21 kN/m^3.

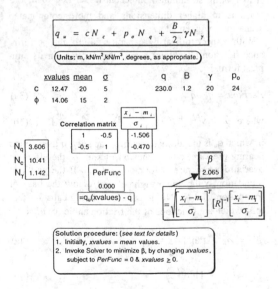

Fig. 1. A simple illustration involving correlation

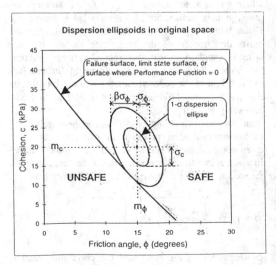

Fig. 2. Graphical equivalent of the case in Fig. 1

In the present example to illustrate reliability-based design, the width B of the base of the retaining wall is to be determined based on a reliability index $\beta = 3.0$ against bearing capacity failure. The parameters c, ϕ, Q_h, and Q_v, will be treated as random variables with mean values equal to those in Tomlinson's deterministic example, and with coefficient of variation equal to 0.20, 0.1, 0.15, 0.10 respectively. The mean and σ are entered in the top left corner of Fig. 3. The random variables are partially correlated, with correlation matrix as shown.

The bearing capacity equation is (e.g. Eq. 2.7 in Tomlinson 1995, or Table 4.1 in Bowles 1996):

$$q_u = cN_c s_c d_c i_c + p_o N_q s_q d_q i_q + \frac{B}{2}\gamma N_\gamma s_\gamma d_\gamma i_\gamma \qquad (5)$$

where the nine factors of s_j, d_j and i_j account for the shape and depth effects of foundation and the inclination effect of the applied load, and other symbols are as defined for Eq. 3b. The lower half of Fig. 3 shows Brinch Hansen's equations, as given in Tables 4.5a-4.5b in Bowles (1996). All boxed cells (except the correlation matrix) contain equations. These equations refer to the xvalues (top left), which are initially set equal to the mean values. Equations for d_q and d_c are entered in Fig. 3 using the "IF" spreadsheet function. The formula for the reliability index β is entered as in Fig. 1. Subsequent

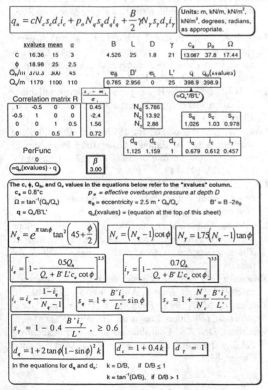

Fig. 3. To determine width B, for a β index of 3.0

steps are:
1. Copy mean values to *xvalues*, and set initial B value such that *PerFunc* > 0.
2. Invoke Solver to minimize β, by changing *xvalues*, subject to *PerFunc* $\leq$ 0 and *xvalues* $\geq$ 0.
3. Repeat (manually, or more conveniently by recording a simple VBA module) steps 1 & 2 until β equals the design value.

A final width B equal to 4.53 m is obtained for a reliability index β of 3.0. Had the c.o.v. of ϕ been equal to 0.15 instead of 0.10, the required width B is 5.51 m to attain the same reliability.

A possible refinement for the analysis in Fig. 3 is to introduce a factor M to allow for the uncertainty in the analytical model.

5. ON USING SOLVER

Solver can handle up to 500 constraints—one upper limit and one lower limit for each changing cell, plus 100 additional constraints—according to Microsoft Excel 7's on-line help. Each changing cell can be constrained by a number, another cell or range reference, or formula.

In the previous section, it is important to select initial width B such that *PerFunc* > 0 initially when *xvalues = mean*. This merely means that the search by the spreadsheet's optimization tool should start from a point that is not within the failure domain in order to obtain a positive reliability index and a correct design width B.

Although the correlation coefficient between two random variables has a range $-1 \leq \rho_{ij} \leq 1$, one is not totally free in assigning any values within this range for the correlation matrix. The correlation matrix has to be positive definite (e.g. Ditlevsen 1981, p85). For the present approach, an inconsistent correlation matrix will manifest itself by causing *Solver* to break down due to "error encountered" when Solver tries to evaluate the square root of a negative quantity—the right hand side of Eq. 2—during its iterative searching for the minimum dispersion ellipsoid and the corresponding reliability index β.

6. RELIABILITY FOR MULTIPLE FAILURE MODES

In addition to the bearing capacity mode of failure, a retaining wall may also fail by sliding along its base and by overturning about its toe. The performance functions for these two failure modes are taken to be:

$$PerFunc(Sliding) = c_a B' + Q_v \tan\phi - Q_h \qquad (6)$$

$$PerFunc(Overturning) = Q_v \frac{B}{2} - Q_h \times 2.5m \qquad (7)$$

where $B' = B - 2e_B$, and is a function of Q_h/Q_v, as given by the equations in Fig. 3.

In Eq. 6, the passive resistance of the soil in front of the wall has been ignored, to allow for the possibility that it may not have been placed during construction, or that it might be excavated away after construction.

1839

With B equal to 4.526 m as shown in Fig. 3, Eqs. 6 and 7 were entered into separate cells in the spreadsheet, and the spreadsheet optimization tool was invoked to determine the reliability indices for these two failure modes. A reliability index of 3.67 was obtained for the sliding mode, and 8.06 for the overturning mode. These, together with the reliability index of 3.00 against bearing capacity failure, give an estimate of the probability of failure as between 0.135% and 0.147%, based on first order bounds.

Monte Carlo simulation can be easily implemented using Microsoft Excel's Visual Basic for Applications (VBA) programming environment, as described in Low (1996). For the statistical parameters given in Fig. 3, and accounting for different failure modes (Eqs. 5, 6, 7), a probability of failure equal to 0.145% was obtained (Fig. 4) in 400,000 Monte Carlo trials, with 518 failures in bearing capacity, 14 in sliding, 46 in combined bearing and sliding, and 0 in overturning. That the bearing capacity failures outnumber sliding failures is consistent with the reliability index (3.0) for the bearing capacity failure mode being smaller than the reliability index (3.67) for the sliding mode. The Monte Carlo failure rate of 0.145% is also consistent with the range (0.135% to 0.147%) indicated by first-order bounds for the reliability indices of 3.0, 3.67, and 8.06 against bearing, sliding, and overturning failures respectively.

(In the VBA code for Monte Carlo simulation, the spreadsheet RANDOM function was used first to generate sets of independent standard normal variates, which were then transformed to correlated normal variates c, ϕ, Q_h, and Q_v.)

7. SUMMARY AND CONCLUSIONS

The ease of implementing reliability-based design using a spreadsheet software and its optimization tool was illustrated, and a useful perspective in the original space of the basic variables was described. The spreadsheet approach obtains the same result as would a first order reliability method (FORM). The concepts of reduced variates and diagonalization of covariance matrix are however not necessary in the spreadsheet procedure, which automatically searches for the smallest dispersion ellipsoid that is tangent to the limit state function in the original space of the random variables.

For the retaining wall example, in addition to the bearing capacity failure mode, the sliding and overturning failure modes were also considered. First order probability bounds based on the reliability indices for these modes are in good agreement with the probability of failure obtained from the Monte Carlo simulation that was implemented using the Microsoft Excel spreadsheet software and its VBA programming environment.

The spreadsheet method is applicable also to correlated nonnormals. The performance function can be highly implicit, incorporate user-defined spreadsheet functions, and reflect spatial autocorrelations (Low and Tang 1997b, 1997c, Low et al. 1998).

REFERENCES

Bowles, J.E. 1996. *Foundation Analysis and Design*, 5th edition, McGraw-Hill.

Ditlevsen, O. 1981. *Uncertainty Modeling*. McGraw-Hill.

Haldar, A., and Mahadevan, S. 1995. First-order and second-order reliability methods. In *Probabilistic Structural Mechanics Handbook*, ed. C. (Raj) Sundararajan, Chapman & Hall.

Hansbo, S. 1994. *Foundation Engineering*, Developments in Geot. Engrg. Series, Elsevier, Amsterdam.

Hasofer, A.M. and Lind, N.C. 1974. Exact and invariant second-moment code format. *J.Engrg.Mech.*, ASCE, 100(1), 111-121.

Low, B.K. 1996. Practical probabilistic approach using spreadsheet. *Proc., Uncertainty in Geologic Environment: from Theory to Practice*, ASCE Geotech. Spec. Pub. #58, Vol. 2, 1284-1302.

Low, B.K. and Wilson H.Tang 1997a. Efficient reliability evaluation using spreadsheet. *J.Engrg.Mech.*, ASCE, 123(7), 749-752.

Low, B.K. and Wilson H.Tang 1997b. Probabilistic Slope Analysis based on Janbu's Generalized Procedure of Slices. *Computers and Geotechnics*, Elsevier Science Ltd., 21(2), 121-142.

Low, B.K. and Wilson H.Tang 1997c. Reliability analysis of reinforced embankments on soft ground. *Canadian Geotechnical Journal.* (*in press*)

Low, B.K., Gilbert, R.B., and Wright, S.G. 1998. Slope Reliability Analysis Using Generalized Method of Slices. *J.Geotech. & Geoenviron. Engrg.*, ASCE. (*in press*)

Shinozuka, M. 1983. "Basic analysis of structural safety." *J. Struct. Engrg.*, ASCE, 109(3), 721-740.

Tomlinson, M.J. 1995. *Foundation Design and Construction*, 6th edition, Longman Scientific & Tech.

Veneziano, D. 1974. Contributions to second moment reliability. *Research Report No. R74-33*. Dept. of Civil Engrg., MIT.

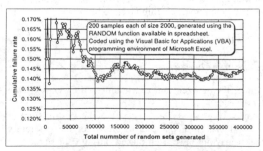

Fig. 4. Monte Carlo simulation for multiple modes

Bridges

Structural Safety and Reliability, Shiraishi, Shinozuka & Wen (eds) © 1998 Balkema, Rotterdam, ISBN 90 5410 978 5

Structural safety of existing road bridges

A. Žnidarič
Slovenian National Building and Civil Engineering Institute, Ljubljana, Slovenia

F. Moses
University of Pittsburgh, Pa., USA

ABSTRACT: Heavily deteriorated bridges can still be safe enough to carry normal traffic. Therefore, the structural safety assessment should play an important role in any bridge management process. Realistic data is essential in any safety evaluation. While the most adequate resistance and dead load data are obtained during an in-depth inspection of the structure, the most appropriate technique for the reliable traffic load acquisition is the use of a weigh-in-motion (WIM) system. WIM results are used either to model the expected traffic loading when calculating the safety index β or to develop the appropriate loading schemes in the rating factor (RF) method. Load factor selection, maximum expected traffic load effects and the rating loading schemes, used in Slovenia for the safety evaluation of road bridges, are also discussed in the paper. The application of the safety analysis is illustrated on a heavily deteriorated viaduct.

1 INTRODUCTION

Adequacy of road bridges should be assessed not only when they are heavily deteriorated or distressed and when the decision about their present condition, future reliability and necessary improvements or interventions has to be supported by an analysis and an in-depth investigation, but also on a regular basis as a part of a bridge management system (BMS). One of the goals of a BMS is to yield quantitative information about the condition of every bridge and to evaluate bridge problems.

There are two main components of the BMS, which is presently under development in Slovenia: the collection and the evaluation of data and the interdependencies between individual functions or procedures.

Collection of data comprises:

- regular inspection of all bridges on state roads and motorways,
- in-depth inspection, investigation and analysis of deteriorated structures,
- measuring the true heavy vehicle weights and the traffic volume on the bridge sites by the weigh-in-motion system.

Evaluation of collected data leads to the assessment of the main performance characteristics of a bridge structure:

- condition rating,

- structural safety,
- remaining service life and
- functionality and/or obsoleteness.

The whole evaluation process consists of series of individual assessments whose accuracy can, if required, be improved by more reliable information and testing data and/or by using more refined methods of analysis.

2 STRUCTURAL SAFETY OF EXISTING STRUCTURES

2.1 General

Realistic structural safety is evaluated when, for any reason, precise evidence about safety, which can not be estimated by the lower level methods, is required. Actions on a deteriorated bridge should not be judged only by its condition which does not include any information about the actual loads. It is even more important to examine its safety based on the actual resistance and on the traffic which is expected over the structure. Only when the results of such analysis are inadequate the bridge manager can with confidence chose between:

- doing nothing,
- implementation of a more detailed analysis; in many cases it is possible to increase the calculated

structural safety by collecting more reliable data or using more complex analytical procedures,

- posting the bridge,
- repairing the bridge or
- closing and replacing the bridge.

Structural safety can be expressed by the *safety index* β or by *the rating factor RF*. Safety index β can be used in normal or log-normal form:

$$\beta = \frac{\overline{R} - \overline{S}}{\sqrt{\sigma_R^2 + \sigma_S^2}} \quad \text{or} \quad \beta = \frac{\ln \overline{R}\big/\overline{S}}{\sqrt{V_R^2 + V_S^2}} \qquad (2.1)$$

where $\overline{R}$ = mean value of the actual carrying capacity of the critical structural element; $\overline{S}$ = mean value of the total load effect in the section; σ_R, σ_S = standard deviations of resistance and total load effect; V_R, V_S = coefficients of variation of resistance and of total load effect.

In a bridge management system safety level of every bridge is important for assessing its adequacy in relation to other structures in the same system. In such a case the structural safety is estimated by the rating factor, *RF*, developed from the ultimate limit state formula:

$$RF = \frac{\Phi \times R_d - \gamma_G \times G_n}{\gamma_Q \times Q_n} \qquad (2.2)$$

where R_d = design resistance of the section, calculated by the load factor design formula; Φ = capacity reduction factor or resistance factor; G_n, Q_n = dead load and traffic load effects in the section; γ_G, γ_Q = partial safety factors of dead and traffic load effects.

While the calculation of β values requires a probabilistic approach and is generally used only in some exceptional cases, there are no limitations to employ the deterministic RF method as widely as possible.

Safety evaluation should be based on the actual rather than on the design values of the *carrying capacity* and the *load effects*. Resistance and dead load information are usually obtained during an in-depth inspection of the structure. On the other hand, the most adequate traffic load effect is modelled from the weigh-in-motion (WIM) data. It is clear from equations 2.1 and 2.2 that coefficients of variation and partial safety factors are strongly related to the quality of the applied data. More reliable the data, higher calculated values of structural safety can be achieved. Generally, for normal service life a target β value 3.5 is used. In exceptional cases, e.g. for limited service life or until the next bridge inspection, target β values can be decreased to 2.5. Values for RF should always be greater than 0.95 to avoid posting or remedial action.

According to the experience, both approaches yield to similar values when the level of structural safety is close to the critical (e.g. β value of 2.5 will usually result in RF around 1.0). It has to be emphasised that experienced engineers should use both approaches to avoid erorrs when selecting parameters in equations 2.1 and 2.2. This is particularly imprtant since quite often all the data can not be achieved with sufficient reliability.

2.2 Carrying capacity of existing bridges

A capacity reduction factor is used to adjust the resistance in equations 2.1 and 2.2. It is based on the information collected during the regular or in-depth inspection of the analysed bridge.

Bridge inspection

A method based on numerical evaluation of all types of damages detected by the regular, principal and in-depth inspections of bridges was developed in Slovenia and has been used regularly since 1989 for all 1700 bridges on Slovenian state roads and motorways. The great majority of them are built of reinforced and prestressed concrete.

Regular inspections take place every two years. Inspection includes visual examination of the whole structure and some simple random testing. Every sixth year the covered and enclosed parts of a bridge, including the areas accessible only by the special inspection vehicle, must be exposed for inspection and examined.

In-depth inspection of a structure is generally required in case of heavier distresses revealed at a

Table 2.1. Damage recording format, its description in the report, and automatic calculation of damage value, V_D

Item	A	A1	B	C	D1	D2	D3	E	F	G	H		
	05	622	41	321	VP-	---	LDe	---	ODL	T75M	PRKO	080810	

A+A1	Main girder - T; top flange		B	corrosion of reinforced bars	Date	05.03.96
C+D1	majority of spans; -		E	spalling of concrete	V_D	1.92
D2+D3	left and right side of member		F	total length 75 m		
			G	corrosion test		

Table 2.2. Deterioration classes, relative condition values, R_c, and deterioration factors, α_R

Class	Inspected condition	Necessary intervention	Condition value R_c	Deterioration factor α_R
1	Very good	No maintenance/repair works required	<5	0.3
2	Good	Regular maintenance works needed	3 to 10	0.4
3	Satisfactory	Intensified maintenance/repair works needed within 6 years	7 to 15	0.5
4	Tolerable	Substantial repair works needed within 3 years	12 to 25	0.6
5	Inadequate	Immediate posting and repair required	22 to 35	0.7
6	Critical	Immediate closing, then repair (strengthening) required	>30	0.8

regular inspection. The deterioration mapping of important defects and systematic in-situ, generally non-destructive testing of materials in the structure are performed. Findings of the site survey are systematically recorded and evaluated. A computer-aided system using a standard condensed description for each detected deterioration is used (Table 2.1). It calculates a numerical value of every recorded damage on a bridge member, the *damage value*, V_D, as a product of type of damage (in the range from 1 to 5), its extent (0 to 1) and intensity (0 to 1), structural member (0 to 1) and urgency of intervention (0 to 10).

The *condition value*, R_C, is then the sum of all V_D values, normalised to the maximum possible condition value on the same structure (Table 2.2). It is expressed in percentage and can be evaluated for entire structure or for any individual major component of the bridge (superstructure, substructure, bridge deck ...)

Capacity reduction factor

For safety purposes, the result of a computer aided damage evaluation is applied in the *capacity reduction factor*, Φ, which accounts for the overall condition of the deteriorated structural element. Its range can be from 0.6 for very heavy deteriorated structures to over 1.0 for structures in very good condition.

The effective carrying capacity of deteriorated concrete bridge members can be determined by multiplying the design resistance, R_d, with Φ:

$$\Phi = B_R \times e^{-\alpha_R \times \beta_c \times V_R} \qquad (2.3)$$

where B_R = bias, i.e. the ratio of existing and designed mean resistance of the critical member section; α_R = deterioration factor, based on the condition of the structural element (Table 2.2); V_R = coefficient of variation of the member resistance recognising also the reliance of the testing data; β_c = target value of the safety index as a function of the expected service life. Selection of Φ is presented in Figure 2.1.

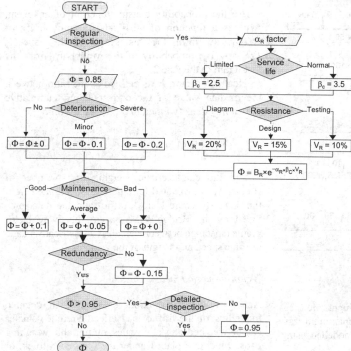

Figure 2.1 - Selection of the capacity reduction factor, Φ

2.3 Traffic load effect on bridges

In the safety evaluation, the influence of traffic loading is taken into account either by the rating loading schemes or by a load model which is based on the WIM results from the road section where the bridge is located.

Rating loading schemes

When safety of a bridge is assessed by the rating factor method, loading schemes are applied to represent the traffic load effect. Since the rating loading schemes, proposed by Moses (1987), are not applicable to the European traffic conditions, a sensitivity study was carried out (Žnidarič J. 1994) to examine the suitability of different design loading schemes for safety analysis. The design scheme PTP-5, used before 1970's, is definitely inappropriate for short span bridges (the lack of multiple axles considerably underestimate the load effect of contemporary traffic). On the other hand, the current design scheme, based on the German code DIN 1072, and the Load Model 1 from Eurocode 1 (Eurocode 1 1994) seem too severe for safety evaluation of bridges under normal traffic conditions. As a result, rating loading schemes SLS 1 and SLS 2, which are based on extensive weigh-in-motion measurements on Slovenian roads, have been proposed and are currently used in Slovenia for rating factor calculation. The analysed design and rating loading schemes are presented in Table 2.3.

Table 2.3. Design and rating loading schemes used in Slovenia

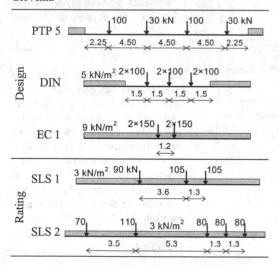

Live load modelling

When the weigh-in-motion measurement are performed, a considerably more realistic maximum traffic load effects on the bridge can be modelled using the formula (Moses 1987):

$$Q = a \times W_{.95} \times H \times m \times I \times g \qquad (2.4)$$

where: Q = predicted (expected) maximum load effect; a = deterministic value relating the load effect to a reference loading scheme; $W_{.95}$ = characteristic vehicle weight, defined as 95th percentile of the weight probability function; H = headway factor, describing the simulated multiple presence of vehicles on the bridge; m = factor, reflecting the variations of load effects of random heavy vehicles, compared to the standard, reference vehicle; I = coefficient of impact; g = girder (lateral) distribution factor.

All parameters except a are random variables and are evaluated from the WIM data. While very basic statistical evaluation is applied to determine $W_{.95}$, m, I and g, the convolution method (Moses 1987) is used to simulate the headway factor H. This assumes that maximum load effect is caused by an event, when two vehicles meet side by side in the middle of the span. It is therefore applicable when probability of having more than 2 trucks on the bridge simultaneously is very low. This can be usually achieved when the span is up to 30 m long and the density of heavy traffic is less than 2 000 vehicles/day. With the supposition of independent traffic in both lanes, the probability of such event can be expressed as:

$$f_Y(y) = \sum P(W_1 = w_n) \times P(W_2 = w_m) \qquad (2.5)$$

where the probability density function of an event, $f_Y(y)$, is a function of: $P(W_1=w_n)$ = probability of weight w_n from the histogram of the lane 1; $P(W_2=w_m)$ = probability of the weight w_m from the histogram of the lane 2.

Headway factor, H, is defined as the ratio between the median value of the corresponding cumulative probability density function, $F_y(Y)$, raised on N:

$$F_{y_{max}}(Y) = \left(F_y(Y) \right)^N \qquad (2.6)$$

and the characteristic weight $W_{.95}$. Number of events, N, in evaluated time period is estimated from the ADT (Average Daily Traffic) and the data, provided by the Bridge WIM system: headway histograms (spacings between vehicles), classification data, average speed and length of the vehicles.

Weigh-in-motion measurements

Actual weight information is essential in detailed modelling of the traffic load effect. Freight vehicles can be weighed on static scales, on portable weighing pads, which are placed under the tyres of a truck, or on low-speed weigh-in-motion (WIM) scales, which are driven over at a speed under 15 km/h. These well known weighing procedures are sufficiently accurate and are comonly used for controlling and fining of the overloaded vehicles. Unfortunately they usually don't operate permanentlyand can be therefore easily avoided. As a result, a great part of the heaviest, most representative trucks is not recorded.

On the other hand, high-speed weigh-in-motion systems provide continuous weighing of high percentage of vehicles passing the system. They are also imperceptible which means that the drivers are not aware of the weighing operation and do not try to avoid it. Today there are approximately 1000 working WIM stations around the world of which approximately 450 in the United States, 300 in Europe and 150 in Australia.

WIM systems are usually divided into the *strip sensor, mat/scale sensor* and *bridge* weigh-in-motion systems. The majority of present WIM systems use strip sensors (Figure 2.2), mostly of the piezo or capacitive type. However, very narrow sensor and dynamic variation of weights of the passing axles restrict the accuracy of these systems. Scales like bending plates or capacitive mats are wider and more accurate but often more expensive.

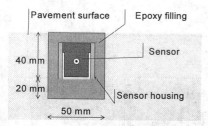

Figure 2.2. Cross section of a strip sensor

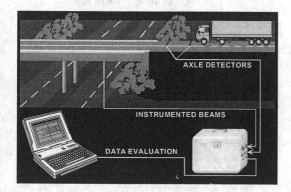

Figure 2.3. Bridge WIM field instrumentation

The *bridge WIM system* (Figure 2.3) was developed in late 70's at the Case Western Reserve University, Cleveland, USA. It uses strain transducers on the main longitudinal members and axle detectors on the pavement. These are placed in each lane approximately 4 m apart and 3 to 10 m before the bridge, to provide vehicle dimensions, velocity and classification. The interface between the user and the system is provided by a portable computer. In each lane, trucks of known weight are used to calibrate the bridge. Since in most cases the measurements are performed through the period in which the whole vehicle is passing over the structure, the system is generally less influenced by the vehicle/bridge interaction. Bridge WIM system also provides important information about impact factor, lateral distribution of loads and strain records which can be used for further bridge analysis. The majority of these systems can be found in the USA, Australia and South Korea, and within Europe, in Ireland and Slovenia.

A more detailed description of WIM systems can be found in (Žnidarič A. 1995).

2.4 Load factors for dead and traffic load effects

Uncertainty in the applied data is taken into account through the load factors. When using actual structural and traffic parameters, it is not reasonable to apply the design load factors (e.g. $\gamma_G/\gamma_Q = 1.6/1.8$ for reinforced concrete in Slovenia).

The dead load factor, γ_G, (Table 2.4) is related to the reliability of the structural data and can be reduced to 1.2 if the analysis is based on an in-depth inspection of the bridge. The selection of the traffic load factor γ_Q depends on:

- uncertainty of the used traffic information (accuracy, level of the overloaded vehicles),
- expected service life of the bridge (the period for which the analysis is deemed to be valid) and
- traffic density.

The value of γ_Q can vary from 1.4 to 2.2. To comply with the design codes, γ_G and γ_Q for prestressed concrete bridges are increased by 15% compared to the reinforced concrete ones. Selection procedure of γ_Q is presented in Figure 2.4.

Table 2.4. Selection of the dead load factor, γ_G

Structural data	γ_G
obtained by an in-depth inspection	1.2
based on the design information (project)	1.4
obtained by any other simplified procedure	1.6

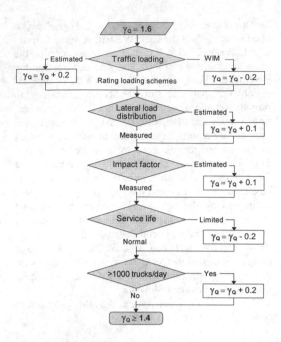

Figure 2.4. Selection of the live load factor γ_Q

3 SAFETY EVALUATION OF THE RAVBERKOMANDA VIADUCT

The safety evaluation procedure is illustrated on the heavy deteriorated Ravbarkomanda viaduct over 17 prestressed 36.3 m long simple spans on the very busy motorway between Ljubljana and Italy. Since the more damaged of the two parallel structures was already under reconstruction, the owner of the bridge wanted to decrease the traffic jams on the other structure by introducing a third traffic lane in the middle of the bridge (Figure 3.1). Unfortunately the in-depth inspection showed that in one of the spans 4 of 11 tendons in the beam 1 were heavy corroded and could not contribute to the carrying capacity of the section. Therefore, the design resistance of this beam was reduced by the number of corroded tendons to estimate the resistance moment $M_R = 16,402\ kNm$. Since the resistance was based on the project, a high coefficient of variation, $V_R = 15\%$, was selected. According to Figure 2.1, a capacity reduction factor $\Phi = 0.87$ was applied for a redundant structure with good maintenance and deterioration factor $\alpha_R = 0.7$. A maximum moment due to dead load, $M_G = 7,034\ kNm$, with the $V_G = 8\%$ was based on the project data and on the in-depth inspection information.

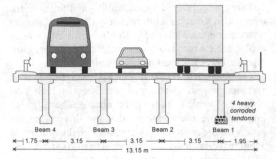

Figure 3.1. Proposed traffic regime on the Ravbarko-manda viaduct

Maximum traffic load effect

Seven days of WIM measurements were performed on the bridge to obtain the necessary traffic load information. Figure 3.1 presents the gross weight histograms of 8,544 heavy vehicles in both directions, which were used to calculate the probability functions, and to determine the characteristic weights $W_{.95}$ (Figure 3.2).

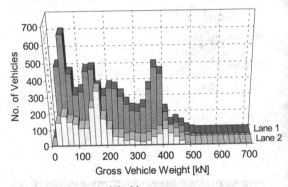

Figure 3.1. Gross weight histograms

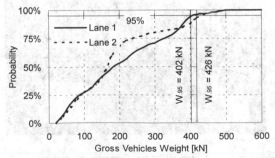

Figure 3.2. Probability functions and $W_{.95}$

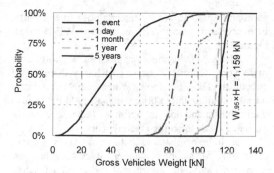

Figure 3.3. Expected maximum gross weight

Using the convolution method, a maximum expected gross weight of 1,159 kN was obtained in the middle of the span for a period of 5 years (Figure 3.3). Such a short period was used since the evaluated structure was planned for reconstruction immediately after the completion of the parallel viaduct.

It was obvious that the extreme loading can be achieved only with the trucks that have more than 3 axles. Therefore, the coefficient a was determined by comparing the weight W_{SLS2} of the reference vehicle from the loading scheme SLS 2 (Table 2.3) with the corresponding bending moment M_{SLS2} on a 36.3 m long simply supported span:

$$a = \frac{M_{SLS2}}{W_{SLS2}} = \frac{3,055 \ kNm}{420 \ kN} = 7.27 \ m$$

All evaluated parameters from equation 2.3 are summarised in Table 3.1. The same vehicle from loading scheme SLS 2 was used as the reference truck in the calculation of the m factor.

Table 3.1. Parameters evaluated from the WIM measurements

Parameter	Mean value	Coeff. of variation
$W_{95} \times H$	1,159 kN	5.7 %
I	1.15	4.6 %
g	0.25	8.4 %
m	0.923	8.4 %

Hence, the maximum expected bending moment in the first beam due to the truck loading was:

$$M_{Q,T} = 7.27 \times 1.159 \times 0.923 \times 1.15 \times 0.25 =$$
$$= 2,236 \ kNm$$

with a coefficient of variation:

$$V_Q = \sqrt{V_{W_{95}}^2 + V_m^2 + V_I^2 + V_g^2} =$$
$$= \sqrt{5.7^2 + 8.4^2 + 8.4^2 + 4.6^2} = 14.0 \ \%$$

A uniform loading of 5 kN/m², which was added in the middle lane to simulate car traffic, yielded the total moment in the critical beam due to traffic, $M_Q = 2,349$ kNm.

Selection of the load factors γ_G and γ_Q was based on the in-depth inspection of the bridge and flow chart of Figure 2.4:

- $\gamma_G = 1.2 \times 1.15 \approx 1.4$
- $\gamma_Q = 1.4 \times 1.15 \approx 1.65$

As a result, the following values of the rating factor RF and safety index β were obtained:

$$RF = \frac{0.87 \times 16,402 - 7,034 \times 1.4}{2,349 \times 1.65} = 1.14 \ \rangle \ 0.95$$

$$\beta = \frac{\ln \dfrac{16,402}{7,034 + 2,349}}{\sqrt{0.15^2 + \left(0.08^2 + 0.13^2\right)}} = 2.54 \ \rangle \ 2.5$$

Both values were just sufficient to permit the additional lane of car traffic in the middle of the bridge. However, to avoid any unexpected events, regular monthly inspections of the critically damaged beams were specified.

Additional analysis showed that if the more conservative rating loading schemes were used instead of the model, based on WIM results, values of RF and β would fall below the acceptable values.

4 FUTURE RESEARCH

The tools described in previous chapters are successfully used for safety evaluation of the *critical sections* of bridges. To extend the methodology to whole structures, Moses and Ghosn (1997) have recently concluded a study that uses the system safety index, β_S, to describe the global safety of different types of bridges as a function of their redundancy. This work leads to a prescribed set of partial system safety factors to be used in checking equations which reflect ultimate capacity, displacement response (serviceability) and damage tolerance.

To verify the new models and due to lack of appropriate experiments of prestressed concrete beams, a set of laboratory tests has been proposed in cooperation between the Slovenian National Building and Civil Engineering Institute and the University of

Pittsburgh. The fact, that in Slovenia there are app. 200,000 m² of bridges using parallel prestressed concrete I or T beams with the RC deck slab over them, some of which are very heavy deteriorated, considerably contributed to the successful application for the national research funds in years 1996 to 1998. Apart from the US-Slovenian *consortium for research cooperation*, the main financial supporters from Slovenia are Ministry for Science and Technology, Ministry for transportation and a construction company extensively producing this type of bridges.

The main goal of the project is to examine the redistribution of loads after potential failure of one or more beams and to evaluate the remaining global safety of such structures. Therefore, laboratory tests in a reduced scale of 1:3 have been designed to investigate simply supported, 3 and 6 beams bridges of 30 m span (10 m in scale 1:3). Side elevation and cross section of the 3-beam model bridge are presented in Figures 4.1 and 4.2 (all units are centimetres). Prototype materials (simple model similarity) are used. Additional 6 beams will be tested to define their individual behaviour. Releasing of the distinctive tendons will simulate the partial deterioration of the beams.

As an alternative tool in current research in civil engineering, the intelligent, neural network-like systems will be used to predict the limit capacity of individual beams as well as of the whole structure.

5 CONCLUSIONS

Safety of structures or structural elements is an important issue in any bridge management process. Its evaluation is strongly dependent on the quality of data that is used in the analysis. While regular and in-depth inspections of the structure can considerably improve the resistance and the dead load information, the most appropriate tool to reduce uncertainties in the traffic load assessment are weigh-in-motion (WIM) measurements.

A Bridge WIM system has been successfully used in Slovenia for safety analysis of heavy deteriorated structures. The new tools, which have been introduced, should help the bridge managers to better plan their investment and to optimise the allocation of available funds for bridge maintenance.

It has to be emphasised that this approach is applicable only for safety evaluation of existing bridges. Engineers sould be aware that reduction of safety factors or implementation of rating loading schemes are not intended and should not be used for new structure design.

Authors wish to thank the U.S.-Slovene Science and Technology Joint Fund in co-operation with Department of Transportation, as well as Ministry for Science and Technology and Ministry of Transportation of Republic of Slovenia to sponsor the research described in this paper.

6 REFERENCES

ASTM 1318-90. 1990. Standard Specification for Highway Weigh-in-Motion (WIM) Systems with User Requirements and Test Method

European pre-standard ENV 1991-3, Eurocode 1 - Basis of design and actions on structures - Part 3: Traffic loads on bridges. 1994. Brussels

Ghosn, M., Moses, F., 1995. Redundancy in Highway Bridge Superstructures, *4th Bridge Engineering Conference, Transportation Research Board*, San Francisco

Moses, F., Verma, D. 1987. Load Capacity Evaluation of Existing Bridges. *National Cooperative Highway Research Program (NCHRP) Report 301.* Washington DC.

Nyman, W.E., Moses, F. 1984. Load Simulation for Bridge Design and Life Prediction. *Case Western Reserve University.* Cleveland.

Žnidarič, J., Žnidarič, A. 1994. Evaluation of the Carrying Capacity of Existing Bridges. *US-Slovene project No. JF 026.* Ljubljana.

Žnidarič, A., Žnidarič, J., Snyder, R.E., Moses, F. 1995. Bridge Weigh-in-Motion Testing of Vehicle Gross Weights in Slovenia, *Proceedings of the 1st European WIM conference.* 323-330. Zürich.

Žnidarič, A. 1995. Weigh-in-Motion Applications for Bridges and Pavements, *Proceedings of the 1st Croatian Road Congress.* 701-708. Opatija.

Žnidarič, J. 1995. Adequacy Rating of Existing Road Bridges in Slovenia, *Presentation of some Slovenian technical papers on roads, Concluding conference OECD/ RTRP.* 178-184. Ljubljana.

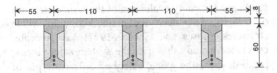

Figure 4.1. Cross section of the 3 beam bridge model

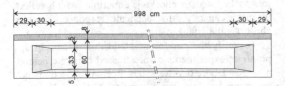

Figure 4.2. Side elevation of the bridge model

Structural Safety and Reliability, Shiraishi, Shinozuka & Wen (eds) © 1998 Balkema, Rotterdam, ISBN 90 5410 978 5

Optimal damage allocation of seismically-isolated elevated bridge system for extremely severe ground motion

Yozo Fujino & Masato Abé
Department of Civil Engineering, The University of Tokyo, Japan

Gaku Shoji
Department of Civil Engineering, Tokyo Institute of Technology, Japan

ABSTRACT: Under extremely severe ground motion such as those recorded in the 1995 Kobe Earthquake, it is reasonable to allow minimum repairable damage to elevated highway bridges. To keep damage under control, earthquake-induced damage must be allocated to each structural element (superstructures, bearings, piers, and foundation) appropriately. In this paper, formulation of the optimal allocation of damage to elevated highway bridges is presented considering not only the seismic performance of each element but also that of the total structural system. First, the relationship between damage to each structural element and its repair cost is established by collecting damage data in the Kobe earthquake, and the relationship between the initial construction cost and seismic damage is also obtained on the basis of experienced engineers' estimate. Then, optimal damage allocation to minimize total cost(initial cost plus repair cost) is obtained by combining these relationships with nonlinear dynamic analysis of a foundation-pier-isolator-superstructure system.

1. INTRODUCTION

The ground motions recorded in the 1995 Kobe earthquake were extremely strong; the elastic acceleration response spectra with 5% critical damping ratio in some of the horizontal ground motions reaches 2.0g or even more in the period from 0.5 sec. to 1.0 sec. Due to the extremely strong ground motion together with inadequate seismic resistance, enormous damage was induced in many civil engineering structures and facilities including elevated urban highway bridges. In 1996, a new seismic bridge design code in Japan adopted a design ground motion equivalent to those recorded in Kobe area(Japan Road Association, 1996). Development of a rational design procedure for existing bridges as well as new bridges to cope with such severe ground motions is an urgent issue in Japan.

In view of the importance of the urban bridges, damage-free elastic design for such severe ground motions is desired. However, considering very infrequent occurrence of earth-quakes near or beneath large cities and economical constraints, damage-tolerant design is a logical choice. The elevated highway bridges is structurally a series system, consisting of foundation-pier-bearing-girder structural elements. Then allocation of seismic damage to each structural element under the Kobe level ground motion has to be carefully studied.

Optimal allocation of damage to the bridge system is a trade-off problem in two folds; one is the trade-off between the initial construction cost and the earthquake-induced damage (Fig. 1). The other is the trade-off in the seismic forces transmitted among each elements(Toki 1993). High elastic strength of one element increases the seismic forces transmitted to the other elements, while yielding of one element reduces the seismic forces to the other elements; consequently the strength of each element changes the distribution of seismic forces in the nonlinear bridge system subject. Hence the optimal allocation of the seismic damage to the bridge system is an interesting problem from the reliability as well as mechanical points of view.

In the present paper, the allocation of the earthquake-induced damage on a typical elevated highway brigde system is studied. An emphasis is placed on utilization of the data, in particular of the data on the repair cost during restoration of the elevated Hanshin Expressway which was heavily damaged during the 1995 Kobe earthquake. Formulation to obtain the optimal allocation of seismic damage to the bridge system is also stressed.

2. DAMAGE CURVE

The damage curve is defined to be a curve which relates a structural damage index to monetary loss. This damage curve was obtained as follows.

First, the repair cost of each bridge elements(girder, bearing, pier and foundation) in a typical elevated bridge damaged/undamaged during the 1995 Kobe earthquake was investigated. The type and dimension of a typical elevated bridge system is presented in Table 1. The repair cost depends on the damage level; as structural damage index, As(collapsed or almost collapsed), A(seriously damaged and unrepairable) B(heavily damaged), C(mild damage) and D(practically no damage) used by the Hanshin Public Expressway Corporation was employed in this study. The repair(replacement for the damage levels, As and A) cost for the bridge elements as well as the initial construction cost are obtained through the interview to engineers of HPEC and Fig. 2 shows the result. In Fig. 2, one can find that the cost of damage to the girders is high when the damage is A or As. Another thing to be noticed is that repair cost of the pile foundation is high even though the damage is not so heavy. In the case of the foundation, repair for heavily damaged piles is not possible and addition of new piles is only the solution, resulting in large cost. Next, the relation between the damage level and the ductility factor was obtained based on the past experiments(Kousa et al. 1993, Usami 1995). The ductility factor is widely used as an index of the damage level, but relating the damage level to the ductility facor is not established and was determined rather based on the authors' subjective judgment. Table 2 shows the relation between the damage level and the ductility ratio in bridge

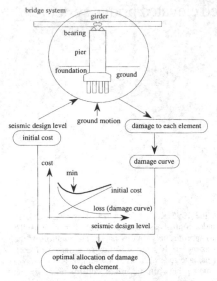

Fig.1 Optimal sesmic design of bridge system

Table 1   Typical Elevated Bridges

Girder	5 I-girder with RC slab
	  Width: 17.6m span: 30m
	  Area: 528m²
	  Weight: 1190ka
	Box girder with RC slab
	  Width: 17.6m span: 50m
	  Area: 880m²
	  Weight: 2590kN:

Bearing	Steel bearing (→Rubber (isolator) bearing)

Pier	T-shape
	Height: 10.8m from footing
	  top
	Section: 2.0m x 2.0m
	RC pier
	  column volume: 55m³, beam
	  column: 55m³
	  re-bar: 216KN
	Steel pier
	  column weight: 314KN,
	  beam weight: 294KN

Foundation	in-site piles II-class ground condition footing: 7.0m x 7.0m x 2.0m 9 piles: φ=1m, length=10m

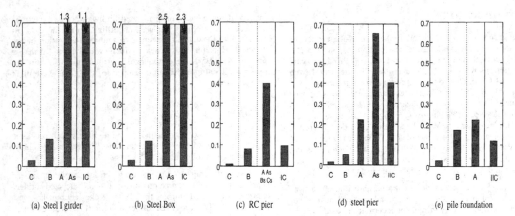

| (a) Steel I girder | (b) Steel Box | (c) RC pier | (d) steel pier | (e) pile foundation |

Fig.2   Damage level versus repair cost & initial construction cost(IC) (unit:100 million yen)

Table 2   Damage level versus ductility ratio

	D	C	B	A	As
Isolator (shear strain)	~ 17 (~ 250%)	17 ~ 34 (250% ~)	17 ~ 34 (~ 500%)	34 ~ (500% ~)	
RC pier	~ 2.0	2.0 ~ 4.0	4.0 ~ 6.0	6.0 ~ 8.0	8.0 ~
Steel pier	~ 4.0	4.0 ~ 6.0	6.0 ~ 8.0	8.0 ~ 10.0	10.0 ~
Pile Foundation	~ 0.9`	0.9 ~ 1.5	1.5 ~ 3.5	3.5 ~	

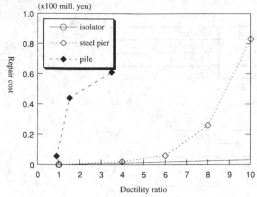

Fig.3 Repair cost curve versus ductility ratio, μ

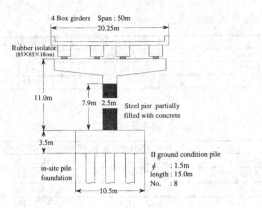

Fig.5 Elevated bridge model

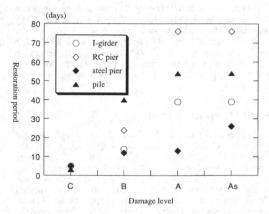

Fig.4 Restoration period versus damage level

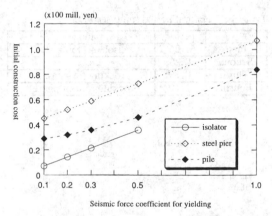

Fig.6 Initial cost versus seismic force coefficient

elements used in the present study. Finally the damage curve was obtained and shown in Fig. 3. The repair cost of the pile foundation is very high even for a small ductility ratio, indicating that the damage to the foundation should be kept small compared with other elements.

The repair cost used is just direct loss and not including the indirect loss. Damage to elevated highway bridge may result in human loss, economic loss due to malfunction of the highway or societal indirect loss. These losses should be theoretically included in the formulation. However, evaluation of these indirect losses is extremely difficult and only the direct loss is considered in the present study. The time required to restoration of the damaged bridge system may be an index of the loss because it partly accounts for the indirect loss. The time for complete restoration for each element was estimated using the data in Hanshin Expressway(Kobe Line) and presented in Fig. 4.

3. INITIAL COST CURVE

Damage to the bridge system is affected by the seismic design. In general, higher allowable strength yields to more material and higher initial construction cost. Seismic force coefficient(=seismic force/gravity force) for the yielding limit state is used as an index of the strength in the present study.

The relation between the seismic force coefficient and the initial cost increase for a typical elevated bridge system(Fig. 5) has to be obtained for the purpose of the present study. Note that the typical elevated bridge system is designed according to the new design guide for highway bridges(Kawashima 1992, 1993). To construct the cost curves of each structural element, a questionnaire was sent to ten experienced engineers of consulting firms, construction companies and so on. The results were very scattered in each element. After reliability of the answers from engineers was examined and, after removing unreliable answers, averaged cost curves for the bridge elements were obtained and presented in Fig. 6.

4. NONLINEAR ELEVATED BRIDGE MODEL

A nonlinear 3-masses 4-degree-of-freedom bridge model corresponding to the model shown in Fig. 7 is employed; sway and rocking are included in the foundation model and rotational inertia is included in the pier model. Nondegrading bi-linear model with nonzero second stiffness is employed for all the elements. The mass, stiffness and damping of each elements are given in Tables 3 and 4. Note that the model used in the present study as the pile foundation accounts for the yielding of the piles, nonlinear soil and uplift of the foundation. Natural periods of the lower modes computed are given in Table 5.

Table 3   Model of elevated bridge

	Weight(KN)	Rotational Inertia	Height
girder	11,760(m_2)	9.445×10^5	14.9(H_2)
piers	980(m_1)	($I_1 + I_2$)	13.5(H_1)
footing	9210(m_0)	9.445×10^4(I_0)	0.0

Table 4   Stiffness and damping

	initial sttifness	second stiffness	damping
Isolator	6.782×10^4	1.402×10^4	0
steel pier	1.547×10^5	6.316×10^3	1
sway	4.212×10^5	1.646×10^3	10
rocking	2.594×10^7	7.313×10^4	10

Table 5   Natural Period (unit: second)

	period	mode
First	1.25	isolator-dominate
Second	0.29	sway
Third	0.19	rocking (in-phase)
Fourth	1.10	rocking (out-of phase)

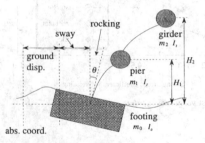

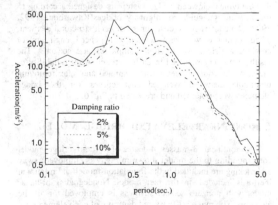

Fig.7 Model of elevated bridge

Fig.8 Response spectra of the ground motion recorded at JMA station, Kobe, 1995

In the nonlinear time history response analysis, the ground motion recorded in Kobe Marine Meterological station, JMA was used. The maximum acceleration was 818 gals and its response spectra(5% critical damping ratio) exceeds 2000 gal in the period range from 0.3 to 0.5 second(Fig. 8). Integration scheme in the nonlinear dynamic analysis, Runge-Kutta with the time step 0.000625 second was used in the numerical simulation.

5. NUMERICAL RESULTS

By changing values of the seismic force coefficient for each bridge element, the total cost(the initial cost plus the repair cost) was computed using the result of the nonlinear dynamic response analysis and the results are presented in Fig. 9. In Fig. 9(a), the yielding strength of the rubber bearing was varied while the other seismic coefficients of the structural elements(pier and pile foundation) were kept constant. A trade-off relation can be clearly shown in Fig. 9; for example, increase of seismic force coefficient of the pier decreases the ductility of the pier whereas the ductility of the rubber bearing as well as that of the foundation are increased(Fig. 9(b)).

Fig. 10 presents the total cost of the bridge system for different values of the seismic coefficients. It should be noted that there is indeed the optimal combination of the coefficients, which minimizes the total cost.

Lower yielding level of the rubber isolator provides lower seismic forces to piers and foundation, but the displacement of the girder becomes larger. The maximum displacement of the girder should be kept not so larger to avoid the pounding to the adjacent girder. If the seimic force coefficient for the isolator is greater than 0.1, the girder displacement is not so large and the shear strain of the rubber is within the allowable limit of 250%.
Fig. 10 indicates that the seismic coefficient for the isolator is chosen to be 0.1 according to the above-mentioned reasons, the optimal coefficient $\alpha_{p,opt}$ for the steel pier partially filled with concrete is between 0.2 and 0.25 and the optimal value $\alpha_{f,opt}$ for the pile foundation is between 0.5 and 0.9. The total cost for $\alpha_{f,opt} = 0.5$ is practically the same to that for $\alpha_{f,opt} = 0.9$ because the former case corresponds to small initial cost with large damage and the latter case is *vice versa*, resulting more or less the same total cost.

6. CONCLUDING REMARKS

The elevated highway bridge is a series system and consists of girder, bearing, pier and foundation. The premise that highway bridges in Japan should be designed for the ground motion experienced during the 1995 Kobe earthquake was adopted in the study. The optimal allocation of the damage to each element, i.e. optimal seismic design of the bridge system, which minimizes the toal cost(inital cost plus repair cost) was discussed. The relation between the damage level and the repair cost was constructed using the extensive data from Hanshin Expressway which was heavily damaged during the 1995 Kobe earthquake , while the relation between the yielding strength and the initial cost were obtained based upon the experienced engineers' judgment. Using these two relations and the nonlinear response analysis of the bridge system, the optimal design of the bridge system was studied.

Determination of the loss due to the damage to bridges is a very difficult issue. In the present study, the repair cost is chosen as a loss in the numerical example. For certain essential bridges, their malfunction due to the damage leads to the essential loss to the society even though the period of the malfunction is short. Development of rational procedure to evaluate the loss including indirect loss is the next step of the study.

ACKNOWLEDGMENT

Useful data and comments were provided by Ishizaki, H., Nanjyo, A. and Hayashi, H., Hanshin Public Expressway Corporation and their assistance is gratefully acknowledged.

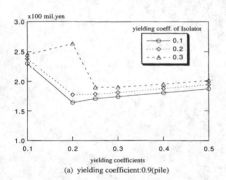

(a) yielding coefficient:0.9(pile)

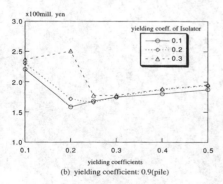

(b) yielding coefficient: 0.9(pile)

Fig.9 Ductility of bridge elements for various combination of yielding coefficients for seismic force

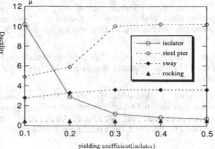

(a) yielding coefficients: 0.2(steel pier), 0.5(pile)

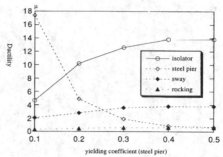

(b) yielding coefficients: 0.1(isolator), 0.5(pile)

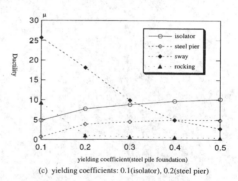

(c) yielding coefficients: 0.1(isolator), 0.2(steel pier)

Fig.10 Total cost

REFERENCES

Kawashima, K. et al., 1992. "*Examples of seismic design of highway bridges,*"Sankaido Pub. Company, pp. 159-180(in Japanese).

Toki, K., 1993. "Allocation of seismic safety to structure-foundation system," Foundation Engineering, Vol. 21, No.12, pp.2-7(in Japanese).

Kawashima, K.(editor), 1993. "Design manual for Menshin (base-isolated) highway bridges," pp. 23-28(in Japanese).

Kousa, K. et al., 1994. "Experimental study on performance of actual grouped piers under large lateral forces, " Journal of Soil and Foundation, vol. 45, No. 3, pp. 43-45(in Japanese).

Usami, T. et al., 1995. "Hybrid experiment on steel pier partially filled with concrete," Journal of Structural Engineering and Earthquake Engineering, JSCE, No. 525, pp. 55-67(in Japanese).

Japan Road Association, 1996. "Design specifications for highway bridges, - Seismic design part V," pp.1-120(in Japanese).

Shoji, G., Fujino, Y. and Abé, M, 1997. "Optimal damage allocation of elevated bridge system under strong ground motion," Journal of Structural Engineering and Earthquake Engineering, JSCE(in Japanese) (to appear).

Structural Safety and Reliability, Shiraishi, Shinozuka & Wen (eds) © 1998 Balkema, Rotterdam, ISBN 90 5410 978 5

Reliability-based integrity assessment of segmental PC box girder bridges

Kae-Hwan Kwak
Department of Civil and Environmental Engineering, Wonkwang University, Iksan, Korea

Hyo-Nam Cho
Department of Civil and Environmental Engineering, Hanyang University, Ansan, Korea

Young-Min Choi
Department of Civil Engineering, Hanyang University, Seoul, Korea

ABSTRACT: The main objective of this study is to suggest practical methods for field load testing and a reliability-based approach for the assessment of safety, durability, and load carrying capacity of PC box girder bridges. The proposed field proof-load and behavior tests such as static and dynamic proof-load tests, crack behavior test, and the test for the measurement of external post-tension forces are proved to be very practical and effective for the integrity assessment of PC box girder bridges. The response ratios acquired from proof-load tests are incorporated into the limit state model for the assessment of realistic safety and load carrying capacity of the type of bridges. This paper also suggests practical strength and crack durability limit state equations for the reliability-based integrity assessment of various types of segmental PC box girder bridges. Especially, linear and interactive non-linear strength limit state models are proposed. Various limit states are considered for the assessment of durability of segmental PC box girder bridges. The AFOSM (Advanced First Order Second Moment) and ISM(Importance Sampling Method) are used as reliability methods for the reliability analysis using the proposed models. The proposed reliability-based approach with the results of extensive field static and dynamic tests are applied for the integrity assessment of the two actual new segmental PC box girder bridges before opening to traffic, namely, New Haengju Grand Bridge over the Han River in Seoul, which have been reconstructed by the ILM erection technique after the collapse during construction 5 years ago and the viaducts of the Seoul Interior Circuit expressway erected by the PSM. Based on the observations, it may be stated that the proposed field load testing and reliability methods and models may be implemented as rational and practical approaches for the integrity assessment of segmental PC box girder bridges.

1 INTRODUCTION

Recently, lots of PC box girder bridges have been widely constructed due to the development of design methods and various advanced erection techniques. Recently in Korea, mainly because of construction simplicity and economic advantages, more and more segmental PC box girders are adopted as main bridge type and constructed by various erection techniques in many construction projects, especially for those of high-speed railroads, inter-island or island-mainland connections and urban expressways.

To guarantee safe and trouble-free transportation on service, segmental PC box girder bridges should ensure high level of QC/QA during construction, and thus it is important to assess the integrity of the bridges based on established static and dynamic field proof-load tests with effective instrumentations for the monitoring of construction control and maintenance before opening to traffic. These field tests are also necessary to obtain initial structural response as the signature needed for effective bridge main-

tenance. In addition, the realistic assessments of reserve capacity and safety of existing segmental PC box girder bridges are also important for proper bridge management. Therefore, the main objective of this study is to suggest practical methods for field proof-load tests and a reliability-based approach for the assessment of safety, durability and load carrying capacity of PC box girder bridges.

The proposed field proof-load tests are proved to be very practical and efficient if such tests as the static and dynamic field load tests using heavy test trucks, the crack behavior test, and the test for the measurement of external post-tension forces are performed effectively in the field.

This paper also proposes practical strength and crack durability limit state equations for the reliability-based integrity assessment of various types of segmental PC box girder bridges. Conventionally, the axial and bending stresses due to effective prestress force are usually considered in the WSR(Working Stress Rating) equation. For more precise assessment, a set of 4-mode strength limit state models are developed based on modified interaction equations.

Various limit states may be considered for the assessment of durability of segmental PC box girder bridges. In this study the limit state model of crack width is adopted as a measure of durability for segmental PC box girder bridges. Thus, the limit state function of crack durability is expressed in terms of random crack width due to applied dead and live loads.

The reliability of the structures with the proposed limit state model is evaluated by using the AFOSM (Advanced First Order Second Moment) method and an ISM(Importance Sampling Method) algorithm developed by the authors.

Based on the results of extensive static and dynamic load tests, the proposed reliability-based approaches are applied for the integrity assessment of the two actual new segmental PC box girder bridges before opening to traffic, namely, New Haengju Grand bridge, which had been collapsed during construction about 5 years ago and recently reconstructed by the ILM(Incremental Launching Method) erection technique, in Seoul, and the viaducts of the Seoul Interior Circuit expressway erected by the PSM(Precast Segmental Method).

2 FIELD LOAD TESTING AND INTEGRITY ASSESSMENT

As stated above, to guarantee safe and trouble-free transportation on service, segmental PC box girder bridges should ensure high level of QC/QA during construction. Therefore, it is imperative to assess the integrity of the bridges based on established static and dynamic field proof-load and behavior tests with effective instrumentations for the monitoring of construction control and maintenance before opening to traffic. These tests are also necessary to obtain initial structural response as the first step of effective maintenance. Also in the case of existing bridges the testings should be performed to evaluate the structural behavior and degradation of the structural stiffness. In Fig. 1, the proposed procedure for the field testing and integrity assessment of a PC box girder bridge is shown as a flow diagram. Some of the key ideas for the field testing are briefly described in what follows.

As shown in Fig. 1, an effective field load testing should starts, on the basis of the results of inspection, NDT and preliminary structural analysis, with the selection of a few critical spans to be tested for the integrity assessment. Then, when sensors had been installed during construction for construction control or monitoring, additional sensors at critical locations may be placed with instrumentation. It should be noted that the determination of the level of optimal test loading is important because a high test load near or above the design live load is a proof of strength capacity since possibilities of lower strength could be effectively eliminated based on test results[Moses et al. 1994]. Next, several critical load cases for the static and dynamic load testing are selected to find maximum responses(stresses, displacements, crack widths and accelerations) and the load testing is performed according to the planned load cases. Additional testings, such as the measurement of actual prestressing forces, may also need to be carried out if necessary.

The response ratio and the impact factor are then obtained from the results of the field load testing together with the uncertainty assessments. The reliability-based assessment of integrity and carrying capacity are evaluated next based on the proper limit state models and capacity rating criteria proposed in the paper. If the assessment results are not satisfactory, some proper repair and/or strengthening is performed to upgrade the structural safety to the design level. As shown in Fig. 1, the field testing and the assessment may be repeated until the results are satisfactory.

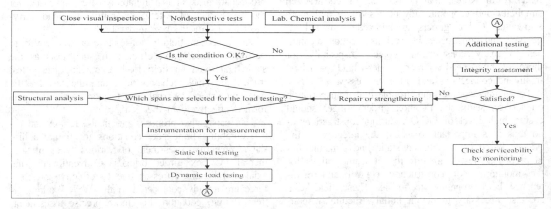

Fig. 1 Flow Diagram of Field Testings and Integrity Assessment

3 LIMIT STATE MODELS

This paper proposes practical strength and crack durability limit state equations for the reliability-based integrity assessment of various types of segmental PC box girder bridges.

3.1 Strength limit state

Since this study is concerned about the assessment of strength integrity of segmental PC box girder bridges, it is conventionally more meaningful to model the linear strength limit states based on the basic bending or shear equation. For more precise assessment, a set of 4-mode combined strength limit state models are developed based on modified interaction equations. The followings are considered in the equations; 1) the combined effects of bending, shear and torsional forces, 2) the difference between transverse reinforcements of decks and webs of box girders, which are modified from the CEB interaction equation, and 3) the capacity of shear connection of segments, which is newly added to the formula.

Thus, the well known linear limit state equation for bending or shear failure becomes[Cho et al. 1989, Moses et al. 1994];

$$g(\cdot) = S_R - (S_D + S_L) \qquad (3.1)$$

where S_R = true resistance such as bending or shear strength; and S_D, S_L = true load effects such as applied moment or shear due to dead and live loads, respectively.

The true resistance S_R may be modelled as

$$S_R = S_n \cdot N_R \cdot D_F \qquad (3.2)$$

where S_n = the nominal resistance such as moment or shear strength specified in the code; N_R = the correction factor adjusting any bias and incorporating the uncertainties such as material strength uncertainty, fabrication and construction errors, and prediction and modelling errors involved in the assessment of S_n.; and D_F = damage factor($= \omega_D^2 / \omega_I^2$), in which ω_D, ω_I = the fundamental natural frequencies of the damaged and intact structures, respectively.

The true applied load effects such as moments and shears may also be expressed in terms of nominal and random variates, respectively, as follows:

$$S_D = s_D \cdot D_n \cdot N_D \qquad (3.3a)$$
$$S_L = s_L \cdot L_n \cdot K \cdot N_L \qquad (3.3b)$$

where s_D, s_L = the influence coefficients of load effects for dead and live loads, respectively; D_n, L_n = the nominal dead and live loads, respectively; N_D, N_L = random variables of the correcting factors for adjusting the bias and uncertainties in the estimated s_D, s_L and D_n, L_n, respectively; and K = response ratio = $K_s(1+i)$, in which K_s = the ratio of the measured stress to the calculated stress, and i = the impact factor.

When the strength limit state in terms of the interactive combined load effects has to be considered, a nonlinear limit state model expressed as an implicit function may be suggested as follows[CEB-FIP, 1991]:

Mode 1 :

$$g(\cdot) = 1 - \left[\frac{F_{yu}}{F_{yl}} \left\{ p_B \left(\frac{T_D + T_L}{T_R} \right)^2 + \left(\frac{V_D + V_L}{V_R} \right)^2 \right\} + \frac{M_D + M_L}{M_R} \right] \qquad (3.4)$$

Mode 2 :

$$g(\cdot) = 1 - \left[p_T \left(\frac{T_D + T_L}{T_R} \right)^2 + \left(\frac{V_D + V_L}{V_R} \right)^2 - \frac{F_{yl}}{F_{yu}} \left(\frac{M_D + M_L}{M_R} \right) \right] \qquad (3.5)$$

Mode 3 :

$$g(\cdot) = \frac{1}{2} \left(\frac{F_{yl}}{F_{yu}} + 1 \right) - \left[p_M \left(\frac{T_D + T_L}{T_R} \right)^2 + 2 \left(\frac{T_D + T_L}{T_R} \right) \left(\frac{V_D + V_L}{V_R} \right) \sqrt{\frac{2h}{u}} + \left(\frac{V_D + V_L}{V_R} \right)^2 \right] \qquad (3.6)$$

Mode 4 :

$$g(\cdot) = 1 - \left(\frac{T_D + T_L}{T_R'} + \frac{V_D + V_L}{V_R'} \right) \qquad (3.7)$$

where M_R, V_R, T_R = true bending, shear, torsion strength of girder, respectively; V_R', T_R' = shear and torsion strength of shear connection, respectively; M_D, V_D, T_D = actual bending moment, shear force, and torsion of dead load, respectively; M_L, V_L, T_L = actual bending moment, shear force, and torsion of live load, respectively; p_B, p_T, p_M = perimeter ratio of bottom and top decks, and combined perimeter ratio, respectively which are $p_B = \{2h(\lambda_B - 1) + u\}/u\lambda_B$, $p_T = \{2h(\lambda_T - 1) + u\}/u\lambda_T$, $p_M = \{2h(\lambda_M - 1) + u\}/u\lambda_M$; λ_B, λ_T = reinforcements ratio of bottom and top decks to web, respectively and $\lambda_M = 2\lambda_B\lambda_T/(\lambda_B + \lambda_T)$ = combined reinforcements ratio; F_{yu}, F_{yl} = yield force of the half of the upper and lower stringer, respectively; h = depth of shear wall(distance between the longitudinal reinforcements enclosed by the stirrups); and u = perimeter connecting the longitudinal stringers of the cross section.

3.2 Durability limit state

In recent years, prediction of the deterioration rate of prestressed concrete structures has become a major research interest. However, there are still many uncertain factors in the deterioration process and the relation between deterioration and durability of structures. This is mainly due to various uncertainties involved in the construction process and the environmental condition which affects the rate of the deterioration of prestressed concrete structures.

Various limit states may be considered for the assessment of durability based on the measure of concrete crack width, the corrosion rate of reinforcement, and the degree of salt penetration or carbonation. In this study a simple limit state model for crack width is adopted as a measure of durability for segmental PC box girder bridges. Thus, the limit state function of crack durability can be written in terms of the allowable crack width W_R and the actual random crack widths due to dead and live loads W_D and W_L, respectively[Zhao et al. 1989, Cho et al. 1995].

$$g(\cdot) = W_R - (W_D + W_L) \qquad (3.8)$$

where

$$W_R = W_{R,W} N_{R,W} \qquad (3.9a)$$
$$W_D = W_{D,n} \cdot N_{D,W} \qquad (3.9b)$$
$$W_L = W_{L,n} \cdot N_{L,W} \qquad (3.9c)$$

in which $W_{R,W}$ = limit crack width -in the code; $W_{D,n}$, $W_{L,n}$ = measured crack widths due to dead and live loads, respectively; and $N_{R,W}$, $N_{D,W}$, $N_{L,W}$ = random variates of the correcting factors for adjusting the bias and uncertainties in the estimated $W_{R,W}$, $W_{D,n}$, $W_{L,n}$, respectively.

In the paper, the measured crack width $W_{L,n}$ due to nominal live load is evaluated based on the code formula in the following way:

$$W_{L,n} = K_W \cdot (1 + i_W) \cdot W_{L,c} \qquad (3.10)$$

where K_W = response ratio of the measured crack width to the calculated; i_W = the impact factor for crack width; and $W_{L,c}$ = calculated crack width due to the live load(mm) as follows

$$W_{L,c} = 10.8 R \sigma_s \sqrt[3]{d_c A} \times 10^{-6} \qquad (3.11)$$

in which R = ratio(= h_1/h_2) of the distances to the neutral axis from the extreme tension fiber and from the centroid of the reinforcement; σ_s = calculated stress in the reinforcement at service loads(kg/cm^2); d_c = thickness of the concrete cover measured from the extreme tension fiber to the center of the bar or wire located closest to it(cm); and A = effective tension area of concrete surrounding the flexural tension reinforcement and having the same centroid as that reinforcement, divided by the number of bars or wires(cm^2).

3.3 Statistical uncertainties

In the paper, most of the uncertainties of the basic random variables of resistance and load effects are obtained from data available in Korea, whereas, if the data is not available, those uncertainties are subjectively estimated based on the judgement and the literatures[Ellingwood et al. 1980, Nowak 1993, Zhao et al. 1993]. The statistical uncertainties such as mean -nominal ratio($\eta = \overline{X}/X_n$) and coefficient of variation (COV, Ω_X) of each resistance and load effects with the assumed distributions for the strength and durab-

ility limit states chosen for this specific study are summarized in Tables 1 and 2.

3.4 Reliability analysis

The structural reliability may be numerically evaluated by the failure probability, P_F. In practice, however, the relative reserve safety of a structural element may be best represented by the corresponding safety index β as the following:

$$\beta = -\Phi^{-1}(P_F) \qquad (3.12)$$

where P_F = probability of failure, and Φ^{-1} = inverse of the standard normal distribution function.

Various available numerical methods can be applied for the reliability analysis of the bridges either at the element or at the system level using the limit state models proposed in the paper. However, in this paper, the reliability analyses are performed only at the element level mainly because the application examples are limited to newly constructed bridges of which the investigations of minimum element reliability are more meaningful for integrity assessment. If the deteriorated and/or damaged existing bridges are considered, the system reliability analysis should be performed for more precise assessment of reserve safety. The AFOSM algorithm[Ang et al. 1984] is used for the linear limit state function of the proposed models and an ISM algorithm is also used to check the applicability of the AFOSM results.

Table 1 Statistical uncertainties for strength limit state

Variables	$\overline{X}/X_n$	Ω_X	Distribution
Bending Resistance M_R	1.05	0.075	normal
Shear Resistance V_R	1.15	0.14	normal
Dead Load Effect S_D	1.05	0.10	normal
Live Load Effect S_L	1.24	0.25	log-normal

Table 2 Statistical uncertainties for durability limit state

Variables	$\overline{X}/X_n$	Ω_X	Distribution
Crack Allowance W_R	1.0	0.10	normal
Dead Load Crack W_D	1.0	0.34	normal
Live Load Crack W_L	0.90	0.44	normal

4 SAFETY ASSESSMENT

The safety factor is conventionally used to assess the deterministic safety of structures based on the concept of allowable stress. However, the uncertainty-based nominal safety factor, n', consistent with reliability index β may be more reasonable to be used in practice in lieu of conventional safety factor, which can be expressed in the well known inverse form of the FOSM formula in terms of reliability index β, the uncertainties Ω_R, Ω_S and the mean-nominal ratios of resistance R and load effect S($\eta_R = \overline{R}/R_n$, $\eta_S = \overline{S}/S_n$). When the ln-ln model is used for the strength limit state,

$$n' = \frac{\eta_S}{\eta_R} \exp\left[\beta \sqrt{\Omega_R^2 + \Omega_S^2} \right] \qquad (4.1)$$

On the other hand, when the normal-normal model is used for the durability limit state,

$$n' = \frac{\eta_S}{\eta_R}\left[\frac{1 + \beta\sqrt{\Omega_R^2 + \Omega_S^2 - \beta^2 \Omega_R^2 \Omega_S^2}}{1 - \beta^2 \Omega_R^2} \right] \qquad (4.2)$$

5 LOAD CARRYING-CAPACITY RATING

In the paper, it is suggested that in order to ensure both serviceability and strength of a segmental PC girder bridge, both stress and strength capacity rating criteria for dominant internal forces as bending, shear, and torsion in the forms of WSR(Working Stress Rating) and LRFR(Load and Resistance Factor Rating) may have to be used in practice. And for more precise rating, the nonlinear combined strength capacity rating(CSCR) criteria based on a modified interaction equations may be derived. It should be noted that the capacity rating factor RF can be defined as the ratio of the nominal load-carrying capacity Pn and the standard design or rating load Pr(RF = Pn/Pr).

For the WSR, the following rating formula may be derived by incorporating the stresses due to prestressing:

$$RF = \min. \ of \begin{cases} RF_t = \dfrac{\sigma_a + \sigma_{pa} + \sigma_{pm} - \sigma_D}{K_s(1+i)\sigma_L} & (ten.) \\[2mm] RF_c = \dfrac{\sigma_a - \sigma_{pa} + \sigma_{pm} - \sigma_D}{K_s(1+i)\sigma_L} & (comp.) \end{cases} \qquad (5.1)$$

For the LRFR,

$$RF = \frac{\phi D_F R_n - \gamma_D D_n}{\gamma_L L_n(1+i)K_s} \qquad (5.2)$$

where σ_a = allowable stress of concrete; σ_{pa}, σ_{pm} = axial and flexural stresses due to effective prestress force, respectively; σ_L, σ_D = flexural stresses due to the live and dead loads, respectively; K_s = response ratio(measured stress/calculated stress); i = impact factor; ϕ = resistance factor; D_F : damage factor; and γ_L, γ_D = factors of live and dead loads; R_n = nominal strength of a PC box girder; and L_n, D_n = live and dead load effects.

And for the CSCR, the following rating formula may be derived from the limit state equations, Eqs. (3.4)~(3.7):

$$RF = \min. \ of \ [RF_1, \ RF_2, \ RF_3, \ RF_4] \qquad (5.3)$$

$$RF_i = \frac{-B_i \pm \sqrt{B_i^2 - 4A_iC_i}}{2A_i} \quad (i = 1, 2, 3) \qquad (5.4a)$$

$$RF_1 = \frac{1 - (t_{kD} + v_{kD})}{t_{kL} + v_{kL}} \qquad (5.4b)$$

where, $A_1 = f(p_B t_L^2 + v_L^2)$, $A_2 = (p_T t_L^2 + v_L^2)$,
$A_3 = (p_M t_L^2 + 2r t_L v_L + v_L^2)$. $\qquad (5.5a)$

$B_1 = 2f(p_B t_D t_L + v_D v_L) + m_L$,
$B_2 = 2(p_T t_D t_L + v_L v_L) - f^{-1} m_L$,
$B_3 = 2(p_M t_D t_L + r(t_D v_L + t_L v_D) + v_D v_L)$, $\qquad (5.5b)$

$C_1 = f(p_B t_D^2 + v_D^2) + m_D - 1$,
$C_2 = p_T t_D^2 + v_D^2 - (f^{-1} m_D + 1)$,
$C_3 = p_M t_D^2 + 2r t_D v_D + v_D^2 - \frac{1}{2}(f^{-1} + 1)$ $\qquad (5.5c)$

,in which

$$f = \frac{F_{yu}}{F_{yl}}, \quad r = \sqrt{\frac{2h}{u}}, \quad n_D = \gamma_D N_D / \phi_n D_F N_{p0},$$

$n_L = \gamma_L K_S(1+i)N_L / \phi_n D_F N_{p0}$ (N=M, V, T),

$t_{kD} = \gamma_D T_D / \phi_t D_F T_{k0}$, $v_{kL} = \gamma_L K_S(1+i) V_L / \phi_t D_F V_{k0}$

For example, RF_1 in mode 1 is derived as Eq. (5.6).

$$1 - \left[\frac{F_{yu}}{F_{yl}}\left\{ p_B\left(\frac{\gamma_D T_D + \gamma_L(1+i)K_S \cdot RF \cdot T_L}{\phi_t D_F T_R} \right)^2 \right. \right.$$
$$\left. + \left(\frac{\gamma_D V_D + \gamma_L(1+i)K_S \cdot RF \cdot V_L}{\phi_t D_F V_R} \right)^2 \right\}$$
$$\left. + \frac{\gamma_D M_D + \gamma_L(1+i)K_S \cdot RF \cdot M_L}{\phi_m D_F M_R} \right] = 0 \qquad (5.6)$$

6 APPLICATIONS

6.1 Example bridges

The models for the reliability-based integrity assessment and capacity rating of segmental PC box girder bridges together with the proposed extensive field testing are applied to the two actual segmental PC box girder bridges before opening to traffic, namely, New Haengju Grand Bridge over the Han River near by Seoul, which was collapsed during construction about 5 years ago and have recently been reconstructed using the ILM erection technique, and the viaducts of the Seoul Interior Circuit expressway erected by PSM. The main spans of the New Haengju Grand bridge were originally constructed as a PC cable-stayed bridge, but after the collapse, it has been reconstructed as a steel cable-stayed bridge, the integrity of which is beyond the scope of this study. The testing spans, the configuration and the typical cross sections of the bridge are shown in Fig. 2. and Fig. 3. The Seoul Interior Circuit expressway is a 4 span continuous curved precast segmental PC box girder bridge with the radius of curvature of 250 meters and each span length of 50 meters. The configuration and the typical cross section of the bridge are also shown in Fig 4.

6.2 Field testing of example bridges

According to the procedure shown as the flow dia-

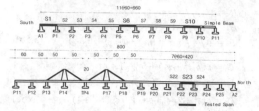

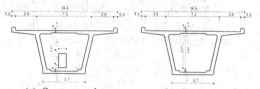

Fig. 2 Configuration and testing spans(The New Haengju Grand Bridge)

(a) Support point   (b) Span center

Fig. 3 Typical cross section(The New Haengju Grand Bridge)

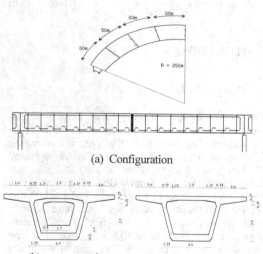

(a) Configuration

(b) support point   (c) span center

Fig. 4 Configuration and typical cross section(The Seoul Interior Circuit expressway)

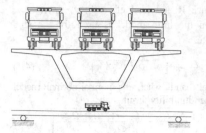

Fig. 5 Field load testing

Table 3 Static test results

Span No. Parameter	New Haengju Grand Bridge				Seoul Interior Circuit expressway
	S1	S6	S10	S23	
Response ratio	0.88	1.02	1.19	0.70	0.72
Impact factor	0.15				0.36

Table 4 Dynamic test results

Span No. Parameter	New Haengju Grand Bridge				Seoul Interior Circuit expressway
	S1	S6	S10	S23	
Natural frequency	3.25	3.25	3.25	3.05	3.05
Damping ratio	0.070	0.060	0.075	0.051	0.051

-24 design load of the Korean Bridge Code, which is equivalent to 1.33 times HS20 lane load of the AASHTO. One of the static load cases of the Seoul Interior Circuit expressway is shown in Fig. 5.

The static and dynamic load tests are performed respectively for 13 loading cases for the New Haengju Grand Bridge and are carried out with 15 static loading cases and 18 dynamic loading cases for the Seoul Interior Circuit expressway, respectively. Especially, the dynamic tests consist of truck running tests, a running impact test and a 30cm-free drop test of truck-wheels. The results of the response ratio and impact factor of each span for each bridge obtained from the static and dynamic load tests are shown in Table 3. The natural frequency and damping ratio evaluated by the results of the dynamic tests are summarized in Table 4. And no damage factor(D_F=1) is used in the paper because the application examples are the newly constructed PC box girder bridges.

The first segment of the New Haengju Grand Bridge has been partially crack-damaged during launching due to punching shear and thus 8 external tendons are installed for retrofitting. And though not presented in the paper, the additional test with the excited external tendons is performed and acquired the acceleration of each tendon in order to measure induced tendon forces. For the Seoul Interior Circuit expressway, there are a lot of hair cracks of the lo-

gram in Fig. 1, the field load testing have been performed for the 4 test spans of the New Haengju Grand Bridge and for the single span of the Seoul Interior Circuit expressway. In addition to the tests for superstructures, the conditions of footing, pile and the interface of footing and pile of the New Haengju Grand Bridge have been also investigated by the endoscopy method. For the field testing, 4 dump-trucks for the New Haengju Grand Bridge and 3 for the Seoul Interior Circuit expressway, each of which weighs about 30-ton at full load are used as the testing loads. This test load is estimated as about 85~96% of the unfactored design live load DL

Table 5 Results of Safety Assessment and Capacity Rating

Position	Content		Linear limit state						Non-linear limit state			
			Rating Factor(RF)		Safety Assessment				Rating Factor (RF)	Safety Assessment		
			WSR	LRFR	Reliability Index(β)		Nominal Safety factor(n')	Conventional Safety factor(n')		Reliability Index(β)		Nominal Safety factor(n')
					AFOSM	ISM				AFOSM	ISM	
New Haengju Grand Bridge	S1	(+) Bending	3.01(t)	3.44				3.85				
		(−) Bending	2.62(c)	2.57	4.61	4.75	2.05	3.13	1.12 (mode 1)	4.73	4.81	N/A
		Shear	-	2.36				-				
	S6	(+) Bending	2.68(t)	2.77				4.21				
		(−) Bending	1.99(t)	1.92	5.81	5.92	2.10	3.15	0.95 (mode 1)	5.69	4.81	N/A
		Shear	-	3.04				-				
	S10	(+) Bending	2.56(t)	2.38				4.05				
		(−) Bending	1.98(c)	2.28	6.36	6.44	2.27	3.62	1.29 (mode 1)	6.47	5.21	N/A
		Shear	-	2.75				-				
	S23	(+) Bending	3.45(t)	3.96				4.36				
		(−) Bending	3.31(t)	2.83	6.50	6.56	2.23	3.41	1.42 (mode 1)	6.39	5.28	N/A
		Shear	-	3.70				-				
Seoul Interior Circuit expressway		(+) Bending	2.50(t)	1.89	5.85	5.71	2.14	3.48	mode 1 1.84	5.32	5.61	N/A
		(−) Bending	4.34(t)	1.88	5.34	5.26	1.97	3.78	mode 1 1.37	5.24	5.16	N/A
		Shear	-	3.57	5.17	5.19	3.49	-	mode 1 2.81	7.61	Not Performed	N/A
		Shear key	N/A	N/A	N/A	N/A	N/A	N/A	mode 1 1.72 / mode 4 1.87	4.58	4.70	N/A

wer cord of upper flange, which are directed to the longitudinal direction due to transport trucks to carry a precast segment box block which weighs about 100t. So, the crack measurement tests are performed.

6.3 Modelling

A grillage model as shown in Fig. 6(a) and Fig. 6(b) is used for practical finite element analysis of the superstructure to evaluate the total static and dynamic responses of bridge system. A FEM analysis for a substructure model for single span box with plate and shell element models as shown Fig. 6(c) is also applied to acquire more precise and detailed response of the bridge deck. However, the analysis results are not presented in the paper due to the limited space.

6.4 Integrity Assessment

The results of the safety assessment and the capacity rating of the New Haengju Grand Bridge and the Seoul Interior Circuit expressway are summarized in Table 5. And then the results of the durability assessment of the two bridges are also summarized in

Table 5. In the case of the integrity assessment of the New Haengju Grand Bridge, the reliability index (β) and the nominal safety factor(n') are evaluated with only dominant limit states whereas the rating factors(RF) of each span are calculated for governing failure modes with both stress and strength rating formula, and then the critical rating factor of each

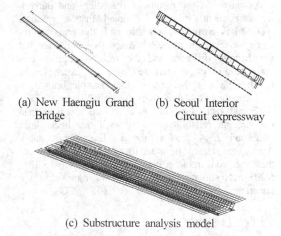

(a) New Haengju Grand Bridge

(b) Seoul Interior Circuit expressway

(c) Substructure analysis model

Fig. 6 Structural analysis model

span is represented as the shaded value. For the int-egrity assessment by non-linear limit state model for the Seoul Interior Circuit expressway, the reliability indices and the rating factors are evaluated with only dominant modes.

It may be observed that the RF results(1.98~3.45) of WSR for serviceable stress limit state and those(1.92~3.96) of LRFR for strength limit state are not significantly different for the New Haengju Grand Bridge, but are different for the Seoul Interior Circ-uit expressway(2.50~4.34 of WSR vs. 1.88~3.57 of LRFR). In most cases except one span(S10) of New Haengju Grand Bridge the bending or shear strength governs the capacity rating of the bridge. It may also be realized that the uncertainty-based nominal safety factor, n', may be used in practice to evaluate the reserve safety of the structure in practice because the results(n'=1.97~3.49) are invariably reasonable compared with those of the conventional safety fact-or(n=3.13~4.36) because the conventional safety fa-ctor n provides unreasonably conservative results com-pared with the uncertainty-based nominal safety fac-tor n'. This apparently means that the conventional safety factor is nothing but pure nominal and cannot be used in practice to assess a realistic reserve stru-ctural safety. For both of the example bridges, the differences in the RF by WSR and LRFR based on the linear limit state do not show any consistent tre-nd. Therefore, it may be stated that the rating meth-ods are not suited for the precise safety assessment and capacity rating.

In all cases, the RF(0.95~2.81) based on non-linear limit states are more dominant than the RF(1.89~3.96) based on linear limit states. From the results, it may be observed that for a precise assessment the safety assessment and capacity rating of the PC box girder bridges must be performed based on the non-linear limit state.

As shown in the results of the safety and durabil-ity assessment, it may be noted that a practical AFOSM is properly applicable with the proposed in-tegrity assessment models because the results are not significantly different and the method requires less computational effort compared with the precise results by the ISM. In the case of the example bridges, it is interesting to note that the reliability(β =3.17~ 4.27) of crack durability is a lot more critical than the strength reliability(β =4.61~6.50 for linear limit state and β =4.73~6.47 for non-linear limit state). Also, the results of durability assessment indicate that the conventional crack safety factors(n=3.81~ 6.20) overestimate the durability far more than the uncertainty-based nominal ones(n'=2.18~2.73).

7 CONCLUSION

This paper suggests practical methods for proof-load field tests and a reliability-based approach for the

Table 6 Results of Durability Assessment

Content / Position		Reliability index(β)		Nominal safety factor(n')	Conventional safety factor(n)
		AFOSM	ISM		
New Haengju Grand Bridge	S1	3.54	3.63	2.38	4.57
	S6	3.93	3.94	2.60	3.83
	S10	4.27	4.40	2.73	3.81
	S23	4.00	4.05	2.67	6.20
Seoul Interior Circuit expressway		3.17	3.25	2.18	3.94

integrity assessment of safety, durability, and load carrying capacity of PC box girder bridges. Based on the observations and the results of the applications, it may be concluded that the proposed field testing methods and integrity assessment models can be eff-ectively used in practice for newly constructed PC box girder bridges, and also for deteriorated existing bridges as well.

ACKNOWLEDGEMENT

The paper is a part of the research results of the KOSEF projects 961-1203-011-2. The financial suppo-rt funded by the KOSEF is greatly appreciated.

REFERENCES

CEB-FIP(1991), "CEB-FIP Model Code," Thomas Telford.

Cho, H. N. and Ang, H-S.(1989), "Reliability Asses-sment and Reliability-based Rating of Existing Road Bridges," Proc. of 5th Int. Conference on Structural Safety and Reliability, ICOSSAR'89, pp. 2235-2238.

Cho, H. N., Lee, S. J. and Ok, S. B.(1995), "Relia-bility-Based Models for Integrity Assessment of High Speed Railroad Bridges," International Symp-osium on Public Infrastructure Systems Research, 25-27 September, Seoul, Korea, pp. 369-378.

Ellingwood, b., Galambos, T. V., MacGregor, J. C. and Cornell, C. A.(1980), "Development of a Pro-bability-Based Load Criterion for the American National Standard A58," National Bureau of Stan-dard SP-577, Washington D.C.

Lee, S. J.(1995), "Reliability-based Integrity Assess-ment Models for Computer Aided Maintenance of High Speed Railroad Bridges," Thesis for the Ph. D. of Hanyang University.

Moses, F., Lebet, J. P. and Bez, R.(1994), "Applica-tions of Field Testing to Bridge Evaluation," J. Struct. Engrg., ASCE, 120(6), pp. 1745-1762.

Nowak, A. S.(1993), "Development of Bridge Load Model for LRFD Code," Natural Hazards Mitigation, pp. 1041-1046.

Zhao, G. F. and Li, Y.(1989), "Reliability Analysis of Reinforced Concrete Structures for Serviceability Limit States," Proc. of ICOSSAR'89, pp. 2067 -2070.

Zhao, G. F. and Wang, Q. X.(1993), "Evaluation of Crack Width of Concrete Structural Members," The Fourth East Asia-Pacific Conference on Structural Engineering & Construction, Sep., pp. 1243 -1248.

Structural Safety and Reliability, Shiraishi, Shinozuka & Wen (eds) © 1998 Balkema, Rotterdam, ISBN 90 5410 978 5

Influence of load effect due to earthquake on reliability of steel piers of highway bridges

Wataru Shiraki
Tottori University, Japan

ABSTRACT: Many highway bridges suffered severe damage by a great earthquake which hit west part of Japan on Jan. 17, 1995. Especially, pier structures designed by the old version of design code were injured. In this study the reliability level of these pier structures is evaluated, and the influence of load effect due to earthquake on the reliability is examined.

1 INTRODUCTION

A great earthquake with M=7.2 hit west part of Japan on January 17,1995. The highest intensity and most severe damage was concentrated in Kobe City and north of Awaji Island. Many highway and railway bridges suffered severe damage, especially pier structures designed by the old versions of the Bridge Standards based on the ASDM had great damage.

In early studies [Shiraki et al.1987, Shiraki et al.1989, Shiraki et al.1990, Shiraki 1993], the author pointed out a shortcoming such that the reliability indices of pier structures differ considerably from each other, depending on the model type of structure. In order to overcome this shortcoming the optimal load factors corresponding to the design formats of the Load Factor Design Model (LRDF) were calculated for various lifetimes of pier structures, for various models of actual load components: dead load(D), traffic live load(L), temperature load(T), and earthquake load(E), and for various target reliability indices.

In this study, the reliability level of steel piers of existing highway bridges designed by the ASDM is evaluated again. The influence of load effect due to earthquake on reliability of pier structures is examined in detail to give some efficient materials for analyzing the characteristics of pier structures injured in Kobe. In analysis twelve typical types of pier structures which were modeled in the early studies mentioned above are considered. The reliability indices of pier structures for two loading directions such as longitudinal and transverse of bridge axis are evaluated.

2 MODELING OF PIER STRUCTURES

A typical structural system of highway bridge is selected out of the existing systems constructed in the Hanshin area as shown in Fig.1[Shiraki1993], where a three -span continuous steel box girder bridge is supported by two steel rigid-frame piers. In this study, the longitudinal direction model as well as transverse direction model are considered in analysis. Twelve pier structures are considered by combining three geometrical parameters such as the span length of superstructure L=40,60,80m, the total height of pier H=10,20m, and the total width of pier W=20,30m [Shiraki1993]. The principal dimensions and configurations of these twelve models are listed in Table1, and demonstrated in Figs.1 through 3 [Shiraki et al 1987, Shiraki1993].

The wall thickness of beam and column sections, t_b and t_c, and t_f of main girders of these twelve piers, are determined by the conventional allowable stress design formulas shown in Table 2 [JARE 1980], in which D_n, L_n, T_n, E_n=the nominal value of each load components D,L,T and E, respectively; α_D, α_L, α_T and α_E =factors which convent each load component into corresponding stress level; and ϕ =the augmentation factor of the allowable stress. The results of design calculations are summarized in Table 3. In the design calculations, seven checking points 1 through 7 (see Fig.3) are considered. For each structural model the larger one between t_b or t_c for transverse and longitudinal directions is selected in structural design. Except the model No.3, t_b and t_c are determined for transverse direction model as shown in Table 3.

The characteristics of steel material used in design of pier structures are as follows: the grade of steel=SM50Y; the allowable stress σ_a=206 GPa; and the yield stress σ_y=353MPa.

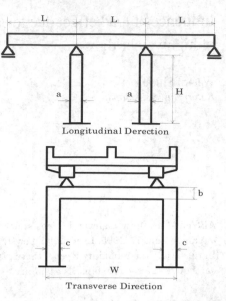

Longitudinal Derection

Fig.1 Typical type of highway bridge structureral system

Table 1 Twelve models of rigid-frame piers

(unit: m)

Model No.	L	H	W	h	l	a	b	c
1	40.0	10.0	20.0	9.17	18.5	2.00	1.67	1.5
2	″	″	30.0	8.75	28.0	″	2.50	2.0
3	″	20.0	20.0	19.17	18.0	″	1.67	2.0
4	″	″	30.0	18.75	27.5	″	2.50	2.5
5	60.0	10.0	20.0	9.17	18.5	3.00	1.67	1.5
6	″	″	30.0	8.75	28.0	″	2.50	2.0
7	″	20.0	20.0	19.17	18.0	″	1.67	2.0
8	″	″	30.0	18.75	27.5	″	2.50	2.5
9	80.0	10.0	20.0	9.17	18.5	4.00	1.67	1.5
10	″	″	30.0	8.75	28.0	″	2.50	2.0
11	″	20.0	20.0	19.17	18.0	″	1.67	2.0
12	″	″	30.0	18.75	27.5	″	2.50	2.5

Transverse Direction

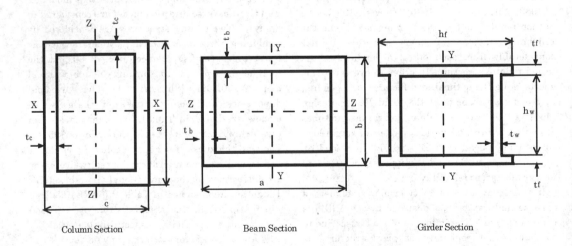

Column Section

Beam Section

Girder Section

Fig.2 Cross-section of rigid-frame pier

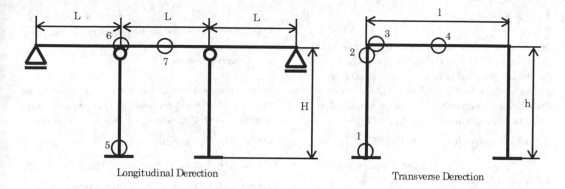

Longitudinal Derection   Transverse Derection

Fig.3 Analytical models

Table 2   Design Formulas

Code	Design Formulas	ϕ
1	$\alpha D \cdot Dn + \alpha L \cdot Ln \leqq \phi \cdot \sigma a$	1.0
2	$\alpha D \cdot Dn + \alpha L \cdot Ln + \alpha T \cdot Tn \leqq \phi \cdot \sigma a$	1.15
3	$\alpha D \cdot Dn + \alpha E \cdot En \leqq \phi \cdot \sigma a$	1.5
4	$\alpha D \cdot Dn + \alpha T \cdot Tn + \alpha E \cdot En \leqq \phi \cdot \sigma a$	1.7

Table 3   Results of design calculation

Model No.	Transverse Direction		Longitudinal Direction	
	Beam Section t_b(mm)	Column Section t_c(mm)	Girder Section t_f(mm)	Column Section t_c(mm)
1	22.4	28.7	17.6	12.8
2	29.0	39.3	17.6	10.8
3	18.5	18.4	17.6	18.7
4	24.0	26.6	17.6	16.0
5	24.3	31.1	26.5	15.9
6	32.4	43.1	26.5	14.2
7	20.4	20.5	26.5	17.5
8	26.6	29.8	26.5	15.3
9	26.0	33.4	36.6	27.8
10	35.3	46.6	36.6	27.7
11	22.3	22.3	36.6	17.7
12	29.0	32.7	36.6	15.9

3   MODELING OF ACTUAL LOAD COMPONENTS

Four actual load components D,L,T and E are modeled by the Borges-Castanheta(B-C) load model [Christensen et al.1982]. Based on extensive investigation on actual conditions of various loads acting on highway bridge in the Hanshin area, the characteristics of the B-C process of each load component are determined as follows [Shiraki 1993].

3.1 Earthquake load, E

Actual earthquake load is modeled by the limiting spike type of the B-C process as $E=S_A/g$, where S_A=linear acceleration response spectrum; and g=acceleratoin of gravity. The cumulative distribution function (CDF) of S_A is expressed as for natural frequency of structure =0.5SEC

$$F_{SA}(x) = 1 - \exp\left[-\left\{(x - 41.28)/34.24\right\}^{0.913}\right]$$

(41.28<x ;unit: cm/sec²)

for natural frequency of structure =0.7SEC

$$F_{SA}(x) = 1 - \exp\left[-\left\{(x - 25.88)/26.12\right\}^{0.879}\right]$$

(25.88<x ;unit: cm/sec²)   (1)

for natural frequency of structure =1.0SEC

$$F_{SA}(x) = 1 - \exp\left[-\left\{(\ddot{x} - 17.19)/18.05\right\}^{0.850}\right]$$

(17.91<x ;unit: cm/sec²)

In evaluation of Eq.(1), the occurrence of earthquake is assumed to be Poisson process, and its average return period is considered to be greater than 2 years. Furthermore, it is assumed that the magnitude is greater than 5.0, the ground condition is Grade 2 and the damping ratio of structure is 0.05. The uncertainty of attenuation law is not considered.

3.2 Dead load, D

As dead load D, only the own weight of structure is considered and it is assumed to be deterministic. To take its variability into consideration, however, the design value of D is calculated by the formula D=D'(1+δ), where D'=actual weight of the structure calculated on the basis of the unit weight of the material and the volume of the members; and δ =0.05 for the superstructure, 0.10 for pier structure.

3.3 Traffic live load, L

The actual traffic live load is modeled by the mixed type of the B-C process as the support reaction on the piers by using the Monte-Carlo simulation technique. The probability of occurrence, p, and the basic time intervals, τ_L, are taken as 0.75 and 6 hours, respectively. Given that the load occurs the CDF of its amplitude, $F_L{}^*(x)$, is expressed as

$$F_L{}^*(x) = 1 - \exp\left[-(x/56.49)^{2.342}\right]$$ (2)

(x>0; unit: ton force)

This CDF is evaluated for two supports on the pier.

3.4 Temperature load, T

Actual temperature load is modeled by the mixed type of the B-C process as the temperature difference such that actual temperature of structure minus 15℃. The parameters p and τ_T are taken as 0.75 and 6 hours, respectively. The CDF of the temperature difference, $F_T{}^*(x)$, is expressed as

$$F_T{}^*(x) = 0.5 + 0.5\Phi\left\{(x - 13.2)/4.4\right\}$$ (3)

(x>0; unit:℃)

where $\Phi(\cdot)$ is the standard normal cumulative distribution function.

4 LOAD COMBINATION ANALYSIS AND RELIABILITY ANALYSYS

In load combination analysis and reliability analysis of the rigid-frame pier structure models under combined action of the earthquake, dead, traffic live and temperature load components, the Turkstra's rule in connection with the B-C processes [Christensen et al. 1982] and the extended level 2 reliability method are used. In this study, seven load combination cases of actual load components shown in Table 4 are considered. The minimum value among the reliability indices at the four checking point 1,2,3 and 4(see Fig.3) for transverse model, and at the three checking points 5,6, and 7(see Fig.3) for longitudinal models is considered to be the reliability index of the pier structures for transverse and longitudinal models, respectively.

Table 4   Combination Cases of Actual Load Component

Case	Actual Load Combination
1	D+L
2	D+T
3	D+L+T
4	D+E
5	D+L+E
6	D+T+E
7	D+L+T+E

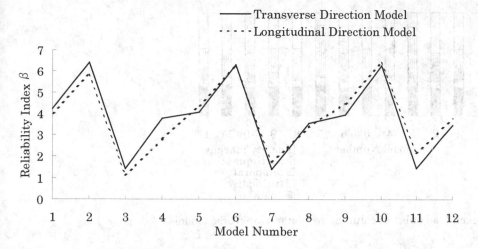

Fig.4 Reliability indices of twelve piers structures β

4.1 *Evaluation of reliability of pier structure*

For the load combination Case 7, the reliability index was calculated for each of twelve pier models shown in Tables 1 and 3. In numerical calculations, the lifetime of structures was assumed to be 50 years. The results obtained are shown in Fig.4 in which the solid and doted lines indicate the results of transverse and longitudinal models, respectively.

The reliability indices β considerably differ from for each model. For the models Nos.3,7 and 11, the reliability indices take very small values which are nearly equal to 1.0, while for the models Nos.2,6 and 10, they take very large values over 6.0. The design code based on the ASDM does not insure consistent level of reliability. This shortcoming inherent the ASDM was already pointed out in the early studies [Shiraki et al. 1990, Shiraki 1993].

For model Nos.1 through 4 with L=40m, the reliability indices of transverse models take large values as compared with those of longitudinal models, for model Nos.5 through 12 with L=60 and 80m, while, this tendency is the opposite. This fact implies that the reliability of pier structure is different from depending on the loading direction of earthquake as well as the structural model types.

4.2 *Influence of load effect due to earthquake on reliability*

The reason for taking different reliability indices for twelve pier models mentioned above lies in the

augmentation factor ϕ=1.50 or 1.70(see Table 2) of allowable stress which is used in considering the load combination with earthquake load. According to the conventional design code which is based on the ASDM, the allowable stress is uniformly augmented without considering the magnitude of the load effect due to earthquake. It is pointed out in early studies [Shiraki et al. 1987, Shiraki et al. 1989] that pier structures with large earthquake load effect have lower reliability in comparison with those with small earthquake load effect.

In order to examine in detail the influence of load effect due to earthquake on the reliability of twelve pier models, the rate of each load effect to the yield stress σ_y is calculated for the results of design calculation shown in Table 3. Fig.5 and Fig.6 show the rate of each load effect such as D,L,T, and E at the bottom sections of each column (points 1 and 5, see Fig.3) for transverse models and longitudinal models, respectively. In these figures the percentage of 100 implies the yield stress. It is seen from Figs.4 through 6 that models with small earthquake load effect as well as large safety margin such as Nos.2,6 and 10 have high reliability. Models of Nos.3,7 and 11 have low reliability and small safety margin with large earthquake load effect. In longitudinal models, dead load effect is small , earthquake and temperature load effect are large comparing with transverse models. Such difference of load effects is reflected in the difference of reliability between longitudinal and transverse models as shown in Fig.4.

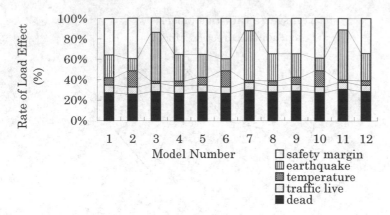

Fig.5 Rate of each load effect at column section of transverse models

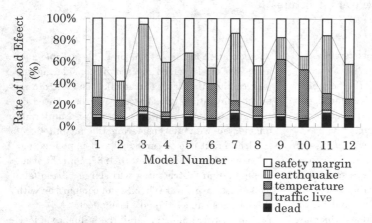

Fig.6 Rate of each load effect at column section of longitudial models

It can be emphasized again that the code based on the ASDM does not insure the consistent level of reliability of different types of pier structures subjected to earthquake load. The ultimate limit state design method based on reliability theory should be introduced into for the design of structures subjected to a great earthquake load.

5 CONCLUDING REMARKS

The main results obtained in this study are as follows:

(1) The earthquake load effect of twelve pier structures designed by the ASDM considerably differ from each other. The reliability indices of piers which have small load effects due to earthquake take large values, while the reliability indices are small for pier which have large load effects due to earthquake.

(2) The reliability indices of pier structures subjected to earthquake load in transverse direction are larger than those of in longitudinal direction. For piers with comparatively large span length of superstructure, the inverse results are obtained.

(3) The results obtained in this study may be used for analyzing the characteristics of damage of pier structures injured in Kobe.

REFERENCES

Christensen,P.T. and Baker,M.J.1982. Structural Reliability and Its Applications. Springer-Verlag.

Japan Association of Road Engineering (JARF) 1980. Specifications for Steel Highway Bridges, Vol. I to V ,Maruzen Book Co.(in Japanese).

Shiraki,W., Matuho,S. and Takaoka,N.1987. Load Combination Analysis and Reliability Analysis of Steel Rigid-Frame Piers Supporting Bridges Constructed on Urban Expressway Network. Proc. of ICASP-5, Vol.1, pp.206-213.

Shiraki,W., Matuho,S. and Takaoka,N.1989. Seismic Risk Analysis of Pier Structures and Pile Foundations of Existing Highway Bridges.Proc. of 9WCEE, Vol.VI, pp.537-542.

Shiraki,W., Matuho,S. and Takaoka,N.1990. Probabilistic Evaluation of Load Factors for Steel Rigid-Frame Piers on Urban Expressway Network. Proc. of ICOSSAR'89, "Structural Safety & Reliability", ASCE, Vol.III, pp.1987-1994.

Shiraki,W.1993. Probabilistic Load Combinations for Steel Piers at Ultimate Limit States. J. of Structural Safety, Vol.13,No.1+2, pp.67-81.

Structural Safety and Reliability, Shiraishi, Shinozuka & Wen (eds) © 1998 Balkema, Rotterdam, ISBN 90 5410 978 5

Optimum repairing of bridge painting systems based upon neural network and genetic algorithms

Hitoshi Furuta – *Department of Informatics, Kansai University, Osaka, Japan*

Masahiro Dogaki – *Department of Civil Engineering, Kansai University, Osaka, Japan*

Norie Nakatsuka – *Bridge Design Division, Harumoto Iron Works Inc., Tokyo, Japan*

Hiroo Kishida – *Consulting Division, Japan Industrial Testing Co., Osaka, Japan*

ABSTRACT : The aim of this paper is to develop an optimum decision supporting system for proposing rational maintenance plan, especially repainting plan, of a group of many existing steel plate- and box-girder bridges. The optimum plan that repaints some steel bridges among many existing ones is determined, selected of a group of many deteriorating bridges by solving the combinatorial optimization problems with discrete variables and a discontinuous objective function within annual budget. A simple Genetic Algorithms(GA), which is used in a method for searching for most suitable repainting program of steel bridges, is adopted to the combinatorial optimization problems. Some numerical examples show to prove the applicability and usefulness of this decision supporting system for searching for the fittest repainting plan of damaged existing bridges.

1 INTRODUCTION

A lot of highway and railway bridges have been constructed during past 50 years after the 2nd World War in Japan. In recent years, as such bridges have been suffering from damage and deterioration due to heavy traffics and severe environment, many bridges need some kinds of maintenance, and the number of such bridges is likely to grow for at least the foreseeable future. Under this situation, it is very important to establish a rational maintenance strategy for many damaged existing bridges, so that they are safely used for a long period.

When determining whether or not a particular bridge should be repainted, common practice is for a expert to inspect the bridge visually or to touch its paint surface. This method is, therefore, time-consuming, and the growing number of bridges requiring attention is making the current approach impractical. Under these circumstances, engineers who are not specialist on repainting are often called upon to judge whether or not bridge maintenance needs.

It is very difficult to determine the appropriate combination of repainting some bridges among many damaged existing bridges within annual budget, because there are extremely many number of combinations for their repainting. In this paper, an attempt is made to develop a practical decision supporting system of bridge maintenance for assisting inexperienced engineers to make appropriate decision on the time of repainting. Taking into account the financial constraints as well as the safety and functional constraints, this system can provide a set of optimum program for repainting some bridges among many damaged existing bridges. The bridge management system will propose a reasonable repainting plan by the application of simple Genetic Algorithms (GA).

2 DEFINITION OF DETERIORATION DEGREE OF BRIDGE PAINT

The damage and deterioration of bridge paint greatly depend on the environment, i.e. air pollution and wetness, at bridge site, and the kinds of paints.

When determining whether or not a particular bridge should be repainted, common practice is for an expert to inspect the bridge visually or to touch its paint surface. This method is, therefore, time-consuming, and the growing of the number of bridges which require attention is making the current approach impractical (Kobori 1990, Miyake 1995).

As more rational method for determining the deterioration degree of paint, it may be considered to apply the neural network technique for the damage assessment. When there are past sufficient records of bridge maintenance, the learning ability of the neural network is useful to save the working time and load necessary in the inspection and analysis. Further reduction of working time can be achieved by utilizing the technique of image processing. The visual information on the corrosion of structures is gained by photos and it is processed by some method of image processing (Fujiwara 1993). Through the image processing, it enables us to assess the damage degree of structural corrosion automatically and independent of the subjectivety of inspector or engineer. In this paper, the deterioration degree of paint judged by such new technique is applied to present the optimum repairing program of bridge painting.

The deterioration degree of bridge paint determined by the above-mentioned technique is classified by the levels specified by some authorities which are established by the goverment and states in Japan. In this paper, the damage and deterioration state of painting of existing steel plate- and box-girder bridges are ranked by four categories of A, B, C, and D corresponding to the corrosion degree on their surfaces, in which the rank A indicates the well-conditioned, i.e. no repainting at all and the rank D is the most severe state of painting, i.e. the need of immediate repainting, as shown in Table 1. The numbers of 0, 1, 2, and 3 are used in the simulating program written by C language, instead of four damage ranks classified by alphabets of A, B, C, and D.

3 FORMULATION FOR COMBINATORIAL OPTIMIZATION PROBLEM OF REPAIRING

With increase in repairing bridges, engineers who are not specialist on repairing are often called upon, to judge whether or not the maintenance of the bridge needs. So as to assist non-special engineers to make appropriate decision on the timing of repairing, we attempt to develop a practical decision

supporting system for the damage assessment of structural corrosion.

In order to establish a rational program for determining the bridges and timing in which repairing should be made among many existing steel bridges, it is necessary to take into account the financial constraints, i.e. annual budget, as well as the safety and functional requirements. The repairing problem, therefore, can be formulated as a combinatorial optimization problem. There are various methods such as linear and nonlinear programming methods for analyzing the optimization problems. Such methods can not apply to the optimization problems such as present repairing, because the objective function is discontinuous and is not differentiated.

The objective function for the fittest repainting program of bridge can be given by

$$OBJ(\{I\}) = \sum_{i=1}^{n}(T_i + A_i)I_i \rightarrow \max \qquad (1)$$

where T_i = the weight for repairing of the ith damaged portion; A_i = the weight by the area of the ith damaged portion; and I_i = the value of variable as

$$\{I\} = \{I_1, I_2, \cdots, I_n\} \qquad (2)$$

where this is 1 for repainting and is 0 for no repainting; and n = the number of repainting portions. The function is optimized so as to maximize its fitness.

The financial constraint condition is given by

$$g(\{I\}) = C - B \leq 0 \qquad (3)$$

where C = the total cost spent on repainting; and B = the annual budget for the maintenance.

In the problem of repairing scheduling, the evaluation for each repairing plan is very complicated and therefore its fitness function should be expressed in terms of special forms such as "If-Then-rules". This means that the objective function is not differential, because the repairing cost is a descrete function of design variable $\{I\}$. If the

Table 1. Definition of corrosion rank of painting and the need of maintenance

Corrosion rank		Condition of painting	Method
A	0	good painting	monitoring
B	1	no rust on painting	appropriate repairing
C	2	much rust on painting	need of repairing as quick as possible
D	3	serious painting	need of immediate repairing

objective function is discontinuous and indifferential, such optimization techniques as linear and nonlinear programming methods can not apply to the optimization problems.

In this paper, it is, therefore, attempted to apply to a simple Genetic Algorithms (GA), in order to determine a practical program of bridge repainting under the financial constraints. GA was invented to solve the combinatorial optimization problems by simulating the same process as the evolution process of living beings (Chikada 1995, Matsui 1986, Natsuaki 1995, Tamura 1994), because GA has such a high ability that it can pursue an optimum solution even for optimization problems with vague and imprecise objective functions.

Fig.1 shows a flow of evaluation process of living beings. That process is as follows:
1. A set of populations, i.e. the combination of repainting of a group of steel plate- and box-girder bridges, is assumed.
2. The evaluation, i.e. the fitness degree, is calculated from Eq.(1) for each population.
3. The process of selection and multiplication is applied to a set of current populations. The populations with evaluation under their average value is put on by new populations.
4. The crossover process for some populations is carried out.
5. The mutation process for some populations is carried out.
6. The value of fitness fuction is calculated.
7. Whether or not the evaluation process is finished is judged.

4 NUMERICAL RESULTS

Numerical computation is comprehensively carried out to confirm the applicability and usefulness of the above-mentioned decision supporting system for providing reasonable repairing program for a group of existing steel bridges. In this paper, maintenance job is especially focused on the repainting of steel plate- and box-girders.

4.1 A group of repairing bridges

As illustrative examples, consider three existing steel bridges which require some maintenance, i.e. 1) bridge A, 2) bridge B, and 3) bridge C. The bridge A is a box-girder bridge with one rectangular cell as shown in Fig.2. The bridges B and C are plate-girder bridges consisting of four and three main I-section girders as shown in Figs.3 and 4,

respectively. The span length and width of bridges, surface areas of box- and I-section girders, and number of girders are given in Table 2 for the bridges A, B, and C.

To estimate repainting cost of main girders, the painting area of the box-girder bridge A are assumed to be 20% up of all surfaces of main box-girder in consideration of the existing of longitudinal and transverse stiffeners, and diaphragms attached at its inside. Also, for the plate-girder bridges B and C, it is assumed that the painting area is 15% up of the surfaces of I-section girders taking into account the presence of lateral bracings. The areas of temporary facilities under painting are assumed to be given by the product of the width and length shown in Figs.2 to 4, in which

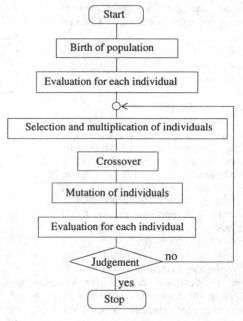

Fig.1. Evaluation process based on simple GA

Table 2. Dimensions of bridge models A, B, and C

	Bridge		
	A	B	C
Span length (m)	30	28	32
Width (m)	10	15	13
Painting area (m^2)	462.00	502.32	529.92
Number of girders	1	4	3

the width is given by the sum of the real width of bridges and additional width 2 m for the temporary facilities.

Figs. 2 to 4 also show the dimensions of three bridges and the portions divided in the direction of bridge axis, at which whether or not the repainting needs is judged. The bridges A and C are divided into three and four blocks with same length respectively. The bridge B is unequally divided into three portions. The deterioration degree at each portion is determined by applying the corrosion rank in Table 1, referring to the results of monitoring. In this paper, the deterioration degree for each portion is assumed to be as in Table 3, in which numeral in this table indicates the deterioration degree of painting defined by referring to Table 1.

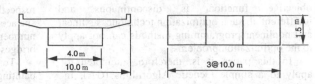

Fig.2. Cross-section and three portions of repainting for bridge A

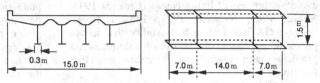

Fig.3. Cross-section and three portions of repainting for bridge B

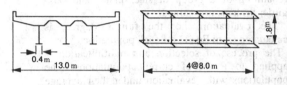

Fig.4. Cross-section and four portions of repainting for bridge C

Table 3. Deterioration degree of bridge painting

(a) bridge A

	in direction of bridge axis		
in-side of box	2	2	3
out-side of box	2	1	2

(b) bridge B

	in direction of bridge axis		
in direction of width	0	1	2
	2	2	3
	1	3	2
	1	2	0

(c) bridge C

	in direction of bridge axis			
in direction of width	1	2	1	0
	2	3	2	1
	0	2	1	1

4.2 Parameters for numerical computation

4.2.1 Annual budget
The scale of repainting is greatly influenced by the amount of annual budget for maintenance. Here, the amount of budget is assumed to be 6.5 million Yen corresponding to 60% of which all three bridges are fully painted at a time. It is also assumed that repainting cost per unit area is 4,000 Yen and cost for temporary painting facilities is 3,500Yen/m².

4.2.2 Selection method
There are various methods for selecting and multiplying the population to evolve them. In this paper, the elite strategy is used to select the populations.

4.3 Numerical examples

4.3.1 Number of populations and crossover rate
To determine appropriate values of Genetic Algorithm operations for searching for the optimum solutions as few number of generation as possible and as high evaluation as possible under evolution process, the simulation is carried out for the cases of which the number of populations is a value between 20 and 50 and the crossover rate is a value between 0.4 and 0.9. The mutation rate is fixed as 0.01.

As a result of numerical simulation, Tables 4 to

7 are obtained to show the maximum evalution for the optimum combination of bridge paintings searched by GA technique, generation at which maximum evaluation is obtained firstly, and total cost at the maximum evaluation for the number of populations of 20, 30, 40, and 50, respectively.

It is obvious that all results are ones that the repairing costs are within the annual budget of 6.5 million Yen. It can be seen that the maximum evaluation and generation of proposed repairing programs differ for the number of populations and crossover rate.

As a result of numerical consideration, the appropriate crossover rates for each number of populations are obtained as in Table 8.

4.3.2 Mutation rate
To demonstrate the effect of the mutation rate on the optimum solution of repainting, the simulation is carried out for the mutation rates of 0.005, 0.01, and 0.015, in which the number of populations and crossover rate are fixed as 30 and 0.6, respectively. Table 9 shows the optimum solutions for each mutation rate.

It is obvious from this table that when the mutation rate is 0.01 the optimum solution is obtained by less number of populations than that in the case of 0.015. Unfortunately, optimum solution could not be obtained in the case that the mutation rate is 0.005.

4.3.3 Appropriate GA operations
As a result of comprehensive numerical computation, optimum combination of GA operations is that the number of populations is 30, the crossover rate is 0.6, and the mutation rate is 0.01 for this combinatorial optimization problem.

4.3.4 Convergence process
Fig.5 shows the convergence process with generation, in which the maximum, average, and minimum evaluations for 30 populations are illustrated. It is found from this figure that the evaluation reaches the maximum value at the 47th generation. It can be also seen from this figure that a reasonable solution is obtained after 160th generation.

Table 4. Maximum evaluation, generation at which the evaluation yields the maximum value firstly, and maintenance cost for number of individuals 20

Crossover rate	Max. Evaluation	Generation	Cost(Yen)
0.4	103.6153	38	6,467,020
0.5	104.6062	61	6,433,240
0.6	103.6821	135	6,206,380
0.7	106.7398	74	6,331,960
0.8	104.6062	132	6,433,240
0.9	103.7291	26	6,312,000

Table 5. Maximum evaluation, generation at which the evaluation yields the maximum value firstly, and maintenance cost for number of individuals 30

Crossover rate	Max. Evaluation	Generation	Cost(Yen)
0.4	104.6062	64	6,433,240
0.5	104.6062	25	6,433,240
0.6	106.7398	47	6,331,960
0.7	103.6586	59	6,155,320
0.8	103.6153	37	6,433,240
0.9	106.7398	60	6,331,960

Table 6. Maximum evaluation, generation at which the evaluation yields the maximum value firstly, and maintenance cost for number of individuals 40

Crossover rate	Max. Evaluation	Generation	Cost(Yen)
0.4	106.7398	104	6,331,960
0.5	106.7398	56	6,331,960
0.6	106.7398	118	6,331,960
0.7	106.7398	139	6,331,960
0.8	106.7398	68	6,331,960
0.9	106.7398	72	6,331,960

Table 7. Maximum evaluation, generation at which the evaluation yields the maximum value firstly, and maintenance cost for number of individuals 50

Crossover rate	Max. Evaluation	Generation	Cost(Yen)
0.4	103.6586	122	6,155,320
0.5	106.7398	48	6,331,960
0.6	106.7398	51	6,331,960
0.7	104.6062	141	6,433,240
0.8	106.7398	99	6,331,960
0.9	106.7398	62	6,331,960

Table 8. Optimum crossover rate for each population

Population	Optimum crossover rate
20	0.7
30	0.6, 0.9
40	0.4 to 0.9
50	0.5, 0.6, 0.8, 0.9

Table 9. Maximum evaluation, generation at which the evaluation yields the maximum value firstly, and maintenance cost for various mutation rates

Mutation rate	Max. Evaluation	Generation	Cost(Yen)
0.005	103.6153	104	6,477,340
0.010	106.7398	47	6,331,960
0.015	106.7398	48	6,331,960

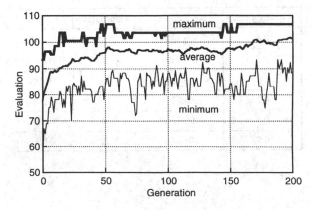

Fig.5. Convergence process

Table 10. Proposed repainting plan

(a) bridge A

	in direction of bridge axis		
in-side of box	2	2	3
out-side of box	2	1	2

(b) bridge B

	in direction of bridge axis		
in direction of width	0	1	2
	2	2	3
	1	3	2
	1	2	0

(c) bridge C

	in direction of bridge axis		
in direction of width	1	2	1	0
	2	1	2	1
	0	2	1	1

4.3.5 *Proposed repainting program*

Table 10 shows the proposed repainting program for the corrosion given by Table 3. The total amount of painting cost is 6,331,960Yen and is within assumed annual budget.

Let us examine how the amount of annual budget effects on the repainting program. As the annual budget increases from 6.5 million Yen to 7.8 million Yen, i.e. it corresponds to 20% up of annual budget, the repainting area increases 15%.

On the other hand, as the annual budget decreases from 6.5 million Yen to 5 million Yen, i.e. it corresponds to 20% down of annual budget, the repainting area decreases 24% in comparison with that for annual budget of 6.5 million Yen.

5 CONCLUSIONS

This paper presents the appropriate decision supporting system for the paint maintenance program of many existing bridges for inexperienced engineers of repairing. Through comprehensive numerical computation, it is concluded that the bridge management system developed here is useful for proposing the optimum repairing program of many existing bridge groups. Using the Genetic Algorithms technique, it is possible to obtain some reasonable plans which are applicable for practical use.

REFERENCES

Chikada, Y., K. Tachibana, T. Siroto & T. Kobori 1995. An aproach to repair planning of existing bridges by Genetic Algorithm. *Proc. of JSCE* 513/I31: 151-159 (in Japanese).

Fujiwara, H., S. Degawa, Y. Kohno & T. Sugano 1993. A study on the system for judgement of deterioration of bridge painting by application of photo processing. *Proc. of the 48th annual meeting of JSCE:* 578-579 (in Japanese) .

Kobori, T., N. Kimata, K. Komai & T. Takemura 1990. A study on supporting system for judgement of corrosion and deterioration of bridges. *Bridge and Foundation Engineering* 24(11): 45-60 (in Japanese).

Matsui, S. & Y. Maeda 1986. A rational evaluation method for deterioration of highway bridge decks. *Proc. of JSCE* 374/I6: 419-426(in Japanese).

Miyake, M., H. Fujiwara & T. Akai 1995. Development of judgement system of deterioration of bridge painting. *Proc. of the 50th annual meeting of JSCE*: 724-725(in Japanese).

Natsuaki, Y., S. Mukanndai, K. Yasuda & H. Furuta 1995. Application of Genetic Algorithms to the problem of determining the laying sequence for a continuous girder reinforced concrete floor system. *Jour. of Structural Engineering* 41A: 627-642(in Japanese).

Tamura, T., H. Sugimoto & T. Uemae 1994. Application of Genetic Algorithms to dicision problems of maintenance scheduling of highways. *Proc. of JSCE* 482/IV: 37-46(in Japanese).

Structural Safety and Reliability, Shiraishi, Shinozuka & Wen (eds) © 1998 Balkema, Rotterdam, ISBN 90 5410 978 5

Reliability models for assessing highway bridge safety

Gongkang Fu
Wayne State University, Detroit, Mich., USA

ABSTRACT: In evaluation and design of highway bridges, their safety often need be assessed, especially when developing requirements for such practice. This paper presents two reliability models for highway bridges, which consider overloads and proof load testing for bridge evaluation, respectively. The former case focuses on live load modeling for overloads, and the latter case concentrates on modeling the resistance to be proof load tested. These models are adapted based on a general model that has been used in developing the new AASHTO design and evaluation codes based on structural reliability.

1. INTRODUCTION

With significant developments in the theory of structural reliability for the past two decades, several structural design codes have been adopted incorporating this concept. These include US highway bridge design and evaluation specifications [1,2]. They cover typical US highway bridges and application cases of design and evaluation. Their issuance marks a new milestone of development of the structural reliability theory.

Modeling and assess structural reliability of bridges was an important step in these developments. Furthermore, there are other cases of bridge evaluation that these specifications do not completely cover. Examples are bridge evaluation or checking considering overloads and using proof load testing. The bridge structure reliability model for more routine cases need be revised or new models need be developed to address these applications. This paper presents two reliability models respectively for these cases, which are adapted based on the model used for routine cases.

2. RELIABILITY MODELING FOR CHECKING OVERLOADS

Heavy vehicle loads on highway bridges exceeding the legal limit are referred to as overloads. Occasionally, overloads are desired or required to cross these bridges. This is because the transported assembled items can avoid high costs of assembly at the destination. They are now accommodated by special permit systems available in many countries, including US. Understanding the reliability of bridges under these loads is often required, for example, for developing a rational procedure of checking overloads. Modeling the reliability for this case is at the component level, and presented below.

For a primary component of highway bridges, its reliability is described here by its probability of failure P_f, i.e. the probability of the load effect exceeding the resistance of the component:

$$P_f = \text{Maximum of } [\, P_{ft} \text{ and } P_{fs}\,] \tag{1}$$

$$P_{ft} = \text{Probability } [R - D - L_t < 0] \tag{2}$$

$$P_{fs} = \text{Probability } [R - D - L_s < 0] \tag{3}$$

where R is the load carrying capacity of the bridge component, D is the dead load effect to the same component, and L_t and L_s are live load effects respectively for traffic load (indicated by the subscript t) and single passage of an overload (indicated by the subscript s). They are modeled by lognormal random variables independent of one another. For the case of dealing with overloads on highway bridges, the live load modeling is particularly important. Using the live model developed by Moses and Ghosn [16]:

$$L_t = m\,M\,g\,I \qquad\qquad (4)$$

$$L_s = m\,M_p\,g\,I \qquad\qquad (5)$$

where all factors are modeled by independent lognormal random variables. m covers variation of load effect due to the configuration of trucks; M represents the total effect of truck loads on the bridge. M_p is the load effect due to an overload. g is a factor distributing the total load effect of the bridge to the interested primary component; and I covers impact effects due to dynamic behavior of the bridge under moving trucks. These random variables in the model are described by their mean and standard deviation based on data collected by weighing-trucks-in-motion [17]. Including the case of single passage of the overload is to ensure that the overload effect is covered, particularly when the overload is extremely high in weight and small in volume.

The statistical parameters of M (mean and standard deviation) are obtained using the following cumulative probability distribution $cpd_M(M')_n$ for passage of n platoons of heavy vehicles:

$$
\begin{aligned}
cpd_M&(M')_n \\
&= \text{Probability } [M<M']_n \\
&= [cpd_M(M')_1]^n = (\text{Probability } [M<M']_1)^n \qquad (6)
\end{aligned}
$$

where $cpd_M(M')_1$ is the cumulative probability distribution for one platoon of vehicles. Note that subscripts 1 and n respectively indicate the number of platoons included. Data needed for estimation of Eq.6 are experimentally obtained as discrete values (e.g. gross vehicle weight), and $cpd_M(M')_n$ thus is also discretized. $cpd_M(M')_1$ was obtained by its corresponding discretized probability distribution function $pdf_M(x)_1$:

$$cpd_M(M')_1 = \sum_{x=0,\ldots,M'} pdf_M(x)_1 \qquad (7)$$

$$
\begin{aligned}
pdf_M&(x)_1 \\
= \sum_i \sum_j \sum_k\ &\text{Prob[Number of Vehicles]} \\
&\times \text{Prob[Vehicle Locations]} \\
&\times \text{Prob[Load Effect due to the Vehicles]} \\
&\qquad\qquad\qquad\qquad\qquad\qquad (8)
\end{aligned}
$$

Note that x is a discretized variable as shown in

Eq.7, and is the total load effect due to the particular combination of number of vehicles on the bridge, the locations of these vehicles, and their contribution to the total load effect. Prob in Eq.8 stand for Probability. These probabilities under the triple summation sign were obtained from field data in a discretized (i.e. histogram) form [6,8,10,16,17].

The above formulation of load effect M simulates the total load effect for the bridge, acknowledging effects of traffic volume (reflected by the number of vehicles in a platoon and n, the number of platoons of vehicles for an interested period of time, which can be explicitly specified). To account for effects of overloaded vehicle traffic, the histogram of vehicle weight is modified by including overloads:

Prob[Load Effect (due to all vehicles)]
= Prob[Load Effect (due to all normal vehicles)]
　+Prob[Load Effect (due to all overload vehicles)]
$$\qquad\qquad\qquad\qquad\qquad\qquad (9)$$

The weight histogram for normal traffic was obtained from [17], and that for overloads is based on overload permits issued in a typical year of 1991 by New York State Department of Transportation, USA. These permits are classified into three groups: annual permits for divisible load (valid for a year), annual permits for nondivisible load (valid for a year), and trip permits for nondivisible load (valid for a trip in a few weeks). Fig.1 shows the histogram of nondivisible trip overloads. These three groups of permit represent 2.65, 0.22, and 0.05 % of total traffic, by equivalent frequency of appearance. An annual permit vehicle, for example, is assumed to be equivalent to a normal vehicle (not needing a permit to travel) for that year, and a vehicle with a trip permit valid for 10 days is equivalent to 10/365 = 0.0274 normal vehicles for that year. Because the divisible loads represent a group of "grandfather-exempted" loads for which permits are issued to an invariable group of truckers, this group of load is always added to the load of normal traffic here in Eq.9. Depending on the case of structural reliability assessment to be discussed below, nondivisible loads were selectively added to the resulting vehicle weight histogram for various cases of permit load groups. Fig.2 shows a case of resulting cumulative histogram of load effect (flexural moment) $cpd_M(M')_n$ for a 150 ft simple span bridge, with n = 100x365x2,

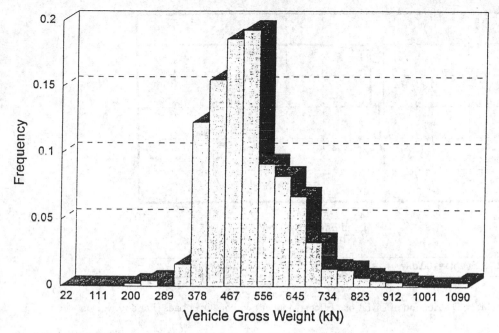

Fig.1 Nondivisible Trip Permit Overloads in New York State, USA

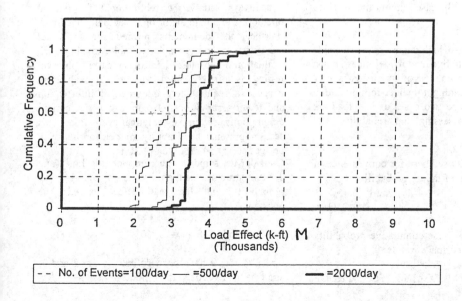

Fig.2 Cumulative Distribution of Live Load Effect (Moment) Including Overloads

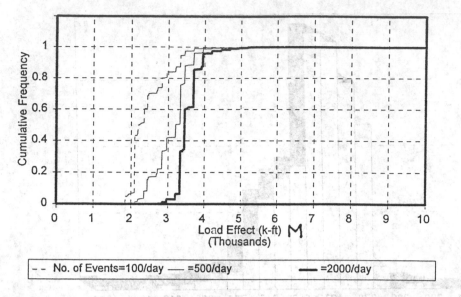

Fig.3 Cumulative Distribution of Live Load Effect (Moment) without Overloads (For comparison with Fig.2)

500x365x2, and 2000x365x2. These cases are interpreted as for sites with 100, 500, and 2000 annual average daily trucks (AADT) for a period of 2 years. Fig.3 shows the case without the overload tail for comparison.

It is important to also include the case of single passage of overload in live load modeling as shown in Eq.5, because the volume of overloads is very small, sometimes leading to under-representation of risk in Eq.4. These two cases of live load are included here in assessing the reliability of bridges.

The safety index β is used here for convenience of numerical calculation of failure probability:

$$\beta = \Phi^{-1} (1-P_f) \qquad (10)$$

where Φ^{-1} (.) is the inverse cumulative probability function of standard normal variable.

3. RELIABILITY MODELING FOR PROOF LOAD TESTING

US highway bridges are now evaluated by analytical methods for safe load-carrying-capacity (load rating, not ultimate capacity), with data from documents (such as design drawings) and obtained through field inspection (such as loss of cross section due to deterioration). This analytical approach is usually based on conservative assumptions. Thus, the resulting evaluation may not always satisfy the requirement for normal operation , although the bridge is actually adequate. Further, the documents needed for analytical evaluation are not always available, making such evaluation impossible. In these cases, physical testing is often desired for bridge evaluation, because it requires less documented information and fewer assumptions. It can also verify certain assumptions used in the analytical evaluation. This section presents a reliability model for highway bridges surviving proof load testing.

Consider the same bridge component in Eqs.2 and 3, its structural reliability is model by the probability that the load effect exceeds the resistance:

$$P_f = \text{Probability} [R - D - L < 0] \qquad (11)$$

where R and D have been defined in Eqs.2 and 3. and L is the live load effect modeled as

$$L = m \, M \, g \, I \qquad (12)$$

m, M, g, and I here have been defined earlier, except in this case M does not include overloads when overloading is not an issue. Proof load testing is to verify that the resistance is equal to or

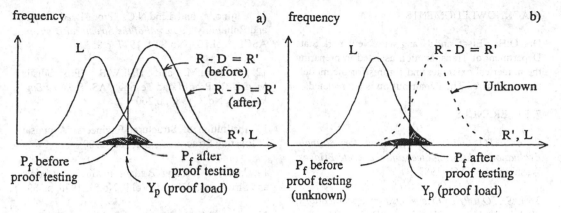

Fig. 4 Effects of Proof Load Testing on Structural Reliability
   a) When Some Knowledge about Resistance Is Available
   b) When No Knowledge about Resistance Is Available

higher than the applied load effect. Namely, the probability that the resistance is lower than the applied load effect will be eliminated. This is modeled here by truncating the distribution function of R at the applied load effect. This is shown graphically in Fig.4, where two cases are included: a) when there is some knowledge about the existing resistance (such as a load rating), and b) when there is no such knowledge. Similar models to this have been used in [11,12,21]. A direct integration method and the method proposed by Fujino and Lind [11] were used to estimate the structural reliability of US highway bridges for Eq.11. Consistency between the two methods was confirmed [6,8].

4. APPLICATION OF THE RELIABILITY MODELS

The reliability model for highway bridges subjected to overloads has been used in a study to develop a new procedure for checking overloads for bridges [10]. The format of load and resistance factors was used in the proposed procedure. The study focused on determining the load and resistance factors. While the resistance and dead load factors were proposed to remain similar to those for routine evaluation (load rating), the live load factor for overload was proposed to be dependent on the overload's magnitude. The heavier the overload, the smaller the live load factor. This is consistent with the understanding that the live load factor is intended to also cover the load to be alongside the overload being checked, and the high the overload, the relatively lower this

possibly alongside load may be compared to the overload [10].

The reliability model for highway bridges surviving proof load testing was used to develop a new set of requirements for the magnitude of proof load. Apparently, the higher the required proof load, the higher the bridge's safetyif surviving, and the higher the probability of bridge damage by the proof load. The required proof load was developed for a target level of safety comparable with that assured by the analytical approach. The proposed requirements allow consideration to the traffic load at the site, current load rating for the bridge if available, and if no load rating can be reasonably estimated. Incorporating these pieces of information, this set of requirements assure relatively uniform safety of the bridge structures covered, which is comparable with that assured by analytical load rating [6].

5. SUMMARY AND CONCLUSIONS

This paper presented two structural reliability models for highway bridges to deal with overloads and proof load testing for their evaluation. The original model used for more routine cases is flexible to be adapted for these two special cases. These two models have been used to develop requirements for overload checking and proof load testing for US highway bridges, targeting at uniform structural reliability. They can serve as effective tools to develop this type of requirements for evaluation specifications of highway bridges.

6. ACKNOWLEDGMENTS

Drs. O.Hag-Elsafi and J.Tang with New York State Department of Transportation assisted in preparing the numerical examples and figures for the models presented here. Their contribution is appreciated.

7. REFERENCES

1. *AASHTO Guide Specifications for Strength Evaluation of Existing Steel and Concrete Bridges*, Washington, D.C., 1989

2. *AASHTO LRFD Bridge Design Specifications*, SI Units 1st Edition, Washington,D.C., 1994

3. Ang,A.H-S. and Tang,W.L. *Probability Concepts in Engineering Planning and Design*, Vol.I and II, John Wiley & Sons, New York, NY, 1984

4. ASCE Committee on Safety of Bridges "*A Guide for the Field Testing of Bridges*", 1980

5.Bakht,B., and Csagoly,P.F. "Bridge Testing", Structural Research Report, SRR-79-10, Research and Development Division, Ministry of Transportation and Communications, Downsview, Ontario, Canada, 1979

6. Fu,G. "Highway Bridge Rating by Nondestructive Proof Load Testing for Consistent Safety", Final Report on R209 to FHWA, FHWA/NY/RR-95/163, Transportation R & D Bureau, New York State Department of Transportation, April 1995

7. Fu,G. and Moses,F. "Overload Permit Checking Based on Structural Reliability", *TRB TRR* 1290,1991, Vol.1, p.279

8. Fu,G., Saridis,P., and Tang,J. "Proof Load Testing for Highway Bridges", FHWA/NY/RR-92/153, Interim Report on R209 to FHWA, Engineering R & D Bureau, New York State Department of Transportation, Dec.1991

9. Fu,G. and Tang,J. "Proof Load Formula for Highway Bridge Rating", *TRB TRR* 1371, p.129, 1992

10. Fu,G. and Hag-Elsafi,O. "New Safety-Based Checking Procedure for Overloads on Highway Bridges", *TRB TRR* 1541, p.22, 1996

11. Fujino,Y. and Lind,N.C. "Proof-Load Factors and Reliability", *Journal of the Structural Division*, ASCE, Vol.103, No.ST4, 1977, p.853

12. Grigoriu,M. and Hall,W.B. "Probabilistic Models for Proof Load Testing", ASCE *J.Stru.Eng.* Vol.110, No.2, 1984, p.260

13. Institution of Structural Engineers "Appraisal of Existing Structures", UK, July 1980

14. Javor,T. "Testing Bridges in Situ", Materials and Structures, RILEM, Vol.9, No.53, 1976, p.369

15. Ladner,M. "In Situ Load Testing of Concrete Bridges in Switzerland", ACI Symposium on Strength Evaluation of Existing Concrete Bridges, SP-88, Detroit, MI, 1985, p.59

16. Moses,F., and Ghosn,M. "A Comprehensive Study of Bridge Loads and Reliability" Report FHWA/OH-85/005, Department of Civil Engineering, Case Western Reserve University, Cleveland, OH, Jan. 1985

17. Moses,F. and Verma,D. "Load Capacity Evaluation of Existing Bridges". Report 301, NCHRP, TRB, 1987

18. Ontario Ministry of Transportation and Communications "*Ontario Highway Bridge Design Code*", Downsview Ontario, Canada, 1983

19. Phillips,M.H., and Wood,J.H. "Proof Loading of Highway Bridges", Proceedings of New Zealand Roading Symposium 1987, National Roads Board, Vol.4, p.803, 1987

20. Thompson,D.M. "Loading Tests on Highway Bridges: A Review", Transport and Road Research Laboratory, Dept. of the Environment and Dept. of Transport, TRRL Laboratory Report 1032, 1981

21. Veneziano,D., Meli,R., and Rodriguez,M. "Proof Loading for Target Reliability", ASCE *J.Stru.Div.* Vol.104, No.ST1, 1978, p.79

Structural Safety and Reliability, Shiraishi, Shinozuka & Wen (eds) © 1998 Balkema, Rotterdam, ISBN 90 5410 978 5

Fatigue reliability assessment of highway bridges using new parameters

I. Okura & T. Ishikawa
Osaka University, Japan

H. Watanabe
Okumura Co. Ltd, Osaka, Japan

ABSTRACT: Two new parameters, called "fatigue resistance" and "fatigue-damage-accumulation", are proposed to make it easy to introduce the results of stress measurement of a monitored bridge into fatigue reliability assessment of highway bridges.

1 INTRODUCTION

Recently there have been many reports on stress measurements of highway bridges. However, a generalized method is not still provided on how to introduce the results of stress measurement into the fatigue reliability assessment. In this paper, two new parameters, called "fatigue resistance" and "fatigue-damage-accumulation", are proposed. The fatigue assessment which is obtained from these parameters is expressed in terms of the design equivalent stress range and the allowable fatigue stress with partial safety factors. The relationship between the reliability index and a lapse of time from opening to traffic is shown. The method to determine the unknown factors involved in the fatigue-damage-accumulation, using a monitoring bridge is given.

2 FATIGUE RESISTANCE AND FATIGUE-DAMAGE-ACCUMULATION

2.1 *Fatigue resistance*

The slope of $S-N$ curves given by integrating the Paris's crack growth law, i.e. the equation for the relation between a propagation rate of a crack and its stress intensity factor range, is almost $-1/3$. As the sample size of fatigue test results is larger, the slope of the $S-N$ curve determined by the least squares method tends to converge into $-1/3$ (Keating 1986). From these facts, the slope of $S-N$ curves may be treated as a constant of $-1/3$, not as a random variable. This gave us the idea of using the variable c defined as

$$c = N(\Delta\sigma)^3 \qquad (2.1)$$

For every pair of stress range $\Delta\sigma$ and number of cycles to failure, N, the values of c are calculated by this equation.

A fatigue test database (Yamada 1988) was used to determine the probability distribution of c. The test data in which fatigue failure occurred before 2 million cycles were adopted for the calculation of c, because it was not clear whether the fatigue test results in the long life region over 2 million cycles were governed by an $S-N$ curve with a slope $-1/3$ or by a fatigue limit.

The probability distribution of c were determined with probability papers. A normal distribution, a lognormal distribution and a Weibull distribution were considered. The cumulative probability p_j at the j-th from the smallest of c is given by

$$p_j = \frac{j}{j_{data} + 1} \qquad (2.2)$$

where j_{data} = number of test data.

As an example, plotting on the probability papers is shown in Figs. 1 and 2 for the finished and non finished cases of transverse butt welds. The probability distributions for the finished and non finished cases are fit for a Weibull distribution and a lognomal distribution, respectively.

Table 1 summarizes the probability distributions of c for various structural details. The probability distributions are expressed by a normal distribution,

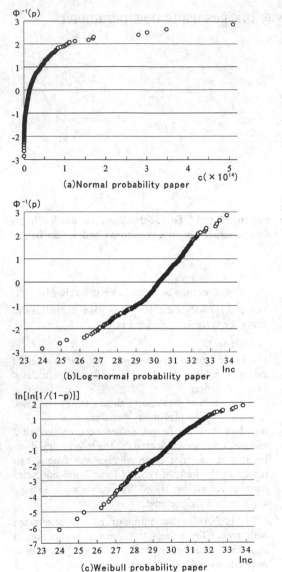

(a)Normal probability paper

(b)Log-normal probability paper

(c)Weibull probability paper

Fig. 1. Transverse butt welds (finished).

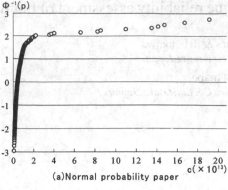

(a)Normal probability paper

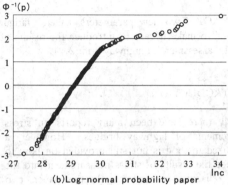

(b)Log-normal probability paper

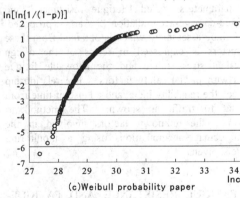

(c)Weibull probability paper

Fig. 2. Transverse butt welds (non finished).

a lognormal distribution or a Weibull distribution, defined as

a) Probability density function and cumulative distribution function for normal distribution

$$f_c(c) = \frac{\phi\left(\dfrac{c - \mu_c}{\mu_c \Omega_c}\right)}{\mu_c \Omega_c} \qquad (2.3)$$

$$F_c(c) = \Phi\left(\frac{c - \mu_c}{\mu_c \Omega_c}\right) \qquad (2.4)$$

where μ_c, Ω_c = mean and coefficient-of-variation of c, respectively; $\phi(\cdot)$, $\Phi(\cdot)$ = probability density function and cumulative distribution function for the standard normal distribution, respectively.

b) Probability density function and cumulative distribution function for lognormal distribution

Table 1. Values of μ_c, Ω_c, λ_c, ξ_c, u and w.

Structural details	Figure No.	Probability distributions	μ_c, λ_c, w	Ω_c, ξ_c, u
Plates (smooth surface, edges finished)	1	Lognormal	30.659	0.769
Plates (mill scale)	1	Lognormal	30.781	0.823
Rolled beams (mill scale)	2	Normal	1.413×10^{13}	0.488
Transverse butt welds (finished)	3	Weibull	2.193×10^{13}	0.995
Transverse butt welds (non finished)	3	Lognormal	29.125	0.549
Beams with transverse butt welds (finished)	4	Weibull	8.656×10^{12}	2.520
Longitudinal butt welds (finished)	5	Lognormal	30.244	0.914
Longitudinal butt welds (non finished)	5	Lognormal	29.974	0.675
Longitudinal fillet welds (non finished)	6	Lognormal	30.478	0.468
Cruciform transverse butt welds (non finished)	7	Lognormal	27.766	0.839
Load-carrying transverse butt welds (non finished)	8	Lognormal	27.056	0.844
Non-load-carrying transverse fillet welds (finished)	9	Lognormal	28.970	0.460
Non-load-carrying transverse fillet welds (non finished)	9	Lognormal	28.684	0.701
Longitudinal attachments (non finished)	10	Lognormal	28.165	0.391
Cover plates in beams (non finished)	11	Lognormal	26.903	0.225
Stud connections (failure in plates)	12	Lognormal	28.594	0.446

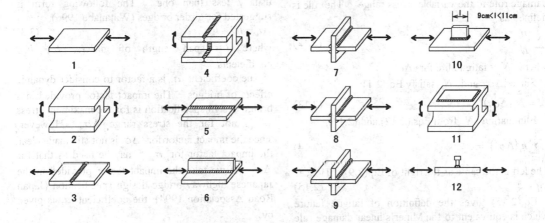

$$f_c(c) = \frac{\phi\left(\dfrac{\ln c - \lambda_c}{\xi_c}\right)}{\xi_c c} \qquad (2.5)$$

$$F_c(c) = \Phi\left(\frac{\ln c - \lambda_c}{\xi_c}\right) \qquad (2.6)$$

where $\lambda_c = \ln \mu_c - \dfrac{\xi_c^2}{2}$; $\xi_c^2 = \ln\left(1 + \Omega_c^2\right)$.

c) Probability density function and cumulative distribution function for Weibull distribution

$$f_c(c) = \frac{u}{w}\left(\frac{c}{w}\right)^{u-1} \exp\left\{-\left(\frac{c}{w}\right)^u\right\} \qquad (2.7)$$

$$F_c(c) = 1 - \exp\left\{-\left(\frac{c}{w}\right)^u\right\} \qquad (2.8)$$

where u, w = parameters to determine the shape of Weibull distribution.

In Table 1 the values on the columns of $\left(\mu_c, \lambda_c, w\right)$ and $\left(\Omega_c, \xi_c, u\right)$ show the values of μ_c and Ω_c for the normal distribution and of λ_c and ξ_c for the lognormal distribution and of u and w for the Weibull distribution. The values are correspondent to the unit (MPa)^3 of c. We call the variable c "fatigue resistance".

2.2 Fatigue-damage-accumulation

For a variable stress range spectrum, we consider the variable q defined as

$$q = \sum_{i=1}^{k} n_i \left(\Delta \sigma_i \right)^3 \qquad (2.9)$$

where $\Delta \sigma_i =$ stress range component; $n_i =$ number of cycles of $\Delta \sigma_i$; $k =$ total number of $\Delta \sigma_i$.

A constant stress range $\Delta \sigma_e$ equal to q at the total number of cycles, $N = \sum_{i=1}^{k} n_i$, is given by

$$q = N \left(\Delta \sigma_e \right)^3 \qquad (2.10)$$

Solving Eqs.(2.9) and (2.10) about $\Delta \sigma_e$,

$$\Delta \sigma_e = \left\{ \sum_{i=1}^{k} \left(\Delta \sigma_i \right)^3 \frac{n_i}{N} \right\}^{\frac{1}{3}} \qquad (2.11)$$

This equation is the same as the equivalent stress range which is given by applying the Miner's linear damage rule to the variable stress range. The rule is defined as

$$\sum_{i=1}^{k} \frac{n_i}{N_i} = 1 \qquad (2.12)$$

where $N_i =$ fatigue life for $\Delta \sigma_i$.

Since $\Delta \sigma_i$ and N_i satisfy Eq.(2.1),

$$c = N_i \left(\Delta \sigma_i \right)^3 \qquad (2.13)$$

Eliminating N_i from Eqs.(2.12) and (2.13),

$$\sum_{i=1}^{k} n_i \left(\Delta \sigma_i \right)^3 = c \qquad (2.14)$$

The left is the same as the right of Eq.(2.9). Hence

$$q = c \qquad (2.15)$$

Eq.(2.15) gives the definition of fatigue failure which is equivalent to the Miner's linear damage rule of Eq.(2.12). Eq.(2.14) shows that when the sum of $n_i \left(\Delta \sigma_i \right)^3$ reaches the fatigue resistance c, fatigue failure occurs. This means that $n_i \left(\Delta \sigma_i \right)^3$ is one component of fatigue damage. From these characteristics, we call the variable q "fatigue-damage-accumulation".

3 GENERAL FORM OF FATIGUE-DAMAGE-ACCUMULATION OF HIGHWAY BRIDGES

For highway bridges, the general form of the fatigue-damage-accumulation q is given by (Watanabe 1996)

$$q = x \psi_1 \psi_2 \left(a_1 a_2 \Delta \sigma_d \frac{P_e}{P_d} \right)^3 V_d \qquad (3.1)$$

where $P_d =$ design fatigue load, which is a concentrated load such as a truck load; $\Delta \sigma_d =$ design stress range produced in the passage of the design fatigue load P_d; $V_d =$ design traffic volume. Other coefficients are stated below.

3.1 Coefficients a_1 and a_2

The coefficient a_1 is a ratio of the actual stress to the stress estimated in practical design, namely

$a_1 =$ (actual stress)/(stress estimated in design)

$$(3.2)$$

The stiffness of secondary members such as parapets, sway bracing and lateral bracing are not taken into account in conventional design, and the effects of lateral load distribution of concrete slabs are not considered either. Thus the coefficient a_1 is usually less than one. The following form is suggested for girder bridges (Watanabe 1996):

$$a_1 = h_1 l + h_2 \qquad (3.3)$$

where $l =$ span length of girders; h_1, $h_2 =$ coefficients.

The coefficient a_2 is a factor to consider dynamic effects of bridges. The impact factor provided in a bridge design specification is for the maximum stress σ_{max}, not for the stress range $\Delta \sigma$. However, since the impact factor for $\Delta \sigma$ is not still made clear, the impact factor for σ_{max} may be used as that for $\Delta \sigma$. If we take the impact factor provided in the Japanese highway bridge design specification (Japan Road Association 1994), the coefficient a_2 is given by

$$a_2 = 1 + i \qquad (3.4)$$

where

$$i = \frac{20}{50 + l} \qquad (3.5)$$

$i =$ impact factor provided in the Japanese highway bridge design specification; $l =$ span length of girders (in m).

3.2 Multiple presence fatigue factor ψ_2

The coefficient ψ_2 is a factor to consider the multiple presence of several vehicles passing through a bridge (Fujino 1986). It is defined by

$\psi_2 =$ (actual fatigue-damage-accumulation for the passage of vehicles)/(fatigue-damage-accumulation for the individual passage of vehicles) (3.6)

The following form is suggested for girder bridges (Watanabe 1996):

$$\psi_2 = h_3 l + h_4 \qquad (3.7)$$

where h_3, h_4 = functions of the mean headway distance of vehicles.

3.3 Equivalent load P_e

The load P_e is the equivalent load defined as

$$P_e = \left\{ \int_0^{P_{max}} P^3 f_P(P) dP \right\}^{\frac{1}{3}} \qquad (3.8)$$

where $f_P(P)$ = probability density function for a load distribution of vehicles; P_{max} – maximum load of vehicles.

Let

$$\alpha = \left(\frac{P_e}{P_d} \right)^3 = \frac{P_e^3}{P_d^3} \qquad (3.9)$$

The coefficient α shows a ratio of the 3rd power of the equivalent load P_e to the 3rd power of the design fatigue load P_d. Hence the coefficient α gives the definition of a truck-mixing-ratio based on the design fatigue load.

With α, Eq.(3.1) becomes

$$q = x \psi_1 \psi_2 (a_1 a_2 \Delta \sigma_d)^3 \alpha V_d \qquad (3.10)$$

3.4 Coefficients x and ψ_1

The coefficient x is a factor to correct any imperfections involved in the coefficients a_1, a_2 and ψ_2. Since those coefficients are usually determined based on a few experimental and analytical studies and some engineering judgment, they are possibly different from the actual ones. Then, the coefficient x is treated as a random variable.

The coefficient ψ_1 is a factor to consider change of traffic load and volume during a design fatigue life. The coefficient ψ_1 is given by a function of time, using a monitoring bridge.

The method to determine x and ψ_1 will be stated in Chapter 5.

4 FATIGUE RELIABILITY ASSESSMENT OF HIGHWAY BRIDGES

4.1 Safety conditions on fatigue failure

The safety conditions on fatigue failure are

established by applying the advanced first-order second-moment method to the state function of

$$g = c - q \qquad (4.1)$$

When the probability distributions for c and q are not normal, they are transformed into an equivalent normal distribution. Next, the safety conditions on fatigue failure will be provided for the case where c and q follow a lognormal distribution and a normal distribution, respectively.

The design point (c^*, q^*), at which the possibility of fatigue failure is highest on the limit state of $g = 0$, is given by

$$c^* = \frac{\exp\left(1 - \frac{1}{r_{cN}}\right)}{\sqrt{1 + \Omega_c^2}} \mu_c \qquad (4.2)$$

$$q^* = r_{qN} \mu_q \qquad (4.3)$$

where

$$r_{cN} = 1 - \frac{\theta (r_{cN} \xi_c)^2 \beta}{\sqrt{\theta^2 (r_{cN} \xi_c)^2 + \Omega_q^2}} \qquad (4.4)$$

$$r_{qN} = 1 + \frac{\Omega_q^2 \beta}{\sqrt{\theta^2 (r_{cN} \xi_c)^2 + \Omega_q^2}} \qquad (4.5)$$

$$\theta = \frac{1 + \beta \sqrt{(r_{cN} \xi_c)^2 + \Omega_q^2 - \beta^2 (r_{cN} \xi_c)^2 \Omega_q^2}}{1 - \beta^2 (r_{cN} \xi_c)^2} \qquad (4.6)$$

μ_q, Ω_q = mean and coefficient-of-variation of q, respectively; β – reliability index.

The safety conditions on fatigue failure are

$$c^* \geq q^* \qquad (4.7)$$

The substitution of Eqs.(4.2) and (4.3) into Eq.(4.7) gives

$$\frac{\exp\left(1 - \frac{1}{r_{cN}}\right)}{\sqrt{1 + \Omega_c^2}} \mu_c \geq r_{qN} \mu_q \qquad (4.8)$$

Let

$$r_c = \frac{\exp\left(1 - \frac{1}{r_{cN}}\right)}{\sqrt{1 + \Omega_c^2}} \qquad (4.9)$$

$$r_q = r_{qN} \qquad (4.10)$$

Then Eq.(4.8) becomes

$$r_c \mu_c \geq r_q \mu_q \qquad (4.11)$$

4.2 Fatigue assessment of highway bridges

When designing a new bridge, the value of ψ_1 must

be evaluated at the design fatigue life. The value will be estimated from load surveys and traffic censuses carried out in the past. Let the evaluated value be denoted by ψ_{1d}. Using it for ψ_1 in Eq.(3.10), the design fatigue-damage-accumulation q_d is expressed by

$$q_d = x\psi_{1d}\psi_2\left(a_1 a_2 \Delta\sigma_d\right)^3 \alpha V_d \qquad (4.12)$$

Since the coefficient x is a random variable, the variable q_d has

$$\mu_{q_d} = \mu_x \psi_{1d}\psi_2\left(a_1 a_2 \Delta\sigma_d\right)^3 \alpha V_d \qquad (4.13)$$

$$\Omega_{q_d} = \Omega_x \qquad (4.14)$$

where μ_{q_d}, Ω_{q_d} = mean and coefficient-of-variation of q_d, respectively; μ_x, Ω_x = mean and coefficient-of-variation of x, respectively.

Eq.(4.14) is used for Ω_q of Eqs.(4.4), (4.5) and (4.6). Let the value of β prescribed in the fatigue design be denoted by β_d. The relationship between β_d and r_{cN} is determined from Eqs.(4.4) and (4.6). The substitution of β_d and r_{cN} into Eq.(4.5) determines r_{qN}.

Substitution of Eq.(4.13) into μ_q of Eq.(4.11) gives

$$r_c\mu_c \geq r_q\left(\Delta\sigma_{ed}\right)^3 N_d \qquad (4.15)$$

where

$$\Delta\sigma_{ed} = \left(\mu_x\psi_2\right)^{\frac{1}{3}} a_1 a_2 \Delta\sigma_d \qquad (4.16)$$

$$N_d = \psi_{1d}\alpha V_d \qquad (4.17)$$

$\Delta\sigma_{ed}$ and N_d are the design equivalent stress range and the design number of cycles, respectively.

The design $S-N$ curves in a fatigue design specification give the following allowable fatigue resistance c_a:

$$c_a = 2\times 10^6 \left(\Delta\sigma_{a200}\right)^3 \qquad (4.18)$$

where $\Delta\sigma_{a200}$ = allowable fatigue stress at 2 million cycles.

Let

$$r_{ca} = \frac{c_a}{\mu_o} \qquad (4.19)$$

Eliminating μ_c from Eqs.(4.15) and (4.19),

$$\left(\frac{r_c}{r_{ca}}\right)^{\frac{1}{3}}\left(\frac{c_a}{N_d}\right)^{\frac{1}{3}} \geq r_q^{\frac{1}{3}}\Delta\sigma_{ed} \qquad (4.20)$$

The term $\left(c_a/N_d\right)^{1/3}$ is the allowable fatigue stress for the design number of cycles, that is

$$\Delta\sigma_a = \left(\frac{c_a}{N_d}\right)^{\frac{1}{3}} \qquad (4.21)$$

Then, let

$$r_R = \left(\frac{r_c}{r_{ca}}\right)^{\frac{1}{3}} \qquad (4.22)$$

$$r_Q = r_q^{\frac{1}{3}} \qquad (4.23)$$

Eq.(4.20) becomes

$$r_R\Delta\sigma_a \geq r_Q\Delta\sigma_{ed} \qquad (4.24)$$

This gives the fatigue assessment of highway bridges. The coefficients r_R and r_Q are partial safety factors.

4.3 $\beta - t/t_d$ relationship

The fatigue-damage-accumulation q_t in a time t after opening to traffic of a bridge designed by Eq.(4.24) is expressed by

$$q_t = x\psi_{1t}\psi_2\left(a_1 a_2 \Delta\sigma_d\right)^3 \alpha \frac{V_d}{t_d} t \qquad (4.25)$$

where t_d = design fatigue life.
Since the variable ψ_1 is a function of time, it is denoted by ψ_{1t}.

The variable q_t has

$$\mu_{q_t} = \mu_x \psi_{1t}\psi_2\left(a_1 a_2 \Delta\sigma_d\right)^3 \alpha \frac{V_d}{t_d} t \qquad (4.26)$$

$$\Omega_{q_t} = \Omega_x \qquad (4.27)$$

where μ_{q_t}, Ω_{q_t} = mean and coefficient-of-variation of q_t, respectively.

Using Eqs.(4.16) and (4.17) for Eq.(4.26),

$$\mu_{q_t} = \left(\Delta\sigma_{ed}\right)^3 N_d \frac{\psi_{1t}}{\psi_{1d}}\frac{t}{t_d} \qquad (4.28)$$

Substituting μ_{q_t} into μ_q of Eq.(4.8),

$$\frac{\exp\left(1-\dfrac{1}{r_{cN}}\right)}{\sqrt{1+\Omega_c^2}}\mu_c \geq r_{qN}\left(\Delta\sigma_{ed}\right)^3 N_d \frac{\psi_{1t}}{\psi_{1d}}\frac{t}{t_d} \qquad (4.29)$$

Eliminating c_a from Eqs.(4.19) and (4.21),

$$\mu_c = \frac{\left(\Delta\sigma_a\right)^3 N_d}{r_{ca}} \qquad (4.30)$$

Using μ_c for Eq.(4.29),

$$\frac{\exp\left(1-\dfrac{1}{r_{cN}}\right)}{r_{ca}\sqrt{1+\Omega_c^2}}\left(\frac{\Delta\sigma_a}{\Delta\sigma_{ed}}\right)^3 \geq \frac{\psi_{1t}}{\psi_{1d}}\frac{t}{t_d} r_{qN} \qquad (4.31)$$

Eq.(4.24) gives

$$\left(\frac{\Delta\sigma_a}{\Delta\sigma_{ed}}\right)^3 \geq \left(\frac{r_Q}{r_R}\right)^3 \qquad (4.32)$$

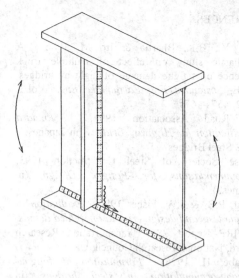

Fig.3.   Crack at the end of a vertical stiffener.

When Eqs.(4.31) and (4.32) are in equality each, elimination of $(\Delta\sigma_a/\Delta\sigma_{ed})^3$ from both equations gives

$$\frac{1}{r_{ca}}\left(\frac{r_Q}{r_R}\right)^3\frac{1}{\sqrt{1+\Omega_c^2}}\exp\left(1-\frac{1}{r_{cN}}\right)=\frac{\psi_{1t}}{\psi_{1d}}\frac{t}{t_d}r_{qN} \qquad (4.33)$$

Eqs.(4.4), (4.5), (4.6) and (4.33) make the relationship between β and t/t_d.

4.4   Numerical example

With a crack at the end of a vertical stiffener as shown in Fig. 3, the partial safety factors r_R and r_Q and the $\beta-t/t_d$ relationship are determined.

The Japanese fatigue design recommendation (Japanese Society of Steel Construction 1993) specifies the allowable fatigue stress of 80 MPa at 2 million cycles for the detail in Fig. 3, with the result of $c_a=1.024\times10^{12}$ (MPa)^3 from Eq.(4.18).   The non-load-carrying transverse fillet welds (non finished) in Table 1 is applied to this detail.   The fatigue resistance c of the non-load-carrying transverse fillet welds (non finished) complies with a lognormal distribution with $\lambda_c=28.68$, $\xi_c=0.7014$, $\mu_c=3.665\times10^{12}$ (MPa)^3 and $\Omega_c=0.7972$. Eq.(4.19) gives $r_{ca}=0.2794$.

The fatigue-damage-accumulation q is assumed to be a normal distribution with $\Omega_q=\Omega_x=0.5$.

The partial safety factors r_R and r_Q are determined for $\beta_d=2$.

With the above values, Eqs.(4.4) and (4.6) give $r_{cN}=0.4429$, resulting in $r_c=0.2223$ from Eq.(4.9). Substitution of $r_{cN}=0.4429$ into Eq.(4.5) gives $r_{qN}=1.443$, resulting in $r_a=1.443$ from Eq.(4.10). Eqs.(4.22) and (4.23) give $r_R=0.93$ and $r_Q=1.13$, respectively.

With $r_R=0.93$ and $r_Q=1.13$, Eqs.(4.4), (4.5), (4.6) and (4.33) make the $\beta-(\psi_{1t}/\psi_{1d})(t/t_d)$ curve as shown in Fig. 4(a).   The curve passes through the point $((\psi_{1t}/\psi_{1d})(t/t_d)=1,\beta=\beta_d(=2))$.   In Fig. 4(b) the logarithm scale is used on the horizontal axis. The $\beta-(\psi_{1t}/\psi_{1d})(t/t_d)$ relationship is expressed in the following form:

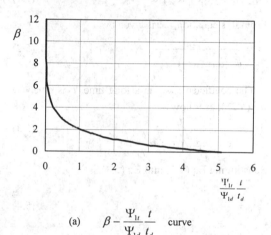

(a) $\beta-\dfrac{\Psi_{1t}}{\Psi_{1d}}\dfrac{t}{t_d}$ curve

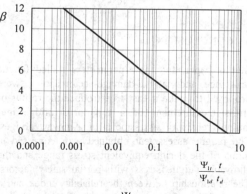

(b) $\beta-\log\dfrac{\Psi_{1t}}{\Psi_{1d}}\dfrac{t}{t_d}$ curve

Fig.4. $\beta-t/t_d$ relationship.

$$\beta = \beta_d - A\log\frac{\psi_{1t}}{\psi_{1d}}\frac{t}{t_d}$$ (4.34)

where A = coefficient.

5 METHOD TO DETERMINE x AND ψ_{1t} USING MONITORING BRIDGE

The coefficient ψ_{1t} is determined by monitoring the stress in a bridge. By application of Eq.(2.9) to the monitored stress, the fatigue-damage-accumulation q_t is obtained. During a short period from $t = 0$ to t_0 at the beginning of the monitoring, ψ_{1t} may be one because of the small variation of traffic load and volume during a short period. Hence, putting $\psi_{1t} = 1$ in Eq.(4.25),

$$q_{t_0} = x\psi_2\left(a_1 a_2 \Delta\sigma_d\right)^3 \alpha\frac{V_d}{t_d}t_0$$ (5.1)

From this equation, x is given by

$$x = \frac{q_{t_0}}{\psi_2\left(a_1 a_2 \Delta\sigma_d\right)^3 \alpha\dfrac{V_d}{t_d}t_0}$$ (5.2)

The coefficient ψ_{1t} in a long time t is given by Eq.(4.25), as follows:

$$\psi_{1t} = \frac{q_t}{x\psi_2\left(a_1 a_2 \Delta\sigma_d\right)^3 \alpha\dfrac{V_d}{t_d}t}$$ (5.3)

Substituting Eq.(5.2) into Eq.(5.3),

$$\psi_{1t} = \frac{\dfrac{q_t}{t}}{\dfrac{q_{t_0}}{t_0}}$$ (5.4)

This equation determines ψ_{1t}.

6 CONCLUSION

In this paper, two new parameters, called fatigue resistance and fatigue-damage-accumulation, were proposed to make it easy to introduce the results of stress measurement of a monitored bridge into fatigue reliability assessment of highway bridges. The fatigue assessment obtained was expressed in terms of the design equivalent stress range and the allowable fatigue stress with partial safety factors. The relationship between the reliability index and a lapse of time from opening to traffic was shown. The method to determine the unknown factors involved in the fatigue-damage-accumulation, using a monitoring bridge was provided.

REFERENCES

Fujino, Y., B.K. Bhartia & Ito M. 1986. A stochastic study on effect of multiple truck presence on fatigue damage of highway bridges. JSCE, *Structural Eng./Earthquake Eng.*, Vol.3, No.2, 457s-467s.

Japan Road Association 1994. *Standard Specification for Highway Bridges* (in Japanese). No.2 Steel Bridges.

Japanese Society of Steel Construction 1993. *Recommendations for Fatigue Design* (in Japanese).

Keating, P.B. & J.W. Fisher 1986. *Evaluation of fatigue tests and design criteria on welded details*. NCHRP Report 286, Transportation Research Board, National Research Council, USA.

Watanabe, H. 1996. *Formulation of fatigue-damage-accumulation in steel bridges* (in Japanese). Thesis for Master degree in Civil Engineering, Osaka University, Japan.

Yamada, K. 1988. *Making fatigue test database and evaluation of allowable fatigue stress* (in Japanese). Research Report 61550327, Grant-in-Aid for Science Research (C), The Ministry of Education, Science, Sports and Culture, Japan.

Structural Safety and Reliability, Shiraishi, Shinozuka & Wen (eds) © 1998 Balkema, Rotterdam, ISBN 90 5410 978 5

Target safety levels for bridges

Andrzej S. Nowak, Maria M. Szerszen & Chan Hee Park
Department of Civil and Environmental Engineering, University of Michigan, Ann Arbor, Mich., USA

ABSTRACT: The development of limit state codes and/or load resistance factor design (LRFD) codes for the design of bridges requires the knowledge of the target reliability level. The optimum safety level depends on the consequences of failure and cost of safety. Selection of the target value can be based on consideration of these two parameters. The analysis is performed for ultimate limit states (ULS) and serviceability limit states (SLS). Serviceability limit states have a lower level of consequences of failure. Therefore, lower values of the target reliability index are selected for SLS than ULS.

1 INTRODUCTION

Recent developments in design codes point to the need for rational criteria in the selection of target safety levels. Safety can be calculated using one of the available methods. The question which has to be considered is how safe is safe enough or what is the minimum acceptable safety. The objective of this paper is to formulate the problem and to provide a summary of a practical procedure for its solution. The analysis is focused on highway bridges and it is demonstrated on the AASHTO Codes (traditional and new LRFD) in the United States and BS-5400 in the United Kingdom.

Load and resistance parameters are random variables. In particular, this applies to frequency of occurrence, magnitude of live loads, material properties, dimensions and geometry. Traditional measurement of structural performance in terms of safety factor is not sufficient. A new generation of design codes is based on quantification of the safety margin measured in terms of the reliability index.

Statistical models of load and resistance for highway bridges are described by Nowak (1995; 1993), Tabsh and Nowak (1992), Nowak and Hong (1992) and Hwang and Nowak (1992). The available parameters can be used to determine the reliability indices for structures designed according to the current code provisions. For bridges designed by AASHTO (1992), the analysis was performed by Nowak (1995). Similarly, for steel bridges designed using BS-5400, the calculations were performed by Nowak, Park and Szerszen (1997). The results indicate a considerable degree of variation (large scatter). It is clear that such a variation is not justified and should be eliminated or at least reduced.

Structural failure can be associated with various limit states. Ultimate limit states are related to loss of load carrying capacity, such as flexural strength, shear capacity, loss of stability, rupture, and so on. Serviceability limit states are related to cracking, deflection and vibration. Fatigue limit states are reached as a result of repeated load applications. Each structural component is designed to satisfy various safety requirements corresponding to different limit states. Therefore, it is practically impossible to avoid over-design. In most cases, only one limit state governs. Therefore, optimum design requires the optimization of the governing limit states.

Reliability indices calculated for existing bridges are reviewed. In most cases, these values can be considered as the lower bounds of safety levels acceptable by the society. A drastic departure from these acceptable limits should be based on a thorough economic analysis. Optimum safety can be determined by minimization of the total expected cost (or maximization of the utility).

2 RELIABILITY INDICES FOR CURRENT DESIGN CODES

Reliability indices were calculated for representative bridges in conjunction with the development of the new LRFD AASHTO bridge design code (Nowak 1995). The analysis was performed for selected existing structures and for idealized structures. The latter were considered without any over-design, it was assumed that the provided resistance is exactly equal to design loads.

For the ultimate limit states of flexural capacity (bending moment) and shear capacity, the results are shown in Fig. 1. The reliability indices are shown for idealized bridges, designed exactly according to the code provisions. However, most of existing structures are over-designed. The ratio of the existing resistance and resistance required by the code varies. The actual values are shown in Fig. 2 (Nowak 1995).

The reliability indices were calculated for selected representative bridges in the United Kingdom. The results are shown in Fig.3 for moment and shear.

The absolute values of β's are rather high. Furthermore, there is a considerable scatter.

Reinforced Concrete T-Beams - Moment

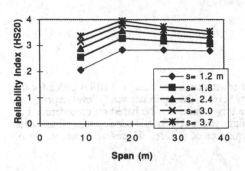

Prestressed Concrete Girder - Shear

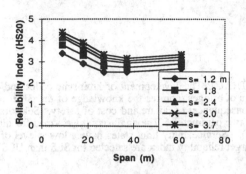

Reinforced Concrete T-Beams - Shear

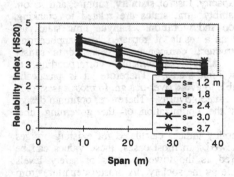

Steel Girder - Moment

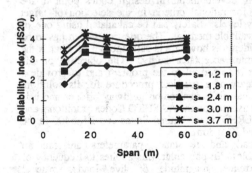

Prestressed Concrete Girder - Moment

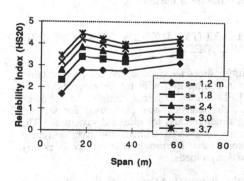

Steel Girder - Shear

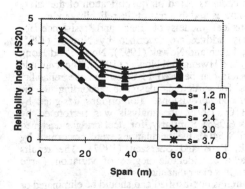

Fig.1. Reliability Indices for ULS in Bridges Designed by AASHTO (1992).

Reinforced Concrete T-Beams - Moment

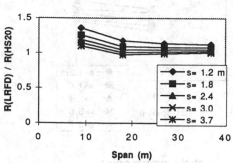

Prestressed Concrete Girder - Shear

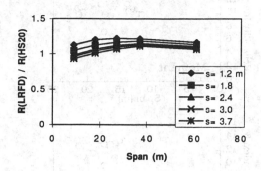

Reinforced Concrete T-Beams - Shear

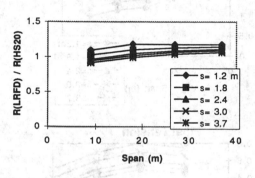

Steel Girder - Moment

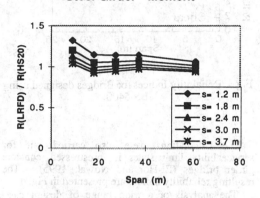

Prestressed Concrete Girder - Moment

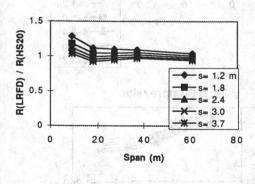

Steel Girder - Shear

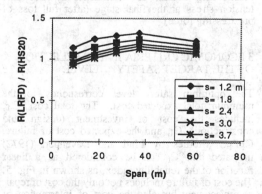

Fig. 2. Ratio of Actual Resistance and Resistance Required by the Code for ULS in Bridges Designed by AASHTO (1992).

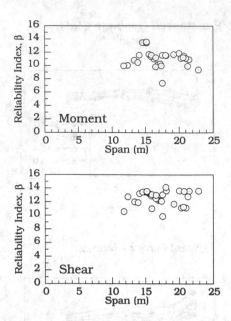

Fig.3. Reliability Indices for Bridges designed using
BS-5400

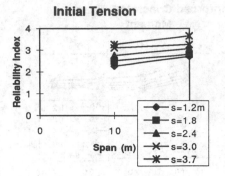

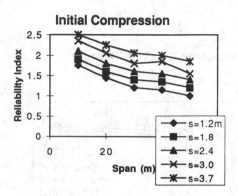

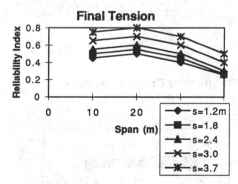

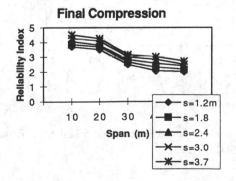

Fig. 4. Reliability Indices for SLS in Prestressed
Concrete Girder Bridges Designed by AASHTO (1992).

The calculations were also carried out for serviceability limit states in prestressed concrete girder bridges (El-Hor and Nowak 1995). The resulting reliability indices are presented in Fig. 4.

The analysis of a wide range of design cases indicates that the ultimate limit state never governs in prestressed concrete girders. The number of prestressing strands is determined by allowable tension stress at the final stage (after full loss of prestressing force).

3 ECONOMIC CRITERIA IN THE SELECTION OF THE TARGET SAFETY LEVEL

The optimum safety level corresponds to the minimum total expected cost. The total cost, C_T, includes the cost of investment (design and construction), C_I, and the expected cost of failure, $C_F P_F$. Studies by Lind and Davenport (1972) indicated that C_I can be considered as a linear function of the reliability index, as shown in Fig. 5. The cost of failure includes not only the cost of repair or replacement but also the cost of interruption of use, and legal costs (liability in case injuries).

In practice, the failure cost, C_F, can be considered as independent of the reliability index. On the other hand, the probability of failure, P_F, decreases with increasing reliability index. Therefore, the expected cost of failure is a function of the reliability index β as shown in Fig. 5.

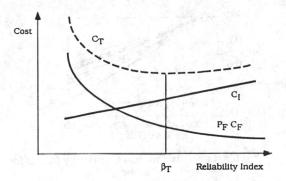

Fig. 5. Cost vs. Reliability Index and Optimum
Safety Level

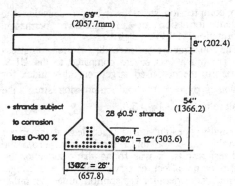

Fig.6. Prestressed concrete AASHTO Type IV
Girder

The optimum safety level, or target reliability index, can be determined by considering the sum of both cost components, i.e. C_I and C_F P_F as shown in Fig. 5. The optimum reliability index corresponds to the minimum of C_T.

4 ULTIMATE LIMIT STATES

For ultimate limit states, the calculated reliability indices (Fig. 1) represent component reliability rather than system. The reliability indices for structural system were calculated by Tabsh and Nowak (1991) and they are larger than β for individual girders by about 2, i.e. instead of $\beta = 3$-4, the system $\beta = 5$-6. The selection of the target reliability level should be directed to consideration of the system. Then, target reliability index for components (girders) can be derived using the appropriate formulas.

In the development of new LRFD Code (AASHTO 1994), the target reliability index for a component (girder) was selected equal to $\beta_T = 3.5$. The load and resistance factors were determined so that the corresponding reliability indices for ULS exceed the target value.

5 SERVICEABILITY LIMIT STATES

The current practice can be considered as representing at least a minimum acceptable limit. For serviceability limit states, reliability indices vary considerably depending on the considered limit state. Serviceability limit states were examined for three types of bridge girder cross-section: prestressed concrete AASHTO type girder, reinforced concrete T-section, and steel girder section. For prestressed concrete AASHTO type girders Fig.6, the lowest values are obtained for tension stress after final loss of prestress.

Tension stress limit is imposed as a protection of prestressing steel. An open crack may cause an accelerated deterioration (corrosion) of steel or concrete. Specific dynamic loading can enlarge the crack opening, even the stresses are in service range.

An exceeding of a compression stress limit in concrete girders may result in an excessive creeping.

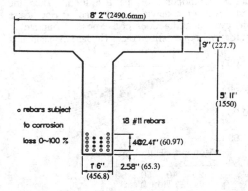

Fig.7. Reinforced Concrete T-Section Girder

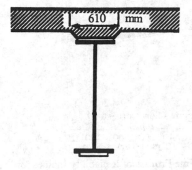

Fig.8. Steel Girder Section

A compression stress limit is also considered to prevent formation of an excessive permanent deformation (kink) in the girder.

The consequences of exceeding the tension stress limit are much less severe compared to the ULS. Therefore, the proposed target reliability index for tension is $\beta_T = 1.0$. For compression stress, the target reliability is $\beta_T = 3.0$.

Usually, design codes specified a maximum allowable deflection under service load. From the field test results, it was found that deflection by itself does not affect the serviceability of the bridge. The main consideration is a comfort of the user rather than structural safety. This does not include excessive deformations preceeding structural failure. These observations were used to develop design criteria. During runs of test vehicles, observers suggested that the vibrations rather than deflections were identified as the main problem. Vibration can be controlled by limiting the dynamic load effect.

Fatigue state can be related to serviceability limit state too. Depending on the major factors like stress range and number of load cycles, fatigue phenomenon can occur, specially for concrete girders. The total fatigue load includes the static and dynamic components of the live load. When the effort level for concrete is under the service stress limit, cycle loading does not expose concrete to degradation, but existing cracks (in case of accidental

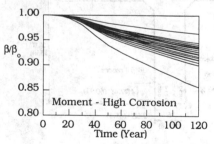

Fig.9a. Life-Time Profiles of Reliability Indices for Moment

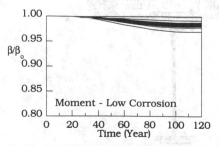

Fig.9b. Life-Time Profiles of Reliability Indices for Moment

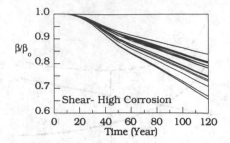

Fig.10a. Life-Time Profiles of Reliability Indices for Shear

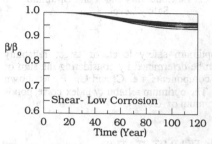

Fig.10b. Life-Time Profiles of Reliability Indices for Shear

overloading) will cumulate due to service live of structure. For the relatively low stress level, an equivalent fatigue live load effect can be derived using Miner's rule. The fatigue capacity of a girder is a random variable. Its distribution may be established on the basis of the available test data, then the fatigue reliability can be calculated.

6 EFFECT OF DETERIORATION

Reliability indices can be reduced due to deterioration, in particular corrosion. The analysis was performed by Nowak, Park and Szerszen (1997) for selected bridges designed using BS-5400.

The initial (as designed) values of β are shown in Fig.3. Two rates of corrosion are considered: high corresponding to marine and chemically aggressive environment, and low corresponding to dry and mild conditions. The relationship between β and time is presented in Fig.9a,b for moment and in Fig.10a,b for shear.

7 CONCLUSIONS

Target reliability index is considered for girder bridges. For the ultimate limit states, the proposed value is determined for components, $\beta_T = 3.5$ and structural systems, $\beta_T = 5.5$.

For the serviceability limit states, stress limits in prestressed concrete girders are considered. The design is governed by tension stress limit at service loads (after final loss of prestress). The corresponding target reliability index is 1.0.

Effect of deterioration caused by corrosion on moment and shear carrying capacity is shown for selected bridges. Low and high rate of corrosion are considered.

It was found the shear capacity is more sensitive to section loss. The target reliability level should be established for the predicted life-time of the structure.

ACKNOWLEDGMENTS

The presented study has been partially supported by NSF, grant MSS-9301387, with Dr. Ken Chong, Program Director, SHRP IDEA Project NCHRP-93-ID002, with K. Thirumalai, Program Manager, and NATO Cooperative Partner Program.

REFERENCES

AASHTO, *Standard Specifications for Highway Bridges*, American Association of State Highway and Transportation Officials, Washington, D.C. (1992).

AASHTO, *LRFD Bridge Design Specifications*, American Association of State Highway and Transportation Officials, Washington, D.C. (1994).

Hwang, E-S. and Nowak, A.S., 1991, "Simulation of Dynamic Load for Bridges", *ASCE Journal of Structural Engineering*, Vol. 117, No. 5, pp. 1413-1434.

Lind, N.C. and Davenport, A.G., 1972, "Towards Practical Application of Structural Reliability Theory", in *Probabilistic Design of Reinforced Concrete Buildings*, ACI SP-31, pp. 63-110.

Nowak, A.S., 1995, "Calibration of LRFD Bridge Code", ASCE *Journal of Structural Engineering*, Vol. 121, No. 8, pp. 1245-1251.

Nowak, A.S. and El-Hor, H.H., 1995, "Serviceability Criteria for Prestressed Concrete

Bridge Girders", *Transportation Research Board*, Conference Proceedings 7, Vol. 2, pp. 181-187.

El-Hor H. H., 1995, *Serviceability Criteria in Prestressed Concrete Bridge Girders*, PhD Thesis, University of Michigan

Nowak, A.S., 1993, "Live Load Model for Highway Bridges", *Journal of Structural Safety*, Vol. 13, Nos. 1+2, December, pp. 53-66.

Nowak, A.S. and Hong, Y-K., 1991, "Bridge Live Load Models", *ASCE Journal of Structural Engineering*, Vol. 117, No. 9, pp. 2757-2767.

Thoft-Christensen, P. and Baker, M.J., *Structural Reliability Theory and Its Applications*, Springer-Verlag, (1982) p. 267.

Tabsh, S.W. and Nowak, A.S., "Reliability of Highway Girder Bridges," *ASCE Journal of Structural Engineering*, Vol. 117, No. 8, (1991), pp. 2373-2388.

Nowak A. S., Park Ch. H., Szerszen M. M., 1997, *Revision of Bridge Assessment Rules Based on Whole Life Performance, Steel Girder Bridges*, Final Report

Structural Safety and Reliability, Shiraishi, Shinozuka & Wen (eds) © 1998 Balkema, Rotterdam, ISBN 90 5410 978 5

Impact factors of steel multigirder highway bridges due to vehicular loadings

Sang-Hyo Kim & Sang-Ho Lee
Department of Civil Engineering, Yonsei University, Seoul, Korea

Jae-Ik Jung
Daewoo Engineering, Korea

ABSTRACT: The dynamic behaviors of multi-girder steel bridges under moving heavy vehicles have been evaluated using 3-dimensional space frame bridge models and 7-DOF nonlinear truck models. The validity of the developed analysis procedure has been demonstrated by comparing with the experimental data. The road surface profiles randomly generated from PSD function models have been modified by a new filtering method to achieve more rational bridge-vehicle wheel interactions. The dynamic responses of various bridges designed according to current design practice are examined, in which important structural parameters(such as span length, girder spacing, etc) are considered systematically. The effect of bridge entrance settlement is evaluated. In addition to the basic loading conditions due to a single truck passing on the bridge, the traffic conditions of multi-truck traveling either consecutively on the same lane or side-by-side on adjacent lanes are also evaluated.

1 INTRODUCTION

The highway bridge superstructures experience dynamic behaviors due to the moving vehicles. The dynamic responses are generally amplified and they result in higher displacements and stresses than the static responses. Therefore, it is vitally needed to accurately estimate the amount of dynamic amplification for the design purpose. However, since the dynamic responses of highway bridges depend on various structural features as well as vehicle characteristics, it is quite difficult for bridge engineers to estimate the dynamic amplification in the design stage.

The bridge design codes specify the dynamic amplification of highway bridges as the impact factor in a very simple format. In most design codes the impact factor is specified as a function of either the loaded length or the natural frequency of the first vibration mode. However, many theoretical and experimental investigations have indicated that the dynamic amplification of a bridge may depend on many other factors, such as bridge type, vehicle characteristics, traveling speed, vehicle weight, road surface profile, etc(Huang 1993, Wang 1996).

The steel plate girder bridge, either composite or non-composite, is the most widely adopted type of highway bridge superstructure throughout the world. The span length of steel girder bridges ranges between 25~80m, which may depends on the span continuity(simple or continuous type). Therefore, the live load portion is generally larger than the dead load portion and then the fatigue damage sustained by bridge superstructure is a significant problem. For mid-span bridge, the ultimate state against structural failure is governed by the passage of a very heavy vehicle, whereas the amount of fatigue damage is accumulated by the moderately loaded trucks.

The objective of this study is to examine the dynamic response characteristics of multi-girder steel bridges under the action of traveling vehicles with various example bridges designed according to current design practice, in which important structural parameters(such as span length, deck width, girder spacing, etc.) are considered systematically. The effect of settlement at the bridge entrance is evaluated. In addition to the basic loading conditions due to a single truck traveling in different speeds as well as different positions, the traffic conditions of multiple trucks traveling either consecutively on the same lane or side-by-side on adjacent lanes are also simulated. The effect of another truck passing away is also examined.

2 ANALYTICAL MODELS

2.1 *Bridge models*

The multi-girder steel bridges have been designed

according to Korean Design Standard for Highway Bridge(1992). The design traffic load applied to the bridge is exactly the same as HS-20 of AASHTO Standard Specification except that the load magnitude is 33% higher. Therefore, the total weight of the design truck is 43.2 tons. The design impact factor is recommended as a function of the loaded length, L, with the upper limit of 0.3:

$$I = \frac{15}{40 + L} \le 0.3 \tag{1}$$

Both 2-lane and 4-lane bridges are designed and the cross sections are shown in **Fig. 1**. The deck width ranges from 8.6m to 8.9m for 2-lane bridges and from 16.0m to 16.3m for 4-lane bridges. In 2-lane bridges 4 identical girders are arranged with equal spacing. The number of girders ranges from 6 to 8 for 4-lane bridges. The girder spacing ranges from 2.0m to 3.6m.

The analytical models for multi-girder bridges have been formulated with the 3-dimensional space frame elements in grillage systems. The section properties of longitudinal elements in the grillage beam system represent the composite sections of the steel plate girders and R.C. slab, while the transverse elements stand for slab and vertical bracings. The vertical bracings are arranged properly depending on the span length.

2.2 *Vehicle model*

A 7-DOF nonlinear vehicle model has been employed to represent the truck with tandem axle, which is the most frequent heavy vehicle type. The model is shown in **Fig. 2**. The basic vehicle model is assumed to have a total weight of 25ton.

The dynamic responses of the bridge and the vehicle are evaluated using the direct integration method, specifically Newmark-β method. The vehicle load effects are assumed to be transferred through the wheel contact and the interaction force between the wheel and bridge is computed as a function of the relative displacement and velocity between the wheel and bridge as well as the stiffness and damping of tire. The negative or upward interaction force is neglected.

The validity of the developed analysis procedure has been examined by comparing the simulated results with the experimental data that have been obtained through the AASHO Road Test. Fenves has performed systematic dynamic tests with a experimental steel girder-R.C. slab composite bridge.

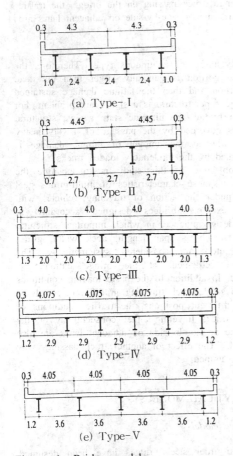

(a) Type-I

(b) Type-II

(c) Type-III

(d) Type-IV

(e) Type-V

Figure. 1 Bridge models

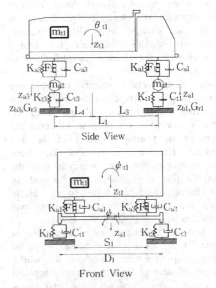

Side View

Front View

Figure. 2 Vehicle model

2.3 Road surface models

2.3.1 Road roughness models

The basic road surface profiles are generated first through Monte Carlo simulation technique using the power spectral density(PSD) function models developed by Dodds and Robson and modified by Wang and Huang(Dodds 1973, Huang 1993). The PSD is defined as the following function:

$$S(k) = A_r(\frac{k}{k_0})^{-2} \qquad (2)$$

in which A_r = roughness coefficient(m³/cycle), k = wave number(cycle/m), k_0 = discontinuity wave number = $1/2 \pi$ (cycle/m).

The roughness coefficient can be selected for different road conditions according to International Organization for Standardization (ISO) specifications, in which the roughness coefficient ranges between the upper and lower bounds. In this study, the median values, 5×10^{-6}, 20×10^{-6}, 80×10^{-6} and 256×10^{-6} m³/cycle, were used for very good, good, average and poor roughness conditions, respectively.

The PSD models adopted are compared with the functions obtained from road survey data in **Fig. 3**(Kawatani,1997). The roughness levels of norma condition decks are found to be between the good and average roughness conditions.

The road surface profile is obtained as a stationary Gaussian random process from the following function:

$$R(s) = \sum_{i=1}^{N} C_i \cos(2\pi ks + \theta_i) \qquad (3)$$

where C_i = amplitude of harmonic curve = $\sqrt{4S(k) \cdot \Delta k}$, θ_i = independent random phase angles distributed uniformly over the range(0, 2π).

The obtained process implies periodicity with a period, $S_0 = 1/\Delta k$, and is asymptotically Gaussian for large N due to the central limit theorem. The basic profiles generated from Eq. (3) are filtered through a new filtering technique to remove high frequency terms and achieve more rational bridge-vehicle wheel interactions. The filtering method generates the modified profile by tracing the wheel moving on the originally generated road surface. As shown in **Fig. 4**, the deep valleys are removed from the originals in the filtered road surface profiles. Otherwise the wheel modeled as a point load may drop into the deep valley, and this can not happen in the real situation.

2.3.2 Settlement models

The road surface may undergo a drastic change of surface elevation due to either settlement of an approaching slab or a gap of an expansion joint, which may increase the dynamic amplification of a bridge. Since the road surface adjacent to such a

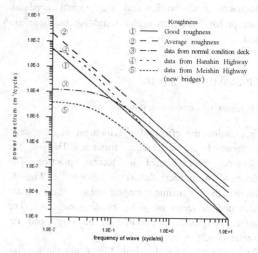

Figure. 3 PSD function

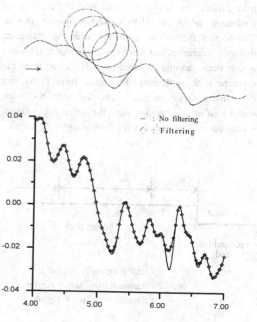

Figure. 4 Filtering method for generated surface

1907

settlement in the direction of vehicle movement experiences more severe damage, the proposed settlement model, shown in **Fig. 5**, consists of four regions: settlement, bad roughness zone, transient zone, and normal condition zone. In this study the bad roughness zone is assumed to be 1m long and the transient zone of 2m. The road surface profile of the transient zone is generated by combining the bad roughness zone profile and the normal condition zone profile, where triangular weighting functions are used.

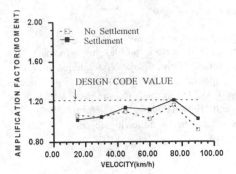

Figure. 6   Effect of settlement
(span 30m, bending moment)

3 PARAMETRIC STUDY

3.1 *Effect of entrance settlement*

To examine the effect of a settlement of 3cm deep is assumed at the bridge entrance. This is the tolerance value limited in Korean practice. The variation of impact factors is shown in **Fig. 6**, where the dynamic magnification factors are calculated in terms of girder bending moments. The surface roughness is assumed to be very good for normal condition zone.

The impact factors shown in **Fig. 6** are the average values of 5 simulation results with the same roughness condition except the randomly generated road surface profiles. It is found that the presence of settlement results in slightly higher impact factors. The impact factors are evaluated with the maximum dynamic response and corresponding static response, which occur around the mid-span far away from the entrance with settlement. Therefore, it is found that the impact factor increase generally with the truck speed and it is assumed that the effect of entrance settlement is diminished with increasing span length.

3.2 *Effect of multi-truck*

3.2.1 *Effect of consecutive traveling trucks*
The traffic conditions that several trucks are traveling together on the bridge may generate different dynamic behaviors of bridges. Previous researches are mainly considering the multi-truck conditions traveling side-by-side without any headway distance(Huang 1993, Wang 1996). In this study multi-truck traffic conditions are assumed to travel either consecutively on the same lane or side-by-side on adjacent lanes with time invariant headway distance as shown in **Fig. 7**. Two statistically independent road surface profiles are generated for two wheels on one lane and the road surface profiles of adjacent lanes are assumed to be different. Very good condition of roughness is considered and the settlement is not placed.

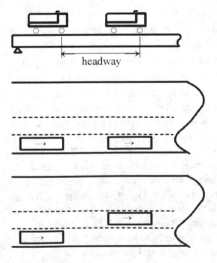

Figure. 7   Consecutive traveling modes

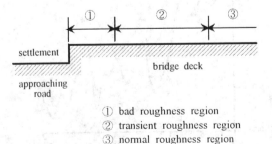

Figure. 5   Settlement model

① bad roughness region
② transient roughness region
③ normal roughness region

Fig. 8 shows the variation of the impact factors, in which the traffic condition of traveling on the same lane with constant headway distance is assumed. **Fig. 8** shows the comparison of two different traveling conditions in **Fig. 7**. In the figures the impact factors evaluated for the 2nd trucks(average value of 5 simulation results) are summarized. The followings are found: For the cases of short headway, the impact factor due to 2nd truck results in the lower value than that caused by a single truck passing on the bridge. This is mainly due to the effect of the interaction between 2 trucks. For certain headways, however, the impact factor caused by 2nd truck increases. This is assumed to be due to the different initial conditions for the dynamic analysis under 2nd truck movement. That is, the bridge is already in vibration condition when the 2nd truck moves in the bridges. It is also found that the multi-truck effect becomes larger in the long span bridges. When the headway distance is same, the traffic condition of traveling consecutively on the same lane causes higher amplification than the condition of traveling side-by-side.

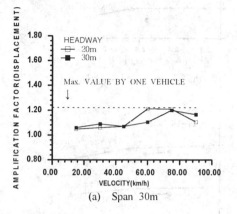

(a) Span 30m

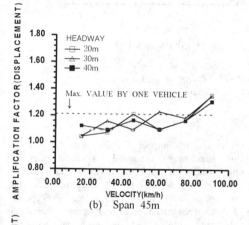

(b) Span 45m

3.2.2 *Effect of passing truck*

The dynamic bridge response due to one moving vehicle may be affected by another vehicle that is passing in the other traffic direction as shown in **Fig. 10**. It is a quite common traveling mode on the bridges that open to 2-way system traffic. In **Fig. 11** the case Ⅰ indicates the impact factor when a truck is moving alone on Lane 1. The case Ⅱ denotes the traffic case of **Fig. 10-(a)**, in which 2 trucks moving in opposite directions are supposed to enter the bridge at the same time and pass each other at the center of span. The case Ⅲ and Ⅳ represent the results for the traveling modes of **Fig. 10-(b)** and **(c)**, respectively.

Based on the results it can be concluded that the dynamic girder response is not much influenced by the truck passing on the adjacent lane.

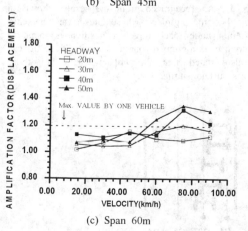

(c) Span 60m

Figure. 8   Variation of impact factors under consecutive traveling mode(displ.)

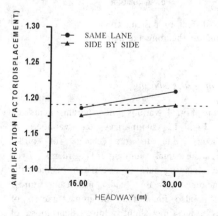

Figure. 9   Effect of traveling condition

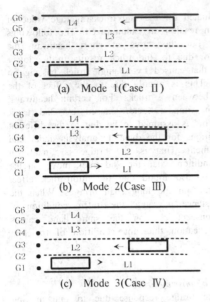

(a) Mode 1(Case II)

(b) Mode 2(Case III)

(c) Mode 3(Case IV)

Figure. 10   Passing traffic modes

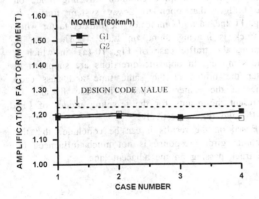

Figure. 11   Effect of passing truck
(30m, 60km/h, bending moment)

3.3 *Effect of girder spacing*

As shown in **Fig. 1** various girder arrangements are examined. **Fig. 12** summarizes the variation of impact factors due to the change of girder spacing(i.e., the total number of girders). Even though the changing rate is not much distinct, the impact factors decrease with increasing girder spacing. It is also found that the impact factors of the 2-lane bridges are slightly lower than those of the 4-lane bridges.

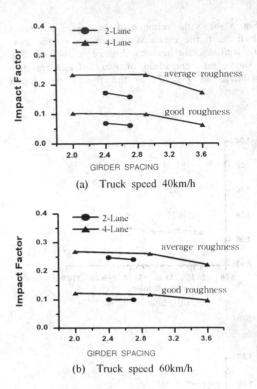

(a)   Truck speed 40km/h

(b)   Truck speed 60km/h

Figure. 12   Effect of girder spacing
(Span length 35m)

3.4 *Effect of traveling position*

The variation of impact factors due to loading positions has been examined as the transverse traveling position of truck moves from outer side to inner side in a lane(**Fig. 13**). The examination has been performed with the 2 lane bridge of Type-II (**Fig. 1**). As recognized from the results shown in **Fig. 14** the girder whose response becomes maximum under each traveling position is found to experience minimum dynamic magnification. It can be also stated that the impact factors of those girders sustain similar level.

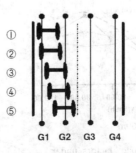

Figure. 13   Traveling positions in a lane

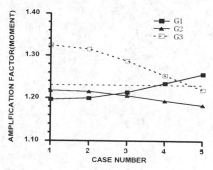

Figure. 14   Effect of traveling position in a lane
(Span 30m, 2-Lane, 60km/h, bending moment)

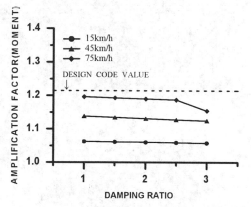

Figure. 15   Effect of damping ratio
(Span length 30m, 4-Lane, bending moment)

3.5 *Effect of damping ratio*

The damping ratio of 2% is selected for the basic bridge models based on experimental results. 5 different values ranging between 1% and 3% are assigned. The results are summarized in **Fig. 15**. The impact factors decrease slightly with increasing damping ratio. However, the difference is not significant as long as the damping ratio remains in reasonable value.

4 CONCLUSIONS

Based on the systematic study on the dynamic behaviors of multi-girder steel bridges the followings are drawn as major conclusions:

(1)   The simulated impact factors are found to remain below the design impact factors except a few cases. Therefore, the design impact factors

may be conservative to be used for fatigue damage assessment, in which normal traffic conditions contribute mainly.

(2)   The entrance settlement causes higher impact factors, especially for short span bridges under high traveling speed.

(3)   Under the multi-truck traffic conditions, the impact factors may increase depending on the relation between span length and headway distance. This effect becomes more significant in long span bridges.

(4)   The dynamic behavior of a girder under one moving truck is not much influenced by another truck passing away from the girder.

(5)   The impact factors decrease with increasing girder spacing.

ACKNOWLEDGEMENT

This research is sponsored by POSCO under the grant No. 96030. This support is greatly acknowledged.

REFERENCES

Dodds, C.J. and Robson, J.D. 1973. *The Description of Road Surface Roughness.* J. Sound and Vibration, 31(2):175-183.

Fenves, S.J., Veletsos, A.S., and Siess, C.P. 1962. "Dynamic Studies of Bridges on the AASHO Road Test," *Highway Research Board*, Report 71, National Academy of Sciences, Washington, D.C..

Huang, D., Wang, T-L., and Shahawy, M. 1993. *Impact Studies of Multigirder Concrete Bridges*, Journal of Standard Engineering, ASCE, Vol. 119, No. 8:2387-2402.

Korean Standard Specifications for Highway Bridges, Department of Construction and Transportation, Korea, 1992.

Standard Specifications for Highway Bridges, American Association of State Highway and Transportation Officials, Washington, D.C., 1992.

Wang, T-L., Huang, D., Shahawy, M., and Huang, K. 1996. Dynamic Response of Highway Girder Bridge, Computers & Structures, Vol. 60, No. 6:1021-1027.

Kawatani, M., et al., "Nonstationary Random Analysis with Coupling Vibration of Bending and Torsion of Simple Girder Bridges under Moving Vehicles", Journal of JSCE, 1997.7

Structural Safety and Reliability, Shiraishi, Shinozuka & Wen (eds) © 1998 Balkema, Rotterdam, ISBN 90 5410 978 5

Nonstationary random vibration analysis of highway bridges with coupling of bending and torsion under moving vehicles

Mitsuo Kawatani
Osaka University, Japan

Yoshikazu Kobayashi
Nichizo Tech Inc., Osaka, Japan

Kazue Takamori
Co., Ltd, Consultants Daichi, Hiroshima, Japan

ABSTRACT: According to experimental results of dynamic field tests, a response of external girder is considerably different from internal one's. This difference is come from influence of torsional vibration coupling with bending vibration of a bridge. In this study, simultaneous nonstationary random vibrations of a bridge and moving vehicles are theoretically analyzed by means of random vibration theory, taking account of roadway roughness and coupling vibration of bending and torsion. RMS values of random response of a girder bridge are calculated and compared with those from simulation analysis.

1. INTRODUCTION

Dynamic response of highway bridges under moving vehicles has been investigated in connection with impact factor used in strength design of bridges. Traffic-induced vibration of highway bridges is affected considerably by not only dynamic characteristics of bridge and vehicle but also roadway roughness. Even assuming that a sequence of roadway roughness is a stationary random process, traffic-induced vibration of bridges shows properties of nonstationary ones, because vibrating vehicles are moving on bridges (Frýba 1976, Hikosaka 1980, Okabayashi 1983, Kawatani & Komatsu 1988). Meanwhile, according to experimental results of dynamic field tests, dynamic response of external girder is considerably different from internal one's (Kawatani 1993). This difference comes from influence of torsional vibration coupled with bending vibration of a girder bridge. Torsional vibration also has a large effect on estimating vibration serviceability of pedestrians because sidewalk is located at the edge of deck.

In this study, simultaneous nonstationary random vibrations of both bridge and moving vehicles are theoretically analyzed by means of random vibration theory, taking account of roadway roughness and coupling vibration of bending and torsion. The validity of this method is investigated by comparing root mean square (RMS) values of dynamic response of a bridge based on the present procedure with those due to simulation analytical method. RMS values of the internal girder are compared with those of the external one. The influence of characteristics of moving vehicles on dynamic response of a highway bridge is investigated. Vibration serviceability of pedestrians is also estimated based on velocity response of a girder bridge.

2. ANALYTICAL PROCEDURE

2.1 *Fundamental equations of motion*

Fundamental equations of motion for a simple girder bridge subjected to loadings of a series of moving vehicles are firstly derived under the following assumptions.

① A simple girder bridge is a plane system, having a certain cross section over the whole length.

② Each moving vehicle is a two-degree-of-freedom damped sprung-mass system which has front and rear axles.

③ A sequence of the roughness of roadway surface is a stationary random process.

As shown in Fig.1, the center of gravity G of a bridge cross section is defined as the origin, the y coordinate axis is taken in the direction of vertical downward. Disregarding vibration of horizontal direction, simultaneous equations for bending vibration and torsional vibration can be written as follows (Kawatani, Komatsu & Sasaki 1988);

$$EI_z \frac{\partial^4 v}{\partial x^4} + mA \frac{\partial^2 v}{\partial t^2} + mAz_s \frac{\partial^2 \varphi}{\partial t^2} = q_y(t,x)$$

$$EC_w \frac{\partial^4 \varphi}{\partial x^4} - GK \frac{\partial^2 \varphi}{\partial x^2} + mAz_s \frac{\partial^2 v}{\partial t^2} + mI_s \frac{\partial^2 \varphi}{\partial t^2} = m_x(t,x)$$

(1)

where,

m :mass per unit volume of a bridge,

A :area of cross section of a bridge,

z_s : z coordinate of the shear center,

EI_z :bending rigidity around z axis,

GK :torsional rigidity,

EC_w :warping rigidity,

$q_y(t,x)$:external force in the direction of
vertical downward,

$m_x(t,x)$:external moment around x axis
(longitudinal axis of a bridge),

I_s :inertia moment around the shear center
$$(= I_G + A(z_s^2 + y_s^2)),$$

I_G :inertia moment around the gravity center.

The dynamic vertical deflection v and torsional deflection φ at an arbitrary point x of longitudinal axis of a bridge and at any time t are expressed by the following equations, employing generalized coordinates $a_n(t)$ and $c_n(t)$, and normal mode functions $v_n(x)$ and $\varphi_n(x)$ satisfied with the boundary conditions of a bridge, respectively.

$$\left.\begin{array}{l} v(t,x) = \sum_n a_n(t) v_n(x) \\ \varphi(t,x) = \sum_n c_n(t) \varphi_n(x) \end{array}\right\} \quad (2)$$

The simultaneous differential equations of bending and torsional vibration of a bridge under moving vehicles on the lane eccentric from the shear center by taking account of viscous damping of a bridge can be written as follows;

$$\left.\begin{array}{l} \ddot{a}_n(t) + 2h_{bn}p_{bn}\dot{a}_n(t) + p_{bn}^2 a_n(t) + z_s\ddot{c}_n(t) \\ \quad = \dfrac{2}{mAl_b}\sum_{j=1}^{h}\sum_{s=1}^{2}\sum_{k=1}^{ax(s)} v_n(x_{jsk})P_{jsk}(t) \\ \ddot{c}_n(t) + 2h_{tn}p_{tn}\dot{c}_n(t) + p_{tn}^2 c_n(t) + \dfrac{z_s}{\gamma_s^2}\ddot{a}_n(t) \\ \quad = \dfrac{2}{mI_s l_b}\sum_{j=1}^{h}\sum_{s=1}^{2}\sum_{k=1}^{ax(s)} \varphi_n(x_{jsk})P_{jsk}(t)e \end{array}\right\} \quad (3)$$

where,

$p_{bn} = \left(\dfrac{n\pi}{l_b}\right)^2 \left[\dfrac{EI_z}{mA}\right]^{1/2}$:the n -th natural circular frequency of bending vibration of a bridge,

$p_{tn} = \left(\dfrac{n\pi}{l_b}\right)\left[\dfrac{GK}{mI_s}\left\{\left(\dfrac{n\pi}{k}\right)^2 + 1\right\}\right]^{1/2}, k = l_b\left[\dfrac{GK}{EC_w}\right]^{1/2}$:the n -th natural circular frequency of torsional vibration,

h_{bn}, h_{tn} :damping constant of bending and torsional vibration,

$\gamma_s^2 = I_s / A$,

e :eccentric distance between the shear center and the loading point of vehicles,

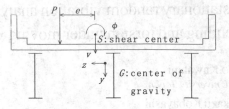

Fig. 1 Cross section of model bridge

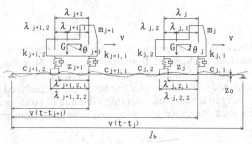

Fig.2 Analytical models of a bridge and moving vehicles

h :number of vehicles,

$x_{jsk} = v(t - t_j) - \lambda_{jsk}$,

$P_{jsk}(t) = \dfrac{1}{ax(s)}P_{js}(t)$, $P_{js}(t)$ are the loading forces of
front and rear wheels,

$ax(s)$:number of axles of front and rear wheels,
where, $ax(1) = 1, ax(2) = 2$.

As shown in Fig.2, if each moving vehicle is idealized in a two-degree-of-freedom sprung-mass system, the motion of the vehicle can be described in terms of the vertical displacement $z_j(t)$ of the center of gravity G and the rotational angle $\theta_j(t)$ about it of the j -th moving vehicle as follows;

$$\left.\begin{array}{l} m_j\ddot{z}_j(t) + \sum_{s=1}^{2} v_{js}(t) = 0 \\ m_j r_j^2 \ddot{\theta}_j(t) - \sum_{s=1}^{2}(-1)^s \lambda_{js} v_{js}(t) = 0 \\ \qquad\qquad (j = 1,2, \dots\dots, h) \end{array}\right\} \quad (4)$$

where,

$$\begin{array}{l} v_{js}(t) = k_{vjs}\{z_j - (-1)^s \lambda_{js}\theta_j - \dfrac{1}{ax(s)}\sum_{m=1}^{ax(s)} y_{vjsm}\} \\ \qquad + c_{vjs}\{\dot{z}_j - (-1)^s \lambda_{js}\dot{\theta}_j - \dfrac{1}{ax(s)}\sum_{m=1}^{ax(s)} \dot{y}_{vjsm}\} \end{array} \quad (5)$$

where,

$m_j r_j^2$: the mass moment of inertia of vehicle.

The other symbols are referred in Fig.2 and the displacement y_{vjsm} of the loading point of the moving vehicle is expressed as follows;

$$y_{vjsm} = v(t, x_{jsm}) + \varphi(t, x_{jsm})e - z_0(x_{jsm})$$
$$= \sum_g a_g(t)v_g(x_{jsm}) + \sum_g c_g(t)\varphi_g(x_{jsm})e - z_0(x_{jsm})$$
$$(j = 1,2\cdots,h, \quad s = 1,2, \quad m = 1, ax(s)) \qquad (6)$$

The loading forces of front and rear wheels are expressed as follows;

$$P_{js}(t) = \left(1 - \frac{\lambda_{js}}{\lambda_j}\right)m_j g + v_{js}(t) \qquad (7)$$

$$(j = 1,2,\cdots,h, \quad s = 1,2)$$

where, g : the acceleration of gravity.

By using Eqs.(5),(6) and (7), simultaneous differential equations of a bridge and moving vehicles on roadway roughness can be derived from Eqs.(3) and (4).

When the mean values of nonstationary random process $a_n(t), c_n(t), z_j(t), \theta_j(t)$ at an arbitrary time t are expressed as $\bar{a}_n(t), \bar{c}_n(t), \bar{z}_j(t), \bar{\theta}_j(t)$, they are dynamic response taking no account of roadway roughness. Expressing centered random values from the mean values as $\tilde{a}_n(t), \tilde{c}_n(t), \tilde{z}_j(t), \tilde{\theta}_j(t)$, nonstationary random process can be expressed as follows;

$$\left. \begin{array}{l} a_n(t) = \bar{a}_n(t) + \tilde{a}_n(t), \quad c_n(t) = \bar{c}_n(t) + \tilde{c}_n(t) \\ z_j(t) = \bar{z}_j(t) + \tilde{z}_j(t), \quad \theta_j(t) = \bar{\theta}_j(t) + \tilde{\theta}_j(t) \end{array} \right\} \qquad (8)$$

The dynamic response of a bridge at an arbitrary point x is expressed as follows;
$$y(t,x) = \bar{y}(t,x) + \tilde{y}(t,x) \qquad (9)$$

Substituting Eqs.(8) and (9) into Eqs. (3) and (4), the differential equations for centered random response are derived as follows;

$$\left. \begin{array}{l} \ddot{\tilde{a}}_n(t) + 2h_{bn}p_{bn}\dot{\tilde{a}}_n(t) + p_{bn}^2\tilde{a}_n(t) + z_s\tilde{c}_n(t) = \\ \qquad \dfrac{2}{mAl_b}\sum_{j=1}^{h}\sum_{s=1}^{2}\sum_{k=1}^{ax(s)} v_n(x_{jsk})\tilde{P}_{jsk}(t) \\[4mm] \ddot{\tilde{c}}_n(t) + 2h_{tn}p_{tn}\dot{\tilde{c}}_n(t) + p_{tn}^2\tilde{c}_n(t) + \dfrac{z_s}{\gamma_s^2}\ddot{\tilde{a}}_n(t) = \\ \qquad \dfrac{2}{mI_s l_s}\sum_{j=1}^{h}\sum_{s=1}^{2}\sum_{k=1}^{ax(s)} \varphi_n(x_{jsk})\tilde{P}_{jsk}(t)e \\[4mm] m_j\ddot{\tilde{z}}_j(t) + \sum_{s=1}^{2}\tilde{v}_{js}(t) = 0, \\[2mm] m_j r_j^2\ddot{\tilde{\theta}}_j(t) - \sum_{s=1}^{2}(-1)^s\lambda_{js}\tilde{v}_{js}(t) = 0 \\ \qquad\qquad (j = 1,2, \ldots, h) \end{array} \right\} \qquad (10)$$

where,

$$\left. \begin{array}{l} \tilde{P}_{jsk}(t) = \dfrac{1}{ax(s)}\tilde{v}_{js}(t) \\[3mm] \tilde{v}_{js}(t) = k_{vjs}\{\tilde{z}_j - (-1)^s\lambda_{js}\tilde{\theta}_j - \dfrac{1}{ax(s)}\sum_{m=1}^{ax(s)}\tilde{y}_{vjsm}\} \\[3mm] \qquad + c_{vjs}\{\dot{\tilde{z}}_j - (-1)^s\lambda_{js}\dot{\tilde{\theta}}_j - \dfrac{1}{ax(s)}\sum_{m=1}^{ax(s)}\dot{\tilde{y}}_{vjsm}\} \\[3mm] \tilde{y}_{vjsm} = \sum_g \tilde{a}_g(t)v_g(x_{jsm}) \\[2mm] \qquad + \sum_g \tilde{c}_g(t)\varphi_g(x_{jsm})e - z_0(x_{jsm}) \end{array} \right\} \qquad (11)$$

2.2 System of linear differential equations

The state vector $w(t)$ associated with both bridge and moving vehicles as well as the external force vector $z(t)$ are defined as Eq.(12).

$$w(t) = \left\{ \bar{a}_1; \bar{a}_2; \cdots; \bar{a}_n; \dot{\bar{a}}_1; \dot{\bar{a}}_2; \cdots; \dot{\bar{a}}_n; \right.$$
$$\tilde{c}_1; \tilde{c}_2; \cdots; \tilde{c}_n; \dot{\tilde{c}}_1; \dot{\tilde{c}}_2; \cdots; \dot{\tilde{c}}_n;$$
$$\tilde{z}_1; \dot{\tilde{z}}_1; \tilde{\theta}_1; \dot{\tilde{\theta}}_1; \cdots; \tilde{z}_h; \dot{\tilde{z}}_h; \tilde{\theta}_h; \dot{\tilde{\theta}}_h \right\}$$
$$= \{w_1; w_2; \cdots; w_{2n}; w_{2n+1}; w_{2n+2}; \cdots;$$
$$w_{4n}; w_{4n+1}; w_{4n+2}; \cdots; w_{4n+4h-1}; w_{4n+4h} \}$$
$$z(t) = \{z_0[v(t - t_{v1})]; z_0[v(t - t_{v1}) - \lambda_{121}];$$
$$z_0[v(t - t_{v1}) - \lambda_{122}]; \dot{z}_0[v(t - t_{v1})];$$
$$\dot{z}_0[v(t - t_{v1}) - \lambda_{121}]; \dot{z}_0[v(t - t_{v1}) - \lambda_{122}];$$
$$\cdots\cdots\cdots\cdots\cdots\cdots;$$
$$z_0[v(t - t_{vh})]; z_0[v(t - t_{vh}) - \lambda_{h21}];$$
$$z_0[v(t - t_{vh}) - \lambda_{h22}]; \dot{z}_0[v(t - t_{vh})];$$
$$\dot{z}_0[v(t - t_{vh}) - \lambda_{h21}]; \dot{z}_0[v(t - t_{vh}) - \lambda_{h22}] \} \qquad (12)$$

Using Eq.(12), Eq.(10) can be expressed in a matrix form as Eq.(13).
$$\dot{w}(t) = A(t)w(t) + B(t)z(t) \qquad (13)$$

Equation(13) is regarded as a linear differential equation, and has the following initial conditions for moving vehicles at time t_{v1}, t_{v2}, ... and t_{vh}.

$$\left. \begin{array}{l} w(t_{v1}) = w_{01} = \{0; \ldots; 0; w_{4n+1}; \ldots; w_{4n+4}; 0; \ldots; 0\} \\ w(t_{v2}) = w_{02} = \{0; \ldots; 0; w_{4n+1}; \ldots; w_{4n+8}; 0; \ldots; 0\} \\ \qquad\qquad\cdots\cdots\cdots\cdots\cdots, \\ w(t_{vh}) = w_{0h} = \{0; \ldots; 0; w_{4n+1}; \ldots\ldots\ldots; w_{4n+4h}\} \end{array} \right\} \qquad (14)$$

According to the theory of a linear differential equation (Soong 1973), the solution of Eq.(13) can be given under the initial conditions of Eq.(14) as follows:

$$w(t) = \Phi(t, t_0)w_{0k} + \int_{t_0}^{t} \Phi(t, \tau)B(\tau)z(\tau)d\tau \qquad (15)$$

where, $\Phi(t, \tau)$ is a transition matrix, and k is the number of moving vehicles entering the bridge by time t.

2.3 Covariance matrix of response

The covariance matrix $R_w(t_1,t_2)$ of the state vector $w(t)$ can be written as Eq.(16).

$$
\begin{aligned}
R_w(t_1,t_2) &= \mathrm{E}\Big[w(t_1)w^T(t_2)\Big] \\
&= \Phi(t_1,t_0)\mathrm{E}\Big[w_{0,k_1}w_{0,k_2}^T\Big]\Phi^T(t_2,t_0) \\
&+ \int_{t_0}^{t_1}\Phi(t_1,\tau)B(\tau)\mathrm{E}\Big[z(\tau)w_{0,k_2}^T\Big]\Phi^T(t_2,t_0)\,d\tau \\
&+ \int_{t_0}^{t_2}\Phi(t_1,t_0)\mathrm{E}\Big[w_{0,k_1}z^T(s)\Big]B^T(s)\Phi^T(t_2,s)\,ds \\
&+ \int_{t_0}^{t_1}\int_{t_0}^{t_2}\Phi(t_1,\tau)B(\tau)\mathrm{E}\Big[z(\tau)z^T(s)\Big]B^T(s)\Phi^T(t_2,s)\,d\tau ds
\end{aligned}
\qquad (16)
$$

Where, $\mathrm{E}[\ ]$ is the linear operator of the mean value and the superscript T denotes the transpose of a vector or a matrix.

The initial conditions for the bridge and each moving vehicle are assumed as follows;

I) The bridge remains at rest till the first vehicle enters its span.

II) Each vehicle has been moving on the roadway having the statistically same surface roughness as those of the bridge roadway. Consequently, it can be expected that a stationary random vibration has been already produced in each vehicle before entering the span of the bridge.

Under the initial conditions mentioned above, the covariance matrix of the state vector $w(t)$ can be given by the following equation based on the Wiener-Khinchine relations between the spectral density and the covariance of a stationary random process.

$$
R_w(t_1,t_2) = \Phi(t_1,t_0)
\begin{bmatrix}
0 & & & 0 \\
 & \mathrm{E}\big[w_{10}w_{10}^T\big] & & \\
0 & & \mathrm{E}\big[w_{k0}w_{k0}^T\big] & \\
 & & & \mathrm{E}\big[w_{h0}w_{h0}^T\big]
\end{bmatrix}
\Phi^T(t_2,t_0)
$$

$$
+\int_{-\infty}^{\infty}\Big\{H^*(t_1,\omega)_{\tau 1}x_{\tau 1,k}^{(T)}+\cdots\cdots+H^*(t_1,\omega)_{\tau k}x_{\tau k,k}^{(T)}\Big\}\hat{S}_{z_0}
\begin{bmatrix}
H_1^T(t_{v1},\omega) & & 0 \\
0 & & H_k^T(t_{vk},\omega)
\end{bmatrix}d\omega\,\Phi^T(t_2,t_0)
$$

$$
+\Phi(t_1,t_0)\int_{-\infty}^{\infty}
\begin{bmatrix}
0 & & \\
H_1(t_{v1},\omega) & & 0 \\
0 & & H_k(t_{vk},\omega)
\end{bmatrix}
\hat{S}_{z_0}\Big\{x_{k,s1}H^{*T}(t_2,\omega)_{s1}+\cdots+x_{k,sk}H^{*T}(t_2,\omega)_{sk}\Big\}d\omega
\qquad (17)
$$

$$
+\int_{-\infty}^{\infty}\Big\{H(t_1,\omega)_{\tau 1}\big[x_{\tau 1,s1}H^{*T}(t_2,\omega)_{s1}+\cdots+x_{\tau 1,sk}H^{*T}(t_2,\omega)_{sk}\big]+\cdots\cdots
$$

$$
+H(t_1,\omega)_{\tau k}\big[x_{\tau k,s1}H^{*T}(t_2,\omega)_{s1}+\cdots+x_{\tau k,sk}H^{*T}(t_2,\omega)_{sk}\big]\Big\}\hat{S}_{z_0}d\omega
$$

where, $\quad H(t_1,\omega)_{\tau m}=\int_{t_{vm}}^{t_{v,m+1}}\Phi_k(t_1,\tau)B(\tau)e^{-j\omega\tau}d\tau,\qquad \mathrm{E}\big[w_{k0}w_{k0}^T\big]=\int_{-\infty}^{\infty}H_k(t_{vk},\omega)x_{ekk}\hat{S}_{z0}H_k^{*T}(t_{vk},\omega)d\omega$

$$
H_k(t_{vk},\omega)=\int_{-\infty+t_{vk}}^{t_{vk}}\Phi_k(t_{vk},\xi)B_ke^{-j\omega\xi}d\xi,\qquad \hat{S}_{z_0}=\frac{1}{2\pi v}S_{z_0}(\frac{\omega}{2\pi v}),\qquad x_{epq}=\begin{bmatrix}x_{pq} & j\omega x_{pq}\\ -j\omega x_{pq} & \omega^2 x_{pq}\end{bmatrix}\exp\big\{j\omega(t_{vp}-t_{vq})\big\}
$$

$$
x_{pq}=
\begin{bmatrix}
1 & \exp\big\{-j\dfrac{\omega}{v}\lambda_{q21}\big\} & \exp\big\{-j\dfrac{\omega}{v}\lambda_{q22}\big\} \\[2mm]
\exp\big\{j\dfrac{\omega}{v}\lambda_{p21}\big\} & \exp\big\{j\dfrac{\omega}{v}(\lambda_{p21}-\lambda_{q21})\big\} & \exp\big\{j\dfrac{\omega}{v}(\lambda_{p21}-\lambda_{q22})\big\} \\[2mm]
\exp\big\{j\dfrac{\omega}{v}\lambda_{p22}\big\} & \exp\big\{j\dfrac{\omega}{v}(\lambda_{p22}-\lambda_{q21})\big\} & \exp\big\{j\dfrac{\omega}{v}(\lambda_{p22}-\lambda_{q22})\big\}
\end{bmatrix}
\qquad (18)
$$

From Eq.(17), mean square values of the deflections of the bridge at an arbitrary point x can be expressed as follows;

$$
R_y(t,t)=\sum_i\sum_k v_i(x)v_k(x)\,\mathrm{E}\big[\tilde{a}_i(t)\,\tilde{a}_k(t)\big]+s^2\sum_i\sum_k\varphi_i(x)\varphi_k(x)\,\mathrm{E}\big[\tilde{c}_i(t)\,\tilde{c}_k(t)\big]+2s\sum_i\sum_k v_i(x)\varphi_k(x)\mathrm{E}\big[\tilde{a}_i(t)\,\tilde{c}_k(t)\big]
\qquad (19)
$$

where, s : the distance between the shear center and noted point.

3. NUMERICAL ANALYSIS

3.1 *Analytical models*

a) *A simple girder bridge*
Structural quantities of a model bridge with span length of 40.4m are listed in Table 1. These quantities are estimated for a full cross section of the bridge with two lanes. The 1st. mode to the 3rd. one of bending and torsional vibration, respectively, are considered in analysis.

b) *A moving vehicle*
The vehicle model of two-degree-of-freedom sprung-mass system with one front axle and two rear axles is used as shown in Fig.2. The geometrical dimensions of the vehicle model is also shown in Fig.3 and its mechanical quantities are listed in Table 2. The mass moment of inertia is calculated based on an assumption of dividing the weight in the ratio 1:4 to the front axle and rear one. The spring constant k_{js} and the damping coefficient c_{js} are calculated on assumptions of the natural frequency $f_v = 3.0$Hz and the damping constant $h_v = 0.03$, respectively, and are divided in the ratio 1:4 to front axle and rear one. Mechanical quantities of 20tf vehicle are modeled appropriately from an actual dump truck. Those of 25tf vehicle are chosen from literature as vehicle length of 11.0m, the farthest distance between front and rear axles of 7.0~8.8m and adjacent distance of the tandem wheels of 1.8m. Table 2 shows the case that the farthest distance between front and rear axles is 7.0m. The vehicles have a constant speed of 10m/s. This bridge model has two traffic lanes and the running position of the vehicle is eccentric at 1.442m from the shear center.

c) *Power spectra of roadway roughness*
The power spectral density function of road surface roughness may be usually expressed by a formula as follows;

$$S_{z0}(\Omega) = \frac{\alpha}{\Omega^n + \beta^n} \qquad (20)$$

where α is the parameter of smoothness, n is the parameter of distribution of the power in frequency domain, β is the shape parameter as for $S_{z0}(\Omega)$ must not become infinity at $\Omega = 0$.

Three kinds of power spectra are used in this analysis as shown in Fig.4, in which broken lines indicate the boundaries of ISO estimate of roadway roughness. Roadway roughness No.① is modeled based on the measurement roughness at Yasugawa

Table 1 Structural properties of a model girder bridge

Span length	(m)	40.4
Weight per unit length	(kN/m)	74.01
Area of section	(m^2)	2.553
Moment of inertia of area	(m^4)	0.2197
Polar moment of inertia		
x Weight per unit length	(kN·m)	579.1
Torsion constant	(m^4)	5.479×10^{-2}
Warping constant	(m^6)	1.126
Damping constant		
for 1st. and 2nd. modes		0.026
Natural frequency		
Bending vibration 1st	(Hz)	2.35
2nd	(Hz)	9.42
3rd	(Hz)	21.19
Torsional vibration 1st	(Hz)	3.86
2nd	(Hz)	10.16
3rd	(Hz)	19.89

Table 2 Dynamic properties of model vehicle

Total weight	(kN)(tf)	196(20)	245(25)
Mass moment of inertia	(kN·m^2)	499.2	1458.6
Spring constant k_{j1}	(kN/m)	1421.2	1776.5
k_{j2}	(kN/m)	5684.9	7106.1
Damping coefficient c_{j1}	(kN·s/m)	4.528	5.655
c_{j2}	(kN·s/m)	18.101	22.618
Natural frequency	(Hz)	3.0	3.0
Damping constant		0.03	0.03

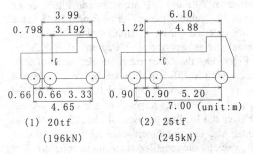

	3.99			6.10	
0.798	3.192		1.22	4.88	
0.66	0.66	3.33	0.90	0.90	5.20
	4.65			7.00 (unit:m)	

(1) 20tf   (2) 25tf
(196kN)   (245kN)

Fig.3 Dimension of moving vehicles

bridge on Meishin Expressway just after completion. No.② is defined in safety side from some measurement roughnesses on Hanshin Expressway. No.③ is defined as the mean value of many measurement roughnesses on the various short or medium-span bridges(Honda 1982).

3.2 *Analytical results*
In the above formulation a series of moving vehicles is considered, however in the following numerical examples, only a single moving vehicle is considered. RMS values of random response are calculated in terms of physical quantities of stress and velocity.

a) *Comparison with simulation method*

A RMS value of stress response is estimated as non-dimensional that dynamic RMS value is divided by the maximum static response, because stress response is related to impact factor used in strength design. Non-dimensional RMS values at the span center of the bridge by the present theory are compared with those by simulation analysis of Monte Carlo method as shown in Fig.5. The result of simulation method is estimated from frequent calculations using 100 samples of roadway roughness. Both results are in good agreement, and the present theoretical procedure is validated.

In Fig.5 the RMS values of the internal and external girder are shown, respectively, and non-dimensional RMS value of the external girder is smaller than that of the internal one. A response of the external girder is larger than that of the internal one due to torsional component added to bending component under an eccentric loading of vehicle. In this analytical result, dynamic RMS response of torsional component does not increase as the static response compared with that of bending component.

b) *Comparison of new and old live load*

Non-dimensional RMS values due to two types of vehicles of 20tf and 25tf are shown in Fig.6. In the case of 20tf vehicle, the non-dimensional RMS value of the external girder is smaller than that of the internal one as described in paragraph a) and shown in Fig.5. On the other hand, in the case of 25tf vehicle with a different distance between front and rear axles, the non-dimensional RMS value of the external one becomes larger than that of the internal one over the loading position of about 3/10 of span length. Also the non-dimensional RMS values due to 25tf vehicle are smaller than those due to 20tf vehicle, and this shows that the increase of dynamic response is smaller than that of static response with increasing of the vehicle's weight. This is also affected that the distance between axles of 25tf vehicle is larger than that of 20tf vehicle.

In Fig.7, the analytical results are shown under the conditions that the farthest distance of axles of 25tf vehicle is changed to 7.0m, 7.8m and 8.8m, respectively. There is no remarkable difference among non-dimensional RMS values, and this shows that effects of the farthest distance defined for new live load on traffic-induced vibration of bridge are small.

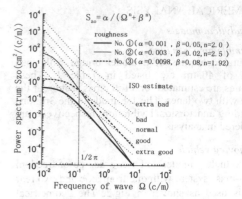

Fig.4 Power spectra of roadway roughness

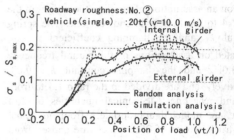

Fig.5 R.M.S value of random response

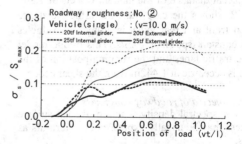

Fig.6 R.M.S value of random response

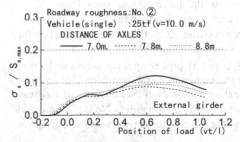

Fig.7 R.M.S value of random response

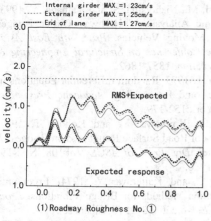

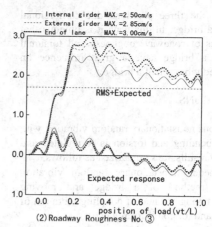

Fig.8 Time history of R.M.S value and expected value of velocity of girder
(Vehicle:weight=20.0tf,velocity=10.0m/s)

(1) Roadway Roughness No. ①

(2) Roadway Roughness No. ③

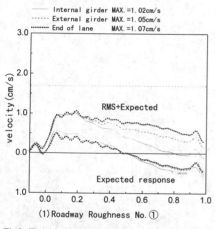

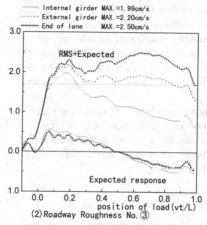

Fig.9 Time history of R.M.S value and expected value of velocity of girder
(Vehicle:weight=25.0tf,velocity=10.0m/s)

(1) Roadway Roughness No. ①

(2) Roadway Roughness No. ③

c) *Velocity response of vibration*

The analytical results of velocity response of the internal girder, the external girder and the position of end of lane at the span center due to 20tf vehicle and 25tf one are shown in Figs.8 and 9, respectively. As the model bridge has two lanes and no sidewalk, it is assumed that the position of sidewalk is at end of lane, where velocity response noticed. RMS value of random response obtained by the presented procedure is concerned with the deviation of the random response from an expected value that is the mean value calculated by usual simulation analysis under the condition of completely smooth roadway surface. In the case of estimating velocity response for vibration serviceability, the summation of the

RMS value and the expected value should be used as shown in Fig.8 and Fig.9.

In comparison between the velocity response due to roadway roughness No.① and that due to No.③, the response due to roughness No.① that is smoother than roughness No.③ is remarkable small. In the case of 20tf vehicle, vibration velocity due to roadway roughness No.③ is almost always exceed 1.7cm/s that is the lower limit of category "lightly hard to walk" in a proposed criterion in reference (Kobori 1974). At the end of lane vibration velocity is exceed 2.7cm/s that is the lower limit of category "extremely hard to walk". In the case of 25tf vehicle, there is a remarkable difference among velocity responses at the three positions due to torsional vibration of a bridge. In this way, it is obvious that characteristics of roadway roughness and torsional vibration of a bridge have a great influence on traffic-induced vibration of a bridge.

4. CONCLUSIONS

Simultaneous nonstationary random vibration with coupling of bending and torsion is formulated and the analytical results are summarized as follows.
(1) Simultaneous nonstationary random vibration analysis method of a bridge and moving vehicles taking account of coupling vibration of bending and torsion is formulated.
(2) RMS value of dynamic response due to the present procedure is in good agreement with that due to simulation analysis method and the validity of the present method is verified.
(3) In the case of 20tf vehicle the non-dimensional RMS value of stress response of the external girder is smaller than that of the internal one. On the other hand, in the case of 25tf vehicle the former one becomes larger than the latter one over the loading position of about 3/10 of span length.
(4) According to the velocity response of a bridge, it is obvious that characteristics of roadway roughness and the torsional component have a great influence on traffic-induced vibration of a bridge.

REFERENCES

Frýba, L. 1976. Non-stationary response of a beam to a moving random force. *J. Sound and Vibration.* Vol.46, No.3:323-338.
Hikosaka, H., Yoshimura, T. and Uchitani, T. 1980. Non-stationary random response of bridges to a series of moving vehicle loads. *Theo. and Appl. Mech.* Vol.28:379-386.
Okabayashi, T. and Yamaguchi, Z. 1983. Mean square response analysis of highway bridges under a series of moving vehicles. *Proc. of JSCE*, No.334: 1-11 (In Japanese).
Kawatani, M. and Komatsu, S. 1988. Nonstationary Random Response of Highway Bridges under a Series of Moving Vehicles. *Structural Eng./Earthquake Eng.* Vol.5, No.2: 285-292. (*Proc. of JSCE*, No.398/I-10).
Kawatani, M., Komatsu, S. and Sasaki, T. 1988. Dynamic Response Characteristics of Plate Girder Bridge subject to Moving Motor Vehicle. *Proc. of JSCE*, No.392/I-9: 351-358 (In Japanese).

Kawatani, M., Nishiyama, S. and Yamada, Y. 1993. Dynamic Analysis of Highway Girder Bridges under Moving Vehicles. *Proc. 4th East Asia-Pacific Conference on Structural Engineering & Construction*: 1857-1862.
Soong, T.T. 1973. Random differential Equations in Science and Engineering. *Academic Press. Inc.* New York:152-179.
Honda, H., Kajikawa, Y. and Kobori, T. 1982. Spectra of Road Surface Roughness on Bridges. *J. of Strict. Div. Proc. of ASCE* Vol.108, No.ST9: 1956-1966.
Kobori, T. and Kajikawa, Y. 1974. Ergonomic Evaluation Methods for Bridge Vibrations. *Proc. of JSCE*, No.230: 23-31 (In Japanese).

Structural Safety and Reliability, Shiraishi, Shinozuka & Wen (eds) © 1998 Balkema, Rotterdam, ISBN 90 5410 978 5

Reliability investigation of prestressed bulb-tee bridge beams

Andrew D. Fisher
University of Tennessee, Knoxville, Tenn., USA

Karen C. Chou
Department of Civil and Environmental Engineering, University of Tennessee, Knoxville, Tenn., USA

ABSTRACT: This paper presents the reliability index analysis for prestressed concrete bulb-tee girders. Prestressed bulb-tee beams are among the standard prestressed concrete beams used in highway bridges in the U.S. The section properties of a prestressed concrete beam change very dramatically when the concrete in the tension zone of the beam cracks. Hence prestressed beams are designed so that the tensile stress of the beam would not exceed the tensile strength of concrete. This criterion is crucial not only for strength requirements, but also for serviceability requirements. Therefore, this limit state was chosen for the reliability index evaluation. Sixty three prestressed bulb-tee beams in 3 different sizes were selected for the study. These beams were designed according to the current AASHTO specifications. It was found that the reliability index of these beams ranges from about 1.1 to 2.6.

1. INTRODUCTION

While the probability based load resistance factored design (LRFD) has been widely adopted and fully implemented in many design codes, there is only limited reliability studies performed in prestressed concrete beams (for example, Naaman and Siriaksorn, 1982; Mirza et al, 1980; Al-Harthy and Frangopol, 1994). Current design practice in prestressed concrete beams still uses working stress approach. With the recently developed LRFD based AASHTO code for bridge design (AASHTO, 1994), it is desirable to update the specifications for prestressed concrete beams as well.

Bulb-tee beams are among the standard prestressed concrete beams specified by the American Association of State Highway and Transportation Officials (AASHTO). Majority of the concrete highway bridges use the standard prestressed concrete beams. The bulb-tee beams were chosen for the study because of their improved efficiency and are gaining popularity. A typical bulb-tee beam is shown in Fig. 1. The standard bulb-tee beams have 3 sizes, 54-in, 63-in., and 72-in., designated according to their section depth.

The objective of this paper is to examine the reliability of some prestressed concrete sections commonly used in highway bridges that are designed based on the current AASHTO design specifications. The reliability index was calculated for each beam designed in which concrete and prestressed tendon stresses, loads, and section properties are considered as independent random variables. The girder spacing and span length chosen for the study are representative of those actually designed and built in the State of Tennessee. The results presented here can be used to develop the resistance factors for future editions of AASHTO LRFD Bridge Design Specifications.

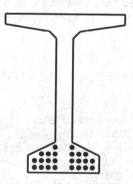

Figure 1. Typical bulb-tee beam section.

2. PRESTRESSED CONCRETE BEAM DESIGN

Stresses in concrete produced by external bending moment, whether due to beam's own weight or any externally applied loads, can be computed by the elastic theory,

$$f = \frac{My}{I} \tag{1}$$

in which f = flexure stress, M = bending moment, y = the distance from the neutral axis, and I = moment of inertia. For a prestressed concrete beam due to external loads, the resulting stress in concrete is given by (Lin, 1963)

$$f = \frac{F}{A} \pm \frac{Fey}{I} \pm \frac{My}{I} \tag{2}$$

in which F = prestressed force, A = area of beam cross section, e = eccentricity of prestressed steel. The first hair cracks in the beam occurs when the stress in concrete exceeds the tensile strength of concrete,

$$f_r < -\frac{F}{A} - \frac{Fey}{I} + \frac{My}{I} \tag{3}$$

in which f_r = tensile strength of concrete which is commonly represented by the modulus of rupture. The negative sign in Eq. 3 denotes compression stress. Since the prestressing increases the capacity of tensile strength of the beam, the critical location where cracks initiated will be in the tension zone induced by bending. The third term on the right hand side of Eq. 3 represents a tensile bending stress.

3. RELIABILITY ANALYSIS OF BULB-TEE BEAMS

The prestressed bulb-tee beams were designed using a commercial software CONSPAN for Windows. This software was written in accordance to the AASHTO bridge design specifications and is used by the Tennessee Department of Transportation.

Since the section properties of a prestressed concrete beam change very dramatically when the concrete in the tension zone of the beam cracks, prestressed beams are designed so that the tensile stress of the beam would not exceed the tensile strength of concrete. This criterion is crucial not only for strength requirements but also for serviceability requirements.

The first order second moment method which was used to develop the LRFD design codes was used to assess the reliability. The reliability index β for the bulb-tee beams is evaluated based on the limit states given by Eq. 3. The performance function becomes,

$$g(\underline{X}) = f_r + \left\{ \frac{A_s f_{ps}}{A} + \frac{A_s f_{ps} e C_b}{I_b} - \frac{D C_b}{I_b} - \frac{(L + I_m) C_c}{I_c} \right\} M_c \tag{4}$$

in which
f_r = tensile strength of concrete
A_s = total area of prestressed tendons
f_{ps} = stress in prestressing steel
A = area of beam section
e = eccentricity of prestressed steel
C_b = distance from neutral axis to the bottom of prestressed beam
I_b = moment of inertia of beam section
D = dead load moment
L = live load moment
I_m = impact moment
I_c = moment of inertia of composite beam section
C_c = distance from neutral axis to the bottom of the composite beam
M_c = model coefficient for stress in a beam
All the variables shown in the performance function are considered as random. They are assumed to be mutually independent. Their statistics are shown in Table 1. The section properties were derived from basic beam dimensions shown in Table 1. All the values shown in the mean value column are to be multiplied by their corresponding nominal values except for model coefficient, eccentricity, beam width, and tensile strength.

The statistics for live load moment were extracted from the model developed by Nowak and Hong (1991). The ratio of the mean truck moment to the calculated HS-20 moment for different spans is shown in Fig. 2. The statistics for strand area are for a single ½-in. diameter prestressed steel. The number of tendons used in the designs varied from

22 to 58. The area for all the tendons are assumed to be independent, identically distributed. The nominal final prestressing stress ranges from 145 ksi to 177 ksi. The concrete tensile strength ranges from 4000 psi to 7000 psi with majority of them in 5000 psi and 6000 psi. Table 2 shows the summary of the mean and standard deviation for most of the random variables used in Eq. 4.

A total of 63 beams were designed with twenty one 54-in. bulb-tees having span length ranging from 70 ft. to 105 ft., twenty two 63-in. sections having span length ranging from 90 ft. to 120 ft., and twenty 72-in section having span length ranging from 100 ft. to 140 ft. The girder spacing ranges from 5

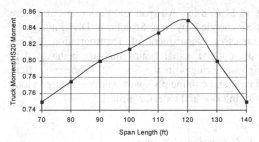

Figure 2. Relationship between truck moment to HS20 moment ratios and span length.

Table 1.   Statistical Properties of Random Variables

Random Variable	Distribution	Mean Value	Coeff. of Variation	Source
Tensile Strength	Normal	$1.002(8.3\sqrt{f'_c})$	0.18	Mirza & MacGregor (1979)
Prestressing Stress:				
Initial stage	Normal	1.0	0.015	Mirza et al. (1980)
Final stage	Normal	1.0	0.04	Mirza et al. (1980)
Beam Dimensions:				
Beam width	Normal	$b_n + (5/32)$	0.25	Al-Harthy & Frangopol (1994)
Overall depth	Normal	1.0	0.25	Al-Harthy & Frangopol (1994)
Wed thickness	Normal	1.0	0.1875	Al-Harthy & Frangopol (1994)
Flange thickness	Normal	1.0	0.15625	Al-Harthy & Frangopol (1994)
Eccentricity, e	Normal	$e_n + 0.125$	0.34375	Mirza & MacGregor (1979)
Strand Area	Normal	0.1548	0.0125	Naaman & Siriaksorn (1982)
Section Properties:				
Area - 54" bulb-tee	Normal	1.0029	0.038	Derived
Area - 63" bulb-tee	Normal	1.0026	0.0372	Derived
Area - 72" bulb-tee	Normal	1.0025	0.0365	Derived
Moment of inertia - 54"	Normal	1.004	0.00791	Derived
Moment of inertia - 63"	Normal	1.004	0.00891	Derived
Moment of inertia - 72"	Normal	1.004	0.00943	Derived
Loads:				
Dead load moment	Normal	1.03	0.08	Tabsh & Nowak (1991)
Live load moment	Type I	Figure 2	0.3	Nowak & Hong (1991)
Impact moment	Type I	0.15(live load)	0.8	Tabsh & Nowak (1991)
Model Coefficients:				
For live load	Normal	1.0	0.12	Nowak & Hong (1991)
For permissible stress	Normal	0.945	0.03	Al-Harthy & Frangopol (1994)

ft. to 11 ft. 8 in. All span and girder spacings were recommended by the Structural Division of the Tennessee Department of Transportation. They represent the actual beams that are being used in highway bridges in the State of Tennessee. Both simple and continuous spans were considered along with interior and exterior girders.

3.1 Discussion of Results

Figures 3-5 show the reliability index for each size bulb-tee beam analyzed. In each figure, the reliability indices were plotted against the beam span lengths and the girder spacings. The lines indicate the trends of β as a function of span length for a given girder spacing. The unconnected data points are the β for multiple beams analyzed using the same girder spacing and span length. Overall, the reliability index ranges from about 1.1 to 2.6. All but 8 of the beams were less than 2.0. In general, with the exception of one 63-in. beam (designated as 63-15 in the study), the reliability index β increases with decreasing girder spacing, and/or decreasing

span length. There is no significant difference in reliability index between simple and continuous spans. Table 3 summarizes the statistics on β for each size beam.

Beam 63-15 is the only 63-in. bulb-tee beam that has a reliability index significantly higher than 2.0. This is contributed by the high concrete strength, 7000 psi, used in the design and over-designed the section. The beam could possibly be designed with 6000 or 6500 psi concrete. The high β value of beam 63-15 also contributed to the high average reliability index for 63-in. bulb-tee beams.

4. CONCLUSIONS

The reliability index was computed for 63 prestressed bulb-tee concrete beams. Three beam sizes, 54-in., 63-in., and 72-in. in overall depth, were considered. The limit state considered was the first cracks of concrete in the tension zone due to externally applied loads. The results showed that the reliability index ranges from about 1.1 to 2.6 with all but 8 beams having a β less than 2.0.

Table 2. Mean and Standard Deviation for the Random Variables used in the Performance Function

Variable	Bulb-tee Beam Size					
	54-in.		63-in.		72-in.	
	Mean	Std. Deviation	Mean	Std. Deviation	Mean	Std. Deviation
A (in^2)	661	25.04	715	26.52	769	28
I_b (in^4)	269149	2040	394209	3499	548078	5148
C_b (in)	27.28	0.344	23.25	0.344	36.73	0.344
I_c (in^4)	515401-659442	3922-5018	733041-912126	6531-8127	990523-1223630	9341-11539
C_c (in)	39.76-46.63	0.358-0.420	45.59-52.53	0.41-0.473	51.11-58.9	0.46-0.53
f_r (ksi)	0.513-0.616	0.092-0.111	0.556-0.653	0.10-0.118	0.556-0.635	0.10-0.114
A_{sp} (in^2)	2.477-6.192	0.031-0.077	3.406-8.359	0.043-0.105	3.715-8.978	0.046-0.112
f_{ps} (ksi)	148.36-173.24	5.934-6.93	145.58-176.63	5.823-7.065	147.04-170.54	5.882-6.882
e (in)	20.425-24.485	0.286-0.343	23.435-28.815	0.328-0.403	26.445-33.055	0.370-0.463
D (k-ft)	967-2140	77.36-171.2	1658-3404	132.64-272.32	2119-4090	169.52-327.2
L (k-ft)	480-1166	144-349.8	701-1493	210.3-447.9	797-1485	239.1-445.5
I (k-ft)	72-174.9	57.6-139.92	105.2-224	84.12-179.16	120-222.8	95.64-178.2

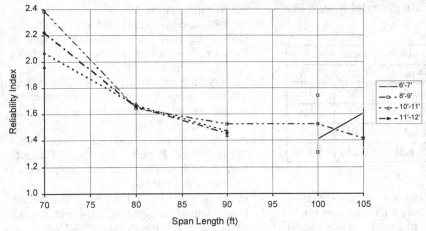

Figure 3 Reliability index for 54-in. bulb-tee beams.

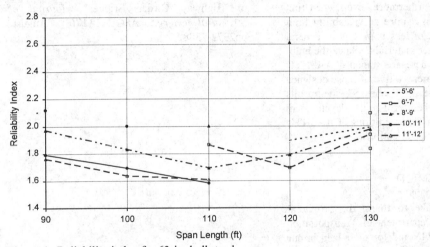

Figure 4 Reliability index for 63-in. bulb-tee beams.

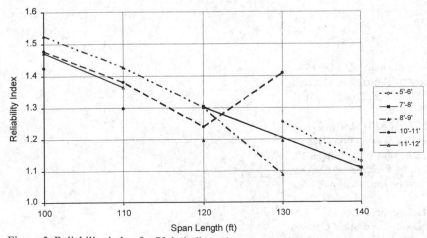

Figure 5 Reliability index for 72-in.bulb-tee beams.

Table 3. Statistics on reliability index for each size of bulb-tee beams.

Statistics	Bulb-tee Beam Size		
	54-in.	63-in.	72-in.
mean	1.641	1.876	1.293
standard deviation	0.297	0.224	0.139
coeff. of variation	0.181	0.119	0.107
range	1.28-2.38	1.61-2.61	1.1-1.53

Although the first cracks of a prestressed beam is considered as a serviceability limit state, the capacity of the beam may change drastically once the section is cracked. Hence, β value of under 2.0 appears to be unconservative. Furthermore, even when first cracks is considered as a pure serviceability limit state, reliability index of less than 2 is in general lower than that for other materials. Since the bulb-tee beams considered here are standard AASHTO beams and they are representative of those designed and built in the State of Tennessee, the results presented here should be useful in the development of resistance factors for future editions of AASHTO LRFD Bridge Design Specifications.

5. ACKNOWLEDGEMENT

The authors would like to thank the Structural Division, Tennessee Department of Transportation for the use of *CONSPAN* and for their help in our beam selections; to David Korda and Chye Eng Yew for his help in some of the figures.

6. REFERENCES

Al-Harthy, A.S. and Frangopol, D.M. 1994. "Reliability Assessment of Prestressed Concrete Beams", *Journal of Structural Engrg.*, ASCE, 120(1), January, pp180-199.

AASHTO 1994. *AASHTO LRFD Bridge Design Specifications,* AASHTO, Washington, DC.

CONSPAN V5.0, LEAP Software Inc., Tampa, FL.

Lin, T.Y. 1963. *Design of Prestressed Concrete Structures*, second edition, John Wiley & Sons, New York.

Mirza, S.A. and MacGregor, J.G. 1979. "Variations in Dimension fo Reinforced Concrete Members", *Journal of Structural Div.*, ASCE, 105(4), April, pp751-765.

Mirza, S.A., Aatzinikolas, M. and MacGregor, J.G. 1979. "Statistical Descritptions of Strength of Concrete", *Journal of Structural Div.*, ASCE, 105(6), June, pp1021-1037.

Mirza, A.S., Kikuchi, D.K., and MacGregor, J.G. 1980. "Flexural Strength Reduction Factor for Bonded Prestressed Concrete Beams", *Journal of ACI*, 77(4), pp237-246.

Naaman, A.E. and Siriaksorn, A. 1982. "Reliability of Partially Prestressed Concrete Beams at Serviceability Limit States", *PCI Journal*, 27(6), pp66-85.

Nowak, A.S. and Hong, Y.K. 1991. "Bridge Live Load Models", *Journal of Structural Engrg.*, ASCE, 117(9), September, pp2757-2768.

Tabsh, S.W. and Nowak, A.S. 1991. "Reliability of Highway Girder Bridges", *Journal of Structural Engrg.*, ASCE, 117(8), August, pp2372-2388.

System reliability and system reliability-based carrying capacity evaluation of cable-stayed bridges

Hyo-Nam Cho
Department of Civil and Environmental Engineering, Hanyang University, Ansan, Korea

Jong-Kwon Lim & Kyung-Hoon Park
Department of Civil Engineering, Hanyang University, Seoul, Korea

ABSTRACT : This paper is intended to propose a practical system reliability-based approach for the safety and load carrying capacity evaluation of cable-stayed bridges. In the paper, an improved interaction LRFR(Load and Resistance Factor Rating) formula is proposed for the codified rating at the element level whereas a new approach is also suggested for the evaluation of system reliability-based load carrying capacity of cable-stayed bridges under vehicle traffic loads in terms of equivalent system-strength which may be defined as a bridge system-strength corresponding to the system reliability index of the bridge. The system reliability of cable-stayed bridges is formulated as a partial ETA(Event Tree Analysis) model considering the major failure paths including combined failures of cables, deck, and pylons.

INTRODUCTION

The optimal decision on the bridge maintenance and rehabilitation involves tremendous economic and safety implication, and heavily depends upon the assessment of reserve safety and load carrying capacity of existing bridges. Thus, it may be necessary to assess the safety and capacity rating of cable-stayed bridges based on system performance and system reliability for the realistic prediction of residual safety and capacity of these bridges(Bruneau 1992). However, it is still extremely difficult to evaluate realistic reserve safety and load carrying capacity especially when these bridges, such as cable-stayed bridges, are highly redundant and deteriorated or damaged to a significant degree.

This paper is intended to propose practical models for the evaluation of system reliability and system reliability-based capacity rating of cable-stayed bridges incorporating the results of field load tests. This paper also proposes rational approaches for the evaluation of carrying capacity both by an improved interaction LRFR formula for the codified rating and in terms of the equivalent system-strength for the non-codified system-level rating.

A practical approach for the assessment of system reliability-based safety and load carrying capacity under vehicle traffics is proposed for the realistic evaluation of safety and rating of cable-stayed bridges. A partial ETA model incorporating major critical failure paths is suggested as a practical tool for the system reliability analysis and system reliability-based capacity rating. The proposed approach for the system reliability analysis and

system reliability-based rating is applied to the safety assessment of the Jindo Bridge which is one of the two existing steel cable-stayed bridges in Korea. The results of analyses at the system level based on the system reliability are compared with those at the element level for the evaluation of load carrying capacity as well as reliability.

Of course, it may be important to consider dynamic effects of wind and earthquake for extensive safety assessment of long span bridges like cable-stayed and suspension bridges. But, the safety assessment of cable-stayed bridges considering dynamic effects of wind and earthquake is beyond the scope of this study. The present study is specifically concerned about the system reliability-based carrying-capacity evaluation of cable-stayed bridges for their rating under vehicle traffic loads. And thus the overall safety assessment will be studied as a future research.

ELEMENT LIMIT STATE MODEL

Since this study is concerned with the assessment of reserve safety and load carrying capacity, only the strength limit state is considered in this paper. Moreover, for more realistic modeling, the code-specified nonlinear interaction limit state model is used for the combined load effects at the critical sections of pylons and stiffened girders of cable-stayed bridges.

Limit State for Cable Failures

For tensile failure of cables, the limit state equation

may be expressed in the following form

$$g(\cdot) = P_{TR} - (P_{TD} + P_{TL})$$ (1)

where P_{TR} = true tensile strength($= P_n N_p D_F$) which is expressed in terms of nominal tensile strength(P_n) and random bias factor(N_p) for uncertainties associated with material strength, fabrication and construction, modeling, and assessment of damage and/or deterioration(D_F), and P_{TD} and P_{TL} = true applied tensile forces for dead and live load, respectively, which, again, can be expressed in terms of nominal load effect and random bias factor for uncertainties involved in applied load, response and modeling.

Combined Interaction Limit State for Pylons and Deck Failures

For the combined axial and bending load effects at all critical sections of stiffened girders and at the fixed ends of pylons of a cable-stayed bridge, the nonlinear interaction strength limit state equation may be expressed as follows(Salmon and Johnson 1995, AASHTO 1994):

$$g(\cdot) = 1 - \left\{ \frac{P_{CD} + P_{CL}}{P_{CR}} + C_m \frac{M_D + M_L}{M_{CR}\left(1 - \frac{P_{CD} + P_{CL}}{P_e}\right)} \right\}$$ (2)

where P_{CR} and M_{CR} = true axial buckling strength and true ultimate moment capacity, respectively, each of which should be expressed in terms of nominal strength and random bias factor for uncertainties similar to P_{TR} of Eq. 1; P_e = Euler buckling load; C_m = modification factor; P_{CD} and P_{CL} = true axial dead and live load effects, respectively; and M_D and M_L = true bending moment due to dead and live load, respectively, each of which, again, can be modeled in terms of nominal load effect and random bias factor for uncertainties. The detailed uncertainty models and statistical uncertainties are referred to the reference(Cho and Ang 1989). It may be noted that true resistance and live load effects in the element strength limit state as expressed above include damage factors and response ratios, respectively, for the more realistic assessment of the reserve strength of the cable-stayed bridges.

Furthermore, reliability analysis of the steel plate deck with open or closed ribs may be evaluated based on the general structural analysis such as orthotropic plate theory, equivalent grillage analysis or approximate methods. In this study, an equivalent grillage structural analysis method was used for the reliability analysis. Boundary conditions in the grillage analysis of the steel plate deck at the most critical panels which are near the center of the side span are obtained from the displacements of two diaphragms at center of the side span of the cable-stayed bridges through the 2-D global structural analysis. Reliability analysis is carried out considering both global and local effects.

SYSTEM RELIABILITY MODEL

Cable-stayed bridges that consist of many cable elements, deck and pylons are generally known to be highly redundant and have multiple potential failure modes(Bruneau 1992). When a structure is redundant, the system failure can occur in more than one path according to multiple limit state failure modes; and consequently there can be several system failure modes. Thus, in general, the system reliability at mechanism or mixed level is expected to be higher than the element reliability(Tabsh and Nowak 1991).

Structural Element Failure Model

In evaluating the system reliability of a structure, mechanical behavior of the potential failure element may be of utmost importance. Reliability modeling depends on whether the element failure characteristics are brittle or ductile. However, the real behavior of element failure is neither perfectly brittle nor perfectly ductile, but rather somewhere in-between. Thus, in this paper, the failure characteristics of cable elements are assumed to be perfectly ductile but those of pylons and deck are assumed as semi-ductile with residual post-buckling strength in the case of strength limit state. The residual strength capacity is given by the parameter γ (= $M_{residual}/M_{cr}$), where $0 \leq \gamma \leq 1$.

Structural System Failure Model

Theoretically, the realization of collapse failure state of a cable-stayed bridge may be defined as the limit state of system performance. Various descriptions for system failure or system resistance are possible based on either theoretical or practical approaches. However, in this study, for practical but efficient applicability of system reliability problems without involving nonlinear structural analysis, it is assumed that the system failure state of a cable-stayed bridge may be defined as the realization of various possible partial failure paths of critical failure sections that may eventually constitute a failure mechanism under little more additional loading. With the definition of system failure as such, the cable-stayed bridges may be virtually collapsed with excessive deflection of the deck. In the system modeling, the system reliability problem for cable-stayed bridges may thus be formulated as a partial ETA model considering only dominant failure paths. It may also be noted that the load effects of each element are obtained from the linear elastic analysis of a three dimensional FEM model.

Reliability Analysis

Various available numerical methods can be applied for the reliability analysis of cable-stayed bridges using the limit state and system reliability models proposed in the paper. The AFOSM(Advanced First Order Second

Moment) method incorporating the equivalent normal transformation(Rackwitz and Fiessler 1978) and an IST(Important Sampling Technique)(Cho and Kim 1991) algorithm are used for reliability analysis in this study.

In the paper, all the uncertainties of resistance and load effects for the reliability analysis are subjectively assessed based on the expert's judgement and the data available in the literature (Ellingwood et al. 1980; Shin et al. 1989; Nowak 1995).

CODIFIED AND NON-CODIFIED BRIDGE RATING

The conventional capacity rating of a bridge have been largely based on the WSR(Working Stress Rating) or LFR(Load Factor Rating) criterions which do not systematically take into account any information on the uncertainties of strength and loading, the degree of damage or deterioration, and the characteristics of actual response or redundancy specific to the bridge to be rated. Thus, unfortunately, the nominal rating load or reserve capacity evaluated by the conventional code-specified formula, in general, fails to predict realistic carrying capacity of deteriorated or damaged bridges. First, an interaction-type rating formula is proposed for the codified rating at the element level. Next, this paper proposes a practical but rational approach for the evaluation of reserve system carrying capacity - system rating load(P_{ns}) or rating factor(RF) - in the form of the equivalent system-strength, which is derived based on the inverse fitting of the conceptual FOSM form of system reliability index.

Codified LRFR Interaction Formula

Since combined load effects compression and bending can not be evaluated in the conventional WSR, LFR and LRFR formula, an improved LRFR(Load and Resistance Factor Rating) criterion is proposed based on the code-specified LRFD interaction equation(AASHTO 1994) considering axial and bending effects for more precise capacity rating of cable-stayed bridges. It may be seen as follows:

For $P_u \geq 0.2\phi P_n$

$$\frac{\gamma_d' P_d + \gamma_l' P_l K_c \, RF}{\phi P_n D_{Fc}} + \frac{8}{9}\left(\frac{\gamma_d' M_d + \gamma_l' M_l K_b RF}{\phi_b' D_{Fb} M_n}\right) = 1$$

(3a)

For $P_u < 0.2\phi P_n$

$$\frac{\gamma_d' P_d + \gamma_l' P_l K_c \, RF}{2\phi P_n D_{Fc}} + \left(\frac{\gamma_d' M_d + \gamma_l' M_l K_b RF}{\phi_b' D_{Fb} M_n}\right) = 1$$

(3b)

where P_d and P_l = nominal compressive forces due to

dead and live load effects, respectively; P_{cr} = compressive buckling strength; M_d and M_l = nominal bending moment due to dead and live load effects, respectively; M_n = nominal bending strength; ϕ_c' and ϕ_b' = strength reduction factor for compression and bending; γ_d' and γ_l' = dead and live load factors, respectively, which should be calibrated but can be used in practice as the values specified in the code; K_c and K_b = response ratio for compressive and for bending stress, respectively; RF(Rating Factor) = P_n / P_r in which P_r and P_n = rating load and nominal strength, respectively; and D_{Fc} and D_{Fb} = damage factors for the compression and bending, respectively.

Note that the rating factor RF can be easily obtained by solving Eq. 3a and Eq. 3b for the RF.

Non-codified Equivalent System Capacity Rating

The precise prediction of the reserve load carrying capacity of an aged cable-stayed bridge as a system is extremely difficult especially when the structure is highly redundant and significantly deteriorated and/or damaged. Therefore, in this paper a practical and rational approach is suggested for the evaluation of realistic load-carrying capacity of cable-stayed bridges as a system in terms of the equivalent system-strength which can be derived from an exponential inverse fitting of the conceptual FOSM (First Order Second Moment) form of system reliability corresponding to a target system reliability index(Cho et al. 1994).

The system reliability index β_s may be conceptually expressed as the ln-ln model of the FOSM form of 2nd moment reliability methods in the following way:

$$\beta_s \simeq \frac{\ln(\overline{R}_s / \overline{Q}_s)}{\sqrt{\Omega_{Rs}^2 + \Omega_{Qs}^2}}$$

(4)

where $\overline{R}_s$ = mean system resistance; and $\overline{Q}_s$ = mean system load effects, Ω_{Rs} and Ω_{Qs} = the COV of system resistance and load effects. Then, noting that mean system load effects $\overline{Q}_s$ may be expressed in terms of system mean dead and live load effects ($\overline{Q}_s = \overline{c}_{Ls} P_{ns} + \overline{c}_{Ds} D_n$ in which $\overline{c}_{Ls}, \overline{c}_{Ds}$ are average unit system mean dead and live load effects, respectively, D_n is nominal dead load effects).

Therefore, Eq. 4 may be solved for P_{ns} as follows:

$$P_{ns} = Z_m \, EXP(-\beta_s \Omega_s) - \eta_s D_n$$

(5)

where Z_m = parameter that conceptually represents the mean resistance safety ratio ($\overline{R}_s / \overline{c}_{Ls}$); Ω_s = parameter that conceptually represents the system uncertainties ($=\sqrt{\Omega_{Rs}^2 + \Omega_{Qs}^2}$); and η_s = ratio of unit system mean dead and live load effects($= \overline{c}_{Ds} / \overline{c}_{Ls}$). The relationship between P_{ns} and β_s can be represented by the exponential curve corresponding to Eq. 5.

Thus, the unknown parameters Z_m and Ω_s of Eq. 5 can be evaluated when the two distinct rating points(P_{R1}, β_{s1}), (P_{R2}, β_{s2}) are substituted into Eq. 5. Note that these may be obtained as the system reliability indices β_{s1} and β_{s2} corresponding to the upper and lower standard rating load P_{R1} and P_{R2}, respectively. Thus, Eq. 5 becomes:

$$P_{R1} = Z_m \ EXP(-\Omega_s\beta_{s1}) - \eta_s D_n \qquad (6a)$$

$$P_{R2} = Z_m \ EXP(-\Omega_s\beta_{s2}) - \eta_s D_n \qquad (6b)$$

The new method for the system reliability-based capacity evaluation in the paper may be conceptually represented in the Fig. 1.

From Eq. 6a and Eq. 6b the parameters Z_m and Ω_s can be derived as follows:

$$Z_m = \left[\frac{(P_{R2} + \eta_s D_n)^{\beta_{s1}}}{(P_{R1} + \eta_s D_n)^{\beta_{s2}}} \right]^{\frac{1}{\Delta\beta}} \qquad (7)$$

$$\Omega_s = -\frac{1}{\Delta\beta} \ln\left(\frac{P_{R1} + \eta_s D_n}{P_{R2} + \eta_s D_n} \right) \qquad (8)$$

where $\Delta\beta = \beta_{s1} - \beta_{s2}$.

Finally, substituting Eq. 7 and Eq. 8 into Eq. 5, P_{ns} may be derived in the following form:

$$P_{ns} = \frac{(P_{R2} + \eta_s D_n)^{\Delta\beta_{s1}/\Delta\beta_{so}}}{(P_{R1} + \eta_s D_n)^{\Delta\beta_{s2}/\Delta\beta_{so}}} - \eta_s D_n \qquad (9)$$

where P_{ns} = nominal equivalent system-strength; P_{R1} and P_{R2} = upper and lower rating loads, respectively; $\Delta\beta_{s1} = \beta_{s1} - \beta_{so}$ and $\Delta\beta_{s2} = \beta_{s2} - \beta_{so}$, in which β_{s1} and β_{s2} = system reliability corresponding to P_{R1} and P_{R2}, respectively; and β_{so} = target reliability.

Hence, system reliability-based load carrying capacity may be evaluated in terms of equivalent system-strength either by curve fitting on the Fig. 1 or by the calculating formula in Eq. 9. Also for the capacity rating at the element level with implicit or interactive limit state, it may be noted that the similar concept can be applied to the derivation of the equivalent element-strength, P_{ne}.

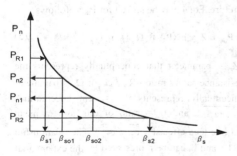

Fig. 1 β_s versus P_n

SYSTEM REDUNDANCY EVALUATION

Probabilistic System Redundancy and Reserve Safety

The collapse of a bridge occurs by taking multiple failure paths involving various intermediate damage or failure state after initial failure. Thus, the definition of system redundancy requires a measurement of the ultimate capacity of a bridge to resist collapse failure following the initial element failure. Thereby, the results of system-reliability analysis in terms of system reliability index may be effectively used either as a probabilistic measure of system redundancy or reserve safety of existing bridges. So far, various approaches to the definition for the measure of the system redundancy or reserve safety have been suggested by several researchers(Fu and Moses 1989; Frangopol and Curley 1987; Frangopol and Nakib 1989).

The following definitions for system redundancy and reserve safety in terms of reliability indices are adopted in the paper as a measure of system redundancy and reserve safety.

$$PSRF = \beta_s / \beta_i \qquad (10a)$$

$$PSR\ eF = \beta_s / \beta_e \qquad (10b)$$

where PSRF = Probabilistic System Redundancy Factor; PSReF = Probabilistic System Reserve Factor; β_s = system reliability index; β_i = reliability index of initial-failure element which can be obtained from the reliability evaluation of the first failure element of the governing failure path; and β_e = element reliability index.

Deterministic System Redundancy and Reserve Strength

Once the ultimate system load carrying capacity in terms of the equivalent system-strength P_{ns} is obtained from Eq. 9, the deterministic measure of system redundancy and reserve strength corresponding to those of probabilistic measure may be defined as follows:

$$DSRF = P_{ns} / P_{ni} \qquad (11a)$$

$$DSR\ eF = P_{ns} / P_{ne} \qquad (11b)$$

where DSRF = Deterministic System Redundancy Factor; DSReF = Deterministic System Reserve Factor; P_{ns} = ultimate system load carrying capacity in terms of equivalent system-strength corresponding to system reliability index obtained from Eq. 9; P_{ne} = nominal element load carrying capacity in terms of equivalent element-strength corresponding to element reliability index; and P_{ni} = nominal initial-failure load carrying capacity in terms of equivalent initial failure strength corresponding to reliability index of initial-failure element. It may be noted that the measure of the system redundancy associated with the deterministic system redundancy and reserve strength may be more familiar to practicing engineers, and thus be more effectively used in practice.

APPLICATION

Description of Example Bridges

The Jindo bridge which is one of the two major steel cable-stayed bridges in Korea was chosen as an application example. As shown in Fig. 2, the bridge has a deck system consisting of 3-span continuous single steel box with a main span of 344m and side spans of 70m. The stay-cables are arranged in a fan configuration that converges at the top of A-frame tower. Each tower carries 34 stay-cables. The two towers reach 69m above their fixed base on piers. The cross section of the single stiffened steel box girder with closed ribs has a hexagonal shape as shown in Fig. 2b. The A-frame towers, stayed cables and girder system constitute a 3-dimensional space structure. Recently, an extensive safety assessment of the bridge was carried out by the authors with extensive and systematic static and dynamic load tests.

The design load of the bridge is the Korean standard of the time, which is equivalent to the AASHTO HS20-44. However, now in Korea, it is essential that the current Korean standard design live loads DB-24(Truck Load) and DL24(Lane Load) which are one and a third as large as DB-/DL-18 have to be used as the rating loads for major highway bridges. Thus, in the paper, the DL-24 design live load is selected as the main rating load.

Reliability and Safety Assessment

The results of reliability and safety assessment for the example cable-stayed bridge are shown in Table 1. It can be seen that the deck girder at support shows the lowest reliability($\beta_e = 3.1$ for DL-24). Although it is not shown in the paper, it has been observed that the element reliability($\beta_e = 6.5$ for DB-24) for local failure of steel deck plate is significantly higher than the reliability of deck girder in general. Based on these observations, it may be stated that the deck girders govern element reliability and thus we don have to consider deck plate reliability in this application.

Note that, as expected, the system reliability($\beta_s = 4.5$ for the rating load DL-24) estimated by the partial ETA model for failure paths model at the Level 2 without considering residual strength for conservative assessment, as shown in Fig. 3, is significantly higher than the element reliability($\beta_e = 3.1$) of the most critical section of steel box deck. This observation suggests that the system reliability has to be considered for more realistic assessment of the reserve system safety and load carrying capacity of cable-stayed bridges.

Capacity Rating

The results of capacity rating of the Jindo bridge are summarized in Table 2. As shown in Table 2, it is interesting to observe that the results of the non-codified rating for target reliability index(β_o=3.0) at the level of SLR(Service Load Rating) and the LRFR are about the same at the element level. Thus, either the non-codified rating or the LRFR can be effectively applied in practice for the rating of critical members of which ultimate strengths are governed by combined axial and bending forces. Also, it can also be observed, as expected, that the rating at the system level(RF= 1.36, DL-32.7) for box deck at support is considerably higher than that at the element level(RF=1.03, DL-24.6).

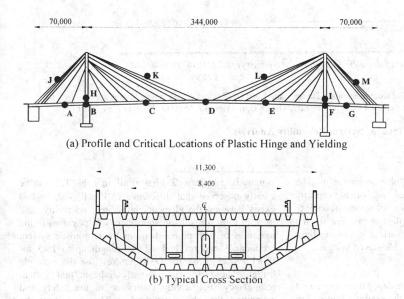

(a) Profile and Critical Locations of Plastic Hinge and Yielding

(b) Typical Cross Section

Fig. 2 Example Bridge (unit:mm)

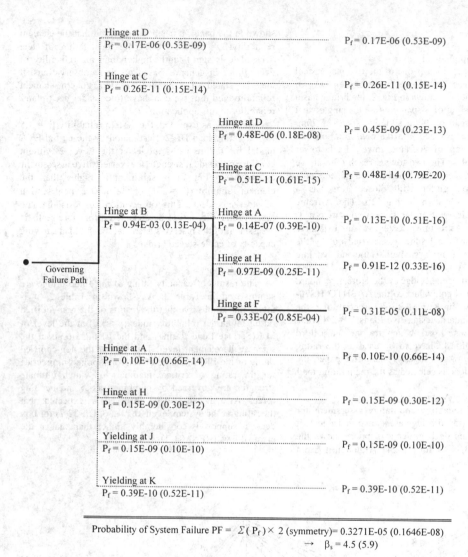

Hinge at D $P_f = 0.17E-06\ (0.53E-09)$		$P_f = 0.17E-06\ (0.53E-09)$
Hinge at C $P_f = 0.26E-11\ (0.15E-14)$		$P_f = 0.26E-11\ (0.15E-14)$
	Hinge at D $P_f = 0.48E-06\ (0.18E-08)$	$P_f = 0.45E-09\ (0.23E-13)$
	Hinge at C $P_f = 0.51E-11\ (0.61E-15)$	$P_f = 0.48E-14\ (0.79E-20)$
Hinge at B $P_f = 0.94E-03\ (0.13E-04)$	Hinge at A $P_f = 0.14E-07\ (0.39E-10)$	$P_f = 0.13E-10\ (0.51E-16)$
	Hinge at H $P_f = 0.97E-09\ (0.25E-11)$	$P_f = 0.91E-12\ (0.33E-16)$
	Hinge at F $P_f = 0.33E-02\ (0.85E-04)$	$P_f = 0.31E-05\ (0.11E-08)$
Hinge at A $P_f = 0.10E-10\ (0.66E-14)$		$P_f = 0.10E-10\ (0.66E-14)$
Hinge at H $P_f = 0.15E-09\ (0.30E-12)$		$P_f = 0.15E-09\ (0.30E-12)$
Yielding at J $P_f = 0.15E-09\ (0.10E-10)$		$P_f = 0.15E-09\ (0.10E-10)$
Yielding at K $P_f = 0.39E-10\ (0.52E-11)$		$P_f = 0.39E-10\ (0.52E-11)$

Governing Failure Path

Probability of System Failure $PF = \Sigma(P_f) \times 2$ (symmetry)$= 0.3271E-05\ (0.1646E-08)$
$$\rightarrow \quad \beta_s = 4.5\ (5.9)$$

Note : Values are obtained by applying Korean Standard Design Lane Load DL-24, and values in parentheses are obtained by applying Korean Standard Design Lane Load DL-18 equivalent to AASHTO HS20-44 Lane Load.

Fig. 3 Results of Partial Event Tree for System Reliability Analysis

Based on these comparative observations it may be suggested that the non-codified equivalent capacity rating method derived on the basis of system reliability analysis can be successfully applied in practice for the rating of bridges that may have various governing limit state equations as in the case of cable-stayed bridges.

System Redundancy Evaluation

The results of the system redundancy measures based on the reliability assessment for the example bridges are summarized in Table 3. First of all, in Table 1, it can be clearly observed that difference ($\Delta\beta = \beta_s - \beta_e = 1.4$) exists between the element and system reliability, and thus, in turn, it results in significantly high values in the measures of both probabilistic and deterministic system redundancy and residual safety/strength up to 1.45 for PSRF/PSReF, 1.63 for DSRF/DSReF for the example bridge. These results apparently indicate that system redundancy significantly contribute to the safety and capacity of the cable-stayed bridges. Therefore, it may be argued that system reliability approaches may have to be used for the evaluation of realistic reserve safety and capacity of highly redundant bridges.

Table 1. Results of Reliability Analyses

Critical Section		Failure Mode	Element Reliability Index	Reliability Index		
				Element (β_e)	System (β_s)	Initial (β_I)
Deck	Center	Combined	6.3 (6.7)	3.1* (4.2)	4.5 (5.9)	3.1 (4.2)
	Support	Combined	3.1 (4.2)			
Pylon		Combined	6.3 (7.2)			
Cable		Single	6.3 (6.7)			

* Governing element reliability index is minimum of the critical sections.
Note : Values are obtained by applying Korean Standard Design Lane Load DL-24, and
values in parentheses are obtained by applying Korean Standard Design Lane Load DL-18.

Table 2. Capacity Rating of Example Bridge

Section		Element Level						System Level (Non-codified)			
		Codified(LRFR)		Non-codified							
				SLR (β_o=3.0)		MOR(β_o=2.0)		SLR(β_{so}=3.0)*		MOR(β_{so}=2.0)**	
		RF	P_{ne}	RF	P_n	RF	P_n	RF	P_{ns}	RF	P_{ns}
Deck	Center	1.75 (2.33)	DL-42.0	1.83 (2.44)	DL-43.9	2.44 (3.25)	DL-58.6	1.36 (1.82)	DL-32.7	1.67 (2.23)	DL-40.1
	Support	1.18 (1.58)	DL-28.4	1.03 (1.37)	DL-24.6	1.33 (1.78)	DL-32.0				
Pylon		2.76 (3.69)	DL-66.4	2.87 (3.83)	DL-68.9	3.95 (5.27)	DL-94.9				

* SLR – Service Load Rating
** MOR = Maximum Overload Rating
Note : Values are obtained by applying Korean Standard Design Lane Load DL-24, and
values in parentheses are obtained by applying Korean Standard Design Lane Load DL-18.

Table 3. System redundancy and reserve safety/strength

Measure of System Redundancy	PSRF	PSReF	DSRF	DSReF
System Redundancy Factor	1.45 (1.41)	1.45 (1.41)	1.63	1.63

Note : Values are obtained by applying Korean Standard Design Lane Load DL-24, and
values in parentheses are obtained by applying Korean Standard Design Lane Load DL-18.

CONCLUSIONS

This paper suggests a practical system reliability-based model and method for the assessment of safety and load carrying capacity of existing cable-stayed bridges. It is demonstrated that the system reliability-based approach is more rational and realistic than the conventional methods, and is also conceivably more preferable to the element reliability-based approach, for more precise assessment of reserve safety and capacity rating of existing cable-stayed bridges. This paper also suggests a LRFR interaction rating formula considering combined effects of compression and bending at the element level, and proposes a new approach for the evaluation of reserve system carrying capacity of cable-stayed bridges in terms of the equivalent bridge strength corresponding to some desirable system target reliability of existing bridges for optimal maintenance. It may be stated that the system reliability and system reliability-based capacity evaluation models can be used in practice for the capacity and safety assessment of the existing cable-stayed bridges under traffic loads.

REFERENCES

AASHTO (1994), "LRFD Bridge Design Specification"

Bruneau, M.(1992), "Evaluation of System-Reliability Methods for Cable-Stayed Bridge Design", Jour. of Structural Engineering, ASCE, Vol. 118, No. 4.

Cho, H. N. and Ang, A. H-S. (1989), "Reliability Assessment and Reliability-Based Rating of Existing Road Bridges", 5th International Conference on Structural Safety and Reliability (ICOSSAR '89), San Francisco, Calif., USA, pp. 2235-2238.

Cho, H. N. and Kim, I. S.(1991), "Importance Sampling Technique for the Practical System Reliability Analysis of Bridge", Proc. of the US-Korea-Japan Trilateral Seminar, Honolulu, pp. 87-100.

Cho, H. N. and Lee, S. J. and Kang, K. K. (1994), "Assessment of System Reliability and Capacity-Rating of Composite Steel Box-Girder Highway Bridges", Jour. of Stru. Mech. And Earthquake Eng., JSCE, No. 495/ I-28, pp. 13-20.

Cho, H. N. and Lim J. K. and Lee, W. K.(1995) "Reliability-Based Safety Assessment and Berth-Capacity Rating of Aged Wharf Structures", Asian-Pacific Symposium on Structural Reliability and its Applications(APSSRA95), Tokyo, Japan, pp.140-147.

Ellingwood, B., Galambos, T. V., MacGregor, J. C. and Cornell, C. A. (1980), "Development of a Probability-Based Load Criterion for the American National Standard A58", National Bureau of Standard SP-577, Washington D. C., June.

Frangopol, D. M. and Curley, J. P. (1987), "Effects of Damage and Redundancy on Structural Reliability", Jour. of Structural Eng., ASCE, Vol. 113, No. 7, pp. 1533-1549.

Frangopol, D. M. and Nakib, R. (1989), "Redundancy Evaluation of Steel Girder Bridges", 5th International Conference on Structural Safety and Reliability (ICOSSAR'89), San Francisco, Calif., USA, pp. 2172-2178.

Fu, G. and Moses, F.(1989), "Probabilistic Concepts of Redundancy and Damage Tolerability for Structural System", 5th International Conference on Structural Safety and Reliability(ICOSSAR'89), San Francisco, Calif., USA, pp. 967-974.

Nowak, A. S. (1995), "Calibration of LRFD Bridge Code", Jour. of Structural Eng., ASCE, Vol. 121, No. 8, pp. 1245-1251.

Rackwitz, R., and Fiessler, B. (1978), "Structural Reliability Under Combined Random Load Sequences", Computer and Structures, Pergamon Press, Vol. 9, pp. 489-494.

Shin, J. C., Cho, H. N., and Chang, D. I. (1989), "A Practical Reliability-Based Capacity Rating of Existing Road Bridges", Proc. of JSCE, No. 398/I-10, Vol. 5, No. 2, pp. 245s-254s.

Tabsh, S. W. and Nowak, A. S. (1991), "Reliability of Highway Girder Bridge", Jour. of Structural Eng., ASCE, Vol. 117, No.8, pp. 2372-2388.

Thoft-Christensen, P. and Murotsu, Y. (1986), "Application of Structural Systems Reliability Theory", Springer-Verlag, Berlin Heidelberg.

Bridges (ongoing research)

Structural Safety and Reliability, Shiraishi, Shinozuka & Wen (eds) © 1998 Balkema, Rotterdam, ISBN 90 5410 978 5

Dynamic loads of bridges for high speed train

E.-S. Hwang & K.-H. Lee
Kyung Hee University, Yongin, Korea

B.-S. Kim & J.-Y. Kang
Korea Institute of Construction Technology, Seoul, Korea

ABSTRACT: The safety of bridges for high-speed train is very important due to its great impact on the economy and industry. Especially, dynamic response of bridges needs attention due to its high speed. To evaluate the dynamic response of bridges for high speed train, computer simulation program was developed and parametric study has been performed for various factors. Based on this parametric study, the dynamic load factors for collected bridges are calculated and compared with design codes. Statistics for dynamic load factors are also calculated.

1 INTRODUCTION

The first high speed train system is now being constructed in Korea. The safety of bridges for high speed train is very important due to its great impact on the industry and economy of the country. Especially, dynamic response of bridges needs attention due to its great speed for the passenger comfort and train safety.

Since the characteristic of loading is very different from the ones for bridges on highways or low speed train system, appropriate design codes should be developed. Also load and resistance factor design method is now widely accepted as a basis for the design of structures. Therefore, probabilistic characteristics of each loading model must be investigated.

The objective of this study is to investigate the dynamic load factors for the design of bridges for high speed train bridges. To accomplish the objective, a computer program to analyze the dynamic response of the bridge is developed and parametric studies are performed. Simulations are performed for various bridges and the results are compared with the design code. Statistics of the dynamic load factor is also calculated.

2 COMPUTER SIMULATION PROGRAM

To analyze the dynamic responses of bridges for high speed trains, computer simulation program has been used, which is basically time history analysis program. The program numerically solves the dynamic equations of motion from the finite element formulation of the bridge and train model by Newmark β method with predictor and corrector scheme. The solution schemes are well explained in the references (Humar 1990, KICT 1991). The programming language is FORTRAN.

Bridges are modeled by finite element method. Three-dimensional, two-nodal point frame elements are used. Each nodal point has 6 degrees of freedom - three translational displacements and three rotational ones. Rayleigh damping is used in the study. Formulations of the equations of motions and the damping matrix are in the references(Holzer 1990, Petyt 1990).

This study considers three types of high speed trains model.

1. Constant force system

When the high speed train pass the bridge, train loading is assumed that its magnitude does not change according to time.

2. Rolling mass system

When the high speed train pass the bridge, train loading is influenced by the vertical acceleration of bridge. This method is known as the very exact solution in case that the mass of bridge is much larger than that of trains.

3. Sprung mass system

The train is modeled as a series of sprung mass

system, which includes the mass and springs representing bodies and the suspension system.

Figure 1 shows the simulation results using three train models mentioned above. Rolling mass system model and sprung mass system show the similar results but constant force model shows less values. As a result, the rolling mass system model is used throughout the analysis.

3 SIMULATION RESULTS

3.1 *Definition of Dynamic Load Factor (DLF) and code specifications*

Dynamic load factor (DLF) is calculated based on the ratio between the maximum static and dynamic response of bridge as in Eq(3.1)

$$i = \frac{y_{max,dynamic}}{y_{max,static}} \quad \text{or} \quad i = \frac{M_{max,dynamic}}{M_{max,static}} \quad (3.1)$$

where, y = displacements; M = positive or negative moments.

On the other hand, the dynamic load or impact load in Korean design code (KHSTP 1991) is defined as a fraction of the live load. The dynamic load factors are specified as below, which is the same as in UIC code (UIC 1994).

(1) for standard lines

$$i_m = \frac{1.44}{\sqrt{L_c - 0.2}} - 0.18 \quad (3.2)$$

$$i_s = \frac{0.96}{\sqrt{L_c - 0.2}} - 0.12 \quad (3.3)$$

(2) for other lines

$$i_m = \frac{2.16}{\sqrt{L_c - 0.2}} - 0.27 \quad (3.4)$$

$$i_s = \frac{1.44}{\sqrt{L_c - 0.2}} - 0.18 \quad (3.5)$$

where, i_m = dynamic load factor for moments; i_s = impact factor for shear; and L_c = characteristic length specified in Table 1.

3.2 *Bridge and Train data*

Collected bridges are prestressed concrete box girder bridges which are being constructed or will be

constructed in Seoul-Pusan Line. 27 different types are used. The list is in the reference (KICT 1996). The mass of the ballast is assumed as 104.5 kN/m.

Trains used in this study are the real train systems which will be operated on Seoul-Pusan Line. There are three types of systems as shown in Figure 2.

3.3 *Comparison with the code*

The positive moments at midspan, negative moments at supports and the shear force at supports are calculated for each span to determine the DLF (Eq(3.1)). The train speed is fixed at 300km/hr and the bridge damping ratio is assumed as 2.5%.

Figure 3(a)~(c) show the DLFs from collected bridges. They show that the values are very scattered, the maximum is about 1.30 and very little correlation between the DLFs and the span length from the regression analysis.

3.4 *Statistics of DLF*

To calculate the statistical characteristics of DLF, the average and the standard deviations for each span are calculated from the values of Eq(3.1) subtracted by 1.0 and showed in Table 2. The average ranges from 0.029 to 0.099, and the standard deviation ranges from 0.024 to 0.080. Also they show that the DLFs for the shear force are less than those for the moments, which the trend are the same as the current code.

3.5 *Effect of Train Speed and Resonance*

To find the effects of train speed, simulations are performed for various train speed from 10km/hr to 350km/hr on a 40m two span continuous bridge. All three types of train are used and results are in Figure 4.

It shows that there is not much effect of train speed. However, for certain speed, DLFs are increased abruptly by the resonance effect.

The resonance is the phenomenon that the response is abruptly increased by the interaction between the structure and the load due to their frequency characteristics. When the series of loads pass the bridge, two types of frequencies are important. One is the frequency that relates to the span length and train speed (Eq(3.6)). The other is the frequency that relates to the spacing of loads and

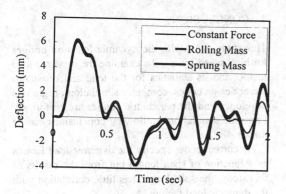

Figure 1. Simulation results for different train models.

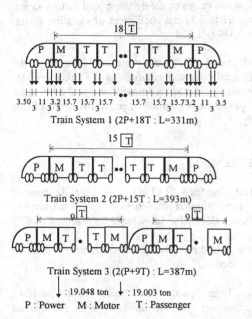

Figure 2. Train systems.

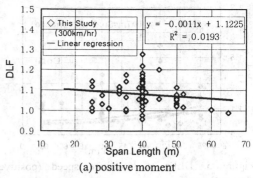

(a) positive moment

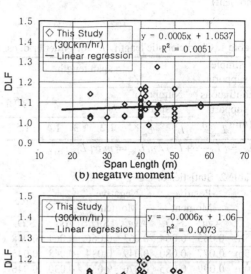

(b) negative moment

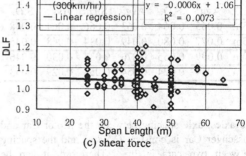

(c) shear force

Figure 3. Dynamic Load Factors from Simulations

the train speed (Eq(3.7)). If the natural frequency of the bridge coincide with these frequencies, the resonance will occur.

$$f_L = \frac{NV}{L} \tag{3.6}$$

$$f_S = \frac{NV}{S} \tag{3.7}$$

where, $N = 1, 2, 3, ...$; V = train speed (m/s); L = span length (m); and S = spacing of load.

Even though the train systems used in this study (Figure 2) don't have the constant spacing between

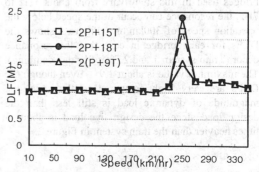

Figure 4. Effect of Train Speed.

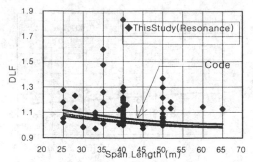

Figure 5. DLFs at resonance speed (positive moment)

Table 1. Characteristic length L_c for girder bridges.

simple supports	L_c = span length			
continuous supports (min L_{max})	Number of spans	2	3	4	≥ 5
	$L_c = L_m \times$	1.2	1.3	1.4	1.5

$L_m = (L_1 + \cdots + L_n) / n, L_{max} = max(L_1, \cdots, L_n)$

Table 2. Statistics of DLF.

	Positive Moment		Negative Moment		Shear Force	
	Avg.	S.D.	Avg.	S.D.	Avg.	S.D.
25m	0.065	0.064	0.063	0.066	0.064	0.048
35m	0.077	0.080	0.049	0.034	0.048	0.035
40m	0.099	0.065	0.076	0.033	0.030	0.046
50m	0.054	0.024	0.054	0.053	0.029	0.053

the axles, axle spacing between the Motor Car and Passenger Car is constant (15.7m) and the spacing between two cars is 3m. Therefore, it can be assumed that the load spacing is 18.7m in average. Therefore, since the natural frequencies of the bridges used in this study vary from about 1Hz to 7Hz, the resonance can occur at the speed below the operation speed of 300km/hr. Figure 5 shows the DLFs for each bridge in case that the resonance occur (Train system 1 and 2.5% of bridge damping). The maximum value is about 1.9. Even though the DLFs are very high compared to the code, the magnitude of dynamic load is still less than the design load since the design live load is about 3 times heavier than the train system in Figure 2.

4 CONCLUSIONS

This study deals with the dynamic loads on bridges for high speed train. To examine the dynamic load factors and its statistics for the load and resistance factor design codes, computer simulation program is developed and the parametric studies are performed. From the simulations, following conclusions can be drawn.

(1) current codes specify the dynamic load factors as a function of span length but from the results of this study, the span length has little correlation with the dynamic load factors.

(2) dynamic load factors for shear force is less than the ones for the moments.

(3) mean values of the dynamic load factors varies from 1.03 to 1.1, and coefficient of variation varies from 0.434 to 1.828.

All results of this study are drawn based on the theoretical computer simulations. Further analysis is required and it is recommended that the full scale test should be performed to prove the result of this study.

REFERENCES

Holzer, Siegfried M. 1985. *Computer Analysis of Structures (Matrix Structural Analysis Structured Programming)*. Elsevier Science Publishing Co.

Humar, J.L. 1990. *Dynamics of Structures.* Prentice Hall Book Co.

Korea High Speed Train Project 1991. *Standard Specifications for Reinforced and Prestressed Concrete Structures.*

Korea Institute of Construction Technology 1991. *Design of Precast Prestressed Concrete Girder Brides for Magnetic Levitated Train System.*

Korea Institute of Construction Technology 1996. *A Study on Loads and Dynamic Characteristics of Bridges for High Speed Train (II).*

Petyt, M., 1990 *Introduction to Finite Element Vibration Analysis*. Cambridge University Press.

UIC 1994. *Union Internationale des Chemins de fer 776-1.*

Structural Safety and Reliability, Shiraishi, Shinozuka & Wen (eds) © 1998 Balkema, Rotterdam, ISBN 90 5410 978 5

Numerical study on the enhancement of earthquake-resistance of reinforced concrete bridge piers

Takahiro Nakayama
Department of Civil Engineering, Hiroshima Institute of Technology, Japan

Michiaki Sakate
Co., Ltd, Consultants Daichi, Hiroshima, Japan

Tsuyoshi Okada
High Technology Research Center, Hiroshima Institute of Technology, Japan

Abstract: In this study, an analysis was made with a view to establishing a reasonable earthquake-resistant design method to prevent reinforced concrete bridge piers from collapsing under an extremely large external force at the time of an earthquake.

Specifically, the "reasonable earthquake-resistant design for reinforced concrete bridge piers" was defined as the "design for maximizing the safety factor as defined by the ratio between load carrying capacity and design external force (force of inertia)", and changes in safety factor for varying arrangements of "main reinforcing bars" and "hoops which confine main reinforcement", which had attracted little attention in the field of civil engineering, were studied. Variations in safety factor were also reviewed for different levels of concrete strength (design strength) and reinforcement strength (yield strength).

As the material strength basically involves unpredictable uncertainty, probabilistic and statistical reviews were made of load carrying capacity and deformation characteristics, taking such uncertainty into consideration. Specifically, the probability of failure was obtained by the Monte Carlo simulation for the bridge pier designed by the existing seismic coefficient method. Then the safety of bridge piers designed by the method, and the effects of variations in material strength on the load carrying capacity were considered.

1. Numerical Study on Earthquake-Resistance of Reinforced Concrete Bridge Piers

1.1 Safety factor

A bridge pier is considered safe during an earthquake if the safety factor (Fs), represented as a ratio between the horizontal load-carrying capacity of the bridge pier in the state of inelastic response (Pa) and the seismic inertia (Pe) (external design force specified based on the construction point and the equivalent natural frequency), exceeds 1.0.

$$F_s = \frac{P_a}{P_e} \qquad (1.1)$$

1.2 Analytical Model and Analytical Cases

The analytical model was created as shown in Figure 1.1 based on an actual reinforced concrete bridge pier. The district, ground type and priority were assumed to be B, I (diluvium) and 1 (national expressway) prescribed in Design Specifications of Highway Bridges of Japan, respectively.

In this study, the bridge pier safety was reviewed for a case in which hoop diameter was changed and for another where the main reinforcement had a varying diameter as shown in Table 1.1. In order to study concrete design strength and reinforcement yield strength in each of the above cases, 15 different cases were assumed as shown in Table 1.2 (a) Changes in Concrete Strength and in (b) Changes in Reinforcement Strength. The rate of variations in concrete strength and in reinforcement strength were represented, considering that the variety of concrete strength was 10 times as

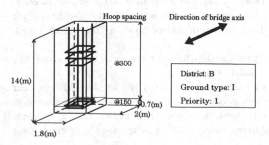

Fig.1.1 Analytical Model

Table 1.1 Analytical Cases
(for different bar diameters)

(a) Variations in Hoop Diameter

Case number	Main reinforcement		Hoop	
	Diameter	Spacing (mm)	Diameter	Spacing (mm)
1-1	D25	133	D19	150
1-2	D25	133	D22	150
1-3	D25	133	D25	150
1-4	D25	133	D29	150

(b) Variations in Main Reinforcement Diameter

Case number	Main reinforcement		Hoop	
	Diameter	Spacing (mm)	Diameter	Spacing (mm)
2-1	D25	133	D25	150
2-2	D29	133	D25	150
2-3	D32	133	D25	150
2-4	D35	133	D25	150

Table 1.2 Analytical Cases
(for different levels of strength)

(a) Variations in Hoop Diameter

Strength (kgf/cm^2)	Ac	Bc	Cc	Dc	Ec
Reinforcement	3000	3000	3000	3000	3000
Concrete	210	240	270	300	350

(b)Variations in Main Reinforcement Diameter

Strength (kgf/cm^2)	As	Bs	Cs	Ds	Es
Reinforcement	2970	3000	3030	3060	3110
Concrete	240	240	240	240	240

large as that of reinforcement strength. This study covered the safety of bridge piers only from a seismic force in the direction of the bridge axis.

1.3 Review of Analytical Results

Analyses were made for a case where concrete strength varied while reinforcement strength was kept fixed as in Table 1.2 (a), and for another where various levels of reinforcement strength were used with concrete strength fixed. The bar diameters shown in Table 1.1 were used.

(1)Relationship between Concrete Strength and The Safety Factor

Variations in the safety factor for different bar diameters and for different levels of concrete strength are shown in Figure 1.2. Figure 1.2 (a) presents different safety factors corresponding to different levels

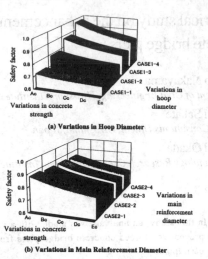

(a) Variations in Hoop Diameter

(b) Variations in Main Reinforcement Diameter

Fig 1.2 Safety Factor Changes According to Bar Diameter and Concrete Strength

of material strength as shown in Table 1.2 (a), where various hoops having a different diameter were used. Figure 1.2 (b) provides similar data when the diameter of main reinforcement varied.

It was found from the above figures that with respect to the bar diameter, a larger hoop diameter lead to a higher safety factor while the safety factor remained almost unchanged when the diameter of main reinforcement was increased. It was also obvious that increases in concrete strength did not contribute to increases in the safety factor but decreased the factor instead. The size of change in the safety factor corresponding to the change in the main reinforcement diameter was almost constant while a greater hoop diameter resulted in a larger change in the safety factor. Thus the analyses made it clear that increasing concrete strength did not help improve safety. It was also found that changes in hoop diameter caused greater changes in the safety factor than those in the main reinforcement diameter.

(2) Relationship between Reinforcement Strength and The Safety Factor

Figure 1.3 shows changes in the safety factor corresponding to changes in the bar diameter and reinforcement strength. Figure 1.3 (a) presents different safety factors corresponding to different levels of material strength as shown in Table 1.2 (b), where various hoops having a different diameter were used. Figure 1.3 (b) provides similar data when the diameter of the main reinforcement varied.

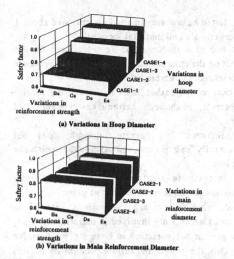

(a) Variations in Hoop Diameter

(b) Variations in Main Reinforcement Diameter

Fig 1.3 Safety Factor Changes According to Bar Diameter and Main Reinforcement Strength

These figures represented the similar trend to that in (1) above with respect to changes in bar diameters. The effects of changes in reinforcement strength are discussed here. As shown in Figure 1.3 (a) and (b), increases in reinforcement strength lead to a slight improvement in the safety factor regardless of whether the hoop or main reinforcement diameter was changed. It was also revealed that changes in the safety factor due to changes in reinforcement strength were smaller that those due to changes in concrete strength described in (1) above.

2. Reliability Evaluation in Relation to Safety of Reinforced Concrete Bridge Piers

In this study, it was assumed that the bridge pier would collapse due to a rupture in bending, which would occur when the concrete strain at the compressive edge in the cross-section of the bridge pier reached the ultimate strain. The Monte Carlo simulation method was used in order to evaluate of its reliability.

2.1 *Probability Distribution for Material Strength*

It was assumed that both concrete compressive strength and reinforcement yield strength, which greatly affect the resisting bending moment and curvature of a cross section of the reinforced concrete bridge pier, were distributed normally. The mean values for concrete compressive strength and reinforcement yield strength were set on the assumption that those characteristic values at the probability of noexceedance 5% were 240

kgf/cm^2 and 3000 kgf/cm^2 ,respectively. As the variation in the concrete compressive strength was substantially larger than that in reinforcement strength, the coefficient of variation was set at 5, 7 and 10%. On the other hand, the variation in reinforcement yield strength was considered smaller than that in concrete, so that the variation coefficient was set at 1, 3 and 5%. It was assumed that yield strength of both compression and tension bars would be distributed under the same coefficient of variation .

2.2 *Review of Safety Level and Calculated Probability Distribution*

The resisting bending moment and curvature, when trials were made 100,000 times, were calculated, using the analytical model described earlier and the assumed distribution of concrete compressive strength and reinforcement yield strength. The probability distribution calculated based on such resisting bending moment and curvature is shown below.

2.2.1 *Safety Level*

(1) Changes According to Variations in Concrete Compressive Strength

Results of an analysis conducted to study the effect of variations in concrete compressive strength on the safety level are shown in Table 2.1. In the analysis, the coefficient of variation for reinforcement yield strength was kept constant at 5% while the coefficient of variation for concrete compressive strength was changed. The tables shows that failure probability P_1 in relation to the resisting bending moment was below 5%. On the other hand, failure probability in relation to curvature was also expected to be below 5% as P_1, but greatly exceeded 5%, and the low safety level was confirmed. It was, therefore, found that the safety level of the bridge pier P_f would extremely decrease.

(2) Changes According to Variations in Reinforcement Yield Strength

Table 2.2 shows the effect of variations in reinforcement yield strength on the safety level. In the analysis, the coefficient of variation for the concrete compressive strength was kept constant at 5% while the coefficient of variation for the reinforcement strength was changed. The failure probability P_1 in relation to the resisting bending moment was below 5% as in (1) above. Moreover, the failure probability increased substantially in proportion to the variation in reinforcement yield strength. The failure probability P_2

Table 2.1 Failure Probabilities in case that Coef. of Variation
for Concrete Strength Was Changed
While Coef. for Reinforcement Strength Kept Fixed at 5%

	Coef. of variation for concrete (%)		
	5	7	10
$P_1(M_{ud}-M_n<0)$	4.5	4.6	4.6
$P_2(\Phi_n-\Phi_i<0)$	36.6	38.2	40.4
P_3 $(P_1 \cap P_2)$	4.4	4.2	3.8
P_f $(P_1+P_2-P_3)$	36.7	38.6	41.2

Table 2.2 Failure Probabilities in case that Coef. of Variation
for Reinforcement Strength Was Changed
While Coef. for Concrete Strength Kept Fixed at 5%

	Coef. of variation for Reinforcement (%)		
	1	3	5
$P_1(M_{ud}-M_n<0)$	0.0	0.3	4.5
$P_2(\Phi_n-\Phi_i<0)$	28.8	32.5	36.6
P_3 $(P_1 \cap P_2)$	0.0	0.2	4.4
P_f $(P_1+P_2-P_3)$	28.8	32.5	36.7

in relation to curvature as well as P_1 increased in proportion to the variation in reinforcement yield strength.

3. Conclusions

In this study, the following two types of review were made with a view to establishing a reasonable earthquake-resistant design method to prevent reinforced concrete bridge piers from collapsing under an extremely large external force at the time of an earthquake.

1) The "reasonable earthquake-resistant design for reinforced concrete bridge piers" was defined as the "design for maximizing the safety factor as defined by the ratio between load carrying capacity and design external force (force of inertia)", and changes in safety were checked for varying arrangements of "main reinforcing bars" and "hoops which confine main reinforcement". Variations in safety were also reviewed for different combinations of concrete compressive strength and reinforcement yield strength which were assumed deterministic.

2) Concepts of probability and statistics were introduced in the material strength, and the probability distribution of the resisting bending moment was obtained by the Monte Carlo simulation for the bridge pier designed by the existing seismic coefficient method. Then the safety of bridge piers designed by the method, and the effects of variations in material strength on the load carrying capacity were considered.

First, listed below are conclusions obtained about 1) bar arrangements and material strength.

(1) The use of a thicker main reinforcement has no effect on the enhancement of earthquake-resistance of reinforced concrete bridge piers.

(2) Thicker hoops rather than a thicker main reinforcement, enhance earthquake-resistance of piers .

(3) An increase in concrete strength does not necessarily lead to improved earthquake-resistance of piers.

(4) An increase in reinforcement strength slightly improves earthquake-resistance of piers.

Second, what follow are conclusions reached in relation to 2) uncertainty involved in material strength.

(1) The greater the variation in concrete compressive strength, the greater the failure probability on was found in bridge pier deformation, and the lower the safety level became.

(2) The greater the variation in reinforcement yield strength, the greater the failure probability in bridge pier load carrying capacity and deformation were found, and the lower the level of safety resulted.

Acknowledgment

This work is a part of the High Technology Research Project of Hiroshima Institute of Technology supported by the Ministry of Education of Japan.

We would like to thank Mr. Kenji Shimizu and Mr. Yousuke Inoue, Hiroshima Institute of Technology, for their aid in this study.

References

Alfredo H-S.Ang and Wilson H. Tang., 1977. Probability Concepts in Engineering Planning and Design, Vol.2 Decision, Risk, and Reliability, Jonh Wiley Pres.

A.Sheikh, 1982. A Comparative Study of Confinement Models, ACI Journal,Vol.79, No.4:296-303.

B.D. Scott et al., 1982. Stress-Strain Behavior of Concrete Confined by Overlapping Hoops at Low and High Strain Rates, ACI Journal, Vol. 79, No.1:13-27.

I. Hirasawa et al.,1994. The Test And Analysis on The Ultimate Strength of Short Columns With Confining Reinforcement Under Biaxal Bending, Proc. Japan Society of Civil Engineers,No.490,V-23:91-100 (in Japanese)

J. Hoshikuma et al.,1995. A Stress-Strain Model For Reinforced Concrete Columns Confined by Lateral Reinforcement, Proc. Japan Society of Civil Engineers, No.520,V-28:1-11 (in Japanese)

Structural Safety and Reliability, Shiraishi, Shinozuka & Wen (eds) © 1998 Balkema, Rotterdam, ISBN 90 5410 978 5

Parameter identification for submerged tubular bridges

Rolf M. Larssen & Svein Remseth
Norwegian University of Science and Technology, Trondheim, Norway

Bernt J. Leira
SINTEF Civil and Environmental Engineering, Trondheim, Norway

ABSTRACT: A structural system identification methodology applicable to structures that respond dynamically to stochastic environmental loading is presented. Identification of structural parameters based solely on response measurements is focused upon. A two step procedure is utilised: Natural frequencies and corresponding modal damping ratios are identified using Block Hankel matrices. Structural model parameters are subsequently estimated by means of a maximum likelihood estimator. Application to measurements from model tests of a submerged floating bridge illustrates the practical implementation of the procedure and the level of accuracy to be expected.

1 INTRODUCTION

The main objective of this work is to establish procedures for assessment of design models for dynamically sensitive structures. The basis for the assessment is measured dynamic response induced by environmental loading.. Based on the identification from the measurements, preselected models are either verified or modified. This also implies that the procedure must be able to handle large multi-degree-of-freedom models.

Surveys on system identification methods are given e.g. in Kozin and Natke (1986) or Ghanem and Shinozuka (1995). Most of these methods are based on measurements of both the input process (the loading) and the system response process. For submerged tubular bridges such as that shown in Figure 1, simultaneous measurements of load and response is generally not feasible.

In this paper a system identification method is presented were measurement can be limited to response quantities only. Application of the method is illustrated by analysing response data from ocean basin experiments for a submerged tubular bridge, Larssen (1996).

2 OUTLINE OF THE METHOD
2.1 *General description*

The procedure for estimation of basic structural parameters is split into two basic steps:

(i) Identification of natural frequencis and modal damping ratios.
(ii) Estimation of basic parameters based on minimization of a given error function.

The procedure for identification of natural frequencies and modal damping ratios is based on representation of the dynamic system by a number of first order differential equations. This requires a reformulation of the more frequently employed second-order equation system employed in structural dynamics.

The random excitation process for a submerged floating bridge can for a suitable period of time be regarded as a Gaussian process. Hence $w(t)$ can be modelled as a linearly filtered, Gaussian white noise process.

By augmenting the state vector process $\mathbf{x}_s(t_k)$ by the load vector process $\mathbf{x}_w(t_k) = \mathbf{w}(t_k)$ the expanded state vector can be expressed in discretized form as

$$\begin{aligned}\mathbf{x}(t_{k+1}) &= \mathbf{F}\mathbf{x}(t_k) + \mathbf{B}_x\mathbf{e}_x(t_k)\\\mathbf{y}(t_k) &= \mathbf{C}\mathbf{x}(t_x) + \mathbf{e}_m(t_k)\end{aligned} \qquad (1)$$

where $\mathbf{e}_x(t_k) = \left[\mathbf{0}, \mathbf{e}_w(t_k)\right]^T$, and $\mathbf{e}_m(t_k)$ is a Gaussian white-noise process representing the random disturbances of the measurements. The second line in Eq(1) represents the discretized measurement process with the vector $\mathbf{y}$ containing the observations.

2.2 *Identification of Natural Frequencies and Damping*

On the basis of the measured response alone, an estimate of the system matrix $\mathbf{F}$ should be obtained. The characteristics of the structural system may subsequently be separated from the load and noise. In step (ii), values of the uncertain structural parameters of the a priori model are determined based on these characteristics.

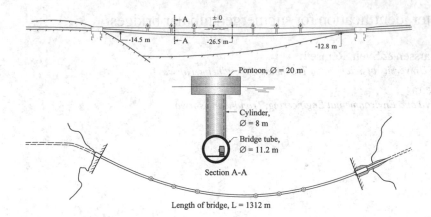

Figure 1 - Possible concept for submerged tubular bridge across Høgsfjorden, Rogaland county, Norway

A procedure that has been found to be efficient for identification of natural frequencies and modal damping ratios employs the so-called Covariance Block Hankel Matrix method, Ho and Kalman (1966), Aoki (1987), Henriksen (1990), Hoen (1991).

The cross-covariance function matrix of the measurements is a matrix of dimension ($ny{\times}ny$). This function can be expressed by the state space matrices F, B_x and C as

$$C_{yy}(t_k) = E\left\{y(t_{j+k})y^T(t_j)\right\}$$
$$= CF^{k-1}\left[FC_{xx}C^T + B_xC_{xm}\right] = CF^{k-1}M \qquad (2)$$

C_{xx} is the cross-covariance matrix of the state vector for zero lag, and C_{xm} correspondingly for the noise processes.

A Block Hankel matrix of order p (later referred to as lag length), $H_1(p)$, may now be constructed based on estimates of a sequence of cross-covariance functions with increasin lag. This is a matrix of dimension ($ny \cdot p{\times}ny \cdot p$) where p is the maximim lag of the cross-covariance functions.

In analogy with the deterministic realization formulation, the block Hankel matrix may be expressed as

$$H_1(p) = Q_o(p)Q_m(p) \qquad (3)$$

where $Q_o(p)$ is designated as the observability matrix of order p and defined as follows

$$Q_o^T(p) = \left[C^T(CF)^T(CF)^T \ldots (CF^{p-1})^T\right] \qquad (4)$$

The matrix $Q_m(p)$, which resembles the so-called reachability matrix, is defined as

$$Q_m(p) = \left[M(FM)(F^2M)\ldots(F^{p-1}M)\right] \qquad (5)$$

It is further assumed that $H_1(p)$ is of rank r, r < ny·p. The system represented by F contains information about the structural, the load and the measurement noise subsystems. Structural frequencies must then be identified among all the frequency indications returned by the method.

Calculations are performed for successively increasing lag lengths. Frequency estimates from the structural subsystem show stable estimates for increasing lag length over a wide range of lags. Neither load nor noise related natural frequencies will exhibit such stability.

2.3 *Estimation of basic structural parameters*

Based on a given pre-established model of the structure, updated values of selected parameters entering the model are then estimated. This is achieved by introducing proper relationships between the selected parameters and the modal properties identified by the procedures above.

In the following, only the over-determined case is considered. This implies that the number of unknown parameters are smaller than number of identified natural frequencies).

The task of parameter estimation can be formulated as a minimization problem for the following criterion function:

$$e(\theta) = [y - h(\theta)]^T W_y[y - h(\theta)] + [\theta - \theta_0]^T W_\theta[\theta - \theta_0] \qquad (6)$$

The first term in e(θ) takes into account the difference between the measured, y, and predicted quantities, $h(\theta)$, multiplied by the measurement weighting matrix W_y. The second term represents the distance of the parameters θ from an a priori mean value of the parameter vector θ_0 weighted by the matrix $\mathbf{W}_\theta$. The minimum of this function may be determined by standard procedures taken from optimization theory.

If no prior information about the parameters exists, i.e. $\mathbf{W}_\theta = 0$ in Eq (7), the maximum likelihood estimator (MLE) is applicable. For the present purpose this estimator is found to be convenient .

Two types of methods are investigated for use here. The first method belongs to the so-called Quasi-Newton methods. It is based on a Taylor series expansion of the criterion function, truncated after the second order. The second method is only applicable for a subset of the cases defined by Eq. (7) where the criterion function must be a sum of squares. This corresponds to diagonal weighting matrices in Eq. (7) can be written as a sum of squares.

For this category the simplest and most effective method is the so-called Gauss-Newton method. The Levenberg-Marquardt method is a modification which can handle significant second order terms in the Taylor expansion.This latter method is applied in the following examples.

3 EXAMPLE OF APPLICATION

3.1 Introduction

An experimental program on tubular bridges was initiated in 1989 by the Norwegian Public Roads Administration. Different configurations were tested in model scale and subjected to regular waves, irregular waves, impulse waves and current. The tests were all carried out in the Ocean Basin at MARINTEK in Trondheim, Dahle et. al. (1990).

A long flexible model representing a scaled-down (scale 1:20) version of a "generic" submerged floating bridge with full-scale diameter 10 m and length 800 m was tested. A straight bridge was tested but with three different support versions, i.e. free-spanning, tension legs or pontoons. Only the free-spanning model is considered here. During the final model tests, it was found that the model had been subjected to an axial tension force of roughly 3 kN during at least some of the tests.

3.2 Structural model

Horizontal and vertical deflections were measured at three locations (1/3-point, midpoint and 2/3-point). Horizontal and vertical accelerations were also measured at two of these locations.

Large variation of the numerical estimates for the natural frequencies are observed. For the first horizontal mode the results varied from 0.16 Hz to 0.223 Hz. The range for the second mode was 0.585 Hz to 0.680 Hz, for the third mode 1.276 Hz to 1.483 Hz, for the fourth mode from 2.208 to 2.584 Hz and for the fifth mode 3.344 Hz to 3.922 Hz.

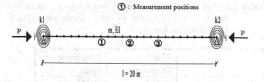

Figure 2 - Computational model for free bridge

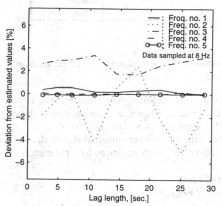

Figure 3 Natural frequency estimates as a function of lag length

3.3 Estimation of natural frequencies and damping ratios

Measurements from one test run are considered. A sea state with irregular waves having a mean direction of $0°$ and a wave spectrum with $H_S = 0.057$ m and $T_P = 1.09$ seconds in model scale is analyzed. The full scale values are $H_s = 2.3$ m and $T_P = 6.89$ seconds. The corresponding wave spectrum has no significant energy for frequencies below 0.5 Hz and above 2.5 Hz.

Time series of displacement are employed, and estimates of the five first horizontal natural frequencies of the bridge are given in Table 1. The influence of lag length on the frequency estimate is shown in Figure 3.

Modes no. 2 and 3 have nodes at some of these points. The results for these modes have a larger scatter than the rest, and are not so easily identified. This is clearly seen in Figure 3.

Stable estimates for increasing lag lengths may be found for frequencies and damping ratios of modes no. 1, 4 and 5. More uncertain frequency and damping estimates may be determined for frequencies no 2 and 3. The results are reported in Table 1.

The measurement at the midpoint was subsequently excluded from the identification. This reduces the variation of frequency no. 2 but the identification is still not satisfactory. This is due to frequency no. 2 being located near the top of the wave spectrum and is hence disturbed by the load process. Selecting sensor locations away from the nodes of the active modes would improve the results.

Table 1.Identified natural frequencies and damping ratios for the free bridge model by the Covariance Block Hankel Matrix method

	Natural frequency	Damping ratio
Horizontal modes	0.224	0.010
	0.676	0.035
	1.309	0.015
	2.348	0.008
	3.579	0.006

3.4 *Estimation of a structural model based on measured response*

A computational model that gives better agreement with the estimated natural frequencies than models excluding the axial force effect is now to be established.

The fundamental computational model is shown in Figure 2. This model is characterized by 7 parameters

- length of beam
- stiffness of beam, EI
- mass of beam, both structural and hydrodynamic
- rotational stiffness of end supports, k1 and k2
- axial force P (compression positive)
- structural and hydrodynamic modal damping

The beam length is taken as fixed. The remaining 4 parameters are then estimated using the maximum likelihood estimator and the Levenberg-Marquardt search procedure.The results are given in Table 2.

Table 2. Estimated parameters of numerical model based on estimated natural frequencies by the CBHM-method.

Model parameters	A priori model (ref. 11)	Posteriori model
Beam stiffness. [kNm2]	133.60	112.5
Support stiffness, [kNm/rad]	4.3	4.37
Support stiffness, [kNm/rad]	4.3	4.36
Axial force P, tension [kN]	3.0	3.70
Calculated natural frequencies from above models		
Mode 1	0.2188	0.2229
Mode 2	0.6883	0.6605
Mode 3	1.4408	1.3675
Mode 4	2.4956	2.3234
Mode 5	3.8519	3.5684

In these calculations, distributed mass is fixed and the beam stiffness is thus determined. Significant reduction in beam stiffness may be an indication that the specified distributed mass is too low.

Allowing both of the support stiffnesses to be free parameters in the optimization may introduce multiple solutions to the minimization problem. This information may be included in Eq.(21) by use of W_θ. This means that a maximum a priori estimator is used instead of a maximum likelihood estimator. The problem of multiple solutions is solved by controlling the termination criterion of the minimization.

4 CONCLUSIONS

A robust method for identification of structural systems has been presented. The procedure is based on a combination of modal parameter identification by the Covariance Block Hankel Matrix method followed by structural parameter estimation by e.g. the maximum likelihood estimator. The primary scope has been to develop a method that can identify the structural properties without the need for measurement of load parameters or processes. However, development of procedures for the inclusion of such additional data is a natural extension of the present study. Application to structural monitoring is another interesting development.

REFERENCES

(1) Aoki, M, (1987): "State Space Modelling of Time Series". Universitext, Springer-Verlag, Berlin
(2) Dahle, L.A., Reed, K., Aarsnes, J.V. (1990) Model tests with submerged floating tubebridge" Proc. of 2. Symp. on Strait Crossings, Trondheim, Ed. Krokeborg, Balkema, Rotterdam, pp. 435-442.
(3) Ghanem, R., and Shinozuka, M. (1995). "Structural System Identification" Journal of Engineering Mechanics, ASCE, Vol. 121, No. 2, pp 255-264.
(4) Henriksen, R., (1990). "Realization of linear systems", Rep. no 90-01-W, Division of Engineering Cybernetics, Norwegian Institute of Technology, Trondheim.
(5) Ho, B.L. and Kalman, R.E. (1966). "Effective construction of linear state-variable models from input/output functions". Regelungstechnik, Vol. 14, No. 12, pp 545-592.
(6) Hoen, C. (1991). "System identification of structures excited by stochastic load processes". Dr.ing. Thesis, Division of Marine Structures, The Norwegian Institute of Technology, Trondheim.
(7) Kozin, F. and Natke, H.G. (1986). "System identification techniques". Structural Safety, Vol 3, No 3, pp 269-316.
(8) Larssen, R.M., (1996). "Response verification of a submerged tubular bridge by instrumentation". Dr. Ing Thesis, Division of Structural Engineering, NTNU.

Structural Safety and Reliability, Shiraishi, Shinozuka & Wen (eds) © 1998 Balkema, Rotterdam, ISBN 90 5410 978 5

Reliability of highway bridges

P.Śniady, R.Sieniawska & S.Żukowski
Technical University of Wrocław, Poland

ABSTRACT: The reliability of highway bridges is considered under following assumptions: the traffic flow is modeled by a point stochastic process, the bridge is modeled by a multispan beam, the bridge's capacity, which is degraded by fatigue and corrosion and on the other hand increases after some inspections and repairs is described by two mathematical models. The reliability is regarded as a first crossing problem. The paper contain both the theoretical and numerical part.

1 INTRODUCTION

Estimation of the reliability of bridges is an important problem in their whole life-period, by design, by the planning their inspections and maintenance, because of the necessity of cost optimization (Madsen, Sorensen, 1990). The problem is not simple, while many various mutable in time factors related to the load and structure capacity should be taken into account. On the one hand the structure is degraded by its exploitation, influence of the environment, corrosion, fatigue of material, aging, creep, overload, etc. and on the other one after some inspections it can be repaired or modernized.

The contents of this work is the reliability analysis of highway bridges with respect to the decreasing of its capacity due to fatigue and corrosion and increasing of its capacity after some repairs. The reliability is formulated as the first passage problem. Two different mathematical models for describing the structure's capacity are proposed.

2 MATHEMATICAL MODELS OF ALTERATION OF STRUCTURE'S CAPACITY

The mathematical model for describing the structure's degradation and repair can be, depending on situation, very simple or very complicated. Usually two opposite tendencies must be reconciled: the model should be so simple that it could be applied in engineering practice and on the other hand the whole complicity of the phenomenon should taken into account. We propose two descriptions of structure's capacity alteration.

1. The first (simplest) model can be described as follows

$$R(t) = f_i(t)\big(H(t - t_{i-1}) - H(t - t_i)\big) \qquad (1)$$

where $f_i(t)$ is a deterministic function, for example
$f_i(t) = A_i e^{\alpha_i(t_{i-1}, t_i)}$, $A_1 \geq A_2 \geq ... \geq A_n$,
$\alpha_1 \leq \alpha_2 \leq ... \leq \alpha_n$ and
$H(t - t_i)$ is the Heaviside function.

Such model can be generalized by assuming the quantities A_i as random variables for which the probability density functions $f_{A_i}(a_i)$ are known.

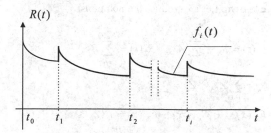

Figure 1. First model of capacity alteration

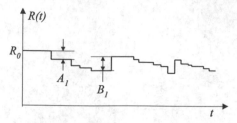

Figure 2. Second model of capacity alteration

2. The second model takes into account the random nature of structure degradation. Usually, the degradation is not a continuous process, the fatigue cracks decrease when some heavy vehicle drive on a bridge. Therefore, the fatigue degradation can be described by a cumulative jump process. Let's assume, that the degradation of the structure's capacity $R(t)$ take place at random times $t_1, t_2, \ldots, t_n$ which constitute a Poisson stochastic process $N_\lambda(t)$ and that the repair process has also jumping character and can be described by a Poisson process $N_\mu(t)$.

In such a case the capacity $R(t)$ can be described by the expression

$$R(t) = R_0 - \sum_{i=1}^{N_\lambda(t)} A_i + \sum_{j=1}^{N_\mu(t)} B_j \qquad (2)$$

where R_0 is the capacity of new structure, $t = 0$. The random positive quantities A_i determine the degradation (for example it could be the capacity connected with the crack size) and the random positive quantities B_j determine the capacity after some repairs. Let the random variables A_i and B_j be mutually independent and their probability density functions $f_A(a)$ and $f_B(b)$ or their cumulative distribution functions $F_A(a)$ and $F_B(b)$ are known. Let's introduce the notations

$$R_1(t) = R_0 - \sum_{i=1}^{N_\lambda(t)} A_i, \quad R_2(t) = \sum_{j=1}^{N_\mu(t)} B_j,$$

$$S_n = \sum_{i=1}^{n} A_i, \quad Z_k = \sum_{j=1}^{k} B_j,$$

$$F_{S_n}(x) = P\{S_n \le x\}, \quad F_{Z_k}(x) = P\{Z_k \le x\}, \qquad (3)$$

$$f_{S_n}(x) = \frac{dF_{S_n}(x)}{dx}, \quad f_{Z_k}(x) = \frac{dF_{Z_k}(x)}{dx}$$

Since we have assumed that the degradations and the repairs constitute Poisson stochastic processes, the probabilities of occurring n jumps of degradation and k jumps of repair are equal to

$$p_n(t) = P\{N_\lambda(t) = n\} = \frac{(\lambda t)^n}{n!} e^{-\lambda t}, \quad n = 0,1,\ldots$$

$$r_k(t) = P\{N_\mu(t) = k\} = \frac{(\mu t)^k}{k!} e^{-\mu t}, \quad k = 0,1,\ldots \qquad (4)$$

respectively.

The cumulative distribution functions and probability density functions of the components in equation (2) have the forms

$$F_{R_1}(x,t) = P\{R_1(t) \le x\} =$$
$$= p_0(t) H(R_0 - x) + \sum_{n=1}^{\infty} F_{S_n}(R_0 - x) p_n(t) \qquad (5)$$

$$F_{R_2}(x,t) = P\{R_2(t) \le x\} =$$
$$= r_0(t) H(x) + \sum_{k=1}^{\infty} F_{Z_k}(x) r_k(t) \qquad (6)$$

$$f_{R_1}(x,t) = p_0(t)\delta(x) + \sum_{n=1}^{\infty} f_{S_n}(R_0 - x) p_n(t) \qquad (7)$$

$$f_{R_2}(x,t) = r_0(t)\delta(x) + \sum_{k=1}^{\infty} f_{Z_k}(x) r_k(t) \qquad (8)$$

where $H(\cdot)$ and $\delta(\cdot)$ are the Heaviside and Dirac delta functions, respectively.

From the assumption of mutually independence of variables A_i and B_j follows that

$$F_{S_n}(x) = \int_0^x F_{S_{n-1}}(x - \xi) f_A(\xi) d\xi \qquad (9)$$

$$f_{S_n}(x) = \int_0^x f_{S_{n-1}}(x - \xi) f_A(\xi) d\xi \quad \text{and} \qquad (10)$$

$$F_{Z_k}(x) = \int_0^x F_{Z_{k-1}}(x - \xi) f_B(\xi) d\xi \qquad (11)$$

$$f_{Z_k}(x) = \int_0^x f_{Z_{k-1}}(x - \xi) f_B(\xi) d\xi \qquad (12)$$

Knowledge of the above probabilistic characteristics allows to calculate the probability density function and the cumulative distribution function of the capacity $R(t)$ described by equation (2) from the expressions

$$f_R(x,t) = \int_0^t f_{R_1}(x-\xi,t)f_{R_2}(\xi,t)d\xi \quad \text{and} \qquad (13)$$

$$F_R(x,t) = \int_0^t F_{R_1}(x-\xi,t)f_{R_2}(\xi,t)d\xi = \qquad (14)$$

$$= \int_0^t F_{R_2}(x-\xi,t)f_{R_1}(\xi,t)d\xi$$

3 RELIABILITY MEASURE

Now, let's consider the bridge's reliability meant as the expected value of its life-time. At first, one should calculate the first crossing rate of the given level of the structure resistance which for the ultimate limit state is the structure's capacity. For calculating the reliability measure one need to known the joint probability density function $p_{\sigma\dot\sigma}(\sigma,\dot\sigma,x,z,t)$ of the stress process $\sigma(x,t)$ and the stress velocity process $\dot\sigma(x,t)$. An approach for calculating this probability density functions was shown in [Sieniawska, Śniady, 1990]

The mean value of crossing rate $\bar{n}_+(r,x,t)$ for the deterministic and constant threshold r can be calculated from the Rice's formula

$$\bar{n}_+(r,x,t) = \int_0^\infty \dot\sigma p_{\sigma\dot\sigma}(r,\dot\sigma,x,t)d\dot\sigma . \qquad (15)$$

If the bridge is a well designed and built construction the probability of upcrossing the given level of its capacity is very small. Since the probability $p(r,x,t)$ of not crossing the level r can be modeled by the Poisson stochastic process and has the form

$$p(r,x,t) = \exp\{-\int_0^t \bar{n}_+(r,x,\tau)d\tau\} \qquad (16)$$

Let T denote the structure's life-time. The probability that the life-time T of some structure is greater than the time t is equal to the probability of not crossing its resistance by the response. Therefore, one can calculate the cumulative distribution $F_T(t)$ of the structure's life-time, its probability density function $f_T(t)$ and its expected value

$$E[T] = \int_0^\infty t\bar{n}_+(r,x,t)\exp\{-\int_0^t \bar{n}_+(r,x,\tau)d\tau\}dt \qquad (17)$$

Assuming the proper level of uprossing in probabilistic dynamical problems is a problem for itself because the expected values of stresses include also the zero values within time periods when there is no traffic. We propose to assume the level r as follows

$$r = \kappa_{1,0}\big|_{t=T_r} + \sqrt{2\kappa_{2,0}\ln(\frac{\kappa_{2,0}^{1/2}}{2\pi\kappa_{0,2}^{1/2}\bar\eta_{0,T_r}})} \qquad (18)$$

where T_r is the designed construction's life time and $\bar\eta_{0,T_r}$ is the number of crossings the given level within the time period $(0,T_r)$ by structure response and $\bar\eta_{0,T_r}$ can be calculated from the expression

$$\bar\eta_{0,T_r}(r,x,T_r) = ln\frac{1}{1-p_f} \qquad (19)$$

in which the value of the probability of failure p_f is assumed. The formula (18) has been obtained from the Rice's formula for calculating the mean value of crossing rate in the case when the structure's response and its velocity have normal distributions.

4 INFLUENCE OF THE ALTERATION OF CAPACITY ON THE RELIABILITY OF BRIDGE

If the structure's capacity is degraded due to fatigue, corrosion etc. the first passage problem can be formulated in two different ways: in the first one the degradation is included into the threshold level $r = r(t)$ and can be for example described by equation (1) or (2). In this case the Rice's formula should be slightly modified
for the first model of the alteration

$$\bar{n}_+(r(t),x,t) = \int_0^\infty (\dot\sigma - \dot r(t))p_{\sigma\dot\sigma}(r(t),\dot\sigma,x,t)d\dot\sigma \qquad (20)$$

and for the second model of alteration (Sieniawska, Śniady, Żukowski, 1993)

$$\bar{n}_+(r(t),x,t) =$$
$$= \int_0^{R_0}\int_0^\infty (\dot\sigma - \dot r(t))p_{\sigma\dot\sigma}(r(t),\dot\sigma,x,t)f_R(r,t)d\dot\sigma \qquad (21)$$

In the second case the threshold level does not change in time and the structure's degradation and repair are included into alteration of their stiffness. This influence on the values of stresses which increases with the degradation and decreases after some repair. In this case the probabilistic characteristics of the stresses are changing in time, also. Such approach seems to be more compatible with the engineering intuition as the first one.

5 NUMERICAL RESULTS

Let the bridge be modeled by a two-span beam of finite length of each span l and I cross section built from steel. The probabilistic characteristic of the structure's response due to traffic flow modeled by a set of concentrated forces, which are moving along the bridge with constant speed and their arrival times constitute a Poisson stochastic process described in (Sieniawska, Śniady, 1990).
As an example the expected value of the stresses for $x = l/2$ in the first span, its standard deviation and the mean values $\bar{\eta}_{0,T_r}$ of crossing the level r as in equation (1) versus time are presented in the figures 3 and 4.
To compare the same quantities are calculated when the structure was not repaired. The results have been obtained for the following parameters: bridge span length $l = 30$ m, bridge mass per unit length m=3000

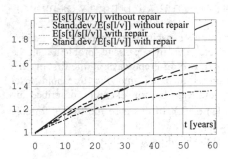

Figure 3.

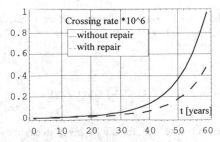

Figure 4.

kg/m, the damping coefficient $c = 0.3$ kg/s, the elasticity modulus of steel E_s=205000000kN/m^2, vehicle speed $v = 20$ m/s, the cross section A_s=0.0118 m^2, the moments of inertia $I_s = 0.005$ m^4, $T_r = 60$ years.

6 CONCLUSIONS

An approach for calculating the reliability of highway bridges due to traffic flow is presented. Two models for describing some kinds of structure degradation such as fatigue, corrosion, aging, etc. for bridges are proposed. The first one is very simple and seems to be good for estimating the bridge's reliability in such cases when its inspection are proceeded periodically and after them, if needed, takes place the repair. The model can be also useful for planning the optimal inspections and repairs time. In the second model, both the degradation and the repair are random. Such model can be good for assuming the reliability of old bridges, of which exploitation and repair history is unknown.
An important conclusion of the investigations seems to be the possibility of estimation the probability of failure when assuming the structure's life time or inverse from the graph of crossing rate $\bar{\eta}_{0,T_r}$ within the time period $(0,T_r)$.

ACKNOWLEDGEMENT

This research work was supported by the Scientific Research Committee in Warsaw under grant number 7 TO7E 01209.

REFERENCES

Madsen H.O., Sorensen J.D., (1990) Probability-Based Optimization of Fatigue Design, Inspection and Maintenance, *Int. Symp. on Offshore Structures*, University of Glasgow

Sieniawska R., Śniady P., (1990) First passage problem of the beam under a random stream of moving forces, *J. of Sound and Vibr.*, 136(2), 177-185.

Sieniawska R., Śniady P., Żukowski S. (1993). "Reliability of Structure Being Fatigue-degraded due to Stochastic Excitation", *Reliability and Optimization of Structural Systems*, **V (B-12)**, pp. 237-244, Thoft-Christensen E. and Ishikawa H., Elsevier Science Publishers B.V., IFIP.

Reliability of reinforced concrete bridge piers

Ichiro Iwaki
Department of Civil Engineering, Tohoku University, Aoba, Aramaki, Sendai, Japan (Formerly: Department of Civil, Environmental, and Architectural Engineering, University of Colorado, Boulder, Colo., USA)

Dan M. Frangopol
Department of Civil, Environmental, and Architectural Engineering, University of Colorado, Boulder, Colo., USA

ABSTRACT: During the past decade, strong earthquakes induced severe damages in many urban highway bridge systems in the U.S. and Japan. The collapses of reinforced concrete bridge piers are the result of different factors including underestimating load demands, insufficient ductility, and insufficient shear resistance due to insufficient confinement reinforcing steel, among others. In this study, the effects of several factors on the reliability of reinforced concrete bridge piers are investigated. In the analysis, the reliabilities of a reinforced concrete bridge pier at the cross section level and at the member level are both examined. The reliability analyses associated with different limit states including ultimate state, yielding of reinforcing steel in tension, and cracking of concrete are performed. The approach is demonstrated on a typical urban highway bridge structure composed of steel girders and reinforced concrete piers. A pier from this bridge is modeled and its reliability under seismic loads is evaluated considering the effects of ductility.

1 INTRODUCTION

During the past decade, the vulnerability of reinforced concrete bridge piers to strong earthquake ground motions was demonstrated in a number of major earthquakes in the U.S. and Japan including the 1989 Loma Prieta earthquake, the 1994 Northridge earthquake, and the 1995 Hyogoken - Nanbu earthquake. The latter earthquake induced damage nearly in every column along the elevated Hanshin Expressway through Kobe. The most spectacular failure where the bridge "rolled over" was a segment of reinforced concrete column supports (EERI 1995). Most of the bridges which suffered severe damages or collapsed were built before modern seismic design provisions were developed for reinforced concrete piers. For example, almost all reinforced concrete bridges which were severely damaged in the Hyogoken - Nanbu earthquake did not have specific detailing requirements to insure a ductile behavior of the piers. However, while most of the failures of reinforced concrete bridge piers may be attributed to insufficient confinement, the damage induced in many piers is still difficult to understand without detailed reliability analyses.

This paper is based on research in progress at the University of Colorado (Ide 1995, Frangopol et al. 1996, Iwaki 1996, Durmus 1996, Milner 1996, and Iwaki and Frangopol 1997) on reliability of reinforced concrete columns and bridge piers. In this study, the reliabilities of reinforced concrete bridge piers are examined at the cross section level and at the member level. The reliability analyses associated with different limit states including cracking of concrete, yielding of steel, and ultimate limit state are performed. The approach is demonstrated on a typical urban highway bridge structure used in Japan. The bridge has steel girders and reinforced concrete piers. A pier from this bridge is modeled and its reliability under seismic loads is evaluated considering the effects of ductility.

2 LIMIT STATES

Recently, Frangopol et al. (1996) used a fiber model formulation to construct failure surfaces of short and slender nondeterministic reinforced concrete columns taking into consideration both load

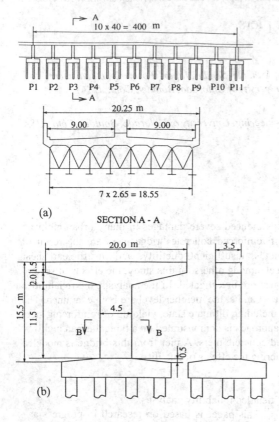

(a)

SECTION A - A

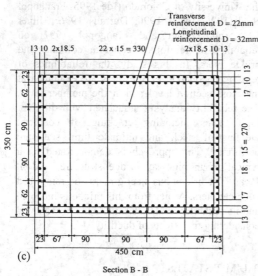

(b)

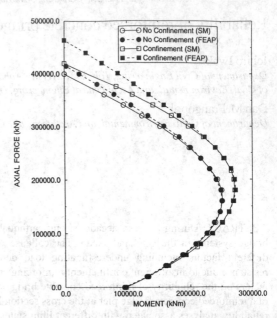

Figure 2. Failure Surfaces for Confined and Unconfined Concrete Models Generated by Finite Element Method (FEAP) and Simplified Method (SM).

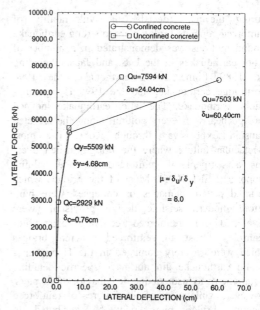

Figure 1. Highway Bridge System (Japan Road Association 1995): (a) Superstructure; and Reinforced Concrete Bridge Pier (b) Elevation, and (c) Cross-section.

Figure 3. Load - Deflection (Q-δ) Relations for Confined and Unconfined Concrete Models.
Note: δ is computed at the center of gravity of the superstructure.

path and load correlation effects. It was shown that this model can adequately represent the nonlinear behavior of a reinforced concrete cross section, member, and structure under nonproportional loads. In this study, the fiber model is used to generate the limit states of a reinforced concrete pier of a typical urban bridge system in Japan (Japan Road Association 1995).

Figure 1(a) shows the typical highway bridge structure. Pier P_3 (see Figure 1(a)) is considered in the numerical example. Its elevation and cross-section are shown in Figures 1(b) and 1(c), respectively (Japan Road Association 1995). Since the stresses of both concrete and reinforcing steel for the transverse direction are more severe than those for the longitudinal direction, the investigation is performed for the transverse direction only. All data associated with the superstructure (Figure 1(a)), substructure (Figures 1(b) and 1(c)), natural period, longitudinal and transverse reinforcing, confined and unconfined concrete models, steel model, and load effects are given in Iwaki (1996). Using two analysis methods, the fiber model method implemented in the general purpose program FEAP described in Zienkiewicz and Taylor (1989, 1991), and the simplified method (SM) described in Ide (1995), three limit states (i.e., cracking of concrete, yielding of steel, and ultimate state) of the reinforced concrete bridge pier P_3 are computed considering both confined and unconfined concrete models. As an example, Figure 2 shows the comparison of ultimate limit states (i.e., failure surfaces of the cross-section under the most severe load combination) between confined and unconfined concrete cases associated with the fiber model (FEAP) and the simplified method (SM). Also, lateral load - lateral deflection (Q-δ) relations for both confined and unconfined concrete cases were computed according to the provisions of the Japan Highway Bridge Design Code (Japan Road Association 1990). These relations are shown in Figure 3. In this figure, Q_c, Q_y, and Q_u are the lateral loads associated with cracking of concrete in tension, yielding of reinforcing steel in tension, and ultimate state, respectively. Their associated lateral deflections are δ_c, δ_y, δ_u, respectively. As expected, in the confined case the ductility factor $\mu = \delta_u / \delta_y$ is improved considerably.

3 RELIABILITY ANALYSIS

In the previous section the bridge pier in Figure 1 was studied from a deterministic viewpoint. In reality, loads, material properties, and dimensions are random. Under seismic loading, however, the uncertainty in earthquake contributes the most to the limit state probability. Assuming seismic and gravity loads as random variables having Type-II and log-normal density distributions with coefficients of variation 0.85 and 0.15, respectively, Figure 4 shows the relation between the reliability index and the mode of acceleration for three limit states (i.e., cracking of concrete, yielding of steel, and ultimate limit state). As indicated, as the mode of acceleration increases the reliability index associated with each limit state remarkably decreases, especially for cracking. Considering the effects of ductility, the design force associated with the seismic load can be reduced according to Japan Highway Bridge Design Code (Japan Road Association 1990). By taking into account the characteristics of the Hyogoken - Nanbu earthquake (Iwaki 1996) and the Japan Highway Bridge Design Code (Japan Road Association 1990) the reliability index of the reinforced concrete bridge pier P_3 was $\beta = 0.46$ for a ductility factor $\mu = 8.0$ and $\beta = 0.92$ for a ductility factor $\mu = 12.9$. Therefore, the reliability of the reinforced concrete bridge pier is very low.

Finally, the shear reliability of the bridge pier in Figure 1 was investigated by considering the seismic load as a Type-II random variable with a coefficient of variation (COV) of 0.85; the gravity load (COV = 0.15), the steel yield strength (COV = 0.10), and the concrete shear strength (COV = 0.18) as log-normal distributed variables; and the concrete compressive strength (COV = 0.12) as a normal distributed variable (Iwaki 1996). For this particular example, it was concluded that the shear reliability was greater than the flexural reliability, which means that bending failure will most probably occur first. However, as the height of the pier decreases, the reliability with respect to bending is approaching that for shear. The results presented in Iwaki (1996) show that the reliabilities with respect to shear and bending are almost the same when the pier height is reduced from 15 m (Figure 1(b)) to 7 m.

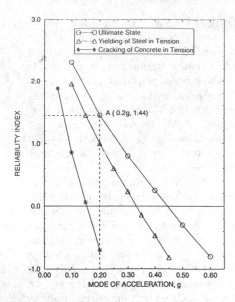

Figure 4. Reliability Index Versus Acceleration for Different Limit States.

4 CONCLUSIONS

In this study, the reliability of a typical reinforced concrete pier of an urban highway bridge system in Japan is investigated. The cross-section under the most severe load combination is considered. The limit states (failure surfaces) of this cross section are examined. Three different limit states are considered as follows: cracking of concrete, yielding of reinforcing steel, and ultimate limit state. These limit states are associated with different levels of damage induced by earthquake. Cracking of concrete corresponds to minimal damage due to a relatively small earthquake, yielding of reinforcing steel corresponds to repairable damage due to a moderate earthquake, and ultimate state corresponds to a significant damage due to a strong earthquake. The failure surfaces are obtained for both confined and unconfined concrete models by using a finite element method and a simplified method. Moreover, the ductility of the pier is also computed for both confined and unconfined concrete models. Under a seismic excitation comparable to that of the Hyogoken - Nanbu earthquake, the bridge pier showed low reliability levels with respect to both bending and shear. While useful results have been obtained in this study at the member (bridge pier) level, questions still remain on the seismic reliabilities of the pier - to - girder joint and of the bridge system. Further research is needed in these areas.

REFERENCES

Durmus, A. 1996. Reliability of reinforced concrete columns under cyclic loading, *MS Thesis*, Dept. of Civil Engr., Univ. of Colorado, Boulder, Colorado.

EERI : Earthquake Engineering Research Institute 1995. The Hyogo-Ken Nanbu Earthquake: Preliminary Reconnaissance Report, Oakland, California.

Frangopol, D.M., Ide, Y., Spacone, E., and Iwaki, I. 1996. A new look at reliability of reinforced concrete columns. *Structural Safety*, 18: 123-150.

Ide, Y. 1995. Reliability of reinforced concrete columns under random loading, *MS Thesis*, Dept. of Civil Engr., Univ. of Colorado, Boulder, Colorado.

Iwaki, I. 1996. Reliability of reinforced concrete bridge piers under seismic loads. *MS Thesis*, Dept. of Civil Engr., Univ. of Colorado, Boulder, Colorado.

Iwaki, I. and Frangopol, D.M. 1997. Reliability based evaluation of reinforced concrete bridge piers under seismic loads, Japan Concrete Institute, Tokyo, submitted.

Japan Road Association 1990. *Japan Highway Bridge Design Code*, Tokyo.

Japan Road Association 1995. *Draft of Guide Specification for Repair and Reconstruction of Highway Bridge which Supported Damage Due to the Hyogoken-Nanbu Earthquake*, Tokyo.

Milner, D. 1996. Reliability of short and slender reinforced concrete columns, *MS Thesis*, Dept. of Civil Engr., University of Colorado, Boulder, Colorado.

Zienkiewicz, O.C. and Taylor, R.L. 1989, 1991. *The Finite Element Method*, 1&2, McGraw-Hill, London.

Structural Safety and Reliability, Shiraishi, Shinozuka & Wen (eds) © 1998 Balkema, Rotterdam, ISBN 90 5410 978 5

Stochastical analysis of highway bridge across Vltava River

Aleš Florian
Department of Structural Mechanics, Technical University of Brno, Czech Republic

Jaroslav Navrátil
Department of Concrete and Masonry Structures, Technical University of Brno, Czech Republic

ABSTRACT: The detailed stochastical time-dependent analysis of the bridge during the construction process is performed. Uncertainties in mechanical, geometrical, environmental, and loading characteristics as well as in construction process and modeling errors are considered. Statistics of input variables are based on in-situ measurements. The concrete creep and shrinkage model is updated based on short-term measurements.

INTRODUCTION

The remarkable long-span structures used in modern design practice require top design methods and construction technology. During the construction the structure utilizes different structural systems; boundary conditions change, new structural members are cast, post-tensioning is applied, and temporary support elements are removed. Concrete structural elements of various age are combined and the concrete is gradually loaded. Rheological properties of concrete and the development of micro cracks can influence behavior of the structure in decisive way. Also the uncertainties in geometrical, physical, mechanical, chemical, climatic, loading, environmental and technical properties as well as in construction process and modeling errors must be taken into account. Only the combination of numerical methods of structural analysis with modern reliability methods provides an effective tool for solution of the problem.

The time-dependent analysis of highway bridge across Vltava River (Czech Republic), see Cieslar et al. 1995, is performed. The main spans (69+125+69 m) have been built using the cantilever construction method. The crucial moment of the construction is the connection of two ends of both double-cantilevers of different age. The cantilevers deflect different each other.

The analysis is based on the time-discretization method which is combined with the finite element analysis. The construction process is respected in detail. The B3 model for concrete creep and shrinkage is used with the extension to cyclic humidity. The input variables are taken as random ones. They describe uncertainties in mechanical properties of materials, geometry of the structure including the position of prestressing steel in cross-section, loading characteristics, environmental properties, changes in time, and especially the uncertainties in construction process and concrete creep and shrinkage. Also uncertainties due to modeling errors are incorporated into the analysis. The simulation technique Latin Hypercube Sampling is used for the statistical analysis. For the purpose of sensitivity analysis, the measure based on the Spearman rank correlation coefficient is used. Reliability analysis is based on the calculation of reliability index β.

1 STRUCTURAL MODEL

The method for time-dependent analysis is based on a step-by-step computer procedure, see Navrátil 1992, in which the time domain is subdivided into discrete time intervals. The finite element analysis is performed in each time node. The element stiffness matrix and load vector terms include the effect of axial, bending and shear deformations. The elements are installed or removed according to the way of construction. The effect of different age of the elements representing the structural members made of concrete is respected. All operations used in the construction such as addition or removal of segments and prestressing cables, changes of boundary

ELEVATION

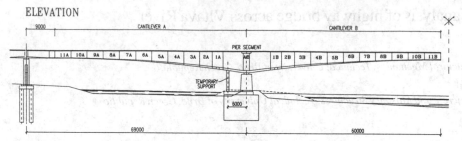

Fig. 1 Bridge across Vltava River

conditions, loads and prescribed displacements are modeled.

The time-dependent analysis has been performed for one double-cantilever, see Fig. 1, until the nominal time of connecting the ends of both double-cantilevers. The structural model consists of 617 elements, which represent concrete box girder, prestressed tendons, reinforcement, diaphragms, piers, temporary anchoring and supports, and the elements representing the formwork traveler.

Individual cast-in place segments are modeled in parts by prismatic finite elements. The centroidal axis of the elements in tapered portion of girder is placed in appropriate eccentricity. Also prestressing tendons and reinforcement are modeled by finite elements in an eccentricity. The geometry, and sequence of stressing of real tendons is respected. Short-term losses of prestressing are calculated in advance, losses caused by relaxation of prestressing steel are applied immediately after jacking, which simplifies the input data. The calculation of long-term losses in prestressed tendons is included in the method itself.

All construction steps are modeled according to designed schedule. The time of casting of bridge piers is considered as the starting point. The changes of structural configuration or loading are performed in 60 time nodes. The finite element analysis of the structure is performed in 148 time nodes to refine the creep analysis. The phases of balanced cantilever construction of one double-cantilever and the construction of side-span end section cast on stage are analyzed.

The linear aging viscoelastic theory is applied for the rheological analysis. Therefore, the creep prediction model is based upon the assumption of linearity between stresses and strains to assure the applicability of linear superposition. The development of modulus of elasticity in time due to the aging of concrete is respected. The numerical solution is based on the replacement of Stieltjes hereditary integral by a finite sum. Thus the general creep problem is converted to a series of elasticity

problems. The shrinkage and creep of structural members is predicted through the mean properties of a given cross-section taking into account the average relative humidity and member size.

The largest source of uncertainty in creep and shrinkage prediction is the dependence of model parameters on the composition and strength of concrete. To reduce this uncertainty the short-time measurements of creep and shrinkage of small size specimens were carried out and were used for the updating of the prediction, see Strásky et al. 1996. The B3 model, see Bažant and Baweja 1995, for creep and shrinkage of concrete is used. The updated parameters were modified for the real bridge structure. The procedure of updating is discussed in Navrátil 1996.

Various permanent or temporary loads are applied step-by-step according to real construction schedule. It is in particular dead weight of concrete, reinforcing bars, prestressing steel, and grouting, weight of temporary ballast and weight of travelers.

2 RELIABILITY ANALYSIS

The Latin Hypercube Sampling technique is used for the purpose of statistical analysis, see McKay et al. 1979, Florian 1992. It theoretically provides estimates of some statistical parameters with lower bias and reduced variance in comparison with Simple Random Sampling or other sampling techniques. Thus the number of simulations needed for reliable estimates of commonly used statistical parameters is generally very low. The number of simulation equals 30 in the presented study.

In the sensitivity analysis the measure based on the Spearman rank correlation coefficient is used, see Florian and Navrátil 1993. The higher the Spearman coefficient, the higher the sensitivity of the output to the random variability of an appropriate input variable. Results of sensitivity analysis are obtained

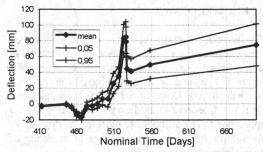

Fig. 2 Deflection of the End of Cantilever

obtained from a reliability analysis depends on these statistics in decisive way. Some of the input variables including e.g. dimensions of cross-section, strength and unit weight of concrete, content of cement, sand, aggregate and water in concrete, modulus of elasticity of tendons, and prestressing force after anchoring etc. were measured experimentally in situ, see Stráský et al. 1996, and were carefully statistically evaluated, see Florian 1996/1. Also other variables including type of curing, cement type and information about humidity and about temporary support were calculated based on available statistical data. The B3 model for concrete creep and shrinkage was updated based on short-term measurements of 6 specimens, see Navrátil 1996. The results of updated models were compared with laboratory measured data and statistically evaluated, see Florian 1996/2. They incorporate the modeling error effect as well. The statistical parameters of rest input variables are based on the professional judgment and information obtained from literature.

as a part of statistical and/or probability analysis. No additional simulations are necessary.

Probability analysis is based on calculation of reliability index β. The probability of failure (or generally probability of exceeding of some prescribed limits) is then calculated as

$$p_f = \Phi(-\beta) \qquad (1)$$

where Φ - cumulative distribution function of standardized normal distribution.

3 BASIC RANDOM VARIABLES

The input variables describing geometrical, physical, mechanical, chemical, climatic, environmental, loading, and technical properties as well as construction process and modeling errors are supposed to be random ones. Totally 67 basic random variables are used in the study. They are described by the assumed cumulative distribution function (generally three-parametric) and by appropriate statistical parameters. A lot of effort was made to obtain statistical parameters exact as most as possible, because the reliability and quality of results

4 RESULTS

For the sake of brevity only some illustrative results are shown in Figs. 2 - 4. The following notation is used: mean - mean value, 0,05 - 5% quantil, 0,95 - 95% quantil.

In Fig. 2 the deflection of the end of cantilever in time is shown.

The results of sensitivity analysis are shown in Fig. 3. There are shown the input variables having generally high influence on deflection of the end of cantilever in time: relative error of prestressing of some tendons (32), anchoring tie strain (45), effective cross-section thickness (51), duration of curing (52), cement content (54), microcracking (60), ambient relative humidity (62), and creep of

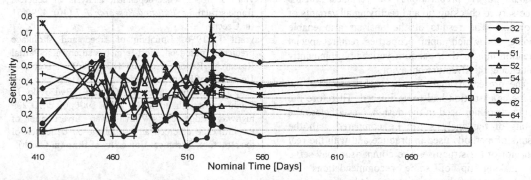

Fig. 3 Sensitivity Analysis of Deflection of the End of Cantilever

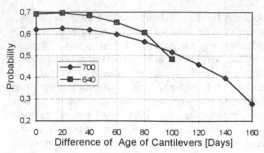

Fig. 4 Connection of Ends of Cantilevers

concrete (64). Also the influence of another 13 input variables is not neglectable. It means, that only a few input variables (from totally 67) have an impact on the deflection and that the influence of concrete creep seems to be the most important. Also this impact is generally different in different time nodes.

The most important moment in the bridge construction is the connection of free ends of both double-cantilevers. The same technology is used for their erection but they can be of different age. Also the nominal time of connection could be different. The acceptable difference between the deflections of both ends was considered ±20mm. The probability that deflections of both ends at the time of connection are within above mentioned limits is presented in Fig. 4. Two variants are supposed - the connection is accomplished (i) at the nominal time 700 days, (ii) at the nominal time 640 days.

CONCLUSIONS

The analysis of a structure using the presented method provides the designer with reliability limits of the response of the structure. It enables the determination of possible critical development in the time-dependent behavior resulting in timely (at the design stage) preparations of technical means necessary to checking up and rectifying all variants of evolution. The results of the analysis also enable finding out which input properties require special attention due to their random variability dominantly influencing the structure behavior.

The presented analysis was performed after the bridge construction had been finished. Therefore the results were not used in the design. Nevertheless the results of the analysis can be compared with the results of methods used in practice and with the real behavior of the structure. The comparison may serve for making up of some recommendations for calculation of deflections of long-span bridges.

ACKNOWLEDGMENTS

The financial support of Grant Agency of Czech Republic under research contract No. 103/95/0048 and Ministry of Education under contract No. FR260773 is greatly acknowledged. The facilities and help by the Dept. of Structural Mechanics and Dept. of Concrete and Masonry Structures is also appreciated. The authors are indebted to Prof. Z. P. Bažant for his support and advices in modeling of concrete creep and shrinkage.

REFERENCES

Bažant Z. P., Baweja S. 1995. Creep and Shrinkage Prediction Model for Analysis and Design of Concrete Structures - Model B3. RILEM Recommendation. *Mater. Struct.* 28: 357-365.

Cieslar P., Landa T., Žurych R. 1995. The bridge across Vltava River near Vepřek. *Concrete and masonry* 4: 5-9 (in Czech).

Florian A. 1992. An Efficient Sampling Scheme: Updated Latin Hypercube Sampling. *J. Probabilistic Engineering Mechanics* 7(2): 123 - 130.

Florian A. 1996/1. Statistical Evaluation of Experimental Data - D8-0802c/SO 209 Highway Bridge across Vltava River. Partial Research Report No. 09-103/0048/95, Technical University of Brno (in Czech).

Florian A. 1996/2. Statistical Analysis of Concrete Creep and Shrinkage Prediction from Short-Term Tests. Partial Research Report No. 08-103/0048/95, Technical University of Brno.

Florian A., Navrátil J. 1993. Reliability Analysis of the Cable Stayed Bridge in Construction and Service Stages, 6th Int. Conf. on Struct. Safety and Reliability ICOSSAR'93, Innsbruck, Austria.

McKay M. D., Beckman R. J., Conover W. J. 1979. A Comparison of Three Methods for Selecting Values of Input Variables in the Analysis of Output from a Computer Code. *Technometrics* 2: 239-245.

Navrátil J. 1992. Time-dependent analysis of concrete frame structures. *Building Research J.* 7 (40): 429-451 (in Czech).

Navrátil J. 1996. Updating of creep and shrinkage prediction based on short-term measurements. Partial Research Report No. 03-103/0048/95, Technical University of Brno (in Czech).

Stráský J., Navrátil J., Zich M., Cikrle P., Bydžovský J., Chalupná M., Chandoga M. 1996. D8-0802 c/SO 209 highway bridge across Vltava River - investigation of the influence of creep and shrinkage on deflection of the structure. Technical University of Brno (in Czech).

Structural Safety and Reliability, Shiraishi, Shinozuka & Wen (eds) © 1998 Balkema, Rotterdam, ISBN 90 5410 978 5

Aseismic assessment of bridge piers

Bo Hu, Wancheng Yuan & Lichu Fan
Tongji University, Shanghai, People's Republic of China

ABSTRACT: A relative simple probabilistic procedure is used to evaluate the seismic reliability of bridge piers. The structure is modelled as a lumped-mass SDOF(Single Degree of Freedom) system and the non-linear relationship in bridge piers is used to get the characteristic of the model. Then by transforming the random process to random variables, the reliability is calculated by FORM(First Order Reliability Method). The relationship of displacement ductility and reliability is discussed and how to make safety level criteria is also discussed.

1. Introduction

The seismic damages of bridges mainly occur in the sub-structures especially in the piers. So the aseismic capacity of bridge piers is of vital importance to the dynamic safety of the whole structure and the proper seismic evaluation of piers is fundamental to the determination of bridge performance.

Usually the most important contents included in seismic evaluation of structures are the method of analysis and the safety criteria. Depending on the nature of the variables considered, the method of analysis can be classified as: deterministic or probabilistic. Because there are important uncertainties existing in earthquake problems such as the input ground motion and properties of the soil, materials and structure, it seems more reasonable to use probabilistic method, but in fact deterministic method is now used widely and the use of probabilistic method is limited. The main reasons are the complex of probabilistic procedure and the lack of computational tools.

In this study, we presented a simplified probabilistic procedure of bridge piers. By analysing the non-linear properties relationship in bridge piers, the dynamic model is derived, then the reliability is calculated using FORM. In the last part the relationship of ductility and reliability and the safety level criteria are discussed.

2. Reliability Calculating

2.1 Modelling

Single column piers (Fig. 1) are often used in beam bridges especially in urban viaducts. Its lateral dynamic characteristic can be modelled as a SDOF oscillator with the lumped mass. In elastic response stage the relationship between the displacement of the mass centre and the curvature at the column base section is :

$$\Delta = \frac{\phi L^2}{3} \tag{1}$$

in which: Δ is the displacement of the centre of the lumped mass; ϕ is the curvature at the column base; L is the distance from the column base to the centre of the mass.

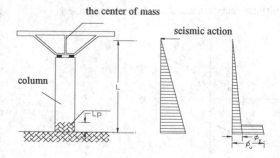

Fig. 1 Bridge piers under severe earthquake

Under severe earthquake, the structure is permitted undergo inelastic deformation. From the moment distribution it could be concluded that the plastic hinge occurs at the column base. So with the plastic hinge assume the total displacement of the centre of the mass can be written as [5]:

$$\Delta = \frac{\phi_y L^2}{3} + (\phi - \phi_y) L_p (L - L_p) \qquad (2)$$

in which: ϕ_y is the curvature at the column base at first yield point; L_p is the equivalent plastic hinge length.

The moment-curvature relationship of RC section subjected to bending and shear forces could be taken as bilinear. The relationship between the displacement of the mass centre and the section curvature at column base is linear in any deformation stage and the column base bending moment is the product of the seismic force acting at the centre of the lumped mass and the distance L, so the displacement-force relationship at the centre of the mass is bilinear (Fig. 2) . The two points which determine the characteristic of bilinear hysteretic system are the yield point and the ultimate deformation point given as:

$$\begin{cases} f_y = M_y \cdot L \\ x_y = \dfrac{\phi_y L^2}{3} \end{cases}$$

$$\text{and} \quad \begin{cases} f_u = M_u \cdot L \\ x_u = \dfrac{\phi_y L^2}{3} + (\phi_u - \phi_y) L_p (L - 0.5 L_p) \end{cases} \qquad (3)$$

in which: f_y is the force at the first yield; x_y is the displacement at first yield; M_y is the bending moment at the column base at first yield; f_u is the force at ultimate deformation; x_u is the displacement at ultimate deformation; M_u is the bending moment at the column base at ultimate deformation; ϕ_u is the ultimate curvature at the column base section.

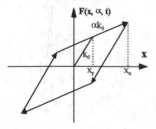

Fig.2 The relationship between displacementand force at the top of piers

So the following reliability analysis could be based on the results of the response of SDOF non-linear oscillator subjected to random seismic excitation.

2.2 Stochastic Response

There are usually two ways to calculate the dynamic reliability: one is to solve the first excursion time directly from the stochastic dynamic equation; the other is to get the moment of response power spectral density first, then use random variables to replace stochastic process to get the reliability index like normal reliability problem. The second one is of wide engineering interest and is used in this study.

Based on a semi-empirical relation developed by Kiureghian [3] for the mean and variance of the peak of a stationary Gaussian process. It is given as:

$$\mu_e = \left(\sqrt{2 \ln \upsilon_e \tau} + \frac{0.5772}{\sqrt{2 \ln \upsilon_e \tau}} \right) \sigma_y \qquad (4)$$

$$\sigma_e = \begin{cases} \left[\dfrac{1.2}{\sqrt{2 \ln \upsilon_e \tau}} - \dfrac{5.4}{13 + (2 \ln \upsilon_e \tau)^{3.2}} \right] \sigma_y, & \upsilon_e \tau > 2.1 \\ 0.65 \sigma_y, & \upsilon_e \tau \le 2.1 \end{cases}$$

in which: μ_e is the mean of the response peak; σ_e is the standard deviation of the response peak; ν_e is the reduced mean zero-crossing rate; τ is the duration of excitation; σ_y is the standard deviation of the response.

When the response steps into inelastic stage, equivalent linearization method [2] is used to get the non-linear response peak moments. Equivalent stiffness is:

$$k_e (\mu) = \frac{k_0}{\mu} [(1 - \alpha)(1 + \ln \mu) + \alpha \mu] \qquad (5)$$

Equivalent damping ratio with initial value 0.05, consist with Chinese design code JTJ004-89, is:

$$\xi_e = 0.05 + 0.15 \cdot \left[1 - \sqrt{\frac{1 + \alpha (\mu - 1)}{\mu}} \right] \qquad (6)$$

where μ is the displacement ductility factor; in stochastic response analysis it is defined as the ratio of the mean of the response peak and the displacement at first yield; α is the hardening coefficient of bilinear system.

In every iteration step equivalent stiffness and damping ratio are calculated again according to the latest calculating value of μ and the moment of non-linear peak could be get with convergence as controlling condition. The seismic excitation is modelled as a mean zero filter white noise stationary Gaussian process.

2.3 Reliability Calculation

Reliability is always corresponding with certain limit states. In structure design, two levels limit states of serviceability limit state and ultimate limit state are mostly used. So in this study two levels limit states are defined as: elastic limit state and ultimate deformation limit state. They are specified by the response displacement and the displacement capacity of bridge piers at first yield and ultimate deformation.

According to results of some experiments and research, it could be assumed that the probability distribution of both seismic response peak and ultimate displacement capacity of RC structures are log-normal, so by FORM method, the reliability of bridge piers under certain seismic intensity could be written as:

$$P_s(S < R|A_d) = \Phi(\beta) \tag{7}$$

in which: $\beta = \dfrac{\ln\left(\dfrac{\sqrt{1+v_s^2}}{\sqrt{1+v_R^2}} \cdot \dfrac{m_R}{m_s}\right)}{\sqrt{\ln(1+v_R^2)(1+v_s^2)}}$, is the reliability index, A_d is the design P.G.A. of ground motion; m_R is the mean of the resistance of structures; m_s is the mean of the seismic action; v_R is the variance coefficient of the resistance of structures; v_s is the variance coefficient of the seismic action.

3. Ductility and Reliability

In seismic design, ductility is now accepted widely as an effective way to improve the seismic capacity of structures. Using energy concept, to improve the ductility of structures is to increase the energy dissipation capacity, so the structure can dissipate more energy by plastic deformation to ensure the safety under severe earthquake. In dynamic reliability, seismic damages are mostly caused by the first excursion of deformation barriers. For this reason, the improvement of ductility could enhances the ultimate deformation capacity of structures and the barrier value turns big, so the seismic reliability will increases greatly with the improvement of structure ductility.

From the analysis above, the moments of non-linear response peak of bridge piers are only concerned with the initial stiffness and the hardening coefficient but have nothing to do with the ultimate deformation capacity, so when the value of variance coefficients is relatively small, the relationship between the displacement ductility factor and the reliability index can be expressed approximately from eq.(7) as:

$$\beta \approx \frac{\ln m_R - \ln m_s}{\sqrt{v_R^2 \mid v_s^2}} = \frac{\ln(\mu \cdot \Delta_y) - \ln m_s}{\sqrt{v_R^2 + v_s^2}}$$
$$= \frac{\ln \mu + \ln \dfrac{\Delta_y}{m_s}}{\sqrt{v_R^2 + v_s^2}} \tag{8}$$

The eq.(8) indicates the log relationship exists between the ductility and the reliability index and could be used to calibrate the seismic design codes or determines the value of ductility factor when the target reliability is given.

Example: a viaduct pier as shown in Fig. 1; the width of the column is 2m; the depth is 1m; the distance from the mass centre to the column base is 10m; the mass is 500000kg; the concrete is R40; the longitudinal steel ratio is 1.5% and the calculating dynamic parameters are: yield strength is 1010kN; yield displacement is 0.03m, the hardening coeffient is 0.16; 0.08 is adopted as the variance coeffient and the design P.G.A. is 0.2g.

Fig. 3 showns the relationship between the ductility factor and the reliability index. It could be concluded that the ductility should be improved as greatly as possible in the range consistent with other structural constraints to incease the dynamic reliability of piers.

4. Safety levels Criteria

In probability-based design codes, target reliability index is used as a quantitative measure of acceptable performance to ensure the safety level of the structure. In theory the selection of target reliability is required in support of life cycle cost analysis and some other socio-economic analysis, but the difficulty is obvious and this fact is often adduced against the use of probabilistic method as a basis for decision-making.

There are three main way to determine the value of target reliability: analogy, calibration and optimisation. and now the calibration method is mostly used to circumvent the problem.

The essence of calibration is to inhere the safety

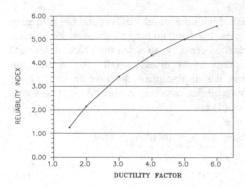

Fig. 3 Reliability and ductility

degree of the existing design code, which suggests that the safety level of the existing design code has been verified, so it can be used as the safety criteria basis. In common structural problems, it could be guaranteed by lots of engineering experience, but in earthquake problems, because of the lack of seismic damage information and unsatisfactory performance in recent several earthquakes of bridge we can conclude that it is not a right way to get the seismic design target reliability from the calibration of the existing bridge design codes.

But the calibration is still a useful tool to select the target reliability. The key of calibration method is to find what the calculating (nominal) reliability really means in engineering practice. So in earthquake problems what we need now is to find such functions or indexes that could reflect the real safety level of structures under seismic loading and at the same time have certain relationship with the calculating (nominal) reliability as the criteria to evaluate the practical engineering safety level of the calculating reliability to get the seismic design target reliability. That is to say the calibration of the verified facts could be used to set up the safety level criteria.

For example, in recent years the Park and Ang[4] damage model based on the maximum displacement and total hysteretic energy dissipation is considered to be a good measurement of damage degrees of structural members or the global structure because of the broad experimental basis.

So we can take the ultimate deformation as the limit state to calibration the damage index with different value in the term of reliability to get the target reliability accord with different damage levels or safety levels. Other verified functions or indexes could be also used. But the fulfilment still needs a lot of further study.

5. Conclusion

Probabilistic analysis method is used in this study to evaluate the aseismic capasity of bridge piers. The following conclusions can be drawn :
1. The non-linear relationship of moment-curvature of the column base section can be used to establish the hysteretic bilinear model of the structure. The modelling procedure can be extended easily to other types bridge piers such as bi-column, multi-column and so on.
2. By transforming the stochastic process to random variables, the dynamic reliability can be relatively simply derived by FORM with the moments of the response peak.
3. The relationship between the displacement ductility factor and reliability index can be expressed as logarithm form and the ductility of piers in seismic design should be improved as greatly as possible in the range consistant with other structural constriants.

Acknowledgement

This study was carried out with the financial support of China National Key Project on Basis and Application Research: Application Research on Safety of Major Construction Projects.

References

(1) Ellingwood, B. R. (1994). Probability-Based Codified Design: Past Accomplishments and Future Challenges, Structural Safety, 13(1994), 159-176
(2) Jiang, Jinren, et al., (1984). Stochastic Seismic Response Analysis of Hysteretic MDF Structures Using Mean Response Spectra, Earthquake Engineering and Engineering Vibration, 4(4), 1-13 (in Chinese)
(3) Kiureghian, A. D. (1980). Structural Response to Stationary Excitation, J. of Engrg. Mech., ASCE, 106(6), 1195-1213
(4) Park, Y. J. and Ang, A. H. S. (1985). Mechanistic Seismic Damage Model for Reinforced Concrete, J. of Struct. Engrg., ASCE, 111(4), 722-739
(5) Priestley, MJN. and Park, R. (1987). Strength and Ductility of Concrete Bridge Columns Under Seismic Loading, J. of ACI, 84(1), 61-76

Structural Safety and Reliability, Shiraishi, Shinozuka & Wen (eds) © 1998 Balkema, Rotterdam, ISBN 90 5410 978 5

Case study of accident due to lateral buckling of a composite girder bridge during demolition

Katsutoshi Ohdo & Shigeo Hanayasu
National Institute of Industrial Safety, Kiyose, Tokyo, Japan

ABSTRACT: On a falling down accident of a composite girder bridge during demolition, structural safety analysis was conducted to determine the causes of this accident. From the analysis, several accident causes including improper work procedures, an inappropriate structural safety examination during the design stage for demolition work, inadequate safety management system, were identified.

1 INTRODUCTION

This paper presents a case study of a recent accident due to lateral buckling of a composite girder bridge during demolition. The bridge analyzed here was constructed in the early 1960's crossing over a 100 m width river. In 1995, a new bridge was constructed nearby, so that removal of the old bridge was planned and carried out.

During the demolition work of the old composite girder bridge, when a part of the concrete slab of the bridge was removed using a concrete breaker, a falling down accident due to lateral buckling of the bridge girder took place. The edges of the main girders of the bridge slid away from the pier and fell down into the river bank together with the workers, concrete breaker, and dump truck. As a result, one worker died and three workers were injured.

A case study of this accident to clarify the main causes that led to the accident including structural safety analyses in terms of the bridge stability during the demolition work were examined.

2 BRIDGE STRUCTURE AND DEMOLITION WORK PROCEDURES

The general elevation and cross section of the bridge is shown in Fig. 1. The bridge is a relatively small structure having a 21.6 m span length, 6.1 m in width, and 1.6 m in height consisting of three 1.2 m height main girders with two inner sub-girders and concrete slab (0.16 m thickness at the center).

The distance between main girders was 2.1 m each.

Lateral braces installed in the cross frames to connect main and sub-girders were set 5 places between a 5.4 m distance each along with the bridge axis. The 5.4 m length and 0.8 m height inner sub-girders were set between main girders and fixed with lateral braces and end plates installed.

The actual demolition work process carried out until the accident occurrence is as follows.

(1) Remove the inner lateral braces between main and sub-girders due to the inconvenience of setting

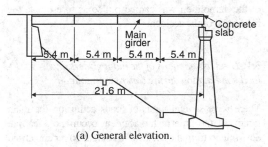

(a) General elevation.

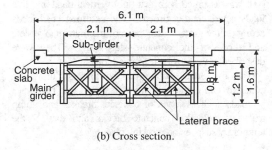

(b) Cross section.

Fig. 1. General elevation and cross section of bridge.

work place beneath the main girder by sub-contractor A.

(2) Set the suspension temporary working place for workers beneath the main girder to catch any destroyed concrete debris by sub-contractor A.

(3) Remove the concrete slab over the main girders using a concrete breaker and a dump truck by different sub-contractor B.

(4) During the course of demolition when one-forth of the total span of concrete slab (5.4m) from the pier side edge of main girders was removed, the falling down accident took place. Prior to the concrete slab demolition work the sub-contractor who carried out the concrete slab demolition had not been informed that lateral braces had already been removed.

3 STRUCTURAL SAFETY ANALYSIS OF FAILURE ACCIDENT

To clarify the cause that led to the accident, in this study, the bending stress acting on the main girders and their corresponding allowable and failure stresses in terms of lateral buckling and local buckling were analyzed in accordance with the work process of the concrete slab demolition. This analysis was examined for two types of girder configuration; i.e.,

(1) Girders fixed with lateral braces (Fig. 1).
(2) Girders without lateral braces (Fig. 2).

A comparison between the analyzed bending stress and corresponding allowable/failure stress for each stage of the demolition was carried out so as to estimate the likelihood of the accident.

3.1 *Load assumptions of the main girders and load combination during concrete demolition*

There were several kinds of loads acting on the main girders at the time of the accident occurrence, that are determined from the accident investigation report carried out by the labour standard office.

It was assumed here that only vertical dead and live loads acted on the girders. The assumed dead loads acting on the girders were those of main and sub-girders and those of the concrete slab deck. They were described as uniformly distributed loads.

The live loads acting on the girders during the concrete slab demolition were classified into two types of loads such as loads of concrete breaker and dump truck with loaded concrete blocks and that of the temporary suspension working place.

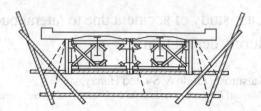

Fig. 2. Analyzed girder configuration without braces.

The temporary suspension work place load was analyzed as a uniformly distributed load and the loads due to the concrete breaker as well as the dump truck, etc. were analyzed as the concentrated loads.

The concrete breaker and the dump truck for demolition were located in the center of the slab deck of the bridge during operations. Therefore the share proportion of concentrated live loads between three main girders was assumed that a half of the concentrated live loads were supported by the central main girder and the rest were supported by two outer girders equally (i.e., 1/4 of live load). The dead loads and the uniformly distributed live load were allocated to the three main girders equally.

In accordance with the progress of concrete slab demolition, the load combination has been changing. Figure 3 shows the five different concrete demolition work stages along with the work process and their corresponding load combination.

3.2 *Failure modes of girder*

From the accident investigation report, the failure modes for the structural safety analysis were assumed as lateral and local buckling of the main girder. However, from only the observational investigation of the accident, it was difficult to identify which types of buckling modes were dominant to the girder collapse. Therefore, both types of buckling failure modes were examined.

Figure 4 shows the assumed failure modes due to lateral buckling of the main girder at the time of the accident occurrence. Figure 4 (a) shows the case for a girder fixed with lateral braces. On the left-side girder edge, both horizontal displacement and torsion have been constrained while only horizontal displacement was constrained on the right edge. This failure mode was observed in the outer main girder in this collapse. Figure 4 (b) shows the case for a girder without lateral braces. In this case, torsion was not constrained on the left-side girder edge. This failure mode was observed at the central main girder in this accident.

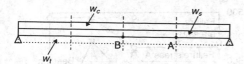

(a) Case 1 : Initial stage before demolition.

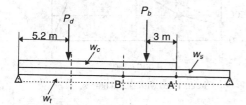

(b) Case 2 : 1/4 concrete slab removed.

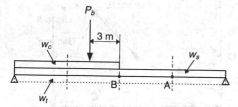

(c) Case 3 : 1/2 concrete slab removed.

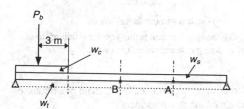

(d) Case 4 : 3/4 concrete slab removed.

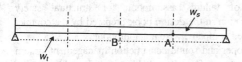

(e) Case 5 : Completion of slab demolition.

where;

P_d : Dump truck with concrete block: 8 tonf.
P_b : Concrete breaker: 10 tonf.
w_c : Concrete slab: 1.179 tonf/m.
w_s : Main and sub-girders: 0.271 tonf/m.
w_t : Temporary suspension working place:
   0.86 tonf/m.

Fig. 3. Load combination during concrete demolition.

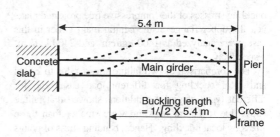

(a) Girder fixed with lateral braces.

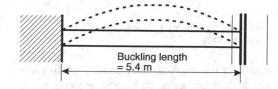

(b) Girder without lateral braces.

Fig. 4. Failure mode due to lateral buckling.

The buckling length is then assumed as the distance between cross frames of 5.4 m for the girder without lateral braces. While the buckling length of girder (a) fixed with lateral braces becomes $1/\sqrt{2}$ times shorter than that of girder (b) without braces.

3.3 Analyses of allowable and failure bending stress

Points A and B, as indicated in Fig. 3 in the central main girder, are considered as the critical points against lateral or local buckling. Therefore, the analyzed bending stress at points A and B, were compared with the corresponding allowable and failure stress against lateral or local buckling.

In this study the allowable bending stresses against lateral buckling as well as local buckling of girders are determined in accordance with the Japanese Specifications for Highway Bridges.

In terms of the lateral buckling, it is prescribed that the calculated allowable bending stress value against lateral buckling should not exceed 1400 kgf/cm². In addition, it is also stated that failure bending stress against lateral buckling should not exceed the standard strength of 2400 kgf/cm². Furthermore, it is required that the allowable and failure bending stress against lateral buckling should not exceed those of allowable and failure stress against local buckling, respectively.

For local buckling, the allowable and failure local

buckling stresses of the compressive free projected plate, i.e., the upper flange of the central main girder in this case, were analyzed as 1400 kgf/cm^2 and 2400 kgf/cm^2 respectively.

The comparison of two failure stresses due to lateral and local buckling for different load cases and for different types of girder conditions showed that failure stress due to lateral buckling were smaller than those stress by local buckling. Hence, bending stress of points A and B were compared with the corresponding lateral buckling failure stress.

4 RESULTS OF STRUCTURAL SAFETY ANALYSES

Results of the structural safety analyses are shown in Fig. 5. In these figures, the bending stresses acting on points A and B and their corresponding failure stresses analyzed are shown for each girder case in accordance with the slab demolition work process.

From Fig. 5 (b) (case of central main girder without lateral braces), we can see that the bending stress at point A exceeds the corresponding failure stress at work stage 2, when one-forth of concrete slab of total span was removed, which is coincident with the situation of the occurrence of the accident.

On the contrary, in the case of a girder fixed with lateral braces as shown in Fig. 5 (a), the bending stresses acting on points A and B did not exceed the corresponding failure stresses against all work stages of concrete slab demolition.

Therefore, it can be concluded that the removal of lateral braces of the cross frames prior to the concrete slab demolition work is the main cause of this accident. If the lateral braces were not removed, the girder would not have fallen down.

5 CONCLUSION

The main conclusions in this case study, including structural safety analyses, are summarized as follows:

1. The structural safety analyses show that the bending stress imposed on the center girder exceeds the corresponding lateral buckling failure stress, for the type of girder without having braces, at the time when one-forth of the concrete slab is removed.

2. On the other hand, the bending stress for the type of girder fixed with lateral braces has not exceeded the corresponding lateral and local buckling failure stress simultaneously for all stages of demolition work. Therefore, removal of lateral braces prior to the concrete

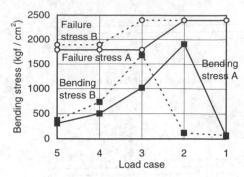

(a) Girders fixed with lateral braces.

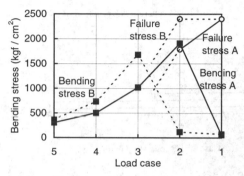

(b) Girders without lateral braces.

Fig. 5. Comparison between acting stress and failure stress for girders during concrete demolition work.

slab demolition is determined as the main contributor of this bridge falling down accident.

3. The assumption of dead and live loads as well as the load distribution for the main girders, including limit state of failures assumption for structural safety verification in the design book prepared by the contract awarded company, were not appropriate.

4. Proper and sound construction management system was not satisfactorily established. In addition, the information processing system within a multistage construction system was not carried out well. For instance, advanced removal of lateral braces have not been announced to the contractor who carried out the concrete slab demolition work.

REFERENCES

Japanese Specifications for Highway Bridges, 1996, 118-150. Japan Road Association (In Japanese).

Itoh, M., 1985. *Steel Structural Engineering*: 163, Corona Press (In Japanese).

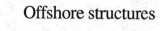
Offshore structures

Structural Safety and Reliability, Shiraishi, Shinozuka & Wen (eds) © 1998 Balkema, Rotterdam, ISBN 90 5410 978 5

Minimum required stiffness of tension leg mooring for large floating structures

T. Hamamoto
Department of Architecture, Musashi Institute of Technology, Tokyo, Japan

M. Inoue & Y. Tanaka
Department of Architecture, Waseda University, Tokyo, Japan

ABSTRACT: A probablistic method is presented to determine the minimum required stiffness of mooring lines of a large floating island for wind waves and earthquakes. The floating island is idealized as an elastic circular plate with uniformly distributed taut mooring lines. The stress in the mooring lines is evaluated by a wet mode superposion approach and stationary random vibration theory, taking account of structural flexibility and fluid structure interaction. The lifetime failure probability of mooring lines is separately calculated by solving a first passage problem for wind waves and earthquakes. The minimum required stiffness of mooring lines is determined in such a way that the summation of the lifetime failure probabilities against both loadings does not exceed a target failure probability. Numerical examples are presented to illustrate how to determine the minimum required stiffness of tension leg mooring for a large floating island at different offshore sites.

1 INTRODUCTION

With the recent trend toward the utilization of ocean space, a number of projects related to artificial large floating islands which serve as floating cities or airports have been proposed. The designs of these large structures demand a rational prediction of structural safety in the hostile ocean environment. One of the key issues of large floating islands is structural deformation. To reduce structural deformation, a tension leg mooring system which is uniformly distributed over the lower surface of the floating island seems to be useful. With the increase of mooring stiffness, the stress in the tension legs decreases for wind waves, whereas it sometimes increases because of seaquake phenomenon as well as direct propagation of seismic waves through mooring system for earthquakes (Hamamoto et al., 1991). Consequently, the determination of appropriate mooring stiffness becomes an important problem to keep structural safety of large floating islands. However, this is not an easy task because of large uncertainties in environmental forces as well as structural behavior.

The motion performance of large floating structures has been studied by a continuum approach for mat-like structures and a discrete approach for module-linked structures. In the former approach, a dry mode or wet mode superposition is used to solve hydro-elastic problems (Bishop and Price, 1976). Wen

(1974) used the dry mode superposition approach for a rectangle plate structure. Hamamoto (1995) used the wet mode superposition approach for a circular plate structure. Mamidipudi and Webster (1994) used a finite difference method to directly solve the equation of motion. The latter approach may be divided into Rigid Module Flexible Connecter method (Wang et al., 1991) and Elastic Module Flexible Connecter method (Ertekin et al., 1994). Very few studies have been carried out on the seaquake response of large floating structures (Babu and Reddy, 1988; Hamamoto, 1995). Little attention has been paid to the safety evaluation of mooring system of large floating structures. Soong (1984) studied the conditional failure probability of a conventional TLP for wind waves.

In this study, a probabilistic approach is presented to determine the minimum required stiffness of a large floating island for wind waves and earthquakes. The stress in the tension legs is calculated by a wet mode superposition approach and stationary random vibration theory. The failure probability of mooring lines which is conditional on load intensity is separately evaluated for wind waves and earthquakes. An unconditional failure probability of each loading per an action is calculated by multiplying the conditional failure probabilities by the corresponding occurrence rates and integrating them with respect to all possible load intensities. The minimum required stiffness of mooring lines is determined in such a way that the summation of the lifetime failure probabilities against both loadings does not exceed a specified target failure probability. Numerical examples are presented to illustrate how to determine the minimum required stiffness of mooring lines for a large floating island at different offshore sites.

2 ANALYTICAL MODEL AND ASSUMPTIONS

The analytical model of a large circular floating island subjected to wind waves and earthquakes is shown in Fig.1. The mooring system is assumed to be a series of tension legs which are uniformly distributed over the lower surface of the floating island. The following assumptions are introduced in this study :

1. The floating island is vertically guided around the circumference without friction.
2. The floating island is linearly elastic, isotropic and of constant thickness.
3. The fluid flow is inviscid, incompressible and irrotatinal.
4. The mooring lines transfer only tensile force and the restoring force is linearly elastic.
5. The mass effect of mooring lines and hydrodynamic force acting on them are disregarded.
6. The sea is of constant depth and extends to infinity in the radial direction.
7. The wind waves propagate in one direction only.
8. Only the vertical ground motion at sea bed due to earthquakes is considered.
9. The wind waves and earthquakes are stationary, ergodic and zero mean gaussian processes.
10. The second order drift and springing forces are disregarded.

3 FRAMEWORK OF METHODOLOGY

The overall methodology is shown in Fig.2 for the determination of mooring stiffness which satisfies safety requirements for both wind waves and earthquakes.

Step1: A target failure probability of tension legs is determined.

Step2: Load intensities of wind waves and earthquakes and the corresponding occurrence rates are evaluated from each extreme value distribution at an offshore site.

Step3: For each load intensity, wave height at sea surface and vertical ground acceleration at sea bed are modeled as stationary random processes and their frequency contents are described by spectral density functions.

Step4: The spatial distribution of stress in the tension legs conditional on load intensity is evaluated

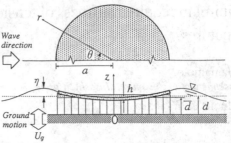

Fig.1 Geometric parameters of floating island

by a stationary random vibration analysis for wind waves and earthquakes.

Step5: The conditional failure probability which exceeds upper and lower limits of tension legs is calculated separately for wind waves and earthquakes.

Step6: An unconditional failure probability against each loading per an action is calculated by multiplying the conditional failure probabilities by the corresponding occurrence rates and integrating them with respect to all possible load intensities.

Step7: The lifetime failure probability of each loading is separately calculated for wind waves and earthquakes.

Step8: The minimum required stiffness is determined in such a way that the summation of the lifetime failure probabilities against both loadings does not exceed a target failure probability.

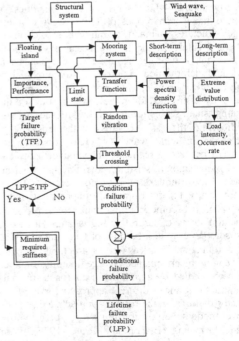

Fig.2 Framework for determining the minimum required stiffness of mooring lines

4 DESCRIPTION OF EXTERNAL LOADINGS

Long term descriptions of wind waves and earthquakes are described by extreme value distributions. Because wind waves are generated by winds above the sea surface, the extreme value distribution of mean wind velocity is used for the long term description of wind waves. The type III extreme value distribution of maximum mean wind velocity, v, in free air (Makino and Watakabe, 1984) is used,

$$F_{V_w}(v) = \exp\left\{-\left(\frac{w-v}{w-u}\right)^k\right\}, \tag{1}$$

where u and k are the size and shape parameters of the distribution, respectively, and w is the upper limit value. The mean wind velocity above the sea surface is followed by the power law. On the other hand, the type II extreme value distribution of vertical ground motion is used for the long term description of earthquakes. Due to lack of sufficient amounts of data of vertical ground motion, the type II extreme value distribution of horizontal peak ground velocity, v, at bed rock (Ozaki et al., 1978) is used,

$$F_{V_g}(v) = \exp\left\{-\left(\frac{\mu}{v}\right)^k\right\}, \tag{2}$$

where μ and k are the size and shape parameters of the distribution, respectively. The maximum vertical ground velocity at bed rock is assumed to be 1/2 of horizontal one.

Short term descriptions of wind waves and earthquakes are described by power spectral density functions. The spectral density function of wave height in a fully developed sea is given by the Pierson -Moskowitz (1964) spectrum,

$$S_{\eta\eta}(\omega) = \frac{\alpha g^2}{\omega^5}\left\{-\beta\left(\frac{g}{\omega V}\right)^4\right\} \quad 0 \le \omega \le \infty, \tag{3a}$$

in which V is the mean wind velocity at $19.5m$ above the sea surface, g is the acceleration due to gravity, and α and β are spectral parameters. Common values $\alpha = 0.0081$ and $\beta = 0.74$ are adopted in this study. On the other hand, the power spectral density function of vertical ground acceleration at sea bed is given by

$$S_{\ddot{U}_g\ddot{U}_g}(\omega) = G_0 \cdot H_h(\omega) \cdot H_l(\omega) \quad 0 \le \omega \le \infty, \tag{3b}$$

where G_0 is the spectral intensity, $H_h(\omega)$ is the Clough-Penzien (1993) high pass filter and $H_l(\omega)$ is the Kanai-Tajimi (1960) low pass filter given as, respectively,

$$H_h(\omega) = \frac{(\omega/\omega_k)^4}{\{1-(\omega/\omega_k)^2\}^2+4\xi_k^2\,(\omega/\omega_k)^2}, \tag{4a}$$

$$H_l(\omega) = \frac{1+4\xi_g^2(\omega/\omega_g)^2}{\{1-(\omega/\omega_g)^2\}^2+4\xi_g^2\,(\omega/\omega_g)^2}, \tag{4b}$$

where ω_k and ξ_k are high pass filter parameters, and ω_g and ξ_g are low pass filter parameters which may be interpreted as the predominant ground circular frequency and ground damping ratio, respectively. In this study, we assume $\omega_k = 3.0\,rad/sec$, $\xi_k = 0.6$, $\omega_g = 30.0\,rad/sec$, $\xi_g = 0.6$.

5 HYDRODYNAMIC PRESSURE

Due to wind waves or earthquakes, the hydrodynamic pressure is generated on the lower surface of the floating island. The hydrodynamic pressure may be evaluated as a linear combination of pressure component, p_f, acting on the motionless island subjected to wind waves or seaquakes and the pressure component, p_m, due to island motion which contains rigid body motion and elastic deformation. Moreover, p_f, may be divided into two components due to incident and scattered waves, respectively. Because of the geometrical simplicity, each pressure component can be obtained in closed form based on a linear potential flow theory (Hamamoto et al., 1991).

6 DYNAMIC MOORING FORCE

The dynamic mooring force acts on the floating island in addition to hydrodynamic pressure. When a series of tension legs are uniformly distributed over the lower surface of the floating island, the dynamic tensile force per unit area is given by

$$p_d(r,\theta,t) = -k_d\{\zeta(r,\theta,t) - U_g(r,\theta,t)\}, \tag{5}$$

where k_d is the mooring stiffness, $\zeta(r,\theta,t)$ is the vertical displacement of the floating island, $U_g(r,\theta,t)$ is the vertical displacement at sea bed due to earthquakes and t is time. It is assumed that the vertical motion at sea bed moves rigidly without phase difference, i.e., $U_g(r,\theta,t) = U_g(t)$. For wind waves, $U_g(r,\theta,t) = 0$.

7 WET MODE SUPERPOSITION APPROACH

Making use of a wet mode superposition approach, the total displacement of the floating island can be expressed as

$$\zeta = \sum_{n=0}^{\infty}\sum_{m=1}^{\infty}\zeta_{nm}(r)\cos n\theta\, q_{nm}(t), \tag{6}$$

where n is the circumferential Fourier wave number, m is the radial mode number, $\zeta_{nm}(r)$ is the nm-th wet mode shape function in the radial direction along $\theta = 0$, and $q_{nm}(t)$ is the nm-th generalized coordinate. The wet mode shape function of the floating island can be obtained by fluid coupled free vibration analysis (Hamamoto et al., 1994).

Having obtained the hydrodynamic pressure and dynamic mooring force induced by wind waves and earthquakes, the equation of motion of the floating island is obtained. The dynamic behavior of the floating island is governed by the Lagrange's equation:

$$\frac{d}{dt}\left\{\frac{\partial T}{\partial \dot{q}_{nm}(t)}\right\} - \frac{\partial T}{\partial q_{nm}(t)} + \frac{\partial S}{\partial q_{nm}(t)} = Q^L_{nm}(t) + Q^D_{nm}(t),$$
(7)

where $\cdot$ denotes time derivative, T and S are the kinetic and strain energy of the floating island, respectively, $Q^L_{nm}(t)$ is the nm-th generalized loading force and $Q^D_{nm}(t)$ is the nm-th generalized damping force of the floating island.

Making use of the orthoganal properties of wet mode shapes of the floating island, the nm-th un-coupled modal equations of motion can be obtained as follows:

For wind waves,

$$(M^P_{nm} + M^W_{nm})\ddot{q}_{nm}(t) + (C^P_{nm} + C^W_{nm})\dot{q}_{nm}(t)$$
$$+ (K^P_{nm} + K^W_{nm} + K^T_{nm})q_{nm}(t) = Q^F_{nm}(t)$$
$$(n = 0, 1, 2, \cdots ; m = 0, 1, 2, \cdots). \quad (8a)$$

For earthquakes,

$$(M^P_{0m} + M^W_{0m})\ddot{q}_{0m}(t) + (C^P_{0m} + C^W_{0m})\dot{q}_{0m}(t)$$
$$+ (K^P_{0m} + K^W_{0m} + K^T_{0m})q_{0m}(t) = Q^F_{0m}(t) + Q^T_{0m}(t)$$
$$(m = 1, 2, \cdots), \quad (8b)$$

where M^P_{nm}, C^P_{nm} and K^P_{nm} are the nm-th generalized mass, damping and stiffness of the floating island, M^W_{nm}, C^W_{nm} and K^W_{nm} are the nm-th generalized added mass, added damping and added stiffness, respectively, due to dynamic interaction between the floating island and sea water, K^T_{nm} is the nm-th generalized added stiffness due to attachment of mooring lines, $Q^F_{nm}(t)$ is the nm-th generalized force associated with the pressure component p_f, and $Q^T_{0m}(t)$ is the $0m$-th generalized added excitation due to direct propagation of seismic waves through mooring lines. It is noted that the generalized added mass and added damping are frequency dependent.

8 STOCHASTIC RESPONSE

On the basis of a linear random vibration theory, for example, the variance of vertical displacement response ζ can be obtained by

$$\bar{\zeta}^2(r,\theta) = \int_0^\infty S_{\zeta\zeta}(r,\theta,\omega)d\omega$$

$$= \sum_{n=0}^\infty \sum_{m=1}^\infty \zeta^2_{nm}(r)\cos^2 n\theta \, \bar{q}^2_{nm}, \quad (9)$$

where $S_{\zeta\zeta}(r,\theta,\omega)$ is the power spectral density function of ζ, $\bar{q}^2_{nm}$ is the variance of the nm-th generali-

zed coordinate given by

$$\bar{q}^2_{nm} = \int_0^\infty |H_{nm}(\omega)|^2 S_{Q_{nm}Q_{nm}}(\omega)d\omega, \quad (10)$$

where $S_{Q_{nm}Q_{nm}}(\omega)$ is the power spectral density function of the summation of $Q^F_{nm}(t)$ and $Q^T_{nm}(t)$, and $|H_{nm}(\omega)|^2$ is the nm-th transfer function given by

$$|H_{nm}(\omega)|^2 = 1/(M^P_{nm} + M^W_{nm})^2\left[(\bar{\omega}^2_{nm} - \omega^2)^2\right.$$
$$\left. + 4(\bar{\xi}_{nm} + \bar{\xi}^*_{nm})^2\bar{\omega}^2_{nm}\omega^2\right], \quad (11)$$

where $\bar{\omega}_{nm}$ is the nm-th wet mode circular frequency, and $\bar{\xi}_{nm}$ and $\bar{\xi}^*_{nm}$ are the nm-th structural damping ratio and hydrodynamic radiation damping ratio, respectively.

The power spectral density function of dynamic stress in the tension legs is given by

$$S_{zz}(r,\theta,\omega) = k_d^2 \cdot S_{\zeta\zeta}(r,\theta,\omega). \quad (12)$$

The variance of dynamic stress in the tension legs can be obtained by

$$\sigma^2_z(r,\theta) = \int_0^\infty S_{zz}(r,\theta,\omega)d\omega = k_d^2\bar{\zeta}^2(r,\theta). \quad (13)$$

9 MINIMUM REQUIRED STIFFNESS

The total stiffness of mooring lines is given by

$$K_m = k_d A_d = \frac{E_m A_m}{d}, \quad (14)$$

where A_d is the lower surface area of the floating island, A_m is the total sectional area of mooring lines and E_m is Young's modulus of mooring lines, respectively. The parameter Λ is defined by

$$\Lambda = \frac{A_m}{A_d}. \quad (15)$$

The relationship between k_d and Λ is given by

$$k_d = \frac{E_m\Lambda}{d}. \quad (16)$$

An initial tensile stress is induced in the tension legs by pulling mooring lines from the freely floating state. The buoyancy associated with pulling is equilibrium with the initial mooring force as

$$\rho_w g s A_d = z_0 A_m, \quad (17)$$

where s is the pull length for initial installment, ρ_w is the mass density of sea water and z_0 is the initial mooring force. The initial mooring force is given by

$$z_0 = \frac{\rho_w g s}{\Lambda}. \quad (18)$$

It is assumed that the failure of one leg occurs when the tensile stress in the tension leg exceeds a yield stress as an upper limit and drops to zero as a lower limit. The lower limit is related to snap load due to slackness of mooring lines (Yoshida et al., 1978). The pull length is determined so that the initial tensile stress keeps the mean value of upper and lower limits.

The average frequency that the stress in the tension legs upcrosses or downcrosses the upper and lower limits respectively are given by

$$\nu_u = f_0 \exp\left[-\frac{(z_u - z_0)^2}{2\sigma_z^2}\right],\qquad(19a)$$

$$\nu_l = f_0 \exp\left[-\frac{z_0^2}{2\sigma_z^2}\right],\qquad(19b)$$

where z_u is the upper limit, σ_z is the standard deviation of dynamic stress induced in the tension legs by wind waves or earthquakes, and f_0 is the apparent frequency given as

$$f_0^2 = \left(\frac{1}{2\pi}\right)^2 \frac{\displaystyle\int_0^\infty \omega^2 S_{zz}(\omega)d\omega}{\displaystyle\int_0^\infty S_{zz}(\omega)d\omega},\qquad(20)$$

where $S_{zz}(\omega)$ is given by Eq.(12).

It is assumed that the tension leg recovers immediately after the failure and the failure occurs independently. The safety probability between time interval $[0, \tau]$ which is conditional on load intensity V is given by

$$P_s(r, \theta \,|\, V) = \exp\left[-(\nu_u + \nu_l)\tau\right],\qquad(21)$$

where τ is the time interval of the maximum load intensity. The failure probability of tension legs which is conditional on load intensity is given by

$$P_f(r, \theta \,|\, V) = 1 - P_s(r, \theta \,|\, V) = 1 - \exp\left[-(\nu_u + \nu_l)\tau\right].\qquad(22)$$

The unconditional failure probability against each loading per an action is calculated by multiplying the conditional failure probabilities by the occurrence rates and integrating them with respect to all possible load intensities.

For wind waves,

$$P_f^W(r, \theta) = \int_0^\infty P_f^W(r, \theta \,|\, v) f_{V_w}(v)\, dv.\qquad(23a)$$

For earthquakes,

$$P_f^E(r) = \int_0^\infty P_f^E(r \,|\, v) f_{V_g}(v)\, dv,\qquad(23b)$$

where $P_f^W(r, \theta \,|\, v)$ and $P_f^E(r \,|\, v)$ are failure probabilities conditional on load intensity, and $f_{V_w}(v)$ and $f_{V_g}(v)$ are probability density functions which are derived from Eqs.(1) and (2).

Assuming that the occurrence of external loadings follows the Poison process, the lifetime failure probability of each loading is given by

$$\tilde{P}_f^i(r, \theta) = 1 - \sum_{k=0}^\infty \{1 - P_f^i(r, \theta)\}^k \frac{(\lambda_i T)^k \exp[-\lambda_i T]}{k!}$$

$$= 1 - \exp\left[\lambda_i T\{1 - P_f^i(r, \theta)\}\right]\exp[-\lambda_i T]$$

$$= 1 - \exp\{-\lambda_i T P_f^i(r, \theta)\},\qquad(24)$$

where subscript i is the kind of external loadings ($i = W, E$; W: wind wave, E: earthquake), k is the number of occurrences of external loadings, T is the lifetime (year) and λ_i is the annual occurrence rate.

In Eq.(24), it is noted that the lifetime failure probability varies with the location of tension legs. The summation of the lifetime failure probabilities against both loadings is calculated at all locations on the floating island. The maximum value is taken as a system failure probability given by

$$P_f = \underset{r,\theta}{\text{Max}}\left[\tilde{P}_f^W(r, 0) + \tilde{P}_f^E(r)\right].\qquad(25)$$

10 TARGET FAILURE PROBABILITY

The target failure probability of a single tension leg is determined by Allen (1981) as

$$P_{fa} = \frac{T A \times 10^{-5}}{W\sqrt{N}},\qquad(26)$$

where N is the maximum number of people who are influenced by the failure of a tension leg, A is the activity factor and W is the warning factor. Setting $T = 100$, $N = 1$, $A = 1.0$ and $W = 0.1$ yields,

$$P_{fa} = \frac{100 \times 1 \times 10^{-5}}{1 \times 10^{-1}} = 1.0 \times 10^{-2}.$$

The lifetime failure probability given by Eq.(24) is separately calculated for wind waves and earthquakes by changing mooring stiffness. The minimum required stiffness of mooring lines is determined in such a way that the summation of the lifetime failure probabilities against both loadings given by Eq.(25) does not exceed the target failure probability.

11 NUMERICAL RESULTS AND DISCUSSION

For numerical computations, dimensions and material constants of a structure-mooring-sea water system are assumed as follows: radius of structure $= 1000m$, thickness of structure $= 50m$, Young's modulus of structure $= 2.0 \times 10^{11} N/m^2$, Poison's ratio of structure $= 0.15$, mass density of structure $= 4.0 \times 10^2\, kg/m^3$, material damping ratio of structure $= 0.05$ for all dry modes, Young's modulus of tension leg $= 2.1 \times 10^{11}$ N/m^2, yield stress of tension leg $= 1.0 \times 10^9\ N/m^2$, water depth $= 200m$ and mass density of sea water $= 1.05 \times 10^3 kg/m^3$. The pull length of the floating island is adjusted so that an initial tension stress in the tension legs keeps the average value, 5.0×10^8 N/m^2, of upper and lower limits. The minimum required stiffness of mooring lines is determined at two different offshore sites.

Figure 3 shows the relationship between return period and its expected load intensity for both wind waves and earthquakes at each site. For both wind waves and earthquakes, the environmental forces at Site A are more severe than at Site B.

Figure 4 shows the relationship between power spectral density functions of wind waves and earthquakes with different return periods and wet mode frequencies of the floating island with $\Lambda = 4.0 \times 10^{-4}$. Although the high frequency content of wave spectra remains almost unchanged in spite of the increase of return period, the peak frequency moves to the low frequency region with the increase of return period. The difference in wave spectra at both sites is relatively small. The earthquake spectra at site A are much larger than those at site B. The contributions of 10 modes are used for wave response and 9 modes for earthquake response.

Figure 5 shows the radial distribution of tensile stress in the tension legs with $\Lambda = 4.0 \times 10^{-4}$ along $\theta = 0$ for different return periods. The response is evaluated as the summation of the initial tensile stress, z_0, and the standard deviation of dynamic stress, σ_z, due to wind waves and earthquakes, i.e., $z_0 \pm \sigma_z$. The upper and lower limits of tensile stress are drawn with dotted lines. At both sites, the increase of wind wave response with return period is relatively small in comparison with that of earthquake response. Both wind wave and earthquake responses at site A are larger than those at site B.

Figure 6 shows the variation in conditional failure probability due to Λ for different return periods at each site. The time interval of maximum load intensity is selected to be 20 minutes for wind waves and 20

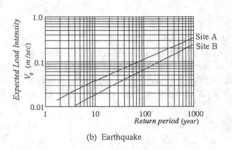

(a) Wind wave

(b) Earthquake

Fig.3 Return period and expected load intensity

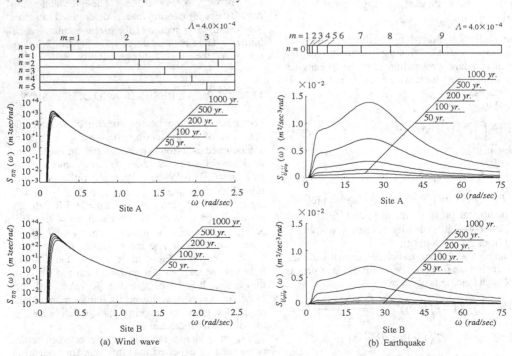

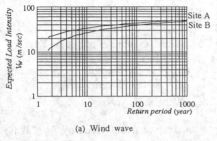

(a) Wind wave

(b) Earthquake

Fig.4 Power spectral density functions of external loadings and wet-mode natural frequencies of floating island

1976

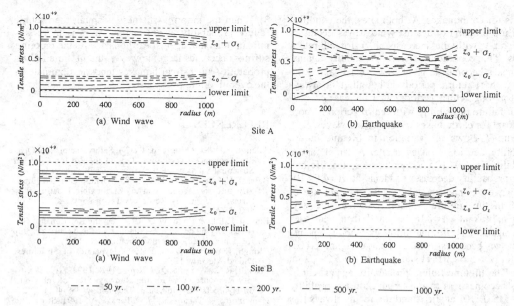

Site A

Site B

$$-----\ 50\ yr. \quad -\ \cdot\ -\ 100\ yr. \quad ------\ 200\ yr. \quad -\ -\ -\ 500\ yr. \quad ————\ 1000\ yr.$$

Fig.5 Standard deviations of tensile stress in mooring lines

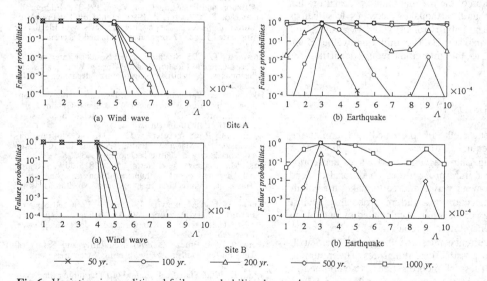

Site A

Site B

$$—\times—\ 50\ yr. \quad —\circ—\ 100\ yr. \quad —\triangle—\ 200\ yr. \quad —\diamond—\ 500\ yr. \quad —\square—\ 1000\ yr.$$

Fig.6 Variation in conditional failure probability due to Λ

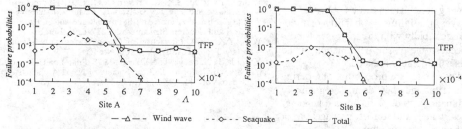

Site A

Site B

$$—\triangle—\ \text{Wind wave} \quad -\ -\diamond-\ -\ \text{Seaquake} \quad —\square—\ \text{Total}$$

Fig.7 Variation in lifetime failure probability due to Λ

seconds for earthquakes. At both sites, the conditional failure probability against wind waves decreases considerably with the increase of Λ for all return periods. The conditional failure probability against earthquakes becomes large at $\Lambda=3.0\times10^{-4}$ and 9.0×10^{-4} for short return periods although it is always large for long return periods. The increase in conditional failure probability with return period is more significant for earthquakes than for wind waves.

Figure 7 shows the variation in lifetime failure probability due to Λ at each site. A target failure probability is 1.0×10^{-2}. At both sites, the lifetime failure probability decreases suddenly at $\Lambda=4.0\times10^{-4}$ wind waves. For earthquakes, with the increase of Λ, the lifetime failure probability increases slowly, attains a peak at $\Lambda=3.0\times10^{-4}$, and then decreases slowly again. The lifetime failure probability against wind waves becomes less than a target failure probability for $\Lambda\geq5.6\times10^{-4}$ at site A and $\Lambda\geq5.2\times10^{-4}$ at site B. The lifetime failure probability against earthquakes becomes less than a target failure probability for $\Lambda\geq5.0\times10^{-4}$ at site A and it remains always less than a target failure probability for any Λ at site B. The summation of the lifetime failure probabilities for wind waves and earthquakes becomes less than a target failure probability for $\Lambda\geq6.0\times10^{-4}$ at site A and $\Lambda\geq5.5\times10^{-4}$ at site B. The minimum value of Λ corresponds to the minimum required stiffness of tension legs.

12 CONCLUSIONS

A probabilistic method is presented to determine the minimum required stiffness of mooring lines of a large floating island against wind waves and earthquakes. The failure probabilities conditional on load intensity for wind waves and earthquakes are calculated. The unconditional failure probability against each loading per an action is calculated by integrating the conditional failure probabilities by the corresponding occurrence rates and integrating them with respect to all possible load intensities. The minimum required stiffness of mooring lines is determined in such a way that the summation of lifetime failure probabilities against both loadings does not exceed a target failure probability. Within the scope of this study, the following conclusions can be obtained.
1. For wind waves, the failure probability of mooring lines decreases rapidly with the increase of mooring stiffness because the elastic deformation of the floating island is considerably reduced.
2. For earthquakes, the failure probability of mooring lines increases at first and then decreases gradually due to the combination effect of seaquake phenomenon through sea water and direct propagation of seismic waves through mooring lines.

3. When the mooring stiffness is small, the lifetime failure probability against wind waves is more significant than that against earthquakes. As the mooring stiffness becomes large, however, the lifetime failure probability against earthquakes tends to dominate in the overall failure probability.

REFERENCES

Allen, D.E. 1981. Criteria for Design Safety Factors and Quality Assurance Expenditure. Proc of the 3rd Int. Conf. on Structural Safety and Reliability: 667-678. Amsterdam.

Babu, P.V.T & Reddy, D.V. 1988. Dynamic Coupled Fluid-Structure Interaction Analysis of Flexible Floating Platforms. J. of Energy Resources Technology, ASME. Vol. 108: 297-304.

Bishop, R.E.D & Price, W.G. 1976. On the Relationship Between Dry-modes and Wet-modes in the Theory of Ship Response. J. of Sound and Vibration. Vol.13(1): 9-25.

Clough, R.W. & Penzien, J. 1993. Dynamics of Structures. 2nd ed, McGrow-Hills.

Ertekin, R.C., Wang, S.Q. & Riggs, H.R. 1994. Hydroelasticity Response of a Floating Runway. Proc. of Int. Conf. on Hydroelasticity in Marine Technology: 389-400.

Hamamoto, T., Takahashi, H. & Tanaka, Y. 1991. Stochastic Response of Anchored Flexible Floating Islands Subjected to Wind-Waves and Seaquakes. Proc. of the 1st Int. Offshore and Polar Eng. Conf. Vol.3: 391-398. Edinburgh.

Hamamoto, T. & Asami, T. 1994. Fluid-Coupled Free Vibration of Floating Elastic Circular Plates with Elastically Supported Edge. Theoretical and Applied Mechanics. Vol. 43: 171-179.

Hamamoto, T. 1995. Stochastic Fluid-Structure Interaction of Large Circular Floating Islands During Wind waves and Seaquakes. Probabilistic Engineering Mechanics. Vol.10: 209-224.

Makino, M. & Watakabe, M. 1984. Extreme Value Distribution of the Annual Maximum Wind Speed Obtained by a Poisson Process (Part 2). Trans. of Architectural Inst. of Japan. No. 338:10-18. (in Japanese)

Mamidipudi, P. & Webster, W.C. 1994. The Motions Performance of Mat-like Floating Airport. Int. Conf. on Hydroelasticity in Marine Technology: 363-375.

Ozaki, M., Kitagawa, Y. & Hattori, S. 1978. Study on Regional Characteristics of Earthquake Motions in Japan (Part 1). Trans. of Architectural Inst. of Japan. No. 266:31-40 (in Japanese).

Pierson, W.J. & Moskowitz, Z. 1964. A Proposed Spectral Form for Fully Developed Wind Seas Based on the Similarity Theory of S.A. Kitaigorodoskii. J. of Geophysical Research. Vol. 69: 5158-5190.

Soong, T.T. & Prucz, Z. 1984. Reliability and Safety of Tension-leg Platforms. Engineering Structures. Vol. 6: 142-149.

Tajimi, H. 1960. Statistical Method of Determining the Maximum Response of Building Structure During an Earthquake. Proc. of the 2nd World Conf. on Earthquake Eng. Vol.2: 781-798. Tokyo.

Wang, M.L., Du, S.X. & Ertekin, R.C. 1991. Hydroelastic Response and Fatigue Analysis of a Multi-Module Very Large Structure. Proc. Int. Symp. Fatigue and Fracture in Steel and Concrete Structures. 2: 1277-1291. Bombay.

Wen, Y.K. 1974. Interaction of Ocean Waves with floating Plate. Proc. of ASCE. Vol.100. No. EM2: 375-395.

Yoshida, K., Yoneya, T. & Oka, N. 1978. Snap Loads in Taut Moored Platforms. J. of the Society of Naval Architects of Japan. Vol.144: 205-213. (in Japanese)

Structural Safety and Reliability, Shiraishi, Shinozuka & Wen (eds) © 1998 Balkema, Rotterdam, ISBN 90 5410 978 5

Probabilistic models of ringing

Kurtis Gurley
University of Florida, Gainesville, Fla., USA

Federico Waisman & Mircea Grigoriu
Cornell University, Ithaca, N.Y., USA

Ahsan Kareem
University of Notre Dame, Ind., USA

ABSTRACT: A probabilistic model is developed to describe the ringing phenomenon observed in the response of tension leg platforms (TLPs) to wave forces. The model is based on the statistical analysis of input–output records of an oscillating column piercing the water surface under the action of viscous hydrodynamic loads. It is shown that wave forces acting on the column can be represented by the sum of a translation and a Poisson white noise process. The statistics of the response of the oscillating column to this probabilistic model and the corresponding simulated records are in good agreement.

1 INTRODUCTION

The response of offshore platforms experience sudden infrequent bursts of short duration but large magnitudes, referred to as ringing. This high frequency transient type response has been observed in offshore systems, particularly in tension leg platforms (TLPs). It is essential to account for ringing in design because it can reduce the fatigue life of TLP tendons. The loading mechanism to ringing response are not fully understood, making the incorporation of the ringing phenomenon in the reliability analysis of offshore platforms difficult. In recent years, significant interest has been shown in identifying the nonlinear mechanisms that induce ringing in complex offshore structural systems (Davies et al., 1994; Jeffreys, E.R. and Rainey, R.C.T., 1994; Natvig, 1994; Faltinsen, 1995; Newman, 1995; Gurley, K. and Kareem, A., 1996). To distinguish between the commonly misused and interchanged terms "ringing" and "springing", some definitions are appropriate (see Fig. 1). Springing is a steady state response in the vertical and/or bending modes of TLPs and gravity based structures (GBS) due to second–order wave effects at the sum frequencies. This behavior is commonly observed in both mild and severe sea states. Ringing is the strong transient response observed in these modes under severe

loading conditions triggered, presumably, by the passage of a high, steep wave event. The transient response decays to steady state at a logarithmic rate that depends on the system damping. Ringing is a rare event, and has been unaccounted for in standard response analysis codes until recent experimental and full–scale observations brought them to light. This has been attributed to the higher–order loading mechanisms leading to its onset. Springing, unlike ringing, is accounted for by current response analysis codes through improved modeling of the second–order wave–structure interaction.

Studies reported in the literature have focused on large volume structures which are dominated by wave diffraction inertial type loading and minimally affected by drag forces (Davies et al., 1994; Jeffreys, E.R. and Rainey, R.C.T., 1994; Natvig, 1994; Faltinsen, 1995; Newman, 1995). These loads are calculated by a slender body theory or diffraction/radiation analysis. Full scale and model test observations (e.g., wave profiles and model behavior and validation of numerical procedures), are utilized in these studies. Natvig (1994) details a number of mechanisms which contribute to ringing such as variable cylinder wetting and added mass, wave profile, wave slapping, and added mass. Using a model based on slender body theory

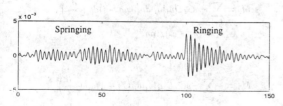

Figure 1: Ringing and Springing events.

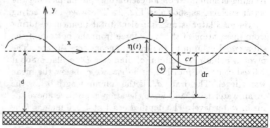

Figure 2: Cylinder in wave train.

with modified Wheeler stretching, Jeffreys and Rainey (1994) show encouraging agreement between model tests and theory. Davies et al. (1994) highlight the nature of loads that cause ringing based on model tests, present at time domain simulation scheme for estimating ringing response, and discuss simple guidelines for reducing the ringing response. Newman (1995) and Faltinsen et al. (1995) discuss second and third–order sum frequency wave loads and their effects on ringing. Gurley and Kareem (1996) have shown that viscous loads are also capable of inducing ringing response of members with large wavelength to diameter ratios, where the instantaneous moment acting on the cylinder is a quartic function of wave elevation. Ringing response in pitching due to viscous loading is simulated on a simple pivoted cylinder which pierces the surface. The major contributing mechanisms are identified, and the system characteristics that influence the onset of ringing are delineated. Ringing behavior is only observed under very specific nonlinear sea states and loading conditions combined with system parameters conductive to large energy build up under these circumstances. Ringing cannot be attributed to general polynomial nonlinear loading, as indicated by other studies of quadratic loading of structures in Gaussian sea states.

The objectives of this paper are (1) the identification of the cause of ringing based on the statistical analysis of the typical wave forces acting on offshore platforms, (2) the development of a practical probabilistic model of wave forces incorporating the ringing phenomenon, and (3) the evaluation of the accuracy of the response of offshore platforms subjected to the wave force model proposed in this study. The wave forces used in the statistical analysis are generated using a model designed to induce ringing on a pitching oscillator due to non–Gaussian waves. The wave forces, in this model, are characterized by infrequent large values of very short duration that can be viewed as impulses of random magnitudes arriving at random times. The wave forces are modeled by the superposition of a non–Gaussian translation process and a Poisson white noise. The statistics of these processes are estimated from wave force records. The offshore platform is modeled as a simple linear oscillator.

2 GENERATION OF WAVE FORCES

Let $\{M(t), t \geq 0\}$ be the wave force process acting on an offshore platform representing the equivalent total moment acting on a cylindrical column piercing the water surface.

2.1 Oscillator Model

Ringing is simulated on an oscillating column piercing the water surface, as shown in Fig. 2. The wave force acting on the oscillator is an equivalent total moment resulting from integration of the wave force from the bottom of the submerged column to the instantaneous free surface. The pivoted cylindrical column of diameter D oscillates about a fixed center of rotation, at a distance c_r below the mean water level. The draft, d_r, is the column length below the mean water level, and wave elevation is positive above the mean water level. The depth d is set at 1,000 meters. The system inertia, damping, and restoring forces are first-order functions of the system acceleration, velocity, and displacement, respectively. The equation of pitching motion is described by

$$m\ddot{\Theta}(t) + c\dot{\Theta}(t) + k\Theta(t) = M(t) \qquad (2.1)$$

where m is the system moment of inertia, c is the system damping, k is the system stiffness, $\ddot{\Theta}(t)$, $\dot{\Theta}(t)$, and $\Theta(t)$ are the rotational displacement, velocity and acceleration, respectively, and $M(t)$ is the moment due to hydrodynamic loads which is detailed later. The fluctuating moment of inertia is not considered in the analysis since its magnitude is small compare to the system moment of inertia m.

2.2 Wave Input Model and Equivalent Moment Calculation

The JONSWAP wave elevation spectrum is applied with a peak frequency of 0.1 Hz throughout this study (Chakrabarti, 1987). Stokes second-order random waves are simulated utilizing a quadratic transfer function (QTF) in the Volterra series framework. The QTF is analytically derived based on Stokes second-order random wave (Hasselmann, 1962; Hudspeth, R.T. and Chen, M., 1979; Kareem et al., 1994). Simulation details can be found in (Gurley et al., 1996). The simulated realization of the surface elevation of gravity waves exhibit non-Gaussian features with characteristic high peaks and shallow troughs. These non-symmetric profiles lead to skewed water particle velocity profiles, with higher probability of occurrence in the extreme tail region than in corresponding Gaussian waves. Both non-Gaussian waves and free surface integration are considered to simulate ringing in this study.

Application of the Morison equation to calculate the force at the mean water level ignores the nonlinear effects of the fluctuating free surface, which is considered to be the dominant ringing mechanism. The wave kinematics up to the instantaneous water surface are used to generate moment input from both linear and second-order waves by integrating the force to the free surface and multiplying by an equivalent moment arm. The water particle velocity at the mean water level is related to the velocity profile on the wetted cylinder using modified Airy stretching theory (Mo, O. and Moan, T., 1985).

The time dependent moments acting on the cylinder are calculated from the water particle velocity using the Morison drag term, $M = LF_lR$, where, $F_l = \rho/2C_dDu|u|$ is the viscous force per unit length on the cylinder, ρ, C_d, and u are the fluid density, coefficient of drag, and water particle velocity, L is the fluctuating wetted cylinder length, and R is the fluctuating equivalent moment arm. The total applied wave moment is a combination of four components,

$$M_1 = \frac{1}{2}\rho C_d D\eta \left(\frac{\eta}{2} - c_r\right) u_{mwl}|u_{mwl}| \qquad (2.2)$$

$$M_2 = \sum_{i=1}^{na} \frac{1}{2}\rho C_d Du_i|u_i|d_l \left((na-i)d_l + \frac{d_l}{2}\right),$$

$$d_l = (n_l - c_r)/na,$$

$$n_l = \begin{cases} 0, & \eta > 0 \\ \eta, & \eta \leq 0 \end{cases} \qquad (2.3)$$

$$M_3 = -\sum_{i=1}^{nb} \frac{1}{2}\rho C_d Du_i|u_i|d_l \left((i-1)d_l + \frac{d_l}{2}\right),$$

$$d_l = (d_r + c_r)/nb \qquad (2.4)$$

$$M_4 = \sum_{i=1}^{nb} \frac{1}{2} \rho C_d D u_i |u_i| d_l \left((i-1)d_l + \frac{d_l}{2} - \eta \right),$$
$$d_l = (d_r + \eta)/\ nb \tag{2.5}$$

where, u_{mwl} is the water particle velocity at the mean water level. The cylinder below the mean water level is discretized to calculate the local force per unit length due to the exponentially decaying velocity profile. The portion below the mean water level and above is divided into na parts, and its moment contribution is given above as M_2. The portion below is divided into nb parts, and its moment contributions are given by M_3 and M_4. The local water particle velocity at the ith discrete portion of the cylinder is u_i, and d_l is the length of the discretized section.

There are three combinations of the four moment expressions in Eqs. 2.2–2.5 for three different combinations of the instantaneous wave elevation η with respect to the center of rotation and the mean water level,

$$\eta > 0, \ \eta > c_r \quad M = M_1 + M_2 + M_3$$
$$\eta < 0, \ \eta > c_r \quad M = M_2 + M_3$$
$$\eta < 0, \ \eta < c_r \quad M = M_4$$

3 PROBABILISTIC MODELS OF WAVE FORCES

Let $M = \{M_i, i = 1, 2, \ldots, n\}$ be a time series giving values of $M(t)$ at equal time intervals $\Delta t > 0$. Figure 3 shows a realization of this time series with $n = 51,200$ and $\Delta t = 1$sec. The series is characterized by large infrequent values of short duration, referred to as impulses. These impulses cause the ringing phenomenon observed in the response of offshore platforms to wave forces. Let M^c be a new time series derived from M by removing the impulses present in the wave force record. The series M^c is called the continuous component of M in this study.

Eleven independent realizations of M of the same duration and time step as the record of Fig. 3 are used to estimate the marginal distribution and the spectral density function of M^c and the statistics of the impulses of the wave force process.

3.1 Marginal distribution of M^c

Let $\hat{F}_m$ be the empirical distribution of the continuous component of M^c of the wave force process. Figure 4 shows with a solid line this empirical distribution estimated from the set of eleven independent realizations of M. This empirical distribution is practically unchanged if the impulses of M are not eliminated from the record prior to estimation because they are very infrequent.

The model

$$\tilde{F}_m(x) = \begin{cases} 0.25 - 0.25\left(1 - \exp(a_1(x + b_1))\right), & x \leq -b_1 \\ 0.46 - 0.24\left(1 - \exp(a_2 x)\right), & -b_1 \leq x \leq 0 \\ 0.5 + 0.25\left(1 - \exp(-a_2 x)\right), & 0 \leq x \leq b_3 \\ 0.7 + 0.3\left(1 - \exp(-a_3(x - b_3))\right), & x \geq b_3 \end{cases}$$
$$\tag{3.1}$$

of $\tilde{F}_m$ with parameters $a_1 = 0.0031$, $a_2 = 0.02$, $a_3 = 0.0046$, $b_1 = 100$. and $b_3 = 80$ is shown with a broken line in Fig 4. The agreement between the empirical distribution and the model of Eq. 3.1 is satisfactory.

3.2 Spectral density of M^c

Figure 5 shows with a solid line the average power spectral density $\hat{g}$ of the continuous component of the eleven independent realizations of M considered in the analysis. The figure shows that (1) the frequency band of the wave force process is $(0, 0.5)$ Hz. and (2) a significant fraction of the wave force energy is concentrated in the frequency range $(0.06, 0.14)$ Hz. Because the impulses of M occur very infrequently, the differences between the power spectral density of Fig. 5 and the one corresponding to the entire record M including the impulses are negligible.

Let $Y(t)$ be a stationary Gaussian process with mean μ_y defined by

$$Y(t) = \mu_y + Z(t), \quad t \geq 0, \tag{3.2}$$

where $\{Z(t), t \geq 0\}$ is a stationary Gaussian process with mean zero and spectral density $\{\tilde{g}(f), f \in (0, 0.5)\text{Hz.}\}$ given by,

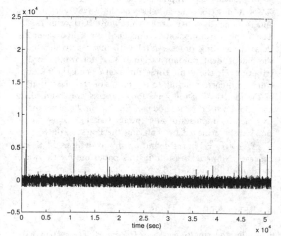

Figure 3.

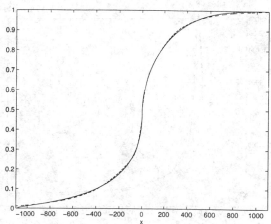

Figure 4: Marginal distribution of $M^c(t)$.

$$\tilde{g}(f) = \frac{g_0\,(f/f_0)^2}{(1-(f/f_0)^2)^2 + (2\zeta_0 f/f_0)^2} \qquad (3.3)$$

with parameters $g_0 = 388.8$, $f_0 = 0.098$ Hz., and $\zeta_0 = 0.565$. The graph of this model is drawn with dotted line in Fig. 5. The covariance function of Y is $EZ(t+\tau)Z(t)$ so that the power spectral density of $Y(t)-\mu_y$ is $\tilde{g}(f)$ (Eq. 3.3).

3.3 Translation model of M^c

The continuous component of the wave force process can be represented by the translation process

$$X^c(t) = \tilde{F}_m^{-1} \circ \Phi\left(\frac{Y(t)-\mu_y}{\sigma_y}\right) = q(Y(t)). \qquad (3.4)$$

where σ_y denotes the standard deviation of $Y(t)$ (Grigoriu, 1995). The marginal distribution of X^c is $\tilde{F}_m$. The mean and correlation function of this process are

$$EX^c(t) = Eq(Y(t))$$
$$EX^c(t)X^c(s) = Eq(Y(t))q(Y(s)). \qquad (3.5)$$

Fig. 5 shows with a broken line the power spectral density of X^c for $\tilde{F}_m$ and $g = \tilde{g}$ given by Eqs. 3.1 and 3.3, respectively.

The resulting model X^c matches the marginal distribution and the correlation structure of the continuous component M^c of the wave force process. Therefore, M^c can be approximated by X^c.

The definition of the continuous component X^c of the wave force process can be modified by replacing the models $\tilde{F}_m$ and $\tilde{g}$ with the estimates $\hat{F}$ and $\hat{g}$, respectively. However, the use of the models $\tilde{F}_m$ and $\tilde{g}$ is more convenient for numerical calculations and they are used in the paper.

3.4 Impulse model

It is assumed that the impulses of the wave force process arrive in time according to a Poisson process. The valid-

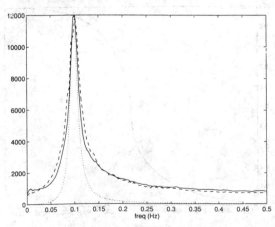

Figure 5: Spectral densities of $M(t)$ (solid line), $Y(t)$ (dotted line), and $X^c(t)$ (broken line).

ity of this assumption is verified by considering the time series realizations of $M(t)$. Figure 6(a) shows with solid line the empirical distribution $\hat{F}_\tau$ of the interarrival times $\tau_i, i=1,\cdots 90$, between consecutive impulses. The broken line in fig. 6(a) is the distribution of an exponentially distributed random variable with parameter $\lambda = 1/\,E\tau$, where E is the expectation operator. The resulting average inter-arrival time between consecutive impulses $E\tau$ is 5.688 sec, so that the estimate of the mean impulse arrival rate is $\hat{\lambda} = 0.000176$. The agreement between the empirical data and the Poisson assumption model is satisfactory.

Figure 6(b) shows with a solid line the empirical distribution, $\hat{F}_i$ of the impulses estimated from the set of eleven independent realizations of $M(t)$. This distribution was obtained using 91 impulses, and can be modeled by a Weibull distribution

$$\tilde{F}_i(x) = 1 - \exp-\left(\left[\frac{x-2,000}{\alpha}\right]^c\right), \quad x \geq 2,000 \quad (3.6)$$

where $\alpha = 3883.79$, and $c = 1$, and is shown as the broken line in Fig. 6(b). The distributions have the same fourth central moment. The agreement between the empirical distribution and the model in Eq.3.6 is satisfactory.

3.5 Probabilistic model of M

The statistical analysis of the wave force data suggests that the process

$$X(t) = X^c(t) + X^i(t) \qquad (3.7)$$

where

$$X^c(t) = \tilde{F}_m^{-1} \circ \Phi\left(\frac{Y(t)-\mu_y}{\sigma_y}\right),$$
$$X^i(t) = \sum_{k=1}^{N(t)} Y_k \delta(t-\tau_k). \qquad (3.8)$$

can be used to approximate $M(t)$. The first term of the definition of X is the model X^c of Eq. 3.4 and corresponds to the continuous component M^c of M. The second term X^i of X describes the impulses of the wave force process and is modeled by a Poisson white noise (Grigoriu, 1995). The impulse component X^i depends on a homogeneous Poisson counting process $N(t)$ with mean arrival rate $\hat{\lambda}$, the independent random variables $\{Y_k\}$ following the distribution $\tilde{F}_i$, the delta Dirac function δ, and the random times $\{\tau_k\}$ corresponding to the jumps of N. The impulses of the model X of the wave force process are assumed to have no duration. The model of Eq. 3.7 can be generalized to generate impulses of any specified shape. This extension can be achieved by replacing the Poisson white noise $\sum_{k=1}^{N(t)} Y_k \delta(t-\tau_k)$ in the definition of X by a filtered Poisson process. Numerical results in this paper are for the wave force model of Eqs.3.7– 3.8.

4 RESPONSE ANALYSIS

Consider the single degree of freedom linear system with moment of inertia m, damping c and stiffness k (Eq. 2.1).

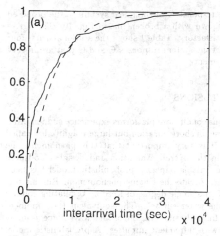

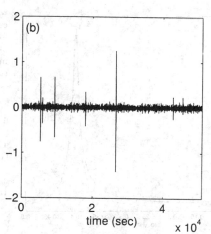

Figure 6: Impulse model for M

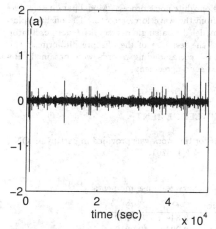

Figure 7: System response to samples of (a) $M(t)$, and (b) $X(t)$

Figure 7 (a) shows the system response $\Theta(t)$ subjected to the wave force record shown in Fig. 3, for $m = 2,876.88$, $c = 181.73$, and $k = 18173.23$.

Let $\tilde{\Theta}$ be the solution of

$$m\ddot{\tilde{\Theta}}(t) + c\dot{\tilde{\Theta}}(t) + k\tilde{\Theta}(t) = X(t), \qquad (4.1)$$

where X is given by Eqs. 3.7–3.8. Let Θ^c and Θ^i be the stationary responses of the linear system of Eqs. 4.1 to X^c and X^i, respectively. Then, the response to the wave force model X is $\tilde{\Theta} = \tilde{\Theta}^c + \tilde{\Theta}^i$. Figure 7 (b) shows the system response $\tilde{\Theta}(t)$ of Eq. 4.1 to a sample of the wave force process $X(t) = X^c(t) + X^i(t)$. Figure 8 shows in more detail the ringing phenomena on the response $\tilde{\Theta}$ of Eq 4.1. This figure details the response of Fig. 7(b) around time $t = 20,000$ sec. The transient response associated with a ringing event can be observed clearly and resembles Fig. 1. The decay rate depends on the system damping.

The response analysis of Eq. 4.1 is performed in three steps. First, the theory of filtered Poisson processes is used to find analytically the response component $\tilde{\Theta}^i(t)$ to the input impulses $X^i(t)$ defined by Eq. 3.8. Second, the Monte Carlo simulation is used to calculate realizations of the response component $\tilde{\Theta}^c(t)$ to the input $X^c(t)$ defined by Eq. 3.8. Third, the total response $\tilde{\Theta}$ as shown in Fig. 7(b) is defined by the superposition $\tilde{\Theta} = \tilde{\Theta}^c + \tilde{\Theta}^i$.

Figure 9 shows the power spectral densities of Θ and $\tilde{\Theta}$. The solid line is the average power spectral density of the response Θ of the system in Eq. 2.1 to the eleven independent realizations of $M(t)$. The broken line in Fig. 9 is the power spectral density of $\tilde{\Theta}$ of the response of Eq. 4.1. The power spectral densities have two distinct peaks. These peaks are located at 0.1 and 0.4 Hz and correspond to the wave force energy content and the oscillator natural frequencies, respectively. The agreement between the response of the system in Eq. 2.1 to the empirical data and the proposed model is satisfactory.

Figure 10 shows with a solid line the marginal distribution of the solution Θ of Eq. 2.1. The marginal distribu-

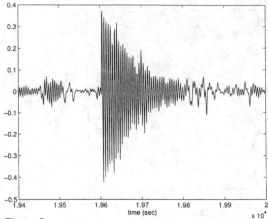

Figure 8.

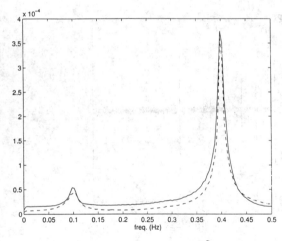

Figure 9: Power spectral densities of Θ and $\tilde{\Theta}$.

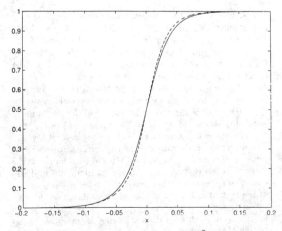

Figure 10: Marginal distribution of Θ and $\tilde{\Theta}$.

tion of the response $\tilde{\Theta}$ of the linear system to the proposed model is shown with a broken line in Fig. 10. The agreement is satisfactory. Table 1 shows the stationary first four moments of the system responses Θ and $\tilde{\Theta}$ that are in very good agreement.

5 CONCLUSIONS

The response of offshore platforms experience sudden infrequent bursts of short duration but large magnitudes, called ringing. It is very important that this phenomenon be included in the overall evaluation and design of offshore platforms. In this paper, a probabilistic model has been used to incorporate the ringing phenomenon. Ringing was simulated on a single degree of freedom oscillating column piercing the water surface. The equivalent total moment resulting from the integration of the wave force is non–Gaussian with infrequent impulses. A probabilistic model has been developed to describe this non–Gaussian behavior. The model consists of a translation process superimposed with a Poisson white noise process. Model parameters were estimated from the wave force records. The offshore platform was modeled as a single degree of freedom oscillator. Statistics of the response of the offshore platform to this model and the corresponding records were obtained. Results showed good agreement.

6 ACKNOWLEDGEMENT

The support for this work was provided in part by an ONR Grant N00014–93–1–0761.

Table 1: Stationary response moments

Statistics	Θ	$\tilde{\Theta}$
$E(.)$	-8.34e-4	8.24e-4
$Var(.)$	0.0020	0.0019
γ_3	0.6772	0.7142
γ_4	88.9081	99.8921

7 REFERENCES

Chakrabarti, S. (1987). *Hydrodynamics of Offshore Structures*. Springer–Verlag, Boston.

Davies, K. et al. (1994). Ringing of tlp and gbs platforms. In *BOSS*.

Faltinsen, O. (1995). Nonlinear wave loads on a slender vertical cylinder. *Journal of Fluid Mechanics*, 268:179–198.

Grigoriu, M. (1995). *Applied Non-Gaussian Processes: Examples, Theory, Simulation, Linear Random Vibration, and MATLAB Solutions*. Prentice Hall, Englewoods Cliffs, NJ.

Gurley, K. et al. (1996). Simulation of a class of non–normal processes. *International Journal of Nonlinear Mechanics*, 31(5):601–617.

Gurley, K. and Kareem, A. (1996). Numerical experiments in ringing of offshore systems under viscous loads. In *15th International Conference on Offshore Mechanics and Artic Engineering*, Florence, Italy. ASME.

Hasselmann, K. (1962). On the nonlinear energy transfer in a gravity wave spectrum, part i. *Journal of Fluid Mechanics*, 12:481–500.

Hudspeth, R.T. and Chen, M. (1979). Digital simulation of nonlinear random waves. *Journal of the Waterway Port Coastal and Ocean Division*, pages 67–85.

Jeffreys, E.R. and Rainey, R.C.T. (1994). Slender body models of tlp and gbs ringing. In *BOSS*.

Kareem, A. et al. (1994). Response analysis of offshore systems to nonlinear random waves part i: wave field characteristics. In *Proceedings of the Special Symposium on Stochastic Dynamics and Reliability of Nonlinear Ocean Systems*, Chicago, IL. ASME.

Mo, O. and Moan, T. (1985). Environmental load effect analysis of guyed towers. *Journal of Energy Resources Technology*, 107:24–33.

Natvig, B. (1994). A proposed ringing analysis model for higher order tether response. In *Proceedings of the Fourth International Offshore and Polar Engineering Conference*, pages 40–51, Osaka, Japan.

Newman, J. (1995). To second order and beyond. In *TLP Technology Symposium*.

Structural Safety and Reliability, Shiraishi, Shinozuka & Wen (eds) © 1998 Balkema, Rotterdam, ISBN 90 5410 978 5

Approximate evaluations on dynamic responses of offshore structures

Kenji Kawano & Venkataramana Katta
Department of Ocean Civil Engineering, Kagoshima University, Japan

Tomoyo Taniguchi
Kawasaki Heavy Industries Ltd, Kakogawa, Hyogo, Japan

Abstract   Offshore structures have the great possibilities to develop ocean spaces such as the power stations, airports and resident area etc. These structures generally experience more severe loads than those on land structures. In order to perform the reliable design such as structures, it is important to clarify dynamic characteristics of the structures subjected to random sea wave forces. In this study, it is examined to evaluate the reliability of the offshore structure with the simplified modeling of the structure. Since the nonlinear responses may be caused by severe wave forces, the dynamic responses are evaluated not only for the linear responses but also nonlinear responses. It is suggested that the relevant evaluation of the nonlinear responses give important roles on the reliability estimation of the offshore structures subjected to severe wave forces.

1. Introduction

While a wave force is one of the most important loads of offshore structures, the dynamic characteristics of wave forces give important contributions on the reliable design of offshore structures. In order to perform the reliable design of the offshore structure, the preliminary design and examination are required to clarify the dynamic characteristics. The wave force has dynamic and stochastic characteristics, and is represented with stochastic approach in which the response quantities are evaluated by their root-mean-square(*rms*) values(J. Penzien et al, 1972). It seems to be important to perform evaluations of the extreme response quantities for a reliable and comprehensive analysis. Since the offshore structures are generally made of lots of members, the governing equation of motion which is used to determined the dynamic responses have very large dimensions and can be solved with much computation time. It is , however, suggested that considering the results on the dynamic responses of the offshore structure due to random sea waves, they are mainly controlled by the dominant vibration modes such as the first few vibration modes(Y. Yamada et al, 1988). The vibration mode can be closely related to the simplified model of the offshore structure. The preliminary design and examination of the offshore structure to random sea wave conditions are required to evaluate the dynamic response characteristics as convenient as it can .

Considering the design wave force has probabilistic and stochastic properties, the dynamic responses have possibility such as exceeding the elastic region. It is, then, important to examine and evaluate the nonlinear response effects on the design level responses of the offshore structure.

In this study, the dynamic response analyses are carried out using the simplified model of the offshore platform. The nonlinear response analysis is performed to examine the contributions on the linear response evaluation because time domain approach with simulated wave forces is useful to analysis the nonlinear responses. Moreover, the random vibration approach is applied to evaluate the dynamic responses due to random sea state, and to perform the reliability estimation of the offshore structure. The nonlinear model of the offshore structure is represented with the versatile model(Y.K.Wen(1976)), and random vibration analyses of the structure is carried out with the equivalent linearization approach.

2. Dynamic Response Analysis

2.1 Time Domain Approach

The offshore structure can be formulated with the finite element method. The dynamic response of the offshore structure is mainly governed by the dominant frequency of a wave force and the first natural frequency. The dynamic characteristics of structures such as an offshore platform may be represented with a simplified dynamic model. In this study, an offshore platform is modeled with an appropriate shape function such as shown in Fig.1. The wave force can be computed with the modified Morison equation. The wave force due to the drag force is proportional to square relative velocity between the structure and water particle. This force can be generally represented with the equivalent linearization method using the assumption of Gaussian process of the relative velocity(J. Penzien et al, 1972). The structure is modeled with two-degree-of-freedom system as shown in Fig.1. Considering the nonlinear characteristics of structure, the governing equation of motion of the simplified structure subjected wave force is given by

$$\begin{bmatrix} m_1 + C_{M1} & 0 \\ 0 & m_2 \end{bmatrix}\begin{Bmatrix} \ddot{x}_1 \\ \ddot{x}_2 \end{Bmatrix} + \begin{bmatrix} C_1 + C_D & -C_2 \\ -C_2 & C_2 \end{bmatrix}\begin{Bmatrix} \dot{x}_1 \\ \dot{x}_2 \end{Bmatrix} +$$

$$\begin{bmatrix} \alpha F_Y / Y + k_2 & -k_2 \\ -k_2 & k_2 \end{bmatrix}\begin{Bmatrix} x_1 \\ x_2 \end{Bmatrix} + \begin{Bmatrix} (1-\alpha)F_Y z \\ 0 \end{Bmatrix} = \begin{Bmatrix} F_W \\ 0 \end{Bmatrix}$$

$$Y\dot{Z} + \gamma|\dot{x}_1||Z|^{n-1}Z + (\beta|Z|^n - A)\dot{x}_1 = 0 \qquad (1)$$

in which

$$C_{M1} = c_m \rho_W A_S$$

$$C_D = \frac{1}{2} c_d \rho_W d \sqrt{\frac{8}{\pi}} \sigma_v$$

The wave force F_W is expressed with an integrated force on the shape function as follows.

$$F_W = \left[(C_M + C_A)\frac{\omega^2}{\sinh(kh)}\eta + C_D\sqrt{\frac{8}{\pi}}\sigma_v\frac{\omega}{\sinh(kh)}\dot{\eta} \right]F_D$$

$$(2)$$

in which F_D is given by the wave number k and depth of water h, and the height of the structure l.

$$F_d = \frac{3}{l^2 k^3}(F_{D1}(h_1) - F_{D1}(0)) -$$

$$\frac{2}{l^3 k^4}(F_{D2}(h) - F_{D2}(0)) \qquad (3)$$

in which

$$F_{D1}(s) = ((ks)^2 + 2)\sinh(ks) - 2(ks)\cosh(ks)$$

$$F_{D2}(s) = ((ks)^3 + 6(ks))\sinh(ks) - (3(ks)^2 + 6)\cosh(ks)$$

where k is the wave number and s is the distance from the sea bottom. The variable η and $\dot{\eta}$ denote motions of a sea surface, and can be simulated with a power spectrum density function such as the Bretschneider type(Chakrabarti S. K., 1987).

$$S_{\eta\eta}(\omega) = \frac{4210}{\omega^5}\left(\frac{H}{T^2}\right)^2 \exp\left(-1052\left(\frac{1}{\omega T}\right)^4\right) \qquad (4)$$

in which H and T denote the mean wave height and mean wave period, respectively. Giving the random sea wave condition with these quantities, the dynamic

responses due to simulated wave forces can be carried out using Eq.(1) and Eq.(2) . However, these differential equations are combined by different orders. These equations can be solved with transform to the first order differential equation as follows.

$$[A]\{\dot{y}\} + [B]\{y\} = \{f\} \qquad (5)$$

in which

$$[A] = Diag[m_1 + C_{M1} \quad m_2 \quad m_1 \quad m_2 \quad 1]$$

$$[B] = \begin{bmatrix} \tilde{C}_1 & -C_2 & ky & -k_2 & kz \\ -C_1 & C_2 & -k_2 & k_2 & 0 \\ -m_1 & 0 & 0 & 0 & 0 \\ 0 & -m_2 & 0 & 0 & 0 \\ F_e & 0 & 0 & 0 & G_e \end{bmatrix}$$

$$\{y\}^T = [\dot{x}_1 \quad \dot{x}_2 \quad x_1 \quad x_2 \quad Z]$$

$$\{f\}^T = [F_W \quad 0 \quad 0 \quad 0 \quad 0]$$

$$ky = k_2 + \alpha F_Y / Y$$

$$kz = (1 - \alpha)F_Y$$

The coefficient F_e and G_e denote the nonlinear effects of the structure as follow

$$F_e = \gamma|\dot{x}_1||Z|^{n-1}$$

$$G_e = (\beta|Z|^n - A_1)/Y \qquad (6)$$

in which γ, β, A_1 and n are parameters which determine the nonlinear characteristics. If the wave force is simulated in time region, the dynamic responses of the nonlinear structure as expressed with Eq.(6) can be solved with Runge Kutta method.

2.2 Random Vibration Approach

If the random vibration approach is applied to Eq.(5) , the nonlinear coefficient as expressed with Eq.(6) requires to represent the constant values. Using the assumption that these responses have Gaussian process, these nonlinear coefficients can be approximately expressed with the equivalent linearization method as follows(Y.K. Wen,1980).

$$F_e = \left(\sqrt{\frac{2}{\pi}}(\beta + \gamma\frac{\langle \dot{x}_1 z \rangle}{\sigma_z \sigma_{\dot{x}_1}})\sigma_z - A_1 \right)/Y$$

$$G_e = \sqrt{\frac{2}{\pi}}(\gamma + \beta\frac{\langle \dot{x}_1 z \rangle}{\sigma_z \sigma_{\dot{x}_1}})\sigma_{\dot{x}_1}/Y \qquad (7)$$

in which σ_z and $\sigma_{\dot{x}_1}$ denote the rms responses of Z and $\dot{x}_1$, respectively, and $\langle \dot{x}_1 z \rangle$ denotes the expectation of Z and $\dot{x}_1$. Being the matrix $[B]$ expressed with these coefficients, the power spectrum of the responses $[S_{yy}(\omega)]$ can be obtained with

$$[S_{yy}(\omega)] = [H(\omega)][S_{ff}(\omega)][H(\omega)]^* \quad (8)$$

in which

$$[H(\omega)] = [i\omega[A] + [B]]^{-1}$$

The covariance matrix of the response $[R_{yy}]$ can be ,then, obtained by

$$[R_{yy}] = \int_{-\infty}^{\infty}[S_{yy}(\omega)]d\omega \quad (9)$$

While the *rms* responses can be given by these results, these responses are closely dependent upon the assumed *rms* responses such as $\sigma_{\dot{x}_1}$ and σ_z . Then, these calculations have to iterate until the calculated values converge to assumed ones in allowable region. When the nonlinear responses are caused by random sea waves, the restoring forces exerted on the structure can be evaluated with these results. The variance of the restoring force is expressed with

$$\sigma_{FQ}^2 = (\alpha F_Y / y)^2 \sigma_{x1}^2 + ((1-\alpha)F_Y)^2 \sigma_Z^2 + \\ (2\alpha F_Y / Y)(1-\alpha)F_Y \sigma_{xz}^2 \quad (11)$$

Assuming F_Q a zero-mean Gaussian process with spectral density function $G_F(\omega)$, the degree of dispersion of the spectral density function about its central frequency is expressed using a bandwidth parameter q_x . If the barrier level λ is taking for a relevant design value, the reliability $R(\lambda)$ of the structure on the first passage probability can be expressed with

$$R(\lambda) = \exp\left(-\frac{1}{\pi}\sqrt{\frac{\alpha_2}{\alpha_0}}t_0 \exp(-\frac{\gamma^2}{2})c_1\right) \quad (12)$$

where

$$c_1 = \frac{1-\exp(\sqrt{\frac{\pi}{2}}q_x\gamma)}{1-\exp(-\frac{\gamma^2}{2})} \quad , \quad \gamma = \frac{\lambda}{\sigma_{FQ}}$$

$$q_x = 1 - \frac{\alpha_1^2}{\alpha_0\alpha_2} \quad ,(0 \le q_x \le 1)$$

$$\alpha_i = \int_0^{\infty} S_{yy}(\omega)d\omega \quad (i = 0,1,2)$$

and the duration time of the input motion is denoted by t_0 .This equation corresponds to the first crossing time of asymmetric barrier for a zero-mean stationary Gaussian process(E. H. Vanmarcke,1975).

Since the nonlinear response is not always symmetric to a barrier, it is useful to evaluate the first passage probability of the offshore structure during the very long duration of wave forces.

3. Numerical Results and Discussions

The dynamic response analyses are carried out for the simplified model of an offshore platform as shown in Fig.1. The depth of water is 50m and the height of structure is 60m. The leg of the simplified model has an outer diameter of 3.0m. The structure is restrained from the base movement because of the simplification of dynamic response characteristics. Modified Morison equation is used to compute the hydrodynamic force due to the surrounding water and sea waves. The values of the inertia coefficient c_M and the drag coefficient c_D are taken as 2.0 and 1.0, respectively. The governing equation of motion is expressed with the first order differential equation. The structure can be transformed to two degrees of freedom system with an appropriate shape function. The structure has the deck loads which occupy almost structure weights. The structural damping is assumed to be 2%, and the natural frequency is 3.9rad/sec. The displacement of the structure is evaluated at the nodal point 1. Surface motion of random sea is represented with Bretschneider type power spectrum by the determination of the mean wave height and mean wave period.

3.1 Dynamic Response to Wave Forces

The example of power spectra of Bretshneider type for the mean wave height 5m is shown in Fig.2 to several mean wave periods. It is shown that since the sea wave motion is a narrow band process, it has the

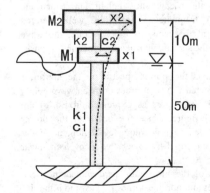

Fig 1. Analytical model of simplified offshore structure

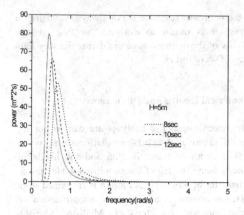

Fig 2. Bretschneider power spectra of wave heights

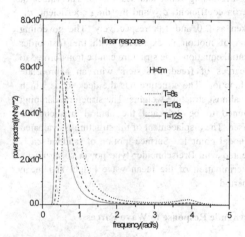

Fig 3. Power spectra of linear response

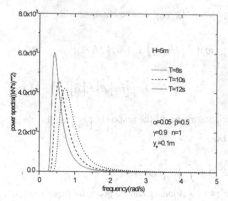

Fig 4. Power spectra of nonlinear responses

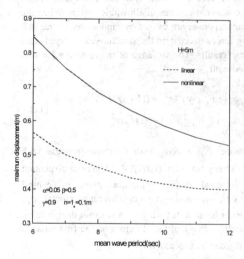

Fig 5. Maximum displacement vs mean wave

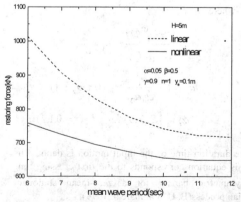

Fig 6. Maximum restoring force vs mean wave period

dominant periods of wave forces. Fig.3 shows the power spectra of responses of the structure subjected to random sea waves of the mean wave height 5m. Since the dominant peak frequency is generally well-separated from the natural frequency of the structure, the wave force provides the significant roles on dynamic responses of the structure.

Fig.4 also shows the power spectra on the nonlinear responses subjected to wave forces of mean wave height 5m. Nonlinear parameters as expressed in Eq.(6) are denoted in the figure. Since the peaks of the power spectra are moved to low frequency region, nonlinear responses are governed by lower frequency than linear responses.

Comparison of the maximum displacement between linear responses and nonlinear ones is shown in Fig.5. It maximum displacements at node 1 to the wave forces of the mean wave height 5m. They gradually decrease as

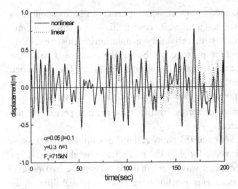

Fig 7. Time histories of displacement responses

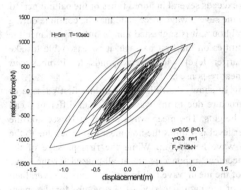

Fig.8 Time history of restoring force

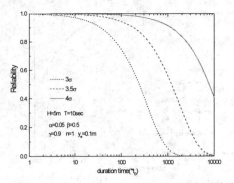

Fig 9a. Reliability on nonlinear responses

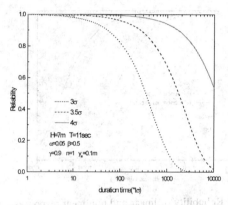

Fig 9b. Reliability of nonlinear responses

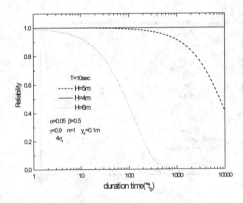

Fig 10. Reliability on mean wave heights

the mean wave period increases, because the dominant frequency of wave forces is separated from the natural frequency of the structure. Nonlinear responses are larger than linear ones. These influences mainly depend on the nonlinear parameters and the sea wave state.

Fig.6 shows similarly comparisons of the maximum restoring forces between linear and nonlinear responses. The wave force and nonlinear parameters are the same situations as in the previous case. The restoring forces of the nonlinear responses become smaller than the linear responses.

Fig.7 shows the time histories both the linear displacement response and nonlinear one due to the wave force of the mean wave height 5m. The nonlinear response is larger than the linear one, and the nonlinear result enlarge as duration exerted of a wave force increases.

Fig.8 shows the relation between the displacement and the restoring force. They are obtained to wave forces of the mean wave height 5m and the mean wave period 10sec. It is suggested that if the nonlinear effects are caused by severe wave state, it provides important contributions on response evaluations.

3.2 Evaluations of the first passage probabilities

It is considered that the wave force parameters such as the mean wave height(or the significant wave height) and the mean wave period give important roles for design of an offshore structure. When the offshore

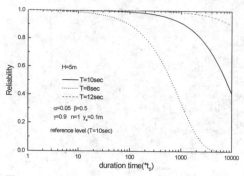

Fig 11. Reliability on nonlinear responses

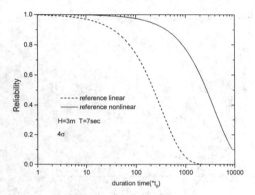

Fig 12. Reliability of linear and nonlinear responses

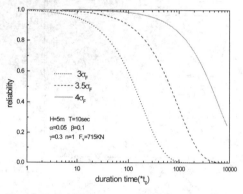

Fig 13. Reliability on restoring force

structure is designed for some wave force situations, the first stage of design may be carried out with the linear response quantities. However, it is suggested that some design level due to severe wave states have the possibilities of excess with respect to the linear dynamic responses of the structure. Considering these

complicated circumstances, it seems to be reasonable to examine to nonlinear contributions on the dynamic responses with reliability evaluations. Thus, reliability on the first passage of the displacement and restoring force can be calculated with Eq.(12). The reference response to the barrier level λ is used to the corresponding *rms* response. The duration t_0 is expressed in terms of the first natural period of the structure.

Fig.9(a) and (b) show reliabilities on the first passage for the wave force of the mean wave height 5m and 7m, and the mean wave period 10sec. When the barrier level is 3 times *rms* nonlinear responses, probability of the first passage increase drastically as the duration of wave force exceeds several hundred times of the natural period. Since the severe wave force state may be continue during several hours, it is suggested that in order to enhance the reliabilities on the first passage, it is reasonable to take the barrier level which corresponds to 4 times *rms* nonlinear responses.

Fig.10 shows the reliabilities on the first passage of the structure due to the wave force with different mean wave heights. The mean wave period is 10 sec and the barrier level is 4 times the nonlinear responses due to the mean wave height 5m. While the first passage of the displacement response is not at all caused for the wave state of the mean wave height 4m, it occurs at several ten times of the natural period of a structure for the mean wave height 6m. Since the severe wave state provides significant contributions on the nonlinear responses, it is important to examine the nonlinear response influences for the reliable evaluations of the offshore structure responses.

Fig. 11 shows the reliabilities on the first passage of the displacement due to the wave force with different mean wave periods. The reference response of the barrier level takes the same one as in the previous case. If the mean wave period is different from the design one, the first passage probability on the nonlinear response is considerably influenced by the mean wave period. If the nonlinear responses of the offshore structure may be caused by severe wave forces, it is suggested that the selection of the mean wave period of the design response provides important roles on the evaluation of the first passage probability.

Fig. 12 shows the first passage probabilities on the barrier level of 4 times *rms* responses which are determined by the linear and nonlinear analyses. It is shown that if the barrier level is determined for the linear response, the first passage probability on the linear response is larger than that on the nonlinear responses.

Fig.13 shows the reliabilities on the first passage of the restoring force of the structure due to the wave force of the mean wave height 5m and the mean wave period 10sec. The reliability on the first passage of the restoring force gives the same tendency as one to the displacements as shown in Fig.9. When the duration of the severe wave force exceeds 1000 times the natural period of the structure, the first passage probabilities increase for the barrier level of 3 times and 3.5 times. It is suggested that in order to perform the reliable design of the offshore structure, it is important to examine and clarify the nonlinear contributions on the dynamic response.

4. Conclusions

The dynamic response characteristics of an offshore structure due to severe sea state are examined. The main results are summarized as follows.
1) In order to perform the reliable design of offshore structures, it is necessary to clarify not only the linear dynamic response characteristics but also the nonlinear dynamic responses. The nonlinear response evaluations provide significant roles on evaluating the first passage probability of the structure.
2) Using a simplified model of an offshore structure, nonlinear effects on the dynamic response estimation can be comprehensively examined at the preliminary stage of design.
3) The reliable evaluation of the dynamic responses of offshore structure can be implemented with the nonlinear dynamic response which is closely related to both the nonlinear parameters and sea wave states.

REFERENCES

Penzien,J., M.K.Kaul and B.Berge, 1972, Stochastic response of offshore towers to random sea waves and strong motion earthquake, Computers and structures, Vol.2, 733-756
Vanmarcke,E.H. 1975. On the distribution of the first passage time for normal stationary random processes,: J.of applied mechanics, ASCE, Vol.42,215-220
Wen Y. K., 1976, Method for random vibration of hysteretic systems, Jour. of Eng. Mech. Div., Proc. of ASCE, Vol.102, EM2, 249-263
Wen Y.K., 1980, Equivalent linearization for hysteretic systems under random excitation, Trannsactions of the ASME, Vol.47, March, 150-154
Yamada Y., K. Kawano, H. Iemura and K. Venkataramana, 1988, Wave and earthquake response of offshore structures with soil-structure interaction, Proc. Of JSCE, Structural Eng./Earthquake Eng.,Vol.5, No.2, 361s-370s
Chakrabarti S. K. ,1987, Hydrodynamics of offshore structures, Computational Mechanics Publications

Structural Safety and Reliability, Shiraishi, Shinozuka & Wen (eds) © 1998 Balkema, Rotterdam, ISBN 90 5410 978 5

Benefits and learnings from the Heidrun Field development risk assessment and safety assurance program

Demir I. Karsan
Bechtel Corporation, Houston, Tex., USA

Fikry R. Botros
Conoco Inc., Houston, Tex., USA

ABSTRACT: Benefits gained from the comprehensive risk assessment and safety assurance and improvement program implemented during the Heidrun Field Development Project in Offshore Norway are outlined. The economic, safety improvement, and learning, benefits from this program far outweighed its costs.

1 INTRODUCTION

The Heidrun Field is located about 175 km off the coast of Norway (Fig. 1) in 350 meters water depth. The field consists of: 1) A light weight aggregate concrete TLP with two concrete MSBs supporting the Living Quarters, Utility, Drillers, Well Bay, and Process modules (Fig. 2) designed to produce 200,000 BOPD, (2) An oil offtake system with two DSL tankers, (3) A 56 slot well template, injection subsea wells, and oil and gas export flowlines. Heidrun RASAP consisted of establishing Heidrun Field RAC, specifying DAE and associated load effects, demonstrating that the Field RAC and the Norwegian Statuary requirements are satisfied, recommending ALARP measures to reduce risks and providing safety advisors to high risk construction sites and offshore operations, motivating, controlling, and improving safety and working environment practices. Fig. 3 outlines the Heidrun RASAP, its sequence, and interrelation between RAC, CSA, DDRA, TRA and the field design, construction, and operations.

The Heidrun RASAP was carried out within a time frame of five years, at a cost of NOK 36 million. This represents 0.15% of the total Heidrun Field Development cost of NOK 25 Billion.

2 DESIGN IMPROVEMENTS AND ECONOMIC BENEFITS

The first step in the Heidrun RASAP was setting up of the Heidrun RAC (HRAC, Karsan 1996). HRAC set annual probability of exceedence limits on the Main Safety Functions *(Escapeways available for 60 minutes, Shelter Area intact for 90 minutes, Evacuation System intact for 90 minutes, Control Center available for 90 minutes, Main Structure available for two hours)*, and Environmental Damage *(Major, Significant, and Minor oil spill effect categories)*. HRAC for loss of life was expressed in terms of FAR. These limits were established to match or improve the offshore oil and gas production operators' safety performance in the North Sea within the 1980-95 period.

Where data was not available, event tree simulations were performed to estimate an operator's implied level of safety (Karsan 1996). Heidrun RASAP results are summarized in Tables 1 through 3.

Operator was allowed to decide on acceptable material damage and production delay limits based on cost of prevention versus cost of consequences analyses, provided that HRAC set for the main safety functions, FAR, and environmental damage and the NPD requirements were satisfied.

2.1 DAE selection

DAE and their load effects were selected to keep the residual events below HRAC and satisfy the NPD PLS requirements:

$$P(HRAC_l) = P(HRAC_l \mid A_{ijk}) \cdot P(A_{ijk}) \leq P_T(HRAC_l)$$
$$i = 1, I; \quad j = 1, J; \quad k = 1, K \qquad \text{Eq. 1}$$

HRAC Requirement (Karsan 1996)

$$P(A_i) = \sum_j \sum_k P(A_{ijk}) \leq 10^{-4}/\text{yr}.$$

$$\qquad \qquad \text{Eq. 2}$$

NPD PLS Requirement (NPD 1992)

$P(HRAC_l)$ represents probability of impairment of safety functions controlled by $HRAC_l$, $P_T(HRAC_l)$ is the target residual event probability set for $HRAC_l$, $P(A_{ijk})$ is the probability of occurrence of the Accidental events j of Class i (vessel impact, blowouts, etc.) at Structural components k. (hull, pontoons, etc.). Given Eq. 2:

$$P(FSYS_i) = P(A_{ijk}) \cdot P(FSYS_i \mid A_{ijk}),$$
$$j = 1, J, \quad k = 1, K \qquad \text{Eq. 3}$$

NPD PLS Case sets the material resistance factor (γ_m) to unity. The fact that the guaranteed material strengths are used and significant redundancy/system action is present to prevent structural system failure when initial failure of a structural component k occurs, for all events j of Class i,

$$P(FSYS_i \mid A_{ijk}) \leq 10^{-2} \qquad \text{Eq. 4}$$

and from Eq. 3

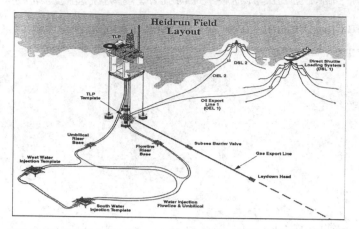

Fig. 1 - Heidrun Field Layout

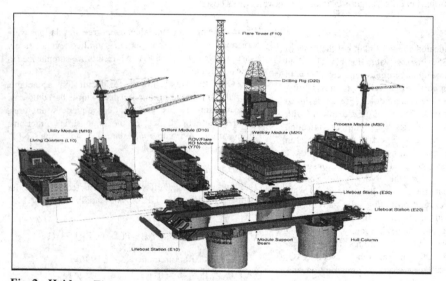

Fig. 2 - Heidrun Field Topsides Facilities

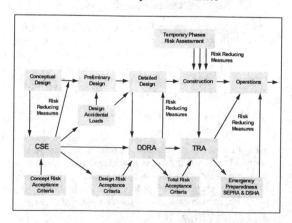

Fig. 3 - Sequence of Heidrun Risk Assessment Activities

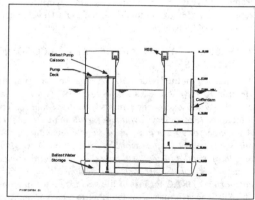

Fig. 4 - Heidrun TLP Concrete Hull Configuration

Table 1 - HRASAP Results for Annual Impairment Frequency of Safety Functions

Safety Function	Annual Safety Function Impairment Frequency			
	Base Case (Peak Blowout Yr)	Sensitivity 1 (Av. Blowout Yr)	Sensitivity 1 plus Additional Module	Acceptance Criteria [*] P_T (HRAC$_j$)
Escape Ways	2.6×10^{-4}	2.2×10^{-4}	2.6×10^{-4}	1 to 5x10^{-4}
Shelter Area	1.9×10^{-4}	1.6×10^{-4}	1.8×10^{-4}	1 to 5x10^{-4}
Evacuation	1.4×10^{-4}	1.2×10^{-4}	1.5×10^{-4}	1 to 5x10^{-4}
Control Room	1.4×10^{-4}	1.2×10^{-4}	1.5×10^{-4}	1 to 5x10^{-4}
Escalation	3.2×10^{-4}	2.9×10^{-4}	3.5×10^{-4}	1 to 5x10^{-4}

[*] Risk is accepted under certain conditions if the sum of residual accidental events fall in the interval 1 to 5×10^{-4} per year with 3.0×10^{-4} as a reference value. Ref. Karsan 1996.

Table 2 - HRASAP Results for Accidental Fatality Risk

Type of Fatality (Ref. Karsan 1996)	FAR, Fatalities per 10^8 Exposed Hours			
	Base Case	Sensitivity 1	Sensitivity 2	Acceptance Criterion
Immediate	1.92	1.60	1.81	No Separate Criterion
Escape & Evacuation	0.75	0.55	0.77	No Separate Criterion
Working	1.15	1.15	1.15	No Separate Criterion
Total	3.82	3.30	3.73	5.0

Table 3 - HRASAP Results for Oil Spill Pollution

Effect Category (Ref. Karsan 1996)	Acceptable Cumulative Frequency of Occurrence	Environmental Risk Assessment Results Without Oil Spill Combat	Environmental Risk Assessment Results With Oil Spill Combat P_T (HRAC$_j$)
Major	10^{-5}/yr.	1.1×10^{-5}/yr.	1.6×10^{-6}/yr.
Significant	10^{-3}/yr.	1.1×10^{-3}/yr.	5.2×10^{-4}/yr.
Minor	10^{-2}/yr.	2.9×10^{-3}/yr.	1.6×10^{-3}/yr.

$$P_T(FSYS_i) \leq 10^{-6}/yr. \qquad \text{Eq. 5}$$

can be taken as the NPD PLS implied target system failure probability for a structure with sufficient redundancy against individual component failures leading to total system failures.

Design generally considers 6 to 10 categories of accidental and extreme events (extreme waves, dropped objects, vessel impacts, blowouts, fires of non-blowout-origin, explosions, unintended flooding, etc.). Assuming 10 or less event categories ($I \leq 10$).

$$P_T(FSYS) = \sum_{i=1}^{10} P(FSYS_i) \approx 10^{-5}/yr. \qquad \text{Eq. 6}$$

is obtained (Moan 1993). In Eq. 6, P_T(FSYS) represents the target failure probability of the structural system under all A_{ijk}. For a component failure with no backup, the system will fail at the first component failure. System action generally results in one order of magnitude lower failure probability. Thus, the conditional probability of failure of a structural system under an event J belonging to event Class I and acting on structural component K, where no backup is provided is:

$$P(FSYS_i|A_{ijk}) \leq 10^{-1}, \; i = I, \; j = J, \; k = K, \qquad \text{Eq. 7}$$

and Eq. 5 may not be satisfied for accidental event Class i

unless the component K is designed for an accidental event J of Class I of an order of magnitude higher probability of occurrence, or the failure probability of the component is decreased by an order of magnitude through use of a higher γ_m.

Fig. 5 outlines the process followed for the DAE selection. DAE derived from this process do not result in an unique A_{ijk} set, providing opportunities for optimizing the design costs while satisfying the constraints given by Eqs. 1 and 6. Table 4 which shows the dropped object DAE selected for the major structural component design is given as an example. HRAC were satisfied as shown in Tables 1 through 3. With the initial assumption of:

$$P(FSYS_i|A_{ijk}) \approx 10^{-2} \qquad \text{Eq. 4}$$

a set of accidental events that satisfy Eq. 2 were selected. Option 1 allows the design of all six major components of the TLP Structural System for accidental events with $0.17.10^{-4}$/yr probability each adding up to 10^{-4}/yr, satisfying the Eq. 2. Option 2 allows design of the column portion between -21 m to -52 m elevations for a lower impact energy of 205 MJ with a higher probability of exceedence, while all the other components are designed against higher impact energies with lower probabilities of exceedence, also adding up to 10^{-4}/yr, satisfying the Eq. 2. This way, high cost components are designed for lower loads with

Table 4 - Design Dropped Object (i) Events and their Probabilities of Impact on Major Structural Components

Event No. j	Target Structural Component k	Design Event A_{ijk}				Design Dropped Objects j
		Design Option 1		Design Option 2		
		Des. Enrgy (kJ)	Target Prob. Lvl	Des. Energy (kJ)	Target Prob. Lvl	
1	Column 0 to -21 m	310/300	$0.17 \cdot 10^{-4}$	370/300	$01 \cdot 10^{-4}$	Drill Riser/Casg 13-5/8"
2	Column -21 to -52 m	240	$0.17 \cdot 10^{-4}$	205	$0.5 \cdot 10^{-4}$	Casing 13-5/8"
3	Column -52 to -77 m	210	$0.17 \cdot 10^{-4}$	235	$0.1 \cdot 10^{-4}$	Casing 13-5/8"
4	Top of Pontoons Including Upper Tether Porches	1550	$0.17 \cdot 10^{-4}$	1800	$0.1 \cdot 10^{-4}$	Tether Tension Insp. Tools or BOPstack
		320/260		340/280		Casing 13-5/8"/ Casing 9-5/8"
5	Side of Pontoons	200	$0.17 \cdot 10^{-4}$	210	$0.1 \cdot 10^{-4}$	Casing 13-5/8"
6	Tethers Incl. Lower Porches	205	$0.17 \cdot 10^{-4}$	220	$0.1 \cdot 10^{-4}$	
	SUM	----	10^{-4}/yr	-----	10^{-4}/yr	----

Note: Elevation 0 represents Mean Sea Level. Negative elevations are below Mean Sea Level.

Table 5 - Actual Vs Design Dur./Accidental Fire Events on TLP Hull & Cost Sav. from Use of Shorter Des. Dur.

Structural Member/Element	Heat Load (kW/m^2)	Actual Dur. (hrs)	Design Dur. (hrs)	Design Accidental Event Reference	NOK 10^6 Savings [4]/ Choice of Des. Dur.
Wellbay trusses: - upper - middle	300	> 2 hrs.	2	Ignited gas blowout at wellhead or BOP	≈5
Columns: ± 0m to + 15m Elevation [1] + 15m Elevation and above	250 200-60 [2]	> 2 hrs. > 2 hrs.	2 2	Fire on sea fed by platform oil blowout	≈22 ≈10
Columns:& MSBS ± 0m to 15m Elevation [2] + 15m Elevation and above	250 [1] 250-60 [3]	< 10 min. < 10 min.	~ 10 min. ~ 10 min.	Jet fire from leak in gas export riser	0 0

[1] ± 0 Elevation is at Mean Water Level (MWL); [2] Linearly decreasing from 200 Kw/m^2 at el. + 15 to 60 Kw/m^2 at column top; [3] Linearly decreasing from 250 Kw/m^2 at el. + 15 to 60 Kw/m^2 at column top, [4] Compared against 4 hour.

higher probability of occurrence, while low cost components are designed for less frequent but higher intensity events, saving cost.

2.2 Hull compartmentation

Dropped objects and boat impacts have the highest potential for damaging the external columns and pontoon walls (Moan 1993). An internal second wall, (cofferdam) is provided between the +10 m to -20 m column elevations (measured from the mean water level) in the ship impact zone (Fig. 4). The pontoons are divided into water tight compartments by means of central bulkheads and accidental flooding of any pontoon compartment will not lead to capsizing. However, compartmenting the columns below the cofferdam would have resulted in a significant weight and cost increase. As per Eqs. 4 and 7, it was decided to increase the γ_m for the uncompartmented column sections lowering P(FSYSi|A_{ijk}) by one order of magnitude to make up for the lack of compartmentation. Studies of the uncertainty in the reinforced concrete strength and associated design equations indicated that a 15% increase in the reinforced concrete γ_m would result in such a decrease in the column wall failure probability (Moan 23). The cost saving from not providing full column compartmentation is estimated to be NOK 80 to 100 million. This design approach does not provide structural robustness (probability of system not to fail following arbitrary removal of any structural component). However, such an approach is in use for a number of weight sensitive structures and judged acceptable when all major accidental events are carefully accounted for.

2.3 Riser and tensioner passive fire protection

Heidrun drilling, production, and export riser systems (Fig. 6) were developed with the consideration that the production tubing, riser pipe wall, the SSV, the ESD valves on the wellhead trees and the PBSV at seabed will always form dual barriers against release of produced hydrocarbons to the environment for all accidental event scenarios. This resulted in the deletion of passive fire protection for risers and tensioners. An NPD request was made to demonstrate that the riser design meets their fire and safety requirements. When this request was made, it was estimated that the passive fire protection for the risers would have cost NOK 700 million. The fact that HRAC was already satisfied, it was agreed to base this decision on a comparison of the cost of protection against fires at sea versus its consequences. Analyses and hydrocarbon fire tests conducted showed that, should fires at sea burn through a riser wall, the small hydrocarbon inventory in the production piping or export risers would not result in any significant escalation of the fires unless a DSV or a PBSV

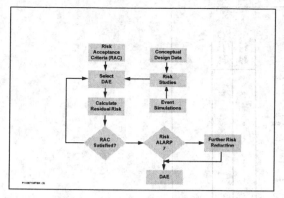

Fig. 5 - Design Accidental Event Selection

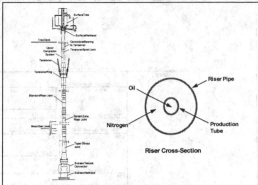

Fig. 6 - Heidrun TLP Production Riser

Table 6 - Target vs. Designed Reliability Levels of Heidrun TLP Tethers (Ref. Wirsching 95)

Target Probability of Failure of Leg Implied by FS = 3 (with inspection) and FS = 10 (no inspection)		
	FS = 3 (inspection)	FS = 10 (no inspection)
Target probability of failure of leg (safety index in parentheses)	185.0E-4 (2.09)	8.00E-4 (3.16)
Prob. of failure of a leg in the present design (safety index in parenthesis)		6.17E-4 (3.23)

Table 7 - Risk Reduc. in % for the Different PBSV Positions Compared to no Valve on P/L (Ref. Technica 91)

RISK FACTOR		% RISK REDUCTION FOR OPTION	
		PSBV AT TEMPLATE	PSBV @ 300m FROM TEMPLATE
Impairmnt Freq	structure	64	99
	shelter area	62	79
	escapeway	63	63
Potential loss of life		35	59
Material damage		30	35
Pollution from escalation to blowout		80	96

fails. Results from DDRA, fire tests and analysis of riser wall strengths, and reliability studies commissioned by the project provided the following information:

$P(FS)$ = Probability of hydrocarbon fires at sea, $= 12 \times 10^{-4}$/yr

$P(FW|FS)$ = Probability of an unprotected riser wall failure, given a major fire at sea longer than 30 minutes, from tests ≈ 0.25

$P(FSSV)$ = On demand failure probability of a SSV $\approx 0.24 \times 10^{-2}$/demand

N = Number of Production Risers = 35

$P(FPBSV)$ = On demand failure probability of a PBSV $\approx 0.50 \times 10^{-2}$/demand

Fig. 7 shows the event tree for cost of consequence calculations for fires at sea escalating into riser wall failures due to lack of passive fire protection. A major loss is represented by a two year loss of production and major platform refurbishment cost of NOK 5 billion. Significant

loss is represented by damaged riser(s) and wells replacement and 30 days or less platform shutdown cost of NOK 100 million. The calculated NOK 11.0 million total cost of consequence (for 50 year platform life) was two order of magnitudes less than the cost of fire-protecting all risers and tensioners. While these calculations were approximate, this large cost difference provided a powerful justification not to provide passive fire protection. Passive fire protection of the risers would have also complicated periodic riser wall inspection at splash zone and caused undetectable crevice corrosion due to potential water ingress between the coating and the riser steel.

2.4 *Limiting hydrocarbon fire durations to 2 hours*

Several North Sea platforms were designed to resist hydrocarbon (HC) fires of 4 hours duration. High intensity HC fires may be caused by blowouts which last much longer than 4 hours causing major damage and sometimes,

1999

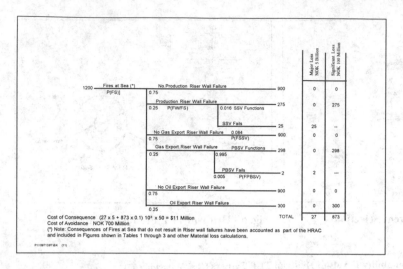

Cost of Consequence (27 x 5 + 873 x 0.1) 10³ x 50 = $11 Million
Cost of Avoidance   NOK 700 Million
(*) Note: Consequences of Fires at Sea that do not result in Riser wall failures have been accounted as part of the HRAC
and included in Figures shown in Tables 1 through 3 and other Material loss calculations.

Fig. 7 - Event Tree for Consequences of Fires at Sea   Escalating to Riser Failures (Probabilities x10⁻⁶/yr)

platform loss. During the concept development phase, 4-hour fire durations were specified for the major structural component design. Studies indicated that the protection of the platform components against these fires will be uneconomical due to increased TLP weight and cost. Objective under these type of fires is the protection of the safety functions for a period allowing safe personnel evacuation (Tables 1 thru 3). Simulations of the platform escape and evacuation systems demonstrated that the process of mustering and launching free fall life boats will take 23 minutes. This was verified by on site simulations after platform installation which indicated that the entire platform personnel can be evacuated within a time frame of 20 to 23 minutes. Further simulations under very adverse conditions demonstrated that probability of not evacuating any live and rescuable personnel from the platform within a 90 minute time frame was less than $1.4 \cdot 10^{-4}$/yr, when all accidental events are taken into consideration (Table 1). Having already satisfied the HRAC, it was decided to limit the design fire durations to 2 hours, providing ample time for evacuation. This decision saved significant hull column and MSB weight (see Table 5).

2.5   Tether Reliability and inspection frequency

The Heidrun TLP Hull is connected to seabed by sixteen (four each corner) 44" OD, 1.5" wall thickness API Gr. X70 tethers. Each tether is made of 26 pipe segments connected by 100% radiographically and NDT inspected and fully grind (inside and outside) girth welds. Extensive tests were conducted to establish the fatigue and ultimate strength of the tether pipes and their welded connections. A detailed fatigue/fracture reliability and maintainability analysis of the tether system was carried out (Wirsching 1995). First the target fatigue failure probability levels $P_T(FSTS_i)$ implied by the NPD fatigue design requirements

with project assumed 4 year weld inspection interval (Fatigue Safety factor FS=3) and with no inspection (FS=10, Refs. NPD 91 and 92) were calculated. These targets were compared against the estimated probability of failure of a tension leg (Table 6). The results demonstrated that the tethers meet the NPD design requirements with a potential for elimination of the periodic internal tether NDT inspection. This potential is now being evaluated and a decision may be made before first tether inspections are due in late 1999. If the tether inspection is eliminated, about NOK 60 million may be saved from the annual inspection costs.   Additionally, the risk from dropped objects during tether inspection and potential flooding and resulting tether internal corrosion will be eliminated.

3   SAFETY IMPROVEMENTS

Many low cost risk reducing measures were recommended and implemented by the Project. Some are listed below.

3.1   Location of the PBSV

The Piper Alpha Disaster Report (Lord Cullen, 1990) recommended that all gas pipelines, that have the potential of becoming major sources and drivers of platform fires, be fitted with PBSV at a sufficient distance from the platform to avoid major loss of life and property. For Heidrun, in the absence of a PBSV, the probability of fires initiated by gas riser wall failures would have increased by three orders of magnitude (Fig. 7). If the PBSV is located too close to the platform, a pipeline failure downstream from the PBSV may result in major gas fires on the platform. Conversely, a PBSV located too far from the platform will leave too much gas in its upstream pipelines portion feeding fires that may initiate at the TLP. Location of the gas PBSV (Fig. 1) was selected by a study (Technica 1991). Probabilities of occurrence of accidental events that involve gas export riser, and pipeline were investigated for several PBSV locations. Table 6 shows the percent risk reduction from locating the PBSV at the subsea template and 300m away from the template, against no PBSV on the pipeline or its riser. These evaluations resulted in locating PBSV about 400m from the template where the risk was lowest (Fig. 2).

3.2 Backup holding device for lowering ballast pumps and caissons into the TLP columns

TLP ballast water is stored in the columns between elevations -64m to -77 m (Fig. 4). Submerged pumps located inside caissons are used for tether tension adjustment and hull trimming. The ballast pumps will be periodically raised out of the caissons for inspection and maintenance, using winches at the column tops. A safety assessment indicated significant probability of dropping a pump or caisson segment during lifting, which may penetrate the bottom concrete slab and may cause column flooding and platform loss. Due to very high consequence of this highly unlikely event, a backup holding device to stop a pump from dropping in case of lifting gear failure was provided. Thick steel plates were also installed at the potential impact points to avoid punching through the base slab. These very low cost measures dropped the probability of these events by about a three orders of magnitude.

3.3 Escape and evacuation studies and associated safety improvements

Heidrun RASAP included studies, simulations, and design of the systems and equipment to ensure safe escape and evacuation of personnel from the platform. During the conceptual development stage, escape and evacuation studies helped select the type, number, and locations of life boats and rafts, escapeways, stairways, and passages to mustering and lifeboat launch areas. Ten free fall lifeboats, each with a capacity of 70 people (Fig. 2), providing 200 percent redundancy for the 350 man maximum platform occupancy scenario were selected as the primary means of evacuation. Six of these lifeboats are installed underside the living quarters and are connected to the remaining 4 located at the southern side of the platform by tunnels through the concrete MSB (Fig. 2). The living quarters, with a smoke free main mustering area connecting to the lifeboat stations was selected as the main shelter area. Configurations and locations of the escapeways, stairways, and corridors were selected to speed up evacuation. After the completion of the detailed design, the escape and evacuation study was updated to confirm the safety of the designed system and to propose further ALARP risk reducing measures. Upon completion of the preliminary design, detailed computer simulations of the designed escape and evacuation systems were conducted to demonstrate residual events will stay below the limits set by HRAC. Modifications for improving the evacuation system safety were proposed:
1. Install smoke free tunnels inside MSBs connecting the North and South life boat stations,

2. Allow lifeboat launches for TLP lists exceeding 2 degrees (for the transportation and installation phases).
3. Improve escape from the mud control room by providing two independent escapeways.
4. Emphasize personnel training to cut down the mustering and boarding time during critical events.
5. Evacuate non-essential personnel first.
6. Establish regular maintenance procedures to ensure lifeboat engine after launch.
7. Lifeboats may be inaccessible or impaired in some accidents. Ensure that lifeboats are effectively filled up before they are launched. Sequential lifeboat launch procedures to avoid collision with each other and life rafts were also established.
8. Eliminate several blind corridors detected in the Living Quarters building.
9. The opening directions of Living Quarters and other module doors were reversed speeding up evacuation.

During the near-shore hook-up and commissioning phase, the number of workers exceeded 1000. Escape and evacuation studies made resulted in several risk reducing improvements:
1. Installation of crush barriers at top of main stairways to avoid a stampede during evacuation,
2. Relocating several escapeways and stairways to allow even personnel distribution during evacuation,
3. Adjusting the size and type of service vessels around the platform to enable fast evacuation.

Simulations of the transportation and installation phases were carried out to demonstrate the adequacy of the escape and evacuation systems and equipment during these operations. After the platform was installed, escape and evacuation drills confirmed the results obtained from the computer simulations conducted during the design phase.

4 LEARNINGS AND TECHNOLOGY TRANSFER

In addition to the economic and risk reduction benefits, a number of industry firsts were achieved and beneficial learnings to future projects were made:

4.1 Risk acceptance criteria (RAC) selection

RAC is an important element that drives the platform design and safety:
1. RAC must be quantitative and should be established early in the design phase. DAE can be quantified and uniform safety levels can be achieved only if quantitative targets are set.
2. RAC must be total and must be set up for the entire production system and entire class of accidental events. Total RAC allows risk tradeoffs, improving the field development economics.
3. RAC must be comparative and should be established to satisfy regularity requirements and in comparison to acceptable safe practices and social, industrial, and ethical standards in the area.
4. RAC and RASAP must be consistent. QRA is influenced by assumptions, databases, analytical tools and safety specialists employed. Most of these influences can

be eliminated by using the same methods, assumptions, databases, tools, and specialists for the entire RASAP.

4.2 Selection of DAE

The methodology for combining the RASAP and the DAE selection to achieve a "risk consistent" design are described in Section 2.1, and Figs. 5 and 6 (Moan 1993, Karsan 1996). This is the first application of such a "risk-consistent" approach to offshore platform design. This process (Figs. 3 and 5) involves following steps:
1. Select RAC.
2. Select DAE and their load effects as those that keep total residual events below RAC, while providing further risk reduction in accordance with the ALARP principle (Eqs 1 and 6, Fig. 5).
3. Perform risk assessment during conceptual, preliminary, and detailed design and after construction completion to demonstrate that RAC are met.

4.3 Discrepancy between the structural safety levels undert environmental events vs. HC design events

The majority of accidental events that lead to loss of life, environmental damage and production loss are observed to be due to drilling, well completion, and maintenance and process accidents. The RASAP estimated a $1.5 \cdot 10^{-3}$/year probability of total platform loss under these events as compared to about 10^{-6}/year for the structural failure under others (environmental loads, dropped objects, vessel impact, material defects, etc.). If a failure rate of $1.5 \cdot 10^{-3}$/year is unavoidable and acceptable for the HC events, designing against environmental events for a three order of magnitude lower failure probability is not consistent.

5 SUMMARY AND CONCLUSIONS

Heidrun RASAP established HRAC, defined DAE and their load effects, and, demonstrated that all HRAC are satisfied.

Cost of consequence vs. consequence avoidance based risk reduction measures were implemented for cases where HRAC are satisfied. Estimated savings are several orders of magnitude higher than the Heidrun RASAP cost which was about 0.15% of the total field development cost.

Methods developed and learnings from the Heidrun RASAP are detailed in Refs. Moan 1993, Wirsching 1995, Karsan 1996, and internal Project documents (Refs. Heidrun Reports 1994/1995, Technica '91).

6 ACKNOWLEDGMENTS

Authors thank the Heidrun Unit Owners Conoco, Statoil, and Neste for allowing the publication of this paper and acknowledge valuable contributions from the Heidrun Project Team and the Project safety contractors Dovre Safetec, QUASAR, a.s., DnV Industry, Sintef, Technica, a.s. and CMR.

7 NOMENCLATURE

ALARP   As Low As Reasonably Practicable
A_{ijk} Accidental event of Class i, type j

within class i, acting at location k
BOPD   Barrels of Oil Per Day
CSA   Concept Safety Assessment
DAE   Design Accidental Events
DDRA   Detailed Design Risk Assessment
DSHA   Defined Situations of Hazard and Accidents
DSL   Direct Shuttle Loading
ESD   Emergency Shut Down
FAR   Fatal Accident Rate = Fatalities per 10^8 hours worked
$FSYS_i$ Failure of System i
HRAC   Heidrun RAC
$HRAC_l$ Heidrun Risk Assessment Criterion l
MSB   Module Support Beam
NDT   Non Destructive Testing
NOK   Norwegian Kroner. 7NOK $\approx$ \$1 at 1991 project kickoff date
NPD   Norwegian Petroleum Directorate
P(X)   Annual Probability of occurrence of event X
PBSV   Pipeline (Subsea) Barrier Safety Valve
QRA   Quantitative Risk Assessment
PLS   Progressive collapse limit state
RAC   Risk Acceptance Criteria
RASAP   Risk and Safety Assessment Program
SEPRA   Specific Emergency Preparedness and Readiness Assessment
SSV   Subsurface Safety Valve
STL   Submerged Tethered Loading
TLP   Tension Leg Platform
TRA   Total Risk Assessment

REFERENCES

NPD, "Regs. Relating to Implementation and Use of Risk Analyses in Petroleum Activities", Rev. February 1991

OLF, 1994, "Guidelines for Establishing Acceptance Criteria for Acute Oil Pollution", June 1994

NPD, "Regs. Relating to Load Bearing Structures in Petroleum Activities", Rev. February 1992

Rt.Hon. Lord Cullen, "The Public Inquiry Into the Piper Alpha Disaster", HMSO, November 1990

Heidrun Project Operating Unit, "CP-S-RS-046, Safety Summary Report", October 1995

Moan T., Karsan D. I., and Wilson T. J., "Analytical Risk Assessment and Risk Control of Floating Platform Subjected to Ship Collisions and Dropped Objects", Proc. OTC 1993, OTC 7123

Wirsching P. H., Karsan D. I. and Hanna S.Y, "Fatigue, Fracture Reliability and Maintainability Analysis of The Heidrun TLP Tether System", Proc. OMAE Conference 1995, Copenhagen

Mitcha J. L., et.al., "The Heidrun Field - Development Overview", Proc. 1996, OTC 8084

Sauer C. W., et.al., "Heidrun TLP Titanium Riser System" Proc. 1996 OTC 8088

Botros, F.R., et.al., "Structural Design and Analysis of the Heidrun TLP". Proc. 1996 OTC 8099

Karsan D. I., et.al., "Risk Assessment and Safety Assurance Program for The Heidrun Field", Proc. 1996 OTC 8103

Technica a.s. HFD-R-201 "Heidrun Safety Barrier Valve Safety Evaluation", June 1991, Norway.

Heidrun Project Operating Unit, "CP-S-RS-029, Total Risk Assessment (TRA)", Dec. 1994

Structural Safety and Reliability, Shiraishi, Shinozuka & Wen (eds) © 1998 Balkema, Rotterdam, ISBN 90 5410 978 5

Reliability analysis of super floating structure and dolphin system against earthquake attack

Takeshi Koike
Kawasaki Steel Corporation, Chiba, Japan

Takashi Hiramoto
Kawasaki Steel Corporation, Tokyo, Japan

ABSTRACT : Seismic response and risk analyses of a super floating structure supported with many dolphins are carried out to study the mutual interaction and its instability of the floating-dolphin system against earthquake attack. The conventional reliability approach is applied to evaluate the structural safety in the various seismic environments. Discussion is also devoted for the risk of the progressive failure which might be triggered by increasing damaged dolphins.

1 INTRODUCTION

The floating type structural system is applicable to large offshore structures including airports, power plants and multi-purpose facilities. Such a large-scale floating structure should be in service at least more than 100 years because of its economical investments and social usage, so it also should be designed to be safe and stable against several natural hazards and accidental loads during its service life.

For the floating structures supported with mooring cables, an earthquake load is not always critical in their structural design, while the super- floating structure which must be supported with many dolphins (FSD) may suffer critical damages during its long period because the severe seismic loads may cause the extreme response of the dolphin enough to break the connecting devices to the floating structures, or may destroy the dolphin itself.

In order to develop the seismic assessment of the FSD, the following major issues should be discussed:
1) prediction of expected maximum earthquakes during its service period,
2) seismic response analysis of dolphin system,
3) seismic response analysis of the FSD system under spatial phase delay of seismic wave arrivals, and
4) assessment of progressive failure of FSD with increasing damaged dolphins.

This study presents and discusses the method how to estimate the seismic response and risk of the FSD supported with many dolphins in the seismic environment.

For the first three issues, several formulations are developed in the frequency domain with the power spectral density of the earthquake motions. The discussion is also focused for the risk of the progressive failure of the FSD which might be triggered by increasing damaged dolphins.

2 SEISMIC ENVIRONMENT

2.1 *Seismic activities in Japan*

Japan is always suffered from severe earthquakes which may originate along the boundary of tectonic plates, or from the active faults widely distributed over the country.

The seismic hazard at the construction site in Japan during its service life is estimated with the maximum acceleration which is calculated on the assumption of magnitude and focal distance through the attenuation formula (Utsu 1984, Boore et al 1982).

Since the 1995 Hyogoken Nanbu Earthquake, several seismic design codes and guidelines have been revised and the others are under study for the revised version, in which the following two classifications on the earthquake motion in the design stage are recommended from the Japan Society of Civil Engineers:

1) seismic design should be assessed with two kinds of accelerations of L1 (for serviceability limit state criterion) and L2 (for ultimate limit state criterion),
2) dynamic analysis for L2-level should be applied for two types of earthquakes: one originated from the tectonic plate boundary, and the other from causative faults.

Since the FSD may have comparatively long typical periods, special attention should be required on the spectral contents of strong earthquake motion to be used for the seismic response analyses.

(1) Far-field event (Plate tectonic type)

The information on the most frequent epicentral points of great earthquakes is necessary when one may select the site of offshore structures in the vicinity of Japan. Fig.1 shows the distribution of epicentral points (1 to 14) in the past 50 years in Japan, in which earthquakes occured along the boundary area of tectonic plates.

(2) Near-field event (Active fault type)

Recent great earthquakes, 1994 Northridge and 1995 Hyogoken Nanbu Earthquakes, attack the modern big cities, because their epicenters are close to or under the city areas.

Such significant disasters are often caused by the active faults which are distributed not only in the countryside but also under the city areas all over the country. The active fault causing severe damages to the structures has its own fault length which can limit the maximum possible magnitude shown in Fig.2 relating with the following formula (Matsuda 1975).

$$\log L = 0.6\ M_{max} - 2.9 \qquad (1)$$

If one may have the information on the active fault of the fault length L and the activity given in Table 1, the annual rate of occurrence of the earthquake can be estimated in the following form:

$$v_0 = \frac{s}{10^{1.9}\ L} \qquad (2)$$

Thus the occurrence rate of the earthquake exceeding the acceleration level (a) which initiates from several active faults surrounding the site is given by

$$v(a) = \sum_i v_{0i} \int f_{x_i}(x)\ P(a\,|\,M_i, x)\ dx \qquad (3)$$

where f_x is the density function of the active faults around the site, and $P(a\,|\,M_i, x)$ is the probability of acceleration under the condition of the magnitude M_i from the i-th fault.

2.2 Prediction of earthquake motions

The seismic response analysis can be conducted with the strong ground motion accelerogram which has been furnished with the actual records measured at the observatory stations or with the numerical data calculated on the basis of statistical or theoretical approaches.

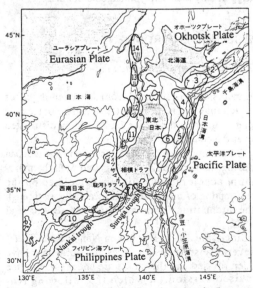

Fig.1 Focal zones of great earthquakes in Japan and its vicinity in the past 50 years (Seno 1996).

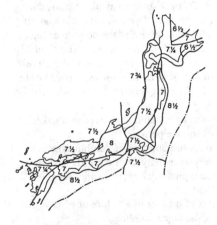

Fig.2 Expected maximum earthquake magnitudes in Japan (Matsuda 1990).

Table 1. Activity of active faults (Matsuda, 1975)

Activity	fault displacement velosity s (m / 1000 years)
A	$1 \leqq s < 10$
B	$0.1 \leqq s < 1$
C	$0.01 \leqq s < 0.1$

(1) Statistical approach

The statistical approach can provide the expression of accelerogram as the nonstationary random process whose spectral content is statistically predicted with historical earthquake database in the following form:

$$\ddot{z}(t,x) = \sum_{k=1}^{n} \sqrt{2\, S(\omega_k, t, x)\, \Delta\omega}\, \exp\left\{ i\left(\omega_k t + \phi_k \right) \right\} \quad (4)$$

where $\omega_k = k\Delta\omega$, $\Delta\omega = \omega_u/n$, and ω_u is the upper bound of frequency, while ϕ_k is the phase angle to be randomly distributed in $(0, \pi)$.

The nonstationary power spectral density function $S(\omega_k,t,x)$ in Eq.4 can be defined (Harada 1995) with

$$S(\omega,t,x) = \frac{1}{2\pi} |W(t,\omega)|^2\, |A(\omega,x)|^2 \quad (5)$$

in which $W(t, \omega)$ is the profile function expressing the temporal nonstationarity of earthquake accelerogram, while $A(\omega,x)$ is the spectral content of the assumed earthquake (Kameda 1975).

Since Kanai (1957) provided the function of $A(\omega,x)$, several ground motion models have been proposed by Kameda (1975), Kamiyama (1986), Sugito (1986) and Harada(1995).

Kameda furnished the regression formula to predict the spectral content of the nonstationary acceleration under the assumptions of magnitude, epicentral distance and site geology. This approach is simple and appropriate for medium size of earthquakes, while, in order to predict the greatest earthquakes more than magnitude of 8 or from the nearest active faults, the power spectrum density of the earthquake must include the informations of fault surface and fracture pattern, wave propagating medium between the focal point and the site, and the site geological and geotechnical characteristics. So the typical expression of the power spectral content should be expressed by

$$|A(\omega,x)| = S(\omega) \cdot P(\omega) \cdot F(\omega,x) \quad (6)$$

where $S(\omega)$:the acceleration spectrum of the seismic source, $P(\omega)$:spectral filter in the wave propagating medium and $F(\omega,x)$:spectral amplification at the site.

(2) Spatial variation of seismic wave propagation

The FSD is applicable to a large airport whose maximum length is several kilometers. Since seismic wave velocity in the hard rock is approximately 1000 to 5000 m/sec, there may be a phase difference at the both ends of the FSD.

Such a phase difference can be caused not only by the propagating wave velocity, but by the spatial randomness of the geological and geotechnical conditions at the site.

The effect of spatial randomness for the spectral content can be estimated with the coherency function $coh(\omega,x)$ in the following form (Hino 1977):

$$S(\omega, t, x) = S_0(\omega, t)\, coh(\omega, x) \quad (9)$$

where $So(\omega,t)$ is the nonstationary power spectral density at the specific site, and the coherency function is given with parameter α and the separate distance Δ by

$$coh(\omega,x) = \exp\left[-\frac{\alpha\,\omega|\Delta|}{2\pi\,c_s} \right] \quad (10)$$

3 STRUCTURAL MODELING

When the FSD is not allowed to exceed the limited displacement, the floating structure must be supported with many dolphins as shown in Fig.3 instead of the mooring cables currently to be used.

The dolphin system is more sensitive for the seismic excitation through the structural piles drived into the baserock than the mooring system.

3.1 Dolphins

The connecting device which is composed of spring and damper is furnished between the dolphin

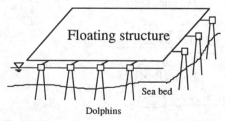

Fig.3 Floating structural system supported with dolphins.

and the floating structure as shown in Fig.4.

The dolphin connected to the FSD can be modeled as the single-degree-of-freedom system whose amplification factor is given by the following equation:

$$H_j(\omega) = \frac{1 + 2ih_{2j}\omega_{2j}/\omega - (\omega_{2j}/\omega)^2}{H_1(\omega)} \quad (11)$$

in which

$$H_1(\omega) = (\omega_{1j}^2 + \omega_{2j}^2 - \omega^2) + 2i(h_{1j}\omega_{1j} + h_{2j}\omega_{2j})\omega \quad (12)$$

where ω_{1j} and ω_{2j} are the characteristic frequencies of the j-th dolphin and its connecting device system, respectively, while h_{1j} and h_{2j} are their damping factors. The symbol "i" is a complex unit to be equal to $(0,1)$.

The characteristic values of the connecting device of the j-th dolphin are given by

$$\omega_{2j} = \sqrt{\frac{k_j}{m_j}} \quad , \quad h_{2j} = \frac{c_j}{2\sqrt{m_jk_j}} \quad (13)$$

where m_j, k_j, c_j are the mass of the top of the dolphin, the spring constant and damping coefficient of the connecting device, respectively.

3.2 Floating structures

The FSD is assumed to move in the horizontal surface and to neglect the local elastic deflection of the floating structure at the applied force point, so that the rigid model is introduced to simulate the motion of the floating structure.

Fig.5 is the configuration of the floating structure, in which the dolphins are arranged along the x-direction (i=1 to n) and along the y-th direction (j=1 to m), respectively.

The earthquake excitation is transmitted to the floating structure from the baserock through the inertia forces F_i and G_j of the dolphins.

The inertia forces are given in the following form:

$$F_i = k_i^*\{v_i - (x_i - x_f)\theta - v\} + c_i\{\dot{v}_i - (x_i - x_f)\dot{\theta} - \dot{v}\}$$

$$G_j = k_j^*\{u_j + (y_j - y_f)\theta - u\} + c_j\{\dot{u}_j + (y_j - y_f)\dot{\theta} - \dot{u}\}$$

$$(14)$$

where u, v, θ are the motion (two dimensional translations and rotation) at the gravity center (x_f, y_f) of the FSD, while u_j is the response in the x-direction at the top of the j-th dolphin, and v_i is the response in the y-direction at the top of the i-th dolphin. Since the global stiffness of the i-th dolphin and its connecting device must be taken into consideration in the response analysis of the following section, the spring constant k_i^* in eq.(14) can be given by

$$k_i^* = m_i\,\omega_{ni}^2 \quad (15)$$

where

$$\omega_{ni} = \frac{\omega_{1i}\omega_{2i}}{\sqrt{\omega_{1i}^2 + \omega_{2i}^2}} \quad (16)$$

The incident seismic wave is assumed herein to propagate into the FSD in the direction of ψ radian from the x-coordinate axis, and its exciting motion is also to be perpendicular to the propagating direction of the seismic shear wave.

The frictional resistance of the FSD induced by the surrounding water is estimated as the damping coefficient of the FSD.

4 FORMULATIONS

The equation of motion of the FSD can be formulated in the following simultaneous equations:

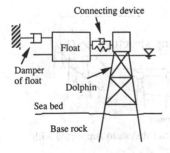

Fig.4 Dolphin structural model.

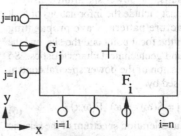

Fig.5 Configuration of the floating structure.

$$M\ddot{u} + C\dot{u} = \sum_j G_j$$

$$M\ddot{v} + C\dot{v} = \sum_i F_i \qquad (17)$$

$$I\ddot{\theta} + C_\theta\dot{\theta} = \sum_i F_i(x_i - x_f) - \sum_j G_j(y_j - y_f)$$

in which M, I, C and C_θ are the mass, inertia mass, and damping coefficients (for translation mode and rotation mode) of the FSD.

Rewriting the eq. (17) in the matrix form, one may obtain the following expression:

$$M\{\ddot{Q}\} + C\{\dot{Q}\} + K\{Q\} = \{W\} \qquad (18)$$

in which

$$\{Q\} = \{u, v, \vartheta\} \qquad (19)$$

where M, C are K are the matrices of eq.(17) and {W} is the force vector, while the rotational variate is converted from θ to ϑ in the following way.

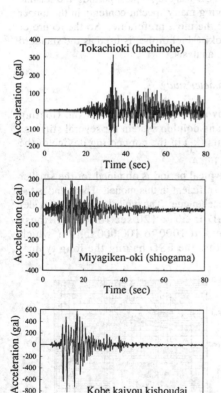

Fig.6 Strong motion earthquake data.

$$\vartheta = L\theta \qquad (20)$$

where $\qquad L = \sqrt{\dfrac{I}{M}} \qquad (21)$

The generalized motion {q(t)} is also converted with the characteristics matrix $[\phi]$ from {Q(t)}:

$$\{Q(t)\} = [\phi]\{q(t)\} \qquad (22)$$

Substituting eq.(22) together with eqs.(4), (9) and (10) into eq.(18), one may obtain the following equation of motion in the generalized coordinates:

$$\{\ddot{q}\} + [2h_n\omega_n]\{\dot{q}\} + [\omega_n^2]\{q\} = [\phi]^T\{W(t)\} \qquad (23)$$

in which ω_n is the characteristic frequency of the n-th mode and the matrix $[\phi]^T$ is the transpose of the matrix $[\phi]$ (Warburton 1976).

The term {W(t)} of the righthand side in eq.(23) can be expanded in the temporal and frequency regions, so that each term is given by the following equations:

$$\{W(t)\} = \begin{Bmatrix} W_x(t) \\ W_y(t) \\ W_\theta(t) \end{Bmatrix}$$

$$= \begin{bmatrix} \sum_k a(\omega_k, t)\left\{\sum_j K_y(\omega_k, y_j, \psi)\right\} \\ \sum_k a(\omega_k, t)\left\{\sum_i K_x(\omega_k, x_i, \psi)\right\} \\ \sum_k \dfrac{a(\omega_k, t)}{L}\left\{\sum_i K_x(\omega_k, x_i, \psi)(x_i - x_f) - \sum_j K_y(\omega_k, y_j, \psi)(y_j - y_f)\right\} \end{bmatrix} \qquad (24)$$

in which

$$a(\omega_k, t) = \sqrt{2S_0(\omega_k, t)\Delta\omega}\,\exp\{i(\omega_k t + \phi_k)\} \qquad (25)$$

and

$$K_x(\omega_k, x_i, \psi) = \frac{m_i}{M}b_x(\omega_k, x_i, \psi)(2ih_i\omega_{n_i} + \omega_{n_i}^2)H_i(\omega_k)$$

$$K_y(\omega_k, y_j, \psi) = \frac{m_j}{M}b_y(\omega_k, y_j, \psi)(2ih_j\omega_{n_j} + \omega_{n_j}^2)H_j(\omega_k)$$

$$b_x(\omega_k, x_i, \psi) = \cos\psi\,\exp\left[-\frac{1}{2}\frac{\omega_k}{2\pi}\frac{\alpha|x_i - x_f|}{\frac{c_s}{\cos\psi}} - i\,\omega_k\frac{x_i - x_f}{\frac{c_s}{\cos\psi}}\right]$$

$$b_y(\omega_k, y_j, \psi) = -\sin\psi\,\exp\left[-\frac{1}{2}\frac{\omega_k}{2\pi}\frac{\alpha|y_j - y_f|}{\frac{c_s}{\sin\psi}} - i\,\omega_k\frac{y_j - y_f}{\frac{c_s}{\sin\psi}}\right]$$

$$(26)$$

5 SYSTEM RELIABILITY UNDER PROGRESSIVE FAILURE

If a severe earthquake produces many damaged dolphins, the system response could be unstable. Once the FSD initiates the rotational motion, the residual dolphins might be damaged one by one, so that the progressive failure of the dolphins occurs.

Let us define the event of the system failure that the rotational response of the FSD exceeds the critical value θ_{cr} given in the following form:

$$\text{event } E = \langle \theta_{D(d1,d2,...,dm)} > \theta_{cr} \rangle \quad (27)$$

where the response $\theta_{D(d1,d2,...,dm)}$ of the FSD is to be controled by the global stiffness which is generated from any combination $D(d_1,d_2,...,d_m)$ of damaged and undamaged dolphins.

When the site S is surrounded in the seismic environment where the i-th fault can initiate the earthquake EQ_i of the maximum magnitude $M^i_{max}(T)$ during the service life T, the conditional probability of the FSD can be formulated by

$$P[E| S,T] = \sum_i P_{EQ}[E_i| S] P[EQ_i, T]$$

$$= \sum_i (1 - \exp[-v_{0i} T]) \int P[E_i| a] \quad (28)$$

$$f_A \{ a | G(S), M^i_{max}(T) \} da$$

where a:acceleration at the baserock, f(· | ·):the conditional probability density function of the random variate A and G(S):geological condition of the site S. ν_{0i} is the occurrence rate of an earthquake EQ_i which is given by eq.(2).

6 NUMERICAL RESULTS

6.1 Conditions

The numerical model is assumed as the same size of Kansai International Airport, so that the length, width and height are 5000m, 1000m and 10m, respectively.

The dolphins are located at each 50m, so that 116 units of the dolphin are arranged along the longer side, while 17 units are set along the shorter side.

The standard type of the dolphin is assumed to have the following parameters:

Term		unit	amount
typical period	$(2\pi/\omega_{1j})$	sec	0.5
damping factor	(h_{1j})	%	5
traveling wave velocity	(c_s)	m/sec	3000
incident angle	(ψ)	degree	45
spring constant	(k_j)	tonf/m	10000
mass of the dolphin	(m_j)	ton	741
damping coefficient	(h_{2j})	%	10
floating damper	(C)	%	2
spatial parameter	(α)		1

The strong motion accelerogram measured at the hard ground are selected from the historical database of severe earthquakes in Japan. The profiles of these data are shown in Fig.6 and each spectral contents are compared each other in Fig.7. The first two earthquakes belong to tectonic type, while the last one is active fault type.

Since the FSD has long typical periods, the seismic record having many spectal contents in the longer periods is the most preferable. So the record of Tokachi-oki (Hachinohe) is used as the standard data in this analysis.

6.2 Parameter study

Fig.8 shows the typical period of the floating structure and dolphin system for several stiffness coefficients (k_j) in the connecting device of the dolphin in Fig.4.

Longer typical period is obtained for the smaller stiffness coefficient in this model. This trend is the same for each mode. The typical period (1st mode) of the FSD is $20 \sim 120$ sec for the stiffness coefficients of 1000 to 100,000 tonf/m which suggests that the FSD having the long typical

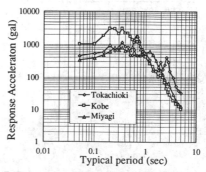

Fig.7 Response spectra of the earthquakes

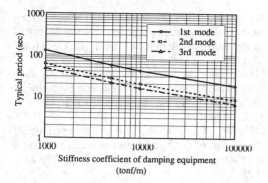

Fig.8 Typical period of floating structure for several stiffness coefficients of the connecting device of dolphin.

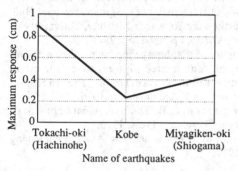

Fig.9 Earthquake response of floating structure.

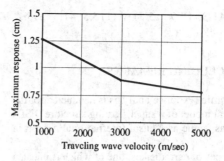

Fig.10 Earthquake response for several traveling wave velosities.

period is insensitive in the earthquake response analyses, because the current strong motion accelerogram does not include such spectral contents of extremely long periods.

Fig.9 is the maximum response of the FSD at the farthest dolphin from its gravity center for those three earthquakes. This figure shows that the response of FSD expressed with the displacement (cm) is less than 1cm for these earthquakes. The response by the record of Kobe kaiyou kishoudai is the smallest among them, while the response by the record of Tokachi-oki is the largest. These difference depends upon the spectral contents of the input earthquakes. The spectrum of the Tokachi-oki's record has the largest especially in the longer period which is appropriate with the amplification of the response of the FSD.

According to the result of the Kobe record, the response of the FSD against the earthquake of the active fault type does not always cause the large amplification of the response, although its maximum amplitude is the largest. This reason is also due to

the spectral content which does not include comparatively longer periods.

The effect of traveling wave velocity is studied in Fig.10, in which smaller velocity makes the response of the FSD largely amplified, while the response for large velocity is decreased because of its small phase delay effect.

The numerical simulation for the progressive failure of the FSD is carried out with the integrand $P[Ei \mid a]$ of eq.(28) for the actual earthquake motion. The rigorous estimation, on the other hand, of structural safety using eq.(28) is not applied because the major concern is placed on the point that the progressive failure of dolphins may occur or not by the severe earthquake ground motion.

In the case study, when the response of a dolphin exceeds the critical level (to be equal to 60% of the maximum response of all the dolphins), the stiffness of that dolphin is assumed to be completely lost.

Fig.11 shows the rotational response of the FSD under progressive failure process, in which the response abruptly increases after 32 seconds which corresponds to the time when the first failure of dolphins occurs. The typical periods (1st, 2nd and 3rd modes in second) of the FSD are also increased

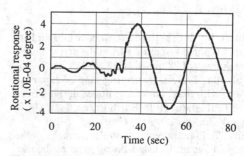

Fig.11 The rotational response under progressive failure process.

to be (41.3, 19.7, 15.5) to (115.5, 41.3, 29.6) , respectively.

7 CONCLUDING REMARKS

The seismic response analysis is conducted for the numerical model of a super floating structure (FSD) almost as same as Kansai International Airport in Japan.

Two types of earthquakes, one of which is initiated from tectonic plate boundary in the Pacific Ocean and the other is from the near-field fault rupture are applied to assess the instability of the structural system.

Numerical results indicate that

(1) the methodology of the seismic response analysis for a very large floating structure can be formulated on the analytical basis, in which the floating structure itself is assumed as the rigid body;

(2) the typical period of the floating structure has a long period of 40 to 120 sec (1st mode), so that the maximum responses of the structural system at the farthest dolphin from the gravity center for those three earthquakes are limited to less than 1cm;

(3) the numerical results reveal that a slow propagating sesmic wave velosity increases the rotational response of the FSD; and

(4) the progressive failure of dolphins can generate the large response of the FSD, and the typical periods under the process are also increased to be two or three times of the original values.

ACKNOWLEDGEMENT

This study was supported with the Technological Association of Mega-float Structure in Japan.

REFERENCE

1)Matsuda, T.:Earthquake magnitude and its repetition period occuring from the active faults, Seismology, Vol.28, pp.269-283, 1975.

2)Matsuda, T.:Seismic zoning map of Japanese Islands, with maximum magnitudes derived from active fault data, Bull. Earthq. Res. Inst. Univ. Tokyo, Vol.65,pp.289-319, 1990.

3)Seno, T.:Plate movement and earthquake in the vicinity of Japan, Hanshin-Awaji great earthquake and future prediction, Iwanami Publishing Inc., pp.295-303, 1996.

4)Kameda, H.:On the consideration of calculating method of nonstationary power spectral density of strong motin accelerogram, JSCE, No.235, pp.55-62, 1975.

5)Kamiyama, M.: Strong motion earthquake wave form of the baserock and its prediction by statistical analysis of strong motion records, JSCE, No.374, pp.557-566, 1986.

6)Harada,T.,T.Tanaka and Y.Tamura:Digital simulation of earthquake ground motions using a seismological model, JSCE,No.507,pp.209-217, 1995.

7)Utsu, T.:Seismology, Kyouritu Zensho,1984.

8)Boore, D.M. and W.B.Joyner:The empirical prediction of ground motion, Bull. Seism. Soc. Am., 72, S43-S60,1982.

9)Kanai, K.:A semi-empirical formula for the seismic characteristics of the ground motions, Bull. of Earthquake Research Institute, University of Tokyo, Vol.35, pp.309-325, 1957.

10)Sugito, M.:Earthquake motion prediction, microzonation, and buried pipe response for urban seismic damage assessment, the doctorial dissertation of Kyoto university,1986.

11)Warburton, G.B.:The dynamical behavior of structures, Pergamon Press, 1976.

12)Hino, M.:Spectral analysis, Asakura Publishing Inc.,1977.

Structural Safety and Reliability, Shiraishi, Shinozuka & Wen (eds) © 1998 Balkema, Rotterdam, ISBN 90 5410 978 5

Reliability of plate elements subjected to compressive loads and accounting for corrosion and repair

C.Guedes Soares & Y.Garbatov

Unit of Marine Technology and Engineering, Instituto Superior Técnico, Lisboa, Portugal

ABSTRACT: A formulation is presented for the assessment of the reliability of a plate element subjected to compressive loads, corrosion and maintenance actions. This paper will examine how the plate collapse strength will vary in time as a consequence of corrosion and associated plate renewal. In the presence of general corrosion, the plate thickness will depend mainly on that effect and this will be the random variable considered here to affect the net section. The collapse strength against compressive loading is described by a function of time and the resulting reliability is quantified. The sensitivity of the reliability estimates with respect to several parameters is also studied. The reliability is predicted by a time variant formulation and the effects of repair and maintenance actions in the reliability assessment are shown.

1. INTRODUCTION

Plates are the main structural components of several important metal structures. Their behaviour under the effect of compressive loads is particularly important because the failure is generally in an unstable mode, which has harmful consequences from the point of view of safety.

Guedes Soares, (1997) has reviewed several approaches to assess the variability of the predictions of the compressive strength of plate elements or the reliability of structures made with these components, and this will not be repeated here. However, an interesting problem not considered in that survey is the change of the compressive strength due to corrosion, which is a potential problem in all metal structures. This problem has attracted the interest of several researchers such as Hart et al., (1986), White and Ayyub, (1992), Shi, (1993), Melchers and Ahammed, (1994).

Guedes Soares, (1988) has studied the effect of general corrosion in decreasing the thickness of the plating and considered that repair actions were performed whenever the plate thickness would decrease below a defined limit value. It was shown that in the steady state situation the expected value of plate thickness depends on the repair criteria and is independent of the corrosion rate, a result that is

very useful in that often corrosion rates are difficult to assess.

In many situations, the expected value at a random point in time is not enough information and the real time variation of reliability is desired. To this objective, a model has been proposed by Guedes Soares and Garbatov, (1996) to describe the time dependent reliability of a ship hull in which the plates are subjected to corrosion and repair actions. However, simple models were adopted to represent the effect of corrosion and of the inspection procedures, which are improved in the present paper.

The paper addresses the strength formulation adopted to represent plate strength, as well as the time variant reliability approach. A model is proposed for the uncertain outcome of inspections and its effect on reliability is quantified.

2. COMPRESSIVE STRENGTH OF PLATES

The most important parameter that governs the compressive strength of plate elements is the slenderness (Timoshenko and Gere, 1986):

$$\lambda = \frac{b}{h} \sqrt{\frac{\sigma_y}{E}} \tag{1}$$

where b and h are the plate breadth and thickness

respectively, σ_y is the yield stress and E is Young's modulus of the material.

These parameters are included in classical formula due to Bryan for the critical elastic buckling stress σ_{cr} of infinitely long thin elastic plate with simply supported edges:

$$\frac{\sigma_{cr}}{\sigma_y} = \frac{4\pi^2}{12(1-v^2)} \frac{1}{\lambda^2} \tag{2}$$

Expression (2) was extended by Faulkner, (1975) adding one extra term and fitting it to data of ultimate strength leading to:

$$\frac{\sigma_u}{\sigma_y} \equiv \phi_b = \frac{a_1}{\lambda} - \frac{a_2}{\lambda^2}, \quad \lambda \geq 1.0 \tag{3}$$

where the constants a_1 and a_2 are given $a_1 = 2.0$ and $a_2 = 1.0$ for simple supports and $a_1 = 2.5$ and $a_2 = 1.56$ for clamped supports. This equation accounts implicitly for average levels of initial deflection and it can be complemented with others that dealt explicitly with the effect of residual stresses.

Guedes Soares, (1988) has derived a strength assessment equation and design formula for the compressive strength of plate elements under uniaxial load which dealt explicitly with initial defects as:

$$\phi = (\phi_b B_b)(R_r B_r)(R_\delta B_\delta) \tag{4}$$

where ϕ_b is given by Eqn (3), B_b, B_r and $B_{r\delta}$ are model uncertainties factors and R_r and R_δ are strength reduction factors which are due to the presence of weld induced residual stresses and initial distortions respectively. The forms of these expressions are:

$$B_b = 1.08 \tag{5}$$

$$R_r = 1 - \frac{\Delta\phi_b}{1.08\phi_b} \tag{6}$$

$$B_r = 1.07 \tag{7}$$

$$R_\delta = 1 - (0.626 - 0.121\lambda)\frac{\delta_o}{h} \tag{8}$$

$$B_{r\delta} = 0.76 + 0.01\eta + 0.24\frac{\delta_o}{h} + 0.1\lambda \tag{9}$$

where the strength reduction due to the residual stress σ_r is:

$$\Delta\phi_b = \frac{\sigma_r}{\sigma_y} \frac{E_t}{E} \tag{10}$$

The residual stress depend on the width $\eta\,h$ of the two strips of tensile yield stress at the edges of the plate:

$$\frac{\sigma_r}{\sigma_y} = \frac{2\eta}{\dfrac{b}{h} - 2\eta} \tag{11}$$

The tangent modulus of elasticity E_t accounts for the development of plasticity. This modulus can be approximated by the expression which was used by Guedes Soares and Faulkner, (1987):

$$\frac{E_t}{E} = \frac{\lambda - 1}{1.5}, \quad \text{for } 1 \leq \lambda \leq 2.5 \tag{12}$$

$$\frac{E_t}{E} = 1, \quad \text{for } \lambda \geq 2.5 \tag{13}$$

This formulation was used for the reliability assessment of plates by Guedes Soares and Silva, (1992), who compared it with of the results of using other formulations. Guedes Soares and Kmiecik, (1993) have shown that assessing the plate strength with non-linear finite elements would lead to the same general type of results although with different numbers. Thus, the use of the present formulation in the following analysis can be justified in view of its analytical character.

3. EFFECT OF CORROSION

A variable that governs the resistance of the plate to buckling is the slenderness, which is dependent on the thickness. The thickness also influences longitudinal stresses since they are the ratio of the applied force by the net section. On its turn the applied stresses will govern the collapse strength of individual plate elements.

In Guedes Soares, (1988) it was shown that the plate collapse is basically insensitive to the uncertainties in plate dimensions except for the thickness which has a small effect. In the presence of corrosion, the uncertainty in plate thickness will depend mainly on that effect and this can be modelled by a random variable.

It is considered that general corrosion will occur and localised pit corrosion will not be accounted for since its effect on plate collapse is not meaningful.

In fact, typical values of the coefficient of variation of plate thickness are of the order of 4% and these will be completely dominated by the uncertainty in the corrosion rates which can have coefficients of variation in a range of 20% to 50%.

For a plate element, the cross section area A is given by the product of its breadth b by thickness h:

$$A(t) = bh(t) \tag{14}$$

The plate thickness starts from an initial value h_o and decreases with time at a rate r:

$$h(t) = h_o - rt \tag{15}$$

The corrosion rate is considered to be time invariant but uncertain, although the formulation could easily account for a time varying corrosion rate, if data on it would be available.

According to Eqns (3) and (15) the ultimate compressive force (P_u), which is a function of time, may be written:

$$P_u\left(h_o, b, \sigma_y, E, r\right) = \phi\left(h_o, b, \sigma_y, E, r\right)\sigma_y A(t) \tag{16}$$

which is a product of the ultimate strength by the yield stress of the material and the net section area.

For simplification this formulation is not considering the effect of initial distortion and residual stresses described in the previous section, which can easily be incorporated?

In many cases, plates are protected with anti-corrosion paints, which are effective during limited period of time. This implies that corrosion is not occurring permanently and that it will only start at the random point in time in which the protection ceases to be effective. Therefore, the effect of corrosion just described is conditional on the initiation of the corrosion process.

4. TIME VARIANT RELIABILITY

The limit state for buckling failure is defined as:

$$P_T > P_u(t) = \varsigma(t) \tag{17}$$

where P_T is the total axial loading, $P_u(t)$ is the ultimate collapse force, which has the threshold limit $\varsigma(t)$.

There will be a failure if Eqn (17) is fulfilled and the probability of the load exceeding $\varsigma(t)$ during the period of the time $[0, T]$ is (Corotis et al., 1972)):

$$P_f[T] = 1 - \exp\left[-\int_o^T v[\varsigma(t)]\,dt\right] \tag{18}$$

where $v[\varsigma(t)]$ is the mean upcrossing rate of the threshold $\varsigma(t)$.

The amplitude of the compressive force P_T is assumed to follow the Weibull distribution and in this case:

$$v[\varsigma(t)] = v_o \exp\left[-\left(\frac{\varsigma(t) - \bar{P}_T}{\gamma_L}\right)^{\alpha_L}\right] \tag{19}$$

where α_L and γ_L are the Weibull parameters and $\bar{P}_T$ is mean value of total compressive force (Naess, (1984).

The scale parameter γ_L is determined from the shape parameter α_L and the force P_{n_o}, exceeded once during the corresponding reference number of the force cycles n_0, determined as the n_0^{-1} probability level:

$$\gamma_L = \frac{P_{n_o}}{\left(Ln(n_o)\right)^{1/\alpha_L}} \tag{20}$$

Considering that during the plate lifetime h_o, b, σ_y, E, r and P_T are random variables and also that the threshold limit can be described by Eqn (17), the upcrossing rate can be calculated by:

$$v\left(t|h_o, b, \sigma_o, E, r, \bar{P}_T\right) =$$
$$\int_o^t v_o \exp\left[-\left(\frac{\varsigma(\tau|h_o, b, \sigma_o, E, r) - \bar{P}_T}{\gamma_L}\right)^{\alpha_L}\right]d\tau \tag{21}$$

The probability of failure $P_f(t)$ is just a conditional probability and may be obtained from:

$$P_f(t) = 1 - \int_0^\infty\int_0^\infty\int_0^\infty\int_0^\infty\int_0^\infty\int_0^\infty f_{\bar{P}_T}(\bar{P}_T)f_r(r)f_E(E)f_{\sigma_y}(\sigma_y)f_b(b)f_{h_o}(h_o)$$
$$\exp\left[-v\left(t|h_o, b, \sigma_y, E, r, \bar{P}_T\right)\right]dh_o\,db\,d\sigma_y\,dE\,dr\,d\bar{P}_T \tag{22}$$

The time dependent reliability after corrosion has started, implying that the corrosion rate is larger than zero, is denoted as reliability after loss of effectiveness of anticorrosion coating $R_a(t)$:

$$R_a(t) = 1 - P_f(t) \quad t > t_o \tag{23}$$

where t_o is the time of failure of the coating protection.

For $t \le t_o$ the metal plate is still intact and the thickness is equal to its value at $t=0$:

$$h(t) = h(0) \quad \text{for} \quad t \le t_o \tag{24}$$

and $\varsigma(t)$, given by Eqn (19) becomes a constant ς_o reducing the upcrossing rate to:

$$\nu(t|h_o, b, \sigma_o, E, r, \bar{P}_T) = \nu_o \exp\left[-\left(\frac{\varsigma(h_o, b, \sigma_o, E, r) - \bar{P}_T}{\gamma_L}\right)^{\alpha_L}\right] t \tag{25}$$

Therefore, the reliability before $R_b(t)$ the time corrosion starts to decrease thickness is modelled substituting Eqn (25) in (22), which is transformed into the reliability formulation of Eqn (23) when $t \le t_o$.

The life of the coating is defined as the duration between the time of its painting and the time when its effectiveness is lost. The life of coating is described as random variable which is governed by normal probability density function (Yamamoto and Ikegami, (1996):

$$f_{t_o}(t_o) = \frac{1}{\sqrt{\pi}\sigma_{t_o}} \exp\left[-\frac{(t - E(t_o))^2}{2\sigma_{t_o}^2}\right] \tag{26}$$

Since the time to loss of effectiveness of the anticorrosion coating is a random variable, the reliability is conditional on the probability of coating time failure, $R(t|t_o)$. Therefore, the unconditional reliability of a plate is given by:

$$R(t) = \int_0^t R(t|t_o) f_{t_o}(t_o) dt_o \tag{27}$$

The total reliability $R(t)$ is given by the reliability of the plate with corrosion plus the reliability of the plate without corrosion, which has a probability of $[1 - F_{t_o}(t)]$. Thus, the final expression is given by:

$$R(t) = [1 - F_{t_o}(t)]R_b(t) + \int_0^t R_b(t_o)R_a(t - t_o)f_{t_o}(t_o)dt_o \tag{28}$$

The first term of this equation represents the probability that no corrosion appears and that failure does not occur in time $[0,t]$. The second term

represents the probability of non-failure under the condition that the corrosion is initiated.

The reliability of the plate can be related with the generalised index of reliability which is calculated from a multinormal distribution (Ditlevsen, 1979). Under this assumption the reliability index (can be related with the probability of failure by:

$$\beta(t) = -\Phi^{-1}[P_f(t)] \tag{29}$$

where Φ is the standardised normal distribution and $P_f(t)$ can be calculated from Eqn (28).

5. MODELLING CORROSION INSPECTION AND REPAIR

The state of general corrosion in a panel is assessed by measuring the plate thickness at several points. There are two sources of uncertainty in this procedure. One results from the precision of the measuring instrument and the other from sampling variability. Measurements are made at few points of a panel and they are considered to be representative of the thickness in the whole plate.

Inspections are routinely made for structures in service and they may result in detection or no detection of a plate that has a mean thickness smaller than the acceptable value that is a fraction k of the original mean value.

$$E[h(t)] \le kE[h_o], \quad k \le 1.0 \tag{30}$$

It is assumed that an element will be inspected every four years. It is further assumed that the method of inspection is such that if a plate thickness is smaller than a limit value it will be replaced and after replacement its thickness will be h_o which is its original value.

The reliability is computed for each period between inspections by using Eqn (28) being a function of the repair time t_r:

$$R(t) = [1 - F_{t_o}(t - t_r)]R_b(t - t_r) + \int_0^{t-t_r} R_b(t_o)R_a(t - t_r - t_o)f_{t_o}(t_o)dt_o \quad \text{for } T_{j-1} \le t < T_j \tag{31}$$

At each repair operation, a value of t_r must be determined. This updated value is substituted in Eqn (31) and the reliability can be evaluated for the next interval between inspections. In Eqn (31) the first term denotes the probability of non-failure when

Table 1. Probabilistic models of the basic variables.

Parameter	Mean value	cov	Distribution
E	207GPa	0.04	Log-normal
h_o	7 mm	0.02	Normal
r	0.12 mm/year	0.3	Normal
σ_y	245MPa	0.08	Log-normal
b	0.6 m	0.01	Normal
$\overline{P}_T$	0.265MPa	0.12	Normal
t_o	5.5years	0.4	Normal

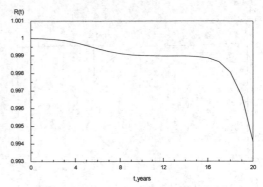

Figure 2 - Reliability of a plate element (without inspection).

corrosion is not initiated in the service interval before $[T_{j-1}, T_j]$ and the second term denotes the probability of non-failure when corrosion appears in the service interval $[T_{j-1}, T_j]$.

6. NUMERICAL EXAMPLE

The proposed approach is applied to assess the reliability of a plate element with corrosion. The plate is simply supported on the edges. The breadth is 0.6 m, and $\eta = 5$. Detailed information on the probabilistic models adopted to describe the random variables is presented in Table 1.

The compressive force (P) is described by an Exponential distribution. The reference probability level is taken of $n_o = 10^{-5}$ with corresponding force $P_{n_o} = 0.183$ MPa. The shape parameter in Eqn (20) is assumed $\alpha_t = 1$.

Figure 1 shows the degradation of the plate parameters as a function of time including ultimate strength, reduction factors and plate slenderness.

The reliability of a plate element without

inspection and repair is calculated by Eqn (28) is presented in Figure 2.

The reliability of a plate with inspection is shown in Figure 3. The restoring action is provided when the thickness of the element is less than 75% of original thickness independently of the time between inspections.

The reliability of the plate element after repair will be equal of the initial value for the new plate. However, in the present example plate replacement was made at 21 years and this brought the reliability to its initial value.

The formulation presented can be used to assess the effect of different parameters in the reliability.

Figure 4 presents results of numerical simulation of inspection taking into account that a repair of an element will be done if the thickness of the element is less than 75, 80 and 85 percent of the original value. The time between inspection is equal to four years.

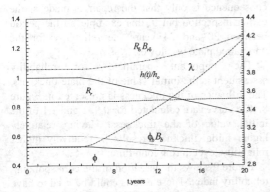

Figure 1 - Degradation of the plate parameters as function of time (without inspection).

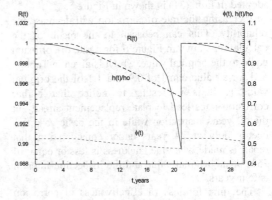

Figure 3 - Reliability of a plate element.

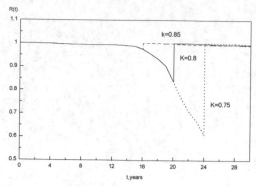

Figure 4 - Influence of the repair criteria
on the reliability.

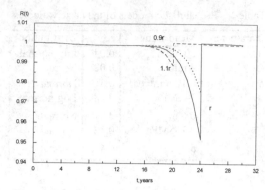

Figure 6 - Influence of the corrosion rate
on the reliability.

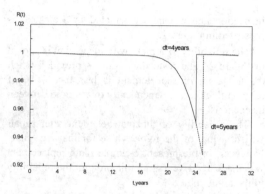

Figure 5 - Influence of the time interval between
inspection on the reliability.

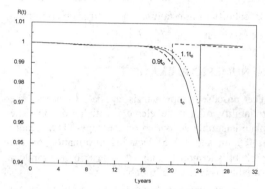

Figure 7 - Influence of the coating time on
the reliability.

The important aspect related with reliability is a time interval between inspection after which the plate will be detected and as result of this it may be replaced or not. The effect of different time interval adopted in Eqn. (31) is shown in Figure 5.

Increasing the rate of corrosion will decrease the reliability. This can be seen in the result of the calculation shown in Figure 6 for a rate of corrosion equal to the original value, which is given in Table 1 and for a value equal of 0.9 and 1.1 of the original value r. It is interesting to notice that higher corrosion rates lead to plate replacement already at the 20 years inspection while in the basic case this occurs only at 24 years under consideration that repair is made when the thickness is less or equal of 75% of its original value and the inspection interval is four years.

The time for loss of effectiveness of corrosion protection has also a significant influence as shown in Figure 7. Its change will directly influence the time that the element will be subjected to corrosion.

It is interesting to note that whenever the time between inspection and repair is fixed, the worst cases of larger corrosion rate or of earlier failure of the coating protection may not lead to lower reliability, as shown in Figure 6 and Figure 7. The consequence is only that the repair is made at the earlier inspection but in this example, in the period between 20 and 24 years the reliability for the unrepaired plate was lower.

The important parameter for reliability assessment is the initial value of the plate thickness. The influence of the thickness is presented in Figure 8. The curves are calculated for 0.9, 1 and 1.1 of the initial value of the thickness. Having relatively higher initial thickness results in relatively higher reliability level during long time.

Figure 9 shows the variation of the corresponding reliability index. These results could be used to have a repair criterion based on a limit value of β. If this limit was set for instance at $\beta=3$, then the plate

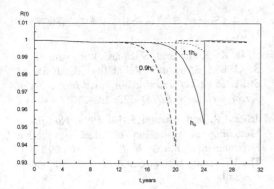

Figure 8 - Influence on the reliability of the initial thickness of a plate element.

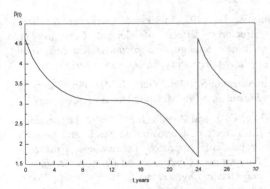

Figure 9 - Reliability index of a plate element.

replacement should be made at about 17 years in the present example, instead of at 24 years.

7. CONCLUSIONS

A model has been presented which can determine the reliability of a plate element considering the effect of corrosion on its ultimate strength.

The reliability is predicted as a time variant reliability, which shows step changes whenever a repair is performed. Different criteria for corrosion detection and for the effect of repair can be easily incorporated.

Different assumptions were made about loading and material properties that are not essential to the method but are needed for the example.

This formulation was used for constant time interval between inspections but if could also be used to determine the time of repair when using a criteria of repairing only at a specified reliability level. Alternatively, keeping the same inspection interval, the requirement of a minimum reliability level can be related with the detection limit of the inspection method.

8. ACKNOWLEDGEMENTS

The present study has been made within the project "Stochastic Methods in Structural and Mechanical Engineering", which is funded partially by the European Union through the Human Mobility programme under contract No. CT94-0565.

9. NOTATION

a_1, a_2	coefficients,
b	breadth of the plate,
$f_*(*)$	probability density function of $*$,
$h(t)$	plate thickness,
h_o	initial plate thickness,
r	corrosion rate,
t	time,
t_o	coating time,
$A(t)$	plate net section,
B_b	bias of the perfect plate strength,
B_r	bias of the strength of plates with residual stresses,
$B_{r\delta}$	bias of the strength of plates with residual stresses and initial distortions,
E	Young modulus of elasticity,
$E(*)$	mean value of $*$,
E_t	tangent modulus of elasticity,
P_T	total compressive force,
$P_u(t)$	ultimate compressive force,
$R(t)$	reliability,
R_r	bias of the strength of plate with residual stresses,
R_δ	strength reduction factor due to initial distortions,
α_L, γ_L	Weibull parameters,
$\beta(t)$	generalised index of reliability,
σ_y	yield stress,
ϕ_b	perfect plate strength,
σ_{cr}	critical stresses,
σ_{t_o}	variance of coating time,
σ_u	ultimate stresses,
δ_o	initial distortion,
$\Delta\phi_b$	reduction of perfect plate strength due to residual stresses.

λ   plate slenderness,
$\varsigma(t)$ threshold limit,
η   width of the weld induced tension zone,
ν   Poisson coefficient.

10. REFERENCES

Corotis, R. B., Vanmarcke, E. H. and Cornell, C. A. 1972. First passage of Non-Stationary Random Processes. *Journal of the Engineering Mechanics Division*. 98: 401-414. ASCE.

Ditlevsen, O. 1979. Generalised Second Moment Reliability Index. *Journal of Structural Mechanics*. 7: 435-451.

Faulkner, D. 1975. A Review of Effective Plating for use in the Analysis of Stiffened Plating in Bending and Compression. *Journal of Ship Research*. 19: 1-17.

Guedes Soares, C. 1988. A Code Requirement for the Compressive Strength of Plate Elements. *Marine Structures*. 1: 71-80.

Guedes Soares, C. 1988. Reliability of Marine Structures. *Reliability Engineering*: 513-559. Amendola, A. & Saiz be Bustamante (eds). Kluwer Academic Publishers: Netherlands.

Guedes Soares, C. 1997. Probabilistic Modelling of the Strength of Flat Compression Members. *Probabilistic Methods for Structural Design*. Guedes Soares, C. (ed). Kluwer Academic Publishers: Netherlands.

Guedes Soares, C. and Faulkner, D. 1987. Probabilistic Modelling of the Effect of Initial Imperfections on the Compressive Strength of Rectangular Plates. *Proceedings of the Practical Design of Ships and Mobile Units*. II: 783-795.

Guedes Soares, C. and Garbatov, Y. 1996. Reliability of Maintained Ship Hull Subjected to Corrosion. *Journal of Ship Research*. 40: 3: 235-243.

Guedes Soares, C. and Kmiecik, M. 1993. Simulation of the Ultimate Compressive Strength of Unstiffened Rectangular Plates. *Marine Structures*. 6: 553-569.

Guedes Soares, C. and Silva, A. G. 1992. Reliability of Unstiffened Plate Elements Under In-Plane Combined Loading. *Proceedings of the 11th International Conference on Offshore Mechanics and Arctic Engineering (OMAE'92)*. II: 265-276.

Guedes Soares, C. et al (eds). ASME: New York, USA.

Hart, D. K., Rutherford, S. E. and Wichham, A. H. S. 1986. Structural Reliability Analysis of Stiffened Panels. *Transaction Royal Institution of Naval Architects (RINA)*. 128: 293-310.

Melchers, R. and Ahammed, M. 1994. Non-linear Modelling of Corrosion of Steel in Marine Environments. *Research Report*. 106.09.1994: The University of Newcastle, New South Wales, Australia.

Naess, A. 1984. On a Rational Approach to Extreme Value Analysis. *Applied Ocean Research*. 6: 3: 173-228.

Shi, W. B. 1993. In-service Assessment of Ship Structures: Effects of General Corrosion on Ultimate Strength *Transaction Royal Institution of Naval Architects (RINA)*. 135: 77-91.

Timoshenko, S. P. and Gere, J. M. 1986. *Theory of Elastic Stability*. McGraw-Hill Book Company.

White, G. J. and Ayyub, B. M. 1992. Determining the Effects of Corrosion on Steel Structures: A Probabilistic Approach. *Proceedings of the 11th International Conference on Offshore Mechanics and Arctic Engineering (OMAE'92)*. II: 45-52. Guedes Soares, C. et al (eds). ASME: New York, USA.

Yamamoto, N. and Ikegami, K. 1996. A Study on the Degradation of Coating and Corrosion of Ships Hull Based on the Probabilistic Approach. *Proceedings of the 15th International Conference on Offshore Mechanics and Arctic Engineering (OMAE'96)*. II: 159-166. Guedes Soares, C. et al (eds). ASME: New York, USA.

Structural Safety and Reliability, Shiraishi, Shinozuka & Wen (eds) © 1998 Balkema, Rotterdam, ISBN 90 5410 978 5

Reliability of plate elements subjected to offshore pool fires

C. Guedes Soares, A. P. Teixeira & J. B. Lopes
Unit of Marine Technology and Engineering, Instituto Superior Técnico, Lisboa, Portugal

ABSTRACT: A reliability formulation is proposed for thermally insulated fire walls subjected to a pool fire. The collapse temperatures of plates are determined with a non-linear finite element code that accounts for the elasto plastic behaviour and for the changes in material properties with temperature. The basic mechanisms that influence the shape of the flame of a pool fire are described and a first order second moment approach is presented to quantify the uncertainty of the heat loads and to describe the importance of the governing variables in the limit state function. The limit state functions is defined terms of steel temperature and the reliability index is determined by a time independent fist order method. An example of the reliability analysis of a fire wall protected with insulation is provided.

1. INTRODUCTION

The regulations in force in Norway and UK concerning the operation of offshore platforms in the North Sea, have adopted a goal setting approach which leaves the operators with the task to demonstrate that their installations have a risk level as low as reasonable practicable. Furthermore the Piper Alfa accident raised the awareness of the community about the risks that fire represents for an offshore platform.

To deal in a consistent way with the design of the structure taking into account the effects of fire, it is necessary to quantify the risk of fire and the structural reliability of the platform under fire conditions.

In the design of offshore structures against fire a fire protection system should be developed, in order to limit the temperature in the structural members and to delay the total collapse of the structure in fire conditions (Shetty et al, 1996).

In the special case of fire walls that exist in platform topsides, the plates are not subjected to external loading since their function is only to serve as a barrier to the propagation of the fire. In this case the plate collapse is only a result of the heat loads, a case that was studied in (Guedes Soares et al., 1996).

The results of that systematic study on plate collapse under heat load showed that the factors governing the collapse temperature were the yield stress of the material, the aspect ratio of the plate and the slenderness. However, for a specific plate those parameters will be specified and one can associate one temperature with the plate collapse. This allows the limit state condition and the reliability problem to be formulated in terms of temperature.

The loading of the plate is produced by the fire and it can be modeled simply as an uncertain value of heat flux.

The two main types of fires that are relevant in offshore structures, are the pool and the jet fires, both of which can be modeled by methods of computational fluid dynamics or by approaches based on empirical formulations, as reviewed in (Guedes Soares, 1993).

This paper deals only with pool fires and their effect on fire walls in the topside of offshore platforms. The basic features of the fire model, of the heat transfer through the passive fire protection and of the collapse temperature of plates will be described. Then an example of the reliability assessment with the first order reliability methods (FORM) is given.

2. POOL FIRES

In hydrocarbon pool fires that can occur in offshore structures, the thermal radiation is the primary mechanism for injury or damage from large open hydrocarbon spill fires and depends on a number of parameters including the composition of hydrocarbon, the size, shape and duration of the fire and its proximity to the object at risk.

2.1 Physical Model

The fire models are based on the assumption that the pool can be described by an effective equivalent diameter D that does not vary with time. The characteristic quantity that describes the pool fire is the mean length of the visible flame H, usually defined as the distance above the fire source where the intermittence has declined from unity to 0.5.

The pool fire is modeled as a flame surface represented by a tilted cylinder shape with an elliptical horizontal base. The thermal radiation intensity $\dot{q}''$ at any point outside the flame surface can be estimated using the following expression,

$$\dot{q}'' = \tau E_f VF \tag{1}$$

where τ is the atmospheric transmissivity, E_f is the emissive power of the flame and VF is the view factor.

The determine the total radiation from one fire requires that in addition to those factors, the geometry of the flame is known, which in turn depends on several factors as discussed in (Guedes Soares, 1993) and summarized here.

2.1.1 Pool Fire Geometry

The flame geometry is generally determined by assuming that the flame is a solid, gray emitter, having a regular well defined shape such as a tilted cylinder. The geometry of the flame for the pool fire model is characterized by the flame base diameter, visible flame height, flame tilt and flame dragged diameter.

The flame diameter is dependent on the spill size and the rate of burning. The visible flame length is predicted by the Thomas correlation (Thomas, 1963) as function of the circular pool size and mass burning rate in non-wind pool fires,

$$\frac{L}{D} = 42\left(\frac{m}{\rho_a \sqrt{gD}}\right)^{0.61} \tag{2}$$

where L is the flame length, D is the pool diameter m is the mass burning rate (kgm^{-2}s^{-1}), ρ_a is the ambient air density (kgm^{-3}) and g is the acceleration of gravity (ms^{-2}).

The estimation of the burning rate for hydrocarbon liquids is given by following relation,

$$m_\infty = 1.27 \times 10^{-6} \rho_L \left(\frac{\Delta H_c}{\Delta H_v - \Delta TC_p}\right) \tag{3}$$

where C_p is the specific heat of the liquid, ΔT is the temperature difference between the liquid at its boiling point and its initial condition, ΔH_c and ΔH_v are respectively the net heat of combustion and the vaporisation at the boiling point of the liquid fuel. If the burning rate of the fuel is known, it can be corrected for use in small fires by an equation given in (Babrauskas, 1983).

To characterise the geometrical properties of the flame in the wind blow situation two additional parameters are required, i.e. the flame drag and the flame tilt angle. The American Gas Association, (1974) has proposed the following expression for estimation of tilt angle of the flame from the vertical,

$$\cos\theta = \begin{cases} 1 & for \quad \dfrac{u_w}{u_c} < 1 \\[2ex] \left[\dfrac{u_w}{u_c}\right]^{0.5} & for \quad \dfrac{u_w}{u_c} \geq 1 \end{cases} \tag{4}$$

where u_w is the wind speed and u_c is given by,

$$u_c = \left[\frac{gmD}{\rho_o}\right]^{\frac{1}{3}} \tag{5}$$

The wind causes the base of the flame to be dragged downwind of the pool, increasing its size. Mudan and Croce, (1988) have proposed the following expression for the extended flame base D' which depends on the Froude number and on the vapor fuel density at the normal boiling point ρ,

$$\frac{D'}{D} = 1.25\left[\frac{u_w^2}{gD}\right]^{0.069}\left(\frac{\rho}{\rho_o}\right)^{0.48} \tag{6}$$

2.1.2 Atmospheric Transmissivity

The atmospheric transmissivity is given by the following relationship:

$$\tau = 1.389 - 0.135 \log_{10}(P_{wv}d) \qquad (7)$$

where P_{wv} is the partial water vapor pressure (N/m^2) and d is the distance from receiver point to flame center (m). The partial water vapor pressure is given by:

$$P_{wv} = \frac{RH}{100}\exp\left(14.4114 - \frac{5328}{T_a}\right), \text{ atm} \qquad (8)$$

where RH is the ambient relative humidity (%) and T_a is the ambient temperature (°K).

2.1.3 Emissivity Power

The emissivity power of a large turbulent fire can be approximated by:

$$E_f = E_b \varepsilon \qquad (9)$$

where E_b is the black body emissive power in KW/m^2 and ε is the emissivity.

The black body emissive power is given by:

$$E_b = \sigma(T_f^4 - T_a^4) \qquad (10)$$

where T_f and T_a are the radiation and ambient temperatures of the flame in °K and σ is the Stefan-Boltzmann constant (in KW/m^{2}K^4).

The emissivity accounts for the fact that the flame is a gray emitter. It has a component due to soot and another from carbon monoxide and water vapor. It is difficult to estimate these values and an empirical relation for the average emissive power is given by:

$$E_f = 140e^{-0.12d} + 20(1 - e^{-0.12d}) \qquad (11)$$

2.1.4 View Factor

The view factor depends on the location of the flame relative to the receiving target. It is calculated by a two-dimensional integral over the flame surface:

$$VF = \int_S \frac{\cos\beta_1 \cos\beta_2}{\pi d^2} dS \qquad (12)$$

where β_1 and β_2 are the angles made by the normal to the fire and the receiving element and d is the distance from receiver point to the flame center. The integration is carried out numerically over the flame surface.

2.2 Probabilistic Model

To estimate the thermal radiation due to a pool fire requires the assessment of the series of equations just described, which makes it cumbersome to include them in the limit state function of a reliability formulation. Thus, an alternative is to model the output of such a model as a function of random variables which can be assessed with first order second moment methods. This formulation is based on describing the random variables by their mean value and standard deviation without specifying the type of probability distribution that governs them.

As in the present case the number of variables that influence the fire model is relatively large and there is not much data for an accurate statistical description of the variability of each one, this probabilistic model is compatible with that type of information.

Whenever one has a function f($\underline{x}$) of several random variables, its first two statistical moments can be approximated by:

$$E[f(\underline{x}^*)] = f(\underline{x}^*)$$
$$V[f(\underline{x}^*)] = \sum_{i=1}^{\infty}\sum_{j=i}^{\infty}\left(\frac{\partial f}{\partial x_i}\right)\left(\frac{\partial f}{\partial x_j}\right)\sigma_i \sigma_j \rho_{ij} \qquad (13)$$

where $E[f(\underline{x}^*)]$ and $V[f(\underline{x}^*)]$ stands for the expected value and variance, respectively, $\underline{x}^*$ is the vector with the linearisation point, σ_i is the standard deviation of the variables x_i and ρ_{ij} is the correlation coefficient between the two variables. This formulation implies linearisation about the value $\underline{x}^*$ of the variables and therefore it is valid only in its vicinity.

The importance of the contribution of each variable to the uncertainty of $f(\underline{x})$ can be assessed by the sensitivity factors which are determined by:

$$\alpha_i = -\frac{1}{\sqrt{\sum_{i=1}^{\infty}\left(\frac{\partial f(x)}{\partial x_i}\right)^2}}\frac{\partial f(x)}{\partial x_i} \qquad (14)$$

Since the pool fire model is not represented by one analytical expression which could be easily differentiated, the partial derivatives indicated in the above expression have to be calculated numerically.

The most relevant variables for modeling are shown in table 1.

Table 1 - The variables for probabilistic modeling.

	Variables	Unit
m	Mass flow rate of spill	Kg/s
m_w	Molecular weight of the fuel	Kg/mol
$\dot{m}''$	Maximum burning rate of the fuel	Kg/m²s
K_β	Burning rate coefficient	m⁻¹
H_v	Heat of vaporisation of the fuel	KJ/Kg
H_c	Heat of combustion of the fuel	KJ/Kg
C_p	Specific heat capacity	KJ Kg⁻¹ K⁻¹
E_α	Max. Emissive power of the fuel	KW/m²
k	Extinction coefficient of the fuel	m⁻¹
u_w	Ambient wind speed	m/s
ϕ	Horizontal wind direction	Degrees
T_a	Ambient air temperature	K
RH	Ambient relative humidity	%
BP	Boiling point of the fuel	K
D	Diam. Of confined or bounded pool	m
H	Module ceiling height	m

The results of a sensitivity analysis performed by Guedes Soares et al., (1997) are described in figure 1. The variables not listed in the figure presented below have negligible influence on the uncertainty of the results.

Figure 1 shows that the most important variables for the pool fire model are the horizontal wind direction and mass flow rate of spill. The maximum burning rate and the boiling point of the fuel are also seen to be important, but not to such a high degree. However, the molecular weight of the fuel does not greatly affect the heat flux. The environmental variables of ambient air temperature, wind speed and relative humidity are not significant terms in the fire model.

3. HEAT TRANSFER MODEL

Since fire walls are protected by insulation material the prediction of the temperature of the steel plate depends on the heat transfer across the insulation material.

The unknown surface temperature of the plate T_s on the inner side of the fire wall can be calculated from the continuity equations for the heat flux through the insulation. The fire wall, with a total thickness of insulation d, is divided into $n+1$ equidistant subintervals of thickness $\Delta d = \dfrac{d}{n+1}$ as shown in figure 2.

The temperature field $T_f(t)$ or flux $F_i(t)$ are assumed to be homogeneous over the exposed side of the fire wall, as is the temperature field $T_a(t)$ at the outward side, which is not exposed to the fire.

The flux into the wall is given as

$$F_i = -k\frac{\partial T_f}{\partial x} \approx \frac{k}{\Delta d}\left(T_f - T_1\right) \tag{15}$$

The temperature at layer j, T_j, is given by the following one-dimensional heat equation,

$$\rho_i c_i \frac{\partial T_j(t)}{\partial T} = k_i \frac{\partial^2 T}{\partial x^2} \approx$$
$$\approx \frac{k_i}{\Delta d_i^2}\left(T_{j-1}(t) - 2T_j(t) + T_{j+1}(t)\right) \tag{16}$$

$$\frac{dT_j(t)}{dt} = \alpha\left(T_{j-1} - 2T_j + T_{j+1}\right) \quad j=1...n \tag{17}$$

$$\alpha = \frac{k}{\rho c \Delta d^2} \tag{18}$$

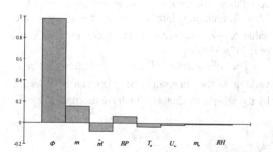

Figure 1 - The sensitivities of the variables used in pool fire model.

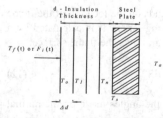

Figure 2 - Discretization of the firewall

where k, ρ and c represent the thermal conductivity, the mass density and the heat capacity of the firewall, respectively.

This equation can be solved by a finite difference approximation in which the boundary conditions $T_o(t)=T_f(t)$ and $T_{n+1}(t)=T_s$ have been applied, as done by Nielsen et al., (1994).

Since the plate temperature increases with time, the temperature T_a will also increase, and may be calculated using:

$$F_i = h\left(T_s - T_a\right) \qquad (19)$$

where h is the average convection heat transfer coefficient of the air.

4. LIMIT TEMPERATURE DIFFERENTIAL FOR STEEL PLATES

In (Guedes Soares et al., 1996) the elasto plastic behavior of plates subjected to heat loads has been studied and curves have been shown with the stresses as a function of temperature. These curves were obtained with a non-linear finite element code which took into account the change of temperature as well as the corresponding changes of material properties.

The curves had a shape similar to the ones obtained for the collapse of plates under in plane loading. They had a clear collapse and a post collapse region in which the strength decreased.

Table 2 summarizes the results of the calculations, considering three different materials with yield stresses of 235MPa, 300MPa and of 355MPa.

Table 2 -Limit temperature differentials for plate collapse (°C).

b/t	σ_o=235 (MPa)			σ_o=300 (MPa)		σ_o=355 (MPa)	
	a/b=1	a/b=2	a/b=3	a/b=1	a/b=3	a/b=1	a/b=3
20	64	56	56	80	70	128	80
40	68	48	40	88	50	160	80
60	80	56	40	100	56	160	80
80	84	56	48	104	56	160	80
100	84	56	48	100	56	160	80
Mean	76.0	54.4	46.4	94.4	57.6	153.6	80.0
C.O.V	0.123	0.066	0.144	0.106	0.128	0.093	0.0

Calculations were performed for plates of aspect ratio (a/b) equal to 1, 2 and 3 and breadth to thickness ratio (b/t) between 20 and 100. The final results for the limit temperature are shown in table 2.

Inspection of the table shows that there is a clear effect of the three governing parameters. As a general observation, it looks as if the most dominant parameter is the yield stress and the less important is the breadth to thickness ratio.

Table 3 - Collapse temperature differentials of the different materials (°C).

(MPa)	σ_o=235	σ_o=300	σ_o=355
Mean	58.93	76.00	116.8
C.O.V	0.25	0.28	0.34

Depending on the level of detail desired in the analysis one can either use the collapse temperature for each set of three parameters, or only the average value for each set of σ_0 and a/b, as shown in table 2 or even use only σ_0 as the governing parameters as indicated in table 3. Note that these values correspond to a differential of temperature, and not to an absolute temperature of collapse.

After attaining the maximum stress at the critical temperature, the plates are still able to carry some load with increasing temperature, but one is generally interested on the maximum load carrying capacity.

In the case of fire walls, even after the collapse, the plate will be in its position and as such it will continue constituting a barrier to the transmission of fire. However, when the plate collapses, it acquires large deformations due to the buckled pattern and it is most likely to cause damage on the adjacent insulation material.

One can expect that whenever the passive fire protection becomes ineffective, although in a localized area, that the plate will have a very quick raise of temperature and will collapse rapidly loosing any load carrying capacity.

Therefore, taking into account the progression of the damaging situation that will occur after the first plate collapse, it is justifiable to adopt this situation as the reference one to establish the limit state function defining failure.

5. RELIABILITY FORMULATION

It was established in the previous section that the differential of temperature in a plate will lead to its collapse whenever it reaches the limit value as given in table 2. Therefore, at a specific point in time, one can define the probability of failure as the probability of the temperature in the plate being higher than its limit temperature.

The limit state function is then:

$$g(\bar{x}) = \Delta T_{\lim} - \Delta T_{steel} \qquad (20)$$

where, $\Delta T_{\lim}$ is the difference of temperature that leads to plate collapse, and ΔT_{steel} is the actual increase of plate surface temperature.

In the formulation of the reliability problem the input thermal radiation intensity is defined as a stochastic variable which is used as input for the steel temperature evaluation.

Since the temperature increase cannot be explained by an analytical expression the limit state equation has to include the numerical scheme that yields the temperature increase as a function of the thickness of the insulation (t_i) the thermal conductivity (k_i), the density (ρ_i) and the specific heat Cp_i of the material, in addition to the input thermal radiation intensity. Thus the limit state equation is written as:

$$g(\underline{x}) = \Delta T_{\lim} - \Delta T_s(\dot{q}'', t_i, k_i, \rho_i, Cp_i) \qquad (21)$$

Having established the form of the limit state equation, the reliability can be assessed by any of the available codes based on first order reliability methods. In the present case use was made of RELIAB (CSR, 1994).

The development of a fire is a time dependent problem and so will be the temperature of the steel plate. However, the change of temperature with time is a monotonic function, and this allows the time variant reliability problem to be studied by a series of time independent formulations at different time steps. The problem is solved here by considering different points in time after the start of the fire and calculating the reliability index at those points.

6. EXAMPLE CALCULATION

The example analyzed here is a wall with dimensions representative of the modules in the topside of offshore platforms, as shown in figure 3. The origin of the pool fire was considered to be 10 m away.

Two values for the horizontal wind direction are analyzed. The first value of 45° was considered in order to obtain the maximum value of radiation in the center of the wall (50.9 KW/m² - 702 °C). The

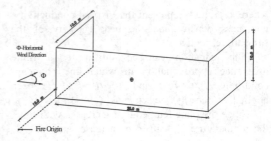

Figure 3 - Model analyzed.

second value of 80° corresponds to a radiation in the center of the wall of 13.9 KW/m² (436 °C).

For the present example all variables are assumed to be normal distributed. Table 4 shows the statistical moments of the random variables considered.

Table 4 - Stochastic variables.

Variables		Mean Value	Std. Dev.
Rad	Radiation	13.9 / 50.9	1.39 / 5.09
t_i	Thick. Of insulation	0.020	0.002
K_i	Thermal conductivity	0.05	0.005
ρ_I	Density	2000.0	200.0
Cp_i	Specific heat	500.0	50.0
$T_{\lim}$	Limit Temperature	58.9	5.89

Figure 4 shows the reliability index that was obtained as a function of time for the two mean values of radiation. For the lower radiation value higher values of β were obtained, as was expected. Figure 5 shows the reliability index obtained with the COV=0.1 and 0.25 to describe the limit temperature. The expected higher values of β were obtained for the curve with COV = 0.1.

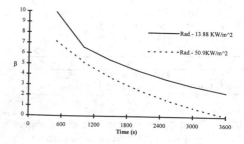

Figure 4 - Time dependent reliability index.

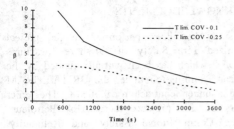

Figure 5 - Influence of T_{lim} COV in the reliability index β

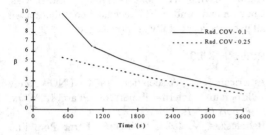

Figure 6 -Influence of radiation COV in the reliability index β

For the radiation a similar result is shown in figure 6. The time dependent reliability index is obtained for the values of 0.1 and 0.25 of the coefficient of variation.

Figure 7 shows the reliability index obtained for two different materials with yield stress, $\sigma_o=235MPa$ and $\sigma_o=355$ MPa, which correspond to the collapse temperatures values $T_{lim} = 58.9°C$ and $T_{lim} =116.8°C$, respectively.

The higher values of β were obtained for the curve with higher yield stress, which decreases smoothly with time. The curve obtained with the other yield stress drops quickly with time.

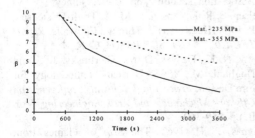

Figure 7 - Influence of material type in the reliability index

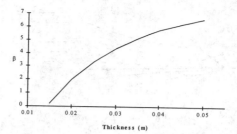

Figure 8 - Influence of insulation thickness in the reliability index.

Figure 8 shows the reliability index that was obtained for the thickness of insulation with mean value changing from 0.015 to 0.045 mm after 1 hour burning. The curve shows the increase of β with the increase of the thickness of insulation, as was expected.

Table 5 presents the elasticities of mean and standard deviation for time 3600s. It is apparent that the important ones are the limit temperature, the thickness of insulation and the thermal conductivity of the insulation.

Table 5 - Elasticities of mean and standard deviations values for time 3600s

Variable	$\dfrac{\partial \beta}{\partial \mu}\dfrac{\mu}{\beta}$	$\dfrac{\partial \beta}{\partial \sigma}\dfrac{\sigma}{\beta}$
Radiation	-0.8212	-0.0281
Thickness of insulation	3.5118	-0.5139
Thermal conductivity	-2.1912	-0.2001
Density	0.6250	-0.0163
Specific heat	0.6250	-0.0163
Limit Temperature	2.3235	-0.2251

Figures 9 to 11 show the sensitivities and time dependent elasticities of the mean and standard deviation values of the reliability index with respect to the different variables. This analysis was made for the higher reliability index curve shown in figure 4.

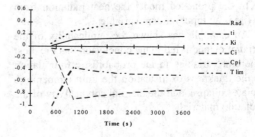

Figure 9 - Time dependence of sensitivity analysis

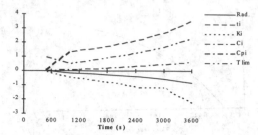

Figure 10 -Time dependence for elasticity of mean values.

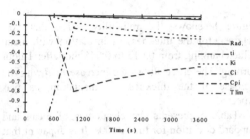

Figure 11 - Time dependence for elasticity of standard deviation values.

The sensitivities show the limit temperature, the thickness of insulation and the thermal conductivity as the more important variables in the determination of the reliability index.

As can be seen in figure 10 the elasticities, of the thickness of insulation of the limit temperature and of the thermal conductivity are the largest ones.

The elasticity of standard deviations are presented in figure 11. It is observed that the most important variable is the thickness of insulation.

7. CONCLUSIONS

A formulation has been presented to determine the reliability of fire walls subjected to a pool fire, based on a temperature limit state.

In the proposed model the heat radiation from the fire is an input random variable.

An example has shown the applicability of the formulation and it led to the conclusion that the most important variables in the probabilistic formulation are the thickness of insulation the limit temperature of plate collapse, and the thermal conductivity of the insulation material.

8. ACKNOWLEDGEMENTS

This study has been performed in the project "Optimized Fire Safety of Offshore Structures (OFSOS)" which has been partially funded by the European Commission under the BRITE/EURAM program, under contract n° 92/0598. The other partners of this project where AEA Petroleum Service, Computational Safety and Reliability, Germanischer Lloyd, Registro Italiano Navale, SNAMPROGETTI, TECNOMARE, and WS Atkins, having as sponsors AGIP, British Gas, Chevron and Amoco. The technical contributions of all partners is gratefully acknowledged.

REFERENCES

American Gas Association 1974. LNG Safety Program - Interim Report on Phase II Work, *Report IS 3-1*.

Babrauskas, V. 1983. Estimation Large Pool Fire Burning Rates, *Fire Technology 19*, p. 251.

CSR 1994. RELIAB01 Version 2.0 - Manual and Software, *CSR ApS*.

Guedes Soares, C. 1993. Review of Modelling Techniques for Hydrocarbon Fires, *Report TEC-C013-01, OFSOS Project*, Instituto Superior Técnico.

Guedes Soares, C., Gordo, J. M., & Teixeira, A. P. 1996. Elasto-Plastic Collapse of Plates Subjected to Heat Loads, *Journal of Constructional Steel Research (submitted for publication)*.

Guedes Soares, C., Teixeira, A. P., & Neves, L. 1997. Probabilistic Modelling of Offshore Pool Fires, *Advances in Safety and Reliability*, C. Guedes Soares (Ed.), Elsevier .

Mudan, K. S. & Croce, P. A. 1988. Fire Hazard Calculations for Open Hydrocarbon Fires, *in The SFPE Handbook of Fire Protection Engineering*, P.J. DiNenno et al (eds), National Fire Protection Association, section 2, pp. 45-97, Quincy.

Nielsen, S. R. K, Jensen, F. M., & Thoft-Cristensen, P. 1994. Heat Transfer Through Firewalls, *Report TEC-C022-03*, OFSOS Project, CSR.

Shetty, N. K., Deaves, D. M., Gierlinsky, J. T. and Dogliani, M., 1996, Unified Methodology for Fire Design, *Proceedings 15th Int. Conference on Offshore Mechanics and Artic Engineering*, Vol. II, pp. 359-369.

Thomas, P. H. 1963. The Size of Flames from Natural Fires, *9th International Combustion Symposium*, Academic Press, pp. 844-859.

Structural Safety and Reliability, Shiraishi, Shinozuka & Wen (eds) © 1998 Balkema, Rotterdam, ISBN 90 5410 978 5

Earthquake response and reliability analysis of offshore structure

Katta Venkataramana, Kenji Kawano & Tomoyo Taniguchi
Department of Ocean Civil Engineering, Kagoshima University, Japan

ABSTRACT: Dynamic response and reliability analysis of offshore structures under wave, current and earthquake loads are investigated. The two structure models considered for study are: (i) a jacket-type offshore structure and (ii) a tension-leg-platform. The ground acceleration due to seismic input is represented by the Kanai-Tajimi spectrum. Response and reliability analysis, using frequency-domain random-vibration approach, are carried out when this spectrum is used in the original form and also when it is used in the modified form to account for the correction at low-frequency range. It is shown that the selection of the suitable value for frequency parameter of the ground acceleration spectrum affects moderately the response and reliability evaluation of jacket structures whereas the response of tension-leg-platforms are highly dependent on the frequency parameter. Since the tethers of tension-leg-platforms are highly flexible in the horizontal direction but are very rigid in the vertical direction due to pretension, their response behavior in the vertical direction is of main interest. When the tethers are perfectly vertical they can be treated as aseismic structures against vertical ground excitations whereas when offset condition is created due to wave or current load, tethers undergo elongation under ground motion. In the present study, the initial offset is created due to current action and then the dynamic response of tethers is investigated for the inputs of earthquake excitations. Studies indicate that the horizontal and vertical components of displacements are strongly influenced both by the amount of initial offset of tether, and by the intensity of earthquake loading.

1 INTRODUCTION

While carrying out the response analysis of offshore structures to earthquake excitations, ground motions for stationary conditions are usually represented by the well-known Kanai-Tajimi spectrum. But this expression does not change the amplitudes as the frequency approaches zero and some difficulty may arise with very low-frequency components. In particular, the natural frequencies of offshore structures such as jacket structures and tension-leg-platforms have generally lower values. The above spectrum is modified by introducing a filter which attenuates low-frequency components. Proper selection of the parameters of this filter is very important because if the attenuation is too small, the responses are over-estimated resulting in an uneconomical and conservative design whereas if the attenuation is too large, the responses are underestimated thus affecting the safety and reliability of the structure. The present study intends to estimate quantitatively the effects of the variations in the parameter of this filter known as frequency parameter on the dynamic response and reliability evaluations of offshore structures. The two models considered for study are (i) jacket-type offshore structure with a first natural frequency of about 1.61 rad/s and (ii) tether of tension-

log platform (TLP) having a first natural frequency of 0.19rad/s. The response of jacket structure is evaluated for wave and earthquake loads whereas the response of the tether of TLP is determined for current and earthquake loads.

2 FORMULATION

The earthquake ground motions are highly random in nature and hence the response analysis is usually carried out using the random vibration approach. The random earthquake ground motions may be represented with a stationary filtered white noise, given by Kanai and Tajimi (This is referred to as KT spectrum in this paper) as

$$\left[S_{\ddot{u}_g \ddot{u}_g}(\omega)\right] = \left[S_1(\omega)\right] S_0 \tag{1}$$

where

$$\left[S_1(\omega)\right] = \frac{1 + 4h_g^2 \left(\omega / \omega_g\right)^2}{\left(1 - \left(\omega / \omega_g\right)^2\right)^2 + 4h_g^2 \left(\omega / \omega_g\right)^2},$$

$$S_0 = \frac{\sigma_{\ddot{u}_g}^2}{\pi \left(1 + 4h_g^2\right) \omega_g / \left(2h_g\right)}$$

in which $\left[S_{\ddot{u}_g \ddot{u}_g}(\omega)\right]$ is the power spectrum of ground acceleration, ω_g and h_g are filter parameters (characteristic ground frequency and characteristic ground damping ratio respectively) , $\sigma_{\ddot{u}_g}$ is the root-mean-square (*rms*) value of ground acceleration, S_0 is the intensity of white noise at the base.

But the above formulation does not change the amplitudes as the frequency approaches zero and some difficulty may arise with very-low frequency components. Therefore Eq.(1) is modified by including another filter which attenuates the very-low frequency components as

$$\left[S_{\ddot{u}_g \ddot{u}_g}(\omega)\right] = \left[S_1(\omega)\right]\left[S_2(\omega)\right] S_0 \qquad (2)$$

where

$$\left[S_2(\omega)\right] = \frac{\left(\omega / \omega_f\right)^4}{\left(1-\left(\omega / \omega_f\right)^2\right)^2 + 4h_f^2\left(\omega / \omega_f\right)^2}$$

in which ω_f and h_f are the filter parameters (frequency parameter and damping parameter respectively) of a second filter, introduced to overcome the limitations of Eq.(1) in the low-frequency region. Eq.(2) is referred to as the modified Kanai-Tajimi spectrum (MKT spectrum) in this paper. Investigations have been carried out in this paper on a jacket-type offshore structure and a tension-leg-platform to assess the influence of the parameters of this spectrum on the dynamic response evaluations.

2.1 Jacket structure (Model 1)

Fig.1 shows the model of a jacket-type offshore structure including pile-soil foundation (Model 1). The structure is discretized by FEM. Morison equation in the linearized form is used for computing the wave force. The dynamic characteristics of the pile-soil foundation system are described using impedance functions. The equation of motion are obtained by the substructure method by formulating the equations of motion for the superstructure and the foundation separately and then combining them using the compatibility condition of displacements and equilibrium equation of forces at the interface nodes. The vibration mode shapes and the natural frequencies are determined by eigenvalue analysis. Next, frequency-domain random-vibration analysis is carried out and the response displacements and stresses are determined. Then using the principles of first passage probabilities, the reliabilities against crossing of design's stress levels are computed.

The equations of motions for the structure-pile-soil system are expressed as (Yamada et al, 1989)

$$[M]\{\ddot{r}\}+[C]\{\dot{r}\}+[K]\{r\}=[F]_w\{v_w\}-[F]_e\{\ddot{u}_g\}$$

$$(3)$$

where

$$[M]=\begin{bmatrix}[\ddots I \ddots] & [\tilde{M}_{ap}] \\ [\tilde{M}_{pa}]^T & [\tilde{M}_p]\end{bmatrix}, \quad [C]=\begin{bmatrix}[\ddots 2\beta_{fj}\omega_{fj}\ddots] & [\tilde{C}_{ap}] \\ [\tilde{C}_{pa}] & [\tilde{C}_p]\end{bmatrix}$$

$$[K]=\begin{bmatrix}[\ddots \omega_{fj}^2\ddots] & [0] \\ [0] & [\tilde{K}_p]\end{bmatrix}, \quad \{r\}=\begin{Bmatrix}\{q\} \\ \{u_p\}\end{Bmatrix}, \quad \{u_a^c\}=[\Phi]\{q\}$$

$$[F]_e=\begin{bmatrix}[\Phi]^T[\tilde{M}_{aa}][L][G] \\ [G]^T[L]^T[\tilde{M}_{aa}][L]+[M_{bb}][G]\end{bmatrix}, \quad \{v_w\}=\begin{Bmatrix}\{\ddot{v}_a\} \\ \{\dot{v}_a\}\end{Bmatrix}$$

$$[F]_w=\begin{bmatrix}[\Phi]^T[K_M] & [\Phi]^T[\overline{K}_D] \\ [G]^T[L]^T[K_M] & [G]^T[L]^T[\overline{K}_D]\end{bmatrix}, \quad [\tilde{M}_{aa}]=[M_{aa}]+[K_m]$$

$$[K_m]=[\ddots \rho(C_M-1)V\ddots], \quad [K_M]=[\ddots \rho C_M V\ddots]$$

$$[\overline{K}_D]=\begin{bmatrix}\ddots \rho C_D A\sqrt{\dfrac{2}{\pi}}\sigma_{v_a-\ddot{u}_a}\ddots\end{bmatrix}$$

in which $[\ddots I \ddots]$ is the unit matrix, subscript a denotes the unrestrained nodal points of superstructure, subscript b denotes the unrestrained nodal points at the base, subscript p denotes the pile-soil foundation, subscript w denotes the wave force, subscript e denotes the earthquake force, $\{v_a\}$ and $\{\dot{v}_a\}$ are water particle velocity and acceleration respectively at the undeflected structure coordinates, V and A are the volume and area respectively of each structural member normal to the wave flow, C_M is the inertia coefficient, C_D is the drag coefficient, $\sigma_{v_a-\ddot{u}_a}$ is the *rms* value of the relative velocity between the water particle and the structure (In the present problem, relative velocity is the difference between the water particle velocity due to the wave motion and the structural velocity due to the wave motion as well as earthquake ground motion), $[\Phi]$ is the modal matrix of the undamped superstructure with fixed-base, ω_{fj} is the natural frequency of the super-structure with fixed-base for jth vibration mode, β_{fj} is the corresponding damping ratio, $\ddot{u}_g$ is ground acceleration, u_p is the displacement of the center of gravity of the pile-soil foundation (which consists of translational and rotational components) , u_a^c is the dynamic displacement of the unrestrained nodal points of the superstructure with fixed-base and q is the modal displacement vector.

Eq.(3) contains nonproportional damping matrix. But, when the natural frequencies are well separated, modal coupling effects due to off-diagonal terms are negligible. In the present paper, simplifying approximation is made considering only the diagonal terms of the damping matrix.

The response quantities in Eq.(3) are expressed as a linear combination of a generalized coordinate $\{y\}$ using a new eigenvector $[\Psi]$ for the structure-pile-soil system. Therefore Eq.(3) can be transformed as

$$\{\ddot{y}\} + \left[\cdot \cdot 2\beta_j \omega_j \right] \{\dot{y}\} + \left[\cdot \cdot \omega_j^2 \cdot \cdot \right] \{y\}$$

$$= [\Psi]^T [F]_w \{v_w\} - [\Psi]^T [F]_e \{\ddot{u}_g\} \quad (4)$$

in which ω_j is the natural frequency for jth mode of vibration of the structure-pile-soil system, β_j is the corresponding damping ratio which includes the structural damping, the radiation damping through the foundation and the hydrodynamic damping.

The ground motion is expressed using the MKT spectrum as given in Eq.(2). The wave motion is represented by the Bretschneider's wave energy spectrum which is a function of mean wave height H and mean wave period T. Then the power spectrum of the generalized modal forces can be obtained. Next, power spectrum and variance of the modal responses, and finally, *rms* response displacements and stresses are determined. Then, using the principles of first passage probabilities (Kiureghian, 1980), reliabilities against the crossing of barrier levels by extreme responses are determined.

2.2 Tension-Leg-Platform (Model 2)

A Tension-Leg-Platform (TLP) consists of buoyant platform moored to the sea bed through vertical tethers. The tethers are kept in tension by extra buoyancy of the platform. The main advantage of the TLP is that the heave motion of the platform is suppressed due to the axial stiffness of tethers. Thus the platform acts like a moored semi-submersible vessel with great flexibility in the horizontal direction but is quite rigid in the vertical direction. Since the tethers of TLPs are highly flexible in the horizontal direction but are very rigid in the vertical direction due to pretension, their response behavior in the vertical direction is of main interest to structural engineers.

A horizontal load such as wind, wave or current will create an offset of the platform. When this platform under offset condition is subjected to a seismic excitation, the response characteristics of the platform and the tethers may deviate from their originally expected values based on a no-offset assumption. When the tethers are perfectly vertical, they can be treated as aseismic structures for vertical excitations whereas when offset condition is created, tethers undergo elongation under earthquake load. Kawanishi et al (1991,1993) investigated the earthquake response of a fixed-base TLP under an offset condition. They examined the tension variation in the tethers and found that the minimum tension of a downstream tether falls remarkably under the offset condition. In their analysis weight, inertia force and hydrodynamic force of tendons were neglected.

In the present study, the offset of the tether of TLP is caused due to the action of current force. The dynamic behavior of this tether, which is in the offset condition, for the inputs of horizontal and vertical seismic excitations is investigated. The effects of the selection of frequency parameter of the ground acceleration spectrum on the response evaluation are investigated. The bending stiffness as well as the hydrodynamic loading due to surrounding water is included in the analysis but the wave force is not considered.

Fig.2 shows the schematic diagram of a tether-TLP system under steady current. Let N be pretension in the tether, l be the length of the tether and p be the horizontal load on the tether due to current. The tether is modeled as a cantilever beam under axial load due to pretension N and the lateral load p due to the current. The load p per unit length of the tether is

$$p = 0.5 C_{dc} \rho A V_c^2 \quad (5)$$

where C_{dc} is a drag coefficient, ρ is the mass density of water, A is the area projected in the direction of flow and V_c is the velocity of steady current.

The governing equation of deflection of tether is

$$EI \frac{d^4 x}{dz^4} - N \frac{d^2 x}{dz^2} = p \quad (6)$$

where x is the deflection at distance z measured up from the base, E is the modulus of elasticity of the tether and I is the moment of inertia of the tether. The general solution of the above equation is

$$x = C_1 \exp(kz) + C_2 \exp(-kz) + C_3 z + C_4 - \frac{p}{2N} z^2 \quad (7)$$

where $k = \sqrt{N/EI}$. The constants C_1, C_2, C_3, C_4 are determined using the boundary conditions at the tether ends. The expression for the deflection is finally obtained as

$$x = \frac{p(1 - kl \exp(-kl))}{Nk^2 \exp(-kl)(1 + \exp(2kl))} \exp(kz)$$

$$+ \frac{p(1 + kl \exp(kl))}{Nk^2 \exp(-kl)(1 + \exp(2kl))} \exp(-kz)$$

$$+ \frac{-2p + plk(\exp(-kl) - \exp(kl))}{Nk^2 \exp(-kl)(1 + \exp(2kl))} + \frac{pl}{N} z - \frac{p}{2N} z^2 \quad (8)$$

The last two terms of the above equation correspond to the solution for a taut tether without bending.

The dynamic analysis for earthquake input is then carried out for this deflected tether. The effective earthquake force which produces the dynamic response of the tether results from the fact that inertia force depends on the total motion, while the damping and elastic force depend only on relative motion. Therefore the equation of motion can be obtained in terms of relative displacements as

$$\left[\tilde{M} \right] \{\ddot{u}\} + \left[\tilde{C} \right] \{\dot{u}\} + [K] \{u\} = -[P] \{\ddot{u}_g\} \quad (9)$$

where

$$[P] = [\tilde{M}]\{C_g\}, \qquad [\tilde{M}] = [M] + [\cdot \cdot \rho C_m V \cdot \cdot],$$

$$[\tilde{C}] = [C] + [\cdot \cdot \rho C_d A \sqrt{\overline{\mathstrut}}_{\kappa} \sigma_{\dot{u}} \cdot \cdot], \qquad [K] = [K_s] + [K_g]$$

in which $\{C_g\}$ is a vector representing a column of ones and zeros depending on the type of excitation, $[M]$ is the lumped mass matrix, $[C]$ is the structural damping matrix, $[K]$ is the stiffness matrix, $[K_s]$ is the elastic stiffness matrix, $[K_g]$ is the geometric stiffness matrix which takes into account the pretension in the tethers, $\{u\}$ is the displacement vector of the tether, C_m is the added mass coefficient, C_d is the hydrodynamic damping coefficient and $\sigma_{\dot{u}}$ is the *rms* value of the structural velocity which is obtained by an iterative procedure. The displacement vector of the tether consists of horizontal displacements (surge), vertical displacements (heave) and rotational displacements (pitch).

Now using eigenvalue analysis of an undamped vibration system and assuming Rayleigh-type damping, Eq.(9) can be transformed as

$$\{\ddot{q}\} + [\cdot \cdot 2\beta_{fj}\omega_{fj} \cdot \cdot]\{\dot{q}\} + [\cdot \cdot \omega_{fj}^2 \cdot \cdot]\{q\} = -[\Phi]^T[P]\{\ddot{u}_g\}$$
(10)

where $\qquad \{u\} = [\Phi]\{q\}$

in which ω_{fj} is the natural frequency for the jth vibration mode of the tether, β_{fj} is the corresponding damping ratio which includes both the structural damping and the hydrodynamic damping, $[\Phi]$ is the undamped eigenvector, $\{q\}$ is the corresponding modal displacement vector.

The ground motion is expressed using the MKT spectrum as given in Eq.(2). The power spectrum of the generalized modal forces is obtained by taking Fourier transform of Eq.(10) and the power spectrum and variance of the modal responses, and finally, rms response displacements are determined.

3 NUMERICAL RESULTS AND DISCUSSIONS

As mentioned earlier, earthquake ground motions are modeled stochastically using the MKT spectrum (Eq.2) for stationary conditions. Numerical results of response analysis of offshore structures are presented for *rms* ground accelerations of 100gal (severe earthquake situation) and 30gal (moderate earthquake situation). Fig.3 shows the ground acceleration spectrum for *rms* ground accelerations of 100gal. The values obtained using the KT spectrum are compared with those obtained using the MKT spectrum for different values of frequency parameter ω_f. The difference is prominent in the low-frequency region which includes the natural frequencies of offshore structure models. Also, in this region, the spectrum values strongly depend on the frequency

parameter ω_f chosen for the calculation.

3.1 *Jacket structure (model 1)*

Fig.1 shows the analytical model of jacket structure with pile-soil foundation. The superstructure is 120m high and the water depth is 110m. The main members have an outer diameter of 2.8m and a thickness of 27mm. The structural members as well as the piles in the foundation are made of steel. The diameter of each pile is 0.6m and there are 10 piles at each base node. The shear wave velocity in the soil is assumed as 100m/sec. The displacement of each nodal point has horizontal, vertical and rotational components in plane.

The wave force is represented with Morison equation using the Airy wave theory. The values of the inertia coefficient and the drag coefficient are taken as 2.0 and 1.0, respectively. The nonlinear drag term is linearized in the classical manner by assuming that the probability density function of the relative velocity is Gaussian. (In the present problem, relative velocity is the difference between the water particle velocity due to wave motion and the structural velocity due to the wave motion as well as earthquake ground motion.) The response analysis is performed with equivalent linearization of the drag force term and reasonable convergence is attained in about three cycles of iteration.

The governing equation of motion is obtained by the substructure method in which the structure-pile-soil system is divided into two substructures: the structure subsystem and the pile-soil foundation system. Natural frequencies and vibration mode shapes are computed by eigenvalue analysis, firstly for the rigidly supported base condition and then for the soil-structure interaction condition. The structural damping for the structure subsystem is assumed to be 2% for first mode of vibration Table 1 shows examples of natural frequencies.

The *rms* displacement of top node is plotted against the frequency parameter of ground acceleration spectrum in Fig.4 for different combinations of sea states and ground motions. It is seen that the responses are mainly controlled by the intensity of wave and earthquake forces, the proximity of wave excitation frequency and the frequency parameter to the natural frequency of the structure. The responses generally increase with the decrease in the value of frequency parameter.

In Fig.5, wave response components, earthquake response components and the total responses are plotted for the *rms* displacement of node 1. Wave force consists of inertia and drag force components. Wave responses are generally larger when the mean wave period is smaller and closer to the natural period of the structure resulting in a higher inertia force component. Wave responses are also larger when the mean wave period becomes longer resulting in a higher drag force component. On the other hand earthquake responses generally decrease with the increasing wave period due to the effect of increasing hydrodynamic damping effects.

Fig.6 to 8 show the reliabilities on the level crossing of the *rms* stresses at the bottom element for different loading conditions. Mainly the results for moderate waves (H=3m, T=7s), and severe earthquake conditions (rms ground acceleration=100gal) are shown. Three cases of barrier level λ i.e., λ=1000 kgf/cm², 1200 kgf/cm² and 1400 kgf/cm² are considered which represent the expected strength of the structure material. The abscissa denotes the duration of excitation as a function of the first natural period of the structure-pile-soil system.

Fig.6 shows the reliability when KT spectrum is used to represent the ground acceleration. Figs.7 and 8 correspond to the cases of MKT spectrum with the frequency parameters 1.0 and 1.5 respectively. It is seen that in addition to the intensity of earthquakes, the variations in the frequency parameter significantly affect the first passage probabilities across the barrier level and hence the reliability of offshore structures. As the duration of wave and earthquake excitation become longer the effects also increase accordingly.

3.2 Tension-leg-platform (Model 2)

The dynamic response analysis is carried out for the tether model shown in Fig.2. The depth of water is 300m from mean sea level. The structural details of the tether are given in Table 2. Its static deflected shape for different current loads is given in Fig.9. The deflections are proportional to the square of the current velocity, as is clear from Eqs.(5) and (8). The maximum deflection of the tether, against a current velocity of 2m/s, is 3.4m which is about 1.3% of its total length. The pretension in the tether has prevented it from undergoing large deflection.

The dynamic analysis is carried out for this deflected tether. The bottom end of the tether is assumed to be fixed to the sea bed whereas the top end is free to move laterally. For analysis purposes, this tether is discretized by lumping masses at selected nodal points into 51 nodes and 50 elements. The effect of platform is included in the top node as a concentrated mass. The displacement of each node has horizontal (sway), vertical (surge) and rotational (pitch) components in plane. The pretension in the tether is taken into account in the form of a geometric stiffness term.

The natural frequencies and vibration mode shapes are computed by eigenvalue analysis. The structural damping is assumed to be 2% for the first mode of vibration. Table 3 shows the natural frequencies for the first five modes for the five cases of current loading i.e., current velocity V_c=0 (undeflected position), 0.5m/s, 1m/s, 1.5m/s and 2m/s. The first natural frequency for all the cases is lower than the dominant wave frequency range (0.314 to 1.256rad/s

or 5 to 20sec) whereas the frequencies corresponding to second and higher modes are higher than the dominant wave frequency range for a water depth of 300m, assumed for the TLP.

The hydrodynamic force on the tether due to the surrounding water is expressed as the sum of an added mass term and a linearized hydrodynamic damping term based on Morison equation. The values of the added mass coefficient C_m and the hydrodynamic damping coefficient C_d are taken as 1.0 and 1.0 respectively. Since the hydrodynamic damping force is coupled to the dynamic response, the linearized damping term is calculated by a cyclic procedure and, reasonable convergence was attained in about four cycles of iteration.

Earthquake ground motions are modeled stochastically using the MKT spectrum (Eq.2) for stationary conditions. Fig.10 shows the variation of *rms* displacement of node 1, in the horizontal direction) as a function of frequency parameter of the earthquake spectrum for horizontal excitations with no-offset condition. As mentioned earlier, the response value is strongly dependent on the frequency parameter ω_f chosen for the calculation as the present offshore structure model has lower natural frequencies compared to jacket structures. Therefore, for reliable response evaluation for earthquake excitation, it is suggested that the value of the parameter must be chosen by studying many typical earthquake records and their characteristics. The value of the frequency parameter usually chosen for earthquake response of onshore structures is around 1.5 rad/s (with characteristic ground frequency ω_g of around 15 rad/s representing firm soil conditions). Since the marine soil is generally soft, in the following analysis, the value of ω_f of 1.0 is assumed (with characteristic ground frequency ω_g of 10 rad/s).

Numerical computations were carried out for horizontal as well as vertical ground excitations and *rms* responses of structural nodes were obtained for *rms* ground accelerations representing severe ground motions. Fig.11 and 12 show the horizontal and vertical displacements respectively of the tether for horizontal ground excitations. The distribution of displacements for different current velocities and *rms* ground accelerations are compared. It is observed that the horizontal displacements increase with the increase in ground acceleration, but are nearly the same for all the cases of current velocities for a given value of ground acceleration, indicating very little effect of initial offset due to current on the earthquake response characteristics in the horizontal direction. Vertical displacements, which are zero in the absence of initial offset with no current, increase rapidly with the increase in initial offset and earthquake forces. Excessive vertical displacements may cause slackening of tethers and may cause serious operational problems.

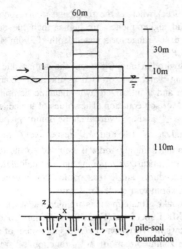

Fig.1 Jacket structure including pile-soil foundation (Model 1)

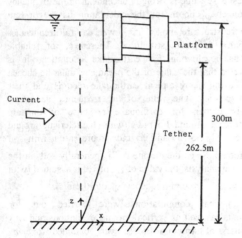

Fig.2 Tether - TLP system (Model 2)

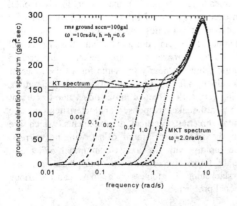

Fig.3 Ground acceleration spectrum

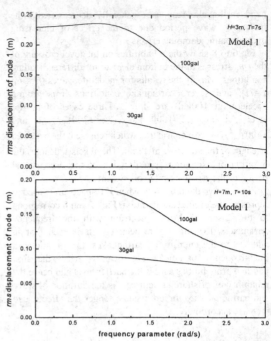

Fig.4 *rms* displacements of node 1 against frequency parameter

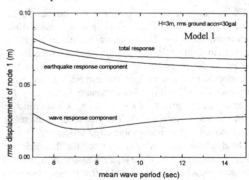

Fig.5 Wave, earthquake and total responses

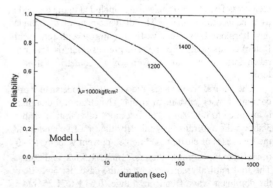

Fig.6 Level crossing probability using KT spectrum

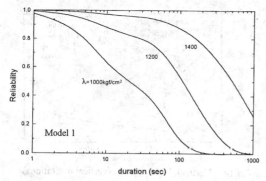

Fig.7   Level crossing probability using MKT spectrum (ω_f=1.0rad/s)

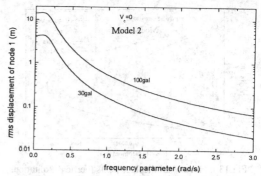

Fig.10   *rms* displacement of node 1 against frequency parameter

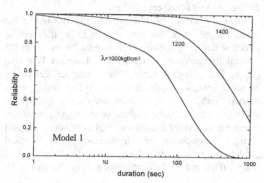

Fig.8   Level crossing probability using MKT spectrum (ω_f=1.5rad/s)

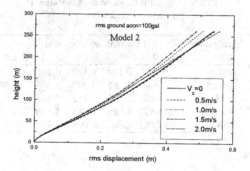

Fig.11   Horizontal displacements (horizontal excitations)

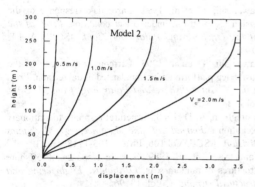

Fig.9   Static deflection of the tether

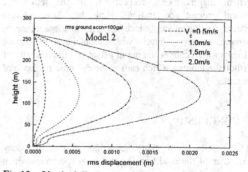

Fig.12   Vertical displacements (horizontal excitations)

Table 1   Natural frequencies of jacket structure (rad/s) (Model 1)

Vibration mode	Rigid base	Including pile-soil foundation
first	2.24	1.61
second	11.88	8.87
third	27.49	25.14

Table 2   Structural details of the tether (Model 2)

Outside diameter of the tether	0.81m
Wall thickness	38mm
Length of tether	262.5m
Pretension	15205.5kN
Weight of platform	14715kN
Self-weight	7.081N/m
Modulus of elasticity	$2.06 \cdot 10^8$ kN / m^2
Modulus of rigidity	$7.94 \cdot 10^7$ kN / m^2
Water depth	300m

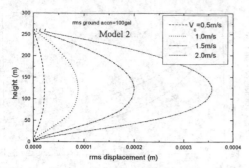

Fig.13 Horizontal displacements (vertical excitations)

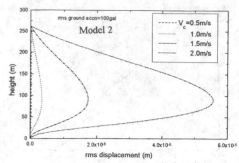

Fig.14 Vertical displacements (vertical excitations)

Table 3   Natural frequencies of vibration (rad/s) of tether (Model 2)

Vibration mode	Current velocity (m/s)				
	0	0.5	1.0	1.5	2.0
first	0.190	0.190	0.192	0.198	0.210
second	1.568	1.568	1.575	1.585	1.614
third	3.160	3.160	3.162	3.162	3.162
fourth	4.885	4.885	4.886	4.886	4.885
fifth	6.788	6.788	6.789	6.789	6.790

Figs. 13 and 14 show the examples of horizontal and vertical displacements respectively of the tether for vertical ground accelerations. Both the horizontal and vertical displacements, which are zero in the absence of currents, increase rapidly with the increase in current velocity which causes the initial offset and the intensity of earthquake loading which causes the dynamic response of the tether.

4 CONCLUSIONS

The results show that the value of the frequency parameter of the modified Tajimi-Kanai spectrum, which attenuates the low-frequency components, should be chosen carefully because the natural frequencies of offshore structures are usually lower than those of structures on land and fall within the low-frequency range. The dynamic response and reliability of offshore structures mainly depend on the intensity of wave and earthquake forces, the lower vibration modes of the structure and on the proximity of the corresponding natural frequencies to the frequencies of the excitation forces. The dominating wave frequencies are usually close to the structural frequencies and strongly affect the response values. The values of the *rms* responses are generally underestimated if a large value of the frequency parameter of MKT spectrum is used. Among the two models considered in the present study, the proper selection of frequency parameter is especially important for the analysis of tethers of TLPs.

Since the tethers of TLPs are highly flexible in the horizontal direction but are very rigid in the vertical direction due to pretension, their response behavior in the vertical direction is of main interest to designers. When the tethers are perfectly vertical, they can be treated as aseismic structures whereas when offset condition is created, tethers undergo elongation under earthquake loading. The vertical components of response displacements for horizontal excitations, and both horizontal and vertical components of displacements for vertical excitations are strongly influenced both by the amount of initial offset, and by the intensity of earthquake load.

REFERENCES

Kawanishi, T. et al. 1991. Earthquake response of the tension leg platform under offset condition, *Proc. of the 1st Int. Offshore and Polar Eng. Conf.*, ISOPE, Vol.1, 80-86.

Kawanishi, T. et al. 1993. Earthquake response of the tension leg platform under unbalanced initial tension, *Proc. of the 3rd Int. Offshore and Polar Eng. Conf.*, ISOPE, Vol.1, 319-325.

Kiureghian, A. D. 1980. Structural response to stationary excitation, *Journal of the Engineering Mechanics Division*, ASCE, Vol 106, EM6, 1195-1213.

Yamada, Y. et al. 1989. Seismic response of offshore structures in random seas, *Earthquake Engineering and Structural Dynamics*, Vol. 18, 965-981.

Structural Safety and Reliability, Shiraishi, Shinozuka & Wen (eds) © 1998 Balkema, Rotterdam, ISBN 90 5410 978 5

Failure probability and expected settlement of breakwater foundation caused by wave force

Y.X.Tang
Kanmon Kowan Kensetsu, Shimonoseki, Japan

T.Tsuchida
Port and Harbour Research Institute, Yokosuka, Japan

ABSTRACT: Distribution uncertainty of soil strength and occurrence characteristic of high waves are considered. First, the failure probability of breakwater foundation is analyzed by use of Monte Carlo simulation, in which variance coefficient for shear strength of the foundation is taken into account. The result shows that the failure probability with respect to the bearing capacity of foundation will be between $50 \sim 60\%$, if the safety factor of 1.0 is used as requirement in design.

Next, it is tried to estimate the settlement of caisson due to foundation failure under high wave force. Wave force which causes ground slip is assumed as single pulse of impaction on upright wall of caisson box.

Then, the stochastic process of high waves is characterized with two steps: (1) wave height, $p(H)$, during a designed storm according to Rayleigh distribution and (2) extreme high wave, $p(H_{max})$, during designed service years according to Gumble's distribution. Meanwhile, critical wave height, $p(H_{cr})$, for the foundation associated with uncertainty of soil strength is confirmed to accord to normal distribution through Monte Carlo simulation.

The analytical result shows that expected settlement maybe less than 10 cm for triangle-formed wave, and less than 60 cm for sine-formed wave.

Finally, discussion is carried out on the current method to examine the bearing capacity for the foundation. It is shown that the current method underestimates the foundation stability by 20% in safety factor.

1 INTRODUCTION

To design a breakwater, for example, a composite type with a caisson box placed on a rubble mound, we have to examine the stability from three aspects: sliding and overturning of the caisson box, and bearing capacity of foundation. The aim of the present study is to consider the failure probability of breakwater foundation and the expected settlement due to foundation failure.

There were some different methods which had been used to examine foundation stability. However, the current *Technical Standards for Port and Harbour Facilities* in Japan (issued in 1989) instructs that the breakwater foundation will remain stable if the safety factor is calculated greater than 1.0, where circular slip analysis of modified Biship's method is recommended to use. Meanwhile, it is also required that the safety factors for both sliding and overturning of caisson be greater than 1.2. It seems that the probability of foundation failure is too large when a designed high wave occurs actually.

In this paper, a breakwater is assumed to be built on a sandy ground. Monte Carlo simulation is conducted

through a series of circular slip analyses, and distribution property of the failure probability for the foundation is obtained. Then the authors present a procedure to estimate the expected settlement of composite type breakwater accumulated as foundation failure progresses, in which the stochastic process of high wave is considered.

2 FAILURE PROBABILITY OF FOUNDATION

2.1 *Monte Carlo simulation*

Monte Carlo simulation was done according to the following procedures:

a) Assume the distributions of soil parameters as normal distribution. Shear strength S for each layer is determined with variance coefficient $V(=\sigma_s/\mu_s)$, which is assigned to be 0.1, 0.15, or 0.2.

b) Conduct a series of circular slip analyses according to Bishop's method (Bishop, 1955), and find out the minimum value of safety factor F_{min}.

c) Add a calculation error to the obtained F_{min}. The calculation error takes place during the circular slip

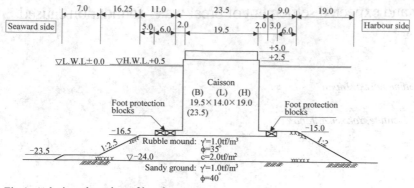

Fig.1 A designed section of breakwater

analysis, and is thought to distribute uniformly within [-0.1, 0.1] (Matsuo, 1984).

d) Repeat steps of a) to c) for 1000 times (N=1000), and count the number of failure cases (N') for which F_{min}<1.0.

Thereby, failure probability was obtained by P_F=N'/N.

2.2 Analyzing condition
Foundation stability was analyzed on a composite breakwater as shown in Fig.1. The forces of wave pressure acting on upright wall was estimated by use of Goda's formula. Wave characteristics used here were determined as blows:

Significant wave height: $H_{1/3}$=6.9 m
Design highest wave height: H_{max}=12.4 m
Wave length: L=263.6 m
Wave period: T=13 sec.
Principle direction of wave: θ=0°.

2.3 Failure probability
Following the *Technical Standard* mentioned, a breakwater was designed as a section in Fig.1, of which safety factor for the foundation was just 1.0 under design highest wave condition. At the same time, sliding and overturning stabilities of this section were examined, resulting in safety factors of 1.25 and 2.10 respectively. These values meet the requirement for sliding and overturning stability of caisson.

Alteration in safety factor was investigated, when ordinary waves appear lower than the design highest wave. Fig.2 shows that safety factor becomes larger than 1.0 as normal high waves act on the breakwater. The relation between safety factor and wave height can be expressed as:

$$F=2.37-0.11H \qquad (1)$$

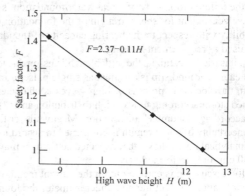

Fig.2 Relation between mean safety factor and wave height

Fig.3 shows the result of failure probability obtained through Monte Carlo simulation. Failure probability P_F decreases exponentially with decreasing high wave height. At the same time, variance coefficient V for shear strength of the foundation is an important parameter to failure probability. The larger the variance coefficient, the greater the failure probability.

Another important fact is that the failure probability under the design highest wave H_{max} seems too large. The result in Fig.3 shows us that it may be as large as 50~60%. Such a large failure probability should be regarded unacceptable by our common sense.

Yet, it must be recognized that highest wave is designed usually for a return period of 50 years, so there exists the possibility for extremely high waves, which exceed the designed highest wave, to occur during that period. But the occurrence of the extreme high waves does not mean the complete failure of the foundation, perhaps settling for several centimeters, but the breakwater

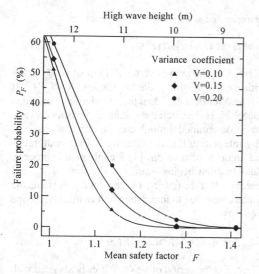

Fig.3 Failure probability varying with mean safety factor and wave height.

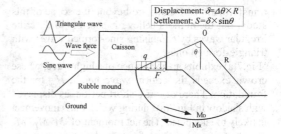

Fig.4 Sketch of the virtual rotating mass.

remains useful in most practical cases. Therefore, it is thought as a meaningful attempt to consider expected settlement during the service years.

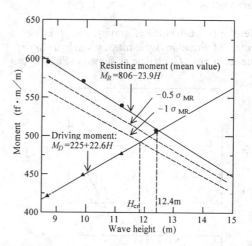

Fig.5 Driving and resisting moments varying with wave height.

3 EXPECTED SETTLEMENT DUE TO FAILURE OF FOUNDATION

3.1 *Estimation of settlement caused by unit high wave*

Fig.4 shows a sketch of caisson box placed on a foundation consisting of mound and ground. To examine the stability of the foundation, let us consider a cylindrical mass virtually, as shown in Fig.4. Virtual movement of this mass is supposed to take place when the driving moment M_D exceeds resisting moment M_R around the center "O". Here, M_D is generated by the gravities of caisson and foundation, and by the wave force as well. On the other hand, M_R is mobilized by the foundation only.

Fig.5 presents the changes of both moments with wave height for the case in Fig.1. Driving moment increases with wave height, while resisting moment is the reverse. If these two moments are equivalent to each other, the wave height is regarded the critical wave height H_{cr} of this foundation.

Certainly, water surface varies with time. In the deep water area, a sine function may express the form of waves fairly well. However, as waves transfer toward shallow area, effects such as diffraction, refraction, reflection, shoaling and breaking of waves shall be taken into account. Fig.6 gives an illustration of these

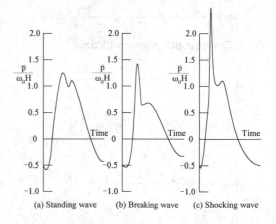

Fig.6 Transformations of wave pressures with change in water depth or existance of structures.

transformations. Details are beyond the scope of this study, but the authors believe it possible to describe irregular waves by combining sine-formed waves with triangle-formed ones.

Fig.7(a) exhibits an occurrence of a high wave, whose crown exceeds the critical wave height H_{cr} for the foundation. There occurs a short period, as displayed with shadow in Fig.7(a), during which mass movement is likely to take place. The net moment of $M=M_D-M_R$ to achieve acceleration of mass rotation is shown in Fig.7(b).

The rotation acceleration can be determined by:

$$\ddot{\theta}=Mg/I \qquad (2)$$

Here, g is acceleration of gravity, and I is inertia moment of virtual movable mass, given by $I=\Sigma m_i r_i^2$. The change of M with time as shown in Fig.7(b) can

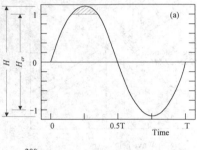

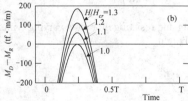

Fig.7 Change in net moment with time.

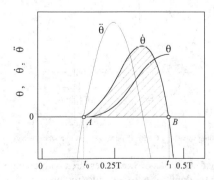

Fig.8 Calculation of rotation angle by integration.

be expressed with the following function:

$$M(t)=M_0(K\sin(2\pi/T)\,t-1) \qquad (3a)$$

Here, K is the ratio of vertex of high wave H_m to the critical wave height for the foundation, $K=H_m/H_{cr}$. If K is smaller than 1.0, then the foundation is regarded stable. M_0 is considered constant approximately, and can be determined through circular slip analysis.

By integrating Eq.(2) twice, we can get both rate $\dot{\theta}$ and angle θ of rotation. Fig.8 explains this process. Mass rotation begins from A at the time of t_0, and ceases by B at the time t_1. Twice integration yields the displacement due to foundation failure induced by one high wave.

$$\delta_{(s)1}=0.5(T/2\pi)^2\{K\sin(2\pi/T\cdot t_1)-1\}^2\cdot\delta_0 \qquad (4a)$$

Here, T is the period of wave, and δ_0 is assigned with $\delta_0=M_0gR/I$. R is radius of the arc in Fig.4.

In addition, K should be limited within $K<1.38$ in Eq.(4a).

Lower and upper boundaries of integration are given by the following relations:

$$t_0=(T/2\pi)\sin^{-1}(1/K)$$
$$t_1=(T/2\pi)\{\sin^{-1}(1/K)+K(\cos t_0-\cos t_1)\} \qquad (5a)$$

It can be seen that the ceasing time t_1 can not be determined directly by Eq.(5a). Nevertheless, the middle term involved in Eq.(4a) could be expressed with the approximate relation of $\{K\sin(2\pi/T\cdot t_1)-1\}^2 \approx 9.4(K-1)^2/K$.

To evaluate the settlement at base of caisson structure, let us consider the angle θ in Fig.4 which usually changes from $45°$ to $60°$, so we have $\sin\theta\approx0.8$. So far, the settlement caused by a single sine-formed wave can be estimated with the following relation:

$$S_{(s)1}=\delta_{(s)1}\cdot\sin\theta\approx0.095T^2(K-1)^2/K\cdot\delta_0 \qquad (6a)$$

Similar analysis is applicable to triangle-fomed waves. The net moment to generate rotating movement in this case can be expressed as below:

$$M(t)=M_0\{Kt/(T/4)-1\} \qquad (0\leq t\leq T/4)$$
$$=M_0\{2K-1-Kt/(T/4)\} \qquad (T/4<t\leq T/2) \qquad (3b)$$

Lower and upper boundaries of integration are given by the following relations:

$$t_0=(T/4)/K$$
$$t_1=(T/4)\{1+(1+\sqrt{2})(1-1/K)\} \qquad (5b)$$

By applying integration on Eq.(3b) from t_0 to t_1 by Eq.(5b), we can obtain the displacement of the failing foundation:

$$\delta_{(\Delta)1}=(1+2\sqrt{2}/3)(T/4)^2(K-1)^3/K^2\cdot\delta_0 \qquad (4b)$$

Also should K be limited within $K<1.71$ in Eq.(4b). Similarly, settlement by a single triangle-formed wave can be estimated as following:

$$S_{(\Delta)1}-\delta_{(\Delta)1}\cdot\sin\theta \approx 0.097T^2(K-1)^3/K^2\cdot\delta_0 \qquad (6b)$$

Based on Eqs.(4) or Eqs.(6), it is clear that the estimated displacement or settlement depends on wave period T and wave height ratio K. Each is directly proportional to T^2, and increases significantly with increasing K. Relations between δ_1 and K for both wave forms are drawn in Fig.9. We can find that the displacement induced by a triangle-formed wave is much smaller than that of sine-formed one. In fact, Fig.9 indicates that $\delta_{(\Delta)1}=(1/10\sim1/4)\delta_{(s)1}$ within the range of $K=1.1\sim1.3$.

3.2 Settlement expected during a high wave storm

To consider the settlement likely to be accumulated by a series of high waves during a storm, we have to presume a train of waves. Usually, for the cases of irregular deep water waves, the Rayleigh distribution is recommended to be used.

$$p(x) = \frac{\pi}{2}x\exp(-\frac{\pi}{4}x^2) \qquad (7)$$

Here, $x=H/\bar{H}$, and $\bar{H}$ is mean height of waves. Since the relation between significant wave height and mean wave height of $H_{1/3}=1.6\bar{H}$ is widely used, and the design highest wave height is usually given with the correlation of $H_{max}=1.8H_{1/3}$, mean wave height can be described as $\bar{H}=H_{max}/2.88$.

It is mostly observed that normal high wave storms continues for 2 to 5 hours. Here, we suppose a high wave storm to continue for 4 hours. Regarding wave period to be 13 seconds, the number of waves to occur during a high wave storm can be counted by $N_0=4\times3600/13\approx1100$.

By integrating the following relation, we can get the expected settlement to accumulate during a high wave storm.

$$S_E = N_0\int_{x_{cr}}^{\infty} p(x)\cdot S_1 dx \qquad (8)$$

Here, x_{cr} is given by $x_{cr}=2.88H_{cr}/H_{max}=2.88\rho$.

When substituting the unit settlements given by Eqs.(6a,b), we get the expected settlements caused by sine-formed and triangle formed waves during a high wave storm.

$$S_{(s)E}=0.095N_0\delta_0\{(1/x_{cr}+\pi/2\cdot x_{cr})/\sqrt{\pi}\cdot\Gamma(1/2,\pi/4\cdot x_{cr}^2)$$
$$-\exp(-\pi/4\cdot x_{cr}^2)\} \qquad (9a)$$

$$S_{(\Delta)E}=0.097N_0\delta_0\{(1/x_{cr}+3\pi/2\cdot x_{cr})/\sqrt{\pi}\cdot\Gamma(1/2,\pi/4\cdot x_{cr}^2)$$
$$-2\exp(-\pi/4\cdot x_{cr}^2)-\pi/4\cdot x_{cr}^2\Gamma(0,\pi/4\cdot x_{cr}^2)\} \qquad (9b)$$

In Eqs.(9a,b), $\Gamma(p,q)$ means the incomplete Gamma function. For they look rather complicated, these results are drawn in Fig.10. Fig.10 tells us that, if a breakwater, as shown in Fig.1, is designed with the standard of $H_D=H_{max}$, and its foundation has a critical

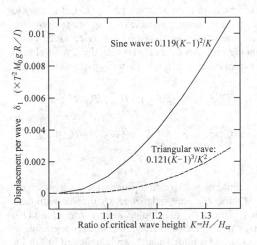

Fig.9 Displacements induced by a single wave

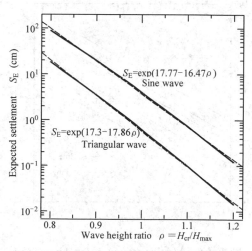

Fig.10 Expected settlements decreasing with wave height ratio $\rho=H_{cr}/H_{max}$.

wave height of $H_{cr}=H_D$ indeed, then settlement caused by a high wave storm with the highest high wave height equal to H_{max} should be from 0.6 cm (triangle-formed) to 3.7 cm (sine-formed). The expected settlement decreases exponentially with increase in the wave height ratio of $\rho=H_{cr}/H_{max}$.

Besides, relations given by Eqs(9a,b) can be fitted with a straight line as shown in Fig.10 with broken lines. They can be expressed as below:

$$S_E(H_{cr}/H_{max}) \approx \exp(a_0-a_1 \cdot H_{cr}/H_{max}) \qquad (10)$$

Here, constants of a_0 and a_1 are both fitting coefficients.

3.3 Estimation of settlement expected during service life

Now, we have to consider the uncertainty of shear strength for the breakwater foundation, and also the occurrence characteristic of the highest high wave.

Distribution of shear strength for the foundation is assumed to conform to normal distribution. Having conducting Monte Carlo simulation, we have found that safety factor appears of normal distribution also. Table.1 presents mean value μ_F and standard deviation σ_F of safety factor under the design highest wave of H_{max}=12.4m. It can be seen that mean value of safety factor μ_F decreases gradually with increasing variance coefficient V, meanwhile, standard deviation σ_F becomes larger and larger.

Since there is a linear relation between safety factor and wave high as given by Eq.(1), it is also reasonable to assume the critical wave height H_{cr} to be of normal distribution, expressed with the following function.

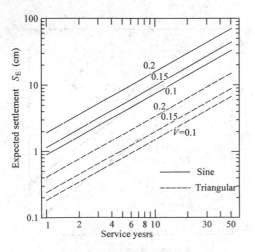

Fig.11 Expected settlements estimated during service years.

$$p(H_{cr}) = \frac{1}{\sqrt{2\pi}\sigma_{cr}} \exp\left(-\frac{(H_{cr}-\mu_{cr})^2}{2\sigma_{cr}^2}\right) \qquad (11)$$

With the help of Eq.(1), it is possible to estimate distribution parameters of critical wave height H_{cr} for the foundation. Estimated mean value μ_{cr} and standard deviation σ_{cr} for critical wave height are presented in Table.1

Table.1 Distribution characteristics of safety factor and critical wave height

Variance coef. of shear strength V	Safety factor (F)		Critical wave height (H_{cr}, m)	
	μ_F	σ_F	μ_{cr}	σ_{cr}
0.10	0.9995	0.0735	12.39	0.669
0.15	0.9893	0.0856	12.27	0.780
0.20	0.9720	0.1057	12.05	0.979

Next, let us think the occurrence characteristic of extreme high waves. For the problems of extreme weather or wave statistics, Gumbel's distribution (FT-I) is one of most useful function, which is described as below:

$$p(H_{max}) = \frac{1}{A}\exp\left\{-\frac{H_{max}-B}{A} - \exp\left(-\frac{H_{max}-B}{A}\right)\right\} \qquad (12)$$

Here, A and B are called scale and location parameters. In the present study, they are assigned as A=1m, and B=8.5m, respectively, so that H_{max}=12.4m corresponds to a extreme high wave with a return period of 50 years.

By integrating the relation of Eq.(13), it is easy to obtain the settlement expected during one service year. If the breakwater is suggested to service for $\bar{L}$ years, then the settlement expected during the $\bar{L}$ years should be estimated by multiplying $\bar{L}$ to S_E given with Eq.(13).

$$S_E = \int_0^\infty \int_0^\infty S_E\left(\frac{H_{cr}}{H_{max}}\right) p(H_{cr})p(H_{max})dH_{cr}dH_{max}$$

$$= \int_0^\infty \exp\left\{a_0-a_1\left(\frac{\mu_{cr}}{H_{max}} - \frac{a_1}{2}\left(\frac{\sigma_{cr}}{H_{max}}\right)^2\right)\right\}p(H_{max})dH_{max}$$

$$(13)$$

It should be realized that probabilistic wave heights of H_{cr} and H_{max} are independent variables with each other. Therefore, the double integrations of Eq.(13) can be performed separately. Numerical integration on Eq.(13) was conducted, and result is plotted in Fig.11. Based on the result shown in Fig.11, we can find that both the variance coefficient V of shear strength parameters for the foundation and the form of high wave (triangle-formed or sine-formed) are important factors. Expected settlement may become double as the variance coefficient V changes from 0.1 to 0.2. Form difference of high waves seems more considerable, sine-formed waves may cause larger settlements by nearly 5 times as compared with triangle-formed ones. The expected settlements for a service period of 50 years is summarized in Table.2.

Table.2 Expected settlements for different variance coefficient of shear strength and different shape of high waves (service years, 50)

Variance coef. of shear strength V	Triangle-formed high waves $S_{(\Delta)E}$	Sine-formed high waves $S_{(s)E}$
0.10	8 cm	38 cm
0.15	10 cm	46 cm
0.20	17 cm	69 cm

Shimosago *et al* (1994) established a method to estimate the displacement induced from sliding failure for composite breakwaters. Their result shows that the caisson is expected to slide about 7.4cm, if the breakwater section is designed with safety factor for sliding equal to 1.2.

Comparing the sliding displacement given by Shimosago's method and that by the present method, two expected values are not different so much. Therefore, the estimation method suggested is giving acceptable expected settlement as regarding a safety factor of 1.0 is used as requirement.

4 REMARKS

Monte Carlo simulation showed a probability of $50\sim60\%$ for foundation failure. Such a failure probability sounds too large. Records of failed breakwaters present that most of breakwater failures occurred in the pattern of sliding, other than foundation failure. Here, we shall review the present standard related with bearing capacity of foundation.

The examination method instructed was adopted on the base of investigations conducted by Kobayashi *et al* (1987). In their investigations, a series of centifuge model and prototype tests were carried out to obtain the bearing capacity of rubble mound. But the loads were applied in a static manner, this situation is different from dynamic condition of wave forces acting on upright wall of caisson. The static loads in these tests should

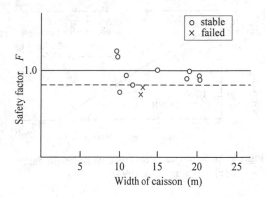

Fig.12 Case study of breakwaters

be more severe than instant loads of actual high wave.

Fig.12 is quoted from the report by Kobayashi *et al*. The result of their case study shows that the breakwater failed actually at $F=0.7\sim0.8$ with respect to foundation stability.

The points mentioned above lead to a suspicion that the examination for bearing capacity of breakwater foundation by use of circular slip analysis is a conservative method. The safety factor obtained by the current method includes extra security margins. Recently, Nagao *et al* (1997) have re-examined the safety factor by the current design method. They have revealed a hidden safety margin more than 20% if 1.0 is set as the allowable safety factor.

In the light of conclusion drawn by Nagao *et al*, the safety factors for foundation stability obtained in present study was enlarged by 20%, and failure probability and expected settlement were assessed again. The result is presented in Table.3. It can been seen that the failure probability drops from $50\sim60\%$ to $0.3\sim5.4\%$, and the expected settlements falls to mere 1/10. On suggestion that the accurrence characteristic of extreme high waves be taken into account comprehensively, failure probability will become much smaller.

Table.3 Failure probability and expected settlement due to foundation failure with arbitrary enlargement of 20% in safety factor.

Variance coef. of shear strength V	Failure probability P_F	Expected settlement (tri. waves) $S_{(\Delta)E}$	(sine waves) $S_{(s)E}$
0.10	0.3 %	0.6 cm	3.3 cm
0.15	0.6 %	0.8 cm	4.4 cm
0.20	5.4 %	1.5 cm	8.0 cm

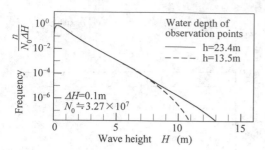

Fig.13 An Example of observed wave height data (after Shimosago, 1994).

Takayama *et al* (1994) investigated the estimation errors of various kinds of sources, and evaluated the degree of breakwater instability. They showed failure probabilities of P_F=0.7% and 0.1% for caisson sliding and overturning, respectively. It can be said that the failure probability for foundation stability is in accordance with the estimate given by Takayama as concerning with sliding and overturning stabilities.

Another importance is how to hindcast extreme high waves. Fig.13 shows wave data observed for 9 years by Shimosago *et al*(1994). Even the data were obtained at the same harbour, there is a considerable discrepancy in the occurrence characteristic, especially within the wave height range of 8~13m, only because the water depth is changed for the observing point. The authors must emphasize that the discrepancy as shown in Fig.13 will influence the estimate of expected settlement to a great extent.

5 CONCLUSION

Monte Carlo simulation has been conducted with the aim to investigate the uncertainty property of breakwater foundation. In compliance with the current *Technical Standard for harbour facilities*, breakwaters under design highest waves have a probability ranging within 50~60% for foundation failure.

A method has been introduced to estimate the expected settlement due to foundation failure during service years. First, the displacement based on virtual circular mass rotation has been analyzed for a single high wave. The result shows that settlement at the base of caisson depends on both period and shape of a high wave. Settlement increases with square of wave period T^2 linearly, and more is expected to take place from a sine-formed wave than from a triangle-formed wave.

Next, with stochastic processes for the uncertainty of shear strength of foundation, wave height distribution

in a high wave storm, and occurence characteristic of extreme high wave been considered, an estimate method has been established. Analysis for the present case yielded that the expected settlement due to foundation failure would be 8~17cm for triangle-formed waves, and 38~69cm for sine-formed waves.

Discussions showed that the safety factor based on the present design method may underestimate the foundation stability by 20%.

REFERENCE

Bureau of Ports and Harbours. 1989. Technical standards for port and harbour facilities. (*in Japanese*)

Bishop, A. W. 1955. The use of the slip circle in the stability analysis of slopes. *Geotechnique*. Vol.5, No.1, pp.7-17

Goda,Y. 1988. Numerical investigations on plotting formulas and confidence intervals of return value in extreme statistics. *Report of PHRI (in Japanese)*. Vol.27, No.1, pp.31-92

Bromhead, E.N. 1986. The stability of slopes. *Surrey University Press, Chapan and Hall*. pp.149-153

Tsuchida, T. and Tang, Y.X. 1996. The optimum safety factor for stability analyses of harbour structures by use of the circular arc slip method. *Report of PHRI (in Japanese)*. Vol.35, No.1, pp.117-146

Matsuo, M. 1984. Theorise and practises for reliability-based designs. *Gihodo press. (in Japanese)*. Chapter 5. pp.27-33

Kobayashi, M., Terashi, M., Takahashi, K., Takashima, K. and Odani, H. 1987. A new mehod for calculating the bearing capacity of rubble mounds. *Report of PHRI (in Japanese)*. Vol.26, No.2, pp.371-411

Takayama, T., Suzuki, Y., Kawai, H. and Fujisaku, H. 1994. Approach to probabilistic design for a breakwater. *Technical note of PHRI (in Japanese)*. No.785, p.36

Shimosago, K. and Takahashi, S. 1994. A method to estimate expected displacement due to sliding failure for composite breakwater. *Proc. Civil Engng. in the Ocean*. Vol.41(2). pp.756-760

Nagao, T., Kadowaki, Y., Tsuchida, T. and Terauchi, K. 1997. Evaluation of safety of breakwater by the reliability based design method. *Report of PHRI (in Japanese)*. Vol.36, No.1, pp.25-57

Structural Safety and Reliability, Shiraishi, Shinozuka & Wen (eds) © 1998 Balkema, Rotterdam, ISBN 90 5410 978 5

Inverse reliability method and applications in offshore engineering

Ricardo O. Foschi & Hong Li
Civil Engineering Department, University of British Columbia, Vancouver, B.C., Canada

ABSTRACT: An inverse reliability algorithm is proposed and applied to two problems in offshore engineering: 1) calculation of wave and iceberg collision forces with a gravity-based platform at a prescribed annual exceedence probability; and 2) calculation of the mean structural weight corresponding to a target probability of failure of sliding on the seabed. Numerical results are compared with applications of FORM as a forward reliability procedure, and advantages of the inverse procedure are discussed.

1 INTRODUCTION

The inverse reliability problem arises when it is desired to find a specified system design parameter corresponding to a given target reliability level. The calculation of the design parameter, for example, the cross-section of a column, can be done by means of a "trial and error" procedure using a forward reliability analysis method such as FORM (Madsen et al., 1986). Recently, more efficient methods of approaching this problem have been proposed (Winterstein et al., 1994; Der Kiureghian et al., 1994) under the name of "inverse reliability procedures". For example, a reliability contour method has been described by Winterstein and applied to problems in offshore environmental loads in the context of limit-state functions of the form

$$G(x, y_{cap}) = y_{cap} - R(x) \qquad (1)$$

where x is the vector of random variables and y_{cap} a given threshold. Based on given environmental parameters, a contour with a prescribed reliability level is constructed first and the maximum R_{max} of the response $R(x)$ is found along the contour. The corresponding vector x provides the variable combination corresponding to the design point and the companion y_{cap} is then obtained from (1) by using the condition $G = 0$. In this case, y_{cap} is treated as a deterministic design variable. Der

Kiureghian et al. (1994) proposed an iterative algorithm to solve the problem, based on the modified Hasofer-Lind-Rackwitz-Fiessler scheme, extending its applicability to general limit-state functions. In this paper, the function G is considered to be dependent on the random vector x and a random vector d, the latter containing the design parameters. Thus, these are considered to have given coefficients of variation, reflecting, for example, expected tolerances. The objective of the inverse procedure is to find, directly, the mean value of a design vector d so that a target reliability level can be satisfied.

For a unique solution to the problem, it is necessary (but not sufficient) that the dimension of the vector d be equal the number of constraints, including those from geometry as well as those reliability-related through specified limit state functions G. When the dimension of d exceeds the number of constraints, the solution to the problem is not unique but an optimum vector d can be obtained by introducing an optimization with an objective function related, for example, to minimum weight or cost. In this article, a direct algorithm is proposed to approach the general inverse reliability problem when no optimization is required. Furthermore, in the examples, only one design parameter is considered but it is treated either as a deterministic or as a random variable.

2 ALGORITHM

Suppose the limit-state function in the Standard Normal space is

$$G = g(u) \tag{2}$$

where u is the random Standard Normal vector containing also d, the design variable. Here we treat d (with mean value $\bar{d}$ and coefficient of variation V) as another random variable. Let x be the vector of original, basic variables, and β the prescribed target reliability. The inverse problem can be stated as:

Given β:

Find: $\bar{d}$ (mean value of d)   (3)

Subject to: $\min(u^T u) = \beta^2$ and $G(u) = 0$

It the forward reliability procedure FORM, the vector u, at the design point, must satisfy the following equation:

$$u = \left(\frac{\nabla G^T u}{\nabla G^T \nabla G}\right) \nabla G \tag{4}$$

and the reliability index β is given by

$$\beta = -\frac{\nabla G^T u}{(\nabla G^T \nabla G)^{1/2}} \tag{5}$$

Combining (4) and (5), one obtains

$$u = -\frac{\beta \nabla G}{(\nabla G^T \nabla G)^{1/2}} \tag{6}$$

Equation (6), together with the constrain $G(u) = 0$, is now used as the basis for the inverse reliability algorithm. Since the statistics for the variable d will influence the function $G(u)$ through the mapping from the Normal to the basic space, the function G can be regarded as a function $G(u, \bar{d})$.

For an initial $\bar{d}$, and a given β, Eq.(6) is used to set up an iterative scheme to find the u which satisfies it. However, the constraint $G(u)=0$ may remain unsatisfied. In order to meet it, the function G has to be modified by changing the variable d. We do this by using a Taylor expansion of G on $\bar{d}$ conditional on u. Thus,

$$G(u, \bar{d}) = G(u, \bar{d}_0) + \frac{\partial G}{\partial \bar{d}}\Big|_{u, \bar{d}_0} (\bar{d} - \bar{d}_0) = 0 \tag{7}$$

from which

$$\bar{d} = \bar{d}_0 - \frac{G(u, \bar{d}_0)}{\left(\frac{\partial G}{\partial \bar{d}}\right)\big|_{u, \bar{d}_0}} \tag{8}$$

Equation (8) is now used to find the new $\bar{d}$ given u and the previous $\bar{d}_0$. With the new $\bar{d}$, (6) and the modified G function permits an upgrade of u. The process is repeated until convergence is achieved.

For non-Normal variables the following transformation is utilized:

$$x_i = F_{x_i}^{-1}(\Phi(u_i)) \quad i = 1, n \tag{9}$$

where F_{x_i} is the cumulative function for the variable x_i, and Φ is the Standard Normal function.

For correlated variables, a vector v of correlated standard Normal variables is obtained first:

$$v = Lu \tag{10}$$

with

$$R_0 = L L^T \tag{11}$$

where R_0 is the correlation matrix decomposed into lower and upper triangular forms L (Der Kiureghian et al., 1986). Equation (9) is then used to obtain the vector x from v.

For a special case, when the limit-state function G is of the form

$$g(x, y_{cap}) = y_{cap} - R(x) \tag{12}$$

with y_{cap}, a deterministic design variable, (6) gives

$$u = \frac{\beta \nabla R}{(\nabla R^T \nabla R)^{1/2}} \tag{13}$$

with y_{cap} directly from

$$y_{cap} = R(x) \tag{14}$$

3 APPLICATIONS

The inverse reliability algorithm was applied to two problems in offshore engineering. Figure 1 shows a gravity-based, reinforced concrete cylindrical platform of radius a in water with a depth d. This platform receives a force F produced either by waves or through collision with an iceberg. Figure 1 shows the assumed shape of the iceberg, with a circular plan and ellipsoidal elevation. The waterline length is D, the draft is h and the maximum radius is R. Two limit states are considered: 1) the exceedence of a force level F_o, with a corresponding annual exceedence probability p_o; and 2) the sliding of the platform on the seabed. Details of the limit state function G, the intervening random variables and the procedures for the calculation of the wave and collision forces are given by Foschi et al.(1996) and Foschi (1994). These applications consider conditions similar to those of the Hibernia platform to be located in the Grand Banks off the Newfoundland coast of Canada.

In the first case, the limit state function is

$$G(x) = F_o - F_M(x) \qquad (15)$$

where $F_M(x)$ is the maximum force corresponding to the vector of random variables x, including a variable quantifying the model error in the calculation of F_M. In this case, we want to find the value of F_o corresponding to a given annual exceedence probability p_o.

In the second case, the limit state function is

$$G(x, W, \phi) = W \tan(\phi) - F_M(x) \qquad (16)$$

where ϕ is the soil friction angle (a random variable) and W is the weight of the platform, also a random variable. In this case, we want to find mean value of W which is required to obtain a prescribed reliability level as a function of the coefficient of variation of W, reflecting the accuracy with which W can be achieved in practice.

Both problems can be solved directly by the forward method (FORM), calculating the reliability index β corresponding to different levels of F_o or of the mean of the weight W. These results can then be interpolated to find that corresponding to the target reliability.

As an alternative, the inverse procedure described here was applied. In this case, after specifying the target reliability, the values of F_o and of the mean weight W were directly obtained without the interpolation required by the forward procedure. Tables 1 and 2 present the results from both methods.

Table 1: Loads (MN) at specified annual exceedence probabilities

Load Case	Annual Risk	Method	
		Forward FORM	Direct Inverse Algorithm
Wave Load	10^{-2}	1431.79	1430.33
	10^{-4}	2230.63	2228.80
Iceberg Load	10^{-2}	1164.67	1163.82
	10^{-4}	3394.89	3395.28

(Iceberg arrival rate = 1.0 collision/year)

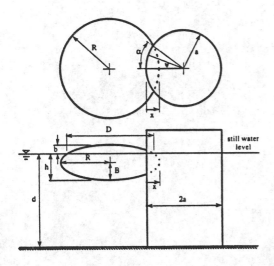

Figure 1. Gravity-based platform and iceberg collision.

Table 2: Mean structure weight for sliding with a 10^{-4} annual failure probability (MN)

Load Case	Coeff. of Variation for W	Method	
		Forward FORM	Direct Inverse Algorithm
Wave Load	0.0	5654.86	5653.20
	0.04	5680.60	5679.53
	0.08	5764.48	5761.28
Iceberg Load	0.0	5997.76	5996.56
	0.04	6018.86	6018.10
	0.08	6086.38	6085.11

(Iceberg arrival rate = 1.0 collision/year)

4 RESULTS AND CONCLUSIONS

Table 1 shows the results for the first case, both for waves and iceberg collision-induced forces, at two annual exceedence probabilities, and obtained by either the forward or the direct inverse method.

The results show that there is agreement between the two methods. However, the inverse procedure offers some advantage as to efficiency and execution time. For example, in the first case, the 10^{-4} iceberg collision force of 3394.89 MN required 6.04 secs. in a Pentium-based 166 Mhz computer when the forward method was utilized. In this case, 50 calculations were done at different F_o levels, increasing this value from 1000 MN to 3500 MN in steps of 50 MN. These results then permitted the interpolation at the desired 10^{-4} exceedence level. For the inverse procedure, the same computer required 2.09 secs. and produced the desired F_o level directly. Apart from some gain in computer time, an advantage of the inverse procedure is that no a-priori guessing of the range for F_o is required, facilitating the implementation of the inverse method within other design software. However, as described, the inverse algorithm requires, for each iteration, the calculation of the basic variables corresponding to a set in the Standard Normal space, a somewhat time-consuming operation. This is needed during the calculation of the gradient of G, which is required in the Standard Normal space, while the G function itself is described in the basic space.

The inverse reliability procedure is thus seen to be an efficient method to estimate directly design parameters corresponding to a target reliability and, in some applications, may provide a cost-saving alternative to the more standard forward approach.

REFERENCES

Der Kiureghian, A., Y. Zhang & C.C. Li. 1994. Inverse Reliability Problem. *J. of Engineering Mechanics, ASCE*, 120: 1154-1159.

Der Kiureghian, A. & P. L. Liu. 1986. Structural Reliability Under Incomplete Probability Information. *J. of Engineering Mechanics, ASCE*, 112: 85-104.

Foschi, R.O., M. Isaacson, N. Allyn & S. Yee. 1996. Combined wave-iceberg loading on offshore-structures. *Canadian Journal of Civil Engineering* 23: 1099-1110.

Foschi, R.O. 1994. Reliability Applications in Iceberg Collision Forces with Offshore Structures. *Proceedings of the Symposium on Risk Analysis,* University of Michigan, Ann Arbor, Michigan, 55-62.

Madsen, H. O., S. Krenk & N.C. Lind. 1986. *Methods of Structural Safety*, Prentice-Hall Inc., Englewood Cliffs, NJ., 44-101.

Winterstein, S.R., T.C. Ude & C.A. Cornell. 1994. Environmental parameters for extreme response: Inverse form with omission factors. *Structural Safety & Reliability,* Schueller, Shinozuka & Yao (eds), Balkema, Rotterdam, 551-557.

Structural Safety and Reliability, Shiraishi, Shinozuka & Wen (eds) © 1998 Balkema, Rotterdam, ISBN 90 5410 978 5

Target levels for reliability-based reassessment of offshore structures

T. Moan
Norwegian University of Science and Technology, Trondheim, Norway

ABSTRACT: The paper deals with approaches for establishing consistent target levels for structural reliability analysis with reference to global ultimate limit states of existing structures. It is emphasised that the target level should depend upon the reliability methodology applied, especially which uncertainties are accounted for, the cause and mode of failure, the consequences of failure as well as the expense and effort to reduce the risk of failure. Therefore, target failure probabilities given in general guidelines for structural reliability analysis should not be applied before they are justified for the relevant application.

1. INTRODUCTION

Adequate structural safety of offshore structures is ensured by design, as well as by load or response monitoring, or inspections; and by taking the necessary actions to reduce loads directly or indirectly by, e.g., removal of marine growth; or by repair, when necessary.

During operation of offshore structures a reassessment of the safety may be necessary, e.g. due to required change of live loads, or occurrence of overload damage, or unexpected subsidence of the seafloor for fixed platforms.

Reliability methods are increasingly used to make optimal decisions regarding safety and life cycle costs of offshore structures (see e.g. Moan, 1994). Such methods deal with the uncertainties associated with design, fabrication and operation, and may be classified as follows:

- classical structural reliability analysis (SRA). The purpose of SRA is to determine the failure probability considering fundamental variability, and natural and man-made uncertainties due to lack of knowledge
- quantitative risk analysis (QRA) which deals with estimation of likelihood of fatalities, environmental damage or loss of assets in a broad sense.

Traditionally, failure probabilities of components and systems calculated by SRA are considered to be notional values. In classical reliability analysis, for example, as applied in connection with electronic components as well as in QRA, component reliability is usually determined by failure data of real components. The corresponding system properties are commonly determined by appropriate systems models. However, SRA is sometimes used to provide input about probabilities of structural failure into quantitative structural risk analysis (QSRA), possibly even QRA (see e.g. Moan, 1994). Care should then be exercised in providing as realistic failure probabilities as possible.

This paper deals with structural reliability methodology applied in connection with ultimate limit states of platforms under permanent, live and environmental loads. The failure probabilities provided by SRA are then compared with the relevant target levels. The remaining part of this paper will be devoted to procedures for establishing consistent target levels for SRA.

2. BASIS FOR ESTABLISHING TARGET LEVELS

2.1 *General*

The target safety level should depend upon the following factors

- method of SRA or QSRA analysis, especially which uncertainties are included
- failure cause and mode
- the possible consequences of failure in terms of risk to life, injury, economic losses and the level of social inconvenience.
- the expense and effort required to reduce the risk

of failure.

The safety level is affected by

- different initiating events (hazards) such as environmental loads, various accidental loads, etc.,. which may lead to
- different structural failure modes of components and system which ultimately may cause
- different consequences such as fatalities, environmental damage and loss of assets.

In principle a target level which reflects all hazards, (e.g. loads) and all failure modes (collapse, fatigue, ...) as well as the different phases (in-place operation and temporary phases associated with fabrication, installation and repair) could be defined with respect to each of the three ultimate consequences and the most severe of them would govern the decisions to be made. If all consequences were measured in economic terms, a single target safety level could be established.

However, in practice it is convenient to treat different hazards, failure modes, consequences and phases separately. A certain portion of the total target failure probability (or risk) may then be allocated to each case, assuming e.g. that the total failure probability (or, risk) is just equal to the sum of the individual probabilities (or, risks). Often the simplification is made to treat the different hazards, failure modes and phases separately. This may be reasonable because rarely do all hazard scenarios and failure modes contribute equally to the total failure probability for a given structure. In particular the principle of establishing target levels for each hazard separately was adopted by NPD for accidental loads; see e.g. Moan (1983). It was also advocated recently by Cornell (1995).

2.2 Method of analysis

As indicated above SRA and QSRA account for different uncertainties, and SRA may in a sense be considered a special case of QSRA. In particular, QSRA accounts for human factors which may lead to accidental loads and abnormal resistance. Even in SRA the various uncertainties may be assessed in different ways as discussed in Section 3.2. Clearly, the corresponding target safety levels will differ.

2.3 Failure cause and mode

The most important distinction of different failure causes is due to whether they are instantaneous or progressive - i.e., take time. Sometimes the notions: failure preceded and not preceded by a warning are used. The most relevant practical examples would be an instantaneous overload failure versus a gradually developing fatigue failure or other deterioration, respectively. The failure development over time may

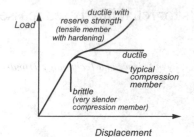

Fig.1   Load-deformation characteristics of components

influence the failure consequences since a warning may initiate escape and evacuation of personnel.

The most important distinction of structural failure modes is between component and system modes. This fact also has a bearing on consequences of failure and is further discussed in Section 2.4.

It is observed that the component characteristic: reserve strength vs. no reserve strength (see Fig. 1a) affects the behaviour of a determinate structural system under static loading. Whether the component behaviour is ideally elasto-plastic (ductile) or brittle (Fig. 1a) does not have any influence on such (static) systems. For a redundant structure, however, the system strength will depend upon the component characteristic (Fig. 1b), as well as the system composition of components. Fig. 2 shows typical behaviour of jackets under broadside static loading . The statically determinate K-braced jacket fails in a "brittle manner" while the X-braced structure is more "ductile" and also yields a reserve strength beyond first member failure.

The implication of the mentioned characteristics of structural behaviour in connection with target safety levels will depend upon whether target reliability measures for components or systems are required. In case of ultimate strength design of components the question of residual strength of the system (or, more precisely conditional system failure probability) overrides the effect of the component characteristics illustrated in Fig. 1. Ultimate systems strength may be discussed with reference to Fig. 2. Obviously, both the ultimate strength and post-ultimate behaviour for the cases S1 and S2 differ. The more ductile post-ultimate behaviour of case S2, would have no impact on the target level if the loading is truly static. However, the ultimate behaviour under dynamic (wave) loading may differ significantly, depending upon the post-ultimate behaviour. This is because the external loads then will be balanced (partly) by inertia forces. Thus, a jacket with ductile overall behaviour may exhibit an ultimate strength which exceeds the static capacity by, say, 10-15%, see e.g. Azadi et al (1995). If the reliability analysis is based on the ultimate strength limit determined by static (pushover) analysis a differentiation in the target level could be made depending upon the mentioned post-ultimate behaviour.

The ultimate limit of a jacket as a whole, is commonly based on load capacity. However, it should be noted that excessive displacement (before ultimate load is reached) may have to be considered as the ultimate limit because of the loads/deformations thereby imposed, e.g., on risers.

2.4 *Failure consequences*

In principle the target safety level is set with respect to consequences in terms of fatalities or human injury, environmental damage and economic losses. However, besides these consequences the platform owner/operator may lose reputation, both towards the public as well as towards the government. This is a consequence which is hard to quantify, but it may affect the potential of future licences for hydrocarbon exploitation and hence the business at large, and is, therefore, sometimes considered part of the economic consequences.

To obtain target levels for SRA and QSRA, the above mentioned consequences need to be related to

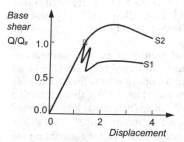

a) Load displacement behaviour. Q_{ff} is base shear at first member failure

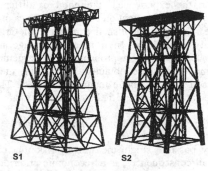

b) Layouts of jackets S1 and S2

Fig. 2   Global behaviour of jacket structures, subject to broadside loading, (Hellan, 1995).

structural failure modes.

Fatalities induced by structural failure of offshore platforms occur primarily when the support of the deck fails or the platform capsizes, i.e. system failure occurs. Failure of individual components (members, joints) commonly does not lead to fatalities. Clearly, the risk of fatalities would depend upon whether platforms will be evacuated before or during the accidental scenario or not. For instance, the likelihood of fatality caused by storm overload in the Gulf of Mexico (GOM) may be less than in the North Sea (NS) because most platforms in GOM can be evacuated in face of a storm (hurricane), while this is not the case in the NS.

Environmental damage may occur due to direct damage to risers/conductors, piping or process equipment; or structural failure. Potential environmental damage depends upon the safety systems (subsea safety valves etc.) available.

Cost-benefit considerations in monetary terms should in principle be applied in connection with setting serviceability limit state criteria. However, the practical implementation may be difficult due to lack of adequate data.

The cost-benefit of increasing the safety would be judged differently depending upon the socio-economic system in the actual geographical region.

2.5 *Reference period for target failure probability*

The target failure probability should be referred to a given time period, i.e., a year or the service time. If the consequence is fatalities, annual failure probabilities are favoured to ensure the same fatality risk of individuals at any time. This principle means that the target level should not depend upon the number of people at risk, i.e., not include risk aversion. This issue is discussed further in Section 3.3. However, in general, as discussed above in Section 2.4 the target level (with respect to environmental damage and economic loss) should depend upon the potential consequences.

3. METHODS FOR ESTABLISHING TARGET LEVELS

3.1 *General*

Various methods may be applied to establish the target level, see e.g. Flint (1976), CIRIA (1977), Faulkner (1983), Jordaan (1988), ISSC (1991), Iwan et al. (1993) and Paté-Cornell (1993). The following approaches will be discussed herein:
a) the implicit safety or risk level implied by existing codes; or in actual structures which are considered acceptable

b) the experienced likelihood of fatalities, environmental damage or property loss associated with operations which are considered acceptable
c) cost-benefit criteria

These methods are first briefly described in general. Then, method a) is pursued to establish target level for existing structures.

3.2 Target level based on the safety level implied by existing codes

In this case the target level is commonly taken to be the probability of structural failure implied by given codes or guidelines which are judged to be acceptable. To achieve a representative target level, several cases of structural geometries, material properties and load conditions should be considered. The implied failure probability will therefore vary and the target level should be based on the mean value or some other measure of the implied failure probability. Obviously, if e.g. a relaxation of safety level is desirable, a higher value than the mean is selected. Different levels may be used depending upon the mode of failure, consequences of failure etc. In particular it is necessary to make a distinction between target level for structural components and system. If a single target value for structural design is applied, the target value could be a weighted mean, with a weight factor which depends upon the consequence of failure for the different components considered.

This approach has been applied in calibration of ultimate limit state criteria for structures. See e.g. Fjeld (1977), Moses (1986-87) , Lloyd and Karsan (1988), Moan (1988) and Jordaan and Maes (1991).

When calculating the failure probability implied by existing codes, the results obviously depend upon the uncertainty measures applied. It is noted in this connection that different uncertainty measures for e.g. wave height, current velocity, hydrodynamic loads as well as resistances have been applied even in various authoritative code calibration studies for marine structures (Moan, 1995).

However, if the same probabilistic models are applied when determining the implied failure probability in an existing code (target value) as used when calculating the inherent failure probability in a new code or a given structure, the sensitivity of the partial safety factors to the mentioned model will be limited. This consistency is therefore crucial. However, it is another matter that the magnitude of uncertainties at the time when the existing code was established, may be different from the uncertainties at the time of application of the target level, say in a reassessment, due to information acquired during fabrication and operation. Moreover, it is important that the reliability-based design is consistent with well-established design practice for commonly occurring cases. Unfortunately, general guidance in NKB (1978, 1987) and other sources is not consistent with reliability measures quantified for different codes for various types of offshore structures (Moan, 1995), and can in general not be recommended for use.

3.3 Target level based on accident experiences

In structural risk assessment the probability of fatalities, pollution and property loss is estimated, and the target level should in principle be referred to each of these consequences. The focus has been on fatalities and the reference value is the annual death rate in the society, which is of the order $p_d = 10^{-4}$ (Flint 1976; Jordaan and Maes 1991). Paté-Cornell (1993) suggests 10^{-3} to 10^{-4} to be an upper bound of acceptable fatality rate. The target structural failure rate, p_{FT} based on death rate may be taken to be

$$p_{FT} = \frac{1}{f(n_r)} K_s \cdot 10^{-4} \qquad (3.1)$$

where K_s is a social criterion factor which should be related to the extent to which the activities associated with the structure is hazardous and voluntary (Flint, 1976). $f(n_r)$ is a risk aversion function of the total number of people, n_r, at risk. $f(n_r)$ has e.g. been proposed to be $f(n_r) = n_r$ (Flint 1976) and $f(n_r) = n_r^{1/2}$ (e.g. Allen 1981). Obviously, if the concern is individual fatality rate, $f(n_r)$ should be set equal to 1.0.

A more detailed picture of the accident rate in offshore operations is displayed in Moan (1997), by considering all kinds of accidents for world-wide operations. It can be inferred from these data that the probability of total (property) loss of fixed platforms world-wide is about $4 \cdot 10^{-4}$. These data may also be analysed to establish the accident rate in different geographical regions. The likelihood of fatalities and environmental damage are also given. Based on the experienced likelihood of different consequences a judgement on acceptable values may be made. Having established a measure of target probability of fatalities, environmental damage and property loss, the target probability for structural failure modes may be obtained by relating these failure modes to the above mentioned targets. This principle is further exemplified by Moan (1997).

3.4 Target level based on economic criteria

The only possible single measure of risk that can include all consequences, is an economic criterion. In this case the cost of failure should, in principle, include that associated with:

• repair or replacement of the facility

- delay in operation (offhire costs)
- pollution damage (including long-term effects)
- fatalities and injury

The controversial issue is obviously to put value on life, but it may be based on *compensation* obtained in courts for loss of life expectancy, see e.g. Jordaan (1988). The economic consideration may then be based on

- cost optimisation, see e.g. CIRIA (1977)
- risk-weighted cash-flow, see e.g. Stahl and Lloyd (1995)

Herein, only the implication of a cost optimisation shall be briefly illustrated.

The initial cost is written as (CIRIA, 1977)

$$C_i = a - b \log_{10} \overline{p} \qquad (3.2)$$

where a and b are constants. Should the structure fail, then the cost (C_f) will be

$$C_f = (C_i + d + e + Kn_L) \cdot pvf \qquad (3.3)$$

where C_i represents the cost of replacement, d is the cost of downtime (lost production), e is the cost of environmental damage, n_L is the number of lives lost and K is the cost associated with a human life. The cost, e of environmental damage will depend upon the reliability of the Down hole safety valve etc., given the failure of the system above the seabed. pvf is a present value function which discounts the future risk costs to present values and depends upon the discount rate and the service period considered.

The failure probability, $\overline{p} = p_{FT}$ for the service period that minimises the expected costs, $E(C) = C_i + \overline{p} C_f$, is approximately

$$p_{FT} \cong \frac{b}{2.3[a + d + e + Kn_L + \lambda \cdot b] \cdot pvf} \qquad (3.4)$$

where λ is a factor which is of the order of $-\log_{10} p_{FT}$.

The annual target failure probability in a service life of T_s years will be $p_{FT} / (\alpha \cdot T_s)$; where the factor α is a function of dependence of failure in each year, and will be $\alpha = 1$ if the annual failure events are independent.

It is noted that if only the costs associated with fatalities are included and n_L is expressed as $n_L = c \cdot n_r$ it is seen that p_{FT} is inversely proportional to n_r as proposed by Flint (1976) and CIRIA (1977).

The cost-benefit analysis which is outlined above, can be refined by including loss of reputation, the expected costs of injuries, limited structural damages - which may imply shutdown, etc.

The cost-benefit analysis as indicated above, may be criticised on the following grounds:

- the approach is sensitive to the method in which the failure probability p_F is estimated, and the fact that p_F should be "real" probabilities and not notional values
- the optimum safety should be established considering the total system and all hazards, including accidental events - and not be limited to the load bearing structure and "normal" functional and environmental hazards.
- the approach is sensitive to the data on marginal cost of increasing the safety level as well as the expected costs of pollution and loss of production.

It is felt that the cost-benefit analysis could be applied to determine target safety levels, especially when failure only implies economic losses. Economic risks which only affect the (oil) company can certainly be dealt with by the company. If potential losses affect the national economy, the authorities would decide about the acceptable risk level in the same way as for risks of life and environmental damage.

Cost-benefit analysis is also considered useful to support decisions regarding the relative safety of new versus existing structures, as illustrated in Section 4.

4. TARGET LEVEL FOR REASSESSMENT OF EXISTING STRUCTURES

4.1 *General*

In this section the target safety level for ultimate strength of existing jacket platforms under sea loads is addressed.

Adequate safety of existing structures may be demonstrated by using semi-probabilistic design procedures similar to those applied during design of new structures, for instance based on component ultimate limit states and a linear global analysis to obtain load effects. More realistic global (system) failure modes of the structure, however, are desirable because significant consequences such as fatalities, are primarily caused by global failure. Moreover recent developments of efficient methods of structural analysis which account for large deflections and plasticity facilitate systems analyses. Such methods are applied in reassessments when the conventional design methods fail to demonstrate adequate safety.

A particular feature of offshore structures is that the calculation of sea loads critically depends upon whether the wave crest does or does not reach the deck. For this reason the use of a semi-probabilitistic design approach based on a load factor on, say, the 100 years load will be inconsistent if the wave height (corresponding to the design point of the reliability analyses) exceeds the lower deck level. This is because the wave load pattern for the 100 year condition and design point are significantly different. In such circumstances probabilistic approaches have proven to be especially attractive.

The relevant target level is then established by

- using the implicit component reliability in the relevant design code for new structures as a reference failure probability
- requiring that the system reliability (failure prob.) is higher (lower) than that for components
- relaxing the target reliability thus established for new structures, to account for the economic and social reasons for accepting increased failure probability for existing structures.

This approach is detailed in the following.

4.2 Implied probability of component failure according to ULS criteria

The component probability of failure, $p_{F,C}$ inherent in the relevant design code is obtained by using relevant measures of uncertainty and reliability methodology - i.e. consistent with the approach to be used to demonstrate compliance with the target level. The emphasis should be placed on primary components in the relevant type of structure and foundation.

Previous studies of implied annual failure probability implied by codes for offshore structures are reviewed by Moan (1995). The values for jackets typically vary in the range $2 \cdot 10^{-3}$ to 10^{-5}, depending on the design code formulation, uncertainty measures and reliability methodology which is applied.

4.3 System versus component reliability

The reliability measure obtained in Section 4.2 for components, needs to be adjusted by a factor α_{cs} to serve as a target level for global failure.

Offshore codes do not have explicit requirements to the systems ultimate strength under wave loads. In principle the target level could therefore be taken to be the reliability level implied by a statically determinate jacket designed to perfectly fulfil design criteria for in-place condition, which is a permissible concept.

However, jackets and other structures may have an ultimate strength which exceeds the load which corresponds to γ times the reference load that gives first component failure. This reserve capacity may be explicit or implicit overdesign, e.g. by using conservative methods for load and resistance calculation, by using materials with reserve strength, and the fact that pre service loads and requirements for buoyancy or space for piles in legs may increase member sizes (of platform legs) beyond what are

required for in-service strength. Such reserve strength is most likely to be present in a system with "redundant" components. For six representative jackets on the Norwegian Continental Shelf Stewart, et al (1993) found that first member failure for the most critical wave direction occurred at a load which was 1.35 to 2.1 times the factored 100 year environmental load for this wave direction (when using a total safety factor of 1.5 according to NPD). It is noted that this «overdesign factor» varies significantly since it is not implied by consistent design requirement. Moreover, it is observed (Stewart, et al, 1993) that the systems collapse load is only slightly larger than the load causing first member failure, implying that the «reserve strength» only to a very limited extent is facilitated by nonlinear load redistribution.

Also in other structural concepts there is normally a small reserve capacity beyond «the component limit state». The hull girder of a production ship possesses a reserve strength beyond first component failure of typically 10-15% for a reasonably well balanced longitudinal strength design (Moan 1988). Cylindrical prestressed concrete monotowers, are also expected to have a reserve ultimate strength beyond the design limit state; at most up to 1.27 (in bending). Other, more complex framed structures may have higher system reserve capacity.

On this background it is felt reasonable to establish a basic target level based on a system strength which is 1.15 times the load which causes first component failure in a statically determinate system. This strength ratio corresponds to an increase of the safety index by 0.3-0.4 units or a target probability for the system which is $\alpha_{cs} = 1/3 - 1/5$ of the component level, for typical reliability levels.

The procedure for setting target level for overall system failure could be refined by accounting for the post-ultimate behaviour as mentioned in Section 2.3.

4.4 Old versus new structure

Up to now reference has been made to new designs. In theory the target level associated with individual fatalities and environmental damage should apply indifferently to old and new facilities. Only the cost-benefit analysis of given safety measures should be different and also reflect the remaining life of the facility. When using the cost-optimisation approach in Section 3.4 it should be noted that the initial costs (b) of reducing the failure probability by a factor of 10 for an existing structure may be several times the costs (b) for a new structure. Eq. (3.4) accordingly implies a probability for existing structures which is a factor α_{CB} times that for new ones.

In practice, however, even the individual risk

criteria (both for workers on-site and for the public off-site) are typically relaxed for existing plants, essentially for economic reasons; upgrading old platforms to reach the basic required levels of individual safety would be too costly. The only alternatives may then be to close the facility, in which case the risk may simply be displaced. The energy (oil and gas) previously produced at the closed facility will be produced elsewhere but not without risks to others. One may also argue that closing a facility, if it increases unemployment, may create a higher risk to life for the fired workers than the occupational risk of working in the facility. Therefore, for a variety of economic and social reasons, there seems to be an agreement that it is appropriate to consider lowering the safety standards related to individual risks for older plants. See Paté-Cornell (1993) for a more detailed expose.

Bea (1993) favours cost analysis to set target levels for existing offshore structures. This approach implies a willingness to accept lower reliabilities for old systems compared to new ones. Iwan, et al. (1993) proposed a target level based on separate considerations of the fatality rate and environmental damage, and arrive at a different target reliability level. However, this also implies slightly lower target reliabilities for existing compared to new platforms.

API (1994) proposes a failure probability which is two times higher for existing than for new designs. The deterministic approach of API for reassessment of platforms is transformed into reliability terms by Krieger et al. (1994).

4.5 Concluding remarks

The desired target level may be expressed by

$$p_{FT} = p_{F,C} \cdot \alpha_{CS} \cdot \alpha_{CB} \qquad (4.1)$$

where $p_{F,C}, \alpha_{CS}$ and α_{CB} are discussed in Sections 4.2, 4.3 and 4.4, respectively.

For jacket platforms within the North Sea regulatory regime the target level could be obtained as follows: α_{CS} is assumed to be 1/3. When consequences primarily involve economic loss: α_{CB} = 4 to 5, totally implying a p_{FT} which is about 2 times that of components of new structures. When fatalities or significant environmental damage may result: α_{CB} = 1 to 2, implying a p_{FT} which is 1/2 of the reference component failure probability.

The resulting target level even for existing, manned platforms, would still represent a relaxation of current criteria used for design of new structures. This is because the global strength analysis methodology applied normally will reveal a reserve strength of more than 15% beyond the value predicted by conventional design analysis methods.

5. CONCLUSIONS

Since the applied structural reliability approach varies, caution should be exercised in using general target values, i.e., without justification of their consistency with the methodology applied in the reliability analysis.

It is proposed to establish the target probability for global failure of existing structures based on the target value for components modified by two multiplicative factors α_{CS} and α_{CB}, described below.

The target level for components obtained as the failure probability implied by acceptable codes and should be calculated using the same methodology as would later be used to determine failure probabilities that should comply with the target value.

The first modification α_{CB} is to transform the target failure probability level for components to that for the system. The second factor, α_{CB} is a cost-benefit factor to possibly permit the target value for an existing structural system to be higher than that for a new one. The actual magnitude of modification factors would depend upon the regulatory regime.

REFERENCES

Allen, D.E.. 1981. Criteria for Design Safety Factors and Quality Assurance Expenditure, *Proc. ICOSSAR*, T. Moan et al (eds), Amsterdam: Elsevier.

API RP2A.WSD. 1994. Sect. 17.0, Draft, Dallas:American Petroleum Institute.

Azadi, M.R.E., Moan, T. and Amdahl, J. 1995. Dynamic Effects on the Performance of Steel Offshore Platforms in Extreme Waves. *Proc. EUROSTEEL 1995.* A.N. Kounadis (ed). Rotterdam: Balkema.

Bea, R.G. 1993. Reliability-based Requalification Criteria for Offshore Platforms. *Proc. 12th OMAE.* Vol. II: 351-361. New York: ASME.

CIRIA. 1977. Rationalisation of Safety and Serviceability Factors in Structural Codes. London: CIRIA(Construction Industry Research and Information Association) Report 63.

Cornell, C.A. 1995. Structural Reliability - Some contributions to Offshore Technology, *Proc. 27th OTC*; 535-542, OTC 7753. Houston: Offshore Technology Conf.

DNV. 1995. Guidelines for Offshore Structural Reliability Analysis - General. Final Draft. Report No. 95-2018, Oslo: Det Norske Veritas.

Faulkner, D. 1983. On Selecting a Target Reliability for Deep Water Tension Leg Platforms. *Proc. 11th IFIP Conf. on System Modelling and Optimization.* Copenhagen: IFIP. Vol. 2: 459-472, OTC 3027. Houston: Offshore Technology Conf.

Fjeld, S. 1977. Reliability of Offshore Structures. *Proc. 9th OTC*: Vol. 2: 459-472, OTC 3027. Houston: Offshore Technology Conf.

Flint, A.R. 1976. Design Objectives for Offshore Structures in Relation to Social Criteria. *Proc. BOSS Conf.*. Trondheim: Tapir.

Hellan, Ø. 1995. Nonlinear Pushover and Cyclic Analysis in Ultimate Limit State Design and Reassessment of Tubular Steel Offshore Structures. Dr.ing. diss., MTA-report 1995: 108, Trondheim, Dept. Marine Technology, Norwegian Inst. of Technology

Iwan, W.D. et al. 1993. A Reliability-based Approach to Seismic Reassessment of Offshore Platforms. *Proc. ICOSSAR*, Structural Safety and Reliability. G.I. Schüller, M. Shinozuka and J.T.P. Yao (eds). Rotterdam: Balkema.

Jordaan, I. 1988. Safety Levels Implied in Offshore Structural Codes: Application to CSA Program for Offshore Structures. Report, Memorial Univ. of Newfoundland, St. John's. Prepared for the USA Program for Fixed Offshore Structures.

Jordaan, I.J. & M.A. Maes. 1991. Rationale for Load Specifications and Load Factors in the New CSA Code for Fixed Offshore Structures. *C.J. Civil Engng*. 18(3): 454:464.

Krieger, W.F. et al. 1994. Process for Assessment of Existing Platforms to Determine their Fitness for Purpose. *Proc. 26th OTC*: OTC 7482. Houston: Offshore Technology Conference.

Lloyd, J.R. & D.I. Karsan. 1988. Development of a Reliability-based Alternative to API RP2A. *Proc. 20th OTC:* Vol. 4: 593-600, OTC 5882. Houston: Offshore Technology Conf.

Moan, T. 1983. Safety of Offshore Structures. *Proc. 4th ICASP*: 41-85. Bologna: Pitagora Editrice.

Moan, T. 1988. The Inherent Safety of Structures designed according to the NPD Regulations. Report No. STF71 F88043. Trondheim: Div. Structural Engineering, SINTEF.

Moan, T. et al. 1991. Report of ISSC Committee IV.1. Design Philosophy. *Proc. 11th ISSC*, Wuxi (1991).

Moan, T. 1994. Reliability and Risk Analysis for Design and Operations Planning of Offshore Structures. *Proc. ICOSSAR, Structural Safety and Reliability*. G.I. Schüller, M. Shinozuka and J.T. P. Yao (eds). Rotterdam: Balkema.

Moan, T. 1995. Safety Level Across Different Types of Structural Forms and Materials - Implicit in Codes for Offshore Structures. Report STF 70 A95210 Trondheim: SINTEF. Prepared for ISO/TC250/SC7.

Moan, T. 1997. Target Levels for Structural Reliability and Risk Analysis of Offshore Structures, in *Risk and Reliability in Marine Technology*, C.Guedes Soares (ed). Rotterdam, Balkema.

Moses, F. 1986. Load and Resistance Factor Design-Recommended Practice for Approval. Final Report, API PRAC 86-22. Dallas: API.

Moses, F. 1987. Load and Resistance Factor Design-Recalibration LRFD Draft Report. API PRAC 87-22. Dallas: API.

NKB 1978, 1987. Recommendations for Loading and Safety Regulations for Structural Design. Report No. 36, 55E. Copenhagen: The Nordic Committee on Building Regulations.

NPD 1992. Regulations Concerning Loadbearing Structures in the Petroleum Activity. Stavanger: Norwegian Petroleum Directorate.

Paté-Cornell, M.E. 1993. Risk Management for Existing Energy Facilities: A Global Approach to Numerical Safety Goals, in *Aging of Energy Production and Distribution Systems*. Applied Mechanics Reviews: Vol. 46, No. 5. New York: ASME.

Stahl, B. and Lloyd, J. 1995. Debate on the Application of Structural Reliability Techniques for Offshore Structural Engineering. London: The Institution of Structural Engineers.

Stewart, G., Moan, T., Amdahl, J. and Eide, O.I. 1993. Nonlinear Re-assessment of Jacket Structures under Extreme Storm Cyclic Loading. Part I - Philosophy and Acceptance Criteria. *Proc. 12th OMAE Conf.*: 491-502 S.K. Chakrabati et al (eds). New York: ASME.

Structural Safety and Reliability, Shiraishi, Shinozuka & Wen (eds) © 1998 Balkema, Rotterdam, ISBN 90 5410 978 5

The role of human and organisational factors (HOF) in the fabrication, installation and modification (FIM) phase of offshore facilities

Ove T. Gudmestad & Wenche K. Rettedal – *Statoil, Stavanger, Norway*

Rachel Gordon – *The Robert Gordon University, Aberdeen, Scotland*

Linda Bellamy – *Save, Apeldoorn, Netherlands*

Bernhard Stahl – *Amoco Corporation, Houston, Tex., USA*

ABSTRACT

Most failures in *Offshore Fabrication, Installation and Modification Phases* can ultimately be attributed to human factors and most failures are not mechanically related as is the general perception of the public. How and to what extent organisational factors influence the human factors are at present not very well understood, but the safety culture and the qualifications of the organisation are prime factors influencing human factors.

This paper will assess the benefit of integrating Human and Organisational Factors (HOF) for analysis of the Fabrication, Installation and Modification (FIM) phases of Offshore Facilities. This will be done by considering the influence of human factors and organisational aspects on human errors and accidents. The role of the individual worker, training of employees, influence of the design phase and specifics of the FIM phases will be discussed.

INTRODUCTION

The offshore oil industry is a young industry. It faces unique technical challenges in a hostile offshore environment. It encompasses large international operators, government owned companies and smaller regional companies. All face the challenge of maintaining and improving safety in an ever changing industrial environment.

Many offshore projects are unique in their size and complexity and as the industry moves to deeper waters, the complexity previously encountered in the design and *fabrication* phases continues into the *installation* phase of an offshore facility. Furthermore, as the industry has matured, several of the offshore facilities are in need of considerable *maintenance* and modification to continue production. However, when the costs of maintenance exceed the income from production, funding for necessary maintenance might be deferred at the expense of reduced safety. On the other hand, an extensive maintenance or modification programme could involve a safety risk, and a "cost-benefit" safety analysis might document the safety effectiveness of a lower maintenance level not involving any modification work. It should be noted that the word "safety" in the context of this paper covers safety with respect to personnel and assets as well as external environmental impacts.

Throughout all activities in the fabrication, installation and modification (FIM) phases of an offshore facility, there is a considerable number of personnel involved, from company management to the persons carrying out the manual work. The behaviour of the personnel is thus the most important factor with respect to the safety in the FIM phases, and the "human factor element" in these phases will be thoroughly reviewed in this paper. Of considerable importance in this respect is the link between the organisation, in particular its safety culture, and the individuals (see also Bea, et al., 1996 and Bea and Roberts, 1995).

For fabrication, installation and modification of offshore facilities there are certain specific problems which distinguish offshore projects from onshore projects, such as the large amount of work being carried out in confined areas, the uniqueness of working in the marine environment, and many complex interfaces and differences in specifications from operator to operator.

Furthermore, a call for increased effectiveness and productivity, cost reduction in all phases and new management principles rewarding outsourcing and use of contractors rather than company personnel influence the personnel involved in the FIM phases. Further insight into how safety can be maintained under such climate represents valuable knowledge.

It should be noted that the paper contains a long list of important factors. The key point is that all these factors ultimately affect the decision making, whether of a front line operator or a manager. See Fig. 1 where the control and monitoring loop for decision making is presented.

DEFINITIONS

The terms *"human factors"* and *"human errors"* are often interchanged in the offshore oil industry. They are often used interchangeably as general terms referring to the cause of an accident related to people as opposed to a technical fault. The traditional definition of *"human factors"* is the scientific study of the interaction between man and machine. This definition has been extended in recent years to encompass the effects which individual groups and organisational factors have on safety (Wilpert, 1995). Human *errors* have been defined by Rasmussen (1993) as *"human acts which are judged by somebody to deviate from some kind of reference act ... they are subjective and they vary with time"*. These are specific acts which can cause an accident (see Fig. 2).

Human errors and human factors are usually studied separately. The human factors could, however, be regarded as those factors which describe the underlying causes and the human errors as the specific acts which are caused by the human factors and are seen as the immediate cause of the accident. The diagram (Fig. 2) indicates that the human factors (which includes organisational, group and individual factors) cause the human errors which cause the accident. This paper particularly refers to the human and organizational factors (HOF) which cause human errors leading to accidents.

ORGANISATIONAL ASPECTS, SAFETY CULTURE AND SAFETY CLIMATE

Definition of Safety Culture/Climate
    Safety Culture can be defined in terms of underlying belief systems about safety which are partly determined by group norms and regulatory frameworks. As defined by ACSNI (1993), safety culture is "the product of individual and group values, attitudes, perceptions, competencies and patterns of behaviour that determine commitment to and the style and proficiency of an organisation's health and safety management. Organisations with a positive safety culture are characterised by

communications founded on mutual trust, by shared perceptions of the importance of safety and by the efficiency of preventative measures".

Safety Climate refers to the perceptions of the current environment or prevailing conditions which impact upon safety. The safety climate of an installation is a product of the combined attitudes of the workforce. This is more easily measured than safety culture.

Both safety culture and safety climate can be related to the physical environment in which the system operates, the work environment and features of the work/management system. The safety culture will underpin and impact upon the safety climate. It has been postulated that without a good organisational safety climate to which everyone contributes, it is inconceivable that any organisation has a safe working environment (Donald & Canter, 1993).

Factors Affecting Organisational Safety Culture
    Factors found to be related to safety culture are management's commitment to safety, safety training, open communication, stable workforce and positive safety promotion policy (Donald & Canter, 1993). In addition, the following factors have been found to discriminate between companies in terms of safety climate: importance of safety training, effects of workplace, status of safety committee, status of safety officer, effect of safe conduct on promotion, level of risk at the workplace, management's attitude towards safety and effect of safe conduct on social status (Zohar, 1980).

Production versus safety: The pressure for production is a drive from the top level of the corporation, through the management levels onto the supervisor and finally directed to the individual at the front line. Although it is widely recognised that ignoring safety can be more costly than giving it attention, it is often the case that production is the main focus. With pressure from the top, production management are driven to stay on schedule even if it could be detrimental to safety. For example, maintenance work may be delayed or work may be continued under severe weather conditions.

Decisions of whether to continue work in bad weather conditions or to have the maintenance work completed must be left up to competent operators at the site. This gives them the responsibility to assess the situation using their knowledge and experience However, it does leave room for errors of judgement (Paté-Cornell, 1990).

The pressure to reduce production costs leads to minimum costs for design, fabrication, installation and modification while long term effects are increased accidental rates and eventually higher costs.

Resource constraints are unavoidable parts of industrial life and the engineers and other workers who are subjected to these constraints must try to satisfy them. This may be done by taking short cuts without having clear ideas of the influence on the safety. Budget constraints, for example, in the design and verification phases, may lead to inaccurate design which may cause a catastrophic collapse in the FIM phases (Paté-Cornell and Rettedal, 1996).

Incentive effects: People are influenced by the type of reward structures, thus it is important that the incentives encourage safe working practices. The safety culture of an organisation can in part be shaped through incentives. However, if incentives are given to complete short term production figures, safety could be threatened.

Time pressures: Production goals and project budgets set by Corporate Management can be stimulating and motivating, but if the pressure is too much, people tend to cut corners in order to complete the goals in time. In order to cut time, people will carry out more than one task at a time, which can be managed only if the tasks are routine and there are few uncertainties. Generally, time pressure increases the probability of errors and decreases the chances that the errors are detected (Paté-Cornell, 1990). To avoid these problems, management must clearly indicate that safety cannot be compromised under any circumstances.

Organisational learning: Organisations need systems by which they can analyse information about past mistakes and positive experiences in order to gradually reconcile past actions with actual experience. It is necessary to record the human and organisational factors which contribute to the cause of accidents as well as near misses to improve the understanding of how to control potential hazards. Paté-Cornell (1990) proposed that the following items be considered for organisations to improve their statistics:

- ensuring the effectiveness of learning mechanism
- maintaining corporate memory and updating databases
- using "probability" in management processes to improve communication/decision making
- adjusting scheduling procedures to include uncertainties/delays
- improving feedback to make managers more aware of consequences of their goals
- having project engineers check that the technical changes don't compromise system safety

New Trends in the Organisation of the FIM Phases of Offshore Facilities

Present trends in the organisation of FIM phases of an offshore facility encompass among others:

- further use of new concepts like production ships and use of maritime regulations
- further emphasis on economical constraints and time pressure whereby "fast track" projects are the key to successful project economy with early oil production as the result
- use of functional rather than prescriptive requirements
- outsourcing, whereby consultants and sub-contractors take over work previously carried out by operators and main contractors
- new contract strategies, e.g., partnering, involving close working relations in integrated teams where the role of Company and Contractor becomes less distinct
- further use of lump sum contracts where contractors take increased financial risks.
- transfer of "old" leases to smaller operators with limited technology base
- further use of smaller contractors (in particular in the modification phase) who may not demonstrate the same commitment to safety as the larger and more experienced contractors
- reduced independent verification work and spot checks

MANAGEMENT ASPECTS

For a discussion of the effect of management factors on human behaviour and how the effect can be modelled in risk analysis, see Murph and Paté-Cornell, 1996.

Management's commitment to safety for personnel

In order to have a positive safety culture, management needs to be committed to safety. For workers to believe that management is committed to safety, the following areas need to be addressed:

Safety equipment: Basic safety equipment (such as gloves) must not be ignored. The role of a tidy working environment to avoid, for example, tripping hazards would also be emphasised.

Contradictory safety standards: It is important for management to keep consistent safety standards even when work load increases in order to show their commitment to safety.

Accident Reporting: The focus must never be put on low accident statistics but on the welfare of the work force. Further to accident reporting, near miss reporting should also be urged.

Role of Safety Officer: If the safety officers are given credibility and authority from management to

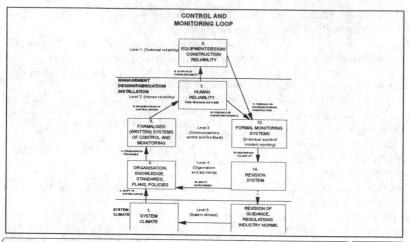

Fig. I CONTROL AND MONITORING LOOP
(Adapted from the AVRIM2 Project, Ministre van Sociale Zaken en Verkgelegenheid, The Netherlands)

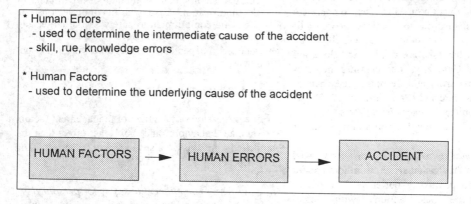

* Human Errors
 - used to determine the intermediate cause of the accident
 - skill, rue, knowledge errors

* Human Factors
 - used to determine the underlying cause of the accident

Fig. 2 Relationship between Human Errors & Human Factors

oversee safety, they are more likely to aid in the improvement of the project's safety.

Management Style: Humanistic approach to management, which focuses on personal and work problems, has been found to be a more effective method. Training in better people-management skills is required.

Openness of management: Senior management is often seen as unapproachable and distant by workers.

Loyalty: The loyalty of management to the workers is determined in numerous ways: job security, wages/salary, pension scheme, shift rotations, holidays, Christmas/New Year holidays, offshore allowances, helicopter flights, schedules, money allocated to catering and accommodation environment.

Regular appearances of management on shop floor: As the workload and workforce increases, it is more difficult for management to make regular appearances to all work sites although such appearances increase the morale of the work force (Peters, 1989). For aspects related to the management's role, see also Paté-Cornell and Bea, 1992.

Communication

Errors can occur from problems in communication, where the necessary information has not been gathered, and where communication channels don't exist or don't function. This may be because of unreliable procedures, failure of the communication equipment, lack of informal communications, or deliberate retention of information (Paté-Cornell, 1990).

Problems of information flow: It is a common problem that redundant or irrelevant information is provided, and that relevant information is mis-represented or ignored (Paté-Cornell, 1990). Organisational boundaries are often communication barriers; an example may be the communication between designers and construction personnel.

Personnel: High turnover of staff is considered a safety risk, as personnel may not have the necessary level of understanding of the system. Selection of personnel is in this respect very important.

Supervisor's Role

The issues: The supervisor has been identified as a key individual in industrial safety. As early as in 1931 Henrick stated: *"The supervisor or foreman is the key man in industrial accident prevention. His application of the art of supervision ... is the factor of greatest influence in accident prevention".* The main *Supervisory skills* required to encourage safe working include: instructing, guiding, coaching, developing workers' talents & abilities, praise for working safely and setting a good example. The supervisor provides in-house quality control of the worksite and the jobs performed by the group he manages.

Methods of *Communication* used by supervisors include, e.g.: tool box talks, site visits, job assignments & clear directions.

- *Tool box talks* are an important part of the job which involve discussing the best methods of carrying out the task and problems that could arise and how they should be solved.
- *Worksite visits:* Infrequent worksite visits often means that the supervisor has poor information about the work that has been carried out, leading to handovers which bear little or no resemblance to the actual worksite or amount of work which had been completed.
- *Relationship with workers:* When workers get on better together, they are more likely to be effective/efficient.

Responsibilities: Supervisors need to be given the freedom to make decisions as to whether a job should go ahead as they are the ones who know the details surrounding the job.

Planning: There is a need to give supervisors time to plan their work more carefully in order to reduce time pressure.

Risk communication: The supervisor should communicate the real risk picture to the field workers by involving everybody in education programmes related to risk perception and assessment of risk avoidance.

Focus on productivity: The focus needs to be put on safety as well as productivity.

Temporary promotion: Individuals temporarily promoted to a position of supervision are less likely to have supervisory experience which may lead to the job being poorly supervised. Since these individuals have taken on new responsibilities, some activities which they did prior to their promotion may furthermore no longer be performed. In addition, a lack of confidence in their own decision-making abilities due to being recently promoted without much training may cause supervisors to be more reluctant to stand up to senior management or to make their own decisions.

Working Environment

Housekeeping: Working in a poorly kept environment is bound to lead to more accidents (Gordon, 1996). This is particularly true in the case of slips, trips and falls, since poor housekeeping increases the workforce's exposure to slipping and tripping hazards. An increase in the number of general assistants would help clean up the site. Furthermore, it should be noted that good housekeeping is a visible indication of rule enforcement. This is why some safety management auditors look to housekeeping.

Density of workers: During FIM phases there are often too many workers located in the same area. As every job is a priority, personnel often are expected to work around each other, in confined spaces with other workers.

Procedures: In the situation where procedures cannot be followed in order to complete the job, the use of procedures in general can be undermined.

THE ROLE OF THE INDIVIDUAL WORKER

Human Errors made by individuals at the "sharp-end" (i.e., those who actually carry out the task) are usually observed as the initial cause of the accident. However, these errors usually have underlying causes, such as lack of training, which need to be addressed. When considering possible problems with persons, the following aspects should be looked into:

- *The capability of the employee:* in terms of their knowledge and skills, experience, training and qualifications to carry out their job.

- *Job Security & Morale*
  Morale: It seems that there could be a link between low morale and an increase in the number of accidents; furthermore, if you highlight the positive, morale will generally be higher.
  Job security: Workers who feel insecure about keeping their job may try and obtain some control in their situation to try and secure their job by becoming more productive, which may compromise their own safety (e.g., by cutting corners). In addition, job insecurity can lead to stress (see below) and low morale.
- *Aspects of their job:* The jobs may include the following items which can be strongly influenced by supervisors/management:
  Level of responsibility: workers should be given a suitable level of responsibility for making decisions of routine operations.
  Clarity of the job: Unclear job directions lead to unsafe work.
  Time pressure: Pressure encourages workers to save time/effort by taking short cuts.
  Co-worker support: Workers are more likely to work effectively if they get along with each other and are encouraging each other to continue to work safely.
  Motivation in the job: Appropriate peer pressure can lead to people acting/working more safely.
  Workload: If the workload is increased, this can lead to workers cutting corners and a reduction in safety monitoring. Management need to highlight the cost of accidents and convince workers that effective performance is important, rather than hasty performance.
  Length of job: When workers during the FIM phases know that it is a short term job and that they are not going to be out there for long, workers pay less attention and care less about the work environment.
- *Stress:* Fatigue, personal problems, frustration, monotony, exposure to hazards and extreme temperature affect risk perceptions.

INFLUENCE OF THE DESIGN PHASE ON THE FIM PHASES

The design phase (including conceptual and detailed design) represents the phase where the decisions about the concept and detailed arrangement are being taken. Thus, an undetected error in the design phase (Ferguson, 1993) might propagate into large errors in the FIM phases of the offshore facility. Risk analysis of the design phase could be carried out (Trbojevic et al., 1996), but in most cases careful independent verification will be sufficient (Paté-Cornell, 1990). In this respect, review routines as well as systems and technical audits carried out by the operator will be helpful.

Safety for workers throughout all subsequent phases should furthermore be designed into the facilities. Of particular importance for later phases is the incorporation in the design phase of "fabrication friendliness" and "fabrication efficiency" through fabrication studies (as well as ergonometric studies related to the operations of the facilities) and constructability reviews. A "fabrication friendly" concept can be fabricated without delay more so than a facility which is very difficult to fabricate.

Furthermore, the facilities must be designed such that the installation phase represents minimum risk to personnel involved. For example, the weather criteria for carrying out the different tasks in the installation phase should be decided in the design phase of the project. This will also make it possible to determine a realistic schedule for the installation phase (Brabazon, et al., 1996).

In the design phase, it is furthermore necessary to assess the future modification needs of the facilities in order to make the facilities easy to maintain and modify. If possible, large equipment should be easy to exchange for later modifications of the platform. Similarly, feedback from fabricators, operators and maintenance is important to improve the goodness of the design.

SPECIFICS OF THE FABRICATION, INSTALLATION AND MODIFICATION (FIM) PHASES OF AN OFFSHORE FACILITY

Contract Format and Contractor Selection

A contract for the FIM phases of an offshore facility must include HOF requirements by fitting the contract to minimise problems. This can be done, for example, by reducing pressure for productivity and by reducing the possibility for schedule constraints causing stress and fatigue of workers.

The selection of contractor to carry out the work is very important. Emphasis must be put on contractor's experience, competence and safety record as on price and schedule. The newer contract models used emphasise the need to carefully review the human factors element of the contractor's organisation.

New Projects vs. Modifications

For modification projects one has to work on what is already installed and the conditions for the workers could only be changed to a limited extent. It is, however, even more important that past experience is incorporated into this phase and therefore company and contractor must involve highly experienced personnel in modification of offshore facilities. This fact should also influence which contractor is chosen for the job.

Furthermore, a "safety benefit analysis" should be carried out prior to upgrading projects to assess whether the upgraded/modified facilities are sufficiently safe to warrant a major modification activity where the risks of accidents would normally be higher than during normal operations with the facility "as is". Of particular concern are un-engineered field modifications where proper design and planning are lacking.

Company In-house Experience

Company's in-house experience in selecting technology, contract format, contractor and in implementing safety climate in the FIM phases of an offshore facility will largely influence the project.

Specific Human Error Sources in the FIM Phases

During the FIM phases there are specific tasks which are more often sources of human oversights and human error related accidents:

- Communication between different groups of personnel
- Simultaneous operations; construction and production as well as construction and drilling
- Hot work (welding and burning)
- Need for communication between field construction work and office
- Construction work performed by drilling rig
- Contingency planning for rough weather
- Operations of cranes on barges as well as platform cranes including their maintenance and possible modifications
- Rigging operations including certification of riggers and responsibility of those involved.
- Tripping hazard
- Decommissioning; noting that the state of the structure is not fully known

It is important to make all personnel involved aware of specific critical tasks where human errors are more likely to occur as compared to other tasks.

Unfamiliar Events

Even when the best planning possible has been exercised, and even when experienced personnel are involved, unfamiliar events are likely to occur in the FIM phases of an offshore facility. It is of importance to prepare for such events through emergency planning and emergency exercises. For certain difficult operations, in particular in the installation phase, simulator training is considered useful (Gudmestad, et al., 1995).

Weather Criteria

The effect of weather on offshore installation work is obvious. Specific criteria should be set in the design phase in order to reduce the pressure for exceedance of the criteria during actual operations in the case of tight schedule or reimbursable contracts.

Regulatory and Official Approvals

This paper points to the fact that the human factors element is particularly important in the FIM phases of offshore facilities. Would there then be scope for increased regulations and further requirements for official approvals?

Although certain provisions could be regulated, like setting competence requirements for those involved in any safety related activities (NPD, 1996), it is generally felt that the human mind can not be regulated to function as one wishes. Working environment objectives could be defined for the various phases and activities (NPD, 1995).

Interfaces between organisations

To improve the understanding of the interfaces between organisations involved in the FIM phases of an offshore facility, influence diagrams can be presented to help identify potential weak links, see Appendix.

CONCLUDING REMARKS

The purpose of this paper is to highlight HOF aspects of the offshore working environment which influence safety during FIM phases.

It is necessary for industry to become involved in the debate about the topic of safety culture as practitioners have first hand experience. The organisation, management, supervisors and individual workers all play a part in the safety culture of an organisation. However, each of these have been addressed separately in this paper.

Management and supervisors have been shown to play a major role in safety improvements and thus the training of them is important. In addition they need to be given the resources (in particular time and money) to carry out their job effectively. In this respect contract format and selection of contractors are particularly important.

The emphasis on the role of the individual in accident causation has been replaced by more emphasis on the responsibility of the organisation for safety. Emphasis is here put on organisational learning and new organisational trends. However, the workers at the front line are directly involved in the accident and they too are part of the overall defense plan against accidents.

Training could be very fruitful in order to improve safety. Particular critical tasks could be identified for specific training programmes.

ACKNOWLEDGEMENTS

Participants at the International Workshop on Human Factors in Offshore Operations, New Orleans, December, 1996 are acknowledged for comments to the draft version of this paper. Reference is also made to Gudmestad and Gordon (1996) where a discussion on quantification of human errors is presented.

REFERENCES

ACSNI; "Human Factors Study Group". Third Report: "Organising for Safety". London. HMSO, 1993.

Bea, R.G. and Roberts, K.H.; "Human and Organisation Factors in Design, Construction and Operation of Offshore Platforms". SPE Paper SPE 30899, Richardson, Texas, Dec. 1995.

Bea, R., Holdsworth, R. and Smith, C.; "Introduction to Human and Organisational Factors in the Safety of Offshore Platforms", Proc. "Int. Workshop on Human Factors in Offshore Operations", New Orleans, 1996.

Brabazon, P., Hopkins, I. and Gudmestad, O.T.; "Estimating the Likelihood of Weather Criteria Exceedance during Marine Operations". Proceedings of OMAE 96, Vol II pp 23-28, Firenze, June 1996.

Donald, J. and Canter, D.; "Employee Attitudes and Safety in the Chemical Industry". Journal of Loss Prevention in Process Industries, 7, 203 - 208, 1994.

Ferguson, E.S., "How Engineers Lose Touch". Invention and Technology, pp. 16 - 24, Winter of 1993.

Gordon, R.; "The Contribution of Human Factors to Accidents in the Offshore Oil Industry". Reliability Engineering & Safety Systems. (In press), 1996.

Gudmestad, O.T. and Gordon, R.; "The role of human and organisational factors (HOF) in the fabrication, installation and modification (FIM) phasees of offshore facilities". Proc. "Int. Workshop on Human Factors in Offshore Operations", New Orleans, 1996.

Gudmestad, O.T., Rettedal, W.K., Sand, S., Brabazon, P., Trbojevic, V. and Helsøe, E.; "Use of Simulator Training to Reduce Risk in Offshore Marine Operations". Proc. OMAE -95, Vol. II, pp 487 - 498. Copenhagen, 1995.

Henrick, H.; "Industrial Accident Prevention: A Specific Approach". 1st Ed., McGraw-Hill Publishing Co., Ltd., London, 1931.

Murph, D.M. and Paté-Cornell,E.; "The SAM Framework: Modelling the Effects of Management Factors on Human Behaviour in Risk Analysis", Risk Analyis, Vol. 16, No. 4, 1996.

NPD (1995); "Regulations Relating to Systematic Follow-up of the Working Environment in the Petroleum Activities". Norwegian Petroleum Directorate, Stavanger, Norway, 1995.

NPD (1996); "Regulations Concerning Offshore Structures". Norwegian Petroleum Directorate, Stavanger, Norway, 1996.

Paté-Cornell, E.;"Organisational Aspects of Engineering System Safety: The Case of Offshore Platforms". Science, Vol. 250, pp. 1210 - 1217, 1990.

Paté-Cornell, E. and Bea, R.G.; "Management Errors and Systems Reliability: A Probabilistic Approach and Application to Offshore Platforms". Risk Analysis Vol. 12, No. 1, pp 1 - 18, 1992.

Paté-Cornell, E. and Rettedal, W.K.; "Management of Resource Constraints and System Safety. Application to the Design and Construction of Concrete Offshore Platforms". Report to Statoil, Stanford University, Sept. 1996.

Peters, R.H.; "Review of Recent Research on Organisational and Behavioural Factors Associated with Mine Safety". A Bureau of Mines Information Circular, United States Department of Interior, 1989.

Rasmussen, J.; "Perspectives on the Concept of Human Error". Invited Keynote Talk given at the "Human Performance and Anaesthesia Technology". Society for Technology in Anaesthesia Conference: New Orleans, February, 1993.

Trbojevic, V., Bellamy, L., Gudmestad, O.T., Aarum, T. and Rettedal, W.; "Assessment of Risk in the Design Phase of an Offshore Project". Proc. OMAE -96, Vol. II pp 431 - 435, Firenze, 1996.

Wilpert, B.; "Psychology in High Hazard Systems - Contributions to Safety and Reliability". Invited Keynote Address given at the IV European Congress of Psychology, Athens, July, 1995.

Zohar, D.; "Safety Climate in Industrial Organisations: Theoretical and Applied Implications". Journal of Applied Psychology, Vol 65, No. 1, pp. 96 - 102, 1980.

APPENDIX INFLUENCE DIAGRAMS

Influence diagram for relations between
Regulator (R) - Operator (O) - Contractor (C) - Subcontractors (SC)

Weak HOF Links:

R ↔ O:
Communication
Trust
Education on regulatory issues
Decommissioning

O ↔ C:
Contract format
- Selection of C
- Incentives
- Stress (schedule/budget)
Goodness of info
Communication
Trust
Experience of operator

Influence diagram for relations between

**Designers (D) - Fabricators (F) - Installation engr. (I) -
Modification (M) - Users (U)**

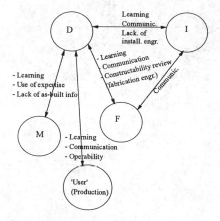

**Influence diagram for relations between
Management (M) - Supervisor (S) - Worker (W)**

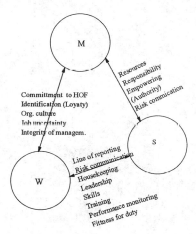

Offshore structures (ongoing research)

Structural Safety and Reliability, Shiraishi, Shinozuka & Wen (eds) © 1998 Balkema, Rotterdam, ISBN 90 5410 978 5

Analysis of nonlinear systems under non-Gaussian hydrodynamic loads

Michael A. Tognarelli & Ahsan Kareem
University of Notre Dame, Ind., USA

ABSTRACT: By casting a nonpolynomial system or excitation nonlinearity (e.g., nonlinear stiffness, Morison drag force) as a statistically equivalent polynomial, the Volterra theory may be employed as an effective frequency-domain analysis tool for approximating the power spectral density, root-mean-square and higher-order cumulants of the dynamic response of the original nonlinear system (tension-leg or jacket-type structure). The focus of this research in progress is to further develop the aforementioned framework to include treatment of nonlinear and non-Gaussian characteristics of the ocean environment which, heretofore, have not been fully considered. In particular, it is proposed to improve the force representations of existing studies to include a third-order representation of potential forces as well as the nonlinearity introduced by the intermittent effects of forces at the ocean free surface. In addition, it is proposed to establish accurate estimation of response statistics up to the fourth order when the ocean environment is modeled by the nonlinear random wave theory (second-order Stokes theory), for which the wave elevation and wave kinematics are non-Gaussian.

1 INTRODUCTION

It has been shown that the methods of equivalent statistical quadratization and cubicization, in tandem with the Volterra theory, can be effective tools for developing the power spectral densities (PSDs), response statistics and probability density functions (PDFs) for systems containing statistically asymmetric or symmetric nonlinearities, respectively, in their excitation, system characteristics or both (Li & Kareem 1990; Spanos & Donley 1991; Kareem & Zhao 1994a&b; Kareem et al. 1995; Tognarelli et al. 1997).

According to this framework, which has been applied to jacket-type and tension-leg platforms (TLPs), the system response is expressed as a Voltcrra functional series containing either first-order and second-order terms (equivalent statistical quadratization) or first-order and third-order terms (equivalent statistical cubicization). Non-polynomial nonlinearities are cast as polynomials and the original equations of motion are cast as a Volterra system from which frequency-domain transfer functions may be obtained. These transfer functions may be employed in integral expressions for the response cumulants up to the fourth-order and the response PSD. The cumulants are utilized to approximate the response PDF via an appropriate model. The ability to estimate higher-order cumulants is critically important in assessing the extremes of the system response.

2 QUADRATIZATION AND CUBICIZATION

In this study, the structure is modeled as a SDOF system as follows,

$$M\ddot{x} + C\dot{x} + Kx + g(x, \dot{x}) = f(t), \qquad (2.1)$$

where M, C, and K are system constants and both $g(\cdot), f(\cdot)$ may be nonlinear. The formalism of the Volterra theory, i.e., the representation of the output of a system as the infinite sum of the outputs of separate systems of increasing order, makes it amenable for situations in which the nonlinearities treated have polynomial forms. As such, in the context of this study, the application of this system analysis technique often requires that nonlinear functions be approximated as polynomials when their original representations do not possess such forms.

In the past, quadratization has been employed to treat statistically asymmetric nonlinearities. For systems containing statistically symmetric nonlinearities, the quadratic term arising from this technique vanishes and cubicization has been employed to treat them. Li et al. (1995) have developed a hybrid technique wherein linear and both quadratic and cubic terms are retained in the analysis of a jacket-type structure.

The present study also employs a hybrid technique, however, the coefficients of the polynomial representation are determined by a constrained matching with a moment-based Hermite representation (Grigoriu 1984; Winterstein 1985) rather than minimization of a mean-square error. This is done in an attempt to match the first four statistical moments of the nonlinearity being modeled, rather than solely its mean-square character. It is suggested that choosing the coefficients in this manner will either eliminate the need to correct the higher-order statistics (Li et al. 1995) or provide a systematic guide for making such a correction by indicating the relative error in each of the statistics.

3 NONLINEARITIES IN THE OCEAN ENVIRONMENT

Throughout this study, it is proposed to use the aforementioned frequency-domain analysis procedures to treat offshore systems in an ocean environment which is characterized by one or a combination of: (1) a third-order wave potential; (2) a nonlinear wave field; (3) a fluctuating free surface. In the literature, these analysis techniques have been developed to their greatest extent (i.e., response power spectrum and first four response cumulants) for only SDOF or MDOF systems in Gaussian (linear) random seas with a first- or second-order wave potential and forces considered only up to the mean water level.

3.1 Third-order wave potential model

Recently, it has been suggested that third-order effects may give rise to extreme response phenomena on TLPs. While springing, a steady-state, resonant effect, has been linked to second-order effects, ringing, characterized by transient bursts of energy, may be attributable to higher-order interactions. Therefore, it has become increasingly important to model and analyze these effects and their possible sources. One area of particular interest is that of potential forces, which have been successfully modeled up to the second order by several authors and used, in some cases, to compute the response of offshore structures. While an accurate representation of the third-order potential forces is not yet available, it is important to establish the computational capability to incorporate such forces into currently available analysis frameworks for future applications. From this point of view, the third-order potential studied is a non-physical model, intended only to demonstrate the capabilities of the analysis technique.

Kareem & Li (1994) have developed second-order response statistics for the response of a 6-DOF TLP model to first- and second-order viscous and potential forces using the boundary element method. Donley & Spanos (1992) have employed the Volterra theory to compute the response PSD and statistics up to the third order for TLPs subjected to viscous and potential loads represented up to the second order.

The development of a third-order transfer function for potential force which relates wave elevation components at three frequencies is presented. The purpose is to use the Volterra theory to establish some understanding of the importance of a potential force of this order even though its exact form is not known. This approach is similar to that of Stansberg (1993) for a two-dimensional wave potential. However, a simplified cubic transfer function, $H_P(\omega_1, \omega_2, \omega_3)$, is devised and systematically analyzed in addition to the quadratic transfer function. Such a representation is useful in a frequency-domain Volterra series approach for cubic-order nonlinearities or nonlinearities which have been approximated to cubic order. As the analytically derived expressions for higher-order potential forces are increasingly complex, the development of an experimental, rather than analytical, set of transfer functions may be more attractive from a practical standpoint. In anticipating such a case, this research provides a sound basis for future analysis.

3.2 Nonlinear random wave field

In practical analyses, the system inputs to the forcing processes, sea surface elevation and wave kinematics, have been modeled as Gaussian processes. In general, this is an inaccurate assumption. Second-order response statistics prediction capability has been developed for a jacket-type structure when the ocean environment is modeled by second-order random Stokes waves which are non-Gaussian (Kareem et al. 1994, 1996). The wave elevation and kinematics themselves have been derived using an implicit second-order perturbation technique along with the Fourier-Stieltjes spectral representation theorem. Also, higher-order statistics and PSDs for each quantity have been derived. The statistics of the wave kinematics are used to express the kinematics themselves as nonlinear functions of Gaussian processes via the moment-based Hermite transformation. Taking this approach, the wave kinematics are also non-Gaussian and this information is incorporated into the expressions for the Morison inertia force and nonlinear Morison drag force. The autocorrelation and PSD for the force have been calculated, from which the PSD of the response of the jacket-type platform system, which has been modeled as linear, may be obtained. This study has been limited, however, to concerns with the mean-square character of the response.

The present task is the incorporation of a representation of the wave kinematics derived from the second-order random wave theory, which are non-Gaussian, into the development of the wave force which is suitable for treatment by the Volterra theory in the frequency domain. Knowing the higher-order statistics of the kinematics (Kareem et al. 1994), they may be expanded in a moment-based series of Hermite polynomials as explained above. Expressing these non-Gaussian processes through nonlinear transformations of a Gaussian process is desirable, since such an assumption (a Gaussian parent process) has been made in the development of the cumulant expressions which are employed. However, when the polynomialization technique has been performed, for example, on a Morison drag force term, we have

$$K_D(u + U - \dot{x})|u + U - \dot{x}| \qquad (3.1)$$
$$= \alpha_0 + \alpha_1(u - \dot{x}) + \alpha_2(u - \dot{x})^2 + \alpha_3(u - \dot{x})^3$$

where u is water particle velocity which is non-Gaussian, U is current velocity and $\dot{x}$ is structure velocity. Now, if we employ the suggested non-Gaussian representation for u, we have in Eq. (3.1) a third-order polynomial in u which is, itself, a third-order polynomial of a Gaussian parent process. Thus, we may now actually have a fourth- or sixth-order polynomial in terms of the parent Gaussian process.

A logical means for reducing the order of this expression must be employed so that it is still representable as a third-order Volterra system, while important information about the frequency-domain character of the response is retained. This may be attainable by inserting the Hermite representation for the wave kinematics into the original force expression first, then using the polynomialization technique to approximate and reduce the order of the expression to two or three. Ultimately, such a representation could be used in tandem with the potential forces described earlier as input to a TLP system and analyzed within the frameworks which have been described.

An alternative approach focuses on the frequency character of the kinematics as the Hermite transformation can distort their PSDs inappropriately. This involves the assumption that the higher-order statistics of these processes are Gaussian, when, in truth, they are not. However, the correct frequency character of the higher-order representation of the PSDs of the kinematic quantities is preserved by using the derivations of Kareem et al. (1994) without increasing the order of the polynomial representation of the nonlinear force. If it is shown that the higher-order statistics of the kinematics are only mildly non-Gaussian, using only the appropriate spectral representations is sufficient to characterize the effect of their nonlinearity on the system response.

3.3 Intermittence of the ocean free surface

The free surface effect has been discussed in separate studies via several methods for Gaussian random

waves to compute force and response statistics up to the second order. Among the methods which have been employed to treat the nonlinearity associated with intermittence of the force near the free surface are stretching, extrapolation, delta stretching, and modified stretching (Mo and Moan, 1985). Huang et al. (1983) have derived a marginal non-Gaussian PDF of the wave elevation based on a third-order Stokes expansion for a narrow-banded wave process without using the troublesome Gram-Charlier distribution. Hu & Zhao (1992) developed fourth-order statistics of wave kinematics based on second-order Stokes theory for general bandwidths using the Gram-Charlier series. Tung (1995) has discussed the importance of the fluctuating free surface on the total wave force on a partially submerged cylinder and developed up to second-order statistics. This analysis, however, has not been extended to computations of the response of an offshore structure. Olagnon et al. (1988) employed a Taylor series expansion of the wave force about the MWL, but concluded that this contribution was insignificant. Li & Kareem (1993) have expanded this intermittent force in terms of trivariate Hermite polynomials and employed their representation in determining second-order response characteristics for a TLP.

The nonlinear force per unit length near the surface, $f_{NS}(z, t)$, on a partially submerged body may be expressed using extrapolation as,

$$f_{NS}(z, t) = f(z, t)\Theta(\eta(t) - z), \qquad (3.2)$$

where $f(z, t)$ is an inertia, viscous drag, or potential force, $\Theta(\cdot)$ is the Heaviside unit step function, $\eta(t)$ is wave elevation, and z is a vertical position which is zero at the MWL. If stretching is employed, z is replaced by the transformed coordinate and the Heaviside function may be eliminated. The forces considered generally depend upon one or more wave kinematic quantities, thus it is desirable to derive or devise a JPDF for these quantities. Having this information, it may be possible to cast these forces as polynomials in terms of the wave elevation and another kinematic quantity, either water particle velocity or acceleration, depending on the particular force in question. Such a formulation is the most conducive for use with the other force descriptions which have been proposed within the context of this study in a frequency-domain Volterra system analysis scheme. Whereas, in previous sections, we have discussed non-Gaussian representations of the wave elevation and wave kinematics, it is advantageous both computationally and academically to begin this study by treating these as jointly Gaussian quantities with appropriate correlations.

In general, the force per unit length must be integrated along the submerged length of the structure,

L_s, as follows, up to the instantaneous wave elevation,

$$F(t) = \int_{-L_s}^{0} f(z,t)dz + \int_{0}^{\eta(t)} f_{NS}(z,t)dz \qquad (3.3)$$

If we choose to express the force near the free surface as a one-term Taylor series, we have,

$$F(t) = \int_{-L_s}^{0} f(z,t)dz + \eta(t)f(0,t). \qquad (3.4)$$

This is an alternate representation which is simpler to incorporate within the Volterra series framework as it already possesses a polynomial form, involving only products of the wave elevation and wave kinematics. Extrapolation and stretching methods would involve hyperbolic functions of the wave elevation due to the forms of the transfer functions which relate it to wave kinematics. Use of the Taylor series approach circumvents this situation.

The presence of the multiplication of the wave elevation in the second term in Eq. (3.4) increases the order of the polynomial representation for the force considered. If the order of the new expression becomes higher than cubic, a reduction or truncation must be performed. This is a subject of further study.

4 CONCLUSIONS

The issues discussed herein are important in gaining a more accurate insight into the extreme character of the responses of offshore structures, thus aiding in design efforts to further ensure their safety. The framework for solving these problems is the Volterra theory of nonlinear systems in the frequency domain. Background information has been provided to give a perspective on the current state of each proposed area of research. This research in progress will further develop the accuracy of each focus area and in its completion will bring them together to form a more complete set of tools for offshore engineering design.

REFERENCES

Donley, M.G. & Spanos, P.D. 1992. Stochastic response of a tension leg platform to viscous and potential drift forces. *Proc. OMAE '92 Conf.*

Grigoriu, M. 1984. Crossings of non-gaussian translation processes. *J. Engrg. Mech.* 110: 610-620.

Hu, S-L. J. & Zhao, D. 1992. Kinematics of nonlinear random waves near the free surface. *J. Engrg. Mech.* 118: 2072-2086.

Huang, N.E., Long, S.R., Tung, C-C., Yuan, Y. & Bliven, L.F. 1983. A non-Gaussian statistical model for surface elevation of nonlinear random wave fields. *J. Geophys. Res.* 88: 7597-7606.

Kareem, A., Hsieh, C.C. & Tognarelli, M.A. 1994. Response analysis of offshore systems to nonlinear random waves: part I -- wave field characteristics. *Proc. '94 ASME Wint. Ann. Mtg.*

Kareem, A., Hsieh, C.C. & Tognarelli, M.A. 1996. Response analysis of offshore systems to nonlinear random waves: response statistics. *Proc. OMAE '96 Conf.* I.

Kareem, A. & Li, Y. 1994. Stochastic response of a tension leg platform to viscous and potential drift forces. *Prob. Engrg. Mech.* 9: 1-14.

Kareem, A. & Zhao, J. 1994a. Stochastic response analysis of tension leg platforms: A statistical quadratization and cubicization approach. *Proc. OMAE '94 Conf.*

Kareem, A. & Zhao, J. 1994b. Analysis of non-gaussian surge response of tension leg platforms under wind loads. *J. Offshore Mech. Arctic Engrg.* 20: 137-144.

Kareem, A., Zhao, J. & Tognarelli, M.A. 1995. Surge response statistics of tension leg platforms under wind and wave loads: A statistical quadratization approach. *Prob. Engrg. Mech.* 10: 225-240.

Li, X-M., Quek, S-T. & Koh, C-G. 1995. Stochastic response of offshore platforms by statistical cubicization. *J. Engrg. Mech.* 121: 1056-1068.

Li, Y. & Kareem, A. 1990. Stochastic resonse of a tension leg platform to wind and wave fields: frequency and time domain analysis. *J. Wind Engrg. Indust. Aero.* 36: 915-926.

Li, Y. & Kareem, A. 1993. Multivariate Hermite expansion of hydrodynamic drag loads on tension leg platforms. *J. Engrg. Mech.* 119: 91-112.

Mo, O. & Moan, T. 1985. Environmental load effect analysis of guyed towers. *J. Energy Res. Tech.* 107: 24-33.

Olagnon, M., Prevosto, M. & Joubert, P. 1988. Nonlinear spectral computation of the dynamic response of a single cylinder. *J. Offshore Mech. Arctic Engrg.* 110: 278-281.

Spanos, P.D. & Donley, M.G. 1991. Equivalent statistical quadratization for nonlinear systems. *J. Engrg. Mech.* 117: 1289-1310.

Stansberg, C.T. 1993. Non-gaussian properties of second-order sum frequency responses in irregular waves: a numerical study. *Proc. OMAE '93 Conf.*

Tognarelli, M.A., Zhao, J., Rao, K.B. & Kareem, A. 1997. Equivalent statistical quadratization and cubicization for nonlinear systems. *J. Engrg. Mech.* 123.

Tung, C.C. 1995. Effects of free surface fluctuations on total wave force on cylinder. *J. Engrg. Mech.* 121: 274-280.

Winterstein, S. 1985. Non-normal responses and fatigue damage. *J. Engrg. Mech.* 111: 1291-1295.

Structural Safety and Reliability, Shiraishi, Shinozuka & Wen (eds) © 1998 Balkema, Rotterdam, ISBN 90 5410 978 5

On the reliability of ship structures in different coastal areas

A. P. Teixeira & C. Guedes Soares
Unit of Marine Technology and Engineering, Instituto Superior Técnico, Lisboa, Portugal

ABSTRACT: This paper aims at quantifying the changes in notional reliability levels that result from ships being subjected to different wave environments in European coastal waters. The probability of failure is calculated using a first order reliability method. An example of the reliability analysis using different formulations of the wave induced and still water load effects is provided. Calculations are performed for different coastal areas showing how the risk levels depend on the area.

1. INTRODUCTION

The risk of shipping in coastal waters results from the contributions of different hazards such as collision, grounding, fire, explosion, structural failure and others.

An overall risk model must account for the different sources of accident as well as their geographical variability. The present work has been made within such a framework, aiming at quantifying the changes in the notional probability of structural failure as a function of the coastal area in which the ship is.

This paper deals with the reliability of the primary ship structure with respect to the ultimate collapse moment and the probability of failure is calculated with a first order reliability method (FORM).

Two stochastic models have been used to describe both still water and wave induced load effects. The results using these two reliability formulations are compared in an example of a tanker. Calculations are then performed for different areas in the North of Europe.

2. STOCHASTIC MODELS

2.1 Limit State Equation

The limit state equation for midship section collapse is:

$$\frac{\left(M_s + \Psi_w \chi_w \chi_{nl} M_w \right)}{\chi_u M_u} \leq 1 \tag{1}$$

where M_u is the random ultimate longitudinal bending strength of the ship, M_s and M_w are the stochastic still water and wave induced bending moments, respectively. Ψ_w is the combination factor between still water and wave induced bending moment; χ_u, χ_w and χ_{nl} are the model uncertainties on ultimate capacity, wave load calculations and nonlinear effects, respectively.

This failure equation includes only the vertical bending because it was shown that the levels of the horizontal bending moment are small and its influence can be neglected for tankers (Guedes Soares et al., 1996).

For tankers three different load conditions, can be defined, i.e. Full load, Ballast and Partial load. The global annual reliability index β was obtained from the probability of failure for each condition,

$$\beta = \Phi^{-1}\left(PF_{BL} + PF_{FL} + PF_{PL} \right) \tag{2}$$

where Φ^{-1} is the standard normal probability distribution function and PF_{BL}, PF_{FL} and PF_{PL} are the failure probability in the different load conditions.

For each loading condition a percentage of ship life can be identified according to an estimate of operational profile for each ship type.

2.2 Stochastic Modeling of Ultimate Strength of the Primary Structure

The ultimate collapse bending moment was evaluated by the HULLCOLL program based on the theory outlined in (Gordo and Guedes Soares, 1996). This variable is used as deterministic in the failure equation. To take into account the uncertainty on the ultimate capacity the stochastic variable χ_u was defined.

2.3 Stochastic Modeling of Load Variables

The stochastic model for the vertical still water bending moment assumes that the still water loads vary monotonically during the voyage, between a departure and an arrival value, according to an uniform distribution, conditional on the departure and arrival Gaussian distributions. For the purpose of reliability analysis, a Gaussian distribution was proposed for the still water load model (Guedes Soares et al., 1996).

The statistical parameters can be calculated either based on the available data from the ships loading manuals or from general ship statistics (Guedes Soares and Moan, 1988).

The extreme distribution of the still water load over the time period T_c that the ship spends in loading case c is obtained by assuming independence of the maximum between different voyages,

$$F_{se}(x_e, T_c) = [F_s(x)]^{n_c} \tag{3}$$

where n_c is the number of voyages in the time period T_c.

When the values μ_s and σ_s of the normal distribution $F_s(x)$ are known, the distribution of the extreme values over the time period T_c can be approximated as a Gumbel law with the following parameters:

$$\mu_{se} = u_n = \Phi^{-1}\left(1 - \frac{1}{n_c}\right) \tag{4}$$

$$\sigma_{se} = [h(u_n)]^{-1} \tag{5}$$

were h is the hazard function and the characteristic largest value u_n is the value of x that, on average, is exceed one in a sample of size n_c.

The evaluation of the wave induced load effects that occur during long-term operation of the ships in the seaway was carried out for different areas in the North of Europe given in Global Wave Statistics (GWS). The resultant probability distribution is fitted to the Weibull model, which describes the distribution of the peaks at a random point in time. The distribution of the extremes values over the time period T is then obtained as a Gumbel law.

The Gumbel parameters x_n and σ can be estimated from the initial Weibull distribution with parameters w and k using the following equation:

$$x_n = w \cdot [\ln(n)]^{\frac{1}{\lambda}} \tag{6}$$

$$\sigma = \frac{w}{\lambda}[\ln(n)]^{\frac{1-\lambda}{\lambda}} \tag{7}$$

where n is the return period associated with one year of operation. The average of wave period is assumed to be 7 s.

2.4 Load Combination Between Still Water and Wave Bending Moment Ψ_w

Guedes Soares, (1992) obtained values for the load combination factors between 0.86 and 0.94 for a series of tankers. Casella et al., (1996) calculated the values given in table 1 for a specific tanker. The values in table 1 lie within the range calculated by Guedes Soares, and hence were adopted for the present example.

2.5 Model Uncertainties

The uncertainty on ultimate capacity χ_U, takes into account both the uncertainty in the yield strength (.08 to.10) and the model uncertainty on the ultimate capacity of the ship. Its stochastic model adopts a log-normal distribution function with mean value equal to one and a coefficient of variation equal to 0.15.

The χ_w random variable was used in the reliability calculations to introduce the uncertainty on the wave induced load calculations. It was assumed a normal distribution function with mean equal to 0.70 and a coefficient of variation equal to 0.15 based on the results of a benchmarking study presented by Shellin et al., (1996).

Table 1 - Values of the load combination factor for tankers

Load Case	Full Load	Ballast Load	Partial Load
Ψ_w	0.95	0.92	0.82

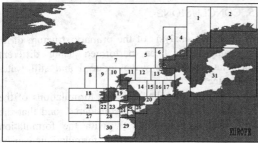

Figure 1 - Sea areas in Europe

3. RELIABILITY FORMULATION

In the present example a 236 m long tanker ship is considered for the reliability assessment. The stochastic model of wave induced bending moment is defined for different areas in the North Europe. ATLN refers to the wave induced bending moment in the North Atlantic calculated based on the world sea areas 8, 9, 11, 15 and 16 which covers the Europe areas 8, 9, 10, 18, 21, 27 and 11 to 17. (Figure 1).

Different formulations can be used for the load variables in eqn (1). The model that has been traditionally used in this field uses the random point in time formulation in which M_s is a normal distribution and M_w a Weibull. However, if one wants to calculate the reliability during a certain period of operation, the extreme loads during that period should be considered i.e. M_{se} and M_{we}, which are then Gumbel distribution. Combination of extreme and random point in time distributions could also be considered in the spirit of the Turkstra rule.

Table 2 summarises the reliability results in the full load condition for the different reliability formulations.

The relationship between the model of the long term distribution of individual waves and extreme model is obtained using the probability $P_e = 1/n$ that the most likely maximum wave occurs in the reference time period, assuming independence between n successive waves.

The probability of failure calculated with the extreme model can be considered as conditional

Table 2 - β-values for the different reliability models

Area	$M_{se}+M_{we}$	M_s+M_{we}	$M_{se}+M_w$	M_s+M_w
ATLN	2.35	2.85	4.26	5.75

Table 3 -Relation between β-value using the initial and the extreme value models (Area-ATLN)

M_w-Gumbel (n= 1.75E6)				M_w-Weibull
β_e	$P_{f|e}$	$P_{f|e} \cdot P_e$	β	β_w
2.85	2.19E-03	1.39E-09	5.94	5.75

($P_{f|e}$) on that maximum (P_e). Thus the total probability of failure is obtained by unconditioning:

$$P_f = P_{f|e} \cdot P_e \tag{8}$$

where $P_{f|e} = \Phi(-\beta_e)$ is the probability of failure considering the extreme wave model.

Table 3 shows the results of these calculations indicating that the two formulations lead to similar values of β (5.94 and 5.75).

It is also possible to estimate the reliability in the reference time period, considering a sequence of n wave peaks for each of which the reliability R_i is calculated with the Weibull model.

$$\beta_e' = \Phi^{-1}\left[1 - (R_i)^n\right] \tag{9}$$

The results in table 4 show that β obtained in both cases is similar.

4. RELIABILITY IN COASTAL WATERS

The probability of failure in a given area was calculated using the extreme reliability formulation, with the model for the wave induced bending moment corresponding to the area.

In figure 2 the long term distribution in full load condition is illustrated for different sea states showing a significant variability in the calculated wave induced loads. Values of the vertical bending moment range from 4668 MN.m to 1637 MN.m, calculated at the $10^{-6.5}$ probability level for the areas 7 and 31, respectively.

Table 5 gives the reliability indices for each loading condition, as well as the resulting global value for one year of operation (β_{1yr}). It can be seen that the most probable mode of failure is in the sagging condition, and that this probability of failure is highest for the full load situation. This is expected,

Table 4 - Relation between β-values using the initial and the extreme value models (Area-ATLN)

M_w-Weibull		M_w-Gumbel	(n= 1.58E6)		
β_w	P_f^b	$R_e = R_i^n$	P_f^e	β_e'	β_e
5.75	4.42E-09	9.93E-01	6.95E-3	2.46	2.85

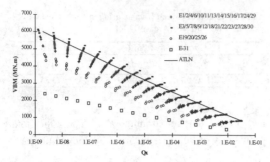

Figure 2 - Long term distribution for different sea areas.

Table 5 -β-values for the different load conditions

Area	L.C.	F.L.	B.L.	P.L.	$\beta_{1\,year}$	P_{fi}
	Sag	2.35	4.82	5.55	9.51E-3	2.34
	Hog	4.77	2.77	3.75	2.86E-3	2.76

because the largest still water bending moment is in sagging. Additionally, the ultimate capacity under vertical bending moment is smaller in sagging than that in hogging.

Table 6 illustrates the probability of failure in full load condition in each area normalized by the maximum value that occurs in sea area 7.

It should be noted that there is significant variability between the probability of failure obtained for the different sea areas as shown in the last column of table 6. Knowing the probability of failure in each area (P_f^A) and the probability that a ship is on that area (P_A), one can estimate the total probability of failure for a particular route.

Table 6 -β-values for the different sea areas

Area	β	P_{fi}	P_{fi}/P_{fmax}	Area	β	P_{fi}	P_{fi}/P_{fmax}
ATLN	2.35	9.51E-3	0.59	E16	2.80	2.56E-3	0.16
E1	2.57	5.07E-3	0.31	E17	2.78	2.73E-3	0.17
E2	2.69	3.55E-3	0.22	E18	2.26	1.18E-2	0.73
E3	2.35	9.44E-3	0.58	E19	3.07	1.07E-3	0.07
E4	2.52	5.87E-3	0.36	E20	3.18	7.34E-4	0.05
E5	2.39	8.45E-3	0.52	E21	2.31	1.05E-2	0.64
E6	2.50	6.19E-3	0.38	E22	2.34	9.69E-3	0.60
E7	2.14	1.63E-2	1.00	E23	2.38	8.56E-3	0.53
E8	2.26	1.19E-2	0.73	E24	2.59	4.74E-3	0.29
E9	2.26	1.19E-2	0.73	E25	3.01	1.30E-3	0.08
E10	2.44	7.36E-3	0.45	E26	3.11	9.51E-4	0.06
E11	2.59	4.83E-3	0.30	E27	2.23	1.27E-2	0.78
E12	2.35	9.51E-3	0.59	E28	2.27	1.15E-2	0.71
E13	2.68	3.70E-3	0.23	E29	2.57	5.16E-3	0.32
E14	2.66	3.93E-3	0.24	E30	2.32	1.02E2	0.63
E15	2.60	4.66E-3	0.29	E31	3.75	9.02E-5	0.01

5. CONCLUSIONS

A reliability analysis of the primary structure of an oil tanker has been performed using different formulations of the wave induced and still water load effects.

It was shown that different formulations of the reliability problem can be considered, and that the results change significantly with the formulation adopted. However, the various formulations can be related to each other and the choice of one or the other is a matter of standardisation in order to allow the ship structures to be compared.

A reliability analysis was carried out for different sea areas in the European coast. It was shown that there is a significant effect of the wave climate in the different European coastal waters.

ACKNOWLEDGEMENTS

This study has been performed in the project "Safety of Shipping in Coastal Waters (SAFECO)" which has been partially funded by the Commission of the European Communities, through the Transport Programme under contract n° WA-95-SC.023.

REFERENCES

Casella, G., Dogliani M. and Guedes Soares, C., (1996), Reliability Based Design of the Primary Structure of Oil Tankers, *Proceedings 15th Offshore Mechanics and Artic Engineering Conference*, Vol II, pp. 217-224.

Gordo, J. M. and Guedes Soares, C., (1996), Approximate Method to Evaluate the Hull Girder Collapse Strength, *Marine Structures*, 1, 9, 449-70.

Guedes Soares, C., (1992), Combination of Primary Load Effects in Ship Structures, *Probabilistic Engineering Mechanics*, Vol. 7, pp. 103-111.

Guedes Soares, C., Dogliani., M., Ostergaard, C., Parmentier, G. and Pedersen, P. T., (1996), Reliability Based Ship Structural Design, *Transactions of the Society of Naval Architects and Marine Engineers*, Vol.104, New York.

Guedes Soares, C. and Moan, T., (1988), Statistical Analysis of Still Water Load Effects in Ship Structures, *Transactions of the Society of Naval Architects and Marine Engineers*, Vol. 96, pp. 129-156, New York.

Shellin, T., Östergaard, C., and Guedes Soares, C., (1996), Uncertainty Assessment of Low Frequency Wave Induced Load Effects for Containerships, *Marine Structures,* Vol. 9, n. 3-4, pp. 313-332.

Structural Safety and Reliability, Shiraishi, Shinozuka & Wen (eds) © 1998 Balkema, Rotterdam, ISBN 90 5410 978 5

Expected sliding distance of caisson type breakwaters

Kenichiro Shimosako & Shigeo Takahashi
Hydraulic Engineering Division, Port and Harbour Research Institute, Yokosuka, Japan

ABSTRACT. Estimating the sliding distance is essential in the future probabilistic design of caisson type breakwaters. In this paper, characteristics of the sliding phenomena are described, and a method to calculate the sliding distance using a Monte Carlo simulation is proposed. The probabilistic property of wave period, wave force, friction coefficient, and wave direction were taken into consideration in this calculation method.

1 INTRODUCTION

Caisson type breakwaters consisting of a rubble mound foundation and upright section have several advantages over conventional rubble mound breakwaters, since they are more stable, can be constructed faster and easier, and also reduce wave transmission.

In the conventional design process of a caisson type breakwater, the sliding stability of the caisson is evaluated by the sliding safety factor (*S.F.*). However, even if the *S.F.* is below 1.0, the breakwater can still maintain its function if the sliding distance is small. Consequently, to ensure economical design, it is necessary to determine the expected sliding distance occurring in the return period of the caisson.

Ito et al. (1966) conducted the research on the stability of breakwaters and proposed the concept of the expected sliding distance. However, it was difficult to estimate the wave pressure precisely, much more the sliding distance at that time.

Goda (1974) developed a new wave pressure formula which included an impulsive pressure. This formula is quite useful and has become the standard method to obtain wave pressure against a vertical wall, although discrepancies arise under some impulsive pressure conditions.

Takayama et al. (1994) carried out the probabilistic estimation of stability of sliding which considered the probabilistic property of wave height, wave pressure and friction coefficient between caissons and rubble mound. However, caisson's sliding distance was not included.

In this study, a method is proposed to calculate the sliding distance using Monte Carlo simulation.

2 PRESENT DESIGN METHOD AND FORMULATION OF CAISSON'S SLIDING

2.1 *Present Design Method*

The design wave forces acting on the caisson's upright section can be obtained using the Goda pressure formula. The present design method for determining the sliding stability is shown as follows:

$$S.F. = \mu \, (W' - U) \, / \, P \qquad (1)$$

The safety factor for sliding *S.F.* is represented by the ratio of the friction resistance $\mu(W' - U)$ to the horizontal wave force P, where μ is the friction coefficient between the caisson and rubble mound, W' is the caisson weight in water, and U is the uplift force. When *S.F.* is less than 1.0, the caisson is considered to be in an unstable condition. However, even if *S.F.* is less than 1.0, the breakwater can still maintain its function providing the sliding distance is small.

In the present design method, *S.F.* must not be less than 1.2 considering the fluctuation of wave force, friction coefficient, and caisson weight. In order to optimize the design from an economical standpoint, we must determine the expected sliding distance occurring in the return period of the caisson. However, the sliding distance cannot be estimated using the present design method.

2.2 *Equation of Motion of Caisson*

Figure 1 shows the forces that act on the caisson when it is sliding. M_a is the added mass, x is the acceleration of the caisson, F_R is the frictional resistance force ($=\mu \, (W' - U)$), and F_D is the force related sliding velocity including the wave-making

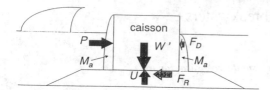

Figure 1 Forces acting on the caisson in sliding.

resistance force.

The equation of motion representing caisson sliding is presented as follows:

$$(W/g + M_a) x = P - F_R - F_D \qquad (2)$$

where W is the caisson weight in the air, g is the gravity.

In our simplified sliding model, it is assumed that μ is constant before and during sliding, and that F_D is small enough to be neglected. Consequently, Eq.(2) is rewritten as follows:

$$(W/g + M_a) x = P + \mu U - \mu W \qquad (3)$$

2.3 Calculation Method of the Sliding Distance

The sliding distance of the caisson can be calculated by integrating the acceleration twice. The displacement x can be calculated from Eq.(3) if the added mass M_a, the horizontal force P, uplift force U, friction coefficient μ, caisson weight in water W' and in the air W are known. In the proposed model, we assumed the added mass M_a is equal to $1.0855 \rho h'^2$, where ρ is the density of the water and h' is the water depth in front of the caisson.

Figure 2 shows the time series of $P(t)$ used to simulate caisson displacement, where $P(t)$ is defined as follows:

$$P(t) = \max \{ P_1(t), P_2(t) \} \qquad (4)$$

$P_1(t)$ indicates the slowly varying component of the wave force, while $P_2(t)$ is the impulsive component.

$U(t)$ is also defined as follows:

$$U(t) = \max \{ U_1(t), U_2(t) \} \qquad (5)$$

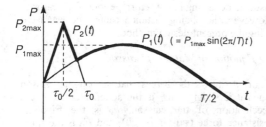

Figure 2 Time-dependent mathematical model.

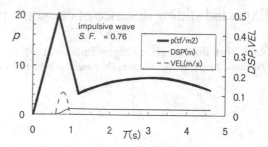

Figure 3(a) Calculated profile of the impulsive wave.

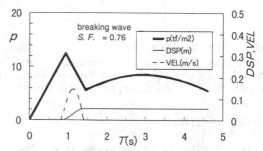

Figure 3(b) Calculated profile of the breaking wave.

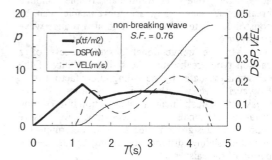

Figure 3(c) Calculated profile of the non-breaking wave.

The caisson begins to slide when $(P + \mu U)$ becomes larger than $\mu W'$. $P(t)$ and $U(t)$ can be obtained by the Goda pressure formula, but we still must determine τ_0 to evaluate sliding distance. We used theoretical analysis and model experiments to determine τ_0. Consequently, τ_0 is represented as follows:

$$\tau_0 = k \, \tau_{0F} \qquad (6)$$
$$k = 1 / \{(\alpha*)^{0.3} + 1\}^2 \qquad (7)$$
$$\alpha* = \max \{\alpha_1, \alpha_2\} \qquad (8)$$
$$\tau_{0F} = \{0.5 - H/(8h)\} T \qquad (0 \leq H/h \leq 0.8) \quad (9)$$

where α_1 is an impulsive pressure coefficient (Takahashi, Tanimoto and Shimosako, 1994), α_2 is a coefficient indicating the effect of impulsive pressure in Goda pressure formula, H is wave height, h is water depth, and T is wave period. In non-breaking

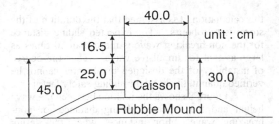

Figure 4   Cross section of the model experiment.

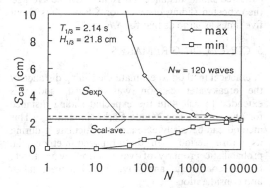

Figure 5 Average of calculated sliding distance as a function of the number of calculations.

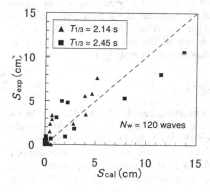

Figure 6 Calculated sliding distance vs. Experimental sliding distance.

wave, τ_0 is almost the same as τ_{0F}, whereas for impulsive wave, τ_0 is 0.1~0.2 s in the model experiment. Note that τ_0 is determined based on the duration time of shear force which is the effective force producing caisson sliding. Actually, the duration time of impulsive pressure is much smaller than τ_0.

Figure 3(a) to 3(c) show the typical calculated time series of the horizontal wave force, the velocity of the caisson, and the displacement for one wave.

Although these three cases are designed by the same condition, e.g. *S.F.* = 0.76, the sliding distance for the non-breaking wave is much larger than that for the breaking or impulsive wave.   This is because the non-breaking wave has longer duration time of the wave force.

The proposed method can be extended to estimate the expected sliding distance of the caisson for a group of waves, or during its return period. Monte Carlo simulation were adopted to reproduce all wave data according to the Rayleigh distribution, and the probabilistic property of wave period, wave force, friction coefficient between the caisson and rubble mound, and wave direction were taken into consideration.

3. MODEL EXPERIMENTS

3.1 *Experimental Procedure*

A series of model experiments were conducted to determine whether the proposed calculation method is good or not.   Figure 4 shows the employed breakwater model.   The horizontal displacement of the caisson was measured.   Irregular waves were used with significant wave periods of 2.14s and 2.45s. Based on the wave force, caisson weight was accordingly adjusted by putting lead weights inside it.

3.2 *Sliding Distance*

Figure 5 shows an example of the relation between the average of calculated sliding distance and the number of calculations.   The experimental value and the average of 10,000 calculations are also shown in this figure.   The margin of error decreases as the number of calculations increases.   In the present study, the calculated sliding distance (the expected sliding distance) is defined as the average of 2,000 calculations.

Figure 6 shows the relation between the calculated sliding distance (S_{cal}) and the experimental one (S_{exp}).   The experimental results are the average of eight measurements.   Note that good agreement exists between the calculated results and the experimental ones.

4 PROTOTYPE CALCULATIONS

4.1 *Calculation Procedure of Expected Sliding Distance*

Prototype calculations based on proposed method were also conducted to investigate the expected sliding distance.   The cross section of the designed breakwater is shown in Figure 7, and the design conditions are listed in Table 1.   The caisson weight and the width B was accordingly adjusted to set the

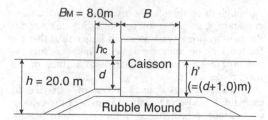

Figure 7 Cross section of the prototype calculation.

Table 1 Structural and wave conditions.

Wave Type	d (m)	h_c (m)	$T_{1/3}$ (s)	$H_{1/3}$ (m)
Non-breaking	13.0	3.9	12.0	6.5
Breaking	11.0	5.1	12.0	8.5
Impulsive	8.0	5.1	12.0	8.5

Table 2 Expected sliding distance for one storm.

	$S.F. = 1.0$	$S.F. = 1.2$
Non-breaking Wave	0.420 m	0.088 m
Breaking Wave	0.219 m	0.043 m
Impulsive Wave	0.021 m	0.004 m

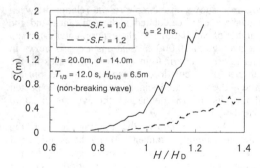

Figure 8 Expected sliding distance vs. wave height.

sliding safety factor ($S.F.$) at 1.0 and 1.2 for the design wave condition.

4.2 *Calculation Results*

As mentioned in 2.3, the sliding distance for the non-breaking wave is much larger than that for the breaking or impulsive wave. Table 2 compares the expected sliding distance for one storm which has the same significant wave height as the design wave. In this calculation, it is assumed that the duration of the storm is two hours. The expected sliding distance for the non-breaking wave is more than 20 times as large as that for impulsive wave. Thus the degree of instability of the designed breakwater cannot be verified quantitatively by the sliding safety factor.

Figure 8 shows the relation between the wave height and the expected sliding distance for non-breaking wave. For instance, when the design safety factor against sliding $S.F. = 1.2$ and the wave height is larger than design wave height by 10 %, the expected sliding distance is 0.16 m. On the average, the expected sliding distance for $S.F. = 1.0$ is about five times as large as that for $S.F. = 1.2$.

5. CONCLUDING REMARKS

A practical method to estimate the sliding distance of the breakwater caisson was derived, and was extended to calculate the expected sliding distance for one storm using Monte Carlo simulation. This method can be easily extended to calculate it during its return period. In the proposed method, the probabilistic property of wave period, wave force, friction coefficient, and wave direction were taken into consideration.

In future breakwater designs, probabilistic design method should be adopted to ensure economical considerations are optimized. Subsequent research will be directed at extending the proposed sliding model to estimate the sliding distance of the caisson during its return period considering the estimation errors of the deep sea wave, the wave transformation, and caisson weight.

REFERENCES

Ito, Y., M. Fujishima, and T. Kitatani (1966): On the stability of breakwaters, *Rept. of Port and Harbour Research Institute,* Vol.5, No.14, 134p (in Japanese).
Goda, Y. (1974): A new method of wave pressure calculation for the design of composite breakwaters, *Proc. of 14th Coastal Engineering Conference, ASCE,* pp. 1702-1720.
Takahashi, S., K. Tanimoto and K. Shimosako (1994): A Proposal of Impulsive Pressure Coefficient for Design of Composite Breakwaters, *Proc. of the International Conference on Hydro-Technical Engineering for Port and Harbor Construction,* pp.489-504.
Takayama, T., Y. Suzuki, H. Kawai, H. Fujisaku (1994): Approach to Probabilistic Design for a Breakwater, *Tech. Note of the Port and Harbour Research Institute,* No. 785, 36p (in Japanese).

Author index